GED

2009–2010 EDITION

Caren Van Slyke and Associates

KAPLAN

PUBLISHING

New York

The GED tests are developed and distributed by the GED Testing Service, a program of the American Council on Education, which neither sponsors nor endorses this product.

This publication is designed to provide accurate and authoritative information in regard to the subject matter covered. It is sold with the understanding that the publisher is not engaged in rendering legal, accounting, or other professional service. If legal advice or other expert assistance is required, the services of a competent professional should be sought.

© 2009 Learning Unlimited

Published by Kaplan Publishing, a division of Kaplan, Inc.
1 Liberty Plaza, 24th Floor
New York, NY 10006

Printed in the United States of America

10 9 8 7 6 5 4 3

ISBN-13: 978-1-4195-5250-2

Kaplan Publishing books are available at special quantity discounts to use for sales promotions, employee premiums, or educational purposes. Please email our Special Sales Department to order or for more information at kaplanpublishing@kaplan.com, or write to Kaplan Publishing, 1 Liberty Plaza, 24th Floor, New York, NY 10006.

WELCOME TO *KAPLAN GED!*

Congratulations. You've selected a powerful and effective self-study guide for the GED produced by Kaplan, the world's leader in test preparation. Each year, Kaplan provides the courses, books, software, and online tools to help hundreds of thousands of people succeed on standardized tests, including the GED.

To provide you with the best possible book for passing the GED, Kaplan has partnered with Caren Van Slyke and Learning Unlimited. Van Slyke and the rest of the Learning Unlimited staff have decades of experience teaching GED classes and preparing GED study materials.

This book has been designed to help you prepare for the tests in the way that best suits your needs and your schedule. Below is a plan to get the most benefit out of *Kaplan GED*.

Step 1: Read the *Overview of the GED Tests*, pages vii–viii, to get an overview of the five test areas.

Step 2: Look over the *Contents*, pages iv–vi, for a general idea of the topics that are covered in this book. You may be surprised at how much of the subject matter you recognize.

Step 3: Read *Kaplan GED Strategies for Success*, pages ix–xvi. You may come back to these proven test-taking strategies several times, especially in the week before you take the test.

Step 4: Take the *GED Pretests* on pages 2–43. These half-length practice tests have been designed to acquaint you with the GED and to help you analyze how to prepare best.

Step 5: Read the answers and explanations that follow the *Pretests*. Use the *Evaluation Charts* in the Pretest Answers and Explanations section to make decisions about how to prioritize your study.

Step 6: Get a schedule of upcoming testing dates for taking the GED in your area. The schedules vary from location to location, so you will need to contact your local GED testing center for times and dates. To find a testing center convenient to you, contact the GED Hot Line at 1-800-62-MY-GED (1-800-626-9433), or contact a local community college or public school adult education program.

Step 7: Look at the results of your *Evaluation Charts* and the schedule of upcoming testing dates, to make a week-by-week study plan for yourself.

Step 8: Work through the book, studying the sections that are most important to you. Use the **Key Ideas, Hints,** and **On the GED** features in the margins of many of the pages to focus on the information and skills that you need to pass the tests. After you finish a practice activity, be sure to read the *Answers and Explanations* so that you can check your mastery of the material and learn from your mistakes.

Step 9: Plan to take the *GED Post-Tests* on pages 530–611 about two weeks before your scheduled testing dates.

Step 10: Use the results of the *Planning Charts* in the Post-Test Answers and Explanations section to plan your study for the last two weeks before you take the GED. Decide where you need to do the most work, and focus your efforts.

In the pages that follow, you will find all that you need to succeed on the GED. The next steps are up to you. Good luck!

CONTENTS

OVERVIEW OF THE GED TESTS

Why Should I Take the GED Tests?

Since you are making the big commitment to study for the GED Tests, keep these goals in mind:

Educational   You may find that you need to further your education. Many technical or vocational schools and training programs now require a high school diploma or the equivalent. Certainly, most two-year and four-year colleges have that requirement.

Employment   Some employers now require a high school diploma or its equivalent to hire new workers. Also, even if you have a job, your employer may require a degree for advancement.

Personal Satisfaction and Growth   Maybe you don't have educational or employment reasons for wanting the GED. You may want to prove to yourself, your family, or your friends that you can do it—that you can achieve a high school diploma or certificate, whether you have been out of school for four years or forty years. You should know you are in good company—many people take and pass the GED just so they can say, "I did it!"

What's on the Tests?

Educational institutions and employers throughout the United States and Canada recognize the GED as a high school equivalency test. Every year, hundreds of thousands of individuals obtain GED diplomas or certificates as their first step toward further education or advancement in the workforce.

The GED is based on the major high school subject areas, as shown on the chart below. However, to pass the GED, you do not have to remember specific facts, dates, or terminology. Rather, you have to demonstrate that you can apply essential knowledge and skills to specific situations. This chart gives you basic information about the five test areas. Each section of this book begins with an "About the Test" overview with more detail and sample questions from each test area.

GED Test	Test Content	Question/Time Limit	Page Numbers
Language Arts, Writing	Sentence Structure • Organization • Usage • Mechanics Essay Writing	Part I: 50 multiple-choice questions in 75 minutes Part II: 1 essay in 45 minutes	61–160
Social Studies	U.S. History • World History • Geography • Economics • Civics and Government	50 multiple-choice questions in 70 minutes	161–228
Science	Life Science • Physical Science • Earth and Space Science	50 questions in 80 minutes	229–282
Language Arts, Reading	Fiction • Nonfiction • Drama • Poetry	40 questions in 65 minutes	283–340
Mathematics	Number Operations and Number Sense • Measurement and Geometry • Data Analysis, Statistics, and Probability • Algebra, Functions, and Patterns	Part I: 25 questions in 45 minutes with a calculator Part II: 25 questions in 45 minutes without a calculator	341–529

What Score Do I Need to Pass the GED?

You need two scores to pass the GED: an individual score for EACH test and an average score for ALL tests. The GED Testing Service has set a minimum passing score of 410 for each test and an average score of 450 for all of the tests. In addition, different jurisdictions (states, territories, and Canadian provinces) can set higher scores than the minimum. Contact your state Department of Education for the passing individual and average scores in your state.

What Do I Need to Know to Pass the GED?

In this book, you will see many skills and topics to study. Some of them may be familiar to you, and some may be new. However, there are four key skill areas that you will be developing in *Kaplan GED* that will help you pass the GED.

Reading and Thinking Skills As in all areas of life, reading is fundamental to passing the GED. On the test, you will have to read passages on the *Social Studies*, *Science*, and *Reading Tests* and answer questions based on them. On the *Writing Test*, you will need to read informational articles and business documents in order to answer questions about how to edit or improve them. On the *Mathematics Test*, you will read many word problems. Besides reading these materials, you will have to demonstrate that you can **think** about what you have read. For example, you may have to analyze a writer's point of view or evaluate whether there is support for a scientific conclusion.

Understanding Graphics The GED Tests recognize that a lot of information in our world is presented in the form of numbers and other data (charts and tables) and pictures (maps, diagrams, graphs, etc.). Because of this, sixty percent of the questions on the *Social Studies Test* are based on graphics alone or in combination with some text, and fifty percent of the questions on the *Science* and *Mathematics Tests* are based on graphics alone or in combination with some text.

Writing and Editing Whether you are planning to go on in school, advance in the workforce, or just keep in touch with family and friends, the ability to communicate effectively in writing is crucial. That's why the GED *Writing Test* requires you to compose an essay to demonstrate that you can organize your ideas, support them, and use correct sentence structure and grammar. The multiple-choice part of the *Writing Test* allows you to show how you can edit or improve a piece of existing writing by using many of the same skills that you needed to write your essay.

Math Problem Solving Because calculators and computers are commonly used to solve complicated problems, the focus of the GED *Mathematics Test* is on problem solving. Therefore, rather than solving complicated calculations, your focus will be on understanding what a given problem is asking for and deciding how to come up with a solution.

KAPLAN *GED* STRATEGIES FOR SUCCESS

In the rest of this book, you will be learning the material and skills for the GED Tests. In order to boost your score, you also need to learn some strategies that will help you succeed on the test. They are:

- **Get in the GED Mind-Set**
- **Learn How to Relax and Reduce Test Anxiety**
- **Take Control**

Get in the GED Mind-Set

Mind-Set 1: Think It Through

The GED tests your thinking skills, not your memory. It tests the analysis and problem-solving abilities that you have been developing all along in school and in life. You've got what it takes to pass the GED, if you use your thinking skills in the right way.

The GED is not like many of the tests you took in school. It is not a test where you recall facts or "write short-answer questions." It is a test that is designed to see whether you can apply the thinking, writing, and problem-solving skills needed to succeed in school or in the work-force. Many people approach the GED with the same mind-set that they had when they took tests in school. They are ready for a "memory" test, rather than a "thinking" test.

The good news is that most of the content of the GED will be pretty familiar. As you work through *Kaplan GED*, you may find that you are reviewing some material that you already know as you are learning some new content and thinking skills.

Just remember, the GED is not testing your ability to remember a lot of picky little facts. If you have prepared with this book, read each question carefully, and thought it through, you should be able to succeed on the GED.

Mind-Set 2: Put the Question into a Form That Makes Sense to You

Because the GED tests your thinking skills and not your memory, each question requires you to figure out what it is asking. Whether you are solving a math word problem or answering a question about a map in social studies, your first job is to make sense of the material and the question.

Look at the science question below and restate it in your own words.

Which of the following would help reduce the level of carbon dioxide in the atmosphere and thus slow the global warming trend?

Did you think something like the following? *What would lower the amount of carbon dioxide in the air—which would then slow down global warming?*

However you restate the question, use words and relate the ideas in a way that makes sense to you.

Mind-Set 3: Use the Material Provided to You

Since the GED isn't a memory test, don't rely on your memory. Use the passages and graphics that you are given to answer the question.

Many test takers jump right to the questions to see if they can answer them. As you know by now, most GED questions contain or are preceded by information that you need to answer the question. The information may be a passage, a graphic, or a combination of the two.

Sometimes more than one question is based on the same material. Your clue to that is a direction line that says something like this:

Questions 4 through 6 are based on the map of Egypt below.

That direction tells you that you will need to use the map for the next three questions.

As you work through this book, you should try the following strategies and see which one works best for you:

Strategy 1: Read passages carefully, and preview graphics to understand what they are telling you. Then work on answering each question. Don't rely on your memory, but refer back to the material provided to you as you try to answer the question.

Strategy 2: Skim the questions first (not the multiple-choice answers) so that you know what you are looking for when you read a passage or interpret a graphic. Then follow the advice in Strategy 1.

Mind-Set 4: Avoid Being Attracted by Misleading Answer Choices

Here's an inside tip. The wrong answer choices for a GED question are based on common errors in reading or in reasoning.

One of the reasons that the GED Tests can be challenging is that there are not "throwaway" answer choices. The correct answer is . . . well . . . correct, but the wrong answer choices have been written to attract your attention if you did not read carefully or if you didn't think through how to answer a question. Here's a common example of the second type of error.

> *Sophia borrowed $1000 for 2 years at 7 percent interest. How much did she have to pay back at the end of the 24 months?*

If you use the interest formula, *Interest = principal* times *rate* times *time*, you will get $140 in interest. You can be sure that would be one of the answer choices.

However, if you read the question carefully and use your common sense, you will know that a person couldn't borrow $1000 and pay back $140. That's only the interest. Sophia would have to pay back the whole amount plus the interest, or $1140.

Which raises another important point. After you have made a choice, ask yourself, *Does that answer make sense?* Your common sense may keep you from making foolish mistakes.

Mind-Set 5: Never Leave Any Answer Choices Blank

An unanswered question is always wrong. Try your best to reason out an answer. If you are stumped, use a process of elimination to narrow your choices.

Unlike some other standardized tests, the GED doesn't have a "wrong answer" penalty. A wrong answer and a blank answer count the same—as nothing. Since you are trying to raise your overall score on the tests as a whole, as well as your score on each individual test, it is important that you record an answer for each question.

Since you are trying to attain the highest possible score, you need to try to improve your score at every turn. Use your thinking skills and common sense, as we have been stressing to this point. But when all else fails, you may need to guess.

Before you take a guess, reread the question, review the answer choices, and eliminate the ones that you are sure are wrong. Then, read the question again and go back to the source material to see if one of your remaining choices seems more correct than others. If so, go with your best instincts. As you work through *Kaplan GED*, practice using the elimination strategy on questions that you are unsure about.

If all else fails, make a guess. You have a 1 in 5 chance of getting it correct—which is better than a 0 in 5 chance if you leave it blank.

The GED Examiner should let you know when you have 10 minutes left to finish a test. Finish up the question that you are working on and then maybe a few more. But in the last minute or two, fill in everything you have left blank.

Mind-Set 6: Be Careful with the Answer Sheet

Here's a scary scenario. Let's say you are ready to bubble in your answer to question 25 on the Writing Test, so you look down to where you are on the answer sheet—and you are not at question 25. Somehow, you got lost.

Your score on the GED is based on the answers that you fill in on the answer grid. Even if you figure out the answers to the questions, your answers won't count if you don't fill in the right bubble.

Make sure that you are filling in the correct question and corresponding answer choice carefully. If you change your mind, be sure to erase completely and mark your new answer completely. Machines, not people, score the answer sheets, and machines will read what they see, not what they think you meant.

If you want to skip a question and then come back to it later, make a <u>light</u> mark next to the number of the question so that you know which question or questions to refer to. Then return to those questions before the end of the test.

Learn to Relax and Reduce Test Anxiety

Adapted from the Kaplan Advantage™ Stress Management System

The countdown has begun. Your date with THE TEST is looming on the horizon. Anxiety is on the rise. The butterflies in your stomach have gone wild. Perhaps you feel as if the last thing you ate has turned into a lead ball. Your thinking is getting cloudy. Maybe you think you won't be ready. Maybe you already know your stuff, but you're going into panic mode already.

Don't panic. It is possible to tame that anxiety and stress—before *and* during the test. We'll show you how. You won't believe how quickly and easily you can deal with your anxiety.

1. Identify the Source of Your Anxiety

In the space provided, jot down anything that you identify as a source of your test-related stress. The idea is to pin down that free-floating anxiety so that you can take control of it. Here are some common examples:

- I always freeze up on tests.
- I haven't studied math for years.
- I have to get my GED to _____.
- I study like crazy, but nothing seems to stick.

Now write down five or six personal "sources of stress."

_____

_____

_____

_____

_____

Take a few minutes to think about what you've just written down. Then, on another sheet of paper, rewrite your ideas in order. Put your biggest sources of anxiety at the top of the list and the lesser items below. As you write the list, you are forming a hierarchy of anxiety producers that bother you the most. Experience shows, as you begin to reduce your stress by taking care of items at the top of the list, you will have gone a long way to relieving your test anxiety, and the problems at the bottom will begin to take care of themselves.

Start at the top of the list and develop a strategy to diffuse that source of stress.

2. Identify Your Areas of Strength and Weakness

There are five test areas on the GED: reading, writing, math, science, and social studies. Based on this list, write the areas in which you are strongest:

_____

Now identify the tests that you expect to be most problematic:

_____

Next, go back to the "strong" list and take two minutes to write why you are strong in those subject areas.

_____

_____

_____

_____

_____

_____

When you have stopped, check how much you wrote in two minutes. Do you think you could have written more? Is it possible that you need to give yourself more credit for what you are good at and what you like to do?

You just took an important step toward helping yourself pass the GED. Notice any increased feelings of confidence? Enjoy them.

Here's another way to think about what you wrote. Every area of strength and confidence is like a savings account that you can draw on. You can use your strengths to answer difficult problems, maintain confidence, and keep stress at a distance. For example, if you are good at reading but are worried about science, know that a lot of the science questions are based on reading science material that is provided on the test. Or if you like math but are worried about social studies, remember that you will use logical thinking on the *Social Studies Test*, as well as on the *Mathematics Test*.

3. Imagine Yourself Succeeding

Forcing relaxation is like asking yourself to flap your arms and fly. You can't do it, and every push and prod only gets you more frustrated. Relaxation is something you don't work at. You simply let it happen. Think about it. When was the last time that you tried to force yourself to go to sleep and it worked?

First, get yourself into a comfortable sitting position in a quiet setting. Wear loose clothing and take off any glasses. Close your eyes and breathe in a deep, satisfying breath of air. Really fill your lungs until your rib cage is fully expanded and you can't take in any more. Then exhale the air completely. Imagine that you are blowing out a candle with a little puff of air. Do this two or three more times, filling your lungs to the maximum and emptying them totally. Keep your eyes closed comfortably but not tightly. Let your body sink deeper into the chair as you become even more comfortable.

With your eyes shut, you can notice something very interesting. You're no longer dealing with the worrisome stuff going on in the world *outside* of you. Now you can concentrate on what happens *inside* of you. The more you recognize your own physical reactions to stress and anxiety, the more you can do about them. You may not realize it, but you've begun to regain a sense of control.

Let images begin to form on the "viewing screens" on the back of your eyelids. You're experiencing visualizations from the place in your mind that makes pictures. Allow the images to come easily and naturally. Imagine yourself in a relaxing situation. Make your picture as detailed as possible, and notice as much as you can. Think about the sights, tastes, and textures associated with this place. See and *feel* yourself in this place.

Stay focused on the images as you sink farther back into your chair. Breathe easily and naturally. You may have the sensations of any stress or tension draining from your muscles and flowing downward and away from you.

Take a minute to notice how comfortable you've become. Imagine how much easier it would be if you could take the GED feeling this relaxed. You've coupled the images of a special place with sensations of relaxation and comfort. You've found a way to relax through visualization.

Close your eyes again, and remember a real-life situation in which you did well on a test. If you can't come up with one, remember a situation in which you did something (in school or otherwise) that you were really proud of—a genuine accomplishment. Make the memory as detailed as possible. Remember how confident you felt when you accomplished your goal. Now start thinking about taking the GED Tests. Keep your thoughts and feelings in line with that successful situation. Don't make comparisons between them. Just imagine taking the GED with the same feelings of confidence and relaxed control.

This exercise is a great way to bring the test down to earth. You should practice this exercise often, especially when the prospect of taking the GED starts to create anxiety. The more you practice it, the more effective it will be for you.

4. Determine to Overcome Your Weaknesses

Let's get back to the list of your weak points on page xii. Take two minutes to expand it, just as you did with your list of strengths. Be honest with yourself without going overboard. It's an accurate appraisal of the test areas that give you trouble. So pick up your pencil, check your clock, and start writing.

_____

_____

_____

_____

_____

_____

_____

How did you do? Were you able to keep writing for the full two minutes? Has making this list helped you become clearer about the specific areas you need to work on?

Facing your weak spots gives you some distinct advantages. It helps a lot to realize that the WHOLE test can be broken down into areas of strengths and weaknesses. This allows you to build on your strengths to improve your scores in your strong areas and to focus on spending extra effort on your areas of weakness. Increased exposure to tough material makes it more familiar and less intimidating. Actually, you'll feel better about facing the test because you know that you're actively strengthening your chances of earning a higher overall score on the GED.

Take Control

Now that you have gotten into the GED mind-set and have practiced relaxing and reducing stress, you have to learn to take control, both in the days just before you take the GED and during the test itself.

Quick Tips for the Days Just Before You Take the GED

- **Ease up as Test Day approaches.**   The best test takers do less and less as "Test Day" approaches. Taper off on your study schedule and take it easy. You want to be ready, but you also want to be relaxed. Give yourself time off, especially the evening before you take the test. By that time, if you've studied well, everything you need to know has been covered.

- **Give yourself positive self-talk.**   Positive self-talk can be extremely liberating and invigorating, especially as the test looms closer. Tell yourself things such as, "I choose to take this test," rather than "I have to" and, "I will do well," rather than "I hope I can pass." Be aware of negative, self-defeating thoughts and images, and immediately counter those you become aware of. Replace them with positive statements that encourage your self-esteem and confidence.

- **Get your act together sooner rather than later.**   Have everything (including choice of clothing) laid out in advance. More importantly, be sure you know where the test will be held and the easiest, quickest way to get there. You will get great peace of mind if you know that all the little details—gas in the car, directions, etc.—are firmly in control on Test Day.

- **Go to the testing center a few days in advance.**   This is very helpful if you are especially anxious. If at all possible, find out what room you will take the test in, and sit in the room. Better still, bring some preparation material with you, and work on it in that room. Familiarity doesn't breed contempt; it generates comfort and confidence.

- **Don't study on the day before the test.**   It is best to marshal your physical and psychological resources for twenty-four hours or so. Even racehorses are kept in the paddock and treated like princes the day before a race. Keep the upcoming test out of your consciousness: go to a movie, take a hike, or just relax. Don't eat junk food or tons of sugar. And, of course, get plenty of rest the night before the test. Just don't go to bed too early. It's hard to fall asleep earlier than you're used to, and you don't want to lie there thinking about the test.

Handling Stress During the Test

The biggest stress monster will be Test Day itself. Fear not; there are methods of quelling your stress during the test.

- **Keep moving forward, instead of getting bogged down with a difficult question.** You don't have to get everything right to achieve a passing score. So don't linger on a question that is going nowhere, even after you have spent considerable time on it. Even the most successful test takers temporarily skip difficult material. You should lightly mark the ones that are left unanswered and be sure to come back to them before the test ends. But remember—before the test ends, make sure you leave no question unanswered.

- **Don't be thrown if other test takers seem to be working more quickly than you.** Continue to spend time patiently, but doggedly, thinking through your answers. This is going to lead to higher-quality test taking and better results. Don't mistake activity for a guarantee of correct test taking.

- **Manage your time.** Wear a watch or keep your eye on the clock. If you have a watch, set it at 12:00 at the beginning of each test so that it is easy to check the time. Even though the GED examiner will tell you how long you have for each test, you need to be in charge of your own time management. Easier questions will take you less time, and you need to be able to spend extra time on the more difficult ones.

- **Keep breathing!** Sometimes people forget to breathe when they are taking a test. No kidding! They start holding their breath without realizing it, or they breathe erratically. Improper breathing hurts confidence and accuracy. Just as importantly, it interferes with clear thinking.

- **Do some quick relaxation exercises during the test.** Do some quick isometrics during the test, especially if concentration is wandering or energy is waning. Try this: Put your palms together and press intensely for a few seconds. Concentrate on the tension you feel through your palms, wrists, forearms, and up into your biceps and shoulders. Then quickly release the pressure. Feel the difference as you let go. Focus on the warm relaxation that floods through the muscles. Now you're ready to return to the task.

  Here's another isometric that will relieve tension in both your neck and eye muscles. Slowly rotate your head from side to side, turning your head and eyes to look as far back over each shoulder as you can. Feel the muscles stretch on one side of your neck as they contract on the other. Repeat five times in each direction.

With what you've learned here, you're ready to face the test. This book and your other studies will give you the information you'll need to answer the questions. It's all firmly planted in your mind. You also know how to deal with any excess tension that might come along when you're studying for and when you're taking the GED Tests. You've practiced what you need to control your test anxiety and stress. Study productively, and you'll pass the GED.

Good luck!

GED Pretests

On the following pages, you will see pretests for the five GED Tests:

- Language Arts, Writing
- Social Studies
- Science
- Language Arts, Reading
- Mathematics

You can use these tests to evaluate your areas of strength and weakness and to make a study plan. Most of the questions will be in multiple-choice format. You may circle or check off your answers in this book or write them on a separate sheet of paper. There are two exceptions to this:

1. You will need to write an essay for Part II of the *Language Arts, Writing Test*.

2. On the *Mathematics Test*, you will need to fill in an answer sheet similar to the one that you will see on the GED Test. It includes three types of items:

- **Answer choices** to "bubble-in" like this:

  ① ② ● ④ ⑤

- A **grid** to be filled in like this:

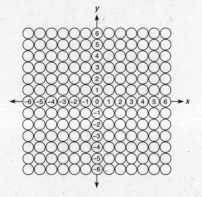

- A **coordinate graph** to be filled in with a plotted point:

Be sure to check your answers with the *Pretest Answers and Explanations* that begin on page 45. At the end of the answers are *Pretest Planning Charts*, which start on page 57. These charts enable you to target your problem areas so that you can plan your study in the most effective manner.

Language Arts, Writing Pretest: Part I

Questions 1 through 6 refer to the following paragraphs.

To: Parents and Guardians
From: Sonia Vasquez, School Nurse

(A)

(1) A student in your child's class have been diagnosed with strep throat. (2) Strep throat is a highly contagious disease and a common illness in children. (3) Unlike most sore throats, which are caused by viruses, strep throat is caused by bacteria and is treatable with antibiotics. (4) The time between exposure to the disease and the appearance of symptoms is usually one to three days. (5) To safeguard your child's health, please take the following precautions. (6) Watch your child for strep symptoms. (7) Such as sore throat, fever, swollen glands, and headache. (8) If your child developed any of these symptoms, take him or her to the doctor. (9) If a throat culture is positive, treatment can be started. (10) It is extremely important to take all the prescribed medicine until it is gone.

(B)

(11) Children should get immediate treatment for several reasons. (12) For one, treatment reduces spread of the disease. (13) In addition antibiotics may prevent rheumatic fever. (14) Treatment also prevents other rare but possibly dangerous complications.

(C)

(15) Your child may return to school after taking medicine for 24 hours and the fever must be gone. (16) Please call us with any questions or concerns you have.

1. Sentence 1: **A student in your child's class have been diagnosed with strep throat.**

   Which correction should be made to sentence 1?

   (1) replace your with you're
   (2) change child's to children
   (3) insert a comma after class
   (4) change have to has
   (5) no correction is necessary

2. Sentences 6 and 7: **Watch your child for strep symptoms. Such as sore throat, fever, swollen glands, and headache.**

   Which is the best way to write the underlined portion of these sentences? If the original is the best way, choose option (1).

   (1) symptoms. Such as
   (2) symptoms such as
   (3) symptoms, the best known are
   (4) symptoms, and such as
   (5) symptoms examples are

3. Sentence 8: **If your child developed any of these symptoms, take him or her to the doctor.**

   Which correction should be made to sentence 8?

   (1) replace your with you're
   (2) change developed to develops
   (3) remove the comma
   (4) replace him or her with them
   (5) change doctor to Doctor

4. Which revision would improve the effectiveness of the memo?

   Begin a new paragraph with

   (1) sentence 3
   (2) sentence 4
   (3) sentence 5
   (4) sentence 6
   (5) sentence 9

5. Sentence 13: **In addition antibiotics may prevent rheumatic fever.**

   Which correction should be made to sentence 13?

   (1) insert a comma after addition
   (2) insert a comma after antibiotics
   (3) change may prevent to are preventing
   (4) change rheumatic fever to Rheumatic Fever
   (5) no correction is necessary

6. Sentence 15: **Your child may return to school after taking medicine for 24 hours and the fever must be gone.**

   The most effective revision of sentence 15 would begin with which group of words?

   (1) After the fever is gone and your child has taken
   (2) Having taken medicine for 24 hours and the fever
   (3) Your child, once having taken medicine for 24 hours, may
   (4) The fever being gone and the medicine being finished,
   (5) Since the fever is gone and your child

Questions 7 through 12 refer to the following paragraphs.

Compulsive Gambling

(A)

(1) Most of us can bet on a football game, or buy a lottery ticket with little damage to our finances. (2) In contrast, compulsive gamblers cannot stop even when their behavior had threatened to ruin their lives.

(B)

(3) Gambling frequently occupies their thoughts. (4) For instance, they may be reliving past gambling experiences or coming up with schemes to get more money for gambling. (5) Although they may have tried several times to stop gambling, their efforts met with failure. (6) When trying to stop gambling, they feel irritable and restless. (7) They need to gamble with more and more money in order to enjoy it, losing money increases their desire to gamble. (8) They may even commit fraud forgery, or theft to get the funds to continue their habit. (9) Many of them have lost jobs, important relationships, or career opportunities because of their involvement with gambling.

(C)

(10) Compulsive gambling is like any other addiction. (11) As gamblers lose control over gambling, they lose control over their lives as well. (12) They may become anxious and depressed, or they may fail to live up to their obligations, causing others to stop trusting them.

(D)

(13) Treatment for compulsive gambling is similar to therapy for other forms of addiction. (14) Gamblers Anonymous, a 12-step program similar to Alcoholics Anonymous, provides a supportive environment for change. (15) Group therapy with recovering gamblers is also helpful because people who have the same problem can easily spot a gambler's denial and defense mechanisms. (17) In addition, some medications are being investigated.

7. Sentence 1: **Most of us can bet on a football game, or buy a lottery ticket with little damage to our finances.**

Which correction should be made to sentence 1?

(1) insert a comma after us
(2) change bet to be betting
(3) remove the comma
(4) insert a comma after ticket
(5) no correction is necessary

8. Sentence 2: **In contrast, compulsive gamblers cannot stop even when their behavior had threatened to ruin their lives.**

Which is the best way to write the underlined portion of this sentence? If the original is the best way, choose option (1).

(1) had threatened
(2) will threaten
(3) threatens
(4) having threatened
(5) threatened

9. Which sentence would be most effective if inserted at the beginning of paragraph B?

(1) Compulsive gamblers have a lot of problems.
(2) Some people engage in compulsive gambling.
(3) Gamblers escape from negative emotions.
(4) Gambling is an addiction.
(5) Compulsive gamblers display a number of consistent traits.

10. Sentence 7: **They need to gamble with more and more money in order to enjoy <u>it, losing</u> money increases their desire to gamble.**

Which is the best way to write the underlined portion of this sentence? If the original is the best way, choose option (1).

(1) it, losing
(2) it but losing
(3) it, now that losing
(4) it and losing
(5) it. Losing

11. Sentence 8: **They may even commit fraud forgery, or theft to get the funds to continue their habit.**

Which correction should be made to sentence 8?

(1) insert a comma after <u>fraud</u>
(2) insert a comma after <u>theft</u>
(3) replace <u>their</u> with <u>there</u>
(4) replace <u>their</u> with <u>they're</u>
(5) no correction is necessary

12. Sentence 12: **They may become anxious and <u>depressed, or they</u> may fail to live up to their obligations, causing others to stop trusting them.**

Which is the best way to write the underlined portion of this sentence? If the original is the best way, choose option (1).

(1) depressed, or they
(2) depressed or they
(3) depressed, they
(4) depressed. Or
(5) depressed and they

Questions 13 through 18 are based on the following paragraphs.

Choosing a Pet

(A)

(1) After seeing an adorable puppy or kitten in a pet store, pets are often selected on impulse. (2) Unhappily, these poor creatures are likely to end up at animal shelters when the owners find he can't care for them. (3) To avoid this outcome, choose your pet wisely. (4) Remember that your pet will become a member of your family and a daily responsibility.

(B)

(5) There's a number of factors to consider when selecting a pet. (6) First of all, do you have the time to care for a pet? (7) While some pets require little care, puppies and kittens need to be housebroken and to train them. (8) If the animal needs exercise, is your home large enough? (9) Would you enjoy taking your pet outdoors for exercise? (10) Do you think people should get a lot of exercise? (11) Can you afford the costs of food, vaccinations, and health checkups? (12) Does your building allow pets? (13) Finally, if you must leave home for a few days, can you find someone to care for your pet?

(C)

(14) Once you choose a pet that is appropriate for your lifestyle, bring the animal to a veterinarian for examination. (15) You should be able to return the pet if he or she was unhealthy.

13. Sentence 1: **After seeing an adorable puppy or kitten in a pet store, pets are often selected on impulse.**

The most effective revision of sentence 1 would begin with which group of words?

(1) The selection of a pet often occurs on
(2) People often select pets on impulse after
(3) After an adorable pet is seen in a
(4) Impulse is often responsible for pet
(5) Having seen a puppy or kitten in a pet

14. Sentence 2: **Unhappily, these poor creatures are likely to end up at animal shelters when the owners find he can't care for them.**

Which correction should be made to sentence 2?

(1) remove the comma
(2) change <u>animal shelters</u> to <u>Animal Shelters</u>
(3) insert a comma after <u>shelters</u>
(4) replace <u>he</u> with <u>they</u>
(5) no correction is necessary

15. Sentence 5: **There's a number of factors to consider when selecting a pet.**

Which correction should be made to sentence 5?

(1) change There's to There are
(2) insert a comma after factors
(3) replace to with too
(4) insert a comma after consider
(5) change selecting to to select

16. Sentence 7: **While some pets require little care, puppies and kittens need to be housebroken and to train them.**

Which is the best way to write the underlined portion of the sentence? If the original is the best way, choose option (1).

(1) be housebroken and to train them
(2) housebreak and train
(3) housebreaking and training
(4) be housebroken and trained
(5) be housebroken and training

17. Which revision should be made to the placement of sentence 10?

(1) move sentence 10 to the beginning of paragraph B
(2) move sentence 10 to follow sentence 6
(3) move sentence 10 to the beginning of paragraph C
(4) remove sentence 10
(5) no revision is necessary

18. Sentence 15: **You should be able to return the pet if the animal was unhealthy.**

Which correction should be made to sentence 15?

(1) change You to One
(2) insert a comma after pet
(3) replace if with and
(4) change was to is
(5) change was to would be

Questions 19 through 25 refer to the following paragraphs.

Kites and Science

(A)

(1) Who doesn't enjoy flying a kite? (2) When you seen people in your community flying kites on a windy day, you might think that kites are just for fun. (3) Kites have been flown in countries around the world and for centuries, by young and old alike. (4) However, kite flying, it may surprise you to know, have been responsible for a number of scientific discoveries.

(B)

(5) In 1752, Benjamin Franklin used a kite to prove the presence of electricity in storm clouds. (6) He did it by flying a kite during a thunderstorm with a brass key attached to the end. (7) When lightning struck the kite line and traveled down to the key, their was a spark of electricity.

(C)

(8) Kites also played a role in learning about the weather. (9) In 1749, Alexander Wilson of Scotland became the first scientist to send a thermometer aloft in a kite. (10) Starting in the 1890s, kites held meteorological instruments that also measured humidity and wind speed. (11) They measured barometric pressure too.

(D)

(12) Kites were an early form of aircraft. (13) The Wright Brothers, inventors of the first plane, experimented with kites. (14) Alexander Graham Bell, the physicist and inventor, used kites to learn about problems of airplane construction.

(E)

(15) So the next time you see some neighborhood children flying kites, just think. (16) You may be watching budding young scientists.

19. Sentence 2: **When you seen people flying kites in your community on a windy day, you might think that kites are just for fun.**

Which is the best way to write the underlined portion of the sentence? If the original is the best way, choose option (1).

(1) seen
(2) saw
(3) see
(4) have seen
(5) seeing

20. Sentence 3: **Kites have been flown in countries around the world and for centuries, by young and old alike.**

Which revision should be made to the placement of sentence 3?

(1) move sentence 3 to the beginning of paragraph A
(2) move sentence 3 to follow sentence 1
(3) move sentence 3 to follow sentence 4
(4) remove sentence 3
(5) no revision is necessary

21. Sentence 4: **However, kite flying, it may surprise you to know, <u>have been</u> responsible for a number of scientific discoveries.**

Which is the best way to write the underlined portion of the sentence? If the original is the best way, choose option (1).

(1) have been
(2) has been
(3) were
(4) been
(5) are

22. Sentence 6: **He did it by flying a kite during a thunderstorm with a brass key attached to the end.**

The most effective revision of sentence 6 would begin with which group of words?

(1) Attaching a brass key to the end of a kite
(2) By flying a kite with a brass key
(3) The kite was flown during a thunderstorm
(4) A brass key was attached to the end
(5) During a thunderstorm, he flew a kite with

23. Sentence 7: **When lightning struck the kite line and traveled down to the key, their was a spark of electricity.**

Which correction should be made to sentence 7?

(1) insert a comma after <u>line</u>
(2) change <u>traveled</u> to <u>travels</u>
(3) remove the comma after <u>key</u>
(4) replace <u>their</u> with <u>there</u>
(5) no correction is necessary

24. Sentences 10 and 11: **Starting in the 1890s, kites held meteorological instruments that measured humidity and wind speed. They measured barometric pressure too.**

The most effective combination of sentences 10 and 11 would include which group of words?

(1) one of the purposes was measuring wind
(2) humidity, wind speed, and barometric pressure
(3) barometric pressure was measured along with
(4) meteorological instruments such as
(5) the measurement of barometric pressure

25. Sentence 14: **Alexander Graham <u>Bell, the physicist and inventor, used</u> kites to learn about problems of airplane construction.**

Which is the best way to write the underlined portion of the sentence? If the original is the best way, choose option (1).

(1) Bell, the physicist and inventor, used
(2) Bell the physicist and inventor, used
(3) Bell, the physicist and inventor used
(4) Bell the physicist and inventor used
(5) Bell, the physicist and inventor, he used

Answers and explanations start on page 45.

LANGUAGE ARTS, WRITING PRETEST: PART II

Following are the directions for writing a GED essay as they appear on the actual test.

Essay Directions and Topic

Look at the box on the next page. In the box are your assigned topic and the letter of that topic.

You must write on the assigned topic ONLY.

You will have 45 minutes to write on your assigned essay topic. You may return to the multiple-choice section after you complete your essay if you have time remaining in this test period. Do not return the Language Arts, Writing Test booklet until you finish both Parts I and II of the Language Arts, Writing Test.

Two evaluators will score your essay according to its overall effectiveness. Their evaluation will be based on the following features:

- ❏ Well-focused main points
- ❏ Clear organization
- ❏ Specific development of your ideas
- ❏ Control of sentence structure, punctuation, grammar, word choice, and spelling

REMEMBER, YOU MUST COMPLETE BOTH THE MULTIPLE-CHOICE QUESTIONS (PART I) AND THE ESSAY (PART II) TO RECEIVE A SCORE ON THE LANGUAGE ARTS, WRITING TEST. To avoid having to repeat both parts of the test, be sure to do the following:

- ❏ Do not leave the pages blank.
- ❏ Write legibly in ink so that the evaluators will be able to read your writing.
- ❏ Write on the assigned topic. If you write on a topic other than the one assigned, you will not receive a score for the Language Arts, Writing Test.
- ❏ Write your essay on the lined pages of the separate answer sheet booklet. Only the writing on these pages will be scored.

TOPIC

What is some important goal you would like to achieve in the next few years?

In your essay, identify that goal. Explain how you plan to achieve it.

Use your personal observations, experience, and knowledge to support your answer.

Part II is a test to determine how well you can use written language to explain your ideas. In preparing your essay, you should take the following steps:

❑ Read the **DIRECTIONS** and the **TOPIC** carefully.

❑ Plan your essay before you write. Use the scratch paper provided to make any notes. These notes will be collected but not scored.

❑ Before you turn in your essay, reread what you have written and make any changes that will improve your essay.

Your essay should be long enough to develop the topic adequately.

Reprinted with permission of the GED Testing Service of the American Council on Education.

Essay evaluation guidelines start on page 46.

GED Social Studies Pretest

Choose the <u>one best answer</u> to each question.

<u>Questions 1 and 2</u> refer to the following map.

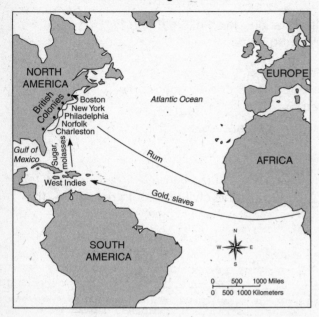

Colonial Triangular Trade

1. Based on this map, what were the three sides of the triangle in the triangular trade?

   (1) Europe to the West Indies; the West Indies to Africa; Africa to the British colonies
   (2) the West Indies to the British colonies; the British colonies to Africa; Africa to the West Indies
   (3) the West Indies to England; England to the British colonies; the British colonies to Africa
   (4) South America to Africa; Africa to the West Indies; the West Indies to the British colonies
   (5) England to Africa; Africa to South America; South America to the West Indies

2. Which statement is a conclusion based on the map rather than a supporting detail from the map?

   (1) Cargo ships never had to sail empty on any leg of a profitable triangular journey.
   (2) The journey of Africans from Africa to the Americas was called the Middle Passage.
   (3) Slaves sometimes sailed on cargo ships from the West Indies to the British colonies.
   (4) Rum was shipped from one of the ports on the east coast of North America.
   (5) Gold was shipped from Africa to the Americas.

<u>Question 3</u> refers to the following information.

Several types of U.S. banking institutions and some of their main services are described below.

Federal Reserve Banks   The central banking system of the United States, used by the federal government to control the money supply.
Commercial banks   Provide checking accounts, savings accounts, and loans for businesses and consumers
Investment banks   Provide long-term financing to businesses by underwriting, distributing, and trading stocks and bonds
Savings banks   Provide savings accounts, checking accounts, and home mortgage loans to consumers
Credit unions   Provide savings accounts, often at a higher rate of interest, and make home mortgage loans, often at a lower rate of interest, to people who are members

3. At which type of banking institution would a consumer probably get the best deal on her home mortgage?

   (1) Federal Reserve Bank
   (2) commercial bank
   (3) investment bank
   (4) savings bank
   (5) credit union

Questions 4 and 5 refer to the following passage from a state agency brochure.

Welcome to the Maximum Recycling Program, which lets you recycle up to 40 percent of your trash. There is no fee for your town to bring recyclables to Smithtown. Your town will save money because your recyclables won't be dumped (for a fee) at the Central Landfill.

Maximum recycling is easy. Here's how:

Blue bin	Glass bottles, metal cans, and plastic containers
Green bin	Paper, thin cardboard, and bagged textiles
Bundles	Newspapers

Put your recycling bins out for pickup on the same day as trash collection.

4. Which incentives to recycle does the state resource recovery agency emphasize?

(1) cleaning up the environment and conserving resources for the future
(2) conserving resources for the future and saving the town money
(3) saving the town money and making recycling convenient
(4) making recycling convenient and reducing the total amount of material put out for pickup
(5) reducing the total amount of trash and increasing the number of trash collection days

5. Which of the following actions would probably increase the rate of household participation the most?

(1) requiring that households bring their recyclables to a collection center
(2) requiring that households remove labels as well as lids from containers
(3) charging the town a fee for bringing recyclables to the Smithtown facility
(4) fining each household that mixes its recyclables in with the regular trash
(5) distributing another brochure about the Maximum Recycling Program

6. Most Americans believe it is their civic duty to take part in the political system.

Which of the following actions represents participation in the political system?

(1) pursuing higher education
(2) displaying the American flag
(3) volunteering at a hospital
(4) starting a local business
(5) serving on a jury

7. In many Latin American countries, control passes back and forth between military and civilian rule. Generally, when a civilian government rules, it tries to improve conditions for the nation's citizens, but these attempts lead to turmoil and civil unrest. In response, the military takes power and imposes strict controls on the populace. Such shifts have taken place in Argentina, Peru, and Chile in recent decades.

Which of the following is highly valued by those who favor military rule?

(1) social welfare
(2) freedom
(3) democracy
(4) law and order
(5) the right to privacy

Questions 8 and 9 refer to the following chart.

Presidential Powers in Several Nations

Constitutional Power	U.S.A.	South Africa	France	Mexico	Egypt
Controls armed forces	✔		✔	✔	✔
Approves legislation	✔	✔	✔	✔	✔
Appoints executive branch officials	✔	✔	✔	✔	✔
Appoints judges	✔	✔	✔	✔	
Appoints prime minister			✔		✔
Dissolves legislature			✔		

8. What is the main difference between the powers of the U.S. and South African presidents?

   (1) The U.S. president controls the armed forces and the South African president does not.
   (2) The U.S. president approves legislation and the South African president does not.
   (3) The U.S. president appoints judges and the South African president does not.
   (4) The U.S. president appoints executive branch officials and the South African president does not.
   (5) The U.S. president can dissolve the legislature and the South African president cannot.

9. Which of the following statements is a conclusion based on the chart rather than a detail?

   (1) The president of Egypt has the power to appoint a prime minister.
   (2) Of all the presidents shown, the French president has the most power.
   (3) The president of Mexico has the power to appoint judges.
   (4) The U.S. president has the power to approve legislation.
   (5) The presidents of both South Africa and France have the power to dissolve the legislature.

Question 10 refers to the following paragraph.

After the Civil War, southern states passed Jim Crow laws, which kept whites and blacks apart in public places like restaurants, buses, and rest rooms. In an 1896 case, *Plessy v. Ferguson,* the U.S. Supreme Court upheld a Louisiana law requiring separate railroad cars for white and black passengers. The court ruled that it was constitutional to have "separate but equal" facilities for whites and blacks and other minorities. The Court reasoned that "Legislation is powerless to eradicate racial instincts or to abolish distinctions." One justice dissented, saying that the decision was "inconsistent with the personal liberty of citizens, white and black."

10. Which of the following statements is an opinion rather than a fact?

   (1) In the late 1800s, many southern states passed Jim Crow laws to keep whites and blacks separate in public places.
   (2) In Louisiana, a law required separate railroad cars for white and black passengers.
   (3) *Plessy v. Ferguson* was an 1896 Supreme Court case that challenged the Louisiana law related to segregated railroad cars.
   (4) The U.S. Supreme Court upheld Louisiana's right to enact laws that provided for separate but equal public facilities.
   (5) The U.S. Supreme Court ruling in *Plessy v. Ferguson* was wrong because it infringed on freedoms guaranteed in the Constitution.

11. The Global Positioning System can pinpoint any location on Earth. Twenty-four GPS satellites orbit Earth, transmitting signals that can be picked up by anyone with a GPS receiver anywhere on the planet. A basic handheld GPS receiver gives its location in terms of degrees of latitude and longitude on the global grid.

Michael bought a basic handheld GPS receiver because he thought it would help him find his way around Los Angeles. Why wasn't this type of GPS receiver very useful for this purpose?

(1) GPS satellites do not orbit over Los Angeles.
(2) The GPS receiver transmitted faulty signals.
(3) The latitude and longitude grid does not extend over urban areas.
(4) Knowing only latitude and longitude does not help a person get around a city.
(5) Los Angeles is a huge city with a complex street pattern.

Questions 12 and 13 refer to the following paragraph and graph.

When the U.S. government cannot cover its expenses, it borrows money by selling bonds. It pays back the principal and interest on the bonds over a period of many years. The national debt is the total amount the U.S. government owes at any particular point in time. In 2000, this was about $5.7 trillion.

One way of measuring the national debt is by computing the per capita national debt. The per capita national debt is total national debt divided by the population of the United States. The graph in column 2 shows figures for the per capita national debt every five years from 1980 to 2000.

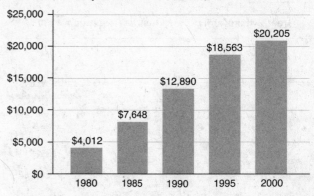

Per Capita U.S. National Debt, 1980–2000

SOURCE: U.S. Bureau of the Census and *Statistical Abstract of the United States.*

12. Which of the following conclusions is supported by the data in the paragraph and the graph?

(1) The per capita national debt tripled between 1980 and 2000.
(2) The nation's debt increased at a faster rate than did the U.S. population during the period shown on the graph.
(3) Every person in the United States owed an average of $20,000 to the government in the year 2000.
(4) In 1980, the U.S. government owed every American about $4,000.
(5) The U.S. government sold about $5.7 trillion worth of bonds in 2000.

13. Which action would enable the U.S. government to pay off the debt?

(1) declare bankruptcy
(2) pay interest to foreign investors
(3) pay interest to U.S. investors
(4) raise taxes
(5) raise social security payments

Question 14 refers to the following map.

Great Britain During the Industrial Revolution, 1830

14. Which of the following is a conclusion based on the map rather than a supporting detail from the map?

   (1) The Industrial Revolution took place in Great Britain around the year 1830.
   (2) More than 300,000 people lived in Sheffield around 1830.
   (3) Many cities had large populations because nearby coal and iron ore deposits meant jobs.
   (4) There was a large area with coal deposits in southern Wales about 1830.
   (5) Glasgow, Scotland, was very close to areas that had coalfields and iron ore deposits.

15. When a nation follows a policy of appeasement, it makes concessions to an aggressor in order to preserve the peace.

   Which of the following is an example of appeasement?

   (1) Italy's support of Spanish Nationalists in the Spanish Civil War in the late 1930s
   (2) Great Britain's acceptance of Germany's takeover of Austria and Czechoslovakia in the late 1930s
   (3) Germany's 1939 invasion of Poland, which started World War II
   (4) Japan's alliance with Germany and Italy in 1940, creating the Rome-Berlin-Tokyo Axis
   (5) The United States moving the Pacific fleet to Pearl Harbor early in 1941 in reaction to Japanese aggression in Asia

Questions 16 through 18 refer to the following poster.

Source: From the poster collection of the Library of the American Legion National Headquarters, Indianapolis, Indiana

16. The person who designed this poster used irony to make a point. Behind this irony was an assumption with which the designer expected viewers to agree.

Which of the following statements summarizes this assumption?

(1) People will give to the war effort because they are doing well economically.
(2) Financing the war requires selling bonds and raising taxes.
(3) During wartime, people have little money to spend on their sons.
(4) People value the lives of their children more than they value money.
(5) A quick end to the war will save soldiers' lives.

17. During which war was this poster part of a government advertising campaign?

(1) the Civil War
(2) World War I
(3) World War II
(4) the Vietnam War
(5) the Persian Gulf War

18. If the government were running a similar advertising campaign today, which medium would probably be most effective?

(1) posters
(2) leaflets and brochures
(3) print ads in financial newspapers
(4) radio ads on classical stations
(5) television ads at prime time

Question 19 refers to the following chart.

The Five Most Populous American Colonies, 1750

Colony	Population (estimate)
Massachusetts	188,000
Pennsylvania	119,700
Connecticut	111,300
Maryland	141,000
Virginia	231,000

SOURCE: U.S. Bureau of the Census.

19. Which of the following statements is supported by the data in the chart?

(1) The population of all of the American colonies was less than 700,000.
(2) Virginia had more than twice as many people as Maryland.
(3) Most of the population of Massachusetts was of English origin.
(4) The two most populous colonies were Massachusetts and Pennsylvania.
(5) The population of the colony of New York was smaller than that of Connecticut.

Questions 20 through 22 refer to the following paragraph and flowchart.

The U.S. Civil Service system is designed to ensure that people are appointed to government positions because of their skills and abilities rather than because of their political affiliation. Over 90 percent of federal jobs are covered by civil service rules. The typical steps in applying for a civil service job are shown below.

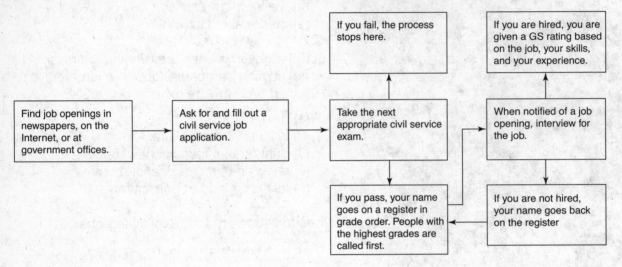

20. Which of the following is the best title for the flowchart?

(1) A History of the Civil Service
(2) The Qualifications of Civil Service Workers
(3) Applying for Civil Service Jobs
(4) Interviewing for a Civil Service Job
(5) The Politics of the Civil Service

21. What does a civil servant's GS rating probably affect most?

(1) salary
(2) length of service
(3) job security
(4) education level
(5) the agency in which the job is located

22. On which of the following values does the structure of the Civil Service system primarily rest?

(1) patriotism
(2) equal opportunity
(3) freedom of speech
(4) respect for seniority
(5) loyalty to one's political party

Questions 23 and 24 refer to the following graphs.

Interest Rates for Conventional Mortgages

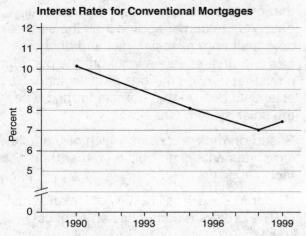

SOURCE: U.S. Bureau of the Census.

U.S. Mortgage Debt Outstanding

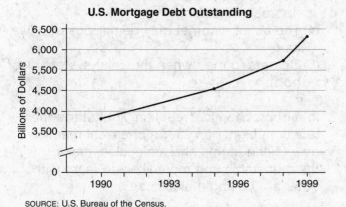

SOURCE: U.S. Bureau of the Census.

23. In 1995, what were the approximate interest rate and approximate total mortgage debt outstanding for a conventional mortgage?

(1) 10 percent and $3,500 billion
(2) 8 percent and $4,500 billion
(3) 7 percent and $5,000 billion
(4) 7 percent and $5,500 billion
(5) 6 percent and $6,000 billion

24. In general, based on the graphs, how do mortgage interest rates and total mortgage debt outstanding compare?

(1) The lower the interest rate, the higher the total mortgage debt outstanding.
(2) The lower the interest rate, the lower the total mortgage debt outstanding.
(3) The higher the interest rate, the higher the total mortgage debt outstanding.
(4) Interest rates rise in direct proportion to increases in total mortgage debt outstanding.
(5) Interest rates fall in direct proportion to decreases in total mortgage debt outstanding.

25. A culture hearth refers to the center of a culture—the source of its ideas, values, customs, fashions, and practices. An example of an ancient culture hearth was the area along the Nile River in Egypt. The agricultural, economic, social, artistic, and religious ideas and practices that grew up there spread through trade to other areas of the ancient world.

Which of the following is an example of a modern culture hearth with worldwide influence?

(1) Pyongyang, capital of North Korea, which has a 95 percent literacy rate
(2) Zaire, which exports gold, diamonds, and other minerals
(3) Ottawa, capital of Canada, with a population of about one million
(4) New Zealand, which exports wool and textiles
(5) Hollywood, California, with its movie and television entertainment industry

Answers and explanations start on page 50.

GED Science Pretest

Directions: Choose the one best answer to each question.

Question 1 refers to the following paragraph and diagram.

A neuron is the basic functional unit of the nervous system. Neurons transmit information throughout the body.

A Neuron

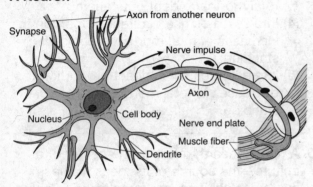

1. Which of the following is implied by the paragraph and the diagram?

   (1) Neurons are part of the endocrine system.
   (2) Oxygen is carried throughout the body by neurons.
   (3) Neurons transmit instructions regarding movement to muscles.
   (4) Nerve impulses travel from the axon to the cell body.
   (5) The cell body of a neuron lacks a nucleus.

2. A comet is a small body made of ice and dust that orbits the sun in an elliptical, or oval, path. As the comet approaches the sun, its core heats up, releasing gas and dust. The gas and dust stream away from the comet in a tail that may be millions of miles long. Some scientists believe that comets formed when the solar system was born.

   Based on the paragraph, which of the following statements is an opinion rather than a fact?

   (1) Comets are small bodies of ice and dust.
   (2) The orbit of a comet has an elliptical shape.
   (3) Comets release gas and dust as they approach the sun.
   (4) The tail of a comet may be millions of miles long.
   (5) Comets formed when the solar system was born.

3. In a photochemical reaction, light starts the reaction. Light can start a chemical reaction by exciting atoms and molecules, making them unstable and more likely to react with other atoms and molecules.

   Which of the following is an example of a photochemical reaction?

   (1) polymerization, in which long-chain organic compounds are formed from repeating units called monomers
   (2) fractional distillation, in which various petroleum products are separated out of crude oil
   (3) neutralization, in which an acid and a base react to form a salt and water
   (4) anodizing, which results in the building up of a protective oxide layer on the surface of a metal
   (5) photosynthesis, in which green plants use the energy from sunlight to make carbohydrates from water and carbon dioxide

Questions 4 through 6 refer to the following chart.

Some Glands of the Endocrine System

Endocrine Gland	Hormone	Function
Pituitary gland	Growth hormone	Promotes bone and muscle growth
Ovary	Estrogen	Stimulates development of female secondary sexual characteristics
Testis	Testosterone	Stimulates development of male secondary sexual characteristics
Adrenal gland	Adrenaline	Increases heart activity, breathing rate, and blood flow to muscles for "fight or flight"
Thyroid	Thyroxine	Regulates metabolism and growth
Pancreas	Insulin	Regulates blood sugar levels

4. What is the function of the hormone thyroxine?

(1) It controls female secondary sexual characteristics.
(2) It controls male secondary sexual characteristics.
(3) It speeds up the pulse and breathing rate for "fight or flight".
(4) It helps control metabolism and growth.
(5) It helps control blood sugar levels.

5. People who have one form of the disease diabetes mellitus do not produce enough insulin. Based on the chart, what is the general effect of this disease?

(1) stunted growth
(2) excess growth
(3) overproduction of estrogen
(4) overproduction of testosterone
(5) uncontrolled blood sugar levels

6. Paul, a child who was not growing as rapidly as he should, was given growth hormone to stimulate his growth. Paul anticipated that the hormone would enable him to reach an adult height of over six feet, even though his parents are both below average height. In fact, Paul's adult height was 5 feet 7 inches. What was wrong with Paul's thinking?

(1) Growth hormone is only one of several factors that determine a person's adult height.
(2) Growth hormone, when administered as a drug, does not affect a person's height.
(3) In order to grow to over six feet tall, Paul would have had to take thyroxine, too.
(4) In order to grow to over six feet tall, Paul would have had to take testosterone, too.
(5) Growth hormone is effective only when given to adults.

7. An emulsion is a mixture of two liquids whose particles are evenly scattered in one another without dissolving. Emulsions are unstable. After a time, the liquids separate.

Which of the following is an emulsion?

(1) tea with sugar
(2) salt water
(3) oil and vinegar salad dressing
(4) food coloring and water
(5) freshly brewed coffee

8. Earth science includes the study of Earth's atmosphere—the layer of gases that surrounds Earth—and Earth's hydrosphere—the oceans, rivers, lakes, and groundwater.

Which of the following scientists would be most likely to apply knowledge from a study of both the atmosphere and hydrosphere to his or her work?

(1) a geologist who studies volcanoes and mountain formation
(2) an astronomer who studies the planets of the solar system
(3) a meteorologist who studies weather patterns and predicts weather
(4) an ecologist who studies the distribution of populations of organisms
(5) an entomologist who studies the effects of pesticides on insects

Question 9 refers to the following chart.

Organisms in a Food Chain

Role	Description
Producer	Green plants, which produce their own food using energy from sunlight
Herbivore	An animal that gets nutrients by eating plants
Carnivore	An animal that gets nutrients by eating other animals
Omnivore	An animal that gets nutrients by eating both plants and animals
Decomposer	An organism that gets nutrients from feeding on dead organisms and returns nutrients to the soil in the process

9. Earthworms break down large pieces of dead organic material in the soil. What role do earthworms play in the food chain?

(1) They are producers.
(2) They are herbivores.
(3) They are carnivores.
(4) They are omnivores.
(5) They are decomposers.

Question 10 refers to the following graph.

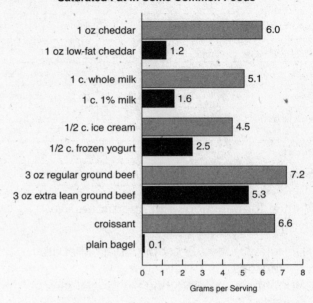

10. Suppose a child's diet usually includes two servings of cheese, four servings of milk, one serving of ice cream or frozen yogurt, one serving of ground beef, and a croissant or bagel every day.

If the child's parent wanted to decrease the amount of saturated fat in the child's diet, which of the following actions would be most effective?

(1) switch from regular to low-fat cheddar
(2) switch from whole milk to 1 percent milk
(3) switch from frozen yogurt to ice cream
(4) switch from regular to extra lean ground beef
(5) switch from croissants to bagels

11. Torque is the ability of a force to produce rotation. The torque of any force is equal to the amount of the force multiplied by the distance from the pivot point to the point where the force is applied. For example, when you go through a revolving door, you are applying force as you push. The torque of your force is equal to the force you apply times the distance between your hand and the axis of the revolving door.

Which of the following actions would decrease torque as you go through a revolving door?

(1) moving your hand closer to the center of the revolving door
(2) moving your hand closer to the outer edge of the revolving door
(3) pushing with two hands rather than one hand
(4) leaning toward the door as you push to increase your force
(5) getting a friend to help you push the door

Question 12 refers to the following graph.

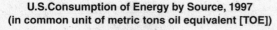

**U.S.Consumption of Energy by Source, 1997
(in common unit of metric tons oil equivalent [TOE])**

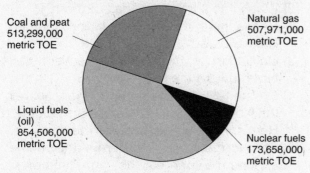

Coal and peat
513,299,000
metric TOE

Natural gas
507,971,000
metric TOE

Liquid fuels
(oil)
854,506,000
metric TOE

Nuclear fuels
173,658,000
metric TOE

SOURCE: World Resource Institute

12. Of the four energy sources shown, which two are the most similar in the proportion of energy they supply in the United States?

(1) coal/peat and natural gas
(2) natural gas and nuclear fuels
(3) nuclear fuels and liquid fuels
(4) liquid fuels and natural gas
(5) oil and coal/peat

Question 13 refers to the following paragraph and map.

In 1620, the eastern half of the United States was covered by virgin forest—forest that has never been cut down. Many parts of this region today are covered by second-growth forest—the ecosystem that eventually grows back after farmland is abandoned.

Virgin Forest of the United States 1620–1990

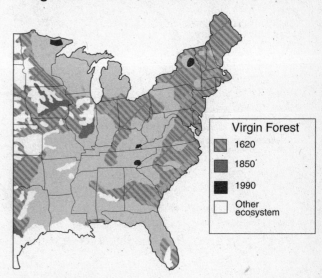

Virgin Forest
1620
1850
1990
Other ecosystem

SOURCE: *National Geographic*

13. Which of the following conclusions is supported by the paragraph and the map?

(1) The western half of the United States had far less forest cover in 1620 than did the eastern half.
(2) As European Americans moved from the East Coast westward between 1620 and 1850, they cut down forests to build farms.
(3) A number of relatively large areas of virgin forest remain in the eastern half of the United States today.
(4) Today's second-growth forests in the eastern United States have fewer species of plants and animals than the virgin forest did.
(5) Cities and suburbs now cover all of the eastern United States except the areas that still have virgin forest.

Questions 14 and 15 refer to the following information and diagram.

The seasons occur because the axis of Earth is tilted. At different times of year, different parts of Earth get more hours of higher-intensity sunlight. As the diagram shows, summer begins in the Southern Hemisphere on December 21, when that hemisphere is tilted toward the sun.

Why Earth Has Seasons

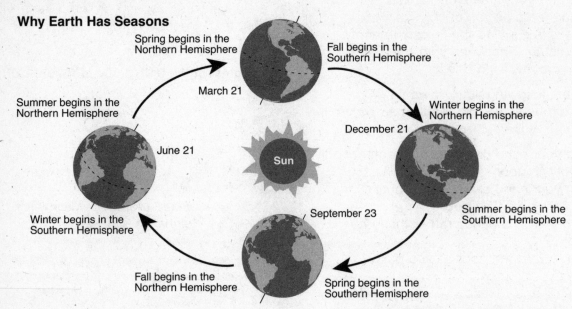

14. Which portion of Earth is tilted toward the sun on June 21?

  (1) the Southern Hemisphere
  (2) the Northern Hemisphere
  (3) the axis
  (4) the equator
  (5) the South Pole

15. Which of the following statements is supported by the information in the diagram?

  (1) The Earth rotates once around its axis each and every day.
  (2) When it is summer in the Northern Hemisphere, it is summer in the Southern Hemisphere.
  (3) On March 21, the Northern Hemisphere is tilted toward the sun.
  (4) On the first day of spring and fall, neither the Northern Hemisphere nor the Southern Hemisphere is tilted toward the sun.
  (5) The Northern and Southern hemispheres experience spring at the same time of year.

16. Ecologists use a tool called a quadrat when doing field studies of plant distribution. A quadrat is an open, four-sided structure about a meter square. It is placed on the ground, whether in a meadow, on a hillside, or at the beach. The ecologist then counts the plants of different species inside the quadrat. By using a quadrat, an ecologist can get a more accurate understanding of species distribution than by doing a random count.

Which of the following statements is a conclusion based on the given facts?

  (1) A quadrat is a tool used by ecologists.
  (2) A quadrat is a frame about a meter square.
  (3) To use a quadrat, the ecologist places it on the ground.
  (4) The plants inside the quadrat are counted.
  (5) A quadrat makes plant distribution estimates more reliable.

17. According to Charles's Law, when the pressure of a gas remains constant, the volume of a quantity of gas varies directly with the temperature. In other words, as the temperature of a gas rises, the volume of the gas increases.

Which of the following graphs illustrates Charles's Law?

(1) **Charles's Law**

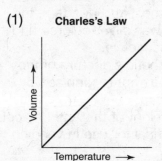

(2)

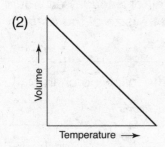

(3)

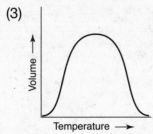

(4)

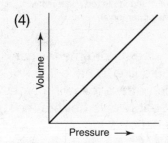

(5)

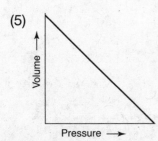

18. At the beginning of the twentieth century, only three subatomic particles were known: protons, neutrons, and electrons. In the last half of the century, dozens of new particles were discovered using new technology. Machines called particle accelerators push particles to tremendous speeds, giving them enormous energy. When they smash into other particles, energy is converted to mass, and new particles form.

Which of the following does the writer take for granted that you know?

(1) Protons, neutrons, and electrons are subatomic particles.
(2) Atoms are composed of subatomic particles.
(3) In particle accelerators, particles are pushed to very high speeds.
(4) Energy is converted to mass when high-speed particles collide with one another.
(5) New particles have been discovered using the technology of particle accelerators.

19. Density is the amount of matter, or mass, in a given volume of a substance. To find the density of an object, you divide its mass by its volume. A student wanted to find the density of a 3-cm cube of lead. First, she used a scale to find the mass of the cube. Next, she calculated the volume by multiplying 3 cm × 3 cm × 3 cm. Finally, she divided the volume by the mass to find the density of the lead cube.

Why was the density the student calculated inaccurate?

(1) A scale cannot be used for finding mass.
(2) Multiplying three sides of the cube will not give the cube's volume.
(3) The student should have found the volume first.
(4) The student should have divided the mass by the volume.
(5) The density of a cube cannot be determined.

Questions 20 and 21 refer to the following passage.

When the U.S. Mint had to design a new dollar coin to replace the old Susan B. Anthony dollar, it faced a problem. It wanted to design an appealing, distinctive golden-color coin that vending machines would recognize as an Anthony dollar, which looks like a quarter. Vending machines identify coins by their weight, size, and electromagnetic signature. They test a coin by passing an electric current through it and measuring the resulting magnetic field. Thus the new Sacagawea dollar coin had to be similar to the Anthony dollar in size, weight, and electromagnetic signature.

Size and weight were easy to imitate, but the electromagnetic signature was not. The Anthony dollar had a copper core covered by a silver-colored copper-nickel alloy. All the golden alloy sample coins had three times as much electrical conductivity as the Anthony dollar. Vending machines did not recognize them. Finally, metallurgists came up with the idea of adding manganese, which has low conductivity, to zinc and copper. The result was a coin consisting of 77 percent copper, 12 percent zinc, 7 percent manganese, and 4 percent nickel. The pure copper core was covered with a golden alloy of manganese, zinc, copper, and nickel. This golden coin has electromagnetic properties similar to those of the Anthony dollar, so it is recognized by U.S. vending machines.

20. What is an alloy?

    (1) a magnetic material
    (2) a material that stops electricity
    (3) a mixture of metals
    (4) the core of a coin
    (5) the outer layer of a coin

21. The U.S. Mint could have solved its technical problems with the Sacagawea dollar by making it out of the same metals as the Anthony dollar. Why did the people at the Mint decide against this?

    (1) The metals in the Anthony alloy were too rare and expensive to use in the new coin.
    (2) Like nickels, dimes, and quarters, the Anthony dollar was silver-colored and therefore not distinctive.
    (3) The electromagnetic signature of the Anthony coin was not recognized by vending machines.
    (4) The size and weight of the Anthony coin made it impractical for use in vending machines.
    (5) A detailed portrait of Sacagawea would not fit on a coin the size of the Anthony dollar.

Question 22 refers to the following chart.

Types of Plants

Type	Characteristics
Annual	Completes life cycle in one growing season
Biennial	Completes life cycle in two growing seasons; flowers during second year
Perennial	Lives for years and flowers each year
Tender	Sensitive to cold (can be annual, biennial, or perennial)
Hardy	Can withstand frosts (can be annual, biennial, or perennial)

22. Marion has little interest in or time for gardening, yet she would like to have flowers in her front yard. Which of the following types of plants would probably give her the most flowers for the least effort?

    (1) annuals
    (2) biennials
    (3) tender plants
    (4) hardy biennials
    (5) hardy perennials

Question 23 refers to the following diagram.

The Reflection of Light

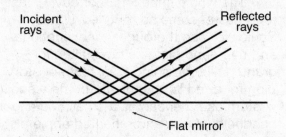

Incident rays

Reflected rays

Flat mirror

23. If the flat mirror were removed from this telescope, what would happen as a result?

   (1) Light rays would not enter the telescope.
   (2) Light rays would not reflect off the curved mirror.
   (3) A viewer could not see anything through the telescope.
   (4) A viewer could see only objects that were in focus.
   (5) A viewer could see only distant things.

24. The discovery of a new drug was once largely the result of trial and error, laboratory experiments on animals, and clinical trials on real patients. Although these methods are still widely used, computer science is being applied to the drug discovery process to refine it and speed it up. For example, computers can analyze genetic material to locate genes that may hold promise in the development of new drugs. Computers can analyze data generated by lab experiments and clinical trials. Computer simulations can even help scientists predict how a particular drug will work under specific circumstances.

What is the main reason that computers are now being used in the drug discovery process?

   (1) They enable scientists to abandon trial-and-error methods.
   (2) They help scientists analyze large amounts of data in a systematic way.
   (3) They have made laboratory experiments unnecessary.
   (4) They have made clinical trials unnecessary.
   (5) They ensure that new drugs will be approved by the federal government.

25. People planning to visit tropical countries may need to be vaccinated against disease. For example, one week to one month before a trip, travelers should be vaccinated against cholera. The vaccine is about 60 percent effective, and its protection lasts about six months. Additional precautions against cholera include avoiding food and water that may be dirty.

If a traveler is vaccinated against cholera a month or two before a brief trip to the tropics, why should he or she take extra precautions against contracting the disease?

   (1) The cholera vaccination is effective for only six months.
   (2) The cholera vaccination is only 60 percent effective.
   (3) The cholera vaccination can cause soreness, fever, and headache.
   (4) Cholera spreads only through air and water.
   (5) It is not always possible to tell whether food and water are dirty.

Answers and explanations start on page 52.

LANGUAGE ARTS, READING PRETEST

<u>Questions 1 through 5</u> refer to the following excerpt from an essay.

DO AMERICANS EAT TOO MUCH FAST FOOD?

A few years ago, in a moment of culinary cross-cultural crisis, the gracious owners of a Japanese restaurant offered my family their house delicacy. With a flourish
(5) and a smile, they placed before us an elegantly sliced and uncooked lobster tail.

Not only was the tail raw, but it shared the plate with the body to which it had so recently been attached. Right above the
(10) creature's eyes were two antennae. Still twitching.

This was the night I came up with Goodman's First Rule for Dining: never eat anything while it's watching you.

(15) Now, however, after reading Eric Schlosser's "Fast Food Nation," I look back on that dining adventure with something akin to nostalgia. He has convinced me that the problem isn't that Americans have too
(20) intimate a relationship with their dinner but rather too distant.

On any given day, one-quarter of adult Americans eat at a fast-food restaurant. In any given week, the typical American
(25) downs three hamburgers and four orders of french fries. In any given month, 90 percent of American children between the ages of 3 and 9 eat at a McDonald's restaurant.

Despite the fact that we spend $110 bil-
(30) lion a year on fast food—more than we do on higher education, software, or new cars—few of us have any idea where the food comes from, how it gets to the plate, or what's in it. We don't raise it, we don't
(35) harvest it, we don't cook it. We just take it wrapped and ready.

"The whole experience of buying fast food has become so routine," writes Schlosser, "so thoroughly unexceptional
(40) and mundane that it is now taken for granted, like brushing your teeth or stopping for a red light. It has become a social custom as American as a small, rectangular, handheld, frozen and reheated apple pie."

(45) It's Schlosser's muck-and-Big-Mac-raking task to deconstruct the food-industrial complex. He shows that American speed cuisine has had "an enormous impact not only on our eating habits but
(50) on our economy, our culture, and our values." The industry has created a cheap, expendable work force and a network of vast factory farms.

From "If we are what we eat, we're in trouble" by Ellen Goodman, Boston Globe, 2/11/01.

1. Why did the author include the example of the lobster at the beginning of the essay?

    (1) to contrast Japanese and American eating habits
    (2) to show her knowledge of other cultures
    (3) to explain what is wrong with eating animals
    (4) to ridicule the eating habits of some people
    (5) to strengthen her argument for more nutritious food

2. Which of the following actions would Schlosser most likely compare to buying a fast-food meal?

    (1) planning a party for Saturday night
    (2) writing a letter to a friend
    (3) building a shelving unit
    (4) flipping a light switch
    (5) teaching a child how to tie his shoe

3. What is meant by the line "It's Schlosser's muck-and-Big-Mac-raking task" (lines 45–46)?

    Schlosser has taken it upon himself to

    (1) compare meals from different fast-food companies
    (2) explain why fast food appeals to so many people
    (3) defend the popularity of fast food
    (4) persuade people never to eat at fast-food restaurants again
    (5) expose the fast-food industry for what it is and its far-reaching effects

4. Which of the following best describes the author's approach toward her topic?

    (1) technical
    (2) informal
    (3) resentful
    (4) objective
    (5) respectful

5. Later in this essay the author writes, "It's 6 P.M. Do you know where your chicken nugget has been? It's probably come off the overdeveloped breast of a new breed of chicken. It's been reconstituted, stabilized, breaded, frozen, reheated, flavored with beef additives, and set on the plate containing twice as much fat per ounce as hamburger."

    Based on this information and the excerpt, if the author were to write Goodman's Second Rule for Dining, which would it most likely be?

    (1) Learn how your food is prepared.
    (2) Eat a variety of healthful foods.
    (3) Always avoid raw lobster.
    (4) Never eat any type of chicken.
    (5) Appreciate the food you have.

WHAT HAPPENS WHEN DIANE CONTINUES TO LOOK FOR TROUBLE?

Except when we were at our jobs, we were together, even if I was just taking a ten-minute trip to the drug store. "You don't think I'm too clingy?" she asked.

(5)   "I love it," I told her. "Don't use that word."

Diane knew from the start how badly I was going to fail her, and her difficult job was to teach me that. She started practi-
(10) cally at once asking whether she disappointed me, whether I was upset with her, as though I were a doctor withholding news of fatal illness.

"You look nervous," she'd say, or "You
(15) look unhappy," when I wasn't aware of feeling those things. If I did tell her something was bothering me, a backache or something from work, she was more upset than I was, as though the trouble were her fault.
(20) She saw things in my expression that I never meant to be there. She heard them in my voice. She heard them in my silence.

And at last it became maddening, when I had been thinking about something, to
(25) look up and see her little smile of guilty fear. "I wasn't being cold," I'd shout, before she had a chance to say it.

But now I began to criticize everything about her. I said she spent too much on
(30) clothes—her dresses filled her closet and half of mine, many more than my mother had owned.

"That's because she threw them out whenever the style changed," said Diane.
(35) And it was true, I had been unfair, most of Diane's clothes were old, I thought I could remember some from the days of Richard Dean—old and unflattering, tight around the stomach and rear. And how strangely
(40) somber. When I saw them by the dozen, packed together on hangers, I realized that she never wore anything vivid.

"You should try bright colors," I told her. But she only looked worried and asked
(45) me, smiling a little, her voice as hopeless as though I'd suggested she leap the moon, "Do you think I should?"

From "Emotion Recollected in Tranquility" from PRIVATE PARTIES, by Jonathan Penner, © 1983. Reprinted by permission of the University of Pittsburgh Press.

6. What does Diane seem to think whenever the narrator is silent?

He is

(1) pleasantly daydreaming
(2) trying to avoid her
(3) thinking of work
(4) lost in thought
(5) upset or angry with her

7. On the basis of the excerpt, which one of the following animals would best represent Diane's character?

(1) a snake
(2) an eagle
(3) a cat
(4) a mouse
(5) a monkey

8. What is the underlying conflict between Diane and the narrator?

(1) Diane makes him act negatively toward her.
(2) He thinks Diane is old-fashioned.
(3) Diane is critical of his mother.
(4) The two have almost nothing in common.
(5) The two argue over budgeting money.

9. Which of the following best describes the narrator's attitude toward Diane?

(1) protective
(2) resentful
(3) proud
(4) concerned
(5) scolding

10. Which of the following best describes how the narrator changes during the time he describes in the excerpt?

(1) He feels free to be more honest with Diane.
(2) He begins to understand Diane better.
(3) He begins to feel toward Diane the way she always feared he did.
(4) He wants to leave Diane.
(5) He changes his mind about the way Diane should dress.

IS THIS MAN SUCCESSFUL
IN HIS PURSUIT OF LOVE?

My Love Is Like to Ice

My love is like to ice, and I to fire:
How comes it then that this her cold so great
Is not dissolved through my so hot desire,
But harder grows the more I her entreat?
(5) Or how comes it that my exceeding heat
Is not allayed by her heart-frozen cold,
But that I burn much more in boiling sweat,
And feel my flames augmented manifold?
What more miraculous thing may be told,
(10) That fire, which all things melts, should harden ice,
And ice, which is congealed with senseless cold,
Should kindle fire by wonderful device?
Such is the power of love in gentle mind,
That it can alter all the course of kind.

By Edmund Spenser

11. What is ice compared to in this poem?

   (1) hatred
   (2) indifference
   (3) frustration
   (4) anger
   (5) destruction

12. Which of the following is the best restatement of lines 2–4?

   (1) Why is my love so cold?
   (2) Why doesn't my desire appeal to her?
   (3) Why does she seem less interested the more I pursue her?
   (4) Why does love make us act the way we do?
   (5) Why does love affect some people but not others?

13. What effect does the attitude of the speaker's love have on him?

   (1) He wants her even more.
   (2) He feels his fire burning out.
   (3) He will seek love elsewhere.
   (4) He is speechless when he is near her.
   (5) He will never love again.

14. According to the speaker, what is the power of love?

   It can

   (1) melt the hardest heart
   (2) bring joy to even the saddest
   (3) change the very nature of things
   (4) confuse and puzzle us
   (5) drive a man to wild desire

15. Which of the following ideas are most clearly contrasted in the poem?

   (1) knowledge and ignorance
   (2) truth and deception
   (3) trust and fear
   (4) desire and disinterest
   (5) openness and secrecy

Questions 16 through 20 refer to the following excerpt from a play.

WHAT IS MARY'S CONFLICT WITH MRS. MOREHEAD?

MRS. MOREHEAD: But the children, Mary. The children—

MARY: What good will it do them to be brought up in a home full of quarreling
(5) and suspicion? They'll be better off just with me.

MRS. MOREHEAD: No, they won't. A child needs both its parents in one home.

MARY: A home without love?

(10) MRS. MOREHEAD: He's terribly fond of you—

MARY: Mother, don't use that word! Oh, Mother, please. Every argument goes round in circles. And, it's too late now—

(15) MRS. MOREHEAD: It's never too late when you love. Mary, why don't you call this thing off? I'm sure that's what Stephen's waiting for.

MARY: [*Bitterly*] Is it? He hasn't made any
(20) sign of it to me. Isn't he the one to come to me?

MRS. MOREHEAD: You're the one, Mary, who insisted on the divorce.

MARY: But don't you see; if he hadn't
(25) wanted it, he'd have fought me—

MRS. MOREHEAD: Stephen's not the fighting kind.

MARY: Neither am I.

MRS. MOREHEAD: Damn these modern
(30) laws!

MARY: Mother!

MRS. MOREHEAD: Damn them, I say. Fifty years ago, when women couldn't get divorces, they made the best of situa-
(35) tions like this. And sometimes, out of situations like this they made very good things indeed! [*Enter* JANE, *right.*]

JANE: Mr. Haines' secretary, ma'am.

MRS. MOREHEAD: Tell her to come in. [*Exit*
(40) JANE] Now, go bathe your eyes. Don't let that adding-machine see you like this. And don't be long. Remember, you have one more unpleasant task.

MARY: Mary?

(45) MRS. MOREHEAD: The child must be told.

MARY: [*Miserably, and a little guiltily*] I have been putting it off. Because—

MRS. MOREHEAD: Because you hope at the last minute a miracle will keep you
(50) from making a mess of your life. Have you thought: Stephen might marry that girl?

MARY: [*Very confident*] He won't do that.

MRS. MOREHEAD: What makes you so
(55) sure?

MARY: Because, deep down, Stephen does love me—But he won't find it out, until I've—really gone away—[*At the door*] You'll take good care of the children,
(60) Mother? And make them write to me to Reno, once a week? And please, Mother, don't spoil them so. [*Exits left.*]

From THE WOMEN by Clare Boothe, copyright 1937 and renewed 1965 by Clare Boothe Luce. Used by permission of Random House, Inc.

16. Why does Mary believe her husband wants a divorce?

   (1) He hasn't tried to stop her from getting one.
   (2) He never shows her that he loves her.
   (3) He is arguing with her constantly.
   (4) He has left her and the children.
   (5) He has asked her for one.

17. How does Mrs. Morehead respond to Mary's situation?

   She generally

   (1) ignores Mary's feelings and concerns
   (2) pokes fun at Mary's mistaken notions
   (3) lets Mary have her way
   (4) criticizes and degrades Mary
   (5) appeals to Mary's duty to her family

18. What is Mary hoping will happen when she goes to Reno?

   (1) She will get a quick divorce.
   (2) She will have time to think things over.
   (3) She will meet someone new and start a new life.
   (4) Her husband will miss her and want her back.
   (5) Mrs. Morehead will help her save her marriage.

19. If Mrs. Morehead was having a disagreement with a friend, what would she probably do?

   (1) talk about the friend behind her back
   (2) discuss the problem with the friend
   (3) forget about the friend
   (4) wait for the friend to apologize
   (5) argue and try to shout her friend down

20. Later in the play, two women are discussing Stephen, and one says, "I don't butt into his private affairs. But I must say knowing her gave him a new interest in his work. Before her, he was certainly going stale."

   Based on this information and the excerpt above, what is the most likely reason Mary and Stephen broke up?

   (1) Mary wants to be free and independent.
   (2) Mary thinks Stephen spent too much time at work and ignored the family.
   (3) Stephen was having an affair with someone at work.
   (4) Stephen wants Mary to take more of an interest in him and his work.
   (5) They both realized they had grown apart.

Answers and explanations start on page 54.

GED Math Pretest

Part I

Mark your answers on the answer sheet provided at the bottom on page 43. You may use the formulas on page 688 of this book on this test.

Directions: Choose the one best answer to each question. You MAY use your calculator.

1. Which point on the number line shown below represents the value $-\frac{16}{6}$?

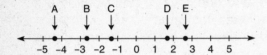

   (1) *A*
   (2) *B*
   (3) *C*
   (4) *D*
   (5) *E*

Questions 2 and 3 refer to the following graph.

Video Warehouse has divided the surrounding community into four advertising zones. The graph shows the total number of customers from each zone for a three-week period.

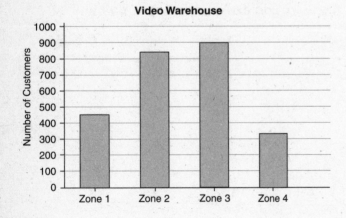

2. During the three weeks, about how many customers came from Zones 3 and 4?

   (1) between 800 and 900
   (2) between 900 and 1000
   (3) between 1000 and 1100
   (4) between 1100 and 1200
   (5) between 1200 and 1300

3. Approximately what is the ratio of customers from Zone 1 to customers from Zone 3?

   (1) 5:3
   (2) 3:5
   (3) 3:2
   (4) 2:1
   (5) 1:2

4. Evaluate the expression $2x - (4y - 3) + 5xz$, when $x = -3$, $y = 2$, and $z = -1$?

   (1)   45
   (2)   16
   (3)   4
   (4) −10
   (5) −22

Question 5 refers to the following drawing.

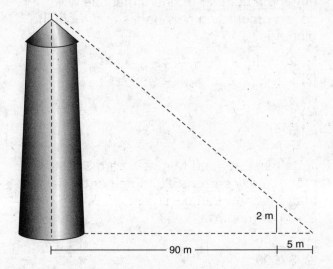

2 m

90 m   5 m

5. To find the height of a tower, a surveyor places a 2-meter pole in the ground so that it is parallel to the tower. Then she finds the point on the ground from which she can sight the top of the tower and the top of the pole. Using the measurements from the diagram, what is the height of the tower in meters?

Mark your answer in the circles in the grid on your answer sheet on page 43.

6. A parallelogram has two obtuse angles and two acute angles. If the measure of one of the obtuse angles is 110°, what is the measure, in degrees, of one of the acute angles?

Mark your answer in the circles in the grid on your answer sheet on page 43.

Questions 7 and 8 refer to the following information.

Designer Furnishings sells premade cabinets and cupboards. The following cabinets are currently discounted from 10% to 40%.

Model	Dimensions (in inches)	Original Price	Discount
411R	32 by 22 by 10	$ 90.00	25%
412R	28 by 36 by 15	$120.00	25%
413S	24 by 72 by 18	$150.00	40%
414S	25 by 24 by 6	$ 80.00	10%

7. Each face of cabinet 413S is in the shape of a rectangle. What is the volume of Model 413S in cubic feet?

(1) 18
(2) 31
(3) 36
(4) 108
(5) 216

8. Sharon wants to buy two cabinets, Models 411R and 412R. What is the total sale price of the two cabinets?

(1) $52.50
(2) $105.00
(3) $157.50
(4) $160.00
(5) $210.00

9. A potter uses $\frac{3}{5}$ pound of clay in making a bowl. How many bowls could the potter make from 10 pounds of clay?

(1) 6
(2) 8
(3) 13
(4) 16
(5) 17

10. Janelle has recently been hired for the job of library assistant. The following graph shows what percent of her time will be spent in each of five tasks each day.

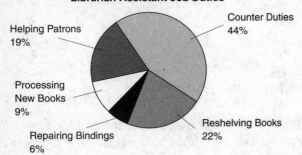

Librarian Assistant Job Duties

Helping Patrons 19%

Counter Duties 44%

Processing New Books 9%

Repairing Bindings 6%

Reshelving Books 22%

The number of hours that Janelle will spend working at the counter is about how many times the number of hours that she will spend processing new books and repairing bindings?

(1) 2
(2) 3
(3) 4
(4) 5
(5) 6

11. Together, Levy and Matthew earn $4680 per month. Levy earns $520 more per month than Matthew earns. How much does Levy earn per month?

(1) $2080
(2) $2600
(3) $3120
(4) $3640
(5) $4160

12. The design for a new drink box container is shown below.

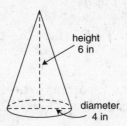

height
6 in

diameter
4 in

Which of the following expressions could be used to find the approximate volume of the container in cubic inches?

(1) $\frac{1}{3}(3.14)(2^2)(6)$

(2) $(3.14)(2^2)(6)$

(3) $\frac{1}{3}(3.14)(4^2)(6)$

(4) $(3.14)(4^2)(6)$

(5) $\frac{1}{3}(4^2)(6)$

13. A rectangle is drawn on a coordinate grid. Three of its four vertices are located at points $(-1,-2)$, $(-1,4)$, and $(2,-2)$. What is the location of the fourth vertex?

Mark your answer on the coordinate plane grid on your answer sheet on page 43.

PART II

Mark your answers on the answer sheet provided at the bottom of page 43.

Directions: Choose the one best answer to each question. You MAY NOT use your calculator.

1. Fifteen percent of the workers at Nationwide Industries earn minimum wage. If 24 workers earn minimum wage, how many are there at Nationwide Industries?

   (1)   4
   (2) 36
   (3) 160
   (4) 360
   (5) Not enough information is given.

2. To get to work each day, Jill drives 8 blocks due south and 9 blocks due west. If the blocks are the same length, which of the following equations could be used to find the straight-line distance, in blocks (x), between Jill's home and her work?

   (1) $8^2 + x^2 = 9^2$
   (2) $9^2 - 8^2 = x^2$
   (3) $x^2 + 9^2 = 8^2$
   (4) $9^2 - x^2 = 8^2$
   (5) $8^2 + 9^2 = x^2$

3. Which of the following expressions is equal to the expression $4x - 2(3x - 9)$?

   (1) $2x + 12$
   (2) $18 - 2x$
   (3) $-10x - 18$
   (4) $-2x - 18$
   (5) $10x + 18$

4. All numbers that are evenly divisible by both 6 and 14 are also divisible by which of the following numbers?

   (1) 8
   (2) 12
   (3) 21
   (4) 28
   (5) 35

Question 5 refers to the following figure.

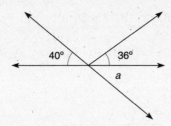

5. What is the measure, in degrees, of angle *a*?

Mark your answer in the circles in the grid on your answer sheet on page 43.

6. Alice, Kathy, and Sheila work as medical assistants at Valley Clinic. Alice has worked 8 years longer than Kathy. Kathy has worked half as long as Sheila. If Sheila has worked at the company for 10 years, how many years has Alice worked there?

Mark your answer in the circles in the grid on your answer sheet on page 43.

Question 7 refers to the following information.

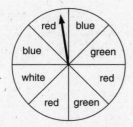

7. The spinner shown in the drawing is divided into eight equal sections. If you spin the spinner one time, what is the probability of not getting blue?

(1) $\frac{1}{8}$

(2) $\frac{1}{4}$

(3) $\frac{3}{8}$

(4) $\frac{3}{4}$

(5) $\frac{7}{8}$

8. A computer monitor is regularly priced at $290. During a 2-day sale, the price was decreased to $260. Which of the following could be used to find the percent of decrease in the monitor's price during the sale?

(1) $\dfrac{\$30(100)}{\$260}$

(2) $\dfrac{\$30(100)}{\$290}$

(3) $\dfrac{\$260(100)}{\$290}$

(4) $\dfrac{\$290(100)}{\$260}$

(5) $\dfrac{\$260(100)}{\$290 - \$260}$

9. For a 10-day period, a bank kept track of the number of new accounts opened each day. The results are shown in the table below. What is the median number of accounts opened per day during this 10-day period?

Day	Accounts	Day	Accounts
May 7	6	May 14	4
May 8	2	May 15	8
May 9	7	May 16	6
May 10	5	May 17	4
May 11	4	May 18	7

    (1) 5
    (2) 5.3
    (3) 5.5
    (4) 6
    (5) Not enough information is given.

10. In the equation $3x^2 - 10x = 8$, which of the following values for x will make the equation true?

    (1) -4
    (2) -3
    (3) 0
    (4) 3
    (5) 4

11. Matt is helping a community group produce a play. He estimates that he will need to have 1500 programs printed. If each program costs 4 cents per page to print, how much should Matt expect to pay for the programs?

    (1) $6.00
    (2) $20.00
    (3) $60.00
    (4) $200.00
    (5) Not enough information is given.

12. On a coordinate graph, a line segment connects points at $(-5,-2)$ and $(1,4)$. Another segment connects points at $(-2,4)$ and $(-2,-5)$. At which point do these line segments intersect?

Mark your answer on the coordinate plane grid on your answer sheet on page 43.

Answers and explanations begin on page 55.

PRETEST ANSWER SHEET

PART I

1. ① ② ③ ④ ⑤
2. ① ② ③ ④ ⑤
3. ① ② ③ ④ ⑤
4. ① ② ③ ④ ⑤
5.

	/	/	/	
·	·	·	·	·
⓪	⓪	⓪	⓪	⓪
①	①	①	①	①
②	②	②	②	②
③	③	③	③	③
④	④	④	④	④
⑤	⑤	⑤	⑤	⑤
⑥	⑥	⑥	⑥	⑥
⑦	⑦	⑦	⑦	⑦
⑧	⑧	⑧	⑧	⑧
⑨	⑨	⑨	⑨	⑨

6.

	/	/	/	
·	·	·	·	·
⓪	⓪	⓪	⓪	⓪
①	①	①	①	①
②	②	②	②	②
③	③	③	③	③
④	④	④	④	④
⑤	⑤	⑤	⑤	⑤
⑥	⑥	⑥	⑥	⑥
⑦	⑦	⑦	⑦	⑦
⑧	⑧	⑧	⑧	⑧
⑨	⑨	⑨	⑨	⑨

7. ① ② ③ ④ ⑤
8. ① ② ③ ④ ⑤
9. ① ② ③ ④ ⑤
10. ① ② ③ ④ ⑤

11. ① ② ③ ④ ⑤
12. ① ② ③ ④ ⑤
13.

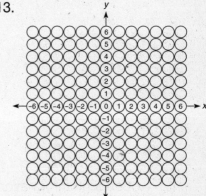

PART II

1. ① ② ③ ④ ⑤
2. ① ② ③ ④ ⑤
3. ① ② ③ ④ ⑤
4. ① ② ③ ④ ⑤
5.

	/	/	/	
·	·	·	·	·
⓪	⓪	⓪	⓪	⓪
①	①	①	①	①
②	②	②	②	②
③	③	③	③	③
④	④	④	④	④
⑤	⑤	⑤	⑤	⑤
⑥	⑥	⑥	⑥	⑥
⑦	⑦	⑦	⑦	⑦
⑧	⑧	⑧	⑧	⑧
⑨	⑨	⑨	⑨	⑨

6.

	/	/	/	
·	·	·	·	·
⓪	⓪	⓪	⓪	⓪
①	①	①	①	①
②	②	②	②	②
③	③	③	③	③
④	④	④	④	④
⑤	⑤	⑤	⑤	⑤
⑥	⑥	⑥	⑥	⑥
⑦	⑦	⑦	⑦	⑦
⑧	⑧	⑧	⑧	⑧
⑨	⑨	⑨	⑨	⑨

7. ① ② ③ ④ ⑤
8. ① ② ③ ④ ⑤
9. ① ② ③ ④ ⑤

10. ① ② ③ ④ ⑤
11. ① ② ③ ④ ⑤
12.

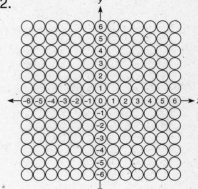

PRETEST ANSWERS AND EXPLANATIONS

Language Arts, Writing

Part I

1. **(4) change have to has (Subject-verb agreement)** The third-person singular subject *student* requires the verb form *have*.

2. **(2) symptoms such as (Sentence fragment)** Option (2) links a fragment to an independent clause to form a complete sentence.

3. **(2) change developed to develops (Verb tense)** The verb should be in the present tense because the action is occurring in the present. Moreover, the present tense is consistent with the majority of verbs in the passage.

4. **(3) sentence 5 (Paragraphing)** Sentences 1–4 explain basic facts about strep throat. Sentences 5–10 explain what parents should do if their child has strep throat.

5. **(1) insert a comma after addition (Comma after introductory element)** Generally, an introductory phrase is followed by a comma.

6. **(1) After the fever is gone and your child has taken (Subordination)** Combining the detail about taking medicine and the second independent clause about the fever into an introductory subordinate clause results in a smooth, effective sentence.

7. **(3) remove the comma (Overuse of commas)** No comma is needed between two verbs in a compound predicate (*bet on a football game or buy a lottery ticket*).

8. **(3) threatens (Verb tense)** The action is always true, so the present tense is correct. Moreover, the present tense is consistent with the majority of verbs in the passage.

9. **(5) Compulsive gamblers display a number of consistent traits. (Topic sentence)** Option (5) is the only topic sentence that sums up the main point and is neither too specific nor too general.

10. **(5) it. Losing (Comma splice)** Option (5), which forms two complete sentences, is the only way to correct the comma splice here. Option (4) is incorrect because a comma must precede *and* in a compound sentence.

11. **(1) insert a comma after fraud (Commas in a series)** Commas are required between items in a series.

12. **(1) depressed, or they (Commas in compound sentences)** The sentence is correct as written. A comma should precede a coordinating conjunction that joins independent clauses.

13. **(2) People often select pets on impulse after (Dangling modifiers)** In the original sentence, it is not clear who has seen an adorable puppy or kitten in a pet store.

14. **(4) replace he with they (Pronoun antecedents)** The antecedent *owners* is plural, so *they* is the correct pronoun to use.

15. **(1) change There's to There are (Subject-verb agreement)** The verb agrees with the subject *number* ("a number of factors"), which is plural.

16. **(4) be housebroken and trained (Parallel structure)** Only option (4) has both verbs in parallel structure and creates a correct sentence.

17. **(4) remove sentence 10 (Logical order/relevance)** The sentence about exercise and people is not relevant to pets, the topic of the article.

18. **(4) change was to is (Verb tense)** The statement is always true, so the present tense is correct. Moreover, the present tense is consistent with the majority of verbs in the passage.

19. **(3) see (Verb form)** The verb form *see* is required with the subject *you*. *Seen* requires the helping verb *have*, but the present perfect tense *have seen* is not needed in the sentence, just the simple present.

20. **(2) move sentence 3 to follow sentence 1 (Logical order/relevance)** With sentence 1, sentence 3 catches the reader's attention and gives background information about the topic of the whole article. Sentences 2 and 4 introduce the main idea of the article.

21. **(2) has been (Subject-verb agreement)** The verb needs to agree with the subject *kite flying*, which is singular.

22. **(5) During a thunderstorm, he flew a kite with (Misplaced modifiers)** In the original sentence, it sounds as if the thunderstorm had a key attached to it.

23. **(4) replace their with there (Spelling/homonyms)** The word *their* is a possessive meaning "belonging to them." Its homonym, *there*, is needed in this sentence.

24. **(2) humidity, wind speed, and barometric pressure (Subordinating ideas/Parallelism)** Option (2) combines two sentences that have related details.

25. **(1) Bell, the physicist and inventor, used (Appositives)** The sentence is punctuated correctly as written.

Language Arts, Writing Pretest

Part II

Scoring Your Essay

Directions: Ask a friend or family member who is a good writer to read your essay and evaluate it using the checklist below.

	Yes	No
Response to the Prompt		
Does the essay answer the question in the topic?		
Is there a clear main idea?		
Does the essay stay on topic?		
Organization		
Are there an introduction, body, and conclusion?		
Does each body paragraph include a topic sentence and supporting details?		
Does the writing flow smoothly from sentence to sentence and from paragraph to paragraph?		
Development and Details		
Do the topic sentences support the main idea of the essay?		
Are topic sentences supported with specific details and examples?		
Conventions of Edited American English		
Are complete sentences used?		
Does the essay have a variety of sentence structures?		
Do subjects and verbs agree?		
Is it clear what each pronoun refers to?		
Are correct verb forms and tenses used?		
Are all words spelled correctly?		
Is correct punctuation used?		
Are capital letters used correctly?		
Word Choice		
Does the essay use specific and clear language?		
Have all unnecessary words been eliminated?		

Scoring:

Essay scorers read an essay and get an overall impression of it. They do not add up points to get a score. Therefore, you should do the same when looking at your chart. Get a general idea of how you stand. If there are many "yes" answers, you are in good shape. After working through the essay sections of this book, you should succeed on the test. If you have mostly "no" answers, you can still do well, but you will have to practice your writing skills.

The checklist is divided into five areas (notice the bold headings). If you have a lot of "no" answers in a particular area, you should devote extra attention to that area.

Essay Scoring Guide

The following scoring guide is used by the evaluators who read test takers' GED essays. You may want to use this chart to evaluate your essay. If you get a score of less than 2 on the essay, you will get *no score at all* for the Language Arts, Writing Test, and you will have to retake the entire test again.

	1	2	3	4
	Inadequate	**Marginal**	**Adequate**	**Effective**
	Reader has difficulty identifying or following the writer's ideas.	**Reader occasionally has difficulty understanding or following the writer's ideas.**	**Reader understands writer's ideas.**	**Reader understands and easily follows the writer's expression of ideas.**
Response to the Prompt	Attempts to address prompt but with little or no success in establishing a focus.	Addresses the prompt, though the focus may shift.	Uses the writing prompt to establish a main idea.	Presents a clearly focused main idea that addresses the prompt.
Organization	Fails to organize ideas.	Shows some evidence of an organizational plan.	Uses an identifiable organizational plan.	Establishes a clear and logical organization.
Development and Details	Demonstrates little or no development; usually lacks details or examples or presents irrelevant information.	Has some development but lacks specific details; may be limited to listing, repetitions, or generalizations.	Has focused but occasionally uneven development; incorporates some specific detail.	Achieves coherent development with specific and relevant details and examples.
Conventions of Edited American English (EAE)	Exhibits minimal or no control of sentence structure and the conventions of EAE	Demonstrates inconsistent control of sentence structure and the conventions of EAE.	Generally controls sentence structure and the conventions of EAE.	Consistently controls sentence structure and the conventions of EAE.
Word Choice	Exhibits weak and/or inappropriate words.	Exhibits a narrow range of word choice, often including inappropriate selections.	Exhibits appropriate word choice.	Exhibits varied and precise word choice.

Reprinted with permission of the GED Testing Service of the American Council on Education.

A High-Scoring GED Essay

To get a better idea of an effective GED essay, read the sample topic assignment below and the essay that follows it.

TOPIC

What is one important goal you would like to achieve in the next few years?

In your essay, identify that goal. Explain how you plan to achieve it. Use your personal observations, experience, and knowledge to support your answer.

Reprinted with permission of the GED Testing Service of the American Council on Education.

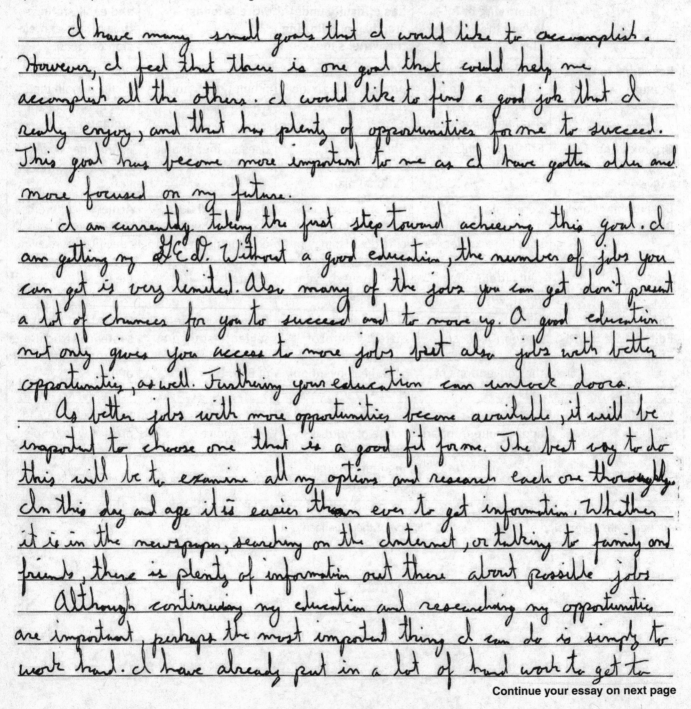

I have many small goals that I would like to accomplish. However, I feel that there is one goal that could help me accomplish all the others. I would like to find a good job that I really enjoy, and that has plenty of opportunities for me to succeed. This goal has become more important to me as I have gotten older and more focused on my future.

I am currently taking the first step toward achieving this goal. I am getting my G.E.D. Without a good education, the number of jobs you can get is very limited. Also many of the jobs you can get don't present a lot of chances for you to succeed and to move up. A good education not only gives you access to more jobs but also jobs with better opportunities, as well. Furthering your education can unlock doors.

As better jobs with more opportunities become available, it will be important to choose one that is a good fit for me. The best way to do this will be to examine all my options and research each one thoroughly. In this day and age it is easier than ever to get information. Whether it is in the newspaper, searching on the Internet, or talking to family and friends, there is plenty of information out there about possible jobs

Although continuing my education and researching my opportunities are important, perhaps the most important thing I can do is simply to work hard. I have already put in a lot of hard work to get to

Continue your essay on next page

this point, but I know there is more to do. If I want to find the right job and then succeed, it will be up to me.

Getting a better job is important to me. A better job would lead to more money, which will help me improve my life in many other way. By working hard and taking one step at a time, I feel confident that I will accomplish my goal.

This paper received a score of 4.

This clearly focused response explains the writer's desire to find a good job. He achieves coherent development with specific and relevant examples of the educational preparation necessary ("I am getting my GED"). He acknowledges the importance of researching his options and explains how his current activities are preparing him to do that. Control of sentence structure and EAE is consistent, and word choice is precise.

Compare this essay with your own. Does your essay show similar strengths in—

- ❏ focus?
- ❏ development?
- ❏ examples?
- ❏ control of sentence structure?
- ❏ control of Edited American English?
- ❏ word choice?

Social Studies

1. **(2) the West Indies to the British colonies; the British colonies to Africa; Africa to the West Indies (Comprehension)** According to the map, the West Indies exported sugar and molasses to the British colonies in North America. The British colonies exported rum to Africa. Finally, Africa exported slaves and gold to the West Indies. The trade routes formed a triangle.

2. **(1) Cargo ships never had to sail empty on any leg of a profitable triangular journey. (Analysis)** This is a general conclusion that is supported by the details of the map, which show goods traveling along each leg of the triangular trade route. Therefore, a very profitable journey must have meant a ship carried cargo on each leg of the route. The remaining options state details that may or may not be confirmed by the map.

3. **(5) credit union (Application)** A consumer looking for a low rate of interest on a mortgage would probably do best at a credit union, which often offers better rates than other types of banking institutions. Note, however, to get the rate the consumer would first have to qualify to join the credit union.

4. **(3) saving the town money and making recycling convenient (Comprehension)** The brochure points out that recycling saves the town dumping fees, which is an incentive to recycle. The other incentive, implied in the chart and the sentence following the chart, is that recycling is easy: sorting the recyclables for the bins and putting the bins out with the regular trash are quite convenient.

5. **(4) fining each household that mixes its recyclables in with the regular trash (Analysis)** If compliance is low, the best way to get more households to participate is to fine those that do not. To avoid future fines, the households that haven't recycled before are likely to begin recycling.

6. **(5) serving on a jury (Application)** Serving on a jury, like voting, is a civic duty of each citizen. It is a way to participate in the judicial branch of government. Note that although option (2), displaying the American flag, is a patriotic act, it does not involve participating in government in any way and so is not a way of participating in the political system.

7. **(4) law and order (Evaluation)** The hallmark of military rule is strict control over the citizenry; in other words, law and order.

8. **(1) The U.S. president controls the armed forces and the South African president does not. (Analysis)** First locate the columns for the U.S. and South African presidents. The checkmarks in those columns differ only in control of the armed forces, with the U.S. president shown to have this power and the South African president shown not to have it.

9. **(2) Of all the presidents shown, the French president has the most power. (Analysis)** This statement is a conclusion, a generalization based on the details in the chart. Options (1), (3), and (4) are specific details from the chart. Option (5) is not true.

10. **(5) The U.S. Supreme Court ruling in *Plessy v. Ferguson* was wrong because it infringed on freedoms guaranteed in the Constitution. (Analysis)** This statement is a rephrasing of the dissenting justice's opinion, or belief, about the case. The other statements are all facts from the paragraph.

11. **(4) Knowing only latitude and longitude does not help a person get around a city. (Evaluation)** Being able to pinpoint precise location in terms of latitude and longitude is not of much value in a city unless this information is translated into streets and highways. A basic receiver such as the one described in the paragraph does not do that; however, other more sophisticated models, such as those built into vehicle dashboards, do just that.

12. **(2) The nation's debt increased at a faster rate than did the U.S. population during the period shown on the graph. (Evaluation)** You can tell this is true because the per capita debt figure increased steadily from 1980 to 2000. This would happen only if the debt increased faster than the number of people in the United States.

13. **(4) raise taxes (Analysis)** By raising taxes, the United States could collect enough revenue to pay off the debt if it wished.

14. **(3) Many cities had large populations because nearby coal and iron ore deposits meant jobs. (Analysis)** Coal and iron ore were among the most important raw materials of the Industrial Revolution. By examining the relationship of the location of the cities to that of the coalfields and iron ore deposits, you can conclude that Great Britain's most populous cities (with the exception of London) were large partly because of their proximity to the important raw materials of the Industrial Revolution. The remaining statements are details from the map.

15. **(2) Great Britain's acceptance of Germany's takeover of Austria and Czechoslovakia in the late 1930s (Application)** Of all the options, this is the only one that has the element of concession without opposition that is the hallmark of appeasement.

16. **(4) People value the lives of their children more than they value money. (Analysis)** This is the underlying assumption of the poster: that Americans have been willing to send their sons into battle where they risk their lives, but haven't been donating money to the war cause with equal willingness. The poster thus plays upon their sense of guilt.

17. **(2) World War I (Comprehension)** The poster is dated 1917, so the war is World War I.

18. **(5) television ads at prime time (Application)** Today the government could probably reach the most people with TV ads rather than print or radio ads (especially on classical stations), because so many people watch TV.

19. **(5) The population of the colony of New York was smaller than that of Connecticut. (Evaluation)** Since the chart shows the five colonies with the largest populations in 1750, it follows that any colony not listed has a population smaller than that of Connecticut, which ranked fifth. The other options are not supported by the data in the table.

20. **(3) Applying for Civil Service Jobs (Comprehension)** This title best describes what the flow-chart shows—the steps in applying for a civil service job.

21. **(1) salary (Analysis)** The GS rating of a job, based on the job description and the candidate's skills and experience, is directly related to the salary level of the position. The other options would not be affected by the GS rating.

22. **(2) equal opportunity (Evaluation)** Since Civil Service jobs are open to all who apply and are awarded on merit, they provide equal opportunity for employment, regardless of gender, race, ethnicity, party affiliation, or other factors.

23. **(2) 8 percent and $4,500 billion (Comprehension)** Locate 1995 on each graph. (Note that each tic mark on the horizontal axis indicates a year, even if it is not labeled.) The first graph shows the mortgage interest rate was about 8 percent in 1995. The second graph shows the total outstanding mortgage debt was about $4,500 billion in 1995.

24. **(1) The lower the interest rate, the higher the total mortgage debt outstanding. (Analysis)** Look at the general trend shown by each graph. Note that as interest rates fell, total mortgage debt rose. This is because consumers tend to borrow more when the cost of borrowing decreases.

25. **(5) Hollywood, California, with its movie and television entertainment industry (Application)** The movies and TV shows that originate in Hollywood are distributed worldwide, helping to spread American popular culture to other nations.

Science

1. **(3) Neurons transmit instructions regarding movement to muscles. (Comprehension)** Since neurons transmit information and the function of muscles is to move, it follows that neurons transmit instructions regarding movement to muscles. The paragraph and the diagrams show that all the other options contain incorrect information.

2. **(5) Comets formed when the solar system was born. (Analysis)** Opinions are usually signaled by words like "believe," "think," or "feel." In this case, the last sentence of the paragraph states that scientists *believe* that comets formed when the solar system was born, showing that option (5) is an opinion.

3. **(5) photosynthesis, in which green plants use the energy from sunlight to make carbohydrates from water and carbon dioxide (Application)** The key element in a photochemical reaction is light. Of the options listed, only photosynthesis involves light.

4. **(4) It helps control metabolism and growth. (Comprehension)** First locate thyroxine in the "Hormone" column, then move along the row to the "Function" column to find the answer.

5. **(5) uncontrolled blood sugar levels (Analysis)** The chart shows that insulin regulates blood sugar levels, so problems with insulin production will cause problems with blood sugar levels.

6. **(1) Growth hormone is only one of several factors that determine a person's adult height. (Evaluation)** Growth hormone alone does not determine height. A person's genetic make-up—the height of his parents and other family members—contributes, as do nutrition and the action of other hormones. Paul's expectations were therefore unrealistic.

7. **(3) oil and vinegar salad dressing (Application)** This is an example of an emulsion—two liquids mixed together but not dis-solving. If you let oil and vinegar dressing stand, the oil will rise to the top. The other options are all solutions, which do not separate over time.

8. **(3) a meteorologist who studies weather patterns and predicts weather (Application)** Knowledge gained from a study of the atmosphere and hydrosphere is closely related to the study of weather, which is influenced by both.

9. **(5) They are decomposers. (Application)** Since earthworms are feeding on dead organic matter, which comes from dead organisms, they must be decomposers.

10. **(2) switch from whole milk to 1 percent milk (Analysis)** The switch from whole milk to low-fat milk reduces fat intake by 3.5 grams/serving. While the difference in saturated fat per serving is greater in cheddar cheese than in milk, since the child drinks 4 servings of milk daily, this would be a reduction of 14 grams per day. The reduction from switching cheeses comes to 9.6 grams, since the child eats two servings of cheese per day.

11. **(1) moving your hand closer to the center of the revolving door (Analysis)** Moving your hand closer to the center of the door decreases distance to the pivot point. Since the force remains the same in this case, when you multiply distance times force you will come up with a lower number, which indicates decreased torque.

12. **(1) coal/peat and natural gas (Analysis)** Look on the circle graph for energy sources occupying wedges of approximately the same size. The only two that are about the same size are coal/peat and natural gas, indicating they provide about the same proportion of energy consumed in the United States.

13. **(2) As European Americans moved from the East Coast westward between 1620 and 1850, they cut down forests to build farms. (Evaluation)** The map shows and the paragraph implies that the virgin forests of the eastern United States were almost all cut down between 1620 and 1850. The paragraph further implies that the forests were cut down for farmland, which has since been abandoned. Based on this information, option (2) is the only conclusion that is supported by the map and the paragraph. The map and the paragraph either lack support for or contradict the other options.

14. **(2) the Northern Hemisphere (Comprehension)** First locate June 21 on the diagram and then examine the tilt of Earth. Note that at that time of year, the Northern Hemisphere tilts toward the sun, and it is summer there.

15. **(4) On the first day of spring and fall, neither the Northern Hemisphere nor the Southern Hemisphere is tilted toward the sun. (Evaluation)** According to the diagram, on March 21 and September 23, Earth's axis is tilted neither toward nor away from the sun, so neither hemisphere is tilted toward the sun. The remaining options are not supported by the diagram.

16. **(5) A quadrat makes plant distribution estimates more reliable. (Analysis)** This option is a conclusion, or a general statement, that is supported by all the details in the paragraph. The other options are specific details paraphrased from the paragraph.

17. **(1) (Comprehension)**

Charles's Law

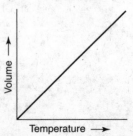

Charles's Law involves the relationship of a gas's volume and temperature. Since volume increases with increases in temperature, the first graph must be correct. Note that you can eliminate options (4) and (5) immediately because they involve changes in pressure, and Charles's Law assumes that pressure remains constant.

18. **(2) Atoms are composed of subatomic particles. (Analysis)** This is an assumption made by the writer of the paragraph. He or she does not explain this but assumes it is common knowledge. All the other options are statements made or strongly implied in the passage.

19. **(4) The student should have divided the mass by the volume. (Evaluation)** The paragraph states that density is calculated by dividing mass by volume. The student did the reverse, which is incorrect. All of the other steps the student followed were correct.

20. **(3) a mixture of metals (Comprehension)** According to the passage, the Anthony dollar was made of a copper-nickel alloy, and the final Sacagawea dollar, of a manganese, zinc, copper, and nickel alloy. From these examples, you can infer that an alloy is a mixture of metals.

21. **(2) Like nickels, dimes, and quarters, the Anthony dollar was silver-colored and therefore not distinctive. (Evaluation)** The Mint wanted to replace the Anthony dollar with a distinctive coin—a coin that looked different from the coins already in circulation. Making the new coin out of the same metals as the silver-colored Anthony dollar would not accomplish this.

22. **(5) hardy perennials (Application)** Hardy plants withstand frost, so they are more likely to survive than tender plants. Perennials come up and flower for many years. Therefore hardy perennials are likely to provide the most flowers with the least effort on the gardener's part.

23. **(3) A viewer could not see anything through the telescope. (Analysis)** The function of the flat mirror is to redirect the light rays toward the eyepiece so the viewer can see the object in the telescope's sights. If the flat mirror were removed, the reflection of the object would no longer be visible through the eyepiece.

24. **(2) They help scientists analyze large amounts of data in a systematic way. (Analysis)** The ability of a computer to process lots of data, far more systematically and quickly than a human being can, has helped speed and refine the drug discovery process although the older methods of running laboratory experiments and clinical trials are still also vitally important.

25. **(2) The cholera vaccine is only 60 percent effective. (Analysis)** Because getting vaccinated against cholera does not completely eliminate the traveler's chance of getting the disease, it makes sense that he or she should take extra precautions against contracting this food- and water-borne disease.

Reading

1. **(1) to contrast Japanese and American eating habits (Analysis)** The live lobster is an example of how close the Japanese are to their food sources. In contrast, the author shows how "distant" Americans are from the sources of the fast food they consume.

2. **(4) flipping a light switch (Application)** Only this option is automatic, routine, and "taken for granted," just as eating fast food, "brushing your teeth or stopping for a red light" are.

3. **(5) expose the fast-food industry for what it is and its far-reaching effects (Analysis)** The phrase "muck-and-Big-Mac-raking" is a play on the word *muckraking*. The rest of the sentence helps you understand what Schlosser's muckraking task is.

4. **(2) informal (Synthesis)** Throughout the excerpt are examples of Goodman's wit on a serious topic, including, "Not only was the tail raw, but it shared the plate with the body to which it had so recently been attached." Also, her choice of words and phrasing are breezy and informal: "We just take it wrapped and ready."

5. **(1) Learn how your food is prepared. (Synthesis)** The statement "few of us have any idea where the food comes from, how it gets to the plate, or what's in it" and Goodman's explanation of how chicken nuggets are processed help you conclude she would support this rule.

6. **(5) upset or angry with her (Comprehension)** The fourth and fifth paragraphs give examples of Diane's fear of what his silence indicates.

7. **(4) a mouse (Application)** Diane is timid and insecure. You might even describe her as "mousy."

8. **(1) Diane makes him act negatively toward her. (Analysis)** When Diane questions the narrator's every thought and expres-sion, she does not let him be him-self; instead, he must constantly reassure her. He therefore begins to feel and act negatively.

9. **(2) resentful (Synthesis)** The tone of the narration is resentful as the narrator describes how Diane "knew from the start how badly I was going to fail her" and in the end begins to criticize her, despite his initial feelings.

10. **(3) He begins to feel toward Diane the way she always feared he did. (Synthesis)** Diane expected the narrator to fail to love her and continually tried to prove her theory. This leads him to begin to "criticize everything about her."

11. **(2) indifference (Analysis)** The object of the speaker's love is cold to him; coldness is a way of expressing indifference, or not caring.

12. **(3) Why does she seem less interested the more I pursue her? (Comprehension)** "How comes it then [Why] that this her cold . . . harder grows [does she seem even less interested] the more I her entreat [the more I pursue her]?"

13. **(1) He wants her even more. (Analysis)** The speaker states, "I burn much more" as a result of her coldness.

14. **(3) change the very nature of things (Comprehension)** The final lines of the poem reveal the speaker's appreciation of love: "it can alter all the course of kind"—in other words, fire and ice, figuratively speaking, do not act as they ordinarily do.

15. **(4) desire and disinterest (Synthesis)** Throughout the poem fire (the speaker's desire) is contrasted with ice (his love's disinterest in him).

16. **(1) He hasn't tried to stop her from getting one. (Comprehension)** In lines 24–25, Mary responds to Mrs. Morehead's observation that Mary is the one who insists on a divorce, not her husband: "if he hadn't wanted it, he'd have fought me—"

17. **(5) appeals to Mary's duty to her family (Analysis)** Mrs. Morehead states that a child needs both parents in one home. Later she argues that fifty years ago women couldn't get divorces and "they made the best of situa-tions like this . . . [and] made very good things indeed!"

18. **(4) Her husband will miss her and want her back. (Analysis)** You can infer this is Mary's motive when she says, "Stephen does love me—But he won't find it out, until I've—really gone away."

19. **(2) discuss the problem with the friend (Application)** Mrs. Morehead seems levelheaded and straightforward in her talk with Mary. She encourages Mary to call off the divorce and go to her husband. She would there-fore probably talk to a friend and try to work things out.

20. **(3) Stephen was having an affair with someone at work. (Synthesis)** In the excerpt Mrs. Morehead says, "Have you thought: Stephen might marry that girl?" That coupled with the information about "his private affairs" and "knowing her" and no longer "going stale" help you conclude that the reason Mary is getting a divorce is that Stephen was having an affair.

Math

Part I

1. (2) B Simplify the fraction: $-\frac{16}{6} = -2\frac{2}{3}$; therefore, the point on the number line must be between -2 and -3. Only point B is at this location.

2. (5) between 1200 and 1300 The bar for Zone 3 is close to 900, and the bar for Zone 4 is between 300 and 400. Use an estimate such as 330. Combine: $900 + 330 = 1230$. Option (5) is correct.

3. (5) 1:2 The bar for Zone 1 seems to be a little less than halfway between 400 and 500; round to 450. The best estimate for the bar for Zone 3 is 900. Make sure you write the ratio in the order stated in the problem.
Zone 1:Zone 3 = 450:900, which simplifies as 1:2.

4. (3) 4 Substitute and simplify.
$2x - (4y - 3) + 5xz$
$2(-3) - [4(2) - 3] + 5(-3)(-1)$
$-6 - [8 - 3] + 15$
$-6 - 5 + 15$
$-11 + 15$
4

5. 36

The tower, the pole, the ground, and the sight line along the tops of the pole and tower form two similar right triangles. Use proportion to find the height of the tower.

$$\frac{\text{base from tower}}{\text{base from pole}} = \frac{\text{height of tower}}{\text{height of pole}}$$
$$\frac{95}{5} = \frac{x}{2}$$
$$95(2) = 5x$$
$$190 = 5x$$
$$x = 38 \text{ meters}$$

6. 70

In a parallelogram, the opposite angles are equal; therefore, if one obtuse angle measures 110°, its opposite also measures 110°. The sum of the interior angles of any quadrilateral is 360°. Thus, the sum of the two acute angles equals $360° - 2(110°) = 360° - 220° = 140°$. Since both acute angles have the same measure, one of the angles measures $140° \div 2 = 70°$.

7. (1) 18 If the face of each cabinet is a rectangle, then the cabinet is in the shape of a rectangular solid. To find the volume, use the formula Volume = length × width × height. To work the problem in cubic feet, change the inch measurements to feet.
$24 \text{ in} \times 72 \text{ in} \times 18 \text{ in} = 2 \text{ ft} \times 6 \text{ ft} \times 1.5 \text{ ft} = 18 \text{ cu ft}$

8. (3) $157.50 Both have the same discount rate. You can find the discounts first and then add the discounted price of each cabinet, or add first and find the discount for the total.
$90 + $120 = $210 original price
$210 × 0.25 = $52.50 discount
Subtract the discount.
$210 − $52.50 = $157.50

9. (4) 16 Divide 10 by $\frac{3}{5}$.
$10 \div \frac{3}{5} = 10 \times \frac{5}{3} = \frac{50}{3} = 16\frac{2}{3}$
Decide what to do with the fraction part of the answer. The answer would round to 17 bowls, but the potter can complete only 16 bowls. There isn't enough left to make a 17th complete bowl.

10. (2) 3 The problem doesn't tell you anything about the actual number of hours Janelle will work, but it does tell you how her time spent at one activity compares to another. If she works 100 hours, she will spend 44 hours working at the counter, 9 hours processing new books, and 6 hours repairing bindings. Compare 44 to 15. The number 44 is about 3 times as great as 15.

11. (2) $2600 Let x = the amount Matthew earns and $x + $520 = the amount Levy earns. Write an equation and solve.
$x + x + $520 = $4680
$2x + $520 = $4680
$2x = $4160
$x = $2080
If Matthew earns $2080, then Levy earns $2080 + $520 = $2600.

12. (1) $\frac{1}{3}(3.14)(2^2)(6)$ The formula for finding the volume of a cone is Volume $= \frac{1}{3} \times \pi \times \text{radius}^2 \times \text{height}$. Substitute the values from the diagram and select the correct option. Since the diameter is 4 inches, the radius is 2 inches. The correct option is $\frac{1}{3}(3.14)(2^2)(6)$.

13. (2,4) Sketch a coordinate grid, and plot the points given in the problem. Then determine the location of the fourth vertex. Plot the correct coordinates.

Part II

1. (3) 160 Using the percent formula (part = rate × base), solve for the total (base). $24 = 0.15b$ Divide. $24 \div 0.15 = 160$

2. (5) $8^2 + 9^2 = x^2$ The distances that Jill drives are the legs of a right triangle. Use the Pythagorean relationship to find the way to solve for the hypotenuse (x).
$a^2 + b^2 = c^2$
$8^2 + 9^2 = x^2$

3. (2) $18 - 2x$ Simplify as follows.
$4x - 2(3x - 9)$
$4x - 6x + 18$
$-2x + 18$, which equals $18 - 2x$

4. (3) 21 One way to solve the problem is to find a number that is evenly divisible by 6 and 14, and then try each answer option. Go through the multiples of 14 until you find one that is divisible by 6: 14, 28, 42. The number 42 is divisible by both 14 and 6. Then review the answer choices. 42 cannot be evenly divided by 8, 12, 28, or 35. It can be evenly divided by 21.

5. 40

Angle a is a vertical angle to the angle that measures 40°, and vertical angles are equal.

6. 13

Work backward through the facts. Sheila has worked 10 years. Kathy has worked half as long as Sheila, which equals 5 years. Alice has worked 8 years longer than Kathy. $5 + 8 = 13$ years

7. (4) $\frac{3}{4}$ Two sections, which equal $\frac{2}{8}$ or $\frac{1}{4}$, are marked "blue." Thus, the chance of not getting blue is $1 - \frac{1}{4} = \frac{3}{4}$.

8. (2) $\frac{\$30(100)}{\$290}$ To find percent of change, divide the amount of change ($290 − $260 = $30) by the original price ($290). Each choice is multiplied by 100 to change the result from a decimal to a percent.

9. (3) 5.5 The median is the middle of the data. Arrange the numbers of accounts in order: 2, 4, 4, 4, 5, 6, 6, 7, 7, 8. The middle numbers are 5 and 6. When there are two numbers in the middle, find the mean of the numbers. $5 + 6 = 11$, and $11 \div 2 = 5.5$

10. (5) 4 This is a quadratic equation. You can factor the equation and solve for x, but the quickest way to solve the problem is to try each answer option in the equation.

$$3x^2 - 10x = 8$$
$$3(4^2) - 10(4) = 8$$
$$3(16) - 40 = 8$$
$$48 - 40 = 8$$
$$8 = 8$$

11. (5) Not enough information is given. You need to know how many pages are in each program in order to multiply the number of pages per program by cost by number of programs. You are not given that information.

12. (−2,1) Try sketching the information on scratch paper, but be sure to be as accurate as possible in your drawing. Or lightly draw the line segments on the coordinate grid. They intersect at point (−2,1). Be sure to erase completely any stray marks on the grid on the answer sheet.

PRETEST PLANNING CHARTS

Language Arts, Writing

Circle the number of the questions that you got correct and total them in the last column of each row.

CONTENT AREA	Correction	Revision	Construction Shift	Correct/Total
Organization (pages 66–83)	17, 20		4, 9	____/4
Sentence Structure (pages 84–105)		2, 6, 10, 16	13, 22, 24	____/7
Grammar and Usage (pages 106–123)	1, 3, 14, 15, 18	8, 19, 21		____/8
Mechanics (pages 124–139)	5, 7, 11, 23	12, 25		____/6
Total				____/25

Use this chart to determine your areas of strength and weakness. If you do not have time to review the entire writing unit of this book, you may want to review the sections in which you need the most work.

Social Studies

Circle the number of the questions that you got correct and total them in the last column of each row.

CONTENT AREA	Comprehension	Application	Analysis	Evaluation	Correct/Total
U.S. History (pages 166–179)	1, 17	18	2, 10, 16	19	____/7
World History (pages 180–193)		15	14	7	____/3
Civics and Government (pages 194–205)	20	6	8, 9, 21	22	____/6
Economics (pages 206–217)	23	3	13, 24	12	____/5
Geography (pages 218–228)	4	25	5	11	____/4
Total					____/25

Use this chart to determine your areas of strength and weakness. If you do not have time to review the entire social studies unit of this book, you may want to focus your study on the areas in which you need the most work.

Science

Circle the number of the questions that you got correct and total them in the last column of each row.

CONTENT AREA	Comprehension	Application	Analysis	Evaluation	Correct/Total
Life Science (pages 234–253)	1, 4	9, 22	5, 10, 16, 24, 25	6, 13	_____/11
Earth and Space Science (pages 254–267)	14	8	2, 12	15	_____/5
Physical Science (pages 268–282)	17, 20	3, 7	11, 18, 23	19, 21	_____/9
Total					_____/25

Use this chart to determine your areas of strength and weakness. If you do not have time to review the entire science unit of this book, you may want to focus your study on the areas in which you need the most work.

Reading

Circle the number of the questions that you got correct and total them in the last column of each row.

CONTENT AREA	Comprehension	Application	Analysis	Synthesis	Correct/Total
Nonfiction (pages 286–303)		2	1, 3	4, 5	_____/5
Fiction (pages 304–317)	6	7	8	9, 10	_____/5
Poetry (pages 318–329)	12, 14		11, 13	15	_____/5
Drama (pages 330–340)	16	19	17, 18	20	_____/5
Total					_____/20

Use this chart to determine your areas of strength and weakness. If you do not have time to review the entire reading unit of this book, you may want to focus your study on the areas in which you need the most work.

Mathematics

Circle the number of the questions that you got correct and total them in the last column of each row.

CONTENT AREA	Test Portion	Using Procedures	Understanding Concepts	Applying Strategies	Correct/Total
Math Basics (pages 346–347)	Part I				
	Part II		4	6	____/2
Decimals and Fractions (pages 368–389)	Part I			9	
	Part II			11	____/2
Ratio, Proportion, and Percent (pages 390–411)	Part I	10		3, 8	
	Part II	8		1	____/5
Data Analysis (pages 412–433)	Part I	2		.	
	Part II	9		7	____/3
Measurement (pages 434–449)	Part I			7	
	Part II				____/1
Algebra (pages 450–495)	Part I	4	1	11	
	Part II	10	3		____/5
Geometry (pages 496–528)	Part I	12	6, 13	5	
	Part II	2	5, 12		____/7
Total					____/25

Use this chart to determine your areas of strength and weakness. If you do not have time to review the entire math unit of this book, you may want to focus your study on the areas in which you need the most work.

Language Arts, Writing

The GED Language Arts, Writing Test consists of two parts. Part I uses multiple choice questions to assess your knowledge of the conventions of written English. Part II requires you to write an essay. The scores for Parts I and II will be combined and reported to you as a single score. You will have a total of two hours for the test.

Part I: 50 questions, 1 hour 15 minutes

On Part I, you will read 6 to 9 documents that are 12 to 22 sentences long. You will answer multiple choice questions about each document.

Part II: 1 essay, 45 minutes

The test directions tell you to plan, make notes, write, revise, and edit an essay on an assigned topic. It is recommended that you take 45 minutes for your essay. If you have time left, you can go back to work on Part I.

Part I: Content Areas

Organization (15 percent) These questions focus on the clarity with which ideas are presented and organized. Organization items ask about choosing effective topic sentences, paragraphing, moving sentences to improve the order of ideas, removing irrelevant sentences, and using transitions. You can review and practice these skills on pages 66–73 and 80–83.

Sentence Structure (30 percent) These questions will test your ability to recognize and correct errors in sentence structure. Topics include correcting sentence fragments, comma splices, and run-on sentences; combining ideas effectively; correctly placing modifying words or phrases; and making sure that parallel parts of a sentence are consistent. You can review and practice these skills on pages 84–97 and 102–105.

Usage (30 percent) These questions ask about the rules governing our use of the English language. Topics include choosing correct verb forms and tenses, making subjects and verbs agree, and correcting common errors in pronoun use. You can review and practice these skills on pages 106–117 and 120–123.

Mechanics (25 percent) Mechanics questions focus on correcting errors in punctuation, capitalization, and spelling. Most of the punctuation questions concern comma use and misuse. Capitalization items apply rules for capitalizing and for avoiding unnecessary capitalization. Spelling questions focus on possessives, contractions, homonyms, and commonly confused words. You can review and practice these skills on pages 124–133 and 136–139.

GED TIP

Don't rush to answer the questions on the writing test. You will have time to read each document carefully, from beginning to end. As you do, think about the corrections or improvements that could be made.

Part I: Multiple Choice

Three Types of Documents

You will read and answer questions about three types of documents:

- **How-to** documents such as instructions and directions
- **Workplace** documents such as business letters and memos
- **Informational** documents such as mailings on tourist destinations or analyses of public transit needs

Read each document before you answer the questions that follow it. As you read, look for errors and other problems, as if you were going to fix them. That way, you will be able to predict many of the questions that follow. You will also be better able to answer questions that ask you to look at the piece as a whole. For example, for some questions you must consider the organization of the piece, such as where you should divide one long paragraph, or the relevance of a detail, such as which sentence could be deleted.

Three Types of Questions

Read the document below. Then choose answers to the questions that follow.

GETTING STARTED WITH EXERCISE

(1) Sooner or later, we all realize that we are not getting any younger. (2) At that point, many of us decide too start an exercise program. (3) For an exercise program to be effective, you need to spend at least 20 minutes, 3 times a week. (4) If you decide to exercise regularly, you should first check with your doctor. (5) Your doctor will tell you what type of exercise is best for you.

Correction Questions

These questions require you to identify an error in a sentence and the best way to fix it. But be aware: some sentences will not contain any errors. For these questions, choose option (5)—no correction is necessary (or no revision is necessary).

Example Sentence 2: At that point, many of us decide too start an exercise program.

Which correction should be made to sentence 2?
(1) remove the comma after point
(2) insert we after us
(3) change decide to decides
(4) replace too with to
(5) no correction is necessary

Answer: (4) replace too with to This spelling correction replaces one word with the correct homonym.

Revision Questions

A revision question shows you an underlined portion of a sentence or sentences and asks you to choose the best revision for it. The first option will always be the same as the underlined words. If the sentence is correct as written, you should choose option (1).

Example Sentence 3: For an exercise program to be <u>effective, you</u> need to spend at least 20 minutes, 3 times a week.

Which is the best way to write the underlined portion of this sentence? If the original is the best way, choose option (1).

(1) effective, you
(2) effective you
(3) effective. You
(4) effective, and you
(5) effective, so you

Answer: (1) effective, you The sentence is correct as written. The other options incorrectly punctuate the sentence or add an unnecessary connecting word.

Construction Shift Questions

These items ask you to recognize writing that may not be technically incorrect, but it is wordy or awkward. When you read the sentence or pair of sentences, you need to think about how you could rewrite to improve them.

Example Sentences 4 and 5: If you decide to exercise regularly, you should first check with your doctor. Your doctor will tell you what type of exercise is best for you.

The most effective combination of sentences 4 and 5 would include which group of words?

(1) If you ever do decide whether or not to,
(2) When you are deciding
(3) At the time at which you decide,
(4) doctor, who will tell you
(5) doctor, and then he or she will

Answer: (4) doctor, who will tell you Option (4) smoothly combines the two sentences to eliminate the repeated phrase *your doctor*. The new sentence would read as follows: *If you decide to exercise regularly, you should first check with your doctor, who will tell you what type of exercise is best for you.* The other options would not solve the problem of repetition or would create an even more awkward sentence.

You will have 45 minutes to write an essay on an assigned topic. The directions encourage you to plan, make notes, draft, revise, and edit your essay. Once you practice writing on the essay topics in this book, you will see that 45 minutes is enough time to plan, write, and edit a well-developed essay of about 250 words.

Essay Topic

You will be given a topic, sometimes called a "prompt," to write about. The topic will be one that you can write about by drawing on your general life experience and observations. Specialized knowledge will not be needed. The essay will ask you to give your opinion or an explanation.

Below is a sample GED essay prompt:

TOPIC

Many people vote in every election. Other people don't vote at all. Do you think that it is important to vote? Why or why not?

In your essay, explain the reasons for your opinion.

Holistic Scoring

Two readers will read your essay; each will assign it a score from 1 to 4. The average of the two scores is combined, through a formula, with your score from Part I.

The essay readers won't take out a red pen and mark mistakes. Rather, each will read the essay once, fairly quickly, to get an impression of your work as a whole. This method of evaluating is called "holistic" scoring. The essay readers will ask themselves the following questions about your paper:

- Is there a clearly focused main idea?
- Does the main idea of the essay address the assigned topic?
- Is the essay clear and logically organized?
- Is the word choice appropriate and effective?
- Does the essay basically contain correct sentence structure, grammar, and mechanics?

Your essay score will reflect one of the general categories shown below:

Level 4—effective
Level 3—adequate
Level 2—marginal
Level 1—inadequate

If your essay receives an average score of less than 2, you will not receive any score for the Language Arts, Writing Test, even if you performed well on Part I.

GED TIP

The best way to write an effective GED essay is to follow a strategy that uses the 45 minutes to plan, write, edit, and revise. You can devise this kind of strategy later in this writing section.

ON THE GED

There is no "right" answer to a GED essay topic question. The essay scorers are looking to see only if you can support your answer with logical, well-written statements.

The essay scorers are trained to expect that your work is a draft written under the pressure of a test. They are not expecting it to be perfect.

The Standards for Your Essay Score

Below is a copy of the scoring guidelines that the essay readers will use when they review your paper: Read the guidelines over carefully, and come back to them to evaluate the essays that you write as you work through this book.

GED Essay Scoring Guide

	1	2	3	4
	Inadequate	**Marginal**	**Adequate**	**Effective**
	Reader has difficulty identifying or following the writer's ideas	**Reader occasionally has difficulty understanding or following the writer's ideas**	**Reader understands writer's ideas**	**Reader understands and easily follows the writer's expression of ideas**
Response to the Prompt	Attempts to address prompt but with little or no success in establishing a focus	Addresses the prompt, though the focus may shift	Uses the writing prompt to establish a main idea	Presents a clearly focused main idea that addresses the prompt
Organization	Fails to organize ideas	Shows some evidence of an organizational plan	Uses an identifiable organizational plan	Establishes a clear and logical organization
Development and Details	Demonstrates little or no development; usually lacks details or examples or presents irrelevant information	Has some development but lacks specific details; may be limited to listing, repetitions, or generalizations	Has focused but occasionally uneven development; incorporates some specific detail	Achieves coherent development with specific and relevant details and examples
Conventions of Edited American English (EAE)	Exhibits minimal or no control of sentence structure and the conventions of EAE	Demonstrates inconsistent control of sentence structure and the conventions of EAE	Generally controls sentence structure and the conventions of EAE	Consistently controls sentence structure and the conventions of EAE
Word Choice	Exhibits weak and/or inappropriate words	Exhibits a narrow range of word choice, often including inappropriate selections	Exhibits appropriate word choice	Exhibits varied and precise word choice

Clear and Organized Writing

Ideas and Paragraphs

Key Ideas

- Each paragraph should have one main idea. Each sentence in the paragraph should relate to the main idea.
- Break long paragraphs into two if possible.
- Join short paragraphs if they both relate to the same main idea.

Effective Paragraphs

A **paragraph** is a group of sentences that relate to one main idea. If the sentences do not help develop the same main idea, the paragraph seems disorganized, and the writer's meaning is unclear.

Incorrect: Group of sentences that do not relate to the same main idea:
Houseplants make a home more beautiful, but many people find them difficult to take care of. I water my houseplants once a week. There are many different kinds of houseplants. If you are buying a houseplant as a gift, consider how much light the person's home gets.

In the example above, each sentence is about houseplants, but there is no main idea. In the paragraph below, however, each sentence supports one idea: *helping houseplants adjust to a new home.*

Correct: Paragraph with sentences that relate to one main idea:
Houseplants need help to adjust to a new environment. Your home is probably less bright and humid than a greenhouse or plant store. Therefore, when you get a new houseplant, keep it near a south-facing window at first. Move it away from the light over a period of four weeks. Use a humidifier to make the air in your home more humid. These actions will help avoid the loss of foliage that often occurs when plants change locales.

One paragraph should stop and a new one begin when the main idea shifts. In the example below, the first four sentences describe what road rage is, while the last four sentences tell how to react to road rage. The writer should have started a new paragraph with sentence 5.

Incorrect: One paragraph that should be divided into two paragraphs:
(1) Road rage is an episode of violent behavior that takes place when one driver's actions anger another driver. (2) Young males are the most likely to lose their cool on the road. (3) Most road rage incidents take place during rush hour, when people often get frustrated. (4) Warm weather is another factor in road rage. (5) If you're a victim of an aggressive driver, try to stay calm. (6) Don't react or make eye contact. (7) Try not to brake or swerve in retaliation. (8) These actions will only infuriate the other driver, and you might lose control of your car.

Sometimes the ideas in two paragraphs really belong in one:

Incorrect: Two paragraphs that should be combined:
To make chicken broth, boil a pot of water. Take some chicken, onions, parsnips, carrots, and herbs, and wrap them up in cheesecloth.

Make sure it is real cotton cheesecloth, or you won't be able to eat the broth! Simmer the cheesecloth-wrapped vegetables and chicken in the water for several hours; then remove them. Add salt and pepper to taste.

GED TIP

If a paragraph is especially long in a GED passage, check to see if the main idea shifts at some point. If so, that is where the paragraph should be divided in two.

A. Directions: Read each group of sentences. If there is a main idea, underline it. If there is no main idea, write "No MI."

_____ 1. The pharmacist at the local drugstore is very helpful. She can always get the medicines we need. She arranges deliveries of our prescriptions when we're sick. When we don't have money, she lets us pay the next time. Many people have written to thank her.

_____ 2. Keep your toolbox well equipped, and you'll always be able to make home repairs. Common home repairs include replacing lighting fixtures and fixing furniture. The community center offers a class on this subject. You can pay someone to do home repairs.

_____ 3. Some people don't vote because they think their vote doesn't count. However, elections have been won by just a few hundred votes. If people don't vote, they are giving up their voice. Every vote counts, so let your voice be heard and vote!

_____ 4. When you are traveling, it's a good idea to mark your luggage clearly. Put a luggage tag on every piece you intend to bring, including hand luggage like backpacks. To recognize your luggage quickly, put a brightly colored ribbon on it.

_____ 5. Listening to music can benefit you in many ways. When you are feeling stress, music can help soothe and relax you. When you need energy, rock 'n' roll or hip-hop can give you a boost. If you have a baby or small child, soft music can help lull the child to sleep.

B. Questions 6 and 7 refer to the following paragraphs.

The Common Cold

(A)

(1) How frequently you get colds depends on your age. (2) The average young adult gets two to four colds a year. (3) Adults over 60 have fewer than one cold a year, while children have six to ten colds annually. (4) Colds are caused by viruses. (5) Contrary to popular belief, being cold will not cause you to get a cold. (6) Vitamin C is thought to prevent colds, but there is no proof.

(B)

(7) Because there is no cure for the common cold, prevention is key. (8) Washing your hands is the best way to avoid getting a cold. (9) Encourage others who have colds to sneeze into a tissue and throw it away immediately.

(C)

(10) Refrain from touching your eyes and nose, and stay far from people who have colds.

6. Which revision would improve the effectiveness of the article?

   Begin a new paragraph with

   (1) sentence 2
   (2) sentence 3
   (3) sentence 4
   (4) sentence 5
   (5) sentence 6

7. Which revision would improve the effectiveness of the article?

   (1) remove paragraph B
   (2) remove paragraph C
   (3) move paragraph B to follow paragraph C
   (4) join paragraphs B and C
   (5) no revision is necessary

Answers and explanations start on page 629.

- A topic sentence states the main idea of a paragraph.
- Each sentence in a paragraph should provide details to support the main idea.
- An essay should have a main idea statement that states the main point of the entire essay.

ON THE GED

The topic sentence will generally be at the beginning of a paragraph. You may need to choose a more effective topic sentence, or you may need to choose a topic sentence for a paragraph that is missing one.

Topic Sentences in Paragraphs

Every paragraph should have a **topic sentence** that states the main idea. The other sentences in the paragraph are **supporting details.** These details tell more about the topic sentence. The topic sentence usually appears at the beginning of the paragraph, though it may appear elsewhere.

A topic sentence must do two things:

- Tell the topic, or subject, of the paragraph
- State the central point that the writer wants to make about the topic

In the paragraph below, the topic sentence is underlined. Notice how the topic sentence tells the subject of the paragraph (*graffiti in the neighborhood*) and states the central point about the topic (*graffiti is a serious problem in the neighborhood and should be addressed*).

EXAMPLE

We need to do more to stop the problem of graffiti in our neighborhood. Recently, several bus stops and the exterior walls of many buildings have been defaced with unsightly graffiti. The neighborhood is fast becoming a much less desirable place to live. As a result, prospective renters feel frightened and look elsewhere.

A topic sentence should not be too specific or too general. If it is, readers won't know what the overall point is. A topic sentence like "The market is covered with gang symbols" would be too specific for the paragraph above. "There is graffiti in our neighborhood" would be too general.

Main Idea Statements in Essays

Just as every paragraph should have a topic sentence, so every essay should have a **main idea statement.** Whereas a topic sentence states the main idea, or "point," of a single paragraph, a main idea statement expresses the central point of all the paragraphs in an essay. In the essay below, the main idea statement is underlined. Notice that while the main idea statement appears in the first paragraph, it is not the first sentence.

EXAMPLE

While graffiti is indeed a serious problem facing our neighborhood, other issues also need to be addressed. Two of the most pressing neighborhood issues are the crime rate and the lack of decent housing.

In recent months, crime has increased. For example, a number of muggings have occurred. As a result, residents are nervous about going out at night. The number of apartment break-ins has increased as well. We need a stronger police presence to combat the crime problem.

In addition, much of the housing in this neighborhood is in poor condition. Every day, residents are put in danger by peeling paint, broken locks, and rundown fences. We must put pressure on landlords to resolve their tenants' complaints, perhaps by showing them that, in the long run, it is in their financial interest to do so.

If we do not act immediately, our neighborhood will decline even more. Therefore, I recommend that we form a community task force to tackle these issues. We should ask our city councilwoman to be an advocate for us. With full participation of community members, we will be on our way to a safer, more livable neighborhood.

A. Directions: Write topic sentences for each of the following paragraphs.

1. _____

Weather satellites send us information about weather around the world. Thanks to satellite TV, we have an ever-widening range of programs to choose from. Satellites even play a role in long-distance telephone communication.

2. _____

First of all, stock prices are falling. Second, home sales have slowed to a crawl. Finally, many consumers have cut back on big purchases such as cars, home improvements, and vacations.

3. _____

According to the new dress code, employees of the library may now wear "semi-casual" clothing. Khakis, blue jeans with no holes, and other slacks are acceptable for men and women. Skirts must be knee-length or longer. Sandals are acceptable in the summer. Employees are requested not to wear gym shoes.

B. Questions 4 and 5 refer to the following paragraphs.

Repetitive Strain Injury

(A)

(1) Repetitive strain injury is a problem. (2) The injury can affect factory workers, computer users, and meatpackers, among others. (3) Anyone who uses his or her hands all day may be affected, even if the work does not seem to require a lot of physical effort. (4) When fine hand movements are repeated for many hours a day, they eventually strain the forearms, wrists, and fingers.

(B)

(5) Maintaining a stiff and constrained posture, as is required for working at a computer, places a lot of stress on the body. (6) Likewise, holding muscles still for long periods causes fatigue and discomfort. (7) In addition, many jobs require workers to work at top speed all day long. (8) Consistently working quickly deprives the body of natural rest breaks, forcing workers to push themselves to the limit.

4. Which is the most effective rewrite of sentence 1?

(1) Some workers get repetitive strain injury.

(2) Just what, you may ask, is repetitive strain injury?

(3) Repetitive strain injury affects many workers.

(4) Workers suffer many injuries on the job, and repetitive strain injury is just one of them.

(5) Repetitive strain injury is a painful condition resulting from repeated use of the hands.

5. Which sentence would be most effective if inserted at the beginning of paragraph B?

(1) Repetitive movements cause muscle strain.

(2) A number of factors contribute to repetitive strain injury.

(3) Watch your posture as you work.

(4) Repetitive strain injury is very common.

(5) Computer users frequently have problems.

Answers and explanations start on page 629.

CLEAR AND ORGANIZED WRITING

Logical Order and Relevance

When you are writing a paragraph, it is important to put your sentences in a logical order. For instance, you may choose to sequence supporting details from most important to least important, from least important to most important, or in time order. All the sentences in the paragraph should follow the same order. If not, your readers may get confused. Look at the sample paragraphs below:

Incorrect: Sentences not in time order:
> To clear a clogged drain using a plunger, fill the sink so that the water covers the plunger cup. Put petroleum jelly on the rim of the cup to form a tight seal. Before you begin, check to make sure that the plunger's suction cup is big enough to cover the drain. Block the sink overflow with rags. Plunge 15 or 20 times.

Correct: Sentences in time order:
> To clear a clogged drain using a plunger, <u>first check to make sure that the plunger's suction cup is big enough to cover the drain</u>. Fill the sink so that the water covers the plunger cup. Put petroleum jelly on the rim of the cup to form a tight seal. Block the sink overflow with rags. Plunge 15 or 20 times.

The reasons and examples you use to support your points should come immediately after you make each point. If they come later, they will be less effective.

Incorrect: Reason far from point:
> Don't make a habit of using chemicals to clear your drain. Always wear rubber gloves to protect your hands when using chemical drain cleaners. These powerful cleaners can damage the pipes.

Correct: Reason close to point:
> Don't make a habit of using chemicals to clear your drain. <u>These powerful cleaners can damage the pipes</u>. Always wear rubber gloves to protect your hands when using chemical drain cleaners.

Sometimes a sentence in a paragraph relates to the topic in a general way but does not support the topic sentence. This mistake is a type of **irrelevant detail**, as shown in the paragraph below:

> In many cultures, blonde is considered a desirable hair color. Perhaps blonde hair is valued because few people are naturally blonde. The practice of bleaching one's hair blonde is very old, dating back to ancient Roman times, and it continues to be popular today. <u>My sister dyed her hair last year</u>. A number of hair-bleaching products are sold in drugstores and supermarkets.

The sentence "My sister dyed her hair last year" is an irrelevant detail. While it relates to the topic of bleaching one's hair, it does not support the idea that blonde is a popular hair color in many cultures. This sentence should be deleted.

Key Ideas

- The sentences in a paragraph should follow a logical order.
- Keep reasons and examples close to the point you are making with them.
- Eliminate any irrelevant details.

ON THE GED

Some items will test your ability to recognize the logical order and relevance of sentences in paragraphs. You also need this skill to write your essay.

A. Directions: Cross out the irrelevant detail in each paragraph.

1. Why do people blame themselves when things go terribly wrong? Some psychologists believe that by blaming themselves, people find a reason for the upsetting event. Getting very ill is one bad thing that could happen. Finding a reason is more comforting than believing that the event took place for no reason at all.

2. It's almost time for the back-to-school rush. This year, come to Carter's to make sure that your child is outfitted with all the things that he or she needs. We have school supplies at rock-bottom prices. Adult students also can use school supplies. Check out our backpacks and lunch boxes in colors your kids will love. At Carter's, we have everything your kids will ever need!

3. Tenants: On Friday, April 23, the boiler in this building will be fixed. This job will be extremely expensive! There will be no water from 8 A.M. to 5 P.M. Please plan in advance, and draw out water the night before to be used the next day. We apologize for the inconvenience.

B. Questions 4 through 6 refer to the following cover letter.

(A)

Dear Mr. Soros:

    (1) Thank you very much for taking the time to speak with me on Thursday. (2) It was a pleasure to meet you and to learn about your organization.

(B)

    (3) As you will see from the enclosed resume, I recently completed a program in carpentry at Dade Community College. (4) I have also worked in the field. (5) In addition, I held a secretarial job.

(C)

    (6) With my education and experience, I believe that I could make a valuable contribution to your company. (7) Thank you for considering me for this position. (8) I look forward to hearing from you soon. (9) I would be honored to take the job if it were offered to me.

Sincerely,

Sandra Barnes

4. Which revision would improve the effectiveness of paragraph A?

  (1) remove sentence 1
  (2) move sentence 1 to follow sentence 2
  (3) move sentence 2 to the beginning of paragraph B
  (4) move paragraph A to follow paragraph C
  (5) no revision is necessary

5. **Sentence 5:** In addition, I held a secretarial job.

Which revision should be made to the placement of sentence 5?

  (1) move sentence 5 to follow sentence 1
  (2) move sentence 5 to follow sentence 3
  (3) move sentence 5 to follow sentence 7
  (4) remove sentence 5
  (5) no revision is necessary

6. **Sentence 9:** I would be honored to take the job if it were offered to me.

Which revision should be made to the placement of sentence 9?

  (1) move sentence 9 to follow sentence 2
  (2) move sentence 9 to follow sentence 3
  (3) move sentence 9 to follow sentence 6
  (4) move sentence 9 to follow sentence 7
  (5) no revision is necessary

Answers and explanations start on page 629.

CLEAR AND ORGANIZED WRITING

Relating Sentences and Paragraphs

Good writing flows smoothly and logically from one sentence to the next and from one paragraph to the next. To make your writing flow, use **transitions** to show how ideas are related. Here are some common transitions and their uses.

Key Ideas

- Use transitions to help your writing flow from sentence to sentence and from paragraph to paragraph.
- Choose the transition that expresses the correct relationship between ideas.

Transitional Word or Phrase	Use it to . . .
for example, for instance	give an example
also, furthermore, in addition, in the same way, likewise, moreover, similarly	compare ideas or add to an idea
however, nevertheless, on the other hand, in contrast	contrast ideas
first, second, then, next, after that, later, at last, finally, in conclusion	show steps in a process or time order
because	show a cause
as a result, consequently	show a result
therefore, thus	draw a conclusion

You can link two sentences using transitions in the following ways:

EXAMPLES

Begin the second sentence with a transition followed by a comma: Raquel has many hobbies. For example, she paints furniture and sews clothes.

Put the transition within the second sentence and set it off with commas: Raquel has many hobbies. She paints furniture, for example, and sews clothes.

Combine the two sentences into one. Put a semicolon before the transition and a comma after it: Raquel has many hobbies; for example, she paints furniture and sews clothes.

Transitions can also be used to link one paragraph to another, highlighting the relationship between the two paragraphs.

EXAMPLE

Top performance in sports depends on "mental economy." Mental economy involves focusing the mind on the task at hand. When athletes think too much about what they're doing or worry about the outcome, they interfere with the communication between the brain and the muscles.

In addition, athletes must strive for "physical economy." Although athletes put forth a tremendous amount of effort, they must take care to pace themselves in order to conserve energy for the end of the event.

To decide which transition to use, see how the paragraph is organized and what you are trying to accomplish. For example, are you comparing two things? If so, you will want to use transitions that compare ideas. Similarly, when choosing transitions to introduce paragraphs, consider the organization of the entire essay.

GED TIP

When you use a transition at the beginning of a sentence, be sure you put a comma after the transition. One exception is the word then. *You generally do not need a comma after it.*

A. Directions: Rewrite each pair of sentences using a transition from the chart on page 72. Change the punctuation if necessary. Write your answers on a separate sheet of paper.

Example: We have worked very hard this year. Sales are at an all-time high.
We have worked very hard this year. As a result, sales are at an all-time high.

1. Our marketing efforts need to be enhanced. We will soon begin another marketing initiative.

2. Sales representatives say their jobs are extremely demanding. The salary is attractive.

3. The marketing director has instructed sales representatives to try some new ideas. Sales representatives can give away free samples.

4. A new ad campaign will be launched in just a few weeks. We expect sales to increase.

B. Questions 5 through 7 refer to the following paragraphs.

Library Cafes

(A)

(1) Until very recently, eating was not something that most people associated with libraries. (2) A patron would likely be chased out for munching on a sandwich in a corner. (3) Times are changing, and these days patrons can even buy coffee and a croissant in some public libraries.

(B)

(4) Following the lead of successful bookstores, libraries across the country are installing cafes. (5) Some library cafes have menus that offer just as much variety as a regular restaurant. (6) In addition, one of them offers 20 varieties of coffee, hot cider, and muffins. (7) These refreshments make going to the library more pleasant and may therefore increase library patronage.

(C)

(8) Having a cafe may benefit a library financially. (9) The income from the cafe adds to library revenues. (10) Also, as more people enjoy coming to the library, they may be more likely to approve tax increases for it.

5. **Sentence 3:** Times are changing, and these days patrons can even buy coffee and a croissant in some public libraries.

Which correction should be made to sentence 3?

(1) insert <u>however</u> after <u>Times</u>
(2) insert <u>however,</u> after the comma
(3) insert <u>, however</u> after <u>these days</u>
(4) insert <u>however</u> after <u>coffee</u>
(5) insert <u>, however</u> after <u>coffee</u>

6. **Sentences 5 and 6:** Some library cafes have menus that offer just as much variety as a regular <u>restaurant. In addition,</u> one of them offers 20 varieties of coffee, hot cider, and muffins.

Which is the best way to write the underlined portion of these sentences? If the original is the best way, choose option (1).

(1) restaurant. In addition,
(2) restaurant, in addition,
(3) restaurant, for example,
(4) restaurant. For example,
(5) restaurant. Nevertheless,

7. **Sentence 8:** Having a cafe may benefit a library financially.

The most effective revision of sentence 8 would begin with which group of words?

(1) In addition, having
(2) On the other hand, having
(3) A cafe, by benefiting a library,
(4) A library, however,
(5) Financially a cafe

Answers and explanations start on page 629.

CLEAR AND ORGANIZED WRITING

Essay Writing Process: Prewriting

Key Ideas

- List or brainstorm to generate ideas about the essay
topic. Listing is a careful
process, whereas brain-
storming is a freer method
that helps if you are having
trouble generating ideas.
- Decide on a main idea for
your essay.
- Cross out ideas that don't fit
your main idea.

Generating Ideas

When you first read an essay topic, you might feel that you have nothing to say about it. Fortunately, there are steps to help you get your ideas flowing. For example, read the essay topic below.

TOPIC
Is it important to develop a network of acquaintances, or is it better to concentrate on just a few close friends?

To get ideas to write about this topic, you could try one of these techniques:

- **Listing:** Think carefully about the topic; then list ideas that come to mind. You may even find yourself creating two or more lists of related ideas. As you list, try to stay on topic as you go. Later, you may decide that an idea is irrelevant. However, listing is a careful, thoughtful process that generally results in usable ideas.
- **Brainstorming:** Think about the topic and write down everything that comes to mind. Write as quickly as possible. Include all ideas. The process of brainstorming is especially helpful if you're experiencing "writer's block." Brainstorming results in a long list of ideas, but you must then evaluate which ideas are useful and which are not.

Listing Ideas

Acquaintances:

good to have some—for variety

need "quantity" sometimes—can't have a
    party with only two best friends

close friends not always free to see you

Friends:

can tell anything to close friends

can be yourself with friends

best friends

Brainstorming Ideas

everyone has friends and acquaintances

acquaintances—help you network, get jobs

can become real friends

close friends always there for you

my family always there for me

fun to know lots of different people

learn about world through acquaintances

people today—no genuine closeness

intimate conversation most satisfying

can confide in close friends

some people can't be trusted

friends' intentions sincere

friends stand test of time

understand when you're grouchy

need more than 2 best friends for party

can't be close friends with boss

can't see close friends every day

can be yourself with close friends

GED TIP

*Generally brainstorming is a
timed activity. However,
because the GED essay is
timed, you also need to time
yourself if you list ideas.
Allow yourself about 5 minutes to generate ideas for
your essay.*

Once you have ideas on paper, your next step is to find your main idea. Look at your ideas, and see what main point most of them lead to. Here is the main idea of the listed ideas and the brainstormed ideas shown above:

Main Idea: A person needs both friends and acquaintances.

Once you write your main idea, go back to your generated ideas and cross off any that do not directly support it. For example, in the brainstormed list of ideas, "can't be close friends with boss" concerns friendship, but it isn't directly related to the main idea. It should be crossed out.

A. Directions: Use listing to generate ideas and find a main idea for each of the following topics.

TOPIC 1

In modern society, people depend on machines for many basic needs. Some believe that our dependence on machines undermines our natural abilities. Do you agree or disagree?

List here:

Main Idea: _____

TOPIC 2

What causes people to overeat?

List here:

Main Idea: _____

B. Directions: On a separate sheet of paper, brainstorm ideas about the following topic. Try to brainstorm in five minutes, but give yourself more time if needed. Then write your main idea, and cross out irrelevant ideas.

TOPIC

What are the advantages and disadvantages of owning a pet?

In your essay, explain the advantages, the disadvantages, or both. Give reasons to support your answer.

Save your work. You will use this list in the next step of the writing process, grouping and ordering your ideas.

Answers and explanations start on page 629.

Key Ideas

- Group and label your ideas.
- Organize your groups by outlining or mapping.
- Put your groups in an order that makes sense and supports the essay's main idea.

GED TIP

It's good to have three groups of ideas for your GED essay, but sometimes two or four will make more sense. Plan to give yourself about 5 minutes to group and order your ideas.

Grouping Your Ideas

After you generate ideas and eliminate irrelevant ones, group related ideas together and label each group. Each group will become a paragraph in your essay. The label will become a topic sentence. For example, look at the brainstormed list on page 74. Those ideas could become two main groups labeled *benefits of close friends* and *reasons to have acquaintances.*

Another way to group ideas is to outline them. An **outline** shows each main group label marked by a roman numeral, followed by the supporting ideas in that group marked by capital letters. Minor details are marked by numbers. In the outline below, notice that the writer divided *reasons to have acquaintances* into two groups, which will be used for two paragraphs. Thus, the writer will have three paragraphs to support the main idea of the essay.

Main idea: A person needs both friends and acquaintances.

If diagrams help you see relationships, you may prefer to map your ideas.

I. Benefits of close friends
    A. Will always be there for you
    B. Can be yourself
    C. Intimate conversation
       1. Is most satisfying
       2. Can confide in
    D. Stand the test of time
II. Acquaintances can be a lot of fun
    A. Add variety to life
    B. Can teach you about the world
III. Acquaintances fulfill some needs
    A. Can't see close friends every day
    B. Can help you network—get jobs
    C. Need more than 2 best friends to have a party

To make a **map,** write your main idea in the center of the page and circle it. Then draw lines going away from the circle. At the end of each line, write the label of a main group of ideas and circle it. Add ideas to each group, like this:

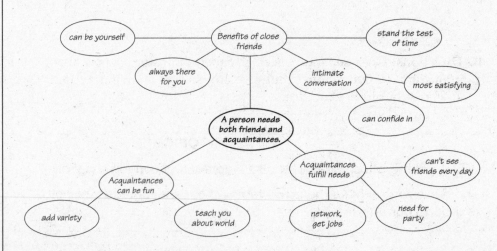

Ordering Your Ideas

Once you have divided your ideas into groups, you must decide how to order the groups in your essay. The order of ideas depends on the purpose of your essay.

- If you are explaining causes and effects or listing reasons, number your groups in **order of importance.** When you write your essay, signal this organization by using transitions such as *first*, *second*, and *third*, or *more important* and *most important*.

- If you are analyzing similarities and differences, number your groups to show this **comparison and contrast**—similarities first and then differences, or vice versa. When you write your essay, signal this organization by using transitions. To show similarities, use *also*, *similarly*, and *in the same way*. To highlight differences, use *however*, *on the other hand*, and *in contrast*.

- If you are discussing **advantages and disadvantages,** number your groups so that you discuss the more significant group last. When you write your essay, signal this organization by using a transition such as *on the other hand* to shift from advantages to disadvantages, or vice versa.

Once you have grouped and ordered your ideas, you have a prewriting plan. You will follow this plan as you write your essay.

CLEAR AND ORGANIZED WRITING ▸ PRACTICE 4.2

A. Directions: Read the main idea and the ideas for the topic below. Cross out the irrelevant ideas. Then, on a separate sheet of paper, group the remaining ideas using a map or an outline.

> ### TOPIC
> Which is a better way to spend free time—going on vacation or staying at home?

Main idea: Staying at home is better than going on vacation.

costs less	can avoid crowds
can see friends	no negotiating unfamiliar territory
can vacation with friends	no asking strangers for directions
more relaxing	less chance of getting ripped off
no planning	opportunity to catch up on reading, knitting,
can play tourist in your home city	other hobbies, home improvement
should buy a new suitcase	

B. Directions: On page 75, you brainstormed a list of ideas for the topic below. Look at that list now. On a separate sheet of paper, group your ideas using a map or an outline. Decide which order to present your ideas. Give yourself five minutes, but take more time if needed.

> ### TOPIC
> What are the advantages and disadvantages of owning a pet?
>
> In your essay, explain the advantages, the disadvantages, or both. Give reasons to support your answer.

Save your prewriting plan. You will use it during the next stage of the writing process, drafting.

Answers and explanations start on page 630.

CLEAR AND ORGANIZED WRITING

Essay Writing Process: Drafting

Your prewriting plan is a blueprint for the next step in the writing process, **drafting.** Use your plan as a guide when you write the first draft of your essay. At this stage, don't worry about grammar and spelling. You will polish your essay later.

A good essay should have the following elements:

- An **introductory paragraph** that states the main idea of the essay and gives the reader a preview of what's to come
- **Body paragraphs** that expand on the main points, each with a topic sentence and supporting details
- A **concluding paragraph** that wraps up the essay

An idea map is shown below. Notice how it becomes a blueprint for an essay. The main idea of the map becomes the basis of the introductory paragraph. The main idea sentence in the introduction, which tells the point of the essay, is underlined.

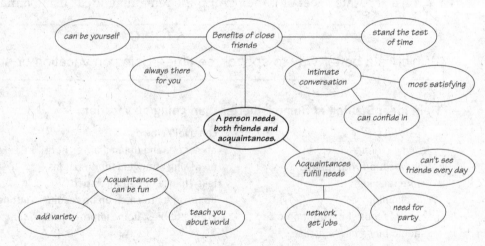

EXAMPLE

Introductory Paragraph: <u>A person needs both close friends and acquaintances because they meet the person's social needs in different ways.</u> The special bond a person has with close friends is irreplaceable. However, there are times when it's helpful to have acquaintances.

Use each group of ideas on your map to develop one body paragraph. For example, the body paragraph on the next page is developed from the group shown on the map above. Notice that the main idea sentence (underlined) comes from the idea in the center of the group and that the supporting details are drawn from the ideas around it.

Key Ideas

- An effective essay has an introduction, a body, and a conclusion.
- Use your outline or idea map to develop topic sentences and supporting details.
- Don't worry about spelling or grammar when you are drafting an essay.

GED TIP

After you plan your essay, allow yourself about 25 minutes to write the draft.

EXAMPLE

Body Paragraph: <u>Close friendships have numerous benefits.</u> For one thing, loyal friends are always there to support each other, no matter what happens. Some friendships last many years, becoming deeper and more meaningful with time. In addition, people can be themselves with friends. No one has to worry about not being perfect when he or she is among friends. Finally, nothing is more satisfying than the intimate conversations that true friends can have. They can confide and trust in each other.

Once you've written an introductory paragraph and your body paragraphs, write your conclusion. A good conclusion summarizes the main idea of the essay. It should also leave readers with something to think about.

EXAMPLE

Concluding Paragraph: In conclusion, although it's wonderful to have close friends, it's also important to have a wide circle of acquaintances. It is worthwhile to cultivate acquaintances, even though our relationships with them may be short and superficial. Acquaintances provide us with some things that we can't get from just a few close friends.

CLEAR AND ORGANIZED WRITING ▸ PRACTICE 5

A. Directions: Below are the body paragraphs of an essay. On a separate sheet of paper, write an introduction and a conclusion.

For one thing, when you teach children to be organized at an early age, they will have less difficulty with this skill later in life. Therefore, it is important to encourage children to put away their toys and to praise them when they do it, especially when they have taken the initiative. Later on, children can help you organize around the house. They'll be improving their organizing skills, and you will have a saner home!

A second point is that being organized helps children succeed in school. Teachers can get very frustrated when their students lose their homework or forget to do assignments. By being organized, your child is likely to avoid these problems.

Finally, when your children are organized, it makes your life easier. How many times have you been late to an appointment yourself because you were running around trying to find something that your child had lost? Do you always find yourself apologizing to friends because your kids make it impossible to keep to any sort of schedule? Improving your children's organizational skills will help you regain control of your own time.

B. On page 77, you grouped and ordered your ideas on the topic below.

> **TOPIC**
>
> What are the advantages and disadvantages of owning a pet?
>
> In your essay, explain the advantages, the disadvantages, or both. Give reasons to support your answer.

Now use your prewriting plan to draft an essay on the topic. Use a separate sheet of paper. Your essay should include an introduction, body paragraphs, and a conclusion. Save your work. You will use it for the next step of the writing process, revising.

Answers and explanations start on page 630

CLEAR AND ORGANIZED WRITING PRACTICE QUESTIONS

Questions 1 through 5 refer to the following paragraphs.

The Effects of Lack of Sleep

(A)

(1) Research shows that about 70 million North Americans have experienced the problem of sleep disruption. (2) Losing sleep is more than just an annoyance. (3) In some cases, it can have catastrophic results. (4) In the United States, sleepy drivers are responsible for at least 100,000 car crashes each year. (5) Most people need at least eight hours of shut-eye a night but get only six or seven. (6) Their fast-paced lives leave them little time for sleep. (7) Another factor is poor bedtime habits. (8) Family stresses may also cause sleep loss.

(B)

(9) A study of high school students showed that students with low grades went to bed 40 minutes later and got 25 minutes less sleep than students with high grades. (10) Similarly, another study shows that when one gets fewer than six to eight hours of sleep, it is harder to learn new skills.

(C)

(11) If you have trouble sleeping, avoid caffeine and alcohol. (12) Get regular exercise during the day, when it won't make you too energized to sleep. (13) Exercise can also help you lose weight.

(D)

(14) Set times for going to bed and getting up each day, and stick to them. (15) Don't watch TV or use a computer late at night, since these stimulate visual response and interfere with sleep. (16) If you find you still can't sleep, get up and do something.

1. Which revision would improve the effectiveness of the article?

Begin a new paragraph with

(1) sentence 3
(2) sentence 4
(3) sentence 5
(4) sentence 6
(5) sentence 7

2. Which sentence would be most effective if inserted at the beginning of paragraph B?

(1) Some high school students get better grades than others.
(2) High-achieving students get more sleep.
(3) Lack of sleep interferes with concentration.
(4) Not getting enough sleep is a big problem.
(5) People need more sleep than they used to.

3. Sentences 9 and 10: **A study of high school students showed that students with low grades went to bed 40 minutes later and got 25 minutes less sleep than students with high grades. Similarly, another study shows that when one gets fewer than six to eight hours of sleep, it is harder to learn new skills.**

Which is the best way to write the underlined portion of these sentences? If the original is the best way, choose option (1).

(1) grades. Similarly,
(2) grades, likewise,
(3) grades. Moreover
(4) grades. As a result,
(5) grades. Therefore,

4. Sentence 13: **Exercise can also help you lose weight.**

Which revision should be made to the placement of sentence 13?

(1) move sentence 13 to follow sentence 9
(2) move sentence 13 to follow sentence 11
(3) move sentence 13 to follow sentence 14
(4) move sentence 13 to follow sentence 15
(5) remove sentence 13

5. Which revision would improve the effectiveness of the article?

(1) join paragraphs B and C
(2) move sentence 11 to the end of paragraph B
(3) remove sentence 14
(4) join paragraphs C and D
(5) no revision is necessary

Questions 6 through 10 refer to the following paragraphs.

Getting Out Those Troublesome Stains

(A)

(1) Have you ever ruined a nice piece of clothing by staining it? (2) If so, the following information on stain removal may interest you. (3) By learning a few simple rules and keeping some household cleaners on hand, you can preserve your clothing. (4) First of all, the faster you act, the better. (5) With time, the stain will set. (6) Be sure to blot the stain rather than scrubbing it. (7) Scrubbing can actually drive the stain into the fabric.

(B)

(8) Use hot water on a grease stain such as salad dressing and cold water on a water-based stain such as wine, pasta sauce, or blood. (9) If you don't know what the stain is or where it came from, use room-temperature water. (10) Otherwise you might set the stain.

(C)

(11) Sometimes other liquids are more effective than water. (12) Lemon juice, for example removes ink, rust, and iodine. (13) White vinegar takes out alcohol, coffee, deodorants, and glue. (14) Liquid shampoo can be used on oil, tar, and grease. (15) Not surprisingly, it works the same way on an oil stain as it does on oil in your hair. (16) Rubbing alcohol removes stains from grass and soft drinks.

(D)

(17) If you find that a stain is not going away or is getting worse, stop and take your clothes to a dry cleaner. (18) Professionals know best. (19) Home remedies may not work on every stain.

6. Which revision would improve the effectiveness of the article?

   Begin a new paragraph with

   (1) sentence 3
   (2) sentence 4
   (3) sentence 5
   (4) sentence 6
   (5) sentence 7

7. Which sentence would be most effective if inserted at the beginning of paragraph B?

   (1) Hot and cold water have many uses.
   (2) Choose the right water temperature for cleaning each stain.
   (3) Try to avoid setting the stain.
   (4) Hot water takes out tough stains.
   (5) The second step is to determine the proper use of hot water.

8. Sentence 12: **Lemon juice, for example removes ink, rust, and iodine**.

   Which is the best way to write the underlined portion of this sentence? If the original is the best way, choose option (1).

   (1) juice, for example removes
   (2) juice, for example. Removes
   (3) juice for example removes
   (4) juice, for example, removes
   (5) juice. For example, removes

9. Which revision would improve the effectiveness of paragraph C?

   (1) remove sentence 11
   (2) move sentence 11 to follow sentence 12
   (3) move sentence 12 to follow sentence 14
   (4) remove sentence 14
   (5) remove sentence 15

10. Sentence 19: **Home remedies may not work on every stain.**

    Which revision should be made to the placement of sentence 19?

    (1) move sentence 19 to the beginning of paragraph C
    (2) move sentence 19 to follow sentence 13
    (3) move sentence 19 to follow sentence 15
    (4) move sentence 19 to the beginning of paragraph D
    (5) no revision is necessary

Questions 11 through 14 refer to the following memo.

To: All Employees
From: Denise Ellis, Benefits Manager

(A)

(1) Starting on January 1, Allcity will no longer be our insurance carrier. (2) Instead, you will have a choice of two other insurance carriers: HealthPlan and Rainbow Insurance Company.

(B)

(3) HealthPlan is an HMO. (4) You will not have to pay any money to doctors in advance with this plan, but you must go to doctors listed with the insurance company. (5) HMOs are becoming increasingly popular. (6) With Rainbow Insurance, you may choose any doctor you wish. (7) However you must pay the health providers when you receive the service. (8) Afterwards, you submit the receipts to Rainbow Insurance. (9) Representatives of both companies will be here on December 2 to discuss the details of their plans. (10) Please sign up for an informational session on that day. (11) The sign-up sheet is on the door of the conference room, where the meetings will take place.

(C)

(12) At the meeting, you will receive a card on which you must indicate your choice of company. (13) Please mark your choice in the appropriate box and submit it to me by December 5.

(D)

(14) If you do not submit your card in time, you may not be insured for the month of January. (15) If you are not able to attend any of the informational sessions, please let me know right away. (16) Feel free to contact me at ext. 2453 with any questions you may have about this process.

11. Which revision would improve the effectiveness of paragraph B?

   (1) remove sentence 3
   (2) move sentence 5 to the beginning of paragraph B
   (3) move sentence 5 to follow sentence 3
   (4) remove sentence 5
   (5) no revision is necessary

12. Sentence 7: **However you must pay the health providers when you receive the service.**

   Which correction should be made to sentence 7?

   (1) insert a comma after However
   (2) change pay to have paid
   (3) insert a comma after when
   (4) change receive to receives
   (5) no correction is necessary

13. Which revision would improve the effectiveness of the memo?

   Begin a new paragraph with

   (1) sentence 6
   (2) sentence 7
   (3) sentence 8
   (4) sentence 9
   (5) sentence 10

14. Sentence 14: **If you do not submit your card on time, you may not be insured for the month of January.**

   Which revision should be made to the placement of sentence 14?

   (1) move sentence 14 to the end of paragraph C
   (2) move sentence 14 to follow sentence 15
   (3) move sentence 14 to follow sentence 16
   (4) remove sentence 14
   (5) no revision is necessary

Questions 15 through 19 refer to the following paragraphs.

Repairing a Flat Bicycle Tire

(A)

(1) The first step in fixing a flat bicycle tire is to remove the wheel. (2) Before you begin, let out any air in the tire. (3) Next, release the brake. (4) If you are removing the back wheel, put the derailleur in high gear. (5) Then take off the axle nuts by unscrewing counterclockwise. (6) If your bike has safety washers, remove these also. (7) Put them on the wheel so that you can keep track of them.

(B)

(8) Remove the tire, and mark the valve stem position on it. (9) If possible, remove the tire without using tools, because the inner tube punctures easily. (10) Use tire levers or the backs of forks and spoons if necessary. (11) When you find the leak, scrape the spot with sandpaper. (12) Remove the inner tube and inflate it, listening and feeling for air leaks. (13) Then apply cement to the tube, and let it dry completely before putting the patch on.

(C)

(14) First, inflate the tube and make sure the leak has been fixed. (15) Next, slip the inner tube back into the tire, and put the tire back on the rim. (16) Then inflate the tube to the correct pressure. (17) The pressure is right when there is enough air to steady the tire but not so much air that the tire cannot be squeezed between the brake pads.

(D)

(18) Put the bike back on its wheels, and then tighten the wheel nuts. (19) Moreover, readjust the tire pressure, and you're ready to ride!

15. Which revision would improve the effectiveness of paragraph A?

   (1) begin a new paragraph with sentence 4
   (2) begin a new paragraph with sentence 5
   (3) move sentence 5 to follow sentence 7
   (4) remove sentence 6
   (5) no revision is necessary

16. Which revision would improve the effectiveness of paragraph B?

   (1) remove sentence 11
   (2) move sentence 11 to follow sentence 9
   (3) move sentence 11 to follow sentence 12
   (4) move sentence 11 to follow sentence 13
   (5) no revision is necessary

17. Which sentence would be most effective if inserted at the beginning of paragraph C?

   (1) All you have to do now is take care of the tire pressure.
   (2) There are a lot of other things you still have to do in order to fix the flat.
   (3) Fixing a flat tire is a long process that requires a lot of patience.
   (4) The next step is to put the tire and tube back onto the rim.
   (5) Patching the leak properly is also very important.

18. Which sentence would be most effective if inserted at the beginning of paragraph D?

   (1) The final step is to reinstall the wheel.
   (2) Fixing a flat tire requires careful planning.
   (3) Whether you are an experienced cyclist or just a beginner, you can fix a flat tire.
   (4) Second, don't forget to tighten the wheel nuts.
   (5) Try not to use sharp tools to fix a flat tire.

19. Sentence 19: **Moreover, readjust the tire pressure, and you're ready to ride!**

   Which correction should be made to sentence 19?

   (1) replace Moreover, with Then
   (2) change readjust to readjusting
   (3) remove the comma after pressure
   (4) replace you're with your
   (5) no correction is necessary

Answers and explanations start on page 630.

SENTENCE STRUCTURE

Complete Simple Sentences

Key Ideas

- Make sure each sentence has a subject and verb and expresses a complete thought.
- If a sentence doesn't express a complete thought, you may need to add a subject, verb, or other words.
- Use correct end punctuation.

A complete simple sentence has at least one subject and one verb. The **subject** is the person, place, or thing that the sentence is talking about. The subject performs an action or is described. The **verb** is the word that tells what action the subject is doing or links the subject to a modifier.

Action verb: Elaine took notes on the meeting.
          subject verb

Linking verb: They were long.
          subject verb modifier

If a sentence is missing either the subject or the verb, it is incomplete. An incomplete sentence is called a **fragment.**

EXAMPLES

No Subject: Typed up her notes.
Complete Sentence: Elaine typed up her notes.

No Verb: The computer in the main office.
Complete Sentence: The computer in the main office crashed several times.

A complete sentence must also express a complete thought. The reader should not be left asking questions.

Incomplete thought: When she lost her work. (What happened when she lost her work?)
Complete thought: Elaine was very frustrated when she lost her work.

Incomplete thought: The person in charge of computer support. (What about that person?)
Complete thought: Elaine called the person in charge of computer support.

Incomplete thought: By replacing the hard drive.
Complete thought: Elaine can fix the computer by replacing the hard drive.

Finally, a complete sentence should have correct end punctuation. A statement should end with a period, and so should a command. A question should end with a question mark. An exclamation should end with an exclamation point.

Statement: Elaine has lost several files this way.
Command: Turn off the computer.
Question: Will the computer ever be fixed?
Exclamation: What a mess we're in!

If you find a fragment in your writing, rewrite to make it a complete sentence.

- If the sentence does not have a subject, add a subject.
- If the sentence does not have a verb, add a verb.
- If the thought is incomplete, add words or combine the incomplete thought with a complete sentence.

GED TIP

Read each sentence in a GED passage to yourself and pause at its end. That may help you "hear" whether the sentence is actually an incomplete thought.

A. Directions: Write *C* if the sentence is complete or *F* if the sentence is a fragment. Rewrite any fragments to make them complete.

EXAMPLES:

Talks all the time on the telephone. *F Dave talks all the time on the telephone.* _____

1. Drives his girlfriend crazy. _____

2. As soon as he comes home from work. _____

3. He calls everyone he knows. _____

4. Dave's sister and his best friend. _____

B. Questions 5 through 7 refer to the following advertisement.

What Is Three-Way Calling?

(A)

(1) Three-way calling is a unique service that enables you to conduct a conference call. (2) From the privacy of your own home. (3) You can talk to your sister in Florida and your mother in Nebraska at the same time. (4) It's even possible to seek a third person's advice when you're in the middle of a regular call. (5) For instance, if you're closing a deal, can bring your lawyer into the conversation.

(B)

(6) Why wait? (7) This useful and convenient service. (8) Can be yours for only pennies a month.

5. Sentences 1 and 2: Three-way calling is a unique service that enables you to conduct a conference <u>call. From</u> the privacy of your own home.

Which is the best way to write the underlined portion of these sentences? If the original is the best way, choose option (1).

(1) call. From
(2) call. And from
(3) call from
(4) call, from
(5) call. It from

6. Sentence 5: For instance, if you're closing a deal, can bring your lawyer into the conversation.

Which correction should be made to sentence 5?

(1) remove the comma after <u>instance</u>
(2) change <u>closing</u> to <u>to close</u>
(3) remove the comma after <u>deal</u>
(4) insert <u>you</u> before <u>can</u>
(5) no correction is necessary

7. Sentences 7 and 8: This useful and convenient <u>service. Can</u> be yours for only pennies a month.

Which is the best way to write the underlined portion of these sentences? If the original is the best way, choose option (1).

(1) service. Can
(2) service, can
(3) service it can
(4) service can
(5) service. That can

Answers and explanations start on page 631.

SENTENCE STRUCTURE

Compound and Complex Sentences

Key Ideas

- You can join two independent clauses into one compound sentence.
- Use a coordinating conjunction preceded by a comma.
- Choose a conjunction that correctly relates the two ideas.

Compound Sentences

The simple sentences described in Lesson 1 are also called **independent clauses.** An independent clause has a subject and a verb and expresses a complete thought. You can join two or more independent clauses in one **compound sentence.** To make a compound sentence, you should:

- Choose a logical **coordinating conjunction** to join the independent clauses. The coordinating conjunctions are *and, but, or, nor, for, so,* and *yet.*
- Insert a comma before the coordinating conjunction.

EXAMPLES

Two independent clauses: Sam saw a design flaw. He wrote a memo.
Joined correctly: Sam saw a design flaw, so he wrote a memo.

No coordinating conjunction: Sam asked his boss, she told him to send it.
Correct: Sam asked his boss, and she told him to send it.

No comma: Sam's boss was busy so she asked Sam to write the memo.
Correct: Sam's boss was busy, so she asked Sam to write the memo.

Be sure the coordinating conjunction expresses the correct relationship between the ideas in the two independent clauses.

Relationship Between Ideas	Coordinating Conjunction
join two equally important ideas	and
contrast two ideas	but, yet
show a cause	for
show an effect	so
give a choice	or
give no choice	nor

Incorrect conjunction: Sam showed initiative, **yet** his boss praised him.
Correct conjunction: Sam showed initiative, **and** his boss praised him.

Be sure that you are actually joining two independent clauses and not just two subjects or two verbs.

Incorrect: The designers, and the builders got the memo.
Correct (no comma): The designers and the builders got the memo.

Incorrect: The designers needed the information, and they appreciated the memo.
Correct (two independent clauses): The designers needed the information, and they appreciated the memo.
Correct (no comma): The designers needed the information and appreciated the memo.

GED TIP

Be sure that a coordinating conjunction is separating two independent clauses before you choose the option that inserts a comma before the conjunction.

SENTENCE STRUCTURE ▶ PRACTICE 2.1

A. Directions: Using the list on page 86, choose a coordinating conjunction for each sentence. On a separate sheet of paper, rewrite the sentence using the conjunction preceded by a comma.

EXAMPLE: I didn't want to seem timid, _so_ _____ I didn't tell anyone about my experience.

1. It was late _____ I was walking home from work.

2. My co-worker, Judy, had offered to drive me _____ I had refused.

3. It was a warm night _____ I decided to get some fresh air.

4. It was really my choice. I could have taken a cab _____ I could have walked.

5. I heard a loud noise _____ I ran the last block to my house. Later, I learned that it was only a car backfiring.

B. Questions 6 through 8 refer to the following paragraph.

Air Couriers

(1) If you want to travel abroad but don't have a lot of money, one option is to be an air courier. (2) An air courier carries shipping documents on an international flight, and gets a cheap ticket in return. (3) Companies use couriers because it often costs less to check freight as baggage than to ship it as cargo. (4) Air couriers fly on the major airlines, so sometimes they can't check any baggage of their own. (5) Couriers usually book their trips in advance but they get their tickets on the day of the flight.

6. **Sentence 2:** An air courier carries shipping documents on an international flight, and gets a cheap ticket in return.

   Which correction should be made to sentence 2?

   (1) change carries to carry
   (2) remove the comma
   (3) replace and with but
   (4) change gets to getting
   (5) no correction is necessary

7. **Sentence 4:** Air couriers fly on the major airlines, so sometimes they can't check any baggage of their own.

   Which is the best way to write the underlined portion of this sentence? If the original is the best way, choose option (1).

   (1) airlines, so
   (2) airlines so
   (3) airlines, but
   (4) airlines but
   (5) airlines, or

8. **Sentence 5:** Couriers usually book their trips in advance but they get their tickets on the day of the flight.

   Which correction should be made to sentence 5?

   (1) replace usually with never
   (2) replace book with will book
   (3) insert a comma after advance
   (4) insert a comma after but
   (5) no correction is necessary

Answers and explanations start on page 631.

- Join a subordinate and an independent clause to form a complex sentence.
- Use a subordinating conjunction that shows the correct relationship between ideas.
- Put a comma after the subordinating conjunction when it comes at the beginning of a sentence.

In a complex sentence, the subordinate clause can go at the beginning or the end, and sometimes more than one conjunction is appropriate. However, for a GED item there will always be only one option that is correct.

Complex Sentences

A **complex sentence** is made up of an independent clause and a **subordinate clause**. A subordinate clause has a subject and verb, but it does not express a complete thought.

EXAMPLES
Subordinate clause: Because their pay was too low.
Complex sentence: Teachers went on strike because their pay was too low.

          independent clause   subordinate clause

Every subordinate clause begins with a **subordinating conjunction** that shows the relationship between the subordinate clause and the independent clause. Below is a list of common subordinating conjunctions.

Relationship Between Clauses	Subordinating Conjunction
cause/reason	because
effect/result	in order that, so that
time	after, as, before, once, since, until, when, whenever, while
place	where, wherever
choice	if, whether
contradiction	although, even though, though

Choose the subordinating conjunction that conveys the meaning you are trying to express.

Incorrect meaning: The strike continued for more than a month once it finally ended.
Correct meaning: The strike continued for more than a month before it finally ended.

When a subordinate clause comes at the beginning of a sentence, put a comma after it. If the subordinate clause comes at the end of a sentence, you generally don't need a comma before it.

At beginning of sentence: While teachers were on the picket line, kids stayed home.
At end of sentence: Kids stayed home while teachers were on the picket line.

However, when a subordinate clause at the end of a sentence begins with *although, though,* or *even though*, put a comma before the clause.

At beginning of sentence: Even though the public supported the teachers, the school board did not concede to the teachers' demands.
At end of sentence: The school board did not concede to teachers' demands, even though the public supported the teachers.

A subordinate clause cannot stand independently. By itself, a subordinate clause is a sentence fragment. Make sure that every subordinate clause is joined to an independent clause.

Incorrect: After the strike finished. The school year began.
Corrected by joining independent and subordinate clauses: After the strike finished, the school year began.

SENTENCE STRUCTURE ▸ PRACTICE 2.2

A. Directions: Join the clauses to form complex sentences. Use the subordinating conjunctions in parentheses.

EXAMPLE
(if) You buy a smoke detector. You can protect your family.
If you buy a smoke detector, you can protect your family.

1. Most fatal fires occur. (when) A family is asleep.

   _____

2. (because) A smoke alarm wakes you up. It can allow you to escape.

   _____

3. Try to replace the smoke detector's battery. (before) It goes dead.

   _____

4. (although) Smoke detectors cost money. The expense is worth it.

   _____

B. Questions 5 through 7 refer to the following paragraph.

Phone Etiquette

(1) When you are making a business call, it's wise to keep a few key rules in mind. (2) First of all, be prepared. (3) Have paper and pencil ready so that you won't have to fumble for them. (4) Whenever you identify yourself, ask the person whether this is a good time to talk. (5) Get to the point quickly. (6) Before you hang up. (7) Thank the person for his or her time. (8) Finally, put the phone down gently. (9) Slamming down the receiver makes a poor impression.

5. Sentence 1: When you are making a business call, it's wise to keep a few key rules in mind.

Which correction should be made to sentence 1?

(1) change are making to is making
(2) replace are with our
(3) remove the comma
(4) change it's to its
(5) no correction is necessary

6. Sentence 4: Whenever you identify yourself, ask the person whether this is a good time to talk.

Which correction should be made to sentence 4?

(1) replace Whenever with After
(2) remove the comma
(3) insert a comma after person
(4) replace the person with them
(5) no correction is necessary

7. Sentences 6 and 7: Before you hang up. Thank the person for his or her time.

Which is the best way to write the underlined portion of these sentences? If the original is the best way, choose option (1).

(1) up. Thank
(2) up thank
(3) up, thank
(4) up and thank
(5) up, thanking

Answers and explanations start on page 631.

SENTENCE STRUCTURE

Run-Ons and Comma Splices

- A run-on sentence is two or more sentences that are connected without correct punctuation.
- In a comma splice, two sentences are joined with only a comma.
- To correct a run-on or comma splice, make a compound or complex sentence, or separate the sentences.

Run-Ons

There are two errors people commonly make when they join independent clauses to form a sentence. The first type of error is called a **run-on.** In a run-on, two independent clauses are combined without proper punctuation.

Run-On: Banks offer many helpful services you should check them out.

You can correct a run-on in one of several ways:
- Break the run-on into two separate sentences.
  Correct: Banks offer many services. You should check them out.
- Make a compound sentence (add a coordinating conjunction and a comma).
  Correct: Banks offer many services, so you should check them out.
- Make a complex sentence (add a subordinating conjunction and, if necessary, a comma).
  Correct: Because banks offer many services, you should check them out.

A run-on can also consist of independent clauses strung together with *and.* Correct this kind of run-on by dividing it into one or more compound sentences or by combining ideas into one sentence.

Run-On: Banking is getting more and more convenient and you can check on your account using bank-by-phone services and it's even possible to do your banking on the Internet.
Correct: Banking is getting more and more convenient. You can check on your account using bank-by-phone services, and it's even possible to do your banking on the Internet.

Run-On: Friday I got paid and I went to the bank and I cashed my check.
Correct: Friday I got paid, went to the bank, and cashed my check.

Comma Splices

The second type of error people sometimes make when joining independent clauses is called a **comma splice.** A comma splice occurs when two sentences are joined with just a comma. To correct a comma splice, add a coordinating conjunction after the comma:

Comma splice: You can check on your account using bank-by-phone services, it's even possible to do your banking on the Internet.
Correct: You can check on your account using bank-by-phone services, and it's even possible to do your banking on the Internet.

You can also correct a comma splice using the methods described above for correcting a run-on.

Comma splice: There are fewer bank tellers today banks do offer other services.
Corrected by creating a complex sentence: Although there are fewer bank tellers today, banks do offer other services.

GED TIP

When you read a run-on sentence, look for places where the reader would naturally pause between ideas. These places are most likely where the sentence needs correction.

SENTENCE STRUCTURE ▸ PRACTICE 3

A. Directions: Correct the following run-ons and comma splices using the methods explained on page 90. Try to use each method at least once.

1. Jeff just got his driver's license, he's very excited.

_____

2. He bought a car that has a lot of miles on it it wasn't very expensive.

_____

3. He doesn't have a lot of free time, he'd like to take a car trip.

_____

4. He needs to find out about car insurance and he needs to get a good map and he needs to join an auto club.

_____

B. Questions 5 through 7 refer to the following paragraphs.

Photography Tips

(A)

(1) It's not hard to take great pictures just keep these tips in mind. (2) For one thing, you need to get close to your subject, or you won't get a good shot. (3) Be patient, wait for the right moment to shoot. (4) Make sure the lighting is sufficient. (5) Even outdoors, you can use a flash to fill in shadows.

(B)

(6) Always keep extra film on hand. (7) You can buy it at a drugstore or discount store and it is also available by mail order. (8) Don't forget to keep extra batteries on hand too.

5. Sentence 1: It's not hard to take great <u>pictures just</u> keep these tips in mind.

Which is the best way to write the underlined portion of the sentence? If the original is the best way, choose option (1).

(1) pictures just
(2) pictures if you just
(3) pictures, if you just
(4) pictures that just
(5) pictures that are just

6. Sentence 3: Be patient, wait for the right moment to shoot.

Which correction should be made to sentence 3?

(1) remove the comma
(2) insert <u>and</u> after the comma
(3) replace <u>wait</u> with <u>weight</u>
(4) insert a comma after <u>moment</u>
(5) no correction is necessary

7. Sentence 7: You can buy it at a drugstore or discount store and it is also available by mail order.

Which correction should be made to sentence 7?

(1) insert a comma after <u>drugstore</u>
(2) insert a comma after <u>store</u>
(3) remove <u>and</u>
(4) replace <u>and</u> with <u>or</u>
(5) no correction is necessary

Answers and explanations start on page 631.

SENTENCE STRUCTURE

Subordinating Ideas

Writing is more effective when it flows smoothly. Therefore, try to eliminate short, choppy sentences whenever possible. You can do this by using **subordination** in a variety of ways.

You already know how to form a complex sentence with a subordinating clause. You also know how to create compound sentences. Either of these methods can be used to combine short sentences.

EXAMPLES
Short and choppy: Carla ran for the bus. She missed it.
Complex sentence: <u>Although</u> Carla ran for the bus, she missed it.
Compound sentence: Carla ran for the bus<u>, but</u> she missed it.

If two sentences have the same subject, you can combine them to form one sentence with a compound predicate. The **predicate** includes the verb plus anything else that is not part of the subject:

Short and choppy: Carla sat on the bench. She looked at her watch.
With compound predicate: Carla <u>sat on the bench and looked at her watch.</u>

Likewise, when two sentences have the same predicate, you can combine them to form one sentence with a compound subject. The resulting sentence will be less repetitive and wordy:

Short, choppy, and repetitive: Carla missed the bus. Dave missed the bus, too.
With compound subject: <u>Carla and Dave</u> missed the bus.

Finally, several short sentences that are related can be combined into one longer and more detailed sentence:

Short and choppy: Carla missed the bus. It was the 7:45 bus. She was on her way to work.
More detailed sentence: Carla missed <u>the 7:45 bus on her way to work.</u>

Sometimes, you can use two methods at the same time. For instance, in the sentence below you can make a complex sentence with combined details:

Short and choppy: Carla found a pay phone near the bus stop. She called her boss. Then she called one of her co-workers.
Complex sentence with combined details: After Carla found a pay phone near the bus stop, she called <u>her boss and one of her co-workers.</u>

Repetitive: Her boss thanked her for calling. Her co-worker thanked her for calling, and they both offered to pass along any messages.
With compound subject and compound predicate: <u>Both her boss and her co-worker</u> thanked her for calling <u>and offered</u> to pass along any messages.

Key Ideas

- Use smooth, flowing sentences rather than short, choppy sentences.
- Form compound or complex sentences from short sentences.
- Combine two predicates to make a compound predicate, or combine two subjects to make a compound subject.

GED TIP

Read the passages on the GED Writing Test to yourself as if you could hear them in your mind. That "silent hearing" will help you notice sentences that are choppy or repetitive.

SENTENCE STRUCTURE ▸ PRACTICE 4

A. Directions: Write each set of short, choppy sentences as one longer, smooth sentence.

EXAMPLE

If you are in a tornado, keep the windows closed. You should go to a safe place.
If you are in a tornado, keep the windows closed and go to a safe place.

1. Tornadoes can cause a lot of damage. Earthquakes are also capable of causing a lot of damage.

   _____

2. Earthquakes are somewhat common in California. Many Californians do not seem to mind.

   _____

3. On May 3, 1999, there was a tornado. It happened in Kansas. Five people were killed. One hundred fifty people were injured.

   _____

4. Tornadoes can occur anywhere in the United States. They can happen any time of year.

   _____

B. Questions 5 through 7 refer to the following warranty.

Limited Warranty

(1) If there is any defect, Pantronics will repair this unit free of charge. (2) Radios and audio components will be repaired. (3) Repairs will take place up to one year after date of purchase. (4) The unit may be brought to the service center. (5) It can also be mailed. (6) A proof of purchase, such as a receipt, must be presented in order to receive service. (7) This warranty does not cover damage due to accidents. (8) It does not cover damage due to mishandling or faulty installation.

5. Sentences 2 and 3: Radios and audio components will be <u>repaired. Repairs will take place up</u> to one year after date of purchase.

Which is the best way to write the underlined portion of these sentences? If the original is the best way, choose option (1).

(1) repaired. Repairs will take place up
(2) repaired and repairs will take place up
(3) repaired, the repairs will take place up
(4) repaired up
(5) repaired, so the repairs will take place up

6. Sentences 4 and 5: The unit may be brought to the service center. It can also be mailed.

The most effective combination of sentences 4 and 5 would include which group of words?

(1) brought or mailed to
(2) once brought to the service center,
(3) units that are mailed to the service center
(4) to the service center, but
(5) bringing it to the service center, or mailing

7. Sentences 7 and 8: This warranty does not cover damage due to accidents. It does not cover damage due to mishandling or faulty installation.

The most effective combination of sentences 7 and 8 would include which group of words?

(1) accidents, and it
(2) accidents, and this warranty
(3) accidents, and, in addition, it
(4) accidents, nor does it
(5) accidents, mishandling, or faulty installation

Answers and explanations start on page 631.

SENTENCE STRUCTURE

Modifying Ideas

Key Ideas

- Modifiers make writing clearer and more interesting.
- Correct a dangling modifier by turning it into a subordinate clause or by making the word that is modified the subject of the sentence.
- Place a modifier as near as possible to the word or phrase it describes.

Modifiers are words and phrases used to add descriptive details. A modifier might be a word like *sweaty*, a verb phrase like *dragging the heavy box*, a prepositional phrase like *from the storage room*, or a clause like *that we packed this morning*. Modifiers make writing clearer, more specific, and more interesting.

EXAMPLES

Without modifiers: Our friends Jack and Tina helped us while we were moving.

With modifiers: Our good friends Jack and Tina helped us while we were moving, watching our baby in their home.

Without modifiers: We realized the weather would not cooperate.

With modifiers: Sweating profusely at 9 A.M., we realized the weather would be uncooperatively hot.

Use modifiers carefully, or your meaning will be unclear. A **dangling modifier** is a word or phrase at the beginning of the sentence that has no clear subject to describe. To correct a dangling modifier, turn it into a subordinate clause, or make the word that the modifier describes into the subject of the sentence.

Dangling modifier: Driving the truck, one of the boxes fell out. (Who was driving the truck—one of the boxes?)
Correct: As we were driving the truck, one of the boxes fell out.
Correct: Driving the truck, we heard one of the boxes fall out.

Dangling modifier: Parking in a tow zone, a police officer gave us a ticket. (It sounds as if the police officer were parking in the tow zone.)
Correct: Because we parked in a tow zone, a police officer gave us a ticket.

Dangling modifier: Never having planned a move before, the real estate agent gave us some tips. (It sounds as if the real estate agent is the one who has never planned a move.)
Correct: Never having planned a move before, we asked the real estate agent for some tips.

ON THE GED

When a modifying phrase is at the beginning of a sentence, use a comma to separate it from the rest of the sentence. Some GED items may test that use of the comma.

A **misplaced modifier** is poorly placed in the sentence. It is not clear which word it modifies, or it modifies the wrong word in the sentence. To correct a misplaced modifier, put the modifier next to the word it describes.

Misplaced modifier: The moving van was just large enough that we rented.
Correct: The moving van that we rented was just large enough.

Misplaced modifier: We hoisted and lugged all our furniture up two flights of stairs panting heavily. (What was panting heavily—*we* or *the stairs*?)
Correct: Panting heavily, we hoisted and lugged all our furniture up two flights of stairs.

SENTENCE STRUCTURE ▸ PRACTICE 5

A. Directions: Revise each sentence, correcting the misplaced or dangling modifier.

1. Trent's sister encouraged him to become a nurse, who is also a health professional.

_____

2. Waking up the patients to take their blood pressure, they get rather annoyed.

_____

3. He writes their temperature and blood pressure on their charts carefully.

_____

4. Talking with the patients, it is hard to make visitors leave at 9 P.M.

_____

B. Questions 5 through 7 refer to the following paragraphs.

Adoption

(A)

(1) Adoption is a legal procedure that gives a person the rights of a son or daughter who is not the birth child of the adopter. (2) This practice dates back to ancient Greece. (3) People without heirs used it to perpetuate their estates.

(B)

(4) Adoptions may be handled through an agency or by independent placement. (5) Going through an agency, a "home study" to decide whether prospective parents will be fit is required. (6) In an independent placement, there is no study. (7) Lawyers handle these adoptions when parents ask them to frequently.

5. Sentence 1: Adoption is a legal procedure that gives a person the rights of a son or daughter who is not the birth child of the adopter.

The most effective revision of sentence 1 would include which group of words?

(1) a legal procedure, adoption that gives
(2) giving legal rights to a person
(3) a person who is not the birth child
(4) the son or daughter of the adopter
(5) the birth child, who is a son or daughter

6. Sentence 5: Going through an agency, a "home study" to decide whether prospective parents will be fit is required.

The most effective revision of sentence 5 would begin with which group of words?

(1) For parents, going through an agency
(2) Requiring a "home study"
(3) An agency requires a "home study"
(4) Deciding whether a parent is fit
(5) When going through an agency

7. Sentence 7: Lawyers handle these adoptions when parents ask them to frequently.

Which correction should be made to sentence 7?

(1) change handle to handles
(2) insert a comma after adoptions
(3) replace to with too
(4) move frequently to follow Lawyers
(5) no correction is necessary

Answers and explanations start on page 631.

Parallel Structure

Key Ideas

- Listed items should be parallel in form and structure.
- Each phrase should have the same elements as other phrases in the series.
- Don't put words and clauses together in the same series.

When you write a sentence that lists two or more words, phrases, or clauses, the elements in the list must be in the same grammatical form. In other words, the sentence must have **parallel structure.** Writing that has parallel structure is clearer and easier to follow.

Examples
Not Parallel: Jim wants to eat less, exercise more, and be getting more sleep.
Parallel: Jim wants to <u>eat</u> less, <u>exercise</u> more, and <u>get</u> more sleep.

Not Parallel: Walking and to swim are good aerobic exercises.
Parallel: <u>Walking</u> and <u>swimming</u> are good aerobic exercises.

Not Parallel: Try to lose weight slowly, sensibly, and in a careful way.
Parallel: Try to lose weight <u>slowly</u>, <u>sensibly</u>, and <u>carefully</u>.

To be sure that your sentences have parallel structure, follow the guidelines below.

Make sure that verbs in a list are in the same form and tense:

Not Parallel: Jim went to the store, bought an exercise mat, and is doing exercises.
Parallel: Jim <u>went</u> to the store, <u>bought</u> an exercise mat, and <u>did</u> exercises.

Be sure that phrases in a list are parallel in form and wording. For example, if one phrase in a list begins with a preposition, the others should, too. If one phrase begins with the word *the*, the others should, too.

Not Parallel: Avoid exercising on busy streets, near traffic jams, and polluted areas.
Parallel: Avoid exercising <u>on busy streets</u>, <u>near traffic jams</u>, and <u>in polluted areas</u>.

Not Parallel: He left the gym shoes, sweatpants, and the shirt in the gym.
Parallel: He left <u>the</u> gym shoes, <u>the</u> sweatpants, and <u>the</u> shirt in the gym.

Each list must have single words, short phrases, or clauses. Don't put single words and clauses together in the same series:

Not Parallel: The most effective fitness programs are low impact, informal, and you can do them at home.
Parallel: The most effective fitness programs are <u>low impact</u>, <u>informal</u>, and <u>home-based</u>.

Finally, notice that a comma separates each item within a list of three or more: *low-intensity, informal, and home-based.*

GED TIP

The comma before the and *in a list of three or more is optional:* hop, skip, and jump *or* hop, skip and jump. *It's best to get in the habit of using that comma, however, so that you don't forget to use commas elsewhere in the series.*

SENTENCE STRUCTURE ▸ PRACTICE 6

A. Directions: Rewrite each sentence to make the structure parallel.

EXAMPLE
Jenna works quickly, carefully, and in a thorough manner.
Jenna works quickly, carefully, and thoroughly.

1. Jenna has worked in a factory, a store, and as a waitress.

2. She would like putting her kids in a better school and to get a better job.

3. She thinks the kids' father is irresponsible, lazy, and doesn't care about them.

4. He doesn't have the time, the energy, or money to give them what they deserve.

B. Questions 5 through 7 refer to the following memo.

TO: All Employees

(A)

(1) A new alarm system has been installed. (2) It is designed to make our workplace safer, more comfortable, and pleasant. (3) However, we need everyone's cooperation.

(B)

(4) If you are the last one to leave, turn off all lights, computers, and check the coffee makers. (5) Then go to the alarm system located by the door. (6) Punch in the secret code, press ON, and be leaving immediately. (7) Lock the door behind you.

5. Sentence 2: It is designed to make our workplace safer, more comfortable, and pleasant.

Which correction should be made to sentence 2?

(1) change is to was
(2) replace our with are
(3) remove the comma after safer
(4) insert more before pleasant
(5) no correction is necessary

6. Sentence 4: If you are the last one to leave, turn off all lights, computers, and check the coffee makers.

Which is the best way to write the underlined portion of the sentence? If the original is the best way, choose option (1).

(1) computers, and check the
(2) computers and checking the
(3) computers, and to check the
(4) and computers, and the
(5) computers, and

7. Sentence 6: Punch in the secret code, press ON, and be leaving immediately.

Which correction should be made to sentence 6?

(1) change punch to punching
(2) change code to codes
(3) remove the comma after ON
(4) change be leaving to leave
(5) insert a comma after leaving

Answers and explanations start on page 632.

SENTENCE STRUCTURE

Essay Writing Process: Revising Your Sentences

Key Ideas

- Read your work as a whole to make sure that it is clear and logical.
- Imagine that you are reading your work for the first time.
- Correct any sentences that have errors in structure or punctuation.

GED TIP

To prepare for the GED essay, practice prewriting, drafting, and revising often. Frequent practice will help you feel more comfortable and confident as a writer.

Revising Unclear and Incorrect Sentences

When you write an essay, your first step is to get your ideas down on paper. To do this, you follow a prewriting and drafting plan like the ones on pages 74–79. When you are finished drafting, go back and reread what you have written. As you read each sentence, ask yourself:

- Do the ideas in the sentence make sense? If not, how can I make the sentence clearer? Add some words? Drop or move a confusing word or phrase? Insert or delete punctuation? Change the words?
- Is the sentence structure correct? If not, how can I correct it?

Read the paragraph below, and think about how you would revise the errors in clarity and sentence structure. Then compare it with the revised paragraph.

Paragraph with unclear and incorrect sentences:

Working outdoors has many advantages over working indoors. When you are outside you are in contact with nature. You can enjoy the sunshine on your face, hear the birds, and to smell the flowers. You don't have to consult the weather forecast on TV. In contrast, sitting in a climate-controlled cubicle, it is not known whether the sky is sunny or cloudy. Also, most outdoor jobs require you to use your body, that can be a huge advantage. Finally, if you work indoors, you might be sitting down at a desk, and typing all day long. After work, instead of relaxing. You'll probably have to go to the gym to work out.

Paragraph with revised sentence structure:

Working outdoors has many advantages over working indoors. When you are <u>outside, you</u> are in contact with nature. You can enjoy the sunshine on your face, hear the birds, and <u>smell</u> the flowers. You don't have to consult the weather forecast on TV. In contrast, <u>when you sit in a climate-controlled cubicle, you don't know</u> whether the sky is sunny or cloudy. Also, most outdoor jobs require you to use your <u>body, and that</u> can be a huge advantage. Finally, if you work indoors, you might be sitting down at a <u>desk and typing</u> all day long. After work, instead of <u>relaxing, you'll</u> probably have to go to the gym to work out.

Use these **revision marks** when you revise your sentences:

- To delete a word or punctuation mark, cross it out.
- To add a word or punctuation mark, insert a caret (^) in the line where you want it to go, and then write it in above the line.
- To change a word, cross it out and write the new word above it.
- To move a word or phrase, circle it and draw an arrow to its new position.
- To capitalize a letter, draw three lines under it.

SENTENCE STRUCTURE ▸ PRACTICE 7.1

A. Directions: Read and revise the sentences. Correct these problems by using revision marks.

☑ fragments, run-ons, and comma splices
☑ incorrect coordination and subordination
☑ misplaced or dangling modifiers
☑ problems in parallel structure

EXAMPLE: It's fun to do a family tree⊙ you can learn a lot.

1. First, write down what you know about your family then interview relatives.
2. Videotaping or to record the interviews is a good idea.
3. Ask relatives to provide exact names, dates, and give other details.
4. Making copies of documents such as birth certificates and marriage licenses.
5. Interviewing older family members, they'll often tell you stories you never heard.
6. Record all the information you get and put it in a three-ring binder carefully.
7. Some people use their computers to do genealogy searches, they get very good results.
8. However, one must have the time, the patience, and know-how to use the Internet.
9. If you decide to learn more about your roots don't be surprised to find yourself at a huge family reunion.
10. The whole process of putting together a family tree and contacting long-lost family members.

B. Directions: Read the paragraphs below. Use revision marks to correct problems with sentences.

It was a beautiful day, the blue ocean sparkled in the sunlight. A perfect day for going to the beach. Looking across the sand, two little girls were building a sandcastle and made a moat next to it. Renelle spread out her towel she anchored it with her shoes and beach bag and began to read a magazine. Suddenly she heard a voice. "Are you going to get in the water, or are you just going to lie there?" Renelle looked up, and saw her friend Terry. She laughed softly and she got up and she greeted Terry. Putting on her sandals, the two of them walked across the burning sand to the water's edge.

Renelle loved going to the beach. Going to the beach relaxed her. Going to the beach helped her forget about her problems. It didn't cost money like most other forms of entertainment. Most of Renelle's friends also spent a lot of time at the beach so that was another incentive.

Answers and explanations start on page 632.

- Revise your essay if so that the organization is clear to the reader.
- Make sure that paragraph breaks fall in the right places.
- Check for faulty transitions and irrelevant details.

GED TIP

When you write the draft of your GED essay, leave wide margins and space between lines so that you can more easily use the revision marks and revise.

Revising Problems in Organization

When you reread your essay, you may also need to make changes in organization to make the essay clearer to the reader. As you read, ask yourself:

- Is my main idea clear?
- Are there a clear introduction, body of support, and conclusion?
- Is the paragraphing correct? Does each paragraph relate to only one main idea? Should any paragraphs be split into two? Should any be combined?
- Does each paragraph have a topic sentence that tells the main idea? Are any of the other sentences in a place that doesn't make sense? Are there any irrelevant details that should be removed?
- Does the writing flow smoothly from sentence to sentence and from paragraph to paragraph? If not, where can I add transitions?

Read the sample paragraph below. Think about how you would correct the errors in organization. Then compare it with the revised paragraph.

Paragraph with problems in organization:

(1) Many people believe that changes in technology have improved our communication with others. (2) I believe that the opposite is true. (3) So-called technological improvements have led to a marked decline in the quality of interpersonal communication. (4) In the old days, when you called someone, the person was likely to pick up the phone to find out who was calling. (5) Nowadays, screening devices make that unnecessary. (6) By listening to your voice on the answering machine or by seeing your phone number pop up on his caller identification box, the other person can decide that he doesn't care to speak to you. (7) This encourages long games of "phone tag." (8) Television is another example—you can barely get a word out of someone who is glued to the tube.

Paragraphs with revised organization:

(1) Many people believe that changes in technology have improved our communication with others. (2) <u>However,</u> I believe that the opposite is true. (3) So-called technological improvements have led to a marked decline in the quality of interpersonal communication.

(*) <u>Phone use is one area in which communication has suffered.</u> (4) In the old days, when you called someone, the person was likely to pick up the phone to find out who was calling. (5) Nowadays, screening devices make that unnecessary. (6) By listening to your voice on the answering machine or by seeing your phone number pop up on his caller identification box, the other person can decide that he doesn't care to speak to you. (7) This encourages long games of "phone tag."

In the revised paragraphs, the transition *however* was added to sentence 2. The piece was divided into two paragraphs—an introductory paragraph and a body paragraph about phone use. A topic sentence (marked with *) was added. Sentence 8 of the original, which was not related to telephones, was deleted.

Use these symbols to revise essay organization:

- To change whole sentences, use the same marks you used to change words.
- To start a new paragraph, use the paragraph symbol (¶).

A. Directions: Using the revision marks, revise the paragraphs below.

EXAMPLE:

We've all heard countless advertising campaigns warning us not to litter. Yet some people still think nothing of throwing a soda can out of their car window onto the highway or dropping a candy wrapper on the sidewalk. Most of us realize that we are upsetting a delicate ecological balance when we don't dispose of our trash properly. Why do people continue to litter? Why do people continue to litter?

One reason people litter is that they just don't care about others. It doesn't bother them to leave their trash in front of someone else's apartment building, forcing another person to deal with the problem.

This inconsiderate attitude is also reflected in the refusal to recycle plastic, glass, and newspapers. People figure that they won't be around in the future when the landfills are used up, so who cares? Another possible reason for littering is low self-esteem. If people don't feel good about themselves, they won't be motivated to keep their environment looking attractive. Low self-esteem can cause many other problems, including depression and lack of self-confidence. People who have high self-esteem believe that it's important to keep their home, the planet Earth, clean and beautiful.

B. Directions: Revise the essay that you wrote on the following topic:

TOPIC

What are the advantages and disadvantages of owning a pet?

In your essay, explain the advantages, the disadvantages, or both. Give reasons to support your answer.

Be sure to check for:

- ☑ clear main idea
- ☑ introduction, body, and conclusion
- ☑ correct paragraphing
- ☑ topic sentences
- ☑ logical placement of sentences
- ☑ irrelevant details that should be removed
- ☑ clear transitions

Save your work. You will use it in the next step of the writing process, editing.

Answers and explanations start on page 632.

SENTENCE STRUCTURE PRACTICE QUESTIONS

Questions 1 through 5 refer to the following paragraphs.

Conserving Household Energy

(A)

(1) According to the Department of Energy, many families spend an average of 14 percent of their yearly income on heating and cooling costs. (2) Although you can't do much about high fuel prices, you can try some energy-saving measures.

(B)

(3) To reduce wintertime energy costs, keep the shades drawn at night. (4) Seal your windows, so that cold air can't get through the cracks. (5) You can use sealing material available at any hardware store. (6) If you have an air conditioner, cover it with thick plastic. (7) Keep your thermostat at 68°F during the day. (8) Keep it at 62°F at night.

(C)

(9) In the summer, use fans and natural breezes rather than air-conditioning whenever possible. (10) If you have windows that get direct sun. (11) Keep the shades down during the day. (12) Don't leave your air conditioner running when you're not at home, change the filter every summer. (13) With a clogged filter, the air conditioner's energy use can go up as much as 5 percent. (14) Put your air conditioner on a low setting. (15) Your home will not cool down when your air conditioner is on full blast any faster.

1. Sentence 4: **Seal your windows, so that cold air can't get through the cracks.**

   Which correction should be made to sentence 4?

   (1) change seal to sealing
   (2) remove the comma
   (3) replace so that with because
   (4) change can't to couldn't
   (5) no correction is necessary

2. Sentences 7 and 8: **Keep your thermostat at 68°F during the day. Keep it at 62°F at night.**

   The most effective combination of sentences 7 and 8 would include which group of words?

   (1) keeping your thermostat at
   (2) during the day, and to keep
   (3) during the day and 62°F
   (4) the day, keeping it at
   (5) at night, it should be kept

3. Sentences 10 and 11: **If you have windows that get direct <u>sun. Keep</u> the shades down during the day.**

   Which is the best way to write the underlined portion of these sentences? If the original is the best way, choose option (1).

   (1) sun. Keep
   (2) sun and to keep
   (3) sun keep
   (4) sun, keep
   (5) sun, keeping

4. Sentence 12: **Don't leave your air conditioner running when you're not at <u>home, change</u> the filter every summer.**

   Which is the best way to write the underlined portion of the sentence? If the original is the best way, choose option (1).

   (1) home, change
   (2) home change
   (3) home and change
   (4) home, so change
   (5) home. Do change

5. Sentence 15: **Your home will not cool down when your air conditioner is on full blast any faster.**

   The most effective revision of sentence 15 would begin with which group of words?

   (1) Your home will not cool down any faster
   (2) Cooling down your home, when your air
   (3) Having the air conditioner on full blast, it
   (4) When your home will not cool down,
   (5) Air-conditioning your home on full blast,

Questions 6 through 10 refer to the following letter of complaint.

Cole Electronics
2514 Broadway
New York, NY 10057

Dear Manager:

(A)

(1) On August 2, I purchased a television at your store. (2) When I got the television home I discovered that the picture was fuzzy. (3) Returning to the store to see if the problem could be fixed easily. (4) I assumed that there would be no problem because I had just purchased the set.

(B)

(5) The customer service personnel said they had no time to handle my complaint. (6) They were extremely rude and unprofessional. (7) Finally, a salesman told me that I would have to send the TV to a service center in Detroit. (8) At that point, I demanded a refund. (9) Claiming that the TV had been used, it could not be returned.

(C)

(10) I am angry about the treatment I received and I am also very frustrated. (11) I would now like to receive a full refund or getting the TV repaired locally. (12) Please contact me to let me know what action will be taken. (13) My phone number is (212) 555-2719.

Sincerely,
Jeffrey Barnes

6. Sentence 2: **When I got the television home I discovered that the picture was fuzzy.**

Which correction should be made to sentence 2?

(1) replace When with Since
(2) change got to gotten
(3) insert a comma after home
(4) insert a comma after discovered
(5) change was to be

7. Sentence 3: **Returning to the store to see if the problem could be fixed easily.**

Which correction should be made to sentence 3?

(1) replace Returning with I returned
(2) add a comma after store
(3) change to see to seeing
(4) change could to can
(5) no correction is necessary

8. Sentence 9: **Claiming that the TV had been used, it could not be returned.**

The most effective revision of sentence 9 would begin with which group of words?

(1) He claimed that because
(2) The TV was claimed to
(3) Returning the TV,
(4) Because of the used TV,
(5) Making a claim about the TV

9. Sentence 10: **I am angry about the treatment I received and I am also very frustrated.**

The most effective revision of sentence 10 would include which group of words?

(1) the treatment I received, and I
(2) angry and frustrated about the
(3) feeling angry about the treatment
(4) being the recipient of such treatment
(5) the manner in which I was treated

10. Sentence 11: **I would now like to receive a full refund or getting the TV repaired locally.**

Which is the best way to write the underlined portion of the sentence? If the original is the best way, choose option (1).

(1) refund or getting
(2) refund, getting
(3) refund, or getting
(4) refund, or get
(5) refund or get

Questions 11 though 15 refer to the following paragraphs.

Workplace Friendships

(A)

(1) Should you make friends at work or keep your distance? (2) Most experts agree that it's not wise to get too chummy with your boss. Relationships with co-workers, however, are a more complex matter. (3) Although workplace friendships between peers can be beneficial, they can also cause problems.

(B)

(4) Workplace friendships have many positive aspects. (5) It's hard to work if you feel alone and in a productive way. (6) Having friends at work can make your day more pleasant, and give you energy. (7) Friends can serve as a sounding board for problems and help you succeed.

(C)

(8) However, like any other friendship, workplace friendships can turn sour. (9) Things get messy, when the friendship unravels in plain view of your boss and co-workers. (10) Discrimination and harassment suits have even been brought in some cases.

(D)

(11) Experts recommend keeping your social life with work friends out of the workplace. (12) For instance, don't exchange presents at work or talking about your evening out. (13) Avoid praising a friend publicly if it could make someone else resentful. (14) Keeping your work life separate from your social life may be hard but it's worth the effort.

11. Sentence 5: **It's hard to work if you feel alone and in a productive way.**

    The most effective revision of sentence 5 would include which group of words?

    (1) work productively if you
    (2) to work, it isn't easy if
    (3) whether working productively or not
    (4) if you feel alone and productive
    (5) work, feel alone, and be productive

12. Sentence 6: **Having friends at work can make your day more pleasant, and give you energy.**

    Which correction should be made to sentence 6?

    (1) change Having to Have
    (2) insert a comma after work
    (3) change make to making
    (4) remove the comma
    (5) change give to giving

13. Sentence 9: **Things get messy, when the friendship unravels in plain view of your boss and co-workers.**

    Which correction should be made to sentence 9?

    (1) change get to are getting
    (2) remove the comma
    (3) change unravels to unravel
    (4) insert a comma after unravels
    (5) no correction is necessary

14. Sentence 12: **For instance, don't exchange presents at work or talking about your evening out.**

    Which is the best way to write the underlined portion of the sentence? If the original is the best way, choose option (1).

    (1) work or talking
    (2) work, or talking
    (3) work or talk
    (4) work, or talk
    (5) working, or talking

15. Sentence 14: **Keeping your work life separate from your social life may be hard but it's worth the effort.**

    Which correction should be made to sentence 14?

    (1) change Keeping to Keep
    (2) insert it after social life
    (3) insert a comma after hard
    (4) insert a comma after but
    (5) replace it's with its

Questions 16 through 19 refer to the following paragraphs.

Computer Virus Hoaxes

(A)

(1) If you use e-mail, you've probably received at least one message warning you of a terrible virus that will ruin your computer. (2) Most of these messages are hoaxes. (3) Designed to scare you. (4) Though some messages about viruses are accurate, most are just inaccurate rumors.

(B)

(5) Virus hoax messages are similar to one another. (6) Frequently, they describe viruses that will destroy your hard drive or computer. (7) These hoaxes also claim that a respected authority, such as a government agency, has issued a warning about the virus. (8) You can check a claim like this. (9) Contacting the agency is a good way to check. (10) Finally, hoaxes urge you to send the message to everyone you know, this just creates panic.

(C)

(11) If you receive a virus warning, don't pass it on. (12) However, you don't have to worry about opening the e-mail message itself. (13) Your computer can't get a virus that way. (14) Don't open any suspicious attachments, though, as you might infect your computer with a real virus. (15) By following these guidelines, you can keep your computer equipment safe, and avoid spreading hysteria.

16. Sentences 2 and 3: **Most of these messages are hoaxes. Designed to scare you.**

Which is the best way to write the underlined portion of these sentences? If the original is the best way, choose option (1).

(1) hoaxes. Designed
(2) hoaxes and they are designed
(3) hoaxes, designing
(4) hoaxes designed
(5) hoaxes and designed

17. Sentences 8 and 9: **You can check a claim like this. Contacting the agency is a good way to check.**

The most effective combination of sentences 8 and 9 would include which group of words?

(1) Checking a claim like this
(2) To check a claim like this, contact
(3) The agency in question can check
(4) A good way to contact the agency
(5) A good way to check, contacting

18. Sentence 10: **Finally, hoaxes urge you to send the message to everyone you know, this just creates panic.**

Which is the best way to write the underlined portion of the sentence? If the original is the best way, choose option (1).

(1) know, this
(2) know and this
(3) know this
(4) know. This
(5) know that this

19. Sentence 15: **By following these guidelines, you can keep your computer equipment safe, and avoid spreading hysteria.**

Which correction should be made to sentence 15?

(1) change by following to to follow
(2) replace these with this
(3) remove the comma after guidelines
(4) change can keep to are keeping
(5) remove the comma after safe

Answers and explanations start on page 632.

GRAMMAR AND USAGE

Nouns and Pronouns

Key Ideas

- A noun names a person, place, thing, or idea.
- A pronoun takes the place of a noun.
- Use subject, object, and possessive pronouns in the proper places.

Using Nouns and Pronouns

A **noun** names a person (such as *woman* or *Anne*), a place (such as *drugstore* or *Florida*), a thing (such as *car* or *Titanic*), or an idea (*truth* or *Buddhism*). A **proper noun** refers to a specific person, place, thing, or idea; a **common noun** is more general. For example, *Anne* is a proper noun; *woman* is a common noun.

A **pronoun** is a word that replaces a noun. The **antecedent** is the noun that is being replaced, as shown below:

EXAMPLE

Steven lost his <u>address book</u>. <u>It</u> held many important phone numbers.
             antecedent   pronoun

There are three types of pronouns: subject, object, and possessive.

EXAMPLES

A **subject pronoun** replaces the subject of a sentence.

<u>Steven</u> called home. <u>He</u> was very worried.
subject   subject pronoun

An **object pronoun** replaces the object of a verb or of a preposition.
His wife called Steven. She asked <u>him</u> what the problem was.
                    object pronoun (object of a verb)

She and Steven looked for <u>it</u>.
         object pronoun (object of a preposition)

A **possessive pronoun** replaces a possessive noun.
Steven needed <u>Kelly's</u> number. He called 411 to get <u>her</u> number.
       possessive noun   possessive pronoun

Use this chart for help in remembering the three types of pronouns:

Subject Pronoun: replaces subject	Object Pronoun: replaces object	Possessive Pronoun: shows ownership
I	me	my, mine
you	you	your, yours
he	him	his
she	her	her, hers
it	it	its
we	us	ours
they	them	their, theirs

GED TIP

To choose the option with the correct pronoun in a compound like "They went to the party with James and I," take out "James and" and ask yourself whether the sentence still sounds correct.

Avoid these mistakes with pronouns in compound subjects and objects:

Incorrect pronoun in compound subject: Linda and <u>me</u> went to the movies.
Correct: Linda and <u>I</u> went to the movies.

Incorrect pronoun in compound object: We saw Kareem and <u>he</u> at the theater.
Correct: We saw Kareem and <u>him</u> at the theater.

A. Directions: Write the correct pronoun to replace each underlined noun.

1. Laurie and Paul just moved to California. _____

2. A neighbor told Laurie and Paul that saving water was important there. _____

3. He said they should turn the water off when brushing their teeth. _____

4. Laurie's sister suggested getting a special shower head that saves water. _____

5. Laurie and Laurie's sister will go shopping for it on Sunday. _____

B. Questions 6 through 8 refer to the following letter.

To Whom It May Concern:

(A)

(1) I am writing to recommend Bonetta Williams for the position of managerial assistant in your firm. (2) I believe that she is highly qualified for the position, and I urge you to strongly consider her candidacy.

(B)

(3) Bonetta and me have worked together for three years. (4) As my secretary, she has proven to be responsible and efficient. (5) She always gets her work done on time and looks for ways to help others. (6) In addition, I find her extremely intelligent and likable. (7) I will be sorry to see her go.

(C)

(8) My supervisor, Walter Constantine, has also worked with Bonetta and would be happy to speak with you if necessary. (9) Please contact Walter or I if you need any further information.

Sincerely,

Carol Rhodes

6. Sentence 3: Bonetta and me have worked together for three years.

Which correction should be made to sentence 3?

(1) replace me with I
(2) replace Bonetta with She
(3) insert a comma after me
(4) change have to has
(5) change have worked to been working

7. Sentence 5: She always gets her work done on time and looks for ways to help others.

Which correction should be made to sentence 5?

(1) replace She with Her
(2) change her to hers
(3) insert a comma after time
(4) change looks to looking
(5) no correction is necessary

8. Sentence 9: Please contact Walter or I if you need any further information.

Which is the best way to write the underlined portion of the sentence? If the original is the best way, choose option (1).

(1) Walter or I
(2) Walter or me
(3) he or I
(4) him or I
(5) he or me

Answers and explanations start on page 633.

- A pronoun should match its antecedent in person and number.
- Make sure it is clear which antecedent a pronoun refers to.
- If necessary, use a noun in place of a pronoun, or construct the sentence differently so that the antecedent is clear.

Pronoun-Antecedent Agreement

Pronouns should agree with their antecedents, or the nouns they refer to. For example, a pronoun and its antecedent must agree in number. If the antecedent is singular, the pronoun should be singular. If the antecedent is plural, the pronoun should be plural.

EXAMPLES

Andy's <u>company</u> is very progressive. <u>It</u> pays for his college classes.
    singular antecedent   singular pronoun

Many <u>employees</u> want to learn more skills, so <u>they</u> take classes.
    plural antecedent   plural pronoun

Incorrect: Any <u>employee</u> who is interested should submit <u>their</u> application.
Correct: Any <u>employee</u> who is interested should submit <u>his or her</u> application.
Correct: <u>Employees</u> who are interested should submit <u>their</u> applications.

Note that for collective nouns (such as *company, jury, family, team, committee, union*), you generally use the singular pronoun *it*.

Incorrect: The <u>committee</u> announced that <u>they</u> will hold weekly meetings.
Correct: The <u>committee</u> announced that <u>it</u> will hold weekly meetings.

A pronoun and its antecedent must agree in person. To agree, they both must be first person (referring to the speaker), second person (the person spoken to), or third person (the person or thing spoken about).

First person	Second person	Third person
I, me, my mine we, us, our, ours	you, your, yours	he, him, his she, her, hers it, its they, them, their, theirs

The indefinite pronoun *one* is like a third-person personal pronoun. A common error in writing (and one that is tested on the GED Test) is an incorrect shift between the third-person *one* and the second-person *you*.

Incorrect shift: If <u>one</u> attends college classes, <u>you</u> can be reimbursed.
Correct: If <u>one</u> attends college classes, <u>one</u> can be reimbursed.
Correct: If <u>one</u> attends college classes, <u>he or she</u> can be reimbursed.
Correct: If <u>you</u> attend college classes, <u>you</u> can be reimbursed.

It must be clear which antecedent a pronoun refers to. If necessary, use a noun in place of the pronoun, or reconstruct the sentence.

Unclear: Carlos spoke to his boss, and he told him about the program.
Clear (noun replaces pronoun): Carlos spoke to his boss, and <u>his boss</u> told him about the program.
Clear (different construction): Carlos spoke to his boss, <u>who told him</u> about the program.

Unclear: Michelle helped Shania fill out the financial aid application that she had picked up.
Correct (different construction): After picking up a financial aid application for Shania, Michelle helped her fill it out.

GED TIP

Take into account the whole passage when you are determining which pronoun is correct. For example, a paragraph may begin in the third-person one, *then incorrectly shift to the second-person* you.

A. Directions: Correct any errors in pronoun use. If there are no errors, write C. You may also have to change some verbs.

EXAMPLE: People who live in small towns know ~~one has~~ fewer amenities than big-city dwellers.

<small>they have</small>

___ **1.** Sally is moving to a small town. Her mother is concerned about the health care options they offer.

___ **2.** Sally tried to reassure her mother, but it was hard for her to believe her.

___ **3.** Sally asked a friend who lives in the town for information about its health care facilities.

___ **4.** The town has a freestanding clinic where a person can go when they are sick.

___ **5.** There is also a nearby hospital, and they have a very good reputation.

___ **6.** If one is concerned about health care, you should sign up for a good insurance plan.

B. Questions 7 through 9 refer to the following paragraphs.

The Best Discipline

(A)

(1) What should parents do when their children act up? (2) Parents often like the idea of punishment, but punishment may not be the most effective solution. (3) If the punishment results from the parent's anger, it won't work. (4) Instead, children will learn only that they shouldn't make one's parents angry.

(B)

(5) One parenting expert feels that they should be clear about their expectations from the outset so that children will not unknowingly violate rules. (6) They should respond to children's misbehavior in a calm and neutral fashion. (7) It's also important to choose a consequence related to the action. (8) If a child hits or bites in a play group, for example, it would be most appropriate not to allow the child to play with them for a short time. (9) He or she will begin to see the connection.

7. Sentence 4: Instead, children will learn only that they shouldn't make one's parents angry.

Which correction should be made to sentence 4?

(1) remove the comma after <u>Instead</u>
(2) change <u>learn</u> to <u>have learned</u>
(3) replace <u>they</u> with <u>you</u>
(4) change <u>shouldn't</u> to <u>should'nt</u>
(5) replace <u>one's</u> with <u>their</u>

8. Sentence 5: One parenting expert feels that <u>they</u> should be clear about their expectations from the outset so that children will not unknowingly violate rules.

Which is the best way to write the underlined portion of this sentence? If the original is the best way, choose option (1).

(1) they
(2) she
(3) we
(4) one
(5) parents

9. Sentence 8: If a child hits or bites in a play group, for example, it would be most appropriate not to allow the child to play with them for a short time.

Which correction should be made to sentence 8?

(1) insert a comma after <u>hits</u>
(2) remove the comma after <u>group</u>
(3) replace <u>the child</u> with <u>them</u>
(4) replace <u>them</u> with <u>the group</u>
(5) no correction is necessary

Answers and explanations start on page 633.

Verb Forms and Tenses

Key Ideas

- Each verb has four forms: present, present participle, past, and past participle.
- Verb forms are used to create different tenses, which show time relationships.
- Use clues in the sentence and paragraph to help decide which tense to use.

Regular Verbs

An important part of writing correctly is using the right verb forms. A **verb** is a word that indicates action or being. Each verb has a base form and four other forms. A **regular verb** follows a consistent pattern to create each verb form.

Base form: look

Tense	Verb Form	How to write it
Present	look/looks	with *I, you, we, they*: use the base form
		with *he, she, it*: add -*s* to the base form
Present participle	looking	add -*ing*
Past	looked	add -*ed* (-*d* if verb ends with *e*)
Past participle	looked	add -*ed* (-*d* if verb ends with *e*)

The forms are used to create different **verb tenses**, or times. The table below shows how verb tense and form are related. Notice that when you use certain tenses, you must also use a **helping verb**—often a form of *be* or *have*.

Tense	Verb Form	Use
Present	look/looks	a habitual action, general truth, or state of being: *I look at the newspaper every day.*
Past	looked	an action that has been completed: *I looked at it this morning.*
Future	will look	an action that has not yet happened: *I will look at it tonight, too.*
Present progressive	am/is/are looking	an action in progress: *I am looking at it right now.*
Present perfect	have/has looked:	an action that began in the past and continues until now: *I have looked at it every day this week.*
Past perfect	had looked	an action that was completed before a specific time in the past: *I had looked at it before it got wet.*
Future perfect	will have looked	an action that will be completed by a specific time in the future: *I will have looked at it by the time I get home.*

Sentences often contain clues that tell you which tense to use. For instance, time words and phrases like *yesterday* or *last week* show that the past should be used, *tonight* and *next month* indicate the future, and *by tonight, since 2000,* and *for seven years* indicate the perfect tenses.

Other verbs in the sentence can be clues: *I look at the newspaper whenever I get the chance.* Finally, verbs in other sentences also can be clues. The verbs in a paragraph or passage are generally in the same tense.

GED TIP

Some passages on the GED Test have a verb-tense question based on the tense of the entire passage. When you read a sentence in a question that sounds correct, make sure the tense matches the tense of the passage.

A. Directions: Rewrite each verb in its correct tense. Use clues in each sentence for help in choosing the tense.

EXAMPLE: Between 1892 and 1924, about 12 million immigrants _entered_ (enter) the U.S. through Ellis Island in New York.

1. By the 1950s, Ellis Island _____ (cease) to be an important immigration checkpoint.

2. The government _____ (close) Ellis Island to immigration in 1954.

3. Now Ellis Island _____ (function) as a national monument.

4. Since the island was reopened as a museum in 1990, many tourists _____ (visit) it.

5. Soon, a genealogical center _____ (open).

6. The island _____ (look) different than it did originally because 24 acres of land-fill have been added.

7. Now we _____ (think) about taking a trip to Ellis Island next month.

B. Questions 8 through 10 refer to the following advertisement.

Don't Miss Your Chance!

(A)

(1) The Express Lane credit card has offered a fantastic deal right now, for a limited time only. (2) If you sign up for Express Lane before April 9, you will receive a 20 percent discount on your first five purchases!

(B)

(3) The Express Lane card carries no monthly charge. (4) You'll pay a low $35 fee just once a year. (5) Become an Express Lane member now. (6) Your savings opportunities will be amazing you!

8. Sentence 1: The Express Lane credit card <u>has offered</u> a fantastic deal right now, for a limited time only.

Which is the best way to write the underlined portion of the sentence? If the original is the best way, choose option (1).

(1) has offered
(2) is offering
(3) offered
(4) offers
(5) will offer

9. Sentence 2: If you sign up for Express Lane before April 9, you will receive a 20 percent discount on your first five purchases!

Which correction should be made to sentence 2?

(1) change <u>sign</u> to <u>have signed</u>
(2) remove the comma after <u>April 9</u>
(3) change <u>you will</u> to <u>one will</u>
(4) change <u>will receive</u> to <u>receive</u>
(5) no correction is necessary

10. Sentence 6: Your savings opportunities will be amazing you!

Which correction should be made to sentence 6?

(1) change <u>Your</u> to <u>You're</u>
(2) change <u>Your</u> to <u>One's</u>
(3) insert a comma after <u>opportunities</u>
(4) change <u>will have amazed</u> to <u>amazed</u>
(5) change <u>will be amazing</u> to <u>will amaze</u>

Answers and explanations start on page 633.

GED TIP

When you choose an answer that changes a verb, read the sentence again, with your choice in it. Doing so may help you "hear" whether the verb form is correct.

Irregular Verbs

Most verbs are regular verbs; their past and participle forms follow the same pattern. Some verbs, however, are **irregular verbs.** Although some irregular verbs follow a pattern, most do not.

A common error with irregular verbs is using the past participle in place of the past—for instance, *I been there* instead of *I was there*. Discover which irregular verb forms, if any, give you problems. Then learn the correct forms. Here are some tips for learning the forms of irregular verbs:

- If you find two verbs that rhyme in the present form (for example, *grow* and *throw*), check to see if they have the same forms in the past and past participles (*grew, grown; threw, thrown*). If so, learn them together.

- Learn which verbs follow the *i, a, u* pattern: *sing, sang, sung; drink, drank, drunk; sink, sank, sunk.* However, be aware that there are exceptions (*bring, brought, brought*).

Here is a list of common irregular verbs.

Present Form	Past Form	Past Participle Form
am, are, is	was, were	been
become	became	become
begin	began	begun
blow	blew	blown
break	broke	broken
bring	brought	brought
buy	bought	bought
choose	chose	chosen
come	came	come
do	did	done
drink	drank	drunk
eat	ate	eaten
fall	fell	fallen
fly	flew	flown
freeze	froze	frozen
get	got	gotten
give	gave	given
go	went	gone
grow	grew	grown
have, has	had	had
know	knew	known
leave	left	left
lose	lost	lost
ride	rode	ridden
run	ran	run
see	saw	seen
shake	shook	shaken
show	showed	shown
speak	spoke	spoken
steal	stole	stolen
take	took	taken
throw	threw	thrown
wear	wore	worn
write	wrote	written

GRAMMAR AND USAGE ▸ PRACTICE 2.2

A. Directions: Write the correct form of the verb shown in parentheses.

EXAMPLE: Since November, the school's heating system _has broken_____ (break) down several times.

1. Yesterday the technician _____ (come) to resolve the problem once and for all.

2. School employees _____ (show) him the boiler.

3. The technician said, "If you _____ (speak) to me about this sooner, it would have been easier to fix."

4. He _____ (take) parts out of the heating system and replaced them with new ones.

5. He said, "I've never _____ (see) such a poorly installed system."

B. Questions 6 through 8 refer to the following paragraphs.

TV Rating Systems

(A)

(1) In 1996, television industry representatives announced that the industry had formed TV Parental Guidelines. (2) This rating system, designed to give parents advance warning about the content of TV shows, begun to appear on TV in 1997. (3) The ratings system was broke down into six different categories, ranging from "All Children" to "Mature Audiences Only."

(B)

(4) Six months later, after pressure from advocacy groups, the television industry agreed to include additional labels to advise viewers if a show they were about to view contained violence, sexual activity, coarse language, or sexually suggestive language. (5) These labels now given viewers more specific and therefore more helpful information about an upcoming show.

6. **Sentence 2:** This rating system, designed to give parents advance warning about the content of TV shows, begun to appear on TV in 1997.

Which correction should be made to sentence 2?

(1) remove the comma after system
(2) change give to be giving
(3) remove the comma after shows
(4) change begun to had begun
(5) change begun to began

7. **Sentence 3:** The ratings system was broke down into six different categories, ranging from "All Children" to "Mature Audiences Only."

Which is the best way to write the underlined portion of this sentence? If the original is the best way, choose option (1).

(1) was broke
(2) broke
(3) was broken
(4) breaking
(5) had broken

8. **Sentence 5:** These labels now given viewers more specific and therefore more helpful information about an upcoming show.

Which correction should be made to sentence 5?

(1) change given to will give
(2) change given to give
(3) insert a comma after specific
(4) insert a comma after information
(5) no correction is necessary

Answers and explanations start on page 634.

Key Ideas

- A verb must match its subject in number.
- Collective nouns are singular when they refer to a group as a single unit.
- Indefinite pronouns may be singular, plural, or both.

If a verb in a GED item is underlined, ask yourself three questions: Does the verb agree with its subject? Is the verb in the right form? Is the verb in the right tense for both the sentence and the passage?

GRAMMAR AND USAGE

Subject-Verb Agreement

Agreement with a Simple Subject

In the present tense, subjects and verbs must agree in number. To understand the basics of subject-verb agreement, study the chart below. Notice that present tense verbs take an -s ending when they are used with the pronoun subjects *he, she,* and *it* or their noun equivalents.

Verb Forms for Singular Subjects	Verb Forms for Plural Subjects
I jump	*we* jump
you jump	*you* jump
he, she, it jumps	*they* jump

To master subject-verb agreement for the GED Test, be aware of these special nouns and pronouns:

Collective nouns are usually singular, even though they may seem plural. A collective noun names a group, such as *army, crew, crowd, staff, family, herd,* or *flock.* If the group is considered to be a single unit, it is singular.

EXAMPLES

The <u>army is</u> a good place to learn discipline.
The <u>church choir sings</u> each Sunday.

Some nouns that end in -s may look plural, but in fact they are not.

EXAMPLE

<u>Politics is</u> an interesting topic.

Indefinite pronouns do not refer to a specific person. Some indefinite pronouns are singular, some are plural, and some may be either.

Singular	anyone, everyone, someone, no one, one anybody, everybody, somebody, nobody anything, everything, something, nothing another, other either, neither, each, much
Plural	many, several, few, both
Singular or plural	all, none, some, any, part, most

EXAMPLES

Singular: These days, it seems as if almost <u>everyone is</u> joining a health club.
Singular: <u>Most</u> of the equipment <u>is</u> easy to use.
Plural: <u>Most</u> of the exercise classes <u>are fun</u>
Plural: <u>A few are</u> advanced classes for those already in great shape.

GRAMMAR AND USAGE ▸ PRACTICE 3.1

A. Directions: Underline the correct verb form to complete each sentence.

EXAMPLE: Every Monday, the National Orchestra (perform, <u>performs</u>) live on the radio.

1. The public (is, are) invited to listen free of charge.

2. Free tickets (becomes, become) available one hour before the performance.

3. The performance (is, are) usually held in Barnes Hall.

4. Many well-known musicians (has, have) played there.

5. Everyone (seem, seems) to enjoy these concerts very much.

6. The concert series (is, are) very popular.

B. Questions 7 through 9 refer to the following article.

The Speed of Sound

(A)

(1) Most of us has heard airplane noise that is so loud it sounds like an explosion. (2) That noise occurs when a plane start to fly faster than the speed of sound. (3) Listeners on the ground hear the noise, but it is not audible to passengers.

(B)

(4) The speed of sound is 1,088 feet per second at 32°F at sea level. (5) It is different at other temperatures and in other substances. (6) For example, sound travels faster in water than in air. (7) Sound takes about one second to move a mile under water, but five seconds to move a mile through air. (8) It travels through ice cold vapor at 4,708 feet per second and through ice cold water at 4,938 feet per second. (9) Surprisingly, some other materials conducts sound very well. (10) For instance, sound travels through glass at speeds up to 19,690 feet per second.

7. Sentence 1: Most of us <u>has heard</u> airplane noise that is so loud it sounds like an explosion.

Which is the best way to write the underlined portion of this sentence? If the original is the best way, choose option (1).

(1) has heard
(2) have heard
(3) has been hearing
(4) having heard
(5) hears

8. Sentence 2: That noise occurs when a plane start to fly faster than the speed of sound.

Which correction should be made to sentence 2?

(1) change <u>occurs</u> to <u>occur</u>
(2) change <u>occurs</u> to <u>occurred</u>
(3) replace <u>plane</u> with <u>plain</u>
(4) change <u>start</u> to <u>starts</u>
(5) replace <u>than</u> with <u>then</u>

9. Sentence 9: Surprisingly, some other materials conducts sound very well.

Which correction should be made to sentence 9?

(1) remove the comma
(2) replace <u>some</u> with <u>any</u>
(3) change <u>conducts</u> to <u>conduct</u>
(4) change <u>conducts</u> to <u>conducted</u>
(5) no correction is necessary

Answers and explanations start on page 634.

Key Ideas

- If a compound subject is joined by *and*, use a plural verb.
- If a compound subject is joined by *or, either . . . or*, or *neither . . . nor*, the verb should agree with the subject closer to it.
- When checking subject-verb agreement, ignore interrupting phrases, and watch for inverted structure.

Agreement with a Compound Subject

A compound subject is made up of two or more subjects joined by *and* or *or*. To make a verb agree with a compound subject, follow these guidelines:

When two or more subjects are joined by *and*, the compound subject is plural. Use the correct verb form for the plural.

EXAMPLE: Tricia and her sister are caring for their mother.

If two subjects are joined by *or*, the verb agrees with the subject closer to it:

EXAMPLE: A health aide or a nurse visits each day.

When subjects are joined by *either . . . or* or *neither . . . nor*, the verb agrees with the subject closer to it.

EXAMPLE: Neither the sisters nor their brother has medical training.

Interrupting Words

Sometimes a word or group of words comes between the subject and the verb. In that case, locate the subject by asking yourself, What is this sentence really about? Mentally cross out the interruptor. Then make the verb agree with the subject.

EXAMPLE: The medicine ~~prescribed by the doctors~~ is on a high shelf.
               subject   interruptor   verb

Interrupting phrases often begin with prepositions, such as *of, in, on, from with, to* and *for*.

EXAMPLE: A pile ~~of medical supplies~~ rests in the front hallway.

Interrupting phrases may be set off by commas. Watch especially for phrases beginning with words like *along with, as well as, besides*, and *in addition to*.

EXAMPLES
Dr. Silva, ~~who is one of the surgeons~~, consults with the family.
The sisters, ~~along with the medical team~~, keep the patient comfortable.

Inverted Structure

Checking subject-verb agreement can be tricky when the sentence structure is **inverted**—that is, when the subject comes after the verb. Most questions and sentences that begin with *here* or *there* are inverted.

EXAMPLES
Does the pharmacy have enough medicine to fill the prescription?
Here are the hospital supplies that Tricia ordered.

Incorrect: What is Tricia and her family going to do?
Correct: What are Tricia and her family going to do?

Incorrect: Do Tricia want to send her mother to a hospital?
Correct: Does Tricia want to send her mother to a hospital?

Incorrect: There's the bandages. (Remember that *There's* is short for *There is*.)
Correct: There are the bandages.

A. Directions: If a sentence contains an interrupting phrase, cross out the interruptor. Then underline the correct verb to complete the sentence.

EXAMPLE: Brushing and flossing ~~with regularity~~ (is, <u>are</u>) key to good dental health.

1. Many toothpastes on the market (carry, carries) a seal of approval from the American Dental Association.

2. Products carrying the seal (are, is) tested to guarantee that they are safe and effective.

3. Fluoride, an important ingredient in many toothpastes, (strengthens, strengthen) teeth and (attacks, attack) bacteria that cause tooth decay.

4. There (is, are) toothpastes that claim to have special benefits, like tartar control or whitening.

5. A few pharmacies and supermarkets (offers, offer) store-brand toothpaste at a low price.

6. Any toothpaste with fluoride and good flavor (is, are) fine to use, even if it's not a brand-name toothpaste.

B. Questions 7 through 9 refer to the following paragraphs.

Unemployment Insurance

(A)

(1) Unemployment insurance provides workers who have lost their jobs with partial replacement of their salary. (2) Each state administers its own program and have its own laws. (3) The amount received is determined by wage level and the length of employment. (4) When the unemployment rate rises above a certain level, states are required to extend the benefits. (5) The state and federal governments share the cost of the additional benefits.

(B)

(6) In most states, employer contributions pay for this program. (7) Unemployed workers who wish to draw benefits reports regularly to their public employment office to learn about job openings.

7. Sentence 2: Each state administers its own program and have its own laws.

Which correction should be made to sentence 2?

(1) change <u>state</u> to <u>State</u>
(2) change <u>administers</u> to <u>administering</u>
(3) change <u>administers</u> to <u>administer</u>
(4) change <u>have</u> to <u>has</u>
(5) replace <u>its</u> with <u>it's</u>

8. Sentence 3: The amount received is determined by wage level and the length of employment.

If you rewrote sentence 3 beginning with

Wage level and the length of employment

the next word(s) should be

(1) determine
(2) determines
(3) is determined
(4) has determined
(5) was determined

9. Sentence 7: Unemployed workers who wish to draw benefits reports regularly to their public employment office to learn about job openings.

Which correction should be made to sentence 7?

(1) insert a comma after <u>workers</u>
(2) change <u>wish</u> to <u>wishes</u>
(3) insert a comma after <u>benefits</u>
(4) change <u>reports</u> to <u>report</u>
(5) replace <u>their</u> with <u>there</u>

Answers and explanations start on page 634.

GRAMMAR AND USAGE

Essay Writing Skills: Editing

After you have written and revised your essay, you will need to edit it. In the editing stage of the writing process, you check for correct grammar, usage, and word choice. You may already have made some organizational changes. The kinds of changes you make when you are editing will be smaller—more like fine-tuning.

You know a lot about grammar and usage from working through the first three lessons in this section. What about word choice? There are several aspects of word choice to look at when you are editing: using precise words, avoiding wordiness, and avoiding slang.

People often use vague terms when they are speaking. They say things like, "It was a great party!" or "The weather is nice today." General words like great and nice are okay in conversation because the listener can ask questions such as, "What was so great about the party?" In writing, however, you should try to write specific words that create a clear picture for the reader.

With vague words: Tim took a <u>long</u> hike in the <u>beautiful</u> mountains.
With precise words: Tim took a <u>12-mile</u> hike in the <u>rocky, snowy</u> mountains.

With vague words: He <u>walked</u> through a forest where the ground was <u>covered</u> with pine needles.
With precise words: He <u>meandered</u> through a forest where the ground was <u>carpeted</u> with pine needles.

It's also helpful to your reader if you write concisely and avoid wordiness. Being brief helps the reader focus on your message. If you notice that you have said the same thing twice, cut out the extra words.

Too wordy: Tim's dream and the thing he hopes for most of all is to make a home for himself and live in a cabin in the woods.
More concise: Tim's most cherished dream is to live in a cabin in the woods.

Too wordy: The only thing getting in the way of his having this dream come true is that his wife isn't so sure that it's such a fantastic idea.
More concise: The only obstacle to realizing his dream is his wife's resistance.

Finally, avoid using slang when writing your essay. Though people sometimes use informal language when speaking, essay writing calls for more formal language. Take care to express yourself appropriately.

With slang: Tim is going to <u>hit the road</u> at seven tonight.
With more formal language: Tim is going to <u>leave town</u> at seven tonight.

With slang: He needs a better map because <u>he's totally clueless about</u> directions.
With more formal language: He needs a better map because <u>he has difficulty understanding</u> directions.

Key Ideas

- Use precise words instead of vague ones.
- Express your ideas in as few words as possible.
- When writing an essay, use formal language instead of slang.

GED TIP

To edit the draft of your essay, use the same marks you used to revise it. Then if you copy your essay over, incorporate the revising and editing changes you made. This version will be the one read by the GED scorers.

GRAMMAR AND USAGE ▸ PRACTICE 4

A. Directions: Replace each of the underlined words or phrases with more appropriate language. Write your answers on a separate sheet of paper.

1. Families International is a <u>non-profit organization that does not make any money</u>.

2. We give aid to <u>many</u> children in the Third World every year.

3. These children must endure <u>lousy</u> living conditions.

4. Your donation, even if it is only five <u>bucks</u>, will help a child get food and clothing.

5. Please send your donation <u>as soon and as quickly as possible</u> to the following address.

B. Directions: Edit the paragraphs below for correct grammar and usage, paying special attention to nouns and pronouns, subject-verb agreement, and regular and irregular verbs.

If you ever order merchandise from a catalog, you should be aware of your rights. All companies, regardless of what state they are located in, is required to ship your order within 30 days unless they have advertise a different shipping time. If a company is unable to meet the shipping deadline, they must send you an "Option Notice." You can choose to wait longer or get a refund.

Some consumers complaining about receiving merchandise that they did not order. They were told that companies that engaged in this practice broken the law. If they send you a product you haven't order, it is yours to keep.

If you receive a package that been damaged, don't open it. Write "REFUSED" on the package, and return it to the seller. There's no need to add new postage as long as the package come by regular mail.

C. Directions: Edit the essay that you wrote on the following topic:

TOPIC

What are the advantages and disadvantages of owning a pet?

In your essay, explain the advantages, the disadvantages, or both. Give reasons to support your answer.

Be sure to check for:

☑ Correct use of nouns and pronouns
☑ Correct use of regular and irregular verbs
☑ Subject-verb agreement
☑ Word choice

Answers and explanations start on page 634.

GRAMMAR AND USAGE PRACTICE QUESTIONS

Questions 1 through 5 refer to the following paragraphs.

Unorthodox Tennis Stars

(A)

(1) Venus and Serena Williams are not your typical tennis stars. (2) For one thing, they are African Americans in a game that few African Americans have played; those who preceded them were Althea Gibson, Arthur Ashe, and Zina Garrison. (3) For another, Venus and Serena are sisters.

(B)

(4) Tennis players often receive hours of instruction from highly paid coaches, but it doesn't happen that way for Venus and Serena. (5) Instead, their father, the former owner of a security-services business, taught them how to play on public courts, after teaching himself through books and films. (6) The family lived in a rough neighborhood, and gang members watched over the girls while they practiced.

(C)

(7) The practice paid off. (8) Venus had won 63 tournaments by the time she turned 12, and she became a professional at 14. (9) In just a few years, she earns millions of dollars in endorsements and prizes. (10) Serena, turning professional a year after Venus, had a slower start. (11) However, experts think she may someday be better than her sister.

(D)

(12) The two sisters, who live in Palm Beach Gardens, Florida, is best friends. (13) Though they sometimes face each other on the court, there been no trace of sibling rivalry.

1. Sentence 4: **Tennis players often receive hours of instruction from highly paid coaches, but it doesn't happen that way for Venus and Serena.**

   Which correction should be made to sentence 4?

   (1) change receive to receives
   (2) replace hours with ours
   (3) remove the comma
   (4) change doesn't to didn't
   (5) no correction is necessary

2. Sentence 6: **The family lived in a rough neighborhood, and gang members watched over the girls while they practiced.**

   Which is the best way to write the underlined portion of the sentence? If the original is the best way, choose option (1).

   (1) they
   (2) the girls
   (3) each
   (4) she
   (5) one

3. Sentence 9: **In just a few years, she earns millions of dollars in endorsements and prizes.**

   Which is the best way to write the underlined portion of the sentence? If the original is the best way, choose option (1).

   (1) earns
   (2) earned
   (3) be earning
   (4) earn
   (5) will earn

4. Sentence 12: **The two sisters, who live in Palm Beach Gardens, Florida, is best friends.**

   Which correction should be made to sentence 12?

   (1) replace two with too
   (2) remove the comma after sisters
   (3) change live to lives
   (4) remove the comma after Florida
   (5) change is to are

5. Sentence 13: **Though they sometimes face each other on the court, there been no trace of sibling rivalry.**

   Which correction should be made to sentence 13?

   (1) change face to faced
   (2) remove the comma after court
   (3) replace there with their
   (4) change been to was
   (5) change been to is

Questions 6 through 10 refer to the following paragraphs.

Getting the Best Service for Your Car

(A)

(1) Have you had trouble finding a good mechanic? (2) By following these tips, you can improve your chances of getting quality service.

(B)

(3) Even before your car breaks down, look for a shop you like and trust. (4) Ask people where they will receive good service at a reasonable price. (5) Don't have picked a shop just because it's close to home, for another shop may have a better deal. (6) Be wary of ads that offer rock-bottom prices. (7) Specials like these often comes with restrictions attached.

(C)

(8) Be as specific as possible when you describe your car's problem to the mechanic. (9) If the technician must spend time trying to determine what's wrong, it will cost more. (10) You also need to request information about both estimates and guarantees before the repair work starts. (11) Ask for a price range rather than an exact estimate. (12) Find out how long the guarantee lasts and whether there's any time or mileage limits.

(D)

(13) If you don't understand a repair explanation, ask for clarification right away. (14) In addition, keep records of all repairs and billing in case of a dispute.

6. Sentence 4: **Ask people where they will receive good service at a reasonable price.**

Which correction should be made to sentence 4?

(1) change Ask to Asking
(2) change Ask to To ask
(3) change will receive to have received
(4) change will receive to receiving
(5) no correction is necessary

7. Sentence 5: **Don't have picked a shop just because it's close to home, for another shop may have a better deal.**

Which correction should be made to sentence 5?

(1) change have picked to pick
(2) change have picked to be picking
(3) replace it's with its
(4) remove the comma
(5) change have to be having

8. Sentence 7: **Specials like these often comes with restrictions attached.**

Which correction should be made to sentence 7?

(1) change Specials to Special
(2) replace these with this
(3) insert a comma after these
(4) change comes to came
(5) change comes to come

9. Sentence 9: **If the technician must spend time trying to determine what's wrong, it will cost more.**

Which correction should be made to sentence 9?

(1) change must spend to spent
(2) change what's to what are
(3) remove the comma
(4) replace it with the repair job
(5) change will cost to costed

10. Sentence 12: **Find out how long the guarantee lasts and whether there's any time or mileage limits.**

Which is the best way to write the underlined portion of the sentence? If the original is the best way, choose option (1).

(1) there's
(2) there be
(3) there are
(4) there were
(5) there will have been

Questions 11 through 15 refer to the following letter.

Taxpayer Notification

(A)

(1) We have received your tax return and have noted some inconsistencies in it. (2) We are therefore proposing a number of changes to your return. (3) These changes and its effect on your refund are outlined below.

(B)

(4) First, the amount you claimed for self-employed income differs from our records. (5) If you wish to contest this change, please send photocopies of one's records. (6) Second, you have made an error in your calculations. (7) Please review our calculations, which is appended to this letter.

(C)

(8) These changes having been made to your return, there is an increase in the amount of taxes you owe. (9) Your refund has therefore been reduced accordingly.

(D)

(10) Contact us if you have any questions about these specific problems or about the documents you must send to contest the changes. (11) Be sure to send the last page of this letter when replying by mail. (12) If we determine that your return was correct as filed, we have credited your account.

11. Sentence 3: **These changes and its effect on your refund are outlined below.**

    Which correction should be made to sentence 3?

    (1) replace These with Them
    (2) insert a comma after changes
    (3) replace its with their
    (4) insert a comma after refund
    (5) change are to is

12. Sentence 5: **If you wish to contest this change, please send photocopies of one's records.**

    Which correction should be made to sentence 5?

    (1) change wish to wishes
    (2) remove the comma
    (3) change send to to send
    (4) replace one's with your
    (5) no correction is necessary

13. Sentence 7: **Please review our calculations, which is appended to this letter.**

    Which correction should be made to sentence 7?

    (1) change review to reviewing
    (2) replace our with are
    (3) remove the comma
    (4) change is to are
    (5) replace to with too

14. Sentence 8: **These changes having been made to your return, there is an increase in the amount of taxes you owe.**

    If you rewrote sentence 8 beginning with

    Because of these changes to your return, the amount of taxes you owe

    the next words should be

    (1) has increased
    (2) have increased
    (3) is increasing
    (4) are increasing
    (5) been increased

15. Sentence 12: **If we determine that your return was correct as filed, we have credited your account.**

    Which is the best way to write the underlined portion of the sentence? If the original is the best way, choose option (1).

    (1) have credited
    (2) will credit
    (3) will have credited
    (4) credited
    (5) had credited

Questions 16 through 20 refer to the following paragraphs.

Disability Etiquette

(A)

(1) Many of us doesn't know how to act when meeting someone who has a disability. (2) The main thing to remember is that people with disabilities has feelings just like everyone else. (3) They want to be treated with respect and dignity. (4) Beyond that, try the following tips.

(B)

(5) When you meet a person with a disability, speak and act with he or she as you would with anyone else. (6) Use your usual tone of voice. (7) A person who has trouble hearing you will let you know. (8) Don't talk down to the person or stare. (9) Refrain from using a term like *handicap,* which focuses on the disability rather than on the person. (10) Instead, use a term such as *physically challenged* or say, "He uses a wheelchair."

(C)

(11) Any assistive equipment, such as a wheelchair, cane, or communication board, is the person's property. (12) Unless you have the person's express permission, you should not touch it. (13) Also, distracting a blind person's guide dog could put the owner in danger, so do not pet it.

(D)

(14) Finally, if you have a child with you, don't prevent him or her from talking to the person or asking questions. (15) Children are often more accepting than adults.

16. Sentence 1: **Many of us doesn't know how to act when meeting someone who has a disability.**

    Which is the best way to write the underlined portion of the sentence? If the original is the best way, choose option (1).

    (1) doesn't
    (2) don't
    (3) didn't
    (4) never does
    (5) never did

17. Sentence 2: **The main thing to remember is that people with disabilities has feelings just like everyone else.**

    Which correction should be made to sentence 2?

    (1) replace main with mane
    (2) add a comma after remember
    (3) change is to are
    (4) change has to have
    (5) no correction is necessary

18. Sentence 5: **When you meet a person with a disability, speak and act with he or she as you would with anyone else.**

    Which is the best way to write the underlined portion of the sentence? If the original is the best way, choose option (1).

    (1) he or she
    (2) he or her
    (3) him or her
    (4) him or she
    (5) them

19. Sentence 11: **Any assistive equipment, such as a wheelchair, cane, or communication board, is the person's property.**

    Which correction should be made to sentence 11?

    (1) remove the comma after wheelchair
    (2) change is to being
    (3) change is to are
    (4) change person's to persons
    (5) no correction is necessary

20. Sentences 13: **Also, distracting a blind person's guide dog could put the owner in danger, so do not pet it.**

    If you rewrote sentence 13 beginning with

    Also, don't pet a blind person's guide dog because distracting

    the next word(s) should be

    (1) a blind person's guide dog
    (2) it
    (3) him
    (4) her
    (5) them

Answers and explanations start on page 634.

MECHANICS

Comma Use

As a general rule, commas indicate where readers would pause in a sentence if they were reading it aloud. Below are specific guidelines for using commas.

Commas in Compound Sentences

In a compound sentence, place a comma immediately before the coordinating conjunction.

EXAMPLES

Some people are insecure about hosting a party, but others are relaxed and confident.

Many hosts have years of practice, and they have some organizational tips.

Watch out, though, for sentences that appear to be compound but are not. Some sentences have one main clause but have a compound subject or a compound predicate. If a sentence does not have two independent clauses, a comma is not needed before the coordinating conjunction.

Incorrect: Planning, and list making are two key organizational techniques.
Correct: Planning and list making are two key organizational techniques.

Incorrect: Making a list reduces disorganization, and helps you feel in control.
Correct: Making a list reduces disorganization and helps you feel in control.

Commas after Introductory Elements

In general, a comma should follow an introductory word, phrase, or clause to separate the introductory element from the main part of the sentence.

EXAMPLES

Introductory words:
Yes, listing your ideas can be very helpful.
However, making a list is only the first step.

Introductory phrases:
Giving it some thought, carefully draw up a guest list.
For a casual feel, have an open house.
On the day of the party, do as much as you can first thing in the morning.
By party time, you should be able to relax.

Introductory clauses:
Before you make a list, decide what kind of party you will have.
If you are a good cook, you might choose to have a dinner party.

Remember that only a subordinate clause at the beginning of a sentence requires a comma after it. A subordinate clause at the end of the sentence generally does not.

No comma: Decide what kind of party you will have before you make a list.

Key Ideas

- In a compound sentence, use a comma before the coordinating conjunction.
- Be careful not to use a comma between two words or phrases joined by *and*.
- Insert a comma after an introductory word, phrase, or clause.

ON THE GED

Commas are the only mark of punctuation directly tested on Part I of the GED Language Arts, Writing Test.

MECHANICS ▸ PRACTICE 1.1

A. Directions: Insert commas where needed in the sentences below. If no commas are required, write *NC*.

_____ 1. Train travel is more pleasant than riding a bus but it can be more expensive.

_____ 2. When you're on a train you can stand up and stretch if you need to.

_____ 3. Most trains have club cars where passengers can get snacks and sometimes even sit at tables.

_____ 4. Unlike buses trains sometimes have seats that face each other.

_____ 5. Traveling through a scenic area you may find that your train has a double-decker car that offers a better view.

_____ 6. Lowered air fares and many people's unwillingness to spend long hours in a train have contributed to the declining popularity of rail travel.

B. Questions 7 through 9 refer to the following paragraphs.

Low-Fat Cooking

(A)

(1) To have a more healthful diet, try cooking with less fat. (2) It's not as hard as you think! (3) For starters use cooking methods that require little or no oil or butter, such as steaming, poaching, or baking. (4) When you do include oil in the preparation of your dish, use less of it. (5) Vinegar can be used without oil in salad dressing, and the flavor can be enhanced with fresh herbs.

(B)

(6) Another tactic is to cut down on dairy fat. (7) Avoid regular milk, cream, and sour cream. (8) Add low-fat dairy products or another liquid to your dish instead. (9) Many dairy foods come in a low-fat version, and though not all of them may be pleasing to the palate, some are.

7. Sentence 3: For starters use cooking methods that require little or no oil or butter, such as steaming, poaching, or baking.

Which correction should be made to sentence 3?

(1) insert a comma after starters
(2) change require to requires
(3) remove the comma after butter
(4) remove the comma after steaming
(5) no correction is necessary

8. Sentence 5: Vinegar can be used without oil in salad dressing, and the flavor can be enhanced with fresh herbs.

Which is the best way to write the underlined portion of the sentence? If the original is the best way, choose option (1).

(1) dressing, and
(2) dressing and
(3) dressing. And
(4) dressing, or
(5) dressing, for example

9. Sentence 9: Many dairy foods come in a low-fat version, and though not all of them may be pleasing to the palate, some are.

Which correction should be made to sentence 9?

(1) change come to comes
(2) remove the comma after version
(3) insert a comma after pleasing
(4) remove the comma after palate
(5) no correction is necessary

Answers and explanations start on page 635.

Key Ideas

- Separate the items in a series with commas.
- Put commas around an appositive only if it gives nonessential details about a noun.
- Don't put a comma between a subject and a verb.
- Don't use a comma between two items joined by *and* or *or*.

GED TIP

When an option involves removing a comma, see if you can apply a specific rule for using a comma in that place. If you cannot, the comma should probably be removed.

Commas in a Series

When three or more items are listed in a series, place commas *between* the items:

EXAMPLES

Keith, Darnelle, Marisol, and Doug are ready to take the GED Test.
They have taken a GED class, studied together, and prepared well.

The comma before the final *and* or *or* is optional (for example, *March 7, March 14,* or *March 21*). Placing a comma there is not tested on the GED Writing Test, but using one there will help you place commas correctly in the series. To use commas between the items in a series, count the number of items listed and subtract one. That is the number of commas you should use.

Commas with Appositives

An **appositive** is a word or group of words that gives more information about a noun by renaming it.

EXAMPLES

Marisol, an experienced writer, feels confident about the GED essay.
Doug's cousin, Gina, was the first in the family to receive a GED.

To decide whether to set off an appositive with commas, mentally cross out the appositive. Then ask, *"Can I still identify the person, place, or thing described in the sentence?"* If you can, use commas around the appositive.

EXAMPLES

Mann College, ~~a local community college~~, offers GED courses.
Keith, ~~who attended GED class for a year~~, has done well there.

Here you can identify the noun without the appositive. Each appositive adds more information, but it is not essential to your understanding. Usually when an appositive is renaming a proper noun, it is not essential.

On the other hand, if you cannot identify the person, place, or thing without the appositive, do not set off the appositive with commas.

EXAMPLES

Keith and his friend ~~Antoine~~ plan to work in construction.
Students ~~who study faithfully~~ usually do well on the test.

In these examples, you cannot identify the nouns without the appositives. You would ask, *"Which friend?"* and *"Which students?"* The appositives are essential to your understanding and should not be set off by commas.

Comma Errors to Avoid

It is easy to overuse commas. Avoid this error by following these guidelines:

Do not use a comma between the subject and the verb.

Incorrect: Park College, is the school Doug hopes to attend.

Do not use a comma between two subjects, two verbs, or two other items joined by *and* or *or.*

Incorrect: Science, and math are hard subjects for Keith.
Incorrect: Darnell writes practice essays, and reads.
Incorrect: They will review his application, and transcript.

A. Directions: Insert commas where needed in the sentences below. If no commas are required, write *NC*.

_____ **1.** Kwanzaa is a week-long African American holiday that celebrates culture community and family.

_____ **2.** Kwanzaa a wintertime holiday is based on an ancient African harvest celebration.

_____ **3.** It was developed in modern times by scholar Maulana Karenga.

_____ **4.** Kwanzaa celebrations include rituals such as singing dancing drumming and poetry reading.

_____ **5.** The family lights one candle every day for each of seven principles: unity self-determination responsibility cooperative economics purpose creativity and faith.

_____ **6.** A day during which people consider their moral worthiness marks the end of Kwanzaa.

B. Questions 7 through 9 refer to the following paragraphs.

Childproofing Your Home

(A)

(1) If you have small children, you no doubt appreciate the need to make your home as safe as possible. (2) It is a fact that home accidents, are responsible for more children's injuries than all childhood diseases combined. (3) Taking a few simple measures might reduce the number of times you take your kids to the emergency room.

(B)

(4) Start by putting childproof locks on all cupboards in which medicines poisons, or fragile objects are stored. (5) To keep babies and toddlers from entering dangerous areas, put baby gates in doorways and install sleeves on doorknobs. (6) Install safety locks on doors and windows. (7) Make sure that older children, those ten and up can open them in an emergency. (8) To prevent burns in the bathtub, keep the water temperature below 120°F. (9) Cover unused outlets with outlet plugs.

7. Sentence 2: It is a fact that home accidents, are responsible for more children's injuries than all childhood diseases combined.

Which correction should be made to sentence 2?

(1) insert a comma after <u>fact</u>
(2) remove the comma
(3) change <u>are</u> to <u>is</u>
(4) insert a comma after <u>injuries</u>
(5) no correction is necessary

8. Sentence 4: Start by putting childproof locks on all cupboards in which medicines poisons, or fragile objects are stored.

Which correction should be made to sentence 4?

(1) change <u>Start</u> to <u>Starting</u>
(2) insert a comma after <u>locks</u>
(3) insert a comma after <u>medicines</u>
(4) insert a comma after <u>objects</u>
(5) change <u>are</u> to <u>is</u>

9. Sentence 7: Make sure that older <u>children, those ten and up</u> can open them in an emergency.

Which is the best way to write the underlined portion of this sentence? If the original is the best way, choose option (1).

(1) children, those ten and up
(2) children those ten and up
(3) children, those ten, and up,
(4) children, those ten and up,
(5) children those ten and up,

Answers and explanations start on page 635.

MECHANICS

Capitalization

Key Ideas

- Capitalize proper nouns and adjectives.
- Capitalize days of the week, months, and names of holidays, but not seasons.
- Capitalize titles if they come before a person's name or are used to address the person.

To recognize capitalization errors on Part I of the GED Writing Test and to use capital letters correctly in your essay, follow these guidelines.

Capitalize proper nouns. A **proper noun** is the name of a specific person, place, thing, or idea. If a proper noun has two or more words, capitalize each word.

EXAMPLES

Claude Normand is a major contributor to Portland Community Hospital.
The hospital is located on Camden Road in Portland, Maine.
The hospital and charities such as the American Cancer Society rely on contributions from citizens.
All major religions, from Islam to Christianity, support giving to charity.

Note that the key words in addresses are proper nouns and are capitalized. The key words include the names of streets, cities, states, and countries.

Do not capitalize common nouns, which do not refer to a specific person, place, or thing.

EXAMPLE
Incorrect: Many Doctors volunteer at Clinics in the City.
Correct: Many doctors volunteer at clinics in the city.

Capitalize the names of proper adjectives. A **proper adjective** is formed from a proper noun.

EXAMPLE
Mr. Normand has a French Canadian heritage.

Capitalize a title before a person's name. Do not capitalize a title when it appears without a person's name unless it is used in direct address.

EXAMPLES
Title before name: Mr. Normand met recently with Dr. Halverson and Mayor Maresky.
Title without name: The doctor and mayor were very receptive to his ideas.
Direct address: He said, "Thank you, Mayor, for listening to my proposal."

Capitalize names of holidays, days of the week, and months. Do not capitalize the names of seasons.

EXAMPLES
Memorial Day is always the last Monday in May and is a paid holiday.
The project will be completed by the end of spring.

Capitalize names of specific school courses and all languages.

EXAMPLE
I am taking Introduction to Computers 101, English, and math.

GED TIP

If you spot a capitalization error as you read a sentence in a GED question, look immediately for the option that corrects it.

MECHANICS ▸ PRACTICE 2

A. Directions: Correct the capitalization errors in the sentences below.

EXAMPLE:

I am writing to thank the ~~S~~taff of the Waterside Physical Therapy ~~c~~enter.

1. Last Spring, I broke my arm in a car accident.

2. My internist, doctor claudia McNally, referred me to Waterside.

3. The center's Director, Ilana Harris, assigned me a physical therapist named Ellie Royce.

4. Ellie studied physical therapy in her native London and used british methods of treatment that relieved my pain quite effectively.

5. She also did therapy with me in the pool at Rainbow health club.

6. I finished my treatments just before labor day, and I feel 100 percent better, thanks to Ellie.

B. Questions 7 through 9 refer to the following paragraphs.

An Unusual Breed

(A)

(1) The akita is a Japanese dog breed that dates to ancient times. (2) The breed has a special spiritual meaning for many. (3) For example, when a child is born, well-wishers give the family small statues of akitas to express hopes for future happiness and health. (4) In the past, only Emperors and nobles were allowed to own this breed.

(B)

(5) Akitas are massive, powerful dogs, used for hunting game and guarding. (6) Starting in the 17th century, they were trained to hunt game and waterfowl in the Mountains of Japan. (7) In 1937, akitas were brought to america by author Helen Keller.

7. **Sentence 4:** In the past, only Emperors and nobles were allowed to own this breed.

Which correction should be made to sentence 4?

(1) remove the comma
(2) change Emperors to emperors
(3) change nobles to Nobles
(4) insert a comma after nobles
(5) change were to are

8. **Sentence 6:** Starting in the 17th century, they were trained to hunt game and waterfowl in the Mountains of Japan.

Which correction should be made to sentence 6?

(1) change Starting to Started
(2) remove the comma
(3) change Mountains to mountains
(4) change Japan to japan
(5) no correction is necessary

9. **Sentence 7:** In 1937, akitas were brought to america by author Helen Keller.

Which correction should be made to sentence 7?

(1) remove the comma
(2) change were to been
(3) change america to America
(4) change author to Author
(5) change Helen Keller to helen keller

Answers and explanations start on page 635.

MECHANICS

Spelling

Key Ideas

- Use apostrophes with possessive nouns but not with possessive pronouns.
- Use an apostrophe to replace the missing letters in a contraction.
- To decide whether to use a possessive or contraction, test to see whether the full form of the contraction makes sense in the sentence.

Possessives and Contractions

Some of the most common spelling errors involve possessives and contractions. Follow these guidelines when spelling these words:

A **possessive** shows ownership. Use apostrophes with possessive nouns. Do not use apostrophes with possessive pronouns.

EXAMPLES

Possessive nouns: friend's car   Marta's map   the dogs' leashes
Possessive pronouns: his, hers, ours, yours, theirs, its
Correct: The car's tires are new. The map is hers.

If a noun is singular or if it is plural but does not end in *s*, add an apostrophe + *s* to form the possessive.

Singular possessive: cat's   boss's   women's

If a noun is plural and ends in *s*, add an apostrophe after the final *s*.

Plural possessive: workers'   ladies'

A singular possessive often sounds like a plural noun. Use an apostrophe only with the possessive.

Correct: My company's benefits (possessive) make it one of the best companies (plural) to work for.

A **contraction** shortens two words by combining the second word with the first and leaving out one or more letters. An apostrophe takes the place of the missing letters. Some contractions combine pronouns with verbs.

EXAMPLES

here is → here's   there is → there's   I am → I'm

Other contractions combine verbs with the word not.

EXAMPLES

have not → haven't   do not → don't   will not → won't

Be careful to use the apostrophe in place of the missing letter or letters. Notice that the correct position is not necessarily the point at which the two words come together.

Incorrect: You do'nt have to come with us tonight. (*do'nt* should be *don't*)

Some possessives and contractions sound the same (*your* and *you're*, *its* and *it's*, *their* and *they're*). To determine whether to use a possessive or a contraction, substitute the two words that make up the contraction. If the substitution makes sense, the contraction is correct. If not, use a possessive.

GED TIP

Contractions are acceptable in informal speech and writing. However, try to avoid them in more formal writing situations, such as the GED essay.

Mechanics ▸ Practice 3.1

A. Directions: Underline the correct word or words to complete each sentence.

EXAMPLE: I'm (your, you're) downstairs neighbor, and (I've, Iv'e) been having trouble sleeping lately because of noise late at night.

1. (Theirs, There's) a noise that sounds like the thumping beat of rock music.

2. I (ca'nt, can't) be sure (who's, whose) responsible, but (its, it's) coming from your apartment.

3. My roommates and I have discussed this, and (were, we're) running out of patience.

4. You should talk to your children if the stereo is (theirs, there's).

5. Please be considerate of your neighbors just as we are considerate of (our's, ours).

B. Questions 6 through 8 refer to the paragraphs that follow.

Sales Trainees Wanted

(A)

(1) Do you have a warm smile? (2) Do people feel comfortable with you? (3) Do you have a friendly phone manner? (4) Do you have good organizational skills? (5) Are you good at solving problems? (6) If you've answered yes to these questions, we need you're skills at Macro Software.

(B)

(7) Macro Software is one of the industry leaders in software distribution. (8) In addition to our chain of stores, were proud to offer a mail order service that was the first of its kind. (9) We pride ourselves on our high-quality products, quick delivery times, and excellent customer service.

(C)

(10) We are currently hiring sales trainees for our Miami office. (11) Interested parties should send they're resumes to Jim Burns, Macro Software, 904 Ocean Drive, Miami, Florida.

6. **Sentence 6:** If you've answered yes to these questions, we need you're skills at Macro Software.

Which correction should be made to sentence 6?

(1) change you've to youve
(2) insert a comma after yes
(3) remove the comma
(4) change need to needs
(5) replace you're with your

7. **Sentence 8:** In addition to our chain of stores, were proud to offer a mail order service that was the first of its kind.

Which correction should be made to sentence 8?

(1) replace our with hour
(2) change were to we're
(3) insert a comma after service
(4) replace its with it's
(5) no correction is necessary

8. **Sentence 11:** Interested parties should send they're resumes to Jim Burns, Macro Software, 904 Ocean Drive, Miami, Florida.

Which correction should be made to sentence 11?

(1) replace parties with party's
(2) replace they're with their
(3) replace resumes with resume's
(4) change Drive to drive
(5) no correction is necessary

Answers and explanations start on page 635.

Key Idea

Homonyms are words that sound the same but have different spellings and different meanings.

ON THE GED

Possessives, contractions, and homonyms are the only kinds of spelling items that appear on the GED Language Arts, Writing Test. Study the ones that give you problems to improve your score.

Homonyms

Homonyms are words that sound alike but are spelled differently and have different meanings. The following chart lists homonyms and other commonly confused words that people often misspell.

Word	Meaning	Word in Sentence
accept	to receive willingly	I <u>accept</u> responsibility for my actions.
except	excluding	Everyone went <u>except</u> Molly.
affect	to have an impact	Did the medicine affect you?
effect	a result	The <u>effects</u> will wear off soon.
board	a piece of wood	Nail that <u>board</u> to the other one.
bored	not interested	Rami was <u>bored</u> in wood shop class.
brake	to stop; something that stops	Put your foot on the <u>brake</u>!
break	to shatter in pieces	Be careful, or you'll <u>break</u> your arm.
close	to shut	Please <u>close</u> that bag.
clothes	something to wear	I'm going to return those <u>clothes</u>.
desert	to leave behind	Don't <u>desert</u> a friend in need.
dessert	sweet food served after dinner	They offer <u>dessert</u> to their guests.
fare	money paid by a passenger	The subway <u>fare</u> was just raised.
fair	just, right	A lot of people think it's not <u>fair</u>.
forth	forward	Let's go <u>forth</u>!
fourth	in the 4th position	It is our <u>fourth</u> trip in three days.
grate	to shred	We need to <u>grate</u> some potatoes.
great	fantastic; of large size	It's going to be a <u>great</u> casserole.
hole	opening	There's a <u>hole</u> in the sweater.
whole	entire	Soon the <u>whole</u> thing will fall apart.
know	to understand	I don't <u>know</u> what's wrong with him.
no	opposite of *yes*	He has <u>no</u> sense.
led	past of the verb *lead*; brought	He <u>led</u> the worker to the supply room.
lead	a material in pencils	They gave her some <u>lead</u> pencils.
lessen	to decrease	Will you <u>lessen</u> the sugar in the recipe?
lesson	something you learn; moral	That will teach him a <u>lesson</u>.
male	a boy or man	There are both females and <u>males</u> in the Army.
mail	to send a message through the post office; a message sent	Send the letter through the <u>mail</u>.
passed	went by	Have you <u>passed</u> the post office?
past	opposite of *future*	Yes, in the <u>past</u>.
peace	opposite of *war*	When will there be world <u>peace</u>?
piece	a part	That's only a <u>piece</u> of the problem.
principal	head of a school	The <u>principal</u> has called a meeting.
principle	a guiding rule; a moral	He has no <u>principles</u>.
than	compared with	I used to have more money <u>than</u> you.
then	after that; at that time	<u>Then</u> I spent most of mine.
there	at that place	The car is over <u>there</u>.
their	belonging to them	It is <u>their</u> car.
they're	they are	<u>They're</u> going to sell it.
to	indicates a direction	Go <u>to</u> the grocery store.
too	also, in addition	Sharmaine will go, <u>too</u>.
two	the number 2	Buy me <u>two</u> loaves of bread.

A. Directions: Underline the correct word to complete each sentence.

EXAMPLE: The chairman of the (board, bored) has called this meeting.

1. This is our (fourth, forth) meeting on the topic of funding.

2. We don't (no, know) any other sources of funding.

3. The director of the organization brought up this (whole, hole) issue.

4. Next (weak, week), we plan to submit a proposal.

5. We worry that a request for funding may (affect, effect) our nonprofit status.

6. In the (past, passed), we could rely on government funding.

B. Questions 7 through 9 refer to the following paragraphs.

Equal Pay for Equal Work?

(A)

(1) In 1963, women earned only 59 percent of the wages men earned. (2) In 1997, the figure was still just 74 percent. (3) Women have logged great achievements in the workforce, so why don't they receive fare pay?

(B)

(4) One explanation is that the statistics include older women. (5) In principal, the age gap could account for the wage gap because older women still work in jobs in which attitudes and conditions of the past prevail. (6) In contrast, women under the age of 25 earn about 92 percent of what men earn. (7) However, upon closer examination, this theory falls flat. (8) Women in entry-level jobs have always earned salaries similar to those of their male peers. (9) The problem is that women don't receive the same raises and promotions that men get. (10) The affect is that, as women get older, the gap between men's and women's salaries becomes greater.

7. **Sentence 3:** Women have logged great achievements in the workforce, so why don't they receive fare pay?

   Which correction should be made to sentence 3?

   (1) change have to has
   (2) replace great with grate
   (3) change achievements to achievement's
   (4) replace fare with fair
   (5) no correction is necessary

8. **Sentence 5:** In principal, the age gap could account for the wage gap because older women still work in jobs in which attitudes and conditions of the past prevail.

   Which correction should be made to sentence 5?

   (1) change principal to principle
   (2) remove the comma after principal
   (3) change work to working
   (4) replace past with passed
   (5) no correction is necessary

9. **Sentence 10:** The affect is that, as women get older, the gap between men's and women's salaries becomes greater.

   Which correction should be made to sentence 10?

   (1) replace affect with effect
   (2) replace salaries with salary's
   (3) change becomes to become
   (4) replace greater with grater
   (5) no correction is necessary

Answers and explanations start on page 635.

MECHANICS

Essay Writing Process: Editing for Correct Mechanics

Key Ideas

- Editing is the final step in the writing process.
- Check your essay for errors in spelling, capitalization, and punctuation.

The final stage of the writing process is editing. You have already practiced editing your work to make sure that your grammar and usage are correct. Now you also need to check for correct mechanics. Ask yourself:

- Did I use commas where needed? Have I removed unnecessary commas?
- Are proper nouns and adjectives, holidays, and days of the week capitalized? Are titles capitalized where appropriate? Did I capitalize any words that should be lowercase?
- Are possessives and contractions used correctly?
- Are homonyms spelled correctly?
- Are there any other misspelled words?

Read the sample paragraph and think about how you would correct the errors in mechanics. Then read the edited paragraph and explanation that follows.

SAMPLE PARAGRAPH

(1) Perhaps I am part of a very small minority but I would much rather live in an apartment than a house. (2) For one thing its much more secure. (3) When you live in an apartment, people pass you're front door all the time, which makes it more difficult for thieves to brake in. (4) Also neighbors can sometimes see your windows from their apartments, so they can be on the lookout for Suspicious Activity. (5) Neighbors can also take in your male when you go to florida for the weak. (6) You do'nt feel bad about asking for their help because they live nearby.

EDITED PARAGRAPH

(1) Perhaps I am part of a very small minority, but I would much rather live in an apartment than a house. (2) For one thing, it's much more secure. (3) When you live in an apartment, people pass your front door all the time, which makes it more difficult for thieves to break in. (4) Also, neighbors can sometimes see your windows from their apartments, so they can be on the lookout for suspicious activity. (5) Neighbors can also take in your mail when you go to Florida for the week. (6) You don't feel bad about asking for their help because they live nearby.

Sentence 1 is a compound sentence, so a comma is required before but. In sentence 2, a comma is needed after the introductory phrase *for one thing*. Also, you can use *it is* in the sentence, so the contraction *it's* is correct. In sentence 3, the door is one you own, so the possessive *your* is needed. Also, *break* should replace *brake*, which refers to stopping a car. In sentence 4, *suspicious activity* is not a proper noun, so it should not be capitalized. In sentence 5, *mail* is the correct word for letters. *Florida* should be capitalized since it is the name of a particular place. *Weak* means *not strong*; *week*, which means *seven days*, is required. Finally, the contraction in sentence 6 should have the apostrophe in place of the missing letter.

GED TIP

Give yourself about ten minutes to edit your GED essay. Read your essay slowly, as if you were reading it aloud. This slow pace will help you catch more errors.

MECHANICS ► PRACTICE 4

A. Directions: Read the paragraphs and correct any errors in spelling, capitalization, or punctuation.

EXAMPLE:

Given the choice of a raise or shorter working hours, I would take the shortened schedule. Even though I ~~do'nt~~ *dont* have a lot of money, I would welcome a ~~brake~~ *break* from my job.

A shorter workday would enable me to accomplish many things that always seem to fall bye the wayside. First and most important is spending time with my family. If I had more time, I could be their when my daughter comes home from School. I could help her with her homework, especially for her spanish class because thats my native language. Perhaps she would spend less time, watching television. I would also like to spend more time with my husband. He works a different shift than I do and we got trouble coordinating our schedules. If I had a less demanding work schedule we'd see each other more.

Second, there are many errands that never seem to get done. For instance it's hard four us to pay bills on time. Once our phone was even cut off! If our lives were'nt so busy, we would sit down and take care of our bills, when they came in.

Finally, I would continue my education. I dropped out of school at 16, and never got my High School Diploma. I was board and had trouble paying attention. Now that I see the negative Affects of not having finished school, I want to get my GED certificate.

B. Directions: Edit the essay that you wrote on the following topic:

TOPIC

What are the advantages and disadvantages of owning a pet?

In your essay, explain the advantages, the disadvantages, or both. Give reasons to support your answer.

Be sure to check for:

- ☑ Correct use of commas
- ☑ Correct capitalization
- ☑ Correct use of possessives and contractions
- ☑ Spelling errors, including homonyms

Answers and explanations start on page 636.

MECHANICS PRACTICE QUESTIONS

Questions 1 through 5 refer to the following paragraphs.

Single Parents and Relationships

(A)

(1) Children of single parents don't exactly cheer their parents on at the start of a new relationship. (2) Instead, children may have tantrums erase phone messages, and generally try to ruin their parents' chances. (3) If you are a parent in this situation, you need to understand, and show your children that you love them. (4) However, also let your kids know that you feel you're doing the right thing.

(B)

(5) Your children may become quickly attached to a new date, even within the course of an evening. (6) Alternatively, they may fear that you plan to marry each potential partner you bring home. (7) For these reasons, it makes sense not to introduce all your dates to your children. (8) Try to see your dates at times when your children are'nt at home.

(C)

(9) Once you become committed to a particular person, it's important to include your partner in family events gradually. (10) Don't be surprised if your children have a negative reaction to your new partner. (11) This time may be difficult for your kids. (12) They're not used to seeing you with a new partner, and they may be realizing that a reconciliation with your ex-spouse is impossible. (13) If communication breaks down consider family counseling. (14) Children may be more willing to share their worries and complaints in that setting.

1. Sentence 2: **Instead, children may have tantrums erase phone messages, and generally try to ruin their parents' chances.**

Which correction should be made to sentence 2?

(1) remove the comma after Instead
(2) insert a comma after tantrums
(3) change try to be trying
(4) change their to they're
(5) no correction is necessary

2. Sentence 3: **If you are a parent in this situation, you need to understand, and show your children that you love them.**

Which is the best way to write the underlined portion of this sentence? If the original is the best way, choose option (1).

(1) understand, and show
(2) understand. And show
(3) understand and show
(4) understand, and you show
(5) understand show

3. Sentence 4: **However, also let your kids know that you feel you're doing the right thing.**

Which correction should be made to sentence 4?

(1) remove the comma after However
(2) replace your with you're
(3) replace you're with your
(4) replace right with write
(5) no correction is necessary

4. Sentence 8: **Try to see your dates at times when your children are'nt at home.**

Which correction should be made to sentence 8?

(1) change Try to Trying
(2) replace your with you're
(3) insert a comma after times
(4) change are'nt to aren't
(5) no correction is necessary

5. Sentence 13: **If communication breaks down consider family counseling.**

Which is the best way to write the underlined portion of this sentence? If the original is the best way, choose option (1).

(1) down consider
(2) down, consider
(3) down. Consider
(4) down, considering
(5) down, and consider

Questions 6 through 10 refer to the following paragraphs.

The History of Daylight Saving Time

(A)

(1) We set our clocks forward every spring and back every fall, but few of us stop to think about why we do this. (2) One of the main reasons for daylight saving time, is to save energy. (3) In the evening, we use lights, TVs, and electrical appliances. (4) Daylight saving time makes the period between sunset and bedtime one hour shorter, and therefore less electricity is used.

(B)

(5) With daylight saving time, each time zone changes it's standard time by an hour. (6) Time zones were introduced by the railroads to make schedules standard across the country. (7) In 1918, congress passed a law making the rail time zones official. (8) That same year, a second law put the country on daylight saving time for the rest of World War I. (9) The law was unpopular, however, and it was repealed seven months later. (10) Daylight saving time was also in force during most of World War II.

(C)

(11) From 1945 to 1966, each state and town could decide whether to observe daylight saving time. (12) The resulting inconsistencies created a great deal of confusion. (13) For example radio and TV stations had to put out new schedules every time a state started or ended daylight saving time. (14) Then came the Uniform Time Act of 1966, which established starting and ending dates for daylight saving time, in the spring and fall. (15) This law was amended in1986, when the starting date was moved almost a month earlier to save energy.

6. Sentence 2: **One of the main reasons for daylight saving time, is to save energy.**

Which correction should be made to sentence 2?

(1) replace main with mane
(2) insert a comma after reasons
(3) remove the comma
(4) change is to are
(5) no correction is necessary

7. Sentence 5: **With daylight saving time, each time zone changes it's standard time by an hour.**

Which correction should be made to sentence 5?

(1) remove the comma
(2) change changes to changed
(3) replace it's with its
(4) replace hour with our
(5) no correction is necessary

8. Sentence 7: **In 1918, congress passed a law making the rail time zones official.**

Which correction should be made to sentence 7?

(1) remove the comma
(2) change congress to Congress
(3) replace passed with past
(4) insert a comma after law
(5) no correction is necessary

9. Sentence 13: **For example radio and TV stations had to put out new schedules every time a state started or ended daylight saving time.**

Which correction should be made to sentence 13?

(1) insert a comma after example
(2) change had to have
(3) change schedules to schedule's
(4) insert a comma after schedules
(5) insert a comma after started

10. Sentence 14: **Then came the Uniform Time Act of 1966, which established starting and ending dates for daylight saving time, in the spring and fall.**

Which correction should be made to sentence 14?

(1) replace Then with Than
(2) change Act to act
(3) replace dates with date's
(4) remove the comma after time
(5) change spring and fall to Spring and Fall

Questions 11 through 15 refer to the following paragraphs.

Rules and Regulations

(A)

(1) Thank you for joining Spring Valley Community center. (2) Before using our facility, please read these rules and regulations carefully.

(B)

(3) Please have your membership card with you at all times when your in the building. (4) When you enter the pool or exercise room, a security guard will request to see your card and will deny you entrance without it.

(C)

(5) Guests are welcome to use the pool and exercise room, but only when accompanied by members. (6) The guest fee is $10 per day. (7) When bringing guests, please have them sign in at the desk in the lobby. (8) They will be given a guest card for the day.

(D)

(9) Pool safety is very important. (10) If you are a week swimmer, life jackets and other flotation devices are available for your use. (11) Do not hesitate to ask lifeguards for help. (12) Children under the age of 12 must swim in the children's pool unless they're supervised by an adult. (13) Swimming classes are available to help both children and adults improve their skills.

(E)

(14) You must register, and pay for any class you wish to take. (15) Members receive a significant discount. (16) Registration may be limited to a certain number of participants.

11. Sentence 1: **Thank you for joining Spring Valley Community center.**

Which correction should be made to sentence 1?

(1) insert a comma after <u>you</u>
(2) replace <u>for</u> with <u>four</u>
(3) change <u>Community</u> to <u>community</u>
(4) change <u>center</u> to <u>Center</u>
(5) no correction is necessary

12. Sentence 3: **Please have your membership card with you at all times when your in the building.**

Which correction should be made to sentence 3?

(1) insert a comma after <u>Please</u>
(2) replace <u>have your</u> with <u>have you're</u>
(3) replace <u>times</u> with <u>times'</u>
(4) insert a comma after <u>times</u>
(5) replace <u>when your</u> with <u>when you're</u>

13. Sentence 10: **If you are a week swimmer, life jackets and other flotation devices are available for your use.**

Which correction should be made to sentence 10?

(1) replace <u>week</u> with <u>weak</u>
(2) remove the comma
(3) change <u>are</u> to <u>is</u>
(4) insert a comma after <u>available</u>
(5) no correction is necessary

14. Sentence 12: **Children under the age of 12 must swim in the children's pool unless they're supervised by an adult.**

Which correction should be made to sentence 12?

(1) insert commas after <u>Children</u> and <u>12</u>
(2) change <u>children's</u> with <u>childrens'</u>
(3) replace <u>they're</u> with <u>their</u>
(4) replace <u>they're</u> with <u>there</u>
(5) no correction is necessary

15. Sentence 14: **You must <u>register, and pay</u> for any class you wish to take.**

Which is the best way to write the underlined portion of this sentence? If the original is the best way, choose option (1).

(1) register, and pay
(2) register and pay
(3) register. And pay
(4) register. Pay
(5) register, paying

Questions 16 through 20 refer to the following paragraphs.

Racial Profiling

(A)

(1) African American and Hispanic motorists are much more likely to be stopped by police then their white counterparts, often for no apparent reason. (2) What's their offense? (3) African Americans have a name for it: DWB, or Driving While Black.

(B)

(4) Blacks and Hispanics, who some police officers believe are more likely to commit crimes, have been systematically targeted by police. (5) Police statistics from 23 states show that this policy, called racial profiling occurs in every geographic location. (6) Motorists, pedestrians, and airline passengers have been searched. (7) The police do not make class distinctions for nonwhites of every station in life have been victims of this practice.

(C)

(8) The statistical evidence shows a clear pattern. (9) On one Maryland highway, 73 percent of those stopped by police were African American, even though blacks represented only 17 percent of all drivers. (10) Hispanics make up only 8 percent of the population in illinois, yet 30 percent of drivers stopped there are Hispanic. (11) However, police superintendents chiefs of police, and other law enforcement officials dispute the studies that document racial profiling. (12) They maintain that the problem has been confined to a small number of officers and can be remedied easily.

16. Sentence 1: **African American and Hispanic motorists are much more likely to be stopped by police then their white counterparts, often for no apparent reason.**

Which correction should be made to sentence 1?

(1) change <u>motorists</u> to <u>Motorists</u>
(2) change <u>are</u> to <u>were</u>
(3) insert a comma after <u>then</u>
(4) replace <u>then</u> with <u>than</u>
(5) replace <u>for</u> with <u>four</u>

17. Sentence 5: **Police statistics from 23 states show that this policy, called racial profiling occurs in every geographic location.**

Which correction should be made to sentence 5?

(1) change <u>states</u> to <u>States</u>
(2) insert a comma after <u>states</u>
(3) insert a comma after <u>profiling</u>
(4) change <u>geographic</u> to <u>Geographic</u>
(5) no correction is necessary

18. Sentence 7: **The police do not make class distinctions for nonwhites of every station in life have been victims of this practice.**

Which is the best way to write the underlined portion of this sentence? If the original is the best way, choose option (1).

(1) distinctions for nonwhites
(2) distinctions, for nonwhites
(3) distinctions moreover nonwhites
(4) distinctions, for, nonwhites
(5) distinctions nonwhites

19. Sentence 10: **Hispanics make up only 8 percent of the population in illinois, yet 30 percent of drivers stopped there are Hispanic.**

Which correction should be made to sentence 10?

(1) change <u>make</u> to <u>makes</u>
(2) change <u>illinois</u> to <u>Illinois</u>
(3) remove the comma
(4) replace <u>yet</u> with <u>and</u>
(5) insert a comma after <u>stopped</u>

20. Sentence 11: **However, police superintendents chiefs of police, and other law enforcement officials dispute the studies that document racial profiling.**

Which correction should be made to sentence 11?

(1) remove the comma after <u>However</u>
(2) insert a comma after <u>superintendents</u>
(3) insert a comma after <u>officials</u>
(4) change <u>studies</u> to <u>studies'</u>
(5) no correction is necessary

Answers and explanations start on page 636.

Approaching the Essay Topic

Key Ideas

- Be aware of who your readers are and why you are writing.
- Don't use slang or nonstandard English in your essay.
- The evaluators will judge your essay on its overall effectiveness.

Knowing Your Audience and Purpose

Whenever you write something that someone else will read, you need to think about your **audience**—who will be reading your work—and your **purpose**—why you are writing.

The audience of your GED essay is the pair of evaluators who will score the essay. Because you don't know them or their background, you need to:

- Use formal language rather than slang.
- Use Standard American English, even if you speak another variant of English.
- Be clear and specific. Explain carefully, include details and background information, and give examples to get your point across.

The essay evaluators are trained to score your essay holistically—on the basis of its overall effectiveness. They will read the essay once, fairly quickly, to get an impression of your work as a whole. The essay readers will be asking themselves the following questions about your paper:

- Is there a clearly focused main idea?
- Is the main idea of the essay about the topic?
- Is the essay clearly and logically organized?
- Is the word choice appropriate and effective?
- Does the essay have correct sentence structure, grammar, and mechanics?

ON THE GED

The evaluators do not judge whether your opinion is right or wrong. Rather, they look to see that you support your opinion well with reasons and examples.

Each reader will assign your essay a score from 1 to 4. The average of the two scores is combined, through a formula, with your score from Part I of the test. Your essay score will reflect one of the general categories shown below:

Level 4—effective   **Level 2**—marginal

Level 3—adequate   **Level 1**—inadequate

You can review the standards for these categories on page 65, **"The Standards for Your Essay Score."**

The purpose of your GED essay will be to give an explanation about a specific situation. To accomplish this purpose, you may need to:

- State and explain your opinion.
- Discuss the causes or effects of a phenomenon.
- Compare or contrast two things.
- List reasons for something.
- List the qualities of something.

The essay topic assignment requires you to know only the types of information, facts, and examples that you would be likely to know from your own experience.

Reading the Directions

Before you begin writing, read the directions carefully. The complete directions for the GED Essay are printed on page 158. Below are excerpts of the directions.

Essay Directions

Look at the box on the next page. In the box are your assigned topic and the letter of the topic.

You must write on the assigned topic ONLY.

You will have 45 minutes to write on your assigned essay topic. You may return to the multiple-choice section after you complete your essay if you have time remaining in this test period. Do not return the Language Arts, Writing Test booklet until you finish both Parts I and II of the Language Arts, Writing Test.

REMEMBER, YOU MUST COMPLETE BOTH THE MULTIPLE-CHOICE QUESTIONS (PART I) AND THE ESSAY (PART II) TO RECEIVE A SCORE ON THE LANGUAGE ARTS, WRITING TEST.

To avoid having to repeat both parts of the test, be sure to do the following:

- Do not leave the pages blank.

- Write legibly in ink so that the evaluators will be able to read your writing.

- Write on the assigned topic. If you write on a topic other than the one assigned, you will not receive a score for the Language Arts, Writing Test.

- Write your essay on the lined pages of the separate answer sheet booklet. Only the writing on these pages will be scored.

Part II is a test to determine how well you can use written language to explain your ideas. In preparing your essay, you should take the following steps:

- Read the DIRECTIONS and the TOPIC carefully.

- Plan your essay before you write. Use the scratch paper provided to make any notes. These notes will be collected but not scored.

- Before you turn in your essay, reread what you have written and make any changes that will improve your essay.

Your essay should be long enough to develop the topic adequately and should be approximately 250 words.

Reprinted with permission of the GED Testing Service of the American Council on Education.

Notice that the directions tell you to plan, write, reread, and improve your essay. These steps make up the writing process. As you work on your essay, be aware of how much time you need for each step. Plan in advance to allot a certain number of minutes for each step, and stick to your plan. For instance, you may use the following plan:

- Prewriting and Organizing: 10 minutes
- Drafting: 25 minutes
- Revising and Editing: 10 minutes

You may need more time for one step and less for another, so analyze your habits and learn what's best for you. Time management is discussed in greater detail on page 156.

Key Ideas

- Read the topic carefully.
- Look for a key phrase that may tell you how to approach the topic.
- Answer the GED essay question on the basis of your life experience, knowledge, and personal observations.

Approaching the Topic

After you read the directions, your next step will be to reread the topic assignment that appears in the box. The topic assignment may include a brief introductory statement. The topic itself often is presented in the form of a question. It is important to answer that question directly. If your essay answers a different question from the one that is asked, it will not be scored.

Here's a sample topic:

TOPIC

What accounts for the popularity of "real life" TV shows, in which real people are placed in a situation so that viewers can see how they act?

In an essay, explain why these shows are so popular. Support your view with reasons and examples.

GED essay topics do not require any specialized knowledge or background information. You will not be asked to provide any specific dates, statistics, or researched factual information. Instead, like the topic shown above, GED topics are meant to be answered on the basis of life experience. Most topics ask you to explain something or to give your point of view.

The topic assignment often includes a "clue phrase" to help you decide which kind of information to include in the essay. Here are some examples:

Clue Phrases:	Information to put in your essay:
Tell how . . . Explain how . . . Identify . . .	Facts or reasons to explain an issue
Present your opinion . . . Explain your answer . . . State your point of view . . .	Your opinion and the reasons for it
State the reasons for . . . Explain why . . . Discuss the effect of . . . How does this affect . . .	Reasons; causes and/or effects
Discuss the similarities and differences . . .	A comparison of two things or a contrast

Now read the sample topic again. What kind of information would you put in an essay on this topic?

TOPIC

What accounts for the popularity of "real life" TV shows, in which real people are placed in a situation so that viewers can see how they act?

In an essay, explain why these shows are so popular. Support your view with reasons and examples.

The essay should include reasons, as indicated by the phrase *explain why. . . .*

Read the next sample topic. What kind of information should you include?

> **TOPIC**
>
> How do you differ from other members of your family, and how are you similar?
>
> In your essay, discuss the similarities and differences. Give specific examples.

The statement *discuss the similarities and differences* indicates that the essay should compare and contrast two things.

Read the next sample topic. What kind of information should you include?

> **TOPIC**
>
> Do you believe it is worthwhile to save for retirement?
>
> State your point of view in an essay. Use your personal observations, experience, and knowledge to support your view.

The directions *state your point of view* indicate that you should give an opinion.

THE GED ESSAY ▸ PRACTICE 1

Directions: Read each topic. Then list the kind of information you should include.

> **TOPIC A**
>
> Many people have hobbies like stamp collecting or knitting. Why do people enjoy hobbies?
>
> Write an essay explaining why people enjoy hobbies. Supply reasons and examples to support your view.

Include what kind of information? _____

> **TOPIC B**
>
> What advice would you give to someone who has trouble controlling his or her anger?
>
> In an essay, suggest ideas for anger management. Tell how they would be helpful. Use your personal observations, experience, and knowledge.

Include what kind of information? _____

> **TOPIC C**
>
> In your opinion, are "No Smoking" sections in restaurants a service to the public, or are they simply a nuisance to smokers?
>
> Present your opinion on the topic. Give reasons and examples to support your view.

Include what kind of information? _____

Answers and explanations start on page 636.

THE GED ESSAY

Prewriting Your Essay

Key Ideas

- Generate ideas by listing or brainstorming. Try to finish in about five minutes.
- After you have generated ideas, look them over and decide on your main idea. Then cross out ideas that don't support your main idea.

Generating Ideas

After you have identified the topic of your essay, you must think of ideas. In Unit 2, you read about two methods of coming up with ideas: listing and brainstorming. When you **list** ideas, you think carefully about the topic and list ideas to include in your essay. Try to stay on topic as much as possible. Create a list of useful ideas that needs little editing.

When you **brainstorm** ideas, you think about the topic and write down everything that comes to mind. Include all ideas, even if they appear to be off-topic. Let your mind go and write as quickly as possible. Create a long list of ideas that you will carefully edit before you move on.

You may find that in a timed essay test such as the GED Writing Test, it is better to generate ideas by listing rather than by brainstorming. If you carefully list ideas, you won't have to spend as much time evaluating them and eliminating irrelevant ones. However, if you have trouble coming up with ideas, brainstorming may be the better method for you.

Read the essay topic below, and look at the ideas generated for it. Note the ideas deleted from the brainstormed list. They do not directly support the main idea.

TOPIC
Is it better to be single or married? Support your opinion in an essay.

GED TIP

Brainstorming is always a timed activity. Listing ideas—for a letter, memo, school essay—usually is not. However, because the GED essay is timed, you must also set a time limit if you use this method.

Idea List

More freedom when single	Different kinds of relationships
Spend money however you want	Have own schedule
~~Stay out late~~	Make own decisions
Support only yourself	Don't have to do another's laundry
Not responsible for another	More self-reliant
Try out new things	

Brainstormed List

More freedom when you're single	Two incomes better than one
Being single—self-reliant	No money hassles with someone else
~~Everyone needs soulmate~~	~~High cost of weddings~~
Partner can be best friend	Don't have to do someone else's chores
~~Can be lonely either way~~	No legal involvement
~~My friends got a divorce~~	Married couples lose feeling for each other
Marriage ties you down	~~Kids have two parents at home~~
Single people choose own friends	

Review your list to find your main idea. Determine the main point that most of your ideas seem to lead to, and cross out the irrelevant ideas. Here is the main idea of both groups of ideas shown above:

Main Idea: The single life is better.

A. Directions: Read each topic and generate ideas as instructed.

TOPIC

Many people have hobbies like gardening or knitting. Why do people enjoy hobbies?

Write an essay explaining why people enjoy hobbies. Supply reasons and examples to support your view.

1a. List ideas. Find your main idea, and cross out irrelevant ones. Time yourself.
 b. It took me _____ minutes to list ideas.

TOPIC

Would you recommend your town as a place for tourists to visit? Why or why not?

Present your opinion in an essay. Support it with observations and experiences.

2a. Brainstorm ideas. Find your main idea, and cross out irrelevant ones. Give yourself five minutes.
 b. Five minutes was ❑ too long ❑ too short ❑ just right

TOPIC

What are the benefits of daily exercise?

In your essay, describe its positive effects. Supply reasons and examples.

3a. Brainstorm or list ideas. Give yourself six minutes.

 b. Six minutes was ❑ too long ❑ too short ❑ just right

B. Directions: Brainstorm or list ideas for the topic below. Give yourself the amount of time you think is best. Save your work. You will use these ideas in the next lesson.

TOPIC

In your opinion, are "No Smoking" sections in restaurants a service to the public, or are they simply a nuisance to smokers?

Present your opinion on the topic. Give reasons and examples to support your view.

C. Directions: After you have finished the exercises above, complete this strategy box. If you need more practice, review Unit 2, Lesson 4, "Essay Writing Process: Prewriting."

MY TEST-TAKING STRATEGY

My favorite technique for generating ideas is _____.

I need about _____ minutes for generating ideas.

Answers and explanations start on page 636.

Grouping Ideas

After you've generated a list and determined your main idea, you need to group similar ideas together and label each group. Each group will become a paragraph in your essay. Earlier in this book, you read about two methods of grouping: mapping and outlining. You will need to decide which method is better for you.

To make an **idea map**, write your main idea in the center of a sheet of paper, and circle the idea. Try to separate your ideas into three main groups and label them. Add these labels to the map, circle them, and attach them to the main idea as shown below. Then add related ideas to each group.

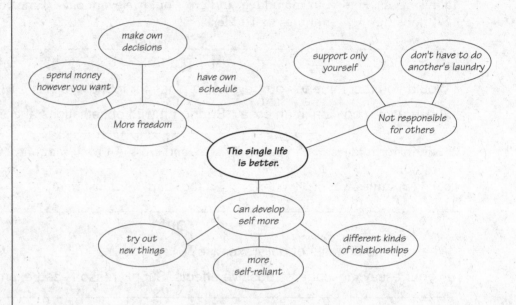

- Effectively grouping your ideas will give you a solid plan to follow as you write your essay.
- Idea maps and outlines are two methods of grouping ideas.
- Be sure to give yourself the time you need to create a well-planned map or outline.

GED TIP

Generating and organizing are not an exact science. New ideas may occur to you as you make an idea map or an outline. If the new ideas support your main idea, add them.

When you make an **outline,** you also put your ideas into groups and label each group. Organize your groups and the ideas within them in an indented list. You may number your groups as shown below, using roman numerals (I, II, III), capital letters, and numbers, or you may devise your own system of numbering.

I. No responsibilities
   A. Support only yourself
   B. Don't have to do someone else's laundry
II. More freedom
   A. Make own decisions
   B. Don't have to adjust to someone else's schedule
      1. Stay out late
      2. No arguments
   C. Do what you want
III. Can develop self more
   A. Try out new things
   B. Have different kinds of relationships

A. Directions: Read the topic and the ideas listed below. Then complete the exercise that follows.

TOPIC

What are the causes of stress? In an essay, explain why people experience stress.

---

working too hard	big changes like moving to a new home
noisy environment	taking a test
waiting for results of medical test	lots of people bothering you
trying to meet tight deadline	being responsible for something important
money troubles	something going wrong, like car breaking down

1. Summarize the ideas in a main idea statement:

   Main idea: _____

2a. Group similar ideas together and label each group. On a separate sheet of paper, create an idea map to organize the ideas. Give yourself five minutes; then answer questions 2b and 2c.

   b. For me, mapping was ❏ very effective ❏ somewhat effective ❏ not effective

   c. Five minutes was ❏ too long ❏ too short ❏ just right

3a. On a separate sheet of paper, make an outline to organize the ideas. Give yourself five minutes; then answer questions 3b and 3c.

   b. For me, outlining was ❏ very effective ❏ somewhat effective ❏ not effective

   c. Five minutes was ❏ too long ❏ too short ❏ just right

B. Directions: To complete your prewriting plan, organize the ideas you generated on page 145, part B. Use mapping or outlining, whichever works better for you. Give yourself five minutes, but take more time if needed. Save your work. You will use your prewriting plan in the next lesson.

TOPIC

In your opinion, are "No Smoking" sections in restaurants a service to the public, or are they simply a nuisance to smokers?

Present your opinion on the topic. Give reasons and examples to support your view.

C. Directions: After you complete the exercise above, complete this strategy box. If you need more practice, review Unit 2, Lesson 4, "Essay Writing Process: Prewriting."

MY TEST-TAKING STRATEGY

The most effective organizing strategy for me is _____.

I need _____ minutes for organizing.

Answers and explanations start on page 636.

THE GED ESSAY

Drafting Your Essay

Key Ideas

- Your essay should have an introductory paragraph, body paragraphs, and a concluding paragraph.
- Consult your prewriting plan as you write.
- Each paragraph, and the essay as a whole, should have a clearly stated main idea.

Using Your Prewriting Plan

As you draft your essay, look back frequently at your prewriting plan. The plan will help you structure your essay and will remind you of ideas to include.

A high-scoring GED essay has:

- An **introductory paragraph** that tells the main idea of the essay and gives a preview of its content
- **Body paragraphs** that expand on main points
- A **concluding paragraph** that summarizes the content of the essay and leaves the reader with something to think about

You will have already determined the main idea of your essay during prewriting. Use the main idea as the basis of your introductory paragraph.

Your idea map or outline should contain two or three main groups of ideas. Each of these groups will be used in a separate body paragraph in the essay. Use the label of each group to develop the topic sentence for that body paragraph. Use the remaining ideas in each group to develop the sentences that help support and explain the topic sentence.

For the concluding paragraph, sum up the main points of the essay. Add a final thought that leaves the reader with something to think about, but do not introduce a new, unrelated idea. Stay on topic.

Writing Topic Sentences

Make sure that each paragraph has a topic sentence that contains the main idea. The other sentences in the paragraph are supporting details—facts, reasons, examples, or anecdotes that help prove your case.

For example, the paragraph below compares listening to the radio and watching TV. The topic sentence is underlined. The writer presents his main idea in that topic sentence and then gives three reasons to support it.

> I find that listening to the radio is preferable to watching TV. Television demands all my attention, but I can listen to the radio and do something else at the same time. Also, programs on the radio are often more interesting and intellectually challenging. Moreover, radio is less addictive—there are only a few shows that I must listen to each week.

Remember the following key facts about main ideas and topic sentences:

- Each topic sentence must clearly state the main idea of the paragraph.
- The topic sentence should be specific enough to focus the reader's attention on the point of the paragraph.
- The topic sentence should be general enough to cover the supporting details.
- An essay should contain a main idea statement in the introductory paragraph that answers the question in the essay assignment.

GED TIP

For your GED essay, it's best to put your topic sentence at the beginning of each paragraph. This placement makes your meaning clearest to the scorer.

THE GED ESSAY ▶ PRACTICE 3.1

A. Directions: Following are three body paragraphs for an essay on the topic below. On separate paper, write an introductory paragraph and a concluding paragraph.

> ## TOPIC
>
> Name a job that you would <u>not</u> like to have. Explain why you think it would be an inappropriate job for you.

First of all, taxi drivers work much more than a regular eight-hour shift. Many drivers are on the road from early morning until night. Most of them work at least six days a week rather than a standard five-day workweek. Not only that, but they often work until very late at night—past midnight in some cases. I would certainly not want to be out on the road then.

Second, although the pay can be good at times, it is not regular. When business is slow, the cabbie suffers. Personally, I would rather have a paycheck that I could count on every two weeks. I have a large family to support, and I would be nervous not knowing whether I'd be able to make the rent payment each month.

Finally, the job is not the safest, especially in large metropolitan areas. There have been a number of cases of taxi drivers that were threatened or assaulted by passengers. It is difficult for drivers to defend themselves because the passengers sit behind them. I would prefer a job that had fewer risks.

B. Directions: Write a topic sentence for each body paragraph below.

1. _____

One reason to avoid it is that eating sugary foods causes cavities. Also, sweet foods are likely to be fattening, and many people are trying to watch their weight. Finally, white sugar does not have any nutritional value, yet it makes you feel full. Therefore, it keeps you from eating nutritious foods.

2. _____

For one thing, advertising entices people to buy things they don't need and can't afford. People become convinced that their lives will not be complete without designer gym shoes or a new car, and little thought is given to budgetary concerns. In addition, many ads depict extremely attractive models living picture-perfect lives. Ads like that make the person watching feel completely inadequate.

3. _____

First of all, be dependable. Always arrive to work on time, and call if you're going to be late. Second, do the very best job you can. Make the extra effort to get all the details right. Third, try to figure things out on your own, but don't be afraid to ask for help when you need it. It's better to ask a question now and again than to make an expensive mistake.

4. _____

One cause of overeating is depression. It's easy to comfort yourself with food. However, you will get even more depressed when you step on the scale! Easy access to food also causes overeating. Homemakers and people who work at home may overeat because the refrigerator is at hand. Also, nobody is home to see them down an entire chocolate cake or bag of chips. Finally, overeating can also be caused by medical problems. People who think they may have physical reasons for overeating should consult a doctor.

Answers and explanations start on page 637.

Strengthening Your Essay

After you have clearly stated your main idea, you need to explain and support it. Work with the ideas from your prewriting plan, and add other ideas as they occur to you. For example, compare the section of the outline shown in the left margin with the body paragraph based on it. Notice how the writer used his prewriting plan while drafting.

II. More freedom
  A. Make own decisions
  B. Don't have to adjust to someone else's schedule
    1. Stay out late
    2. No arguments
  C. Do what you want

> Another great thing about being single is that you have more freedom. For example, you can make your own decisions. If you want to make a large purchase or even move across the country, you don't have to ask permission or negotiate with anyone. It's nobody's business except yours. Also, you don't have to adjust to anyone else's schedule. When you want to go dancing until 4 A.M. or watch the late show on TV, you can just do it. You don't have to answer to anyone. There are no arguments or differences of opinion. You are free to do what you want.

As you compared this section of the outline and the paragraph based on it, you probably saw that some ideas in the paragraph don't appear in the outline. The writer thought of them later and added them. Changes like these are a natural part of the writing process. When you are writing a paragraph, feel free to add ideas—as long as they support the topic sentence.

Using Examples, Specific Details, and Anecdotes

In the paragraph above, the writer developed his ideas by writing them in complete sentences and by adding examples. An **example** is something that illustrates a point. For instance, on the outline the writer used the phrase "Make your own decisions." In the essay, he gave two examples of decision making: making a large purchase and moving across the country.

A **detail** is specific information about your idea. In the paragraph below, the writer added specific details to explain the idea "can develop self more" from the outline. The details he added are underlined.

III. Can develop self more
  A. Try out new things
  B. Have different kinds of relationships

> When you are single, you have more time to focus on yourself. <u>Monday through Friday after 5 P.M. and each weekend</u>, time is yours alone—to think about who you are and what you want from life. It's easier <u>to make career changes</u> and to take <u>spur-of-the-moment trips to places you've always wanted to go</u>. You can have a wider variety of relationships too. <u>Every year, I list more and more friends, acquaintances, and co-workers in my address book</u>.

You can also include **anecdotes,** or short real-life stories, to support your point. Sometimes, the best way to illustrate an idea is by telling a story. The paragraph below contains an anecdote.

> Sometimes, relaxing can help you with your career. I know that from personal experience. A few years ago, I was very nervous about an upcoming job interview. I prepared for it carefully, but I was still worried. My wife said, "Relax!" The night before the interview, I didn't think about the interview at all. She and I went to a movie instead. The next day, I was completely relaxed, and I got the job!

A. Directions: On a separate sheet of paper, rewrite each paragraph. Add examples, details, or anecdotes.

1. If I had a choice, I would rather live in the country than in the city. First of all, the countryside is beautiful. Also, the air is clean. Finally, the cost of living is lower.

2. My father is the most influential person in my life. He's a very caring person, and he always seems to know the right thing to do in a situation.

3. Winning a lot of money would definitely change my life. The first thing I would do is hire someone to clean our apartment. Then I'd have time to spend on activities I really enjoy.

B. Directions: Read the main idea and the groups of ideas listed below. Then write three body paragraphs based on them. Use a separate sheet of paper.

Main idea: I would rather own my own home than rent a home.

More control	Better financial investment	More privacy
Can turn heat up or down	When you leave, you sell—get some money back	No landlord marching through your apartment to see how clean it is
Can make changes (like build bookcase)	All home improvements benefit you, not the landlord	No prospective tenants coming through
No fear that the rent will be raised sky high		

C. Directions: Draft an essay on the topic below Try and complete your draft in 25 minutes, but take more time if needed. Use the prewriting plan that you developed on page 147. Save your work. You will use this draft again in the next lesson.

TOPIC

In your opinion, are "No Smoking" sections in restaurants a service to the public, or are they simply a nuisance to smokers?

Present your opinion on the topic. Give reasons and examples to support your view.

D. Directions: Check your answers to the exercises above. Then complete the strategy box below. If you need more practice, review Unit 2, Lesson 5, "Essay Writing Process: Drafting."

MY TEST-TAKING STRATEGY

I need to pay special attention to these areas of drafting. (Check all that apply.)

❏ Writing an introductory paragraph
❏ Writing a concluding paragraph
❏ Writing body paragraphs
❏ Clearly stating the main idea in a topic sentence
❏ Using examples, specific details, and anecdotes to support my ideas
❏ Remembering to look back at my prewriting plan

I need _____ minutes for drafting.

Answers and explanations start on page 637.

THE GED ESSAY

Revising and Editing Your Essay

Key Ideas

- Revise your work to make sure that the GED scorers can understand it.
- A revision checklist can help you improve your essay as you practice for the GED.

Revising Your Work

After drafting your essay, you must revise it. Reread your draft to see if any part of it might be unclear. Check both the organization and the sentence structure.

To decide how to revise your essay, ask yourself:
- Is there an introductory paragraph that states the main idea of the essay?
- Is there a concluding paragraph that sums up the main idea?
- Does each paragraph in the body have a clear topic sentence?
- Is there enough support for each topic sentence?
- Are all the sentences in logical places?
- Are paragraph breaks in the right places?
- Does the writing flow smoothly? Have I used transitions?
- Have I removed any irrelevant details?
- Do the ideas in each sentence make sense?
- Are there any short, choppy sentences that could be combined?

Read the essay below, and notice how it has been revised.

ON THE GED

You are given some "scratch paper" pages to plan your essay. There will be other pages on which to write your draft.

As you draft your GED essay, be sure to leave a wide margin on both sides of the page so that you can make corrections in the revising and editing stages of the writing process.

A job is much more pleasant when you like and admire your supervisor. A good supervisor must have excellent communication skills and must make it a priority to help workers get ahead.

Communication is a key part of management.
Supervisors need to give clear directions to spare the workers many hours of frustration. In addition, supervisors should be confident *and decisive.* ~~They should also be decisive.~~ Finally, supervisors should be as honest as possible. Once they make a decision, they should stick to it, so *that* everyone knows what the policy is.

Good bosses want to see their workers progress. Therefore, supervisors should give lots of encouragement and reward workers who display initiative and problem-solving abilities. *Also,* Supervisors should offer opportunities for workers to improve their skills *and education.*

¶ Knowing the qualities of a good supervisor is important for both bosses and workers. The next time you apply for a job, think about whether your prospective boss is a clear communicator who wants you to succeed.

THE GED ESSAY ▸ PRACTICE 4.1

A. Directions: Read the essay below, and revise the problems in sentence structure and organization. Try to complete your revisions in five minutes, but use more time if needed.

Most of us are aware of the consequences of speeding, which range from receiving a speeding ticket to getting into an accident. A quick survey of any highway will show that many drivers exceed the speed limit. Why do people speed? One common reason is that people do not think they will suffer any consequences. If they have never been stopped by the police or crashed their car, they don't see any reason to worry.

People simply need to get somewhere in a hurry. They realize that they are speeding but they have such a need to arrive on time that they don't care. They've got ants in their pants. A final reason is lack of respect for other drivers, one driver who is speeding makes road conditions less safe for everyone. Drivers who act as though they are in the Indy 500 they have no regard for the safety of others.

We know that people speed because of impatience and they don't fear the consequences. Another reason is no respect. Let's figure out what will make them stop.

B. Directions: Revise the essay that you wrote on the topic below. Time yourself. Try to complete the revision in five minutes. Save your work. You will use the essay again.

TOPIC

In your opinion, are "No Smoking" sections in restaurants a service to the public, or are they simply a nuisance to smokers?

Present your opinion on the topic. Give reasons and examples to support your view.

C. Directions: After you check your answers to the exercise above, complete the strategy box below. If you need more practice with specific skills and concepts, review Unit 2, "Clear and Organized Writing."

MY TEST-TAKING STRATEGY

I need to pay special attention to these areas of revising. (Check all that apply.)

❏ Writing introductory paragraphs   ❏ Putting in paragraph breaks
❏ Writing concluding paragraphs   ❏ Remembering to use transitions
❏ Writing topic sentences   ❏ Deleting irrelevant details
❏ Adding support to body paragraphs   ❏ Combining short, choppy sentences
❏ Putting sentences in logical places   ❏ Making sure each sentence makes sense

I need _____ minutes for revising.

Answers and explanations start on page 637.

ON THE GED

As long as your corrections are neat and readable, you can make corrections. Making changes will not count against you.

Editing Your Work

Once you're satisfied with the organization and clarity of your essay, check for other errors in sentence structure, as well as errors in grammar, usage, and mechanics. To edit your essay, ask yourself these questions:

- Are all the sentences complete?
- Are there any run-ons or comma splices that should be corrected?
- Are all lists parallel in structure?
- Are nouns and pronouns used correctly?
- Are verb forms and tenses used correctly?
- Does the subject of each sentence match the verb?
- Is the punctuation correct?
- Is capitalization used correctly?
- Are all words correctly spelled?
- Are there any inappropriate word choices?

► Read the paragraph below, and notice how the errors were corrected.

A job is much more pleasant when you like and admire your supervisor. A good supervisor must have excellent communication skills, and must make it a priority to help workers get ahead. In addition, a supervisor should be a fair and moral person.

Clear communication is a key part of Management. Supervisors need to give clear directions, To spare the workers many hours of frustration. In addition, supervisors should be confident and decisive. Once they made a decision, they should stick to it so everyone knows what the policy is. Finally, supervisors should be as honest as possible.

Good bosses want to see their workers progress. Therefore, supervisors should give lots of encouragement and reward workers who display initiative, and problem-solving abilities. Also, supervisors should offer opportunities for workers to improve their skills, and education.

Top-notch supervisors *have* has a high level of moral character. They reward honesty and fire workers who have lied or cheated. Some bosses keep on employees who lie if *their* his skills are valuable to the Company, *but* I feel that this is an example of poor management.

Knowing the qualities of a good supervisor is important for both bosses and workers. The next time you apply for a job, think about whether *your* you're prospective boss is a moral person and a clear communicator who want you to succeed.

THE GED ESSAY ▶ PRACTICE 4.2

A. Directions: Read the body of the essay. Correct errors in sentence structure, grammar, usage, mechanics, and word choice. Try to finish editing in five minutes, but use more time if needed.

One common reason for speeding is that people don't think they will suffer any consequences. If they have never been stopped by the Police or crashed there car they don't see any reason too worry.

Another reason is that people simply are needing to get somewhere in a hurry. They realize that they are speeding, but they have such a need to arrive on time that they dont care. There impatience get the better of them.

A final reason is lack of respect for other drivers, one driver who is speeding make road conditions less safe for everyone. Drivers who act as though they are in the indy 500 got no regard for the safety of others.

B. Directions: Edit the essay that you wrote on the topic below. Time yourself and try to complete the edit in five minutes.

TOPIC

In your opinion, are "No Smoking" sections in restaurants a service to the public, or are they simply a nuisance to smokers?

Present your opinion on the topic. Give reasons and examples to support your view.

C. Directions: After you check your answers to the exercise above, complete the strategy box below. If you need more practice with specific skills and concepts, review Unit 3, "Sentence Structure," Unit 4, "Grammar and Usage," and Unit 5, "Mechanics."

MY TEST-TAKING STRATEGY

I need to pay special attention to these areas of editing. (Check all that apply.)

❏ Making sure my sentences are complete

❏ Correcting run-ons and comma splices

❏ Using parallel structure

❏ Using nouns and pronouns correctly

❏ Using verb forms and tenses correctly

❏ Matching subjects and verbs

❏ Making sure punctuation is correct

❏ Using capitalization correctly

❏ Making sure words are spelled correctly

❏ Choosing appropriate words

Answers and explanations start on page 638.

THE GED ESSAY

Your Plan of Attack

Key Ideas

- Figure out what you must do during every step of the writing process.
- Make a plan to use your time wisely.

When you take the GED essay test, you will have only 45 minutes for all the steps in the writing process. Therefore, you need to walk into the testing center with a plan for how to organize your time wisely.

To create your plan, think about what you need to accomplish during each step of the writing process and how much time it will take you. Ask yourself the following questions:

Prewriting

- How long does it take me to generate ideas? What method of generating ideas works best for me?
- How long does it take me to organize ideas? What method of organizing works best for me?

Drafting

- How quickly can I write three to five good paragraphs?
- Do I usually remember to leave space in the margins for additions?
- Which parts of drafting to I need to focus on the most?

Revising and Editing

- Do I make a lot of changes, or is my first draft usually similar to the final draft?
- Are there certain parts of revising and editing that are especially hard for me? What are they?
- How much time does it take me to revise an essay? How long does it take me to edit?

GED TIP

Remember: Individual writers may spend different amounts of time on each stage of the writing process. Find out how much time you need.

When trying to decide how much time you need for each step, consider the guidelines on the chart below. The chart shows a suggested time frame for each step of the writing process and a general range—the minimum and maximum amounts of time that should be used.

	General Guidelines	Range
Prewriting (generating ideas and organizing)	10 minutes	5–15 minutes
Drafting	25 minutes	20–30 minutes
Revising and editing	10 minutes	5–10 minutes
Total	45 minutes	

The final step is to fill in a chart that outlines your plan of attack. To get an idea of what you need to do, look at one student's chart on the following page.

My Plan of Attack

- **Prewriting**
  I need _5_ minutes.
  To come up with ideas, I will _brainstorm_ _____
  To organize ideas, I will _make an outline_ _____

- **Drafting**
  I need _30_ minutes.
  I will focus on _writing three to five good paragraphs, writing a good topic_ ___
  sentence for each paragraph, leaving wide margins, and staying on topic. ___

- **Revising and Editing**
  I need _10_ minutes.
  I will focus on _including enough support, avoiding run-ons and comma splices,_ ___
  matching subjects and verbs, and using commas correctly. ___

THE GED ESSAY ▸ PRACTICE 5

A. Directions: Complete the chart below to form your essay-writing strategy. Use the page numbers in parentheses to check what you wrote earlier in "My Test-Taking Strategy" boxes.

My Plan of Attack

- **Prewriting** (page 145)
  I need _____ minutes.
  To come up with ideas, I will _____
  To organize ideas, I will _____

- **Drafting** (page 151)
  I need _____ minutes.
  I will focus on _____
  _____

- **Revising and Editing** (pages 153 and 155)
  I need _____ minutes.
  I will focus on _____
  _____
  _____

B. Directions: Follow your essay-writing strategy as you write an essay on the topic below.

TOPIC

"If you are told to keep a secret, you shouldn't break that confidence under any circumstances." Do you agree or disagree with this statement?

Present your opinion and explain why you feel that way.

Answers and explanations start on page 638.

Essay Directions and Topic

Below are the essay directions in the exact form that they will appear on the GED test. Read them over and familiarize yourself with them.

Essay Directions and Topic

Look at the box on the next page. In the box are your assigned topic and the letter of the topic.

You must write on the assigned topic ONLY.

You will have 45 minutes to write on your assigned essay topic. You may return to the multiple-choice section after you complete your essay if you have time remaining in this test period. Do not return the Language Arts, Writing Test booklet until you finish both Parts I and II of the Language Arts, Writing Test.

Two evaluators will score your essay according to its overall effectiveness. Their evaluation will be based on the following features:

- Well-focused main points

- Clear organization

- Specific development of your ideas

- Control of sentence structure, punctuation, grammar, word choice, and spelling

REMEMBER, YOU MUST COMPLETE BOTH THE MULTIPLE-CHOICE QUESTIONS (PART I) AND THE ESSAY (PART II) TO RECEIVE A SCORE ON THE LANGUAGE ARTS, WRITING TEST.
To avoid having to repeat both parts of the test, be sure to do the following:

- Do not leave the pages blank.

- Write legibly <u>in ink</u> so that the evaluators will be able to read your writing.

- Write on the assigned topic. If you write on a topic other than the one assigned, you will not receive a score for the Language Arts, Writing Test.

- Write your essay on the lined pages of the separate answer sheet booklet. Only the writing on these pages will be scored.

IMPORTANT:
The essay that you write is the property of the GED Testing Service (GEDTS) and is considered confidential and secure. GEDTS policy prohibits your discussing or publicizing the topic or content of your essay. This policy also prohibits returning the essay to you, your family, or any other individual or program.

TOPIC F

If you could make one positive change to your daily life, what would that change be?

In your essay, identify the change you would make. Explain the reasons for your choice.

Part II is a test to determine how well you can use written language to explain your ideas. In preparing your essay, you should take the following steps:

- Read the **DIRECTIONS** and the **TOPIC** carefully.

- Plan your essay before you write. Use the scratch paper provided to make any notes. These notes will be collected but not scored.

- Before you turn in your essay, reread what you have written and make any changes that will improve your essay.

Your essay should be long enough to develop the topic adequately.

Reprinted with permission of the GED Testing Service of the American Council on Education.

Additional Essay Topics

The essay topics on this page may be used for extra practice.

TOPIC A

"It's all right to break a law that is unfair and oppressive." Do you agree or disagree with this statement?

Discuss the statement above. Give details to support your ideas.

TOPIC B

What are some ways to develop and support a child's ethnic identity?

In your essay, explain how ethnic identity can be cultivated and supported. Include specific details and examples.

TOPIC C

Is it better to live for the moment or plan for the future?

Explain which is the better overall approach and why. Base your answer on your own life experience and personal observations.

TOPIC D

Why do some people seek attention and enjoy the spotlight?

Discuss the reasons why people seek attention. Use your own life experience, knowledge, and personal observations.

TOPIC E

What are some of the results of taking risks?

Discuss the effects that risk taking can have on a person. Discuss positive effects, negative effects, or both.

TOPIC F

What is the definition of a successful person?

Describe the qualities of a person who has truly succeeded in life. Use specific examples in your essay.

TOPIC G

Do you agree or disagree with the idea that education is the key to freedom?

In your essay, give reasons for your opinion. Use specific details and examples to support your point of view.

Social Studies

The GED Social Studies Test evaluates your ability to understand and interpret social studies information. You will have 70 minutes to answer 50 questions that are based on reading passages or graphics such as maps, graphs, diagrams, tables, political cartoons, posters, or photographs. You will also answer questions based on an excerpt from an important document in U.S. history (for example, the U.S. Constitution) and one practical document (such as consumer information about buying a product).

The questions are based on material in the areas of U.S. History, World History, Civics and Government, Economics, and Geography.

Content Areas

U.S. History (25 percent) Questions cover such topics as exploration and colonization of the New World, the American Revolution and the founding of the new nation, westward expansion, the Civil War and Reconstruction, industrialization and urbanization, the Progressive Era, the Great Depression, World Wars I and II, and contemporary social, environmental, and technological challenges.

World History (15 percent) Questions are based on major topics in early civilizations, feudalism, the Renaissance, nation states, revolutions, world wars, and contemporary global issues.

Government and Civics (25 percent) Questions cover topics in federalism, three branches of government, the U.S. Constitution and the Bill of Rights, political parties and elections, and the rights and responsibilities of citizens.

Economics (20 percent) Questions include topics such as production, consumption, supply and demand; basics of our economic system, the role of the government in the economy (budget, taxes, regulation, and consumer protection), and labor and consumer issues.

Geography (15 percent) Questions cover such topics as hemispheres, continents, and oceans, the relationship between humans and the environment, protecting natural resources, and reading and interpreting maps.

In addition to reviewing material in this chapter, prepare for the GED Social Studies Test by reading newspapers and magazines and listening to news programs on the radio and television. Pay special attention to graphs, maps, and diagrams that you see in the media because 30 out of 50 questions on the test are based on graphics alone or graphics and text together.

Four Types of Questions

Comprehension

Some questions on the GED Social Studies Test require you to recognize an implication, restatement, or summary of information that you read.

Example

Starting in the 1890s, a group of Republicans known as the Progressives sought to use the federal government to curb the excesses of monopolies. Former Republican President Theodore Roosevelt was the presidential candidate of the Progressive (Bull Moose) Party. His candidacy split the Republican vote and helped Wilson to defeat Republican presidential candidate William Howard Taft in 1912.

Which is the best summary of this passage?

(1) Republicans opposed the Progressive movement.
(2) Theodore Roosevelt was President of the United States.
(3) The Progressives, a splinter group of the Republican Party, helped defeat Taft in 1912.
(4) William Howard Taft was the Republican presidential candidate in 1912.
(5) William Howard Taft was elected president in 1912.

Answer: (3) The Progressives, a splinter group of the Republican Party, helped defeat Taft in 1912. This summarizes the main idea of the passage. Options (1) and (5) are contradicted by the passage, and options (2) and (4) are specific facts, not a summary of the main point of the paragraph.

Application

Some of the questions on the Social Studies Test require you to apply given information to a new or specific situation.

Example

Political Systems

aristocracy   power held by a small group of people

democracy   rule by the people or their elected representatives

military dictatorship   rule by the leadership of the armed forces

monarchy   rule by one person

theocracy   government in which laws are seen as divinely ordained

The government of England from 1714 through the 19th century, where king and Parliament alike were under the control of a few families, was an example of which type of system?

(1) aristocracy
(2) democracy
(3) military dictatorship
(4) monarchy
(5) theocracy

Answer: (1) aristocracy In this question, you apply the definitions to the given situation. Even though the example mentions a king (monarchy), the situation describes rule by a few families (aristocracy)

GED TIP

If you are reading a passage that is hard for you to understand, slow down and try to restate it, sentence by sentence, in your own words.

Analysis

Many of the questions require you to see the relationships between ideas such as distinguishing facts from opinions, recognizing unstated assumptions, comparing and contrasting, and seeing causes and their effects.

Example

The prices of goods and services are determined by the relationship of supply to demand. When supply exceeds demand, sellers must lower prices to stimulate sales; on the other hand, when demand exceeds supply, consumers bid prices up as they compete to make purchases.

Based on the theory of supply and demand, what causes prices to rise?

(1) The supply of a product exceeds the demand for it.
(2) Sellers try to stimulate sales.
(3) The demand for a product exceeds its supply.
(4) Consumers make major purchases.
(5) Corporations try to make profits for their stockholders.

Answer: (3) The demand for a product exceeds its supply. This question asks you to analyze a cause/effect relationship. According to the paragraph, when demand exceeds supply, prices tend to rise. Options (1) and (2) relate to decreasing prices; options (4) and (5) are not based on the paragraph at all.

Evaluation

Some of the questions involve making judgments about the validity or accuracy of social studies material. These questions also require evaluating the role that values, beliefs, and convictions play in decision making.

Example

One of the main controversies in the 2000 presidential election was the issue of drilling for oil in the Arctic National Wildlife Reserve. On the one hand, Republican candidate George W. Bush advocated drilling for oil in the Arctic Reserve in order to decrease America's dependence on foreign oil. Democratic candidate Al Gore opposed oil drilling in the Arctic Reserve in order to preserve its environmental purity as a wildlife refuge untainted by modern development.

According to the passage, the controversy over drilling for oil in the Arctic Reserve represented a conflict between which values?

(1) Democratic and Republican issues
(2) oil and animals
(3) drilling and not drilling
(4) economic independence and environmental protection
(5) animal protection and wildlife preservation

Answer: This question asks you to evaluate the role that values and beliefs play in decision making. Only option **(4) economic independence and environmental protection** represents competing sets of beliefs about priorities. Options (1), (2), and (3) relate to details in the passage, not values, and option (5) is the same thing said two different ways.

Interpreting Graphics
Charts

Social studies information is often organized in charts. You need to read down the columns and across the rows to locate information in a chart.

Example

Year	Average Hours Worked per Week	Average Hourly Wages*
1910	56.6	$ 3.63
1930	NA	$ 4.61
1950	40.5	$ 9.91
1970	39.8	$11.32
1990	40.8	$10.83
*Adjusted for inflation, in 1990 constant dollars		

GED TIP

Carefully read all titles and labels on charts and graphs.

Between which years did average hours worked rise while average hourly wages fell?

(1) 1900–1910
(2) 1910–1930
(3) 1930–1950
(4) 1950–1970
(5) 1970–1990

Answer: (5) 1970–1990 The chart shows that between 1970 and 1990, there was a one-hour increase in average hours worked and a $0.49 drop in average hourly wages. The chart doesn't give complete information on options (1), (2), or (3). Option (4) is contradicted by the chart.

Circle Graphs

Circle graphs are used to show how a whole is divided into parts. Often they are divided into percents or fractions.

Example

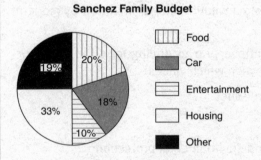

The greatest portion of the Sanchez family's budget is spent on which two items?

(1) housing and food
(2) housing and entertainment
(3) food and car
(4) entertainment and food
(5) entertainment and other

Answer: (1) housing and food The Sanchez family spends a total of 53% of their budget on housing and food. All of the other options have totals less than 53%.

Line and Bar Graphs

You can read line and bar graphs by reading up from the labels on bottom **axis** (line) and across from values on the side axis. Be sure to read all titles and labels carefully.

Example

Divorce Rates for Five Countries in the Western Hemisphere*

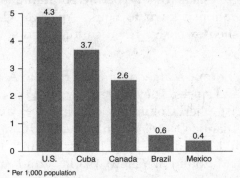

* Per 1,000 population

Which of the following statements is supported by the graph?

(1) Cuba has the highest divorce rate in the hemisphere.
(2) Mexico has the lowest divorce rate in the hemisphere.
(3) The divorce rate in the U.S. is increasing.
(4) Mexico has a higher divorce rate than Brazil.
(5) Brazil has a higher divorce rate than Mexico.

Answer: The graph supports option **(5) Brazil has a higher divorce rate than Mexico.** Options (1) and (4) are contradicted by the graph. Option (2) is the lowest on this graph, but that doesn't mean it is the lowest of all of the countries in the hemisphere; option (3) may be true, but it is not supported by the graph.

Maps

You will need to interpret information from maps on the GED Social Studies Test. It is important that you use any map **legend** (also called the **key**) to interpret symbols, **compass rose** to find directions, and **scale** for distances.

Example

According to the map, what is England's climate?

(1) hot and humid
(2) mild and humid
(3) cold and humid
(4) dry
(5) alpine

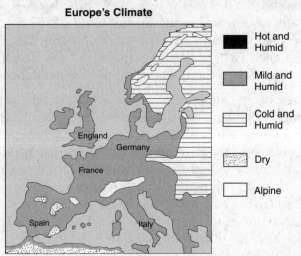

Answer: The map key shows that the medium gray color stands for **(2) mild and humid** climate.

GED TIP

Bar graphs help you make comparisons; line graphs help you see trends over time.

U.S. HISTORY

Exploration, Colonialism, and the American Revolution

The first Americans traveled from Asia across the Bering Strait into North America and, over many generations, down to South America. Called **Native Americans,** they established extensive tribal cultures and several advanced civilizations.

In the late 1400s, **explorers** from Europe searched for a sea route to Asia so they could trade for Asian gold and spices. They traveled around the tip of Africa. However, in 1492 Christopher Columbus convinced Spain to finance a trip west, across the Atlantic Ocean. When he reached land, he thought he had found India and called the inhabitants Indians. Later explorers realized that they had found a "New World," and many European nations set out to establish **colonies** there. The first explorers were searching for valuable resources and for the glory of conquest. This colonization led to tragedy for many Native Americans who died from diseases or were killed, enslaved, or forced off their lands.

In the 1500s and 1600s, European nations, including Spain, France, England, and the Netherlands, established settlements in North America. One type of settlement was established to gain power and wealth. The other was established for permanent residence. The first such English settlement was established in Jamestown, Virginia in 1607. In 1620, the **Pilgrims** sailed to the Americas aboard the *Mayflower* and established a second English colony in Massachusetts. Beginning about 1675, colonists began importing a large number of slaves who had been forcibly taken from Africa. Many were put to work on the plantation system in the Southern colonies.

The colonies grew rapidly in the early 1700s. With France's defeat in the French and Indian War (1754–1763), England acquired France's American colonies. After the war, England sought to regain more control over the Thirteen Colonies. It also sought to recover economically from the debts caused by the costly war. New British taxes and policies troubled the colonists; however it was not until 1775 that a war for independence seemed inevitable. After a series of skirmishes, the **Continental Congress** assigned George Washington to lead the Continental Army and ordered publication of the **Declaration of Independence** on July 4, 1776.

Despite the superiority of the well-trained British forces, the Americans had the advantage of defending their own land and eventually forged a fighting force with strong military leaders. The **American Revolution** lasted until the surrender of the British at Yorktown in 1781. In 1783, the final treaty to end the war resulted in the recognition of American independence. The new nation initially formed a weak national government through the **Articles of Confederation.** This first effort stressed a loose confederation of the states with strong local control. Over time, many colonial leaders recognized the need for a centralized government. The principles of this government were established in the **U.S. Constitution,** which was ratified in 1788. To counter fears of an overly powerful government, the first ten amendments to the Constitution, the **Bill of Rights,** promised many individual freedoms, such as freedom of speech and assembly.

Key Ideas

- European explorers sought wealth and conquest in the New World from the 1400s to the 1600s.
- The Thirteen Colonies declared independence from England in 1776.
- America won its independence in 1783 and ratified the U.S. Constitution in 1788.

GED TIP

Reviewing key vocabulary can help you prepare for the GED test. As you review, look up any words that you do not understand. Pay special attention to the words in **bold** *type.*

Choose the one best answer to each question.

Questions 1 and 2 refer to the following map.

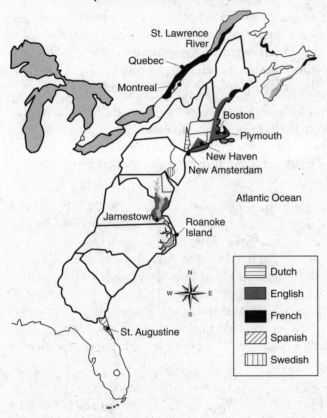

European Colonial Settlements, 1650

1. Based on the map, which European power had the southernmost colony in 1650?

   (1) the Dutch
   (2) the English
   (3) the French
   (4) the Spanish
   (5) the Swedish

2. Which of the following conclusions is supported by the map?

   (1) By 1650, Spain had conquered most of North America.
   (2) Sweden was a major power in the New World.
   (3) The English established several colonies in the New World.
   (4) The Dutch established their colonies in the western part of North America.
   (5) French colonies extended along the East Coast between Boston and Jamestown.

3. Some of the early colonists did not come to the New World to gain power and wealth. These groups came seeking freedom from persecution.

   Which immigrant group is most similar to those early colonists?

   (1) African slaves who were involuntarily brought to work on plantations
   (2) Mexican workers who came to the U.S. to earn better wages than they could at home
   (3) Chinese students who came to the U.S. to study math and science
   (4) British businessmen who visited the U.S. to invest in media companies
   (5) Haitian refugees who fled to the U.S. to escape a dictatorship

4. According to the passage on page 166, which of the following was a cause of the American Revolution?

   (1) France's defeat in the French and Indian War
   (2) increased British taxes and restrictions on the colonies
   (3) the signing of the Articles of Confederation
   (4) Britain's acquisition of France's colonies in North America
   (5) the publication of the Declaration of Independence

5. The first amendment to the U.S. Constitution states: "Congress shall make no law abridging the right of the people peaceably to assemble, and to petition the government for a redress of grievances."

   What is the most likely reason the framers of the Constitution included these guarantees?

   (1) They did not like Congress.
   (2) They were planning to organize assemblies.
   (3) They were concerned about the government becoming tyrannical.
   (4) They were hoping to petition the government.
   (5) They were attempting to prevent a redress of grievances.

Answers and explanations start on page 638.

U.S. HISTORY

Westward Expansion and the Civil War

Key Ideas

- The economy of the South was based on slavery. The Northern economy was based on free labor.
- Conflict over whether slavery should be allowed in the nation's new western territories led to the Civil War.
- The North won the war and ended slavery. During Reconstruction, the South was rebuilt.

GED TIP

As you study for the GED Social Studies Test, focus on analyzing events to understand causes and effects, rather than memorizing names and dates.

Early on in the history of the United States, the North and the South diverged economically. The North developed a varied economy that included industry and commerce as well as agriculture. Slavery had been legal throughout the North during the colonial period. However, by the early 1800s, it was **abolished** in all Northern states. Women and **immigrants,** as well as men, provided labor for the growing economy in the North.

The Southern economy was based largely on agriculture. By the 1800s, there was one major crop in the South: cotton. Planting and harvesting cotton required a lot of labor. Southern farmers came to depend more and more on slaves to do the work, and the number of enslaved persons grew in the South.

As the United States expanded during the early 1800s, the North and the South worked to maintain a balance of power. New states were generally added in pairs, one slave and one free. But there was increasing tension over the vast western territory that had become part of the United States by the mid-1800s. In the 1850s, Congress voted that the territories themselves should decide whether or not to allow slavery. This soon led to war in Kansas. People from both the North and the South rushed to settle the territory. Vote fraud in the 1855 elections led to the set up of two warring governments. The violence in Kansas foreshadowed the violence that soon tore up the nation.

In the late 1850s, political parties fractured over the slavery issue. Four candidates ran for president in 1860. Abraham Lincoln, who promised to halt the spread of slavery (although not abolish it where it already existed) won. Opposed to Lincoln's policies, most slave states **seceded** from the United States. They set up their own government, called the **Confederacy.** By April 1861, the United States (called the **Union**) and the Confederacy were at war.

At first it seemed as if the Confederacy might win. They had well-trained military leaders and soldiers who were willing to fight hard to hold onto their way of life; so the Confederacy won many early battles. However, by the summer of 1863, the Confederacy began to wear down. Because the South lacked industry, ammunition, uniforms, and shoes were in short supply for Confederate soldiers. There were food shortages for soldiers and civilians alike. The war was fought mostly in the South and the destruction was terrible. After four long years, in 1865, Confederate general Robert E. Lee surrendered to Union general Ulysses S. Grant. The Civil War ended.

For the next 12 years, federal troops oversaw the rebuilding of the South. This period was called **Reconstruction.** Schools were established for former slaves, who were all freed when the war ended. However, the **sharecropping** system, which kept black farmers enslaved economically, soon came into being. Whites who came back to power in the South in the 1870s prevented African Americans from exercising their right to vote. The Civil War ended slavery, but it did not end racism. And the entire nation has suffered for it.

U.S. HISTORY ▸ PRACTICE 2

Choose the <u>one best answer</u> to each question.

1. Based on the passage, which of the following disagreements was a main cause of the Civil War?

    (1) whether cotton should be the main crop in the South
    (2) whether the North should become more agricultural
    (3) whether slavery should continue to exist
    (4) whether the United States should expand westward
    (5) whether slavery should be permitted in territories in the West

2. In 1820, Missouri proposed to enter the Union as a slave state. Based on the passage, what do you think was the response of Northerners in Congress?

    (1) They supported having another slave state join the Union.
    (2) They lobbied against having Missouri join the Union as a slave state.
    (3) To balance the admission of Missouri, they lobbied to have Maine admitted as a free state.
    (4) They proposed adding a western territory to the Union instead.
    (5) They started a war to prevent Missouri from attaining statehood.

3. In the mid-1900s, the country of Vietnam was divided. There was a communist government in the North and a noncommunist government in the South. The two fought for control of Vietnam. In 1975, the communists won. Vietnam was united under this form of government.

    Based on this information, how was the war in Vietnam similar to the U.S. Civil War?

    (1) Both wars involved racial conflict.
    (2) Other nations sent soldiers to fight in both wars.
    (3) In both wars, the addition of new territory had upset the balance of power.
    (4) At the end of each of these wars, the nation was reunified.
    (5) At the end of each of these wars, two separate, new nations were formed.

Questions 4 and 5 refer to the following photographs of people who served in South Carolina's state government in 1868.

Photography by Katherine Wetzel. Reprinted with the permission of The Museum of the Confederacy, Richmond, Virginia.

4. Which of the following is a fact confirmed by information in the photographs?

    (1) Politicians in power in the South during Reconstruction were called Radical Republicans.
    (2) Southern Democrats were treated very well during Reconstruction.
    (3) It was unfair that former Confederate soldiers could vote during Reconstruction.
    (4) In 1868, many African Americans served in the government of South Carolina.
    (5) The most qualified leaders in South Carolina government in 1868 were African Americans.

5. Which of the following conclusions is supported by the photographs and the passage on page 168?

    (1) Over the course of Reconstruction, blacks in the South gained and then lost political power.
    (2) Over the course of Reconstruction, blacks in the South lost and then gained political power.
    (3) Over the course of Reconstruction, whites in the South gained and then lost political power.
    (4) In the early years of Reconstruction, blacks served in government in each Southern state.
    (5) In the early years of Reconstruction, blacks served only in South Carolina's government.

Answers and explanations start on page 638.

U.S. HISTORY

Industrialization, Immigration, and the Progressive Era

Key Ideas

- The U.S. underwent rapid industrialization starting in the mid-1800s.
- Immigrants came from many places to work in the expanding American industries.
- Rapid industrialization brought problems, which labor unions and reformers tried to solve, especially during the Progressive Era.

ON THE GED

The GED Social Studies Test examines your ability to interpret graphs, charts, maps, and other visual sources of information.

In the mid-1800s, American industries, which had been growing steadily since the late 1700s, began a period of extremely fast growth. This rapid **industrialization** occurred for several interconnected reasons. With the addition of the vast western territories, the United States gained plentiful **natural resources.** Among these resources were materials, such as metals, needed to manufacture new products and machines, and fuels, such as coal, needed to run these machines. Another reason for rapid industrialization was the invention of many new machines and new industrial processes. With these new inventions and processes, manufactured goods could be produced more easily, more efficiently, and less expensively. A third reason for the rapid industrialization was the nation's booming population. The U.S. population more than doubled in the last forty years of the 1800s. There were more people to buy more goods, spurring commerce and further industrial growth.

Rapid industrialization meant that many new factories were built in the mid- and late 1800s. Most were built in or near the nation's large cities, including New York, Boston, Chicago, Philadelphia, and Pittsburgh. These urban centers had large groups of people who could work in the factories and large groups of people who would buy the goods the factories produced.

U.S. factory jobs drew many **immigrants** to American cities. Although the United States has always been a "nation of immigrants," the late 1800s saw a sharp rise in the number of people moving here from foreign countries. The majority came from Europe, including Germany, Italy, Russia, and Eastern European countries. Many also came from Mexico and Central America. Asian immigration was declining because the government had passed laws barring Chinese from moving to the United States. However, thousands of Japanese came to this country, taking jobs in farm fields and mines.

America's factory workers, whether native- or foreign-born, worked very hard at grueling, dangerous work. Many received low pay for long hours on the job. Over time, workers began to unionize. By joining a **union,** workers pledged to work together for better and safer working conditions and higher wages. They called **strikes** when their employers cut their pay or refused to grant raises. Many of the laws we have today, including the eight-hour workday and the five-day workweek, came about through the bitter struggles for better working conditions that unions waged in the late 1800s and the early 1900s.

Unions weren't the only groups working to solve problems brought on by America's rapid industrialization. Some reformers worked to clean up slums, improve the health care, and stop child labor. Others worked to preserve the nation's natural beauty by creating National Parks. Still others worked to give more people a voice in government. For example, many women lobbied to gain the right to vote. In the early 1900s, groups were working toward so many sweeping social and political improvements that the time is called the **Progressive Era.**

U.S. History ▸ Practice 3

Choose the one best answer to each question.

1. Which of the following always occurs during a period of rapid industrialization?

   (1) the annexation of new territory
   (2) an increase in manufacturing
   (3) an increase in population
   (4) an increase in immigration
   (5) increased unionization of the labor force

2. Which event directly contributed to the growth of American industries in the mid-1800s?

   (1) the passage of the Chinese Exclusion Act, which banned Chinese immigration
   (2) the passage of the Sherman Antitrust Act, which helped prevent businesses from forming monopolies
   (3) the development of the Bessemer process, which made it easier to produce steel
   (4) the development of settlement houses to aid impoverished immigrants and city dwellers
   (5) the adoption of the direct primary, which allowed voters, rather than political parties, to choose candidates

3. Based on the passage, which of the following would early union workers have valued the most?

   (1) productivity in the workplace
   (2) contact with people of all different backgrounds
   (3) cooperation with others to improve worker safety
   (4) the freedom of self-expression
   (5) the freedom to work whenever they pleased

4. What was a strong ideal held by people working toward reforms during the Progressive Era?

   (1) efficiency
   (2) wealth
   (3) artistic beauty
   (4) scholarship
   (5) fairness

Questions 5 and 6 refer to the following graphs.

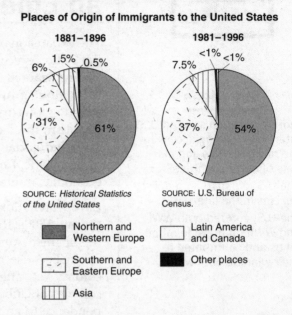

Places of Origin of Immigrants to the United States

1881–1896

1981–1996

SOURCE: *Historical Statistics of the United States*

SOURCE: U.S. Bureau of Census.

Northern and Western Europe

Southern and Eastern Europe

Asia

Latin America and Canada

Other places

5. Based on the first graph, in the late 1800s, where did most immigrants to the United States come from?

   (1) Northern and Western Europe
   (2) Southern and Eastern Europe
   (3) Asia
   (4) Latin America and Canada
   (5) Australia and Antarctica

6. Based on the graphs, what was a major difference between U.S. immigration in the late 1800s and U.S. immigration in the late 1900s?

   (1) There was a smaller percentage of immigrants from Northern and Western Europe in the late 1800s than in the late 1900s.
   (2) There was a smaller percentage of immigrants from all of Europe in the late 1800s than in the late 1900s.
   (3) There was a smaller percentage of immigrants from Asia in the late 1800s than in the late 1900s.
   (4) There was a larger percentage of immigrants from the Americas in the late 1800s than in the late 1900s.
   (5) There was a larger percentage of immigrants from Russia in the late 1800s than in the late 1900s.

Answers and explanations start on page 638.

U.S. HISTORY

The United States as an Emerging World Power

Key Ideas

- Industrialization spurred U.S. interest in gaining access to the raw materials and markets of other countries.
- The U.S. pursued imperialist policies in the late 1800s.
- The U.S. entered both WWI and WWII on the side of the Allies and contributed to their winning both wars.

GED TIP

When weighing answer choices, immediately eliminate ones that are directly contradicted by information in the passage or graphic.

The expansion of U.S. industries in the mid-1800s had an effect not only on the nation's economy but also on its politics. Business and government leaders wanted access to more natural resources, which industries needed to continue growing. They also wanted to be able to sell more goods overseas. Regions in Africa, Asia, and Latin America had rich natural resources. People in these regions might buy what Americans wanted to sell. To promote industrial growth and increase its power, the United States became imperialistic. **Imperialism** is the policy by which a stronger nation extends economic, military, and/or political control over a weaker nation or region.

European nations had been engaging in imperialism for many centuries. In the late 1800s, the United States joined in. In 1898, the United States fought the Spanish-American War. Ostensibly, the United States declared war on Spain because of Spain's mistreatment of Cuba, which was a Spanish colony. Yet, after winning the war, the United States took over Spain's colonies of Cuba, Puerto Rico, the Philippines, and Guam. It granted independence to none of them.

The next war the United States was involved in was World War I, which began in Europe in 1913. It pitted two groups of nations against each other. One group was called the **Allies;** the leading Allied nations included Great Britain, Russia, and France. The other group was called the **Central Powers,** which included Germany, Austria-Hungary, and the Ottoman Empire. The Allies and Central Powers fought for three years in what fast became a deadly stalemate. Then, in 1917, the United States, alarmed over Germany's sinking of American ships, joined the Allies. With American help, in November 1918 the Allies defeated the Central Powers and World War I ended.

Because the destruction was so terrible, some people called World War I "the war to end all wars." However, this was not to be. Within twelve years, by 1929, the world had fallen into a serious economic downturn, which Americans called the **Great Depression.** Economic problems aided the rise of **fascism** in Europe and elsewhere. Fascist nations squelched democracy and advocated the takeover of other nations. Germany, led by fascist dictator Adolf Hitler, started attacking smaller nations in Europe in the mid-1930s. Italy fought to take over Ethiopia, in Africa. Japan attacked China. Hitler built an alliance with Italy and Japan, which came to be called the **Axis.** By 1939, war again broke out between the Axis and the Allies.

The United States did not enter World War II until 1941, when the Japanese bombed the U.S. naval base at Pearl Harbor in Hawaii. This time, Americans fought not only in Europe but also in Africa and Asia as well. With its horrific battles, the fire-bombing of cities, the **Holocaust,** and the dropping of two atomic bombs on Japan, World War II led to the greatest destruction and despair the world has ever known. The United States, which played a major part in the Allied victory in World War II in 1945, also played a major part in helping to rebuild war-scourged nations after the war was over.

Choose the one best answer to each question.

Question 1 refers to the following chart.

Factors Related to the Growth of Imperialism

Economic: Focusing on Resources	Desire for greater access to raw materials and fuels
Economic: Focusing on Markets	Desire for more places to sell agricultural or industrial goods
Military: Focusing on Refueling	Desire for control of ports that could serve as refueling stations for long sea voyages or air flights
Military: Focusing on Defense	Desire for control of places that could aid in national defense
Political	Desire to spread the institutions of democracy or other political systems
Religious	Desire to spread Christianity or other faith
Cultural/Racial	Lack of respect for different cultures or races

1. Cuba lies about 90 miles off the coast of Florida. After the United States freed Cuba from Spanish rule in 1898, the U.S. Navy built an important base there.

   Which factor related to imperialism does this situation best illustrate?

   (1) economic/resources
   (2) military/refueling
   (3) military/defense
   (4) political
   (5) cultural

2. What assumption do you need to make to fully understand the last sentence in paragraph 4 on page 172?

   (1) In World War I, the Allies fought the Central Powers.
   (2) In World War II, the Allies included England, France, and Russia.
   (3) In World War II, the Allies included the Germans, Austrians, and Ottoman Turks.
   (4) In World War II, the Axis included Germany, Italy, and Japan.
   (5) World War II lasted longer than World War I did.

3. Franklin D. Roosevelt became president during the height of the Great Depression, in 1933. He soon instituted a set of federal programs called the New Deal to try to lower unemployment.

   Which conclusion about the effectiveness of New Deal programs does the graph below support?

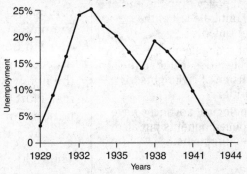

U.S. Unemployment Rate, 1929–1944

SOURCE: *Historical Statistics of the United States*

   (1) Within a year, the New Deal had raised unemployment to its pre-Depression level.
   (2) Within a year, the New Deal had lowered unemployment to its pre-Depression level.
   (3) The New Deal had no effect on unemployment.
   (4) The New Deal lowered unemployment, but U.S. entry in World War II lowered it further.
   (5) The New Deal lowered unemployment, but Allied victory in World War II lowered it further.

4. Which statement best summarizes the main idea of paragraph 5 on page 172?

   (1) America entered World War II in 1941.
   (2) Americans fought in Europe, Africa, and Asia.
   (3) World War II involved more nations than any other war ever fought.
   (4) America took a strong leadership role during and after World War II.
   (5) People have learned from the worldwide conflicts of the 1900s how horrible war can be.

Answers and explanations start on page 639.

U.S. HISTORY

Facing Enduring Challenges

Key Ideas

- The Cold War dominated U.S. foreign policy from the end of WWII until the fall of the Soviet Union.
- Social changes in the U.S. in the mid-1900s included the expansion of civil rights for minorities.
- Technological advances have introduced benefits but also caused problems.

ON THE GED

The GED Social Studies Test will include some questions that focus on the role of the United States in the world.

After World War II ended, the capitalist and communist nations soon began engaging in a power struggle called the **Cold War.** Leading the capitalist nations was the United States; leading the communist nations was the Soviet Union. The Cold War never led to direct fighting between these two superpowers, although there was a constant threat of nuclear war. Clashes between communism and capitalism did lead to numerous smaller conflicts. These included the Korean War of the early 1950s and the Vietnam War, which lasted from 1954 to 1975. The United States sent soldiers to both. The Vietnam War was long and difficult and caused deep division among Americans. The United States sent massive military aid to the noncommunist South Vietnamese, but they kept losing to the communist North Vietnamese. Although a few Americans wanted to continue fighting, in 1973 America pulled out of Vietnam. In 1975, the communists took over the country.

The Cold War ended in 1991 with the breakup of the Soviet Union and the end of communism there. In the late 1980s, Soviet leader Mikhail Gorbachev had tried to reform the communist government. But, the loosening of Soviet control had led to the collapse of many communist governments of Eastern Europe. The Berlin Wall, which had separated East and West Germany, was torn down. With communism no longer so threatening, world politics became less tense but also more unpredictable.

During the second half of the twentieth century, the United States continued to face many challenges. In the 1950s, African American leaders launched the **civil rights movement** to try to end segregation and discrimination in the United States. Among their victories included the integration of public schools and other public facilities, the passage of laws protecting the voting rights of minorities, and the striking down of laws that permitted overt discrimination based on race or cultural background. However, minority groups and people of all backgrounds concerned about fair application of the law have continued to be vigilant in insisting that civil rights laws be upheld.

Another area of challenge in recent decades has been **technology.** Technology has led to many advances in science, medicine, and our personal lives. Computers, for instance, make many jobs easier and more productive. They allow almost instantaneous communication with co-workers, family, and friends. Furthermore, they allow people from around the world to share information quickly and easily, giving us the sense that we live in a "global village." However, our reliance on the use of technology has led us to pollute the air with exhaust from a growing number of cars. It has led us to pollute the water with acid rain, resulting from burning coal to generate increased electricity. It has led us to pollute our land with mountains of trash and tons of hazardous wastes.

American ingenuity and spirit have led to great advances in technology and in building a just society. Americans can continue to use creativity and skills to solve the problems we face in this new millennium.

Choose the one best answer to each question.

1. Why was the conflict between the United States and the Soviet Union called the Cold War?

   (1) It involved communists and capitalists.
   (2) It involved Korea and Vietnam.
   (3) It occurred in the Northern Hemisphere.
   (4) There was a constant threat of nuclear war.
   (5) The two superpowers never actually fought.

2. Which of the following best summarizes the message of the cartoon below?

   © 1980 Mark Alan Stamaty. Reprinted with permission of Mark Alan Stamaty.

   (1) Holding a bomb over someone's head is difficult.
   (2) Nuclear bombs are extremely destructive.
   (3) Expanding U.S. nuclear capabilities is a good idea.
   (4) The build-up of nuclear arms increases fear and instability, not peace.
   (5) The threat of nuclear war is lessened if both superpowers have equally powerful weapons.

3. Which of the following statements about the Vietnam War is a false generalization?

   (1) Some Americans served in both Korea and Vietnam.
   (2) The Vietnam War was a clash between communists and noncommunists.
   (3) The United States sent massive military aid to South Vietnam
   (4) Americans were in complete agreement about pulling out of Vietnam.
   (5) The Vietnam War lasted much longer than the Korean War.

4. What caused the Cold War to end?

   (1) the destruction of the Berlin Wall
   (2) the fall of communism in the Soviet Union
   (3) the threat of communism in Eastern Europe
   (4) the separation of East and West Germany
   (5) the death of Mikhail Gorbachev

5. Which of the following goals would a civil rights activist be most likely to pursue?

   (1) getting the courts to uphold laws that restrict access to personal computer files
   (2) getting Congress to enact laws to restrict the sale of firearms
   (3) working for a city law requiring realtors to sell property to anyone who is able to buy it
   (4) getting local companies to stop polluting the environment
   (5) working with local clergy to publicize a worship service open to people of all religions

6. Which of the following is a conclusion about technology rather than a supporting detail?

   (1) Reliance on technology has increased pollution.
   (2) Cars cause air pollution.
   (3) Coal-generating power plants cause acid-rain pollution.
   (4) The ease of manufacturing disposable items has led to land pollution at landfill sites.
   (5) Hazardous wastes generated from increased manufacturing have polluted the land.

Answers and explanations start on page 639.

U.S. History Practice Questions

Choose the one best answer to each question.

Questions 1 and 2 refer to the time line below.

Important Events in Early Cherokee History

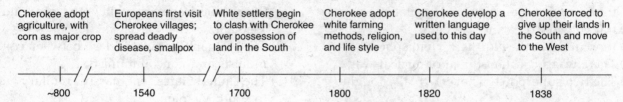

Cherokee adopt agriculture, with corn as major crop	Europeans first visit Cherokee villages; spread deadly disease, smallpox	White settlers begin to clash with Cherokee over possession of land in the South	Cherokee adopt white farming methods, religion, and life style	Cherokee develop a written language used to this day	Cherokee forced to give up their lands in the South and move to the West
~800	1540	1700	1800	1820	1838

1. Which of the following is a conclusion based on the time line?

   (1) The Cherokee had begun farming around 800, before Europeans came to America.
   (2) Clashes between Cherokee people and white settlers coming into the South started in the 1700s.
   (3) Although the Cherokee adopted many aspects of white culture, they were driven off their ancestral lands.
   (4) The Cherokee traditionally considered land ownership to be a tribal matter rather than a right of individuals acting on their own.
   (5) The Bible was one of the first books the Cherokee translated into their written language.

2. When President Andrew Jackson mandated that the Cherokee move west in 1830, he claimed that the U.S. government would be better able to protect the Cherokee from whites who might try to get their new land in the West. The Cherokee considered this to be illogical.

   Which of the following summarizes the logical fallacy?

   (1) If the government can't protect us from white settlers here, now, how could it protect us from whites moving west in the future?
   (2) If you ask us to move to the West now, how do we know you won't ask us to move back to the South in the future?
   (3) If the land we have in the South is good, why wouldn't the land in the West be better?
   (4) If the state governments are protecting us now, why can't the U.S. government help later?
   (5) If we have our own farms now, why wouldn't we have bigger farms later?

3. In the late 1700s, Abigail Adams—wife of John Adams, who was our nation's second president—wrote the following in a letter to her sister:

   I will never consent to have our sex considered in an inferior point of light. Let each planet shine in their [its] own orbit . . . if man is Lord, woman is *Lordess*—that is what I contend for.

   Based on this letter, which of the following principles was Abigail Adams advocating?

   (1) the separation of church and state
   (2) the abolition of slavery
   (3) the promotion of scientific learning
   (4) equal rights and opportunities for women
   (5) freedom of expression

Questions 4 and 5 refer to the following map.

The Union and the Confederacy

4. Which of the following sets of states had slavery but did not join the Confederacy?

(1) Maine, Vermont, Ohio, Iowa, and Oregon
(2) Pennsylvania, West Virginia, Tennessee, and Texas
(3) Delaware, West Virginia, Kentucky, and Missouri
(4) Arkansas, Missouri, Indian Territory, and Kansas
(5) Dakota Territory, Nebraska Territory, New Mexico Territory, and Arizona Territory

5. The loyalty of Maryland was of crucial importance to the Union. Based on the map, which statement best explains why this was so?

(1) The nation's capital was located nearby.
(2) The Confederate capital was located there.
(3) It was close to Fort Sumter, where the Civil War began.
(4) It was close to Pennsylvania, where the Battle of Gettysburg was fought.
(5) Important rail lines ran through Baltimore.

6. In the Emancipation Proclamation, issued in 1863, President Lincoln freed all people enslaved in the states that had seceded from the Union. This proclamation was explicitly not to be put into effect in slave states that had remained in the Union. The proclamation went on to say:

I hereby enjoin upon the people so declared to be free to abstain from all violence . . . and make known that such persons of suitable condition will be received into the armed services of the United States to garrison forts, positions, stations, and other places, and to man vessels of all sorts.

Based on the information given about the Emancipation Proclamation and the text of the order itself, which of the following was a major reason Lincoln issued the proclamation?

(1) to encourage states to secede from the Union
(2) to abolish slavery in the Union
(3) to punish slaveholders throughout the South
(4) to weaken the North by enlisting former slaves in the Confederate army
(5) to weaken the South by enlisting former slaves in the Union army

Questions 7 through 9 refer to the following chart.

Civil Rights Amendment and Laws

14th Amendment (1868)	Granted citizenship and equal protection of the law to all persons born in the United States (not applied to American Indians)
15th Amendment (1870)	Granted voting rights to African Americans
Civil Rights Act of 1875	Gave African Americans the right to serve on juries Banned racial segregation in public places
Civil Rights Act of 1964	Outlawed segregation by race in public places and racial discrimination in employment
Voting Rights Act of 1965	Prohibited literacy tests for voting Allowed the federal government to register voters
Civil Rights Act of 1968	Outlawed discrimination in the sale or rental of homes

7. Based on the chart, in which situation would the civil rights law passed in 1965 apply?

   (1) An Asian American registers to vote and is given a reading test.
   (2) An African American family is asked to give up their seats on a bus to a white family.
   (3) An American Indian applies for a job but is told that dark-skinned people will not be hired.
   (4) A Haitian man goes to a restaurant in a Cuban neighborhood but is told that he will not be served.
   (5) An Hispanic couple wants to buy a house in an African American neighborhood but they are told to look elsewhere.

8. Which statement best summarizes what this chart shows about voting rights?

   (1) African Americans were granted the vote five years after the Civil War ended.
   (2) African Americans were granted the vote 100 years after the Civil War ended.
   (3) African Americans were granted the vote soon after the Civil War, but laws enforcing these rights had to be passed a century later.
   (4) African Americans were granted the vote in 1870 but American Indians were never granted these same rights.
   (5) Literacy tests to prove a person was qualified to vote began to be used in 1965.

9. How are the Civil Rights Act of 1875 and the Civil Rights Act of 1964 similar?

   (1) They both guaranteed African Americans citizenship rights.
   (2) They both prohibited the legal separation of people by race in public places.
   (3) They both ensured that African Americans could serve on juries.
   (4) They both make job discrimination illegal.
   (5) They both protected voters by allowing the federal government to take charge of voter registration.

10. Alexander Graham Bell invented the telephone in the spring of 1876. In the fall, he exhibited it at an exposition in Philadelphia. When leading scientists saw Bell's invention, they said, "Here is the greatest marvel ever achieved in electrical science."

   Which of the following statements related to the passage is an opinion, not a fact?

   (1) Alexander Graham Bell was the inventor of the telephone.
   (2) Bell invented the telephone in 1876.
   (3) Bell exhibited the telephone at an exposition in Philadelphia.
   (4) Scientists admired Bell's invention.
   (5) The telephone was the greatest electrical invention ever.

Questions 11 through 13 are based on the paragraph and the political cartoon below.

In 1974, President Richard Nixon resigned from office. He had been involved in a scandal known as Watergate. The Watergate scandal implicated Nixon in covering up crimes committed by members of his reelection committee. These crimes ranged from illegally harassing political opponents to burglary and bribery. With Congress investigating him, he was sure to be impeached. This cartoon was published before Nixon resigned to avoid impeachment.

Hey guys, do you really think we need that clause about impeachment in there?

Cartoon by Robert Lawlor. Reprinted with permission of the "Philadelphia Daily News."

11. In this cartoon, whom is Nixon addressing?

  (1) the writers of the Declaration of Independence
  (2) the framers of the U.S. Constitution
  (3) the past presidents of the United States
  (4) the present session of Congress
  (5) the Watergate burglars

12. Which value was Congress furthering by investigating Nixon and Watergate?

  (1) the search for happiness
  (2) the pursuit of justice
  (3) the duty of obedience
  (4) loyalty to a friend
  (5) love of mercy

13. About Watergate one historian has written, "In a society in which distrust of leaders and institutions of authority was already widespread, the fall of Richard Nixon seemed to confirm the most cynical assumptions about the character of American public life."

What was a main reason for Americans' growing distrust of their government in the years just prior to Watergate?

  (1) the horrors of the Civil War
  (2) mismanagement of the New Deal
  (3) the beginning of rock music
  (4) the escalation and failure of the Vietnam War
  (5) the scandals of previous presidents, including John Kennedy and Bill Clinton

Questions 14 and 15 refer to the graph below.

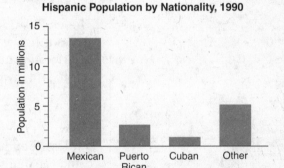

Hispanic Population by Nationality, 1990

SOURCE: U.S. Census Bureau

14. In 1990, about how many people of Cuban nationality lived in the United States?

  (1) 100
  (2) 270
  (3) 100,000
  (4) 1,000,000
  (5) 5,000,000

15. A Hispanic family moves into the apartment next door to you. Based only on the bar graph, which place is the family most likely to be from?

  (1) Cuba
  (2) Mexico
  (3) Puerto Rico
  (4) Spain
  (5) Peru

Answers and explanations start on page 639.

WORLD HISTORY

Early Civilizations

One of the earliest known **civilizations** is ancient Egypt. By 5000 B.C., people who lived along the **Nile River** had begun to take advantage of the fertile soil left behind by floods. The river and irrigation systems allowed the Egyptians to grow enough food to support a large population. Around 3000 B.C., Egyptian civilization grew under the rule of Egypt's kings, or **pharaohs.** Believing their pharaohs to be part god, Egyptians built the famous **pyramids** to house these rulers in their next lives. Many who built the pyramids and did the hard work to build this civilization were slaves.

Around the same time, in the **Fertile Crescent**—an area northeast of Egypt—**Sumerian** city-states were also developing irrigation and flood control methods. They also created a system of writing. In about 1800 B.C., the Sumerians were conquered by the Babylonians. One of the Babylonian kings, Hammurabi, is remembered for codifying laws. The **Code of Hammurabi** was written on a huge stone in a public place so all Babylonians could know and follow the law.

The civilization of **ancient Greece** did not develop around a river, but around the sea. The Greeks built an **empire:** they established colonies on the Mediterranean Sea and the Black Sea; then they imported food from the colonies. However, Greece itself was not politically unified. As its city-states fought for control of each other's land, Sparta, a particularly warlike state, took over a number of other city-states. Athens, another city-state, is known as the first political **democracy.** All Athenian citizens could vote—but less than half of Athenians were citizens. Women could not vote; nor could the many slaves. The Greek Empire lasted only a few hundred years, but its original ideas, such as democracy, and its stunning arts, including architecture and literature, remain influential even now.

Eventually the Greek Empire fell to **Roman** conquerors. Rome began as a city on the Italian Peninsula, governed by its wealthy citizens through an elected Senate. Roman law has been very influential in the modern United States. For example, the Romans believed that a person accused of a crime was innocent until proven guilty. The power of Rome grew, and the Romans took over many lands surrounding the Mediterranean Sea, pushing north as far as England and east into Asia by about A.D. 100. Roman leaders built systems and infrastructure to make their empire strong: schools, roads and bridges, hospitals, a tax system, and an army. The ancient Roman Empire lasted until A.D. 476.

Ancient Egypt, Greece, and Rome were only a few of the early civilizations in which people made important scientific discoveries and developed enduring ideas. In Central America, the **Maya,** whose culture was strongest from A.D. 300 to 900, invented a pictographic writing system in which they recorded remarkable discoveries in mathematics and astronomy. The **Inca Empire** in South America had a sophisticated system of government. The Incas built amazing roads and bridges in their rugged mountain lands. In Mexico, the **Aztecs** invented a written language and a calendar system and expanded their farmlands by dredging mud from lakes.

Choose the <u>one best answer</u> to each question.

1. Which of the following Central American civilizations is particularly noted for achievements in mathematics and astronomy?

   (1) the Egyptians
   (2) the Sumerians
   (3) the Maya
   (4) the Aztecs
   (5) the Incas

2. Which of the following civilizations had systems of government and law that strongly influenced the form of government adopted by the United States?

   (1) Sumer and ancient Egypt
   (2) Sumer and Babylonia
   (3) Babylonia and ancient Greece
   (4) ancient Greece and ancient Rome
   (5) ancient Rome and the Incas

3. What did the ancient civilizations of Egypt and the Fertile Crescent have in common?

   (1) Both developed flood control and irrigation technologies to boost food production.
   (2) Both had a public code of law engraved on a huge stone.
   (3) Both were centered on the shores of the Mediterranean Sea.
   (4) Both developed systems of political democracy in which citizens could vote.
   (5) Both extended their influence throughout Europe as well as the Middle East.

4. Once a society developed agriculture and domesticated animals, food surpluses and rising populations made possible which of the following developments?

   (1) hunting and gathering
   (2) a nomadic lifestyle
   (3) towns
   (4) stone tools
   (5) stone carvings

Questions 5 and 6 refer to the following map.

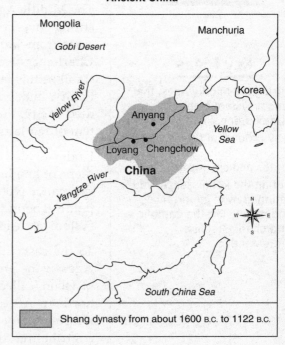

5. In the Yellow River valley, floods deposit a fertile yellow soil called loess that is easily worked by farmers.

   Which of the following civilizations arose under geographic conditions similar to those in ancient China?

   (1) the Incas
   (2) the Aztecs
   (3) ancient Greece
   (4) ancient Rome
   (5) ancient Egypt

6. Which of the following statements is supported by the information in the map?

   (1) The Yellow River is the only major river in China.
   (2) The Shang dynasty, or ruling family, controlled China for almost a thousand years.
   (3) The Yellow River was probably the main trade route between Loyang and Chengchow.
   (4) The Shang civilization traded more with Korea than with Manchuria.
   (5) Later Chinese dynasties located their capital city along the Yangtze River.

Answers and explanations start on page 640.

WORLD HISTORY

Feudalism to Nation States

Key Ideas

- During the Middle Ages, the feudal system helped to stabilize Europe.
- A by-product of the Crusades was the opening up of trade routes and city growth.
- During the Renaissance, education grew in importance and people left the Catholic Church to establish Protestantism.

GED TIP

To summarize a graph such as the one on page 183, ask yourself: What is the topic of the graph? What is the main point of the data? How could I say this in a sentence or two?

The **Middle Ages** in Europe lasted from about A.D. 500 to 1500. As the once strong government of Rome weakened, Europe became vulnerable to invasions from warring groups called barbarians. One barbarian ruler named **Charlemagne** conquered most of Europe by 800. Charlemagne was able to stabilize this large territory for a time. He established laws, spread Christianity, and encouraged education and commerce. When Charlemagne died in 814, the territories of Europe became unstable again, and the system of **feudalism** emerged.

Under feudalism, kings granted control of land to nobles. A noble's soldiers, or knights, protected the noble's estate, or manor. **Peasants** farmed at the manor. Nobles paid taxes to kings; peasants paid taxes to nobles. As the political boundaries among the kings' lands became established, the feudal system made life in Europe more peaceful over several hundred years' time.

To the east, the religion of **Islam** was founded during the early Middle Ages by the prophet Muhammad, who was born in A.D. 570. The followers of Islam, called **Muslims,** conquered large territories in the Middle East, northern Africa, Spain, Persia, and India. They established the Muslim Empire. Many people in these conquered lands converted to Islam while contributing their own knowledge and arts to the Muslim culture. Although the Muslim Empire itself did not last, its religion and culture have remained strong.

During the late Middle Ages, Christians and Muslim Turks fought over the holy city of Jerusalem in a series of wars called the **Crusades.** Christians gained control of Jerusalem from the Turks, but they ruled the city for less than 90 years. A more lasting effect of the Crusades was to open up trade between Europe and the Middle East and even China. As trade, money, and merchants grew in importance in Europe, feudalism declined. People left the manors and went to live and work in cities, where opportunities were greater. Cities gained political, economic, and cultural importance.

During the Middle Ages, European nations began to form as **monarchs** combined territories of small rulers and took advantage of the wealth of cities. England's monarchy was established by 1100. France won the Hundred Years' War against England and emerged as a strong nation under its monarch. Spain united through the marriage of two rulers, Ferdinand and Isabella, who had each controlled smaller states.

The **Renaissance,** which spread from Italy across Europe between 1300 and 1600, brought growth in education, science, and the arts. The Renaissance also led to changes in the Catholic Church. During the **Reformation** in the 1500s, reformers criticized the church for abusing its power. Those who believed that people should read the Bible themselves rather than follow the pope split from the Catholic Church and formed the **Protestant** religion. King Henry VIII of England broke from the Catholic Church and formed the Church of England so he would not have to obey the pope.

Choose the **one best answer** to each question.

1. What was the role of the knights in feudal Europe?

   (1) to farm the manor
   (2) to collect taxes for the king
   (3) to take care of livestock
   (4) to protect their noble's land from attack
   (5) to administer justice

2. In which modern European nation would you expect to find evidence of the arts and culture of the Muslim Empire?

   (1) Great Britain
   (2) France
   (3) Spain
   (4) Italy
   (5) Greece

3. During the late Middle Ages, the growth of trade spurred a migration of peasants from the manors to the towns. To which of the following events is this most similar?

   (1) the migration of Puritans to the New World to escape religious persecution in the 1600s
   (2) the migration of people from farms to industrial cities in the 1800s
   (3) the migration of political refugees to the United States in the 1900s
   (4) the migration of individuals with health problems from cold, damp regions to warm, dry regions
   (5) the growth of trade with nations along the Pacific Rim in the late 1900s

4. At the time of the Reformation, which of the following was one of the main differences between Roman Catholics and Protestants?

   (1) Roman Catholics accepted the authority of the pope and Protestants did not.
   (2) Roman Catholics lived on the manors and Protestants lived in the towns.
   (3) Roman Catholics supported the monarchies in their nations and Protestants did not.
   (4) Roman Catholics consolidated their nations from feudal units and Protestants did not.
   (5) Roman Catholics led the Church of England under Henry VIII and Protestants did not.

5. In England in the 1100s, any free man could bring a case before a royal court headed by a circuit judge, who formed juries of local people. The decisions of these courts were recorded and formed the basis for common law, which was applied to everyone in the kingdom. In contrast, justice in the manor courts, which were run by the nobles, could be fickle. There were few written laws, and the verdicts could be overturned by the lord.

   People usually preferred to be tried in royal courts rather than manor courts because the royal courts valued which of the following?

   (1) accepted legal principles
   (2) harsh punishment
   (3) justice for the nobles
   (4) power for the local lord
   (5) fines rather than imprisonment

Question 6 refers to the following graph.

Population of Western Europe, 500–1500

SOURCE: Carlo M. Cippola, ed. *The Fontana Economic History of Europe: The Middle Ages* and Carlo M. Cippola *Before the Industrial Revolution: European Society and Economy, 1000–1700*

6. Which of the following best summarizes the information shown on the graph?

   (1) The population of western Europe almost doubled.
   (2) The population of western Europe showed the most growth between the years 750 and 1000.
   (3) There were fewer than 50 million people living in western Europe at any given time.
   (4) The population of western Europe showed almost constant growth with only brief periods of decline.
   (5) The population of western Europe fell to its lowest around the year 1450.

Answers and explanations begin on page 640.

WORLD HISTORY

Expansion and the Global Age

Key Ideas

- European explorers sought new sailing routes to make trading easier with India and Asia.
- European rulers set up colonies in order to extend their territories and gain new wealth.
- Native peoples and cultures were exploited by colonization.

ON THE GED

Some questions will ask, "Which of the following statements is supported by the graph (or the map)?" Read the choices and carefully check each against the graphic.

Europeans had many reasons for leaving the shores of their own continent. Starting around 1500, explorers from European nations such as Spain and France sailed on risky voyages all over the world. Some were looking for trade routes and valuable goods, such as spices, to bring back. Others were missionaries bent on spreading the Christian religion. Still others were paid by their rulers to find new lands to conquer. No matter what the reasons for their journeys, they faced real dangers and uncertain rewards.

Vasco da Gama, a Portuguese explorer, sailed south around Africa to reach India. His journey took two years, but it was profitable: his four ships returned full of spices. Most Americans know the story of Christopher Columbus, who sailed west, expecting to reach Asia. Instead, he found the **New World**—the Americas. A different Spanish explorer, Magellan, led the first around-the-world expedition. In 1519, Magellan and his crew left Spain to sail around the southern tip of South America en route to India. Of Magellan's five ships, only one made it back to Spain; Magellan himself died in the Pacific. Not long after, a French explorer, Jacques Cartier, tried and failed to find a river route through North America to the Pacific. These explorers greatly expanded the Europeans' knowledge of geography.

European rulers turned to distant lands to expand their own power and resources, primarily for economic gain. **Colonies** offered a number of advantages to their ruling nations. Colonies could be required to **import** goods only from the ruling nation, and they could be forced to **export** their products and natural resources only to the ruling nation. Furthermore, anything in the colonized area was considered the property of the ruling nation. In the 1500s, Spain gained great wealth from its colonies in the New World by stealing valuable objects from the native civilizations and by mining and removing gold, silver, and other minerals from their lands. Colonialism could be utterly devastating to native cultures, economies, and populations, as colonizers brought not only weapons but also deadly diseases.

Historians distinguish among different types of colonies, depending on the relationship between the ruling nation and the particular colony. In colonies of **settlement,** people from the ruling nation migrated to the colony and established a government under the authority of the ruling nation. The English colonies in North America were colonies of settlement. Although American Indians had long-established societies and territories of their own, these were irrelevant to the English settlers. From the point of view of the British government, the lands belonged to England, and the American Indians were subject to British law and had to obey the British colonial government.

Colonies of **exploitation** were common in tropical climates, where Europeans did not want to establish their own settlements. In these colonies, the ruling nation established a government to exploit the local labor force and natural resources. Although the native people were forced to produce goods and crops to benefit the ruling nation, their own populations and cultures were not usually wiped out.

Choose the one best answer to each question.

1. For what is Magellan best known?

   (1) discovering a route north of North America to the Pacific Ocean
   (2) discovering a route to India around the southern tip of Africa
   (3) being the first European to see the Indian Ocean
   (4) exploring North America's rivers
   (5) leading the first around-the-world expedition

2. According to the passage, what is the main reason European rulers explored the New World and established colonies?

   (1) to convert people to Christianity
   (2) to establish democratic governments
   (3) to gain economic benefits
   (4) to find a river route through North America
   (5) to learn how people in distant lands lived

3. Which of the following is an example of a colony of exploitation?

   (1) Pennsylvania, where Quakers and other religious minorities settled to escape religious persecution in Europe
   (2) Malaya, where the British set up and ran rubber plantations worked by the native peoples
   (3) the island of Manhattan and areas north along the Hudson River, where the Dutch established the settlement of New Netherlands
   (4) Iceland, which was settled by the Norse and came under the rule of Norway and later under the rule of Denmark
   (5) Brazil, where the King of Portugal gave large parcels of land to loyal subjects, who enlisted others to settle on the land

4. Based on the passage, what was the main cause of population decline among native colonized peoples?

   (1) emigration to the colonizing nations
   (2) emigration to other colonies
   (3) slavery
   (4) war and disease
   (5) low birthrate

Question 5 refers to the following map.

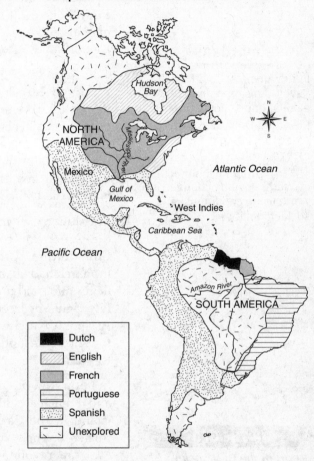

European Claims in the Americas About 1700

5. Which of the following statements is supported by information on the map?

   (1) In 1700, most of the Amazon River valley was claimed by Portugal.
   (2) The Dutch had the smallest claim in the Americas in 1700.
   (3) By 1700, the English had claimed the west coast of North America.
   (4) In 1700, Mexico was claimed by both the Portuguese and the Spanish.
   (5) By 1700, the pope had divided South America between the Spanish and the Portuguese.

Answers and explanations begin on page 641.

The Age of Revolutions

Key Ideas

- In the American and French Revolutions, people fought against unjust governments.
- Revolution spread to Latin America, ending many colonial governments there.
- The Industrial Revolution caused sweeping changes in work, living conditions, and social mobility.

ON THE GED

As part of the GED Social Studies test, you may be provided with basic historic information and asked to make comparisons—such as the similarities and differences between two revolutions.

Political revolutions often happen when people are unhappy about the conditions resulting from their system of government. Political revolutions may also be fueled by new ideas about who is best suited to govern. In the Age of Revolutions, many people wanted more political power.

One important cause of the **American Revolution** was British taxation. Although British citizens in England were represented in government through **Parliament,** the American colonists did not have representatives in that body. The colonists believed that they should not have to pay the special taxes levied on them, since they had had no voice in determining the tax laws. Although the colonists began by arguing for representation in the British government, by 1776, they declared themselves a sovereign nation, the United States of America.

Revolutionaries in France were inspired by democratic ideas expressed in the American colonies' **Declaration of Independence** and the **U.S. Constitution.** Unlike England, France had no Parliament; the French monarch had absolute power. The nobility and the Church had many privileges and paid no taxes, while ordinary citizens paid heavy taxes and had few rights or freedoms. In 1789, the French people organized a National Assembly—a law-making body to represent them. When King Louis XVI fought against the establishment of the National Assembly, the **French Revolution** began. Its turmoil lasted for ten years.

In Latin America, many colonized people, inspired in part by the American and French Revolutions, began to shake off European rule. In Haiti, an island in the Caribbean Sea, slaves led by Toussaint L'Ouverture overturned French rule and established an independent nation in 1804. Mexican revolutionaries finally won their independence from Spain in 1821. In South America, revolutions rocked the continent until 1824, by which time most countries had gained their independence.

Important revolutions are not always political. The **Industrial Revolution** started in the late 1700s in the textile industry, when new equipment was invented for spinning thread and weaving cloth. Instead of workers using their own tools at home, factories could house many workers using machines to produce much greater quantities. This factory model for large-scale production spread along with **steam engines** and electricity. Workers moved into factory towns and cities to work for wages. The Industrial Revolution brought a mixture of benefits and problems—useful inventions, increasing wealth, and new **social mobility** were offset by dangerous factory jobs, **child labor,** crowded cities, and **pollution.**

The Industrial Revolution also brought sweeping social changes. The economic mainstay of the European **aristocracy** had been farmland. After the Industrial Revolution, manufacturing and trade became more important economically than agriculture. Thus, the merchant classes became more powerful. New ideas about political equality affected how people thought about social equality as well.

Choose the **one best answer** to each question.

1. Which of the following had a great influence on the French Revolution?

   (1) the Industrial Revolution
   (2) the Mexican Revolution
   (3) the U.S. Declaration of Independence
   (4) the British monarchy
   (5) Toussaint L'Ouverture's revolution in Haiti

Question 2 refers to the following paragraph and graph.

Before the French Revolution, the French were divided into three groups by law, each with different privileges. In the First Estate were the higher clergy, who were nobles, and the parish priests, who were commoners. The Second Estate consisted of nobles who were not members of the clergy. The Third Estate was made up of commoners, including the middle class and peasants.

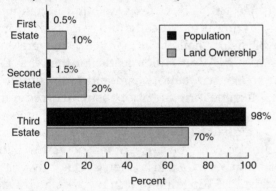

Population and Land Ownership in France, 1789

First Estate: 0.5%, 10%
Second Estate: 1.5%, 20%
Third Estate: 98%, 70%

Legend: Population, Land Ownership
Percent: 0, 20, 40, 60, 80, 100

2. Which of the following statements is supported by the paragraph and the graph?

   (1) The First Estate made up most of the population.
   (2) All members of the nobility belonged to the First Estate.
   (3) The members of the First Estate owned more property than members of the Second Estate.
   (4) The distribution of wealth in prerevolutionary France favored the Third Estate.
   (5) Members of the Third Estate owned the least amount of land per person.

3. According to the passage on page 186, what was a main difference between the English and French governments before 1789?

   (1) England had a Parliament, and France did not.
   (2) England had a monarchy, and France did not.
   (3) England had a class called the nobles, and France did not.
   (4) England levied taxes, and France did not.
   (5) England had colonies, and France did not.

4. On what was the economic power of the aristocracy based in eighteenth-century Europe?

   (1) moral superiority
   (2) attaining a high level of education
   (3) possessing large landholdings
   (4) belonging to the Church bureaucracy
   (5) personal acquaintance with the king

5. Which of the following does the writer of the passage take for granted that you know, and so does not state outright?

   (1) The American colonists demanded representation in the British government before they declared independence.
   (2) A sovereign nation is independent, having the power to control itself.
   (3) Many colonies were influenced by the American and French revolutions to seek independence.
   (4) The Industrial Revolution brought sweeping social changes.
   (5) As manufacturing and trade became more important, the merchant classes gained power.

6. The Information Revolution of the late twentieth century, spurred by the availability of personal computers and the Internet, is most similar to which of the following revolutions?

   (1) the American Revolution
   (2) the French Revolution
   (3) the revolution for Haitian independence
   (4) the Mexican Revolution
   (5) the Industrial Revolution

Answers and explanations start on page 641.

WORLD HISTORY

The Twentieth Century

World War I resulted from **nationalism** and **imperialism**—the desire of nations to extend their empires. This desire for expansion led to military buildup. When war broke out in 1914 between Serbia and Austria-Hungary over the assassination of an Austrian leader visiting Serbia, a chain reaction started as other countries also declared war. Germany and Austria-Hungary were the mainstays of the **Central Powers,** who fought against the **Allies**—England, France, Russia, Serbia, and eventually the United States. When the Central Powers finally lost the war, millions of people had been killed. The war had devastated Europe, leaving many people jobless and homeless. In the 1918 **Treaty of Versailles,** Germany was blamed for the war and forced to pay **reparations** to the Allies.

Revolution in Russia began during World War I. The Russian **Czar** refused to pull out of the war, even though most Russians did not support involvement. In 1917, the Czar and his family were assassinated, and the **Russian Revolution** ended with Bolshevik leader Vladimir Lenin in power. The Bolsheviks founded the Soviet Union as a **communist** nation with one political party—the Communist Party.

The Great Depression, which began in the United States when the stock market crashed in 1929, affected many countries. One hard-hit nation was Germany, which was still suffering economically and politically from its defeat in World War I. By 1933, nearly half of German workers were unemployed, and people were starving. Adolf Hitler, leader of the Nazi Party, rose to power by appealing to German nationalism and promising to put people back to work. Hitler's terrible form of nationalism involved imprisoning and killing people who were not part of "the Aryan race." Jews were the main targets of Hitler's campaign, now called the **Holocaust.** Hitler wanted to take over all Europe, and because other powerful nations wanted to avoid war, they let him annex Austria, then Czechoslovakia. But when Hitler invaded Poland in 1939, England and France declared war on Germany, and **World War II** began. Many nations went to war, including the United States. Once again, Germany and the other **Axis Powers** (including Italy and Japan) were defeated by the Allies. The United States dropped the first **atomic bomb** on Hiroshima to end the war.

After World War II, the United States and the Soviet Union emerged as **superpowers.** Former allies, they each led opposing groups of countries, one group democratic, the other group communist. The two groups of nations so distrusted each other that the period following World War II was called the **Cold War**—a war fought through political and diplomatic contests instead of battles. To catch up with the United States, the Soviet Union started to build its own nuclear weapons, and the **arms race** began, soon followed by the "space race."

However, by 1990 the Soviet bloc was falling apart. The Soviet Union itself split into 15 countries in 1991. People who had lived under repressive governments for many years struggled to establish democracy—not only in the former Soviet bloc, but also in Africa, Latin America, and Asia.

Choose the <u>one best answer</u> to each question.

1. As a result of the 1918 Treaty of Versailles, what did Germany have to do?

   (1) pay the Allies money to repair war damages
   (2) develop its military forces to protect Europe
   (3) adopt a communist government
   (4) promote nationalism among its people
   (5) replace Hitler with a freely elected leader

2. What event was the immediate cause of England and France declaring war on Germany at the beginning of World War II?

   (1) the killing of non-Aryan people
   (2) the annexation of Austria
   (3) the annexation of Czechoslovakia
   (4) the invasion of Poland
   (5) the invasion of France

3. Before the atomic bomb was dropped on Hiroshima, the Allies warned Japan they would suffer "complete and utter destruction" unless they surrendered. Despite the fact that 80,000 people were killed and 40,000 wounded by the bombing of Hiroshima, Japan still refused to surrender. The United States then dropped a second atomic bomb on the city of Nagasaki, killing 40,000 more people. After the second bombing, the Japanese surrendered.

   Japan's refusal to surrender after the bombing of Hiroshima suggests that the Japanese placed a high value on which of the following?

   (1) technological innovation
   (2) independence
   (3) national pride
   (4) the lives of military personnel
   (5) a lasting peace

4. Which of the following is a similarity between World War I and World War II?

   (1) Both were started by Germany.
   (2) Both were confined to Europe.
   (3) Both occurred after the Russian Revolution.
   (4) Both involved the use of atomic weapons.
   (5) Both were won by the Allies.

Questions 5 and 6 refer to the following chart.

Casualties in World War II

Nation	Military Dead	Military Wounded	Civilian Dead
Great Britain	398,000	475,000	65,000
Soviet Union	7,500,000	14,102,000	15,000,000
United States	292,000	671,000	very few
Germany	2,850,000	7,250,000	5,000,000
Japan	1,576,000	500,000	300,000

SOURCE: *The Second World War* by Henri Michel

5. What was the main difference between the casualties sustained by the United States and those sustained by other nations in World War II?

   (1) The United States had more military dead than wounded.
   (2) The United States sustained only a few civilian casualties.
   (3) The United States had the fewest wounded.
   (4) The United States had more civilian than military casualties.
   (5) The United States had few military dead.

6. The main reason that the Soviet Union had so many casualties is that it was invaded by the German army, which got as far as the outskirts of Moscow and Leningrad. There the Germans halted in 1941. Severe winters, long supply lines back to Germany, and stiff resistance from the Soviets ultimately defeated the Germans.

   Which of the following events is most similar to the German invasion of the Soviet Union?

   (1) the 1812 French invasion of Russia, which failed due to harsh weather and lack of supplies
   (2) the occupation of Singapore by Japan in World War II, which gave Japan control of Malaya
   (3) the 1941 Japanese attack on Pearl Harbor, which drew the United States into World War II
   (4) the 1945 Allied invasion of Europe, which liberated Europe from German control
   (5) the 1950 attack by North Korean forces on South Korea, which started the Korean War

Answers and explanations start on page 641.

WORLD HISTORY PRACTICE QUESTIONS

Choose the <u>one best answer</u> to each question.

1. The Germanic tribes that invaded the Roman Empire had relatively simple governments. There were few government officials and taxes. Rulers depended on the loyalty of their warriors rather than on a government bureaucracy. Germanic laws were based on custom and designed to prevent warfare between families.

   Which of the following is the best title for this passage?

   (1) Government in Germany
   (2) How Germanic Tribes Governed
   (3) Germanic Tribes and the Roman Empire
   (4) The Invasion of the Roman Empire
   (5) Loyalty Among the Germanic Tribes

2. By the 500s, Hindu beliefs and practices were deeply rooted in Indian culture. In the 900s, Muslim invaders gained control of most of India. There were many points of conflict between the Muslims and the Hindus. The Muslims, who believed in one God, considered the Hindu belief in many gods evil. Muslims also thought that all believers were equal before God, and Hindus believed in a strict caste system in which people's rank in society reflected their spiritual advancement. As a result of these and other differences, Muslims were not absorbed into Hindu society, as previous invaders had been.

   Which of the following statements is a conclusion rather than a supporting statement?

   (1) Hindu traditions had become part of the Indian social fabric by the 500s.
   (2) Muslims overran India, gaining political control of the country in the 900s.
   (3) Cultural differences prevented Muslim assimilation into Hindu society.
   (4) A caste system with firm social ranking was characteristic of Hindu society.
   (5) Muslims and Hindus differed in their belief in one God or many gods.

Questions 3 and 4 refer to the following map.

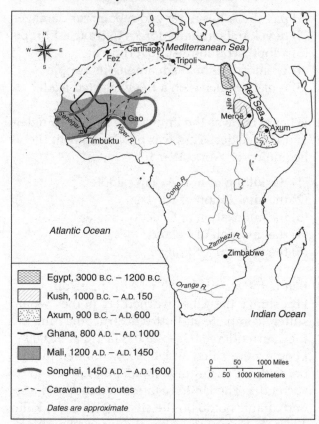

Early Civilizations in Africa

3. Where did the earliest civilizations in Africa develop?

   (1) along the Congo River
   (2) along the Niger River
   (3) along the Nile River
   (4) along the Orange River
   (5) along the Atlantic coast

4. Which of the following statements is supported by information on the map?

   (1) Over 800 years, several civilizations succeeded one another in western Africa.
   (2) The longest river in Africa is the Zambezi.
   (3) The Kingdom of Mali dominated western Africa for more than 500 years.
   (4) Timbuktu was an important center of learning in Songhai.
   (5) Gold and salt were transported along caravan trade routes in western Africa.

5. Toward the end of World War II, delegates from fifty nations met and formed the United Nations, an international organization devoted to peace. Member nations agreed to submit disputes to the United Nations for peaceful settlement.

In terms of goals, to which of the following is the United Nations most similar?

(1) the World Health Organization, formed to coordinate international health activity
(2) the World Trade Organization, formed in 1994 to enforce trade laws and regulations
(3) the International Bank for Reconstruction and Development, formed to further international economic development
(4) the Marshall Plan, a program of loans designed to help Western European nations rebuild after World War II
(5) the League of Nations, formed at the end of WWI to maintain international peace

6. The mechanization of the textile industry, the invention of the steam engine, and the development of the coal and iron industries contributed to Great Britain's lead in the Industrial Revolution. However, after 1850, other nations began to challenge Great Britain's lead. Belgium, France, and Germany all industrialized quickly. By 1900, natural resources and railroad building helped make the United States the leading industrial nation.

Which of the following is the best summary of this passage?

(1) The development of natural resources made Great Britain the leader in the Industrial Revolution.
(2) Many nations, such as Belgium, France, and Germany, industrialized in the 1800s.
(3) The Industrial Revolution started in Great Britain and spread throughout the world.
(4) The Industrial Revolution started in Great Britain and spread to Europe, but by 1900 the United States was the leading industrialized nation.
(5) Plentiful natural resources and a vast railroad system were the underpinnings of the Industrial Revolution in the United States.

7. Gandhi was the popular leader of India's struggle for independence from Great Britain. He backed a policy of nonviolent resistance, boycotting British goods and leading peaceful demonstrations.

Which of the following people was most influenced by Gandhi?

(1) Charles de Gaulle, French general who set up a government in exile after the Nazi's took over France and led French soldiers to victory against the Germans
(2) Martin Luther King, Jr., who led peaceful demonstrations to further the cause of civil rights in the United States
(3) Ho Chi Minh, who led the Vietnamese armed fight for independence from the French and became the leader of North Vietnam
(4) Soviet leader Mikhail Gorbachev, who was the last leader of the Soviet Union
(5) Fidel Castro, who led a guerrilla war and took over Cuba, turning it into a communist state

Question 8 refers to the following chart.

Chinese Governments Since 1271

Government	Description	Years
Yuan	China ruled by Mongol invaders from the northwest.	1271–1368
Ming	China reunified under ethnic Chinese rule.	1368–1644
Ch'ing	China ruled by Manchu invaders from the northeast.	1644–1911
Republic	Provincial rulers, warlords.	1912–1949
People's Republic	Communist revolution led by Mao Zedong.	1949–present

8. What did the Yuan and Ch'ing governments have in common?

(1) They were led by non-Chinese peoples.
(2) They lasted 500 years.
(3) They were overturned by Mongols.
(4) They were overturned by Manchus.
(5) They were followed by periods of provincial rule.

Questions 9 through 12 refer to the following time line.

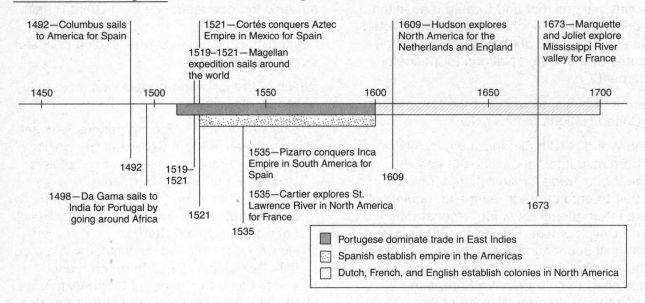

9. Da Gama's voyage opened up trade routes for the Portuguese. Based on the time line, which of the following was a result of his voyage?

(1) Portugal established large settlements in Africa.
(2) Portugal established a colony in Brazil.
(3) Portuguese trade in the East Indies grew.
(4) The Spanish established an empire in the Americas.
(5) The French claimed the St. Lawrence River valley.

10. Which of the following statements is supported by information on the time line?

(1) Spanish and Portuguese domination of exploration gave way to that of the Dutch, French, and English.
(2) Henry Hudson discovered more places in North America than did Marquette and Joliet and Cartier.
(3) Both Cartier and Da Gama explored North America on behalf of France.
(4) French explorers cooperated with American Indians in establishing trade.
(5) Spain dominated the New World for more than three hundred years.

11. Instead of financing expeditions themselves, the rulers of Spain allowed conquistadors to establish outposts in the Americas. The conquistador financed his own expedition, but if he succeeded, he was allowed to keep four-fifths of any treasure he found. Cortés was a conquistador who became rich by conquering the Aztecs in Mexico.

Which of the following explorers was also a conquistador?

(1) Da Gama
(2) Pizarro
(3) Cartier
(4) Hudson
(5) Marquette

12. Which of the following is the best title for this time line?

(1) The Spanish Explorers and Empire
(2) The Age of Exploration
(3) History of the Sixteenth and Seventeenth Centuries
(4) European Colonies in the Americas
(5) Voyages to the New World

Question 13 refers to the following graph.

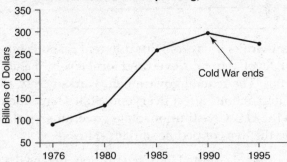

U.S. National Defense Spending, 1976–1995

13. Which of the following statements is supported by the graph?

    (1) Before the Cold War began, defense spending was at an all-time high.
    (2) Defense spending remained steady throughout the Cold War.
    (3) Defense spending declined steadily during the period 1976 to 1990.
    (4) After the Cold War ended, defense spending began to fall.
    (5) Defense spending was almost 4 percent of the Gross Domestic Product in 1995.

14. When establishing colonies, European nations wanted their colonies to be economically self-sufficient. That meant that each colony paid for its government salaries and the cost of building and maintaining roads, railroads, and government buildings. To do this, European colonists or the colonial governments exported natural resources like gold or copper or grew cash crops like sugar or rubber.

    Which of the following statements is an opinion rather than a fact?

    (1) European countries had similar goals in governing their colonies.
    (2) Colonies should be economically independent.
    (3) European nations built railroads, roads, and government buildings in their colonies.
    (4) Colonies provided natural resources that colonists could export.
    (5) Europeans grew cash crops in their colonies.

Questions 15 and 16 refer to the following passage.

During Japan's feudal period, which began during the 1100s, warriors called samurai developed a strict code of conduct. The samurai code, called bushido, emphasized loyalty and obedience to the samurai's lord. It also called for a samurai to lead a simple, courageous, and honorable life. A samurai who violated bushido brought disgrace on himself and his family. To make up for this disgrace, he was expected to commit seppuku, ritual suicide.

15. Which of the following is most similar to bushido?

    (1) chivalry, the way of life of European knights that emphasized personal valor and honor
    (2) appeasement, a process by which an aggressor is satisfied in order to maintain peace
    (3) common law, a system of laws based on the decisions of English royal courts
    (4) conservatism, a philosophy that supports the traditional social and political order
    (5) nirvana, in Hinduism and Buddhism, the ultimate goal of life that consists of the condition of wanting nothing

16. Which of the following did a samurai warrior in feudal Japan probably value the most?

    (1) wealth
    (2) education
    (3) leisure
    (4) recognition of service
    (5) peace

Answers and explanations start on page 642.

CIVICS AND GOVERNMENT

Levels and Branches of Government

Key Ideas

- Under our Constitution, the federal government must share power with the states.
- The federal government has three major branches—executive, legislative, and judicial.
- The three branches of the government balance each other's power.

ON THE GED

Editorial cartoons like the one on page 195 use pictures and humor to make a political point.

The United States government works in layers with different responsibilities at the national, or **federal**, level; the state level; and local levels, including cities, villages, and counties. The federal government works across all fifty states, and its decisions and actions affect everyone. States have their own constitutions, similar to the U.S. Constitution. State governments also are quite powerful in shaping the lives of people in their states.

Federalism, which is a basic principle of the U.S. Constitution, means that power is shared between the national and state levels of government. Dividing power between federal and state government protects the rights of individual states, but also allows our national government to enforce certain rights of citizenship. The Constitution gives some powers only to the national government, some only to state government, and some to both. For example, only the federal government can declare war. States are given the power to establish schools. Both federal and state governments can levy taxes and set up court systems.

There are three branches of government at the federal level, each with different roles to play. The powers of each branch are described in the Constitution. The **executive branch** consists of the president and various advisors (including the president's cabinet) and government departments. The executive branch enforces the nation's laws and provides national leadership, setting goals and policies. The **legislative branch** consists of two houses of **Congress:** the **Senate** and the **House of Representatives.** Congress is responsible for making laws that all citizens, organizations, and businesses must follow. The **judicial branch,** made up of the federal court system including the Supreme Court, decides disputes related to laws, including the U.S. Constitution.

U.S. citizens vote for the president and all members of Congress. As a result, these politicians have a responsibility to represent and serve their **constituents**—the people who elected them. The president may be elected to only two terms of four years each. Representatives are elected for two years and Senators for six years; these members of Congress may be reelected for any number of terms.

Federal judges, in contrast, are appointed by the president and **confirmed** by the Senate. They can serve in these positions for life. As citizens, we have a right to expect our federal judges to make **impartial** decisions based on the Constitution and the laws of the United States.

The people who wrote the U.S. Constitution were afraid to give any government body too much power. Therefore, the Constitution limits the power of each branch of the federal government. Each branch has separate powers. Each branch also has the power to act in ways that affect the other branches, in a system called **checks and balances.** For example, the president can **veto** laws made by Congress. Congress can override a presidential veto by repassing the law with a two-thirds majority. Federal judges can review laws and declare them **unconstitutional.**

CIVICS AND GOVERNMENT ▸ PRACTICE 1

Choose the <u>one best answer</u> to each question.

1. What is the key characteristic of federalism?

   (1) division of power between national and state governments
   (2) concentration of power in one government
   (3) concentration of power at the local level
   (4) an elected legislature representing citizens
   (5) a judicial system with trial, appellate, and supreme courts

2. Which of the following is an example of a government entity that is part of the executive branch?

   (1) the Cattlemen's Action Legislative Fund
   (2) the Democratic National Committee
   (3) Congress's House Rules Committee
   (4) the U.S. Court of Appeals
   (5) the State Department

3. Why do lifetime appointments help ensure that federal judges rule impartially on legal issues?

   (1) Only people who have demonstrated great legal knowledge are appointed.
   (2) Federal judges need not worry about pleasing their constituents in order to be reelected.
   (3) Only people who demonstrate loyalty to the ruling political party are appointed.
   (4) Lifetime appointments mean that federal judges acquire a great deal of experience.
   (5) A federal judge must be impartial or he or she will not be reelected.

4. Which of the following is the system of checks and balances designed to prevent?

   (1) abuse of power
   (2) more than one political party
   (3) voter fraud
   (4) minority rule
   (5) the presidency and Congress controlled by the same party

Question 5 refers to the following cartoon.

"Let's never forget that the constitution provides for three equally important branches of government; the legislative and the other two."

5. Which of the following people is most likely depicted in the cartoon?

   (1) the president
   (2) a presidential advisor
   (3) a member of Congress
   (4) the head of a government department
   (5) a federal judge

6. Although the states have the power to make their own laws in many areas, in practice they cooperate with one another to a great extent. For example, when a person travels, his or her driver's license, which was issued by one state, will be honored in other states.

   On which of the following principles is this type of cooperation based?

   (1) mutual respect and convenience
   (2) centralization of authority
   (3) democracy
   (4) common law
   (5) division of power

Answers and explanations start on page 642.

Civics and Government

Constitutional Government

Key Ideas

- The U.S. Constitution is the basis for our government structure and legal system.
- The Bill of Rights—the first ten Constitutional amendments—define the rights of citizens.
- Amendments to the Constitution require wide support. But many important amendments have gained enough support to be ratified.

ON THE GED

The GED Test will include one passage from or about the Declaration of Independence and one passage from or about the U.S. Constitution.

The Constitution of the United States is the foundation of our national government and legal system. The United States is a **republic,** a form of government in which citizens elect the people who will govern them. A republic is very different from a government system in which citizens do not choose their political leaders, such as a **monarchy** or **dictatorship.**

The people who wrote the Constitution set particular goals for the new nation, which they stated in the **preamble,** or introduction. They wanted to unite the states under one government, establish a nation where people could live peacefully and safely under the rule of law, and make prosperity and freedom possible for all citizens.

Following the preamble are the original seven **articles** of the U.S. Constitution. These articles provide for the three branches of government (see page 194), establish the rights of states, and set forth procedures for ratifying and amending the Constitution. Article 6 states that all government officials must uphold the Constitution as "the supreme law of the land," and that no other laws can contradict any part of the Constitution.

According to Article 5, a Constitutional **amendment** can be proposed by Congress if it is supported by two-thirds majorities in both the House and Senate. The proposed amendment then must be ratified by three-fourths of the states. This process ensures that amendments have very broad national support.

The original Constitution did not specifically describe citizens' rights. Even as the Constitution was being written, some political leaders insisted that a bill of rights was needed to help develop citizens' trust in the new government. However, they agreed to wait to make amendments to the Constitution until after it was **ratified.** As a result of this compromise, the first ten amendments to the U.S. Constitution, passed in 1791, became the **Bill of Rights.** These rights are well known to many Americans. The First Amendment, for example, guarantees freedom of religion, freedom of speech, and freedom of the press. The Second Amendment gives citizens the right to own firearms. The Sixth and Seventh Amendments guarantee citizens' rights to trial by jury.

As Americans' ideas about citizenship and government have evolved, the amendment process has allowed the Constitution to evolve as well. The Thirteenth Amendment (1865) outlawed slavery; the Fifteenth Amendment (1870) established that the rights of citizens "shall not be denied or abridged . . . on account of race, color, or previous condition of servitude."

A number of Constitutional amendments have extended voting rights to citizens. The Nineteenth Amendment (1920) gave women the right to vote. The Twenty-fourth Amendment (1964) banned poll taxes, which some states were using to prevent African Americans from voting. The Twenty-sixth Amendment (1971) lowered the voting age to 18.

Choose the one best answer to each question.

1. Which of the following is the main characteristic of a republic?

   (1) voting rights extended to few adult citizens
   (2) power allocated among executive, legislative, and judicial branches
   (3) elected representatives exercising government power on behalf of citizens
   (4) people governing themselves by voting directly on all issues
   (5) power concentrated among a small group

2. The Constitution is a relatively brief document containing only about seven thousand words. It establishes the structure and powers of the U.S. government, but does not give many specifics.

   What assumption were the drafters of the Constitution working under as they kept the document general and brief?

   (1) There was not enough time to draft a long, detailed document before the states had to ratify it.
   (2) The citizens of the United States could not understand a detailed document.
   (3) Most of the power of the federal government would be reserved to the president, who could govern as he saw fit.
   (4) The details of government would be worked out in the future, as the need arose, within the framework of the Constitution.
   (5) Written constitutions were an untested basis for democratic government, so it was better to keep such a document brief.

3. Franklin Delano Roosevelt was elected to the presidency four times between 1933 and 1945. In reaction to this, the Twenty-second Amendment, ratified in 1951, allowed presidents a maximum of two terms in office.

   People who favored presidential term limits would most likely have valued which of the following?

   (1) responsibility but no authority
   (2) authority but no responsibility
   (3) both authority and responsibility
   (4) the power of an office, not an individual
   (5) the power of an individual, not an office

4. The third paragraph of the passage on page 196 includes a summary of Article 6 of the Constitution, also called the supremacy clause.

   Which of the following is an example of the supremacy clause in action?

   (1) Congress votes to appropriate $2 billion for a federal highways program.
   (2) Congress imposes certain conditions before admitting a new state to the union.
   (3) The Environmental Protection Agency issues new regulations on a pollutant.
   (4) The U.S. Supreme Court refuses to hear a case.
   (5) The U.S. Supreme Court declares an Illinois state law unconstitutional.

Question 5 refers to the following chart.

Methods of Amending the Constitution

Proposal	Ratification Method	When Used
Two-thirds vote in both houses of Congress	By three-quarters of the state legislatures	For every amendment except one.
	By special conventions in three-fourths of the states	Twenty-first Amendment (repealing Prohibition)
Two-thirds of states request Congress to call a constitutional convention	By three-quarters of the state legislatures	Never used
	By special conventions in three-fourths of the states	Never used

5. Which is the most likely reason that the third and fourth methods of amending the Constitution have never been used?

   (1) State governments do not usually act together.
   (2) Only Congress can propose amendments.
   (3) State legislatures can vote on an amendment.
   (4) Conventions meet more frequently than Congress and state legislatures do.
   (5) State legislators have short terms of office.

Answers and explanations start on page 643.

CIVICS AND GOVERNMENT

The Electoral System

Key Ideas

- U.S. politics are dominated by the Democratic and Republican parties.
- Political parties hold primaries to select candidates for the general election.
- Political campaigns are very expensive, and many people believe that we must reform our campaign finance laws.

GED TIP

When you are asked a question about a circle graph, remember that it represents a whole, or 100%.

At the national level in particular, two **political parties** dominate the political arena in the United States: the **Democrats** and **Republicans.** These parties represent different ideas about the role of government in our nation. In each election season, the parties and candidates work to promote their views, or **platforms**—their positions on issues like tax reform, Social Security, education spending, environmental protection, and so on.

The political parties have developed large organizations for raising money and getting their candidates elected. Each party runs its own **primary** election, in which candidates within the party compete with each other for the party's **nomination.** After the primary elections, the winners from each party's primary face off in the general election. In presidential elections, the primary season ends with a party **convention,** where delegates from each state gather to select the party's candidate. Citizens vote in a general election and the results are tallied by state. Following the general election, electors from each state cast their state's votes in the **Electoral College.** The electors generally must cast their votes for the candidate who won the general election in their state. The candidate who wins the greatest number of electoral votes becomes president.

Although Democrats and Republicans are by far the largest political parties, there are small parties as well. At times, a "third-party candidate" like Ralph Nader or Ross Perot attracts enough support to influence the outcome of the national election. Even when small parties offer interesting new ideas or solutions to problems, they have great difficulty attracting money and public attention because the Democratic and Republican parties are so well established.

Although many voters consider themselves to be either Republicans or Democrats, many others are **independent.** Candidates and their political parties rely heavily on **opinion polls** to find out what voters think; they try to tailor their campaign messages to appeal to large numbers of voters. Groups of voters who might "swing" an election one way or another are particularly important targets for political campaigns. Sometimes opposing candidates participate in public **debates.**

Political campaigns can be very expensive, and the higher the office, the more expensive the campaign. To reach the public, candidates pay for mailings, TV ads, and events, including personal appearances. They need campaign staff and offices; they must pay for travel expenses. As a result, fund-raising has become a very important part of running for office.

In recent decades, Americans have become more and more concerned about the high cost of running for office. Many Americans believe that a candidate should not have to be wealthy to begin with, or be overly obligated to contributors, in order to gain political office. We now have laws that restrict the size of campaign contributions. We also have restrictions on how **Political Action Committees** (PACs) operate. However, many people believe that more reforms are needed.

Choose the one best answer to each question.

1. In order to win the presidency, a candidate <u>must</u> have which of the following?

   (1) a majority of primary wins
   (2) a majority of the popular vote
   (3) a majority in the Electoral College
   (4) no third-party opponent
   (5) experience in elected office

2. An exit poll is one that surveys people as they leave a voting location. Instead of waiting for votes to be counted, the media often announce the winners of elections based on exit polls.

   Which of the following is an important draw-back of using exit polls?

   (1) Exit polls may be inaccurate if the people polled are not representative of the political unit as a whole or if the election is very close.
   (2) Exit polls allow the media to present election results during prime time on election night instead of waiting until later in the evening.
   (3) Exit polls have undue influence on the way politicians running for office conduct their campaigns.
   (4) Exit polls are likely to be unreliable when there is a wide margin between the candi-dates.
   (5) Exit polls are usually unreliable because they involve surveying so many people.

3. Which of the following is an example of a pri-mary election?

   (1) A Democrat and a Republican oppose one another in a race for the U.S. Senate.
   (2) A Republican and an independent candidate oppose one another in a race for the state senate.
   (3) The delegates at a party convention vote for the presidential candidate they favor.
   (4) Once presidential candidates are chosen, they select their running mates.
   (5) Two city council members are on a ballot to determine which one will run for mayor as a Democrat.

Questions 4 and 5 refer to the following graphs.

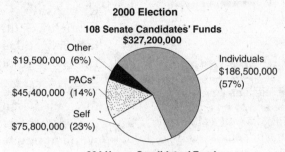

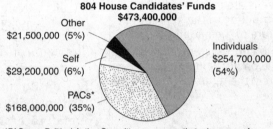

*PACs are Political Action Committees — groups that raise money for candidates.
SOURCE: Federal Election Commission.

4. How do the campaign funding sources of Senate and House candidates compare?

   (1) Senate candidates got the most money from individuals, and House candidates from PACs.
   (2) Senate and House candidates raised money from sources in about the same proportions.
   (3) Senate and House candidates received similar proportions of donations from individuals.
   (4) Senate candidates contributed far less to their own campaigns than House candidates.
   (5) Senate candidates got a greater proportion of money from PACs.

5. Which of the following statements is supported by the graphs?

   (1) More funds were raised for the congressional election of 2000 than for the 1998 election.
   (2) PACs donated far more money to Senate can-didates than to House candidates.
   (3) On average, a Senate candidate raises more money than a candidate running for the House.
   (4) An incumbent candidate usually raises more money than his or her opponents.
   (5) Fund-raising accounts for most of the work of a congressional campaign.

Answers and explanations start on page 643.

CIVICS AND GOVERNMENT

The Role of the Citizen

- U.S. citizens have the right to vote and to hold public office, as well as to enjoy many freedoms.
- Citizens are responsible for contributing to the general welfare of the nation.
- In our court system, citizens serve on juries in order to protect the rights of other citizens.

ON THE GED

The Social Studies Test will include questions about "practical documents," which may include voter registration or election information.

Citizenship is a special relationship between a person and a nation: the nation owes the person certain rights and guarantees; the person has certain obligations to the nation. Thus citizens of the United States have both rights and responsibilities.

People born in the United States, no matter what the circumstances, automatically become U.S. citizens. Regardless of where you were born, if one of your parents was a U.S. citizen, then you are also a U.S. citizen. People who **immigrate** to the United States from other countries can become U.S. citizens through a legal process called **naturalization;** underage children are naturalized along with their parents.

Our rights of citizenship are established in the first ten amendments to the U.S. Constitution—the Bill of Rights (see page 196) and in other sections of the Constitution. The most fundamental right of U.S. citizens is our right to participate in our nation's political life. We are eligible to vote and to hold public office, and we elect representatives to govern us. In a famous phrase in the Gettysburg Address, Abraham Lincoln said that we have a government "of the people, by the people, and for the people."

As Lincoln's famous remark implies, a government "by the people" requires that citizens take responsibility. First and foremost, we must uphold the laws of our country. As citizens, we also make contributions to the national welfare. Our taxes pay for services that the government provides to benefit everyone. By voting, we not only choose our government representatives, but we also help to make the political process meaningful for everyone. Through national service—such as military service, holding public office, or participating in intensive volunteer programs like Teach for America—citizens may devote years of their lives to the responsibilities of citizenship.

Our **jury** system is an important example of the give-and-take of citizenship. We are all guaranteed the right to a fair and speedy trial, heard by "a jury of peers," if we are accused of a crime. However, we are also obligated to serve on a jury or as a **witness** when we are called by the court system. The fairness of our legal system depends on citizens participating in that system. Therefore, our employers are obligated to release us from work at the request of the courts.

In addition to the rights and responsibilities established by law, many citizens contribute their time and money in other ways that serve society as a whole. People volunteer to serve organizations in their communities or within their professions—serving meals in shelters, fund-raising for schools, offering free medical services, etc. People also give money to causes they think are important, from political campaigns to food pantries to environmental organizations. Many citizens also work hard to conduct their daily lives in ways that contribute to the general welfare: by recycling, cleaning up trash, and looking out for their neighbors and family members.

Choose the <u>one best answer</u> to each question.

1. Which of the following documents outlines the rights of U.S. citizens?

   (1) the Declaration of Independence
   (2) the U.S. Constitution
   (3) the Gettysburg Address
   (4) a U.S. passport
   (5) a person's naturalization papers

<u>Questions 2 and 3</u> refer to the following information.

Noncitizens can be classified into five groups:

Resident alien   A foreigner who has established permanent residence in the United States.

Nonresident alien   A foreigner who is staying in the United States for a brief, specified period.

Enemy alien   A foreigner who is a citizen of a nation at war with the United States.

Refugee   A foreigner fleeing his or her country to escape persecution or danger.

Illegal alien   A foreigner who comes to the United States without legal documentation.

2. Louvina married an American and moved to the United States from Trinidad in 1998. Three years later she filed a legal petition requesting U.S. citizenship. In what category of alien does Louvina belong?

   (1) resident alien
   (2) nonresident alien
   (3) enemy alien
   (4) refugee
   (5) illegal alien

3. What would happen to the legal status of noncitizens living in the United States if their country declares war on the United States?

   (1) They would become nonresident aliens.
   (2) They would become resident aliens.
   (3) They would become enemy aliens.
   (4) They would become refugees.
   (5) They would become illegal aliens.

4. The United States must balance the right of society to protect itself against the rights of an accused criminal. One aspect of this tension is the Fourth Amendment guarantee of "the right of people to be secure in their persons, houses, papers, and effects, against unreasonable searches and seizures."

   Which of the following values is supported by the Fourth Amendment?

   (1) free speech
   (2) privacy
   (3) civic duty
   (4) neighborliness
   (5) law and order

Question 5 refers to the following graph.

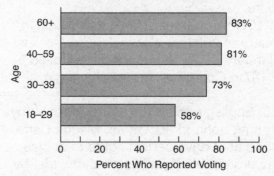

Reported U.S Voter Turnout by Age, 1996 Presidential Election

SOURCE: National Election Studies, 1996.

5. Which of the following is a conclusion based on the graph rather than a detail of the graph?

   (1) About 81 percent of people aged 40 to 59 reported voting in the 1996 presidential election.
   (2) Those aged 60 and above reported the highest voter turnout in the 1996 presidential election—83 percent.
   (3) Only about 58 percent of young people reported voting in the 1996 presidential election.
   (4) In the United States, voter turnout increases with age.
   (5) About 73 percent of people aged 30 to 39 reported voting in the 1996 presidential election.

Answers and explanations start on page 643.

CIVICS AND GOVERNMENT PRACTICE QUESTIONS

Choose the one best answer to each question.

Question 1 refers to the following chart.

Political Divisions in the 107th Congress, January 2001

Party	House	Senate
Republicans	221	50
Democrats	211	50
Other	2	In case of tie, Vice President Dick Cheney (R.) votes
Vacant	1	—

1. Which of the following is the best summary of the chart above?

   (1) The Congress is made up of the House and the Senate.
   (2) The Senate is split equally between the two major parties.
   (3) The House has far more members than the Senate.
   (4) The 107th Congress started its session in January of 2001.
   (5) In January 2001, Republicans controlled the 107th Congress by a small margin.

2. In 1215, English nobles limited royal power by forcing King John to accept the Magna Carta. This document gave certain rights to nobles, such as protection of private property, trial by jury, and religious freedoms.

   Which of the following documents has the most in common with the Magna Carta?

   (1) the Mayflower Compact, establishing a government for Plymouth colony
   (2) the Bill of Rights of the U.S. Constitution, guaranteeing citizens certain rights
   (3) the Albany Plan of Union, calling for a colonial confederation
   (4) the Declaration of Independence, justifying America's break with England
   (5) the Federalist Papers, persuading people to ratify the U.S. Constitution

Questions 3 and 4 refer to the following passage.

In 1979, Congress passed legislation to allow political parties to raise unlimited amounts of money for general purposes, not designated for particular candidates. In 1991, a lawsuit forced disclosure of such "soft money" contributions, and concern grew about the size of individual donations, the extent of total donations, and the ways in which the money was being spent. During the presidential elections of 1996 and 2000, campaign fund-raising, especially the raising and spending of soft money, was an issue, with the candidates promising reform. Finally, in 2001, after several years of hearings, the Senate passed the McCain-Feingold bill, which would eliminate the unregulated soft money contributions that make up a large proportion of the parties' budgets.

3. Which of the following is an example of a soft money contribution?

   (1) a $250 ticket to a fund-raising dinner-dance to benefit a mayoral candidate
   (2) a $3,000 donation to the campaign fund of an incumbent senator
   (3) a $3,000 contribution to a party fund for TV ads on political issues
   (4) a $750 donation to the primary campaign of a would-be congressional representative
   (5) a $1,000 gift to a senator's campaign fund in response to a direct mail solicitation

4. Which of the following is the most likely reason soft money was not a major issue in the 1980s?

   (1) The political parties spent very little money trying to win elections in the 1980s.
   (2) People were less aware of soft money because disclosure was not required.
   (3) Political campaigns were publicly financed, so soft money was not needed.
   (4) Most candidates spent part of their campaign funds on television ads.
   (5) McCain and Feingold had not submitted their campaign finance reform bill.

Questions 5 and 6 refer to the following paragraph and graphs.

In order to win a presidential election, a candidate must win a majority of the vote in the Electoral College. Each state has as many electors as it has senators and representatives in Congress. In most states, the winner of the popular vote gets all the electoral votes of the state. These graphs show the popular and Electoral College votes in the election of 1992.

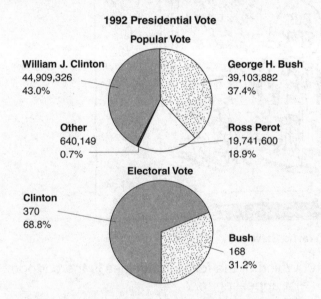

1992 Presidential Vote

Popular Vote

William J. Clinton
44,909,326
43.0%

George H. Bush
39,103,882
37.4%

Other
640,149
0.7%

Ross Perot
19,741,600
18.9%

Electoral Vote

Clinton
370
68.8%

Bush
168
31.2%

5. Which of the following statements is supported by the information in the paragraph and the graphs?

(1) Third party candidates like Perot have never succeeded in winning a majority of the Electoral College vote.
(2) Bush won a greater percentage of the Electoral College vote than the popular vote in the 1992 election.
(3) In most Presidential elections, the winner of the popular vote is also the winner of the Electoral College vote.
(4) Perot won a greater percentage of the popular vote than the Electoral College vote in the 1992 election.
(5) Clinton won a majority of the popular vote as well as a majority of the Electoral College vote.

6. Which of the following would be the best title for the paragraph and the graphs?

(1) The 1992 Election
(2) The Bush-Clinton Election
(3) A Third-Party Presidential Race
(4) Winning the Electoral College
(5) The Popular and Electoral Votes

Question 7 refers to the following passage.

Where do I vote? Your voting district is determined by your place of residence. Watch your local newspaper for an announcement indicating polling locations and times, or contact your local board of election to determine your voting location.

You may also obtain your polling place location by accessing the web site of the Office of the Secretary of State at www.anystate.us. You may also call the Office of the Secretary of State for assistance.

7. Which of the following is assumed but not stated outright in the voter guide above?

(1) The board of election is the county, city, or town office responsible for local voting.
(2) A voter's polling place is determined by his or her address.
(3) Polling locations appear in newspapers.
(4) A voter can find his or her polling place on the Internet.
(5) A voter can call the Office of the Secretary of State to find out where to vote.

8. An interest group is an organization with specific goals that seeks to influence government policies.

Which of the following is an interest group?

(1) the Democratic Party, which nominates candidates and tries to win elections
(2) the National Association of Manufacturers, which lobbies for businesses
(3) the Federal Communications Commission, which regulates broadcasters
(4) the U.S. Department of Agriculture, which oversees American farming
(5) the Cabinet, which is an advisory body for the president

© Wayne Stayskal. Reprinted by permission of Wayne Stayskal.

9. What is the main idea of this cartoon?

(1) Most voters are working people.
(2) Most registered voters don't vote.
(3) Voters should establish another political party.
(4) A non-voters' party would lose every election.
(5) People should register to vote.

10. Which of the following values is the cartoonist appealing for?

(1) the work ethic
(2) majority rule
(3) civic duty
(4) national pride
(5) religious tolerance

11. An oligarchy is a system of government in which a small group of people holds power.

Which of the following is an oligarchy?

(1) France, with a president and an elected legislature
(2) China, where the top leaders of the Communist party control the government
(3) Iraq, which has a dictator, Saddam Hussein
(4) Great Britain, with a monarch, a prime minister, and an elected Parliament
(5) Greece, with a prime minister and an elected Parliament

12. Three typical laws from the code of Hammurabi, written about 1700 B.C., are "If a son strike his father, his hands shall be hewn off. If a man put out the eye of another man, his eye shall be put out. If he break another man's bone, his bone shall be broken."

What principal underlies these laws?

(1) retribution
(2) rehabilitation
(3) incarceration
(4) mercy
(5) mediation

Question 13 and 14 refer to the following map and table.

The Death Penalty in the United States

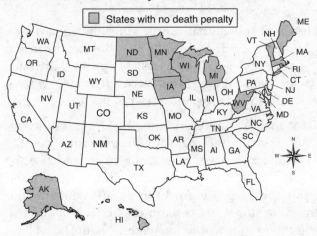

States with no death penalty

Homicide Rate per 100,000 Population

Highest	Lowest
Louisiana, 12.8	North Dakota, 1.1
Mississippi, 11.4	South Dakota, 1.4
New Mexico, 10.9	New Hampshire, 1.5
Maryland, 10.0	Iowa, 1.9
Nevada, 9.7	Massachusetts, 2.0

SOURCE: National Center for Health Statistics and U.S. Bureau of the Census.

13. How many states have the death penalty?

(1) 12
(2) 18
(3) 24
(4) 38
(5) 46

14. People who favor capital punishment usually argue that it prevents serious crimes like homicide. Based on the map and chart, what is a logical flaw with this argument?

(1) When the state puts an inmate to death, it diminishes the respect for life.
(2) A life sentence without parole costs taxpayers more than executing an inmate.
(3) Some executed inmates have turned out to be innocent based on new evidence.
(4) Most states in the Upper Midwest do not have the death penalty.
(5) Three of the five states with the lowest homicide rates do not have the death penalty.

15. The U.S. Constitution gives the president the power to make treaties with foreign nations, and it gives the Senate the power to "advise and consent" on all treaties. Thus a two-thirds majority of the Senate must ratify any treaty presented by the president. In 1978, President Jimmy Carter persuaded the Senate to ratify treaties with Panama that transferred control of the Panama Canal from the United States to Panama. Many Americans were outraged and believed that U.S. interests had been given away.

Which of the following is an opinion rather than a statement of fact?

(1) Presidents have the power to enter into treaties with foreign nations.
(2) The Senate has the power to reject or ratify treaties with foreign nations.
(3) A two-thirds majority of the Senate is needed to ratify a treaty.
(4) The Panama treaties sold out U.S. interests to Panama.
(5) The Panama treaties gave control of the Panama Canal to Panama.

16. In the mayor-council form of city government, voters elect both a mayor and a city council. The mayor is the city's chief executive, operating the city on a day-to-day basis and also serving a ceremonial function. The city council is a legislative body, in charge of the city's finances and passing city laws. In the council-manager form of city government, voters elect a city council that makes city policies and laws. The council may elect a mayor who has a largely ceremonial function. It appoints a professionally trained city manager to oversee day-to-day operations.

What is the main similarity between the mayor's role in the mayor-council and in the council-manager forms of city government?

(1) The mayor sets policy.
(2) The mayor runs day-to-day operations.
(3) The mayor is elected by voters.
(4) The mayor has ceremonial duties.
(5) The mayor passes city laws.

Answers and explanations start on page 644.

ECONOMICS

Basic Economics Concepts

Key Ideas

- Businesses utilize capital, labor, and materials to create goods and services to sell.
- Markets are systems that bring sellers' goods and services to buyers.
- The prices of goods and services are determined in part by supply and demand.

In economics, *capital* is a term for things that can produce income. Money can be capital; so can equipment, land, and buildings. Businesses invest capital in order to create **goods** and **services** to sell for profit. However, capital by itself cannot create value. **Labor,** the work of human beings, transforms capital and materials into goods and services that can be sold.

For example, a business that makes computers must make capital investments to build a factory and install equipment for **production.** Then the business must hire workers and managers to run the plant and use the equipment. The business must also buy the materials and parts to build the computers. The materials and parts are **producer goods,** while the finished computers, ready to sell in stores, are **consumer goods.** Not all businesses make or build objects. Some businesses create value by selling intangible services to their customers—such as an employment agency that offers the service of matching people with jobs.

Markets are established routines and networks for selling and buying goods and services. There are producers' markets for producer goods; there are **retail** and **wholesale** markets for consumer goods; there are markets for **raw materials** such as minerals; there are financial markets for selling stocks and bonds. Some markets are more highly organized than others, and all markets are regulated by law to some extent. But markets, by definition, are not completely under the control of any government or agency.

Goods and services are **distributed** through markets so that they can be **consumed** where they are wanted. Through the market system, sellers and buyers negotiate prices and contracts; they **compete** for the best terms possible in that market. For example, a computer manufacturer might enter the consumer electronics market, competing with other manufacturers to sell its goods at a fair price to retailers. The retailers negotiate contracts specifying how many computers they are willing to buy and distribute to consumers through their stores or catalogs.

How are prices determined in the market system? In economics, price is related to **supply** and **demand.** Sellers need to earn money on the goods they have produced. Buyers want to spend as little as possible. When the supply of something is large, buyers shop around looking for the best price, and sellers lower their prices in order to move their **inventory.** On the other hand, if a product is **scarce,** buyers are less able to shop around, and sellers can raise their prices. When Florida has a hard freeze and fruit growers lose their citrus crops, the price of oranges goes up. That is because there are fewer oranges to buy and fewer sellers to buy them from, so those sellers can charge more.

Supply and demand most clearly influence price in a **free market economy.** The U.S. economy operates primarily, but not completely, as a free market. For example, governmental **price supports** ensure that farmers can sell certain agricultural products at prices that allow them to earn a profit.

ECONOMICS ▶ PRACTICE 1

Choose the one best answer to each question.

1. What is the main role of labor in an economy?

   (1) to provide capital to start new businesses
   (2) to convert capital and raw materials into products and services
   (3) to purchase all the goods and services that are produced
   (4) to perform manual tasks in factories and offices
   (5) to purchase raw materials in retail and wholesale markets

2. Which of the following is an example of a producer good rather than a consumer good?

   (1) a pencil
   (2) a can opener
   (3) a cell phone
   (4) a lawn chair
   (5) a plastic material

3. When there are very few houses for sale in an area, the real estate market is said to be a seller's market.

   Why is this name appropriate?

   (1) When the supply of houses is less than the demand, sellers can raise their prices.
   (2) When the supply of houses is less than the demand, sellers will offer less than list price.
   (3) Sellers are always at an advantage in the real estate market.
   (4) Competition among buyers lowers prices.
   (5) Competition among sellers raises prices.

4. Why might the U.S. government offer price supports to farmers but not to toy manufacturers?

   (1) Toy manufacturers change most of their product line each year.
   (2) Toy sales vary widely, depending on the appeal of a particular toy.
   (3) Toys are not critical to a nation's economic and political well-being.
   (4) Toys are sold to adults for use by children.
   (5) Toys are distributed through conventional wholesale and retail channels.

Questions 5 and 6 refer to the following graph.

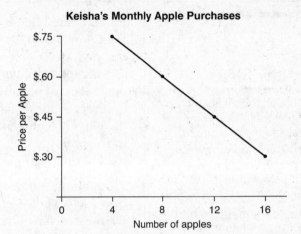

Keisha's Monthly Apple Purchases

5. When apples cost 30 cents each, how many apples does Keisha buy each month?

   (1) 0
   (2) 4
   (3) 8
   (4) 12
   (5) 16

6. Which of the following conclusions is supported by the data on the graph?

   (1) As the supply of apples rises, Keisha buys fewer apples.
   (2) As the supply of apples rises, the demand for apples falls.
   (3) As the price of apples rises, Keisha buys fewer apples.
   (4) As the price of apples falls, Keisha buys the same number of apples.
   (5) Keisha will buy the same number of apples regardless of the price per apple.

7. Which of the following is a service business?

   (1) a tool manufacturer
   (2) a paper mill
   (3) a bicycle repair shop
   (4) a microchip factory
   (5) an oil company

Answers and explanations start on page 644.

ECONOMICS

The U.S. Economic System

In the United States, the economic activity of individual people and businesses primarily determines our economic health and growth. We make our own decisions about how to save and spend most of our income. We can accept employment as we choose, become **entrepreneurs** and build businesses of our own, and seek education and training to whatever level best serves our goals. These freedoms are based on **laissez-faire capitalism,** the ideas of eighteenth-century economist Adam Smith, who believed that if individuals are free to act in their own best interests economically, the sum total of their actions will be in the best interests of the society as a whole.

Throughout the history of the United States, **free enterprise** and **competition** have played important roles in the development of our economy. Businesses have incentives to grow larger—either by expanding their **capacity** or by integrating a broader set of functions into their **operations**—in order to make more **profit.** However, businesses are expected to compete with each other on the merits of their products and operations. Businesses are not allowed to form **monopolies**—single companies that control whole industries; they also are not allowed to form **oligopolies**—tight-knit groups of companies that control whole industries.

Because the U.S. economy is not under government control, no one can predict or control exactly how the economy will behave. Our economy tends to move through a **business cycle** with identifiable phases, but the length and strength of a cycle and its phases vary greatly. The first phase of a cycle is the growth phase, in which businesses invest and expand optimistically. At some point, growth is slowed or stopped by one or more factors—limited resources, limited production capacity, tight employment, or market **saturation**—and the economy enters a slowdown phase. As businesses lay off workers, stop investing their capital, and cut back production, the economy enters a **recession** or **depression** phase. Unemployment rises, consumer spending slows down, and businesses act very conservatively, holding down wages and prices, avoiding risks, and managing cash flow tightly. Eventually, the economy moves into a recovery phase, perhaps initiated by a government action. Recovery may be slow or uneven across economic sectors, but eventually the economy moves into a new growth phase. **Inflation,** in which the combined price of goods and services rises over time, is only partly related to these business cycle phases.

Banking and investment services, like most U.S. industries, are conducted on principles of free enterprise. A major role of **banks** and **savings and loan associations** is to create pools of savings in order to make money available as credit to businesses and consumers. **Stock exchanges** have a similar purpose; they allow investors to purchase shares of stock, which represent part ownership of a business. Both saving and investing make funds available for businesses to use to grow. When people invest in stock, they take risks because the value of the stock depends on the success of the business. However, the potential **return** is generally much higher than the **interest rate** on a savings account.

ECONOMICS ▸ PRACTICE 2

Choose the one best answer to each question.

1. Based on the passage on page 208, why are monopolies not permitted in the United States?

   (1) Monopolies are too efficient.
   (2) Monopolies are part of laissez-faire capitalism.
   (3) Monopolies result from free enterprise.
   (4) Monopolies buy up smaller businesses.
   (5) Monopolies shut out competition.

2. According to the passage, which of the following is characteristic of a recession?

   (1) job growth
   (2) large investments of capital
   (3) increased consumer spending
   (4) rising unemployment
   (5) wage increases

3. Private ownership of property (land or buildings) is a key characteristic of the free enterprise system. Owning property gives people a strong incentive to take care of it and use it productively.

   What is the basis for this incentive?

   (1) Property owners have a stake in the future value of the property.
   (2) Property owners work harder than tenants do.
   (3) Property owners can do whatever they like with their property.
   (4) Property owners are given tax incentives by the federal government.
   (5) Property owners must pay real estate taxes to local government.

4. Which of the following investments carries the most risk?

   (1) Opening a savings account at a local bank.
   (2) Buying a certificate of deposit at a savings and loan institution.
   (3) Depositing money in a checking account.
   (4) Buying stock in a new company, such as an Internet startup.
   (5) Buying stock in an established company, such as General Motors.

Question 5 refers to the following paragraph and graph.

At different times during the business cycle, the gross domestic product—the total value of goods and services produced in a year—rises and falls.

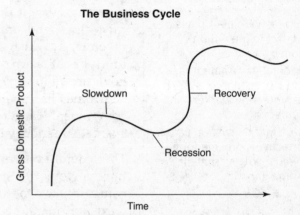

5. Which of the following conclusions is supported by the paragraph and the graph?

   (1) High points in the business cycle are generally followed by recoveries.
   (2) Low points in the business cycle are generally followed by slowdowns.
   (3) During recessions, the rate of unemployment drops.
   (4) Despite ups and downs, the gross domestic product generally increases over time.
   (5) The gross domestic product is a measure of the value of manufactured goods alone.

6. What do saving and investing in stocks have in common?

   (1) They provide capital for businesses to grow.
   (2) They provide a sure rate of return.
   (3) They pay a fixed rate of interest.
   (4) They are without risk.
   (5) They are part of a company's profit.

Answers and explanations start on page 645.

ECONOMICS

The Economy and the U.S. Government

Although the United States has primarily a free market economy, the U.S. government does have important economic functions. Both the executive and the legislative branches of government are involved in setting the U.S. government **budget.** The government has considerable impact on our economy, since it determines our taxes, employs many people, and borrows and spends much money. The federal budget may have a **surplus** of **revenue,** in which case elected leaders may either spend the additional funds or cut taxes; or the budget may have a revenue **deficit,** requiring the government to borrow money to cover its expenses. Government spending sometimes has a very direct impact on the economy. For example, if the government wants to boost the national economy out of a recession, it may spend extra money on projects that create new jobs.

The federal government is also responsible for maintaining good conditions for our free market system. The government must have laws and courts in place to maintain property rights. It must enforce fair legal standards for operating a business. The federal government provides a stable **currency** and operates the U.S. Mint, which makes coins and prints paper money. Our central banking system, the **Federal Reserve System,** manages the total amount of money available for lending and borrowing in the private banking system and partially controls interest rates. The **Federal Deposit Insurance Corporation** (FDIC) insures the money in individual bank accounts in case of bank fraud or failure.

One of the fundamental purposes of the federal government is to promote the general welfare of the nation. Therefore, the government takes over many functions that the free market system does not provide. For example, the free market does not distribute wealth according to what people need to live on, so the government collects taxes to redistribute some money to people who don't earn enough. The government also provides **infrastructure,** such as interstate highways, that indirectly supports economic activity.

Another role for government in the economy is protecting workers from health dangers and exploitation. The **Occupational Safety and Health Administration** (OSHA) is a special federal agency charged to protect workers on the job, particularly in hazardous industries. Many federal and state laws also protect the interests of workers. For example, all states regulate the hours and types of work that children may perform. A number of agencies are involved in enforcing safe and fair working conditions; they visit businesses, investigate reports of problems, identify violations, and initiate prosecution in some cases.

Another group of agencies protects consumers from fraudulent business practices and unsafe products. The **Food and Drug Administration** (FDA) is responsible for making sure that food products are safe, drugs are effective, and cosmetics and drugs are labeled properly. The **Federal Trade Commission** (FTC) ensures that product claims in advertising and on package labels are true and complete.

ECONOMICS ▸ PRACTICE 3

Choose the one best answer to each question.

1. When does the U.S. government have a budget surplus?

   (1) when the U.S. Treasury issues bonds
   (2) when the national debt is rising
   (3) when the government boosts the economy
   (4) when expenditures exceed revenues
   (5) when revenues exceed expenditures

2. Which of the following legislative actions would lead to a direct increase in consumer spending?

   (1) raising Social Security contributions
   (2) funding the Food and Drug Administration
   (3) decreasing spending on federal work projects
   (4) cutting the federal income tax
   (5) ratifying an international trade agreement

3. Which of the following is an example of infra-structure that supports economic activity?

   (1) federal regulatory agencies
   (2) the annual federal budget
   (3) local sales taxes
   (4) the air traffic control system
   (5) the Federal Reserve System

4. The federal government has two main ways to manipulate the economy. The first is fiscal policy, in which the government increases or decreases taxes and spending to influence the economy. The second is monetary policy, in which the government increases or decreases the supply of money in order to stimulate or slow the economy.

   What is the main similarity between fiscal and monetary policy?

   (1) Both involve raising taxes.
   (2) Both involve lowering taxes.
   (3) Both involve raising expenditures.
   (4) Both are budgetary tools of state governments.
   (5) Both affect the amount of money circulating in the economy.

Questions 5 and 6 refer to the following paragraph and chart.

Monetary policy affects the amount of money in circulation. When there is rapid economic growth and a risk of inflation, the Federal Reserve System (the "Fed") slows it down by tightening the money supply. This makes it more difficult for people and businesses to borrow and spend money. When the economy is sluggish, the Fed increases the money supply to stimulate borrowing and spending.

The Fed's Monetary Policy Options

To Take Money Out of Circulation	To Put Money into Circulation
Sell government securities (bonds and Treasury bills)	Buy government securities
Raise the discount rate member banks are charged to borrow from the Fed	Lower the discount rate
Raise the reserve requirement, the amount banks must keep on hand to cover deposits	Lower the reserve requirement

5. Which of the following Fed actions would stimulate the economy?

   (1) selling government securities
   (2) buying government securities
   (3) raising the discount rate
   (4) raising the reserve requirement
   (5) tightening the money supply

6. Since the Fed's monetary policy options have such specific effects, why does the Fed sometimes fail to head off recession or stimulate recovery?

   (1) The Fed's board meets only four times a year.
   (2) The people on the Fed's board lack experience.
   (3) The Fed usually makes poor policy decisions.
   (4) Our complex economy takes time to respond.
   (5) Our economy can be controlled only by international economic forces.

Answers and explanations start on page 645.

ECONOMICS

Labor and Consumer Issues

Key Ideas

- Workers earn wages and some benefits and protections in exchange for their labor.
- The U.S. economy is now in a time of rapid change, and workers must prepare themselves to adapt.
- Consumers must protect themselves by being aware of risks and by spending their money wisely.

ON THE GED

Some of the economics questions on the test will be based on everyday topics faced by workers and consumers.

As workers, we earn **wages** and other **benefits** in exchange for our labor. People who are paid hourly wages are paid only for the number of hours they work. Their earnings may fluctuate depending on how much their labor is needed. People who earn salaries typically receive the same constant pay all the time, although their hours worked may fluctuate. Some people are paid for "piecework"—that is, for each piece of work they complete. Many workers receive benefits in addition to their wages, such as health insurance, vacation pay, and special savings plans. A worker's total **compensation** for a job is the combined value of wages and benefits.

Workers and their employers must pay taxes and buy insurance to cover work-related problems, including injury, disability, and **unemployment.** Workers who lose their jobs because they are fired or laid off usually can receive unemployment benefits for a time or until they find new jobs. Sometimes workers lose their jobs because of major economic changes. For example, rapid changes in the steel industry drove out much of the steel manufacturing in the United States. Plants closed, and workers who thought they would spend their lives making good wages in steel mills suddenly found their skills worthless. In most cases, these workers had to learn new skills. This kind of rapid change is common in our modern times. Because so many markets are international, and because transportation, communication, and shipping are possible even over very long distances, businesses can change strategies very quickly and change their workforce as a result. Workers need to anticipate changes in their industries and continually seek new training in order to be prepared for change.

Most workers have direct, individual agreements with their employers. However, **labor unions** are common in certain industries and professions. Through **collective bargaining,** unions negotiate contracts for wages and working conditions on behalf of all union members. If these negotiations fail, the union can call a **strike,** in which workers refuse to work. When labor-management negotiations break down, federal **mediators** may be asked to intervene. The National Labor Relations Board helps companies and unions resolve disputes.

We all participate in the U.S. economy as **consumers.** The free market system offers U.S. consumers an amazing array of choices for the goods and services we want. As retailers and marketers woo our business relentlessly, we should all remember the maxim, "Let the buyer beware." Although government agencies must protect consumers, consumers must also protect themselves. For example, federal laws require that potentially hazardous products have special labeling and instructions. But these will not protect us as consumers unless we read them. Parents are required by law to strap their small children into automobile safety seats. But if the seats are incorrectly installed, the children are still at risk. Retailers who offer credit payment plans are required to disclose the interest rate, payment amount, and number of payments, but it's up to consumers to work out the total expense and compare the total with the purchase price of the item.

ECONOMICS ▶ PRACTICE 4

Choose the one best answer to each question.

1. What is a worker's total compensation?

    (1) wages only
    (2) benefits only
    (3) wages and benefits
    (4) a form of insurance
    (5) the amount received in unemployment benefits

2. Reread the second paragraph on page 212. Which of the following statements is a conclusion rather than a supporting detail related to the paragraph?

    (1) Workers must learn skills throughout their lives to be prepared for changes in their industries.
    (2) Most steel manufacturing moved out of the United States.
    (3) Many steelworkers found themselves unemployed.
    (4) Many steelworkers had to retrain themselves and learn new skills.
    (5) Workers sometimes lose their jobs because of major economic restructuring.

3. Which of the following people is acting as a consumer?

    (1) a person working in a shopping mall
    (2) a young adult enrolled in a community college
    (3) a woman buying a computer
    (4) a teen starting a babysitting cooperative
    (5) a man collecting unemployment insurance

4. Which of the following proverbs expresses the principle that underlies labor unions?

    (1) All for one and one for all.
    (2) The bad worker always blames his tools.
    (3) Strike while the iron is hot.
    (4) Work expands to fill the time available.
    (5) Many hands make light work.

Questions 5 and 6 refer to the following graph.

SOURCE: *Statistical Abstract of the United States, 2000.*

5. When was civilian unemployment at its lowest during the decade shown on the graph?

    (1) in 1990
    (2) in 1992
    (3) in 1994
    (4) in 1996
    (5) in 2000

6. Which of the following statements is supported by the data in the graph?

    (1) People who have stopped looking for work are not counted among the unemployed.
    (2) As the number of employed civilians rose steadily from 1990 to 2000, the number of unemployed slowly declined.
    (3) The rate of civilian unemployment during the 1990s exceeded the rate of civilian employment.
    (4) Unemployed civilians made up about 25 percent of the total civilian workforce from 1990 to 2000.
    (5) As civilian employment rose from 1990 to 2000, the number of unemployed civilians also rose.

Answers and explanations start on page 645.

ECONOMICS PRACTICE QUESTIONS

Choose the <u>one best answer</u> to each question.

<u>Questions 1 through 3</u> refer to the following passage.

In order to produce goods and services, a free market economy must have four factors of production: (1) land, including natural resources; (2) capital, including money, factories, and machinery; (3) labor, the people who produce goods and services; and (4) entrepreneurs, business people who take risks to organize the other factors of production into businesses that will produce a profit.

1. Which of the following best defines the factors of production?

   (1) the political organizations that support an economy
   (2) the various types of resources needed for an economy to produce goods and services
   (3) the way in which the work flow is organized in a factory or office
   (4) the amount of money and equipment needed to produce goods
   (5) all the transactions involved in producing goods and services

2. In a communist economy, a central government makes all of the economic decisions.

   Which factor of production is not part of a communist economy?

   (1) land
   (2) natural resources
   (3) capital
   (4) labor
   (5) entrepreneurs

3. Which of the following is an example of capital?

   (1) an office building
   (2) a deposit of iron ore
   (3) rich agricultural soil
   (4) a skilled engineer
   (5) the founder of a publishing business

4. Many fiscal conservatives believe that the U.S. budget should be balanced, with spending equal to income. They think it is wrong for the government to influence the economy by manipulating taxes or by borrowing. Instead, they feel that a balanced budget reassures business leaders that the economy is solid.

   Which of the following statements is a fact?

   (1) Our country needs a balanced budget.
   (2) In a balanced budget, revenues equal expenditures.
   (3) The government should not use the budget to tinker with the economy.
   (4) The government should not borrow money to balance the budget.
   (5) A balanced government budget is the best indicator that the economy is healthy.

<u>Question 5</u> refers to the following graph.

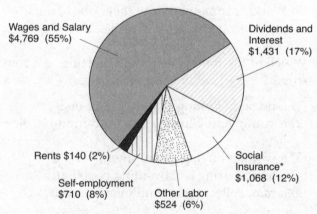

U.S. Personal Income Sources, 2000
(Billions of Dollars)

Wages and Salary $4,769 (55%)
Dividends and Interest $1,431 (17%)
Rents $140 (2%)
Self-employment $710 (8%)
Other Labor $524 (6%)
Social Insurance* $1,068 (12%)

*Social insurance includes Social Security and other government benefits.
SOURCE: U.S. Department of Commerce.

5. Which of the following statements is supported by the data on the graph?

   (1) More than half of all personal income was earned through work in 2000.
   (2) Social insurance payments accounted for one-quarter of personal income in 2000.
   (3) Interest and dividends accounted for one-third of personal income in 2000.
   (4) Per capita income was $25,379 in 2000.
   (5) U.S. personal income rose steadily in the five years prior to 2000.

Questions 6 and 7 refer to the following cartoon.

Reprinted with permission of the *Green Bay Press-Gazette*, Green Bay, Wisconsin.

6. Who does the man in the plaid shorts repre-sent?

(1) a retiree
(2) an American taxpayer
(3) a corporate executive
(4) an investor
(5) a member of a labor union

7. Why is the man in the plaid shorts calm about his ride on the roller coaster?

(1) He enjoys riding on roller coasters.
(2) He makes his living repairing roller coasters.
(3) He has made money buying bonds.
(4) He is accustomed to stock market ups and downs.
(5) All of his retirement savings are in stocks.

8. Employers withhold, or take out, federal income tax from their employees' paychecks. However, some people need to make estimated tax payments. According to the Internal Revenue Service, "Estimated tax is the method used to pay tax on income that is not subject to withholding (for example, earnings from self-employment, interest, dividends, rents, alimony, etc. . . .)"

Which of the following people is most likely to need to make estimated tax payments?

(1) a factory worker
(2) a student working part-time at the university
(3) a person who runs a home day-care center
(4) a gas station attendant
(5) a receptionist in a medical office

9. In a free market economy, people make their own decisions about working, buying goods and property, and starting businesses. Which of the following is most likely to be highly val-ued in nations with free market economies?

(1) cooperation
(2) individualism
(3) job security
(4) economic equality
(5) family values

Questions 10 and 11 refer to the following graph.

U.S. Revenues and Expenditures, 1996–2000

SOURCE: U.S. Department of Commerce.

10. Which of the following conclusions does the data on the graph support?

   (1) In 1998, government revenues declined.
   (2) In 1998, government expenditures declined.
   (3) The United States had a budget surplus in 1998.
   (4) The United States had a budget deficit in 2000.
   (5) The United States increased its borrowing rate between 1996 and 2000.

11. If a family wanted to make a graph of its economic situation similar to this graph of U.S. revenues and expenditures, what documents for the years 1996 to 2000 would be most useful?

   (1) records showing all family members' sources of income
   (2) income tax returns and expense records
   (3) expense records and credit card bills
   (4) credit card bills and rent or mortgage statements
   (5) records showing the value of the family's possessions

12. The Interstate Highway System, begun in 1956, consists of more than 45,000 miles of four- to eight-lane highways connecting most large U.S. cities. The federal government pays for almost 90 percent of the building and maintenance of interstate highways out of receipts from excise taxes on gasoline, tires, truck parts, and other related products.

Which of the following best summarizes this information?

   (1) In 1956, the federal government established the Interstate Highway System.
   (2) The Interstate Highway System links most major cities.
   (3) The Interstate Highway System consists of thousands of miles of large highways.
   (4) The federal government collects excise taxes on transportation-related items.
   (5) The national network of interstate highways is paid for mostly by federal excise taxes.

13. In recent years, the United States has lowered protective tariffs (charges on goods imported from other countries), arguing that lower tariffs encourage free trade and benefit consumers by decreasing the cost of imported goods.

From the perspective of a U.S. factory worker, what is the flaw in this argument?

   (1) When cheaper imported goods force out U.S.-made goods, U.S. factory workers often lose their jobs.
   (2) Free trade leads to cheaper imported goods because the cost of labor is less in many other nations.
   (3) Factory workers cannot afford to buy imported consumer goods even if they are cheaper than U.S.-made goods.
   (4) Lower protective tariffs actually raise the prices of all goods whether they are made in the United States or in foreign countries.
   (5) The U.S. economy has shifted from an agricultural to an industrial to a service economy.

Question 14 refers to the following chart.

U.S. Consumer Protection

Agency	Function
Food and Drug Administration	Protects public from poorly processed and improperly labeled foods and drugs
Federal Trade Commission	Protects consumers from misleading and/or fraudulent advertising
Consumer Product Safety Commission	Protects consumers from risk of injury or death from hazardous products
Securities and Exchange Commission	Protects investors from being misled about stocks and bonds
National Highway Traffic Safety Administration	Protects consumers by testing vehicle safety and monitoring nationwide speed limits

14. Which agency would be involved in a dispute over a commercial that implied something about a product that was not true?

(1) the Food and Drug Administration
(2) the Federal Trade Commission
(3) the Consumer Product Safety Commission
(4) the Securities and Exchange Commission
(5) the National Highway Traffic and Safety Administration

15. Equilibrium occurs when the supply of a product or service equals the demand for it. A product tends to be priced at the equilibrium point. When the price is greater than the equilibrium point, demand decreases and there is an oversupply of the product on the market.

What is the result of the price falling below the equilibrium point?

(1) Demand decreases.
(2) There is a shortage of the product.
(3) There is a surplus of the product.
(4) The equilibrium point decreases.
(5) The equilibrium point increases.

16. One approach to the study of economics is called macroeconomics. Macroeconomics deals with economies as a whole. For instance, a macroeconomist might study the causes of inflation or the factors that determine why some national economies grow quickly and others do not.

Which of the following is most likely to be studied by a macroeconomist?

(1) how a firm prices its products or services
(2) what causes high rates of unemployment
(3) how a company makes a profit
(4) what determines consumer demand for a product
(5) how a factory makes production decisions

Question 17 refers to the following graph.

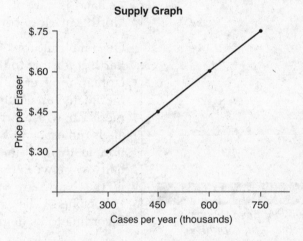

17. Which of the following conclusions is supported by the data on the graph?

(1) As the price per eraser decreases, manufacturers supply more erasers.
(2) As the price per eraser increases, manufacturers supply fewer erasers.
(3) As the price per eraser increases, manufacturers supply more erasers.
(4) As the supply of erasers increases, the demand for erasers decreases.
(5) As the supply of erasers decreases, the demand for erasers decreases.

Answers and explanations start on page 646.

GEOGRAPHY

Basic Geography Concepts

Geography focuses on the relationships between human culture and the natural features of Earth, including how those relationships vary among different regions of the world. Since interactions between people and Earth are complicated and have far-reaching implications, geography is a very broad field of study.

Oceans cover 71 percent of the surface of Earth. The three major oceans are the Atlantic, Pacific, and Indian Oceans. The Arctic Ocean is sometimes also included as a major ocean. The **continents,** including Eurasia (sometimes separated into Europe and Asia), Africa, North America, South America, Antarctica, and Australia, separate the oceans. Each continent also includes a continental shelf—the shallow ocean floor that extends to a depth of about 600 feet and surrounds the continent. Islands that sit on the continental shelf are considered part of the main continent. For example, England, Ireland, and Japan are all part of the Eurasian continent. New Zealand is part of the Australian continent, and Greenland is part of the North American continent.

Over the centuries, people have devised a system for locating places on Earth according to lines of **latitude** and **longitude.** Study these sets of horizontal and vertical lines on the maps below. Note that the longitude meridians run north and south. They are measured in relation to the prime meridian, which runs through Greenwich, England. Note that latitude parallels run east and west in circles around Earth. They are measured in relation to their distance from the **equator,** a circle marking the position halfway between the North and South poles. The area north of the equator is the Northern Hemisphere; south of the equator is the Southern Hemisphere. The exact position of any location on Earth can be identified according to its **degrees** of latitude and longitude.

Geographers identify **regions** based on both natural and man-made features. For example, the Great Plains of North America have a particular set of natural characteristics. They are flat or gently rolling, fairly dry, and covered mainly with grasses with only limited areas of forest. They also have a specific set of man-made characteristics, relating to how people use the land for farming and grazing livestock. Cultural and economic factors can be extremely important in defining a geographic region. For example, a geographer might distinguish an **agricultural** region from an **urban** region even though both are within the Great Plains.

Latitude and Longitude

  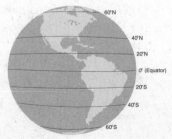

Choose the one best answer to each question.

1. To what continent do England, Ireland, and Japan belong?

   (1) Europe
   (2) Asia
   (3) Eurasia
   (4) Australia
   (5) South America

2. What is the main difference between lines of latitude and longitude?

   (1) Lines of latitude form circles and lines of longitude form ovals.
   (2) Lines of latitude are measured in miles, and lines of longitude are measured in degrees.
   (3) Lines of latitude are measured in degrees, and lines of longitude are measured in miles.
   (4) Lines of latitude run north-south, and lines of longitude run east-west.
   (5) Lines of latitude run east-west, and lines of longitude run north-south.

3. A branch of the military wants to pinpoint a target site for bombing practice.

   Which of the following describes the location of the target site most accurately?

   (1) the distances from two nearby cities
   (2) the distance from the nearest city
   (3) the latitude and longitude
   (4) the prime meridian
   (5) the distance from the equator

4. How do geographers define a region?

   (1) by its natural and man-made features
   (2) by its size
   (3) by its location
   (4) by its distance from the nearest ocean
   (5) by its distance from the North and South poles

Questions 5 and 6 refer to the following paragraph.

Some geographers argue that it makes more sense to divide the United States into cultural regions than into states. According to these geographers, many political state boundaries are meaningless. For example, North and South Dakota are part of a single cultural region with similar terrain and agriculture. In fact, before North and South Dakota became separate states, they formed the Dakota Territory. Many metropolitan regions provide examples of cultural regions that are more meaningful than local state boundaries. For example, a person who lives in northeastern New Jersey is actually part of the New York metropolitan region and probably has more in common with other people in the metro region than with people who live in the southern, rural part of New Jersey.

5. Which of the following statements is an opinion rather than a fact?

   (1) North and South Dakota have similar physical and economic characteristics.
   (2) North and South Dakota were formerly united in the Dakota Territory.
   (3) The southern part of New Jersey is rural, and the northeastern part is urban.
   (4) The United States should be divided into cultural regions rather than states.
   (5) The New York metropolitan region encompasses areas from neighboring states.

6. Which of the following is an example of a cultural region rather than a political unit?

   (1) the state of Pennsylvania in the United States
   (2) the island of Greenland, a possession of Denmark
   (3) the St. Louis metropolitan region, which includes portions of Missouri and Illinois
   (4) the Sudan, a nation in Africa with a Muslim majority in the north and a Christian majority in the south
   (5) the nation of Canada in North America

Answers and explanations start on page 647.

GEOGRAPHY

Humans and the Environment

Key Ideas

- When populations grow, decline, or shift, changes in geographic regions occur.
- Populations change as a result of many different political and economic factors.
- Population growth and urbanization have a negative impact on the environment.

GED TIP

Some questions give a definition and ask you to apply it. To answer an application question such as number 2 on page 221, check each of the answer options against the given definition.

Populations—particularly the movement and growth of population groups—play a major role in defining and altering geographic regions. A population may be **native** to a geographic area, as the Taino, for example, were native to the Caribbean when Columbus arrived there. Sometimes population groups **migrate** over long distances, as did many Irish people who came to the United States during the Potato Famine in the mid-1800s. However, when people feel strong ties to a place, they may stay there even when conditions are unfavorable; they may even develop new economic and cultural strategies that strengthen their population. The **distribution** of population within a region depends on many factors, not all of which humans can control. People tend to move where there are resources, jobs, and other favorable conditions. But these conditions are ever changing, depending on politics, climate, economic development, and so on.

Urban and **rural** development have a strong impact on the distribution of a population. Industrialized regions generally see their populations shift away from rural areas into cities and towns. **Suburban** development very often follows urban growth. As cities become crowded, the urban population spreads into the countryside, often taking up agricultural lands for housing and commercial development. Agriculture also changes in most industrialized regions. Farming is done on an larger scale by fewer people using more mechanized tools. Industrialized regions usually can support a larger population at a higher standard of living than nonindustrialized regions. However, these regions also may lose some of their distinctive traditional cultures, arts, farming methods, and so on.

When political boundaries are in dispute, or ethnic groups declare war on each other, local population shifts may dramatically change the character of a region. For example, during World War II, Hitler depopulated Europe of millions of Jews through deportation and death camps. After World War II, the state of Israel was established in the Middle East, drawing many Jews to the region. Continuing conflicts within the Middle East have led to further population shifts of different Arab and Jewish groups there.

When human populations grow, they significantly affect the natural environment. **Manufacturing** and **urbanization** cause air and water **pollution**. Commercial agriculture tends to degrade both soil and water. Eventually food and water supplies become endangered. For example, these problems, along with a loss of farmland to urbanization, are very prominent in China today, where the government has been trying since the 1970s to reduce population growth.

Overall, government policies and international agreements have not been strong enough nor widely enforced when it comes to reducing the destructive impact of growing populations, large cities, and damaging agricultural methods in many parts of the world. Learning to live in harmony with one another and with the natural processes of the environment will be important as we strive to keep Earth a healthy, livable planet.

Choose the <u>one best answer</u> to each question.

1. What is migration?

   (1) a form of society in which people move on after they consume an area's resources
   (2) temporary travel to another geographic region to scout for resources
   (3) the move of an individual or population from one geographic area to settle in another
   (4) the concentration of populations in urban areas worldwide
   (5) the relative distribution of populations in urban and rural areas

2. Migration within a country's borders is called internal migration. Which of the following is an example of internal migration?

   (1) the movement of the Irish to the United States during the Potato Famine in the 1800s
   (2) the westward movement of the American population from the 1700s to the present
   (3) the movement of Mexican workers into the southwest United States during the 1900s
   (4) the forced movement of Africans from West Africa to the Americas to become slaves
   (5) the movement of people from former British colonies to Great Britain

3. What is a key difference between urban and suburban areas?

   (1) Urban areas are more densely populated.
   (2) Urban areas are more recently settled.
   (3) Urban areas lack commercial development.
   (4) Urban areas contain remnants of farms.
   (5) Urban areas have more agricultural workers.

4. Which of the following technologies was the most likely contributor to the rapid growth of suburbs in the United States?

   (1) the telephone
   (2) the telegraph
   (3) the airplane
   (4) the automobile
   (5) the computer

Questions 5 and 6 refers to the following graph.

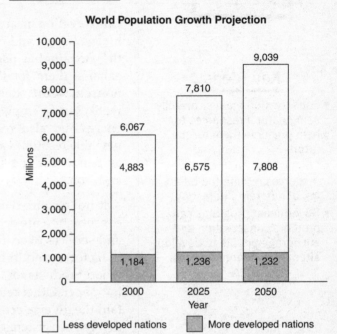

World Population Growth Projection

5. What does the figure 9,039,000,000 represent?

   (1) the total world population in 2000
   (2) the projected population of less developed nations in 2025
   (3) the projected population of less developed nations in 2050
   (4) the projected population of more developed nations in 2050
   (5) the projected total world population in 2050

6. Which of the following conclusions is supported by the data on the graph?

   (1) The total world population will double in the next 50 years.
   (2) About half the world's population lives in the more developed nations.
   (3) Most of the population growth in the next 50 years will occur in the less developed nations.
   (4) Most of the population growth in the next 50 years will occur in the more developed nations.
   (5) At present, the death rate exceeds the birthrate in more developed nations.

Answers and explanations start on page 647.

GEOGRAPHY

Using Resources Wisely

Conservation means using natural resources—such as soil, plant and animal life, water, air, and mineral reserves—carefully. Conservationists encourage the **sustainable use** of resources—using resources in ways that do not exhaust them for the future. Natural resources are either **renewable** or **nonrenewable.** Renewable resources can be sustained through replacement. For example, harvested plants can be replanted. Solar and wind energy are also renewable, since their supply never runs out. Nonrenewable resources are materials that humans use but cannot replace—such as petroleum and natural gas, as well as minerals such as coal, copper, and iron.

Natural resources need to be protected for many reasons. Some reasons for conservation are economic: natural resources are needed to produce goods and services of economic value. Petroleum provides fuel to run equipment in factories and to transport materials and goods. We also need wood and wood products for building structures, making furniture, and manufacturing paper. Other reasons for conserving resources relate to our need to sustain the diverse **ecosystems** of Earth to help keep the planet healthy. These diverse ecosystems help maintain the following resources: water; air; and plant, animal, and human life. Finally, natural resources inspire our sense of beauty and wonder; natural areas and materials play important roles in people's cultural and spiritual traditions.

When natural resources are **scarce** or become threatened, different people's interests can come into conflict. For example, water resources in a region might not be adequate to provide clean drinking water, irrigate local farms, sustain wildlife, and supply water for industrial development. If these interests are not balanced, some people will lose what they need. These problems become even more difficult when political boundaries are involved. Perhaps one nation's water supply comes from a river that flows through another nation; if the second nation builds a dam on the river, it could cut back the flow of water to the first nation. Such conflicts can be very difficult to negotiate. Industry, agriculture, natural ecosystems, clean air and water, and historical and cultural preservation—all these factors influence how people decide to allocate natural resources.

Many countries have laws that protect **endangered species** of plants and animals. Industrial and agricultural interests have to be balanced against **biodiversity**—the maintenance of many different species of organisms. New international agreements attempt to protect the **ozone layer** in the atmosphere, which is critical to maintaining Earth's climate patterns. In some nations—although not in the United States—high taxes on gasoline pay for clean air programs and encourage people to reduce their use of cars. **Fossil fuels** are relatively inexpensive and available, so industrialized regions are highly dependent on them. But they are nonrenewable and cause a great deal of pollution. Globally, we will have to develop more sustainable sources of energy on a large scale—such as **solar** and **wind energy**—to keep our planet healthy in the long run.

Choose the <u>one best answer</u> to each question.

1. What are renewable resources?

   (1) materials that will never run out or can be replaced if used
   (2) materials that are found underground
   (3) materials that we do not use and so can use at a later date
   (4) materials that we use but cannot replace
   (5) an incentive to conserve materials

2. Which of the following is an example of the sustainable use of a resource?

   (1) burning fossil fuels
   (2) depleting an oil field
   (3) strip mining
   (4) overgrazing livestock
   (5) rotating crops

3. Since conflicts over scarce or polluted resources sometimes cross national boundaries, which of the following methods would be most likely to solve problems related to these resources?

   (1) using force
   (2) negotiating in an international forum
   (3) taking unilateral action
   (4) importing resources
   (5) selling resources

4. In the United States, there is disagreement about how to reduce dependence on foreign oil. Some favor exploiting domestic sources of oil even if that means polluting the environment. Others prefer to concentrate on developing alternative, renewable sources of energy.

   Which of the following best characterizes the underlying difference in points of view between the pro-oil and pro-alternative energy factions?

   (1) self-sufficiency versus interdependence
   (2) competition versus cooperation
   (3) isolationism versus foreign involvement
   (4) short-term benefit versus long-term benefit
   (5) patriotism versus internationalism

5. Which of the following actions could a family take to conserve nonrenewable resources?

   (1) incinerate the trash
   (2) carpool to work and school
   (3) plant trees in the yard
   (4) eat less food
   (5) burn more firewood

Questions 6 and 7 refers to the following chart.

Current Natural Gas Resources and Reserves (in trillion cubic feet)

Region	Current Production	Proved Reserves	Reserves to Production Ratio
N. America	25.5	312.7	12/1
S. America	2.1	189.1	90/1
Europe	9.2	216.3	24/1
Former U.S.S.R.	25.7	2057.5	80/1
Africa	2.6	341.6	131/1
Middle East	3.9	1594.3	409/1
Asia/Oceania	6.5	350.6	54/1

SOURCE: Congressional Research Service.

6. Which of the following world regions currently produces the most natural gas?

   (1) South America
   (2) Europe
   (3) the former U.S.S.R.
   (4) the Middle East
   (5) Asia/Oceania

7. If each region keeps up its current rate of production and does not locate any new reserves, which will run out of natural gas first?

   (1) North America
   (2) Europe
   (3) the former U.S.S.R.
   (4) Africa
   (5) the Middle East

Answers and explanations start on page 647.

GEOGRAPHY

Maps and Their Uses

Key Ideas

- Maps are tools used for a wide variety of purposes.
- Topographic maps show both natural and cultural features of an area.
- A map's key, compass rose, and scale give important information about what the map shows.

Most people are familiar with road maps, globes and world maps that show the borders of modern nations, and the historical maps found in text-books. These display different information because they have different uses. Although some maps are used to help people get from one place to another, many maps are used as reference tools as well. Such maps reveal how certain data relates to **location.** People who make maps are called **cartographers.**

The most common types of maps are **topographic** maps. These maps usually show both natural features of the landscape, such as rivers and mountains, and "cultural" features, such as towns, cities, roads, and political boundaries. Some road maps are topographic maps. More specialized topographic maps are often used by hikers and others interested in the natural contours of the land. Such topographic maps have **contour lines** to show elevation with respect to sea level. The farther apart the contour lines, the flatter the land. Contour lines drawn close together show steep slopes.

Special-purpose maps record specialized information, often as a tool to suit the needs of a particular audience. Aviation charts include topographic information as well as flight paths and radio beacons. Political maps detail political boundaries, such as county lines, state lines, or the borders of nations, without showing natural features. Historical maps reconstruct earlier political boundaries, trade routes, or other types of historical data, often showing change over time. Other special-purpose maps show rainfall, population distribution, land use, and so on.

GED TIP

Map reading skills are an important part of the Social Studies test. Before answering questions, get an overview of the map by reading any titles, captions, and categories on the map's key.

Maps usually have a **key,** or **legend,** which explains symbols used on the map. For example, the legend on the map at right has a special symbol to show the national capital. Many maps also have a **compass rose,** which helps map users orient the map in terms of direction—north, south, east, and west. The map's **scale** tells how the map represents distances. On the map at right, one inch represents 267 miles. Many maps also have a grid representing latitude and longitude.

Legend
★ Capital   ∼ River
● City   _ International Boundary

GEOGRAPHY ▸ PRACTICE 4

Choose the <u>one best answer</u> to each question.

1. What is the basic function of any map?

   (1) to provide a photographic image of a place
   (2) to help people navigate from one place to another
   (3) to show the political borders of a country
   (4) to show how various types of information relate to location
   (5) to show the physical features of a nation or region

Questions 2 through 5 refer to the map on page 224.

2. What type of map is the map of France?

   (1) political
   (2) topographic
   (3) historical
   (4) aviation
   (5) climate

3. According to the map, approximately how far is Bordeaux from Marseilles?

   (1) 100 miles
   (2) 175 miles
   (3) 250 miles
   (4) 325 miles
   (5) 400 miles

4. The Loire River empties into the Atlantic Ocean. Based on this information and the map, in what direction does the Loire River flow?

   (1) northeast
   (2) southwest
   (3) south
   (4) east
   (5) west

5. According to the map, what do Le Havre and Paris have in common?

   (1) Both are capital cities.
   (2) Both are on the English Channel.
   (3) Both are south of Bordeaux.
   (4) Both are on the Seine River.
   (5) Both are on the Mediterranean Sea.

Questions 6 and 7 refer to the following map.

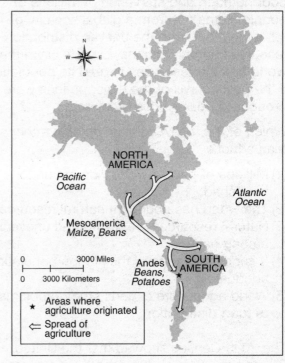

6. What does this map show?

   (1) political boundaries in the ancient Americas
   (2) physical features of the Americas
   (3) how agriculture spread in the Americas
   (4) the history of colonization in the Americas
   (5) all the ancient civilizations of the Americas

7. Which of the following statements is supported by the information on the map?

   (1) Both the Andes civilization and Mesoamerica domesticated maize.
   (2) Both the Andes civilization and Mesoamerica domesticated beans.
   (3) Agriculture developed in the Andes civilization before it did in Mesoamerica.
   (4) Agriculture spread more rapidly northward than southward.
   (5) The centers of Mesoamerican and Andean civilizations were about 6,000 miles apart.

Answers and explanations start on page 648.

GEOGRAPHY PRACTICE QUESTIONS

Choose the <u>one best answer</u> to each question.

1. According to experts in world agriculture, the poor nutrition and starvation of millions of people stems not from a global scarcity of resources, but from the uneven distribution of resources among nations. Experts claim the world has the resources to feed its population if the political will of the richer nations were brought to bear on this problem.

Which of the following is an opinion rather than a fact?

(1) Millions of people worldwide are under-nourished.
(2) The world has abundant natural resources.
(3) Natural resources are distributed unevenly among nations.
(4) It is possible to feed the human population adequately.
(5) World agriculture experts study problems of food distribution.

2. The 2000 Census showed that the United States has 281,421,906 people, an increase of 13.2 percent over the 1990 census. Population growth and immigration accounted for this increase. The state population counts showed the largest relative gains in the South and West, with Nevada's population increase the highest at 66.3 percent. Because state population figures are used to allocate seats in the House of Representatives, every ten years a shift in political power occurs. In 2000, states in the Northeast and Midwest lost seats, and states in the West and South picked up seats.

Which of the following is implied by the paragraph?

(1) Nevada had a 66.3 percent population increase.
(2) Nevada lost seats in the House.
(3) People moved from the Northeast and Midwest to the West and South.
(4) The U.S. population in 2000 was about 281 million people.
(5) The Census was taken in 1990 as well as 2000.

Questions 3 and 4 refer to the following map.

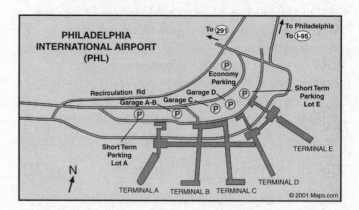

3. Which of the following people is most likely to use the map above?

(1) a geologist surveying land features in the Philadelphia area
(2) a visitor to Philadelphia
(3) an employee of the Federal Aviation Administration
(4) a commercial airline pilot
(5) a meteorologist who works for a Philadelphia TV station

4. Which of the following statements is supported by the data on the map?

(1) Philadelphia International Airport serves a region with over two million people.
(2) More than twenty airlines have landing rights at Philadelphia International Airport.
(3) Route 95 borders the south side of Philadelphia International Airport.
(4) It is possible to get to Philadelphia International Airport by plane, car, or rail.
(5) Labels for terminals and parking areas are coordinated to provide convenient parking.

Questions 5 and 6 refer to the following paragraph and map.

The earliest maps we have were etched on clay tiles and consisted primarily of land and property surveys in Mesopotamia. The map below, made in about 1300 B.C., shows the property boundaries of the king's estate.

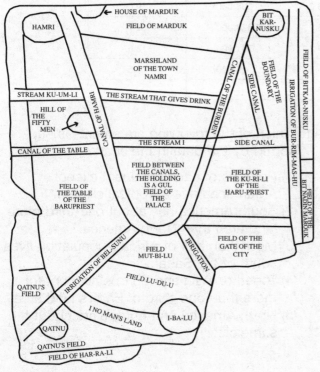

SOURCE: University of Pennsylvania

5. Which of the following formed many of the field boundaries shown on the map?

   (1) mountains
   (2) the sea
   (3) a large river
   (4) irrigation canals
   (5) roads and paths

6. The king's property map is most similar to which of the following modern maps?

   (1) a town tax assessor's tax map
   (2) a U.S. Geological Survey topographic map
   (3) a map showing tourist attractions
   (4) an automobile club's road map of a city
   (5) a U.S. census map of population density

Questions 7 and 8 refer to the following passage.

Desertification, the spread of deserts, is usually caused in part by human activity. Agricultural practices, such as clearing trees and brush, depleting the soil through plowing and planting, overgrazing, and irrigation, contribute to the sterilization and erosion of the land. A period of drought is often enough to tip the balance toward a desert ecosystem.

For example, in the 1930s excessive plowing, overgrazing, and well-digging left the American Great Plains vulnerable to desertification. A lengthy drought led to conditions so severe the topsoil was blown away, creating what is known as the Dust Bowl. Formerly valuable farmland became almost worthless in a period of years. The area was spared permanent desertification only because normal rainfall eventually resumed.

7. Which of the following was the most likely result of the Dust Bowl?

   (1) the drought that began in the early 1930s and lasted for several years
   (2) the Great Depression of the 1930s, an economic downturn
   (3) the migration of thousands of farm families to other regions
   (4) the permanent cessation of agriculture in the Great Plains
   (5) restoration of the Great Plains ecosystem as it was before agriculture

8. Which of the following is an example of desertification?

   (1) the shrinking of the Greenland ice sheet
   (2) the rise in sea level during the 1900s
   (3) the shifting sandbars along the coast of Lake Michigan
   (4) the extension of grazing onto land that is part of the National Forest system
   (5) the spread of the Sahara into the grazing land on its southern border

Questions 9 through 11 refer to the following chart.

Area and Population of the Continents

Continent	Area (thousands of sq. mi.)	Percent of Earth's Area	Estimated Population, 1998 (thousands)	Percent of Total World Population
North America	9,400	16.2	301,000	5.3
South America	6,900	11.9	508,000	9.0
Europe	3,800	6.6	508,000	9.0
Asia	17,400	30.1	3,528,000	62.6
Africa	11,700	20.2	761,000	13.5
Australia/Oceania	3,300	5.7	30,000	0.5
Antarctica	5,400	9.3	—	—

9. On what continent, aside from Antarctica, do the fewest people live?

(1) North America
(2) South America
(3) Asia
(4) Africa
(5) Australia/Oceania

10. Which continent has the greatest population density (the most people per square mile)?

(1) North America
(2) South America
(3) Asia
(4) Africa
(5) Australia/Oceania

11. Which of the following statements is supported by the data in the chart?

(1) Portions of each continent except Antarctica have a tropical climate.
(2) South America has about one-third more land area than North America.
(3) More than half of Africa's population lives south of the Sahara.
(4) Together, Asia and Europe account for more than one-third of Earth's land area.
(5) North America and Europe are about the same size.

12. The Nile River flows down from the mountains of East Africa, north through Egypt, to the Mediterranean Sea. A student looking at a map of Africa could not understand why the map showed the Nile River flowing up, rather than down, to the Mediterranean.

What was wrong with this student's thinking?

(1) The compass direction north does not mean "up" in terms of elevation.
(2) The map of Africa was turned the wrong way, with south at the top.
(3) The Nile River really flows south to the Mediterranean.
(4) North and south have no real meaning on a topographic map.
(5) North and south have opposite meanings south of the equator.

Answers and explanations start on page 648.

Science

The GED Science Test evaluates your ability to understand and interpret science information. You will have 80 minutes to answer 50 questions that are based on brief reading passages or graphics such as diagrams, tables, graphs, and maps.

The questions are based on content in the areas of life science, earth and space science, and physical science (chemistry and physics). They are all in multiple-choice format.

Content Areas

Life Science (45%) Almost half the questions on the Science Test cover life science topics. These topics may include cell structures and processes, the human body, health and nutrition, heredity and reproduction, genetics and DNA, evolution and natural selection, and ecosystems.

Earth and Space Science (20%) One-fifth of the questions are based on major topics such as the structure of Earth, plate tectonics, geological cycles and processes, renewable and nonrenewable natural resources, weather and climate, the solar system, and the universe.

Physical Science (35%) About one-third of the questions cover important topics in chemistry and physics. These topics may include atoms and molecules, the properties and states of matter, chemical reactions, energy and work, motion and forces, waves, electricity, and magnetism.

Many of the questions on the test are based on themes that apply across the science content areas:

- The history and nature of science
- Science in personal and human perspectives
- Science as inquiry—especially focusing on the scientific method
- Science and technology
- Unifying concepts and processes, such as constancy and change

In addition to studying this book, you can prepare for the GED Science Test by paying attention to news programs on the radio and television and by reading newspapers and news magazines. There are often stories in the news that involve science topics, especially new developments in genetics, health, space exploration, and astronomy. Pay special attention to graphs, diagrams, and maps that you see in the media because 25 out of 50 questions on the test are based on graphics alone or graphics and text together.

Four Types of Questions

Comprehension

Some questions on the GED Science Test require you to recognize an implication, restatement, or summary of information that you read.

Example

A nebula is a region of gas and dust in space. There are three main types of nebulae. An emission nebula is bright, giving off light and other radiation. A reflection nebula is also bright, but its light comes from nearby stars. The light from the stars is reflected and scattered by particles of dust in the nebula. A dark nebula does not shine. Instead, its gas and dust absorb light from nearby stars, and the nebula appears as a dark patch in the sky.

Which is the best summary of this passage?

(1) Emission nebulae give off light and other forms of radiation.
(2) There are three types of nebulae—regions of gas and dust in space.
(3) Reflection nebulae scatter the light from nearby stars.
(4) Nebulae are regions of gas and dust surrounding a star.
(5) The gas and dust in a dark nebula absorb light from nearby stars.

Answer: (2) There are three types of nebulae—regions of gas and dust in space. This summarizes the main idea of the passage. Option (4) is contradicted by the passage, and options (1), (3), and (5) are specific facts in the passage, not a summary of the passage's main point.

Application

Some of the questions on the Science Test require you to apply given information to a new or specific situation.

Example

Symbiosis is a relationship between members of two species in which both organisms receive some benefit. Which of the following is an example of symbiosis?

(1) Mistletoe growing on the branches of trees takes water and minerals from the trees.
(2) Ticks living in the fur of a deer feed on the deer's blood, weakening the deer.
(3) Sea anemones living on the shell of a hermit crab get food from the crab and protect it from predators.
(4) Flukes living in the intestines of humans get nourishment from substances there.
(5) Cowbirds leave their eggs in the nests of other bird species to be hatched, fed, and raised by the other birds.

Answer: (3) Sea anemones living on the shell of a hermit crab get food from the crab and protect it from predators. In this question, you apply the definition of symbiosis to the examples in each option. The key element you are looking for in the relationships is that *both species benefit*.

Analysis

Many questions require you to distinguish facts from opinions, recognize unstated assumptions, compare and contrast, or identify causes and their effects.

Example

Plasma is one of the states of matter. It is an ionized gas found only at very high temperatures, as in the sun, other stars, and nuclear reactions.

Which of the following does the writer take for granted that you already know?

(1) what a state of matter is
(2) what plasma is
(3) that plasma exists at high temperatures
(4) that plasma is found in the sun and other stars
(5) that plasma is produced in nuclear reactions

Answer: (1) what a state of matter is. The writer does not explain what a state of matter is; she assumes that this is common knowledge. The other options are all stated explicitly in the passage.

Evaluation

Some questions involve making judgments about the validity or accuracy of material or whether data can support a hypothesis, conclusion, or other statement. Some involve identifying the logical flaw in an argument. These questions also require evaluating the role that values and beliefs play in decision making.

Example

When a sick patient agrees to participate in an experimental drug study, he accepts the risk and hopes to benefit from the drug. In contrast, the researchers want to gather information about the participants' reactions to the drug in the hope of eventually benefiting future patients.

According to the passage, the goals of a drug study participant and those of a drug researcher differ. What does each of them value?

(1) The participant values scientific inquiry and the researcher values caring for others.
(2) The participant values future benefit to others and the researcher values curing people now.
(3) The participant values the potential personal benefit and the researcher values the potential future benefit for others.
(4) The participant values caution and the researcher values risk taking.
(5) The participant values risk taking and the researcher values profit.

Answer: This question asks you to evaluate the role that values play in decision making. Only option **(3) The participant values the potential personal benefit and the researcher values the potential future benefit for others**, represents the values that participants and researchers bring to experimental drug studies.

Interpreting Graphics

Diagrams

The title of a diagram tells you the general topic. The labels name and point out specific things of interest. Science diagrams can show the parts of a structure, the steps in a process, or how something works.

Example

Dry Cell Battery

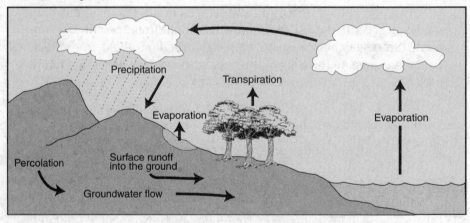

Zinc can (anode)

Ammonium chloride

Carbon rod (cathode)

Porous separator

Manganese dioxide

What is the anode made of?

(1) zinc
(2) carbon
(3) manganese dioxide
(4) ammonium chloride
(5) a porous separator

Answer: (1) zinc. First find the label that says *anode*. The label indicates that the anode is the can, which is made of zinc.

Cycle Diagrams

A cycle diagram shows a process that repeats itself. Arrows are usually used to show changes from one stage or phase to the next.

GED TIP

When reading a cycle diagram, pay careful attention to the arrows. Note that in some cycle diagrams, several different arrows may point to the same place or indicate the same phase of a process.

Example

The Water Cycle

Precipitation

Transpiration

Evaporation

Evaporation

Percolation

Surface runoff into the ground

Groundwater flow

What process moves water from the atmosphere to the land?

(1) evaporation   (4) the flow of groundwater
(2) surface runoff   (5) precipitation
(3) transpiration

Answer: (5) precipitation. The labels and arrows show that water flows from the atmosphere to Earth's surface by means of precipitation.

Line and Bar Graphs

You can read line and bar graphs by reading up from the labels on the bottom **axis** (line) and across from values on the side axis. Also read any titles, labels, and keys or legends carefully.

GED TIP

Line graphs usually show trends over time, and bar graphs show comparisons.

Example

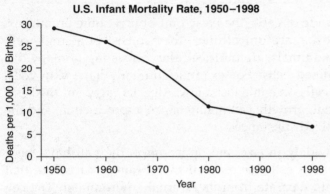

U.S. Infant Mortality Rate, 1950–1998

SOURCE: Centers for Disease Control

Which of the following statements is supported by the graph?

(1) In 1950, the infant mortality rate was 20 deaths per 1,000 live births.
(2) In 1970, about 30 infants died per 1,000 live births.
(3) The infant mortality rate peaked in 1960 and then dropped.
(4) In the year 2000, the infant mortality rate increased.
(5) The U.S. infant mortality rate has declined steadily since 1950.

Answer: The graph supports option **(5) The infant mortality rate has declined steadily since 1950.** Options (1), (2), and (3) are contradicted by the graph. Option (4) may be true, but the graph gives no data for the year 2000.

Circle Graphs

Circle graphs are used to show how a whole is divided into parts. Often they are divided into percents or fractions.

Example

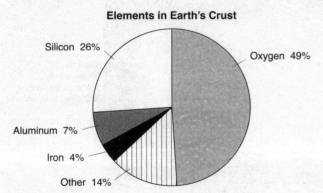

Elements in Earth's Crust

Silicon 26%
Oxygen 49%
Aluminum 7%
Iron 4%
Other 14%

How does the amount of silicon in Earth's crust compare with the amount of oxygen?

(1) There is about half as much silicon as oxygen.
(2) There is about twice as much silicon as oxygen.
(3) There is 26 times as much silicon as oxygen.
(4) There is 49 times as much silicon as oxygen.
(5) There is the same amount of silicon as oxygen.

Answer: Option **(1) There is about half as much silicon as oxygen** is the correct answer as the silicon "wedge" is about half the size of the oxygen "wedge."

LIFE SCIENCE

Cell Structures and Functions

Key Ideas

- The basic unit of all living things is the cell, which carries out the life functions, including movement, growth, and reproduction.
- All cells have a cell membrane, cytoplasm, and genetic material.
- Unlike an animal cell, a plant cell contains a cell wall—a structure that gives the cell rigidity and shape.

All living things are made of **cells,** the basic unit of life. Some organisms, like bacteria and protozoa, are **unicellular**—they consist of a single cell. Others, like plants and animals, are **multicellular,** consisting of many different types of specialized cells. For example, humans have skin cells, blood cells, and nerve cells, to name just a few. All cells carry out the basic life functions: movement, growth, cell maintenance, reproduction, and the manufacture of specialized substances.

Although cells differ widely in size and appearance, they all have basic structures in common. All cells have a **cell membrane,** a structure that keeps the cell's contents separate from its external environment. The cell membrane is selectively permeable, which means that it allows certain substances, such as water, nutrients, and wastes, to pass between the cell's interior and the surrounding environment. Inside the cell membrane is the **cytoplasm,** a watery, jellylike substance that can include other cell structures. Finally, all cells have **genetic material,** which contains coded instructions for carrying out the cell's activities. In bacteria cells, the genetic material consists of a single molecule suspended in the cytoplasm. These cells are called **prokaryotes.** In all other cells, the genetic material is more complex and is contained within a **nucleus.** These cells are called **eukaryotes.** All plant and animal cells are eukaryotes. A typical plant cell is shown below. Note that a plant cell has a **cell wall,** which gives the cell shape and rigidity, and an animal cell does not.

GED TIP

The title and labels of a diagram usually tell you the main idea of the diagram. Here, the main idea is that plant cells have cell structures with specialized functions.

A Plant Cell

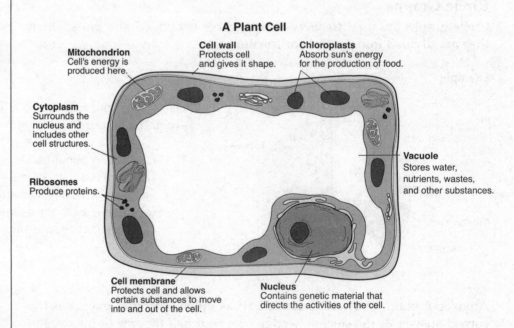

Mitochondrion
Cell's energy is produced here.

Cell wall
Protects cell and gives it shape.

Chloroplasts
Absorb sun's energy for the production of food.

Cytoplasm
Surrounds the nucleus and includes other cell structures.

Ribosomes
Produce proteins.

Vacuole
Stores water, nutrients, wastes, and other substances.

Cell membrane
Protects cell and allows certain substances to move into and out of the cell.

Nucleus
Contains genetic material that directs the activities of the cell.

LIFE SCIENCE ▸ PRACTICE 1

Directions: Choose the <u>one best answer</u> to each question.

1. According to the diagram on page 234, which structure supplies energy to the cell?

   (1) the cell wall
   (2) the nucleus
   (3) the ribosomes
   (4) the mitochondrion
   (5) the vacuole

2. In addition to the cell wall, the water stored in a plant cell's vacuole helps give the plant firmness and shape. When a plant is not taking in enough water from the soil through its roots, it uses up its stored water and its vacuoles shrink. When the vacuoles shrink, the plant wilts.

   Which of the following is a conclusion based on the paragraph above rather than a given fact?

   (1) Cell walls help give a plant cell firmness and shape.
   (2) Vacuoles help give a plant cell firmness and shape.
   (3) Plants take in water from the soil through their roots.
   (4) A plant wilts when it does not get enough water to fill its vacuoles.
   (5) Cell walls cannot maintain a plant's shape and rigidity when the plant lacks water.

3. A student is examining a cell using a microscope. She is able to identify the cell membrane, cytoplasm, a small vacuole, and the nucleus, but she does not see a cell wall or any chloroplasts. She concludes that the cell is a eukaryote.

   Which of the following is evidence that her conclusion is correct?

   (1) the presence of a cell membrane
   (2) the presence of a nucleus
   (3) the presence of cytoplasm
   (4) the absence of chloroplasts
   (5) the absence of a cell wall

4. Cells were first seen during the 1600s, when English scientist Robert Hooke observed cork cell walls through a microscope that could magnify a specimen a couple of hundred times its original size. In the 1800s, the compound light microscope, which magnifies up to a thousand times, was developed. Electron microscopes, which can magnify up to a million times, were invented during the 1900s.

   Why has our knowledge of cells grown with improvements in microscope technology?

   (1) Each time the microscope is improved, scientists can see cell structures more clearly.
   (2) With the first microscopes, all cell structures were clearly visible.
   (3) Compound light microscopes can magnify cells up to a thousand times.
   (4) Robert Hooke's microscope only allowed him to see the largest cell structures.
   (5) Microscopes allow scientists to observe unicellular organisms.

5. Diffusion is a process by which particles move from an area of higher concentration to an area of lower concentration. For example, oxygen diffuses through the cell membrane of a unicellular pond organism from the water, where there is lots of oxygen, into the cell, where there is less oxygen. Eventually, the concentration of oxygen inside and outside the unicellular organism is the same.

   What would happen if the concentration of oxygen were greater in the unicellular organism than in its watery environment?

   (1) Water would diffuse from the unicellular organism into the pond water.
   (2) Oxygen would diffuse from the unicellular organism into the pond water.
   (3) Oxygen would diffuse from the pond water into the unicellular organism.
   (4) Diffusion of oxygen between the organism and the pond water would stop entirely.
   (5) The organism would move to another area of the pond.

Answers and explanations start on page 649.

LIFE SCIENCE

Cell Processes and Energy

All cells need energy to carry out the life functions, such as growth and reproduction. The ultimate source of energy for all living things on Earth is sunlight. Green plants, some algae, and some bacteria use energy from sunlight to make food in a process called **photosynthesis.**

In photosynthesis, plants use sunlight to power chemical reactions that convert carbon dioxide gas and water into oxygen and the simple sugar **glucose.** In the first stage of photosynthesis, light energy is captured by chloroplasts inside plant cells. Chloroplasts contain **chlorophyll,** a pigment that gives plants their green color. Chlorophyll absorbs light energy for photosynthesis. In the second stage, water (H_2O) that the plant gets from the soil and carbon dioxide (CO_2) that the plant gets from the air undergo a complex series of chemical reactions inside the chloroplasts. The products of these reactions are oxygen (O_2) and glucose ($C_6H_{12}O_6$). Plant cells use the energy that is stored in glucose to power cell processes. Photosynthesis can be summarized in the chemical equation shown below:

$$\text{light energy}$$
$$6CO_2 + 6H_2O \rightarrow C_6H_{12}O_6 + 6O_2$$

In words, this means: carbon dioxide plus water, in the presence of light energy, yields glucose plus oxygen.

As a result of photosynthesis, energy is stored in sugars and other **carbohydrates** in the plant. To meet their energy needs, other organisms eat plants or eat organisms that eat plants. When energy is needed in a cell, carbohydrates are broken down to release the energy in a process called **cellular respiration.** In this process, oxygen from the air reacts with glucose from food to yield carbon dioxide, water, and energy. Cellular respiration can be summarized in the following chemical equation:

$$C_6H_{12}O_6 + 6O_2 \rightarrow 6CO_2 + 6H_2O + \text{energy}$$

In words, this means: glucose plus oxygen yields carbon dioxide, water, and energy.

If you examine the two equations, you will notice that the products of photosynthesis are the raw materials of cellular respiration, and the products of cellular respiration are the raw materials of photosynthesis. These two processes are part of a cycle. Plants release oxygen, a waste product of photosynthesis, into the atmosphere. Animals breathe in the oxygen and use it in cellular respiration. They breathe out carbon dioxide, a waste product of cellular respiration. The carbon dioxide is then used by plants in photosynthesis, and the cycle repeats. Between them, photosynthesis and cellular respiration help keep the amounts of oxygen and carbon dioxide in the atmosphere fairly constant.

LIFE SCIENCE ▸ PRACTICE 2

Directions: Choose the one best answer to each question.

1. Which of the following are the products of cellular respiration?

   (1) glucose and light energy
   (2) carbon dioxide and oxygen
   (3) glucose, oxygen, and energy
   (4) glucose, carbon dioxide, and energy
   (5) carbon dioxide, water, and energy

2. A horticulturist wants to grow large healthy plants by maximizing the rate of photosynthesis.

   Which of the following actions would be most likely to get the results she wants?

   (1) increasing the amount of light the plants receive each day
   (2) decreasing the amount of light the plants receive each day
   (3) increasing the amount of oxygen the plants receive each day
   (4) decreasing the amount of oxygen the plants receive each day
   (5) decreasing the amount of carbon dioxide the plants receive each day

3. Carbon dioxide is one of the "greenhouse gases" that help keep Earth warm by trapping radiated heat in the atmosphere. Global warming is thought to be caused in part by increased amounts of carbon dioxide in the atmosphere.

   Which of the following would help reduce the level of carbon dioxide in the atmosphere and thus perhaps slow the global warming trend?

   (1) increasing the human population
   (2) increasing the population of domestic animals
   (3) increasing the number of green plants
   (4) increasing the harvest of trees
   (5) increasing the amount of glucose in our food

Questions 4 and 5 refer to the following information and diagram.

In most plants, photosynthesis takes place primarily in the palisade cells of leaves.

Cross Section of a Leaf

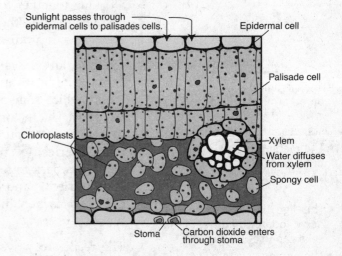

4. A stoma is an opening in the lower surface of the leaf through which gases can pass.

   According to the diagram, which gas passes from the atmosphere into the leaf's chloroplasts?

   (1) xylem
   (2) oxygen
   (3) carbon monoxide
   (4) carbon dioxide
   (5) sunlight

5. Which of the following statements is supported by the information in the diagram?

   (1) Palisade cells provide a means of transporting water through a plant.
   (2) Most of a leaf's chloroplasts are found in its palisade cells.
   (3) The spongy cells are soft, like a sponge.
   (4) The epidermis blocks light from reaching the palisade cells.
   (5) Most leaves have a large surface area to maximize exposure to sunlight.

Answers and explanations start on page 649.

LIFE SCIENCE

Human Body Systems

There are four levels of organization in the human body: (1) cells, the smallest unit of life, (2) **tissues,** groups of similar cells that perform a special function, such as muscle tissue, (3) **organs,** groups of tissues that perform a function, such as the stomach, and (4) body systems, groups of organs working together to perform a function, such as digestion. Human body systems include the circulatory, respiratory, digestive, nervous, immune, endocrine, reproductive, urinary, skeletal, and muscular systems.

The **circulatory system,** sometimes called the cardiovascular system, consists of the heart and the blood vessels. Its main function is to move the blood, which transports substances like oxygen and nutrients, throughout the body. The major **organ** of the circulatory system is the **heart,** a muscle that contracts to pump blood. Blood moves through the blood vessels from large **arteries,** to smaller arteries, to **capillaries,** to small **veins,** to large veins and back to the heart. Through the thin walls of the capillaries, oxygen, nutrients, and other substances pass from the blood into the body's cells and carbon dioxide and other wastes pass from the cells into the blood.

The **respiratory system** consists of the nose, throat, **trachea** (windpipe), and **lungs.** Its function is to take oxygen from the air into the body when we inhale, and to get rid of waste carbon dioxide when we exhale. The trachea branches into two tubes called the **bronchi,** one of which goes into each lung. The bronchi branch into smaller tubes called **bronchioles,** each of which ends in an **alveolus,** a tiny spherical sac. Inside the capillaries of the alveoli, oxygen diffuses into the blood and carbon dioxide diffuses out of the blood.

The **digestive system** consists of the mouth, **esophagus, stomach, small intestine,** and **large intestine.** Its function is to break down food into nutrients, which are used for cell processes including the production of energy, and to get rid of digestive wastes. Digestion begins in the mouth, where the teeth grind food into smaller pieces and **saliva** begins to break it down chemically. Food is pushed by muscular action down through the esophagus into the stomach, where it is churned and further broken down by **enzymes** and stomach acids. From the stomach it travels to the small intestine, where most of the nutrients are absorbed into the blood through tiny capillaries in the **villi.** What remains goes to the large intestine, which removes water, leaving solid waste to be excreted through the rectum.

The **nervous system** consists of the **brain, spinal cord,** and **nerves.** Its function is to receive, process, and transmit information, controlling body activities. The brain has three main parts: the **cerebrum,** which controls functions such as thinking, seeing, and speaking; the **cerebellum,** which coordinates movement and position; and the **brainstem,** which controls breathing and heart rate. Information is transmitted to and from the brain through the nerves, which are bundled in the spinal cord and branch out from there into all parts of the body.

Key Ideas

- The circulatory system moves blood around the body, delivering and taking away substances.
- The respiratory system brings oxygen into the body and gets rid of carbon dioxide.
- The digestive system breaks down food into nutrients that cells can use.
- The nervous system controls body activities.

ON THE GED

*On the GED Science Test, key science words appear in regular, not **bold,** type. As you read a passage, you can underline the key terms. That way, you can easily find them when you are answering a question.*

LIFE SCIENCE ▸ PRACTICE 3

Directions: Choose the one best answer to each question.

1. Which human body system interacts with each cell of the body?

    (1) the circulatory system
    (2) the respiratory system
    (3) the digestive system
    (4) the muscular system
    (5) the skeletal system

2. How are the alveoli in the lungs and the villi in the small intestine similar?

    (1) Both are structures located in the respiratory system.
    (2) Both are structures located in the digestive system.
    (3) Both are structures in which substances pass through capillary walls into the blood.
    (4) Both are structures involved in the control of the body's activities.
    (5) Both are structures involved in coordination and movement.

3. In the 17th century, English physician William Harvey concluded that blood in the veins flows toward the heart.

    Which of the following facts helps support Harvey's conclusion?

    (1) The heart pumps about 1,800 gallons of blood per day.
    (2) The heart has four chambers: two atria and two ventricles.
    (3) Blood circulates in blood vessels called arteries, veins, and capillaries.
    (4) Large veins branch into smaller blood vessels called capillaries.
    (5) Veins have valves that allow blood to flow in one direction only.

Questions 4 and 5 refer to the following information and diagram.

   The kidneys of the urinary system remove cellular wastes and excess water from the blood. This material, called urine, is stored in the bladder until it is excreted from the body.

The Urinary System

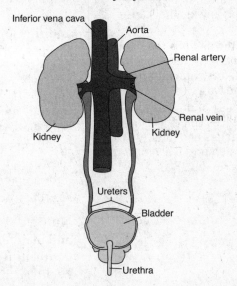

4. Through which structure(s) does urine pass from the kidneys to the bladder?

    (1) the urethra
    (2) the ureters
    (3) the renal vein
    (4) the renal artery
    (5) the aorta

5. A urologist is a doctor who specializes in disorders of the urinary system.

    Which of the following patients is most likely to be treated by a urologist?

    (1) a patient with low levels of iron in her blood
    (2) a patient with high blood pressure
    (3) a patient with a painful kidney stone
    (4) a patient with swollen veins in the anus, called hemorrhoids
    (5) a patient with chronic indigestion

Answers and explanations start on page 649.

LIFE SCIENCE

Health Issues

Health can be affected by infections, nutrition, and substance abuse.

An **infection** is the invasion of the body by germs—microorganisms that cause disease. It is often characterized by fever and other symptoms. Germs can enter the body through breaks in the skin (for example, tetanus), with air (influenza), in contaminated food and water (food poisoning), by contact with contaminated blood or saliva (rabies), or through sexual activity (gonorrhea). Infections can be grouped according to the type of microorganisms that cause them. The most common germs are **bacteria** and **viruses,** although infections can also be caused by fungi, protozoans, and worms.

The body has natural defenses against infection, such as the skin, the mucous membranes in the nose, tears, and acid in the stomach. If germs get past these defenses, the **immune system** produces **antibodies** that destroy the germs. In developed nations, infectious diseases are less common than they used to be because of better nutrition and living conditions, safer water and sewage systems, **immunization** (which provides protection against specific infectious diseases), and **antibiotics,** drugs that fight bacteria.

Nutrients are substances that are needed for growth, normal functioning, and maintenance of cells. The body does not produce nutrients; instead we get them from the food we eat. The nutrients that humans need for good health include **proteins, carbohydrates** (sugars and starches), **fats, vitamins, minerals,** and water. In a well-balanced diet, people get enough nutrients to provide energy as well as the right nutrients needed for all the body's functions. Too much or too little of a nutrient can cause problems. For example, a diet with too much fat can lead to obesity and contribute to heart disease. Too little vitamin C can cause scurvy, a painful disease.

Drugs are substances that affect the structure or function of the body. They are usually used to treat disease or relieve its symptoms, although some drugs, like nicotine in tobacco, have no medicinal purpose. The nonmedical use of a drug to the point that it interferes with a person's normal functioning is called **drug abuse,** or substance abuse. Drug abuse can lead to **addiction,** a severe form of dependence that causes physical changes in the body so that when the drug wears off or is stopped, withdrawal symptoms such as nausea and pain occur. Heroin, speed, alcohol, nicotine, and barbiturates are frequently abused addictive drugs. A milder form of dependence than addiction is **psychological dependence,** or **habituation.** In this type of dependence, the urge to take the drug is strong, even though there are no withdrawal symptoms. Examples of drugs that can cause habituation in humans are marijuana and hallucinogens. People also abuse substances that are not drugs, like glue, gasoline, and aerosols. Most of these substances are **inhalants**—they are sniffed for their effect on the nervous system. Inhalants generally depress, or slow, the functioning of the nervous system, sometimes causing their users to lose control or become unconscious.

Key Ideas

- Infections occur when the body is invaded by germs—microorganisms that cause disease.
- A healthy diet has the right nutrients—proteins, carbohydrates, fats, vitamins, minerals, and water.
- The abuse of drugs and other substances can cause physical changes and interfere with a person's daily functioning.

ON THE GED

All the questions on the GED Science Test are in multiple-choice format. For each question, you must pick the one correct answer from the five options that are given.

LIFE SCIENCE ▸ PRACTICE 4

Directions: Choose the one best answer to each question.

1. Which of the following is among the body's first barriers against germs?

   (1) the immune system
   (2) antibiotics
   (3) antibodies
   (4) the skin
   (5) fever

2. Each evening, Sara has a glass of wine. If there is no wine in the house, she feels a strong urge to get some, although she feels no ill effects if she does not.

   What is Sara's relationship to alcohol?

   (1) addiction
   (2) physical dependence
   (3) habituation
   (4) withdrawal
   (5) abuse

Nutrients in the Diet

Nutrient	Description	Function	Source
Proteins	Complex molecules (amino acids) made of oxygen, carbon, nitrogen, hydrogen	Growth and maintenance of cells and metabolism	Meat, fish, eggs, dairy products, legumes, nuts, seeds
Carbohydrates	Molecules containing oxygen, carbon, and hydrogen	Body's main energy source, providing 4 calories of energy per gram; roughage for digestion	Bread, pasta, cereal, rice, fruits, potatoes
Fats	Fatty acids containing oxygen, carbon, and hydrogen	Concentrated source of energy, providing 9 calories of energy per gram; insulation; cell maintenance	Fish oils, vegetable oils, and animal fats
Vitamins	Substances used in very small quantities that are vital for body chemistry	Growth maintenance, repair of cells; protein synthesis; metabolism; and other functions	Various foods, daylight on skin (Vitamin D), microorganisms in the bowel (Vitamin K)
Minerals	Substances, such as iron and calcium, necessary for normal development	Many functions, including making red blood cells and building strong bones	Various foods
Water	A liquid made of oxygen and hydrogen atoms	involved in almost all body processes	Beverages, soups, foods

3. Which of the following statements is supported by the information in the table?

   (1) Fats are a more concentrated source of energy than carbohydrates.
   (2) Water is necessary for only a few body processes.
   (3) Vitamins are more important in the diet than minerals.
   (4) A good source of Vitamin C is citrus fruits.
   (5) Minerals provide a low-fat source of energy.

4. Which of the following is a fact, rather than an opinion, based on the table?

   (1) Eating meat is the best way to get sufficient protein in your diet.
   (2) Carbohydrates come from fruits and vegetables as well as from bread and rice.
   (3) Fats are always bad to include in your diet.
   (4) Iron is the only mineral you need.
   (5) Everyone should drink eight glasses of water each day.

Answers and explanations start on page 650.

LIFE SCIENCE

Reproduction and Heredity

Organisms reproduce so that their **species** may continue. There are two types of reproduction. In **asexual reproduction,** an individual organism produces offspring identical to the parent. For example, in a type of asexual reproduction called budding, a tiny freshwater animal called a hydra grows buds that develop into offspring. In **sexual reproduction,** a male and a female parent combine their specialized sex cells, called **sperm** and **ova,** to produce unique offspring with characteristics from both parents.

Physical characteristics of organisms are called **traits.** The passing of traits from parents to offspring in sexual reproduction is called **heredity.** The first person to study heredity in a systematic way was an Austrian monk, **Gregor Mendel** (1822–1884). He bred plants and observed that sometimes offspring plants had the same traits as the parents and sometimes they did not. Mendel experimented with **purebred** pea plants—plants that always produced offspring with the same form of a trait as the parent. For example, purebred short plants always produced short offspring. First he crossed purebred short plants with purebred tall plants. In the first generation of offspring, all the plants were tall—the shortness trait had vanished. When the first-generation offspring reproduced, about three-quarters of the next generation of plants were tall, and one-quarter were short. The shortness trait had reappeared.

Mendel repeated his pea plant experiments with other traits over a ten-year period. Eventually he concluded that individual factors from each parent plant control the **inheritance** of specific traits. An offspring plant inherited one factor from the female parent and one from the male parent. Mendel concluded that one factor in a pair can hide the other factor. For example, the tallness factor hid the shortness factor in the first generation of offspring.

The factors that control traits are called **genes.** Different forms of a gene are called **alleles.** The gene that controls pea plant height, for example, has one allele for tallness and one allele for shortness. Each pea plant inherits one allele for the height gene from each parent. Therefore any particular pea plant may have (1) two alleles for tallness, (2) two alleles for shortness, or (3) one allele for shortness and one for tallness. In the third case, the **dominant allele,** the tallness allele, controls the appearance of the trait. The **recessive allele,** the shortness allele, is hidden. For a recessive trait to appear in an individual, the individual must inherit two recessive alleles.

In Mendel's original experiment, the parent plants were purebred tall and purebred short. Thus, one parent had two dominant alleles for tallness, and the other parent had two recessive alleles for shortness. All the offspring in the first generation were **hybrid**—each had one allele for tallness and one for shortness. Because the tallness allele is dominant, all of the first generation plants were tall. In the next generation, some plants inherited two dominant alleles, some inherited two recessive alleles, and some inherited one dominant and one recessive allele, producing a mix of plants.

LIFE SCIENCE ▸ PRACTICE 5

Directions: Choose the <u>one best answer</u> to each question.

Questions 1 through 3 refer to the following paragraph and diagram.

The Punnett square below shows all the possible combinations of alleles for height in offspring pea plants when two tall hybrid pea plants are crossed. A capital *T* represents the dominant tallness allele, and a lowercase *t*, the recessive shortness allele. One parent's alleles are shown along the top of the square; the other's are shown on the left side. The **genotypes** of the offspring are shown in the boxes.

	T	t
T	TT	Tt
t	Tt	tt

1. What do the parent pea plants look like?

(1) Both are tall.
(2) Both are short.
(3) One is tall and one is short.
(4) Both are medium-sized.
(5) One is tall and one is medium-sized.

2. What chance is there that an offspring will be short?

(1) 0 out of 4
(2) 1 out of 4
(3) 2 out of 4
(4) 3 out of 4
(5) 4 out of 4

3. If you wanted to grow only tall pea plants in your garden over several growing seasons, which of the following genotypes would give you the best results?

(1) tt
(2) Tt
(3) tT
(4) TT
(5) Ttt

4. According to the passage on page 242, in order to show a recessive trait, how many recessive alleles for that trait must an organism inherit?

(1) 0
(2) 1
(3) 2
(4) 3
(5) 4

5. Why are organisms that reproduce sexually more genetically diverse than organisms that reproduce asexually?

(1) Organisms that reproduce sexually tend to produce more offspring than those that reproduce asexually.
(2) Organisms that reproduce asexually tend to produce more offspring than those that reproduce sexually.
(3) Organisms that reproduce sexually produce offspring that inherit diverse traits from only one parent.
(4) Organisms that reproduce sexually produce offspring with entirely new traits unlike those of either parent.
(5) Organisms that reproduce sexually produce offspring that have inherited a mix of traits from their parents.

6. A student is trying to repeat Mendel's experiments using the trait of fur color in rabbits. Black fur is dominant, and white fur is recessive. She starts with what she assumes is a purebred white female rabbit and a purebred black male rabbit. She crosses them and is surprised when one of the offspring has white fur.

What probably was wrong with the student's experiment?

(1) The white female was actually a hybrid.
(2) The black male was actually a hybrid.
(3) Most of the offspring were hybrids.
(4) Most of the offspring were purebred.
(5) White fur is actually dominant over black fur.

Answers and explanations start on page 650.

LIFE SCIENCE

Modern Genetics

Key Ideas

- Chromosomes are structures in a cell's nucleus that are composed mostly of genes, which are located on long molecules of DNA.
- DNA contains the genetic code for making proteins in the cell.
- Knowledge of genetics has led to advances in many fields but especially in medicine.

ON THE GED

Some questions on the GED are based entirely on a graphic. You must interpret the diagram, graph, or chart correctly in order to answer these questions.

Years after Mendel died, scientists identified **chromosomes,** rod-shaped structures in the nucleus of each cell, as responsible for carrying genes from parent organisms to their offspring. Reproductive cells have half the number of chromosomes of an organism's other cells. When a sperm cell and an ovum unite, the resulting offspring has a full set of chromosomes. For example, human sex cells have 23 chromosomes and our other cells have 46.

One chromosome can contain thousands of genes on a single, long molecule of **deoxyribonucleic acid (DNA).** A DNA molecule is shaped like a spiral ladder. The sides of the ladder are made of deoxyribose—a sugar—and phosphate. Each rung of the ladder is made of a pair of nitrogen bases. There are four of these bases: adenine (A), guanine (G), thymine (T), and cytosine (C). The four bases pair up in a specific way: *A* always pairs with *T*, and *C* always pairs with *G*.

DNA

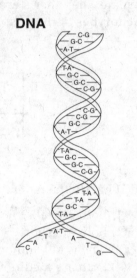

DNA controls the cell's production of proteins, which help determine all the characteristics and processes of the organism. During **protein synthesis,** the information from a gene in the cell's nucleus is used to produce a protein on ribosomes in the cytoplasm. Messenger **ribonucleic acid (RNA),** transmits the code from the DNA. Each set of three base pairs on the messenger RNA, called a **codon,** codes for an amino acid—a protein building block. The sequence of codons determines the sequence of amino acids in the protein and thus the specific protein to be made. So, the order of bases on the gene forms a **genetic code** for the synthesis of a particular protein.

There have been many recent advances in genetics, some controversial. Dolly the sheep and other animals have been cloned from single cells. Cloning bypasses sexual reproduction, raising the possibility that one day humans will be cloned—an idea that many find unethical. Through genetic engineering, the DNA of one organism is introduced into the DNA of another organism, changing the second organism's traits. Genetic engineering has been used to produce medicines, such as insulin. It has been more controversial when used to improve foods. Finally, the entire **human genome,** or genetic code, has been decoded, making possible many advances in medicine. Scientists have identified genes involved in genetic disorders such as cystic fibrosis. They have also identified genes that predispose people to diseases such as breast cancer and Alzheimer's disease. Through genetic testing, people can find out whether they have any of these disease-related genes. In some cases, they can take steps to prevent the disease or to seek early treatment. In the future, scientists may also be able to correct genetic disorders through gene therapy.

LIFE SCIENCE ▸ PRACTICE 6

Directions: Choose the <u>one best answer</u> to each question.

1. Which of the following provides the code needed for a cell to make proteins?

   (1) the number of chromosomes in the cell
   (2) the amino acids in the cytoplasm
   (3) the sequence of base pairs in a gene
   (4) the pairing of adenine with thymine
   (5) the pairing of cytosine with guanine

2. A mutation is any change in the DNA of a gene. Which of the following is the most likely result of a mutation?

   (1) the loss of one or more chromosomes
   (2) an extra chromosome
   (3) too much RNA in the cytoplasm
   (4) a problem with protein synthesis
   (5) a change in the organism's appearance

3. Some farm animals have been genetically engineered to grow larger. Plants have been engineered to resist diseases or insects. Some fruits have been engineered to ripen more slowly. Genetic engineering of domesticated plants and animals is controversial. According to some people, these foods pose a risk because their effects on consumers and the environment are unknown. Others claim that genetically engineered foods are safe.

   Which of the following statements is an opinion about genetic engineering rather than a fact?

   (1) Scientists have used genetic engineering to produce animals that grow larger.
   (2) Disease-resistant plants have been produced by genetic engineering.
   (3) Genetically engineered fruit takes longer to ripen than unaltered fruits.
   (4) Some people think that we shouldn't experiment with genetic engineering.
   (5) Genetically engineered foods are safe for consumers and the environment.

4. When a cell reproduces through cell division, scientists call the reproducing cell the parent cell; the cells that result from the division are called daughter cells. The parent cell and the daughter cells are genetically identical. Before a parent cell starts to divide, the DNA in its nucleus replicates, or makes a complete copy of itself.

   Why is this process necessary?

   (1) so that the parent cell will stop synthesizing proteins
   (2) so that the parent cell will have an extra copy of DNA
   (3) so that each daughter cell receives a complete set of DNA
   (4) so that each daughter cell will not need to synthesize proteins
   (5) so that each daughter cell will receive half its DNA from each parent cell

5. Which of the following statements is supported by the diagram and the passage on page 244?

   (1) The DNA molecule unzips between the sugar and phosphate segments.
   (2) The base guanine pairs only with the base cytosine.
   (3) In a sequence of DNA bases, guanine always comes before adenine.
   (4) DNA is the largest molecule in an organism's body.
   (5) About 10 percent of DNA contains genes; the remainder is "junk" DNA.

6. Each individual's DNA is unique to that individual, unless the person has an identical twin.

   Which of the following uses for DNA does this fact suggest?

   (1) synthesizing human proteins
   (2) cloning an individual
   (3) identifying genetic disorders
   (4) identifying a person
   (5) identifying changes in the genetic code

Answers and explanations start on page 650.

LIFE SCIENCE

Evolution and Natural Selection

Key Ideas

- Charles Darwin's observations in the Galápagos Islands led him to formulate the theory of evolution.
- Adaptations are traits that help an organism survive in its environment.
- Natural selection is the process by which individuals with favorable variations survive, reproduce, and pass the variations to their offspring.

ON THE GED

An occasional passage on the GED Science Test will cover the history of science. This information about evolution is an example of this, although it is much longer than any passage on the GED science test.

In 1831, the British ship the *Beagle* set sail with naturalist Charles Darwin (1809–1882) aboard. Darwin's job was to observe living things they encountered. His observations during this five-year trip around the world led him to formulate an important scientific theory, the theory of **evolution.**

One of the *Beagle*'s stops was the Galápagos Islands, a group of islands in the Pacific Ocean off the South American coast. There Darwin saw great diversity in life forms. He noticed that many of the plants and animals resembled those he had seen on the South American mainland. However, there were also important differences between mainland and island organisms. For example, the iguanas on the mainland had small claws that allowed them to climb trees to eat leaves. On the Galápagos, iguanas had large claws that allowed them to grip wet, slippery rocks and eat seaweed. As Darwin traveled among the Galápagos Islands, he also observed that similar species of organisms sometimes differed from island to island. For example, small birds called ground finches had strong, wide beaks well-suited for breaking and eating seeds. However, different species of ground finches had different sized beaks, depending on which island they lived on. The sizes of the iguanas' claws and the birds' beaks are examples of **adaptations,** traits that help an organism survive in its environment. From these observations, Darwin concluded that organisms had originally come from the mainland and had changed, or evolved, over many generations to become better adapted to their new, island environments.

Darwin explained that species evolve because of **natural selection.** By this process, individuals that are better adapted to their environments are more likely to survive and reproduce, passing their favorable adaptations to their offspring. Several factors are involved in natural selection:

1. Most species produce far more offspring than can survive.
2. These offspring compete with one another for scarce resources in their environment.
3. Members of a species have different traits, called **variations.** Some variations make individuals better adapted to survive in their environment.
4. Individuals with favorable variations are more likely to survive, reproduce, and pass the favorable traits to their offspring.
5. Over generations, helpful variations spread through a species, causing the species to change, or evolve.

Evolution through natural selection explains how species change over time. But how do new species evolve? Geographic isolation seems to play a big role in the evolution of new species. When a group of individuals remains separated from the rest of its species long enough, it may become a new species. This means that members of the new species will be unable to interbreed with members of the original species. For example, there are 13 species of finches on the various Galápagos Islands. They all probably evolved from a single ancestral species.

Directions: Choose the one best answer to each question.

1. What are adaptations?

   (1) traits that make an organism better able to survive in its environment
   (2) the process by which traits are passed to off-spring
   (3) traits that all members of a species possess
   (4) traits that are learned and not inherited
   (5) traits that appear only when two recessive alleles are inherited

2. The more similar the DNA of two species, the more closely related they are. Scientists have used modern DNA analysis to trace the evolutionary relationships among Darwin's 13 species of finches. DNA analysis revealed that the finch species all had very similar DNA. Thus, Darwin was correct when he proposed that they had evolved from a common ancestor.

   Why does DNA analysis provide better evidence to support the hypothesis that Darwin's finches evolved from a common ancestor than the scientific methods that Darwin used?

   (1) DNA analysis takes less time than observation.
   (2) DNA analysis is easier to do than observing birds in the wild.
   (3) DNA analysis provides more objective data than observation does.
   (4) DNA analysis is always right, and observation is rarely reliable.
   (5) Technological methods of obtaining evidence are inferior to observation.

   Questions 3 and 4 refer to the following paragraph and diagram.

   The forelimbs of humans, penguins, birds that fly, and alligators are similar. The similar pattern of the bones is evidence that these animals evolved from a common ancestor. Similar structures that organisms have inherited from a common ancestor are called homologous structures.

Homologous Structures

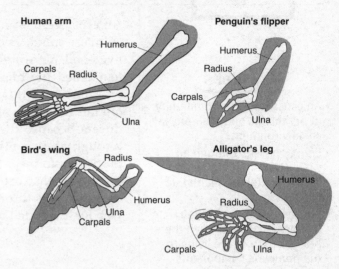

3. Which of the following organisms is most likely to have structures similar to the ones shown in the diagram, and thus be more closely related to birds, humans, and alligators?

   (1) a frog
   (2) a starfish
   (3) a worm
   (4) a spider
   (5) a butterfly

4. Which of the following statements is supported by the paragraph and the diagram?

   (1) The tip of a bird's wing is homologous to a human's upper arm.
   (2) Penguins are more closely related to humans than they are to birds.
   (3) Alligators are more closely related to fish than they are to birds.
   (4) In penguins, flying birds, humans, and alligators, the forelimbs have evolved to perform different functions.
   (5) Homologous structures have similar functions in modern organisms but had different functions in their ancestors.

Answers and explanations start on page 650.

LIFE SCIENCE

Organization of Ecosystems

Key Ideas

- An ecosystem is a community of organisms and their physical environment.
- Energy passes through an ecosystem from the sun, to producers (green plants), to consumers.
- Carbon, oxygen, nitrogen, and water cycle through the biosphere from the living to the nonliving components and back again.

An **ecosystem** is an area consisting of a community of organisms—plants, animals, fungi, bacteria—and the physical environment in which they live—soil, air, water, and climate. Earth as a whole is an enormous ecosystem called the **biosphere.** Smaller ecosystems include meadows, ponds, wetlands, and tidal zones. A healthy ecosystem contains a diversity of organisms. Some of the organisms, such as green plants, are called **producers** because they use energy from the sun to make their own food through photosynthesis. Other organisms, called **consumers,** depend on producers to meet their energy needs. These organisms eat plants, or eat organisms that eat plants, to get energy. The complex pattern in which energy passes through an ecosystem is called a **food web.** A simple food web for a wooded area is shown here.

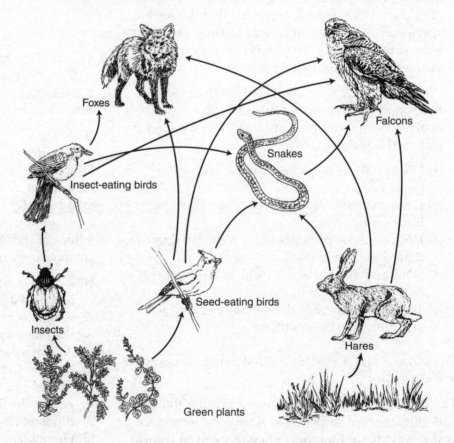

Foxes
Falcons
Snakes
Insect-eating birds
Seed-eating birds
Hares
Insects
Green plants

ON THE GED

On the test, you may answer questions based on a short passage or graphic about a science topic.

Carbon, oxygen, nitrogen, and water also cycle through ecosystems from the living to the nonliving components and back again. As discussed in Lesson 2, carbon and oxygen cycle through the biosphere as a result of photosynthesis and cellular respiration. Nitrogen cycles between the land, organisms, and the air through chemical processes. Water cycles between the oceans and other surface water, the air, land, and organisms through evaporation, condensation, precipitation, and transpiration from plants.

LIFE SCIENCE ▸ PRACTICE 8

Directions: Choose the one best answer to each question.

1. According to the passage, what is the ultimate source of energy for the food web on page 248?

   (1) green plants
   (2) mammals
   (3) insects
   (4) soil, air, and water
   (5) the sun

2. Suppose most of the foxes in the woodland ecosystem on page 248 were hunted and killed. Which of the following is most likely to happen as a result?

   (1) The amount of plant life in the woodland would increase.
   (2) The population of falcons would decrease.
   (3) The populations of hares and seed-eating birds would increase.
   (4) The populations of insects and insect-eating birds would decrease.
   (5) The population of snakes would decrease.

3. Which of the following is most similar to a naturally occurring ecosystem?

   (1) a diorama with dried vegetation and stuffed animals
   (2) an aquarium with aquatic plants and tropical fish
   (3) an animal shelter with stray dogs, cats, and other pets
   (4) a house with central air conditioning and heating
   (5) a supermarket with a large section of fresh fruits and vegetables

4. In most cases, changes in one aspect of an ecosystem result in reactions in other parts of the ecosystem, restoring balance. In some cases, however, changes can be so great that the original ecosystem is replaced with another. When this occurs naturally, as when grasslands replace woods because of drier conditions and lightning fires, it is called succession.

   Which of the following statements is supported by the information above?

   (1) Minor changes often put an ecosystem out of balance.
   (2) When changes are introduced into an ecosystem, its balance is permanently disrupted.
   (3) Succession is usually caused by human destruction of an ecosystem.
   (4) The replacement of a wooded area by a field of cultivated wheat is an example of succession.
   (5) The replacement of oak and hickory forests by red maple forests is an example of succession.

5. Although more than three-quarters of the atmosphere is nitrogen, atmospheric nitrogen cannot be used directly by plants and animals. Instead, certain bacteria and blue-green algae take nitrogen from the air and through a process called nitrogen fixation, turn it into compounds that plants can use. Nitrogen-fixing bacteria are found in the roots of some plants such as peas and beans. When these plants are present, the nitrate content of the soil is increased. Nitrates are absorbed by plants, which are eaten by consumers. Eventually the nitrogen returns to the soil in excrement and when organisms die.

   What is the role of nitrogen-fixing bacteria in the nitrogen cycle?

   (1) to decompose dead plants and animals
   (2) to add nitrogen to the atmosphere
   (3) to turn atmospheric nitrogen into compounds plants and animals can use
   (4) to change nitrogen compounds into pure nitrogen
   (5) to take nitrogen from blue-green algae and turn it into compounds plants can use

Answers and explanations start on page 651.

LIFE SCIENCE PRACTICE QUESTIONS

Directions: Choose the <u>one best answer</u> to each question.

1. Cell membranes are selectively permeable, allowing some substances to pass through and blocking others. The movement through the cell membrane takes place by means of passive or active transport. In passive transport, materials like water move through the membrane without using any of the cell's energy. In active transport, the cell uses energy to move substances in and out. For example, transport proteins use energy when they carry molecules into and out of the cell.

What is the main difference between passive transport and active transport?

(1) Active transport involves the passage of water, and passive transport does not.
(2) Active transport requires the cell to move, and passive transport does not.
(3) Active transport requires the cell to use energy, and passive transport does not.
(4) Active transport is used by animal cells, and passive transport is used by plant cells.
(5) Active transport takes substances out of the cell, and passive transport brings them in.

2. An ecologist is a scientist who studies the relationship between living things and their environment.

Which of the following is most likely to be studied by an ecologist?

(1) biochemical processes involved in producing energy in a cell
(2) classification of organisms according to evolutionary relationships
(3) structure and function of mammalian reproductive systems
(4) role of the immune system in organ transplants
(5) species interactions in saltwater marshlands

Questions 3 and 4 refer to the following information and diagram.

A pedigree shows the pattern of inheritance of a trait in a family. In a pedigree, circles represent females; squares represent males. A completely shaded shape indicates that the person has the trait. A half-shaded shape indicates the person carries the recessive form of the gene for the trait but does not have the trait. An unshaded shape indicates the person neither has nor carries the trait. In the following pedigree, Megan is a carrier of the genetic disorder cystic fibrosis, although she is healthy.

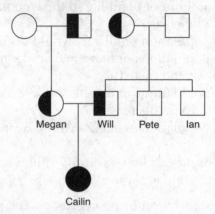

3. Which of the following people is a carrier of cystic fibrosis?

(1) Megan's mother
(2) Megan's father
(3) Will's father
(4) Pete
(5) Ian

4. Which of the following best explains why Megan's and Will's families were surprised to learn Cailin had inherited cystic fibrosis?

(1) Megan and Will are carriers of cystic fibrosis.
(2) Pete and Ian are not carriers of cystic fibrosis.
(3) Will's parents do not have cystic fibrosis.
(4) Megan's father and Will's mother are carriers of cystic fibrosis.
(5) No one in either family has cystic fibrosis except Cailin.

Questions 5 through 7 refer to the following diagram and paragraph.

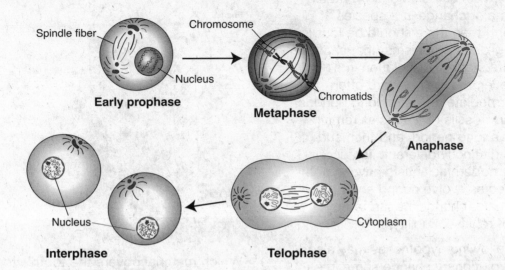

Mitosis is a type of cell division in which two daughter cells that have the same genetic material as the parent cell. Before mitosis starts, each chromosome in the nucleus duplicates itself to produce two sections, called chromatids, that are linked.

5. During which stage do the chromosomes line up across the middle of the cell?

(1) early prophase
(2) metaphase
(3) anaphase
(4) telophase
(5) interphase

6. What is the function of the spindle during mitosis?

(1) to duplicate the chromosomes
(2) to control the movement of chromosomes
(3) to dissolve the nuclear membrane
(4) to pinch the cell membrane
(5) to help divide the cytoplasm for the two daughter cells

7. Bacteria divide by mitosis. Which of the following gives the best evidence for how a bacterial infection can spread quickly when the body's immune system cannot control it?

(1) Bacterial cells are very mobile and can move quickly through the cytoplasm.
(2) Bacterial cells are transported throughout the body in the blood.
(3) Mitosis occurs in geometric progression: 1 cell, 2 cells, 4 cells, 8 cells, 16 cells, etc.
(4) Cell division takes place more rapidly in bacteria than in other types of cells.
(5) Cell division occurs when a bacterial cell gets too large to function properly.

8. A distinction is sometimes made between preserving an ecosystem in its natural state and conserving an ecosystem, or managing it to balance the needs of wildlife and the local human population.

When would conservation be more likely to be used than preservation in an ecosystem?

(1) if humans needed to make a living there
(2) if there were no local human population
(3) if the human population were very small
(4) if the ecosystem were unique
(5) if the ecosystem were far from human settlements

9. Charles Darwin thought that evolution took place gradually, with tiny changes eventually adding up to major change in a species. If this view is right, then there should be fossils, remains of long-dead organisms, that show the intermediate stages of evolution in a species. However, the fossil record often shows no intermediate forms for long periods of time. Instead, fossils of a species remain the same over a long period, and then suddenly become distinctly different. To account for this, some modern scientists have hypothesized that species evolve during short periods of rapid, major change, separated by long periods of relative stability.

Which of the following hypotheses may also explain why evolutionary change sometimes seems to occur rapidly and dramatically?

(1) Organisms with soft tissues rarely form fossils.
(2) Fossils usually form in layers of sedimentary rock.
(3) Genetic change occurs only slowly in most species.
(4) The fossil record for any given species may be incomplete.
(5) Fossils do not provide evidence for evolution.

10. Blood consists of blood cells and proteins suspended in a yellowish liquid called plasma. Red blood cells carry oxygen to the cells. White blood cells protect the body against infection. Plasma transports nutrients and hormones to the body's cells and removes waste.

What are the main functions of blood?

(1) hormone and energy production
(2) energy production and movement
(3) movement and cell repair
(4) cell repair and transport
(5) transport and defense

Questions 11 and 12 refer to the following diagram.

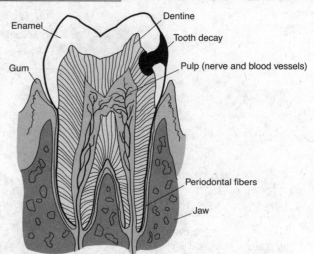

11. Which material covers the tooth's top surface?

(1) enamel
(2) decay
(3) nerve fibers
(4) blood vessels
(5) periodontal fibers

12. Tooth decay can eat away at the structure of a tooth. Which part of the tooth must decay reach to cause extreme pain?

(1) the surface
(2) the enamel
(3) the dentine
(4) the crown
(5) the pulp

13. The carrying capacity of an ecosystem is the maximum number of organisms it can support. If the carrying capacity is exceeded, there will not be enough resources, and one or more species will decline until a balance of organisms and resources is reached.

Which of the following is an example of people overloading the carrying capacity of an ecosystem?

(1) using a park for recreation
(2) grazing too many cattle on grassland
(3) hiking the length of the Appalachian trail
(4) adding a room to a suburban house
(5) banning shellfishing in polluted waters

14. Classification is the grouping of organisms based on similarities in their traits and their evolutionary histories. In the past, scientists classified organisms based primarily on a visual analysis of their structures and on the fossil record. Today, DNA analysis of selected genes is overturning many traditional classifications. For example, it was thought that sperm whales and dolphins, both of which have teeth, were closely related. However, DNA analysis revealed that sperm whales are actually more closely related to baleen whales, which do not have teeth.

What is the reason that DNA analysis has led to changes in the classification of organisms?

(1) DNA analysis provides more fundamental, accurate data than does a visual analysis of structures and fossils.
(2) Traditional classification was based on the erroneous assumption that organisms could be grouped by similarities.
(3) The fossil record is not a reliable source of information about organisms in the past.
(4) When organisms possess similar structures, it always means that they are closely related.
(5) When data from DNA analysis conflicts with data from structural analysis, usually the structural data is correct.

15. Homeothermy refers to the maintenance of a constant body temperature in warm-blooded animals, such as dogs and human beings. Warm-blooded animals have specific body processes that help them gain or lose heat.

Which of the following body processes are involved in homeothermy?

(1) cell repair and growth
(2) resting and sleeping
(3) panting and sweating
(4) eating and digesting
(5) mating and reproducing

Question 16 refers to the following graph.

Leading Causes of Death in the United States, 1980 and 1998

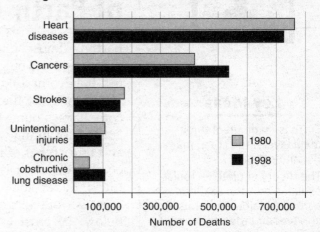

SOURCE: National Center for Health Statistics

16. For which cause did the number of deaths double between 1980 and 1998?

(1) heart diseases
(2) cancer
(3) strokes
(4) unintentional injuries
(5) chronic obstructive lung diseases

17. Ben set up an experiment to prove that ivy plants take in water through their roots. He took a jar, filled it with water, and put an ivy plant in the open jar. After a week, he checked the water level in the jar and found it had gone down. Ben concluded the plant absorbed water through its roots.

Why does Ben have insufficient proof for his conclusion?

(1) Ben should have put more ivy plants in the open jar.
(2) Ben should have put several plants of different species in the open jar.
(3) The water level in the jar might have gone down because of evaporation.
(4) The water level in the jar might have been misjudged the second time.
(5) There should have been soil in the jar rather than water.

Answers and explanations start on page 651.

EARTH AND SPACE SCIENCE

Structure of Earth

Key Ideas

- Earth is made up of three main layers: the crust, mantle, and core.
- The theory of plate tectonics explains how the seafloor spreads, major landforms are created, and the continents move.
- At the margins between plates, plates move away from or toward each other, or they slide past each other.

GED TIP

When you read a multiple-choice question, try to answer it before you read the five choices. If one of the choices is similar to your answer, it is probably correct.

Earth is almost spherical, flattened at the poles and bulging at the equator. It is composed of three main layers: the crust, the mantle, and the core. Earth's outer layer, the **crust,** is made of granite, basalt, gabbro, and other types of rock. Under the oceans, the crust is 3 to 6.8 miles thick; under the continents, the crust is from 12 to 40 miles thick. Below the crust is the **mantle;** it consists of silica and metal-rich minerals. The **core** has two layers: the outer core, which is mostly liquid iron, and the inner core, which is mostly solid iron. Extreme heat and pressure characterize the core.

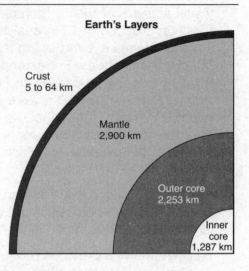

Earth's Layers

Crust 5 to 64 km

Mantle 2,900 km

Outer core 2,253 km

Inner core 1,287 km

The **theory of plate tectonics** explains phenomena of Earth's crust: seafloor spreading, the formation of major landforms, and the movement of continents. According to this theory, Earth's crust is made up of **tectonic plates** that fit together like a crude jigsaw puzzle. These plates move relative to one another at a rate of up to 15 centimeters (6 inches) a year. At the boundaries between plates, major landforms such as mountain ranges, volcanoes, ocean trenches, and mid-ocean ridges form, and earthquakes occur. There are three types of plate boundaries, or **margins.**

- At a **constructive margin,** two plates are moving apart and new crust is forming. Molten material from the mantle below wells up in the space between the plates, hardens, and forms new crust, usually at a mid-ocean ridge. For example, at the Mid-Atlantic Ridge, new crust is forming, causing the seafloor to spread and grow by about 5 centimeters (2 inches) a year.

- At a **destructive margin,** two plates are colliding and crust is being destroyed. When a continental plate collides with an oceanic plate, the denser oceanic crust may be forced under the other plate, forming a deep trench. When two plates consisting of continental crust collide, the crust crumples to form mountain ranges such as the Andes.

- At a **transform,** or **conservative, margin,** two plates are sliding by one another, and no crust is created or destroyed. For example, the San Andreas fault in California is the boundary between the North American plate and the Pacific plate, which is sliding northwest, causing many earthquakes.

As the plates move, they carry the continents with them. Scientists believe that a single large continent, **Pangaea,** existed about 250 million years ago. It gradually broke apart, and over millions of years the pieces (which are today's continents) drifted into the locations they are in today.

EARTH AND SPACE SCIENCE ► PRACTICE 1

Directions: Choose the <u>one best answer</u> to each question.

1. What does the theory of plate tectonics explain?

   (1) changes in Earth's crust
   (2) changes in Earth's mantle
   (3) changes in the composition of Earth's layers
   (4) why there is extreme heat and pressure in Earth's core
   (5) how Earth originally formed

2. According to the information and the diagram on page 254, what is the main difference between the inner and outer core?

   (1) The inner core is made of iron, and the outer core is made of rock.
   (2) The inner core is made of rock, and the outer core is made of iron.
   (3) The inner core is solid, and the outer core is liquid.
   (4) The inner core is liquid, and the outer core is solid.
   (5) The inner core is much thicker than the outer core.

3. The Japan Trench off the coast of Japan is part of the boundary between an oceanic plate called the Pacific plate and a continental plate called the Eurasian plate. The islands of Japan are volcanic in origin, and they experience many earthquakes.

   The Japan Trench is an example of which type of crustal feature?

   (1) a tectonic plate
   (2) a mid-ocean ridge
   (3) a constructive margin
   (4) a destructive margin
   (5) a transform, or conservative, margin

4. Which of the following provides evidence that the present-day continents were once one large continent that broke apart?

   (1) The Andes mountains of South America formed at a destructive margin.
   (2) Australia is a large, continent-sized island.
   (3) Eurasia is the largest land mass on Earth today.
   (4) Australia and Antarctica are located in the Southern Hemisphere.
   (5) The west coast of Africa seems to fit into the east coast of the Americas.

5. Which of the following is implied by the fact that seafloor spreading at the Mid-Atlantic Ridge is causing the Atlantic Ocean to widen by about 5 centimeters a year?

   (1) The Mid-Atlantic Ridge is thousands of miles long.
   (2) The Mid-Atlantic Ridge is the largest underwater structure in the Atlantic Ocean.
   (3) Shallow earthquakes frequently occur along the Mid-Atlantic Ridge.
   (4) The continents of North America and Europe are moving apart.
   (5) The continents of North America and Europe are growing larger at the Mid-Atlantic Ridge.

6. Which of the following is a theory rather than a fact?

   (1) The San Andreas fault is the boundary between the North American and Pacific plates.
   (2) New crust forms at constructive margins where material from the mantle wells up.
   (3) A single large landmass called Pangaea existed about 250 million years ago.
   (4) The Earth's crust is composed of rocks like granite, basalt, and gabbro.
   (5) Earthquakes often occur along tectonic plate boundaries.

Answers and explanations start on page 652.

EARTH AND SPACE SCIENCE

Earth's Resources

Key Ideas

- Natural resources include air, water, soil, minerals, and energy.
- Resources are either renewable (having an endless supply) or nonrenewable (having a limited supply).
- Conservation efforts limit the consumption, overuse, and pollution of the natural environment.

A **resource** is anything that is needed by humans to survive. Natural resources include air, water, soil, minerals, and energy. Air is involved in respiration, climate, and weather. Water is used for drinking, cooking, bathing, agriculture, and industrial processes. Less than 3 percent of the world's water is fresh water. **Soil** is the layer of loose disintegrated rock, organic matter, living organisms, air, and water in which rooted plants, including agricultural plants, grow. **Minerals** are the naturally forming inorganic substances with a crystalline structure of which rocks are made; they have many uses—from talcum powder to uranium fuel rods to diamond drill bits. **Energy resources** include fossil fuels, flowing water, wind, **solar energy,** and **geothermal energy.**

Resources can be classified as nonrenewable or renewable. **Nonrenewable resources** are those that take millions of years to form naturally; when they are used up, there is no replacement for them. For example, fossil fuels, including peat, coal, natural gas, and oil, are nonrenewable resources because they form over millions of years from decaying plant remains. Fossil fuels are our main source of energy for heating, transportation, and the generation of electricity. Soil and minerals are also nonrenewable resources.

Renewable resources are those whose supply will not run out, either because there is an unlimited supply, as is the case with **solar energy** (energy from the sun), or because the resource cycles through the environment, as is the case with water. In addition to solar energy, renewable energy resources include the water power of flowing rivers; tidal and wave power from the movement of ocean water; wind power from the movement of air; and geothermal power from the heat in the Earth's crust. All of these are used as alternative sources of energy to generate electricity.

People harm or destroy natural resources through consumption, overuse, and pollution. For example, some scientists estimate that we have already consumed between one-tenth and one-quarter of the world's supply of oil. Soil is subject to agricultural overuse and erosion. Air is polluted by fossil fuel emissions and its **ozone layer** is depleted by the release of compounds called chlorofluorocarbons (CFCs) into the atmosphere. Water is polluted by sewage, industrial waste, and agricultural and urban runoff.

Conservation is any action taken to preserve natural resources and protect the natural environment. Conservation involves a wide range of activities, including building more efficient combustion engines to reduce gasoline consumption; using catalytic converters to reduce the harmful emissions of burning fossil fuels; developing technologies to exploit renewable sources of energy; recycling glass, plastic, and metal wastes; using agricultural methods that protect the soil; building water treatment and sewage treatment plants; safely disposing of radioactive wastes; and cleaning up sites heavily polluted by industry.

ON THE GED

Some earth and space science questions may deal with the impact of humans on natural resources and the environment.

Directions: Choose the <u>one best answer</u> to each question.

<u>Questions 1 and 2</u> refer to the following graph.

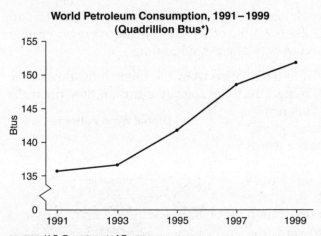

World Petroleum Consumption, 1991–1999 (Quadrillion Btus*)

SOURCE: U.S. Department of Energy
* Btus (British thermal units) are a measure of energy.

1. Approximately how many quadrillion Btus of petroleum were consumed in 1999?

   (1) 130
   (2) 137
   (3) 142
   (4) 148
   (5) 152

2. Which of the following sentences best summarizes the information in the graph?

   (1) During the 1990s, the industrialized nations used most of the world's petroleum.
   (2) World petroleum consumption increased by about 16 quadrillion Btus between 1991 and 1999.
   (3) World petroleum consumption doubled between 1991 and 1999.
   (4) World petroleum consumption quadrupled between 1991 and 1999.
   (5) World petroleum consumption was less than production from 1991 to 1999.

3. Which of the following proverbs best expresses the views of a conservationist?

   (1) All that glitters is not gold.
   (2) Easy come, easy go.
   (3) Every cloud has a silver lining.
   (4) Oil and water don't mix.
   (5) Waste not, want not.

4. The overall demand for water in the developed nations is rising. But it is not rising as quickly as people had predicted it would. In fact, the rate of water consumption per person per year in developed nations has actually dropped. This means that even though population has increased and industrial output has grown, the rate at which people withdraw water from reservoirs, rivers, and aquifers has slowed.

   Which of the following is a likely reason for the drop in demand for water in developed countries?

   (1) Vast new supplies of water have been found in the developed nations.
   (2) Developed nations have started using water more efficiently than they did in the past.
   (3) Developed nations are sharing water resources with each other.
   (4) Some developed nations export fresh water to other nations that lack it.
   (5) The drop in population in developed nations causes a decreased demand for water.

5. Soil erosion occurs when soil is worn away by the natural action of wind, water, and ice or by deforestation and poor farming practices. If soil erosion continues for a long time, it can lead to the formation of deserts. Some scientists estimate that the world lost about 20 percent of its farm topsoil between 1950 and 1990. Contour plowing, planting trees to serve as windbreaks, and other techniques can all reduce soil erosion.

   Which of the following statements is supported by the information above?

   (1) All deserts originally formed as a result of soil erosion.
   (2) Most soil erosion is caused by poor farming practices.
   (3) In some nations, soil erosion is the major environmental problem.
   (4) Improved farming techniques can completely halt soil erosion.
   (5) Soil erosion is caused by both natural forces and the actions of people.

Answers and explanations start on page 652.

EARTH AND SPACE SCIENCE

Weather and Climate

Key Ideas

- Weather is the day-to-day change in atmospheric conditions at a particular place. Climate is the average long-term weather conditions in a region.
- Weather and climate are influenced by global air patterns and ocean currents.
- Daily weather is caused by the movement of air masses and is predicted by meteorologists.

ON THE GED

About 20% of the questions on the GED Science Test will cover earth and space science topics.

Weather is the day-to-day change in conditions in the **atmosphere** at a particular place on Earth. **Climate,** on the other hand, is the average weather conditions of a large region over a long period of time.

All weather and climate ultimately arise from the uneven heating of the Earth. The sun's rays fall more directly at the equator than they do at the North and South Poles. This resulting uneven heating causes global wind circulation patterns: the warm air at the equator rises, creating an area of low pressure, and moves toward the poles. Cold air at the poles sinks, creating an area of high pressure, and moves toward the equator. The result is a pattern of **prevailing winds** in both the Northern and Southern hemispheres.

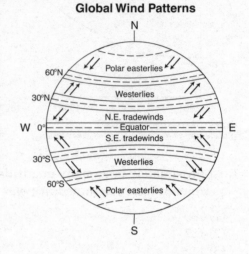

Global Wind Patterns

Another major influence on weather and climate, also caused by the uneven heating of Earth, is the worldwide pattern of **ocean currents.** Ocean currents are caused by the wind and by variations in the density of water (warm water is less dense than cold water). Ocean currents help transfer heat from the equatorial regions to the poles.

Daily weather patterns are caused by the movements of **air masses,** large bodies of air with similar temperature, humidity, and pressure. The boundary between two air masses is called a **front.** A **cold front** occurs where a cold air mass overtakes and displaces a warm air mass. A **warm front** occurs where a warm air mass rises over a cold air mass. An **occluded front** occurs when a cold front catches up with a warm front and the two weather systems merge. Clouds and **precipitation** are characteristic of fronts.

Meteorologists study the short-term weather patterns and data of particular areas. At meteorological stations around the world, temperature, humidity, cloud cover, wind, and other weather data are collected. Satellites and radar are also used to collect weather data. Weather predictions are based on comparing present weather conditions to computer models of previous weather conditions and storm systems in an area. When hurricanes, tornadoes, blizzards, or floods are forecast, meteorologists issue storm watches and warnings. For example, if a hurricane might reach an area in 24 to 36 hours, a hurricane watch is issued. If a hurricane is expected in an area in less than 24 hours, a hurricane warning is issued, and people are urged to take precautionary measures against the storm.

Directions: Choose the <u>one best answer</u> to each question.

1. The diagram of global wind patterns on page 258 suggests that weather systems between 30°N and 60°N generally move in which direction?

   (1) northeast to southwest
   (2) northwest to southeast
   (3) south to north
   (4) southeast to northwest
   (5) southwest to northeast

2. Based on the diagram on page 258, how do the prevailing winds in the Northern Hemisphere compare to the prevailing winds in the Southern Hemisphere?

   (1) The winds in the Northern Hemisphere blow faster than those in the Southern Hemisphere.
   (2) The winds in the Northern Hemisphere are a mirror image of those in the Southern Hemisphere.
   (3) The winds in the Northern Hemisphere hold more moisture than those in the Southern Hemisphere.
   (4) The winds in the Northern Hemisphere blow east and those in the Southern Hemisphere blow west.
   (5) The winds in the Northern Hemisphere blow west and those in the Southern Hemisphere blow east.

3. Hurricanes are violent storms with high winds and rain that form over the ocean. They cover an area 300 to 600 miles across, and move relatively slowly—between 5 and 15 miles per hour. Meteorologists can now predict their paths with a great deal of accuracy.

   Which of the following technologies best accounts for better hurricane tracking?

   (1) anemometers, which measure wind speed
   (2) barometers, which measure air pressure
   (3) thermometers, which measure air temperature
   (4) the Beaufort wind scale, a method of estimating wind speed
   (5) satellites, which transmit cloud photos and weather data

4. Which of the following help even out the unbalanced heating of Earth as a whole?

   (1) precipitation associated with fronts
   (2) local air masses
   (3) tornadoes, blizzards, and floods
   (4) global wind and ocean current patterns
   (5) satellite and radar systems

Questions 5 and 6 refer to the following chart.

Layers of the Atmosphere

Layer	Altitude	Temperature
Troposphere	0 to 6 miles	Average 59°F
Stratosphere	6 to 31 miles	−76°F to 32°F
Mesophere and ionosphere	31 to 50 miles	32°F to −212°F
Thermosphere	50 to 435 miles	Up to thousands of degrees

5. For which of the following statements does the chart provide evidence?

   (1) The higher you go in the atmosphere, the colder it gets.
   (2) The higher you go in the atmosphere, the less oxygen there is to breathe.
   (3) The highest layer of the atmosphere is the stratosphere.
   (4) The highest temperatures in the atmosphere are in the thermosphere.
   (5) The ozone layer is located within the stratosphere.

6. In which layer of the atmosphere does most human activity take place?

   (1) the troposphere
   (2) the stratosphere
   (3) the mesosphere
   (4) the ionosphere
   (5) the thermosphere

Answers and explanations start on page 652.

EARTH AND SPACE SCIENCE

Earth in the Solar System

The **solar system** consists of the sun, a star; the **planets;** their **satellites,** or moons; the **asteroids,** sometimes called the minor planets; and the comets. The sun contains more than 99 percent of the **mass** (amount of matter) in the solar system, and all the other celestial bodies revolve around it, held by the force of **gravity.**

The eight planets of the solar system include (in order from the sun) Mercury, Venus, Earth, Mars, Jupiter, Saturn, Uranus, and Neptune. Mercury, Venus, Earth, and Mars are called the **inner planets** because they are relatively close to the sun. They are all small, rocky planets. Jupiter, Saturn, Uranus, and Neptune are called the **outer planets** because of their great distance from the sun. The outer planets are gas giants. Some facts about the planets are presented in the following chart.

The Planets of Our Solar System

Planet	Distance from sun	Diameter	Number of moons	Rotation period (day)	Revolution period (year)
Mercury	36 million mi	3,030 mi	None	59 Earth days	88 Earth days
Venus	67 million mi	7,500 mi	None	243 Earth days	225 Earth days
Earth	93 million mi	7,923 mi	1	23 hr 56 min 4.1 sec	365 days 5 hr 48 min 46 sec
Mars	142 million mi	4,210 mi	2	24 hr 37 min	687 Earth days
Jupiter	484 million mi	88,700 mi	16	9 hr 51 min	11.86 Earth years
Saturn	0.9 million mi	75,000 mi	18	10 hr 14 min	29.46 Earth years
Uranus	1.8 million mi	31,600 mi	17	17 hr 12 min	84 Earth years
Neptune	2.8 million mi	30,200 mi	8	16 hr 7 min	164.8 Earth years

Earth is unusual among the planets in that about 70 percent of its surface is covered by water. It is the only celestial body in the solar system on which life is known to exist. Earth's rocky satellite, the moon, is the fifth largest satellite in the solar system. It has no atmosphere, but it does have some surface ice, which was discovered in 1998. The moon revolves around Earth once every 27 days. During the lunar month, the moon appears to go through a series of **phases**—changes in the proportion of its surface that is in shadow. U.S. astronauts landed on the moon in several missions from 1969 to 1972, making it the only celestial body visited by crewed spacecraft.

Directions: Choose the <u>one best answer</u> to each question.

1. According to the chart on page 260, which of the planets takes the shortest to revolve, or complete its orbit, around the sun?

   (1) Mars
   (2) Saturn
   (3) Uranus
   (4) Neptune
   (5) Mercury

2. According to the chart, which of the following planets is most similar to Earth?

   (1) Mercury
   (2) Venus
   (3) Jupiter
   (4) Neptune
   (5) Mars

3. Before 1781, the only planets that were known were the ones visible to the naked eye: Mercury, Venus, Mars, Jupiter, and Saturn. In 1781, William Herschel, an astronomer who made his own superb and powerful telescopes, discovered a strange "star" that appeared as a greenish disk rather than a point of light. A few nights later he observed that this "star" had moved relative to the background of the other stars. Herschel realized he had discovered another planet. It was named Uranus, after the Greek sky god. Later it was found that Uranus had actually been observed at least 20 times before, as far back as 1690, but each time it had been identified as a star.

   Which of the following is an unstated assumption that could help account for the fact that Uranus was misidentified as a star prior to 1781?

   (1) Uranus was visible to the naked eye only under good conditions.
   (2) Uranus takes 84 earth years to revolve around the sun.
   (3) The length of a day on Uranus is about 17 hours.
   (4) Uranus was not clearly visible with the telescopes generally in use at the time.
   (5) Uranus was not visible when it was on the other side of the sun.

4. According to the chart on page 260, which of the following planets has the most moons?

   (1) Mercury
   (2) Jupiter
   (3) Saturn
   (4) Uranus
   (5) Neptune

5. According to some estimates, it would cost about ten times more to send a crewed mission to Mars to collect geologic samples and look for life than it would cost to send a robotic mission. Some people think that a human mission would yield much more relevant data, justifying the additional cost. Others think there is no scientific reason to send crewed missions, which are costly and risky, when robotic missions will do.

   Which of the following values is most likely to provide the motivation to send a crewed mission to Mars despite the risk and the additional cost?

   (1) a desire to provide equal opportunities for astronauts of all nationalities
   (2) a desire for economic development
   (3) a love of technology for technology's sake
   (4) a desire to demonstrate the superiority of computers over humans
   (5) faith in human judgment and decision-making skills

6. The structure of the solar system, with the massive sun at the center and many objects revolving around it, is most similar to the structure of which of the following?

   (1) a DNA molecule, with its twisted spiral shape
   (2) an atom, with a dense nucleus and electrons orbiting the nucleus
   (3) the electromagnetic spectrum, with waves of different lengths and frequencies
   (4) the human circulatory system, with the heart pumping blood through the blood vessels
   (5) the planet Earth, with its layers of crust, mantle, and core

Answers and explanations start on page 653.

EARTH AND SPACE SCIENCE

The Expanding Universe

Key Ideas

- Stars are globes of hydrogen and helium that produce their own heat and light through nuclear reactions.
- The sun is one star in the Milky Way galaxy, a large group of stars.
- The Big Bang theory helps explain the origin of the universe. According to this theory, the universe began as a compact spot of matter that exploded.

ON THE GED

Some questions on the GED Science Test require that you understand cause-and-effect relationships.

Our sun is a medium-sized yellow **star,** a globe of helium and hydrogen gas that produces its own heat and light through nuclear reactions. Stars like our sun generally have a 10-billion-year life cycle. They begin as **protostars,** which form from clouds of condensing gases and dust called **nebulae.** As a protostar reaches a certain density and temperature, nuclear reactions begin, releasing huge amounts of energy. At this point the star is known as a **main-sequence star,** the longest stage in the stellar life cycle. After billions of years, the star begins to run out of hydrogen fuel. It may become a **red giant.** In time, the red giant becomes unstable and collapses, either exploding as a **supernova** and leaving behind a **neutron star** or losing mass slowly to become a **white dwarf.** A neutron star can be very dense, and gravity sometimes causes it to collapse in on itself, producing a **black hole.** Black holes are so called because their gravity is so great that light cannot escape from them.

The sun is just one star in a huge group of stars called the **Milky Way** galaxy. **Galaxies** consist of between one million and one trillion stars, along with clouds of gas and dust, which are held together by the force of gravity. Galaxies are classified according to their shape: spiral, barred-spiral, elliptical, and irregular. The Milky Way is a spiral galaxy. A spiral galaxy has a dense circular center with arms spiraling out from the core. Our solar system is located in one of the arms, called the Orion arm, of the Milky Way galaxy.

The Milky Way galaxy is part of a group of galaxies called the **Local Group.** There are 27 known galaxies in the Local Group, of which the Milky Way and the Andromeda galaxy are the largest.

The **universe** consists mostly of empty space with galaxies scattered throughout. Besides galaxies with stars at every stage of the life cycle, the universe has other bodies: **brown dwarfs** are objects that are less massive than a star but more massive than a planet; **pulsars** are thought to be rotating neutron stars that emit pulses of energy at regular intervals; and **quasars** are distant, starlike objects that emit more energy than a hundred galaxies.

Cosmologists study the origin, properties, and evolution of the universe. One theory about the beginning of the universe is called the **Big Bang.** According to this theory, the universe began in a hot, superdense state smaller than an atom. The Big Bang caused all this compacted material to be flung outward, accounting for the still-expanding universe. There is evidence to support the Big Bang theory. First, galaxies appear to be moving away from us in every direction, as if they all originated at the same point. Second, scientists have detected cosmic background radiation left over from the Big Bang. Cosmologists do not know what caused the Big Bang, but from the current rate of expansion of the universe, they estimate its age to be between 10 and 20 billion years.

Directions: Choose the <u>one best answer</u> to each question.

<u>Questions 1 through 3</u> refer to the following paragraph and chart.

In astronomy, magnitude is an indication of the brightness of a celestial body. Magnitudes are measured along a scale from positive to zero to negative, with brightness increasing as magnitude decreases. Apparent magnitude is the brightness as seen from Earth, either by the naked eye or photographically. Absolute magnitude is a measure of the actual brightness of an object. It is defined as the apparent magnitude of the object as seen from 32.6 light-years from Earth.

The Five Brightest Stars

Star	Distance from Earth (light-years)	Apparent magnitude	Absolute magnitude
Sirius	8.7	−1.47	+1.41
Canopus	180	−0.71	−4.7
Alpha Centauri	4.3	−0.1	+4.3
Arcturus	36	−0.06	−0.2
Vega	26	+0.03	+0.5

1. As seen from Earth, which of the following is the brightest star?

(1) Sirius
(2) Canopus
(3) Alpha Centauri
(4) Arcturus
(5) Vega

2. If all the stars listed in the chart were 32.6 light-years away from Earth, which would be the brightest?

(1) Sirius
(2) Canopus
(3) Alpha Centauri
(4) Arcturus
(5) Vega

3. A magazine article makes the following statement about stars: A star's apparent magnitude and its absolute magnitude must always be close in value.

Which of the following explains why the magazine's statement is incorrect?

(1) Stars form from huge masses of dust and gas.
(2) The absolute magnitude of a star indicates how bright the star looks to viewers on Earth.
(3) The apparent magnitude of a star is a measure of the amount of light the star puts out.
(4) In measuring brightness, absolute magnitude takes the star's distance from Earth into account but apparent magnitude does not.
(5) The brightness of different stars cannot be accurately measured even with today's most modern equipment.

4. The sun is about 4.7 billion years old. Based on the information on page 262, at which stage of its life cycle is the sun?

(1) It is a protostar.
(2) It is a main-sequence star.
(3) It is a red giant.
(4) It is a neutron star.
(5) It is a white dwarf.

5. Pluto has a diameter of just 1,438 miles. It is made mostly of ice and frozen rock. It is very small and has an irregular orbit. According to scientists, it should no longer be classified as a planet.

Which of the following is not a factual detail about Pluto?

(1) Pluto has a diameter of 1,438 miles.
(2) Pluto is much smaller than many planets.
(3) Pluto is made mostly of ice and frozen rock.
(4) Pluto has an irregular orbit.
(5) Pluto should be classified as one of the minor planets.

Answers and explanations start on page 653.

EARTH AND SPACE SCIENCE PRACTICE QUESTIONS

Directions: Choose the one best answer to each question.

1. Tides are the twice-daily rise and fall of water along the shores of the oceans. Tides are caused mainly by the gravitational pull of the moon, and secondarily by the gravitational pull of the sun. The highest tides, called spring tides, occur when the sun, moon, and Earth are in line. Other high tides, called neap tides, occur when the sun and moon are at right angles with respect to Earth.

Which of the following statements is supported by the information above?

(1) In most places, high tide occurs once a day, and low tide occurs once a day.
(2) The moon and the sun exert the greatest pull on Earth's oceans when these bodies are all in a line.
(3) When the moon is at right angles to the sun with respect to Earth, tides do not occur along the ocean shore.
(4) Spring tides occur only in the spring and neap tides occur only in the fall.
(5) Neap tides are generally higher than spring tides.

2. Geothermal energy is energy extracted from naturally occurring steam, hot water, or hot rocks in Earth's crust. It is used to heat buildings and generate electricity in areas where hot magma (melted rock) is close to the surface.

In which of the following places is geothermal energy most likely to be used?

(1) Arizona, a state where abundant sunshine provides solar energy
(2) Cape Cod, a peninsula formed from glacial deposits of sand
(3) Iceland, an island nation in the Atlantic with active volcanoes
(4) Greenland, an island in the Atlantic covered with a deep ice sheet
(5) Saudi Arabia, a Middle Eastern nation with ample oil and gas reserves

Questions 3 and 4 refer to the following paragraph and graph.

Scientists think there may be more matter and energy in the universe than has been directly observed because of some gravitational effects that cannot be explained otherwise. Dark matter and dark energy, so-called because they do not interact with light, may account for most of the stuff of the universe. In fact, ordinary matter, made of the chemical elements, may form only 4 percent of the universe.

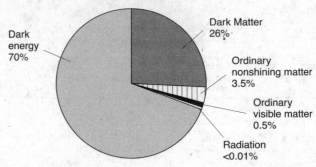

SOURCE: Ostriker, Jeremiah and Paul Steinhardt, "The Quintessential Universe." *Scientific American*, January, 2001

3. According to the graph, about what percentage of the universe may consist of matter that does not interact with light?

(1) less than 0.01 percent
(2) 0.5 percent
(3) 3.5 percent
(4) 4 percent
(5) 26 percent

4. Which of the following statements is a fact rather than a hypothesis about the makeup of the universe?

(1) Dark energy may account for 70 percent of the universe.
(2) Dark matter may account for 26 percent of the universe.
(3) Dark energy causes gravitational effects.
(4) Dark matter causes gravitational effects.
(5) Ordinary matter is made of the chemical elements.

Questions 5 through 7 refer to the following map.

World Climate Zones

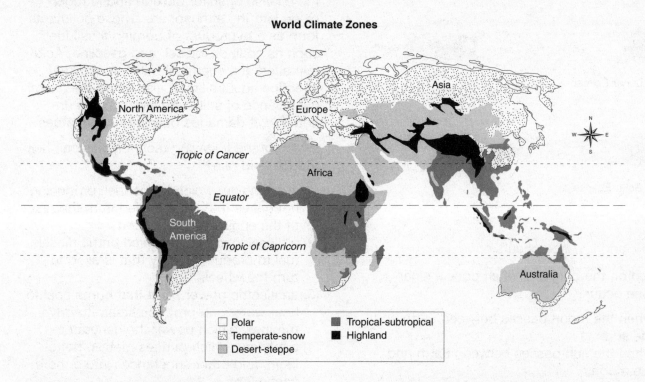

Key:
- ☐ Polar
- ▦ Temperate-snow
- ▨ Desert-steppe
- ▧ Tropical-subtropical
- ■ Highland

5. Which type of climate is characteristic of areas along the equator?

(1) polar
(2) temperate-snow
(3) desert-steppe
(4) tropical-subtropical
(5) highland

6. Which of the following statements is supported by information on the map?

(1) The continent with the least area of desert-steppe climate is South America.
(2) Australia's climate is entirely tropical-subtropical.
(3) Africa and South America do not have areas with highland climate.
(4) Central Asia is characterized by tropical-subtropical climate.
(5) Only North America has a large temperate-snow climate zone.

7. Although only one-third of the world's people live in temperate-snow climate zones, they produce about two-thirds of the world's wealth.

Which of the following is most likely to account for this?

(1) Temperate-snow zones have higher farm output than other zones, allowing for more food production.
(2) Temperate-snow zones have four seasons, and other climate zones have only two or three seasons.
(3) Temperate-snow zones are located mostly in North America, Europe, and Asia.
(4) Temperate-snow zones are located along the equator where it is warm all year round.
(5) Temperate-snow zones have most of Earth's tropical rain forests.

Questions 8 and 9 refer to the following diagram.

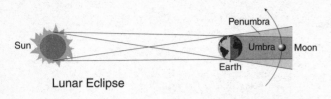

Lunar Eclipse

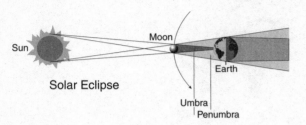

Solar Eclipse

8. Based on the diagram, when does a lunar eclipse occur?

   (1) when the moon passes between Earth and the sun
   (2) when the sun passes between Earth and the moon
   (3) when Earth passes between the moon and the sun
   (4) when the moon's umbra falls across Earth
   (5) when the moon's penumbra falls across Earth

9. Which of the following statements is supported by the information in the diagram?

   (1) During a solar eclipse, the moon passes through Earth's umbra.
   (2) During a lunar eclipse, the sun passes through the moon's umbra.
   (3) The moon's umbra is larger than Earth's umbra.
   (4) A lunar eclipse can be seen only at night and a solar eclipse can be seen only during the day.
   (5) A maximum of five solar eclipses and thirteen lunar eclipses are possible during each year.

10. Acid rain is a form of precipitation caused by the release of sulfur dioxide and nitrogen oxide into the atmosphere. These pollutants form as a byproduct of burning fossil fuels, such as coal, oil, diesel, and gasoline. Acid rain alters the chemical balance of lakes, affecting aquatic life. It also alters the chemical balance of soil, harming plant life. In addition, it damages buildings and statues.

Which of the following technologies can help reduce acid rain?

   (1) a jet engine, which burns fuel, producing hot gases that are expelled from the rear of the engine at high speed
   (2) a diesel locomotive, which burns diesel fuel to produce energy that is used to turn the wheels
   (3) an electric power plant that burns coal to heat water and produce steam to drive turbines, which power the generator
   (4) a refinery, which purifies metals, petroleum, and other substances into a more useful form
   (5) a catalytic converter, a device in the exhaust system of a vehicle that reduces harmful emissions from the engine

11. Tornadoes are swirling, funnel-shaped clouds that descend from a storm cloud. When they touch the ground, they pick up dirt and dust and become dark-colored. The fastest wind ever recorded occurred in a tornado: 134 meters (440 feet) per second. Tornadoes can tear the roof off a building, toss cars into the air, and even cause buildings to explode.

Which of the following is an unstated assumption related to the paragraph?

   (1) Tornadoes are swirling, funnel-shaped clouds.
   (2) Tornadoes are extremely destructive storms.
   (3) The dark color of a tornado is due to the dirt it picks up from the ground.
   (4) Tornadoes have the fastest wind speeds ever recorded.
   (5) Wind speed in a tornado can reach 134 meters per second.

Questions 12 through 14 refer to the following diagram.

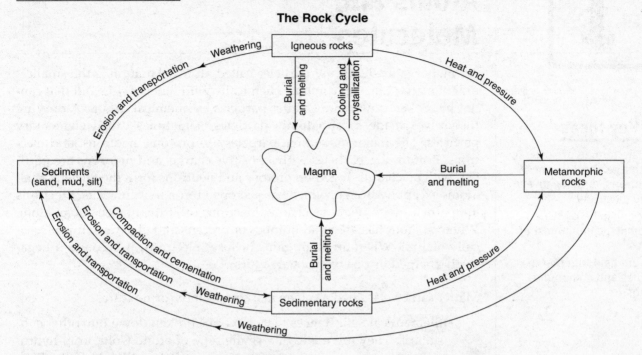

The Rock Cycle

12. Which of the following statements is supported by the information in the diagram?

    (1) The rock cycle is a continuous process of rock formation, destruction, and reformation.
    (2) Sedimentary rocks form under conditions of heat and pressure.
    (3) Metamorphic rocks form under conditions of compaction and cementation.
    (4) Igneous rocks form from the crystallization of metamorphic rocks.
    (5) Sediments form only from sedimentary rocks.

13. Fossils can form when plant or animal remains are buried under sand, mud, or silt. These materials can be compacted to form rock.

    A girl found a rock with a fossilized imprint of a starfish. Which type of rock was it?

    (1) igneous
    (2) sedimentary
    (3) magma
    (4) a crystal
    (5) volcanic ash

14. What is magma?

    (1) melted sediments
    (2) melted rock
    (3) crystallized rock
    (4) mud, sand, and silt
    (5) eroded rock

15. In open-pit mining, surface layers of soil and rock are stripped to obtain coal, ores, or minerals. It is cheaper than shaft mining because there is no underground work.

    Which of the following is the most likely reason that some countries restrict open-pit mining?

    (1) There are no surface deposits.
    (2) There are no underground deposits.
    (3) Open-pit mining is more dangerous than shaft mining.
    (4) Open-pit mining destroys valuable land.
    (5) Open-pit mining yields low-grade coal, ores, and minerals.

Answers and explanations start on page 653.

PHYSICAL SCIENCE

Atoms and Molecules

Key Ideas

- Atoms are formed of positively charged protons, neutral neutrons, and negatively charged electrons.
- All matter can be classified as elements, compounds, or mixtures.
- Atoms are held together in molecules and compounds by bonds.

GED TIP

If you are having trouble choosing the correct answer to a question, eliminate the options that are clearly wrong. Of the remaining options, choose the one that makes the most sense.

All matter is made of tiny particles called atoms. An **atom** is the smallest unit of matter that can combine chemically with other matter and that cannot be broken down into smaller particles by chemical means. Atoms are themselves made of **subatomic particles,** sometimes called elementary particles. The major subatomic particles are protons, neutrons, and electrons. **Protons** are particles with a positive charge, and **neutrons** are particles with no charge. Together, protons and neutrons form the nucleus of all atoms except hydrogen, which has just one proton in its nucleus. **Electrons** are particles with negative charge. Electrons orbit the nucleus of an atom. When an atom has an equal number of protons and electrons, it is electrically neutral. When an atom gains or loses electrons, it becomes a negatively charged or positively charged **ion.**

Matter can be classified as elements, compounds, or mixtures.

- **Elements** are substances that cannot be broken down into other substances. They are made of a single type of atom. Gold, iron, hydrogen, sodium, oxygen, and carbon are some familiar elements. Each element has a **chemical symbol.** For example, gold is Au, iron is Fe, hydrogen is H, sodium is Na, oxygen is O, and carbon is C.
- **Compounds** are substances formed of two or more elements chemically combined in a definite proportion. Compounds have properties that differ from the properties of the elements that they contain. For example, at room temperature, water is a liquid compound made of the elements hydrogen and oxygen, which, uncombined, are both gases. Compounds are represented by **chemical formulas.** The chemical formula for water is H_2O, indicating that a water molecule is made of two atoms of hydrogen and one atom of oxygen.
- **Mixtures** are physical combinations of two or more substances that keep their own properties. For example, salt water is a mixture.

When elements combine to form **molecules** or ionic compounds, their constituents are held together by **bonds.** There are two main types of bonds: covalent and ionic. In a **covalent bond,** atoms share a pair of electrons, each atom contributing one electron. For example, the compound water is held together by covalent bonds. In an **ionic bond,** atoms gain or lose electrons to become ions, and the attraction between positively (+) and negatively (−) charged ions holds the compound together. For example, sodium chloride (NaCl), commonly called table salt, is an ionic compound.

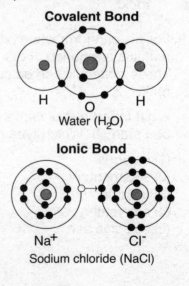

Covalent Bond

H   O   H

Water (H_2O)

Ionic Bond

Na^+ Cl^-

Sodium chloride (NaCl)

Directions: Choose the <u>one best answer</u> to each question.

1. Sodium is represented by the chemical symbol Na and chlorine is represented by the chemical symbol Cl. According to the diagram on page 268, what happens when sodium chloride forms?

   (1) The sodium atom loses an electron, becoming positively charged, and the chlorine atom gains an electron, becoming negatively charged.
   (2) The sodium atom gains an electron, becoming negatively charged, and the chlorine atom loses an electron, becoming positively charged.
   (3) The sodium atom gains an electron, becoming positively charged, and the chlorine atom loses an electron, becoming negatively charged.
   (4) The sodium and chlorine atoms share a pair of electrons, becoming ions and forming a covalent bond.
   (5) The sodium and chlorine atoms dissolve in water, breaking the covalent bonds.

2. Water is composed of two atoms of hydrogen and one atom of oxygen and has the formula H_2O. Glucose, a simple sugar, consists of six atoms of carbon, twelve atoms of hydrogen, and six atoms of oxygen.

   Which of the following is the chemical formula for glucose?

   (1) CHO
   (2) $_6C_{12}H_6O$
   (3) $C^6H^{12}O^6$
   (4) $C_6\,H_6O_6$
   (5) $C_6H_{12}O_6$

3. What is the main difference between atoms and ions?

   (1) Atoms are made of elementary particles, and ions are made of ionic particles.
   (2) Atoms are the building blocks of elements, and ions are the building blocks of compounds.
   (3) Atoms are neutral in charge, and ions have either a positive or a negative charge.
   (4) Atoms have more neutrons in their nuclei than ions do.
   (5) Atoms have more protons in their nuclei than ions do.

4. In 1911, British scientist Ernest Rutherford performed experiments that increased our knowledge of atomic structure. He bombarded an extremely thin sheet of gold foil with helium nuclei. (Helium nuclei, also called alpha particles, consist of two protons and two neutrons). He found that most of the helium nuclei passed right through the foil. Only a few were deflected back toward the source. On the basis of this experiment, Rutherford concluded that an atom has a dense nucleus with electrons orbiting it, but consists mostly of empty space.

   Which of the following is evidence that atoms consist mostly of empty space?

   (1) Helium nuclei consist of two protons and two neutrons.
   (2) Gold foil was bombarded with helium nuclei, also called alpha particles.
   (3) Most of the alpha particles passed right through the gold foil.
   (4) A few alpha particles were deflected off the gold foil and bounced back toward the source.
   (5) Electrons orbit a dense nucleus consisting of protons and neutrons.

5. The number of protons in the nucleus of an atom is called the atomic number. Each element has a unique number of protons in its nucleus and therefore a unique atomic number. Since atoms are neutral, the number of protons and electrons in an atom is the same.

   The atomic number of the element sodium is 11. How many electrons does a sodium atom have?

   (1) 10
   (2) 11
   (3) 12
   (4) 21
   (5) 22

Answers and explanations start on page 654.

PHYSICAL SCIENCE

Properties and States of Matter

Key Ideas

- Matter has mass and occupies space.
- The three states of matter include solid, liquid, and gas. A substance's state of matter can be changed by adding or removing heat.
- Solutions are a type of mixture. The solute is the dissolved substance. The solvent is what the solute is dissolved in. Solvents and solutes can be any of the states of matter.

ON THE GED

Approximately one-third of the questions on the GED Science Test are about physical science topics.

Matter is anything that has mass and takes up space. The **mass** of an object is the amount of matter that it contains, and its **weight** is a measure of the gravitational force exerted on it. The mass of an object like a shovel never changes, but its weight can change. For example, a shovel weighs less on the moon than it does on Earth because the gravitational pull of the moon is less than that of Earth.

Under most conditions, there are three **states of matter,** as described below:

- **Solids** have a definite shape and volume because the molecules of which they are made occupy fixed positions and do not move freely. In some solids, such as minerals, the molecules form an orderly pattern called a **crystal.**
- **Liquids** have a definite volume but no definite shape because the molecules in a liquid are loosely bound and move freely. For this reason, a liquid conforms to the shape of its container.
- **Gases** have no definite shape or volume. The attraction between the molecules of a gas is very weak. In consequence, the molecules of a gas are far apart and are always in motion, colliding with one another and with the sides of the container.

The states of matter can be changed by adding or removing heat energy. When heat is applied to a solid, it melts. This happens because the motion of the solid's molecules increases until the bonds between them are loosened, allowing them to flow freely. The temperature at which a solid becomes a liquid is its **melting point.** When heat is applied to a liquid, it boils and evaporates, turning into a gas as the motion of its molecules increases. The temperature at which a liquid becomes a gas is called its **boiling point.** When heat is removed from a gas, the motion of its molecules decreases and it turns into a liquid. The temperature at which a gas becomes a liquid is its **condensation point.** When heat is removed from a liquid, the motion of its molecules slows until it solidifies. The temperature at which a liquid becomes a solid is its **freezing point.** The temperatures at which a substance changes state are unique properties of that substance. For example, water boils at 100°C (212°F) and freezes at 0°C (32°F). Water is also the only substance that is found naturally in all three states on Earth.

As you learned in Lesson 1, mixtures are physical combinations of two or more substances that keep their original properties. A **solution** is a mixture (such as salt water) that is uniform throughout and that contains ions, atoms, or molecules of two or more substances. The substance in a solution that is dissolved is called the **solute.** The substance in which the solute is dissolved is the **solvent.** In salt water, for example, salt is the solute and water is the solvent. Water is called the universal solvent because so many substances dissolve in it. However, solutions are not always liquids. They can be solids, as when two or more metals are combined in an **alloy,** or they can be gases, as when oxygen and nitrogen are combined in the air.

Directions: Choose the one best answer to each question.

1. Which of the following physical changes involve adding heat to a substance?

   (1) melting and boiling
   (2) boiling and condensing
   (3) condensing and freezing
   (4) freezing and evaporating
   (5) evaporating and condensing

2. Density is the amount of mass in a particular volume of a substance. It can be expressed in kilograms per cubic meter. The chart shows the densities of some common substances.

   Densities of Substances

Substance	Density (g/cm³)
Solids	
Lead	11.35
Iron	7.87
Aluminum	2.70
Liquids	
Chloroform	1.49
Water	1.00
Ethyl alcohol	0.79
Gases	
Oxygen	0.0013
Nitrogen	0.0012
Helium	0.0002

   Which of the following statements is supported by the information provided?

   (1) Water is the least dense liquid on Earth.
   (2) Solids are usually denser than liquids and gases.
   (3) When aluminum melts, it is more dense than lead.
   (4) Density increases as the volume of a substance increases.
   (5) Density decreases as the force of gravity decreases.

3. Water is different from most other substances. It changes from gas to liquid to solid at temperatures that are common on Earth. When it freezes, its molecules form a crystal lattice, so that its solid form is less dense than its liquid form. It is the most common solvent.

   Which of the following is a conclusion about water rather than a supporting statement?

   (1) Water is a unique substance on Earth.
   (2) Water changes state at temperatures typical on Earth.
   (3) When water freezes, its molecules form a crystal lattice.
   (4) Frozen water is less dense than liquid water.
   (5) Water is Earth's most common solvent.

4. When a solute is dissolved in a liquid solvent, the freezing point of the solution is lower than the freezing point of the pure liquid.

   In which of the following situations is this property of liquid solutions applied?

   (1) A Zamboni is used to smooth the surface of ice in a rink between skating sessions.
   (2) Sugar dissolves in water more quickly if the solution is heated.
   (3) Antifreeze added to water in a car's radiator lowers the freezing point below 0°C.
   (4) The oil and vinegar in salad dressing is mixed more thoroughly by shaking.
   (5) Spherical ice "cubes" freeze more quickly than regular ice cubes do.

5. A suspension is a mixture in which the distributed particles are larger than those of the solvent and in which the particles, in time, will settle out.

   Which of the following is a suspension?

   (1) pure gold
   (2) pure oxygen
   (3) salt water
   (4) vinegar
   (5) dusty air

Answers and explanations start on page 654.

Key Ideas

- In a chemical reaction, the atoms or ions of one or more reactants are rearranged, yielding one or more products. Mass is conserved during chemical reactions.
- Chemical reactions can be represented by chemical formulas.
- Chemical reactions are either endothermic or exothermic.

GED TIP

There is no penalty for getting the wrong answer on questions on the GED Test. Therefore, even if you don't know the answer to a question on the test, you should make your best guess.

PHYSICAL SCIENCE

Chemical Reactions

In a **chemical reaction,** the atoms or ions of one or more substances, called the **reactants,** are rearranged, resulting in one or more different substances, called the **products.** For example, iron, water, and oxygen react to form hydrated iron oxide, or rust. Matter is neither created nor destroyed during a chemical reaction, so the mass of the products always equals the mass of the reactants. This principle is known as the **law of conservation of mass.**

Chemical reactions can be represented by **chemical equations.** Chemical equations show the reactants on the left side and the products on the right side. They also show the proportions of the reacting substances—how many units of each reactant and each product are involved. Because of the law of conservation of mass, a chemical equation must balance. That is, the total number of atoms of an element on the left side must be equal to the total number of atoms of the element on the right side. Here is the chemical equation that represents the burning of hydrogen in oxygen to yield water.

$$2H_2 + O_2 \rightarrow 2H_2O$$

Restated in words: two molecules of hydrogen (H_2) combine with one molecule of oxygen (O_2) to form two molecules of water (H_2O). The equation balances because there are four hydrogen atoms on the left side and four on the right; there are two oxygen atoms on the left side and two on the right. To balance a chemical equation, you can change the coefficients—the number of units of any reactant or product. However, you *cannot* change the subscripts of any reactant or product.

Energy is involved in all chemical reactions. A reaction in which the reactants absorb energy from their surroundings is an **endothermic reaction.** For example, when you scramble an egg, you add heat energy and the egg solidifies. A reaction in which energy is given off with the products, usually in the form of heat or light, is an **exothermic reaction.** When you burn wood in a fireplace, for example, heat and light energy are given off. **Activation energy** is the amount of energy needed to get a reaction going. These energy relationships can be shown in graphs like those below.

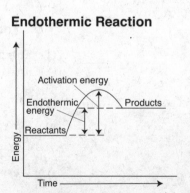

Endothermic Reaction

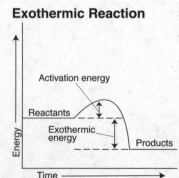

Exothermic Reaction

PHYSICAL SCIENCE ▸ PRACTICE 3

Directions: Choose the <u>one best answer</u> to each question.

1. Which of the following chemical formulas represents the reaction in which copper (Cu) and oxygen gas (O_2) combine to form copper oxide (CuO)?

   (1) $2CuO \rightarrow Cu + 2O_2$
   (2) $2CuO \rightarrow 2Cu + O_2$
   (3) $Cu + O_2 \rightarrow 2CuO$
   (4) $2Cu + O_2 \rightarrow 2CuO$
   (5) $Cu + 2O_2 \rightarrow 2CuO$

2. Which of the following procedures would provide evidence for the law of conservation of mass?

   (1) Weigh the reactants, conduct the reaction in an open container, and weigh the products.
   (2) Weigh the reactants, conduct the reaction in a sealed container, and weigh the products.
   (3) Measure the volume of the reactants, conduct the reaction in a sealed container, and measure the volume of the products.
   (4) Write the chemical formula for the reaction without balancing it.
   (5) Write the chemical formula for the reaction and balance it.

3. When you turn on a burner on a gas stove, the electronic ignition produces a spark that sets the gas burning. In this reaction, what is the spark?

   (1) activation energy
   (2) endothermic energy
   (3) exothermic energy
   (4) a reactant
   (5) a product

4. In the graphs on page 272, what does the horizontal axis represent?

   (1) the instant the reaction starts
   (2) the instant the reaction stops
   (3) the time during which the reaction occurs
   (4) the substances in the reaction
   (5) the energy level in the reaction

5. Organic compounds are those containing linked carbon atoms that form bonds with other atoms, usually hydrogen, oxygen, nitrogen, and/or sulfur. Organic compounds consist of chains, branching chains, rings, and other complex arrangements of carbon atoms with which other atoms bond. One type of organic compound is a polymer, a large long-chain or branching structure made up of many repeated simple units, called monomers. Natural polymers include cellulose. Synthetic polymers include polyethylene and other types of plastics.

   Which of the following is taken for granted and not stated by the writer of the paragraph above?

   (1) Compounds are substances consisting of two or more elements chemically combined in a definite proportion.
   (2) Organic compounds have linked carbon atoms forming bonds with other atoms, usually hydrogen, oxygen, nitrogen, and/or sulfur.
   (3) Chains are among the arrangements carbon atoms in an organic compound can take.
   (4) A polymer is a compound made up of many repeated simple units, called monomers.
   (5) Plastics are synthetic polymers and cellulose is a natural polymer.

6. An acid is a compound that releases hydrogen ions (H^+), or protons, in the presence of water. Strong acids, like battery acid and stomach acid, are corrosive. Most dilute acids, like tomato juice, have a sour taste.

   A base is a compound that accepts hydrogen ions, or protons. Household cleaners like ammonia, lye, and bleach are bases. When an acid reacts with a base, the product is a salt and water. This reaction is called neutralization.

   Which of the following is the best title for this passage?

   (1) Hydrogen Ions
   (2) Corrosive Substances
   (3) Acids and Bases
   (4) Acids and Bases in the Lab
   (5) Neutralization Reactions

Answers and explanations start on page 655.

PHYSICAL SCIENCE

The Nature of Energy

Key Ideas

- Anything that can force matter to move, change direction, or change speed has energy.
- Energy comes in many forms and can be converted from one form to another.
- The law of conservation of energy states that energy can neither be created nor destroyed, only changed in form.

ON THE GED

While the U.S. version of the GED Science Test gives measurements in the English system, the Spanish- and French-language versions usually give measurements in the metric system.

Energy is defined as the capacity to do work. **Work** is done whenever a force is applied to an object to set it in motion. Thus anything that can force matter to move, change direction, or change speed has energy.

Energy comes in many forms. **Heat energy** can change a solid to a liquid and a liquid to a gas. It is also involved in most chemical reactions. **Light energy** can create an image by causing the chemicals on a piece of film to react. It provides the energy needed for the process of photosynthesis in green plants. **Electrical energy** can turn a motor, plate a set of flatware with a layer of silver, or store data on a hard drive. **Chemical energy** in food provides the energy humans need for life functions. It heats our buildings when we burn oil, gas, coal, or wood. Chemical energy in batteries provides electricity when the batteries are connected in a circuit. **Nuclear energy** from breaking apart the nuclei of atoms provides energy to produce electricity or power a submarine. **Mechanical energy** turns the axles of a car or the blades of a fan.

Energy can be converted from one form to another. Consider the production and use of electricity. In most electric plants, a fossil fuel (chemical energy) is burned, producing heat energy that turns water to steam. The energy in the steam turns the blades of a turbine, producing mechanical energy. The turbine powers the generator, which produces electrical energy. Electrical energy is used in homes to provide heat energy (in stoves and toasters), light energy (in light bulbs), sound energy (in the stereo), and mechanical energy (in a blender). Even though energy undergoes changes in form, the amount of energy in a closed system remains the same. This principle is known as the **law of conservation of energy.**

Two basic types of energy are **potential energy** and **kinetic energy.** An object has potential energy because of its position; it has kinetic energy when it moves. For example, when you raise a hammer, at the top of your upswing the hammer has potential energy. When you lower the hammer to hit a nail, the hammer has kinetic energy, the energy of motion. When the hammer hits the nail, it transfers energy to the nail. The energy transferred is equal to the work done by the hammer on the nail, and it can be measured in **joules.** The rate of doing work or consuming energy is called **power,** and it can be measured in horsepower (in the English system) or **watts** (joules per second in the metric system).

Physicist Albert Einstein discovered the relationship between energy and mass and expressed it in the equation $E = mc^2$, in which E represents energy, m represents mass, and c represents the speed of light. Since the speed of light is a very large number, the equation indicates there is a great deal of energy in even the tiniest bit of matter. So, for example, in nuclear bombs and nuclear power plants, mass is changed to energy when large atoms are split into two or more smaller atoms with less mass than the original large atom.

PHYSICAL SCIENCE ▸ PRACTICE 4

Directions: Choose the <u>one best answer</u> to each question.

1. Which of the following states the law of conservation of energy?

   (1) Potential energy is the energy of position; kinetic energy is the energy of motion.
   (2) Potential energy is the energy of motion; kinetic energy is the energy of position.
   (3) Energy can be created and destroyed as well as changed in form.
   (4) Energy cannot be created or destroyed, but can only change in form.
   (5) Energy cannot be created, destroyed, or changed in form.

2. A flashlight has batteries, wires, and a light bulb enclosed in a case.

   What forms of energy are involved when you turn on a flashlight?

   (1) sound, mechanical, and chemical energy
   (2) chemical, electrical, and nuclear energy
   (3) chemical, electrical, and light energy
   (4) electrical, light, and sound energy
   (5) light, sound, and mechanical energy

3. An oak tree may grow very tall very slowly. It may take the tree a hundred years to absorb light energy and store it as chemical energy, yet only a single winter to be turned into heat energy in someone's wood stove. Which concept does this fact best relate to?

   (1) matter
   (2) work
   (3) power
   (4) potential energy
   (5) kinetic energy

4. What does Einstein's equation $E = mc^2$ express?

   (1) the relationship between electricity and magnetism
   (2) the relationship between energy and mass
   (3) the speed of light in a vacuum
   (4) the force that holds subatomic particles together
   (5) the relationship between electrical energy and nuclear energy

Question 5 refers to the following diagram.

A Pendulum's Energy

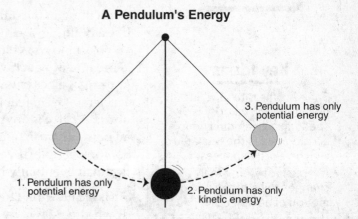

1. Pendulum has only potential energy
2. Pendulum has only kinetic energy
3. Pendulum has only potential energy

5. Which of the following statements is supported by the information in the diagram?

   (1) At the high point of its swing, a pendulum has kinetic energy.
   (2) At the high point of its swing, a pendulum has potential energy.
   (3) As a pendulum swings through one arc, it loses all its energy.
   (4) A pendulum slows gradually because of air resistance.
   (5) A pendulum can swing forever because of kinetic energy.

6. Heat energy is present in all matter in the form of the kinetic energy of its atoms and molecules. Heat energy can pass from one place to another through conduction: the transfer of kinetic energy from molecules in greater motion (hot areas) to molecules of lesser motion (cold areas). Solid metals like silver and copper are good conductors of heat energy; gases like air are poor conductors.

   What is the reason that air is a poor conductor of heat?

   (1) Heat cannot pass through air.
   (2) The molecules in air are far apart.
   (3) The molecules in air are in random motion.
   (4) The molecules in air do not move.
   (5) The molecules in air are very small.

Answers and explanations start on page 655.

PHYSICAL SCIENCE

Motion and Forces

Everything in the universe is in motion. Even objects that seem to be at rest, like a building, are moving with Earth's rotation. **Speed** is the rate at which an object moves; **velocity** is its speed in a particular direction. **Acceleration** is the rate at which velocity changes. So a car's speed may be 40 miles per hour; its velocity may be 40 miles per hour toward the north; and it may accelerate by 10 feet per second until its velocity is 50 miles per hour to the north. A **force** is anything that tends to change the state of rest or motion of an object. A push or a pull on an object is a force, as are gravity and friction. So, for example, if you allow a car to coast on a level road, the force of friction will eventually bring it to a stop.

Sir Isaac Newton (1642–1727), an English physicist and mathematician, set down three laws by which the planets and all other objects move when acted upon by a force. These are called the **laws of motion.**

Newton's first law of motion, the **law of inertia,** states that an object at rest will stay at rest until a force acts upon it, and an object in motion will stay in motion at a constant speed in a straight line until a force acts upon it. Objects moving on Earth eventually slow down and stop because of the forces of friction and gravity. A bullet, for example, would continue its forward motion in a straight line, but friction from the air slows it down and the force of gravity pulls it toward the ground.

The second law of motion is the **law of constant acceleration.** This states that if a constant force acts on an object, the object will move with constant acceleration in the direction of the force. The greater the force, the greater the acceleration. The more massive the object, the more force it takes to accelerate it. This is why truck engines are more powerful than car engines: it takes more force to accelerate an object with more mass (a truck) than an object with less mass (a car).

Newton's third law of motion is the **law of conservation of momentum. Momentum** is related to the amount of energy that a moving object has, and it depends on the mass of the object and its velocity. In fact, momentum is defined as an object's mass multiplied by its velocity. Newton's third law states that when an object is given a certain amount of momentum in a particular direction, some other object must receive an equal momentum in the opposite direction. This law is often stated as "For every action there is an equal and opposite reaction." So, for example, when a bullet is fired out of a gun, the bullet's forward momentum causes the gun to recoil, or move backward.

Key Ideas

- Speed is the rate at which an object moves; velocity is speed in a given direction; acceleration is the rate at which velocity changes.
- A force is anything that changes the state of rest or motion of an object.
- Newton stated three laws of motion that explain the inertia, acceleration, and momentum of objects.

GED TIP

If you are asked to apply a general law or principle of science to a particular situation, ask yourself: "What is similar about this situation and the general principle?"

PHYSICAL SCIENCE ▸ PRACTICE 5

Directions: Choose the <u>one best answer</u> to each question.

1. What is a force?

   (1) the rate at which an object moves in a particular direction
   (2) any change in an object's acceleration or deceleration
   (3) the inertia and momentum of an object at rest
   (4) anything that changes the rest or motion of an object
   (5) the mass of an object moving in a vacuum

2. What is inertia?

   (1) the speed at which an object is moving
   (2) the direction in which an object is moving
   (3) changes in an object's speed or direction
   (4) the force needed to move an object a certain distance
   (5) the tendency of an object to remain at rest or in motion

3. The force that is needed to keep an object moving in a circular path is called centripetal force.

   Which of the following is an example of centripetal force?

   (1) the tides occurring as a result of the moon's gravitational pull
   (2) the International Space Station orbiting Earth
   (3) a parachute slowing as it falls to the ground
   (4) a truck shifting gears as it ascends a hill
   (5) a gun recoiling as a bullet is fired

4. A car is going 30 miles per hour across a narrow bridge when it is approached on a collision course by another car traveling at 30 miles per hour.

   Why will the impact be less severe if both drivers slow their vehicles?

   (1) A car at rest will stay at rest until a force acts upon it.
   (2) A car in motion will stay in motion until a force acts upon it.
   (3) The momentum of a car decreases when its velocity decreases.
   (4) The momentum of a car increases when its velocity increases.
   (5) The momentum of a car is related to its mass.

<u>Question 5</u> refers to the following graph, the paragraph below, and the information on page 276.

Graphs are often used to convey information about motion. One type of motion graph shows distance and time. Distance is measured from a particular starting point. If the distance graph has a straight, horizontal line, the distance is unchanging and object is not moving. If the distance graph has a straight line with an upward slope, the distance is changing at a constant rate; this means that the object is moving at a constant speed. If the distance graph is a curve, the object is accelerating or decelerating, depending on the shape of the curve.

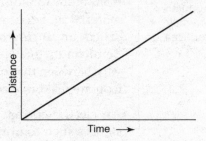

5. What does the graph above show?

   (1) an object that is not moving
   (2) an object that has a constant speed
   (3) an object that has changing velocity
   (4) an object that is accelerating
   (5) an object that is decelerating

6. A machine is a device that transmits a force, changing the direction or size of the force and doing work. The force applied to a machine is the effort force; the force it overcomes is the load. Types of simple machines include the inclined plane, wedge, lever, pulley, and wheel-and-axle.

   Which of the following statements is supported by the information given?

   (1) The force a machine overcomes is called the effort force.
   (2) Work can be done only with machines.
   (3) Some machines simply change the direction of a force.
   (4) All machines change both the direction and size of a force.
   (5) Any simple machine contains a lever.

Answers and explanations begin on page 655.

PHYSICAL SCIENCE

Electricity and Magnetism

Key Ideas

- Particles with like electric charge repel one another, and particles with unlike electric charge attract one another.
- The flow of electrons through a substance is called an electric current.
- An electric current produces a magnetic field, and a moving magnetic field produces an electric current.

GED TIP

You can use your knowledge of everyday things like electricity and motors to help you answer questions on the GED Science Test.

As you recall from your study of atoms, electrons have a negative charge (–), and protons have a positive charge (+). This **electric charge** causes them to exert forces on one another. Particles with like charges repel one another, and particles with unlike charges attract one another. Sometimes electrons are temporarily pulled away from atoms, creating stationary areas of positive and negative charge. This can happen when two objects, like a balloon and a rug, are rubbed together, creating **static electricity.**

The movement of charged particles, usually electrons, is an **electric current.** Direct current flows in one direction only, and it is used in battery-operated devices. Alternating current flows back and forth rapidly, and it is used in household wiring. A material that allows electrons to move freely from atom to atom is called a **conductor.** Metals are good conductors. A material that does not allow electrons to move freely from atom to atom is called an **insulator.** Rubber and plastic are examples of insulators. **Semiconductors** are substances whose ability to conduct electricity is midway between that of a conductor and an insulator. Semiconductors like silicon are used in electronic devices.

An electric current produces a **magnetic field** that affects magnetic substances such as iron in the same way a permanent magnet does. Magnetic fields are produced by moving charged particles. In an **electromagnet,** the charged particles move along a coil of wire connected to a battery or other power source. In a **permanent magnet,** the spinning of electrons creates a magnetic field. Every magnet has two ends, called the north and south poles. The north pole of one magnet attracts the south pole of another magnet; like poles repel one another.

Just as an electric current produces a magnetic field, a moving magnetic field produces an electric current. This principle underlies electric motors, generators, and transformers. In an electric motor, for example, magnetic fields are produced by electric currents. The magnetic fields push against one another, turning the shaft of the motor. In a generator, a moving magnetic field produces electric current. In a transformer, an incoming electric current in coiled wire produces fluctuating magnetic fields, which in turn produce an outgoing electric current of a different **voltage.** The difference in voltage is caused by the differing sizes of the wire coils.

Magnetic Fields

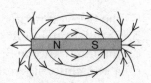

Bar magnet

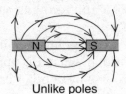

Unlike poles

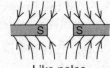

Like poles

Directions: Choose the one best answer to each question.

1. Suppose a drawing of two magnets with their north poles facing one another were added to the diagram on page 278. What would the new drawing show?

   (1) two poles attracting one another
   (2) two poles repelling one another
   (3) magnetic lines of force connecting the poles
   (4) magnetic lines of force flowing northward
   (5) magnetic lines of force flowing southward

2. What is the reason copper and aluminum are used for electrical wiring?

   (1) Copper and aluminum are conductors.
   (2) Copper and aluminum are insulators.
   (3) Copper and aluminum are semiconductors.
   (4) Copper and aluminum are magnetic.
   (5) Copper and aluminum are generators.

3. Based on the passage, which of the following devices is most likely to use direct current?

   (1) a washing machine
   (2) a desktop computer
   (3) a toaster
   (4) a flashlight
   (5) a chandelier

4. In an electric power plant, generators may produce electric current at about 10,000 volts. The current may be stepped up and transmitted along high voltage lines at 230,000 volts, and then stepped down to about 2,300 volts for transmission in a city. Finally, before it enters houses, the current is stepped down to 110 volts.

   Based on the information above and the passage, which of the following devices steps current up and down for efficient transmission?

   (1) a conductor
   (2) an electromagnet
   (3) an electric motor
   (4) a permanent magnet
   (5) a transformer

Questions 5 and 6 refer to the following paragraph and diagram.

An electric circuit is a complete pathway for the flow of electric current. It consists of a source of electricity, such as a battery, wires along which the current travels, devices called resistors powered by the current, and often a switch to start and stop the flow of current.

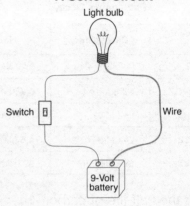

A Series Circuit

5. In the circuit shown above, which of the following is a resistor?

   (1) the battery
   (2) the wire
   (3) the light bulb
   (4) the switch
   (5) the current

6. A student was asked how the current in the circuit shown above could be stopped without using the switch. He answered that the only way to stop the current was to disconnect the battery.

   What was wrong with the student's response?

   (1) A circuit is a complete pathway along which electric current travels.
   (2) Disconnecting the battery will not stop the current.
   (3) Removing the fuse will also stop the current.
   (4) Disconnecting the light bulb will also stop the current.
   (5) There is no way to stop the current without using the switch.

Answers and explanations start on page 655.

PHYSICAL SCIENCE PRACTICE QUESTIONS

Directions: Choose the <u>one best answer</u> to each question.

<u>Questions 1 and 2</u> refer to the following paragraph and chart.

When the nuclei of unstable elements disintegrate, emitting radioactive radiation, the unstable elements change into other elements, becoming more stable. The amount of time it takes for half of a sample of a radioactive element to decay into its stable product is called the radioactive element's half-life.

Radioactive Decay

Radioactive element	Decays into	Half-life
Radon-222	Polonium-218	3.82 days
Carbon-14	Nitrogen-14	5,730 days
Uranium-235	Lead-207	713 million years
Uranium-238	Lead-206	4.5 billion years
Rubidium-87	Strontium-87	50 billion years

1. What is the half-life of carbon-14?

   (1) 3.82 days
   (2) 5,730 years
   (3) 713 million years
   (4) 4.5 billion years
   (5) 50 billion years

2. Uranium is used as fuel in nuclear power plants, resulting in radioactive waste, which is dangerous to living things.

Which of the following arguments is likely to be used by opponents of nuclear power?

   (1) Uranium is a plentiful source of fuel for generating electricity.
   (2) When we run out of uranium, we can use another fuel for nuclear power plants.
   (3) Uranium is a renewable resource, and therefore its use is limitless.
   (4) During the three days that radioactive waste is unstable, it may harm living things.
   (5) Uranium produces radioactive waste that may harm living things for millions of years.

<u>Questions 3 and 4</u> refer to the following paragraph and diagram.

An oscillation is a back-and-forth or up-and-down movement. When an oscillation travels through matter or space transferring energy, it is called a wave.

Longitudinal Wave

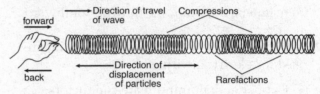

Transverse Wave

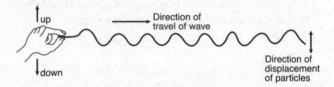

3. What is the main similarity between longitudinal and transverse waves?

   (1) Both involve up-and-down displacement of particles.
   (2) Both involve back-and-forth displacement of particles.
   (3) Both involve rarefactions in which particles are pulled apart.
   (4) Both involve compressions in which particles are pushed together.
   (5) Both involve the transfer of energy through matter or space.

4. After a transverse wave passes through a substance, no particle ever ends up far from its original position.

Which of the following illustrates this principle?

   (1) A cork in water bobs up and down as waves pass.
   (2) Sound waves travel through air.
   (3) Light waves travel through outer space.
   (4) When two waves overlap, they interfere with one another.
   (5) A stone dropped into a pond causes ripples to radiate outward.

5. According to the kinetic theory of matter, all matter is made up of molecules in a state of constant motion. The motion of molecules can be inferred by observing particles in a fluid (a liquid or a gas) as they are hit by molecules of the fluid. The random, zigzag movement of the particles is called Brownian motion.

Which of the following is an example of Brownian motion?

(1) dust motes dancing in a shaft of sunlight
(2) the ground vibrating as a truck passes
(3) water evaporating from a puddle
(4) a helium balloon rising in the air
(5) an inflatable raft floating on a lake

6. In a chemical reaction, the surface area of the reactants affects the rate at which the reaction occurs. The greater the surface area of the reactants, the faster the reaction rate is.

When dilute sulfuric acid reacts with marble, carbon dioxide gas is produced. Which of the following actions will increase the rate of reaction?

(1) using a larger container
(2) using a smaller container
(3) using powdered marble
(4) using large chunks of marble
(5) diluting the sulfuric acid with more water

7. Boyle's Law states that at a constant temperature, the volume of a fixed amount of gas varies inversely with the pressure exerted on the gas.

Which of the following is implied by Boyle's Law?

(1) As pressure on a gas increases, volume decreases.
(2) As pressure on a gas decreases, volume decreases.
(3) The higher the temperature of a gas, the greater the pressure.
(4) The higher the temperature of a gas, the greater the volume.
(5) The higher the temperature of a gas, the smaller the volume.

Questions 8 and 9 refer to the following paragraph and chart.

All of the elements are arranged in the periodic table according to atomic number—the number of protons in an atom of each element. The rows of the periodic table show elements according to the structure of their electron orbits. The columns, or groups, show elements with similar properties. A portion of the periodic table is shown below.

Part of the Periodic Table

					18
					He 2
13	14	15	16	17	
B 5	C 6	N 7	O 8	F 9	Ne 10
Al 13	Si 14	P 15	S 16	Cl 17	Ar 18
Ga 31	Ge 32	As 33	Se 34	Br 35	Kr 36
In 49	Sn 50	Sb 51	Te 52	I 53	Xe 54
Tl 81	Pb 82	Bi 83	Po 84	At 85	Rn 86

8. Group 18 is also called the noble gases. Their electron orbits are completely filled, and they rarely react with other elements. Which of the following is a noble gas?

(1) nitrogen (N)
(2) oxygen (O)
(3) chlorine (Cl)
(4) xenon (Xe)
(5) fluorine (F)

9. Which of the following statements is supported by the information given?

(1) Germanium (Ge) is used in computer chips.
(2) Silicon (Si) is a very common element.
(3) Chlorine (Cl) and iodine (I) have similar properties.
(4) Arsenic (As) and antimony (Sb) have very different properties.
(5) Arsenic (As) has 85 protons in its nucleus.

Electromagnetic radiation consists of electric and magnetic fields that oscillate back and forth. There is a wide range of types of electromagnetic radiation, which together form the electromagnetic spectrum.

The Electromagnetic Spectrum

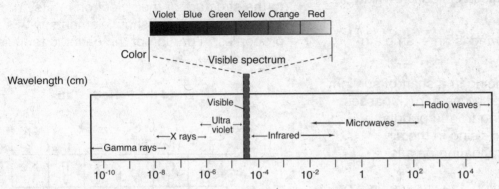

10. Which of the following types of electromagnetic radiation has a wavelength longer than that of the visible spectrum?

    (1) microwaves
    (2) ultraviolet light
    (3) X rays
    (4) gamma rays
    (5) colored light

11. Which of the following generalizations is supported by the diagram?

    (1) Unlike people, some insects can see ultraviolet light.
    (2) Warm colors like yellow have a shorter wavelength than cool colors like blue.
    (3) People can see only a small portion of the electromagnetic spectrum.
    (4) Microwaves are more useful than radio waves.
    (5) In medicine, X rays are used to make images of bones.

12. Objects are attracted to one another by the force of gravity. Gravity is proportional to the mass—the amount of matter—objects have; gravity decreases as the distance between the objects increases. An object's weight is the gravitational attraction of Earth to the object.

    What happens to the mass and weight of a rocket as it travels beyond Earth's orbit?

    (1) Its mass remains the same and its weight increases.
    (2) Its mass remains the same and its weight decreases.
    (3) Its mass decreases and its weight increases.
    (4) Its mass decreases and its weight decreases.
    (5) Its mass increases and its weight remains the same.

13. Heat energy can be transferred from one object to another. In summer, when you hold an ice-cold can of soda against your face, your face feels cooler. However, what is really happening is that the can is being warmed by heat from your body. You are actually losing a little body heat.

    Which of the following is an unstated assumption related to the paragraph?

    (1) Heat can be transferred.
    (2) Cold cannot be transferred.
    (3) Holding something cold against your face makes your face feel cooler.
    (4) A cool object can be warmed by your body.
    (5) You can lose body heat.

Answers and explanations start on page 656.

Language Arts, Reading

The GED Language Arts, Reading Test assesses your ability to understand and interpret a variety of reading materials.

Format

The test consists of seven selections from these areas of literature:

- **Nonfiction**—Two selections of 200–400 words. These selections will be drawn from business documents (for example, training handbooks and personnel policies), informational or persuasive texts (newspaper or magazine articles, biographies, encyclopedias, speeches, diaries) or critical reviews of the fine or performing arts.

- **Fiction**—Three selections of 200–400 words: one written before 1920, one written from 1920 to 1960, and one written after 1960. These fiction selections may be taken from novels or short stories.

- **Poetry**—One poem or excerpt from a poem, 8 to 25 lines.

- **Drama**—One excerpt from a play.

As you will see on the next page, every reading passage is preceded by a "purpose question." This is not the title of the passage, but a question to spur your interest in reading the selection. You can use it as a clue to the topic of the passage and as a guide for your reading.

Some questions on the GED Reading Test ask about a specific line or lines. You will see line numbering to the left side of the selection. Every fifth line of text is numbered: (5), (10), (15), and so on. You can use the line numbers in the passage to locate the word or phrase referred to in the question.

Questions

You will have 65 minutes to read passages and answer 40 multiple-choice questions. Most of the questions about each passage follow the order of information in the passage. There may be a question or two at the end that requires you to think about the passage as a whole, apply something from the passage to a new situation, or combine some new information about the author or the work with what you have read.

Reading and Critical Thinking Skills

The questions on the GED Reading Test are based on four types of reading and critical thinking skills: comprehension, application, analysis, and synthesis. The next two pages show examples of each type of question and demonstrate the type of thinking required to answer them.

Below is a passage similar to one you might find on the GED Language Arts, Reading Test. Think about the purpose question as you read the passage below.

WHY HAS DESMOND TUTU RECEIVED AN AWARD?

On a broad front a campaign is being fought with the weapons of the spirit and reason—a campaign for truth, freedom and justice. In recognition of the fact that it is this alternative which must succeed, the South African bishop, Desmond Tutu, has been selected as this year's
(5) Peace Prize laureate.

The contribution he has made, and is still making, represents a hope for the future, for the country's white minority as well as the black majority. Desmond Tutu is an exponent of the only form for conflict solving which is worthy of civilized nations.
(10) It is today twenty-three years since the Nobel Peace Prize was last awarded to a South African. On that occasion it was Albert Luthuli, then president of the African National Congress, who was presented with the Prize. It is the Committee's wish that this year's award should be seen as a renewed recognition of the courage and heroic patience
(15) shown by black South Africans in their use of peaceful means to oppose the *apartheid* system. This recognition is also extended to all who, throughout the world, stand in the forefront of the campaign for racial equality as a human right.

It is unfortunately not only in South Africa that human rights are vio-
(20) lated. Another former prizewinner, Amnesty International, informs us that such violations are known to occur in 117 countries, and that prisoners of conscience are tortured in 60 countries. Too frequently, the brutal features of power and violence mar the face of our times. But if we are willing to look for it, we can also see the face of peace—even if
(25) we have to peer through prison bars and barbed wire to find it. And, in spite of everything, new hope is raised on each occasion we see how the spirit of man refuses to be conquered by the forces of hate.

© The Nobel Foundation 1984.

Comprehension Skills

To answer comprehension questions successfully, you will need to know how to (1) restate ideas, (2) summarize information, and (3) understand what is implied.

Example 1: Which of the following is the best description of Desmond Tutu's approach to solving the conflict in South Africa?

(1) to fight any group that violates the fundamental right of equality
(2) to win a campaign and gain power over the white minority
(3) to free prisoners and end torture
(4) to work for racial equality by peaceful means
(5) to accept the separation of blacks and whites

Answer: (4). From the passage, you understand that Tutu won a peace prize for working against racial inequality with "the weapons of the spirit and reason."

Application

To answer application questions correctly, you need to understand the ideas in the passage and then use these ideas in a situation not described in the passage.

Example 2: With which of these sayings would Desmond Tutu <u>disagree</u>?

    (1) Turn the other cheek.
    (2) No act of kindness, however small, is wasted.
    (3) All men are created equal.
    (4) Treat others as you would have others treat you.
    (5) The end justifies the means.

Answer: (5). This saying means that any method—including violence—can be used to achieve a goal that is good. Tutu does not believe this.

Analysis

To answer analysis questions, you need to look at specific parts of the passage in order to (1) identify elements of the author's craft and how the author achieved certain effects, (2) identify cause-and-effect relationships, or (3) recognize the author's unstated assumptions.

Example 3: Why does the speechmaker refer to Amnesty International (lines 20–22)?

    (1) to honor another group that has worked for equality
    (2) to support the statement that human rights violations exist worldwide
    (3) to name another recipient of the Peace Prize
    (4) to show that Tutu is not alone in his work
    (5) to question statistics that have been reported

Answer: (2). The writer makes a statement in lines 19–20; then he supports that statement with the information reported by Amnesty International.

Synthesis

To answer synthesis questions, you need to integrate, or put together, elements from different parts of the passage. This process may involve (1) identifying the overall structure, tone, or purpose of the passage, (2) comparing and contrasting ideas, or (3) taking new information and combining it with what you know.

Example 4: What is the tone of this speech?

    (1) light-hearted
    (2) fiery
    (3) solemn
    (4) sarcastic
    (5) friendly

Answer: (3). The topic of the speech (awarding a prize to a man who is working for racial equality) and the choice of words and formal expression ("It is today twenty-three years") all work together to create a solemn tone. If you imagined the man giving the speech, you would hear a solemn tone of voice.

GED TIP

Be sure you select the option that answers the question. Some choices may contain facts from the passage or other true statements, but do not answer the question. They are therefore incorrect.

One of the best ways to prepare for the GED Reading Test is to read as often as you can. The better you are at reading in general, the more successful you will be on the test.

NONFICTION

Identifying Main Ideas and Supporting Details

Key Ideas

- The most important point of a passage is called the main idea.
- Sometimes a main idea is stated, but often you must figure it out.
- Supporting details point to and explain the main idea.

The Main Idea

A writer has a message, or **main idea,** to get across. Sometimes the main idea is stated directly; often you have to figure it out yourself. You can find the main idea by asking, "What is the *most important* point the writer is making?" Most of the information in a passage will point to and explain the main idea.

As you read this passage, ask yourself what *main* point the writer is making. The answer will be the main idea.

> When I am reading a poem, I rarely feel alone in the room. The poet and I are together. It's as if the poet wrote a secret diary years ago. I am unlocking it as I sit alone and read.
>
> At times I don't understand what a poem means. I just like the way it sounds, or the strange images that it provokes. The world is so peculiar in a poem. At the same time, it is so enticing. Sometimes I understand exactly, as if the poet is whispering to me, as if we shared the same experience.
>
> I must be fully concentrated on reading, or I cannot enter the world of a poem. There are too many daily tasks to attend to; tasks that are very far removed from the magic and imagination involved in a poem.
>
> On a cold, snowy day, I cuddle up inside my apartment and read and read. Then, I'm free to ride through the imagination of all those who came before me.

► Which of the following statements expresses the main idea?
  (1) The writer has a love of poetry.
  (2) The writer cuddles up on cold days to read.

You are correct if you chose **(1).** While the passage mentions that the writer reads on cold days, the main point of all the information is how much the writer enjoys and loves reading poetry.

Each paragraph has a main idea. To find the main idea of a passage with more than one paragraph, put together the ideas from all the paragraphs.

Supporting Details

A writer explains the main idea of a passage with supporting details. **Supporting details** include facts, examples, descriptions, and specific pieces of information. When you read, you need to identify details that support the main idea.

► Which detail helps you understand the writer's main point?
  (1) At times, the reader does not understand a poem.
  (2) The writer feels poetry is filled with magic and imagination.

You are correct if you chose **(2).** That detail helps you see that the main idea is the writer's love of poetry. The fact that the writer doesn't always understand a poem is true, but it alone does not support the main idea.

GED TIP

On the GED Reading Test, be sure you don't confuse a supporting detail of a passage with the main idea. If you are asked for the main idea, choose the most important, general point.

NONFICTION ▸ PRACTICE 1

Questions 1 through 5 refer to the following passage from a diary.

WHERE IS THIS WOMAN'S HOME?

I feel I have never had a home. All my life moving from place to place. The only thing that remained the same, that was stable, was Oklahoma. Even the landscape never changed. The
(5) towns there never grew up into cities. The people were the same each year, wearing the same clothing, saying the same things.

The search for a homeland is part of the Chickasaw migration legend. It was ordained by
(10) the deities and began in the past when the people lived in the land of the "setting sun." During the days they would walk over the land, searching for their home. The priests carried a pole. They carried it in their hands by day and planted it
(15) each night. During the night it moved about and by morning it would be pointing the direction they were to travel. For a while it commanded the people to journey east, toward the morning sun. They crossed the Mississippi River eventually,
(20) and on the other side, the pole finally ceased to move during the night. The land was settled, crops were planted. It became known as the Old Fields. But one morning the pole leaned westward. The people gathered together and began
(25) the long journey back. They abandoned their village but did not feel sorrow because the pole had commanded it.

And I am still moving, looking for a home. I don't know if I will ever escape my tradition, my
(30) past. It goes with me everywhere, like a shadow.

By Linda Hogan from *Ariadne's Thread*, edited by Lyn Lifshin, New York: Harper & Row, 1982.

1. How does the author describe herself?

She feels as if she is

(1) searching for a place to call home
(2) doomed to stay in Oklahoma
(3) tired of the sameness in her life
(4) living in the past
(5) being shadowed by failure

2. Who do the Chickasaw believe is responsible for making them move?

(1) the priests
(2) white people
(3) themselves
(4) the gods
(5) Oklahomans

3. Why did the Chickasaw not feel sad when they left their homes in the east?

(1) They knew they were headed to a better place to live.
(2) They had been forced to move east to begin with.
(3) They were returning to their ancient homeland.
(4) Their fields had become too old and worn out.
(5) It was simply part of their beliefs to follow the pole.

4. Which of the following best summarizes the main idea?

The writer

(1) has always lived in Oklahoma and plans to stay there
(2) feels trapped by tradition and wants to move far away
(3) understands that her sense of search is part of her Chickasaw heritage
(4) thinks the most important thing is to find a stable home
(5) believes that people in Oklahoma are all the same

5. How does the statement "I don't know if I will ever escape my tradition" (lines 28–29) support the main idea?

It shows that the writer

(1) accepts that she is Chickasaw
(2) is trying to escape by moving around
(3) lives in a more modern time
(4) believes in the power of Indian legends
(5) does not know what will happen

Answers and explanations start on page 657.

NONFICTION

Restating and Summarizing

Key Ideas

• To restate an idea, put it in your own words.
• To summarize, choose the most important details that explain the main idea of a piece.

Restating Ideas

Restating an idea means putting it into your own words. For example, a friend may tell you that a movie wasn't worth the eight dollars she spent on it. You might then tell a co-worker that your friend said the movie was no good.

As you read the passage below, restate in your mind what you are reading.

> In Canton, Ohio, we take our desserts seriously. There are two local candy stores that receive over 90 percent of the city's candy business: Heggy's and Baldwin's. Those who prefer Heggy's won't befriend anyone who buys their sweets at Baldwin's.
>
> My family has always patronized Heggy's. At the Heggy's factory, Gerty wraps by hand each large chocolate candy in clear cellophane wrap. She's in the back of the store with her hairnet, seated at a table filled with hundreds of chocolates. My favorite chocolates at Heggy's are the dark chocolate creams, peanut clusters, and caramels.
>
> Heggy's aficionados point out that their candy of choice is a larger size and therefore superior. The rivalry runs deep . . . at Easter, Hanukkah, Christmas, Thanksgiving, and all occasions. Baldwin's loyal followers claim its sweets are sweeter. It's a feud over the best chocolate in town.

▶ How do the people of Canton feel about chocolate candy?
  (1) They consider it a serious health issue.
  (2) They feel it's important enough to take a stand on.

You are correct if you chose **(2)**. The phrase "take our desserts seriously" means that the candy is important to the people.

On the GED the correct answer will not always use the exact words from the passage. You will have to recognize that the idea has been restated.

Summarizing

If you want to tell a friend about a movie you liked, you might **summarize** what happens in the movie. You certainly will not give all the details—that would take too long. A summary includes only the most important facts and ideas.

▶ Which of the following statements best summarizes the difference in opinion over the candy?
  (1) Some people prefer Heggy's candy because it's bigger, while others prefer Baldwin's because it's sweeter.
  (2) People argue whether to buy Heggy's or Baldwin's candy for different holidays.

You are correct if you chose **(1)**. The last paragraph sums up the difference in people's opinions. Statement (2) merely misstates a detail in the last paragraph.

GED TIP

As you read a GED passage, check your understanding by pausing occasionally to see if you can restate and summarize what you are reading.

Questions 1 through 3 refer to the following business letter.

WHY IS THE CUSTOMER COMPLAINING?

Dear Richard,

Attached is a copy of my June 8th letter to Customer Service. After having my car serviced on June 30th, the list of problems has grown.
(5) These matters need your immediate attention.

1. Although I did finally receive my copy of the warranty after waiting two months, it is not bumper-to-bumper as Mr. Schecht promised. It also requires service at your facility unless the
(10) warranty administrator waives that requirement. I purchased the car from you at a premium price with the expectation that I would have a bumper-to-bumper warranty that I could use at any dealer. I never would have bought this car from you if I
(15) knew about these limitations. I expect two things: A written waiver from the warranty administrator that allows me to have warranty service performed at any dealer, and a wrap-around warranty, provided at your cost, that turns this lim-
(20) ited warranty into the promised "bumper-to-bumper" warranty.

2. I expect an itemized list of registration costs, and the exact amount of credit I received from the Department of Motor Vehicles for the
(25) canceled plates voucher I gave to Mr. Schecht. If there is a refund due, I expect it within 15 days.

3. I expect a proper bill of sale that itemizes and describes the payments for the alarm system and the extended warranty, and includes all the
(30) items on the original bill of sale.

4. Your mechanic was unable to locate a cause for the burning smell. The smell persists. I expect your written assurance that if and when the cause for this smell becomes known, you will repair the
(35) problem at your cost.

5. The mechanic did *not* repair the left front marker light, although he promised he would. Enclosed is a copy of your invoice for this repair, which wasn't made, as well as an invoice from
(40) another dealer who actually made the repair. I expect reimbursement for $22.90.

cc: Joe Smith, Department of Consumer Affairs

From The Encyclopedia of Business Letters, Fax Memos, and Email © 1999 Robert Bly. Published by Career Press, Franklin Lakes, NJ. All rights reserved.

1. The problems that the writer mentions in the first paragraph and outlines in his letter include which of the following?

(1) overcharges on repairs
(2) rude treatment
(3) lack of proper paperwork
(4) a burning smell that was not present before
(5) the premium price paid for the car

2. What does the customer want done about the burning smell?

(1) written assurance that nothing is wrong
(2) the mechanic to find the cause of the smell
(3) the car to be repaired free if the cause of the problem is discovered
(4) a refund of the money that was paid to have the problem fixed
(5) reimbursement for having the problem fixed by another dealer

3. Which of the following statements best summarizes this letter?

(1) A letter to customer service was never responded to and is being attached.
(2) Mechanics have been unable to fix one problem and did not fix a second.
(3) A bumper-to-bumper warranty is better than a limited warranty.
(4) The service and warranty on the customer's car have been unacceptable.
(5) Some dealers and garages are better than others.

Answers and explanations start on page 657.

3

Key Ideas

- Applying ideas means using information in a new but similar situation.
- To apply ideas, ask yourself, "How is this new situation just like the situation in the passage?"

GED TIP

Remember that you can go back to the passage to find information you need to answer a question.

NONFICTION

Applying Ideas

When you apply ideas, you use information you already know in a new but similar situation. For example, suppose you know that a friend loves country music. When you need to buy a gift for that friend, you walk past the jazz and rock sections in the music store and head straight for the country. You're applying what you've learned about your friend to help you choose a gift.

To apply ideas when reading, look for elements in the new situation that are similar to elements in the passage you have read. Read this selection and then see if you can apply some of the ideas in it.

> When the delivery truck pulled up to my house the day before my mother's birthday, I knew her gift had finally arrived. I was excited. Not only had I ordered a beautiful art book for her, but I'd also ordered a mystery novel for myself and a book each for my nephew and niece. (I couldn't resist buying them while I was choosing my mother's gift from an online bookstore.) The carton looked bigger than I expected, but perhaps it had a lot of filler to keep the books from becoming damaged.
>
> I lugged the huge box into the kitchen so I could open it and begin wrapping my mother's gift. I tugged at the industrial staples and then tore open the carton. To my surprise, it was filled with many copies of the same book. To make matters worse, it was a book I had not ordered. *Who Moved My Cheese?* What kind of book was that? And who would order *one* copy of that book, let alone eleven? I certainly didn't want these books. I knew my family wouldn't want them either. They wanted *The Art of Diego Rivera, Harry Potter,* and Dr. Seuss. So much for buying online. I'm sticking to in-store buying.

► Which of the following situations is most like the situation that happened to the writer?
  (1) buying groceries only to discover you brought someone else's bag home
  (2) buying eleven boxes of the same pasta at the store

Option (1) is correct. It shares the elements of intending to buy something and getting the wrong thing by mistake. The second option is wrong because the writer did not intentionally buy eleven copies of the book. Now try this question.

► If the writer attended an auction, she would be most likely to
  (1) decide which item to bid on and how much she will bid
  (2) get involved in the excitement and bid on many things

You are correct if you chose **(2)**. The writer states that she couldn't resist buying additional items when she was online shopping. Therefore, she seems the type to get caught up in buying things. If she had carefully chosen which book to buy her mother and had ordered only that one, then option (1) would be correct.

Questions 1 through 4 refer to the following excerpt.

WHAT IS THE BEST WAY TO GET OUT OF DEBT?

Once you stop using credit cards, three things will happen.

1. You will buy less—and whatever you do buy will probably be a less expensive model or
(5) make. Studies have found that people spend more when they pay with plastic, because it doesn't feel like real money. When it is real money, you're more sensible.

2. Your total debt will shrink rapidly. You are
(10) paying *off* back bills, you are not adding new ones, and you have extra money (because you're buying less). That surplus cash will reduce your debt faster than you could imagine.

3. You will grow incredibly smug. You're the
(15) first on your block to get out of debt. Others will follow, but you'll be the first.

I'm not against credit cards. They're easy to use. They're handy. If your card has a low annual fee and a 25-day, interest-free grace period for
(20) paying your bills, you're getting monthly loans for practically nothing. What I'm against is buying more on your credit cards than you can pay for at the end of the month.

Once you've fought your way out of debt you
(25) can start using credit cards again—but only for the convenience of not carrying cash. Your days of debt are done. A big expense may sometimes drive you over the limit. A stereo. A llama. A hot-air balloon. Whenever you limp home, back in
(30) debt, recite your mantra: "From now on, I'm not going to put down a charge card for anything." Stick with it until you're free again.

From *Making the Most of Your Money* by Jane Bryant Quinn, New York: Simon & Schuster, 1991.

1. What kind of behavior is becoming debt-free an example of?

(1) overcoming a bad habit
(2) learning a new trick
(3) doing the impossible
(4) following a daily routine
(5) setting a good example

2. If you have five credit cards with high interest rates and no grace periods, how can you become debt free?

(1) buy more expensive items so that they last longer
(2) pay your debt off slowly so that you have extra cash for necessities
(3) never use the credit cards
(4) use them only when it is not convenient to carry cash
(5) cut up four of the credit cards right away

3. Which of the following situations is most like the process of becoming debt free?

(1) buying a winning lottery ticket
(2) saving loose change in a jar each day
(3) wearing a patch to give up smoking
(4) giving up rich foods and losing weight
(5) running a marathon race

4. Earlier in the book, the author made the statement "It's so simple that I'm almost embarrassed to mention it. Don't borrow any more."

Based on this information and the information in this passage, with which of the following statements would the author most likely agree?

(1) "Money is the root of all evil."
(2) "You can never have enough money."
(3) "Live within your means."
(4) "Try to keep up with the Joneses."
(5) "You deserve only the best."

Answers and explanations start on page 657.

NONFICTION

Relating Cause and Effect

When one event or idea influences another, there is a cause-and-effect relationship. For example, if you forget to fill your car with gas, the car will stall. The lack of gas is the **cause**, or the reason. The stalled car is the **effect**.

As you read this passage, look for cause-and-effect relationships.

> He is deceptively sweet upon waking up, and lets out a large yawn, showing his thin pink puppy tongue, and simultaneously letting out a high-pitched squeaking sound. Not two minutes later, he's eaten my favorite magazine and stuffed his entire head in the kitchen wastebasket to find a leftover turkey bone. The pup searches under the bed, on top of the dresser, and beside the nightstand for anything to chew. He's on a rampage in the morning—it's just his puppy nature.
>
> To calm him down, we head to the park for one hour of exercise with the other neighborhood dogs. Afterwards, he plays with his stuffed animal squeaky toy, sleeps for an hour, then finds his favorite bone. He lies down like an angel, chewing with contentment.

▶ What causes the puppy's owner to take him to the park?
  (1) They like to see the other neighborhood dogs.
  (2) The puppy is acting too wild and energetic.

You are correct if you chose **(2)**. The first paragraph describes wild behavior, and the second paragraph says, "To calm him down, we head to the park. . . ."

▶ Why is the puppy so wild and energetic?
  (1) It is just the way a puppy is.
  (2) He has a behavior problem.

You are correct if you chose **(1)**. The writer doesn't indicate that the puppy's behavior is a problem. In fact, she clearly states that it's just the puppy's nature.

▶ What effect does the activity in the park have on the puppy?
  (1) It calms him and tires him out.
  (2) It teaches him to obey his owner.

You are correct if you chose **(1)**. When they get back from the park, the puppy plays quietly, sleeps for an hour, and then lies down to chew.

▶ Why does a walk in the park have a calming effect on the puppy?
  (1) because the puppy enjoys seeing the other dogs
  (2) because the puppy gets plenty of exercise

You are correct if you chose **(2)**. The exercise brings on the effect—calm behavior. This cause is not directly stated. You have to apply what you know about exercise and its effects in order to understand the relationship.

Key Ideas

- To determine the cause of an event, answer the question, "Why did this happen?"
- To determine an effect, ask yourself, "What was the result?"

ON THE GED

In a GED passage, a writer might discuss one cause and all its effects, one effect and all its causes, or a chain of events in which each effect becomes the cause of another event.

Questions 1 through 5 refer to the following excerpt from an essay.

WHAT DID THE DEPRESSION TEACH US?

Some events are so important that their influence cuts across class lines, affects all races and ethnic groups, and leaves no region untouched. The depression of the 1930s was such an event. No
(5) one who lived through those years in the United States could ever completely forget the bread lines, the millions of unemployed, or the forlorn and discouraged men and women who saw their mortgages foreclosed, their dreams shattered,
(10) their children hungry and afraid.

The depression was precipitated by the stock market crash in October 1929, but the actual cause of the collapse was an unhealthy economy. While the ability of the manufacturing industry
(15) to produce consumer goods had increased rapidly, mass purchasing power had remained relatively static. Most laborers, farmers, and white-collar workers, therefore, could not afford to buy the automobiles and refrigerators turned
(20) out by factories in the 1920s, because their incomes were too low. At the same time, the federal government increased the problem through economic policies that tended to encourage the very rich to over-save.

(25) Herbert Hoover, a sensitive and humane engineer, had the misfortune of being President when the depression began. Even though he broke with the past and used the power of the federal government to stem the tide of depres-
(30) sion, especially through loans to businesses and banks, his efforts proved to be too little and too late.

From "The Depression" from *Generations: Your Family in Modern American History*, 2nd ed., edited by James Watts and Allen F. Davis, New York: Alfred A. Knopf, 1974, 1978.

1. According to the authors, why was the depression of the 1930s so important?

   (1) It could have been prevented.
   (2) It was a time of economic hardship.
   (3) It hurt the working class.
   (4) It affected nearly everyone.
   (5) It was unforgettable.

2. According to the passage, which of the following was an effect of the depression?

   (1) A small percentage of people became unemployed.
   (2) Many people lost the mortgages on their homes.
   (3) The stock market collapsed in October 1929.
   (4) Herbert Hoover was elected president.
   (5) The rich began to save too much of their money.

3. According to the passage, which of the following was one cause of the depression?

   (1) poor farm crops
   (2) a static stock market
   (3) low worker incomes
   (4) not enough productivity
   (5) laborers refusing to buy products

4. In the early part of the depression, what effect did government policies have on the economy?

   (1) Unemployment was reduced.
   (2) Banks and businesses began to need loans.
   (3) There was little or no effect.
   (4) Some of the poorer people were helped.
   (5) The very rich were helped.

5. One person who lived during the depression stated, "I can remember one time, the only thing in the house to eat was mustard. . . . And we can't stand mustard till today."

   This account supports which of the following ideas from the passage?

   (1) Farmers were not producing enough.
   (2) Workers should have been paid more.
   (3) The depression touched everyone.
   (4) Herbert Hoover could have done more to help the economy.
   (5) The depression left people emotionally scarred.

Answers and explanations start on page 657.

NONFICTION

Comparing and Contrasting

You are probably familiar with comparing and contrasting whenever you go shopping. If you are looking at two cars or even two bottles of aspirin, you want to know if the price of the two is the same or different.

Writers **compare** to point out what is similar and **contrast** to point out what is different about ideas or things.

As you read this passage, look for things being compared and contrasted.

> In December it seems everyone is hurrying to bake holiday treats, decorate, and buy gifts. Some holiday shoppers trek through store after store, while others prefer catalog or online shopping. Just two of the holidays that keep everyone so busy this time of year are Christmas and Hanukkah.
>
> These holidays are, of course, times of celebration. People plan parties and family get-togethers. Both involve gift giving. Both also coincide with the winter solstice in the Northern Hemisphere, a time when many ancient cultures rejoiced.
>
> Christmas is a celebration of the birth of Jesus, though celebrating Christmas on December 25 did not become common until the fourth century.
>
> Hanukkah, the Jewish Festival of Lights, is linked with a tiny amount of oil that is believed to have miraculously burned for eight days in a temple in the second century B.C. That's why on Hanukkah an additional candle is lit each evening until, on the eighth night of the holiday, eight candles are burning.

► What is the writer comparing and contrasting?
  (1) methods of shopping
  (2) Christmas and Hanukkah

You are correct if you chose **(2)**. The similarities and differences between the two holidays are the focus of the discussion. Two methods of shopping are merely mentioned.

► What is one basis on which the writer compares the two?
  (1) time of year celebrated
  (2) kinds of meals served

You are correct if you chose **(1)**. The similarities discussed in this passage include the time of the winter solstice in the Northern Hemisphere, near which each holiday is celebrated.

► What is one basis on which the writer contrasts the two?
  (1) gift giving
  (2) their histories

The correct answer is **(2)**. The two holidays have very different histories. Both holidays involve gift giving, so that is not a point of contrast.

Key Ideas

- To compare ideas or things, find out how they are alike.
- To contrast ideas or things, find out how they differ.
- A writer might compare two things, contrast two things, or compare and contrast in one passage.

ON THE GED

In a GED passage, a writer may (1) compare in one paragraph and contrast in the next or (2) go back and forth, discussing similarities and differences on different points.

Questions 1 through 5 refer to the following excerpt from a diary.

WHO IS TRAVELING ON THIS TRIP?

Mr. West from Peoria, Ill. had another man, his wife, a son Clay about 20 years of age and his daughter, America, eighteen. Unfortunately Mr. West had gone to the extreme of providing him-
(5)   self with such a heavy wagon and load that they were deemed objectionable as fellow argonauts. After disposing of some of their supplies they were allowed to join us. They had four fine oxen. This wagon often got stalled in bad roads much
(10) to the annoyance of all, but as he was a wagon maker and his companion a blacksmith by trade and both were accommodating there were always ready hands to "pry the wheel out of mire."

A mule team from Washington, D.C. was very
(15) insufficiently provisioned . . . [by] a Southern gentlemen "unused to work. . . ." They deserted the train at Salt Lake as they could not pro-ceed with their equipment and it was easier to embrace Mormonism than to brave the
(20) "American Desert."

Much in contrast to these men were four batchelors Messers Wilson, Goodall, Fifield and Martin, who had a wagon drawn by four oxen and two milch cows following behind. The latter
(25) gave milk all the way to the sink of the Humboldt where they died, having acted as draught ani-mals for several weeks after the oxen had per-ished. Many a cup of milk was given to the chil-dren of the train and the mothers tried in every
(30) way possible to express their gratitude.

By Catherine Haun from *Women's Diaries of the Westward Journey,* edited by Lillian Schlissel, New York: Schocken Books, 1982.

1. What did Mr. West do that allowed his group to join the wagon train?

(1) make wagons for the others
(2) bring four fine oxen
(3) offer milk to the children
(4) leave some of his possessions behind
(5) stop his objectionable behavior

2. What purpose did the cows serve?

(1) They led the oxen through rough terrain.
(2) They carried children when wagons were full.
(3) They provided milk and pulled wagons.
(4) They provided food and replaced the mules.
(5) They pulled stalled wagons from the mud.

3. Which of the following is contrasted in this excerpt?

(1) the provisions of each group of travelers
(2) the stability of each of the wagons
(3) the number of people in each group
(4) the health of each of the animals
(5) the ability of each group to feed the children

4. Suppose the writer were comparing a woman with five children who could sew and cook to one man with an old ox. Which of the follow-ing would be her most likely response?

The writer would

(1) worry that the woman's children would weigh down their wagon
(2) be happy to have people who could cook and sew
(3) prefer to add fewer people to the group of travelers
(4) feel sorry for the man and welcome him
(5) offer the man one of her own animals

5. Based on the information in this excerpt, how is this trip similar for all the travelers?

(1) They are looking for excitement and adventure.
(2) They must cooperate and work together.
(3) They will be rewarded for their efforts.
(4) They have similar backgrounds and relate to each other.
(5) They have all been forced to go on the journey.

Answers and explanations start on page 657.

Drawing Conclusions

A detective draws a conclusion when he looks at different pieces of evidence and figures out who committed a crime. A doctor draws a conclusion when she looks at different symptoms and figures out what illness a patient has. You, as a reader, can draw a conclusion when you take pieces of information and put them together to figure out something that the writer has not directly stated.

See what conclusions you can draw from this notice sent by an employer.

> Thank you for sending your resume in response to our newspaper advertisement. We consider our company—and especially our employees—to be the best. And we want to keep it that way. For that reason, we carefully review each resume that is sent to us. We want to ensure that our company and the new employee we hire are a perfect match.
>
> This process, of course, takes some time. We want to assure you that your resume is part of this process and will be reviewed. If we feel we have an opening that matches your qualifications, we will contact you. If you have not heard from us within ten business days of the postmark of this notice, be assured that we will keep your resume on file for one year and review it when future openings arise.

▶ If a job applicant has not heard from this company three weeks after reading this notice, what can she conclude?
  (1) The review process is taking longer than expected.
  (2) She did not get the job that she applied for.

Option (2) is correct. The notice says that the review process takes some time. It also says that the company will contact the applicant if it feels she matches the opening. Finally, if she doesn't hear from it within ten business days, her resume will go on file. You can conclude that the review process takes about ten business days, and if she hasn't been contacted in that time, she didn't get the job.

▶ What kind of notice can you conclude this is?
  (1) a personal note sent to this individual applicant
  (2) a form notice sent to all applicants

Again, you're correct if you chose **(2)**. The way the notice is worded, with no personal references, lets you conclude this. You can also use your knowledge of the real world and businesses form letters to conclude that this, too, is a form.

▶ What conclusion can you draw about the company's attitude?
  (1) It cares about its employees and their job satisfaction.
  (2) It cares only about profits and employee productivity.

You are correct if you chose **(1)**. The fact that the company not only states that it considers its employees the best, but it also takes the time to communicate sincerely with potential employees, lets you conclude that.

Key Ideas

- A conclusion is an idea figured out from different pieces of information.
- You can use your knowledge of the real world to help you draw conclusions when you read.

GED TIP

Be sure to read an entire passage before answering the questions about it. That way, you'll take all the information into account and won't "jump to conclusions."

NONFICTION ▸ PRACTICE 6

Questions 1 through 5 refer to the following excerpt from an autobiography.

WHY IS HELEN INTERESTED IN THE TADPOLES?

Once there were eleven tadpoles in a glass globe set in a window full of plants. I remember the eagerness with which I made discoveries about them. It was great fun to plunge my hand
(5) into the bowl and feel the tadpoles frisk about, and to let them slip and slide between my fingers. One day a more ambitious fellow leaped beyond the edge of the bowl and fell on the floor, where I found him to all appearance more dead than
(10) alive. The only sign of life was a slight wriggling of his tail. But no sooner had he returned to his element than he darted to the bottom, swimming round and round in joyous activity. He had made his leap, he had seen the great world, and was
(15) content to stay in his pretty glass house under the big fuchsia tree until he attained the dignity of froghood. Then he went to live in the leafy pool at the end of the garden, where he made the summer nights musical with his quaint love-song.

(20) Thus I learned from life itself. At the beginning I was only a little mass of possibilities. It was my teacher who unfolded and developed them. When she came, everything about me breathed of love and joy and was full of meaning. She has
(25) never since let pass an opportunity to point out the beauty that is in everything, nor has she ceased trying in thought and action and example to make my life sweet and useful.

It was my teacher's genius, her quick sympa-
(30) thy, her loving tact which made the first years of my education so beautiful.

From *The Story of My Life* by Helen Keller, reprinted in *The Norton Book of American Autobiography*, edited by Jay Parini, New York: W. W. Norton, 1999.

1. What can you conclude about the writer's view of learning?

(1) It is a constant struggle for perfection.
(2) It is rewarding and one of life's joys.
(3) It is better with a strict teacher.
(4) It happens very slowly, if at all.
(5) It happens most often when you are alone.

2. What conclusion can you draw about the writer's character?

The writer is

(1) self-centered and demanding
(2) innocent and helpless
(3) confused and searching
(4) fearful and shy
(5) insightful and grateful

3. If Helen's teacher was trying to teach her addition, what method would the teacher most likely use?

(1) make Helen stand and recite addition facts for one hour every day
(2) assign an abundance of addition homework
(3) allow Helen to learn on her own from books
(4) show Helen how addition is used in everyday life
(5) ask a well-known mathematician to teach the subject

4. How are the thoughts in this personal account organized?

(1) from most important to least important
(2) as a comparison with a frog followed by a contrast
(3) as a problem followed by its solution
(4) in chronological order, or time sequence
(5) as an anecdote followed by a generalization based on the anecdote

5. Later in her story, Helen compares a child's mind to a shallow brook "which ripples and dances merrily over the stony course of its education. . . ." Based on this information and the excerpt above, what is similar about the tadpole and a child?

(1) They learn from others.
(2) They are eager to grow into adulthood.
(3) They begin ambitious but then give up.
(4) Youth can make them do dangerous things.
(5) Their development is not entirely smooth.

Answers and explanations start on page 658.

NONFICTION

Determining Tone and Point of View

Key Ideas

- The author's attitude toward a subject is conveyed by the tone of the writing.
- To determine tone, look at word choice and manner of expression. How would the author sound reading the piece?
- The author's point of view is the position he or she is writing from.

ON THE GED

Some kinds of tone you might see in GED passages are formal or informal, positive or negative, objective, sarcastic, arrogant, concerned, affectionate, and nostalgic.

Tone

A writer usually has a certain attitude toward the subject he or she is writing about. This attitude is the **tone** of the piece. The tone is not directly stated. You have to sense it by the writer's choice of words and manner of expression.

As you read this drama review, ask yourself, "What tone of voice would the author have if he or she were reading this aloud to me?"

Watching actor Brian Dennehy as Willy Loman in the stage production of *Death of a Salesman* was transforming. I know intellectually that live theater is better than movies. Movie actors reshoot scenes until they are perfect. An actor on stage has one chance to get it right. It is immediate. The actors are breathing human beings in the same room with you. Theater provides the opportunity for strong emotions to surface, right there, in the moment. Seeing a play often envelops me in energy.

But I've never gone so far as to cry at a theater performance until now. I cried because Dennehy's Loman reminded me of my father, of the brevity of our lives, of how easy it is to waste our lives. This was not an intellectual response. I suddenly heard what this man on stage was saying—his life wasn't worth living, though he had tried hard, had a devoted wife and two sons. It didn't matter that this play was written in the 1940s. Mr. Dennehy stood on stage and roared at us about our lives now. It was hard-hitting, emotional drama.

▶ Which of the following best describes the tone of this piece?
(1) positive and somewhat awed
(2) cool and objective

The correct response is **(1)**. The writer states positive opinions. He also chooses short, clipped expressions ("It is immediate," "right there, in the moment,") that by themselves create a sense of drama and awe. If the tone were cool and objective, you would not sense the writer's emotional attitude toward the play.

Point of View

The **point of view** of a piece is "where the author is coming from"—that is, the writer's background and experiences that may affect his or her opinions. For example, when you read a column in a newspaper, you can usually tell whether the writer has a liberal or a conservative point of view.

▶ What point of view does the writer of the review above have?
(1) that of a person who prefers sitting at home watching TV
(2) that of an enthusiastic theatergoer

You are correct if you chose **(2)**. You can conclude that the writer goes to the theater ("Seeing a play often envelops me") and enjoys it ("theater is better than movies"). Knowing this helps you evaluate the merits of the review.

Questions 1 through 5 refer to the following review.

IS REALITY TELEVISION HERE TO STAY?

CBS delivered a television low mark called *Big Brother*. Focusing on 10 fame-seeking, people-pleasing, hair-teasing losers willing to submit to surveillance by a nation of snoops for three

(5) months, it was so bad that it wasn't even good. Forget about camp reversals that transform trash into the perversely fascinating, forget about the Cheese Factor, which allows a pop-cultural product to be moldy and musty and stinky and still

(10) taste good. *Big Brother* was so bad that even Jean-Paul Sartre would have yawned, and the dude wrote hundreds of pages about useless passion in *Being and Nothingness*.

But something good did come of *Big Brother*,

(15) something wicked and warped and witty, something created by people with way too much time on their hands and way too much venom in their bite. While the reality series was channeling banality through the cable cords and over the air-

(20) waves six nights a week, a small crew of writers were deconstructing and eviscerating the tedium on the Internet. They were taking hours and hours of prime-time dross and turning it into decadent, amoral, sharp, electronic gold.

(25) Internet sass.

You gotta love it, if only because it keeps razor-tongued fanatics and uncensored savants off the streets and out of trouble.

Not only was there a site devoted entirely to

(30) the ridiculing of CBS, *Big Brother*, its 10 cast members, their families, host Julie Chen, and the gaseous *Big Brother* house pug, but a number of other general interest sites, notably Salon.com, spent the summer providing wry daily updates

(35) on the non-goings-on of the non-people in the non-house. They, too, took the non-pulse of a DOA television series and gave it a semblance of life on the Internet.

Excerpt from "Talking Back to the Tube," by Matthew Gilbert. Reprinted courtesy of the Boston Globe.

1. Who is being referred to as "razor-tongued fanatics and uncensored savants" (line 27)?

   (1) the television writers
   (2) the television cast of Big Brother
   (3) the television audience
   (4) the Internet writers
   (5) the Internet audience

2. Which of the following best summarizes the reviewer's point about *Big Brother*?

   (1) With a little work, it could have been a good "campy" TV show.
   (2) The Internet reviews were much more interesting than the TV show.
   (3) The TV show was so bad that it was funny.
   (4) Internet writers are better than TV writers.
   (5) The main problem was with the ten people on the TV show.

3. What main idea is supported by the statement "even Jean-Paul Sartre would have yawned, and the dude wrote hundreds of pages about useless passion" (lines 10–12)?

   (1) The show was boring.
   (2) The show should have been longer.
   (3) The show needed more passion.
   (4) The show was incomprehensible.
   (5) The show put intellectuals to sleep.

4. Which of the following best describes the tone of this review?

   (1) apologetic
   (2) nostalgic for earlier shows
   (3) informal and hip
   (4) objective
   (5) harsh and technical

5. From whose point of view is this piece likely written?

   (1) a television script writer
   (2) a person who hates watching TV
   (3) someone knowledgeable about the media
   (4) an Internet site writer
   (5) a disgruntled fan

Answers and explanations start on page 658.

NONFICTION PRACTICE QUESTIONS

Questions 1 through 4 refer to the following excerpt from an autobiography.

ARE LECIA AND HER SISTER GOOD STUDENTS?

That fall my school career didn't go much better. I got suspended from my second-grade class twice, first for biting a kid named Phyllis who wasn't, to my mind,
(5) getting her scissors out fast enough to comply with the teacher, then again for breaking my plastic ruler over the head of a boy named Sammy Joe Tyler, whom I adored. A pale blue knot rose through the blond stub-
(10) ble of his crew cut. Both times I got sent to the principal, a handsome ex-football coach named Frank Doleman who let Lecia and me call him Uncle Frank. (Lecia and I had impressed Uncle Frank by both learning to
(15) read pretty much without instruction before we were three. Mother took us each down to his office in turn, and we each dutifully read the front page of the day's paper out loud to him, so he could be sure it wasn't
(20) just some story we'd memorized.)

He let me stay in his office playing chess all afternoon with whoever wandered in. He loved pitting me against particularly lunkheaded fifth- and sixth-grade boys
(25) who'd been sent down for paddlings they never got. He'd try to use my whipping them at chess to make them nervous about how dumb they were. "Now this little bitty old second-grader here took you clean in
(30) six plays. Don't you reckon you need to be listening to Miss Vilimez instead of cutting up?" When Mrs. Hess led me solemnly down the hall to Frank Doleman's office, I would pretend to cry, but thought instead
(35) about Brer Rabbit as he was being thrown into the briar patch where he'd been born and raised, and screaming *Please don't throw me in that briar patch!*

From *The Liar's Club* by Mary Karr, New York: Penguin Books, 1995.

1. If the writer had attended an elementary school dance, which of the following might she have done?

   (1) created a scene just to be funny
   (2) made fun of everyone as they danced
   (3) sat and played chess with the boys
   (4) been too shy to dance with anyone
   (5) hit a boy in the arm to get his attention

2. What is meant by the statement "I . . . thought instead about Brer Rabbit as he was being thrown into the briar patch where he'd been born and raised and screaming *Please don't throw me in that briar patch!*" (lines 33–38)?

   (1) She was so upset that she wanted to scream.
   (2) She was just pretending she didn't want to go to the principal's office.
   (3) She was thinking of stories she might read in the principal's office.
   (4) She hoped the teacher would let her back in class if she pleaded with her.
   (5) She was afraid of what would happen in the principal's office.

3. What type of principal was Frank Doleman?

   (1) strict
   (2) fair
   (3) ineffective
   (4) unusual
   (5) mean

4. Later in the autobiography, the narrator describes herself as "small-boned and skinny, but more than able to make up for that."

   Based on this description and the excerpt, which of the following best describes the narrator?

   (1) confident
   (2) serious
   (3) happy-go-lucky
   (4) friendly
   (5) hopeful

Questions 5 through 9 refer to this review.

WHAT MAKES THIS ARTWORK UNIQUE?

Sol LeWitt's work doesn't look the way radical art is supposed to look. Many of the wall drawings in his retrospective at the Whitney are exuberant and lush, even gor-
(5) geous. "Splotch," the title of a recent series, has a comic-book sound, and each of these gooey fiberglass clusters suggests a family, forest, city, or cave dwelling mod- eled by a class of intent and unpredictable
(10) kids. Even the ascetically spare white cubic sculptures that helped establish LeWitt's reputation in the seventies as a pioneering Conceptual artist are as much jungle gyms as they are geometers' tools. Fantasy and
(15) play are no less welcome here than analysis and rigor. Children and adults, hedonists and mathematicians have a place in LeWitt's universe.

These works do not exclude. This
(20) expansiveness is, in fact, essential to LeWitt's radical ambition. He studied early- twentieth-century modernist developments such as Russian Constructivism, De Stijl, and the Bauhaus, all driven by a utopian
(25) hope that art could change the world. Kasimir Malevich and Piet Mondrian believed their stripped-down geometrical abstractions could initiate new ways of see- ing—and with them, new ways of being.
(30) LeWitt, born in Hartford in 1928, the child of Russian Jews, also wanted to begin again. "Our idea was to re-create art, to start from square one," he told former museum direc- tor Martin Friedman. For him and other
(35) members of his generation, the emo- tionalism and grandiosity of Abstract Expressionism were dead ends. He knew that the impact of European abstract art was limited because it was accessible only
(40) to a select few.

From "High Concept" by Michael Brenson, *New York*, January 1, 2001.

5. According to the review, which of the follow- ing is the best description of LeWitt's art- work?

(1) playful yet skilled
(2) immature and amateurish
(3) emotionally dead
(4) impractical
(5) appreciated by the few

6. If LeWitt's art "doesn't look the way radical art is supposed to look" (lines 1–2), then how can you conclude that most radical art looks to the reviewer?

(1) gorgeous and lush
(2) childlike and light-hearted
(3) spare and serious
(4) realistic and traditional
(5) intricate and detailed

7. What is "LeWitt's radical ambition" (line 21)?

(1) to criticize other artists for trying to change the world
(2) to transform wall drawings from the usual dull and lifeless art
(3) to create lively and shocking titles for his artwork
(4) to study other artists and copy their style
(5) to make a new kind of art that is available to everyone

8. Which of the following is the best description of the tone of this review?

(1) sarcastic
(2) uncaring
(3) hysterical
(4) arrogant
(5) respectful

9. How is this excerpt organized?

(1) pros and cons of modern art
(2) examples of works followed by discussion of artist's philosophy
(3) defense of the artist's work followed by criticism of it
(4) discussion of the artist's works in chrono- logical order
(5) comparison and contrast of the artist's work with others

Questions 10 through 12 refer to the following business document.

SHOULD THE GOVERNMENT MANDATE THAT EMPLOYERS PROVIDE HEALTH COVERAGE TO TEMPORARY WORKERS?

The National Association of Temporary Services (NATS), which represents the nation's temporary help employers, testified today before the House Ways and Means
(5) Committee on the employer mandate and related provisions of the President's Health Security Act (H.R. 3600).

Edward A. Lenz, NATS senior vice president, legal and government affairs, said that
(10) the temporary help industry supports the principle of universal coverage, but has serious concerns that the cost of mandates could weaken the ability of the temporary help industry to act as a "jobs bridge" to
(15) regular, full-time employment.

According to Lenz, the temporary help industry has recently "assumed a new and vital role—by helping to ease the burden on individuals during the current restructuring
(20) of the American work force. Temporary work offers displaced workers a critical safety net of income, benefits, and skills training and often provides a bridge back to regular, full-time employment."
(25) In addition, the Association is concerned that the mandates, as currently structured, would "also impose enormous administrative burdens" due to annual temporary employee turnover in the range of
(30) 400 to 600 percent. If employer mandates are adopted, Lenz urged Congress to create a mechanism that relates premium payments to hours worked, such as a simple payroll tax.

Excerpt from *Independent Consultant's Brochure and Letter Handbook* by Herman Holtz. Copyright © 1995. Reprinted by permission of John Wiley & Sons, Inc.

10. Which of the following states one of the main concerns of NATS?

(1) Temporary workers already get health benefits elsewhere, so NATS does not need to provide them.
(2) NATS won't be able to offer skills training to temporary employees if the government mandates coverage.
(3) There will be an increase in turnover of temporary employees if the government mandates coverage.
(4) The cost of mandated coverage will lessen the ability of NATS to hire and supply temporary workers.
(5) Restructuring the work force is a burden to all Americans.

11. According to the press release, why have businesses supplying temporary help become even more necessary?

(1) More and more businesses want to hire only temporary help.
(2) Many workers are losing their jobs and need temporary jobs until they find permanent work again.
(3) There is not enough work for everyone to have a full-time permanent job.
(4) The job turnover rate has gone as high as 400 to 600 percent.
(5) More and more workers do not want permanent full-time work.

12. What is the overall purpose of this piece?

(1) to raise awareness of one side of an issue
(2) to stimulate debate over universal health insurance coverage
(3) to impress both the Congress and the president
(4) to describe various alternatives to mandated coverage
(5) to persuade Congress to guarantee health benefits

Questions 13 through 16 refer to the following excerpt from a historical feminist speech.

WHAT CONCERNS THIS SPEAKER?

We have met here today to discuss our rights and wrongs, civil and political, and not, as some have supposed, to go into the detail of social life alone. We do not pro-
(5) pose to petition the legislature to make our husbands just, generous, and courteous, to seat every man at the head of a cradle, and to clothe every woman in male attire. None of these points, however important they
(10) may be considered by leading men, will be touched in this convention. As to their costume, the gentlemen need feel no fear of our imitating that, for we think it in violation of every principle of taste, beauty, and dig-
(15) nity; notwithstanding all the contempt cast upon our loose, flowing garments, we still admire the graceful folds, and consider our costume far more artistic than theirs. Many of the nobler sex seem to agree with us in
(20) this opinion, for the bishops, priests, judges, barristers, and lord mayors of the first nation on the globe, and the Pope of Rome, with his cardinals, too, all wear the loose flowing robes, thus tacitly acknowl-
(25) edging that the male attire is neither dignified nor imposing. No, we shall not molest you in your philosophical experiments with stocks, pants, high-heeled boots, and Russian belts. Yours be the glory to dis-
(30) cover, by personal experience, how long the kneepan can resist the terrible strapping down which you impose, in how short time the well-developed muscles of the throat can be reduced to mere threads by the
(35) constant pressure of the stock, how high the heel of a boot must be to make a short man tall, and how tight the Russian belt may be drawn and yet have wind enough left to sustain life.
(40) But we are assembled to protest against a form of government existing without the consent of the governed—to declare our right to be free. . . .

From a speech at a woman's-rights convention by Elizabeth Cady Stanton, as reprinted in *A Treasury of the World's Great Speeches,* edited by Houston Peterson, New York: Simon & Schuster, 1954, 1965.

13. Which of the following best restates the lines "Yours be the glory to discover . . . how long the kneepad can resist the terrible strapping down which you impose" (lines 29–32)?

   (1) Men do not understand how uncomfortable women's clothes are.
   (2) Women will not resort to wearing pants or other restrictive men's clothing.
   (3) Men will only understand women when women dress like them.
   (4) Men and women will be equal only when they both wear belts and collars.
   (5) Men and women should not be concerned with how they dress.

14. What is a "stock" (lines 28 and 35)?

   (1) a man's jacket
   (2) a wooden frame holding a prisoner
   (3) a tight belt
   (4) a loose shirt
   (5) a cloth worn around the neck

15. If the speaker attended a fancy tea party, which of the following would she be most likely to do?

   (1) be on her best behavior
   (2) speak up about current events
   (3) treat the hostess like royalty
   (4) gossip about men
   (5) comment on everyone's clothing

16. Later in the speech, Stanton states that "over the horns of bigotry and prejudice will be our way." Based on this and the excerpt, you can conclude that Stanton is giving this speech for what reason?

   (1) Women are fighting for the right to vote.
   (2) Women are tired of being made to wear dresses.
   (3) Husbands need to be made just and generous.
   (4) All types of prejudice must be fought.
   (5) Many people mistakenly judge others by their appearance.

Answers and explanations start on page 658.

FICTION

Understanding Plot Elements

Plot refers to the events in a story. Generally, the events are told in order—what happened first, next, and so on. Understanding the order of events can help you see which events caused or affected others.

A story usually contains at least one **conflict**, or problem. The conflict may be between characters, within a character, or between a character and nature. Conflict creates tension. When it is resolved, the tension ends.

The following excerpt is about a brother and sister whose mother has a tumor. As you read it, look for the order of events and the conflict.

> Robert didn't phone until evening. His voice was fatigued and thin. "I've moved her to the university hospital," he said. "They can't deal with it at home."
>
> Kate waited, saying nothing. She concentrated on the toes of her shoes. They needed shining. *You never take care of anything*, her mother would say.
>
> "She has a tumor in her head." He said it firmly, as though Kate might challenge him.
>
> "I'll take a plane tomorrow morning," Kate answered, "I'll be there by noon."
>
> Robert exhaled. "Look," he said, "don't even come back here unless you can keep your mouth shut and do it my way."
>
> "Get to the point."
>
> "The point is they believe she has a malignancy and we're not going to tell her. I almost didn't tell you." His voice faltered. "They're going to operate but if they find what they're expecting, they don't think they can stop it."
>
> For a moment there was no sound except an oceanic vibration of distance on the wire. Even that sound grew still. Robert breathed. Kate could almost see him, in a booth at the hospital, staring straight ahead at the plastic instructions screwed to the narrow rectangular body of the telephone. It seemed to her that she was hurtling toward him.

From "Souvenir" by Jayne Anne Phillips, from *Black Tickets*, N.Y.: Delacorte Press, 1979. Reprinted with permission of Jayne Anne Phillips.

▶ When did Robert decide not to tell his mother about the tumor?
  (1) before talking to Kate   (2) after discussing the issue with Kate

(1) is correct. Robert has already decided what to do when he calls Kate.

▶ Which of the following identifies a conflict in this excerpt?
  (1) Kate tells Robert she will fly there tomorrow.
  (2) Robert tells Kate that she must do as he says.

(2) is correct. Robert challenges Kate. That creates tension.

Questions 1 through 4 refer to the following excerpt from a short story called "The String."

WHAT IS THE PEASANT ACCUSED OF?

The countryman looked at the Mayor in astonishment, already terrified by this suspicion resting on him without his knowing why.

"Me? Me? I picked up the pocket-book?"

(5) "Yes, you, yourself."

"On my word of honor, I never heard of it."

"But you were seen."

"I was seen, me? Who says he saw me?"

"Monsieur Malandain, the harness-maker."

(10) The old man remembered, understood, and flushed with anger.

"Ah, he saw me, the clodhopper, he saw me pick up this string, here, Mayor." And rummaging in his pocket he drew out the little piece of (15) string.

But the Mayor, incredulous, shook his head.

"You will not make me believe, Maître Hauchecorne, that Monsieur Malandain, who is a man we can believe, mistook this cord for a pocket-(20) book."

The peasant, furious, lifted his hand, spat at one side to attest his honor, repeating:

"It is nevertheless God's own truth, the sacred truth. I repeat it on my soul and my salva-(25) tion."

The Mayor resumed:

"After picking up the object, you stood like a stilt, looking a long while in the mud to see if any piece of money had fallen out."

(30) The old fellow choked with indignation and fear. . . .

He was confronted with Monsieur Malandain, who repeated and maintained his affirmation. They abused each other for an hour. At his (35) own request, Maître Hauchecorne was searched. Nothing was found on him.

Finally the Mayor, very much perplexed, discharged him with the warning that he would consult the Public Prosecutor and ask for further (40) orders.

From COLLECTED NOVELS AND STORIES by Guy de Maupassant, translated by Ernest Boyd, copyright 1922 and renewed 1950 by Alfred A. Knopf, a Division of Random House, Inc. Used by permission of Alfred A. Knopf, a division of Random House, Inc.

1. What was the peasant doing when he "lifted his hand, spat at one side to attest his honor" (lines 21–22)?

   (1) thinking of striking the Mayor
   (2) showing his disgust at the accusation
   (3) swearing that he was telling the truth
   (4) pleading to the mayor for mercy
   (5) performing a peasant ritual

2. How did the peasant react when confronted with Malandain, the harness-maker?

   He

   (1) became choked with fear and indignation
   (2) swore that he did not do it
   (3) tried to explain what had actually happened
   (4) became respectful and subdued
   (5) confronted him and then asked to be searched

3. Which of the following statements best describes the conflict in this excerpt?

   (1) A town mayor is abusing his authority.
   (2) Two townspeople do not like each other.
   (3) A peasant leads a harsh life and is often at odds with others.
   (4) A peasant is accused of taking a pocket-book.
   (5) Someone has lost a pocket-book with a great deal of money in it.

4. What is the most likely reason the harness-maker is believed?

   (1) A string can't be mistaken for a pocket-book.
   (2) The peasant was looking in the mud for money.
   (3) The harness-maker is the Mayor's friend.
   (4) The harness-maker is higher in social status than the peasant.
   (5) Other people saw the peasant pick up a pocket-book.

Answers and explanations start on page 659.

FICTION

Making Inferences

To understand a story, you can't just rely on what is directly stated. You also need to "read between the lines," or make **inferences**. An inference is based on information you are given *plus* what you have learned about the real world—the way things happen and the way people act.

As you read this excerpt from a story, look for suggested meanings behind people's actions and words.

> "Last night?" The old blue eyes looked blank, then brightened. "Ah no, I must have taken one of my Seconals. Otherwise I'd have heard it surely. 'Auntie,' my niece always says—'what if there should be a fire, and you there sleeping away?' Do what she says, I do sometimes, only to hear every pin drop till morning." She shook her head, entering the elevator. "Going up?"
>
> "N-no," said Mrs. Hazlitt. "I—have to wait here for a minute." She sat down on the bench, the token bench that she had never seen anybody sitting on, and watched the car door close on the little figure still shaking its head, borne upward like a fairy godmother, willing but unable to oblige. The car's hum stopped, then its light glowed on again. Someone else was coming down. . . .
>
> The car door opened. "Wssht!" said Miss Finan, scuttling out again. "I've just remembered. Not last night, but two weeks ago. And once before that. A scream, you said?"
>
> Mrs. Hazlitt stood up. Almost unable to speak, for the tears that suddenly wrenched her throat, she described it.

From "The Scream on Fifty-Seventh Street" by Hortense Calisher, from *Tales for the Mirror*, reprinted in *Women and Fiction*, edited by Susan Cahill, New York: New American Library, 1975.

▶ What happened before the beginning of this excerpt?
  (1) Mrs. Hazlitt heard a scream the night before and asked Miss Finan if she heard it too.
  (2) Mrs. Hazlitt asked Miss Finan about her health and whether she is sleeping well.

The correct answer is **(1)**. You can infer it from details such as "Last night?" and "Not last night, but two weeks ago. And once before that. A scream, you said?"

▶ What is the most likely reason that "tears suddenly wrenched" Mrs. Hazlitt's throat?
  (1) She was upset at Miss Finan's inability to remember.
  (2) She was relieved that Miss Finan had heard a scream too.

You are correct if you chose **(2)**. Mrs. Hazlitt is so relieved that someone else heard the scream that she has to fight back tears.

Questions 1 through 4 refer to the following excerpt from a short story.

WHAT DOES THE WOMAN THINK HAS HAPPENED TO HER HUSBAND?

She knew that she would weep again when she saw the kind, tender hands folded in death; the face that had never looked save with love upon her, fixed and gray and dead. But she
(5) saw beyond that bitter moment a long procession of years to come that would belong to her absolutely. And she opened and spread her arms out to them in welcome.

There would be no one to live for during
(10) those coming years; she would live for herself. There would be no powerful will bending her in that blind persistence with which men and women believe they have a right to impose a private will upon a fellow creature. A kind intention
(15) or a cruel intention made the act seem no less a crime as she looked upon it in that brief moment of illumination.

And yet she had loved him—sometimes. Often she had not. What did it matter! What
(20) could love, the unsolved mystery, count for in face of this possession of self-assertion, which she suddenly recognized as the strongest impulse of her being!

"Free! Body and soul free!" she kept whisper-
(25) ing . . .

Some one was opening the front door with a latchkey. It was [her husband] Brently Mallard who entered, a little travel-stained, composedly carrying his grip-sack and umbrella. He had been
(30) far from the scene of accident, and did not even know there had been one. He stood amazed at [his wife] Josephine's piercing cry; at Richards' quick motion to screen him from the view of his wife.
(35) But Richards was too late.

When the doctors came they said she had died of heart disease—of joy that kills.

From "The Story of an Hour" by Kate Chopin.

1. How did Brently Mallard generally feel toward his wife?

He

(1) had always loved her
(2) kept her at arm's length
(3) wanted to get away from her
(4) liked to play practical jokes on her
(5) had cruel intentions toward her

2. Which detail best expresses Josephine's vision of her future?

(1) that bitter moment
(2) she'd weep again
(3) spread her arms out in welcome
(4) blind persistence
(5) to impose a private will

3. What was the doctors' meaning when they said that Josephine died of "joy that kills" (line 37)?

They thought that

(1) she was overcome and thrilled to see her husband
(2) she was excited about her upcoming life of freedom
(3) she was relieved that Brently was back from his trip
(4) her heart was worn out from giving so much love
(5) her heart was weakened from the strain of living

4. Why did Josephine die?

(1) She was overcome with relief.
(2) She was shocked that she would not be free.
(3) She was confused by feelings of love and hate.
(4) She had been weakened by her grief.
(5) She thought there would be no one to live for.

Answers and explanations start on page 659.

Analyzing Character

Characters are the people who inhabit a story. The personalities and motivations of characters are often stated directly by the **narrator**—the person telling the story. Sometimes you can also infer characters' personalities or motivations by what they do, what they think, and what they say.

As you read this excerpt, look for details that describe each character.

> Axel Olsen was going to paint Helga Crane. Not only was he going to paint her, but he was to accompany her and her aunt on their shopping expedition. Aunt Katrina was frankly elated. Uncle Poul was also visibly pleased. Evidently they were not above kow-towing to a lion. Helga's own feelings were mixed; she was amused, grateful, and vexed. It had all been decided and arranged without her, and, also, she was a little afraid of Olsen. His stupendous arrogance awed her.
>
> The day was an exciting, not easily to be forgotten one. Definitely, too, it conveyed to Helga her exact status in her new environment. A decoration. A curio. A peacock. Their progress through the shops was an event; an event for Copenhagen as well as for Helga Crane. Her dark, alien appearance was to most people an astonishment. Some stared surreptitiously, some openly, and some stopped dead in front of her in order more fully to profit by their stares. "*Den Sorte*" dropped freely, audibly, from many lips.
>
> The time came when she grew used to the stares of the population. And the time came when the population of Copenhagen grew used to her outlandish presence and ceased to stare. But at the end of that first day it was with thankfulness that she returned to the sheltering walls of the house on Maria Kirkplads.

From "Quicksand" by Nella Larsen, in *The Norton Anthology of African American Literature,* edited by Henry Louis Gates, Jr., and Nellie Y. McKay, New York: W.W. Norton, 1997.

▶ Which of the following describes Helga?
  (1) attractive, down-to-earth, embarking on a new life
  (2) self-centered, smug, enjoys being watched

Option (1) is correct. An artist is painting her, suggesting she is attractive. Yet she prefers not to be the center of attention (see the end of the last paragraph).

▶ Which of the following would Olsen most likely do at a party?
  (1) snub the hostess if the wine was below his expectations
  (2) offer to drive anyone home who needed a ride

Option (1) is correct. Apply what you know about people with "stupendous arrogance" (see the end of the first paragraph) to answer this question.

Key Ideas

- Characters are the people in the story.
- You can understand a character by noting what the narrator tells you directly as well as by inferring from the character's appearance, actions, words, and thoughts.

ON THE GED

On the GED Reading Test, a common kind of application question asks you to choose how a character would act in a different situation, based on what you know about the character's personality.

FICTION ▸ PRACTICE 3

Questions 1 through 3 refer to the following excerpt from a short story.

WHAT IS THE WITCH, SPEAKING AS YAJI'S DEAD WIFE, TRYING TO ACCOMPLISH?

"I shall never forget it," the witch went on. "When you were ill you gave your sickness to me. Our only child, who had to carry on our name, grew weak and thin because there was no
(5) rice to fill his empty stomach. Every day the bill collectors were knocking at the door and the rent remained unpaid. Yet I did not complain—not even when I slipped in the dogs' dirt in the lane."

"Don't talk of it," said Yaji. "You'll break my
(10) heart."

"And then, when through my labors I had saved enough money to buy a kimono, I had to pawn it for your sake and never saw it again. Never again did it come back to me from the
(15) pawnbroker's."

"At the same time you must remember what a pleasant place you are in now," said Yaji, "while I have to worry along down here."

"What? What is there pleasant about it? It is
(20) true that by the help of your friends you erected a stone over my grave, but you never go near it, and you never contribute to the temple to get the priests to say prayers for my soul. I am nothing to you. The stone over my grave has been taken
(25) away and put into the wall, where all the dogs come and make water against it. Not a drop of water is ever placed on my grave. Truly in death we suffer all sorts of troubles."

"True, true," said Yaji.

(30) "But while you thus treat me with neglect," the witch went on, "lying in my grave I think of nobody but you and long for the time when you will join me in the underworld. Shall I come to meet you?"

(35) "No, no, don't do that," said Yaji. "It's really too far for you."

"Well then, I have one request to make."

"Yes, yes. What is it?"

"Give this witch plenty of money."

(40) "Of course, of course."

"How sad the parting!" cried the witch. "I have yet much to tell you, countless questions to ask you, but the messenger of Hell recalls me!"

(45) Then, recovering from her trance, the witch twanged her bow.

From "Hizakurige" by Jippensha Ikku in *The Longwood Introduction to Fiction*, Boston: Allyn and Bacon, 1992.

1. Why does Yaji say, "No, no, don't do that . . . It's really too far for you." (lines 35–36)?

   (1) He does not want to die and go to the underworld.
   (2) He has no real interest in seeing his wife again.
   (3) He is frightened about seeing the ghost of his wife.
   (4) His wife shouldn't have to go to any more trouble.
   (5) His wife can't really travel to him anyway.

2. Which of the following is the best description of the witch?

   (1) caring
   (2) straightforward
   (3) talented
   (4) untrustworthy
   (5) thoughtful

3. Earlier in the story the witch, speaking as Yaji's wife, says, "Ah, what agony I went through when I was married to you—time and again suffering the pangs of hunger and shivering with cold in the winter."

   Based on this information and the excerpt, what kind of husband did Yaji seem to be?

   (1) angry
   (2) kind-hearted
   (3) timid
   (4) responsible
   (5) neglectful

Answers and explanations start on page 659.

FICTION

Interpreting Theme

Every story has a subject. The subject might be about fighting a war or growing up in poverty. But there is more to a story than its subject. As a reader, look for what the author is trying to say about the subject. That is the **theme**—the message the author wants the reader to understand. In fiction, the theme is often a statement about life. For example, the theme might be that fighting in a war changes a person's life forever.

The theme may be directly stated. If it is not, you can infer the theme from the characters' thoughts and actions and from the things that happen in the story.

As you read the following excerpt, ask yourself what message about the people and their lives the author is trying to tell you.

> While the boys were getting the Doctor's horse, he went to the window to examine the house plants. "What do you do to your geraniums to keep them blooming all winter, Mary? I never pass this house that from the road I don't see your windows full of flowers."
>
> She snapped off a dark red one, and a ruffled new green leaf, and put them in his buttonhole. "There, that looks better. You look too solemn for a young man, Ed. Why don't you git married? I'm worried about you. : . ."
>
> Sometimes the Doctor heard the gossipers in the drugstore wondering why Rosicky didn't get on faster. He was industrious, and so were his boys, but they were rather free and easy, weren't pushers, and they didn't always show good judgment. They were comfortable, they were out of debt, but they didn't get much ahead. Maybe, Doctor Burleigh reflected, people as generous and warmhearted and affectionate as the Rosickys never got ahead much; maybe you couldn't enjoy your life and put it into the bank, too.

From "Neighbor Rosicky" by Willa Cather, from *Obscure Destinies*.

▶ Which of the following statements is the theme of the story?
  (1) A good life is measured in terms of love, not money.
  (2) People should not gossip about others.

You are correct if you chose **(1)**. Doctor Burleigh's thoughts at the end of the excerpt help you understand that this is the author's main message.

▶ Which of the following details supports the theme?
  (1) Mary Rosicky lovingly "worries" about the doctor.
  (2) The Rosickys keep out of debt.

Again, you are correct if you chose **(1)**. The flowers Mary grows, the fact that she snaps off one to give the doctor, and her expressed concern for him all show her warmth and happiness. They help support the theme that the doctor reflects on.

Key Ideas

- The subject of a story is what the story is about.
- The theme of a story is different from the subject. The theme goes beyond the subject and expresses a point of view about life.

GED TIP

Read the whole passage carefully but not too slowly before you begin to answer the questions. If you read a question that really stumps you, skip it and go on. You can come back to it. But be sure you also skip that question on your answer sheet.

FICTION ▸ PRACTICE 4

Questions 1 through 5 refer to the following excerpt from a short story.

WHAT IS MORNING COMPARED TO?

Early morning is the best time. You're fully rested but not awake enough to remember how hard it all is. Morning is like being a child again, and morning before the sun is out is like those
(5) magic times that you hid under the bed and in between the clothes hanging in your mother's closet. Times when any kind of miracle could come about just as normal as a spider making her web.
(10) I remember waking up in the dark once when I was very small. I jumped right out of bed and went up next to the screen door on the back porch to see what kind of fantastic thing was going on outside. At first I couldn't see anything but there
(15) was a clopping sound, nickering, and a deep voice that made me feel calm and wondering. Slowly, coming out from the darkness, I saw a gray shimmering next to a tall black pillar. The shimmer turned into a big horse and the pillar
(20) became my father holding out an apple and cooing in his bass voice, "Ho! Yeah, boy," even though the horse was tame and eating from his hand.

I drifted into sleep thinking that we were
(25) poor and didn't own a horse. When I woke up it was light and there was no horse to be seen. I asked my father about it but he told me that I was dreaming—where were poor people like us going to find big gray stallions?
(30) But there were horse chips behind the barn and hoofprints too.

I decided that it was a magic horse and man that I'd seen. From that day on I believed that magic hides in the early morning. If you get up
(35) early enough you might find something so beautiful that it would be all right if you just died right then because nothing else in life could ever be better.

From "Gone Fishin'" by Walter Mosley, Baltimore: Black Classic Press, 1997.

1. What effect does the father's explanation have on the boy?

The boy

(1) believes his father
(2) feels confused
(3) finds a new explanation
(4) no longer trusts his father
(5) tries to convince his father

2. Which of the following is the best description of the boy?

(1) hard-hearted
(2) imaginative
(3) skeptical
(4) chatty
(5) lonely

3. What is the most likely reason the boy decides he saw a magic horse and man?

(1) He wants to believe his dream.
(2) He enjoys magic and magicians.
(3) He wants to prove his father wrong.
(4) The hoofprints prove that he saw a horse.
(5) This kind of miracle can happen.

4. Which of the following would the father probably enjoy most?

(1) daydreaming about the future
(2) having enough money to pay some bills
(3) keeping his son's hopes up about getting a new bicycle for his birthday
(4) telling his son about the tooth fairy
(5) sharing ghost stories around a campfire

5. Which of the following statements fits the theme of this story?

(1) False hopes will not get you anywhere.
(2) Dreams really can come true.
(3) Adults cannot see what children see.
(4) Beauty is in the eye of the beholder.
(5) Morning and youth are full of possibility.

Answers and explanations start on page 659.

FICTION

Interpreting Style and Point of View

Key Ideas

- The style of a piece of writing is determined by the choices a writer makes in words, sentence structure, images, and other devices.
- A story is written from a narrator's point of view. The narrator may be an "outsider" or a character who can reveal only what he or she sees and thinks.

Style

A writer has many choices when deciding how to write a story. A writer may use long, complex sentences; short, clipped sentences; or anything in between. A writer may use flowery or formal language, slang or spoken dialect. One writer may use vivid images or symbols, while another writes a plain, spare story. The individual characteristics that a writer chooses— sentence structure, choice of words, use of images, and other devices—are all part of the writer's **style.**

As you read this excerpt, look for the characteristics that this particular author chose. Ask yourself what effect they have on your understanding of the writing.

> The only part of the night I recall without feeling anger or sadness is loading the horses. Andy and I hardly had the fencing up before Brett came along with the first ten or twelve. . . . A couple of roans and an Appaloosa stood out in that first bunch in the starlight, and a bay with a roached mane. Then Ed brought up a second bunch, about fifteen mostly dark but a palomino and two paints in there, I remember. Andy and I shooed them up the ramp, which clattered and thundered under their hooves. It was a cool night, still. I could feel the horses on my skin, their body heat swirling around us. I could . . . hear their nostrils fluttering. I felt hard muscle ripple under my hand when I clapped a hip to steer them around. I felt their tails slap my back, and caught a glint in their bared eyes.

From "Stolen Horses" by Barry Lopez, from WRITER'S HARVEST 3, edited by Tobias Wolff, copyright © 2000 by Share Our Strength. Used by permission of Dell Publishing, a division of Random House, Inc.

► What is the effect of the author's description of the horses?
    (1) It creates a depth of feeling for the horses' vitality.
    (2) It provides insight into what the characters are doing.

You are correct if you chose **(1).** The vivid, descriptive details allow you to imagine the horses and sense their vitality and strength.

Point of View

Another choice a writer makes is which **point of view** to write from. Will the narrator be outside the story, watching and revealing the characters' actions and perhaps even their thoughts and feelings? If so, the writer will use *third person* point of view. Or will the narrator be a character in the story, able to report only what he or she thinks? In that case, the writer will use *first person* point of view.

► Which of the following indicates that the narrator is a character and so we can know only his thoughts?
    (1) "The only part of the night I recall. . . ."
    (2) "Then Ed brought up a second bunch. . . ."

(1) is correct. The narrator tells his own thoughts. A clue is the word *I.*

ON THE GED

The GED Reading Test will not ask you to identify and use terms such as third person *and* first person, *but you should be able to understand and appreciate the effect these writers' choices have.*

FICTION ▸ PRACTICE 5

Questions 1 through 4 refer to the following excerpt from a short story called "Coach."

DOES THIS COACH GET ALONG WITH HIS PLAYERS?

"This apartment your mom found is like an office or something. A studio for her to go to and get away every now and then. . . ."

"She wants to get away from us," Daphne
(5) said.

"Definitely not. She gave me a list, is how this whole thing started. She's got stuff she wants to do, and you with your school problems and me with the team—we're too much for her, see? She
(10) could spend her entire day on us, if you think about it, and never have one second for herself. If you think about it fairly, Daphne, you'll agree." . . .

She made a sigh and marched over to a trash can to deposit her slumping cone. Then she
(15) washed up at the children's drinking fountain and rejoined Coach, who had finished his Brown Cow but had kept the plastic spoon in the mouth.

"What was on this list of Mom's?" Daphne asked.

(20)   "Adult stuff," Coach said.

"Just give me an example."

Coach removed the plastic spoon and cracked it in half.

"Your mother's list is for five years. In that
(25) time, she wants to be speaking French regularly. She wants to follow up on her printmaking."

"This is adult stuff?" Daphne said.

Coach raised a hand to Bobby Stark. Stark had three malt cups in a cardboard carrier and he
(30) was moving toward the parking lot.

"Hey, those all for you?" Coach called out.

"I got a month to get fat, Coach. You'll have five months to beat it off me," the boy called back.

The people at some of the tables around
(35) Coach's lit up with grins. Bobby Stark's parents were grinning.

"Every hit of that junk takes a second off your time in the forty—just remember that!" Coach shouted.

(40)   Stark wagged his head ruefully, his cheeks blushing. He pretended to hide the malts behind his arm.

From AN AMATEUR'S GUIDE TO THE NIGHT by Mary Robison, copyright © 2001, reprinted with the permission of The Wylie Agency, Inc.

1. What is Bobby Stark's attitude?

   (1) He dislikes the coach's outlook.
   (2) He worries about his weight problem.
   (3) He takes things in stride.
   (4) He is looking forward to the sports season.
   (5) He feels unfairly criticized by the coach.

2. Because of the narrator's point of view, what does the reader know?

   (1) only Coach's thoughts and feelings
   (2) only Bobby Stark's actions
   (3) thoughts and feelings of all the characters
   (4) the actions and speech of the characters
   (5) only Daphne's thoughts and feelings

3. Through their dialogue, what kind of relationship can you conclude the characters have with each other?

   (1) informal
   (2) tense
   (3) professional
   (4) suspicious
   (5) deteriorating

4. Later in the story, Coach has this discussion with his wife, Sherry: " 'It's like my apartment,' Sherry said. 'A place apart.' Coach cut her off. 'Don't go on about how much you love your apartment.' "

   Based on this information and the excerpt, which of the following best describes Coach in his discussion with Daphne?

   (1) brutally frank
   (2) concerned for Daphne's feelings
   (3) angry and hostile
   (4) loving and warm
   (5) not entirely honest about his feelings

Answers and explanations start on page 659.

FICTION PRACTICE QUESTIONS

Questions 1 through 3 refer to the following excerpt from a story.

HOW DID LEROY REACT TO HIS INJURY?

Leroy Moffitt's wife, Norma Jean, is working on her pectorals. She lifts three-pound dumbbells to warm up, then progresses to a twenty-pound barbell.
(5) Standing with her legs apart, she reminds Leroy of Wonder Woman.

"I'd give anything if I could just get these muscles to where they're real hard," says Norma Jean. "Feel this arm. It's not as
(10) hard as the other one."

"That's cause you're right-handed," says Leroy, dodging as she swings the barbell in an arc.

"Do you think so?"
(15) "Sure."

Leroy is a truckdriver. He injured his leg in a highway accident four months ago, and his physical therapy, which involves weights and a pulley, prompted Norma Jean to try
(20) building herself up. Now she is attending a body-building class. Leroy has been collecting temporary disability since his tractor-trailer jackknifed in Missouri, badly twisting his left leg in its socket. He has a
(25) steel pin in his hip. He will probably not be able to drive his rig again. It sits in the backyard, like a gigantic bird that has flown home to roost. Leroy has been home in Kentucky for three months, and his leg is
(30) almost healed, but the accident frightened him and he does not want to drive any more long hauls. He is not sure what to do next. In the meantime, he makes things from craft kits. He started by building a
(35) miniature log cabin from notched Popsicle sticks. He varnished it and placed it on the TV set, where it remains. It reminds him of a rustic Nativity scene. Then he tried string art (sailing ships on black velvet), a macramé
(40) owl kit, a snap-together B-17 Flying Fortress, and a lamp made out of a model truck, with a light fixture screwed in the top of the cab. At first the kits were diversions,
(45) something to kill time, but now he is thinking about building a full-scale log house from a kit. It would be considerably cheaper than building a regular house, and besides, Leroy has grown to appreciate how things are put together. He has begun to realize
(50) that in all the years he was on the road he never took time to examine anything. He was always flying past scenery.

Excerpt from SHILOH & OTHER STORIES by Bobbie Ann Mason. Reprinted by permission of International Creative Management, Inc. Copyright © 1982 by Bobbie Ann Mason.

1. Which of the following best describes Leroy's wife, Norma Jean?

   (1) worried
   (2) shy
   (3) loving
   (4) self-concerned
   (5) grumpy

2. Why is Leroy's truck compared to a bird flying home to roost?

   It suggests that Leroy

   (1) comes and goes as he pleases
   (2) always preferred to be at home "nesting"
   (3) won't be driving his truck for a while
   (4) is a bit "flighty" and unpredictable
   (5) is large and heavy like a big bird

3. Why might Leroy be continually making things from craft kits?

   because he

   (1) is impatient with his leg healing
   (2) has bad taste in art
   (3) has always enjoyed working with his hands
   (4) grew tired of bodybuilding
   (5) doesn't want to face what to do next

Questions 4 through 7 refer to this excerpt from a story.

WHAT DOES THE SAILOR-BOY LEARN?

A small sailor-boy, named Simon, stood on the wet, swinging deck, held on to a shroud, and looked up towards the drifting clouds, and to the upper top-gallant yard of
(5) the main-mast.

A bird, that had sought refuge upon the mast, had got her feet entangled in some loose tackle-yarn of the halliard, and, high up there, struggled to get free. The boy on
(10) the deck could see her wings flapping and her head turning from side to side.

Through his own experience of life he had come to the conviction that in this world everyone must look after himself, and
(15) expect no help from others. But the mute, deadly fight kept him fascinated for more than an hour. He wondered what kind of bird it would be. These last days a number of birds had come to settle in the barque's
(20) rigging: swallows, quails, and a pair of peregrine falcons; he believed that this bird was a peregrine falcon. He remembered how, many years ago, in his own country and near his home, he had once seen a
(25) peregrine falcon quite close, sitting on a stone and flying straight up from it. Perhaps this was the same bird. He thought: "That bird is like me. Then she was there, and now she is here."
(30) At that a fellow-feeling rose in him, a sense of common tragedy; he stood looking at the bird with his heart in his mouth. There were none of the sailors about to make fun of him; he began to think out how
(35) he might go up by the shrouds to help the falcon out. He brushed his hair back and pulled up his sleeves, gave the deck round him a great glance, and climbed up. He had to stop a couple of times in the swaying
(40) rigging.

It was indeed, he found when he got to the top of the mast, a peregrine falcon. As his head was on a level with hers, she gave up her struggle, and looked at him with a
(45) pair of angry, desperate yellow eyes.

He had to take hold of her with one hand while he got his knife out, and cut off the tackle-yarn. He was scared as he looked down, but at the same time he felt
(50) that he had been ordered up by nobody, but that this was his own venture, and this gave him a proud, steadying sensation, as if the sea and the sky, the ship, the bird and himself were all one.

From WINTER'S TALES by Isak Dinesen, Random House, Inc.

4. What can you infer about the boy's decision to climb the rig?

   (1) It took some courage.
   (2) It was a familiar task.
   (3) It felt like a chore.
   (4) He was afraid he would die.
   (5) He was ordered to do it.

5. Which of the following best describes both the boy and the bird at the beginning of the excerpt?

   (1) confident
   (2) alone
   (3) scared
   (4) self-reliant
   (5) wary

6. Which ideas are most clearly contrasted in this excerpt?

   (1) love and hate
   (2) truth and falsehood
   (3) youth and experience
   (4) fear and fearlessness
   (5) loneliness and sense of belonging

7. Which of the following best describes the mood created by this excerpt?

   (1) mournful
   (2) nostalgic
   (3) peaceful
   (4) triumphant
   (5) suspenseful

WHO IS CHASING ICHABOD?

"Who are you?" He received no reply. He repeated his demand in a still more agitated voice. Still there was no answer. Once more he cudgelled the sides of the inflexi-
(5) ble Gunpowder, and, shutting his eyes, broke forth with involuntary fervor into a psalm-tune. Just then the shadowy object of alarm put itself in motion, and, with a scramble and a bound, stood at once in the
(10) middle of the road. Though the night was dark and dismal, yet the form of the unknown might now in some degree be ascertained. He appeared to be a horseman of large dimensions, and mounted on a
(15) black horse of powerful frame. He made no offer of molestation or sociability, but kept aloof on one side of the road, jogging along on the blind side of old Gunpowder, who had now got over his fright and waywardness.
(20)   Ichabod, who had no relish for this strange midnight companion, and bethought himself of the adventure of Brom Bones with the Galloping Hessian, now quickened his steed, in hopes of leaving
(25) him behind. The stranger, however, quickened his horse to an equal pace. Ichabod pulled up, and fell into a walk, thinking to lag behind,—the other did the same. His heart began to sink within him; he endeav-
(30) ored to resume his psalm-tune, but his parched tongue clove to the roof of his mouth, and he could not utter a stave. There was something in the moody and dogged silence of this pertinacious com-
(35) panion, that was mysterious and appalling. It was soon fearfully accounted for. On mounting a rising ground, which brought the figure of his fellow-traveller in relief against the sky, gigantic in height, and muf-
(40) fled in a cloak, Ichabod was horror-struck, on perceiving that he was headless!—but his horror was still more increased, on observing that the head, which should have rested on his shoulders, was carried before
(45) him on the pommel of the saddle: his terror rose to desperation; he rained a shower of kicks and blows upon Gunpowder, hoping, by a sudden movement, to give his companion the slip,—but the spectre started full
(50) jump with him.
Away then they dashed, through thick and thin; stones flying, and sparks flashing at every bound. Ichabod's flimsy garments fluttered in the air, as he stretched his long
(55) lank body away over his horse's head, in the eagerness of his flight.

From "The Legend of Sleepy Hollow" by Washington Irving.

8. What is meant by "he endeavored to resume his psalm-tune" (lines 29–30)?

Ichabod Crane tried to

(1) remind himself to stay calm
(2) ride more steadily
(3) start singing again
(4) say his prayers
(5) think of a realistic solution

9. What is the effect of the author's use of words such as "dashed," "stones flying," and "sparks flashing" (lines 51–52)?

to create a feeling of

(1) panic
(2) clumsiness
(3) playfulness
(4) magic
(5) mystery

10. Which of the following best describes the mood of this excerpt?

(1) angry
(2) lighthearted
(3) sorrowful
(4) suspenseful
(5) sentimental

11. Later in the story, Ichabod discovers that the horseman had a pumpkin on the pommel of his saddle. Based on this information, which of the following describes Ichabod in this excerpt?

(1) brave in the face of great danger
(2) too scared to think rationally
(3) unable to see in the dark
(4) moving too quickly
(5) quick-thinking in his escape

WHAT DOES HENRY THINK OF HIS STUDENTS?

Those sprawling universities Henry left behind long ago. America, with its mass-produced undergraduates processed through seedy lecture halls where, under
(5) flickering lights, they slump with their knees up and take in lectures as they might see movies. Where the familiar passes into the wide pupils of their eyes and the rest dribbles down the aisles to collect with the dirt
(10) and candy wrappers at the professor's feet. Has he not been a professor at Queens College and then NYU? And the graduate students. Hasn't he seen them at Princeton clustering at the office doors? Young
(15) Calibans eager for praise. They can tear open the Italian Renaissance before lunch, strangle a Donne sonnet and crush its wings, battering away with blunt instruments. As for the older scholars—like stu-
(20) dents at a cooking school, they cook up Shakespeare, serve him up like roast goose, stuffed with their political-sexual agendas, carve and quarter him with long knives. For Henry, reading had always been
(25) a gentle thing, a thing as delicate as blowing eggs. Two pinpricks and the meaning came, whole, unbroken, into the bowl. Now reading is a boiling and a breaking, something to concoct. It's a deviling of art, his-
(30) tory, social theory, politics—all mixed and piped back in and served up on a platter. These are the scholars in the journals now. They are at war with the beautiful. . . .

Excerpt from "The Wedding of Henry Markowitz" from THE FAMILY MARKOWITZ by Allegra Goodman. Copyright © 1996 by Allegra Goodman. Reprinted by permission of Farrar, Straus and Giroux, LLC.

12. Which of the following is Henry most interested in?

    (1) teaching
    (2) reading
    (3) students
    (4) politics
    (5) history

13. What is Henry's opinion of the younger college students?

    They are

    (1) bright
    (2) too energetic
    (3) open to new ideas
    (4) a dime a dozen
    (5) insightful about literature

14. What is suggested about the older students who "cook up Shakespeare, serve him up like a roast goose, stuffed with their political-sexual agendas, carve and quarter him with long knives" (lines 20–24)?

    The older students

    (1) dissect literature too much and ruin the meaning
    (2) enjoy literature as they would a fine meal
    (3) criticize and turn up their noses at what they read
    (4) throw Shakespeare back in Henry's face
    (5) have trouble finding meaning in literature

15. What is the tone of this excerpt?

    (1) upbeat
    (2) scholarly
    (3) unpleasant
    (4) sentimental
    (5) satisfied

16. Later, Henry refers to his brother as a "shaper himself of the tawdry yellow thing they sell now as the humanities."

    Based on this information and the excerpt, what is Henry's attitude toward college education?

    (1) indifferent
    (2) appreciative
    (3) analytical
    (4) admiring
    (5) disapproving

Answers and explanations start on page 660.

POETRY

Understanding Rhyme and Rhythm

Rhyme and rhythm are the parts of the poem you *hear*. **Rhyme** repeats the sounds at the ends of words. Poets sometimes rhyme the last words in their lines of poetry. For example, in lines 3 and 4 in the poem below, the rhyming words are *leap* and *sleep*. Poets use patterns of rhyme. They might rhyme the first and third line of each stanza, or group of lines. Rhymed poetry is generally pleasing to hear.

Rhythm is like the beat of a drum. In poetry, rhythm is created by the stresses you hear as you read the words aloud. Some words or parts of words are stressed, while others are not. Poets use rhythm as one way to emphasize the poem's meaning. Rhythm can also help create a feeling, or mood. For example, a constant, fast rhythm may be used if the poem is about someone hurrying or running away. You may feel tense as you read the poem.

As you read this poem, hear its rhyme and rhythm.

Meeting at Night

> The grey sea and the long black land;
> And the yellow half-moon large and low;
> And the startled little waves that leap
> In fiery ringlets from their sleep,
> As I gain the cove with pushing prow,
> And quench its speed i' the slushy sand.
>
> Then a mile of warm sea-scented beach;
> Three fields to cross till a farm appears;
> A tap at the pane, the quick sharp scratch
> And blue spurt of a lighted match,
> And a voice less loud, thro' its joys and fears,
> Than the two hearts beating each to each!

By Robert Browning.

► What is the rhyming pattern of the second stanza?
   (1) first and sixth, second and fifth, third and fourth lines
   (2) first and second, third and fourth, fifth and sixth lines

You are correct if you chose **(1)**: *beach/each*, *appears/fears*, and *scratch/match* rhyme. Because of the pattern, the rhyme in this poem is subtle.

► Which of the following describes the rhythm of the first stanza?
   (1) lively—to create excitement about the meeting
   (2) steady—to convey that the boat is moving at an even pace

You are correct if you chose **(2)**. Try reading the poem out loud and notice how the rhythm is like a steady approach of the boat moving toward land.

Questions 1 through 5 refer to the following poem.

WHERE DOES THIS MAN SEE HIS LOVE?

Secret Love

I hid my love when young till I
Couldn't bear the buzzing of a fly;
I hid my love to my despite
Till I could not bear to look at light:
(5)   I dare not gaze upon her face
But left her memory in each place;
Where'er I saw a wild flower lie
I kissed and bade my love good-bye.

I met her in the greenest dells,
(10)   Where dewdrops pearl the wood bluebells;
The lost breeze kissed her bright blue eye,
The bee kissed and went singing by,
A sunbeam found a passage there,
A gold chain round her neck so fair;
(15)   As secret as the wild bee's song
She lay there all the summer long.

I hid my love in field and town
Till e'en the breeze would knock me down;
The bees seemed singing ballads o'er,
(20)   The fly's bass turned a lion's roar;
And even silence found a tongue,
To haunt me all the summer long;
The riddle nature could not prove
Was nothing else but secret love.

By John Clare.

1. Which of the following is the best restatement of "I hid my love to my despite / Till I could not bear to look at light: / I dare not gaze upon her face" (lines 3–5)?

   (1) Even though her smile lights up her face, I would not tell her I loved her.
   (2) Even though it was painful, I told her I loved her.
   (3) Even though I was shy, I looked her in the eye anyway.
   (4) Because I told her my feelings, I felt ashamed to face her.
   (5) Because I kept my feelings secret, it would be painful to look her straight in the eye.

2. Why does the speaker keep repeating, "I hid my love"?

It shows that

   (1) he had no other choice
   (2) he wants the woman to hear him
   (3) his life is monotonous
   (4) he deeply feels his failure to speak
   (5) the woman is uninterested in him

3. If the speaker attended a large party, which of the following would he most likely do?

   (1) profess romantic feelings to a woman he just met
   (2) hope a friend introduces him to someone special
   (3) dance all night with different partners
   (4) sit and think of a woman he once loved
   (5) bring a date who is wearing a gold necklace

4. In the last stanza, which of the following helps convey that the speaker's undeclared love did not fit in with the harmony of nature?

   (1) an uneven and disturbing rhythm
   (2) a fast-paced, upbeat rhythm
   (3) a slow, mournful rhythm
   (4) the lack of any rhyme or rhythm
   (5) the disruption of the rhyme pattern

5. Which word best describes the speaker's tone?

   (1) regretful
   (2) irritated
   (3) hopeful
   (4) confident
   (5) skeptical

Answers and explanations start on page 660.

POETRY

Interpreting Figurative Language

Key Ideas

- Poets use figurative language—words that do not have their literal meaning— to compare different things.
- Some comparisons are introduced by *like* or *as*; others are not. Some comparisons give human characteristics to nonhuman things.

Figurative language refers to words that are being used to mean something other than their actual, literal meaning. Poets use figurative language to help paint a mental picture in the reader's mind. Instead of saying, "His voice was soothing and pleasing," for example, a poet might say, "His voice was like velvet."

Figurative language often compares two different things. Sometimes the comparison is signaled by the words *like* or *as*, but not always. A poet might also say, "His voice was velvet." Another favorite technique of poets is to give a human characteristic to something nonhuman, such as, "The wind sighed."

As you read this poem, look for figurative language and what it might mean.

The School Children

The children go forward with their little satchels.
And all morning the mothers have labored
to gather the late apples, red and gold,
like words of another language.

And on the other shore
are those who wait behind great desks
to receive these offerings.

How orderly they are—the nails
on which the children hang
their overcoats of blue or yellow wool.

And the teachers shall instruct them in silence
and the mothers shall scour the orchards for a way out,
drawing to themselves the gray limbs of the fruit trees
bearing so little ammunition.

From THE HOUSE ON MARSHLAND from THE FIRST FOUR BOOKS by Louise Gluck. Copyright 1968, 1971, 1972, 1973, 1974, 1975, 1976, 1977, 1978, 1980, 1985, 1995.

▶ What is suggested by comparing apples to "words of another language" in the fourth line?
   (1) a sense of strangeness, not a part of one's world
   (2) useless things that have no meaning

You are correct if you chose **(1)**. A language different from your own can seem strange and removed. The mothers feel removed from the world of teachers and schoolchildren.

▶ What does the word *shore* in the fifth line refer to?
   (1) the farthest edge of a lake
   (2) the world of the classroom

You are correct if you chose **(2)**. The mothers in the poem think of school as far away from them.

GED TIP

You are not penalized for wrong answers on the GED Test, so try not to leave any answer blank. If you return to a skipped question and still cannot determine the answer, mark your best guess.

POETRY ► PRACTICE 2

Questions 1 through 5 refer to the following poem.

WHAT HAPPENS ON THIS FERRY TRIP?

**Dejeuner sur l'Herbe
(Lunch on the Grass)**

It's pleasant to board the ferry in the sunscape
As the late light slants into afternoon;
The faint wind ruffles the river, rimmed with
  foam.
We move through the aisles of bamboo
(5)   Towards the cool water-lilies.

The young dandies drop ice into the drinks,
While the girls slice the succulent lotus root.
Above us, a patch of cloud spreads, darken-
  ing
Like a water-stain on silk.

(10)   *Write this down quickly, before the rain!*

Don't sit there! The cushions were soaked by
  the shower.
Already the girls have drenched their crimson skirts.
Beauties, their powder streaked with mascara,
  lament their ruined faces.

The wind batters our boat, the mooring-line
(15) Has rubbed a wound in the willow bark.
The edges of the curtains are embroidered by
  the river foam.
Like a knife in a melon, Autumn slices
  Summer.

It will be cold, going back.

Excerpt from "Dejeuner sur L'Herbe" by Tu Fu, translated by Carolyn Kizer, from *Carrying Over: Poems from the Chinese, Urdu, Macedonian, Yiddish, and French African.* Copyright © 1998 by Carolyn Kizer. Reprinted with the permission of Copper Canyon Press, P.O. Box 271, Port Townsend, WA 98368-0271, USA.

1. What is compared to "a water-stain on silk" (line 9)?

(1) foam on the edge of the river
(2) rain clouds approaching
(3) lotus root juice on a tablecloth
(4) a light rain or drizzle
(5) ice cubes dropping into cold drinks

2. What is meant by the statement "lament their ruined faces" (line 13)?

(1) They could no longer smile.
(2) They were growing old.
(3) The rain caused their makeup to run.
(4) The wind was chapping their faces.
(5) They were unhappy the ferry ride ended.

3. Why is "The edges of the curtains are embroidered by the river foam" (line 16) an effective use of figurative language?

It helps the reader see that

(1) the people forgot to close the windows and curtains
(2) the wind is so strong that it is blowing spray from the river into the boat
(3) the curtains are beautifully edged with lace
(4) the river is rising quickly
(5) the people on the boat are in danger

4. According to the speaker, how was the change from summer to autumn (line 17)?

(1) quick and easy
(2) halting and uncertain
(3) sneaky and quiet
(4) slow and predictable
(5) pleasant and smooth

5. Which of the following words best describe the tone of this poem?

(1) scared and threatened
(2) gentle and calm
(3) humorous and playful
(4) wry and observant
(5) dry and formal

Answers and explanations start on page 661.

POETRY

Analyzing Symbols and Images

- A symbol is something that is used to represent something else.
- An image is a mental picture that appeals to one or more of the five senses.

Symbols

A **symbol** represents something else—usually a concept or idea that is universal, such as love or betrayal. For example, a blossoming cherry tree may symbolize life. It has some of the qualities that life has. However, you must read an entire poem before deciding what a symbol stands for. A cherry tree cannot symbolize life, for example, unless other details in the poem also lead to that conclusion.

As you read this poem, look for clues that tell what the garden seat represents.

The Garden Seat

Its former green is blue and thin,
And its once firm legs sink in and in;
Soon it will break down unaware,
Soon it will break down unaware.

At night when reddest flowers are black
Those who once sat thereon come back;
Quite a row of them sitting there,
Quite a row of them sitting there.

With them the seat does not break down,
Nor winter freeze them, nor floods drown,
For they are as light as upper air,
They are as light as upper air!

By Thomas Hardy.

► What does the seat symbolize?
   (1) the passage of time
   (2) the beginning of winter

You are correct if you chose **(1)**. The seat is described as formerly firm but now sinking in; its paint is discolored. Soon it will break down. These are changes that take place over time.

Images

Images are the pictures a poem creates in your mind. Images are based on the five senses: smell, taste, touch, hearing, and especially sight.

► What does the image of "quite a row of them sitting there," "light as upper air" refer to?
   (1) ghosts of people who used to sit on the garden seat
   (2) the flowers growing around the garden bench

You are correct if you chose **(1)**. If you can imagine "quite a row" of ghosts sitting on the garden bench, "light as upper air," you can understand and appreciate the poet's image.

GED TIP

Pay attention to the title of the poem on the GED Reading Test. The title often offers important clues about the poem's meaning.

POETRY ▶ PRACTICE 3

Questions 1 through 6 refer to the following poem.

WHERE ARE THE BEAVERS LIVING?

The Beaver Pool in December

The brook is still open
where the water falls,
but over the deeper pools
clear ice forms; over the dark
(5)   shapes of stones, a rotting log,
and amber leaves that clattered down
after the first heavy frost.

Though I wait in the cold
until dusk, and though a sudden
(10)   bubble of air rises under the ice,
I see not a single animal.

The beavers thrive somewhere
else, eating the bark of hoarded
saplings. How they struggled
(15)   to pull the long branches
over the stiffening bank . . .

but now they pass without
effort, all through the chilly
water; moving like thoughts
(20)   in an unconflicted mind.

Excerpt from "The Beaver Pool in Winter" copyright © 1996 by the Estate of Jane Kenyon. Reprinted from *Otherwise: New & Selected Poems* with the permission of Graywolf Press, Saint Paul, Minnesota.

1. What is the speaker describing when she says "clear ice forms; over the dark / shapes of stones, a rotting log, / and amber leaves that clattered down / after the first heavy frost" (lines 4–7)?

   (1) the winter home of the beavers
   (2) an icy waterfall
   (3) the path she is walking on
   (4) the forest floor
   (5) things in the pool under the ice

2. What is symbolized by the image "a sudden / bubble of air rises under the ice" (lines 9–10)?

   (1) the eventual coming of spring
   (2) the survival instinct animals have
   (3) the danger that lurks beneath
   (4) the speaker's hope for life
   (5) the death of the animals in the icy water

3. Which of the following descriptions best fits the beavers in winter?

   (1) busy as usual
   (2) relaxed and peaceful
   (3) fighting for survival
   (4) hibernating
   (5) playing by a waterfall

4. What is being described as "like thoughts / in an unconflicted mind" (lines 19–20)?

   (1) the smooth motion of the beavers
   (2) the difficult work of the beavers
   (3) the uncomplicated life of animals
   (4) the slow moving water in winter
   (5) the eagerness for the ease of summer

5. Which of the following terms best describes the mood of this poem?

   (1) excited
   (2) contemplative
   (3) tragic
   (4) exaggerated
   (5) comical

6. Which of the following activities might the speaker of the poem also enjoy?

   (1) playing cards
   (2) working on a computer
   (3) walking along an empty beach
   (4) watching a TV comedy
   (5) attending a football game

Answers and explanations start on page 661.

POETRY

Interpreting Theme

Key Ideas

- The theme is the most important idea the poet wants to express.
- To determine the theme of a poem, consider the subject of the poem and the elements used—images, symbols, rhyme, rhythm, and choice of words and ideas.

To understand the **theme** of a poem, ask, "What is the most important idea the poet is trying to get across?" The theme is not quite the same thing as the subject.

For example, the subject of a poem might be clouds, but what is the poet trying to tell you about clouds? Does the poem talk about the beauty of passing clouds? Or about the fleeting passage of time represented by clouds? The images, symbols, rhyme, rhythm, and choice of words and ideas in a poem all combine to help express the theme about its subject.

As you read this poem, consider all those elements to determine the theme.

The Summer Day

Who made the world?
Who made the swan, and the black bear?
Who made the grasshopper?
This grasshopper, I mean—
the one who has flung herself out of the grass,
the one who is eating sugar out of my hand,
who is moving her jaws back and forth instead of up and down—
who is gazing around with her enormous and complicated eyes.
Now she lifts her pale forearms and thoroughly washes her face.
Now she snaps her wings open, and floats away.
I don't know exactly what a prayer is.
I do know how to pay attention, how to fall down
into the grass, how to kneel down in the grass,
how to be idle and blessed, how to stroll through the fields,
which is what I have been doing all day.
Tell me, what else should I have done?
Doesn't everything die at last, and too soon?
Tell me, what is it you plan to do
with your one wild and precious life?

House of Light by Mary Oliver. Copyright © 1990 by Mary Oliver. Reprinted by permission of Beacon Press, Boston, MA.

▶ What is the subject of this poem?
   (1) a grasshopper and other aspects of nature
   (2) the creation of the earth and the need for prayer

You are correct if you chose **(1)**. Most of the images in the poem are of the grasshopper and other aspects of nature, such as fields and grass.

▶ What is the theme of the poem?
   (1) Take the time to observe and appreciate life.
   (2) We must preserve nature in all its forms.

You are correct if you chose **(1)**. The poet may agree with (2), but the theme is reflected in the last eight lines of the poem.

Questions 1 through 6 refer to the following poem.

WHAT DO THE CHILDREN FIND?

A Postcard from the Volcano

Children picking up our bones
Will never know that these were once
As quick as foxes on the hill;

And that in autumn, when the grapes
(5)   Made sharp air sharper by their smell
These had a being, breathing frost;

And least will guess that with our bones
We left much more, left what still is
The look of things, left what we felt

(10)   At what we saw. The spring clouds blow
Above the shuttered mansion-house,
Beyond our gate and the windy sky

Cries out a literate despair.
We knew for long the mansion's look
(15)   And what we said of it became

A part of what it is . . . Children,
Still weaving budded aureoles,
Will speak our speech and never know,

Will say of the mansion that it seems
(20)   As if he that lived there left behind
A spirit storming in blank walls,

A dirty house in a gutted world,
A tatter of shadows peaked to white,
Smeared with the gold of the opulent sun.

From THE COLLECTED POEMS OF WALLACE
STEVENS by Wallace Stevens, copyright © 1954 by
Wallace Stevens. Used by permission of Alfred A. Knopf,
a division of Random House, Inc.

1. What is the meaning of "these were once /
as quick as foxes on the hill" (lines 2–3)?

(1) The bones used to belong to living people.
(2) The bones belonged to foxes on the hill.
(3) The children are as quick as foxes.
(4) The children don't realize the hill is steep.
(5) The days used to go by very fast.

2. Who is the speaker in this poem?

(1) a child who has found some bones
(2) a man watching children play
(3) a person who dreams about the past
(4) an abandoned house
(5) the dead owner of the house

3. What is being likened to a person because of
its cries?

(1) the volcano
(2) the bones
(3) the mansion
(4) the wind
(5) the sun

4. What will the children say is in the house?

(1) their ancestors
(2) bones
(3) a ghost
(4) nothing but shadows
(5) dirt and dust

5. Which of the following is the theme of this
poem?

(1) Children don't realize who and what came
    before them.
(2) Children can play and find joy in anything.
(3) Time passes and damages houses and
    other buildings.
(4) A house is only a home when people live
    there.
(5) Spirits sometimes live in old houses.

6. What is the mood of the poem?

(1) forgiving
(2) scary
(3) sad
(4) grieving
(5) angry

Answers and explanations start on page 661.

POETRY PRACTICE QUESTIONS

Questions 1 through 6 refer to the following poem.

WHAT IS THE CEMETERY BEING COMPARED TO?

Cemetery in the Snow

Nothing is like a cemetery in the snow.
What name is there for the whiteness upon
  the white?
The sky has let down insensible stones of
  snow
upon the tombs,
(5) and all that is left now is snow upon snow
like a hand settled on itself forever.

Birds prefer to cut through the sky,
to wound the invisible corridors of the air
so as to leave the snow alone,
(10) which is to leave it intact,
which is to leave it snow.

Because it is not enough to say that a
  cemetery in the snow
is like a sleep without dreams
or like a few blank eyes.

(15) Though it is something like an insensible
  and sleeping body,
like one silence fallen upon another
and like the white persistence of oblivion,
nothing is like a cemetery in the snow!

Because the snow is above all silent,
(20) more silent still upon bloodless slabs:
lips that can no longer say a word.

"Cemetery in the Snow" by Xavier Villarrutia, translated by Donald Justice, from NEW POETRY OF MEXICO by Octavio Paz, edited by Mark Strand, copyright © 1970 by E. P. Dutton & Co, Inc. Copyright © 1966 by Siglo XXI Editores, S. A. Used by permission of Dutton, a division of Penguin Putnam, Inc.

1. What is the "white" in the question "What name is there for the whiteness upon the white" (line 2)?

   (1) snow
   (2) tombstones
   (3) rocks
   (4) clouds
   (5) frost

2. What observation about birds does the speaker make?

   Birds

   (1) don't want to disturb the snow
   (2) will not fly when it is snowing
   (3) will not fly over the cemetery
   (4) have a hard time during winter
   (5) become invisible in the snow

3. What is one quality on which a cemetery is being compared to snow?

   (1) coldness
   (2) emptiness
   (3) silence
   (4) wetness
   (5) beauty

4. Why is the first line repeated later in the poem (line 18)?

   (1) It seeks to persuade the listener.
   (2) It reveals the speaker is unsure.
   (3) It creates tension behind what the speaker is saying.
   (4) It shows that the speaker's belief has strengthened.
   (5) It helps further describe the scene.

5. Which of the following statements can you conclude the speaker would make?

   (1) There is nothing as beautiful as a cemetery in the snow.
   (2) Wintertime is more beautiful than summertime.
   (3) Birds are the most interesting animals to observe.
   (4) Silence is an unsettling experience to be avoided.
   (5) Some beautiful things are difficult to explain.

6. What is the mood of the poem?

   (1) quiet
   (2) stormy
   (3) romantic
   (4) contented
   (5) eerie

Questions 7 through 10 refer to the following poem.

WHAT DECISION DOES THIS MAN MAKE?

Traveling Through the Dark

Traveling through the dark I found a deer
dead on the edge of the Wilson River road.
It is usually best to roll them into the canyon:
that road is narrow; to swerve might make more dead.

(5) By glow of the tail-light I stumbled back of the car
and stood by the heap, a doe, a recent killing;
she had stiffened already, almost cold.
I dragged her off; she was large in the belly.

My fingers touching her side brought me the reason—
(10) her side was warm; her fawn lay there waiting,
alive, still, never to be born.
Beside that mountain road I hesitated.

The car aimed ahead its lowered parking lights;
under the hood purred the steady engine.
(15) I stood in the glare of the warm exhaust turning red,
around our group I could hear the wilderness listen.

I thought hard for us all—my only swerving—,
then pushed her over the edge into the river.

"Traveling through the Dark" copyright © 1962, 1988 by the Estate of William Stafford. Reprinted from *The Way It Is: New & Selected Poems* with the permission of Graywolf Press, Saint Paul, Minnesota.

7. What is the situation with the two deer when the speaker first comes upon them?

   (1) A mother and her fawn are both dead.
   (2) An unborn fawn is alive in its dead mother.
   (3) An unborn fawn has been killed inside its mother.
   (4) A live fawn is lying by its dead mother.
   (5) A dying mother has given birth to a live fawn.

8. If the poet were reading this poem to an audience, which of the following introductions would he most likely use?

   (1) It was the worst decision I ever made
   (2) Once upon a time
   (3) The purpose of this poem
   (4) A funny thing happened
   (5) It was a night I'll never forget

9. If the speaker were faced with a difficult decision, what would he most likely do?

   (1) be unable to make a choice and agonize over the indecision
   (2) ask friends for their opinion, then follow their advice
   (3) think for a while, then make a determined choice
   (4) worry he would regret his choice, but do it anyway
   (5) take the easiest way out and as quickly as possible

10. What kind of person does the speaker appear to be?

   (1) cold-hearted
   (2) frivolous
   (3) giving
   (4) anxious
   (5) mindful

Questions 11 through 14 refer to the following poem.

WHAT HAPPENED WITH THE FAMILY THAT MORNING?

Macular Degeneration

Something like radiance is crossing my wife's face.
She won't admit it. I won't press her.
Now, while they happen, here are the facts:
my son is staring up into his mother's eyes;
(5) we are standing in the kitchen at the day's beginning,
half-asleep over mugs of chicory swirling with cream;
he has just barreled in, five today, demanding
a cup of juice from her, not me. Not you,
he repeats. Of course, she fetches it, obedient.
(10) Of course, I awakened the same slavery in my mother,
the need to be commanded by a man-child who is other,
forty years back. What boy could ask his father
with a glance to be maidservant and Queen of Heaven?
Tonight I will type my mother a short letter
(15) since she has written me the facts about her vision—
that there is no cure for progressive scarring
of the retina from five years back and now she reads
slowly with a magnifying glass. I will detail
the feats of her grandson at his birthday party,
(20) leaving out this morning's epiphany. Of course,
the instant he was born she could foresee this moment
because in her eyes he is her son, diminished,
and it is no one's business now how she relinquished me.

Excerpt from THE ASTONISHED HOURS by Peter Cooley, Carnegie Mellon University Press, 1993. Reprint courtesy of *The Iowa Review*.

11. Which of the following can you infer the speaker wants?

   (1) to have his son ask him for help with everyday things
   (2) to have his wife pay him more attention
   (3) to tell his wife to stop waiting on their son
   (4) to teach his son to be self-sufficient
   (5) to do things differently so that his own mother will forgive him

12. What did the speaker realize that morning?

   (1) His son loves his mother more than his father.
   (2) His wife has a radiant beauty about her.
   (3) Mothers want to do things for their children.
   (4) His son is now old enough to be more independent.
   (5) His mother is having problems seeing.

13. Which of the following best describes the tone of the speaker?

   (1) irritated
   (2) hysterical
   (3) concerned
   (4) detached
   (5) sarcastic

14. Macular degeneration is an eye disease that causes a decreasing ability to see. Based on this information and the poem, what is the meaning of the title?

   It refers not only to the grandmother's vision problems but also to the

   (1) son's refusal to let his father help
   (2) grandmother's focus on her grandson
   (3) wife's inability to see her husband's pain
   (4) wife's inability to see her son as spoiled
   (5) speaker's inability to see that his mother needs help

Questions 15 through 18 refer to the following poem.

WHAT SHOULD HAPPEN BEFORE SUNSET?

Before Sunset

In the lower lands of day
On the hither side of night,
There is nothing that will stay,
There are all things soft to sight;
(5) Lighted shade and shadowy light
In the wayside and the way,
Hours the sun has spared to smite,
Flowers the rain has left to play.

Shall these hours run down and say
(10) No good thing of thee and me?
Time that made us and will slay
Laughs at love in me and thee;
But if here the flowers may see
One whole hour of amorous breath,
(15) Time shall die, and love shall be
Lord as time was over death.

By Algernon Charles Swinburne.

15. What is being referred to by "In the lower lands of day" (line 1)?

    (1) in the shade
    (2) in a valley
    (3) toward the end of the day
    (4) during feelings of sadness
    (5) at dawn

16. What does the speaker mean when he says, "Time that made us and will slay" (line 11)?

    (1) Time has given us a strong love, but it may take it away.
    (2) Just as we were born and live, sooner or later we will die.
    (3) Time waits for no one; it goes on endlessly.
    (4) It is time that we face death.
    (5) We should not waste the time we have on earth.

17. To whom is the speaker talking?

    (1) his lover
    (2) the world in general
    (3) the reader
    (4) a woman he wants to get acquainted with
    (5) an old friend

18. Which of the following is the best restatement of "But if here the flowers may see / One whole hour of amorous breath, / Time shall die, and love shall be / Lord as time was over death." (lines 13–16)?

    (1) Time and love are the two most constant elements in life.
    (2) As long as we live life for even a short while, then love is the winner, not time.
    (3) If the flowers live, then time will not laugh at us.
    (4) If the lovers share their love, then their love will last.
    (5) If time dies, then all that is left to us is love.

Answers and explanations start on page 661.

DRAMA

Reading Dialogue and Stage Directions

- Dialogue refers to the lines of speech that the characters in a play say. Dialogue moves the plot forward and reveals something about the characters.
- Stage directions are usually in italics and parentheses or brackets. Stage directions give information about the characters' expressions, feelings, and actions.

Plays can be read on the page as well as performed on the stage. When you read a play, you notice the **dialogue**—the lines that the characters speak. Dialogue moves the plot along by bringing to light the conflict in the play and how it is resolved. The dialogue also reveals—either by stating directly or by implying—how each character thinks or why he or she acts a certain way.

Stage directions are set off in some way. They can be enclosed in parentheses ( ) or brackets [ ] and are often also in *italic* type. They provide additional information about how a character is feeling, speaking, or moving.

Use the dialogue and stage directions to understand this scene from a play.

SAM: You can speak loud. Your Mom's not here.
HALLY: Out shopping?
SAM: No. The hospital.
HALLY: But it's Thursday. There's no visiting on Thursday afternoons. Is my Dad okay?
SAM: Sounds like it. In fact, I think he's going home.
HALLY: [*Stopped short by Sam's remark*] What do you mean?
SAM: The hospital phoned.
HALLY: To say what?
SAM: I don't know. I just heard your Mom talking.
HALLY: So what makes you say he's going home?
SAM: It sounded as if they were telling her to come and fetch him.
   Hally thinks about what Sam has said for a few seconds.
HALLY: When did she leave?
SAM: About an hour ago. She said she would phone you. Want to eat?
   Hally doesn't respond.

From "MASTER HAROLD" . . . AND THE BOYS by Athol Fugard, copyright © 1982 by Athol Fugard. Used by permission of Alfred A. Knopf, a division of Random House, Inc.

GED TIP

When you read the excerpt from a drama on the GED Test, visualize what you read. Imagine you are hearing and seeing actors speak and act out the lines.

▶ What is revealed when Hally says, "There's no visiting on Thursday afternoons. Is my Dad okay?"
   (1) His father is in the hospital, and Hally is worried something has happened to him.
   (2) Hally fears his parents have been hospitalized.

Option (1) is correct. You can conclude that Hally's father is in the hospital, and that Hally fears something is wrong since his mother went on a nonvisiting day.

▶ What do the stage directions tell you about Hally?
   (1) He is surprised by what Sam has told him.
   (2) He thinks carefully about what he says before he says it.

Again, the correct answer is **(1)**. He is "stopped short" and needs to think a few seconds. Those directions tell you he is surprised by what Sam has told him.

DRAMA ▸ PRACTICE 1

Questions 1 through 4 refer to the following excerpt from a play.

ARE BEN AND GUS SATISFIED WITH THEIR WORK?

BEN: You get your holidays, don't you?

GUS: Only a fortnight.

BEN: [*lowering the paper*] You kill me. Anyone
would think you're working every day. How
(5)   often do we do a job? Once a week? What are
you complaining about?

GUS: Yes, but we've got to be on tap though,
haven't we? You can't move out of the house
in case a call comes.

(10) BEN: You know what your trouble is?

GUS: What?

BEN: You haven't got any interests.

GUS: I've got interests.

BEN: What? Tell me one of your interests.

(15) *Pause.*

GUS: I've got interests.

BEN: Look at me. What have I got?

GUS: I don't know. What?

BEN: I've got my woodwork. I've got my model
(20)   boats. Have you ever seen me idle? I'm never
idle. I know how to occupy my time, to its best
advantage. Then when a call comes, I'm ready.

GUS: Don't you ever get a bit fed up?

BEN: Fed up? What with?

(25) *Silence. BEN reads. GUS feels in the pocket of his
jacket, which hangs on the bed.*

GUS: You got any cigarettes? I've run out.

The lavatory flushes off left.

There she goes.

(30) GUS *sits on his bed.*

No, I mean, I say the crockery's good. It is. It's
very nice. But that's about all I can say for this
place. It's worse than the last one. Remember
that last place we were in? Last time, where
(35)   was it? At least there was a wireless there. No,
honest. He doesn't seem to bother much
about our comfort these days.

BEN: When are you going to stop jabbering?

GUS: You'd get rheumatism in a place like this, if
(40)   you stay long.

BEN: We're not staying long. Make the tea, will
you? We'll be on the job in a minute.

From THE DUMB WAITER by Harold Pinter. Used by
permission of Grove/Atlantic, Inc. Copyright © 1960 by
Harold Pinter.

1. What do Ben and Gus generally do on the job?

    (1) feel under pressure to work hard
    (2) think of ways to ask for more money
    (3) look for better jobs
    (4) sit and wait for work
    (5) meet to discuss each week's work

2. According to Ben, what is Gus's problem?

    (1) He has no outside interests.
    (2) He has been on this job too long.
    (3) The boss doesn't like him.
    (4) The job is too hard for him.
    (5) He talks too much.

3. Which of the following can be inferred about
   Ben's behavior?

    He is

    (1) pacing back and forth
    (2) paying only partial attention to Gus
    (3) trying to quit smoking
    (4) making tea to spend the time
    (5) trying to avoid work

4. How does Ben feel about his job?

    (1) overjoyed
    (2) impatient
    (3) angry
    (4) unconcerned
    (5) content

Answers and explanations start on page 662.

DRAMA

Understanding Dramatic Action

Key Ideas

- Dramatic action moves the plot of a play.
- The dramatic action is revealed in the dialogue and the actions of the characters.
- Sometimes characters' actions are stated in stage directions. Often you have to infer their actions.

GED TIP

When you read a question on the GED Test, try to answer it yourself first. Look back at the passage if you need to. Then look for an option that says basically the same thing as your answer.

Like a novel or other story, a play has a **plot.** The plot is the series of events that involves a conflict and produces tension. It eventually ends with a resolution of the conflict.

Dramatic action refers to the events that move the plot along. In a play, dramatic action is revealed in the dialogue and in the actions of the characters. Sometimes the stage directions tell you the characters' actions. When they do not, you need to picture for yourself how characters would move and act as they were saying their lines.

As you read the following excerpt from a play, focus on what is happening and the conflict that is occurring.

> MRS. WARREN [*distracted, throwing herself on her knees*]: Oh no, no. Stop, stop. I am your mother: I swear it. Oh, you can't mean to turn on me—my own child! it's not natural. You believe me, don't you? Say you believe me.
>
> VIVIE: Who was my father?
>
> MRS. WARREN: You don't know what you're asking. I can't tell you.
>
> VIVIE [*determinedly*]: Oh yes you can, if you like. I have a right to know; and you know very well that I have that right. You can refuse to tell me, if you please; but if you do, you will see the last of me tomorrow morning.
>
> MRS. WARREN: Oh, it's too horrible to hear you talk like that. You wouldn't—you couldn't leave me.
>
> VIVIE [*ruthlessly*]: Yes, without a moment's hesitation, if you trifle with me about this.

Excerpt from MRS. WARREN'S PROFESSION by George Bernard Shaw, reprinted courtesy of The Society of Authors on behalf of the Bernard Shaw Estate.

▶ What initially upsets Mrs. Warren?
  (1) Her daughter asks who her father is.
  (2) Her daughter questions whether Mrs. Warren is her real mother.

You are correct if you chose **(2)**. Mrs. Warren is so upset that she throws herself to her knees and begs for her daughter to believe her.

▶ What does Vivie do that increases the tension?
  (1) She threatens to leave her mother.
  (2) She threatens to go find her father.

You are correct if you chose **(1)**. Vivie's words "you will see the last of me tomorrow morning" make the conflict between her mother and herself even more tense. Mrs. Warren calls the words "horrible," and Vivie responds "ruthlessly."

Questions 1 through 3 refer to the following excerpt from a play.

WHAT NEWS IS
EVERYONE GOSSIPING ABOUT?

TIM CASEY: Some dispute I suppose it was that rose between Jack Smith and Bartley Fallon, and it seems Jack made off, and Bartley is following him with a hayfork!

(5) MRS. TARPEY: Is he now? Well, that was quick work! It's not ten minutes since the two of them were here, Bartley going home and Jack going to the Five Acre Meadow; and I had my apples to settle up, that Jo Muldoon of the

(10) police had scattered, and when I looked round again Jack Smith was gone, and Bartley Fallon was gone, and Mrs. Fallon's basket upset, and all in it strewed upon the ground—the tea here—the two pound of sugar there—

(15) the eggs-cups there—Look, now, what a great hardship the deafness puts upon me, that I didn't hear the commencement of the fight! Wait till I tell James Ryan that I see below; he is a neighbour of Bartley's, it would be a pity

(20) if he wouldn't hear the news!

[*She goes out. Enter* SHAWN EARLY *and* MRS. TULLY.]

TIM CASEY: Listen, Shawn Early! Listen, Mrs. Tully, to the news! Jack Smith and Bartley

(25) Fallon had a falling out, and Jack knocked Mrs. Fallon's basket into the road, and Bartley made an attack on him with a hayfork, and away with Jack, and Bartley after him. Look at the sugar here yet on the road!

(30) SHAWN EARLY: Do you tell me so? Well, that's a queer thing, and Bartley Fallon so quiet a man!

MRS. TULLY: I wouldn't wonder at all. I would never think well of a man that would have

(35) that sort of a mouldering look. It's likely he has overtaken Jack by this.

[*Enter* JAMES RYAN *and* MRS. TARPEY.]

JAMES RYAN: That is great news Mrs. Tarpey was telling me! I suppose that's what brought

(40) the police and the magistrate up this way. I was wondering to see them in it a while ago.

SHAWN EARLY: The police after them? Bartley Fallon must have injured Jack so. They wouldn't meddle in a fight that was

(45) only for show!

MRS. TULLY: Why wouldn't he injure him? There was many a man killed with no more of a weapon than a hayfork.

JAMES RYAN: Wait till I run north as far as

(50) Kelly's bar to spread the news!

[*He goes out.*]

From *Spreading the News* by Lady Augusta Gregory.

1. What conclusion does Tim Casey jump to about Mrs. Fallon's basket turning over?

   (1) The police overturned it.
   (2) Mrs. Tarpey accidentally upset it.
   (3) Mrs. Fallon threw it at Jack Smith.
   (4) It happened during a fight.
   (5) The basket was too heavy to carry.

2. What effect has Mrs. Tully's comment "There was many a man killed with no more of a weapon than a hayfork" (lines 47–49)?

   (1) It gives Bartley the idea to kill Jack.
   (2) It persuades people that hayforks are unsafe.
   (3) It gets the others excited enough to run and tell more people.
   (4) It makes the others realize that the police should be called to prevent a murder.
   (5) It recalls what a violent village they live in.

3. Later in the play, Shawn Early reports to Mrs. Tarpey that he saw Jack Smith's wife "laying out a sheet on a hedge" to dry it. Mrs. Tarpey misunderstands and thinks he said "laying out a sheet for the dead."

   Based on Mrs. Tarpey's behavior in this excerpt, what will she likely do next?

   (1) ask Shawn if she heard him correctly
   (2) mind her own business
   (3) say a silent prayer
   (4) tell people that Jack Smith is dead
   (5) go to Jack Smith's wife to sympathize

Answers and explanations start on page 662.

DRAMA

Analyzing Characters

Key Ideas

• Characters are the people in a play.

• The thoughts, feelings, motives, and personalities of characters are revealed through dialogue and stage directions.

Characters are, of course, the people in a play. Through the dialogue and the stage directions, you learn what each character says and does. You can also learn of the characters' thoughts, feelings, motives, and personalities by reading the lines or by reading "between the lines"—that is, by inferring. Pay attention, too, to what other characters say about a particular character. Their words will give you insight into that character's motives and personality.

As you read the following excerpt from a play, decide what kind of people the two characters are.

> WAITER: No one eats here who cannot pay for his food.
> WORKMAN: [*Opening his wallet.*] Feast your eyes on that wad. Is that the real cabbage, or isn't it? The real lettuce, the real spinach, the real scratch?
> [*Allowing the* WAITER *to remove some bills and examine them.*]
> WORKMAN: [*Cont'd.*] Well, what do you say? Is it good enough for you, or do you want me to pick myself up and walk out of here? Plenty of other restaurants I could go to.
> WAITER: No need to raise your voice, sir. I can tell the genuine from the fraud.
> WORKMAN: Then get me what I want to eat! I'm hungry and I want to eat!
> WAITER: [*Clicking his heels.*] Of course. I am at your service.
> WORKMAN: I've been driving all morning in from the border, and my stomach is empty.
> WAITER: I understand. You have the money to pay and I am at your service.

From *Cannibal Masque* by Ronald Ribman. Used by permission of Flora Roberts, Inc.

▶ What does the statement "Feast your eyes on that wad" suggest about the workman?
  (1) He is brash and boorish.
  (2) He is friendly and inviting.

Option (1) is correct. The workman demands that the waiter admire the money in his wallet. That tells you the workman is boldly confident and proud of himself, or brash. That action is also an example of bad manners, or boorish behavior.

▶ Which of the following best characterizes the waiter?
  (1) reserved and obedient
  (2) bitter and resentful

You are correct if you chose **(1)**. The waiter clicks his heels and responds to the workman's demands by agreeing that he, the waiter, is there to serve him. He also speaks in a formal, reserved manner (for example, "No need to raise your voice, sir" and "I am at your service").

GED TIP

Before you read the GED drama excerpt, glance down the left side to see the characters' names. This will tell you how many characters you'll read about and will familiarize you with the excerpt.

DRAMA ▶ PRACTICE 3

Questions 1 through 5 refer to the following excerpt from a play.

HOW DOES SHEILA REACT TO AYAMONN'S INTEREST IN HER?

AYAMONN: . . . Refuse to let yourself be like a timid little girl safely ensconced in a clear space in a thicket of thorns—safe from a scratch if she doesn't stir, but unable to get to (5) the green grass or the open road unless she risks the tears the thorns can give.

SHEILA: Oh, Ayamonn, for my sake, if you love me, do try to be serious.

AYAMONN [*a little wildly*]: Oh, Sheila, our time is (10) not yet come to be serious in the way of our elders. Soon enough to browse with wisdom when Time's grey finger puts a warning speck on the crimson rose of youth. Let no damned frosty prayer chill the sunny sighs (15) that dread the joy of love.

SHEILA [*wildly*]: I won't listen, Ayamonn, I won't listen! We must look well ahead on the road to the future. You lead your life through too many paths instead of treading the one way (20) of making it possible for us to live together.

AYAMONN: We live together now; live in the light of the burning bush. I tell you life is not one thing, but many things, a wide branching flame, grand and good to see and feel daz- (25) zling to the eye of no-one loving it. I am not one to carry fear about with me as a priest carries the Host. Let the timid tiptoe through the way where the paler blossoms grow; my feet shall be where the redder roses grow, (30) though they bear long thorns, sharp and piercing, thick among them!

SHEILA [*rising from the chair—vehemently*]: I'll listen no more; I'll go. You want to make me a spark in a mere illusion. I'll go!

1. What does Sheila think about Ayamonn?

He

(1) doesn't love her enough
(2) doesn't listen to her
(3) is impractical and passionate
(4) is too demanding
(5) is too rough with her

2. Why does Ayamonn say life is "not one thing, but many things" (lines 22–23)?

He believes that life

(1) has no right or wrong answers
(2) has too many choices
(3) has both good and bad in it
(4) is chaotic and interesting
(5) provides safety in numbers

3. Which of the following best describes the conflict between Ayamonn and Sheila?

(1) They have different ideas about love and life.
(2) Sheila seeks to control Ayamonn.
(3) Ayamonn thinks Sheila cares too much what other people think.
(4) Ayamonn refuses to admit Sheila has fallen out of love.
(5) The two have nothing in common.

4. Based on Ayamonn's words, what kind of occupation does he seem best suited for?

(1) lawyer
(2) doctor
(3) accountant
(4) businessman
(5) poet

5. Earlier in the scene, Sheila tells Ayamonn about her mother: "I've told you how she hates me to be near you. She chatters red-lined warnings and black-bordered appeals."

How does this information help explain Sheila's actions in this excerpt?

(1) She sees Ayamonn only because she wants to rebel against her mother.
(2) She is fighting her true feelings for Ayamonn because of her mother's feelings.
(3) She fears Ayamonn will hurt her mother.
(4) She knows her mother is correct about Ayamonn.
(5) She fears harm will come to Ayamonn.

Answers and explanations start on page 662.

Drawing Conclusions

Key Ideas

- Drawing conclusions while reading a play means using the information in the dialogue and stage directions to decide something is true.
- You can draw a conclusion about an event in the play as well as about characters' actions, motives, and personalities.

When you use all the available information to decide something is true, you **draw a conclusion.** For example, if you see a man getting down on one knee while out to dinner with a woman, you could conclude that he is proposing.

When you read a play, you can likewise draw conclusions about the events as well as about characters' actions, motives, and personalities. To draw conclusions, pay attention to the dialogue and stage directions. Consider information that is directly stated as well as inferences you can make. Ask yourself why a character says what she says. Determine what must have happened to explain why a character acts as he does.

As you read this excerpt from a play, see what conclusions you can draw.

> LYDIA: Is she still unhappy, Joe?
> KELLER: Annie? I don't suppose she goes around dancing on her toes, but she seems to be over it.
> LYDIA: She going to get married? Is there anybody. . . ?
> KELLER: I suppose . . . say, it's a couple years already. She can't mourn a boy forever.
> LYDIA: It's so strange . . . Annie's here and not even married. And I've got three babies. I always though it'd be the other way around.
> KELLER: Well, that's what a war does. I had two sons, now I got one. It changed all the tallies. In my day when you had sons it was an honor. Today a doctor could make a million dollars if he could figure out a way to bring a boy into the world without a trigger finger.

Excerpt from ALL MY SONS by Arthur Miller. Reprinted by permission of International Creative Management, Inc. Copyright © 1947 by Arthur Miller.

► What is the most likely reason that Annie is not married?
  (1) Her boyfriend was killed in a war.
  (2) She is basically an unhappy, withdrawn person.

Option (1) is correct. Lydia does ask if Annie is "still unhappy," but other clues help explain why. The lines "seems to be over it," "it's a couple years already," "mourn a boy," and "that's what a war does" help you draw the conclusion that Annie had a boyfriend who was killed in a war.

► What type of person does Joe Keller seem to be?
  (1) angry and negative
  (2) accepting and down to earth

The correct answer is **(2)**. Although you might conclude that a man who lost a son in a war would be angry, Keller accepts it as a matter of fact ("that's what a war does. I had two sons, now I got one"). He expresses other thoughts in the same down-to-earth manner—"I don't suppose she goes around dancing on her toes" and "say, it's a couple years already. She can't mourn a boy forever."

Questions 1 through 3 refer to the following excerpt from a play.

WHAT HAPPENED IN THIS HOUSE?

COUNTY ATTORNEY: Well, that's interesting, I'm sure. [*Seeing the birdcage.*] Has the bird flown?

(5) MRS. HALE: [*Putting more quilt pieces over the box.*] We think the—cat got it.

COUNTY ATTORNEY. [*Preoccupied.*] Is there a cat?

[*MRS. HALE glances in a quick covert way at MRS. PETERS.*]

(10) MRS. PETERS: Well, not now. They're superstitious, you know. They leave.

COUNTY ATTORNEY: [*To SHERIFF PETERS, continuing an interrupted conversation.*] No sign at all of anyone having come from the out-(15) side. Their own rope. Now let's go up again and go over it piece by piece. [*They start upstairs.*] It would have to have been someone who knew just the—

[*MRS. PETERS sits down. The two women sit there (20) not looking at one another, but as if peering into something and at the same time holding back. When they talk now it is in the manner of feeling their way over strange ground, as if afraid of what they are saying, but as if they can not help say-(25) ing it.*]

MRS. HALE: She liked the bird. She was going to bury it in that pretty box.

MRS. PETERS: [*In a whisper.*] When I was a girl— my kitten—there was a boy took a hatchet, (30) and before my eyes—and before I could get there—[*Covers her face an instant.*] If they hadn't held me back I would have— [*Catches herself, looks upstairs where steps are heard, falters weakly.*]—hurt him.

(35) MRS. HALE: [*With a slow look around her.*] I wonder how it would seem never to have had any children around. [*Pause.*] No, Wright wouldn't like the bird—a thing that sang. She used to sing. He killed that, too.

(40) MRS. PETERS: [*Moving uneasily.*] We don't know who killed the bird.

MRS. HALE: I knew John Wright.

MRS. PETERS: It was an awful thing was done in this house that night, Mrs. Hale. (45) Killing a man while he slept, slipping a rope around his neck that choked the life out of him.

MRS. HALE: His neck. Choked the life out of him. [*Her hand goes out and rests on the bird-(50) cage.*]

MRS. PETERS: [*With rising voice.*] We don't know who killed him. We don't know.

MRS. HALE: [*Her own feeling not interrupted.*] If there'd been years and years of nothing, (55) then a bird to sing to you, it would be awful—still, after the bird was still.

Excerpt from TRIFLES, by Susan Glaspell, published by Penguin Putnam, Inc.

1. Who does Mrs. Hale think killed the bird?

   (1) John Wright
   (2) Mrs. Peters
   (3) a strange woman
   (4) the cat
   (5) Mrs. Wright

2. Based on the excerpt, which of the following best describes John Wright?

   (1) a person who is loving and attentive
   (2) someone who smothers all the joy in another person
   (3) a person capable of murder
   (4) an individual who loves animals
   (5) someone devoted to law and order

3. Which of the following conclusions can you draw about Mrs. Peters and Mrs. Hale?

   (1) Together they committed murder.
   (2) Each one thinks the other one is the murderer.
   (3) They are eager to tell the police all they know.
   (4) They are afraid the police suspect them.
   (5) They understand how someone could be driven to murder.

Answers and explanations start on page 662.

DRAMA PRACTICE QUESTIONS

Questions 1 through 5 refer to the following excerpt from a play.

WHAT IS SADIE TELLING O'HARA?

O'HARA: What's to hinder you repenting in Sydney—just as well as in San Francisco—if you've got to repent?

SADIE: You don't understand. I've got to go
(5)   back and be punished for what I've been—there's no other way out. I've got to serve my time—then God will forgive me. It's the sacrifice I've got to offer up for the life I've led. Oh, if it would only
(10)   begin at once. It's this waiting for it to start, that's so bad—all these days and days I'll be alone on the boat. I'm weak. I'm afraid. I'm dreadfully afraid. You've got to be very strong, Handsome, to live
(15)   at all. [*Almost as if to herself.*] It will be much easier in the penitentiary.

O'HARA [*in a strange, shocked voice*]: What's that you're saying? The penitentiary?

(20) SADIE [*with a curious smile*]: When I get to San Francisco, Handsome, I've got to go to the penitentiary for—three years.

O'HARA [*staring back; under his breath*]: God!

(25) SADIE: Reverend Davidson says it doesn't make any difference whether I was innocent or guilty, of what they framed me for. He says that is God's way of letting me square myself. He says I've got to
(30)   accept an unjust punishment by man as a sacrifice to God.

O'HARA: You just listen to me. Get into your room and throw your clothes on as fast as you can. [*He pulls her from her*
(35)   *chair.*]

SADIE: Let go of me—let go! [*She frees herself ferociously; turns on him angrily.*] Don't you dare do that again! I want you to go away. Do you hear? Get right out!

(40) O'HARA [*brokenly*]: Sadie—Sadie!

SADIE [*wildly, going R.*]: I mean it! Get right out! Go away—go away.

From *Rain* by John Colton and Clemence Randolph. Used with permission of American Play Company, Inc. (Est. 1898) a subsidiary of American Entertainment Holding Company, LLC.

1. What reason does Sadie give for her insistence on going to the penitentiary?

(1) She was guilty of a crime.
(2) She has no choice in the matter.
(3) She will be forgiven for her misdeeds.
(4) Reverend Davidson has forced her.
(5) She wants to get away from O'Hara.

2. What is the main conflict between Sadie and O'Hara?

(1) O'Hara has learned about Sadie's past.
(2) O'Hara thinks Sadie is making a mistake.
(3) Sadie no longer loves O'Hara.
(4) Sadie distrusts Reverend Davidson.
(5) O'Hara is too rough with Sadie.

3. What attitude is motivating O'Hara?

(1) admiration for Sadie's choice
(2) curiosity about Sadie's past
(3) interest in being Sadie's boyfriend
(4) concern for Sadie's welfare
(5) concern for his own welfare

4. What would O'Hara's reaction likely be if he met Reverend Davidson?

(1) argue with him
(2) try to trick him
(3) ask him to explain
(4) turn and walk away
(5) laugh at him

5. What mood is created as this scene moves along?

(1) eeriness
(2) formality
(3) resignation
(4) finality
(5) tension

Questions 6 through 8 refer to the following excerpt from a play.

DOES BESSIE THINK LIFE IS EASY?

BESSIE: Ralphie, I worked too hard all my years to be treated like dirt. It's no law we should be stuck together like Siamese twins. Summer shoes you didn't
(5) have, skates you never had, but I bought a new dress every week. A lover I kept— Mr. Gigolo! Did I ever play a game of cards like Mrs. Marcus? Or was Bessie Berger's children always the cleanest on
(10) the block?! Here I'm not only the mother, but also the father. The first two years I worked in a stocking factory for six dollars while Myron Berger went to law school. If I didn't worry about the family
(15) who would? On the calendar it's a different place, but here without a dollar you don't look the world in the eye. Talk from now to next year—this is life in America.

RALPH: Then it's wrong. It don't make
(20) sense. If life made you this way, then it's wrong!

BESSIE: Maybe you wanted me to give up twenty years ago. Where would you be now? You'll excuse my expression—bum
(25) in the park!

RALPH: I'm not blaming you, Mom. Sink or swim—I see it. But it can't stay like this.

BESSIE: My foolish boy . . .

RALPH: No, I see every house lousy with
(30) lies and hate. He said it, Grandpa— Brooklyn hates the Bronx. Smacked on the nose twice a day. But boys and girls can get ahead like that, Mom. We don't want life printed on dollar bills, Mom!

(35) BESSIE: So go out and change the world if you don't like it.

RALPH: I will! And why? 'Cause life's different in my head. Gimme the earth in two hands. I'm strong. There . . . hear him?
(40) The airmail off to Boston. Day or night, he flies away, a job to do. That's us and it's no time to die.

[*The airplane sound fades off as* MYRON *gives alarm clock to* BESSIE, *which she*
(45) *begins to wind.*]

BESSIE: "Mom, what does she know? She's old-fashioned!" But I'll tell you a big secret: My whole life I wanted to go away too, but with children a woman
(50) stays home. A fire burned in *my* heart too, but now it's too late. I'm no spring chicken. The clock goes and Bessie goes. Only my machinery can't be fixed. [*She lifts a button: the alarm rings on the*
(55) *clock; she stops it, says "Good night,"* *and exits.*]

From *Awake and Sing!* by Clifford Odets.

6. What is Bessie trying to express to her son?

(1) She wasn't perfect, but she worked hard for her children.
(2) She is too old-fashioned to understand young people like him.
(3) She feels she should have done more for her children.
(4) The world has always been on their side.
(5) He is a fine young man and should not let his past hold him back.

7. Which of the following best describes Ralph's attitude toward life?

(1) Be content with who you are and what you have.
(2) Money is the most important thing.
(3) Life can be better.
(4) Look out for number one—yourself.
(5) Love of money is the root of all evil.

8. What does Bessie mean when she says, "Only my machinery can't be fixed" (line 53)?

(1) When the alarm rings, she is ready to work.
(2) An old alarm clock can keep going, but not her aging body.
(3) She can't set her life to a specific time or task, like an alarm clock.
(4) She knows she lives in the past.
(5) She would like to change, but she can't.

Questions 9 through 11 refer to the following
excerpt from a play.

WHY IS BERTA UPSET WITH FIDEL?

FIDEL: Last night on the plaza the Celestina
happened to mention it. With a bit of flattery I soon gained the whole story from
her.

(5) BERTA: So that is what you were talking
about as you walked around the plaza?
[*Stands*] It must have taken a great deal
of flattery to gain so much knowledge
from her.

(10) FIDEL [*stands*]: Do you not realize what it
means? They will need someone to carve
the new doors.

[*He strikes a pleased attitude, expecting her
to say, "But how wonderful, Fidel."*]

(15) BERTA [*knowing very well what* FIDEL
*expects, promptly turns away from him,
her hand hiding a smile, as she says with
innocent curiosity*]: I wonder whom Don
Nimfo will get? [*With the delight of dis-*
(20) *covery*] Perhaps the Brothers Ochóa from
Monterrey.
FIDEL [*crestfallen*]: He might choose me.
BERTA: You? Hah!
FIDEL: And why not? Am I not the best
(25) wood carver in the valley?
BERTA: So you say.
FIDEL: It would take three years to carve
those doors, and he would pay me every
week. There would be enough to buy you
(30) a trousseau and enough left over for a
house.
BERTA: Did you tell all that to the
Celestina?
FIDEL: Of course not! Does a girl help a
(35) man buy a trousseau for another girl?
That was why it had to appear as though
I were rolling the eye at her. [*He is very
much pleased with his brilliance.*]
BERTA: Your success was more than per-
(40) fect. Today all the world knows that the
Celestina has won Berta's man.
FIDEL: But all the world does not know that
Fidel Durán, who is I, myself, will carve
those doors so as to buy a trousseau
(45) and house for Berta, my queen.

BERTA: Precisely. All the world does not
know this great thing. . . . [*Flaring out at
him*] And neither do I!
FIDEL: Do you doubt me, pearl of my life?
(50) BERTA: Does the rabbit doubt the snake?
Does the tree doubt the lightning? Do I
doubt that you are a teller of tremendous
lies? Speak not to me of cleverness. I
know what my own eyes see, and I saw
(55) you flirting with the Celestina. Last night I
saw you . . . and so did all the world!

From *Sunday Costs Five Pesos* by Josephina Niggli.

9. What reason does Fidel give for flattering
Celestina?

(1) to make Berta jealous
(2) to win Celestina's affection
(3) to get the work carving doors
(4) to make people think he loved her
(5) to get money from her

10. What does Berta mean when she says,
"Does a tree doubt the lightning?" (line 51)?

(1) There is a spark between Fidel and
Celestina.
(2) The two have nothing in common.
(3) Fidel is special and compelling, and she
is ordinary.
(4) She distrusts Fidel and fears he will hurt
her.
(5) Fidel will probably cause a disaster.

11. Later in the play Berta says, "My heart is
with Fidel. My life is ruined."

Based on this line and the excerpt, which of
the following best describes how Berta acts
with Fidel in this scene?

(1) chatty
(2) playful
(3) straightforward
(4) innocent
(5) dishonest

**Answers and explanations start on
page 663.**

Math

The GED Mathematics Test evaluates your ability to understand and apply math concepts and procedures to solve problems. You will have 90 minutes to answer 50 questions. Problems generally do not require a straightforward calculation such as "What is 45 + 65?" Instead, most of the test consists of word problems or problems based on a graphic, such as a table, graph, or diagram. Many of the problems are based on realistic life situations.

The GED Mathematics Test is divided into two parts:

Part I: 25 questions

On this part of the test, you will be provided with a *Casio fx-260* scientific calculator at the testing center. This calculator has many advanced functions and is programmed with the order of operations.

Part II: 25 questions

You will <u>not</u> be able to use a calculator on this part of the test.

The main difference between the two parts of the test is that you can use the calculator for Part I. At the end of the time for Part I, the calculator and Part I booklet will be collected, and you will be given Part II of the test to work on.

Content Areas

Number Operations and Number Sense (20 to 30 percent) Just like common sense, number sense implies a basic understanding of problem solving and whether answers make sense. Estimation is often useful with many of these problems. Questions in this category involve solving problems with whole numbers, decimals, fractions, integers, ratio, proportion, and percents.

Data Analysis, Statistics, and Probability (20 to 30 percent) Almost everyone has daily encounters with statistics (sports), data analysis (news), and probability and chance (weather). Questions on the test may ask you to interpret data in a table or graph, find the average of a set of numbers, and recognize conclusions based on data. You may also need to find the probability of certain outcomes.

Algebra, Functions, and Patterns (20 to 30 percent) Don't let the word *algebra* worry you. Algebra is a way of looking at something and then applying what you know to similar situations. GED questions may ask you to solve equations, identify patterns, and apply formulas in a variety of situations.

Measurement and Geometry (20 to 30 percent) Measurement uses math to answer questions on everything from distance to weight to volume. The GED Math Test features measurement problems as well as geometry problems based on figures such as angles, triangles, quadrilaterals, and circles.

Three Types of GED Math Questions

The GED Math Test uses three types of questions. Review these problems to become aware of the type of mathematical thinking expected on the GED.

Math Procedures These questions measure your ability to apply the correct math procedure to solving a problem.

Example 1: To upholster a chair cushion, Sofia needs $4\frac{1}{2}$ yards of fabric. How many yards does she need to cover 4 cushions?

(1) $\frac{1}{2}$ (4) 18

(2) $1\frac{1}{8}$ (5) 28

(3) $8\frac{1}{2}$

Answer: (4) 18 You need to know to multiply to get the answer.

$$4\frac{1}{2} \text{ yards} \times 4 \text{ cushions} = 18 \text{ yards}$$

You can estimate to get the answer or to check your calculation.

Estimate: 4 yards $\times$ 4 cushions would be 16, so 18 cushions makes sense.

Math Concepts These questions measure your knowledge of math concepts. Many of these questions require you to demonstrate your knowledge of how math works, rather than to find a specific, numeric answer.

Example 2: The formula for finding distance is $d = rt$, where d = distance, r = *rate*, and t = *time*. Which of the following expressions could be used to find the time (t) of a trip?

(1) $\dfrac{d}{r}$ (4) $\dfrac{rd}{2}$

(2) $\dfrac{r}{d}$ (5) $2rd$

(3) rd

Answer: (1) $\dfrac{d}{r}$ To solve, you need to know how to isolate a variable (t) in a formula or equation. In this problem, divide both sides by the variable r.

$$d = rt$$
$$\frac{d}{r} = \frac{\cancel{r}t}{\cancel{r}}$$
$$\frac{d}{r} = t$$

Application/Modeling/Problem Solving These questions require you to analyze a situation and then apply a strategy for solving the problem.

Example 3: To win a prize, Sarah's daughter has to sell 75 boxes of cookies in 3 days. If she sold 16 boxes on day 1 and 34 boxes on day 2, how many boxes does she need to sell on day 3 to win a prize?

(1) 16   (4) 34

(2) 18   (5) 50

(3) 25

Answer: (3) 25 You have to reason that two steps are needed.

1. Find the total number of boxes of cookies sold so far. $16 + 34 = 50$

2. Find the number of boxes to be sold on the last day. $75 - 50 = 25$ boxes

ON THE GED

Wrong answer choices are based on common errors in thinking. For instance, in Example 3, option (5) is based on calculating just the first step but not finishing the problem.

Using the Scientific Calculator

When you take the GED Mathematics Test, you will be provided with a *Casio fx-260* calculator for Part I of the test. Below is a picture of the calculator you will use and some issues to keep in mind.

Casio fx–260
SOURCE: Courtesy of Casio, Inc.

GED Calculator Tips

- Purchase this calculator or a similar scientific calculator from an office supply store while you are preparing to take the test.

- Every model of scientific calculator is slightly different, but it is important to prepare for the GED Math Test by knowing how a scientific calculator works in general. There will be many opportunities to work with a calculator throughout this book.

- You will not be able to take your calculator into the test. You will be provided with one at the time of the test.

- At the testing center, you will be given directions on how to use the *Casio fx-260* calculator. Even if you have used one before, go over the directions carefully.

- Try your calculator before you begin the test. If you experience any difficulties with it, let the GED Examiner know right away.

General Principles for Calculator Use on the GED

- You may use the calculator on Part I of the test, but it will be collected before you start Part II.

- A calculator is being provided on the test so that you can work with realistic numbers. An important focus of the test is problem solving. Be sure to work through the Problem Solving lessons in this book.

- You <u>do not</u> have to use the calculator to solve problems. Some problems will be easier for you to solve with paper and pencil or even mental math. Some problems will not require a computation at all. Make the calculator a useful tool, not an unnecessary burden.

It is possible to make mistakes when you "key in" numbers, signs, or functions. Always use common sense to see if your answer seems reasonable. Many people use this process when they use a calculator to solve problems:

1. Estimate the answer.

2. Use the calculator to find the answer.

3. Compare the calculator answer to the estimate to catch possible "keying" errors.

Special Types of Questions

You will see many different types of questions on the GED Math Test. There are two special types that you should be familiar with.

Set-Up Items These questions measure your ability to recognize the correct procedure for solving a problem. These questions ask you to choose an expression that represents how to "set up" the problem.

Example 1: Russ makes $24,000 per year at his new job. Which expression below shows how much he earns per month?

      (1) $24,000 + 12
      (2) $24,000 − 12
      (3) $24,000 × 12
      (4) $24,000/12
      (5) 12/$24,000

Answer: (4) $24,000/12 You know that there are 12 months in a year. To find Russ's monthly income, you would divide the total ($24,000) by the number of months (12). Option (5) is incorrect because it means 12 divided by $24,000.

Not Enough Information Is Given Occasionally you will see problems with the answer choice (5) Not enough information is given.

This can be the right answer, but more often than not, it is not. In the example above, you might think at first that there is not enough information to solve the problem. However, you should know that there are 12 months in the year, so you have enough information to solve Example 1. Look at Example 2 below.

Example 2: Selena drives 2 miles to drop off her son at day care and 20 miles to work. How many minutes does it take her to get from home to work?

      (1) 10
      (2) 18
      (3) 22
      (4) 40
      (5) Not enough information is given.

Answer: (5) Not enough information is given. The question asks, "How many minutes does it take?" Since you don't know how fast she is driving, you can't figure out how long it takes. All of the incorrect choices are based on using the numbers in the problem; option (1) divides 20/2, option (2) subtracts 20 − 2, option (3) adds 20 + 2, and option (4) multiplies 20 × 2. However, none of these answer the question that was asked.

Alternative Format Questions

Most of the questions on the GED are multiple-choice questions. However, about 10 of the 50 questions are not. These questions are generally referred to as alternative-format questions because they are an alternative to multiple choice. These questions require you to find an answer and to fill in circles on a grid or on a coordinate axis.

Standard Grid When you are directed to fill in a grid like the one below, keep these guidelines in mind:

- First write your answer in the blank boxes at the top of the grid. This will help keep you organized as you "grid in" the bubbles.

- You can start in any column, but leave enough columns for your whole answer.

- You do not have to use all of the columns. If your answer only takes up two or three columns, leave the others blank.

Example 1: Sam estimates that he spends $\frac{1}{2}$ of his take-home pay on food and rent and 25% on his car—payment, gas, and repair. What part of his pay does he have left for other expenses?

Answer: You could find the answer by using either fractions or decimals. $1 - (\frac{1}{2} + \frac{1}{4}) = 1 - \frac{3}{4} = \frac{1}{4}$ OR $1 - (.50 + .25) = 1 - .75 = \textbf{.25}$

ON THE GED

When your answer is a mixed number, it must be represented on the standard grid in the form of an improper fraction. For example, for an answer of $2\frac{1}{2}$, grid in 5/2.

Whole number, fraction, and decimal forms can be depicted on the grid, as shown in the three examples below. As long as you have the correct answer, you can represent it in either decimal or fraction form.

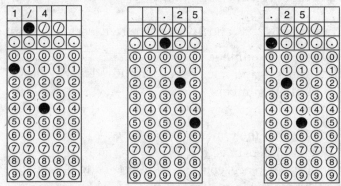

Coordinate Graph When directed to plot a point on a coordinate grid such as the one below, fill in the bubble where the point should appear.

Example 2: Plot the point $(3, -4)$ on the coordinate graph below.

Answer:

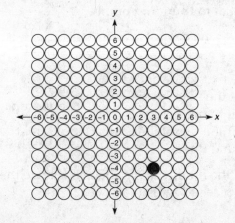

MATH BASICS

Whole Number Review

Place Value

Numbers are part of your everyday life. Whether you're paying with cash, reading bus schedules, or changing television channels, you're using whole numbers.

The value of a number depends on the **place value** of its digits. On the place-value chart below, note that the value of a digit increases as you move to the left.

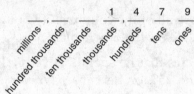

In the whole number shown on the chart, 1 has the greatest value. The number would be read as "one thousand four hundred seventy-nine."

Comparing and Ordering Values

To **order** numbers, you need to compare the value of their digits. Align the place values of the numbers you are comparing. Start at the left and compare the value of the first digit of each number.

Example 1: Place the numbers 342, 98, and 317 in order from <u>least to greatest.</u>

1. Compare the first digit in each number. Since 98 is a two-digit number, and the other numbers are three-digit numbers, 98 has the smallest value.

   hundreds tens ones
   342
   98
   317

2. Next, compare the first digit of the remaining numbers. Since both numbers have the same digit (3) in the hundreds place, compare the digits in the tens place. Since 10 is less than 40, 317 is less than 342.

   From least to greatest: **98, 317, 342**

Rounding Numbers

Place value is also essential to **rounding** numbers.

Example 2: Round 2451 to the nearest hundred.

2451

1. Locate the place value that you want to round to. Then look at the place value to the right. If the digit to the right is 5 or greater, round up. If the digit to the right is less than 5, round down.

   The value to the right of the hundreds place is a 5. Round up.

   2451 rounds up to **2500**

2. Round up the digit in the hundreds place. Then change the digits to the right of the hundreds place to zeros.

Key Ideas

- When ordering numbers, compare the same place values between numbers.
- Round numbers to estimate answers or eliminate answer choices in multiple-choice questions.

GED TIP

It's important to know the inequality symbols below.
< *means* is less than.
≤ *means* is less than or equal to.
> *means* is greater than.
≥ *means* is greater than or equal to.

WHOLE NUMBER ▸ PRACTICE 1

A. **Write the digit from the number below that corresponds to the listed place value. The first one is done for you.**

1,436,879

__4__ **1.** hundred thousands   ____ **5.** thousands

____ **2.** hundreds   ____ **6.** tens

____ **3.** ones   ____ **7.** ten thousands

____ **4.** millions

B. **Round these numbers as directed.**

8. Round 544 to the nearest hundred.   **11.** Round 11,632 to the nearest thousand.

9. Round 76 to the nearest ten.   **12.** Round 1525 to the nearest thousand.

10. Round 1058 to the nearest hundred.   **13.** Round 84 to the nearest hundred.

C. **In each of the following pairs, which number is greater?**

14. 100 or 89   **16.** 1099 or 1145

15. 339 or 341   **17.** 125,391 or 119,450

D. **Write these numbers in order from <u>least to greatest.</u>**

18. 23   18   45   39   **21.** 1429   1420   1432   1425

19. 111   89   109   91   **22.** 12,071   11,098   12,131

20. 1087   932   909   1139   **23.** 15,356   15,309   15,298

E. **Choose the <u>one best answer</u> to each question.**

24. When stacking items, the heaviest items should be placed at the bottom. Starting at the bottom, in what order should items weighing 45 pounds, 40 pounds, 50 pounds, and 48 pounds be stacked?

    (1) 40, 50, 45, 48
    (2) 40, 45, 48, 50
    (3) 45, 50, 40, 48
    (4) 50, 48, 45, 40
    (5) 50, 40, 45, 48

25. Which of the following correctly shows 1,543,976 rounded to the nearest hundred thousand?

    (1) 2,000,000
    (2) 1,600,000
    (3) 1,500,000
    (4) 1,540,000
    (5) 1,544,000

Answers and explanations begin on page 663.

MATH BASICS

Operations Review

Addition and Subtraction

You use **addition** when you need to combine amounts. The answer in an addition problem is called the **sum**, or **total**. When adding, it's helpful to stack the numbers in a column. Be sure to line up the place-value columns and then work from right to left, starting with the ones column.

Sometimes the digits in a place-value column add up to 10 or more. When this happens, you will need to **regroup** to the next place value.

Example 1: Add 40 + 129 + 24.

1. Align the numbers you want to add on the ones column. Working from right to left, add the ones column first. Since the ones column totals 13, write the 3 in the ones column and regroup, or **carry,** the 1 ten to the tens column.

$$
\begin{array}{r}
1 \\
40 \\
129 \\
+\ 24 \\
\hline
3
\end{array}
$$

2. Add the tens column, including the regrouped 1.

$$
\begin{array}{r}
1 \\
40 \\
129 \\
+\ 24 \\
\hline
93
\end{array}
$$

3. Then add the hundreds column. Since there is only one value, write the 1 hundred in the answer.

$$
\begin{array}{r}
1 \\
40 \\
129 \\
+\ 24 \\
\hline
\mathbf{193}
\end{array}
$$

You **subtract** when you want to find the **difference** between amounts. Write the greater number on top, and align the amounts on the ones column. You may also need to regroup as you subtract.

Example 2: If Sue is 57, and Kathy is 38, how many years older is Sue?

1. Find the difference in their ages. Start with the ones column. Since 7 is less than the number being subtracted (8), regroup, or **borrow,** 1 ten from the tens column. Add the regrouped amount to the ones column. Now subtract 17 − 8 in the ones column.

$$
\begin{array}{r}
4\ 17 \\
\cancel{57} \\
-\ 38 \\
\hline
9
\end{array}
$$

2. Regrouping 1 ten from the tens column left 4 tens. Subtract 4 − 3, and write the result in the tens column of your answer. Check: 19 + 38 = 57.

$$
\begin{array}{r}
4\ 17 \\
\cancel{57} \\
-\ 38 \\
\hline
\mathbf{19}
\end{array}
$$

Sue is **19 years older** than Kathy.

Key Ideas

- Add when combining amounts and subtract when finding the difference.
- Align place-value columns when adding or subtracting.
- Always look to the next place-value column first to regroup.

GED TIP

Another way to check answers is to round the numbers in a problem and find an appropriate answer.

Example 3: Find the difference between 205 and 67.

1. Subtract. Start with the ones column. Since 5 is less than the number being subtracted (7), regroup. Since there are 0 tens in the tens column, regroup 1 hundred from the hundreds column. From 10 tens, regroup 1 ten to the one column. Now subtract $15 - 7$ in the ones column.

$$\begin{array}{r} 9 \\ 1\ \cancel{10}\ 15 \\ 2\cancel{0}\cancel{5} \\ -\ \ 6\ 7 \\ \hline 8 \end{array}$$

2. Regrouping 1 ten from the tens column left 9 tens. Subtract $9 - 6$, and write the result in the tens column of your answer.

$$\begin{array}{r} 9 \\ 1\ \cancel{10}\ 15 \\ 2\cancel{0}\cancel{5} \\ -\ \ 6\ 7 \\ \hline 3\ 8 \end{array}$$

3. Subtract the hundreds column: $1 - 0$. Check: $138 + 67 = 205$.

$$\begin{array}{r} 9 \\ 1\ \cancel{10}\ 15 \\ 2\cancel{0}\cancel{5} \\ -\ \ 6\ 7 \\ \hline 1\ 3\ 8 \end{array}$$

WHOLE NUMBER ▸ PRACTICE 2.1

A. Solve.

1. 54
  $+ 23$

2. 46
  $+ 54$

3. 73
  $- 21$

4. 55
  $- 19$

5. 105
  $+ 85$

6. 2386
  $+ 1692$

7. 100
  $- 57$

8. 2500
  $- 383$

B. Rewrite the problems in columns before solving.

9. $20 + 12 + 33 =$

10. $245 - 131 =$

11. $30 + 75 + 75 =$

12. $378 - 85 =$

13. $144 + 238 + 101 =$

14. $545 - 89 =$

15. $2095 + 324 =$

16. $1250 - 350 =$

17. $10,326 + 982 =$

18. $15,890 - 705 =$

19. $108,755 + 22,442 =$

20. $44,789 - 13,890 =$

C. Choose the <u>one best answer</u> to each question.

21. What is the total weight of the boxes below?

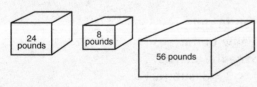

(1) 24
(2) 78
(3) 88
(4) 150
(5) 160

22. Celia's share for lunch is $7. If she pays with a $20 bill, how much change should she get?

(1) $3
(2) $7
(3) $13
(4) $20
(5) $27

Answers and explanations begin on page 663.

Multiplication and Division

You **multiply** to combine the same amount multiple times. For example, instead of adding 24 + 24 + 24, you could multiply 24 by 3. If a problem asks you to find the **product** of two or more numbers, you should multiply.

Example 4: Find the product of 24 and 63.

1. Align place values as you rewrite the problem in a column. Multiply the ones place of the top number by the ones place of the bottom number: $4 \times 3 = 12$. Write the 2 in the ones place in the first partial product. Regroup the 1 ten.

$$\begin{array}{r} 1 \\ 24 \\ \times\ 63 \\ \hline 2 \end{array}$$

2. Multiply the tens place in the top number by 3: $2 \times 3 = 6$. Then add the regrouped amount: $6 + 1 = 7$. Write the 7 in the tens place in the partial product.

$$\begin{array}{r} 1 \\ 24 \\ \times\ 63 \\ \hline 72 \end{array}$$

3. Now multiply by the tens place of 63. Write a **placeholder** 0 in the ones place in the second partial product, since you're really multiplying by 60. Then multiply the top number by 6: $4 \times 6 = 24$. Write 4 in the partial product and regroup the 2. Multiply $2 \times 6 = 12$. Add the regrouped 2: $12 + 2 = 14$.

$$\begin{array}{r} 1 \\ 24 \\ \times\ 63 \\ \hline 72 \\ 1440 \\ \hline \mathbf{1512} \end{array}$$

4. Add the partial products to find the total product: $72 + 1440 = 1512$.

To **divide** means to find how many equal parts an amount can be divided into. The amount being divided is called the **dividend.** The number you are dividing by is the **divisor,** and the answer to a division problem is the **quotient.**

Example 5: At a garage sale, 3 children sold their old toys for a total of $54. If they share the money equally, how much money should each child receive?

1. Divide the total amount ($54) by the number of ways the money is to be split (3). Work from left to right. How many times does 3 go into 5? Write the answer 1 directly above the 5 in the dividend. Since $3 \times 1 = 3$, subtract $5 - 3 = 2$.

$$\begin{array}{r} 1 \\ 3\overline{)\$54} \\ -\ 3 \\ \hline 2 \end{array}$$

2. Continue dividing. Bring down the 4 from the ones place in the dividend. How many times does 3 go into 24? Write the answer 8 directly above the 4 in the dividend. Since $3 \times 8 = 24$, subtract $24 - 24 = 0$.

$$\begin{array}{r} \mathbf{18} \\ 3\overline{)\$54} \\ -\ 3 \\ \hline 24 \\ -\ 24 \\ \hline 0 \end{array}$$

Example 6: Divide $1006 \div 4$.

1. Divide the total amount (1006) by 4. Work from left to right. Since 4 doesn't divide into 1, use the next place value in the dividend. How many times does 4 go into 10? Write the answer 2 directly above the first 0 in the dividend. Since $4 \times 2 = 8$, subtract $10 - 8 = 2$.

$$\begin{array}{r} 2 \\ 4\overline{)1006} \\ -\ 8 \\ \hline 2 \end{array}$$

2. Continue dividing. Bring down the 0 from the tens place in the dividend. How many times does 4 go into 20? Write the answer 5 directly above the second 0 in the dividend. Bring down the 6 from the ones place in the dividend. How many times does 4 go into 6? Write the answer 1 above the 6 in the dividend. Since $4 \times 1 = 4$, subtract $6 - 4 = 2$. Write the **remainder** of 2 as part of the quotient.

$$
\begin{array}{r}
251\ \text{r2} \\
4\overline{)1006} \\
-8 \\
\hline
20 \\
-20 \\
\hline
06 \\
-4 \\
\hline
2
\end{array}
$$

By reviewing and memorizing the multiplication tables, you can save yourself precious time on the GED Math Test.

WHOLE NUMBER ▸ PRACTICE 2.2

A. Solve.

1. 121
    $\times\ 4$

2. 250
    $\times\ 4$

3. 342
    $\times\ 8$

4. $5\overline{)65}$

5. $7\overline{)735}$

6. $9\overline{)189}$

7.   45
    $\times\ 30$

8.   105
    $\times\ 25$

9.   211
    $\times\ 16$

10. $10\overline{)280}$

11. $15\overline{)225}$

12. $19\overline{)114}$

B. Solve. If multiplying more than two numbers, find the product of two numbers before multiplying by the next number, and so on.

13. $50 \times 5 =$

14. $179 \div 4 =$

15. $5 \times 6 \times 10 =$

16. $1004 \div 5 =$

17. $25 \times 3 \times 2 =$

18. $7452 \times 9 =$

19. $10,760 \div 20 =$

20. $12 \times 8 \times 4 =$

21. $144,140 \div 12 =$

C. Choose the <u>one best answer</u> to each question.

22. A fruit juice container holds 16 servings. If the serving size is 6 ounces, how many ounces does the container hold in all?

    (1)   10
    (2)   22
    (3)   76
    (4)   96
    (5) 102

23. A cashier has fifteen \$5 bills. How much does he have in \$5 bills?

    (1)   \$3
    (2)   \$15
    (3)   \$25
    (4)   \$75
    (5) \$150

24. How many 2-foot boards can be cut from the board shown below?

|————— 12 ft —————|

    (1)   6
    (2) 10
    (3) 12
    (4) 14
    (5) 24

Answers and explanations begin on page 663.

MATH BASICS

Distance and Cost Formulas

The Distance Formula

When a relationship remains constant, you can use a **formula** to show how the different parts relate to each other. For example, distance is a product of the rate at which something travels and the amount of travel time. Therefore, we can use the following formula:

$$\text{distance} = \text{rate} \times \text{time, or } d = rt$$

Notice that letters, or **variables,** can be used to represent the different parts of a formula. A formula allows you to substitute known values for certain variables and solve for the unknown variable.

Example 1: How many miles can you travel if you drive at an average speed of 55 miles per hour for 3 hours?

1. You know the rate (55 miles per hour) and the time (3 hours). Substitute the values in the distance formula.

$$d = rt$$
$$\text{distance} = 55 \times 3$$

2. Multiply to find the distance.

$$55 \times 3 = \textbf{165 miles}$$

The Cost Formula

Another helpful formula is the cost formula. It expresses the relationship between cost, the number of units, and rate (price per unit). Note: The word *per* means for every one unit. The cost formula can be written as:

$$\text{total cost} = (\text{number of units}) \times (\text{price per unit}), \text{ or } c = nr$$

Example 2: At a bakery a package of frosted cookies is priced at $3 per package. If a teacher treats her class by buying 4 packages, how much would the cookies cost before tax?

1. You know the number of units (4 packages) and the price per unit ($3 per package). Substitute the values in the cost formula.

$$c = nr$$
$$\text{total cost} = 4 \times \$3$$

2. Multiply to find the total cost.

$$4 \times \$3 = \textbf{\$12}$$

If you know any two of the three variables in a formula, you can solve for the third variable.

Example 3: Max bought a set of 4 floor mats for $44. How much is the price per floor mat?

1. You know the total cost ($44) and the number of units (4 floor mats). Rewrite the formula to solve for the price per unit (r).

$$c = nr$$
$$\frac{c}{n} = r$$

2. Substitute the known values in the cost formula. Divide to find the price per unit.

$$\frac{\$44}{4} = \textbf{\$11}$$

Key Ideas

- The following all indicate multiplication:

  $n \times r \quad nr \quad n(r) \quad n \cdot r$
- The following indicate division:

  $c \div n \quad \frac{c}{n} \quad n\overline{)c}$

- A formula can be rewritten to solve for each of its variables.

  $c = nr \quad \frac{c}{n} = r \quad \frac{c}{r} = n$

  $d = rt \quad \frac{d}{r} = t \quad \frac{d}{t} = r$

GED TIP

Substitute all of the values for variables back into a formula to check your answer.

A. Each problem below includes two of the three variables from either the distance formula or the cost formula. Write the missing variable you need to solve for. Then decide which of the following formula variations you would use in each situation. The first one is done for you.

$$c = nr \qquad \frac{c}{n} = r \qquad \frac{c}{r} = n \qquad d = rt \qquad \frac{d}{r} = t \qquad \frac{d}{t} = r$$

1. Given: distance and time

    Solve for: rate

    Formula: $\frac{d}{t} = r$

2. Given: rate and time

    Solve for: _____

    Formula: _____

3. Given: distance and rate

    Solve for: _____

    Formula: _____

4. Given: cost and number of units

    Solve for: _____

    Formula: _____

5. Given: number of units and price per unit

    Solve for: _____

    Formula: _____

6. Given: cost and price per unit

    Solve for: _____

    Formula: _____

B. Use the formulas provided in part A above to help you set up the problems. Solve for the unknown variable.

7. Find the total cost of 4 flats of plants at $12 each.

8. Find the total cost of 12 boxes of cookies if each box costs $3.

9. If 4 tires cost $320, how much does a single tire cost?

10. How many tickets would you get for $25 if raffle tickets cost $5 apiece?

11. If you paid $20 for 10 bus transfer tickets, how much did you pay per ticket?

12. Find the distance traveled by a car averaging 60 miles per hour for 3 hours.

13. Find the distance traveled by a train averaging 50 miles per hour for 4 hours.

14. How long does it take for a bus to travel 25 miles at an average rate of 25 miles per hour?

15. If a train travels 270 miles in 3 hours, what is the train's speed?

16. How long does it take to complete a delivery route of 75 miles at a rate of 25 miles per hour?

C. Choose the <u>one best answer</u> to each question.

17. A company sold a total of $640 in gift boxes. If the gift boxes cost $20 apiece, how many gift boxes did the company sell?

    (1) 32
    (2) 320
    (3) 620
    (4) 660
    (5) 1280

18. A truck driver traveled 275 miles in 5 hours. What was his average speed in miles per hour?

    (1) 1375
    (2) 280
    (3) 270
    (4)   60
    (5)   55

Answers and explanations begin on page 664.

MATH BASICS

Calculators on the GED

First Function Keys

Calculator use is allowed on Part I of the GED Math Test. The calculator distributed at the testing centers is the *Casio fx-260*. This is a scientific calculator that is programmed with the order of operations (see page 362). Below is an introduction to some of the calculator keys that you will be most likely to use on the GED Math Test. You should buy this calculator or another scientific calculator while you study for the test. While the instruction below applies to the *Casio fx-260*, any scientific calculator will have similar functions.

Key Ideas

- Purchase a scientific calculator to prepare for the GED Math Test.
- Practice the operations shown in this book even if your calculator uses slightly different keys. You will be able to practice with the *Casio fx-260* at the testing center.
- Always clear the calculator before starting a new problem.

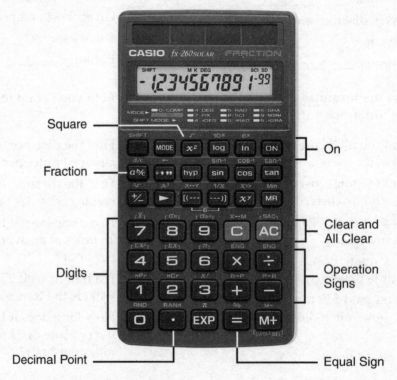

SOURCE: Courtesy of Casio, Inc.

GED TIP

If you make a mistake when entering a number, press the key that will clear only the last entry.

Use a calculator when it will save you time or improve accuracy. For example, use the calculator when numbers are large or the calculation is complicated.

Example 1: Add 63 + 97 + 58 + 32 + 81.

1. Always clear a calculator before starting a new computation. On the *Casio*, use the AC key. $\boxed{AC}$
2. Enter each number followed by the plus sign. $63\boxed{+}97\boxed{+}58\boxed{+}32\boxed{+}81$
3. Press the equal sign to find the total. $\boxed{=}\boxed{\quad 331.}$

The total **331** will appear in the display.

Example 2: Find the difference between 15,789 and 9,332.

1. Always clear a calculator before starting a new computation.   AC

2. Enter the greater number first, followed by the minus sign.   15789 $\boxed{-}$

3. Enter the number being subtracted.   9332

4. Press the equals key to find the total. $\boxed{=}$ 6457.

The answer **6457** will appear in the display.

Example 3: Find the product of 309 and 68.

1. Always clear a calculator before starting a new computation.   AC

2. Enter the first number, followed by the multiplication sign.   309 $\boxed{\times}$

3. Enter the next number.   68

4. Press the equals key to find the product. $\boxed{=}$ 21012.

The answer **21012** will appear in the display.

Example 4: Divide 12,456 by 12.

1. Always clear a calculator before starting a new computation.   AC

2. Always enter the number to be divided first.   12456

3. Enter the division sign and the number you are dividing by. $\boxed{\div}$ 12

4. Press the equals key to find the quotient. $\boxed{=}$ 1038.

The answer **1038** will appear in the display.

WHOLE NUMBER ▸ PRACTICE 4.1

A. Practice solving the following problems on your calculator.

1. $19 + 26 + 85 + 23 =$ 4. $2568 \div 107 =$ 7. $209 \times 56 =$

2. $2579 - 1392 =$ 5. $12,356 + 14,728 =$ 8. $972 \div 18 =$

3. $4 \times 28 \times 7 =$ 6. $107,899 - 93,457 =$ 9. $20,540 \div 13 =$

B. Choose the one correct answer to each question.

10. Dan bought a used car with 16,741 miles on it. If the car now has 42,920 miles on it, how many miles has Dan put on the car?

    (1) 16,741
    (2) 26,179
    (3) 41,246
    (4) 42,920
    (5) 59,661

11. A shipment of 20 computers arrived at a warehouse. If each computer is valued at $995, what is the total value of the shipment?

    (1) $995
    (2) $1,015
    (3) $1,990
    (4) $1,900
    (5) $19,900

Answers and explanations begin on page 664.

Second Function Keys

To access some of the keys on the *Casio fx-260,* you need to press the shift key in the upper left corner of the keypad. This will activate the function shown in yellow above the corresponding key. Highlighted below are the second function keys that you will be most likely to use on the GED Math Test. If you do not currently have the *Casio fx-260,* find out how your calculator finds square roots and percents.

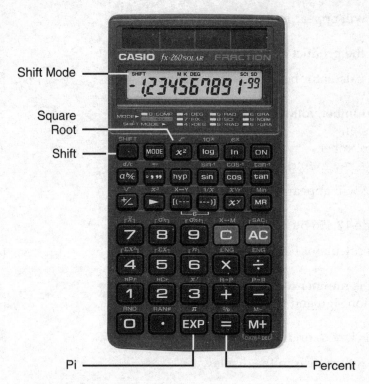

Shift Mode

Square Root

Shift

Pi

Percent

SOURCE: Courtesy of Casio, Inc.

Example 5: Find the square root of 169.

1. Always clear a calculator before starting a new computation. $\boxed{\text{AC}}$
2. Enter the number you want to find the square root of. 169
3. Press the shift key. Note that the word *SHIFT* now appears in the upper left of the display. $\boxed{\text{SHIFT}}$
4. Press the x^2 key, which activates the square root key shown in yellow above the x^2 key on the calculator. $\boxed{\sqrt{}}$

The answer **13** will appear in the display.

Notice that it was not necessary to press the equals key after the square root key. For more information about square roots, see page 458.

Points to remember:

- Use the shift key to help you find square roots and percents on the *Casio fx-260* calculator.

- If you do not have the *Casio fx-260,* see how your calculator finds square roots and percents.

- Always clear the display before beginning a new problem.

Example 6: Find the part if you are given the percent and the whole. Find 10 percent of 500.

1. Always clear a calculator before starting a new computation.
2. Enter the number you want to find the percent of.   500
3. Press the multiplication sign.
4. Enter the percent number.   10
5. Press the shift key, and then press the equals key, which activates the percent key.   SHIFT %

The answer **50** will appear in the display. Ten percent of 500 is 50.

Example 7: Find the percent if you are given the whole and the part. What percent of 240 is 60?

1. Always clear a calculator before starting a new computation.   AC
2. Enter the part.   60
3. Press the division sign.   ÷
4. Enter the whole.   240
5. Press the shift key, and then press the equals key, which activates the percent key.   SHIFT %

The answer **25** will appear in the display. 60 is 25 percent of 240.

For more information about percents, see pages 390–411 .

WHOLE NUMBER ▸ PRACTICE 4.2

A. Practice solving the following problems on your calculator.

1. $\overline{)625}$ =

2. $\overline{)324}$ =

3. $\overline{)1225}$ =

4. Find 20% of 680.

5. Find 10% of 1250.

6. 15 is what percent of 300?

7. Find 5% of 40.

8. Find 30% of 450.

9. 20 is what percent of 400?

B. Choose the <u>one best answer</u> to each question.

10. Tanya paid 20% of $1680 as a down payment. How much was the down payment?

    (1) $20
    (2) $32
    (3) $168
    (4) $336
    (5) $840

11. Aaron received a credit of $48 in interest on $960. What percent of $960 is $48?

    (1)   5%
    (2)   20%
    (3)   48%
    (4) 912%
    (5) 2000%

Answers and explanations begin on page 664.

Filling in the Standard Grid

The GED Math Test features question formats other than multiple choice. One such format is the **standard grid.** After solving some problems, you will be asked to fill in the circles on a standard grid provided on the GED Math Test answer sheet.

The standard grid can be used for answers that are in whole number, decimal, or fraction form. For further information on using standard grids with decimals and fractions, refer to page 382. Below are examples of using standard grids with whole number answers.

Example 1: Mario drove 280 miles on Monday, 320 miles on Tuesday, and 75 miles on Wednesday. How many total miles did he drive for the 3 days?

1. Decide which operation to use. Since you need to find a total amount, add the three values.
$280 + 320 + 75 = 675$

2. Write your answer in the blank boxes provided at the top of the standard grid.

3. Darken in the matching circle in the column under each digit in your answer.

When filling in a standard grid, you can start your answer anywhere as long as the complete answer fits in the grid.

Example 2: Angela worked 40 hours every week for 51 weeks. How many hours did she work in all?

1. Decide which operation to use. Since you need to find the total of the same amount multiple times, multiply.
$40 \times 51 = 2040$

2. Write your answer in the blank boxes provided at the top of the grid.

3. Darken in the matching circle in the column under each digit in your answer.

Key Ideas

- Some questions on the GED Math Test require you to generate an answer and fill in a standard grid.

- Always write your answer at the top of the grid before filling in the circles.

- Fill in only one circle per column. Columns that you do not need should be left blank.

GED TIP

When filling in your answers in a standard grid, fill in the appropriate circles carefully. If you change an answer, erase the first choice completely.

---

1. A veterinary clinic treated 435 cats over a 3-month period. At this rate, how many cats will the clinic treat in a 12-month period?

   Mark your answer in the circles in the grid.

2. A quick oil change shop recommends changing a car's oil and filter every 3,500 miles. If a car is driven 35,000 miles, how many times should the oil and filter have been changed?

   Mark your answer in the circles in the grid.

3. Attendance at a local play was 348 Friday night, 366 Saturday night, and 280 Sunday afternoon. What was the total attendance for the 3 days?

   Mark your answer in the circles in the grid.

4. A restaurant sells cookies 3 for $1. How many cookies could you buy for $5?

   Mark your answer in the circles in the grid.

5. How many sheets of paper would 4 copies of a 617-page document use?

   Mark your answer in the circles in the grid.

6. How many months would it take to pay back $1050 at $50 per month?

   Mark your answer in the circles in the grid.

1.

	/	/	/	
.	.	.	.	.
0	0	0	0	0
1	1	1	1	1
2	2	2	2	2
3	3	3	3	3
4	4	4	4	4
5	5	5	5	5
6	6	6	6	6
7	7	7	7	7
8	8	8	8	8
9	9	9	9	9

2.

	/	/	/	
.	.	.	.	.
0	0	0	0	0
1	1	1	1	1
2	2	2	2	2
3	3	3	3	3
4	4	4	4	4
5	5	5	5	5
6	6	6	6	6
7	7	7	7	7
8	8	8	8	8
9	9	9	9	9

3.

/	/	/		
.	.	.	.	.
0	0	0	0	0
1	1	1	1	1
2	2	2	2	2
3	3	3	3	3
4	4	4	4	4
5	5	5	5	5
6	6	6	6	6
7	7	7	7	7
8	8	8	8	8
9	9	9	9	9

4.

/	/	/		
.	.	.	.	.
0	0	0	0	0
1	1	1	1	1
2	2	2	2	2
3	3	3	3	3
4	4	4	4	4
5	5	5	5	5
6	6	6	6	6
7	7	7	7	7
8	8	8	8	8
9	9	9	9	9

5.

	/	/	/	
.	.	.	.	.
0	0	0	0	0
1	1	1	1	1
2	2	2	2	2
3	3	3	3	3
4	4	4	4	4
5	5	5	5	5
6	6	6	6	6
7	7	7	7	7
8	8	8	8	8
9	9	9	9	9

6.

	/	/	/	
.	.	.	.	.
0	0	0	0	0
1	1	1	1	1
2	2	2	2	2
3	3	3	3	3
4	4	4	4	4
5	5	5	5	5
6	6	6	6	6
7	7	7	7	7
8	8	8	8	8
9	9	9	9	9

Answers and explanations begin on page 664.

MATH BASICS

Problem Solving: Estimation

Estimation and Problem Solving

Not every problem on the GED requires an exact calculation. Read problems carefully to determine whether or not your answer needs to be exact. When you can estimate, use techniques like those shown below.

Example 1: Approximately how many people attended the 3-game series if attendance was 33,541, 35,045, and 34,092?

1. The problem asks "approximately" how many people; therefore, you can estimate. Notice that all three amounts are close to 35,000.

$33,541 \approx 35,000$
$35,045 \approx 35,000$
$34,092 \approx 35,000$

2. Multiply 35,000 by 3 to find the approximate attendance for the 3-game series.

$35,000 \times 3 = \textbf{105,000}$

Example 2: If Ambrose wanted to save enough money to make a $1159 purchase in a year's time, about how much should he put away per month?

1. The problem asks "about" how much; therefore, you can estimate. Divide to find how many equal parts are in one amount. Since 1 year = 12 months, the numbers you need to solve the problem are 12 and $1159.

1 year = 12 months
$1159 \approx \$1200$

2. Round one or both of the numbers so that they are easy to divide. Round $1159 to $1200. Then divide.

$\$1200 \div 12 = \textbf{\$100 per month}$

Reasonable Answers and Estimation

Estimation can also be used to help you narrow down answer choices in multiple-choice problems or to check your calculations.

Example 3: Souvenir sales are $389, $205, and $276 at each of three booths. What is the total amount in sales?

(1) $92   (4) $870
(2) $615   (5) $2621
(3) $828

Strategy 1: You can estimate an answer by rounding values to the nearest hundred. That eliminates options (1), (2), and (5). 900 is closest to option **(4) $870**.

$\$400 + \$200 + \$300 = \$900$

Strategy 2: You can calculate an answer and then check it against an estimate to see if your answer makes sense. The solution **(4) $870** is close to an estimate of $900.

$\$389 + \$205 + \$276 = \textbf{\$870}$

WHOLE NUMBER ▸ PRACTICE 6

A. Round each number below to the two highest place values. The first is done for you.

1. 259 rounds to 300 and 260.

2. 4698 rounds to _____ and _____ .

3. 11,580 rounds to _____ and _____ .

4. 327 rounds to _____ and _____ .

5. 6204 rounds to _____ and _____ .

6. 23,478 rounds to _____ and _____ .

B. Round one or both of the following numbers in each problem to create a compatible pair for easy division. The first one is done for you. (There may be more than one correct pair.)

7. 35 ÷ 13

   Compatible pair: 36 ÷ 12 or 30 ÷ 10 or 39 ÷ 13

8. 50 ÷ 8

   Compatible pair:

9. 42 ÷ 15

   Compatible pair:

10. 105 ÷ 22

    Compatible pair:

11. 364 ÷ 4

    Compatible pair:

12. 450 ÷ 8

    Compatible pair:

C. Choose the <u>one best answer</u> to each question.

13. To get to work, Marcus drives 7 minutes to the train station, rides the train for 65 minutes, and then walks 19 minutes to the office. <u>About</u> how many minutes does it take Marcus to get to work?

    (1) 20
    (2) 70
    (3) 90
    (4) 140
    (5) 200

14. A shipment of 21 crates like the one shown below is delivered. <u>Approximately</u> how many pounds did workers unload?

    (1) 20
    (2) 60
    (3) 80
    (4) 120
    (5) 1200

15. A cheese shop receives a 78-ounce block of cheese. <u>About</u> how many ounces would each piece weigh if it were packaged into 10 separate pieces?

    (1)   8
    (2) 70
    (3) 80
    (4) 90
    (5) 800

16. If you drove 324 miles on 11 gallons of gasoline, <u>about</u> how many miles per gallon did the car get? (*Hint:* Divide the miles by the number of gallons.)

    (1) 3200
    (2) 330
    (3) 300
    (4)   30
    (5)   10

Answers and explanations begin on page 664.

MATH BASICS

Problem Solving: Set-Up Problems

Order of Operations

A set of rules called the **order of operations** exists to ensure that there is only one correct answer when more than one operation is used in a math solution. Perform operations in the order in which they are listed below, working from left to right.

Key Ideas

- Always apply the order of operations when finding a solution.
- Use this order:
  - Grouping symbols
  - Multiplication and division
  - Addition and subtraction
- Use your knowledge of formulas to recognize different variations of the same formula.

Order of Operations

Step 1. Perform any operations within grouping symbols such as parentheses OR over or under a fraction (division) bar.

Step 2. Perform multiplication or division, working from left to right.

Step 3. Perform addition or subtraction, working from left to right.

Example 1: Solve $3 + 4 \times 2$.

1. Since there are no grouping symbols, perform any multiplication or division first.	$3 + 4 \times 2$
2. Perform any addition or subtraction.	$3 + 8 = \mathbf{11}$

Example 2: Solve $(3 + 4) \times 2$.

1. Perform any operations within parentheses.	$(3 + 4) \times 2$
2. Perform any multiplication or division.	$7 \times 2 = \mathbf{14}$

Example 3: Solve $\dfrac{4 \times 5}{2(4 + 1)}$.

1. Perform any operations within parentheses.	$\dfrac{4 \times 5}{2(4 + 1)}$
2. Perform any multiplication or division above and below the fraction, or division, bar.	$\dfrac{4 \times 5}{2(5)}$
3. Think of the fraction bar as a division sign. Divide the top number (20) by the bottom number (10).	$\dfrac{20}{10} = \mathbf{2}$

GED TIP

If at first you don't see your answer in the options provided, try rewriting your answer until it matches one of the set-up solutions provided.

Set-Up Problems

Knowing and recognizing how to solve a problem is important to your success on the GED Math Test. You will encounter questions that ask you to choose the option that shows the correct way to solve the problem.

Example 4: Marissa drove 185 miles in 3 hours. Which of the following could be used to determine her average rate of speed?

(1) $185 + 3$

(2) $185 - 3$

(3) 3×185

(4) $\dfrac{185}{3}$

(5) $\dfrac{3}{185}$

Option (4) is correct. To find the rate, divide the distance by the time.

A. Follow the order of operations to solve.

1. $6 + 20 \times 2 =$
2. $18 - 6 + 1 =$
3. $4 + 5 \times 7 =$
4. $48 \div 8 + 4 =$
5. $3(24 - 19) =$
6. $(34 - 24)(2 + 5) =$
7. $9 + 6/3 =$
8. $6 \times 10 \times 4 \div 8 =$

9. $\dfrac{2(2 + 8)}{1 + 4} =$

10. $\dfrac{105 - 55}{30 - 5} =$

11. $\dfrac{8 \times 9}{3 \times 4} =$

12. $\dfrac{4(2 + 5)}{2(3 + 4)} =$

B. Choose the _one best answer_ to each question.

13. It is recommended that a person drink six 8-ounce glasses of water a day. Which expression shows how many ounces of water a person should drink over a 7-day period?

    (1) $6 + 8 + 7$
    (2) $6 \times 8 \div 7$
    (3) $6 \times 8 \times 7$
    (4) $8 \times 7 \div 6$
    (5) $8 \times 7 - 6$

14. Driving to and from work, Ahmed pays a $3 toll twice a day, 5 days a week. Which expression shows how much he has to pay in tolls in 1 week?

    (1) $\$3 \times 5$
    (2) $\$3 \times 2$
    (3) $\$3 \times \dfrac{5}{2}$
    (4) $\$3 \times \dfrac{2}{5}$
    (5) $\$3 \times 2 \times 5$

15. Five co-workers bought a bouquet of flowers for $25 and a box of candy for $15 for a co-worker in the hospital. If they divided the cost equally, which expression shows how much each co-worker paid?

    (1) $\$25 + \$15$
    (2) $\$25 + \$15 \div 5$
    (3) $5(\$25 + \$15)$
    (4) $\dfrac{(\$25 + \$15)}{5}$
    (5) $\$25 + \$15 \times 5$

16. Aaron gave $10 toward a dinner bill of $78. If the bill is evenly divided among the remaining 7 people in the group, which expression shows how much each person should pay?

    (1) $\dfrac{\$78 - \$10}{7}$
    (2) $\$78 \div 7$
    (3) $\$78 - \$10 \times 7$
    (4) $\$78 - \$10$
    (5) $\$78 - (\$10 \times 7)$

17. Every day at lunch, Andrea buys a sandwich for $4 and a cup of coffee for $1. Which expression shows how much Andrea spends on lunch over a 5-day period?

    (1) $\$4 + \$1$
    (2) $\$4 \times \$1$
    (3) $\dfrac{\$4 + \$1}{5}$
    (4) $5(\$4) - 5(\$1)$
    (5) $5(\$4 + \$1)$

18. A company offers a discount of $5 off an $85 bill for early payment. If this is a monthly bill, which expression shows how much could be saved yearly by always paying the bill early?

    (1) $12 \times \$5$
    (2) $\$85 - (12 \times \$5)$
    (3) $12 \times \$85$
    (4) $12(\$85 - \$5)$
    (5) $\dfrac{12(\$85)}{5}$

Answers and explanations begin on page 664.

MATH BASICS PRACTICE QUESTIONS
PART I

Directions: Choose the <u>one best answer</u> to each question. You <u>MAY</u> use your calculator.

1. A beverage container holds 12 servings. If the serving size is 8 ounces, how many ounces does the container hold in all?

   (1) 4
   (2) 20
   (3) 32
   (4) 48
   (5) 96

2. Sales at 3 concession stands are $839, $527, and $726. What is the total amount in sales?

   (1) $242
   (2) $1581
   (3) $2092
   (4) $2178
   (5) $2517

3. If you want to cut 24 two-foot braces, how many boards of the length shown below would you need?

   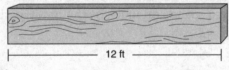
   12 ft

   (1) 4
   (2) 6
   (3) 12
   (4) 24
   (5) Not enough information is given.

4. What is the value of $\sqrt{441}$?

   (1) 11
   (2) 21
   (3) 221
   (4) 441
   (5) 882

5. Angelo bought a used car with 39,451 miles on it. If the car now has 70,040 miles on it, how many miles has Angelo driven the car?

   (1) 30,000
   (2) 30,589
   (3) 39,459
   (4) 70,040
   (5) 109,491

6. If Emory paid 20% of $3280 as a down payment, how much was the down payment?

   (1) $164
   (2) $328
   (3) $656
   (4) $3300
   (5) $6560

7. Inventory shows that a warehouse has 45 printers in stock. If each printer is valued at $125, what is the total value of the printer inventory?

   (1) $5625
   (2) $170
   (3) $80
   (4) $55
   (5) $45

8. Lydia traveled 180 miles in 3 hours. Which of the following expressions shows how far she could drive over a period of 7 hours at the same rate?

   (1) $\dfrac{180}{3}$
   (2) $7 \times 3 \times 180$
   (3) $7\left(\dfrac{180}{3}\right)$
   (4) 180×3
   (5) $7\left(\dfrac{3}{180}\right)$

9. Janelle wants to drive from Danville to Brownsville. If she averages 60 miles per hour, which expression shows how many hours it will take her to drive the distance?

480 miles

Danville   Brownsville

- (1) $480 + 60$
- (2) $480 - 60$
- (3) 480×60
- (4) $\dfrac{480}{60}$
- (5) $\dfrac{60}{480}$

10. A company sold a total of $1440 in gift bears for Valentine's Day. If the gift bears cost $15 apiece, how many gift bears did it sell?

- (1) 15
- (2) 96
- (3) 144
- (4) 1440
- (5) 1455

11. In addition to interest charges, Richard's credit card company charges a $25 late fee for payments made after the payment due date. If he was charged a late fee for 8 different monthly bills, how much could he have saved by paying the bills on time?

- (1) $200
- (2) $96
- (3) $80
- (4) $33
- (5) $25

12. A waiter has seven $5 bills and eighteen $1 bills from tips. In all, how much does he have in tips?

- (1) $5
- (2) $18
- (3) $25
- (4) $35
- (5) $53

13. A car manufacturer recommends an oil and filter change every 3,500 miles. If April took her car in for an oil change at 43,286 miles, what was the odometer reading at her last oil change?

- (1) 50,286
- (2) 46,786
- (3) 43,286
- (4) 39,786
- (5) Not enough information is given.

14. A clinic treated 536 children over a 4-month period. At this rate, how many children did the clinic treat in 1 month?

- (1) 134
- (2) 532
- (3) 536
- (4) 540
- (5) 2144

15. Attendance at a local play was 438 Friday night, 820 Saturday night, and 636 Sunday afternoon. How many more people attended the play on Sunday than on Friday?

Mark your answer in the circles on the grid at the bottom of the page.

16. Raquel has 4 payments left on her car. If each payment is $268, how much does she still owe on her car?

Mark your answer in the circles on the grid at the bottom of the page.

15.

⊘	⊘	⊘	
·	·	·	·	·
⓪	⓪	⓪	⓪	⓪
①	①	①	①	①
②	②	②	②	②
③	③	③	③	③
④	④	④	④	④
⑤	⑤	⑤	⑤	⑤
⑥	⑥	⑥	⑥	⑥
⑦	⑦	⑦	⑦	⑦
⑧	⑧	⑧	⑧	⑧
⑨	⑨	⑨	⑨	⑨

16.

⊘	⊘	⊘	
·	·	·	·	·
⓪	⓪	⓪	⓪	⓪
①	①	①	①	①
②	②	②	②	②
③	③	③	③	③
④	④	④	④	④
⑤	⑤	⑤	⑤	⑤
⑥	⑥	⑥	⑥	⑥
⑦	⑦	⑦	⑦	⑦
⑧	⑧	⑧	⑧	⑧
⑨	⑨	⑨	⑨	⑨

PART II

Directions: Choose the <u>one best answer</u> to each question. You <u>MAY NOT</u> use your calculator for these questions.

17. In what order should items weighing 51 pounds, 40 pounds, 48 pounds, and 44 pounds be stacked if you want them in order from <u>heaviest to lightest</u>?

    (1) 51, 44, 40, 48
    (2) 40, 44, 48, 51
    (3) 51, 48, 44, 40
    (4) 48, 44, 40, 51
    (5) 51, 40, 44, 48

18. Which of the following correctly shows 2,354,769 rounded to the nearest ten thousand?

    (1) 2,400,000
    (2) 2,355,000
    (3) 2,354,800
    (4) 2,350,000
    (5) 2,000,000

19. What is the total weight in pounds of the packages below?

    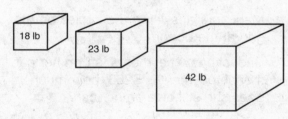

    (1) 83
    (2) 65
    (3) 60
    (4) 42
    (5) 41

20. Jason paid a $14 dinner bill with a $20 bill. How much change should he receive?

    (1) $6
    (2) $7
    (3) $14
    (4) $20
    (5) $34

21. Maria spent 8 minutes installing a new showerhead, 33 minutes rodding out a drain, and 18 minutes fixing a leaking faucet. <u>About</u> how many minutes did it take Maria to complete the plumbing job?

    (1) 90
    (2) 60
    (3) 30
    (4) 20
    (5) 10

22. Carla drove 250 miles in 4 hours. Which of the following could be used to determine her average rate of speed?

    (1) $\dfrac{4}{250}$
    (2) 250 + 4
    (3) 250 − 4
    (4) $\dfrac{250}{4}$
    (5) 4 × 250

23. A bulk bag of nuts weighs 144 ounces. If the nuts are packaged in smaller 8-ounce bags, how many bags will there be?

    (1) 8
    (2) 12
    (3) 18
    (4) 136
    (5) 152

24. If you drove 299 miles on 9 gallons of gasoline, <u>about</u> how many miles per gallon did the car get?

    (1) 10
    (2) 30
    (3) 270
    (4) 300
    (5) 320

25. A shipment of 33 crates like the one shown below is delivered. <u>Approximately</u> how many pounds did workers unload?

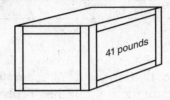

41 pounds

(1)   30
(2)   40
(3)   120
(4)   1200
(5)   2000

26. Four friends bought a birthday cake for $21 and balloons for $15. If they divided the cost equally, how much did each friend pay toward the birthday party?

(1) $4
(2) $5
(3) $9
(4) $20
(5) $36

27. David paid $8 toward a dinner bill of $84. If the bill is divided equally among the remaining 9 people in the group, which of the following expressions shows how much each person should pay?

(1) $84 − $8 − 9

(2)   9 × $8

(3) $\dfrac{\$84}{9}$

(4) $\dfrac{\$84 - \$8}{9}$

(5) $84 − ($8 × 9)

28. A driver traveled 4 hours at an average rate of 65 miles per hour. How many miles did the person drive?

(1)   16
(2)   61
(3)   65
(4)   69
(5)   260

29. Using the following information, how much would a large pizza with 3 toppings cost?

| Large 1-Topping Pizza for $14 |
| $2 for Each Additional Topping |

(1) $20
(2) $18
(3) $16
(4) $14
(5) $10

30. Bagels are 2 for $1. How many bagels could you buy for $7?

(1)   3
(2)   7
(3)   10
(4)   14
(5)   15

31. How many months would it take to pay back $1800 at $75 per month?

Mark your answer in the circles on the grid at the bottom of the page.

32. How many 45-page documents would a binder hold if its maximum capacity is 630 sheets of paper?

Mark your answer in the circles on the grid at the bottom of the page.

31.

32.

Answers and explanations begin on page 664.

DECIMALS AND FRACTIONS

Decimal Basics

The Decimal System

Decimals are numbers that use place value to show amounts less than 1. You already use decimals when working with money. For example, in the amount $10.25, you know that the digits to the right of the **decimal point** represent cents, or hundredths of a dollar.

The first four decimal place values are labeled on the chart below.

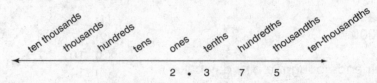

Key Ideas

- The decimal point separates the whole number from the decimal part.
- To round decimals, use the same rules as with rounding whole numbers.
- Adding zeros to the right of the last digit after the decimal does not change the number's value.

The number 2.375 is shown on the chart. Read *and* in place of the decimal point. After reading the decimal part, say the place value of the last decimal digit. This number would be read "two *and* three hundred seventy-five *thousandths*."

Rounding

Round decimals the same way you round whole numbers.

Example 1: A calculator display reads 3.62835. Round to the hundredths place.

1. Look at the digit to the right of the hundredths place.   3.62⬚8⬚35

2. If the digit to the right is 5 or greater, round up. If the digit is less than 5, don't change the number. Then drop all digits to the right of the place you are rounding to.

    Since 8 is greater than 5, round up. 3.62835 rounds to **3.63**

GED TIP

The GED Math Test may show a zero written before the decimal point. The zero does not change the value of the number. Example: 0.75 = .75

Comparing and Ordering

Comparing decimals is similar to comparing whole numbers.

Example 2: Matt ran the 400-meter race in 45.8 seconds. Alonzo ran the same race in 45.66 seconds. Which runner had the faster time?

1. Line up the decimal points. Add a zero at the **end** of 45.8 so that both times have the same number of digits after the decimal.   45.**80**   45.66

2. Compare the decimal parts of the numbers as though they were whole numbers. **Alonzo's time was faster.**   80 is greater than 66, so 45.8 is greater than 45.66

When you compare more than two numbers, it is helpful to compare one place-value column at a time, working from left to right.

Example 3: Arrange the numbers 0.85, 1.8, 0.8, and 0.819 in order from greatest to least.

1. Write the numbers in a column, lining up the decimal points. Add zeros so that the numbers have the same number of decimal places.

```
0.850
1.800
0.800
0.819
```

2. Compare the digits, working from left to right. Only 1.8 has a whole number part, so it is greatest. The remaining numbers each have 8 in the tenths column. Looking at the hundredths column, 0.85 is next, followed by 0.819. The least number is 0.8.

In order: **1.8**
0.85
0.819
0.8

DECIMALS AND FRACTIONS ▸ PRACTICE 1

A. Round these numbers as directed.

1. Round 3.75 to the tenths place.
2. Round 5.908 to the ones place.
3. A calculator display reads 0.4285714. Round to the nearest hundredth.
4. Round 0.66667 to the nearest thousandth.
5. Round 8.125 to the nearest tenth.
6. A calculator display reads 2.7142857. Round to the nearest thousandth.

B. In each of the following pairs, which number is greater?

7. 0.45 or 0.449
8. 0.008 or 0.08
9. 4.68 or 4.086
10. 0.75 or 1.85
11. 1.0275 or 1.029
12. 0.14 or 0.104

C. Write these numbers in order from <u>least to greatest.</u>

13. 5.6   5.08   5.8   5.802
14. 0.1136   0.12   0.2   0.115
15. 14.005   4.52   4.8   4.667
16. 0.8023   0.8   0.803   0.823

D. Choose the <u>one best answer</u> to each question.

17. In a circuit board assembly, the weights of three parts are 0.572 gram, 0.0785 gram, and 0.6 gram. Which of the following lists the weights in order from <u>greatest to least?</u>

    (1) 0.0785 g, 0.572 g, 0.6 g
    (2) 0.572 g, 0.0785 g, 0.6 g
    (3) 0.6 g, 0.0785 g, 0.572 g
    (4) 0.6 g, 0.572 g, 0.0785 g
    (5) 0.572 g, 0.6 g, 0.0785 g

18. Which of the following correctly shows 1.3815 rounded to the nearest hundredth?

    (1) 1.4
    (2) 1.39
    (3) 1.382
    (4) 1.381
    (5) 1.38

Answers and explanations begin on page 665.

DECIMALS AND FRACTIONS

Decimal Operations

Addition and Subtraction

Adding decimals is much like adding whole numbers. The trick is to make sure you have lined up the place-value columns correctly. You can do this by writing the numbers in a column and carefully lining up the decimal points.

Example 1: Add 0.37 + 13.5 + 2.638.

1. Write the numbers in a column, lining up the decimal points.

2. You may add placeholder zeros so that the decimals have the same number of decimal places.

3. Add. Start on the right and add each column. Regroup, or carry, as you would with whole numbers.

4. Place the decimal point in the answer directly below the decimal points in the problem.

$$\begin{array}{r} 0.370 \\ 13.500 \\ + 2.638 \end{array}$$

$$\begin{array}{r} \scriptstyle 1\ 1 \\ 0.370 \\ 13.500 \\ + 2.638 \\ \hline \mathbf{16.508} \end{array}$$

To subtract decimals, write the numbers in a column with the greater number on top. Make sure the decimal points are in a line.

Example 2: Find the difference between 14.512 and 8.7.

1. Write the numbers in a column, lining up the decimal points. Add placeholder zeros so that the numbers have the same number of decimal places.

$$\begin{array}{r} 14.512 \\ -8.700 \end{array}$$

2. Subtract. Regroup, or borrow, as needed. Place the decimal point in the answer directly in line with the decimal points in the problem.

$$\begin{array}{r} \scriptstyle 13\ 15 \\ 1\cancel{4}.\cancel{5}12 \\ -8.700 \\ \hline \mathbf{5.812} \end{array}$$

The greater number may have fewer or no decimal places. In the next example, a decimal is subtracted from a whole number.

Example 3: What does 9 minus 3.604 equal?

1. Line up the place-value columns. Put a decimal point after the whole number 9 and add placeholder zeros.

$$\begin{array}{r} 9.000 \\ -3.604 \end{array}$$

2. Subtract, regrouping as needed. Place the decimal point in the answer.

$$\begin{array}{r} \scriptstyle 8\ 9\ 9\ 10 \\ \cancel{9}.\cancel{0}\cancel{0}\cancel{0} \\ -3.6\ 0\ 4 \\ \hline 5.3\ 9\ 6 \end{array}$$

DECIMALS AND FRACTIONS ▸ PRACTICE 2.1

A. Solve.

1.	4.025 + 3.971	**4.**	8.04 − 2.19	**7.**	17.294 + 0.8	**10.**	3.8 − 2.905

2.	6.5 + 4.008	**5.**	8.5 − 1.074	**8.**	4.07 + 1.047	**11.**	14.64 − 10.8

3.	2.8 + 9.46	**6.**	10 − 7.89	**9.**	17.52 + 3.8	**12.**	100.5 − 98.15

13. 0.236 + 2.4 + 2.87 =

14. 38.06 − 16.9 =

15. 0.006 + 0.09 + 0.549 =

16. 8.5 − 6.074 =

17. 1.02 − 0.87 =

18. 0.45 + 1.8 + 0.07 + 2.56 =

19. 12.5 − 0.7 =

20. 25 − 10.984 =

21. 0.01 + 2.052 + 0.96 + 1.5 =

22. 12.9 − 10.54 =

23. 0.68 + 12.3 + 4.9 =

24. 32.9 − 15.675 =

B. Choose the one best answer to each question.

25. James ran 3 miles. His times for the individual miles were 7.2 minutes, 6.8 minutes, and 8.25 minutes. How long did it take him, in minutes, to run the 3-mile distance?

(1) 9.65
(2) 22.25
(3) 22.7
(4) 23.35
(5) 96.5

26. Claudia earns overtime pay when she works more than 40 hours in one week. How many hours of overtime pay did she work for the week of March 4?

Work Record for March 4–10

March 4	8.5
March 5	Off
March 6	9.25
March 7	8.75
March 8	10
March 9	Off
March 10	7.75

(1) 44.25
(2) 40.0
(3) 8.85
(4) 4.25
(5) 2.25

27. A plumber cut two lengths of pipe measuring 2.8 and 1.4 meters from a 6-meter length.

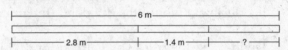

Assuming there was no waste when the cuts were made, what is the length in meters of the remaining piece?

(1) 1.8
(2) 3.2
(3) 4.2
(4) 7.4
(5) 10.2

28. Mona purchased the following art supplies: a storage box for $16.98, a set of art markers for $31.78, and a pad of paper for $6.50. What was the cost of the three items?

(1) $31.78
(2) $48.76
(3) $53.26
(4) $55.26
(5) $61.76

Answers and explanations begin on page 665.

MULTIPLICATION AND DIVISION

The rules you used to multiply whole numbers can be used to multiply decimals. You don't have to line up the decimal points. You will wait until you are finished multiplying before you place the decimal point in the answer. The number of decimal places in the answer equals the total number of decimal places in the numbers you are multiplying.

Example 4: Find the product of 2.6 and 0.45.

1. Set up the problem as though you were multiplying the whole numbers 26 and 45.

$$\begin{array}{r} 2.6 \\ \times\ .45 \\ \hline \end{array}$$

2. Ignore the decimal points while you multiply.

3. Now count the decimal places in the numbers you multiplied. The number 2.6 has one decimal place, and 0.45 has two decimal places, for a total of three.

$$\begin{array}{r} 2.6 \\ \times\ .45 \\ \hline 130 \\ 1\ 040 \\ \hline 1.170 \end{array}$$

4. Starting from the right, count three places to the left and insert the decimal point.

When you divide decimals, you must figure out where the decimal point will go in the answer <u>before</u> you divide.

Example 5: Divide 14.4 by 6.

1. Set up the problem. Since the divisor (the number you are dividing by) is a whole number, place the decimal point in the answer directly above the decimal point in the dividend (the number you are dividing).

$$\begin{array}{r} 2.4 \\ 6\overline{)14.4} \\ -\ 12 \\ \hline 24 \\ -\ 24 \\ \hline 0 \end{array}$$

2. Divide. Use the rules you learned for dividing whole numbers.

If the divisor is a decimal, you must move the decimal points in both the divisor and the dividend before you divide.

Example 6: Divide 4.9 by 0.35.

1. Set up the problem. There are two decimal places in the divisor. Move the decimal point in *both* the divisor and the dividend two places to the right. Note that you need to add a zero in the dividend in order to move the decimal two places.

$$.35\overline{)4.90}$$

2. Place the decimal point in the quotient directly above the decimal point in the dividend.

$$\begin{array}{r} 14. \\ 35\overline{)490.} \\ -\ 35 \\ \hline 140 \\ -\ 140 \\ \hline 0 \end{array}$$

3. Divide.

Note: You may not need to finish dividing in order to choose the correct answer. You may be able to eliminate all but one of the answer choices after only one or two division steps.

A. Solve.

1. $\begin{array}{r} 5.3 \\ \times\ 0.5 \\ \hline \end{array}$

2. $\begin{array}{r} 64 \\ \times\ 0.2 \\ \hline \end{array}$

3. $\begin{array}{r} 12.4 \\ \times\ 0.04 \\ \hline \end{array}$

4. $6\overline{)3.12}$

5. $8\overline{)28.8}$

6. $5\overline{)20.45}$

7. $\begin{array}{r} 6.25 \\ \times\ 1.4 \\ \hline \end{array}$

8. $\begin{array}{r} 13.5 \\ \times\ 0.25 \\ \hline \end{array}$

9. $\begin{array}{r} 9.62 \\ \times\ 1.005 \\ \hline \end{array}$

10. $1.25\overline{)30}$

11. $2.8\overline{)39.76}$

12. $0.003\overline{)47.4}$

13. $15.5 \times 2.2 =$

14. $0.944 \div 0.4 =$

15. $2.05 \times 0.32 =$

16. $1.32 \div 0.5 =$

17. $2.75 \times 0.6 =$

18. $12.825 \div 3 =$

19. $3.36 \times 1.1 =$

20. $15.03 \div 15 =$

21. $0.12 \times 0.06 =$

B. Choose the <u>one best answer</u> to each question.

22. One container of floor cleaner holds 3.79 liters. If Zachary bought 4 containers, how many liters of cleaner did he buy?

    (1) 0.9475
    (2) 7.79
    (3) 9.48
    (4) 12.83
    (5) 15.16

23. Ribbon costs $0.45 per foot. A sewing project calls for 20.5 feet of ribbon. To the nearest cent, what will be the cost of the ribbon for the project?

    (1) $0.92
    (2) $9.23
    (3) $9.90
    (4) $45.56
    (5) $92.25

24. Armando drove 278.7 miles over a 3-day period. On average, how many miles did he drive each day?

    (1)   9.3
    (2)   90.3
    (3)   92.9
    (4) 107.6
    (5) 836.1

Questions 25 and 26 are based on the following information.

Cereal	Net Weight	Servings per Box
Toasted Oats	22.8 oz	19
Crisp Rice	16.9 oz	13
Honey Mix	12.5 oz	10

25. A box of Toasted Oats cereal is priced at $4.94. What is the cost per serving? (*Hint:* Divide the price by the number of servings.)

    (1) $0.49
    (2) $0.38
    (3) $0.29
    (4) $0.26
    (5) $0.22

26. Lee buys 4 boxes of Honey Mix cereal. How many ounces of cereal did she buy?

    (1)   31.25
    (2)   50.0
    (3)   67.6
    (4)   91.2
    (5) 208.8

Answers and explanations begin on page 665.

DECIMALS AND FRACTIONS

Fraction Basics

Understanding Fractions

A **fraction** uses two numbers to represent part of a whole. The bottom number, called the **denominator**, tells how many equal parts are in the whole group or item. The top number, called the **numerator**, tells how many parts you are working with.

There are 4 equal parts in this rectangle. Since 3 are shaded, we say that $\frac{3}{4}$ of the rectangle is shaded.

In a proper fraction, the numerator is less than the denominator. A **proper fraction** represents a quantity less than 1. *An improper fraction* is equal to or greater than 1.

There are 6 equal parts in the figure, and 6 are shaded; therefore, $\frac{6}{6}$ of the figure is shaded. $\frac{6}{6} = 1$

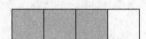

In this grouping, each figure is divided into 2 equal parts. A total of 3 parts are shaded, so $\frac{3}{2}$ are shaded.

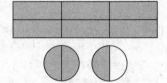

A **mixed number** is another way to show an amount greater than 1. It consists of a whole number and a proper fraction. Another name for the shaded portion in the last figure is $1\frac{1}{2}$. The improper fraction $\frac{3}{2}$ equals $1\frac{1}{2}$.

You can also change an improper fraction to a whole or mixed number.

Example 1: Change $\frac{16}{5}$ to a mixed number.

1. Divide the numerator (16) by the denominator (5). Since 16 is not evenly divisible by 5, there is a remainder of 1. $16 \div 5 = 3\ r1$

2. The answer becomes the whole number, and the remainder becomes the numerator of the proper fraction. The denominator is the same as the original fraction. $\frac{16}{5} = 3\frac{1}{5}$

You can also change a mixed number to an improper fraction.

Example 2: Change $7\frac{2}{3}$ to an improper fraction.

1. Multiply the whole number (7) by the denominator of the fraction (3), and add the numerator (2). $7 \times 3 = 21$ $21 + 2 = 23$

2. Write the sum over the denominator of the original fraction. $7\frac{2}{3} = \frac{23}{3}$

Key Ideas

- The bottom number of a fraction tells how many parts the group or object has.
- The top number tells how many parts you are working with.
- When the top number is greater than the bottom number, the fraction is greater than 1.

ON THE GED

If you have trouble visualizing the fractions in a problem, draw a quick sketch of the information presented in the problem.

To perform operations with fractions, you need to be able to write equal fractions in higher or lower terms. The **terms** are the numerator and the denominator. A fraction is **reduced to lowest terms** when the two terms do not have any common factor except 1.

To **raise** a fraction, multiply both terms by the same number: $\frac{3}{4} = \frac{3 \times 3}{4 \times 3} = \frac{9}{12}$

To **reduce** a fraction, divide both terms by the same number: $\frac{10}{15} = \frac{10 \div 5}{15 \div 5} = \frac{2}{3}$

DECIMALS AND FRACTIONS ▸ PRACTICE 3

A. Write a proper fraction for the shaded portion of each figure.

1.   2.   3.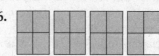

B. Write an improper fraction and a mixed number for the shaded portion of each figure.

4.   5.   6.

C. Write improper fractions as mixed numbers and mixed numbers as improper fractions.

7. $\frac{17}{3} =$ 9. $\frac{24}{6} =$ 11. $\frac{19}{4} =$ 13. $\frac{43}{9} =$ 15. $\frac{33}{7} =$

8. $3\frac{3}{5} =$ 10. $5\frac{2}{9} =$ 12. $2\frac{5}{12} =$ 14. $1\frac{3}{4} =$ 16. $5\frac{7}{10} =$

D. Write an equal fraction with the given denominator.

17. $\frac{3}{4} = \frac{}{16}$ 18. $\frac{1}{3} = \frac{}{21}$ 19. $\frac{4}{5} = \frac{}{60}$ 20. $\frac{3}{8} = \frac{}{40}$ 21. $\frac{6}{25} = \frac{}{100}$

(*Hint:* $4 \times ? = 16$)

E. Reduce each fraction to lowest terms.

22. $\frac{21}{28} =$ 23. $\frac{4}{24} =$ 24. $\frac{12}{20} =$ 25. $\frac{26}{30} =$ 26. $\frac{60}{90} =$

F. Choose the <u>one best answer</u> to each question.

27. Eighteen out of every 24 people surveyed say they went to at least one movie in December. What fraction of the people surveyed went to a movie in December?

(1) $\frac{3}{4}$

(2) $\frac{2}{3}$

(3) $\frac{1}{2}$

(4) $\frac{1}{3}$

(5) $\frac{1}{4}$

28. Which of the following fractions equals $\frac{2}{5}$?

(1) $\frac{15}{100}$

(2) $\frac{30}{100}$

(3) $\frac{40}{100}$

(4) $\frac{65}{100}$

(5) $\frac{80}{100}$

Answers and explanations begin on page 665.

DECIMALS AND FRACTIONS

Fraction Operations

Addition and Subtraction

You can add or subtract **like fractions**. Like fractions have a **common denominator.** In other words, their denominators are the same.

Example 1: Add $\frac{3}{10} + \frac{5}{10}$

Key Ideas

- You can add or subtract fractions, but they must be like fractions.
- If denominators are not the same, find a common denominator and raise one or both fractions.
- Always reduce answers to lowest terms and change improper fractions to mixed numbers.

1. Since the denominators are the same, add the numerators.

$$\frac{3}{10} + \frac{5}{10} = \frac{8}{10}$$

2. Reduce the answer to lowest terms.

$$\frac{8}{10} = \frac{8 \div 2}{10 \div 2} = \frac{4}{5}$$

Example 2: Subtract $\frac{2}{9}$ from $\frac{7}{9}$.

Subtract the numerators. The answer is already in lowest terms.

$$\frac{7}{9} - \frac{2}{9} = \frac{5}{9}$$

If the denominators are not the same, raise one or both fractions to higher terms so that they become like fractions.

Example 3: Add $\frac{5}{6} + \frac{1}{4}$.

1. One way to find a common denominator is to think of the multiples of both denominators. The lowest is 12.

Multiples
of 6: 6, $\boxed{12}$, 18
of 4: 4, 8, $\boxed{12}$, 16

2. Raise each fraction to higher terms with a denominator of 12.

$$\frac{5 \times 2}{6 \times 2} = \frac{10}{12}, \frac{1 \times 3}{4 \times 3} = \frac{3}{12}$$

3. Add the like fractions. Rewrite the sum as a mixed number.

$$\frac{10}{12} + \frac{3}{12} = \frac{13}{12} = 1\frac{1}{12}$$

GED TIP

If your solution to a GED fraction problem is not one of the given answer choices, make sure that you reduced your answer to lowest terms. GED answer choices are always written in lowest terms.

Use the same process to add or subtract mixed numbers. Example 4 shows how to regroup when subtracting mixed numbers.

Example 4: Subtract $4\frac{1}{16} - 1\frac{3}{8}$.

1. Raise the second fraction so that it also has a denominator of 16.

$$\frac{3 \times 2}{8 \times 2} = \frac{6}{16}$$

2. Set up the problem. To subtract the fractions, you need to regroup 1 from the whole number column and add it to the top fraction.

$$4\frac{1}{16} = 3\frac{16}{16} + \frac{1}{16} = 3\frac{17}{16}$$
$$-1\frac{6}{16} \qquad\qquad -1\frac{6}{16}$$
$$\overline{\qquad\qquad\qquad 2\frac{11}{16}}$$

3. Subtract the fractions and then the whole numbers.

A. Solve. Reduce answers to lowest terms. Simplify improper fractions as mixed numbers.

1. $\frac{3}{8}$
   $+\ \frac{1}{8}$

3. $\frac{8}{9}$
   $-\ \frac{5}{9}$

5. $\frac{1}{4}$
   $+\ \frac{2}{3}$

7. $\frac{9}{10}$
   $-\ \frac{3}{5}$

9. $2\frac{1}{5}$
   $+\ 1\frac{2}{3}$

2. $\frac{1}{6}$
   $+\ \frac{5}{6}$

4. $\frac{7}{12}$
   $-\ \frac{5}{12}$

6. $\frac{1}{2}$
   $+\ \frac{5}{8}$

8. $\frac{7}{9}$
   $-\ \frac{1}{2}$

10. $4\frac{1}{2}$
    $-\ 2\frac{3}{4}$

11. $5\frac{5}{6} + 2\frac{2}{3} =$

12. $6\frac{7}{8} + 4\frac{3}{4} =$

13. $12\frac{1}{10} + 9\frac{3}{5} =$

14. $2\frac{2}{9} + \frac{2}{3} + 4\frac{5}{6} =$

15. $3\frac{1}{3} + 5\frac{2}{5} + 3\frac{5}{6} =$

16. $\frac{3}{8} + \frac{7}{12} + 1\frac{2}{3} =$

17. $16\frac{2}{3} + 25\frac{3}{4} =$

18. $10\frac{1}{2} + 8\frac{4}{5} + 3\frac{1}{4} =$

19. $8\frac{1}{2} - 3\frac{4}{9} =$

20. $15 - 3\frac{7}{8} =$

21. $14\frac{1}{4} - 10\frac{3}{7} =$

22. $9\frac{11}{12} - 8\frac{5}{8} =$

23. $6 - 3\frac{4}{7} =$

24. $13\frac{1}{3} - 4\frac{4}{9} =$

25. $5\frac{5}{7} - 4\frac{4}{5} =$

B. Choose the <u>one best answer</u> to each question.

26. To make the top of a dining room table, Craig glues a piece of oak that is $\frac{5}{16}$ inch thick to a piece of pine that is $\frac{7}{8}$ inch thick. What is the total thickness, in inches, of the tabletop?

    (1) $\frac{1}{2}$

    (2) $\frac{9}{16}$

    (3) $1\frac{3}{16}$

    (4) $1\frac{1}{4}$

    (5) $1\frac{9}{16}$

27. Carol will use the two bolts shown below to assemble a book cart. How much longer, in inches, is bolt A than bolt B?

    A $2\frac{7}{8}$ in

    B $1\frac{1}{4}$ in

    (1) $\frac{5}{8}$

    (2) $1\frac{3}{8}$

    (3) $1\frac{5}{8}$

    (4) $1\frac{3}{4}$

    (5) $2\frac{1}{2}$

28. At a fabric store, Melissa sold $8\frac{7}{8}$ yards of cloth to a customer. If the material was cut from a bolt of fabric containing $23\frac{1}{4}$ yards, how many yards are left on the bolt?

    (1) $14\frac{3}{8}$

    (2) $15\frac{1}{4}$

    (3) $15\frac{3}{8}$

    (4) $15\frac{3}{4}$

    (5) $31\frac{7}{8}$

29. A batch of salad dressing requires $1\frac{2}{3}$ cups of olive oil, $\frac{1}{2}$ cup of vinegar, and $\frac{3}{4}$ cup of water. How many cups of salad dressing will this recipe produce?

    (1) $1\frac{2}{3}$

    (2) $1\frac{5}{6}$

    (3) $2\frac{5}{6}$

    (4) $2\frac{11}{12}$

    (5) $3\frac{7}{12}$

Answers and explanations begin on page 666.

Multiplication and Division

It isn't necessary to find a common denominator to multiply and divide fractions. To multiply fractions, simply multiply the numerators and then the denominators. Reduce the answer, if necessary.

Example 1: What is the product of $\frac{7}{8}$ and $\frac{1}{2}$?

Multiply the numerators together, and then the denominators. The answer is in lowest terms.

$$\frac{7}{8} \times \frac{1}{2} = \frac{7 \times 1}{8 \times 2} = \frac{7}{16}$$

Before multiplying a mixed number, change it to an improper fraction.

Example 2: What is $\frac{1}{3}$ of $3\frac{3}{4}$?

1. Change $3\frac{3}{4}$ to an improper fraction.

$$3\frac{3}{4} = \frac{15}{4}$$

2. Multiply the numerators and the denominators.

$$\frac{15}{4} \times \frac{1}{3} = \frac{15 \times 1}{4 \times 3} = \frac{15}{12}$$

3. Change to a mixed number and reduce to lowest terms.

$$\frac{15}{12} = 1\frac{3}{12} = \mathbf{1\frac{1}{4}}$$

You can use a shortcut called **canceling** to reduce the fractions as you work the problem. To cancel, divide both a numerator and a denominator by the same number. The numerator and the denominator can be in different fractions.

Example 3: Multiply $1\frac{1}{2}$ by $1\frac{1}{5}$.

1. Change to improper fractions.

$$1\frac{1}{2} = \frac{3}{2} \text{ and } 1\frac{1}{5} = \frac{6}{5}$$

2. Set up the multiplication problem. Both 6 (a numerator) and 2 (a denominator) are evenly divisible by 2. Divide them by 2. Then multiply using the new numerator and denominator. Finally, change the improper fraction to a mixed number.

$$\frac{3}{2} \times \frac{6}{5} = \frac{3}{\underset{1}{2}} \times \frac{\overset{3}{6}}{5} = \frac{9}{5} = \mathbf{1\frac{4}{5}}$$

The slash marks show that the numbers have been divided.

You will need one additional step to divide fractions. Before dividing, **invert** the divisor (the fraction you are dividing by). To invert the fraction, switch the numerator and the denominator. Finally, change the division symbol to a multiplication symbol and multiply.

Example 4: Jim has an 8-pound bag of nuts. He wants to fill smaller, $\frac{1}{2}$-pound bags using the nuts. How many small bags can he make?

1. Divide 8 by $\frac{1}{2}$. Set up the division problem. Always write whole or mixed numbers as improper fractions.

$$8 \div \frac{1}{2} = \frac{8}{1} \div \frac{1}{2} =$$

2. Invert the fraction you are dividing by, and change the operation sign to multiplication. Multiply, following the rules for multiplying fractions. **Jim can make 16 small bags.**

$$\frac{8}{1} \times \frac{2}{1} = \frac{16}{1} = \mathbf{16}$$

Note: When you multiply by a fraction, the answer is smaller than the number you started with because you are finding a "part of." When you divide by a fraction, the answer is greater than the number.

A. Solve. Reduce answers to lowest terms. Simplify improper fractions as mixed numbers.

1. $\frac{2}{3} \times \frac{1}{4} =$

2. $1\frac{5}{6} \times \frac{1}{2} =$

3. $\frac{2}{3} \times 21 =$

4. $50 \times \frac{3}{8} =$

5. $3\frac{1}{2} \times \frac{1}{4} =$

6. $\frac{3}{4} \times 2\frac{7}{8} =$

7. $2\frac{1}{3} \times 3\frac{2}{5} =$

8. $15 \times 2\frac{3}{4} =$

9. $\frac{5}{8} \times 3\frac{1}{4} =$

10. $\frac{7}{8} \div \frac{1}{16} =$

11. $\frac{4}{5} \div \frac{4}{9} =$

12. $12 \div \frac{1}{4} =$

13. $6 \div 2\frac{1}{2} =$

14. $3\frac{3}{4} \div 1\frac{2}{3} =$

15. $9 \div \frac{1}{3} =$

16. $26\frac{2}{3} \div 3\frac{1}{3} =$

17. $40\frac{3}{8} \div 4\frac{1}{4} =$

18. $3\frac{7}{8} \div 5\frac{1}{6} =$

B. Choose the one best answer to each question.

19. A city is considering raising taxes to build a football stadium. A survey of registered voters yielded the following results:

Position	Fraction of Those Surveyed
Against Tax Hike	$\frac{7}{16}$
For Tax Hike	$\frac{3}{16}$
Undecided	$\frac{3}{8}$

If 400 people were surveyed, how many support the tax hike?

(1) 25
(2) 48
(3) 75
(4) 133
(5) 150

20. A tailor has 20 yards of shirt fabric. How many shirts can she __complete__ if each shirt requires $2\frac{3}{4}$ yards of fabric?

(1) 6
(2) 7
(3) 8
(4) 10
(5) 14

21. An insurance agent estimates that it takes $\frac{2}{3}$ hour to process a customer's claim. If the agent spends 22 hours per week processing claims, about how many claims does he process in a week?

(1) $14\frac{2}{3}$
(2) 26
(3) 33
(4) 44
(5) 66

22. A fluorescent lighting panel is $12\frac{5}{8}$ inches wide. If three of the panels are installed as shown below, what will be the width in inches of the combined panels?

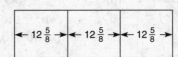

(1) $4\frac{5}{24}$
(2) $13\frac{7}{8}$
(3) $36\frac{5}{8}$
(4) $37\frac{7}{8}$
(5) $42\frac{7}{8}$

Answers and explanations begin on page 666.

DECIMALS AND FRACTIONS

Solving Problems Using a Calculator

Decimals and Fractions on the Calculator

You can solve both decimal and fraction problems using a scientific calculator. Decimal operations are performed in the same way that you have learned to enter operations with whole numbers. Study the following examples.

To solve this problem:	Press these keys:	The display reads:
3.89 + 2.5	3.89 $+$ 2.5 $=$	6.39
5.2 − 0.78	5.2 $-$ .78 $=$	4.42
0.9 × 15	.9 $\times$ 15 $=$	13.5
1.7 ÷ 2	1.7 $\div$ 2 $=$	0.85

When you divide using a calculator, any remainder is expressed as a decimal.

Example 1: For her students, Monica buys 144 heart-shaped erasers for $8.85. To the nearest cent, what is the cost of each eraser?

1. Divide $8.85 by 144. Press: 8.85 $\div$ 144 $=$

   Display: 0.061458333

2. Round the answer to the hundredths place to express the answer in cents. 0.061458333 rounds to **$0.06**.

Although not all scientific calculators will perform operations with fractions, the *Casio fx-260* scientific calculator that you will use when you take the GED Math Test can. To enter a fraction, enter the numerator, press $a^b/_c$, and enter the denominator. If you press $=$, the calculator will reduce the fraction to lowest terms.

Example 2: Reduce $\frac{56}{448}$ to lowest terms.

Press these keys: 56 $a^b/_c$ 448 =

The display reads: 1 ⌐ 8.

The ⌐ symbol separates the numerator and denominator in the answer. Therefore, $\frac{56}{448}$ reduces to $\frac{1}{8}$.

To show a mixed number, the calculator uses the ⌐ symbol twice. The mixed number $3\frac{1}{2}$ would be displayed as 3 ⌐ 1 ⌐ 2

Example 2: Find the sum of $1\frac{7}{8}$ and $3\frac{1}{2}$.

Press these keys: 1 $a^b/_c$ 7 $a^b/_c$ 8 $+$ 3 $a^b/_c$ 1 $a^b/_c$ 2 $=$

The display reads: 5 ⌐ 3 ⌐ 8.

Written as a mixed number, the correct answer is $5\frac{3}{8}$.

A. Solve the following problems using your calculator.

1. $3.5 + 1.87 + 2.009 =$

2. $3\frac{2}{3} - 1\frac{5}{12} =$

3. $\$25.34 \times 15 =$

4. $10\frac{1}{2} \div \frac{1}{4} =$

5. Linda earns $95 per day. If she works $\frac{8}{9}$ of a day, how much will she earn?

6. Aaron bought a refrigerator for $956.88. The price includes tax and interest charges. If he makes 12 equal monthly payments, how much will he pay each month?

7. A plastic pipe that is $20\frac{5}{8}$ feet long is to be cut into pieces measuring $1\frac{3}{8}$ feet. How many pieces can be cut from the longer pipe?

8. An insurance agent estimates the annual cost of insurance on a home by multiplying the sale price of the home by 0.0125. What will be the yearly cost of insurance on a home priced at $118,000?

9. In a recipe, the total liquid added to a mixture is $1\frac{1}{2}$ cups of water and $2\frac{3}{4}$ cups of chicken broth. How many cups of liquid are used in the recipe?

B. Choose the <u>one best answer</u> to each question. You <u>MAY</u> use your calculator.

<u>Questions 10 and 11</u> refer to the following information.

Ordering Information—Bedspreads

Size	Weight (pounds)	Price
Twin	4.13	$49.99
Full	4.81	$69.99
Queen	5.56	$84.99
King	6.88	$94.99

10. Silas buys a total of three quilts: two twin-sized quilts and one king-sized quilt. What is the total cost of his purchase?

   (1) $99.98
   (2) $144.98
   (3) $189.98
   (4) $194.97
   (5) $239.97

11. The shipping charge for an order is $1.20 per pound. To the nearest cent, what would be the shipping charge on a queen-sized quilt?

   (1) $4.96
   (2) $5.56
   (3) $6.67
   (4) $8.26
   (5) $10.20

12. Karen estimates that she spends $\frac{1}{3}$ of her take-home pay on rent and $\frac{1}{4}$ on food. What fraction of her take-home pay is left after these expenses?

   (1) $\frac{3}{4}$
   (2) $\frac{5}{7}$
   (3) $\frac{2}{3}$
   (4) $\frac{7}{12}$
   (5) $\frac{5}{12}$

13. A state park contains 64 acres. The state legislature recently set aside $\frac{3}{8}$ of the park as a wildlife preserve. How many acres will be set aside for wildlife?

   (1) 8
   (2) 21
   (3) 24
   (4) 27
   (5) 38

Answers and explanations begin on page 666.

Filling in the Answer Grid

Key Ideas

- Write your answer in the top row of boxes; then fill in the grid.
- Always write mixed numbers as improper fractions.

Working with Alternative Format Questions

Some of the questions on the GED Math Test are not multiple-choice questions. Instead, you must solve the problem and record the answer by filling in a grid.

In the examples below, you will see how to enter decimals and fractions on the grid. Remember, you should write your answer in the top row of boxes, but this part of the grid will not be scored. You must correctly fill the circles in the grid to receive credit for your answer.

Example 1: John needs $\frac{3}{4}$ cup of brown sugar for a recipe. If he wants to make only one-half the number of servings, how many cups of brown sugar will he need?

1. Multiply to find the answer. $\frac{3}{4} \times \frac{1}{2} = \frac{3}{8}$ **cup**

2. Enter the fraction on the grid. Fill in a slash to represent the fraction bar.

You may not enter mixed numbers on the grid. If the answer to a problem is a mixed number, change the mixed number to an improper fraction.

Example 2: Elaine exercised for $1\frac{3}{4}$ hours on Monday and $1\frac{1}{2}$ hours on Tuesday. How many hours did she exercise in all?

1. Add. $1\frac{3}{4} + 1\frac{1}{2} = 1\frac{3}{4} + 1\frac{2}{4} = 2\frac{5}{4} = 3\frac{1}{4}$ hr

2. Change the answer to an improper fraction.
   $3\frac{1}{4} = \frac{13}{4}$ Enter the answer on the grid.

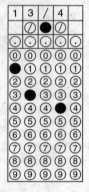

To enter a decimal, fill in a circle on the third row of the grid to show the location of the decimal point.

Example 3: A chemical compound weighs 12.8 kilograms. If the compound is divided equally into five portions, how many kilograms will each weigh?

1. Divide. 12.8 ÷ 5 = **2.56 kilograms**

2. Write the answer in the blank boxes. Then fill in the appropriate circles in the grid. You can start your answer anywhere on the grid as long as the answer fits.

DECIMALS AND FRACTIONS ▸ PRACTICE 6

Solve. Mark your answers in the grids on the right side of the page. You <u>MAY</u> use your calculator.

1. On a business trip, Alex had to buy gasoline three times. He bought 12.6, 9.8, and 13.2 gallons of gasoline. How many gallons did he buy in all?

2. Aubrey withdraws $150 from her bank account and pays $100 to her day-care provider. What fraction of the withdrawal did she spend on day care?

3. Colleen worked $9\frac{1}{2}$ hours on Monday and $7\frac{3}{4}$ hours on Tuesday. How many hours more did she work on Monday than on Tuesday?

4. A bottle holds 2.6 ounces of food coloring. How many bottles can be filled from 100 ounces of food coloring?

5. For a youth picnic, Leah bought 18 cases of soft drinks: 9 were root beer, 6 were lemon-lime, and 3 were cherry cola. Reduced to lowest terms, what fraction of the cases were cherry cola?

6. A sheet of foam board is 0.5 centimeter thick. How many sheets of the board can be stacked in a space that is 12.5 centimeters high?

Answers and explanations begin on page 666.

DECIMALS AND FRACTIONS

Problem Solving: Fraction and Decimal Equivalencies

Use Fraction and Decimal Equivalents

Fractions and decimals are two ways to show part of a whole. You can change fractions to decimals by dividing.

Example 1: Change $\frac{3}{8}$ to a decimal.

The fraction $\frac{3}{8}$ means $3 \div 8$. Use a calculator to divide. $\qquad 3 \div 8 = \mathbf{0.375}$

You can also change a decimal to a fraction.

Example 2: Change 0.35 to a fraction.

Write the decimal number over the place value name of the last decimal digit on the right. The last digit, 5, is in the hundredths column. Reduce to lowest terms.

$$\frac{35}{100} = \frac{35 \div 5}{100 \div 5} = \frac{7}{20}$$

You will find it useful to memorize the most common fraction and decimal equivalents. These equivalents will also help you solve percent problems.

Decimal	Fraction		Decimal	Fraction		Decimal	Fraction
0.1	$\frac{1}{10}$		0.375	$\frac{3}{8}$		0.7	$\frac{7}{10}$
0.125	$\frac{1}{8}$		0.4	$\frac{2}{5}$		0.75	$\frac{3}{4}$
0.2	$\frac{1}{5}$		0.5	$\frac{1}{2}$		0.8	$\frac{4}{5}$
0.25	$\frac{1}{4}$		0.6	$\frac{3}{5}$		0.875	$\frac{7}{8}$
0.3	$\frac{3}{10}$		0.625	$\frac{5}{8}$		0.9	$\frac{9}{10}$
$0.\overline{333}$	$\frac{1}{3}$		$0.\overline{666}$	$\frac{2}{3}$			

The decimal equivalents for $\frac{1}{3}$ and $\frac{2}{3}$ are marked with a bar. The bar shows that the decimal repeats indefinitely.

You can use fraction and decimal equivalents to save time when solving math problems.

Example 3: Each dose of cough medicine contains 0.25 ounce of medication. How many ounces of medication are in 48 doses?

To solve the problem, you need to multiply 48 by 0.25, a time-consuming calculation. However, since $0.25 = \frac{1}{4}$, you can find $\frac{1}{4}$ of 48 to solve the problem. The answer is **12 doses.**

$$48 \times \frac{1}{4} = \frac{48}{4} = 12$$

Key Ideas

- To change a fraction to a decimal, divide the numerator by the denominator.
- To change a decimal to a fraction, write the number without the decimal point over the place value of the last decimal digit. Reduce.
- Avoid time-consuming calculations by using fraction-decimal equivalents.

GED TIP

Look at the answer choices before you begin working a problem. Knowing whether you need an answer in fraction or decimal form may affect how you approach the problem.

Knowing fraction-decimal equivalents can also help you interpret remainders when using a calculator.

Example 4: Ray inspects machine assemblies. He must inspect 12 assemblies during his 40-hour workweek. On average, how many hours can he spend on each inspection?

Using a calculator, divide 40 by 12: 40 $\boxed{\div}$ 12 $\boxed{=}$ $\boxed{3.333333333}$

Since you know that $0.33\overline{3} = \frac{1}{3}$, the answer is **$3\frac{1}{3}$ hours.**

DECIMALS AND FRACTIONS ▸ PRACTICE 7

Solve. When possible, use fraction and decimal equivalents to make the work easier. You MAY use a calculator on questions 5 and 6.

1. During a 25%-off sale, store clerks find the amount of the discounts by multiplying the regular price by 0.25. What is the discount on an item with a regular price of $80?

   (1) $32.00
   (2) $20.00
   (3) $16.40
   (4) $3.20
   (5) $2.00

2. At Linton Products, $\frac{3}{10}$ of the workers are in the company's ride-share program. If there are 480 workers, which of the following expressions could be used to find the number in the ride-share program?

   (1) 480 × 0.7
   (2) 480 ÷ 0.7
   (3) 480 × 0.4
   (4) 480 × 0.3
   (5) 480 ÷ 0.3

3. Sharon is using a calculator to find out how many hours she has spent on a certain job. She divides, and her display reads:

   $\boxed{4.666666666}$

   Assuming her calculations are correct, how many hours did she spend on the job?

   (1) $4\frac{1}{6}$
   (2) $4\frac{2}{3}$
   (3) $4\frac{6}{7}$
   (4) 46
   (5) 466

4. A gourmet candy company charges the following prices per pound.

Jelly Beans	$9.60
Peanut Brittle	$12.00
Almond Toffee	$28.50

   How much would a customer pay for 1.5 pounds of peanut brittle?

   (1) $6.00
   (2) $9.00
   (3) $14.40
   (4) $18.00
   (5) $42.75

5. At 1 P.M., the amount of rain in a rain gauge is 1.125 inches. At 3 P.M., the gauge holds 1.875 inches. What fraction of an inch of rain fell between 1 P.M. and 3 P.M.?

   (1) $\frac{7}{8}$
   (2) $\frac{3}{4}$
   (3) $\frac{7}{10}$
   (4) $\frac{1}{8}$
   (5) Not enough information is given.

6. A steel rod, 3 meters in length, is cut into 8 equal pieces. What is the length in meters of each piece?

   (1) 0.125
   (2) 0.333
   (3) 0.375
   (4) 2.333
   (5) 2.667

   Answers and explanations begin on page 667.

DECIMALS AND FRACTIONS PRACTICE QUESTIONS PART I

Directions: Choose the <u>one best answer</u> to each question. You <u>MAY</u> use your calculator.

1. A wooden flooring strip is $20\frac{1}{2}$ inches long. If you cut off $4\frac{3}{4}$ inches from one end, what will be the new length of the strip in inches?

   (1) $\frac{1}{2}$
   (2) $16\frac{3}{4}$
   (3) $16\frac{1}{4}$
   (4) $15\frac{3}{4}$
   (5) $15\frac{1}{4}$

2. A box of cereal costs $4.69. The package label says that the box contains 19 servings. What is the cost of 1 serving to the nearest cent?

   (1) $0.02
   (2) $0.25
   (3) $0.47
   (4) $0.89
   (5) $2.46

3. How much would a computer system cost if it is priced as shown below?

   > **Pay $200 down and make 12 monthly payments of only $98.85.**

   (1) $3586.20
   (2) $2400.00
   (3) $1386.20
   (4) $1186.20
   (5) Not enough information is given.

4. Unleaded gasoline sells for $1.469 per gallon. How much would $10\frac{1}{2}$ gallons cost? Round your answer to the nearest cent.

   (1) $10.50
   (2) $14.69
   (3) $15.42
   (4) $16.89
   (5) $25.10

5. Three packages weigh $1\frac{1}{2}$ pounds, $4\frac{3}{4}$ pounds, and $2\frac{3}{10}$ pounds. What is the average weight, in pounds, of the packages? (*Hint:* Add the weights, then divide by the number of packages.)

   (1) 2.14
   (2) 2.85
   (3) 4.75
   (4) 8.55
   (5) Not enough information is given.

6. Gina is paid $8 an hour. If she earned $258 in 1 week, how many hours did she work?

   (1) $34\frac{1}{2}$
   (2) $32\frac{1}{2}$
   (3) $32\frac{1}{3}$
   (4) $32\frac{1}{4}$
   (5) $32\frac{1}{5}$

7. A developer plans to build homes on $20\frac{1}{2}$ acres. She estimates that $6\frac{1}{4}$ acres will be used for roads. The remaining land will be divided into $\frac{1}{4}$-acre lots. How many lots can the subdivision include?

   (1)   7
   (2) 31
   (3) 57
   (4) 81
   (5) 107

8. A school buys 1000 white-board markers. Below is the price per marker for two brands. How much did the school save by buying Brand A instead of Brand B?

   Brand A: $0.27 each
   Brand B: $0.36 each

   (1) $0.09
   (2) $0.90
   (3) $9.00
   (4) $90.00
   (5) $900.00

Questions 9 and 10 refer to the following information.

Madison Small Animal Clinic Scheduling Guidelines	
New-Patient Appointment	$\frac{3}{4}$ hr
Immunizations	$\frac{1}{4}$ hr
Routine Physical	$\frac{1}{3}$ hr
Dental Scaling	$\frac{3}{4}$ hr
Sick Animal Visit	$\frac{1}{2}$ hr
Serious-Injury Visit (includes X rays)	$1\frac{1}{4}$ hr

9. Ray is a veterinarian at the small-animal clinic. He has four appointments scheduled for Monday morning: two new-patient appointments, a serious-injury visit, and a dental scaling. In hours, how much time should these appointments take?

    (1) $2\frac{3}{4}$
    (2) $3\frac{1}{2}$
    (3) $3\frac{3}{4}$
    (4) 4
    (5) $5\frac{1}{2}$

10. Jennifer works $3\frac{1}{2}$ hours each morning at the clinic. How many routine physicals could she complete in one morning?

    (1) 1
    (2) 4
    (3) 9
    (4) 10
    (5) 11

11. A minor-league baseball stadium has 6000 seats. On Beach Towel Night, the stadium sold 5500 of its available seats. What fraction of the seats were sold?

    (1) $\frac{5}{6}$
    (2) $\frac{7}{8}$
    (3) $\frac{8}{9}$
    (4) $\frac{9}{10}$
    (5) $\frac{11}{12}$

12. The City Center parking garage charges $3.50 for the first hour and $1.25 for each additional $\frac{1}{2}$ hour. How much would it cost to park at the garage for $2\frac{1}{2}$ hours?

    (1) $4.75
    (2) $6.25
    (3) $7.25
    (4) $8.75
    (5) $12.25

13. Susan scheduled 84 appointments for patients at a hospital outreach clinic. Only 56 patients kept their appointments. What fraction of the scheduled appointments were kept?

    Mark your answer in the circles on the grid at the bottom of the page.

14. This portion of a gas bill compares a household's natural gas usage for December of this year and last year.

Gas Bill Comparison Average Daily Usage			
This Year		Last Year	
Dec	3.13 therms	Dec	3.97 therms

How many more therms of natural gas did the household use in December of last year than December of this year?

Mark your answer in the circles on the grid at the bottom of the page.

13.

14.

PART II

Directions: Choose the <u>one best answer</u> to each question. You <u>MAY NOT</u> use your calculator for these questions.

15. Jim and Carl have until 1 P.M. to load 250 boxes. By 12:30 P.M., 175 of the boxes are loaded. What fraction of the boxes has <u>not</u> been loaded?

    (1) $\frac{1}{5}$

    (2) $\frac{3}{10}$

    (3) $\frac{3}{5}$

    (4) $\frac{7}{10}$

    (5) Not enough information is given.

16. Kim has two jobs. She earns $8.90 per hour as a landscaping assistant and $7.50 per hour as a clerk at a clothing store. In one week, she works 12 hours at her landscaping job and 15 hours at the clothing store. Which of the following expressions could be used to find her earnings for the week?

    (1) $(12 \times 15) + (\$8.90 + \$7.50)$
    (2) $27 \times \$8.90 \times \$7.50$
    (3) $(15 \times \$8.90) + (12 \times \$7.50)$
    (4) $(12 + 15) \times (\$8.90 + \$7.50)$
    (5) $(12 \times \$8.90) + (15 \times \$7.50)$

17. Scott is driving about 380 miles from Los Angeles to San Francisco. He plans to cover $\frac{3}{4}$ of the distance before noon. How many miles does he plan to drive before noon?

    (1) 285
    (2) 254
    (3) 126
    (4) 95
    (5) 32

18. A cookie recipe calls for $1\frac{2}{3}$ cups of sugar. If you wanted to make half the quantity shown in the recipe, how many cups of sugar would you use?

    (1) $\frac{2}{5}$

    (2) $\frac{2}{3}$

    (3) $\frac{3}{4}$

    (4) $\frac{5}{6}$

    (5) $1\frac{1}{6}$

19. Which of the following shows the drill bits arranged in order from least to greatest in size?

Carbide Steel Drill Bits		
Description	**Size (inches)**	**Price**
Cutter	$\frac{9}{16}$	$6.19
Core Box	$\frac{5}{32}$	$16.40
Classic	$\frac{3}{8}$	$17.85
Bevel	$\frac{1}{2}$	$10.50

    (1) cutter, bevel, classic, core box
    (2) core box, bevel, classic, cutter
    (3) core box, cutter, classic, bevel
    (4) bevel, classic, cutter, core box
    (5) core box, classic, bevel, cutter

20. A cable installer cuts two 12.75-foot lengths of coaxial cable from a 50-foot length of cable. Which of the following expressions could be used to find out how many feet of cable are left?

    (1) $12.75 + 12.75 - 50$
    (2) $50 - (2 \times 12.75)$
    (3) $50 - 2 - 12.75$
    (4) $2(50 - 12.75)$
    (5) $50 - 12.75$

21. A project should take no more than 60 hours. If John can spare 7.5 hours per day to work on the project, how many workdays should it take him to finish?

    (1) 5
    (2) 6
    (3) 7
    (4) 8
    (5) 9

22. How many miles would a map distance of $\frac{5}{8}$ inch represent if 1 in = 240 mi?

    (1) 40
    (2) 90
    (3) 130
    (4) 150
    (5) 200

23. A survey shows that $\frac{2}{3}$ of all homeowners have a pet. Of those, $\frac{3}{4}$ have either a dog or cat. Of the homeowners surveyed, what fraction has either a dog or a cat?

(1) $\frac{5}{12}$
(2) $\frac{1}{2}$
(3) $\frac{3}{4}$
(4) $\frac{5}{7}$
(5) $\frac{6}{7}$

24. At Wyman Shipping, 140 employees work during the day shift. At night, the crew is $\frac{2}{5}$ the size of the day shift. How many workers are scheduled to work the night shift?

(1) 28
(2) 56
(3) 70
(4) 94
(5) 98

Question 25 refers to the following map.

The map below shows the distance, in miles, between four stores.

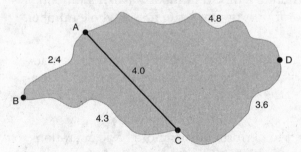

25. Maya drives a van that delivers supplies to each of the stores. On Friday, she traveled the following route.

Store A to Store B
Store B to Store C
Store C to Store D
Store D to Store C
Store C to Store A

How many miles did she drive in all?

(1) 13.9
(2) 14.3
(3) 15.1
(4) 17.9
(5) 19.1

26. From a wooden dowel $12\frac{1}{2}$ feet long, Jamie cut two pieces, each $3\frac{3}{4}$ feet long. How long, in feet, is the remaining piece?

(1) $9\frac{1}{2}$
(2) $8\frac{3}{4}$
(3) $7\frac{1}{2}$
(4) $6\frac{1}{2}$
(5) 5

27. Luis bought 20 shares of stock, priced at $26.38 per share. He also paid an $8 transaction fee. How much did he pay?

(1) $687.60
(2) $535.60
(3) $527.60
(4) $519.60
(5) $54.38

28. A mat board is 60 inches wide. How many strips measuring 0.75 inch wide can be cut from the board? (Assume no waste from the cuts.)

Mark your answer in the circles on the grid at the bottom of the page.

29. Of his take-home pay each month, Jerry spends $\frac{1}{6}$ on a car payment and $\frac{1}{4}$ on food. What fraction of his take-home pay is left after paying for these two items?

Mark your answer in the circles on the grid at the bottom of the page.

28.

29.

Answers and explanations begin on page 667.

RATIO, PROPORTION, AND PERCENT

Using Ratio and Proportion to Solve Problems

Ratio

A **ratio** compares two numbers. You can write a ratio using the word *to*, using a colon (:), or using fraction form.

Example 1: A softball pitcher strikes out four batters for every one batter that she walks. What is the ratio of strikeouts to walks?

Always write the numbers in the ratio in the same order in which they appear in the question.   **4 to 1   4:1 $\dfrac{4}{1}$**

Ratios are similar to fractions. They have two terms, and they can be simplified by reducing to lowest terms.

Example 2: Frank manages a small drugstore. During a two-hour period, he counts 25 cash sales and 15 credit card sales. What is the ratio of credit card to cash sales?

1. Write the ratio as a fraction with the terms in the correct order: credit card to cash sales. $\dfrac{\text{credit card sales}}{\text{cash sales}}\quad\dfrac{15}{25}$

2. Reduce to lowest terms. The ratio of credit card to cash sales is **3 to 5.** $\dfrac{15 \div 5}{25 \div 5} = \dfrac{3}{5}$

There are some fraction rules that ratios do not follow. Do not change a ratio that is an improper fraction to a mixed number. Also, if a ratio in fraction form has a denominator of 1, <u>do not</u> write it as a whole number. Leave it in fraction form.

Another important difference is in the use of labels. The terms in a fraction have the same unit labels: *5/6 of a pie means 5 slices out of 6 slices.* Ratios <u>may</u> have different labels: *The sale advertised 6 cans for $1, a 6:1 ratio.*

To write a ratio, you may need to perform one or more basic operations to find one of the terms.

Example 3: A football team won 12 games and lost 8. What is the ratio of games won to games played?

1. The problem does not tell you the number of games played. Add the games won to the games lost to find the games played.   12 won + 8 lost = 20 played

2. Write the ratio in the correct order and simplify. **The team won 3 games for every 5 games it played, a 3:5 ratio.** $\dfrac{\text{games won}}{\text{games played}}\quad\dfrac{12}{20} = \dfrac{12 \div 4}{20 \div 4} = \dfrac{3}{5}$

Key Ideas

- A ratio has two terms and can be written in words, with a colon, or as a fraction.
- Ratios are simplified by reducing to lowest terms.
- The terms in a ratio can have different labels.

GED TIP

The terms in a ratio must be written in the order given by the words of the question. Don't be fooled by an answer choice that reverses the order of the numbers.

RATIO, PROPORTION, AND PERCENT ▸ PRACTICE 1.1

A. Write each ratio as a fraction in lowest terms.

1. Stan made 24 sales in 6 hours. What is the ratio of sales to hours?

2. Carol's monthly take-home pay is $1500. She spends $250 a month on food. What is the ratio of food costs to take-home dollars?

3. A toy rocket travels 180 ft in 15 sec. What is the ratio of feet to seconds?

4. At Phil's work, there are 12 part-time workers and 18 full-time workers. What is the ratio of part-time workers to total workers?

5. Juanita drove 336 miles on 14 gallons of gasoline. What is the ratio of miles to gallons?

6. Lynn estimates that a roofing job will cost $1500. Bo estimates that the same job will cost $2400. What is the ratio of Lynn's estimate to Bo's estimate?

7. A basketball player attempted 32 free throws and made 20. What is the ratio of free throws made to free throws missed?

8. There are 10 men and 14 women in Kathleen's math class. What is the ratio of women to the total number of students in the class?

9. To paint his apartment, Alex bought 6 gallons of paint to cover 1440 square feet. What is the ratio of square feet to gallons of paint?

B. Choose the one best answer to each question.

Questions 10 through 12 refer to the following information.

Three candidates are running for mayor. Below are the results of a survey of 600 registered voters.

Candidate	Number of Supporters
Stothard	220
Mesa	180
Newmark	50
Undecided	150

10. What is the ratio of Mesa's supporters to Stothard's supporters?

    (1) 2:11
    (2) 9:11
    (3) 11:9
    (4) 11:20
    (5) 20:11

11. What is the ratio of voters who prefer Mesa to the total number surveyed?

    (1) 2 to 5
    (2) 3 to 7
    (3) 3 to 10
    (4) 3 to 13
    (5) 11 to 30

12. What is the ratio of undecided voters to voters who have made a decision?

    (1) $\frac{1}{4}$
    (2) $\frac{1}{3}$
    (3) $\frac{3}{1}$
    (4) $\frac{4}{1}$
    (5) Not enough information is given.

13. Soan made a $400 down payment on a washer and dryer that cost a total of $1200. What is the ratio of the amount paid to the amount owed?

    (1) 1 to 4
    (2) 1 to 3
    (3) 1 to 2
    (4) 2 to 3
    (5) 3 to 4

14. After playing 77 games, a team won 56 games. What is the ratio of wins to losses?

    (1) 3:8
    (2) 8:19
    (3) 8:11
    (4) 11:8
    (5) 8:3

Answers and explanations begin on page 668.

Proportion

A **proportion** is an equation that shows that two ratios are equal. The cross **products** in a true proportion are equal. In other words, when you multiply diagonally across the equals sign, the products are equal.

Example 1: The directions on a can of powdered drink mix say to add 3 cups of water to every 2 scoops of drink mix. Matt adds 12 cups of water to 8 scoops of drink mix. Did he make the drink correctly?

1. Write a proportion, making sure the terms of the ratios are in the same order.

$$\frac{\text{cups}}{\text{scoops}} \qquad \frac{3}{2} \diagup\!\!\!\!\diagdown \frac{12}{8}$$

2. Cross multiply and compare the products. Since the products are the same, the ratios are equal. **Matt made the drink correctly.**

$$3 \times 8 = 24$$
$$2 \times 12 = 24$$

In most proportion problems, you are asked to solve for a missing term.

Example 2: A map scale says that 2 inches = 150 miles. What actual distance would a map distance of 5 inches represent?

1. Write a proportion with both ratios in the same form: inches to miles. The variable x represents the unknown distance.

$$\frac{\text{inches}}{\text{miles}} \qquad \frac{2}{150} = \frac{5}{x}$$

2. Locate the term in the first ratio that is diagonal from the known term in the second ratio. Cross multiply.

$$\frac{2}{150} \diagup\!\!\!\!\diagdown \frac{5}{x}$$

$$150 \times 5 = 750$$

3. Divide the result by the remaining known term to find the value of x.

$$750 \div 2 = \textbf{375 miles}$$

Some proportion problems ask you to find a **rate.** A rate compares a quantity to 1. When a rate is written in fraction form, its denominator is always 1. In word form, rates are often expressed using the word *per*.

Example 3: Connie drove 276 miles on 12 gallons of gasoline. How many miles per gallon did she get on the trip?

1. Gas mileage is one kind of rate. You need to find how many miles Connie drove on one gallon of gasoline.

$$\frac{\text{miles}}{\text{gallons}} \qquad \frac{276}{12} = \frac{x}{1}$$

2. Solve.

$$276 \times 1 = 276$$
$$276 \div 12 = \textbf{23 miles per gallon}$$

Using your calculator, you can solve proportion problems in one series of calculations.

Example 4: Find the value of x in the proportion $\dfrac{6}{16} = \dfrac{21}{x}$.

You need to multiply 16 and 21, then divide by 6.
Press: 16 $\boxed{\times}$ 21 $\boxed{\div}$ 6 = $\boxed{56.}$
The missing term is **56.**

Note: When working a problem, ask yourself if it can be solved using proportion. This may be possible when two quantities are compared or when three values are given and you are asked to find a fourth.

A. Solve for the missing term in each proportion problem. Use your calculator for questions 9 through 16. *Note*: Answers will not always be whole numbers.

1. $\frac{2}{3} = \frac{x}{18}$

2. $\frac{3}{5} = \frac{27}{x}$

3. $\frac{6}{5} = \frac{3}{x}$

4. $\frac{15}{2} = \frac{x}{8}$

5. $\frac{4}{\$2.12} = \frac{7}{x}$

6. $\frac{25}{6} = \frac{400}{x}$

7. $\frac{7}{30} = \frac{x}{9}$

8. $\frac{0.5}{12} = \frac{3}{x}$

9. $\frac{20}{2.5} = \frac{100}{x}$

10. $\frac{\$5.96}{2} = \frac{x}{3}$

11. $\frac{12}{5} = \frac{3}{x}$

12. $\frac{4}{60} = \frac{2.5}{x}$

13. $\frac{3}{19} = \frac{x}{114}$

14. $\frac{9}{\$80.10} = \frac{x}{\$284.80}$

15. $\frac{\$26.00}{4} = \frac{x}{7}$

16. $\frac{24}{96} = \frac{7}{x}$

B. Choose the <u>one best answer</u> to each question. You **MAY** use your calculator for questions 20 through 22.

17. A store is advertising the following sale:

> Tomato Soup
> 4 cans for $0.98

To the nearest cent, how much would five cans of tomato soup cost?

(1) $0.25
(2) $1.23
(3) $2.45
(4) $3.92
(5) $12.25

18. The Bay City Cardinals have won 5 out of 8 games. At the same rate, how many games will they have to play to win 60 games?

(1) 190
(2) 180
(3) 120
(4) 96
(5) 12

19. Carla drove her truck 414 miles on 18 gallons of gasoline. How many miles did she drive per gallon?

(1) 18
(2) 23
(3) 74
(4) 95
(5) Not enough information is given.

20. The scale on a map reads, "2 cm = 150 km." How many kilometers would be represented by a distance of 4.6 centimeters?

(1) 92
(2) 300
(3) 345
(4) 690
(5) 1380

21. Two ingredients in a recipe are $2\frac{1}{2}$ cups of flour and $1\frac{1}{2}$ cups of sugar. If June keeps the proportion the same, how many cups of flour should she add to 4 cups of sugar?

(1) 10
(2) $6\frac{2}{3}$
(3) 6
(4) 5
(5) $3\frac{3}{4}$

22. Claudia drove 155 miles in 2.5 hours. Which of the following expressions could be used to find how many miles she can drive in 7 hours?

(1) $155 \times 7 \div 2.5$
(2) $2.5 \times 7 \div 155$
(3) $155 \times 2.5 \div 7$
(4) $2.5 \div 7 \times 155$
(5) $7 \times 2.5 \times 155$

Answers and explanations begin on page 668.

RATIO, PROPORTION, AND PERCENT

Understanding Percents

Breaking Down Percent Problems

Percent **means** "per hundred" or "out of one hundred." For example, if you have $100 and you spend $25, you spent $25 out of $100, or 25% of your money.

Since percent is a way of showing part of a whole, it has much in common with fractions and decimals. To convert a percent to a fraction, write the percent over 100 and reduce. To convert percents to decimals, drop the percent symbol and move the decimal point two places to the left.

Percent to Fraction   **Percent to Decimal**
$$25\% = \tfrac{25}{100} = \tfrac{1}{4}$$ $$25\% = .25 = 0.25$$

In any percent problem, there are three elements: the base, the part, and the rate. The **base** is the whole quantity, or amount, that the problem is about. The **part** (also called a **percentage**) is a portion of the base. The **rate** is a number followed by the percent symbol (%).

Example 1: At a restaurant, Janice's bill is $20. She gives the waiter a tip of $3, which is 15% of her bill. Identify the base, part, and rate in this situation.

The entire bill of $20 is the base. The $3 tip is part of the base, and the rate is 15%.

One way to think of a percent problem is as a proportion. In Example 1, there are two ratios. The $3 tip is part of the $20 total bill, and 15% is the same as $\tfrac{15}{100}$. Since the two ratios are equal, they can be written as a proportion.

$$\frac{\text{part}}{\text{base}} \cdot \frac{3}{20} = \frac{15}{100}$$

Cross multiply to prove the ratios are equal.

$$20 \times 15 = 300$$
$$3 \times 100 = 300$$

You can solve percent problems by setting up a proportion and solving for the missing elements. Just remember to express the percent as a number over 100.

Example 2: At a plant that manufactures lighting fixtures, it is expected that about 2% of the fixtures assembled each day will have some type of defect. If 900 fixtures are completed in one day, how many are expected to be defective?

1. Write a proportion. Remember that 2% means 2 out of 100. Use the variable x to stand for the number of defective fixtures.

$$\frac{\text{part}}{\text{base}} = \frac{\text{rate}}{100}$$

$$\frac{x}{900} = \frac{2}{100}$$

2. Solve for x. Cross multiply and divide by the remaining number. **The company can expect about 18 defective fixtures.**

$$900 \times 2 = 1800$$
$$1800 \div 100 = 18$$

Key Ideas

- The percent symbol (%) means "out of 100."
- The three elements of a percent problem are the base, the part, and the rate.
- Percent problems can be solved by writing a proportion that has a percent ratio with a denominator of 100.

GED TIP

The word of often comes before the base in a percent problem. For example, if you are asked to find 75% of 250, you know that 250 is the base.

A. For each situation, identify and label the base, part, and rate.

1. Victor owes his uncle $1000. Recently, he gave his uncle $200. The payment was 20% of the money he owes.

2. On a test with 80 problems, Sophie got 72 problems right. In other words, she answered 90% of the problems correctly.

3. The Kang family made a down payment of $2,740 on a new car. The down payment was 20% of the purchase price of $13,700.

4. Zoe's take-home pay each month is $2000. She spends $500 on rent each month, which is 25% of her take-home pay.

5. This year, Rafael has 60 regular customers, which is 150% of the 40 regular customers he had last year.

6. Kayla bought a dress for $38. She paid $3.23 in sales tax. The sales tax rate in her state is 8.5%.

7. Misako's employer withholds 15% of her salary each paycheck for taxes. Misako earns $900 each week, and her tax withholding is $135.

8. Harrison got a 10% raise. Before the raise, his hourly wage was $10.70. Now he earns an additional $1.07 per hour.

9. Kim Industries has 800 employees. Of those, 200 workers, or 25%, work part-time.

10. In an election, 5,000 of the 12,500 registered voters actually voted. Only 40% of the registered voters actually voted.

B. Choose the <u>one best answer</u> to each question. Use the proportion $\frac{\text{part}}{\text{base}} = \frac{\text{rate}}{100}$ to solve each problem.

Questions 11 and 12 refer to the following information.

A local newspaper printed the following high school basketball standings:

Team	Wins	Losses
Fairfax	9	3
Hamilton	8	4
Bravo	6	6
Mountain View	4	8
Lincoln	3	9

11. Which of the following expressions could be used to find what percent of its total games Fairfax has won?

   (1) $\dfrac{9 \times 100}{12}$

   (2) $\dfrac{3 \times 100}{12}$

   (3) $\dfrac{12 \times 100}{9}$

   (4) $\dfrac{12 \times 100}{3}$

   (5) $\dfrac{6 \times 100}{12}$

12. What percent of its games did Bravo win?

   (1) 100%
   (2) 75%
   (3) 60%
   (4) 50%
   (5) 25%

13. A jacket with a price tag of $128 is on a rack with the following sign:

   > All Items:
   > 25% off marked price
   > Discount taken at register

   By how much will the price be reduced when the jacket is taken to the register?

   (1) $4
   (2) $25
   (3) $32
   (4) $96
   (5) Not enough information is given.

Answers and explanations begin on page 668.

RATIO, PROPORTION, AND PERCENT

Using the Percent Formula

Key Ideas

- You can use a formula to solve percent problems: *Base × Rate = Part*.
- To change a percent to a decimal, drop the % sign and move the decimal point two places to the left.
- To change a decimal to a percent, move the decimal point two places to the right and add the % sign.

Solving for Part

You have seen how to use proportion to solve percent problems. You can also solve percent problems using the formula ***Base × Rate = Part***.

Study the diagram at the right to learn how to use the formula. To use the diagram, cover the element you need to solve for: B = Base, R = Rate (percent), and P = Part. Then perform the operation that connects the remaining elements.

Example 1: A company offers its employees two health plans. In a recent newsletter, the personnel department stated that 70% of the employees chose Plan A. If the company has 320 workers, how many chose Plan A?

1. The rate is 70%, and the base is 320, the total number of workers. You need to solve for the part. Using the diagram, cover P for part. You can see that you need to multiply to solve the problem.

2. Change the percent to a decimal and multiply.
   Out of 320 workers, 224 chose Plan A.

   $70\% = 0.7$
   $320 \times 0.7 = 224$

Solving for Rate

Rewrite the percent formula to solve for rate. Use the formula ***Part ÷ Base = Rate***. You can use the diagram to help you remember the formula.

Example 2: A computer system is regularly priced at $1600. On Friday the manager reduced the price by $640. By what percent did the manager discount the computer system?

1. The base is $1600, the regular price. The part is $640, the amount the price was reduced. You are asked to find the rate of the discount. Cover R for rate (percent). You need to divide the part by the base to solve the problem.

2. Divide 640 by 1600.

3. Convert the decimal answer to a percent by moving the decimal point two places to the right and adding the percent sign. The price reduction was a **40% discount.**

$$\begin{array}{r} .4 \\ 1600\overline{)640.0} \\ \underline{640\ 0} \end{array}$$

$0.4 = 40 = 40\%$

Always ask yourself whether your answer seems reasonable. For example, you know that 40% is a little less than $\frac{1}{2}$, and $\frac{1}{2}$ of $1600 is $800. Since $640 is a little less than $800, it is a reasonable answer.

GED TIP

When you take the GED Math Test, make a quick sketch of the percent diagram on scratch paper to help you analyze percent problems.

A. Solve. You <u>MAY</u> use a calculator for questions 7 through 17.

1. What is 20% of $25?

2. Find 90% of 200.

3. What is 35% of 400?

4. What percent is 19 out of 20?

5. 42 is what percent of 168?

6. What percent is $18 out of $600?

7. Find $33\frac{1}{3}$% of 51. (*Hint:* $33\frac{1}{3}\% = \frac{1}{3}$)

8. What is 125% of $48?

9. 240 is what percent of 120?

10. What percent is 3 out of 60?

11. $52 is what percent of $650?

12. Find $8\frac{1}{2}$% of $46.

13. $0.65 is what percent of $10.00?

14. Find 28% of $1300.

15. What percent is 2.5 out of 4?

16. Find $66\frac{2}{3}$% of 108. (*Hint:* $66\frac{2}{3}\% = \frac{2}{3}$)

B. Choose the <u>one best answer</u> to each question. You <u>MAY</u> use your calculator.

17. Pat called 120 customers to offer a software upgrade. Of those he called, 72 purchased the upgrade. What percent agreed to the purchase?

    (1) 6%
    (2) 40%
    (3) 48%
    (4) 60%
    (5) $66\frac{2}{3}$%

18. Douglas received a 6% raise. If his old monthly salary was $2,250, what is his monthly salary now? (*Hint:* Find the amount of the raise. Then add the raise to the previous monthly salary.)

    (1) $1,125
    (2) $2,256
    (3) $2,385
    (4) $3,600
    (5) $13,500

19. At a restaurant Levy's total bill is about $46. Which of the following expressions could he use to calculate a 15% tip?

    (1) $46 × 15
    (2) $46 ÷ 15 × 100
    (3) $46 × 15 × 100
    (4) $46 ÷ 0.15
    (5) $46 × 0.15

20. The following advertisement for sporting goods appeared in the newspaper. What percent of the original price is the sale price?

Little League Package
Magnum bat, tote bag, and youth cleats
Only $45.50
Originally $65
You SAVE $20!

    (1) 20%
    (2) 31%
    (3) 44%
    (4) 70%
    (5) Not enough information is given.

21. Lydia pays $3 sales tax on a $50 purchase. Which of the following expressions could be used to find the sales tax rate in her state?

    (1) $\dfrac{\$3 \times 100}{\$50}$

    (2) $\dfrac{\$3 \times \$50}{100}$

    (3) $3 × $50 × 100
    (4) $3 ÷ $50
    (5) $3 × $50

Answers and explanations begin on page 668.

Solving for Base

Some problems on the GED Math Test may require you to solve for the base in a percent situation. Remember, the base represents the whole item or group. Read each situation carefully to figure out which element is missing. Then choose the correct method for solving the problem.

Example 3: In a math class, 75% of the students got at least a B grade on the final exam. If 18 students got at least a B, how many students are in the class?

1. Analyze the situation. The 18 students are part of the larger class. You know that the 18 students are 75% of the whole group, so 75% is the rate and the base is unknown.

   Use the diagram. Cover B for base. You need to divide the part by the rate to solve the problem.

2. Convert the rate to a decimal (75% = 0.75) and divide. There are **24 students** in the class.

$$\begin{array}{r} 24 \\ 0.75\overline{)18.00} \\ \underline{15\,0} \\ 300 \\ \underline{300} \end{array}$$

Most of the time we work with percents that are less than 100%. When a percent is less than 100%, the part is less than the base. However, it is possible to have a situation in which the part is greater than the base. When this occurs, the percent will be greater than 100%.

Example 4: The workforce at Eastland Inc. is growing rapidly. The number of employees this year is 225% of the number last year. If there are 135 employees this year, how many employees did the company have last year?

1. The base is the number of employees the company had last year. This year's number is a percent of last year's number. Therefore, the rate is 225%, the part is 135, and the base is unknown.

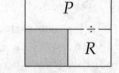

$$225\% = 2.25 = 2.25$$

2. Convert 225% to a decimal. Drop the % sign and move the decimal point two places to the left.

3. Divide the part (135) by the rate (2.25). Last year there were only **60 employees**.

$$\begin{array}{r} 60 \\ 2.25\overline{)135.00} \\ \underline{135\;0} \end{array}$$

Some problems on the GED Math Test are set-up problems. Instead of finding a solution, you have to choose the correct method for solving the problem. (See problems 19 and 21 on page 397.) These choices may be based on the percent formula shown in this lesson or on the proportion method shown in Lesson 2.

Both of these set-up choices show a correct method for solving Example 4.

Formula method: $\dfrac{135}{2.25}$ Proportion method: $\dfrac{135 \times 100}{225}$

If you evaluate both methods using a calculator, both expressions equal 60, the correct solution.

Note: Don't begin calculations before you completely analyze a situation. Every percent problem has three elements. Make sure you know which one is missing before you multiply or divide.

A. Find the missing element in each set.

1. $35 is 20% of what amount?

2. 5% of what number is 14?

3. 3.2 is 50% of what number?

4. $170 is 85% of what amount?

5. 24 is 80% of what number?

6. $105 is 125% of what amount?

7. 190 is 95% of what number?

8. What number is 15% of 60?

9. 90% of $15 is what number?

10. $42 is what percent of $168?

11. $150 is 200% of what amount?

12. 15% of $62 is what amount?

13. 9 is 1% of what number?

14. What percent is 126 of 140?

15. 65% of $1200 is what amount?

16. 5% of an amount is $156. What is the amount?

17. $2\frac{1}{2}$% of a number is 100. What is the number?

18. What percent is $15.60 of $156.00?

B. Choose the one best answer to each question. You MAY use your calculator.

19. Kevin's total payroll deductions are 30% of his earnings. If his deductions add up to $369 for a two-week period, how much were his earnings for the period?

    (1) $110.70
    (2) $123.00
    (3) $1,230.00
    (4) $11,070.00
    (5) Not enough information is given.

20. City council established the following budget to improve public transportation.

	Project Budget
Salaries	50%
Office lease	35%
Equipment	6%
Supplies	2%
Miscellaneous	7%

    If $72,000 is allotted for equipment, what is the total budget for the project?

    (1) $94,000
    (2) $432,000
    (3) $940,000
    (4) $1,200,000
    (5) $120,000,000

21. Jack earns a 5% commission on each sale. If he is paid a $160 commission, which of the following expressions could be used to find the amount of the sale?

    (1) $\dfrac{5 \times 100}{160}$

    (2) $\dfrac{160 \times 100}{5}$

    (3) $\dfrac{5 \times 160}{100}$

    (4) $5 \times 100 \times 160$

    (5) $5 \div 160 \times 100$

22. American Loan Company mailed 3600 customers an application for a new credit card. Only 20% of the customers returned the application. Which of the following expressions could be used to find how many customers returned the application?

    (1) $3600 \times 2 \times 100$

    (2) $\dfrac{12}{5} = \dfrac{3}{x}$

    (3) $\dfrac{3600 \times 100}{0.2}$

    (4) 3600×0.2

    (5) $3600 \div 0.2$

Answers and explanations begin on page 669.

LESSON

4

RATIO, PROPORTION, AND PERCENT

Solving Problems Using a Calculator

Key Ideas

- To use the % key to solve problems, multiply or divide as you would normally, pressing the percent key last. The display will show the answer.

- Do not change the percent to a decimal or a fraction if you are using the percent key.

Using the Percent Key

You already know how to solve problems with fractions and decimals on a calculator. By changing a percent to either a fraction or decimal, you can use a calculator to solve a percent problem.

Example 1: What is 25% of 120?

Change 25% to a decimal and multiply. 25% = 0.25
Press: 120 $\boxed{\times}$ .25 $\boxed{=}$ $\boxed{\qquad 30}$

Change 25% to a fraction and multiply. 25% = $\frac{25}{100}$ = $\frac{1}{4}$
Press: 120 $\boxed{\times}$ 1 $\boxed{a^b/_c}$ 4 $\boxed{=}$ $\boxed{\qquad 30}$

Using either method, you find that **30 is 25% of 120.**

You can also use the percent key $\boxed{\%}$ on your calculator. On the *Casio fx-260* (the calculator provided with the GED), the percent key is the second function above the equals key $\boxed{=}$. To access a second function, you must first press the shift key located in the upper left corner of the calculator and then press the function key.

When you use the percent key, there is no need to convert the percent to either a fraction or decimal. Study the examples below to learn how to use this key. Notice that you must press the % key last in each example.

Example 2: What is 65% of $360?

Multiply the base ($360) and the rate (65%) to find the part.

Press: 360 $\boxed{\times}$ 65 $\boxed{\text{SHIFT}}$ $\boxed{\%}$ The display reads $\boxed{\quad 234.}$
The amount **$234** is 65% of $360.

Example 3: Ned paid $150 for a sound system. The amount was 20% of the total cost of the system. What was the total cost of the system?

Divide the part ($150) by the rate (20%) to find the base.

Press: 150 $\boxed{\div}$ 20 $\boxed{\text{SHIFT}}$ $\boxed{\%}$ The display reads $\boxed{\quad 750.}$
The cost of the system was **$750.**

Example 4: Mona spends $400 of her monthly earnings on child care. If she earns $2500 per month, what percent does she spend on child care?

Divide the part ($400) by the base ($2500) to find the rate.

Press: 400 $\boxed{\div}$ 2500 $\boxed{\text{SHIFT}}$ $\boxed{\%}$ The display reads $\boxed{\quad 16.}$
Mona spends **16%** of her salary on child care.

GED TIP

You may find it easier to solve a problem with a fraction instead of a percent. For example, it is easier to find $\frac{1}{3}$ of some numbers than to find $33\frac{1}{3}\%$ of a number.

RATIO, PROPORTION, AND PERCENT ▶ PRACTICE 4

A. Solve these problems using a calculator.

1. Find 46% of $130.

2. 14% of what amount is $13.44?

3. What is 12% of $126?

4. What number is $62\frac{1}{2}$% of 64?

5. 12 is what percent of 400?

6. A number is 32% of 6500. What is the number?

7. 36 is what percent of 144?

8. 90% of what number is 63?

9. Find 7% of 360.

10. What number is $33\frac{1}{3}$% of 237?

11. 25 is what percent of 1000?

12. What is $12\frac{1}{2}$% of 384?

13. 390 is what percent of 500?

14. Find 2% of $800.

15. 32% of what number is 80?

16. What number is $87\frac{1}{2}$% of 16?

17. $112 is what percent of $1600?

18. A number is $66\frac{2}{3}$% of 414. What is the number?

B. Choose the one best answer to each question. You MAY use your calculator.

Questions 19 and 20 refer to the following chart.

Shipping and Handling Information	
For items costing:	**% of order + handling:**
$20 or less	3% + $1.50
$20.01 to $50	4% + $2.50
$50.01 to $100	5% + $4.00
$100.01 or more	8%

19. Chanel placed an $84 order. How much shipping and handling will she be charged on her order?

   (1) $4.20
   (2) $4.40
   (3) $7.56
   (4) $8.20
   (5) $8.36

20. Jason placed an order totaling $110. Zola placed a $90 order. How much more did Jason pay in shipping and handling than Zola?

   (1) $0.30
   (2) $4.30
   (3) $4.50
   (4) $4.60
   (5) $20.00

21. In an election, 3190 out of 3625 registered voters voted against a tax increase. What percent of the registered voters voted against the increase?

   (1) 43%
   (2) 83%
   (3) 88%
   (4) 98%
   (5) 113%

22. A baseball player has the following statistics. To the nearest percent, what percent of the player's at bats were strikeouts?

At Bats	Hits	Home Runs	Walks	Strikeouts
410	108	2	70	63

   (1) 90%
   (2) 85%
   (3) 58%
   (4) 26%
   (5) 15%

Answers and explanations begin on page 669.

RATIO, PROPORTION, AND PERCENT

Simple Interest

Solving Simple Interest Problems

Interest is a fee paid for the use of someone else's money. If you put money in a savings account, you receive interest from the bank. If you borrow money, you pay interest. In each case, the amount that you invest or borrow is called the **principal.**

Simple interest is a percent of the principal multiplied by the length of the loan. The formula for finding simple interest is given on the formulas page of the GED Math Test (see page 688). It reads:

> **simple interest**   interest = principal × rate × time

You may find it easier to remember the formula using **variables** (letters that stand for numbers): $i = prt$, where i = interest, p = principal, r = rate, and t = time. Writing variables next to each other means that they are to be multiplied.

Example 1: Asher borrows $2500 from his uncle for three years at 6% simple interest. How much interest will he pay on the loan?

1. Write the rate as a decimal.   6% = 0.06

2. Substitute the known values in the $i = prt$
   formula. Multiply. $= \$2500 \times 0.06 \times 3$
                                                   $= \$450$

Asher will pay **$450** in interest.

Some problems ask you to find the **amount paid back.** This adds an additional step to an interest problem. In Example 1, Asher will owe $450 in interest at the end of three years. However, he will pay back the interest ($450) plus the principal ($2500): $2500 + $450 = $2950. When he has finished paying the loan, Asher will have paid his uncle $2950.

In a simple interest problem, the rate is an annual, or yearly, rate. Therefore, the time must also be expressed in years.

Example 2: Eva invests $3000 for 9 months. She will be paid 8% simple interest on her investment. How much interest will she earn?

1. Write the rate as a decimal.   8% = 0.08

2. Express the time as a fraction of a year   9 months $= \frac{9}{12} = \frac{3}{4}$ year
   by writing the length of time in months
   over 12, the number of months in a
   year.

3. Multiply. $i = prt$
                                           $= \$3000 \times 0.08 \times \frac{3}{4}$
Eva will earn **$180** in interest. $= \$180$

Key Ideas

- Simple interest is found by multiplying principal, rate, and time: $i = prt$.
- The time must be written in terms of years. Write months as a fraction of a year.
- To find the amount paid back, add the principal and the interest.

GED TIP

A formulas page (see page 688) is provided when you take the GED Math Test. Try to memorize some of the formulas as you work through this book so you can save time on the test.

A. Solve these problems using the formula for simple interest. You MAY use your calculator.

1. Leah borrows $1500 for 2 years at a 12% interest rate. Find the interest on the loan.

2. How much interest would you pay on a loan of $800 for 6 months at 14% interest?

3. Dominica invested $2000 for 3 years at an interest rate of 7%. How much interest did she earn on her money?

4. How much interest would you earn on an investment of $600 for 8 years at 10% interest?

5. Todd invests $6500 for $3\frac{1}{2}$ years at 5% interest. How much interest will he be paid at the end of the time period?

6. Ricardo borrows $1850 for 8 months at 12% interest. What is the amount he will pay back at the end of the loan period?

7. Yanira puts $5000 in an investment account for 4 years. If she is paid $8\frac{1}{2}$% simple interest, how much interest will she earn?

B. Choose the one best answer to each question. You MAY use your calculator.

8. Jean borrowed $1300 to buy tools for her job as an auto mechanic. The loan is for 1 year 6 months at 9% simple interest. Which of the following expressions could be used to find the amount she will pay back at the end of the loan period?

   (1) $1300 × 1.5 × 0.09
   (2) $1300 × 1.6 × 0.09
   (3) $1300 × 1.5 × 9
   (4) $1300 + ($1300 × 9 × 1.5)
   (5) $1300 + ($1300 × 0.09 × 1.5)

9. Noah borrows $8000 for 5 years to make improvements to his home office. If the simple interest rate is 13%, how much will he pay in interest?

   (1) $5200
   (2) $4000
   (3) $1040
   (4) $420
   (5) $400

10. Caleb borrowed $1500 from his aunt. He plans to pay his aunt back in 9 months. If he pays 4% interest on the loan, what is the total amount he will pay back in 9 months?

   (1) $540
   (2) $1455
   (3) $1545
   (4) $1560
   (5) $2040

Questions 11 and 12 refer to the following information.

Option	Length of Loan	Simple Interest Rate
A	$2\frac{1}{2}$ years	12%
B	3 years	10%
C	4 years	9%

11. Charlotte needs to borrow $2400. She is considering the three loan options shown above. How much more interest would Charlotte pay if she takes loan option C instead of option A?

   (1) $72
   (2) $108
   (3) $144
   (4) $720
   (5) $864

12. Charlotte chooses Option B, but she decides to borrow $2800. What is the total amount she will pay back when the loan is due?

   (1) $2830
   (2) $2884
   (3) $3240
   (4) $3556
   (5) $3640

Answers and explanations begin on page 669.

RATIO, PROPORTION, AND PERCENT

Percent of Change

Key Ideas

- The amount of change is the difference between the new number and the original number.
- Find the percent of change by dividing the amount of change by the original number.
- Percent of increase may be greater than 100%.

Finding Percent of Increase or Decrease

Percent is often used to show change.

Example 1: Michelle recently started her own business. Last month she earned $1000. This month she earned $2000. How could she describe the increase in her earnings?

All of the following statements accurately describe the change.

- Michelle's earnings doubled from last month to this month.
- This month her earnings increased by 100%.
- This month's earnings are 200% of last month's earnings.

Percent of change compares a new number, which shows an increase or a decrease, to the original number—the number before the change.

Example 2: Before her raise, Lisa earned $10.50 per hour. Now she earns $11.34 per hour. What percent raise did her boss give her?

1. Subtract to find the amount of change.

$11.34 - $10.50 = $0.84

2. Divide the amount of change by $10.50, Lisa's wage before the change. Convert the decimal to a percent. Lisa's hourly wage **increased by 8%**.

$$\frac{$0.84}{$10.50} = 0.08 = 8\%$$

GED TIP

You can work backward to check your answers. For example, if a price has decreased by 25%, the new price should be 75% of the original price, since 25% + 75% = 100%.

Think carefully about a situation to decide which number is the original amount.

Example 3: A jacket is on sale for $90. Three days ago, the jacket was on sale for $120. By what percent was the price of the jacket reduced?

1. Subtract to find the amount of change.

$120 - $90 = $30

2. The price of the jacket was $120 before it was $90, so $120 is the original price. Divide the amount of change by $120. The new price is **25% less** than the price three days ago.

$$\frac{$30}{$120} = 0.25 = 25\%$$

Percent of increase may be greater than 100%.

Example 4: Calvin started his business with 10 employees. Now he has 60 employees. By what percent has his workforce increased?

1. Subtract to find the amount of change.

60 − 10 = 50

2. Divide by the original number. Convert the number to a percent. Calvin's workforce has **increased by 500%**.

$$\frac{50}{10} = 5.0 = 500\%$$

RATIO, PROPORTION, AND PERCENT ▸ PRACTICE 6

A. Solve as directed. If necessary, round your answer to the nearest percent. You **MAY** use your calculator for questions 7 through 12.

1. Find the percent of increase from 2000 to 3000.

2. Find the percent of decrease from $2.00 to $1.25.

3. What is the percent of increase from 30 to 90?

4. Find the percent of decrease from 20 to 11.

5. Find the percent of increase from $25 to $30.

6. What is the percent of decrease from 500 to 340?

7. Find the percent of increase from $1.89 to $2.29.

8. What is the percent of decrease from 21 to 3?

9. Find the percent of increase from 65 to 338.

10. What is the percent of decrease from $1550 to $1025?

B. Choose the <u>one best answer</u> to each question. You **MAY** use your calculator.

11. Justin recently moved from a part-time to a full-time job. Because of the change, his weekly pay increased from $280 to $448. To the nearest percent, by what percent did his income increase?

    (1) 17%
    (2) $37\frac{1}{2}$%
    (3) 60%
    (4) 168%
    (5) 267%

12. David bought a computer game on sale for $36. The game was originally $48. What was the percent of decrease in the game's price?

    (1) 12%
    (2) 25%
    (3) $33\frac{1}{3}$%
    (4) $66\frac{2}{3}$%
    (5) 75%

13. The Utleys' rent increased from $600 to $636 per month. By what percent did the rent increase?

    (1) 3%
    (2) 4%
    (3) 5%
    (4) 6%
    (5) 7%

Questions 14 and 15 refer to the following information.

Marc sells computer equipment. He buys printers at wholesale and sells them at retail price. Customers who join his discount club pay the member's price.

Printer Pricing Chart

Model Number	Wholesale Price	Retail Price	Member's Price
L310	$63.00	$141.75	$92.15
L1430	$86.00	$150.50	$105.35

14. What is the percent of increase from wholesale to retail price of the L310 model?

    (1) 44%
    (2) 56%
    (3) 78%
    (4) 125%
    (5) 225%

15. For the L1430 model, what is the percent of decrease from retail price to member's price?

    (1) 26%
    (2) 30%
    (3) 43%
    (4) 45%
    (5) 53%

Answers and explanations begin on page 669.

RATIO, PROPORTION, AND PERCENT

Problem Solving

Too Much or Not Enough Information

Many GED math problems contain more information than you need to solve a problem. For example, a table or diagram may show numbers that relate to the subject of the problem but have nothing to do with answering the question.

Knowing what information you need to answer a question is an important problem-solving skill. To solve any problem, follow these steps:

- Read the problem carefully. Think about the question asked in the problem.
- Decide what facts and operations you will need to answer the question.
- Find the facts you need.
- Work the problem carefully.
- Think about whether your answer makes sense and seems reasonable.

A few problems on the GED Math Test (probably 2 or 3) will not provide all the information needed to solve them. If it isn't possible to answer the question, choose the option "Not enough information is given." This answer choice will also appear in problems that do contain enough information, so you must only choose it when you are sure it is impossible to answer the question.

Example: A department store determines that 80% of the customers on its mailing list live more than 40 miles from the store. Of those, 30% visit the store less than 10 times per year. How many customers on the mailing list live more than 40 miles from the store?

    (1)   32
    (2)   300
    (3) 2000
    (4) 3200
    (5) Not enough information is given.

The correct answer is **(5) Not enough information is given.** The question asks for the number of customers who live more than 40 miles from the store. You know the <u>percent</u> of customers referred to, but you don't know the <u>number</u> of customers on the mailing list. The other numbers in the problem have nothing to do with the question. You don't have enough information to solve the problem.

Problems like the one above can be tricky. For example, if you find 80% of 40 in the example above, you will get the number 32, which is one of the answer options. However, there isn't any reason to find 80% of 40. Eighty percent refers to customers and the number 40 refers to miles. Always avoid calculations that don't make sense. Notice that incorrect answer choices on the GED are often based on common errors in logic.

Key Ideas

- After thinking about the question asked in the problem, look for the facts you need.
- Ignore information that has nothing to do with answering the question.
- If a question cannot be answered with facts given in the problem, choose option (5) Not enough information is given.

GED TIP

If you can't solve a problem, try to eliminate options by using common sense. Then make a reasonable guess. This is better than leaving a blank on the answer sheet; a blank will count against you.

Choose the <u>one best answer</u> to each question. You <u>MAY</u> use your calculator for questions 3 through 6.

<u>Questions 1 through 3</u> refer to the following information.

A state has 286 species of wildlife that have been identified by the federal government as either threatened or endangered. The following table lists several dangers to these species and the number of species affected by each danger.

Danger	Species Affected
Outdoor recreation	123
Road construction	95
Pollution of air, water, and soil	44
Logging	24
Mining	64
Disease	15

1. To the nearest whole percent, what percent of the identified species are affected by road construction?

   (1) 3%
   (2) 26%
   (3) 33%
   (4) 35%
   (5) Not enough information is given.

2. What is the ratio of the number of species affected by logging to the number affected by disease?

   (1) $\frac{3}{22}$
   (2) $\frac{5}{8}$
   (3) $\frac{5}{13}$
   (4) $\frac{8}{5}$

   (5) Not enough information is given.

3. To the nearest tenth percent, what percent of the identified species are threatened by water pollution?

   (1) 4.4%
   (2) 5.1%
   (3) 12.1%
   (4) 15.4%
   (5) Not enough information is given.

<u>Questions 4 and 5</u> refer to the following information.

Corey's Hardware has the following discounts:

All utility ladders:	30% off marked price
Drop cloths:	$2.49 per package
All paintbrushes:	15% off marked price
All interior paint:	10% off marked price

4. What is the total discount for a utility ladder with a price tag of $32.50 and two gallons of interior paint, regularly priced at $19 each?

   (1) $7.05
   (2) $11.65
   (3) $13.55
   (4) $21.15
   (5) Not enough information is given.

5. What is the ratio of the price of a can of interior paint to the price of a paintbrush?

   (1) 2 to 3
   (2) 3 to 2
   (3) 10 to 19
   (4) 19 to 10
   (5) Not enough information is given.

6. Using the Internet, Roy finds the driving distance from his home to several landmarks.

Landmark	Distance in Miles
Baseball Hall of Fame	182
Niagara Falls	95
Finger Lakes	31

   Which of the following best represents the ratio of the distance to Niagara Falls to the distance to Finger Lakes?

   (1) 10:1
   (2) 9:1
   (3) 6:1
   (4) 3:1
   (5) Not enough information is given.

Answers and explanations begin on page 670.

RATIO, PROPORTION, AND PERCENT
PRACTICE QUESTIONS
PART I

Directions: Choose the <u>one best answer</u> to each question. You <u>MAY</u> use your calculator.

1. From a total yearly budget of $360,000, the Kimball Foundation spends $30,000 on leasing office space. What is the ratio of dollars spent on office space to dollars spent on other costs?

   (1) 12:1
   (2) 11:1
   (3) 11:12
   (4) 1:11
   (5) 1:12

2. A worker can assemble 5 motors in 2 hours. Which of the expressions below could be used to find how long it would take the worker to assemble 50 motors?

   (1) $2 \times \dfrac{50}{5}$

   (2) $\dfrac{5 \times 50}{2}$

   (3) $\dfrac{2}{5 \times 50}$

   (4) $\dfrac{5}{2 \times 50}$

   (5) $2 \times 5 \times 50$

3. Frank owns a discount music store. The table below shows how much Frank pays for certain merchandise items.

Item	Wholesale Price
CDs	$7.20
Cassette tapes	$5.60

   To find his selling price, Frank increases each price by 35%. What is the selling price of a cassette tape?

   (1) $9.72
   (2) $7.56
   (3) $5.95
   (4) $3.64
   (5) $1.96

4. Neva's car is now worth $12,000. This is 60% of what she paid for it. How much did she pay for the car?

   (1) $7,200
   (2) $18,000
   (3) $19,200
   (4) $20,000
   (5) Not enough information is given.

5. At a shop, the ratio of union to non-union workers is 7 to 3. If there are 18 nonunion workers at the shop, how many union workers are there?

   (1) 8
   (2) 21
   (3) 25
   (4) 42
   (5) 126

6. Camilla earned $954 in commission on $15,900 in sales. What is her rate of commission?

   (1) 6%
   (2) 9%
   (3) $16\frac{2}{3}$%
   (4) 35%
   (5) 60%

7. John spent the following amounts of time building a workbench:

drawing the plans:	2 hours
cutting the wood:	$1\frac{1}{2}$ hours
assembling the workbench:	2 hours
sanding and sealing:	$3\frac{1}{2}$ hours

   What is the ratio of time spent cutting wood to total time spent on the project?

   (1) 1:9
   (2) 1:6
   (3) 1:5
   (4) 3:7
   (5) 3:4

Questions 8 and 9 refer to the following information.

Ford County Farmland Usage Total Acreage: 40,000	
Usage	**Number of Acres**
Dairy	22,000
Nursery/greenhouse	3,600
Vegetables/fruits	5,200
Grains	9,200

8. What percent of Ford County farmland is used for the growing of grains, vegetables, or fruits?

    (1) 13%
    (2) 23%
    (3) 36%
    (4) 57%
    (5) 64%

9. Last year the total farmland acreage in Ford County was 25% less than the amount shown in the table. What percent of the last year's total acres were used for dairy production?

    (1) 30%
    (2) 41%
    (3) 55%
    (4) 73%
    (5) Not enough information is given.

10. A serving of peanut butter contains 3 grams of saturated fat and 13 grams of unsaturated fat. This amount of fat is 25% of the recommended amount of fat in a 2000-calorie diet. What is the ratio of grams of saturated fat to total fat in a serving of peanut butter?

    (1) $\frac{3}{16}$
    (2) $\frac{3}{13}$
    (3) $\frac{13}{16}$
    (4) $\frac{13}{3}$
    (5) $\frac{16}{3}$

11. A drawing of a company logo is 4 inches wide and 5 inches long. If the drawing is enlarged so that it is 12.5 inches long, how many inches wide will the enlargement be?

    (1) 7.5
    (2) 10.0
    (3) 15.625
    (4) 20.0
    (5) 32.5

12. A local hospital currently has 184 male patients. If the ratio of male to female patients is 4:3, how many female patients are there in the hospital?

    Mark your answer in the circles on the grid at the bottom of the page.

13. A newspaper advertisement contains the following information.

Busy Body Fitness Center Inventory Reduction Blowout! All sale prices are 20% off original price!	
Equipment	**Sale Price**
Treadmill	$1512
Upright bike	$720
Home gym	$3148

In dollars, what was the original price of the upright bike?

Mark your answer in the circles on the grid at the bottom of the page.

12.

13.

PART II

Directions: Choose the <u>one best answer</u> to each question. You <u>MAY NOT</u> use your calculator for these questions.

14. The Tigers' ratio of wins to losses is 5 to 4. If the team continues winning at the same rate, how many games will the Tigers win in a 72-game season?

    (1) 20
    (2) 40
    (3) 37
    (4) 52
    (5) 58

15. A television station called 400 adults and asked the following question: "Do you approve of the governor's new education program?" The table below shows the results of the survey:

Response	Percent
Undecided	16%
Yes	32%
No	52%

    Of the people called, how many did <u>not</u> answer "no"?

    (1) 64
    (2) 128
    (3) 192
    (4) 208
    (5) Not enough information is given.

16. The price of a carton of computer paper decreased from $24 to $19. Which of the following expressions could be used to find the percent of decrease in the price?

    (1) $\dfrac{\$24}{\$24 - \$19} \times 100$

    (2) $\dfrac{\$19}{\$24 - \$19} \times 100$

    (3) $\dfrac{\$19}{\$24} \times 100$

    (4) $\dfrac{\$24 - \$19}{\$19} \times 100$

    (5) $\dfrac{\$24 - \$19}{\$24} \times 100$

17. Six months ago, Sandra had 55 regular customers. Now the number of customers has increased by 220%. How many customers does she have now?

    (1) 121
    (2) 90
    (3) 66
    (4) 25
    (5) Not enough information is given.

18. If 1 gram of fat equals 9 calories, what percent of the calories in a Munchies roast beef sandwich come from fat?

Munchies Sandwich Facts		
Sandwich	Fat (grams)	Calories
Roast Beef	6	300
Club Classic	5	335

    (1) 2%
    (2) 3%
    (3) 6%
    (4) 18%
    (5) 54%

19. For every $8 in their budget, the Parks spend $3 on food. If their weekly budget is $704, how much do they spend on food each week?

    (1) $88
    (2) $188
    (3) $192
    (4) $235
    (5) $264

20. Suddeth Travel estimates that 80% of its employees have more than 12 days of unused sick leave. If 140 employees have more than 12 days of unused sick leave, how many employees work at the agency?

    (1) 112
    (2) 164
    (3) 175
    (4) 700
    (5) Not enough information is given.

21. The Gladstone Theater has 900 seats. At a recent show, the ratio of tickets sold to tickets unsold was 11 to 1. How many tickets were sold to the show?

(1) 75
(2) 82
(3) 810
(4) 818
(5) 825

22. Matthew put $2200 in a savings account for one year six months. If he earns simple interest at an annual rate of 8%, how much will he have in the account at the end of the time period?

(1) $1936
(2) $2212
(3) $2376
(4) $2464
(5) $2640

23. A television set that is regularly priced at $410 is on sale for 20% off. Which of the following expressions could be used to find the sale price of the television set?

(1) $410 − ($410 × 0.2)
(2) $410 − $\dfrac{\$410}{0.2}$
(3) $410 − $\dfrac{0.2}{\$410}$
(4) $410 × 0.2 × 100
(5) ($410 × 0.2) + $410

24. On a county map shown below, the map scale reads, "0.5 in = 60 mi."

What is the actual distance in miles between Lakeview and Riverside?

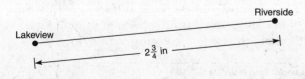

(1) 23
(2) 82$\frac{1}{2}$
(3) 165
(4) 300
(5) 330

Question 25 refers to the following information.

Leo's Bookstore kept track of the number of customers who visited the store over a 3-day period. They also recorded the number of sales for each day during the same period.

Day	Number of Customers	Number of Sales
Friday	112	83
Saturday	138	45
Sunday	140	91

25. Which of the following could be used to find what percent of Sunday's customers did <u>not</u> make a purchase?

(1) 91/140
(2) 91/140 × 100
(3) (140 − 91)/140 × 100
(4) (140 − 91)/91 × 100
(5) 140/91 × 100

26. A school admits 9 out of every 14 who apply. At that rate, how many students will be admitted if 420 apply?

Mark your answer in the circles on the grid at the bottom of the page.

27. In a 40-hour workweek, Marcie spends 15 hours answering telephones. What is the ratio of hours spent answering telephones to hours doing other types of work? (Record your answer as a fraction.)

Mark your answer in the circles on the grid at the bottom of the page.

26.

27.

Answers and explanations begin on page 670.

DATA ANALYSIS

Tables and Pictographs

Working with Tables

Key Ideas

- Tables and graphs are often used to display data.
- Always read all labels to understand what data is presented in the table or graph.
- If symbols are used in a graph, a key will tell what each symbol represents.

Data is facts and information. By analyzing data, we can make predictions, draw conclusions, and solve problems. To be useful, data must be organized in some way. A **table** organizes data in columns and rows. The labels on the table will help you understand what the data means.

Example 1: The table below shows population figures for selected counties in 1990 and 2000 and the land area in square miles for each county.

County	1990 Pop.	2000 Pop.	Land Area in sq. mi.
Adams	11,128	15,295	4,255
Bell	25,199	22,707	2,523
Cook	6,532	6,518	2,398
Davis	82,204	90,834	1,139
Evans	139,510	130,748	921

Which county showed the greatest percent of increase in population from 1990 to 2000?

1. **Read the labels.** The first column shows the county names. The second and third columns show population figures. The fourth column shows land area data. You don't need land area to answer this question.

2. **Analyze the data.** Only Adams and Davis counties show increases from 1990 to 2000.

3. **Use the data.** Find the percent of increase for Adams and Davis counties.

Adams: $\dfrac{15,295 - 11,128}{11,128} \approx 0.374 \approx 37\%$ Davis: $\dfrac{90,834 - 82,204}{82,204} \approx 0.105 \approx 10\%$

Adams County shows the greatest percent of increase in population from 1990 to 2000.

GED TIP

The numbers in a table may be "messy," or difficult to work with. Try using simpler numbers when possible. In Example 1, rounding to the thousands place provides the same result.

A **pictograph** is another way to display data. Pictographs use symbols to compare data. A key shows what value each symbol represents.

Example 2: A city has three public library branches. A librarian kept track of the numbers of books checked out from each branch in a week. He used the data to create the pictograph below.

Branches	Books checked out from 3/4 to 3/10.
North	📖 📖 📖 📖 📖 📖 📖
South	📖 📖 📖 📖 📖
West	📖 📖 📖 📖 📖 📖 📖 📖 📖 📖

Key
📖 = 150 books

From March 4 to March 10, how many books were checked out from the South and West branches combined?

1. There are $4\frac{1}{2}$ symbols for the South Branch and 9 symbols for the West branch. Add.
   $4\frac{1}{2} + 9 = 13\frac{1}{2}$ symbols

2. Find the value of the symbols. The key states that each symbol equals 150 books. Multiply by 150. $13\frac{1}{2} \times 150 = \textbf{2025 books}$

DATA ANALYSIS ▸ PRACTICE 1

A. **Use the table on page 412 to answer questions 1 and 2. Use the pictograph on page 412 to answer questions 3 and 4. You <u>MAY</u> use a calculator.**

1. On average, how many people were there per square mile in Bell County in 2000?

2. To the nearest percent, what was the percent of decrease in Evans County's population from 1990 to 2000?

3. How many more books were checked out from North Branch than from South Branch during the week of March 4?

4. How many books were checked out from all three branches combined?

B. **Choose the <u>one best answer</u> to each question.**

Questions 5 and 6 refer to the following table.

Percent of 3-year-old children with school-readiness skills for the years 1994 and 2000		
	1994	2000
Recognizes all letters	13%	15%
Counts to 20 or higher	37%	41%
Writes own name	22%	24%
Reads or pretends to read	68%	70%

5. How many more children were able to count to 20 or higher in 2000 than in 1994?
   - (1) 2
   - (2) 4
   - (3) 37
   - (4) 63
   - (5) Not enough information is given.

6. A community had 350 three-year-old children in 2000. Based on the table, how many were able to write their own names?
   - (1) 22
   - (2) 77
   - (3) 84
   - (4) 140
   - (5) 273

Questions 7 and 8 refer to the following graph.

Mayfair Parking Garage
Daily Average of Parked Cars by Timed Period

Time of Day	Average Number of Cars
8:00 A.M. – noon	🚗🚗🚗🚗🚗🚗
12:01 – 4:30 P.M.	🚗🚗🚗🚗🚗🚗🚗🚗
4:31 – 8:00 P.M.	🚗🚗🚗🚗

Key 🚗 = 50 cars

7. How many cars are parked in the garage from 12:01 to 4:30 P.M.?
   - (1) 275
   - (2) 350
   - (3) 375
   - (4) 650
   - (5) Not enough information is given.

8. How many more cars are parked from 8 A.M. to noon than are parked after 4:30 P.M.?
   - (1) 75
   - (2) 100
   - (3) 175
   - (4) 200
   - (5) 475

Answers and explanations begin on page 671.

DATA ANALYSIS

Bar and Line Graphs

Key Ideas

- A bar graph uses bars to represent numbers.
- To find the value of a bar, compare its length to the scale shown on one of the axis lines. Estimate the value.
- A double-bar graph compares groups of data. Read the key to find the meaning of the bars.

Working with Bar Graphs

A **bar graph** uses bars to represent values. Bar graphs have two axis lines. One line shows a number scale, and the other shows labels for the bars. By comparing the length of a bar to the scale, you can estimate what value the bar represents.

Example 1: A national corporation made a bar graph (shown below) to show the number of discrimination complaints made by employees during a six-year period. About how many more complaints were made in 1999 than in 1998?

1. **Read the labels.** Each bar represents the number of complaints made within a year. The years are shown beneath the bars.

2. **Analyze the data.** Compare the bars for 1998 and 1999 to the scale. There were 20 complaints in 1998 and about 32 complaints in 1999.

3. **Use the data.** Subtract: 32 − 20 = 12. There were **about 12 more** complaints in 1999 than in 1998.

Employee Discrimination Complaints
Number Per Year

GED TIP

You may not be able to find the exact value of a bar. If the bar falls about halfway between two numbers on the scale, use a whole number that lies in the middle.

A **double-bar graph** compares more than one type of data.

Example 2: A studio released four films in one year. The graph below compares the cost of making each movie to its box-office receipts, or ticket sales. Film B's cost is what percent of its box-office receipts?

1. **Read the labels.** Read the key to find the meaning of the bars. Notice that the scale represents millions of dollars.

2. **Analyze the data.** Film B's cost is about $30 million. It brought in about $65 million in receipts.

3. **Use the data.** Find what percent $30 is of $65.
$\frac{\$30}{\$65} \approx 0.462 \approx 46\%$

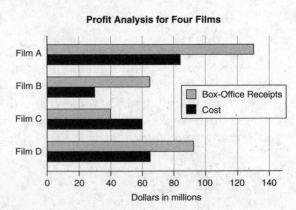

Profit Analysis for Four Films

DATA ANALYSIS ▸ PRACTICE 2.1

A. For questions 1 through 3, use the bar graph entitled "Employee Discrimination Complaints" on page 414. For questions 4 through 6, use the bar graph entitled "Profit Analysis for Four Films" on page 414.

1. To the nearest ten, how many employee discrimination complaints were there in 1995 and 1996?

2. About how many more complaints were there in 2000 than in 1995?

3. By what percent did the number of complaints decrease from 1997 to 1998?

4. About how much more did it cost to make Film A than Film D?

5. Which film made the greatest amount of profit? (profit = receipts − cost)

6. Film C's cost was what percent of its box-office receipts?

B. Choose the <u>one best answer</u> to each question.

<u>Questions 7 and 8</u> refer to the following graph.

<u>Questions 9 and 10</u> refer to the following graph.

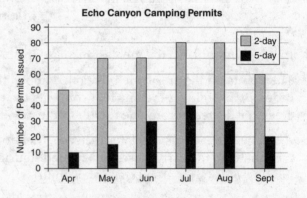

7. Approximately how many more CDs were sold than videos and DVDs combined?

    (1) 24
    (2) 32
    (3) 41
    (4) 70
    (5) 88

8. One-half of the games sold during the week of September 20 were on sale for $16. The rest sold for the full price of $24. Approximately how much money did the store take in for games sold during the week of September 20?

    (1) $400
    (2) $500
    (3) $750
    (4) $1000
    (5) $2000

9. In May, what was the ratio of the number of 2-day permits to the number of 5-day permits?

    (1) 2:5
    (2) 3:14
    (3) 3:17
    (4) 14:3
    (5) 14:17

10. In which month was there a <u>total</u> of 80 permits issued?

    (1) May
    (2) June
    (3) July
    (4) August
    (5) September

Answers and explanations begin on page 671.

Working with Line Graphs

A **line graph** is useful for showing changes over time. By analyzing the rise and fall of the line, you can tell whether something is increasing, decreasing, or staying the same. Like a bar graph, a line graph has two axis lines. One is marked with a scale; the other is marked in regular time intervals.

Example 1: The graph below shows the number of patients who visited an emergency room for the treatment of scooter-related injuries.

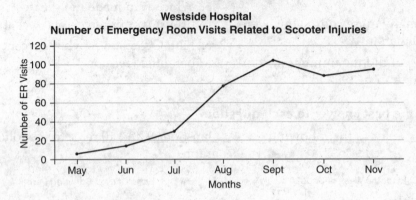

In which month did the greatest increase in scooter-related injuries occur?

The points on the graph are positioned above the months, which are arranged in calendar order. By examining the line that connects the points, you can tell whether there was an increase or decrease from one month to the next.

A steeper line shows a greater increase; therefore, the **greatest increase was during July.** In fact, there were nearly 80 scooter-related injuries by the end of July and about 30 at the beginning of July, for an increase of 50 injuries.

If a line graph has more than one line, a key will tell you what the lines represent.

Example 2: The graph below shows the changes in ticket prices for two amusement parks.

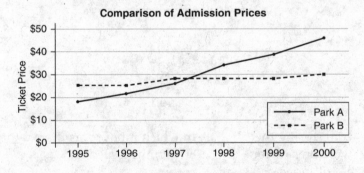

What was the last year in which the admission price to Park B was greater than the admission price to Park A?

The admission prices for Park A are represented by a solid line. Park B's prices are shown with a dotted line. The graph begins in 1995. In 1995, Park B's ticket price is greater than Park A's. Follow the two lines to the right. Between 1997 and 1998, the lines cross, and Park A's prices climb higher than Park B's. **The year 1997** was the last time that Park B charged more than Park A for a ticket.

Note: The steepest line shows the greatest increase or decrease, but it may not show the greatest <u>percent</u> of change. When the original value is small, a small change may result in a high percent of change.

A. For questions 1 through 3, use the graph from Westside Hospital on page 416. For questions 4 through 6, use the graph "Comparison of Admission Prices" on page 416.

1. In which month did the number of scooter-related injuries decrease?

2. To the nearest ten, how many emergency room visits were due to scooter injuries in August, September, and October?

3. Which of the following shows the greatest percent of increase: the change in injuries from June to July or the change from August to September?

4. About how much more did it cost to buy a ticket to Park A than a ticket to Park B in 1999?

5. What was the percent of increase in the ticket prices at Park B from 1995 to 2000?

6. To the nearest ten, how much more did it cost to buy a ticket to Park A in 2000 than in 1995?

B. Choose the one best answer to each question.

<u>Questions 7 and 8</u> refer to the graph below.

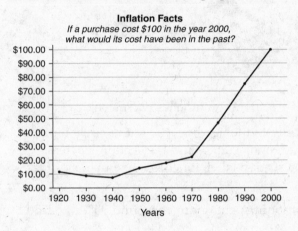

7. Over what period of time did the price of goods actually decrease?

   (1) 1930 to 1940
   (2) 1940 to 1950
   (3) 1960 to 1970
   (4) 1970 to 1980
   (5) 1990 to 2000

8. Goods purchased in 1970 were about what fraction of their cost in the year 2000?

   (1) $\frac{4}{5}$
   (2) $\frac{1}{2}$
   (3) $\frac{1}{3}$
   (4) $\frac{1}{5}$
   (5) $\frac{1}{20}$

<u>Questions 9 and 10</u> refer to the graph below.

Lamp Depot has two stores. The graph shows the sales data from the two stores for an 8-week period.

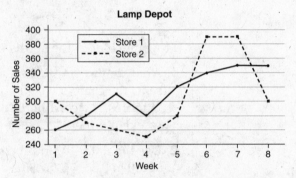

9. About how many more sales were there at Store 2 than at Store 1 in week 6?

   (1) 110
   (2) 50
   (3) 40
   (4) 25
   (5) 20

10. During which week did Store 1 experience the greatest increase in sales from the week before?

   (1) Week 2
   (2) Week 3
   (3) Week 4
   (4) Week 5
   (5) Week 6

Answers and explanations begin on page 671.

DATA ANALYSIS

Circle Graphs

Working with Circle Graphs

Key Ideas

- In a circle graph, the circle represents a whole amount and the sections represent parts of the whole.
- Sections are usually labeled with percents, but they can show amounts.
- The size of each section of a circle graph is equal to the fraction or percent it represents.

A **circle graph** is used to show how a whole amount is broken into parts. The sections of a circle graph are often labeled with percents. The size of each section corresponds to the fraction it represents. For example, a section labeled 25% is $\frac{1}{4}$ of the circle.

Example 1: A graph below shows how a children's sports camp spends its weekly budget.

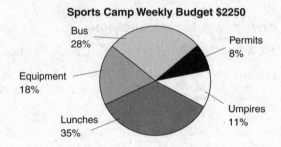

Sports Camp Weekly Budget $2250

How much does the sports camp spend on lunches each week?

1. **Analyze the graph.** According to the heading, the entire circle represents the camp's weekly budget of $2250. Find the section labeled "lunches." According to the section label, lunches make up 35% of the weekly budget.

2. **Use the data.** To find the amount spent on lunches, find 35% of $2250.
   $2250 × 0.35 = **$787.50**

A circle graph may also be labeled using fractions or decimals. One common kind of circle graph labels each section in cents to show how a dollar is used.

GED TIP

Since a circle graph represents a whole, or 100%, amounts can easily be converted to percents. For example, $0.05 on a circle graph can also represent 5%.

Example 2: According to the graph, what percent of the average energy bill is spent on drying clothes, lighting, and heating water?

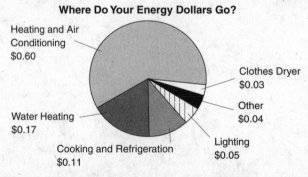

Where Do Your Energy Dollars Go?

1. **Analyze the graph.** The entire circle represents $1. The amounts in the sections mentioned in the problem are $0.03, $0.05, and $0.17.

2. **Use the data.** Add the amounts: $0.03 + $0.05 + $0.17 = $0.25. Since $0.25 is 25% of a dollar, then **25%** of an average bill is spent on these items.

DATA ANALYSIS ▸ PRACTICE 3

A. For questions 1 through 3, use the sports camp budget on page 418. For questions 4 through 6, use the circle graph on energy on page 418.

1. What percent of the total sports camp budget is spent on equipment and umpires?

2. What <u>fraction</u> of the sports camp budget is spent on permits?

3. What amount does the camp spend each week on busing?

4. A family's energy bill is $180. According to the graph, how much did the family spend on water heating?

5. Which section is greater than 50% of an energy dollar?

6. Which energy cost is about $\frac{1}{10}$ of the energy dollar?

B. Choose the <u>one best answer</u> to each question.

<u>Questions 7 and 8</u> refer to the following graph.

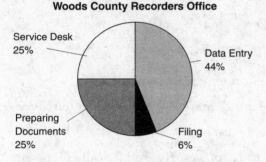

**Records Clerk Tasks
Woods County Recorders Office**

Service Desk 25%

Data Entry 44%

Preparing Documents 25%

Filing 6%

7. During a 40-hour workweek, how many hours does a records clerk spend preparing documents?

   (1) 10
   (2) 15
   (3) 25
   (4) 30
   (5) Not enough information is given.

8. What percent of a records clerk's time is spent on tasks other than data entry?

   (1) 9%
   (2) 25%
   (3) 28%
   (4) 44%
   (5) 56%

<u>Questions 9 and 10</u> refer to the following graph.

The employees of National Bank are given the following graph to explain how their retirement fund is invested.

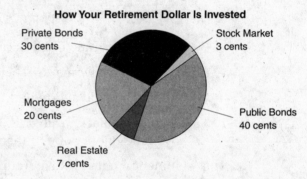

How Your Retirement Dollar Is Invested

Private Bonds 30 cents

Stock Market 3 cents

Mortgages 20 cents

Public Bonds 40 cents

Real Estate 7 cents

9. What percent of each retirement dollar is invested in real estate and the stock market?

   (1) 4%
   (2) 10%
   (3) 40%
   (4) 90%
   (5) 100%

10. Steve contributes $120 of each paycheck to his National Bank retirement fund. How much of his contribution is invested in public bonds?

   (1) $36
   (2) $40
   (3) $48
   (4) $84
   (5) Not enough information is given.

Answers and explanations begin on page 671.

DATA ANALYSIS

Frequency and Central Tendency

Key Ideas

- A frequency table is used to show how often data occurs.
- Tally marks are made next to a list to record the data.
- Numerical data is often grouped in intervals.

Using a Frequency Table

A **frequency table** shows how often an item appears in a data set. The data is in the form of tally marks next to a list of items.

Example 1: The sales manager at Montana Motors asked her sales staff to keep a record of the color of the cars that were chosen for test-drives in one month. Then she combined the data to make the frequency table shown below.

Montana Motors—Car Color Preferences	
white	ΗΗ ΗΗ ΗΗ ΗΗ ΗΗ ΗΗ
black	ΗΗ ΗΗ ΗΗ ΗΗ ΗΗ II
red	ΗΗ ΗΗ ΗΗ
green	ΗΗ ΗΗ I
silver	ΗΗ IIII
other	ΗΗ ΗΗ ΗΗ I

What was the ratio of black cars driven to silver cars driven?

1. Count the tally marks. There are 27 marks for black and 9 for silver.

2. Write the ratio and reduce to lowest terms. $\frac{27}{9} = \frac{3}{1}$

The ratio of black to silver is **3 to 1.** You can also say that the black cars are 3 times more popular than the silver cars.

Numerical data is often grouped in intervals. The table below shows data grouped in intervals of 18 to 24, 25 to 40, and so on. This way of presenting data is called a **grouped frequency table.**

Example 2: The table below shows the ages of the customers at Louise's Diner for a three-day period. What percent of the customers were from 25 to 40 years old?

Louise's Diner Customers by Age Group, February 19–22	
under 18	ΗΗ I
18–24	ΗΗ ΗΗ ΗΗ III
25–40	ΗΗ ΗΗ ΗΗ ΗΗ ΗΗ III
41–55	ΗΗ ΗΗ
over 55	ΗΗ III

1. Find the data you need. There are 28 marks for the 25–40 age group. Add the tally marks for all age groups to find the total number of customers for the three-day period. 6 + 18 + 28 + 10 + 8 = 70

2. Find the percent. The base is 70, the total number of customers. The part is 28, the number of customers in the desired age group. Solve for the rate. $\frac{28}{70} = \frac{4}{10} = 0.4 = \textbf{40\%}$

GED TIP

If several problems refer to a frequency table, you may want to count the tally marks for each line and record the numbers on scratch paper. Then use the numbers to solve all related problems.

DATA ANALYSIS ▸ PRACTICE 4.1

A. For questions 1 through 3, use the frequency table from Montana Motors on page 420. For questions 4 through 6, use the frequency table from Louise's Diner on page 420.

1. What was the total number of drivers who preferred white or black cars?

2. How many more drivers chose red than silver cars?

3. What was the ratio of red cars to white cars chosen for test-drives?

4. What is the ratio of customers under 18 to those over 55?

5. What was the total number of customers from 18 to 40 years of age?

6. What percent of the total customers were from 41 to 55 years of age? (Round your answer to the nearest whole percent.)

B. Choose the <u>one best answer</u> to each question.

<u>Questions 7 and 8</u> refer to the following information.

The frequency table shows the reasons customers gave for returning clothing merchandise to a store.

Reason	Number
Wrong color	卌 卌 卌	
Wrong size	卌 卌 卌	
Unwanted gift	卌 卌 卌 卌
Found flaw after purchase	|||
Changed mind	卌

7. What is the ratio of customers saying the clothes were the wrong size to all other reasons given?

   (1) $\frac{4}{15}$

   (2) $\frac{4}{11}$

   (3) $\frac{4}{9}$

   (4) $\frac{4}{5}$

   (5) Not enough information is given.

8. What percent of the customers who returned clothing said that the clothes were an unwanted gift?

   (1) 5%

   (2) 20%

   (3) 25%

   (4) $33\frac{1}{3}$%

   (5) 50%

<u>Questions 9 and 10</u> refer to the following information.

A personnel office gives keyboarding tests to people applying for a job. The test shows how many words per minute (wpm) a job applicant can enter correctly. After testing 90 applicants, the manager made the following table.

Speed	Number of Applicants
Under 30 wpm	卌 卌 卌 卌 卌 卌 卌
30–45 wpm	卌 卌 卌 卌 卌
46–60 wpm	卌 卌 卌 |||
Over 60 wpm	卌 卌 ||

9. What percent of the applicants had a speed of exactly 40 wpm?

   (1) 14%

   (2) 25%

   (3) 28%

   (4) 38%

   (5) Not enough information is given.

10. What is the ratio of applicants who could keyboard at a speed above 45 wpm to those who could keyboard at a speed of 45 wpm or less?

   (1) 1:3

   (2) 1:2

   (3) 2:3

   (4) 3:2

   (5) 6:5

Answers and explanations begin on page 671.

Mean, Median, and Mode

Suppose you were asked how much money you usually spend on groceries in a week. Some weeks you may spend a great deal; other weeks, much less. You would probably choose an amount in the middle to represent what you typically spend. This middle value is called an **average,** or **measure of central tendency.**

The most common type of average is the **mean,** or the arithmetic average.

Example 1: In five football games, a team scored 14, 21, 3, 20, and 10 points. What is the mean, or average, score per game?

1. Add the values. $14 + 21 + 3 + 20 + 10 = 68$

2. Divide by the number of items in $68 ÷ 5 =$ **13.6 points per game**
   the data set.

Although it is impossible for a football team to score 13.6 points in a game, the number represents the center of the scores from the five games.

A calculator is useful for finding the mean. Do the calculations in two steps. Enter the addition operations and press $\boxed{=}$. Then enter the division operation. Try Example 1 above with a calculator.

Another measure of average is the median. The **median** is the middle value in a set of data.

Example 2: During a 7-hour period, a bookstore recorded the following numbers of sales. Find the median number of sales.

Hour 1	Hour 2	Hour 3	Hour 4	Hour 5	Hour 6	Hour 7
43	28	24	36	32	37	48

1. Arrange the values by size.   24, 28, 32, 36, 37, 43, 48

2. Find the middle number.   24, 28, 32, $\boxed{36}$, 37, 43, 48

If there is an even number of values, the median is the mean of the two middle values.

Example 3: Robert has the following test scores in his math class: 90, 72, 88, 94, 91, and 80. What is the median score?

1. Arrange the values by size and find the   72, 80, $\boxed{88, 90,}$ 91, 94
   middle.

2. Find the mean of the two middle values. The   Add: $88 + 90 = 178$
   median score is **89.**   Divide by 2: $178 ÷ 2 = $ **89**

The **mode** is the value that occurs most often in a set of data. A set of data could have more than one mode if several items occur the same number of times. If each item of data occurs only once, there is no mode.

Example 4: Six weather stations recorded the following temperatures at 3 P.M.: 45°, 44°, 45°, 47°, 46°, and 45°. What is the mode of the data?

The temperature 45° occurs the most often (3 times). The mode is **45°.**

Note: In a set-up problem, the expression used to represent the mean will either be written with parentheses: $(14 + 21 + 3 + 20 + 10) ÷ 5$ or as a fraction:

$$\frac{14 + 21 + 3 + 20 + 10}{5}$$

DATA ANALYSIS ▸ PRACTICE 4.2

A. For each data set, find the mean, median, and mode. Round calculations to the nearest hundredth or cent. You <u>MAY</u> use a calculator.

1. Golf scores for 18 holes:
   76, 82, 75, 87, 80, 82, and 79

2. Sales totals for 6 weeks:
   $5,624; $10,380; $8,102; $6,494; $12,008; and $8,315

3. Cost of lunch for 8 days:
   $4.50, $5.25, $4.50, $3.75, $4.50, $5.25, $6.10, and $4.25

4. Miles driven per day for 5 days:
   330, 286, 342, 300, and 287

5. Grocery bills for 4 weeks:
   $97.48, $106.13, $110.98, and $92.74

6. Scores on 7 quizzes:
   90, 72, 86, 100, 88, 78, and 88

7. High temperatures for 10 days:
   96°, 103°, 98°, 101°, 98°, 100°, 100°, 97°, 98°, and 100°

8. Inches of rainfall over 3-day period:
   2.5, 1.8, and 1.4

9. Attendance figures at a play:
   305, 294, 328, 296, 305, 315, and 292

10. Hours worked per week for 5 weeks:
    36, 40, 38, 40, and 40

B. Choose the <u>one best answer</u> to each question. You <u>MAY</u> use your calculator.

<u>Questions 11 and 12</u> refer to the following information.

Homes Sold in Fairfield Heights in June		
Home	**Asking Price**	**Selling Price**
#1	$124,600	$116,500
#2	$132,400	$124,800
#3	$118,900	$116,500
#4	$98,500	$103,600
#5	$105,800	$109,000
#6	$122,400	$118,400

11. What was the mean asking price of the homes sold in Fairfield Heights in June?

    (1) $120,650
    (2) $117,100
    (3) $116,500
    (4) $115,450
    (5) $114,800

12. What was the median selling price of the homes sold in Fairfield Heights in June?

    (1) $112,750
    (2) $114,200
    (3) $114,800
    (4) $116,500
    (5) $117,450

13. The numbers of patients enrolled at four health clinics are 790, 1150, 662, and 805. Which expression could be used to find the mean number of patients per clinic?

    (1) $\dfrac{790 + 1150 + 662 + 805}{4}$

    (2) $790 + 1150 + 662 + 805$

    (3) $\dfrac{662 + 1150}{2}$

    (4) $\dfrac{790 + 805}{2}$

    (5) $(790 + 1150 + 662 + 805) \div 2$

14. What is the median value of $268, $1258, $654, $1258, $900, $1558, and $852?

    (1) $1258
    (2) $960
    (3) $900
    (4) $913
    (5) $852

15. What is the mode of the following points scored: 14, 17, 14, 12, 13, 15, 22, and 11?

    (1) 13.5
    (2) 14
    (3) 14.75
    (4) 16.5
    (5) Not enough information is given.

Answers and explanations begin on page 672.

DATA ANALYSIS

Probability

Key Ideas

- Probability is a ratio. It can be expressed as a ratio, fraction, decimal, or percent.
- Theoretical probability is the ratio of favorable outcomes to possible outcomes.
- Experimental probability is the ratio of favorable outcomes to the number of trials in an experiment.

Simple Probability

Probability tells whether something is likely or unlikely to happen. The probability of any event can be expressed by a number from 0 to 1. If an event has a 0 probability, the event is impossible. An event with a probability of 1 is certain to happen. Most events are somewhere in between.

To find the probability of a simple random event, we must identify favorable and possible outcomes. A **favorable outcome** is the event that we are interested in. The **possible outcomes** are all the possible events that could occur. **Theoretical probability** (sometimes called **simple probability**) is the ratio of favorable outcomes to possible outcomes.

Example 1: The spinner is divided into 8 equal sections. What is the probability of spinning a 4 on the spinner?

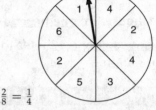

1. There are two sections labeled 4 on the spinner, and 8 sections in all.

2. Use the probability ratio: $\frac{\text{favorable outcomes}}{\text{possible outcomes}}$ $\frac{2}{8} = \frac{1}{4}$

The probability of spinning a 4 on the spinner is **1 out of 4, $\frac{1}{4}$, 0.25, or 25%.**

In Example 1, probability was based on what we knew could happen. Another type of probability, called **experimental probability,** is based on what actually happens during the trials of an experiment. The number of trials are the number of times you try the experiment.

Example 2: Ricardo and Scott used the same spinner to play a game. They kept track of the numbers that they got on each spin for 20 spins. The numbers are shown below.

2, 4, 4, 6, 4, 3, 4, 6, 4, 3, 1, 6, 2, 2, 5, 2, 4, 2, 1, 2

Based on their results, what is the experimental probability of spinning a 4?

1. Ricardo and Scott spun a 4 six times out of twenty.

2. Use this ratio: $\frac{\text{favorable outcomes}}{\text{number of trials in experiment}}$ $\frac{6}{20} = \frac{3}{10}$, **0.3, or 30%**

Notice that experimental probability is close to, but not necessarily equal to, theoretical probability. Theoretical probability can tell you what will probably happen, but it can't predict what will actually happen.

GED TIP

In a GED probability problem, skim the answer choices to see if they are in fraction, percent, or ratio form. Knowing the answer form will help you decide how to do your calculation.

DATA ANALYSIS ▸ PRACTICE 5.1

Express probability as a fraction, decimal, <u>and</u> percent for questions 1 through 5. <u>Do not</u> use a calculator.

1. A game has 50 wooden tiles. Players draw tiles to spell words. If 20 of the tiles are marked with vowels, what is the probability of drawing a vowel from the tiles?

2. A spinner has five equal sections colored either red, white, or blue. After 40 spins, a player has the following results:

Color	Frequency
red	卌
white	卌 II
blue	卌 卌 卌 卌 卌 III

   What is the probability of not spinning blue on the spinner?

3. There are four red, four blue, and two green marbles in a bag. If one marble is chosen from the bag, what is the probability that the marble will be green?

4. A movie theater sells 180 adult tickets and 60 children's tickets to a movie. As part of a special promotion, one ticket will be chosen at random, and the winner will receive a prize. What is the probability that the winner will be a child?

5. A spinner has six equal sections numbered from 1 to 6. What is the probability of spinning either a 5 or 6?

B. Choose the <u>one best answer</u> to each question. You <u>MAY</u> use your calculator.

<u>Questions 6 and 7</u> refer to the following information.

A deck of twelve cards is marked with the following symbols.

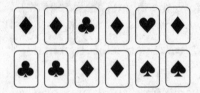

6. If a card is chosen at random, what is the probability of selecting a diamond (♦)?

   (1)   6%
   (2)   12%
   (3)   50%
   (4)   60%
   (5) 100%

7. If a card is chosen at random, what is the probability of selecting something other than a club (♣)?

   (1) $\frac{3}{4}$
   (2) $\frac{2}{3}$
   (3) $\frac{1}{3}$
   (4) $\frac{9}{100}$
   (5) Not enough information is given.

<u>Questions 8 and 9</u> refer to the following information.

Erin flipped a coin forty times and made this table to show how many outcomes were "heads" and how many were "tails."

heads	卌 卌 卌 卌 IIII
tails	卌 卌 卌 I

8. Based on Erin's data, what is the experimental probability of getting tails on a coin flip?

   (1) 3 out of 5
   (2) 3 out of 4
   (3) 2 out of 3
   (4) 2 out of 5
   (5) 1 out of 2

9. What is the theoretical probability of getting heads on a coin flip?

   (1) 3 out of 5
   (2) 3 out of 4
   (3) 2 out of 3
   (4) 2 out of 5
   (5) 1 out of 2

Answers and explanations begin on page 672.

Dependent and Independent Probability

You know how to find the probability of a single event. You can use this knowledge to find the probability of two or more events.

Example 1: Brad tosses two quarters into the air. What is the probability that both will land so that the heads' sides are showing?

One way to solve the problem is to list or diagram all the possible outcomes.

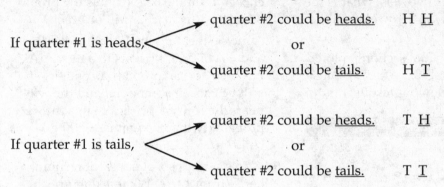

If quarter #1 is heads,
quarter #2 could be <u>heads</u>.   H <u>H</u>
or
quarter #2 could be <u>tails</u>.   H <u>T</u>

If quarter #1 is tails,
quarter #2 could be <u>heads</u>.   T <u>H</u>
or
quarter #2 could be <u>tails</u>.   T <u>T</u>

There are four possible outcomes, and only one is favorable (HH). Therefore, the probability of having both land with the heads side up is $\frac{1}{4}$, or **25%**.

You can also use multiplication to find the probability.

1. Find the probability of the individual events. The probability that one coin will be heads is $\frac{1}{2}$, and the probability that the other will be heads is $\frac{1}{2}$.

2. Multiply to find the probability of both events. $\frac{1}{2} \times \frac{1}{2} = \frac{1}{4}$

The two coin tosses in Example 1 are **independent events.** When events are independent, one does not affect the probability of another. In Example 2 below, the events are **dependent.** Once the first event takes place, the probability of the second event is changed.

Example 2: A box contains four blue marbles and two red marbles. If you select two marbles, what is the probability that both will be blue?

(*Hint:* Even though the marbles in the box are taken out at the same time, think of one as the first marble and the other as the second marble.)

1. There are six marbles in the box, and four are blue. The probability that the first marble will be blue is $\frac{4}{6}$, which reduces to $\frac{2}{3}$.

2. Assume the first marble selected is blue. Now there are only five marbles in the box, and three are blue. The probability that the second marble will be blue is $\frac{3}{5}$.

3. Multiply to find the probability of the two events. $\frac{2}{3} \times \frac{3}{5} = \frac{6}{15}$, or $\frac{2}{5}$

The probability that both marbles will be blue is **2 out of 5.**

Note: The events in Example 2 would not be dependent if the first marble were replaced before the second marble was selected. Always think carefully about the situation to decide whether two events are dependent or independent.

Note: Many probability problems involve randomly choosing two items from a group. A situation is dependent if the first item is not returned to the group before the second item is chosen.

DATA ANALYSIS ▸ PRACTICE 5.2

Solve as directed. Express answers as fractions.

1. Kim rolls two standard six-sided dice. What is the chance that both will be 4s?

2. Ten cards are numbered from one to ten. Toni draws out a card, replaces it, and then draws another card. What is the probability that both cards will be numbers greater than 5?

3. A spinner has four equal sections. Two sections are red, one is green, and one is blue. If the spinner is spun three times, what is the probability that all three spins will be red?

4. Twenty marbles are placed in a bag. Ten are red, and ten are black. One marble is drawn from the bag and set aside. Another marble is drawn from the bag. What is the chance that both marbles will be red?

5. Allison tosses a coin four times. What is the chance that the coin will be heads all four times?

6. If you roll two standard dice, what is the probability that both will be an odd number?

B. Choose the one best answer to each question. You MAY use your calculator.

<u>Questions 7 and 8</u> refer to the following information.

In a game a player rolls a die, numbered from 1 to 6, and spins a spinner. The spinner is shown below.

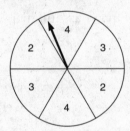

7. What is the probability of rolling a 5 and then spinning an even number?

   (1) $\frac{1}{9}$

   (2) $\frac{1}{6}$

   (3) $\frac{5}{12}$

   (4) $\frac{2}{3}$

   (5) $\frac{5}{6}$

8. What is the chance that a player will get the same number on both the die and the spinner?

   (1) $\frac{5}{6}$

   (2) $\frac{2}{3}$

   (3) $\frac{1}{3}$

   (4) $\frac{1}{6}$

   (5) Not enough information is given.

Daniel uses the ten cards below in a magic trick.

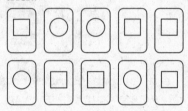

9. Daniel shuffles the cards and asks an audience member to choose and hold two cards. If the cards are chosen randomly, what is the chance that both will be marked with a square?

   (1) 11 out of 19

   (2) 8 out of 14

   (3) 3 out of 5

   (4) 1 out of 3

   (5) 1 out of 5

10. There are fifteen colored chips in a bag. Eight are green, and seven are white. Five white chips are removed. What is the probability that the next chip selected will be green?

   (1) 100%

   (2) 80%

   (3) 75%

   (4) 53%

   (5) 25%

Answers and explanations begin on page 672.

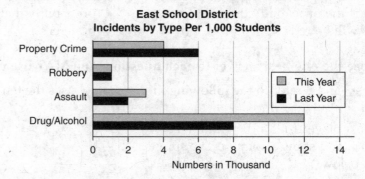

DATA ANALYSIS

Problem Solving

Key Ideas

- An item set has two or more questions based on the same data.
- Read the data carefully to make sure you understand how it is organized.
- Find the facts you need quickly, and ignore any unnecessary information.

Working with Item Sets

An **item set** is a group of GED problems based on the same information. The information may be organized in a paragraph, a chart or table, a graph, or a diagram. To do well on an item set, read the information carefully, then work each problem. Use only the facts you need for each problem, and ignore the rest.

Example: Questions 1 and 2 refer to the following graph:

East School District
Incidents by Type Per 1,000 Students

1. If East School District has about 32,000 students, how many assault incidents occurred last year?

   (1)   2
   (2)   3
   (3)   64
   (4)   96
   (5) 2,000

ON THE GED

About $\frac{1}{4}$ of the questions on the GED Math Test will be part of an item set.

2. Which of the following shows the percent of change in property crimes from last year to this year?

   (1) $66\frac{2}{3}$ increase
   (2) 50% increase
   (3) 50% decrease
   (4) $33\frac{1}{3}$% increase
   (5) $33\frac{1}{3}$% decrease

As you study the graph, note that the upper bar in each set represents this year's data, and the lower bar represents last year's. Also, notice that the scale at the bottom of the graph shows the number of incidents *per 1,000 students*.

To answer question 1, read the lower bar next to assault incidents. There were 2 incidents per 1,000 students. There are 32,000 students in the district. Use proportion to solve the problem. $\frac{2}{1000} = \frac{x}{32,000}$; $2 \times 32,000 \div 1,000 = \textbf{64}$

The answer to question 1 is **(3) 64**.

To answer question 2, you need to compare the two bars for property crimes. The upper bar (this year's data) is shorter than the lower bar (last year's data). Therefore, there has been a decrease in property crimes. Now find the percent of decrease. Subtract. $6 - 4 = 2$ Divide by the original (last year's) number. $\frac{2}{6} = \frac{1}{3} = 33\frac{1}{3}\%$ The correct answer is **(5) $33\frac{1}{3}\%$ decrease.**

Although the questions in an item set relate to the same data, you will never need the answer from one question to solve another. If you are having trouble with the first question in an item set, go on to the next question. Then come back to the other question later.

DATA ANALYSIS ▸ PRACTICE 6

Choose the <u>one best answer</u> to each question. You <u>MAY</u> use your calculator for questions 1 and 2.

<u>Questions 1 and 2</u> refer to the following information.

The city animal shelter surveyed 573 people who own either a dog or a cat to find out where they obtained their pet.

Source	Number of Pet Owners
Breeder	142
Animal shelter	160
Pet store	77
Friend	84
Adopted stray	110

1. What is the ratio of pet owners who adopted a stray to those who bought their dog or cat at a pet store?

(1) $\frac{7}{11}$

(2) $\frac{7}{10}$

(3) $\frac{10}{7}$

(4) $\frac{11}{7}$

(5) $\frac{17}{7}$

2. To the nearest whole percent, what percent of the pet owners surveyed got their pet from either a friend or an animal shelter?

(1) 15%

(2) 28%

(3) 43%

(4) 72%

(5) 85%

<u>Questions 3 and 4</u> refer to the following graph.

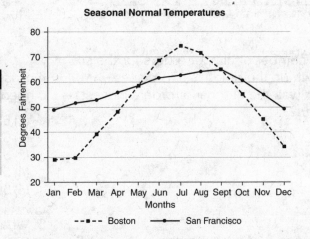

3. During which month is it about 20° colder in Boston than it is in San Francisco?

(1) January

(2) April

(3) July

(4) September

(5) November

4. In May, what is the approximate normal temperature for both Boston and San Francisco?

(1) 42°

(2) 46°

(3) 58°

(4) 65°

(5) 72°

Answers and explanations begin on page 672.

DATA ANALYSIS PRACTICE QUESTIONS
PART I

Directions: Choose the <u>one best answer</u> to each question. You <u>MAY</u> use your calculator.

<u>Questions 1 and 2</u> refer to the following graph.

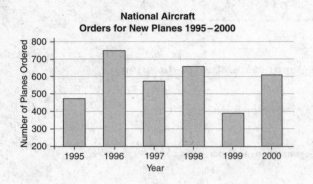

National Aircraft
Orders for New Planes 1995–2000

1. The mean number of aircraft orders for the six years shown on the graph is 573 planes. In which year was the number of orders closest to the mean?

   (1) 1995
   (2) 1996
   (3) 1997
   (4) 1998
   (5) 1999

2. By about what percent did orders at National Aircraft decrease from 1998 to 1999?

   (1) 26%
   (2) 30%
   (3) 40%
   (4) 68%
   (5) 75%

3. At a convention, Jim and his three friends each bought three raffle tickets. At the time of the drawing, 400 tickets had been sold. What is the probability that either Jim or one of his friends will win?

   (1) $\frac{3}{100}$
   (2) $\frac{1}{25}$
   (3) $\frac{3}{50}$
   (4) $\frac{9}{100}$
   (5) $\frac{3}{25}$

<u>Questions 4 through 6</u> are based on the following table.

Southland Weather March 9			
Area	High Temp.	Low Temp.	Precipitation (in inches)
Downtown	65° F	53° F	0.45
Airport	62° F	50° F	0.63
Woodland Hills	68° F	50° F	1.34
East Village	56° F	48° F	3.53
Ventura	62° F	49° F	2.57
Highland Park	64° F	55° F	0.84

4. Based on the data in the table, what was the median low temperature for March 9?

   (1) 63°
   (2) 62.8°
   (3) 51.5°
   (4) 50.8°
   (5) 50°

5. What was the mean amount of precipitation (in inches) on March 9 for the areas listed in the table?

   (1) 0.65
   (2) 1.09
   (3) 1.56
   (4) 1.99
   (5) 2.44

6. For which area on the table was there the greatest range, or difference, between the high and low temperatures?

   (1) Highland Park
   (2) Ventura
   (3) East Village
   (4) Woodland Hills
   (5) Downtown

Platinum Cinemas Ticket Sales

7. Platinum Cinemas opened its first theaters in 1991. The company's ticket sales increased relatively steadily until what year, when there was a large drop in sales?

(1) 1993
(2) 1994
(3) 1995
(4) 1998
(5) 1999

8. Which time period showed the sharpest increase in ticket sales?

(1) 1995 to 1996
(2) 1996 to 1997
(3) 1997 to 1998
(4) 1998 to 1999
(5) 1999 to 2000

9. At Nelson Stationers, the first twenty-five customers who visited the store on Monday morning received their choice of a gift. The table below shows how many customers chose each gift.

pen and pencil set	₶₶
calculator	₶₶ ₶₶ 11
mouse pad	₶₶ 111

What percent of the customers chose a mouse pad?

(1) 8%
(2) 17%
(3) 25%
(4) 32%
(5) $33\frac{1}{3}$%

10. A standard deck of playing cards has 52 cards, with 13 cards each of hearts, diamonds, clubs, and spades. If a card is drawn randomly from the deck, what is the probability that it will be either hearts or diamonds?

(1) 1 in 2
(2) 1 in 4
(3) 1 in 8
(4) 1 in 16
(5) 1 in 52

11. Nita worked the following overtime hours over a six-week period.

Week 1: 5 hours
Week 2: $3\frac{1}{2}$ hours
Week 3: 4 hours
Week 4: 0 hours
Week 5: $1\frac{1}{2}$ hours
Week 6: 7 hours

What is the mean number of overtime hours Nita worked each week?

Mark your answer in the circles on the grid at the bottom of the page.

12. A spinner has five equal sections, and they are numbered from 1 to 5. What is the probability of spinning a number greater than 3? (Express the answer as a fraction or decimal.)

Mark your answer in the circles on the grid at the bottom of the page.

11.

⊘	⊘	⊘	
·	·	·	·
⓪	⓪	⓪	⓪	⓪
①	①	①	①	①
②	②	②	②	②
③	③	③	③	③
④	④	④	④	④
⑤	⑤	⑤	⑤	⑤
⑥	⑥	⑥	⑥	⑥
⑦	⑦	⑦	⑦	⑦
⑧	⑧	⑧	⑧	⑧
⑨	⑨	⑨	⑨	⑨

12.

⊘	⊘	⊘	
·	·	·	·
⓪	⓪	⓪	⓪	⓪
①	①	①	①	①
②	②	②	②	②
③	③	③	③	③
④	④	④	④	④
⑤	⑤	⑤	⑤	⑤
⑥	⑥	⑥	⑥	⑥
⑦	⑦	⑦	⑦	⑦
⑧	⑧	⑧	⑧	⑧
⑨	⑨	⑨	⑨	⑨

PART II

Directions: Choose the <u>one best answer</u> to each question. You <u>MAY NOT</u> use your calculator for these questions.

<u>Questions 13 through 15</u> refer to the following graph.

In a recent election, five candidates ran for the city council seat from District 11. The results of the race are shown in the graph below.

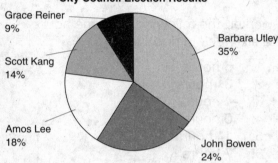

City Council Election Results

Grace Reiner 9%
Scott Kang 14%
Amos Lee 18%
Barbara Utley 35%
John Bowen 24%

13. The three city council candidates who received the fewest votes received what percent of the total vote?

(1) 23%
(2) 41%
(3) 56%
(4) 77%
(5) Not enough information is given.

14. Which two candidates combined received about $\frac{3}{5}$ of the votes cast?

(1) Grace and Utley
(2) Kang and Utley
(3) Lee and Utley
(4) Bowen and Utley
(5) Lee and Bowen

15. If 5100 votes were cast in the election, which of the following expressions could be used to find out how many votes Grace Reiner received?

(1) 5100×0.9
(2) $\dfrac{5100}{0.9}$
(3) $\dfrac{5100}{0.09}$
(4) $5100 - (5100 \times 0.09)$
(5) 5100×0.09

<u>Questions 16 through 18</u> refer to the following graph.

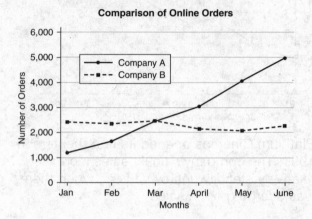

16. In which month did Company A and Company B receive about the same number of online orders?

(1) January
(2) February
(3) March
(4) April
(5) May

17. Based on the trends shown by the data, what would be the best prediction for the number of online orders in July for Company A?

(1) 7200
(2) 5900
(3) 5200
(4) 4900
(5) 4200

18. About 18% of the online orders at Company A are returned for credit or exchange. What percent of the orders at Company B are returned for credit or exchange?

(1) 15%
(2) 18%
(3) 36%
(4) 82%
(5) Not enough information is given.

A basketball player's statistics for an 8-game series are shown in the table below.

Game	Shots Attempted	Shots Made
1	25	10
2	23	12
3	26	10
4	24	13
5	29	15
6	18	7
7	24	12
8	27	10

19. What was the median number of shots attempted in the series?

(1) 23
(2) 24
(3) 24.5
(4) 25
(5) 26.5

20. What is the mode of the shots made during the series?

(1) 12
(2) 11
(3) 10 and 12
(4) 10
(5) Not enough information is given.

21. A bag contains 24 marbles. Eight are red, six are blue, and ten are white. A marble is drawn from the bag and replaced. A second marble is chosen at random from the bag. What is the probability that the first marble is red and the second is white?

(1) $\frac{2}{5}$
(2) $\frac{1}{6}$
(3) $\frac{5}{36}$
(4) $\frac{5}{48}$
(5) $\frac{1}{48}$

22. A company has 36 employees. For three months, the owner has kept track of the number of sick days used by her employees per month.

Month	Sick Days
Sept.	34
Oct.	31
Nov.	42

Which expressions could be used to find the average number of sick days taken each month?

(1) $\dfrac{34 + 31 + 42}{36}$

(2) $\dfrac{34 + 31 + 42}{3}$

(3) $\dfrac{34 + 31 + 42 + 36}{4}$

(4) $\dfrac{34 + 31 + 42 + 36}{3}$

(5) $(34 + 31 + 42) \times 3$

23. Andy rolls two standard six-sided dice. What is the probability of rolling two ones?

Mark your answer in the circles on the grid at the bottom of the page.

24. Kate drove 158 miles on Monday, 276 miles on Tuesday, 54 miles on Wednesday, 305 miles on Thursday, and 210 miles on Friday. In miles, what was the median distance she drove for the five days?

Mark your answer in the circles on the grid at the bottom of the page.

23.

24.

Answers and explanations begin on page 672.

Key Ideas

- Multiply to change from a larger unit of measure to a smaller one.
- Divide to change from a smaller unit of measure to a larger one.
- When dividing, the remainder is the same unit of measure as the number you are dividing by.

The measurement facts shown in the table on this page will not be given to you anywhere on the GED Math Test. You must memorize them in order to answer the measurement questions correctly.

MEASUREMENT

The English System of Measurement

Standard Units of Measure

Measurements are used to describe an object's length, weight, or volume. We also use measurement to describe a quantity of time. The United States uses the English, or standard, system of measurement. Study the table below to learn the common standard units and their abbreviations.

Measurement Equivalencies

Length
1 foot (ft) = 12 inches (in)
1 yard (yd) = 3 ft
1 mile (mi) = 5280 ft

Weight
1 pound (lb) =16 ounces (oz)
1 ton (t) = 2000 lb

Volume
1 cup (c) = 8 fluid ounces (fl oz)
1 pint (pt) = 2 c
1 quart (qt) = 2 pt
1 gallon (gal) = 4 qt

Time
1 minute (min) = 60 seconds (sec)
1 hour (hr) = 60 min
1 day = 24 hr
1 week = 7 days
1 year (yr) = 12 months (mo) = 365 days

To solve problems, you will need to change from one unit of measure to another. If you need to *change a larger unit of measure to a smaller one*, you need to *multiply*. Use the measurement equivalencies above.

Example 1: A picture frame is 3 ft 8 in long. What is the length of the frame in inches?

1. Change 3 feet to inches using the fact that $\qquad$ $3 \text{ ft} \times 12 = 36 \text{ in}$
   1 foot = 12 inches.

2. Add the remaining 8 inches. $\qquad$ $36 + 8 = 44 \text{ in}$

The picture frame is **44 inches** in length.

To change a *smaller unit of measure to a larger one, divide* using the appropriate measurement equivalency.

Example 2: A package weighs 84 ounces. What is the weight of the package in pounds?

1. Change 84 ounces to pounds. Since 1 pound = 16 ounces, divide by 16.

$$\begin{array}{r} 5 \\ 16\overline{)84} \\ -80 \\ \hline 4 \end{array}$$

2. The remainder is in ounces, the same unit you started with. Therefore, the package weighs **5 lb 4 oz,** or you can express the remainder as a fraction. $5\frac{4}{16} = 5\frac{1}{4}$ **lb**

You may need to do a series of conversions.

Example 3: A container holds 1.5 gallons. How many cups does the container hold?

1. Change 1.5 gallons to quarts. (Use the fact 1 gal = 4 qt.)   1.5 gal $\times$ 4 = 6 qt

2. Change 6 quarts to pints. (Use the fact 1 qt = 2 pt.)   6 qt $\times$ 2 = 12 pt

3. Change 12 pints to cups. (Use the fact 1 pt = 2 c.)   12 pt $\times$ 2 = 24 c

The container holds **24 cups.**

MEASUREMENT ▸ PRACTICE 1.1

A. Solve.

1. How many inches are equal to 4 feet?

2. How many minutes are equal to 420 seconds?

3. How many hours are in 3 days?

4. Convert 40 fluid ounces to pints.

5. Five gallons are equal to how many quarts?

6. 11,000 pounds equal how many tons?

7. Four yards equal how many inches?

8. How many hours are equal to 720 minutes?

9. How many cups are in two gallons?

10. How many pounds equal 128 ounces?

11. Eight yards equal how many feet?

12. How many feet equal $1\frac{1}{2}$ miles?

B. Choose the <u>one best answer</u> to each question. You may use a calculator.

<u>Questions 13 through 15</u> refer to the following information.

> **Portable Air Cooler**
> Duracool R612
> 3.75 gallon capacity
> Runs 6 hours without refilling
> width: 27 in; depth: 16 in
> height: 13 3/4 in
> shipping weight: 26 lb

13. Bob wants to buy an air cooler. He knows the capacity of several other models in quarts. Which of the following expressions could he use to find the capacity for this model in quarts?

(1) 3.75 $\times$ 2
(2) 3.75 $\div$ 2
(3) 3.75 $\times$ 4
(4) 3.75 $\div$ 4
(5) 3.75 $\times$ 8

14. Which of these measurements is equal to the width of the Duracool R612?

(1) 2 ft 1 in
(2) 2 ft 3 in
(3) $2\frac{1}{3}$ ft
(4) $2\frac{1}{2}$ ft
(5) 2 ft 7 in

15. Another model, the R500, claims to run 250 minutes without refilling. How many minutes longer will the R612 run?

(1)   50
(2)   60
(3) 110
(4) 360
(5) Not enough information is given.

Answers and explanations begin on page 673.

Solving Measurement Problems

In a measurement problem, you may need to add, subtract, multiply, or divide measurements. When finding a sum or a difference, remember that you can only add or subtract like measurement units.

Example 1: A deck requires pieces of railing that are 5 ft 9 in, 15 ft 4 in, and 8 ft 6 in. What is the total length of railing needed?

1. Write the measurements in a column, aligning like units of measure.

2. Add like units.

3. Simplify the answer. (Change 19 in to 1 ft 7 in, and add to 28 ft.)

$$\begin{array}{r} 5\text{ ft}\quad 9\text{ in} \\ 15\text{ ft}\quad 4\text{ in} \\ +8\text{ ft}\quad 6\text{ in} \\ \hline 28\text{ ft}\ 19\text{ in} \end{array}$$

28 ft + 1 ft 7 in = 29 ft 7 in

The deck requires **29 ft 7 in** of railing.

When you subtract, you may need to regroup, or borrow.

Example 2: How much more is 4 lb 3 oz than 2 lb 8 oz?

1. Align the problem. Since you cannot subtract 8 oz from 3 oz, regroup 1 pound from the pounds column, rewrite it as 16 ounces, and add it to the ounces column. (16 + 3 = 19)

2. Subtract. The difference is **1 lb 11 oz.**

$$\begin{array}{r} {}^{3}\ \ {}^{19}\ \ \\ \cancel{4}\text{ lb}\ \cancel{3}\text{ oz} \\ -2\text{ lb}\ 8\text{ oz} \\ \hline 1\text{ lb }11\text{ oz} \end{array}$$

To multiply a measurement by a whole number, multiply the units of measure separately. Then simplify the result.

Example 3: Tony has five lengths of plastic pipe, each measuring 6 ft 10 in. What is the combined length of the pipe?

1. Multiply each part of the measurement by 5.

2. Simplify using the fact 1 ft = 12 in.

$$\begin{array}{r} 6\text{ ft }10\text{ in} \\ \times\quad 5 \\ \hline \end{array}$$

30 ft 50 in = 30 ft + 4 ft 2 in = 34 ft 2 in

The combined length is **34 ft 2 in.**

To divide a measurement, you can divide each part of the measurement and then add the results. However, it will usually be faster to rewrite the measurement in terms of the smallest unit of measure. Then divide and simplify.

Example 4: John has 1 pt 8 fl oz of liquid lawn fertilizer. He plans to mix one-third of the liquid with two gallons of water and apply it to his lawn. How many ounces of fertilizer will he use?

1. Change the amount to ounces.

2. To find one-third, divide by 3.

1 pt = 2 c = 16 fl oz
1 pt 8 fl oz = 16 + 8 = 24 fl oz
24 fl oz ÷ 3 = 8 fl oz

John will use **8 fluid ounces** of lawn fertilizer.

Note: On the GED Math Test, measurements in the answer choices are not usually labeled. Read the question carefully to know what measurement unit the answers represent.

MEASUREMENT ▸ PRACTICE 1.2

A. Solve as directed. Simplify if necessary.

1. 6 lb 10 oz
    + 2 lb 14 oz

2. 3 hr 30 min
    4 hr 20 min
    + 2 hr 45 min

3. 10 ft 10 in
    +5 ft 8 in

4. 3 gal 1 qt
    − 1 gal 3 qt

5. 2 yd 2 ft 2 in
    −   4 ft 8 in

6. 2 lb 5 oz
    ×   6

7. 8 min 10 sec
    ×   10

8. $\dfrac{11\ ft\ 8\ in}{2}$

9. $\dfrac{5\ min\ 45\ sec}{5}$

B. Choose the one best answer to each question.

Questions 10 and 11 refer to the following diagram.

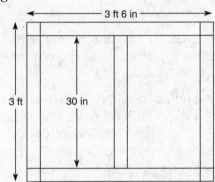

10. Scott is building a platform for a play production. The diagram shows the measurements of the wood frame for the platform. How many feet of wood will Scott need to build the frame?

    (1)   9
    (2) $10\frac{1}{2}$
    (3) 13
    (4) $15\frac{1}{2}$
    (5) 108

11. The theater company buys the wood in 16-foot lengths. How many lengths measuring 30 inches can be cut from one 16-foot board?

    (1) 7
    (2) 6
    (3) 5
    (4) 4
    (5) 3

12. Nydia works in a photo lab. She uses 1 pt 6 fl oz of film developer from a full container. If the capacity of the container is 3 qt, how much developer is left in the container?

    (1) 2 qt 10 fl oz
    (2) 2 qt 6 fl oz
    (3) 2 qt 2 fl oz
    (4) 2 qt
    (5) 1 qt 10 fl oz

13. Max needs to ship six identical packages, each weighing 3 lb 12 oz. What is the total weight of the shipment?

    (1) 19 lb 2 oz
    (2) 22 lb 5 oz
    (3) 22 lb 8 oz
    (4) 24 lb 12 oz
    (5) 25 lb 2 oz

14. On Monday Jean spent 1 hr 45 min doing data entry. On Tuesday she spent 2 hr 30 min, and on Wednesday she worked 3 hr 45 min at the same task. How many hours did Jean spend doing data entry during the three days?

    (1) $6\frac{1}{3}$
    (2) 7.2
    (3) $7\frac{1}{4}$
    (4) $7\frac{1}{2}$
    (5) 8

Answers and explanations begin on page 674.

MEASUREMENT

The Metric System

Common Metric Units

The **metric system** is the measurement system used in most of the countries of the world. The main unit of length in the metric system is the **meter** (m). All other measurements are related in some way. The **gram** (g) is the basic metric measure of **mass** (or weight). The basic unit of volume is called the **liter** (*l*).

To form units of measure, add prefixes to the basic units described above. You will have an easier time learning the metric system if you memorize the meaning of the prefixes.

milli- (m) means one-thousandth   *deka-* (dam) means ten

centi- (c) means one-hundredth   *hecto-* means one hundred

deci- (d) means one-tenth   *kilo-* means one thousand

Therefore, a kilometer (km) equals 1000 meters, a milligram (mg) equals one one-thousandth gram, and a centiliter (cl) equals one one-hundredth liter.

You may find it helpful to memorize the following chart. As in our decimal place-value system, each column on the chart is 10 times the column to its right. To convert between metric units, count the spaces from the unit you are converting from to the unit you are converting to. Then move the decimal point that number of place values in the same direction.

kilo- (km)	hecto- (hm)	deka- (dam)	meter (m)	deci- (dm)	centi- (cm)	milli- (mm)
1000 m	100 m	10 m	1 m	0.1 m	0.01 m	0.001 m

Note: Although the chart uses the meter as the basic unit, the chart can also be used with liters (*l*) and grams (g).

Example 1: How many millimeters (mm) are equal to 3 centimeters (cm)?

1. Find *milli-* and *centi-* on the chart. The prefix *milli-* is one place to the right of the prefix *centi-*; therefore, you need to move the decimal point one place to the right to convert from centimeters to millimeters.

2. For example, 3 cm = 3.0 cm = **30 mm.**

Example 2: How many grams (g) are equal to 6400 milligrams (mg)?

1. Start in the *milli-* column. The basic unit (or ones column) is three columns to the left. Move the decimal point three place-value columns to the left.

2. For example, 6400 mg = 6400. mg = **6.4 g.**

Key Ideas

- The metric system is based on the decimal place-value system.
- Each place-value column is named using a prefix and a standard unit of measure: meter, liter, or gram.
- To make conversions, use the prefixes to determine the relationship between units and move the decimal point.

ON THE GED

On the GED Math Test, you will not be asked to make conversions between the standard and metric systems.

If this is one of your first experiences with the metric system, it may seem confusing. You may want to memorize the following common conversions. You can use these facts to make conversions in the same way that you do in the English system of measurement.

1000 meters = 1 kilometer
1 meter = 100 centimeters
1 meter = 1000 millimeters
1 centimeter = 10 millimeters

← You can replace the word *meter* with either *liter* or *gram* in each conversion.

MEASUREMENT ▸ PRACTICE 2.1

A. Solve.

1. How many meters equal 5 kilometers?

2. 600 centimeters equal how many meters?

3. How many milligrams equal 4 grams?

4. Eight kilograms equal how many grams?

5. 40.5 liters equal how many centiliters?

6. How many liters are equal to 1500 ml?

7. 250 milligrams is equal to how many grams?

8. How many meters are in 30 kilometers?

9. 0.75 *l* is equal to how many cl?

10. 50 grams equal how many kilograms?

11. 35,200 milliliters equal how many liters?

12. How many centimeters are in 15 meters?

B. Choose the one best answer to each question.

Question 13 refers to the following drawing.

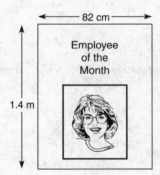

82 cm

Employee of the Month

1.4 m

13. A store manager is creating a display in the hall to reward outstanding employees. The measurements of the display are shown in the diagram. What is the height of the display in centimeters?

(1)   0.014
(2)   0.14
(3)   14
(4)   140
(5)   1400

14. A can of machine oil holds 118.3 ml. How many liters of machine oil does the can hold?

(1)   0.01183
(2)   0.1183
(3)   1.183
(4)   11.83
(5) 1183

15. In a vitamin supplement, each capsule contains 500 milligrams of vitamins. How many <u>grams</u> of vitamins are found in each capsule?

(1) 5000
(2)   500
(3)   50
(4)   5
(5)   0.5

Answers and explanations begin on page 674.

Solving Problems with Metric Measurement

Metric measurements are written as decimal numbers. Therefore, you can perform operations with metric measurements using the rules for adding, subtracting, multiplying, and dividing decimals.

Example 1: Three metal rods measure 1.5 meters, 1.85 meters, and 450 centimeters. What is the total length of the rods in meters?

1. Read the question carefully. You are asked to find the total length in *meters*.

2. The first two measures are written in meters. Convert the third measure to meters. 450 cm = 4.5 m

3. Add using the rules for adding decimals. The total is **7.85 m.**

$$\begin{array}{r} 1 \\ 1.5 \\ 1.85 \\ +4.5 \\ \hline 7.85 \end{array}$$

Follow the same steps to subtract.

Example 2: Tanya is jogging in a city park. The park has a path for joggers that is 2 kilometers in length. When she reaches the 750-meter checkpoint, how many kilometers does she have left to run?

1. You need to find the distance she has left in kilometers.

2. Change 750 meters to kilometers. 750 m = 0.75 km

3. Subtract using the rules for subtracting decimals.

$$\begin{array}{r} 1\ \ 9\ 10 \\ \cancel{2.00} \\ -\ 0.75 \\ \hline 1.25 \end{array}$$

Tanya has **1.25 km** left to run.

Multiplying and dividing is much easier in the metric system. Follow the rules for multiplying and dividing decimals.

Example 3: Alex is a buyer at Rugs Plus. He plans to order 25 acrylic rugs to sell in the store. The shipping weight for each rug is 7.8 kilograms. What is the shipping weight in kilograms of the entire order?

1. Multiply the weight of one rug (7.8 kg) by 25.

2. The weight of 25 rugs is **195 kilograms.** Notice that the answer has the same unit of measure as the number you multiplied.

$$\begin{array}{r} 7.8 \\ \times\ 25 \\ \hline 390 \\ 1560 \\ \hline 195.0 \end{array}$$

Example 4: At a food-processing plant, a tank holds 92.4 liters of a fruit drink. It takes three hours for a machine to empty the tank into small containers. How many liters of fruit drink are processed per hour?

1. To find the number per hour, divide 92.4 liters by 3.

2. The machine can process **30.8 liters** per hour.

$$\begin{array}{r} 30.8 \\ 3\overline{)92.4} \\ 9 \\ \hline 2\ 4 \\ 2\ 4 \end{array}$$

You could also have solved this problem by writing and solving a proportion. $\dfrac{92.4}{3} = \dfrac{x}{1}$; $92.4 \times 1 \div 3 = 30.8$ liters

Note: A common mistake when solving metric problems is putting the decimal point in the wrong place. To avoid errors, estimate before you work the problem. Compare your answer to the estimate.

MEASUREMENT ▸ PRACTICE 2.2

A. Solve as directed. You MAY use a calculator. Pay special attention to the label given for each answer.

1. 5.4 cm + 19 cm + 2.85 cm = _____ cm

2. 12 kg + 10.5 kg + 120 g = _____ g

3. 2.4 m + 150 cm + 4.28 m = _____ m

4. 2 *l* − 1.4 *l* = _____ *l*

5. 2.4 kg − 180 g = _____ kg

6. 3.5 km − 370 m = _____ m

7. 4.3 cl × 30 = _____ cl

8. 1.6 mm × 15 = _____ cm

9. 150 g × 250 = _____ kg

10. 16 g ÷ 64 = _____ g

11. 25.8 m ÷ 4 = _____ cm

12. 3 kl ÷ 15 = _____ *l*

B. Choose the one best answer to each question. You may use a calculator.

<u>Question 13</u> refers to the following diagram.

Russ has been asked to landscape the following area with drought-resistant plants.

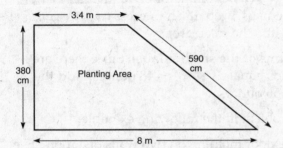

13. Russ decides to edge the entire planting area with cedar. What is the distance in <u>meters</u> around the planting area?

   (1)   10.84
   (2)   12.37
   (3)   21.1
   (4) 123.70
   (5) 211

14. To make a carbonated punch, Kay Lynn adds six cans of club soda to 2 liters of cranberry juice. If each can holds 355 ml, how many liters of punch has Kay Lynn made?

   (1)   4.13
   (2)   4.26
   (3)   5.55
   (4) 23.3
   (5) 37.5

15. A type of bonding gel comes in a small container that holds 4 g of the gel. How many of the small containers could be filled from 2.5 kg of the gel?

   (1) 6250
   (2)   625
   (3)   62
   (4)   6
   (5) Not enough information is given.

16. Sharon buys 4.8 meters of ribbon to use as trim on a set of kitchen curtains. She actually uses 350 centimeters. How many centimeters of the ribbon are left?

   (1)   13
   (2)   44.5
   (3) 130
   (4) 302
   (5) 476.5

17. A map scale reads 1 cm = 3.6 km. If the distance between two cities on the map is 4.2 centimeters, what is the actual distance between the cities in kilometers?

   (1)   0.6
   (2)   1.17
   (3)   7.8
   (4) 12.6
   (5) 15.12

Answers and explanations begin on page 674.

MEASUREMENT

Using a Calculator

Key Ideas

• If a measurement has more than one unit of measure, convert it to one unit before entering it on the calculator.
• Use fractions or decimals to represent smaller units.

Entering Measurements on a Calculator

Most calculators, including the one you will use on the GED Math Test, cannot process a measurement written with more than one unit label. For example, before you can enter the measurement 3 lb 8 oz, you must write it with only one label, either pounds or ounces.

There are several ways to do this quickly.

• **Enter the measurement as a decimal:** You know that 8 ounces = $\frac{1}{2}$ pound, and the fraction $\frac{1}{2} = 0.5$. Therefore, 3 lb 8 oz equals 3.5 pounds.

• **Enter the measurement as a mixed number:** The number of pounds is the whole number part of the mixed number, and the number of ounces is the numerator of a fraction with a denominator of 16 (the number of ounces in a pound). 3 lb 8 oz equals $3\frac{8}{16}$ lb. It isn't necessary to reduce the fraction before entering it into the calculator.

• **Enter the measurement in terms of the smaller label:** Since there are 16 ounces in 1 pound, 3 pounds equals 3×16, or 48 ounces. Add the remaining 8 ounces. $48 + 8 = 56$ ounces

Try each method to solve the problem in the following example.

Example: Janira is replacing the floor molding on two walls of a room. She needs one piece measuring 15 feet 9 inches and one measuring 13 feet 6 inches. How many feet of molding does Janira need?

Enter the measurements as decimals:

9 inches is $\frac{3}{4}$ or 0.75 ft, and 6 inches is $\frac{1}{2}$ or 0.5 ft.
Enter: 15.75 $\boxed{+}$ 13.5 $\boxed{=}$ $\boxed{29.25}$

Enter as mixed numbers:

Enter: 15 $\boxed{a^b/_c}$ 9 $\boxed{a^b/_c}$ 12 + 13 $\boxed{a^b/_c}$ 6 $\boxed{a^b/_c}$ 12 $\boxed{=}$ $\boxed{29 ⌐ 1 ⌐ 4.}$

Enter using the smallest unit of measure:

Since 1 ft = 12 in, multiply the feet in each measurement by 12.

Enter: 15 $\boxed{\times}$ 12 $\boxed{+}$ 9 $\boxed{+}$ 13 $\boxed{\times}$ 12 $\boxed{+}$ 6 $\boxed{=}$ $\boxed{351}$

Change to feet. 351 ÷ 12 $\boxed{=}$ $\boxed{29.25}$

Janira needs **29.25 feet**, or **29$\frac{1}{4}$ feet**, of molding. Since $\frac{1}{4}$ of 12 inches is 3 inches, you can also write the answer as 29 ft 3 in.

Which method do you prefer? The first method, entering the measurements as decimals, is probably the best method for most circumstances. To use this method, you need to have memorized the common fraction/decimal equivalencies on page 384.

GED TIP

Since measurement conversions are time-consuming, choose the method of working the problem that requires the fewest conversions.

MEASUREMENT ▸ PRACTICE 3

A. Solve as directed using a calculator.

1. 3 lb 8 oz + 2 lb 4 oz = _____ lb

2. 2 c 6 fl oz + 1 c 12 fl oz = _____ fl oz

3. 3 min 15 sec − 2 min 45 sec = _____ sec

4. 4.5 l − 350 cl = _____ cl

5. $\frac{3}{4}$ mi + 2640 ft = _____ mi

6. 10 oz × 30 = _____ lb

7. 2.76 km ÷ 3 = _____ m

8. 4 ft 9 in + 2 ft 6 in + 8 ft 4 in = _____ ft _____ in

9. 15 lb 4 oz − 9 lb 8 oz = _____ oz

10. 55 cm × 20 = _____ m

11. 3 yd 2 ft 9 in × 4 = _____ yd _____ ft

12. 2 m + 30 cm + 35 mm = _____ m

13. 3 gal 3 qt ÷ 5 = _____ qt

14. 2.5 tons − 1500 lb = _____ lb

15. 15 g ÷ 100 = _____ mg

16. 2 min 30 sec × 30 = _____ hr _____ min

17. 4 pints ÷ 8 = _____ fl oz

18. 600 mg × 120 = _____ g

19. 100 yd ÷ 150 = _____ ft

20. 4 gal − 12 pt = _____ pt

B. Choose the one best answer to each question. You MAY use a calculator.

Question 21 refers to the following information.

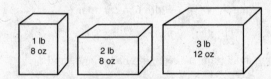

21. What is the combined weight, in ounces, of the three packages shown in the drawing?

    (1)   7.75
    (2)   96
    (3) 123.52
    (4) 124
    (5) 544

22. At a restaurant, a kettle holds $1\frac{3}{4}$ gallons of soup. If a soup bowl holds $1\frac{3}{4}$ cups of soup, how many bowls can be filled from the soup in the kettle?

    (1) 80
    (2) 32
    (3) 16
    (4)   8
    (5) Not enough information is given.

23. A pediatrician estimates that she spends an average of 14 minutes with each patient. Which of the following is the best estimate of how many patients the doctor could see in a 40-hour time period?

    (1)   20
    (2) 170
    (3) 210
    (4) 230
    (5) 560

Answers and explanations begin on page 674.

MEASUREMENT

Problem Solving

Using Benchmarks

A **benchmark** is a common object that can help you estimate the length, weight, or volume of a unit of measure. Using benchmarks, you can perform informal measurements and analyze whether an answer to a math problem makes sense.

The benchmarks in the table below have been used by many people. You may want to learn these or think of some of your own. Remember that benchmarks are not exact measurements. Their purpose is to help you make better estimates.

Key Ideas

- A benchmark is an ordinary object used to represent the approximate size of a unit of measure.
- Learn common benchmarks for metric and English units of measure. Then use the benchmarks to make sure your answers make sense.

Useful Measurement Benchmarks

English System		Metric System	
inch	length of the tip of your thumb	millimeter	the thickness of a penny
foot	length of a sheet of paper	centimeter	width of the tip of your little finger
yard	a long stride	meter	width of a car door
ounce	weight of a first-class letter	kilometer	about $\frac{1}{2}$ mile
pound	weight of a loaf of bread	milligram	weight of a grain of sand
fluid ounce	a dose of cough medicine	gram	weight of a large paper clip
cup	a measuring cup	kilogram	weight of a hardcover book
pint	a little more than a can of soda pop	liter	half of a large plastic soda pop bottle
quart	bottle of motor oil	milliliter	a few drops from an eye dropper
gallon	large milk container		

GED TIP

Your ability to estimate and use common sense to eliminate incorrect choices is important to your GED success. Many items can be answered on the GED Math Test using these skills.

You can answer some GED math problems using benchmarks.

Example: Which of the following would be the best estimate of the length of a living room?

(1) 1.5 kilometers
(2) 4.8 meters
(3) 50 centimeters
(4) 2 yards
(5) 150 feet

Think about your own living room. You can quickly eliminate option (1), which uses kilometers, a large unit of measure, and option (3), which uses centimeters, a very small unit of measure. You can eliminate option (4) because two yards is only six feet, too small for a living room. You know from experience that option (5) 150 feet is too long for a room in a house. Only **option (2) 4.8 meters** makes sense.

MEASUREMENT ▶ PRACTICE 4

A. Choose the best estimate for each of the following objects.

1. the length of an unsharpened pencil
   a. 19 mm
   b. 19 cm
   c. 19 m

2. the weight of a hardcover book
   a. 4 oz
   b. 2 lb
   c. 10 lb

3. the height of a two-story building
   a. 9 m
   b. 90 m
   c. 900 m

4. the volume of the gas tank of a car
   a. 14 pt
   b. 14 qt
   c. 14 gal

5. the width of a television screen
   a. 40 mm
   b. 40 cm
   c. 40 m

6. the capacity of a bottle of eye drops
   a. 2 fl oz
   b. 2 c
   c. 2 pt

7. the width of a rug
   a. 220 mm
   b. 220 cm
   c. 220 m

8. the height of a basketball player
   a. 3 m
   b. 4 ft
   c. 78 in

9. the amount of medicine in one pill
   a. 25 mg
   b. 25 kg
   c. 25 oz

10. the length of thread on a new spool of thread
    a. 175 mm
    b. 175 in
    c. 175 yd

B. Choose the one best answer to each question. You MAY NOT use a calculator.

11. Matt knows that his 12-year-old son weighs a little more than 100 pounds. However, when he took his son to the doctor, he noticed that the doctor recorded his son's weight as 47. What unit of measure did the doctor most likely use to record the boy's weight?

    (1) ounces
    (2) milligrams
    (3) meters
    (4) grams
    (5) kilograms

12. Stephanie measures the length of a dollar bill as 15.7 on a ruler. What unit of measure is Stephanie using?

    (1) inches
    (2) feet
    (3) millimeters
    (4) centimeters
    (5) meters

13. A can of frozen juice concentrate has the following label.

    > **Cranberry Juice Concentrate**
    >
    > Contents: 11.5 fl oz (340 ml)
    >
    > To Serve: Mix with $4\frac{1}{2}$ cups of cold water. Stir or shake briskly

    Kayla mixes two cans of the frozen concentrate with the appropriate amount of water. How much juice has she made?

    (1) 95 fl oz
    (2) 95 c
    (3) 95 ml
    (4) 9.5 pt
    (5) 9.5 qt

Answers and explanations begin on page 674.

MEASUREMENT PRACTICE QUESTIONS

PART I

Directions: Choose the <u>one best answer</u> to each question. You <u>MAY</u> use a calculator.

<u>Questions 1 and 2</u> refer to the following diagram.

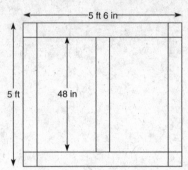

1. James is building a steel platform. The diagram shows the measurements of the frame for the platform. How many feet of pipe will James need to build the frame?

   (1) $14\frac{1}{2}$
   (2) 20
   (3) 21
   (4) 25
   (5) 29

2. The factory buys the pipe in 20-foot lengths. How many lengths measuring 48 inches can be cut from one 20-foot pipe?

   (1) 6
   (2) 5
   (3) 4
   (4) 3
   (5) 2

3. Carla runs a commercial cleaning business. She uses $1\frac{1}{2}$ gallons of industrial-strength cleaner from a full container. If the capacity of the container is 5 gallons, how many <u>quarts</u> of cleaner are left in the container?

   (1) $1\frac{1}{2}$
   (2) $3\frac{1}{2}$
   (3) 5
   (4) 14
   (5) 20

4. Rosanne needs to ship five promotional packages, each weighing 1 lb 9 oz. What is the total weight of the shipment?

   (1) 5 lb
   (2) 5 lb 13 oz
   (3) 7 lb 13 oz
   (4) 8 lb
   (5) 10 lb 5 oz

5. On Monday, Malcolm spent 3 hours 15 minutes updating patient files. On Tuesday, he spent 1 hour 30 minutes at the same task. If Malcolm spent 6 hours updating patient files last week, how many more hours did he spend on the task last week than this week?

   (1) 6
   (2) $4\frac{3}{4}$
   (3) $3\frac{1}{4}$
   (4) $1\frac{1}{2}$
   (5) $1\frac{1}{4}$

Question 6 refers to the following drawing.

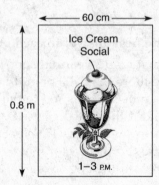

6. A nursing home aide is creating a display to encourage participation in activities. The measurements of the display are shown in the diagram. What is the height of the display in centimeters?

   (1)   0.008
   (2)   0.8
   (3)   80
   (4)   800
   (5) 8000

7. A can of olive oil holds 3000 ml. How many liters of oil does the can hold?

   (1)   0.003
   (2)   0.3
   (3)   3.0
   (4)   30.0
   (5)   300.0

8. In a vitamin supplement, each capsule contains 1000 milligrams of vitamins. How many *grams* of vitamins are found in each capsule?

   (1) 1000
   (2)   100
   (3)   10
   (4)   1
   (5)   0.1

Question 9 refers to the following diagram.

Carter has been hired to install edging around the area shown below.

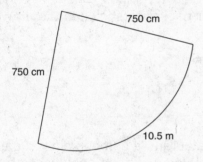

9. What is the distance in *meters* around the planting area?

   (1)   10.5
   (2)   12.0
   (3)   25.5
   (4)   1510.0
   (5)   1605.0

10. A punch recipe calls for 2 liters of club soda and 1 liter of pineapple juice. How many glasses of punch will the recipe make?

   (1) 10
   (2) 20
   (3) 30
   (4) 40
   (5) Not enough information is given.

11. A tube of toothpaste holds 170 grams of paste. If approximately 1500 milligrams are used at each brushing, <u>about</u> how many brushings can a person get from the tube of toothpaste?

   (1) 10,000
   (2) 1,000
   (3)   100
   (4)   10
   (5) Not enough information is given.

12. Aaron buys a roll of plastic sheeting that is 5 meters long. If he uses 3.5 meters, how many <u>centimeters</u> of the plastic are left?

   (1)   1.5
   (2)   15
   (3) 150
   (4) 350
   (5) 500

13. What is the combined weight in kilograms of packages weighing 15.8 kg, 13.5 kg, and 19.3 kg?

   Mark your answer in the circles on the grid at the bottom of the page.

14. A coffee café brews 5 gallons of coffee at a time. How many 8-ounce cups could the café fill using the 5 gallons?

   Mark your answer in the circles on the grid at the bottom of the page.

13.

/	/	/	
.	.	.	.	.
0	0	0	0	0
1	1	1	1	1
2	2	2	2	2
3	3	3	3	3
4	4	4	4	4
5	5	5	5	5
6	6	6	6	6
7	7	7	7	7
8	8	8	8	8
9	9	9	9	9

14.

/	/	/	
.	.	.	.	.
0	0	0	0	0
1	1	1	1	1
2	2	2	2	2
3	3	3	3	3
4	4	4	4	4
5	5	5	5	5
6	6	6	6	6
7	7	7	7	7
8	8	8	8	8
9	9	9	9	9

PART II

Directions: Choose the <u>one best answer</u> to each question. You <u>MAY NOT</u> use your calculator for these questions.

<u>Questions 15 through 17</u> refer to the following information.

> **Humidifier**
> 11 quart capacity
> width: 27 in
> height: 24 in
> depth: 18 in
> Model Number: RQ481

15. Elizabeth bought the humidifier described above. Which of the following expressions could she use to find the capacity of the humidifier in gallons?

    (1) 11×2

    (2) $\dfrac{11}{2}$

    (3) 11×4

    (4) $\dfrac{11}{4}$

    (5) 11×8

16. Which of these measurements is the minimum amount of space needed for the width of the humidifier?

    (1) 2 ft 1 in
    (2) 2 ft 3 in
    (3) $2\frac{1}{3}$ ft
    (4) $2\frac{1}{2}$ ft
    (5) 2 ft 7 in

17. If the humidifier is guaranteed to run 270 minutes without refilling, how many hours will it run before Elizabeth needs to refill it?

    (1) 4
    (2) $4\frac{1}{2}$
    (3) 60
    (4) 90
    (5) Not enough information is given.

18. A map scale reads 1 in = 50 mi. If the distance between two cities on the map is $3\frac{1}{2}$ inches, what is the actual distance between the cities in miles?

    (1) 2.5
    (2) 25
    (3) 50
    (4) 150
    (5) 175

<u>Question 19</u> refers to the following information.

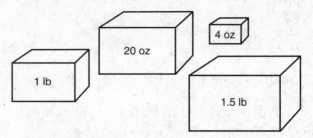

19. What is the combined weight, in ounces, of the four packages shown in the drawing?

    (1) 4
    (2) 26.5
    (3) 49
    (4) 64
    (5) 128

20. At a restaurant, a can contains $2\frac{1}{2}$ gallons of spaghetti sauce. If the cook uses about 5 cups of sauce per hour when cooking, how many cooking hours will 1 can of sauce last?

    (1) 40
    (2) 10
    (3) 8
    (4) 7.5
    (5) Not enough information is given.

21. A veterinarian estimates that she spends an average of 20 minutes with each patient. Which of the following is the best estimate of how many patients the doctor could see if she spends 33 hours a week on office visits?

(1) 20
(2) 33
(3) 60
(4) 99
(5) 660

22. Jan weighs a little more than 160 pounds. During a routine checkup, she sees her current weight is recorded as 74. What unit of measure did the nurse most likely use to record Jan's weight?

(1) ounces
(2) milligrams
(3) meters
(4) grams
(5) kilograms

23. A standard sheet of paper measures about 28 units on a ruler. What unit of measure is being used?

(1) inches
(2) feet
(3) millimeters
(4) centimeters
(5) meters

24. A soup recipe calls for 45 ounces of kidney beans and 30 ounces of navy beans. If 1 can contains 15 ounces of beans, which expression shows how many cans of beans are needed for this recipe?

(1) $\dfrac{(45 + 30)}{15}$

(2) $45 \times \dfrac{30}{15}$

(3) $45 + 30$

(4) $\dfrac{45}{15}$

(5) $\dfrac{30}{15}$

25. A can of frozen lemonade concentrate has the following label.

Lemonade Concentrate
Contents: 9 fl oz (260 ml)
To Serve: Mix with $4\frac{1}{2}$ cups of cold water. Stir.

Andrew mixes two cans of the frozen concentrate with the appropriate amount of water. How much lemonade has he made?
(1) 90 fl oz
(2) 90 c
(3) 90 ml
(4) 9.0 pt
(5) 9.0 qt

26. How many inches are in 4 feet?

Mark your answer in the circles on the grid at the bottom of the page.

27. Marco goes on service calls. He spent $2\frac{1}{2}$ hours on the first call, 45 minutes on the second call, and 70 minutes on the third call. How many <u>minutes</u> did he spend in all on the 3 service calls?

Mark your answer in the circles on the grid at the bottom of the page.

26.

27.

Answers and explanations begin on page 674.

Key Ideas

- If numbers have like signs, add and keep the same sign.
- If numbers have unlike signs, find the difference and use the sign from the larger number.
- To subtract signed numbers, change the operation to addition and change the sign of the number you are subtracting.

ALGEBRA

The Number Line and Signed Numbers

Understanding Signed Numbers

Signed numbers include zero, all positive numbers, and all negative numbers. Zero is neither positive nor negative. On a number line, the positive numbers are shown to the right of zero, and the negative numbers are shown to the left.

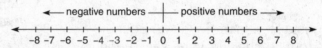

A positive number may be written with a plus (+) symbol. If a number has no symbol at all, we assume that it is positive. A negative number *must* be preceded by a minus (−) symbol.

A signed number provides two important facts. The sign tells the direction from zero, and the number tells you the distance from zero. For example, −5 lies five spaces to the left of zero, and +4 lies four spaces to the right of zero.

Adding and Subtracting Signed Numbers

You can use a number line to model the addition of signed numbers.

Examples: $1 + (-4) = -3$ Begin at +1; move 4 in a negative direction (left).

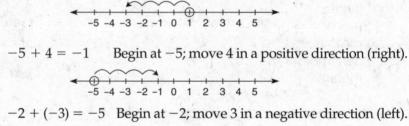

$-5 + 4 = -1$ Begin at −5; move 4 in a positive direction (right).

$-2 + (-3) = -5$ Begin at −2; move 3 in a negative direction (left).

To add without a number line, follow these steps:

- If numbers have like signs, add the numbers and keep the same sign.
- If the numbers have unlike signs, find the difference between the two numbers and use the sign of the larger number.

Example 1: Add $15 + (-25)$.

1. Since the numbers have unlike signs, subtract. $25 - 15 = 10$

2. Use the sign from the larger number. $15 + (-25) = \mathbf{-10}$

Subtraction is the opposite of addition. To rewrite a subtraction problem as an addition problem, change the operation symbol to addition and change the sign on the number you are subtracting. Then apply the rules for adding signed numbers.

Example 2: Subtract $3 - 8$.

1. Change the operation symbol and the sign of the number you are subtracting.

   $3 - 8$ becomes $3 + (-8)$.

2. Add. $3 + (-8) = \mathbf{-5}$

You can use the same rules to combine several signed numbers.

Example 3: $(-5) + 6 - 4 - (-2) = ?$

1. Rewrite each subtraction as addition. $(-5) + 6 + (-4) + 2$

2. Add the positive terms. $6 + 2 = 8$ Add the negative terms. $-5 + (-4) = -9$

3. Combine the results. $8 + -9 = \mathbf{-1}$

ALGEBRA ▸ PRACTICE 1.1

A. Solve.

1. $8 + (-3)$	**9.** $(-7) - (-3)$	**17.** $7 + (-3) + (-5) - 10$
2. $50 - (+5)$	**10.** $(-4) + 6$	**18.** $66 + (-22) - 33$
3. $11 - (-2)$	**11.** $-15 + (-7)$	**19.** $-14 - (-6) + 18$
4. $-1 + 2$	**12.** $(+36) - 4$	**20.** $80 - (-15) - 20$
5. $-4 - (-5)$	**13.** $-60 - (-10)$	**21.** $6 - (-3) + (-5) + 8$
6. $8 - (-2)$	**14.** $-5 - (+6)$	**22.** $-23 + (-11) - (-15) + 21$
7. $6 - (+9)$	**15.** $12 + (+13)$	**23.** $3 + 9 - 5 + 12 - 9 - 11$
8. $2 + (+11)$	**16.** $-55 + (+20)$	**24.** $-7 - 20 - (-14)$

B. Choose the <u>one best answer</u> to each question.

<u>Question 25</u> refers to the following number line.

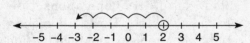

25. The number line above shows which of the following expressions

   (1) $-2 - 5$
   (2) $2 + (-3)$
   (3) $2 + (-5)$
   (4) $-3 + 2$
   (5) $-3 - (+2)$

26. At noon the temperature in the high desert was 92° F. A scientist observed the following temperature changes over the course of the next two hours: $+12°$, $-5°$, $+6°$, $-3°$, and $+13°$. What was the temperature at the end of the two-hour period?

   (1) 53°
   (2) 95°
   (3) 103°
   (4) 115°
   (5) 131°

Answers and explanations begin on page 675.

Multiplying and Dividing Signed Numbers

In algebra, multiplication is not shown using the times sign ($\times$) because the symbol could be easily mistaken for the variable x. Instead, multiplication is shown using a dot or by placing two numbers next to each other. To avoid confusion, one or both of the numbers will be enclosed in parentheses. For example, the expressions $-5 \cdot 6$ and $-5(6)$ and $(-5)(6)$ all mean "-5 times 6."

In algebra, division can be written with the $\div$ symbol, but it is usually shown with a line that means "divided by." The expression $\dfrac{20}{-5}$ means "20 divided by -5," as does $20/-5$. When multiplying or dividing signed numbers, use the following rules:

- If the signs are the same, the answer is positive.
- If the signs are different, the answer is negative.

Example 1: Multiply $4(-25)$.

1. Multiply the numbers only. $4 \times 25 = 100$

2. Determine the sign. Since the signs on the numbers are different, the answer is negative. $4(-25) = \mathbf{-100}$

Example 2: Divide $\dfrac{-160}{-8}$.

1. Divide the numbers only. $160 \div 8 = 20$
2. Determine the sign. Since the signs on the numbers are the same, the answer is positive.

$$\dfrac{-160}{-8} = \mathbf{20}$$

A problem may contain more than two factors. Remember that each pair of negative factors will equal a positive product. Therefore, if there is an even number of negative terms, the product will be positive. If there is an odd number of negative terms, the product will be negative.

Example 3: $(-5)(6)(-1)(-2)(2) = ?$

1. Multiply. $5 \times 6 \times 1 \times 2 \times 2 = 120$

2. There are three negative terms. Since 3 is an odd number, the product is negative. $\mathbf{-120}$

When a problem contains more than one operation, follow this **order of operations.** Do multiplication and division operations first, working from left to right. Do addition and subtraction operations last, also working from left to right. If a problem contains division presented with a division bar, do any operations above and below the bar first, then divide.

Example 4: $(-4)(6) - \dfrac{3 + (-9)}{-2} = ?$

1. Multiply. $-24 - \dfrac{3 + (-9)}{-2}$

2. Do the operation above the fraction bar. $-24 - \dfrac{-6}{-2}$

3. Divide. $-24 - (+3)$

4. Subtract. $-24 - (+3) = -24 + (-3) = \mathbf{-27}$

Note: *Notice how parentheses clarify meaning:* $4 - 5$ *means "four minus five" but* $4(-5)$ *means "four times negative five."*

A. Solve. You MAY NOT use a calculator.

1. (5)(4)
2. (7)(−3)
3. (−8)(6)
4. (−2)(−9)
5. (−10)(1)

6. $9 \div 3$
7. $12 \div (−4)$
8. $−25 \div 5$
9. $(−18) \div (−9)$
10. $\dfrac{40}{−8}$

11. (14)(−2)
12. $(−75) \div 25$
13. $13 \div (−13)$
14. (−5)(15)
15. $\dfrac{18}{3}$

B. Solve. You MAY use a calculator.

16. $\dfrac{25(4)}{−5}$
17. (−3)(−5)(2)(−10)
18. $20 \div (−5) \div (−2)$
19. $\dfrac{6(5)}{(−3)(2)}$

20. (−11)(2)(−5)(6)
21. $(12)(−2) \div (−2)$
22. (−4)(−6)(−5)
23. $50 \div (2)(−5)$

24. (−1)(2)(−3)(2)(−1)
25. $\dfrac{(3)(−4)(2)(5)}{−6}$
26. $\dfrac{4(−4)}{−8(−2)}$
27. (−5)(−2)(0)(−1)

C. Choose the one best answer to each question.

28. Janice is creating a computer spreadsheet. A portion of her work is shown below.

	A	B	C
1	−3	4	7
2	2	−5	−8
3	−1	3	−2

Using the information from the spreadsheet, what is the value of the expression A1*C1*A3/B3*A3? (*Hint*: In a spreadsheet, the symbol * means multiplication.)

(1) −21
(2) −7
(3) −1/7
(4) 7
(5) 21

29. The product of 2 and 8 is divided by −8. Which of the following expressions could be used to find the value of the statement?

(1) $2 \div 8 \div −8$
(2) 2(8)(−8)
(3) $2(8) \div (−8)$
(4) $2(−8) \div 8$
(5) $2(8)(−8) \div (−8)$

30. Which of the following is a true statement about the value of the expression (52)(−103)(−45)(−8)(3)?

(1) The result is a fraction.
(2) The result equals 0.
(3) The result is greater than 1.
(4) The result is a negative number.
(5) The result is a positive number.

Answers and explanations begin on page 675.

ALGEBRA

Powers and Roots

Key Ideas

- In the expression 2^3, the base is 2, and the exponent is 3.
- To raise a number to a certain power, write the base the number of times shown by the exponent and multiply.
- To find a square root, think, "What number times itself equals this number?"

GED TIP

Make a list of common square roots by squaring the numbers from 1 to 15. Memorize them. You will need to know common square roots to solve geometry problems about area and right triangles.

Evaluating Powers and Roots

Powers are a special way to show repeated multiplication. For example, suppose you need to multiply $5 \times 5 \times 5 \times 5$. This series of operations can be expressed as "five to the fourth power." In other words, the number 5 appears in the multiplication problem four times.

We can write the operations algebraically using **exponents**. In the expression $5 \times 5 \times 5 \times 5$, the number 5 is the base. The exponent, a small number written slightly above and to the right of the base, tells how many times the base is repeated: $5 \times 5 \times 5 \times 5 = 5^4$.

To evaluate an expression, perform the multiplication indicated by the exponent.

Example 1: Find the value of 2^5.

Write the base the number of times indicated by the exponent and multiply.

$$2^5 = 2 \times 2 \times 2 \times 2 \times 2 = \mathbf{32}$$

There are some special uses of exponents that you may encounter on the GED Math Test. An exponent can be 1, 0, or a negative number. Memorize the situations described below.

1. A number raised to the first power equals itself. $8^1 = 8$

2. A number other than zero that is raised to the zero power equals 1. $6^0 = 1$

3. A number raised to a negative exponent is equal to a fraction with a numerator of 1. $4^{-2} = \dfrac{1}{4^2} = \dfrac{1}{4 \times 4} = \dfrac{1}{16}$

You can use a calculator to raise numbers to any power. Use the $\boxed{x^2}$ or $\boxed{x^y}$ keys.

Example 2: Find the square of 24.

A number is squared when it is multiplied by itself. In other words, the square of a number is the number raised to the second power.

Press: $24\boxed{x^2}$ The display reads: $\boxed{ 576.}$

The square of 24 is **576**.

Example 3: Find the value of 9^4.

Enter the base, press $\boxed{x^y}$, and enter the exponent. Then press equals.

Press: $9\boxed{x^y}4\boxed{=}$ The display reads: $\boxed{6561.}$

Nine raised to the fourth power is **6561**.

To square a number, multiply the number by itself. For example, $6^2 = 6 \times 6 = 36$. In the expression $6 \times 6 = 36$, the number 36 is the square, and the number 6 is the **square root** of 36.

The symbol for square root is $\sqrt{}$. To find a square root, think, "What number multiplied by itself is equal to the number in the bracket?"

Example 4: Find the value of $\sqrt{144}$.

You know that $12 \times 12 = 144$, so the square root of 144 is **12**.

You may have to approximate the value of a square root.

Example 5: What is the square root of 90?

You know that $9 \times 9 = 81$ and $10 \times 10 = 100$. Therefore, the square root of 90 is **between 9 and 10**.

You can always use your calculator to find a square root. On the *Casio fx-260*, you must first press the SHIFT key to access the square root function. The $\sqrt{}$ function is directly above the $\boxed{x^2}$ key in the top row of keys. (Other calculators may not require the use of the SHIFT key.)

Example 6: Find $\sqrt{90}$ to the nearest tenth.

Press: 90 $\boxed{\text{SHIFT}}$ $\boxed{x^2}$ The display reads: $\boxed{9.486832981}$

Rounding to the tenths place, $\sqrt{90} \approx \textbf{9.5}$.

ALGEBRA ▸ PRACTICE 2

A. Solve each expression. You <u>MAY NOT</u> use a calculator.

1. 3^2
2. 4^1
3. $\sqrt{9}$

4. 25^0
5. $(-3)^2$
6. $\sqrt{49}$

7. 5^3
8. 4^{-2}
9. 2^4

10. $\sqrt{64}$
11. 10^{-3}
12. $\sqrt{121}$

B. Use your calculator to solve each expression. When finding square roots, round your answer to the nearest tenth.

13. 3^8
14. $(-6)^4$
15. $\sqrt{150}$

16. 20^3
17. 1^{15}
18. $(-4)^{-2}$

19. $\sqrt{242}$
20. $(3.3)^2$
21. $\sqrt{57}$

22. $\sqrt{536}$
23. 112^0
24. $(-2)^8$

C. Choose the <u>one best answer</u> to each question.

25. The cube shown below measures 6 inches on each side. You can find the volume of the cube by multiplying length × width × height. Which of the following expressions represents the volume of the cube?

    (1) 6^0
    (2) 6^1
    (3) 6^2
    (4) 6^3
    (5) 6^6

    6 in
    6 in
    6 in

26. Which of the following expressions has the least value?

    (1) 3^{-3}
    (2) 4^0
    (3) 4^1
    (4) $\sqrt{4.4}$
    (5) 2^{-4}

    Answers and explanations begin on page 676.

ALGEBRA

Scientific Notation

Using Scientific Notation

Scientific notation uses the powers of ten to express very small and very large numbers. In scientific notation, a decimal number (greater than or equal to 1 and less than 10) is multiplied by a power of ten.

Look for patterns as you review these powers of ten.

$10^1 = 10$ $10^2 = 100$ $10^3 = 1,000$ $10^4 = 10,000$ and so on.

$10^{-1} = 0.1$ $10^{-2} = 0.01$ $10^{-3} = 0.001$ $10^{-4} = 0.0001$ and so on.

Did you find the patterns? In the row with positive exponents, the exponent is the same as the number of zeros in the number written in standard form. In the row with negative exponents, the exponent is the same as the number of decimal places in the number.

You can use these patterns to change scientific notation to standard form.

Example 1: Write 6.2×10^5 in standard form.   6.20000

Move the decimal point five places to the *right* (the same number as the exponent). Add zeros as needed.   **620,000**

Example 2: Write 3.82×10^{-3} in standard form.

Move the decimal point three places to the *left* (the same number as the exponent). Add zeros as needed.   .00382

Work backward to write large and small numbers in scientific notation.   **0.00382**

Example 3: To reach Mars, the Viking 2 spacecraft traveled 440,000,000 miles. What is the distance traveled in scientific notation?

1. Move the decimal point to the left until there is only a single digit in the ones place.   4.40000000

2. Multiply by 10 raised to a power equal to the number of places you moved the decimal point.   **4.4×10^8**

Example 4: Scientists find that a kind of bacteria moves at a rate of 0.00016 kilometers per hour. Write the measurement in scientific notation.

1. Move the decimal place to the right until there is a single digit in the ones place.   0001.6

2. Multiply by 10 raised to a negative exponent equal to the number of places you moved the decimal point.   **1.6×10^{-4}**

You may be asked to compare numbers in scientific notation.

Example 5: Which is greater: 4.5×10^3 or 9.8×10^4?

You don't need to change the numbers to standard notation. Simply consider the powers of ten. Multiplying by 10^4, or 10,000, must have a greater result than multiplying by 10^3, which equals 1,000. In scientific notation, the number with the greater power of 10 has the greater value. Therefore, **9.8×10^4 is greater than 4.5×10^3.**

ALGEBRA ▸ PRACTICE 3

A. Write each number in scientific notation.

1. 2300
2. 0.00042
3. 12,400,000

4. 14,320,000,000
5. 36,000,000
6. 0.0095

7. 0.00000058
8. 150,000,000,000
9. 0.000000009

B. Convert from scientific notation to standard notation.

10. 5.173×10^{-4}
11. 3.7×10^6

12. 4.8×10^8
13. 1.7×10^{-5}

14. 7.2×10^{-3}
15. 9.16×10^5

16. 8.591×10^7
17. 9.56×10^{-6}

C. Answer the following questions.

18. Many domestic satellites maintain an orbit approximately 23,500 miles above the earth. What is that distance in scientific notation?

19. Modern technology measures very fast transactions in nanoseconds. One nanosecond equals 1.0×10^{-9} of a second. Write the unit of time in standard notation.

20. The average distance of Neptune from Earth is 2.67×10^9 miles. Write the distance in standard notation.

21. Light in the vacuum of space travels at a speed of nearly 300 million meters per second. Write the speed in scientific notation.

D. Choose the one best answer to each question.

Questions 22 and 23 refer to the following table.

Unit	U.S. Equivalent	Metric Equivalent
1 ton	2,000 lb	0.907 metric ton
1 acre	43,560 sq ft	4,047 square m

22. What is the number of square feet in an acre, written in scientific notation?
    (1) 0.4356×10^6
    (2) 4.356×10^4
    (3) 4.356×10^3
    (4) 43.56×10^3
    (5) 43.56×10^2

23. A shipment of goods weighs 5 tons. Which of the following expressions could be used to express the weight in metric tons?
    (1) $5 \times 0.907 \times 10^{-1}$
    (2) $5 \times 9.07 \times 10^1$
    (3) $5 \times 9.07 \times 10^0$
    (4) $5 \times 9.07 \times 10^{-2}$
    (5) $5 \times 9.07 \times 10^{-1}$

Answers and explanations begin on page 676.

ALGEBRA

The Order of Operations

Working with Grouping Symbols, Powers, and Roots

When a mathematical expression contains more than one operation, its value may depend upon the order in which the operations are performed. To avoid confusion, mathematicians have agreed to perform operations in a certain order.

The Order of Operations

1. Parentheses or any other grouping symbols that enclose operations
2. Exponents and roots
3. Multiplication and division, working from left to right
4. Addition and subtraction, working from left to right

Study the following example to see how to apply the order of operations. Notice that parentheses are used in two places in the expression; however, only the first set of parentheses encloses an operation.

Example 1: Evaluate the expression $\dfrac{(5 + 3)^2}{4} + 3(-1)$.

1. Perform the addition operation in parentheses. $\qquad$ $\dfrac{(8)^2}{4} + 3(-1)$

2. Raise 8 to the second power. $\qquad$ $\dfrac{64}{4} + 3(-1)$

3. Divide, then multiply. $\qquad$ $16 + (-3)$

4. Add. $\qquad$ 13

The value of the expression $\dfrac{(5 + 3)^2}{4} + 3(-1)$ is **13.**

In more complicated expressions, one set of grouping symbols may be nested within another set. To avoid confusion, you can also use brackets [ ] or braces { } to group operations. To evaluate an expression with more than one set of grouping symbols, work from the inside to the outside.

Example 2: Evaluate the expression $4[5(-4 + 3) + 2]$.

1. Perform the operation in the inner set of grouping symbols: $(-4 + 3)$. $\qquad$ $4[5(-4 + 3) + 2]$
   $4[5(-1) + 2]$

2. Do the operations in the brackets. Since multiplication comes before addition in the order of operations, multiply 5 and -1, then add 2. $\qquad$ $4[-5 + 2]$
   $4[-3]$

3. Multiply 4 and -3. $\qquad$ **-12**

The division bar is also a grouping symbol. Before you divide, perform any operations shown above and below the bar.

Key Ideas

- To evaluate an expression correctly, you must follow the order of operations.
- If an expression uses more than one set of grouping symbols, start with the inside set and work to the outside.
- The division bar may be used as a grouping symbol.

GED TIP

When you evaluate an expression, write down each step as you work. If you cannot find your answer among the answer choices, you will be able to review the steps quickly to find your mistake.

Example 3: Evaluate the expression $\dfrac{15 + 25}{2\,(5)} + 6$.

1. Perform the operations above and below the fraction bar.

$$\dfrac{15 + 25}{2\,(5)} + 6$$

$$\dfrac{40}{10} + 6$$

2. Divide, then add.

$$4 + 6 = \mathbf{10}$$

ALGEBRA ▸ PRACTICE 4

A. Solve. You <u>MAY NOT</u> use a calculator.

1. $4(3) - 2 + (6 + 4 \cdot 2)$

2. $16 \div (10 - 6)^2$

3. $5^2 - (5 - 7)(2)$

4. $3(-3) + (7 + 4)$

5. $\dfrac{3^3}{5 - 2} - \dfrac{(4 - 2)^2}{2} \cdot 5$

6. $\dfrac{25}{(4 + 1)} \cdot 3 + (6 - 1)$

7. $2^3 + (8 - 5)^2 - 3$

8. $(4 - 12)(-6) + (10 - 3)$

9. $30 \div 3(5 - 4)$

10. $15 + (4)(3) - 2^2$

11. $(4 + 2)^2 + (7 - 2)^3$

12. $7^2 \div (11 - 4) + (9 + 14)$

13. $2\left[(17 - 11)^2 \cdot \dfrac{(15 - 5)}{2}\right]$

14. $(5^2 + 6 - 3) \div (16 - 3^2)$

15. $150 - 4\left[\dfrac{3 + 9}{4 - 1} \cdot (14 - 11)^2\right]$

B. Choose the <u>one best answer</u> to each question.

<u>Question 16</u> refers to the following information.

Susan is in charge of planning Midvale Hospital's parent education classes. She uses the table below to determine the cost of each class to the hospital.

Midvale Hospital Parenting Workshops	
Type of Workshop	Cost per Participant
Childbirth Classes	$35 per couple
Infant Care	$30 per person
Teaching Your Child to Read	$60 per person

16. A local foundation has offered to pay 75% of the cost of infant care classes. The hospital will cover any remaining costs. There are 28 parents enrolled in the upcoming class. Which of the following expressions could be used to find the amount the hospital will pay?

    (1) $(75)(28)(30)$
    (2) $(28)(30) - 75$
    (3) $(28)(30) - (0.75)(30)$
    (4) $(1 - 0.75)(28)(30)$
    (5) $(1 - 0.75)(30) + 28$

17. In the expression

$$5 + 2\left[7\left(\dfrac{10^2}{10}\right) + (6 - 2)(3)\right],$$

what is the last operation you should perform to find the value of the expression?

    (1) Multiply by 3.
    (2) Subtract 2 from 6.
    (3) Add 5.
    (4) Multiply by 2.
    (5) Find the square of 10.

18. Find the value of the expression $22 + 6[(14 - 5) \div 3(17 - 14)]$.

    (1) 2.73
    (2) 28
    (3) 76
    (4) 97
    (5) 102

Answers and explanations begin on page 676.

ALGEBRA

Algebraic Expressions

Key Ideas

- Algebraic expressions show mathematical relationships using numbers, symbols, and variables.
- Variables are letters that take the place of unknown numbers.

Writing Algebraic Expressions

An **algebraic expression** uses numbers, operations, and variables to show number relationships. **Variables** are letters (such as x and y) that represent unknown numbers. Each time a letter is used within the same expression, it represents the same number.

To solve algebra problems, you will need to be able to translate number relationships described in words into algebraic expressions. Study the following examples.

Algebraic expressions in words	In symbols
the product of 5 and a number	$5x$
a number decreased by 12	$x - 12$
the sum of 3 and the square of a number	$3 + x^2$
6 less than the quotient of a number and 2	$\frac{x}{2} - 6$
one-half a number increased by 15	$\frac{1}{2}x + 15$
4 times the difference of -3 and a number	$4(-3 - x)$
a number less another number	$x - y$
10 less the square root of a number plus 3	$10 - \sqrt{x} + 3$

To do well on the algebra portion of the GED Math Test, you must be able to translate a common life situation into mathematical symbols. You will use this skill to write equations and functions, to apply formulas, and to solve word problems.

Example: Kyle processes sales for an online bookstore. The shipping and handling on an order is equal to 4% of the total cost of the order plus $0.95 per book. If c represents total cost and n represents the number of books in an order, which of the following expressions could be used to find the shipping and handling for an order?

(1) $\frac{4}{100}nc + 0.95$

(2) $(0.04 + 0.95)n + c$

(3) $4c + n$

(4) $0.04n + 0.95c$

(5) $0.04c + 0.95n$

GED TIP

To check if the expression you have chosen is correct, substitute easy numbers into the expression and complete the operations. Then see if the result is reasonable for the situation.

This kind of problem is called a **set-up problem.** You need to recognize the correct way to find the shipping and handling based on the total cost and number of items. The relationship is described in the second sentence.

shipping and handling = 4% of total cost (c) plus $0.95 per book ($n$)

$\qquad\qquad\qquad = \qquad 0.04c \qquad + \qquad 0.95n$

The correct answer is option **(5) $0.04c + 0.95n$.**

A. Write an algebraic expression for each description. Use the variables x and y.

1. a number decreased by seven

2. the product of 3 and the square of a number increased by that number

3. the product of 8 and a number less 10

4. the difference of -3 multiplied by a number and the product of 2 and another number

5. 5 less than the quotient of 10 and a number

6. the sum of -8 and the product of 7 and a number

7. the sum of 16 times a number and the number less another number times 3

8. a number squared plus the number raised to the fourth power

9. the sum of the square of a number and 4 divided by 7

10. 6 subtracted from the sum of 15 and the square root of a number

11. a number less the sum of another number and 13

12. the square of the sum of a number and 6

13. 17 less the sum of 2 times a number plus another number

14. a number increased by the quotient of 24 and the number

15. the difference of the product of 2 and a number and 15

16. 4 times the difference of two different numbers

17. 5 multiplied by the difference of a number squared and 3

18. the product of a number and the difference of 11 and the square root of 100

B. Choose the one best answer to each question.

19. A minor-league baseball team is giving a local charity the sum of $1500 and $0.50 for each ticket over 2000 sold for one game. Let x represent the number of tickets sold. Which of the following expressions could be used to find the amount of the donation?

    (1) $1500 + 0.50x$
    (2) $1500 + $0.50(2000)
    (3) $1500 + $0.50(2000 − x)
    (4) $1500 + $0.50($x$ − 2000)
    (5) $1500(2000 − x)($0.50)

20. The sum of 3 times a number and 4 times another number is divided by the sum of 2 and a third number. Which of the following expressions represents this series of operations?

    (1) $(3x + 4y) \div (2 + z)$
    (2) $3x + 4y \div (2 + z)$
    (3) $3x + 4y \div 2 + z$
    (4) $(3x + 4y) \div 2z$
    (5) $3x + 4y \div 2z$

Question 21 refers to the following information.

Appliance City employees earn an hourly wage plus commission. Wage options are shown below.

Option	Hourly Wage	Commission on Sales
A	$7.50	1%
B	$6.00	3%

21. Chandra is paid under Option B. If h represents the number of hours worked and s represents Chandra's total sales, which of the following expressions could be used to find her weekly pay?

    (1) $6 + h + 0.03s$
    (2) $6h + 0.03s$
    (3) $6s + 0.03h$
    (4) $6(h)(s)$
    (5) $0.03(h)(s)$

Answers and explanations begin on page 676.

Simplifying and Evaluating Expressions

Simplifying an expression means to perform all the operations you can within an expression. When working with variables, you must remember an important rule: You can add or subtract like terms only.

A **term** is a number, a variable, or the product or quotient of numbers and variables. A term cannot include a sum or a difference.

Examples: $5x$ $3y^2$ 13 x^3 $\dfrac{x}{2}$

Like terms have the same variable raised to the same power. For example, $3x^2$ and $5x^2$ are like terms. $8y$ and $4y$ are also like terms. However, $6x$ and $2x^2$ are not like terms because the variables are not raised to the same power.

To simplify an expression, combine like terms.

Example 1: Simplify $2x - 5 + 4x^2 - 8 + 6x$.

Combine like terms. It is customary to write the term with the greatest exponent first and to continue in descending order.

$$2x - 5 + 4x^2 - 8 + 6x$$
$$= (2x + 6x) + (-5 + -8) + 4x^2$$
$$= 8x + (-13) + 4x^2$$
$$= \mathbf{4x^2 + 8x - 13}$$

The **distributive property** allows you to remove grouping symbols to simplify expressions. We can state the distributive property using symbols.

$$a(b + c) = ab + ac \quad \text{and} \quad a(b - c) = ab - ac$$

In other words, each term inside the parentheses is multiplied by the term outside the parentheses, and the results are added or subtracted depending on the operation inside the parentheses. Example 2 applies the distributive property.

Example 2: Simplify $4x - 3(x + 9) + 15$.

1. Change subtracting to adding a negative number.
2. Use the distributive property. Multiply -3 by each term in the parentheses.
3. Combine like terms.
   (**Note:** $1x$ means x.)

$$4x - 3(x + 9) + 15$$
$$= 4x + -3(x + 9) + 15$$
$$= 4x + (-3x) + (-3)(9) + 15$$
$$= 4x + -3x + -27 + 15$$
$$= (4x + -3x) + (-27 + 15)$$
$$= 1x - 12$$
$$= \mathbf{x - 12}$$

Evaluating an expression means finding its value. To evaluate an expression, substitute a given number for each variable. Follow the order of operations.

Example 3: Find the value of the expression $\dfrac{3x + 2y}{4}$ when $x = 6$ and $y = 5$.

1. Replace the variables with the values given in the problem.

$$\frac{3x + 2y}{4} = \frac{3(6) + 2(5)}{4}$$

2. Perform the operations above the fraction bar. Then divide.

$$\frac{3(6) + 2(5)}{4} = \frac{18 + 10}{4} = \frac{28}{4} = 7$$

Note: To remove parentheses from an operation that follows a minus sign, imagine that the parentheses are preceded by 1. Then use the distributive property.

$$- (2x + 3)$$
$$= -1(2x + 3)$$
$$= -1(2x) + (-1)(3)$$
$$= -2x + (-3) \text{ or } -2x - 3$$

A. Simplify.

1. $5 + x^2 - 3 + 3x$

2. $2y + 5 + 17y + 8$

3. $3x - 6(x - 9)$

4. $6x^3 + 4 + 2x^2(15) + x^2$

5. $4(y + 8) + 3(y - 6)$

6. $5 - (x - 3) + 4x$

7. $16x + 6(x - 2)$

8. $5y^2 + 4 - 3y^2 + 5 + y$

9. $-3(x + 3) - 2(x + 4)$

10. $5x - (x + 4) - 3$

B. Evaluate each expression as directed.

11. Find the value of $6(x + 2) + 7$ when $x = 2$.

12. Find the value of $3x^2 + 3(x + 4)$ when $x = 3$.

13. Find the value of $\dfrac{(x + y)^2}{2} - 10$ when $x = 2$ and $y = 4$.

14. Find the value of $y^2 + 16 - (y - 5)^2$ when $y = 3$.

15. Find the value of $8x + 9y - (2x + y)$ when $x = 4$ and $y = 6$.

16. Find the value of $x^2 + 3y - 4 + 2(x - z)$ when $x = 7$, $y = 5$, and $z = -3$.

17. Find the value of $(14 - x)^2 + 2\sqrt{x}$ when $x = 9$.

18. Find the value of $\dfrac{3(2x - y)}{3} + 6(y - 5)$ when $x = -2$ and $y = 3$.

19. Find the value of $x^2 - (x^3 + 3)$ when $x = -2$.

20. Find the value of $30x + 2 + 2y^2 - 3(x - 2)^2$ when $x = 1$ and $y = 4$.

C. Choose the <u>one best answer</u> to each question.

21. Which of the following expressions is equal to $3x^2 + 3(x - 3) + x + 10$?

    (1) $x^2 + 9x + 1$
    (2) $3x^2 + 4x + 19$
    (3) $3x^2 + 2x - 19$
    (4) $3x^2 - 2x + 19$
    (5) $3x^2 + 4x + 1$

22. Given the expression $4x^2 - 3(y + 6)$, which of the following values for x and y will result in a value of -11?

    (1) $x = 2, y = 3$
    (2) $x = -2, y = 4$
    (3) $x = -1, y = 2$
    (4) $x = 4, y = 1$
    (5) $x = 1, y = 0$

<u>Question 23</u> refers to the following information.

Temperature Conversion Formulas	
To convert Fahrenheit (F) to centigrade (C)	$C = \dfrac{5}{9}(F - 32)$
To convert centigrade (C) to Fahrenheit (F)	$F = \dfrac{9}{5}C + 32$

23. If the temperature is $68°$ Fahrenheit, what is the temperature in centigrade?

    (1) $5.8°$
    (2) $20°$
    (3) $36°$
    (4) $154.4°$
    (5) $180°$

Answers and explanations begin on page 676.

ALGEBRA

Algebraic Expressions and the Calculator

Using a Calculator to Evaluate Expressions

When you take the GED Math Test, you will be given a scientific calculator (*Casio fx-260*) to use on the first half of the test items. This calculator, like most scientific calculators, uses algebraic logic, which means that it follows the order of operations that you saw on page 458.

You need to practice using a scientific calculator with algebraic logic. You can find out whether your calculator uses algebraic logic by running this simple test.

Press: $4 \boxed{\times} 3 \boxed{x^2} \boxed{=}$

If the display reads $\boxed{36.}$, your calculator uses algebraic logic.

If the display reads $\boxed{144.}$, your calculator does not use algebraic logic. You should find another calculator to practice for the GED Math Test.

You can use a calculator to evaluate an expression that contains several operations.

Example 1: Find the value of the expression $2x^2 + 3x - 5$ when $x = -4$.

Whenever you come to the variable x, enter -4 by pressing $\boxed{4} \boxed{+/-}$. The $\boxed{+/-}$ key is called the **change sign key.**

Press: $2 \boxed{\times} 4 \boxed{+/-} \boxed{x^2} \boxed{+} 3 \boxed{\times} 4 \boxed{+/-} \boxed{-} 5 \boxed{=} \boxed{15.}$

The value of the expression is **15.**

Expressions sometimes contain grouping symbols to show a different order of operations. You can enter grouping symbols on a scientific calculator. On the *Casio fx-260*, the grouping symbols $\boxed{[(\text{---}}$ and $\boxed{\text{---})]}$ are found in the third row of keys. When you enter $\boxed{[(\text{---}}$, the calculator waits until you enter the closing brackets $\boxed{\text{---})]}$ before it calculates what is inside the symbols.

Example 2: Find the value of the expression $2(x + 4) + 5x/3$ when $x = 6$.

Press: $2 \boxed{\times} \boxed{[(\text{---}} 6 \boxed{+} 4 \boxed{\text{---})]} \boxed{+} 5 \boxed{\times} 6 \boxed{\div} 3 \boxed{=} \boxed{30}$

The value of the expression is **30.**

You can also use your calculator for only part of an expression.

Example 3: Find the value of the expression $\dfrac{3x + 6}{2} + \sqrt{225}$ when $x = 4$.

Substitute 4 for x in the first part of the expression.
$$\frac{3(4) + 6}{2} = \frac{12 + 6}{2} = \frac{18}{2} = 9$$
Use your calculator to find the square root of 225.

Press: $225 \boxed{\text{SHIFT}} \boxed{x^2}$ The display reads $\boxed{15.}$

Add the results of the two steps. $15 + 9 = $ **24**

A. Use a calculator as needed to find the value of the expressions as directed.

1. What is the value of $5x^2 - 3x + 5$ when $x = 2$?

2. Find the value of $\sqrt{7x} + 2x$ to the nearest tenth when $x = 5$.

3. If $x = -3$, what is the value of $7x^2 + 2x - 6$?

4. What is the value of $\frac{1}{2}x + 15$ when $x = 3$?

5. Find the value of $3(2x + 3 + y) - 14$ when $x = -2$ and $y = 9$.

6. If $y = -3$, what is the value of $4y^3 + 2(y^2 - 4)$?

7. What is the value of $2(x^2 + 6) + 3(x - 1)$ when $x = 5$?

8. If $x = 4$ and $y = -4$, what is the value of the expression $6x^2 + 3y^2 + 2$?

9. Find the value of $-2(x^3 + 3) + 16x + 2$ when $x = 2$.

10. If $x = 7$, what is the value of the expression $7 + 3(x - 2) - 2x^2$?

11. Find the value of $-(x + y) + 3(2z - y)$ if $x = -5, y = -7$, and $z = 4$.

12. What is the value of the expression $x^2 - 7(3 - y) + 4$ when $x = 5$ and $y = 4$?

13. If $x = -2$ and $y = 8$, what is the value of $\dfrac{x^2 + y}{4} - \dfrac{6(x + 3)}{-3}$?

14. What is the value of $\sqrt{760 - 4x^2}$ to the nearest tenth when $x = 6$?

15. If $x = 20$, what is the value of the expression $4(x + 7) - 3(x - 2)$?

16. Find the value of $\dfrac{x(25 + 2x - y)}{-z}$ when $x = -3, y = 4$, and $z = -1$.

17. What is the value of $5y^2 + 4x^2 - 6(x - y)$ when $x = 5$ and $y = -2$?

18. Find the value of $3x^2 \cdot \dfrac{2(x - 3y)}{6}$ when $x = 6$ and $y = 1$.

19. What is the value of the expression $(x^2 + 5)(x^2 - x + 2) - 3$ when $x = -4$?

20. Find the value of $(x + y)(x - y)(2x + y)$ when $x = 9$ and $y = 4$.

B. Choose the one best answer to each question.

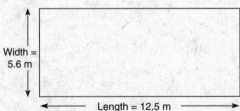

Width = 5.6 m

Length = 12.5 m

21. Jake has to buy enough fencing to enclose the rectangular garden shown below.

    The formula for finding the perimeter of (or distance around) a rectangle is $P = 2l + 2w$, where P = perimeter, l = length, and w = width. Using the values from the drawing, what is the perimeter in meters of the garden?

    (1) 18.1
    (2) 36.2
    (3) 70
    (4) 140
    (5) 280

22. If $x = -5$ and $y = 2$, which of the following expressions has the greatest value?

    (1) $x + y$
    (2) $-x + y$
    (3) $-x - y$
    (4) xy
    (5) $-2xy$

23. What is the value of the expression $2 \div x^{-4}$ when $x = 2$?

    (1) 32
    (2) 16
    (3) 8
    (4) -16
    (5) -32

Answers and explanations begin on page 677.

Algebra

Equations

Writing and Solving One-Step Equations

An **equation** is a mathematical statement that two expressions are equal.

Examples: $3 + 5 = 4 \cdot 2$ $\qquad$ $10 - 1 = 3^2$ $\qquad$ $5(3 + 4) = 35$

An equation can contain one or more variables. Solving an equation means finding a value for the variable that will make the equation true.

Examples: $4 + x = 11$ $\qquad$ $3x = 24$ $\qquad$ $x - 5 = -2$

$\qquad\qquad\quad x = 7$ $\qquad\quad x = 8$ $\qquad\quad x = 3$

The basic strategy in solving an equation is to isolate the variable on one side of the equation. You can do this by performing **inverse,** or opposite, operations. However, you must always follow one basic rule: Whatever you do to one side of the equation, you must also do to the other side.

Example 1: Solve $x - 23 = 45$.

$$x - 23 = 45$$

On the left side of the equation, the number 23 is subtracted from x. The inverse of subtraction is addition. Add 23 to both sides of the equation.

$$x - 23 + \mathbf{23} = 45 + \mathbf{23}$$
$$x = 68$$

To check your work, replace the variable with your solution and simplify.
When $x = \mathbf{68}$, the equation is true.

$$\text{Check: } x - 23 = 45$$
$$68 - 23 = 45$$
$$45 = 45$$

The following examples use the inverse operations of multiplication and division.

Example 2: Solve $\dfrac{x}{2} = 17$.

The variable x is divided by 2. Since multiplication is the inverse of division, you must multiply each side of the equation by 2.

$$\frac{x}{2} = 17$$
$$2\left(\frac{x}{2}\right) = 2(17)$$
$$x = 34$$

When $x = \mathbf{34}$, the equation is true.

$$\text{Check: } \frac{34}{2} = 17$$
$$17 = 17$$

Example 3: Solve $5x = 75$.

$$5x = 75$$

Since the variable x is multiplied by 5, divide both sides of the equation by 5.

$$\frac{5x}{5} = \frac{75}{5}$$
$$x = 15$$

When $x = \mathbf{15}$, the equation is true.

$$\text{Check: } 5(15) = 75$$
$$75 = 75$$

A. Solve for the variable in each equation.

1. $7x = 63$

2. $23 + m = 51$

3. $-13 = y - 12$

4. $\dfrac{x}{4} = -16$

5. $5a = 625$

6. $y - 17 = -30$

7. $x + 6 = 33$

8. $4c = 28$

9. $\dfrac{12}{x} = -3$

10. $26 = b + 33$

11. $93 = 3x$

12. $s + 16 = 8$

13. $36 = \dfrac{x}{3}$

14. $t + 14 = 53$

15. $\dfrac{x}{6} = 8$

16. $16y = -48$

17. $r - 35 = 75$

18. $24 = \dfrac{120}{x}$

19. $5y = -45$

20. $d + 45 = 20$

21. $16 = 4x$

22. $-4x = 24$

23. $19 = h - 7$

24. $\dfrac{x}{11} = 6$

25. $m + 24 = 14$

26. $5y = 45$

27. $14 - w = 42$

28. $18 = \dfrac{y}{4}$

B. Choose the one best answer to each question.

Questions 29 and 30 refer to the following table.

April Time Sheet Summary
Hours Worked per Week

Week	1	2	3	4
Kayla Sax	36	40	40	
Erin Grady		24	28	38

29. Kayla and Erin worked a total of 77 hours during Week 1. Let x = Erin's hours for Week 1. Which of the following equations could be used to solve for Erin's hours during Week 1?

(1) $x - 36 = 77$
(2) $x + 77 = 36$
(3) $x + 36 = 77$
(4) $x - 77 = 36$
(5) $36x = 77$

30. Erin worked twice as many hours as Kayla did during Week 4. Let y = Kayla's hours for Week 4. Which of the following equations could be used to solve for Kayla's hours during Week 4?

(1) $\dfrac{2}{y} = 38$

(2) $\dfrac{y}{2} = 38$

(3) $38y = 2$
(4) $2y = 38$

(5) $\dfrac{1}{2}y = 38$

31. The quotient of a number divided by 4 is 32. What is the number?

(1) 8
(2) 28
(3) 36
(4) 128
(5) 512

32. The solution $x = -5$ makes which of the following equations true?

(1) $14 - x = 9$

(2) $\dfrac{x}{5} = 1$

(3) $x + 3 = 8$

(4) $\dfrac{30}{x} = 6$

(5) $12x = -60$

33. Mike had $572.18 in his checking account. After writing a check, he had $434.68. Which of the following equations could be used to find the amount of the check (c)?

(1) $\$572.18 + c = \$434.68$
(2) $\$572.18 - c = \$434.68$
(3) $\$572.18c = \$434.68$

(4) $\dfrac{\$572.18}{c} = \$434.68$

(5) $\dfrac{c}{\$572.18} = \$434.68$

Answers and explanations begin on page 677.

Solving Multi-Step Equations

Most equations require more than one operation in order to find a solution. Follow these basic steps:

• Simplify by combining like terms.

• Perform addition and subtraction steps.

• Perform multiplication and division steps.

Example 1: Solve $6x + 5 - 2x = 25$.

1. Combine like symbols ($6x - 2x = 4x$).

$$6x + 5 - 2x = 25$$
$$4x + 5 = 25$$

2. Subtract 5 from both sides.

$$4x + 5 - 5 = 25 - 5$$
$$4x = 20$$

3. Divide both sides by 4.

$$\frac{4x}{4} = \frac{20}{4}$$
$$x = 5$$

4. Check by substituting the solution for x in the original equation.

$$6(5) + 5 - 2(5) = 25$$
$$30 + 5 - 10 = 25$$
$$25 = 25$$

In this example, the distributive property is used to simplify an expression. Notice that not every step is written out. As you gain experience, you can perform an operation on both sides of an equation mentally.

Example 2: Solve $-4(x - 6) = 2x$.

1. Use the distributive property to remove the grouping symbols.

$$-4(x - 6) = 2x$$
$$-4x + 24 = 2x$$

2. Add $4x$ to each side.

$$24 = 6x$$

3. Divide each side by 6.

$$4 = x$$

4. Check.

$$-4(4 - 6) = 2(4)$$
$$-4(-2) = 8$$
$$8 = 8$$

Some of the time you will be expected to write an equation from information given in the problem. The problem will describe two expressions that are equal. Write each expression in symbols and connect the expressions with the equals sign (=). In many problems, the word *is* indicates the = symbol.

Example 3: The product of a number and 6 is 44 more than twice the number. What is the number?

1. Write an equation. The word *is* represents the equals sign.

$$6x = 44 + 2x$$

2. Subtract $2x$ from both sides.

$$4x = 44$$

3. Divide both sides by 4.

$$x = 11$$

4. Check.

$$6(11) = 44 + 2(11)$$
$$66 = 44 + 22$$

The number described in the problem is **11**.

$$66 = 66$$

Note: Subtraction and division operations must be written in the order indicated by the words. "The difference between x and y" must be written $x - y$, <u>not</u> $y - x$. "The quotient of x and y" must be written $\frac{x}{y}$, <u>not</u> $\frac{y}{x}$.

A. Solve for the variable in each equation.

1. $3x - 20 = 130$
2. $2y - 8 = -3y - 18$
3. $6m = 14m - 16$
4. $2x + 5 + 6x = -27$
5. $5y + 3(y + 2) = 54$
6. $17 - 4z + 2z = 13$
7. $6m - 4 = m + 11$
8. $35 = x + 7 + 6x$
9. $5p - 2 = 6p - 9$
10. $50 = 3(s + 16) - 2(s - 2)$

11. $\dfrac{5(2x - 10)}{2} + 14 = 19$
12. $3(3 + r) = 2r + 4$
13. $5y = 2y + 22 + y$
14. $38 = 5(2b - 3) + 3b + 1$
15. $-5 - x = 2x - (4x + 6)$
16. $\dfrac{3h}{2} = 30$
17. $4(3 + 2x) + 8 = 92$
18. $-5(3 - z) = z + 1$
19. $10 - 3b + 3 = -1 + (b + 2)$
20. $5n + 8 - n = 6(n - 1)$

B. Choose the one best answer to each question.

21. Three times a number increased by 9 is 15 less than six times the number. Let x = the unknown number. Which of the following equations could be used to find the value of x?

    (1) $3(9x) = 6(15x)$
    (2) $3x(9) = 6x - 15x$
    (3) $3x + 9 = 15 - 6x$
    (4) $3x + 9 = 6x - 15$
    (5) $3x + 9 = 15 - 6x$

22. Dave has 500 baseball cards, which is as many as Eric and Travis have combined. Eric has three times as many cards has Travis has.

Dave	Eric	Travis
500	$3x$	x

    From the information, you can write the equation $3x + x = 500$. How many cards does Eric have? (*Hint:* Solve for x. Then find how many cards Eric has.)

    (1) 125
    (2) 150
    (3) 250
    (4) 350
    (5) 375

23. The difference of 4 times a number and 7 is the quotient of the number and 3 plus 15. Which of the following equations could be used to find the value of x?

    (1) $4x - 7 = \dfrac{x}{3} + 15$

    (2) $7 - 4x = \dfrac{x}{3} + 15$

    (3) $7 - 4x = \dfrac{3}{x} + 15$

    (4) $4x - 7 = \dfrac{3}{x} + 15$

    (5) $7 - 4x = \dfrac{3}{x} + 15$

24. Kim earned x dollars at his part-time job on Friday. His wife earned \$12 more than twice Kim's pay ($2x + 12$). Together, they earned \$174. How much did Kim earn on Friday?
    (*Hint:* Use the equation $x + (2x + 12) = \$174$.)

    (1) \$54
    (2) \$87
    (3) \$108
    (4) \$120
    (5) \$162

    Answers and explanations begin on page 677.

Common Algebra Word Problems

Key Ideas

- To solve a word problem, decide what quantity will be represented by *x*. Then write expressions for the other quantities in terms of *x*.
- Write and solve an equation. Answer the question asked in the problem.

Approaching Algebra Word Problems

Algebra problems describe how several numbers are related. One number is the unknown, which you will represent with a variable. Using the relationships described in the problem, you can write an equation and solve for the variable.

Example 1: There are twice as many women as men in a class on auto repair. If there are 24 students in the class, how many are women?

1. Express the numbers in the problem in terms of the same variable. Let *x* represent the number of men. Since there are twice as many women, let 2*x* represent the number of women.

2. Write and solve an equation. The total number of men and women is 24, so $x + 2x = 24$. Solve:
$$x + 2x = 24$$
$$3x = 24$$
$$x = 8$$

Since $x = 8$, $2x = 2(8) = 16$. There are 8 men and **16 women** in the class.

Consecutive numbers are numbers that follow in counting order. For example, 1, 2, and 3 are consecutive numbers. The numbers 2, 4, and 6 are consecutive even numbers, and 1, 3, and 5 are consecutive odd numbers.

Example 2: The sum of three consecutive numbers is 105. What is the greatest of the three numbers?

1. Let *x* represent the first number, and $x + 1$ and $x + 2$ represent the other numbers.

2. Write an equation and solve:
$$x + (x + 1) + (x + 2) = 105$$
$$3x + 3 = 105$$
$$3x = 102$$
$$x = 34$$

3. Find the answer. The variable *x* represents the first number in the sequence, so the three numbers are 34, 35, and 36. The problem asks for the greatest number, which is **36.**

You may need to use the difference between numbers to write equations.

Example 3: The ticket prices for a play are $12 for adults and $8 for children. One evening, the box office sold 200 tickets. If the total box office receipts were $2240, how many adult tickets were sold?

1. Let *x* represent the number of adult tickets. Since 200 tickets were sold, the number of children's tickets sold can be written as $200 - x$.

GED TIP

The value of x *may not be the answer to the problem; however, it may be listed as an answer choice. Reread the question. You may need the value of* x *to calculate the final answer in a multi-step problem.*

2. Multiply each term by the cost for that type of ticket. Set the total equal to $2240, and solve for x.

$$12x + 8(200 - x) = 2240$$
$$12x + 1600 - 8x = 2240$$
$$4x + 1600 = 2240$$
$$4x = 640$$
$$x = 160$$

3. There were **160 adult tickets** sold.

ALGEBRA ▸ PRACTICE 8

A. Solve.

1. Two houses are for sale on the same street. The second house has 1000 square feet less than twice the square feet of the first house. Together the houses have 4400 square feet. What is the square footage of the first house?

2. Julia has 24 coins in her pocket. The coins are either dimes or quarters. The total value of the coins is $4.50. How many coins are dimes? [*Hint:* The value of the dimes is $0.10x$, and the value of the quarters is $0.25(24 - x)$.]

3. The Bulldogs won twice as many games as they lost. If they played a total of 36 games, how many did they win?

4. The sum of four consecutive even numbers is 212. What is the third number? (*Hint:* Let x = the first number, $x + 2$ = the second number, $x + 4$ = the third, and so on.)

5. A children's store is selling pants for $6 each and shirts for $4. Brenda bought 13 items and paid $62. How many shirts did she buy?

6. The sum of three consecutive numbers is 180. What is the least number in the series?

7. In a month Andrew spends twice as much on rent as he does on food for his family. Last month he spent $1650 on rent and food. How much did he spend on rent?

8. George spends four times as much time helping customers as he does stocking shelves. Last week he spent 35 hours on the two tasks. How many hours were spent helping customers?

B. Choose the one best answer to each question.

9. Sylvia scored 10 points better than Wiley on their science exam. Greg scored 6 points less than Wiley. Altogether the students earned 226 points. How many points did Sylvia earn?

   (1) 68
   (2) 74
   (3) 78
   (4) 84
   (5) 94

10. Two adults and four children paid $48 to get into the fair. A child's ticket is $6 less than an adult's ticket. What is the cost of an adult's ticket?

   (1) $18
   (2) $15
   (3) $12
   (4) $9
   (5) $6

11. Jenny is four times as old as her niece Tina. In 12 years, Jenny will be only twice as old as Tina. The chart shows expressions for Tina and Jenny's ages now and in 12 years.

	Jenny's Age	Tina's Age
Now	$4x$	x
In 12 Years	$4x + 12$	$x + 12$

How old is Tina now?

   (1) 4
   (2) 6
   (3) 8
   (4) 12
   (5) 16

Answers and explanations begin on page 677.

ALGEBRA

Patterns and Functions

Key Ideas

- A pattern is a sequence of numbers determined by an algebraic rule.
- A function is an algebraic rule that shows how one set of numbers is related to another set of numbers.
- To use a function, substitute values for variables and solve.

Recognizing Patterns and Functions

A **pattern** is a series of numbers or objects whose sequence is determined by a particular rule. You can figure out what rule has been used by studying the terms you are given. Think: What operation or sequence of operations will always result in the next term in the series? Once you know the rule, you can continue the pattern.

Example 1: Find the seventh term in the sequence: 1, 2, 4, 8, 16, . . .

1. Determine the rule. Each number in the sequence is two times the number before it.

2. Apply the rule. You have been given five terms and must find the seventh. Continue the pattern. The sixth term is $16 \times 2 = 32$, and the seventh term is $32 \times 2 = \mathbf{64}$.

A **function** is an algebraic rule that shows how the terms in one sequence of numbers are related to the terms in another sequence. For example, a sidewalk vendor charges $1.50 for a slice of pizza. The chart below shows how much it would cost to buy one to six slices.

Number of Pizza Slices	1	2	3	4	5	6
Cost	$1.50	$3.00	$4.50	$6.00	$7.50	$9.00

Each number in the first row corresponds to a price in the second row. We could say that the amount a customer will pay is a function of (or depends upon) the number of slices the customer orders. This function could be written:

Cost = number of slices $\times$ $1.50, or $C = n(\$1.50)$.

If you know the function and a number in the first set of numbers, you can solve for its corresponding number in the second set.

Example 2: Using the function $y = 3x + 5$, what is the value of y when $x = -3$?

1. Substitute the given value of x. $y = 3(-3) + 5$
2. Solve for y. $y = -9 + 5$
                                           $y = \mathbf{-4}$

Example 3: Using the function $n = 100 - 4(3 + m)$, what is the value of n when $m = 6$?

1. Substitute the given value of m. $n = 100 - 4(3 + 6)$
2. Solve for n. $n = 100 - 4(9)$
                                           $n = 100 - 36$
                                           $n = \mathbf{64}$

GED TIP

To figure out what rule has been used to form a pattern, begin by finding the difference between each term and the term that follows it in the sequence.

ALGEBRA ▸ PRACTICE 9

A. Solve.

1. Which number should come next in the following pattern?

   $-12, -9, -6, -3,$ _____

2. What is the next number in the sequence?

   $21, 26, 31, 36,$ _____

3. In the function $y = 4x + 10$, if $x = -2$, what is the value of y?

4. In the function $y = 2x(4 + x) - 2$, if $x = 3$, what is the value of y?

5. Each term in the second row is determined by the function $y = 2x - 1$.

x	1	2	3	4	5	...	12
y	1	3	5	7	9	...	

   What number belongs in the shaded box?

6. In the function $y = \dfrac{x+3}{6} - 8$, if $x = 21$, what is the value of y?

7. What is the next term in the pattern below?

   $1000, 500, 250, 125, 62.5,$ _____

8. What is the next number in the sequence?

   $3, -5, 7, -9, 11,$ _____

9. Each term in the second row is determined by the function $y = 3x + 5$.

x	-2	-1	0	1	2	...	9
y	-1	2	5	8	11	...	

   What number belongs in the shaded box?

10. In the function $y = (x - 7) + 12$, if $x = -10$, what is the value of y?

B. Choose the one best answer to each question.

Question 11 refers to the following drawing.

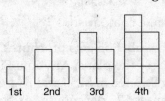

11. How many blocks would be needed to build the 25th construction in the sequence?

    (1) 47
    (2) 49
    (3) 51
    (4) 55
    (5) Not enough information is given.

12. What is the 6th term in the sequence below?

    $$-14, -8, -2, 4, \ldots$$

    (1) 8
    (2) 10
    (3) 14
    (4) 16
    (5) 22

13. The price per scarf is a function of the number of scarves purchased. The table shows the price per scarf for purchases of up to four scarves.

number (n) of scarves	1	2	3	4
cost (c) per scarf	$5.00	$4.75	$4.50	$4.25

    Which of the following functions was used to determine the prices shown in the table?

    (1) $c = n(\$5.00 - \$0.25)$
    (2) $c = \$5.00 - \$0.25(n - 1)$
    (3) $c = \$5.00 - \$0.25n$
    (4) $c = \$5.00n - \$0.25$
    (5) $c = \$5.00n - \$0.25n$

14. Which of the following sequences could be created using the function $y = 4x - 3$?

    (1) $1, 4, 7, 10, 13, \ldots$
    (2) $1, 5, 9, 13, 17, \ldots$
    (3) $1, 4, 8, 13, 19, \ldots$
    (4) $1, -1, -3, -5, -7, \ldots$
    (5) $1, -2, -5, -8, -11, \ldots$

Answers and explanations begin on page 678.

ALGEBRA

Function Applications

Solving Function Word Problems

Functions are used in many business applications. For instance, they can be used to calculate profit, cost, employee wages, and taxes. On the GED Math Test, you will read about common work and life situations. The problems may contain or describe a function that you can use to solve the problem.

Example 1: Anderson Advertising is finishing a series of print ads for a client. Finishing the project will cost $2,000 per day for the first seven days, and $3,500 per day after seven days. The finishing costs can be found using the function $C = \$2,000d + \$1,500(d - 7)$, where C = the cost of finishing the project and d = the number of days. If the project takes 12 days to complete, what will the project cost?

Use the function to solve the problem.
$$\begin{aligned} C &= \$2,000d + \$1,500(d - 7) \\ &= \$2,000(12) + \$1,500(12 - 7) \\ &= \$24,000 + \$1,500(5) \\ &= \$24,000 + \$7,500 \\ &= \mathbf{\$31,500} \end{aligned}$$

You may be asked to use functions to make comparisons.

Example 2: Nita decides to join a health club. She gets brochures from two health clubs and compares the plans. Anytime Fitness charges a one-time membership fee of $250 and $8 per month. Freedom Health Center charges $25 per month. At both health clubs, the price (P) Nita will pay is a function of the number of months (m) she attends the club. The functions are:

Anytime Fitness $\qquad P = \$250 + \$8m$

Freedom Health Center $\qquad P = \$25m$

Nita plans to move in 18 months. If she attends a health club until she moves, which one offers the better price?

1. Find the price at Anytime Fitness:
$$\begin{aligned} P &= \$250 + \$8m \\ &= \$250 + \$8(18) \\ &= \$250 + \$144 \\ &= \$394 \end{aligned}$$

2. Find the price at Freedom Health Center:
$$\begin{aligned} P &= \$25m \\ &= \$25(18) \\ &= \$450 \end{aligned}$$

3. Compare the results. Even though Nita will have to pay a large amount up front, **Anytime Fitness** offers the better price.

A. Solve. You <u>MAY</u> use a calculator.

1. The Chimney Sweep charges $25 for a chimney inspection. If the customer purchases additional services, $15 of the inspection fee is deducted. Let s = the cost of any additional services. The total cost (C) of an inspection and services can be determined by the function $C = \$25 + (s - \$15)$.

   a. Jan has her chimney inspected and purchases a smoke guard for $89. How much will she be charged?

   b. After an inspection, Ahmed decides to have a new damper installed for $255. How much will he pay?

2. Ricardo does a great deal of driving for his work. He generally estimates his driving time (t) using the function $t = \dfrac{m}{60}$, where m = the number of miles.

   a. How many hours will it take Ricardo to drive 330 miles?

   b. How many hours will it take Ricardo to drive 255 miles?

3. A customer's phone charges are a function of the number of minutes of long-distance calls made. The graph shows a comparison of two plans available.

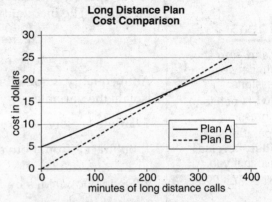

   a. Michelle looks at her previous phone bills and finds that she makes about 350 minutes of long-distance calls per month. Which plan is better for her?

   b. Craig usually makes about 150 minutes of long-distance calls per month. Which plan is better for him?

B. Choose the <u>one best answer</u> to each question. You <u>MAY</u> use a calculator.

<u>Questions 4 and 5</u> refer to the following information.

Alicia is considering three job opportunities. At all three jobs, weekly pay (P) is a function of the number of hours (h) worked during the week. The functions are shown below:

Job 1	$P = \$9.75h$
Job 2	$P = \$70 + \$8.40h$
Job 3	$P = \$380 \times \dfrac{h}{38}$

4. If Alicia works 30 hours in a week, how much more will she earn at Job 2 than at Job 1?

   (1) $5.33
   (2) $29.50
   (3) $40.50
   (4) $59.00
   (5) Not enough information is given.

5. If Alicia works 40 hours per week, which of the following is a true statement?

   (1) Alicia will earn the most at Job 1.
   (2) Alicia will earn the least at Job 3.
   (3) Job 1 will pay more than Job 3.
   (4) Job 3 will pay more than Job 2.
   (5) Alicia will earn the most at Job 2.

6. A company is awarded a $95,000 job that will cost $5,400 per day in expenses. Profits (P) can be calculated using $P = \$95,000 - \$5,400d$, where d = days worked. How much profit is in a job that takes 14 days?

   (1) $10,800
   (2) $19,400
   (3) $66,100
   (4) $75,600
   (5) Not enough information is given.

Answers and explanations begin on page 678.

ALGEBRA

Inequalities

Key Ideas

- Use $<$, $>$, $\leq$, and $\geq$ to show the relationship between two unequal expressions.
- The symbol always points to the smaller expression.
- Use inverse operations to solve inequalities. Reverse the inequality sign if you multiply or divide by a negative number.

Solving Inequalities

An **inequality** is a mathematical statement that connects two unequal expressions. The inequality symbols and their meanings are:

$$> \text{ greater than} \qquad \geq \text{ greater than or equal to}$$
$$< \text{ less than} \qquad \leq \text{ less than or equal to}$$

An inequality is solved much like an equation. Use inverse operations to isolate the variable.

Example 1: Solve for x in the inequality $3x + 2 < 8$.

1. Subtract 2 from both sides.

$$3x + 2 < 8$$
$$3x < 6$$

2. Divide both sides by 3.

$$x < 2$$

The solution $x < 2$ states that any number less than 2 makes the inequality true. Check by substituting 1 (a number less than 2) for x: $3(1) + 2 < 8$, which simplifies to $5 < 8$, a true statement.

There is one important difference between solving equalities and inequalities. Whenever you multiply or divide both sides of an inequality by a <u>negative</u> number, you must <u>reverse</u> the inequality symbol.

Example 2: Solve for n in the inequality $-2n - 5 \geq 3$.

1. Add 5 to both sides to remove -5 from the left side of the equation.

$$-2n - 5 + 5 \geq 3 + 5$$
$$-2n \geq 8$$

2. Divide both sides by -2 and *reverse the inequality symbol.*

$$-2n/-2 \geq 8/-2$$
$$n \leq -4$$

GED TIP

Avoid the most common mistake with inequalities: reversing the symbol accidentally. Always check your work by substituting any number that fits the solution into the original inequality.

Check your work by substituting a number that is less than or equal to -4 into the <u>original</u> inequality. Here -5 is used for n. Since $5 \geq 3$ is a true statement, the answer is correct.

$$-2n - 5 \geq 3$$
$$-2(-5) - 5 \geq 3$$
$$5 \geq 3$$

When an inequality contains a variable, there are usually several numbers that make the inequality true. For that reason, we often graph the solution. In the examples below, a closed dot means that the number is included in the solution set. An open dot means the number is not included.

Examples: $x < 2$

$x > -3$

$x \leq 1$

$x \geq -2$

A **compound inequality** combines two inequalities. To solve a compound inequality, separate the inequalities and solve both. Then combine the solutions.

Example 3: Solve $3x + 4 < 5x < 16 + x$.

1. Write two inequalities and solve each separately.

$$\begin{array}{ll} 3x + 4 < 5x & 5x < 16 + x \\ 4 < 2x & 4x < 16 \\ 2 < x & x < 4 \end{array}$$

2. Write the result as a compound inequality. **$2 < x < 4$**

In other words, any quantity that is greater than 2 *and* less than 4 will make the compound inequality true.

ALGEBRA ▶ PRACTICE 11

A. Solve.

1. $3x - 7 > 5$

2. $13 < 2x - 1$

3. $4 + 2x \le -2$

4. $\dfrac{4 + x}{5} \le 8$

5. $2(x + 3) < 4$

6. $3 + 9x \ge 4(x + 7)$

7. $-4(x + 2) < 24$

8. $-2x + 9 < 1$

9. $\dfrac{x - 2}{3} > 2x + 11$

10. $6x < 5x + 2$

11. $x + 6 \le 8x - 15$

12. $5x + 14 > 2 + 7x$

13. $13x - 7 \ge 25 - 3x$

14. $x - 6 < 2(x + 2)$

15. $-5 + 3x \ge 4(3x - 8)$

16. $36 > 4(x - 12)$

17. $6 \le 3(x + 3)$

18. $\dfrac{4x}{3} > 8x - 20$

19. $x - 2 < \dfrac{2x + 6}{4}$

20. $x \ge 4x - 9$

21. $30 \ge 5(x + 4) \ge 10$

22. $-7x > -2(x + 15) < 10$

23. $3 < 5x - 27 < 53$

24. $22 \le 6x - 2 \le 4x + 16$

B. Choose the one best answer to each question.

25. The perimeter of a square can be found using the formula $P = 4s$, where s is one side of the square.

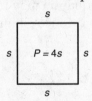

The perimeter of a square is less than or equal to 64 inches. Which of the following represents the possible measures of the side of the square in inches?

(1) $s \le 16$
(2) $s \ge 16$
(3) $s \le 8$
(4) $s \ge 8$
(5) $s \le 64$

26. Three added to the product of -4 and a number (x) is less than 5 added to the product of -3 and the number. Which of the following is a graph of the solution set of x?

(1)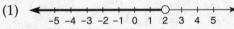

(2)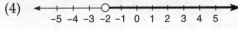

(3)
```
-5 -4 -3 -2 -1  0  1  2  3  4  5
```

(4)
```
-5 -4 -3 -2 -1  0  1  2  3  4  5
```

(5)
```
-5 -4 -3 -2 -1  0  1  2  3  4  5
```

Answers and explanations begin on page 678.

ALGEBRA

Quadratic Equations

Key Ideas

- A quadratic equation can have two solutions.
- Set the quadratic equation equal to 0 and factor.
- Find the values for x that will make each factor equal 0.

Solving by Factoring

A **quadratic equation** contains a squared variable, for example, $x^2 - 3x = 4$. One way to solve quadratic equations is by factoring. This is the simplest method and the one you should use on the GED Math Test. When you factor an expression, you find the terms that divide evenly into the expression.

Example 1: Factor the expression $15x^2 + 9x$.

1. Look for a term that divides evenly into both $15x^2$ and $9x$. Both terms can be divided by $3x$.

$15x^2 \div 3x = 5x$
$9x \div 3x = 3$

2. Factor out $3x$. Write the terms as factors.

$15x^2 + 9x = \mathbf{3x(5x + 3)}$

Study Example 2 to learn how to multiply factors with more than one term.

$$\overset{\text{(factor)}}{} \quad \overset{\text{(factor)}}{}$$

Example 2: Multiply $(2x + 3)(x - 4)$.

$$\underset{\text{four terms}}{}$$

1. Multiply each term in the first factor by each term in the second factor.

$2x \cdot x = 2x^2$
$2x \cdot -4 = -8x$
$3 \cdot x = 3x$
$3 \cdot -4 = -12$
$2x^2 + (-8x) + 3x + (-12) =$

2. Combine the results.

$\mathbf{2x^2 - 5x - 12}$

GED TIP

Trial and error can help you factor quadratic equations. You will get better at it, the more you practice.

This method of multiplying factors is called the FOIL method. The letters in FOIL stand for First, Outer, Inner, and Last. Use the word FOIL to make sure you have performed all the necessary operations.

You factor a quadratic equation to solve it. A quadratic equation may have two solutions. Find values that make the factors equal to 0. Since a number multiplied by 0 is 0, each of the values is a solution.

Example 3: Solve $x^2 - 3x = 4$.

1. Set the equation equal to 0 by subtracting 4 from both sides.

$x^2 - 3x = 4$
$x^2 - 3x - 4 = 0$

2. Factor by trial and error. Think: What factors of the last term, -4, when added, will equal -3, the number part of the middle term?
$-4 \cdot 1 = -4$ and $-4 + 1 = -3$

$(x \quad)(x \quad) = 0$
$(x + 1)(x - 4) = 0$

3. If either one of the factors equals 0, then the product of the factors will be zero. Set each factor equal to 0 and solve for x.

$x + 1 = 0$
$x = \mathbf{-1}$
$x - 4 = 0$
$x = \mathbf{4}$

The solutions to the quadratic equation are **−1 and 4.**

A. Multiply.

1. $(x + 4)(x + 2)$
2. $(x - 3)(x + 5)$
3. $(x - 1)(x + 4)$
4. $(x - 6)(x - 3)$
5. $(x + 8)(x - 2)$

6. $(2x + 1)(x - 2)$
7. $(x - 9)(x - 5)$
8. $(x + 1)(3x - 2)$
9. $(x - 2)(x + 7)$
10. $(3x + 8)(x + 2)$

11. $(x - 6)(x + 5)$
12. $(x - 10)(x - 3)$
13. $(2x + 1)(2x + 2)$
14. $(x + 9)(x - 4)$
15. $(x - 5)(x - 5)$

B. Factor each expression.

16. $x^2 + 4x + 3$
17. $x^2 + 4x - 5$
18. $x^2 + 8x + 12$
19. $x^2 - x - 6$
20. $x^2 + 5x - 14$

21. $x^2 - x - 12$
22. $x^2 + 2x - 35$
23. $x^2 - 12x + 36$
24. $x^2 - 6x - 7$
25. $x^2 + 4x - 32$

26. $2x^2 + 5x - 3$
27. $2x^2 - 8x - 10$
28. $x^2 + 5x - 50$
29. $4x^2 + 4x - 3$
30. $x^2 + x - 56$

C. Choose the one best answer to each question.

31. What are two solutions for the equation $x^2 - x = 20$?

    (1) 4 and 5
    (2) −4 and 5
    (3) 4 and −5
    (4) −10 and 2
    (5) −2 and 10

32. For which of the following equations is $x = -4$ a solution?

    (1) $2x^2 - 8 = 0$
    (2) $x^2 - 8x + 64 = 0$
    (3) $x^2 - 2x - 15 = 0$
    (4) $x^2 + 2x - 24 = 0$
    (5) $2x^2 + 2x - 24 = 0$

33. What is the only positive solution for the equation $2x^2 - 7x - 30 = 0$?

    (1) 4
    (2) 5
    (3) 6
    (4) 7
    (5) 8

34. The area of a rectangle is found by multiplying the length by the width. In the rectangle below, the area of the rectangle is equal to the expression $2x^2 - 27x + 70$.

    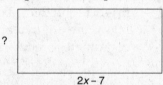

    $2x - 7$

    An expression equal to the length is shown on the diagram. Which of the following expressions is equal to the width of the rectangle?

    (1) $x + 10$
    (2) $x - 10$
    (3) $2x + 10$
    (4) $2x - 10$
    (5) $2x - 5$

    Answers and explanations begin on page 678.

ALGEBRA

The Coordinate Plane

Plotting Points

A **coordinate grid** is a way to locate points that lie in a **plane,** or flat surface. The grid is formed by two intersecting lines, an x-axis and a y-axis. The x-axis is actually a horizontal number line, and the y-axis is a vertical number line. The point at which the two axes intersect is called the **origin.**

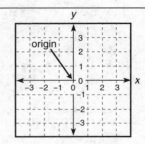

Each point on the grid can be named using two numbers called an **ordered pair.** The first number is the distance from the origin along the x-axis. The second number is the distance from the origin along the y-axis. The numbers are written in parentheses and are separated by a comma: (x,y).

Example 1: Write the ordered pairs for points M and P.

1. Point M lies 2 spaces to the right of the origin along the x-axis and 3 spaces above the origin along the y-axis. The coordinates are **(2,3).**

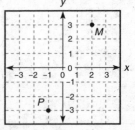

2. Point P lies 1 space to the left along the x-axis and 3 spaces down along the y-axis. The coordinates are **(−1,−3).**

To plot points on the grid, use the number lines located at the axes. Remember that right and up are the directions for positive numbers, and left and down are the directions for negative numbers.

Example 2: Point A is located at (−2,1), and point B is located at (3,−2). Plot these points on a coordinate grid.

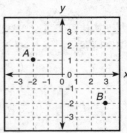

1. To plot point A, start at the origin. Count 2 spaces left along the x-axis. Count 1 space up along the y-axis.

2. To plot point B, start at the origin. Count 3 spaces right along the x-axis. Count 2 spaces down along the y-axis.

A. Write the ordered pair for each point.

1. Point A

2. Point B

3. Point C

4. Point D

5. Point E

6. Point F

7. Point G

8. Point H

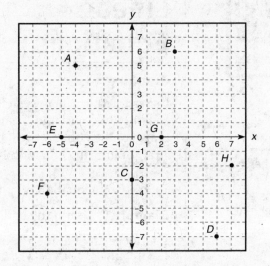

B. Plot the points on the coordinate grid.

9. Plot the following points:

J at (−3,−2)

K at (4,0)

L at (1,−3)

M at (−4,2)

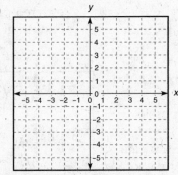

10. Plot the following points:

N at (0,−1)

O at (−4,−4)

P at (3,1)

Q at (−3,0)

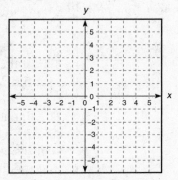

C. Choose the <u>one best answer</u> to each question.

11. On the coordinate grid below, a line passes through points A and B.

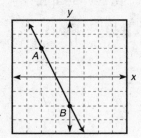

Which of the following ordered pairs also lies on the line?

(1) (1,0)

(2) (1,−1)

(3) (0,1)

(4) (0,−1)

(5) (−1,0)

12. Two of the corners of a triangle are located at (3,−3) and (2,3). What is the location of the third corner as shown in the diagram below?

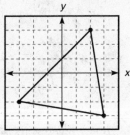

(1) (−3,−2)

(2) (−3,2)

(3) (−2,−2)

(4) (−2,−3)

(5) (3,−2)

Answers and explanations begin on page 679.

Key Ideas

- A linear equation has two variables, x and y.
- When the solutions to a linear equation are graphed on a coordinate grid, the graph forms a line.
- To find a point on the line, substitute a value for x and solve for y.
- You must solve for at least two points in order to draw the line.

GED TIP

If a linear equation is not written with y on one side of the equation, use inverse operations to isolate y. Example: 2x + y = 15 Subtract 2x from each side. y = −2x + 15

ALGEBRA

Linear Equations

Graphing a Line

Using the coordinate system, we can graph equations. When an equation has only two variables, x and y, and neither are raised to a power, the graph of the equation will be a line. When the graph of an equation is a straight line, the equation is a **linear equation.**

To graph an equation, you need to solve for two points on the line.

Example 1: Graph the equation $y = 3x - 4$.

1. Choose any value for x and solve for y. Let $x = 1$.

   $y = 3(1) - 4$
   $y = 3 - 4$
   $y = -1$

   If $x = 1$, then $y = -1$. The ordered pair for the first point is $(1,-1)$.

2. Choose another value for x and solve for y. Let $x = 2$.

   $y = 3(2) - 4$
   $y = 6 - 4$
   $y = 2$

   If $x = 2$, then $y = 2$. The ordered pair for the second point is $(2,2)$.

3. Plot the points on a coordinate grid and draw a line through them.

The line is the graph of all the possible solutions for the equation $y = 3x - 4$. Arrows at both ends of the line indicate that the line continues in both directions. From this you can see that there are an infinite number of solutions to a linear equation.

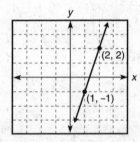

Some linear equation problems don't require you to draw a graph.

Example 2: Point A lies at $(5,-6)$ on a coordinate grid. The graph of which of the following equations passes through point A?

   (1) $y = -5x + 18$
   (2) $y = -4x + 14$
   (3) $y = -2x - 13$
   (4) $y = x - 7$
   (5) $y = 2x - 15$

Use the ordered pair given in the problem. Substitute the x-coordinate, 5, for x in each equation and solve for y. If $y = -6$, the value of the y-coordinate from the ordered pair, you have found the correct equation.

Option (2) is correct.

$y = -4x + 14$
$y = -4(5) + 14$
$y = -20 + 14 = -6$

A. Fill in the y column in each table and graph the equation.

1. $y = \dfrac{1}{2}x + 3$

If $x =$	then $y =$
-2	
0	
2	

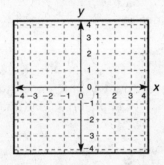

3. $-2 + y = -x$

If $x =$	then $y =$
1	
2	
3	

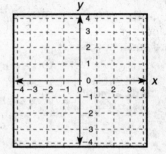

2. $y + 3x = -1$

If $x =$	then $y =$
-1	
0	
1	

4. $y = 3 - 2x$

If $x =$	then $y =$
0	
1	
2	

B. Choose the one best answer to each question.

Questions 5 and 6 refer to the following coordinate grid.

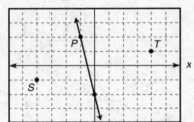

5. The graph of the equation $y = \frac{1}{4}x$ will pass through which of the following pairs of points?

(1) point S and $(-1,2)$
(2) point S and $(0,-2)$
(3) point T and $(0,0)$
(4) point T and $(-1,2)$
(5) point T and $(0,-2)$

6. Line P is the graph of which of the following equations?

(1) $y = 4x + 1$
(2) $y = -4x - 1$
(3) $y = 4x + 2$
(4) $y = -4x - 2$
(5) $y = -x + 2$

7. Point C is located at $(-3,5)$. A graph of which of the following equations would pass through point C?

(1) $3x + 2y = 5$
(2) $2x + 3y = 9$
(3) $4x - 2y = 8$
(4) $5x - 3y = 0$
(5) $3x - 3y = 6$

Answers and explanations begin on page 679.

ALGEBRA

Slope of a Line

Calculating Slope

Slope is the measurement of the steepness of a line. Imagine a road going up a hill. If the road must climb upward over a short forward distance, the road will be very steep. Slope measures the relationship between **rise** (how high the road must climb) and **run** (the distance the road goes forward).

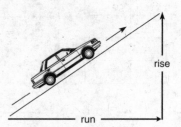

Key Ideas

- Slope is the ratio of rise to run.
- Moving from left to right, a line that goes upward has a positive slope, and a line that moves downward has a negative slope.
- You can find slope by counting spaces and writing a ratio or by using the slope formula.

On a coordinate grid, a line that moves upward from left to right has a **positive slope.** A line that moves downward from left to right has a **negative slope.** You can find the slope of a line on a coordinate grid by writing the ratio of rise to run.

Example 1: What is the slope of line P shown on the coordinate grid?

1. Find two points on line P. Count to find the rise and run. The line moves up 1 space for every 2 spaces it goes to the right.

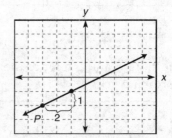

2. Write the ratio: $\dfrac{\text{rise}}{\text{run}} = \dfrac{1}{2}$. The slope is $\frac{1}{2}$.

Example 2: What is the slope of line S shown on the coordinate grid?

1. Find any two points on line S. The line moves down 6 spaces (a negative direction) and 2 spaces to the right.

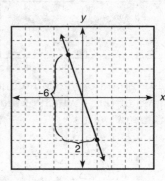

GED TIP

Think of the slope formula this way: Write the difference of the y's over the difference of the x's. Just make sure that you always subtract the coordinates in the same order.

2. Write the ratio: $\dfrac{\text{rise}}{\text{run}} = \dfrac{-6}{2} = -3$.

The slope of line S is **−3.**

You can also find slope using the slope formula on the GED formulas page. The formula will appear as follows:

slope of a line $= \dfrac{y_2 - y_1}{x_2 - x_1}$, where (x_1,y_1) and (x_2,y_2) are two points on a line.

Example 3: A line passes through points at coordinates (1,4) and (−5,2). What is the slope of the line?

1. Choose one point to be (x_1,y_1). The other will be (x_2,y_2). It doesn't matter which you choose. For this example, $(x_1,y_1) = (1,4)$ and $(x_2,y_2) = (-5,2)$.

2. Substitute the values into the slope formula and solve:

$$\frac{y_2 - y_1}{x_2 - x_1} \qquad \frac{2 - 4}{-5 - 1} = \frac{-2}{-6} = \frac{1}{3} \qquad \text{The slope is } \tfrac{1}{3}.$$

Since the slope is positive, you know that the line rises from left to right. You also know that it goes up 1 space for every 3 spaces it moves to the right.

In working with slope, there are a few special circumstances that you should memorize. A horizontal line, just like a flat stretch of roadway, has a slope of 0. The slope of a vertical line is undefined; in other words, our definition of slope will not work for a line that has no run at all.

ALGEBRA ▸ PRACTICE 15

A. Find the slope of each line.

1.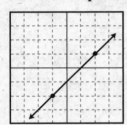

2.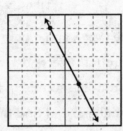

3.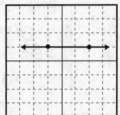

B. Use the slope formula to find the slope of a line that passes through the following pairs of points.

4. (3,5) and (−1,2)

5. (0,2) and (4,0)

6. (4,2) and (2,2)

7. (6,1) and (0,3)

8. (1,4) and (−2,−2)

9. (4,−2) and (2,4)

C. Choose the <u>one best answer</u> for each question.

Question 10 refers to the following graph.

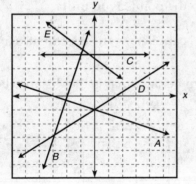

10. Which of the following lines shown on the graph has a slope of −⅓?

   (1) line A
   (2) line B
   (3) line C
   (4) line D
   (5) line E

11. Line N passes through the following points: (0,4), (1,2), (2,0), and (3,−2). What is the slope of line N?

   (1) −4
   (2) −2
   (3) 1
   (4) 2
   (5) 4

12. Line L passes through point (1,0) and has a slope of 3. Which of the following points also lies on line L?

   (1) (0,3)
   (2) (1,4)
   (3) (1,3)
   (4) (2,3)
   (5) (2,5)

Answers and explanations begin on page 679.

ALGEBRA

Distance Between Points

Using a Formula to Find the Distance Between Points

When solving problems using a coordinate grid, you may need to find the distance from one point to another. If two points are on the same vertical or horizontal line, you find the distance by counting spaces. To find the distance between points that are not on the same line, you need to use a formula. You can find this formula on the GED formulas page:

distance between points = $\sqrt{(x_2 - x_1)^2 + (y_2 - y_1)^2}$, where (x_1,y_1) and (x_2,y_2) are two points in a plane

Follow these steps to use the formula to find the distance between two points.

1. Choose a point to be (x_1,y_1) and a point to be (x_2,y_2).

2. Subtract the first x from the second x, and square the difference.

3. Subtract the first y from the second y, and square the difference.

4. Add the squared numbers, and find the square root of the sum.

Example 1: Find the distance between points located at $(1,3)$ and $(7,-5)$.

1. Let $(1,3) = (x_1,y_1)$ and $(7,-5) = (x_2,y_2)$.

2. Subtract the first x from the second, and square. $7 - 1 = 6$, and $6^2 = 36$

3. Subtract the first y from the second, and square. $-5 - 3 = -8$, and $-8^2 = 64$

4. Add the squares, and find the square root of the sum. $36 + 64 = 100$, and $\sqrt{100} = 10$ The distance between the points is **10 units.**

In the example below, the same process is applied as the coordinates are substituted directly into the formula.

Example 2: In the coordinate grid shown below, what is the distance between points A and B, to the nearest tenth?

1. Point A is located at $(5,2)$ and point B is located at $(1,-3)$. Let $(5,2) = (x_2,y_2)$ and $(1,-3) = (x_1,y_1)$.

2. Use the formula:

$$distance = \sqrt{(x_2 - x_1)^2 + (y_2 - y_1)^2}$$
$$= \sqrt{(5 - 1)^2 + (2 - -3)^2}$$
$$= \sqrt{4^2 + 5^2}$$
$$= \sqrt{16 + 25}$$
$$= \sqrt{41}$$

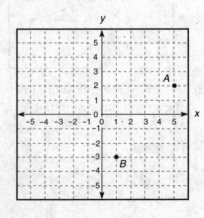

Key Ideas

- To find the distance between points, you can use a formula from the GED formulas page.
- You may need to use a calculator to find the square root in the last step of the formula.

GED TIP

To estimate the distance between points, count the spaces of the rise and run of a line connecting the points. The distance must be greater than the rise or run but less than the sum of the rise and run.

3. Use a calculator to find the square root. On the *Casio fx-260*,

Press: 41 [SHIFT] [x^2]   The display reads: [6.403124237]

4. Round to the nearest tenth. 6.4 The distance between points *A* and *B* is approximately **6.4 units.**

ALGEBRA ▸ PRACTICE 16

A. **Use the distance formula to find the distance between each pair of points. You <u>MAY</u> use a calculator. If necessary, round to the nearest tenth.**

1. (3,4) and (−2,1)   4. (−3,−1) and (−5,3)   7. (−2,−2) and (4,5)
2. (0,1) and (2,4)   5. (5,−2) and (0,0)   8. (4,0) and (−3,1)
3. (4,6) and (5,10)   6. (−1,0) and (8,9)   9. (0,−4) and (1,−6)

B. **Choose the <u>one best answer</u> for each question.**

<u>Questions 10 and 11</u> refer to the following graph.

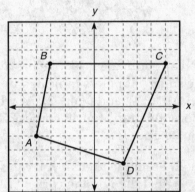

<u>Questions 12 and 13</u> are based on the graph.

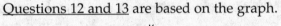
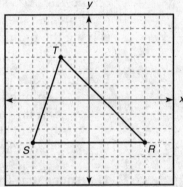

10. Figure *ABCD* is a quadrilateral. If a diagonal is drawn from point *A* to point *C*, what will the length of the diagonal be to the nearest whole unit?

(1) 8
(2) 9
(3) 10
(4) 11
(5) 12

11. Point *E* will be drawn at the midpoint, or center, of the segment connecting points *B* and *C*. At what ordered pair will point *E* be located?

(1) (−1,3)
(2) (0,3)
(3) (0.5,3)
(4) (1,3)
(5) (2,3)

12. If each square on the grid represents one square centimeter, what is the length, to the nearest one-tenth centimeter, of the segment connecting points *S* and *T*?

(1) 6.0
(2) 6.3
(3) 6.8
(4) 7.2
(5) 8.1

13. Suppose point *V* is drawn at the origin of the coordinate grid. What is the distance in units from point *V* to point *S*?

(1) 5
(2) 6
(3) 7
(4) 8
(5) 9

Answers and explanations begin on page 680.

ALGEBRA

Special Coordinate Grid Items

Key Ideas

- Two questions on the GED Math Test will require you to plot points on a special grid.
- The grid will have rows of circles to represent the gridlines formed by the x-axis and y-axis lines.
- Fill in the correct circle to plot your answer on the grid.

Using the Coordinate Grid on Your Answer Sheet

The GED Math Test contains two questions that must be answered on coordinate grids printed on the answer sheet. This grid is shown below.

Each row of circles represents a gridline on a standard coordinate grid. The x-axis and y-axis circles are labeled so that you can easily find the correct coordinates.

To use the grid, carefully fill in the circle at the coordinates of your answer. Make sure you do not make any stray marks on the grid. You should not draw lines or figures on the grid while you are solving the problem.

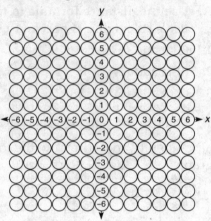

Example: Kate is drawing a square on a coordinate grid. She has already plotted three corners of the square at points indicated by the following ordered pairs: (−4,4), (2,4), and (−4,−2). At what point should she plot the location of the fourth corner? Graph your answer on the coordinate grid.

1. A square has four sides of equal length. Make a rough sketch to find the location of the ordered pairs given in the problem.

2. From the sketch, you can see that the missing corner will be located at (2,−2). Fill in the circle that corresponds with this point on the coordinate grid.

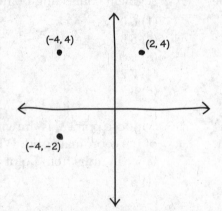

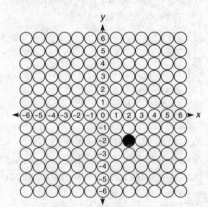

GED TIP

Making a quick sketch of a coordinate grid can help you solve problems. Draw the x-axis and y-axis, and estimate the placement of points.

Special grid questions test your ability to plot points correctly on a coordinate grid. Before filling in a circle, check both the x-axis and y-axis to make sure you have chosen the correct circle. Erase any mistakes or changes completely.

A. Solve.

1. Bea uses a coordinate grid to plan designs for quilt squares. She begins by drawing a rectangle. Three of the corners are located at $(-5,1)$, $(2,1)$, and $(-5,5)$. At what point is the fourth corner of the rectangle located?

   Graph your answer on the coordinate grid.

3. A company logo has a shaded background in the shape of a rectangle. When the rectangle is drawn on a coordinate grid, three of the corners are located at $(-2,4)$, $(5,4)$, and $(5,-4)$. At what ordered pair should the final corner be located?

   Graph your answer on the coordinate grid.

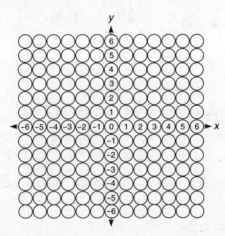

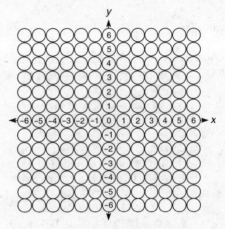

2. A line with a slope of $\frac{1}{2}$ is drawn through point P at $(-2,2)$. Moving from left to right, what is the next ordered pair of whole numbers on the line?

   Graph your answer on the coordinate grid.

4. A city map is placed on a coordinate grid. On the grid, a school is located at $(4,-6)$. Another school is located 9 spaces upward and 5 spaces to the left. What are the coordinates of the second school's location?

   Graph your answer on the coordinate grid.

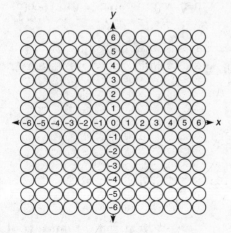

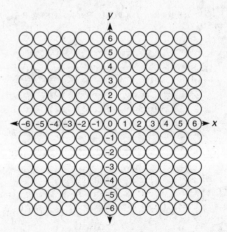

Answers and explanations begin on page 680.

ALGEBRA

Problem Solving

Key Ideas

- Guess and check is a strategy for answering complicated multiple-choice problems.
- Choose an answer from the options, and try the value in the problem. If it works, you have found the correct answer.

Using Guess and Check

One strategy that can help you save time on the more complicated algebra problems is **guess and check.** Guess and check means selecting one of the answer choices and trying that value in the problem. If you guess correctly, you can move on to the next question. If not, guess again. Guess and check is a good strategy for problems involving quadratic equations and expressions.

Example 1: Which of the following is a solution for the equation
$2x^2 - 12 = 2x$?

    (1)   4
    (2)   3
    (3)   0
    (4) −1
    (5) −3

To solve the problem, you would have to rewrite the equation so that the quadratic expression equals zero, factor the expression, and solve.

Instead, substitute each answer choice into the equation.

Option (1): $2x^2 - 12 = 2x$ Option (2): $2x^2 - 12 = 2x$
             $2(4)^2 - 12 = 2(4)$ $2(3)^2 - 12 = 2(3)$
                        $20 \neq 8$ $6 = 6$

Option (2) 3 makes the equation true.

GED TIP

Use your judgment. Do not use guess and check if you can quickly see how to solve the problem. Trying each answer choice may take longer than simply solving the problem.

Guess and check can also save time when writing an equation seems difficult.

Example 2: Terry is ten years older than his brother Tomas. Twenty years ago, Terry was twice as old as Tomas. How old is Terry now?

    (1) 25
    (2) 30
    (3) 40
    (4) 45
    (5) 60

Instead of writing an equation, try each age in the answer choices for Terry.

   (1) If Terry is 25 now, Tomas is 15. Twenty years ago, Tomas would not have been born.
   (2) If Terry is 30 now, Tomas is 20. Twenty years ago, Tomas would have been 0 years old, and Terry would have been 10.
   (3) If Terry is 40 now, Tomas is 30. Twenty years ago, Tomas would have been 10, and Terry would have been 20, which is twice as old as 10.

Therefore, **option (3) 40** is correct.

ALGEBRA ► PRACTICE 18

A. Use guess and check to solve the following problems.

1. A number divided by 2 is equal to 12 less than the original number. What is the number?

   (1) 12
   (2) 20
   (3) 24
   (4) 28
   (5) 36

2. For a fund-raiser, Sandra raised three times as much money as Barbara, and Barbara raised $50 more than Matt. Together they raised $950. How much money did Barbara raise?

   (1) $100
   (2) $150
   (3) $175
   (4) $200
   (5) $325

3. The three packages below weigh a total of 15 pounds.

   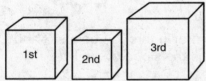

   The first package weighs twice as much as the second package. The third package weighs three times as much as the second package. How many pounds does the first package weigh?

   (1) $1\frac{1}{2}$
   (2) 2
   (3) 4
   (4) 5
   (5) $6\frac{1}{2}$

4. Hannah scored a total of 170 points on two math tests. The score of the first test was 6 points lower than the score of the second test. How many points did Hannah score on the first test?

   (1) 76
   (2) 82
   (3) 88
   (4) 90
   (5) 94

5. Nelson is twice as old as Maria. Six years ago, Nelson was five times as old as Maria. How old was Nelson six years ago?

   (1) 5
   (2) 10
   (3) 15
   (4) 20
   (5) 25

6. Which of the following is a solution for the quadratic equation $2x^2 + x - 15 = 0$?

   (1) −3
   (2) −1
   (3) 2
   (4) 3
   (5) 5

7. An amusement park sells adults' and children's passes. An adult's pass is $25, and a child's pass is $15. A group spent $440 on 20 passes. How many children's passes did the group purchase?

   (1) 3
   (2) 5
   (3) 6
   (4) 9
   (5) 14

8. The rectangular garden below is twice as long as it is wide. If the total distance around the garden is 120 feet, what is the width of the garden in feet?

   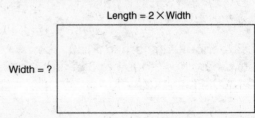

   (1) 10
   (2) 15
   (3) 20
   (4) 30
   (5) 40

   Answers and explanations begin on page 680.

Algebra Practice Questions

Part I
Directions: Choose the <u>one best answer</u> to each question. You <u>MAY</u> use your calculator.

1. Which of the following expressions is equal to $6 - 4(x + 3)$?

   (1) $4x + 3$
   (2) $4x - 9$
   (3) $-4x + 9$
   (4) $-4x - 3$
   (5) $-4x - 6$

2. Three increased by the product of four and a number is equal to the same number decreased by six. What is the number?

   (1) -3
   (2) -1
   (3) 0
   (4) 1
   (5) 3

3. What is the product of 700 and 180,000 written in scientific notation?

   (1) 126×10^9
   (2) 12.6×10^9
   (3) 1.26×10^8
   (4) 1.26×10^9
   (5) 1.26×10^{10}

4. The ordered pair $(-2, -1)$ is a solution to which of the following equations?

   (1) $4x + y = 7$
   (2) $-4x - y = 7$
   (3) $4x + y = -7$
   (4) $4x - y = -7$
   (5) $-4x + y = -7$

5. For a two-week period, Jan earned $150 less than twice Tom's earnings. Together Jan and Tom earned $1380. How much did Tom earn?

   (1) $870
   (2) $720
   (3) $660
   (4) $510
   (5) $360

Questions 6 and 7 refer to the following graph.

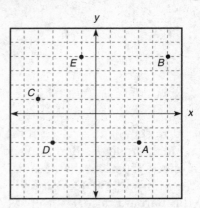

6. If the graph of the equation $y = -x - 5$ were drawn on the grid, which of the points would be on the line?

   (1) A
   (2) B
   (3) C
   (4) D
   (5) E

7. If a line were drawn through points B and C, what would be the slope of the line?

   (1) -3
   (2) $-\frac{1}{3}$
   (3) $\frac{1}{3}$
   (4) $\frac{2}{3}$
   (5) 3

8. Samuel is paid $350 per month plus a 10% commission on his total sales for the month. If he needs to earn at least $2,100 per month, which of the following expressions represents the total sales (s) Samuel needs to achieve?

   (1) $s \geq \$17,500$
   (2) $s \leq \$17,500$
   (3) $s \leq \$21,000$
   (4) $s \geq \$21,000$
   (5) $s \geq \$35,000$

9. For its Checking Plus account, a bank charges $3.95 per month plus $0.10 per check written over ten. The function to find the total monthly fee (F) is $F = \$3.95 + \$0.10(n - 10)$, where n = number of checks written.

Greg writes 24 checks in March. How much will he pay in fees for the month?

(1) $6.35
(2) $5.35
(3) $2.55
(4) $2.40
(5) $1.40

10. The sum of four consecutive odd numbers is 104. What is the largest number?

(1) 21
(2) 23
(3) 25
(4) 27
(5) 29

11. Which value for x makes the inequality $x > 400$ true?

(1) 7^3
(2) 4^4
(3) 3^6
(4) 5^3
(5) 6^3

12. Four less than the product of a number (x) and five is equal to eight more than two added to three times the number. Which of these equations could be used to find the value of x?

(1) $4 - 5x = 8 + 2 + 3x$
(2) $5x - 4 = 8 + 2 + 3x$
(3) $5x = 4 - 8 + 2 + 3x$
(4) $5x - 4 = 8 + 2 + 3$
(5) $4 - 5x = 8 + x(2 + 3)$

13. What is the value of the expression $6(x - y) - 8x$ when $x = -2$ and $y = 5$?

(1) -58
(2) -26
(3) -16
(4) 2
(5) 34

14. What is the next number in the sequence?

$1, 7, 14, 22, \ldots$

(1) 29
(2) 30
(3) 31
(4) 32
(5) 33

15. What is the value of the expression shown below?

$$4^3 - \frac{3(12 + 2^2)}{6} + 5(4) - 15$$

Mark your answer in the circles on the grid below.

16. The graphs of the equations $y = x + 3$ and $y = -2x - 3$ are drawn on a coordinate grid. At which point do the two lines intersect?

Graph your answer on the coordinate grid below.

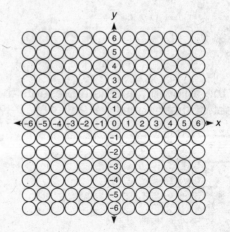

PART II

Directions: Choose the <u>one best answer</u> to each question. You <u>MAY NOT</u> use your calculator for these questions.

17. Which of the following shows the product of -7 and x decreased by the sum of 8 and y?

    (1) $-7x - (8 + y)$
    (2) $-7x - 8 + y$
    (3) $(8 + y) - 7x$
    (4) $7x - 8y$
    (5) $(7 + x) - (8 + y)$

18. What are the possible solutions for the quadratic equation $x^2 - 5x = 24$?

    (1) -8 and 3
    (2) -6 and 4
    (3) 8 and -3
    (4) 4 and -6
    (5) -12 and 2

19. Cynthia is 6 times as old as Rebecca. In 6 years, Cynthia will be only 3 times as old as Rebecca. How old is Rebecca now?

    (1) 3
    (2) 4
    (3) 8
    (4) 12
    (5) 24

20. The graph of which equation will pass through points $(0, -3)$ and $(5, 7)$?

    (1) $y = \frac{1}{2}x - 3$
    (2) $y = \frac{4}{5}x - 3$
    (3) $y = 2x - 3$
    (4) $y = 2x + 7$
    (5) $y = -2x + 3$

21. Which of the following graphs represents the solution set of the inequality $-2(x - 6) > 8$?

    (1)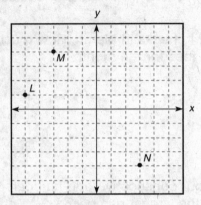
    (2)
    (3)
    (4)
    (5)

Questions 22 and 23 refer to the following graph.

22. Which of the following ordered pairs shows the location of point L?

    (1) $(-5, -1)$
    (2) $(-5, 1)$
    (3) $(-1, -5)$
    (4) $(-1, 5)$
    (5) $(1, -5)$

23. What is the distance in units from point N to point M?

    (1) 6
    (2) 8
    (3) 10
    (4) 12
    (5) 14

24. Bob, Celia, Sam, and Daniel contributed money to buy their boss a retirement gift. Sam and Daniel each gave the same amount of money. Celia gave $12 more than Daniel. Bob gave half as much as Celia gave. If the four workers gave a total of $81, how much did Sam give?

    (1) $9
    (2) $15
    (3) $18
    (4) $21
    (5) $30

25. What is the solution set of the inequality $-7x - 4 \geq x - 28$?

(1) $x \leq 3$
(2) $x \geq 3$
(3) $x \leq -3$
(4) $x \geq -4$
(5) $x \leq 4$

26. What is the value of the expression $5x^2 - xy + 7y^2$ when $x = 3$ and $y = -4$?

(1) -79
(2) -55
(3) 79
(4) 145
(5) 169

27. In a recent election, Perez got 5,512 more votes than 1/3 of the leading candidate's votes. Together the two candidates received 18,072 votes. How many people voted for Perez?

(1) 768
(2) 6,024
(3) 8,652
(4) 9,420
(5) 12,560

28. What is the value of x in the equation $-4(x + 2) - 10 = 5x$?

(1) $x = -18$
(2) $x = -2$
(3) $x = 0$
(4) $x = 2$
(5) $x = 18$

29. Marcia counts the $5 bills and $10 bills in her cash register drawer. She counts a total of 35 bills with a total value of $240. If $x =$ the number of $5 bills in the drawer, which of the following equations could be used to find the number of $5 bills in the drawer?

(1) $\$5x + \$10x = 35$
(2) $\$5x + \$10(35) = \$240$
(3) $\$5x + \$10x + 35 = \$240$
(4) $\$5(35 - x) + \$10x = \$240$
(5) $\$5x + \$10(35 - x) = \$240$

30. The total of five consecutive numbers is 370. What is the fourth number in the sequence?

(1) 72
(2) 73
(3) 74
(4) 75
(5) 76

31. A baseball pitcher's earned run average (E) is a function of the number of earned runs (r) given up and innings pitched (i). The function is written $E = \dfrac{9r}{i}$. What is the earned run average of a pitcher who gives up 8 runs in 18 innings?

Mark your answer in the circles on the grid below.

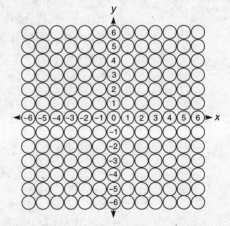

32. Point B is located halfway between $(-1,5)$ and $(-1,-3)$. Name the location of point B.

Graph your answer on the coordinate grid below.

Answers and explanations begin on page 681.

GEOMETRY

Points, Lines, and Angles

Key Ideas

- Most geometric figures are named by points that lie on the figure.
- Angles are measured in degrees and are classified by their measures.
- The sum of two complementary angles is 90°. The sum of two supplementary angles is 180°.

Basic Definitions

A **point** is a single location in space. We assign a name to a point by writing a letter next to it. A **plane** is a collection of points that extends to form a flat surface. In the drawing, point A lies on plane P.

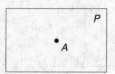

Much of your work in geometry will be concerned with lines and angles. A **line** is a straight pathway of points that extends indefinitely in two directions. A line may be named by a single letter or by two points on the line.

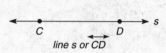

A **ray** is part of a line that begins at an endpoint and extends indefinitely in one direction. A portion of a line with two endpoints is called a **line segment.** Both rays and line segments are named using two points.

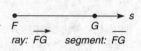

When two rays share an endpoint, they form an **angle.** The shared endpoint is the vertex of the angle. An angle can be named in different ways: by a number written in degrees inside the angle, by the vertex, or by the points on the angle. The symbol ∠ means angle.

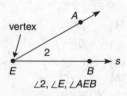

Angles are measured in degrees, indicated by a number and the symbol °. We classify angles by their measurement.

GED TIP

A geometric drawing may show several figures at once. As you read a problem, find each figure named in the problem.

A **right angle** forms a square corner and measures 90°. A right angle is often identified by a small square drawn inside it (see below).

An **acute angle** is less than 90°.

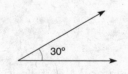

An **obtuse angle** is greater than 90° but less than 180°.

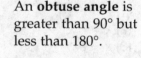

A **straight angle** measures 180°.

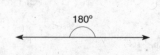

A **reflex angle** has a measure greater than 180° but less than 360°.

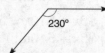

Some GED math problems are about angle relationships. When the sum of two angles is 90°, a right angle, the angles are **complementary.** When the sum of two angles is 180°, a line or straight angle, the angles are **supplementary.** You can use this information to solve for a missing angle measure.

Example 1: In the drawing, ∠AOB and ∠BOC are complementary. What is the measure of ∠AOB?

$$m\angle AOB + 23° = 90°$$
$$m\angle AOB = 90° - 23°$$
$$m\angle AOB = 67°$$

The measure of angle *BOC* is given as 23°, or $m\angle BOC = 23°$. The sum of the angles is 90°. Therefore, ∠AOB measures **67°**.

Example 2: In the drawing, ∠1 and ∠2 are supplementary. What is the measure of ∠1?

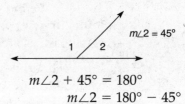

∠2 measures 45°. The sum of the angles is 180°. ∠1 measures **135°**.

$$m\angle 2 + 45° = 180°$$
$$m\angle 2 = 180° - 45°$$
$$m\angle 2 = 135°$$

GEOMETRY ▸ PRACTICE 1

A. Classify each angle based on its angle measure.

1. 55° 3. 180° 5. 270° 7. 30°
2. 95° 4. 18° 6. 90° 8. 110°

B. Choose the <u>one best answer</u> to each question.

<u>Questions 9 and 10</u> refer to the drawing below.

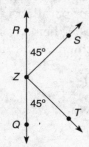

9. ∠QZR is a straight angle. What is the measure of ∠QZS?

(1) 135°
(2) 125°
(3) 90°
(4) 60°
(5) 45°

10. What kind of angle is ∠SZT?

(1) acute
(2) obtuse
(3) right
(4) straight
(5) reflex

<u>Questions 11 and 12</u> refer to the following drawing.

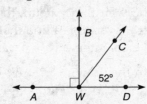

11. ∠AWD is a straight angle. What is the measure of ∠BWC?

(1) 38°
(2) 52°
(3) 128°
(4) 142°
(5) Not enough information is given.

12. What type of angle is ∠AWC?

(1) right
(2) acute
(3) obtuse
(4) reflex
(5) straight

Answers and explanations begin on page 682.

GEOMETRY

Parallel Lines and Transversals

Key Ideas

- Vertical angles, which are equal in measure, are formed when two lines intersect.
- When a transversal crosses two parallel lines, special angle relationships form.
- You can find the measure of any angle formed by the transversal if the measure of one angle is known.

Working with Vertical Angles and Transversals

When two lines intersect, they form two pairs of vertical angles. **Vertical angles** have the same angle measure. In the drawing, $\angle 1$ and $\angle 3$ are vertical angles, as are $\angle 2$ and $\angle 4$.

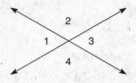

Intersecting lines also form adjacent angles. **Adjacent angles** share the same ray. For example, $\angle 1$ and $\angle 2$ are adjacent angles. The adjacent angles in this figure are supplementary angles because their sum is 180°, the measure of a straight angle. If you know the measure of one angle, you can find the measures of the other three angles.

Example 1: In the figure above, $m\angle 1 = 35°$. What are the measures of $\angle 2$, $\angle 3$, and $\angle 4$?

1. $\angle 1$ and $\angle 2$ are supplementary so their sum equals 180°. Solve for $\angle 2$.

   $m\angle + 35° = 180°$
   $m\angle 2 = 145°$

2. Angles 1 and 3 are vertical, so both measure 35°. Angles 2 and 4 are vertical, so both measure 145°.

   $m\angle 1 = 35°, m\angle 3 = 35°,$
   $m\angle 2 = 145°, m\angle 4 = 145°$

Parallel lines are lines that are exactly the same distance apart. No matter how far they extend, they will never touch. The symbol for parallel is ‖. A **transversal** is a line that intersects two or more other lines. When a transversal intersects two parallel lines, special angle relationships are formed.

In the drawing, $M \parallel N$. The transversal, line P, forms eight angles.

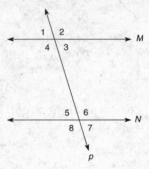

Each angle matches another angle in the same position on the transversal. These angles, called **corresponding angles,** always have the same measure. The corresponding angles are $\angle 1$ and $\angle 5$, $\angle 2$ and $\angle 6$, $\angle 3$ and $\angle 7$, and $\angle 4$ and $\angle 8$.

Alternate exterior angles, which are also equal in measure, are on opposite sides of the transversal and are on the outside of the parallel lines. One pair of alternate exterior angles is $\angle 1$ and $\angle 7$. The other is $\angle 2$ and $\angle 8$.

Alternate interior angles are on opposite sides of the transversals and are inside the parallel lines. One pair of alternate interior angles is $\angle 3$ and $\angle 5$. The other is $\angle 4$ and $\angle 6$. Alternate interior angles are always equal in measure.

Example 2: In the figure, $C \parallel D$. If $m\angle 4 = 48°$, what is the measure of $\angle 5$?

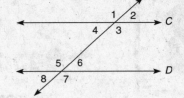

1. There are many ways to solve the problem. Here is one way: $\angle 4$ and $\angle 8$ are corresponding angles, so $m\angle 8 = 48°$.

2. $\angle 8$ and $\angle 5$ are supplementary angles, so $m\angle 5 + 48° = 180°$, and $m\angle 5 = 132°$.

GEOMETRY ▸ PRACTICE 2

A. Using the figure shown at the right, solve as directed.

1. List one pair of alternate interior angles.
2. Which angle corresponds to $\angle 7$?
3. If $m\angle 3 = 80°$, what is $m\angle 8$?
4. List one pair of alternate exterior angles.
5. List one pair of vertical angles.
6. Which angle corresponds to $\angle 8$?

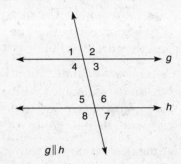

B. Choose the <u>one best answer</u> to each question.

Question 7 refers to the following figure.

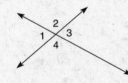

7. The measure of $\angle 3$ is 75°. What is the measure of $\angle 1$?

   (1) 50°
   (2) 75°
   (3) 105°
   (4) 115°
   (5) Not enough information is given.

8. Which of the following is a true statement about corresponding angles?

   (1) They are also vertical angles.
   (2) They are also supplementary angles.
   (3) They are in the same position from one parallel line to the other.
   (4) They are also alternate interior angles.
   (5) They are also alternate exterior angles.

Questions 9 and 10 refer to the following figure.

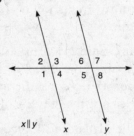

9. The measure of $\angle 7$ is 115°. What is the measure of $\angle 4$?

   (1) 25°
   (2) 65°
   (3) 115°
   (4) 245°
   (5) Not enough information is given.

10. Which of the following angles is equal in measure to $\angle 2$?

    (1) $\angle 1$
    (2) $\angle 3$
    (3) $\angle 5$
    (4) $\angle 7$
    (5) $\angle 8$

Answers and explanations begin on page 682.

GEOMETRY

Quadrilaterals

The Properties of Quadrilaterals

A **quadrilateral** is a closed shape with four sides. To prepare for the GED Math Test, learn the properties of each shape. You will need to identify the characteristics of different types of quadrilaterals and draw conclusions about their angles and sides.

Key Ideas

- Quadrilaterals are classified by the properties of their sides and angles.
- The sum of the interior angles of any quadrilateral is 360°.
- By using the properties of quadrilateral and algebraic reasoning, you can find missing angle measures.

You are already familiar with rectangles and squares. A **rectangle** is a four-sided figure with four right angles. The opposite sides (sides across from each other) are the same length, and they are parallel.

A **square** is actually a kind of rectangle. It, too, has four right angles with parallel opposite sides. However, a square has one additional property: its four sides are all the same length.

A **parallelogram** is a four-sided figure whose opposite sides are parallel and the same length. In addition, its opposite angles (the angles diagonally across from each other) are also equal in measure. A special parallelogram, called a **rhombus** (not shown), has four sides of equal length.

A **trapezoid** is a four-sided figure with exactly one pair of parallel sides. The definition of a trapezoid does not dictate the measure of the angles nor the lengths of the sides.

Sides with the same markings are equal.

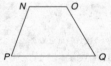

All quadrilaterals have one important property in common. The sum of the measures of the interior angles is 360°. You can use this fact to find a missing angle measure.

Example: In figure *ABCD*, the opposite sides are parallel. What is the measure of ∠*A*?

1. Identify the figure. The notation on the drawing tells you that the opposite sides are equal in measure. Since they are also parallel, the figure is a parallelogram.

2. Find the measure of ∠*C*. The opposite angles of a parallelogram are equal in measure; therefore, $m\angle C = m\angle B$. Both ∠*B* and ∠*C* measure 110°.

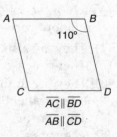

$\overline{AC} \parallel \overline{BD}$
$\overline{AB} \parallel \overline{CD}$

3. Find the measure of $\angle A$. You know the measures of $\angle A$ and $\angle D$ are equal and that the sum of all four angles equals 360°. Let $x = m\angle A$. Therefore, $2x$ = the sum of $m\angle A$ and $m\angle D$. Write an equation and solve.

$$2x + 100° + 110° = 360°$$
$$2x + 220° = 360°$$
$$2x = 140°$$
$$x = 70°$$

The measure of $\angle A$ is **70°**.

GEOMETRY ▸ PRACTICE 3

A. List the names of quadrilaterals with the following properties. Write *None* if no quadrilateral has the given property.

1. four right angles
2. opposite sides are equal in length
3. exactly one pair of parallel sides
4. all angles are equal in measure
5. only three right angles
6. opposite angles are equal in measure
7. all four sides are equal in length
8. sum of interior angles is 360°
9. sides are all of different lengths
10. four equal angles and four equal sides

B. Choose the <u>one best answer</u> to each question.

Questions 11 and 12 refer to the following figure.

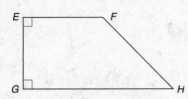

11. Angle *F* is 20° more than three times the measure of $\angle H$. What is the measure of $\angle F$?

    (1) 40°
    (2) 60°
    (3) 120°
    (4) 140°
    (5) 180°

12. In order for figure *EFGH* to be a trapezoid, which of the following must be a true statement?

    (1) *EF* is the same length as *FH*
    (2) *EF* ∥ *GH*
    (3) $m\angle F = m\angle H$
    (4) $m\angle G = m\angle F$
    (5) All sides must be of equal length.

Question 13 refers to the following figure.

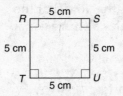

13. If the opposite sides in figure *RSUT* are parallel, what is the measure of $\angle R$?

    (1)   5°
    (2) 20°
    (3) 90°
    (4) 270°
    (5) Not enough information is given.

14. A quadrilateral has sides measuring 10, 15, 10, and 15. The opposite angles are equal, but there are no right angles. What is the figure?

    (1) square
    (2) rhombus
    (3) rectangle
    (4) parallelogram
    (5) trapezoid

Answers and explanations begin on page 682.

Geometry

Triangles

The Properties of Triangles

A **triangle** is a closed three-sided figure. From the definition, we can infer other properties. Since a triangle has three sides, it must also have three interior angles and three vertices.

A triangle is named by writing its vertices in any order. The triangle shown at right could be named ΔDEF. Its sides are DE, EF, and DF.

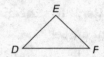

Triangles can be classified by the lengths of their sides and by the measures of their angles. In the figures below, sides with the same number of marks are equal.

Classified by Side Lengths

equilateral triangle	**isosceles triangle**	**scalene triangle**
All sides are equal in length. Note that the angles also are equal.	Exactly two sides are equal in length. Note that the two angles opposite these sides are equal.	No sides are equal in length, and no angles are equal.

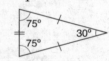
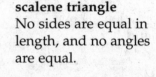

Classified by Angle Measures

right triangle	**acute triangle**	**obtuse triangle**
One angle measures 90°.	All angles measure less than 90°.	One angle is greater than 90°.

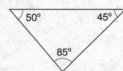
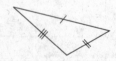
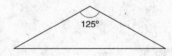

Each triangle can be classified in two ways.

Example 1: What kind of triangle is ΔPQR?

1. Classify by its sides: Two sides have the same length, so ΔPQR is an isosceles triangle.

2. Classify by its angles: $\angle P$ is a right angle, so ΔPQR is a right triangle.

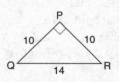

ΔPQR is a **right isosceles triangle.**

Key Ideas

- Triangles are named by their vertices.
- They are classified in two ways: by their side lengths and by their angle measures.
- The sum of the interior angles of any triangle is 180°.

GED TIP

Classify triangles by their properties, not by how they look. For example, the triangle in Example 1 may not look like a right triangle because the right angle is at the top.

The sum of the measures of the interior angles for any triangle is 180°. We can use this fact to solve for a missing angle.

Example 2: In △ABC, ∠A measures 55° and ∠B measures 100°. What is the measure of ∠C?

Write an equation and solve. $55° + 100° + ∠C = 180°$
$$155° + ∠C = 180°$$
$$∠C = 25°$$

The measure of ∠C is **25°**.

GEOMETRY ▸ PRACTICE 4

A. Classify each triangle in two ways.

1.

2.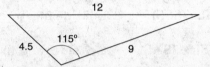

3.

B. Find the measure of the unknown angle in each triangle.

4.

5.

6.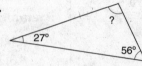

C. Choose the one best answer to each question.

Questions 7 and 8 refer to the following figure.

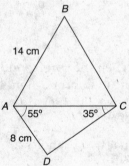

7. If ∠DAB measures 115° and ∠DCB measures 95°, what is the length of side AC in centimeters? (*Hint:* Use the facts in the problem to find m∠BAC and m∠BCA.)

  (1)   6
  (2)   8
  (3) 14
  (4) 22
  (5) Not enough information is given.

8. What kind of triangle is △ACD?

  (1) equilateral
  (2) isosceles
  (3) acute
  (4) right
  (5) obtuse

9. One angle in a scalene triangle measures 38°, and another angle measures 56°. What is the measure of the third angle?

  (1)   38°
  (2)   56°
  (3)   86°
  (4) 124°
  (5) 142°

Answers and explanations begin on page 683.

GEOMETRY

Congruent and Similar Triangles

Key Ideas

- Congruent figures are the same size and shape. Similar figures are the same shape, but they do not have to be the same size.
- Prove triangles are congruent using the rules SSS, SAS, or ASA.
- Triangles are similar if two angles are congruent or if all corresponding sides are in proportion.

Comparing Triangles

Figures are **congruent** (indicated by the symbol ≅) when they have exactly the same size and shape. In other words, two figures are congruent if their corresponding parts (the angles and sides) are congruent. You can often tell that two geometric shapes are congruent by looking. However, in geometry, you must be able to prove that figures are congruent.

Two triangles are congruent if the following corresponding parts are congruent:

Side-Side-Side (SSS)   The side measures for both triangles are the same.

Side-Angle-Side (SAS)   Two sides and the angle between them are the same.

Angle-Side-Angle (ASA)   Two angles and the side between them are the same.

Example 1: Are triangles *ABD* and *BCD* congruent?

1. Find the known corresponding parts: $\angle ABD \cong \angle CBD$ and $\angle ADB \cong \angle CDB$. Both triangles share side *BD*.

2. Is this enough information to prove the triangles are congruent? Yes, two angles and the side between them are equal. Using the ASA rule, **Δ *ABD* ≅ Δ*BCD*.**

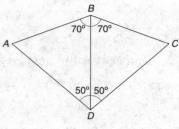

Understanding Similarity

Figures are **similar** (shown by the symbol ~) when the corresponding angles are congruent and the corresponding sides are in proportion. In other words, similar figures always have the same shape, but they do not have to be the same size.

There are two rules that you can use to prove that two triangles are similar:

Rule 1: If two angle measures in the first triangle are equal to two angle measures in the second triangle, the triangles are similar.

Rule 2: If all corresponding sides have the same ratio, the triangles are similar.

Example 2: Are triangles *JKL* and *MNO* similar?

1. Compare corresponding angles. Since only one angle measure is given, you cannot use Rule 1 to prove the triangles are similar.

2. Write ratios comparing the sides in the first triangle to the corresponding sides in the second triangle. Each ratio is equal to $\frac{1}{2}$.

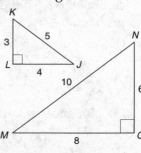

Since the ratios are equal, the triangles are similar: **ΔJKL ~ MNO.**

$$\frac{\Delta JKL}{\Delta MNO} \qquad \frac{3}{6} = \frac{4}{8} = \frac{5}{10} = \frac{1}{2}$$

GED TIP

When a figure is flipped or turned, it may be difficult to identify corresponding parts. Try redrawing one of the figures so that it is turned to match the first figure. Always label your sketch carefully.

If you know that two triangles are similar, you can use proportion to find an unknown measure.

Example 3: $\triangle XYZ \sim \triangle STU$. What is the measure of side ST?

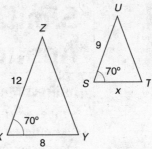

Side SU corresponds to side XZ, and side ST corresponds to side XY. Set up a proportion and solve.

$$\frac{SU}{XZ} = \frac{ST}{XY} \qquad \frac{9}{12} = \frac{x}{8} \qquad 12x = 72 \qquad x = 6$$

Side ST measures **6 units**.

GEOMETRY ▸ PRACTICE 5

A. For these items, the figures are not drawn to scale. Decide whether the triangles are congruent. Write *Yes, No,* or *Not Enough Information.*

1. 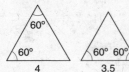 2. 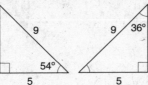 3.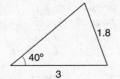

B. Choose the **one best answer** to each question.

Questions 4 and 5 refer to the following figure.

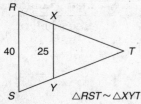

$\triangle RST \sim \triangle XYT$

4. What is the measure of side ST if side YT measures 30 units?

(1) 30
(2) 40
(3) 45
(4) 48
(5) 55

5. If $m\angle S = 68°$ and $m\angle T = 48°$, what is the measure of $\angle TXY$?

(1) 48°
(2) 64°
(3) 68°
(4) 116°
(5) Not enough information is given.

Question 6 refers to the following figure.

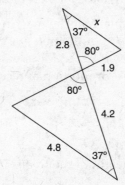

6. What is the measure of the side labeled x?

(1) 2.5
(2) 2.9
(3) 3.2
(4) 3.8
(5) 4.7

Answers and explanations begin on page 683.

GEOMETRY

Similar Triangle Applications

Key Ideas

- Use triangle relationships to indirectly measure distances.
- Objects and their shadows form similar triangles because the sun strikes both at the same angle.
- Use the corresponding angles and sides in similar triangles to measure the distance across a large object.

Indirect Measurement

Similar triangles are often used to measure objects that would be impossible to measure using ordinary tools. This process is called **indirect measurement**.

One common application involves using shadows to find the height of a tall object. In the diagram, both a man and a tree cast shadows at the same time of day. Since the angle of the sun is the same for both the man and tree, two similar triangles are formed.

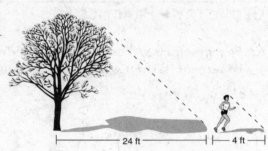

We can easily measure the two shadows using ordinary tools. We can also measure the man's height. Using these facts, we can solve for the height of the tree.

Example 1: If the man in the diagram is 6 feet tall, what is the height of the tree?

Write a proportion and solve. $\dfrac{\text{man's shadow}}{\text{tree's shadow}}$ $\dfrac{4}{24} = \dfrac{6}{x}$ $\dfrac{\text{man's height}}{\text{tree's height}}$

$$24(6) = 4x$$
$$144 = 4x$$
$$36 = x$$

The height of the tree is **36 feet.**

We also use indirect measurement to measure distance across a large object.

Example 2: An engineer needs to know the width of a small lake. Using surveyor's tools, she marks off two similar triangles. She measures the distances shown on the diagram. Using her findings, what is the width of the lake?

The 10-ft side corresponds to the 25-ft side. The 24-ft side of the small triangle corresponds to the lake's width.

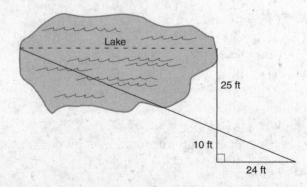

$$\frac{10}{25} = \frac{24}{x} \qquad 25(24) = 10x$$
$$600 = 10x$$
$$60 = x$$

The lake is **60 feet wide.**

GED TIP

Sometimes you can easily see the scale used in a problem. In Example 1, the tree's shadow is six times the man's shadow; therefore, the tree's height must be six times the man's height: 6 × 6 = 36 ft.

Choose the <u>one best answer</u> to each question.

1. An 8-foot-tall street sign casts a 6-foot shadow at the same time that a building casts a 48-foot shadow. How many feet tall is the building?

   (1) 36
   (2) 54
   (3) 64
   (4) 96
   (5) 100

Question 2 refers to the following diagram.

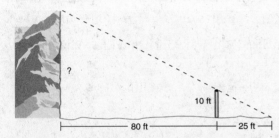

2. To find the height of a cliff, a surveyor puts a 10-foot pole in the ground, 80 feet from the base of the cliff. He then determines the point on the ground from which he can sight both the top of the pole and top of the cliff. Using the distances shown in the diagram, what is the height of the cliff?

   (1) 32
   (2) 42
   (3) 105
   (4) 200
   (5) Not enough information is given.

3. A meter stick is placed in the ground near a flagpole. At the time that the meter stick casts a shadow 2.5 meters in length, the flagpole casts a shadow 22.5 meters long. Which of the following proportions can be used to find the height of the flagpole (x) in meters?

   (1) $\frac{2.5}{22.5} = \frac{1}{x}$
   (2) $\frac{2.5}{22.5} = \frac{x}{1}$
   (3) $\frac{22.5}{2.5} = \frac{1}{x}$
   (4) $\frac{1}{2.5} = \frac{22.5}{x}$
   (5) $\frac{22.5}{1} = \frac{x}{2.5}$

Question 4 refers to the following diagram.

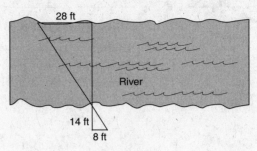

4. To find the distance across a river, a surveyor marks off two similar right triangles. Using the distances shown in the diagram, what is the distance, in feet, from one bank of the river to the other?

   (1) 32
   (2) 36
   (3) 39
   (4) 42
   (5) 49

5. Phil is building a frame to hold a hammock. He wants to place a metal brace across the frame as shown in the drawing below. If he places the brace as shown in the diagram, what will be the length of the brace in feet?

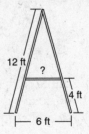

   (1) 3
   (2) 4
   (3) 5
   (4) 6
   (5) 8

Answers and explanations begin on page 683.

GEOMETRY

Perimeter and Area

Key Ideas

- Perimeter is the distance around a figure.
- Area is the measure of the space inside a flat figure. It is measured in square units.
- Area and perimeter formulas are listed on the GED formulas page.

Perimeter and Area of Common Figures

Perimeter is the distance around a figure. To find perimeter, simply add the lengths of the sides. For common figures, you can apply a formula to find the perimeter. On the GED formulas page (see page 688), the formulas are written in words. They can also be written using variables. Both are shown below.

square	Perimeter = $4 \times$ side	$P = 4s$
rectangle	Perimeter = $2 \times$ length + $2 \times$ width	$P = 2l + 2w$
triangle	Perimeter = side$_1$ + side$_2$ + side$_3$	$P = a + b + c$

Example 1: A rectangle is 16 inches long and 9 inches wide. What is the perimeter of the rectangle?

Use the formula: Perimeter = $2 \times$ length + $2 \times$ width
$$= 2 \times 16 + 2 \times 9$$
$$= 32 + 18$$
$$= \textbf{50 in}$$

Area is the measure of the space inside a flat figure. Area is measured in square units. For example, if the sides of a figure are measured in inches, its area will be measured in square inches. The formulas for finding area are shown below.

square	Area = side^2	$A = s^2$
rectangle	Area = length $\times$ width	$A = lw$
parallelogram	Area = base $\times$ height	$A = bh$
triangle	Area = $\frac{1}{2} \times$ base $\times$ height	$A = \frac{1}{2}bh$
trapezoid	Area = $\frac{1}{2} \times$ (base$_1$ + base$_2$) $\times$ height	$A = \frac{1}{2}(b_1 + b_2)h$

GED TIP

To better understand area formulas, study what they have in common. Squares, rectangles, and parallelograms all multiply base and height.

A triangle is $\frac{1}{2}$ a parallelogram, so multiply the area formula for a parallelogram by $\frac{1}{2}$ to find the area of a triangle. To find the area of a trapezoid, multiply the average of the bases by height.

Three of the formulas mention two new measures: base and height. The **base** is one side of the figure. The **height** is the length from the vertex to the base, forming a right angle to the base.

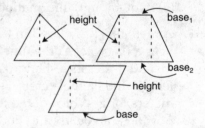

Example 2: Find the area of figure *ABCD*.

1. Identify the figure. *ABCD* is a parallelogram.

2. Find the facts you need. To use the formula for finding the area of a parallelogram, you need to know the height and the length of the base. Ignore the length of side *BD*.

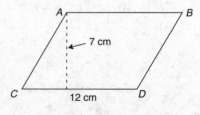

3. Use the formula Area = base $\times$ height.

Area = 12×7
$$= \textbf{84 sq cm or 84 cm}^2$$

A. Find the area and perimeter of each figure.

1.

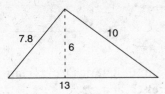

2.

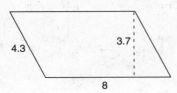

3.

4.

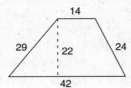

5.

6.

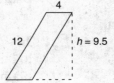

B. Choose the <u>one best answer</u> to each question.

<u>Question 7</u> refers to the following figure.

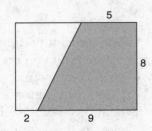

7. What is the area in square inches of the shaded portion of the rectangle?

- (1) 28
- (2) 38
- (3) 40
- (4) 56
- (5) 88

8. The four sides of a parallelogram measure 9 feet, 6 feet, 9 feet, and 6 feet. What is the area of the parallelogram in square feet?

- (1) 30
- (2) 36
- (3) 54
- (4) 81
- (5) Not enough information is given.

9. Martin is building a rectangular patio centered on one side of his yard. The rest of his yard, shown in the diagram, is planted in grass.

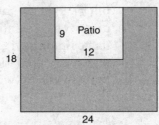

If the measurements in the diagram are in feet, what is the square footage of the grass portion of Martin's yard?

- (1) 108
- (2) 162
- (3) 288
- (4) 324
- (5) 432

10. A square measures 6 centimeters on one side. What is the perimeter of the square in centimeters?

- (1) 12
- (2) 24
- (3) 36
- (4) 216
- (5) Not enough information is given.

Answers and explanations begin on page 683.

GEOMETRY

Circles

Key Ideas

- On the GED Math Test, pi (π) ≈ 3.14.
- To find circumference, multiply pi by the diameter (distance across) the circle.
- The radius is the distance from the center to the edge of the circle. To find area, multiply pi by the square of the radius.

Circumference and Area

A **circle** is a closed set of points that are all the same distance from a single point, the center of the circle. The **circumference** of a circle is its perimeter, or the distance around the circle. The area of a circle is the space inside the circle.

To find perimeter and area of a circle, you need to know two other measures of a circle. The **diameter** is a line segment with endpoints on the circle that passes through the center of the circle. The **radius** is a line segment that connects the center of the circle to any point on the circle. As you can see from the diagram, the radius is one-half the diameter.

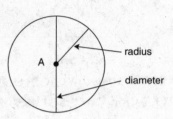

The formulas for circumference and area use a special quantity called **pi** (π). Pi is the ratio of the circumference to the diameter. If you push the pi key on a scientific calculator, the display will show a long string of digits beginning with 3.14. As far as we know, the digits for pi continue infinitely, so calculations with pi are always approximations. For the GED Math Test, you will use 3.14 as the value of pi. Below is the formula for finding the circumference of a circle.

Circumference = $\pi \times$ diameter, or $C = \pi d$

Example 1: A china plate has a gold rim. If the plate's diameter is 10.5 inches, what is the distance around the rim to the nearest tenth of an inch?

Use the formula: $\quad C = \pi d$
$\quad\quad\quad\quad\quad\quad = 3.14(10.5)$
$\quad\quad\quad\quad\quad\quad = 32.97$, which rounds to **33.0 inches**

Use this formula to find the area of a circle: Area = $\pi \times$ radius^2, or $A = \pi r^2$.

Example 2: The circular surface of a satellite component must be covered with heat-resistant tiles. If the radius of the component is 4 meters, what is the area in square meters?

Use the formula: $\quad A = \pi r^2$
$\quad\quad\quad\quad\quad\quad = 3.14(4^2)$
$\quad\quad\quad\quad\quad\quad = 3.14(16)$
$\quad\quad\quad\quad\quad\quad = $ **50.24 square meters**

In some situations, you may need to solve for either the diameter or radius. Remember, the diameter is twice the radius ($d = 2r$), and the radius is one-half the diameter: $r = \frac{1}{2}d$.

GED TIP

To estimate the area or circumference of a circle, use 3 for pi. You may be able to eliminate most incorrect answer choices using only an estimate. Estimating is also a good way to check your work.

Example 3: What is the circumference of circle *B* to the nearest tenth of a centimeter?

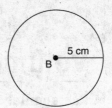

1. The radius of the circle is 5 cm. Therefore, the diameter is 2 × 5, or 10 cm.

2. Use the formula: $C = \pi d$
$$= 3.14(10)$$
$$= \textbf{31.4 cm}$$

GEOMETRY ▸ PRACTICE 8

A. Find the circumference and area of each circle. Round answers to the nearest tenth.

1.
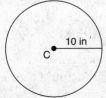

2.
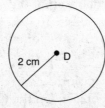

3.
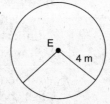

B. Choose the <u>one best answer</u> to each question.

<u>Questions 4 and 5</u> refer to the following drawing.

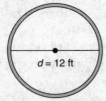

4. If workers lay a tile border around the edge of the fountain shown in the diagram, how many feet long will the border be to the nearest foot?

   (1) 19
   (2) 36
   (3) 38
   (4) 57
   (5) 113

5. Which of the following expressions could be used to find the area of the bottom surface of the fountain?

   (1) 3.14 × 6
   (2) 3.14 × 6^2
   (3) 3.14 × 12
   (4) 3.14 × 12^2
   (5) Not enough information is given.

6. The radius of a circle is 6.5 cm. What is the diameter of the circle in centimeters?

   (1) 3.25
   (2) 13.0
   (3) 33.16625
   (4) 40.82
   (5) 132.665

7. On the target below, the 5- and 10-point bands are each 2 inches wide, and the inner circle has a diameter of 2 inches.

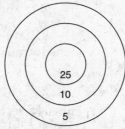

To the nearest inch, what is the outer circumference of the 10-point band?

   (1) 6
   (2) 13
   (3) 19
   (4) 113
   (5) Not enough information is given.

Answers and explanations begin on page 683.

GEOMETRY

Volume

Rectangular Solids, Cubes, and Cylinders

Volume, also called **capacity,** is the measure of space inside a three-dimensional object. You measure volume in cubic units. In other words, if the sides of an object are measured in inches, the volume is the number of cubes (one inch per side) you would need to fill the object.

Many common three-dimensional objects have at least two identical and parallel faces. Think of a cereal box or a soup can. Both objects have identical faces at the top and bottom of the container. Either of these faces can be called the base of the object. To find the volume of any container with identical bases, multiply the area of one base by the height of the object: Volume = Area of base × height.

Another way to find the volume of an object is to use the formula that applies specifically to that object. On the GED formulas page (see page 688), you will be given the following volume formulas:

rectangular solid	Volume = length × width × height	$V = lwh$
cube	Volume = edge³	$V = e^3$
cylinder	Volume = pi × radius² × height	$V = \pi r^2 h$

In the examples below, formulas are used to find the answers, but the problems can also be solved by simply multiplying the area of the base by the height.

A **rectangular solid** has two identical rectangular bases. The remaining sides of the solid are also rectangles.

Example 1: A cardboard box has the dimensions shown in the diagram. What is the volume of the box in cubic feet?

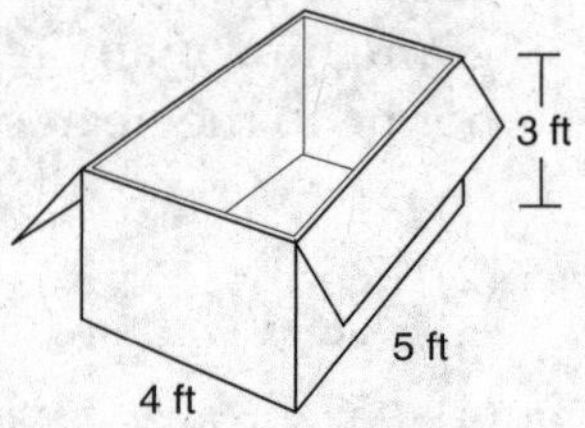

Use the formula: $V = lwh$

$$= 5(4)(3) = \textbf{60 cubic feet}$$

A **cube** is a rectangular solid with six identical faces. In a cube, each edge (where the sides meet) is the same length.

Example 2: A wood block measures 2 inches per edge. What is the volume of the block?

Use the formula: $V = e^3$

$$= 2^3 = \textbf{8 cubic feet}$$

A **cylinder** has two circular bases. The bases are connected by a curved surface. Cans, barrels, and tanks are often in the shape of cylinders.

Key Ideas

- Volume is measured in cubic units that may be written using an exponent: 6 cubic inches or 6 in³.
- Find volume by multiplying the area of one base by the height of the object.
- You can also use formulas to find volume.

GED TIP

Learn which area formula goes with which shape. Once you know the area formulas, you can change them to volume by putting an h at the end. Compare:
Area of circle: πr^2
Volume of circle: $\pi r^2 h$

Example 3: A storage tank has a radius of 1.5 meters. What is the volume of the tank to the nearest cubic meter?

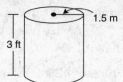

Use the formula: $V = \pi r^2 h$

$$= 3.14(1.5^2)(3) = 21.195 \text{ m}^3,$$

which rounds to **21 cubic meters**

GEOMETRY ▸ PRACTICE 9.1

A. Find the volume of each object to the nearest whole unit.

1.

3.

5.

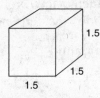

2.

4.

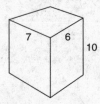

6.

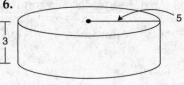

B. Choose the <u>one best answer</u> to each question.

Question 7 refers to the following drawing.

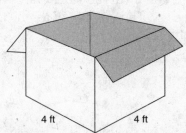

7. A rectangular box with a volume of 80 cubic feet has the length and width shown in the drawing. What is the height of the box?

(1) 5
(2) 10
(3) 16
(4) 20
(5) Not enough information is given.

8. A wooden crate measures 5 feet along each edge. What is the crate's volume in cubic feet?

(1) 15
(2) 25
(3) 125
(4) 150
(5) Not enough information is given.

Question 9 refers to the following drawing.

9. Linda adds a water stabilizer to her children's swimming pool once a week. The instructions tell her to add one scoop of the product for every 20 cubic feet of water. About how many scoops should she add per week?

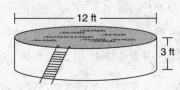

(1) 2
(2) 3
(3) 6
(4) 17
(5) 36

Answers and explanations begin on page 684.

Volume of Pyramids and Cones

A **pyramid** is a three-dimensional object with three triangle faces that connect to the same vertex. The base of a pyramid can be any closed figure, but the pyramids that you will see on the GED Math Test will all have square bases.

The rectangular solid and the pyramid shown here both have identical square bases and the same height. Compare the two figures. As you can see, the pyramid holds much less than the rectangular solid. In fact, it holds only one-third of the rectangular solid's volume.

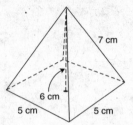

On the GED formulas page (see page 688), the formula for finding the volume of a pyramid is as written below. Notice that (base edge)^2 equals the area of the square base. The height of a pyramid is the perpendicular distance from the base to the vertex at the top.

square pyramid   Volume = $\frac{1}{3} \times$ (base edge)$^2 \times$ height

Example 1: Find the volume of the pyramid shown below.

The length of a base edge is 5 cm. The height of the pyramid is 6 cm. Ignore the diagonal edges.

Apply the formula: $V = \frac{1}{3}e^2h$

$\qquad = \frac{1}{3}(5^2)(6)$

$\qquad = \frac{1}{3}(25)(6)$

$\qquad = \textbf{50 cm}^3$

A **cone** is similar to a cylinder. Both have a circular base and a curved side. The curved side of a cone slants inward so that it meets at a point, or vertex. The volume of a cone is $\frac{1}{3}$ of the volume of a cylinder with the same size base and height.

On the GED formulas page, the formula for volume of a cone is as follows. Notice that the formula contains the formula for finding the area of a circle (πr^2).

cone   Volume = $\frac{1}{3} \times \pi \times$ radius$^2 \times$ height

Example 2: Find the volume of the cone shown below.

The radius of the base is 2 inches, and the height is 9 inches.

Apply the formula: $V = \frac{1}{3}\pi r^2 h$

$\qquad = \frac{1}{3}(3.14)(2^2)(9)$

$\qquad = \frac{1}{3}(3.14)(4)(9)$

$\qquad = \textbf{37.68 in}^3$

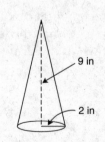

Note: In volume formulas for cones and square pyramids, the factor $\frac{1}{3}$ is shown first. Don't begin with this factor. Multiply the other factors first and then divide by 3, unless the numbers are easily divided by 3.

GEOMETRY ▶ PRACTICE 9.2

A. Find the volume of each object to the nearest unit.

1.
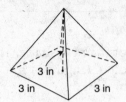
3 in
3 in   3 in

3.
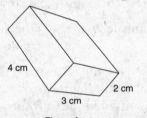
5 cm
12 cm

5.
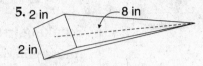
2 in   8 in
2 in

2.
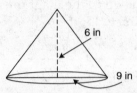
6 in
9 in

4.
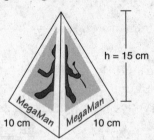
10 m
13.1 m
12 m   12 m

6.
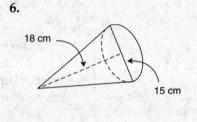
18 cm
15 cm

B. Choose the one best answer to each question.

7. Advertisers have designed this pyramid-shaped package to hold action figures.

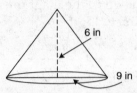

h = 15 cm

MegaMan   MegaMan
10 cm   10 cm

After testing the design, the manufacturer decides to increase both the length and width of the base by 4 cm. How many more cubic centimeters will the new package hold than the package shown above?

(1) 2940
(2) 980
(3) 500
(4) 480
(5)   96

8. The height of a cone is $\frac{1}{2}$ the diameter of its base. If the cone's height is 4 inches, what is the cone's volume to the nearest cubic inch?

(1)   21
(2)   48
(3)   67
(4) 268
(5) Not enough information is given.

9. Which of the following is a true statement about the figures shown below?

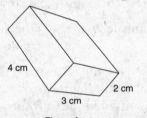   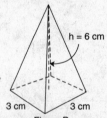
4 cm   h = 6 cm
2 cm
3 cm   3 cm   3 cm
Figure A   Figure B

(1) The volume of A equals the volume of B.
(2) The volume of B is greater than the volume of A.
(3) The volume of A is twice as great as the volume of B.
(4) Both A and B have a volume greater than 20 cubic centimeters.
(5) The volume of B is less than the volume of A.

10. A cone's base is a circle with a radius of 8 inches. The cone's height is 15 inches. What is the cone's estimated volume in cubic inches?

(1) 125
(2) 250
(3) 500
(4) 1000
(5) 4000

Answers and explanations begin on page 684.

GEOMETRY

Irregular Figures

Key Ideas

- Irregular figures are made from two or more regular figures.
- To find the perimeter of an irregular figure, add the lengths of all the sides.
- To find area or volume of an irregular figure, break the figure into parts, and find the area or volume of each part; then combine the results.

Breaking Irregular Figures Into Parts

An irregular figure combines geometric figures to form a new shape. To find the perimeter of an irregular figure, simply add the lengths of the sides. You may need to solve for one or more missing lengths.

Example 1: A family room has the dimensions shown in the diagram. All measures are in feet. What is the perimeter of the room?

1. Find the missing measures. Measurement x equals the combined lengths of the two opposite walls: $x = 8 + 4 = 12$ ft. You also know that $18 - 10 = y$, so $y = 8$ ft.

2. Add all distances to find the perimeter.
   $12 + 18 + 8 + 8 + 4 + 10 = $ **60 ft**

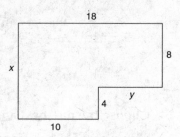

To find the area or volume of an irregular figure, break the figure into parts. Then apply the correct formula to each part.

Example 2: What is the area of the figure in square centimeters?

1. Divide the figure into two shapes, and find any missing measurements. Here the figure is divided into a trapezoid and a rectangle.

2. Calculate the area of each shape.
   Rectangle: $A = lw$
   $\qquad\quad = 2(5) = 10$ sq cm

   Trapezoid: $A = \frac{1}{2}(b_1 + b_2)h$
   $\qquad\quad = \frac{1}{2}(5 + 7)(3) = 18$ sq cm

3. Combine. $10 + 18 = $ **28 sq cm**

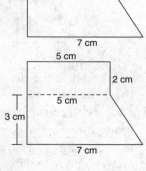

GED TIP

There is usually more than one way to break down an irregular figure. Solve the problem the way that seems easiest to you. The answer will be the same.

Example 3: Find the volume of the container shown below.

Break the figure into a cylinder and a cone, and find the volume of each.

1. Cylinder: $V = \pi r^2 h$
   $\qquad\quad = (3.14)(1^2)(2) = 6.28$ m^3
2. Cone: $V = \frac{1}{3}\pi r^2 h$
   $\qquad\quad = \frac{1}{3}(3.14)(1^2)(1.5) = 1.57$ m^3

3. Combine. $6.28 + 1.57 = $ **7.85 m^3** or **7.85 cu m**

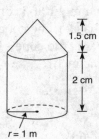

A. Find the perimeter and area of each figure.

1.

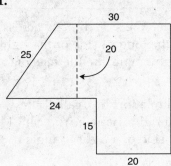

30
25
20
24
15
20

2.

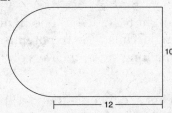

10

|← 12 →|

(*Hint:* Think of the figure as
a rectangle and a half circle.)

3.

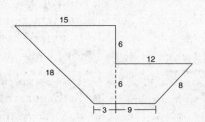

15
6
12
18
6
8
|←3→|←9→|

B. Find the volume of each figure to the nearest cubic unit.

4.

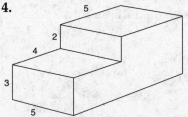

5
2
4
3
5

5.

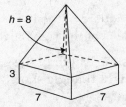

$h = 8$
3
7   7

6.

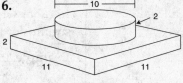

|← 10 →|
2
2
11   11

C. Choose the <u>one best answer</u> to each question.

7. A slab of concrete will have four concrete
blocks in each corner as shown in the
drawing below.

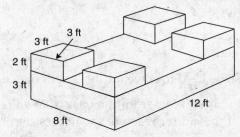

3 ft
3 ft
2 ft
3 ft
12 ft
8 ft

If each corner block has the same dimensions, what is the volume of the structure
in cubic feet?

(1) 360
(2) 288
(3) 168
(4) 72
(5) Not enough information is given.

8. A candy package is in the shape of a
cylinder with a cone on each end.

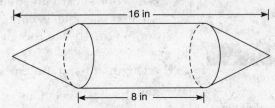

|← 16 in →|

|← 8 in →|

If the radius of the cylinder is 2 inches
and the cones are identical, what is the
capacity of the container to the nearest
cubic inch?

(1) 201
(2) 134
(3) 128
(4) 100
(5) 33

**Answers and explanations begin on
page 684.**

GEOMETRY

Pythagorean Relationship

Key Ideas

- The hypotenuse is the longest side of a right triangle. It is found opposite the right angle.
- The sum of the squares of the legs of a right triangle equals the square of the hypotenuse.

As you know, a right triangle has one right angle. The side directly across from the right angle, called the **hypotenuse,** is the longest side of the right triangle. The remaining sides, the rays of the right angle, are the **legs** of the triangle.

Thousands of years ago, people found a special relationship, called the **Pythagorean relationship,** among the sides of a right triangle. You can use this relationship to find the measure of any side of a right triangle if the other two side measures are known.

Pythagorean relationship $a^2 + b^2 = c^2$; a and b are legs, and c the hypotenuse of a right triangle

In other words, the square of the hypotenuse is equal to the sum of the squares of the two legs of the right triangle.

Example 1: What is the length of the hypotenuse of the right triangle shown in the diagram?

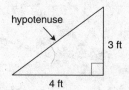

1. The lengths of the legs are 3 ft and 4 ft. Let one leg equal a and the other equal b.

2. Solve for c. Substitute the values.

$$a^2 + b^2 = c^2$$
$$3^2 + 4^2 = c^2$$

3. When one side of an equation equals a squared variable, isolate the variable by finding the square root of both sides.

$$9 + 16 = c^2$$
$$25 = c^2$$
$$\sqrt{25} = c$$
$$5 = c$$

The length of the hypotenuse is **5 feet.**

The Pythagorean relationship can also be used to solve for the length of a leg.

Example 2: If John places a 13-foot ladder 3 feet from the base of a wall, how far up the wall will the ladder reach to the nearest tenth foot?

The wall, ground, and ladder form a right triangle. The hypotenuse is 13 ft in length. One leg is 3 ft. You need to find the length of the other leg.

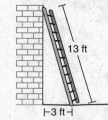

$$a^2 + b^2 = c^2$$
$$3^2 + b^2 = 13^2$$
$$9 + b^2 = 169$$
$$b^2 = 160$$
$$b = \sqrt{160}$$
$$b \approx 12.6$$

The ladder will extend **12.6 feet** up the wall. Note: Most of the time, you will need to use your calculator for the final step when using the Pythagorean relationship. To find the square root of 160 on the *Casio fx-260* calculator , press: 160 $\boxed{\text{SHIFT}}\boxed{x^2}$.

A. The lengths of two sides of a right triangle are given. Find the length of the remaining side to the nearest tenth unit. You may use a calculator.

1. leg *a*: 8 in
   leg *b*: 8 in
   hypotenuse *c*: ? in

2. leg *a*: 9 yd
   leg *b*: 12 yd
   hypotenuse *c*: ? yd

3. leg *a*: 1.5 cm
   leg *b*: 2 cm
   hypotenuse *c*: ? cm

4. leg *a*: ? m
   leg *b*: 3 m
   hypotenuse *c*: 6 m

5. leg *a*: 6 mm
   leg *b*: ? mm
   hypotenuse *c*: 10 mm

6. leg *a*: ? ft
   leg *b*: 5 ft
   hypotenuse *c*: 18 ft

7. leg *a*: 7 cm
   leg *b*: 10 cm
   hypotenuse *c*: ? cm

8. leg *a*: 15 in
   leg *b*: ? in
   hypotenuse *c*: 30 in

9. leg *a*: 4 km
   leg *b*: 5 km
   hypotenuse *c*: ? km

B. Choose the one best answer to each question.

10. On a coordinate plane, points *A*, *B*, and *C* can be connected to form a right triangle.

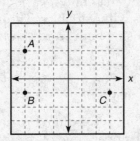

What is the distance from *A* to *C*, to the nearest tenth unit? (*Hint:* Count units to find the lengths of the sides, and use the Pythagorean relationship to find the distance between the points.)

    (1) 5.2
    (2) 6.7
    (3) 8.4
    (4) 10.1
    (5) 22.5

11. The two shorter sides of a right triangle measure 18 ft and 24 ft. What is the measure in feet of the third side?

    (1) 25
    (2) 28
    (3) 30
    (4) 42
    (5) Not enough information is given.

12. Jan has built a rectangular frame out of wood to use for the bottom of a platform. He wants to add a diagonal brace as shown in the drawing below.

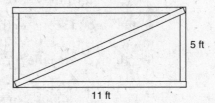

What will the length of the brace be to the nearest tenth foot?

    (1) 16.0
    (2) 13.7
    (3) 12.8
    (4) 12.1
    (5) 11.5

13. The hypotenuse of a right triangle measures 39 inches. If one leg measures 15 inches, what is the measure of the other leg?

    (1) 42
    (2) 36
    (3) 24
    (4) 18
    (5) 12

Answers and explanations begin on page 684.

Using the Formulas Page

Key Ideas

- The GED formulas page will contain all the formulas you might need on the GED Math Test.
- The formulas on the page are written in words and are organized by purpose.
- Memorize as many formulas as you can in case you don't have time to look up every formula.

Using Formulas on the GED Math Test

The GED formulas page lists all the formulas you might need to solve some of the questions on the test. For your convenience, this page is reprinted on page 688 of this book. Look at the page now, and pay close attention to how the formulas are organized. As you can see, the formulas are grouped by purpose. For example, all the area formulas are contained in the first group.

To get the best score possible, you should have the formulas on this page memorized. However, if you forget a formula or are unsure during the test, you can quickly check this list to find the right formula.

The formulas on the GED formulas page are written with words instead of with variables. This eliminates the confusion of knowing what each variable represents. On the other hand, you may find it easier to memorize the formulas if you replace the words with variables. Throughout this book, the formulas have been presented using both words and variables.

To get a good score on the GED Math Test, you need to use the right formula at the right time. Think about the situation presented in the problem; then choose the formula that makes sense.

Example: Ryan plans to put crown molding in his dining room. The molding will be attached to the upper edge of the four walls of the room. The room is 14 ft by 12 ft. The walls are 7 ft high. Which of the following expressions could be used to find the amount of molding Ryan should buy?

(1) 14(12)
(2) 2(14) + 2(12)
(3) 4(14)
(4) (14)(12)(7)
(5) $\frac{1}{2}$(14)(7)

GED TIP

To memorize the formulas, think about what they have in common. For example, the area formulas for squares, rectangles, and parallelograms all multiply base and height.

1. Choose the correct formula. The distance around the upper edge of the four walls is the perimeter of the room. (You don't need to use the height of the ceiling to find the perimeter.) Since the room is rectangular, use the formula: Perimeter = 2 × length + 2 × width.

2. Compare the answer choices to the formula. Only option (2) multiplies both the length and the width by 2 and then adds the products. The correct answer is **(2) 2(14) + 2(12).**

Now look at the incorrect options. All apply incorrect formulas for this situation. Option (1) finds the area of the ceiling. Option (3) finds the perimeter of a square. Option (4) finds the volume in cubic feet of the rectangular room, and option (5) finds the area of a triangle with a base of 14 ft and a height of 7 ft.

Choose the <u>one best answer</u> to each question.

<u>Questions 1 and 2</u> refer to the drawing.

├──── 15 ft ────┤

1. Don is installing the fishpond shown in the diagram at a children's health clinic. If the pond is 1.5 feet deep, which of the following expressions could be used to find how many cubic feet of water the pond will hold?

   (1) $1.5(15)$
   (2) $1.5(7.5^2)$
   (3) $\pi(15)$
   (4) $\pi(15)(1.5)$
   (5) $\pi(7.5^2)(1.5)$

2. A local artist plans to paint an ocean scene on the bottom of the pond. Which of the following expressions could be used to find the number of square feet the painting will cover?

   (1) $(15)(7.5)$
   (2) $(15)(15)$
   (3) $\pi(15^2)$
   (4) $\pi(7.5^2)$
   (5) $\pi(15)$

3. A satellite dish is secured to a house with a diagonal metal brace, as shown below.

   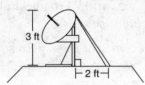

   3 ft
   ├─2 ft─┤

   Which of the following expressions could be used to find the length of the brace?

   (1) $2^2 + 3^2$
   (2) $3^2 - 2^2$
   (3) $\sqrt{3^2 - 2^2}$
   (4) $\sqrt{3^2 + 2^2}$
   (5) $\sqrt{3^2 - 2^2}$

4. Which of the following expressions could be used to find the area of the shaded portion of the figure?

   8 cm

   8 cm

   (1) $8^2 - (4^2 \times \pi)$
   (2) $8^3 - (4^2 \times \pi)$
   (3) $8^2 - 8\pi$
   (4) $8^2 - (8^2 \times \pi)$
   (5) $8^3 - 8\pi$

5. Alicia wants to buy a portable air conditioner for her bedroom. Each air conditioner is rated according to the maximum number of cubic feet it can cool. Alicia's bedroom measures 14 by 15 feet. The ceiling height is 7 feet. Which of the following expressions could she use to find the cubic footage of her bedroom?

   (1) $2(15) + 2(14)$
   (2) $2(15)(14)$
   (3) $4(14)(7)$
   (4) $7(15 + 14)$
   (5) $15(14)(7)$

6. Marc is installing custom sliding doors. A metal molding will go across the top of the doors and down the two sides.

   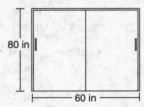

   80 in

   ├──── 60 in ────┤

   Which expression could be used to find how many inches of metal molding is needed?

   (1) $60(80)$
   (2) $60 + 2(80)$
   (3) $80 + 2(60)$
   (4) $2(60) + 2(80)$
   (5) $2(80 \cdot 60)$

   Answers and explanations begin on page 684.

GEOMETRY

Using the Calculator

Key Ideas

- When a problem involves many calculations, use the order of operations to decide what operation to do first.
- Check your work by estimating an answer or by quickly repeating the keystrokes to see if the result is the same.

Using the Calculator with Formulas

When solving problems with formulas, you can generally save time by performing some or all of the operations on a calculator. Remember the order of operations when solving formulas and always check your work, either by re-entering the key sequence or by estimating an answer and comparing your answer to the estimate.

Example 1: A pyramid has a height of 81 feet. The base is in the shape of a square with each side measuring 40 feet. What is the volume in cubic feet of the pyramid?

Use the formula: Volume $= \frac{1}{3} \times$ (base edge)$^2 \times$ height

Substitute: Volume $= \frac{1}{3} \times (40^2) \times 81$

Find the value. In the table below, each step is calculated separately.

Steps	Key Sequence	Display
Evaluate the exponent.	40 $\boxed{x^2}$	1600.
Multiply by 81.	$\boxed{\times}$ 81	129600.
Divide by 3.	$\boxed{\div}$ 3 $\boxed{=}$	43200.

In the last step, you divided by 3 instead of multiplying by $\frac{1}{3}$. Both operations give the same result.

Using the *Casio fx-260*, you can enter the calculation in one series of keystrokes. This sequence uses the fraction key to multiply by $\frac{1}{3}$.

Press: 1 $\boxed{a^b/c}$ 3 $\boxed{\times}$ 40 $\boxed{x^2}$ $\boxed{\times}$ 81 $\boxed{=}$ $\boxed{43200.}$

The volume of the pyramid is **43,200 square feet.**

You need your calculator to find the exact answer to problems that involve the Pythagorean relationship. These problems can also be done in one series of keystrokes.

Example 2: A right triangle has legs 10 inches and 24 inches in length. What is the length of the hypotenuse?

Use the formula: $a^2 + b^2 = c^2$. You will need to add the squares of the legs and then find the square root of the total.

Press: 10 $\boxed{x^2}$ $\boxed{+}$ 24 $\boxed{x^2}$ $\boxed{=}$ $\boxed{SHIFT}$ $\boxed{x^2}$ The display reads: $\boxed{26}$

The hypotenuse is **26 inches** in length.

GED TIP

When calculating a multi-step problem, write down the results of each step as you work. Then if you make an error entering, you can go back to the most recent step instead of starting over.

GEOMETRY ▸ PRACTICE 13

A. Use your calculator to evaluate each formula.

1. Find the perimeter of a rectangle with a length of 16 inches and a width of 5 inches.
Perimeter = 2 × length + 2 × width

2. Find the area of a triangle with a base of 26 centimeters and a height of 15 centimeters.
Area = $\frac{1}{2}$ × base × height

3. What is the volume of a cube if the edge measures 3.5 feet? Round to the nearest cubic foot.
Volume = edge³

4. What is the measure of the hypotenuse of a right triangle when the legs measure 13 cm and 9 cm? Round your answer to the nearest tenth.
Pythagorean relationship: $a^2 + b^2 = c^2$

5. Find the circumference of a circle with a diameter of 12 inches. Round to the nearest tenth.
Circumference = π × diameter

6. Find the volume of a cone with a radius of 12 cm and a height of 20 cm. Round to the nearest cm³.
Volume = $\frac{1}{3}$ × π × radius² × height

B. Choose the one best answer to each question.

Question 7 refers to the following drawing.

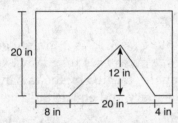

7. For a woodworking project, Paul cuts the shape shown above from plywood. What is the area in square inches of the piece? (*Hint:* Think of the shape as a triangle removed from a rectangle.)

    (1) 240
    (2) 400
    (3) 480
    (4) 520
    (5) 640

8. To the nearest cubic meter, what is the volume of a cylinder with a radius of 1.5 meters and a height of 5 meters?

    (1) 25
    (2) 35
    (3) 45
    (4) 141
    (5) 254

Questions 9 and 10 refer to the drawing.

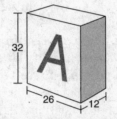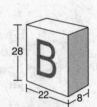

All measurements are in centimeters.

9. How many cubic centimeters greater is the volume of Box A than the volume of Box B?

    (1)   64
    (2) 1,448
    (3) 4,928
    (4) 5,056
    (5) 14,912

10. An advertiser plans to print advertisements on one side panel of each of the boxes (the shaded faces in the drawing). What is the total area, in square centimeters, that the advertiser will cover?

    (1) 1448
    (2) 1200
    (3) 608
    (4) 208
    (5) 160

Answers and explanations begin on page 685.

Problem Solving

Key Ideas

- You need logical reasoning to draw a true conclusion from the facts given in a problem.
- You can use logical reasoning to determine missing measures in a figure.
- You can also use logical reasoning to eliminate incorrect answer choices.

Using Logical Reasoning

Some questions on the GED Math Test will require you to draw a conclusion from the information given. These questions often ask you to determine which of five statements is true (or not true). **Logical reasoning** is step-by-step thinking. You start with the facts in the problem, and then use these facts to find new facts until you have enough information to draw a final conclusion.

Example 1: If point *D* lies on line *AC*, which of the following statements must be true?

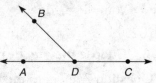

(1) ∠*ADB* is a right angle.
(2) ∠*BDC* is an acute angle.
(3) *m*∠*ADB* + *m*∠*BDC* = 180°
(4) ∠*ADB* and ∠*BDC* are congruent.
(5) ∠*ADB* and ∠*BDC* are complementary.

Since a line passes through points *A*, *D*, and *C*, ∠*ADC* is a straight angle with a measure of 180°. From the drawing, you can see that a ray extends from point *D*. Therefore, the sum of the angles formed by the ray and the line, ∠*ADB* and ∠*BDC*, must be supplementary and equal 180° The correct choice is **(3) *m*∠*ADB* + *m*∠*BDC* = 180°.**

If you cannot see how to solve a problem directly, you can often use logical reasoning to eliminate incorrect choices. As you work, remember that a statement cannot be considered true unless it can be proved using the information included in the problem.

GED TIP

Don't assume facts that are not stated. In Example 2, the triangles look congruent. However, since no sides in △DEF are given, you cannot know the triangles are congruent.

Example 2: Triangles *ABC* and *DEF* are similar triangles, and ∠*F* corresponds to ∠*C*. Which of the following must be a true statement?

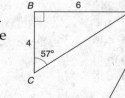

(1) ∠*A* is a right angle.
(2) The measure of *ED* is 6 units.
(3) *EF* measures 12 units.
(4) △*DEF* is an isosceles triangle.
(5) *m*∠*D* = 33°

Option (1) is incorrect because a triangle can have only one right angle. Since ∠*B* measures 90°, ∠*A* cannot be a right angle.

Both options (2) and (3) could be true, but you cannot prove they are true from the information in the problem. You know that the two triangles are similar, but you do not know any sides' measures in △*DEF*. You need at least one side measure in △*DEF* to write a proportion.

Option (4) must be incorrect because an isosceles triangle has two congruent sides and two congruent angles. The angles in △ABC have different measures. Two are known: 57° and 90°. Since the sum of the angles in a triangle equals 180, the measure of ∠A is 33°. Since the triangles are similar, the angles in △DEF also measure 33°, 57°, and 90°. By process of elimination, **option (5)** must be correct. ∠D corresponds to ∠A, so **m∠D = 33°**.

GEOMETRY ▸ PRACTICE 14

Choose the <u>one best answer</u> to each question.

<u>Questions 1 and 2</u> refer to the following figure.

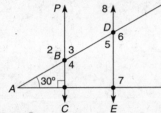

line *P* ∥ line *Q*

1. Which of the following is a true statement about the figure?

   (1) $m\angle 2 + m\angle 7 = 180°$
   (2) $m\angle 4 = m\angle 7$
   (3) $m\angle 3 + m\angle 4 = 90°$
   (4) $m\angle 3 + m\angle 6 = 180°$
   (5) $m\angle 2 = m\angle 3$

2. Which of the following conclusions can you draw based on the information given in the drawing?

   (1) $m\angle 5 = 60°$
   (2) ∠7 is an obtuse angle.
   (3) $m\angle 3 = 30°$
   (4) ∠7 and ∠5 are alternate interior angles.
   (5) ∠2 must be a right angle.

3. Two sides of Triangle *A* measure 4 and 5 inches. Two sides of Triangle *B* measure 8 and 10 inches. Which of the following conclusions can you draw about the two triangles?

   (1) △*A* and △*B* are similar triangles.
   (2) Both are isosceles triangles.
   (3) Neither contains a right angle.
   (4) △*A* and △*B* are not congruent.
   (5) △*A* is an acute triangle, but △*B* is not.

<u>Question 4</u> refers to the following figure.

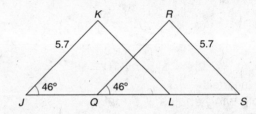

4. The distance from *J* to *L* is 8 units, and the distance from *Q* to *S* is 8 units. Which of the following conclusions can you draw?

   (1) $m\angle JLK = m\angle QRS$
   (2) △*JKL* and △*QRS* are congruent.
   (3) ∠*K* measures 46°.
   (4) The distance from *J* to *S* is 16 units.
   (5) ∠*JLK* measures 44°.

5. In a parallelogram, an angle measures 65°. What are the measures of the remaining three angles?

   (1) Each measures 65°.
   (2) Each measures about 98°.
   (3) 115°, 115°, and 65°
   (4) 115°, 90°, and 90°
   (5) Not enough information is given.

6. Two sides of a triangle measure 6 and 10 inches. If the triangle is a right triangle, which of the following could be the measure, in inches, of the third side?

   (1) 4
   (2) 6
   (3) 8
   (4) 10
   (5) 12

Answers and explanations begin on page 685.

GEOMETRY PRACTICE QUESTIONS

PART I

Directions: Choose the <u>one best answer</u> to each question. You <u>MAY</u> use your calculator.

<u>Questions 1 through 3</u> refer to the figure.

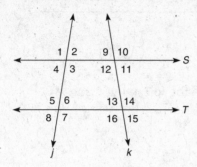

$S \parallel T$ $m\angle 1 = 77°$ $m\angle 10 = 95°$

1. Which of the following angles is equal in measure to $\angle 3$?

   (1) $\angle 13$
   (2) $\angle 9$
   (3) $\angle 8$
   (4) $\angle 5$
   (5) $\angle 2$

2. Classify the figure containing interior angles 3, 6, 12, and 13.

   (1) scalene triangle
   (2) trapezoid
   (3) parallelogram
   (4) rectangle
   (5) square

3. What is the measure of $\angle 15$?

   (1) 103°
   (2) 95°
   (3) 85°
   (4) 77°
   (5) Not enough information is given.

4. In an isosceles triangle, the largest angle is equal to the sum of the two smaller angles. What is the measure of the largest angle?

   (1) 120°
   (2) 100°
   (3) 90°
   (4) 60°
   (5) Not enough information is given.

5. The floor of a walk-in closet measures 7 feet by 4 feet. If the ceiling height is 8 feet, what is the volume in cubic feet of the closet?

   (1) 28
   (2) 56
   (3) 112
   (4) 168
   (5) 224

<u>Question 6</u> refers to the following drawing.

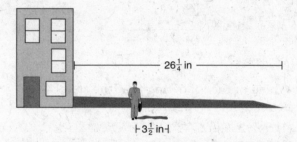

6. The diagram shows the length of the shadows of a man and a building at 4 P.M. If the man in the drawing is 6 feet in height, what is the height of the building in feet?

   (1) 37
   (2) 42
   (3) 45
   (4) 56
   (5) 91

<u>Question 7</u> refers to the following figure.

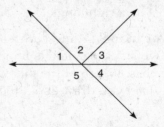

7. If $m\angle 1 = 35°$, what is the measure of $\angle 3$?

   (1) 35°
   (2) 55°
   (3) 75°
   (4) 145°
   (5) Not enough information is given.

PART II

Directions: Choose the <u>one best answer</u> to each question. You <u>MAY NOT</u> use your calculator.

8. Given the information in the diagram, what can you conclude about △LMN and △JKL?

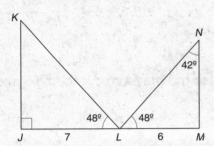

(1) △JKL and △LMN are congruent.
(2) △JKL and △LMN are similar.
(3) △JKL and △LMN are isosceles.
(4) △JKL and △LMN have the same area.
(5) △JKL and △LMN have the same perimeter.

9. Using a compass, Max hikes 300 yards due north of his campsite. From that point, he hikes 400 yards due east. If he walks directly to his campsite from this point, how many yards would he have to hike?

(1) 400
(2) 500
(3) 600
(4) 700
(5) Not enough information is given.

10. The rectangular base of a container measures 9 by 7 inches. By how many cubic inches will the volume of the container increase if you increase the length of the base by 2 inches?

(1) 18
(2) 84
(3) 126
(4) 168
(5) 216

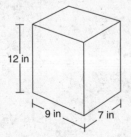

11. In a right triangle, the hypotenuse measures 15 inches. If one leg of the triangle measures 6 inches, which of the following equations could be used to find the length of the other leg (x) in inches?

(1) $x = \sqrt{15 + 6}$
(2) $x = \sqrt{15 - 6}$
(3) $x = 15 - 6$
(4) $x^2 = 15^2 + 6^2$
(5) $x^2 = 15^2 - 6^2$

12. The length of a rectangle is three times its width. If the perimeter of the rectangle is 96 inches, what is its length in inches?

(1) 12
(2) 24
(3) 32
(4) 36
(5) 48

Questions 13 and 14 refer to the following figure.

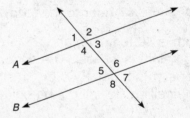

13. If A ∥ B, which of the following pairs of angles have the same measure?

(1) ∠1 and ∠6
(2) ∠2 and ∠3
(3) ∠2 and ∠8
(4) ∠3 and ∠6
(5) ∠4 and ∠7

14. You can draw the conclusion that angles 5 and 7 are equal in measure because they are what kind of angles?

(1) vertical angles
(2) alternate interior angles
(3) corresponding angles
(4) complementary angles
(5) alternate exterior angles

Question 15 refers to the following diagram.

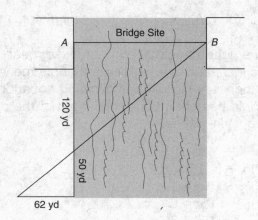

15. A city plans to build a bridge across a local river. To find the width the bridge will span, an engineer stakes out two similar triangles. Which equation could be used to find the distance from point *A* to point *B*?

(1) $\frac{50}{120} = \frac{\overline{AB}}{62}$

(2) $\frac{120}{50} = \frac{\overline{AB}}{62}$

(3) $\frac{120}{\overline{AB}} = \frac{62}{50}$

(4) $\frac{120}{50} = \frac{62}{\overline{AB}}$

(5) $\frac{50}{62} = \frac{\overline{AB}}{120}$

Questions 16 and 17 refer to the following.

A classroom is 40 feet long and 25 feet wide. The ceiling height is 12 feet. The school district plans to repaint the room and put in air conditioning. The ceiling tile will not be painted.

16. What is the approximate total square footage of the four walls of the room? Ignore space taken up by windows and doors.

(1) 1,200
(2) 1,560
(3) 1,920
(4) 4,000
(5) 12,000

17. To choose an air conditioning system, the school district must know the volume of the room. What is the volume in cubic feet?

(1) 1,000
(2) 3,120
(3) 12,000
(4) 15,625
(5) 64,000

Question 18 refers to the following figure.

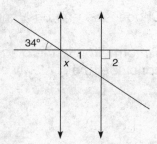

18. What is the measure of the angle marked *x*?

(1) 34°
(2) 45°
(3) 56°
(4) 146°
(5) Not enough information is given.

19. A parallelogram has a base of 6 centimeters and a height of 10 centimeters. This parallelogram has the same area as a triangle with a height of 5 centimeters. What is the measure, in centimeters, of the base of the triangle?

Mark your answer in the circles on the grid below.

20. Angles *R* and *S* are supplementary angles. If ∠*R* measures 16°, what is the measure, in degrees, of ∠*S*?

Mark your answer in the circles on the grid below.

19.

20.

Answers and explanations begin on page 685.

GED POST-TESTS

On the following pages, you will see practice tests for the five GED Tests:

- Language Arts, Writing
- Social Studies
- Science
- Language Arts, Reading
- Mathematics

You should use these full-length tests to see where you stand before you take the actual GED. As on the test, most of the questions will be in multiple-choice format. You may circle or check off your answers in this book or write them on a separate sheet of paper. There are two exceptions to this:

1. You will need to write an essay for Part II of the *Language Arts, Writing Test*.

2. On the *Mathematics Test*, you will need to fill in an answer sheet similar to the one that you will see on the GED Test. It includes three types of items:

- **Answer choices** to "bubble-in" like this:
  ① ② ● ④ ⑤

- A **grid** to be filled in like this:

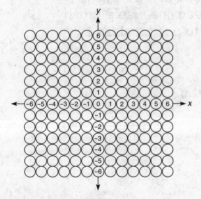

- A **coordinate graph** to be filled in with a plotted point:

Be sure to check your answers with the *Post-Test Answers and Explanations* that begin on page 612. At the end of each set of answers is a *Post-Test Evaluation Chart*. These charts enable you to target your problem areas. You can use the "Total Correct" for each test to estimate your Post-Test score and relate it to passing scores on the actual GED Tests. Use your scores to work with the *Kaplan GED Post-Test Score Conversion Charts* on the inside back cover of this book.

LANGUAGE ARTS, WRITING POST-TEST: PART I

Questions 1 through 7 refer to the following paragraphs.

Painting a Room

(A)

(1) Would you like to redecorate a room in your home? (2) Painting is a fast and inexpensive way to give that room a hole new look. (3) First, remove the furniture, or move it to the center of the room and cover it with drop cloths. (4) Prepare the room by stripping paint and extra layers of wallpaper, filling cracks, and add a coat of primer if necessary.

(B)

(5) Now you're ready to paint. (6) Using a brush, a clean line is painted along all edges where paint stops, such as where the wall meets the door frame, and in places where the ceiling meets a wall of a different color. (7) This is called "cutting in."

(C)

(8) The next step was to paint the room in the following order: ceiling, walls, trim, doors, windows. (9) Put no more than 3/4 of an inch of paint in the paint pan. (10) Run your roller through the paint, being careful not to overload the roller. (11) Apply paint to the ceiling and walls in a "W" or "Z" zigzag pattern.

(D)

(12) Spread the paint evenly by rolling either side to side or up and down, using gentle strokes so as not to leave roller marks. (13) After finishing an area, look for spots you missed, go over them with your relatively dry roller.

(E)

(14) To paint the window trim, raise the bottom sash and lower the top sash. (15) Paint the outer sash first, then the inner sash. (16) Next, reverse the position of the sashes without closing either one completely, and paint the parts of the sashes that you can reach. (17) Keep the window open, until the paint dries to the touch. (18) Then, finally, you can paint the sill and casing.

1. Sentence 2: **Painting is a fast and inexpensive way to give that room a hole new look.**

Which correction should be made to sentence 2?

(1) change is to are
(2) insert a comma after fast
(3) change to give to giving
(4) replace hole with whole
(5) no correction is necessary

2. Sentence 4: **Prepare the room by stripping paint and extra layers of wallpaper, filling cracks, and add a coat of primer if necessary.**

Which correction should be made to sentence 4?

(1) change Prepare to Preparing
(2) insert a comma after paint
(3) remove the comma after wallpaper
(4) change add to adding
(5) insert a comma after primer

3. Sentence 6: **Using a brush, a clean line is painted along all edges where paint stops, such as where the wall meets the door frame, and in places where the ceiling meets a wall of a different color.**

The most effective revision of sentence 6 would begin with which group of words?

(1) A clean line, with a brush, is painted
(2) The painting of a clean line is brushed
(3) Paint by using and brushing
(4) Painting a clean line, use a brush
(5) Use a brush to paint a clean line

4. Sentence 8: **The next step was to paint the room in the following order: ceiling, walls, trim, doors, windows.**

   Which is the best way to write the underlined portion of this sentence? If the original is the best way, choose option (1).

   (1) was
   (2) being
   (3) is
   (4) had been
   (5) will be

5. Sentence 13: **After finishing an area, look for spots you missed, go over them with your relatively dry roller.**

   Which is the best way to write the underlined portion of this sentence? If the original is the best way, choose option (1).

   (1) missed, go
   (2) missed, and go
   (3) missed, and going
   (4) missed go
   (5) missed, but go

6. Which revision would improve the effectiveness of the text?

   (1) join paragraphs A and B
   (2) begin a new paragraph with sentence 10
   (3) join paragraphs C and D
   (4) begin a new paragraph with sentence 13
   (5) join paragraphs D and E

7. Sentence 17: **Keep the window open, until the paint dries to the touch.**

   Which correction should be made to sentence 17?

   (1) change Keep to Keeping
   (2) remove the comma
   (3) change dries to been dried
   (4) replace to with too
   (5) no correction is necessary

Questions 8 through 14 refer to the following paragraphs.

Sick Building Syndrome

(A)

(1) Do you often feel sick when you're at work? (2) Do you experience symptoms such as coughing, sneezing, nausea, and difficulty breathing? (3) Do you have frequent headaches? (4) Do these symptoms seem to disappear once you leave work magically? (5) If so, you may be working in a sick building.

(B)

(6) "Sick building syndrome" is a term that referred to working in a building that makes you sick. (7) The syndrome may be caused by improper building design. (8) Over the past 20 years, architects have designed office buildings with an eye to saving energy. (9) The buildings are tightly sealed so that little heat escapes, and the air inside the buildings are recirculated to avoid the cost of heating fresh air. (10) Although this design reduces energy costs, the lack of ventilation causes a buildup of toxins in the air. (11) On the other hand an older building isn't necessarily immune to the syndrome. (12) Even if they originally opened to let in fresh air, adding insulation, caulking, and weather stripping at a later date may have made the windows airtight.

(C)

(13) Toxins in the air come from a variety of sources. (14) Biological agents including bacteria, viruses, fungi, and pollen, may be found in poorly maintained air circulation systems and dirty washrooms. (15) The deadly gas carbon monoxide can seep into a building's air through an improperly ventilated garage or a leaky duct. (16) Formaldehyde is frequently found in furniture, paneling, draperies, glues, and upholstery. (17) Other toxins come from volatile organic compounds (VOCs), which are released from certain solids and liquids as gases at room temperature. (18) Secondhand tobacco smoke is yet another source of toxins. (19) Sources of VOCs include copy machine toners, spray cans, felt tip markers, and correction fluid.

(D)

(20) It is possible to "cure" a sick building. (21) Steps to take include eliminating tobacco smoke, providing good ventilation, keeping the ventilation system in good repair, and removing all sources of pollution.

8. Sentence 4: **Do these symptoms seem to disappear once you leave work magically?**

The most effective revision of sentence 4 would include which group of words?

(1) disappear magically once you leave
(2) symptoms, seeming to disappear
(3) once you disappear magically
(4) upon leaving work magically
(5) seem to disappear, once you leave

9. Sentence 6: **"Sick building syndrome" is a term that referred to working in a building that makes you sick.**

Which correction should be made to sentence 6?

(1) insert a comma after term
(2) change referred to refers
(3) change working to having worked
(4) insert a comma after building
(5) change makes to made

10. Sentence 9: **The buildings are tightly sealed so that little heat escapes, and the air inside the buildings are recirculated to avoid the cost of heating fresh air.**

Which correction should be made to sentence 9?

(1) change are tightly to been tightly
(2) change escapes to escaped
(3) remove the comma
(4) change are recirculated to is recirculated
(5) no correction is necessary

11. Sentence 11: **On the other hand an older building isn't necessarily immune to the syndrome.**

Which correction should be made to sentence 11?

(1) insert a comma after hand
(2) change isn't to is'nt
(3) change isn't to aren't
(4) insert a comma after immune
(5) replace to with too

12. Sentence 12: **Even if they originally opened to let in fresh air, adding insulation, caulking, and weather stripping at a later date may have made the windows airtight.**

Which is the best way to write the underlined portion of this sentence? If the original is the best way, choose option (1).

(1) they
(2) them
(3) it
(4) the building
(5) the windows

13. Sentence 14: **Biological agents including bacteria, viruses, fungi, and pollen, may be found in poorly maintained air circulation systems and dirty washrooms.**

Which correction should be made to sentence 14?

(1) insert a comma after agents
(2) change bacteria to Bacteria
(3) change may be to has been
(4) insert a comma after systems
(5) no correction is necessary

14. Which revision would improve the effectiveness of the text?

(1) join paragraphs A and B
(2) move sentence 7 to follow sentence 8
(3) begin a new paragraph with sentence 9
(4) move sentence 12 to the beginning of paragraph C
(5) move sentence 18 to follow sentence 16

Questions 15 through 21 refer to the following advertisement.

Clothing Unlimited Buyers Club

(A)

(1) At Clothing Unlimited, we offer the highest quality merchandise at the best prices. (2) Now you can save even more money by joining our buyers club. (3) Benefits of membership are including discounts, free gifts, year-end rebates, and much more. (4) You may be aware that in the past, buyers club members got a 10 percent discount on all items purchased. (5) Well, times have changed. (6) We now offer discounts ranging from 10 percent to 75 percent. (7) Rather than giving a blanket discount, we assessed the discount for each item individually. (8) This change translates into bigger savings for members.

(B)

(9) Many of our customers live in other states. (10) They will be pleased to hear that one benefit of the buyers club is free shipping. (11) All orders over $99 are shipped free of charge. (12) In addition, local customers may arrange for delivery at reduced prices.

(C)

(13) If you join the buyers club now, you will receive a free gift with every order. (14) That you place with our Website, clothes.com. (15) This offer is valid while supplies last.

(D)

(16) Buyers club membership fees are $20 per year or $40 for a lifetime membership. (17) Many of our customers report that they're membership fees pay for themselves several times over. (18) To join, simply fill out the form on the back of this page and return it to any Clothing Unlimited employee. (19) You'll be glad you did!

15. Sentence 3: **Benefits of membership are including discounts, free gifts, year-end rebates, and much more.**

Which is the best way to write the underlined portion of this sentence? If the original is the best way, choose option (1).

(1) are including
(2) include
(3) is including
(4) includes
(5) have included

16. Sentence 4: **You may be aware that in the past, buyers club members got a 10 percent discount on all items purchased.**

Which is the best way to write the underlined portion of this sentence? If the original is the best way, choose option (1).

(1) got
(2) gotten
(3) get
(4) had got
(5) getting

17. Which revision would improve the effectiveness of the advertisement?

Begin a new paragraph with

(1) sentence 3
(2) sentence 4
(3) sentence 5
(4) sentence 6
(5) sentence 7

18. Sentence 7: **Rather than giving a blanket discount, we <u>assessed</u> the discount for each item individually.**

Which is the best way to write the underlined portion of this sentence? If the original is the best way, choose option (1).

(1) assessed
(2) had assessed
(3) assess
(4) are assessing
(5) would have assessed

19. Sentences 9 and 10: **Many of our customers live in other states. They will be pleased to hear that one benefit of the buyers club is free shipping.**

The most effective combination of sentences 9 and 10 would include which group of words?

(1) free shipping to customers who live in
(2) living in other states, customers will
(3) one of the benefits, free shipping, is
(4) free shipping is a benefit of the club for
(5) customers who live in other states will be

20. Sentences 13 and 14: **If you join the buyers club now, you will receive a free gift with every <u>order. That</u> you place with our Website, clothes.com.**

Which is the best way to write the underlined portion of these sentences? If the original is the best way, choose option (1).

(1) order. That
(2) order, and that
(3) order that
(4) order, that
(5) order, so that

21. Sentence 17: **Many of our customers report that they're membership fees pay for themselves several times over.**

Which correction should be made to sentence 17?

(1) insert a comma after <u>customers</u>
(2) change <u>report</u> to <u>reports</u>
(3) replace <u>they're</u> with <u>their</u>
(4) insert a comma after <u>themselves</u>
(5) no correction is necessary

Starting a Community Garden

(A)

(1) In many cities, neighborhood groups are forming community gardens in vacant lots, parks, or on rooftops. (2) These gardens is an ideal way for both children and adults to work with nature while making the neighborhood more beautiful.

(B)

(3) If you would like to start a community garden first determine whether people are truly interested in the project. (4) If they are, then decide what will be planted in the garden and who the garden is intended to serve. (5) Organize a meeting of interested people. (6) Choose someone to be the garden coordinator. (7) Form committees for tasks like finding money for the garden and developing youth activities.

(C)

(8) Once your group is organized, approach a sponsor—a group or individual who can support your garden. (9) Keep in mind that contributions of seeds, tools, and land are just as important as money. (10) Schools, churches, citizen groups, and private businesses are all potential sponsors.

(D)

(11) Find out how the land has been used in the past to avoid places that may be contaminated. (12) Pick a site that gets at least six hours of direct sunlight a day, and make sure that water is available. (13) Contact the owner of the site try to get a lease that allows you to use the land for at least three years.

(E)

(14) After choosing a site, the group of gardeners need to decide how to organize the garden. (15) What size should each plot be, and how will plots be assigned? (16) Will the group charge dues, and if so, how will the money be used? (17) Will the group plan certain activities together, such as composting? (18) How will watering and weeding be handled?

(F)

(19) Finally, remember that angry neighbors spell trouble for a community garden. (20) Neighbors often complain to city officials when a garden is unkempt or when the gardeners exhibited rowdy behavior. (21) Therefore, establish a procedure to follow so that the garden stays tidy and peaceful.

22. Sentence 1: **In many cities, neighborhood groups are forming community gardens in vacant lots, parks, or on rooftops.**

Which is the best way to write the underlined portion of the sentence? If the original is the best way, choose option (1).

(1) in vacant lots, parks, or on rooftops
(2) in vacant lots, parks, or rooftops
(3) in vacant lots, parks, rooftops
(4) in vacant lots, in parks, or on rooftops
(5) in the vacant lots, in the parks, on the rooftops

23. Sentence 2: **These gardens is an ideal way for both children and adults to work with nature while making the neighborhood more beautiful.**

Which correction should be made to sentence 2?

(1) change gardens to garden
(2) change is to are
(3) replace way with weigh
(4) insert a comma after children
(5) change nature to Nature

24. Sentence 3: **If you would like to start a community garden first determine whether people are truly interested in the project.**

Which correction should be made to sentence 3?

(1) change <u>would</u> to <u>will</u>
(2) insert a comma after <u>garden</u>
(3) replace <u>whether</u> with <u>weather</u>
(4) change <u>are</u> to <u>is</u>
(5) no correction is necessary

25. Sentences 5 and 6: **Organize a meeting of interested <u>people. Choose</u> someone to be the garden coordinator.**

Which is the best way to write the underlined portion of these sentences? If the original is the best way, choose option (1).

(1) people. Choose
(2) people, choose
(3) people having chosen
(4) people, then choosing
(5) people, and choose

26. Which sentence would be most effective if inserted at the beginning of paragraph D?

(1) Next, choose a site for the garden.
(2) Land use is a very significant factor.
(3) We all know that you are going to need land for your garden.
(4) It's critical to have a site that gets lots of sunlight.
(5) Learn about the history of your site.

27. Sentence 13: **Contact the owner of the <u>site try</u> to get a lease that allows you to use the land for at least three years.**

Which is the best way to write the underlined portion of the sentence? If the original is the best way, choose option (1).

(1) site try
(2) site, try
(3) site trying
(4) site, you should try
(5) site, and try

28. Sentence 14: **After choosing a site, the group of gardeners <u>need</u> to decide how to organize the garden.**

Which is the best way to write the underlined portion of the sentence? If the original is the best way, choose option (1).

(1) need
(2) needs
(3) needed
(4) needing
(5) will be needing

29. Sentence 20: **Neighbors often complain to city officials when a garden is unkempt or when the gardeners <u>exhibited</u> rowdy behavior.**

Which is the best way to write the underlined portion of the sentence? If the original is the best way, choose option (1).

(1) exhibited
(2) exhibits
(3) did exhibit
(4) exhibit
(5) will be exhibiting

Questions 30 through 36 refer to the following flyer.

Save Compton Point!

(A)

(1) Compton Point, home to many animal species that are threatened with extinction, now face a threat of its own. (2) Developers are in the process of acquiring the rights to part of this beautiful area. (3) They attempted to change the zoning in order to build a hotel, a tourist center, and an observation tower.

(B)

(4) If developers succeed in getting the rights to build, construction will begin next August. (5) The planned 30-story observation tower will be visible from a great distance. (6) Perhaps tourists will get a beautiful view of our area, but the tower will be a blight on our landscape.

(C)

(7) Sam Wanamaker, director of the Society for the Protection of Nature, warns that construction of the development is likely to drive out more than 30 animal species that live on the point. (8) Air pollution from tourist traffic will further reduce the animals' chances for survival. (9) Not to mention litter left behind by floods of tourists wandering through the area.

(D)

(10) The Compton Point area is zoned as natural parkland. (11) There are several other areas in the county that are zoned as natural parkland. (12) However, because this project is potentially so lucrative for the city, the zoning board seems to be bending to the will of the developers.

(E)

(13) Developers argue that the new jobs resulting from their development would boost the region's sagging economy. (14) The influx of tourism would too. (15) Certainly, everyone in the community agree that the economy around here could use a lift. (16) Development is, in fact, necessary, but it must be carried out carefully.

(F)

(17) Register your opposition to the development of Compton Point! (18) Come to a demonstration at 10 A.M. on Saturday, May 7, in front of the mayor's office, 34 Wilton road. (19) Bring signs with slogans that tell how you feel. (20) A strong turn out at this demonstration will send a message to developers.

30. Sentence 1: **Compton Point, home to many animal species that are threatened with extinction, now face a threat of its own.**

Which correction should be made to sentence 1?

(1) change Point to point
(2) remove the comma after Point
(3) change are to is
(4) remove the comma after extinction
(5) change face to faces

31. Sentence 3: **They attempted to change the zoning in order to build a hotel, a tourist center, and an observation tower.**

Which is the best way to write the underlined portion of the sentence? If the original is the best way, choose option (1).

(1) attempted
(2) attempt
(3) are attempting
(4) attempting
(5) will have attempted

32. Sentences 8 and 9: **Air pollution from tourist traffic will further reduce the animals' chances for survival. Not to mention litter left behind by floods of tourists wandering through the area.**

The most effective combination of sentences 8 and 9 would include which group of words?

(1) Tourism increases both air pollution and litter, which will
(2) Litter, which tourists leave behind, and besides
(3) Animals will have less chance for survival when air pollution
(4) Air pollution and litter, having been caused by tourists,
(5) Tourists pollute the air, and they also leave litter behind them

33. Which revision would improve the effectiveness of paragraph D?

(1) remove sentence 10
(2) remove sentence 11
(3) move sentence 10 to follow sentence 11
(4) move sentence 10 to follow sentence 12
(5) no revision is necessary

34. Sentences 13 and 14: **Developers argue that the new jobs resulting from their development would boost the region's sagging economy. The influx of tourism would too.**

The most effective combination of sentences 13 and 14 would include which group or words?

(1) the development, with an influx of jobs,
(2) new jobs and the influx of tourism resulting
(3) an influx of new jobs, say the developers, plus an influx of tourism,
(4) To boost the sagging economy,
(5) The region, to have an influx,

35. Sentence 15: **Certainly, everyone in the community agree that the economy around here could use a lift.**

Which correction should be made to sentence 15?

(1) remove the comma after Certainly
(2) change agree to agrees
(3) replace here with hear
(4) change could use to could be using
(5) no correction is necessary

36. Sentence 18: **Come to a demonstration at 10 A.M. on Saturday, May 7, in front of the mayor's office, 34 Wilton road.**

Which correction should be made to sentence 18?

(1) insert a comma after demonstration
(2) remove the comma after Saturday
(3) change mayor's to mayors
(4) change mayor's to Mayor's
(5) change road to Road

Questions 37 through 43 refer to the following paragraphs.

Chocolate: A Treat Throughout the Ages

(A)

(1) Few people can resist the charms of chocolate. (2) This luscious, creamy treat not only gives an instant boost of energy, but it also brings a sense of emotional comfort. (3) Touted as an aphrodisiac, chocolate is a common romantic gift. (4) Some people, self-proclaimed "chocoholics," are obsessed with this sweet pleasure. (5) Where, then, does chocolate come from?

(B)

(6) The Aztecs were the first to use cacao beans, turning them into a frothy beverage that was supposed to be stimulating and healthful. (7) Only nobility, warriors, and clergy were permitted to have this drink. (8) One rumor has it that the emperor Montezuma used to drink this chocolate beverage before a romantic evening with one of his wives.

(C)

(9) Chocolate first made its appearance in England and Italy in the 1600s, and by 1765, it had made its way to the colonies in North America. (10) The Swiss, now world famous for their chocolates, begun their fascination with the sweet in the mid-1800s. (11) Two Swiss men, Henry Nestle and Daniel Peter, figured out how to mix sweetened condensed milk with chocolate to get chocolate milk. (12) The chocolate bar was invented in 1879 when Rudolph Lindt added cocoa butter to chocolate.

(D)

(13) The Spanish Explorer Hernán Cortés brought the drink to Spain in 1519, but the public did not learn of it for another hundred years. (14) However, it became popular after Anne of Austria, wife of Louis XII declared it the drink of the French court in 1615.

(E)

(15) Chocolate has become a multibillion dollar industry. (16) As a result, each company's chocolate recipes are closely guarded. (17) In 1980, an apprentice of a Swiss company was caught trying to sell secret chocolate recipes to China, Saudi Arabia, and Russia.

(F)

(18) A recent study of 8,000 college graduates showed that chocolate eaters live longer than those who refrain. (19) Researchers believe that this affect is due to the fact that chocolate contains high levels of polyphenol, a substance that protects against heart disease.

37. Sentence 2: **This luscious, creamy treat not only gives an instant boost of energy, but it also brings a sense of emotional comfort.**

Which correction should be made to sentence 2?

(1) remove the comma after luscious
(2) change gives to give
(3) remove the comma after energy
(4) insert a comma after but
(5) no correction is necessary

38. Sentence 6: **The Aztecs were the first to use cacao beans, turning them into a frothy beverage that was supposed to be stimulating and healthful.**

Which is the best way to write the underlined portion of this sentence? If the original is the best way, choose option (1).

(1) beans, turning
(2) beans turning
(3) beans. Turning
(4) beans, and turning
(5) beans, and by turning

39. Sentence 10: **The Swiss, now world famous for their chocolates, begun their fascination with the sweet in the mid-1800s.**

Which is the best way to write the underlined portion of this sentence? If the original is the best way, choose option (1).

(1) begin
(2) beginning
(3) begun
(4) began
(5) had began

40. Sentence 13: **The Spanish Explorer Hernán Cortés brought the drink to Spain in 1519, but the public did not learn of it for another hundred years.**

Which correction should be made to sentence 13?

(1) change Spanish to spanish
(2) change Explorer to explorer
(3) insert a comma after Cortés
(4) change brought to brung
(5) remove the comma after 1519

41. Sentence 14: **However, it became popular after Anne of Austria, wife of Louis XII declared it the drink of the French court in 1615.**

Which correction should be made to sentence 14?

(1) remove the comma after However
(2) change Austria to austria
(3) remove the comma after Austria
(4) insert a comma after XII
(5) change court to Court

42. Which revision would improve the effectiveness of the article?

(1) join paragraphs A and B
(2) remove paragraph B
(3) move paragraph C to follow paragraph D
(4) remove paragraph D
(5) join paragraphs E and F

43. Sentence 19: **Researchers believe that this affect is due to the fact that chocolate contains high levels of polyphenol, a substance that protects against heart disease.**

Which correction should be made to sentence 19?

(1) replace affect with effect
(2) insert a comma after fact
(3) change contains to contain
(4) remove the comma
(5) change protects to protected

Questions 44 through 50 refer to the following letter.

Dr. Calvin R. Simotas
904 East 79th Street
Chicago, IL 60626

Dear Patient:

(A)

(1) I will soon be joining the faculty of Holworth University Hospital in the downtown area of Chicago. (2) In addition to teaching at the medical school, I continue to see private patients.

(B)

(3) We will all benefit from this move to Holworth. (4) First and foremost are its excellent facilities. (5) A spacious, comfortable waiting room is only the start. (6) Numerous examining rooms will help make your visit as pleasant and time efficient as possible, not to mention that they are state of the art. (7) Consultations with different specialists at Holworth will now be possible as well.

(C)

(8) The move to the new office will take place on October 13. (9) No patients will be seen from October 11 to October 15. (10) If you know that you will need medical care before October please make your appointment right away. (11) It might be hard to get an appointment during the holiday season as well.

(D)

(12) The new office is located in the faculty practice building of the Hospital at 180 N. Commerce Avenue, Suite 700. (13) The office is conveniently located close to several bus and train lines and is accessible from all parts of the city. (14) In addition, a large underground parking lot is located across the street.

(E)

(15) Iv'e enjoyed serving you over the years at my 79th Street office. (16) If you would like to see me at my new office, it is necessary for you to sign the enclosed form to release you're files. (17) Please fill out the form and return it to me at the 79th Street address. (18) I look forward to seeing you soon.

All the best,
Calvin R. Simotas, M.D.

44. Sentence 2: **In addition to teaching at the medical school, I <u>continue</u> to see private patients.**

Which is the best way to write the underlined portion of the sentence? If the original is the best way, choose option (1).

(1) continue
(2) will continue
(3) continued
(4) have continued
(5) continuing

45. Sentence 6: **Numerous examining rooms will help make your visit as pleasant and time efficient as possible, not to mention that they are state of the art.**

The most effective revision of sentence 6 would begin with which group of words?

(1) Numerous state-of-the-art examining rooms
(2) A pleasant and time efficient visit will be had
(3) Numerous, pleasant examining rooms that are
(4) Examining rooms that are numerous and
(5) Helping make your visit pleasant and time efficient

46. Sentence 10: **If you know that you will need medical care before October please make your appointment right away.**

Which is the best way to write the underlined portion of the sentence? If the original is the best way, choose option (1).

(1) October please
(2) October, and please
(3) October, please
(4) October, then please
(5) October. Please

47. Which revision would improve the effectiveness of the letter?

(1) move sentence 3 to the end of paragraph A
(2) move sentence 5 to follow sentence 7
(3) remove sentence 8
(4) move sentence 9 to follow sentence 11
(5) remove sentence 11

48. Sentence 12: **The new office is located in the faculty practice building of the Hospital at 180 N. Commerce Avenue, Suite 700.**

Which correction should be made to sentence 12?

(1) change is to being
(2) change located with locating
(3) insert a comma after building
(4) change Hospital to hospital
(5) change Avenue to avenue

49. Sentence 15: **Iv'e enjoyed serving you over the years at my 79th Street office.**

Which correction should be made to sentence 15?

(1) change Iv'e to I've
(2) change enjoyed to been enjoying
(3) insert a comma after years
(4) change office to Office
(5) no correction is necessary

50. Sentence 16: **If you would like to see me at my new office, it is necessary for you to sign the enclosed form to release you're files.**

Which correction should be made to sentence 16?

(1) remove would
(2) remove the comma
(3) replace for with four
(4) insert a comma after form
(5) change you're to your

Answers and explanations begin on page 612.

LANGUAGE ARTS, WRITING POST-TEST: PART II

Essay Directions and Topic

Look at the box on the next page. In the box are your assigned topic and the letter of that topic.

You must write on the assigned topic ONLY.

You will have 45 minutes to write on your assigned essay topic. You may return to the multiple-choice section after you complete your essay if you have time remaining in this test period. Do not return the Language Arts, Writing Test booklet until you finish both Parts I and II of the Language Arts, Writing Test.

Two evaluators will score your essay according to its overall effectiveness. Their evaluation will be based on the following features:

- Well-focused main points
- Clear organization
- Specific development of your ideas
- Control of sentence structure, punctuation, grammar, word choice, and spelling

REMEMBER, YOU MUST COMPLETE BOTH THE MULTIPLE-CHOICE QUESTIONS (PART I) AND THE ESSAY (PART II) TO RECEIVE A SCORE ON THE LANGUAGE ARTS, WRITING TEST. To avoid having to repeat both parts of the test, be sure to do the following:

- Do not leave the pages blank.
- Write legibly in ink so that the evaluators will be able to read your writing.
- Write on the assigned topic. If you write on a topic other than the one assigned, you will not receive a score for the Language Arts, Writing Test.
- Write your essay on the lined pages of the separate answer sheet booklet. Only the writing on these pages will be scored.

Reprinted with permission of the GED Testing Service of the American Council on Education.

TOPIC

What is the secret to staying young at heart, even as your body grows older?

In your essay, describe things that help people to continue feeling young. Use your personal observations, experiences, and knowledge.

Part II is a test to determine how well you can use written language to explain your ideas. In preparing your essay, you should take the following steps:

- Read the **DIRECTIONS** and the **TOPIC** carefully.
- Plan your essay before you write. Use the scratch paper provided to make any notes. These notes will be collected but not scored.
- Before you turn in your essay, reread what you have written and make any changes that will improve your essay.

Your essay should be long enough to develop the topic adequately.

Essay evaluation guidelines start on page 614.

GED SOCIAL STUDIES POST-TEST

Directions: You will have 70 minutes to answer 50 questions on the Social Studies Test. Choose the one best answer to each question.

Question 1 refers to the following paragraph and graph.

When the value of exported goods—those sold abroad—is greater than the value of imported goods—those bought from foreign nations—there is a favorable balance of trade. On the other hand, when imports are greater than exports, there is an unfavorable balance of trade.

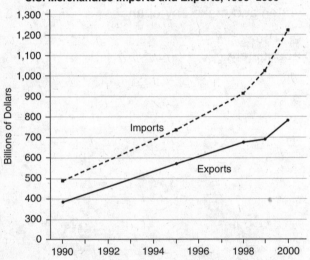

U.S. Merchandise Imports and Exports, 1990–2000

SOURCE: *Statistical Abstract of the United States.*

1. Which of the following statements is supported by the paragraph and the graph?

   (1) Exports equaled imports at the start of the 1990s.
   (2) Exports exceeded imports throughout the 1990s.
   (3) The United States had a favorable merchandise balance of trade during the 1990s.
   (4) The United States had an unfavorable merchandise balance of trade during the 1990s.
   (5) The unfavorable merchandise balance of trade steadily decreased during the 1990s.

2. The Second Amendment to the U.S. Constitution was ratified in 1791. It states: "A well-regulated militia being necessary to the security of a free state, the right of the people to keep and bear arms shall not be infringed."

   Which of the following modern organizations cites this amendment to support its goals and political positions?

   (1) the Council of State Governments
   (2) the National Right to Life Political Action Committee
   (3) the National Taxpayers' Union
   (4) the National Rifle Association
   (5) the United States Chamber of Commerce

3. In the late 1800s, industrialization caused a large-scale migration from rural to urban areas in the United States. Parents who moved to cities with their children left behind the social support of their extended families. In addition, city families found that children, who were an asset on the farm because they could work at an early age, were more of an economic drawback in the city. As a consequence, the birthrate dropped during this period and average family size shrank.

   Which of the following is the best summary of this passage?

   (1) Industrialization led to increased urbanization in the late 1800s.
   (2) City families lost the social support of their extended families back on the farm.
   (3) Industrialization and urbanization caused many changes in family life in the late 1800s.
   (4) The U.S. birthrate dropped in the late 1800s.
   (5) In the late 1800s, average family size shrank due to the fall in the birthrate.

Questions 4 through 6 refer to the following map.

Percentage of Undernourished People Worldwide

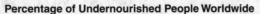

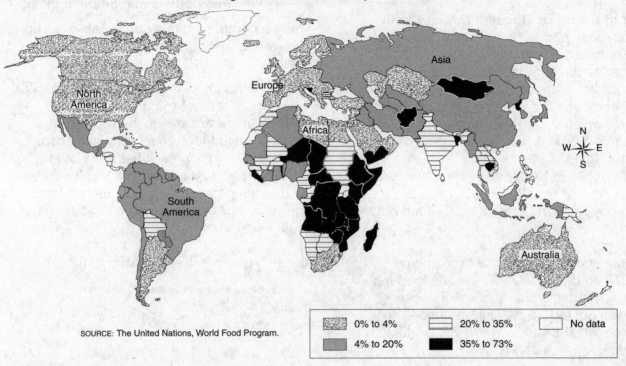

| | 0% to 4% | | 20% to 35% | | No data |
| | 4% to 20% | | 35% to 73% | | |

SOURCE: The United Nations, World Food Program.

4. According to the map, what is the percentage range of people in the United States who do not get enough food and nutrients?

   (1) 0% to 4%
   (2) 4% to 20%
   (3) 20% to 35%
   (4) 35% to 73%
   (5) more than 73%

5. Which of the following people would have the greatest use for this map?

   (1) a nutritionist in a hospital
   (2) a person who heads a relief organization
   (3) a person traveling around the world
   (4) a farmer in the United States
   (5) a math professor from Central America

6. Which of the following statements is supported by the information on the map?

   (1) All areas with more than 35% of the population undernourished are inland nations.
   (2) World hunger would disappear if food were distributed more fairly.
   (3) There are approximately 830 million undernourished people worldwide.
   (4) There are no areas of hunger in Europe or Australia.
   (5) Hunger is a major problem in many countries in Africa.

Question 7 refers to the following excerpt from a credit card bill.

In Case of Errors or Questions About Your Bill If you think your bill is wrong, or you need more information about a transaction, write us on a separate sheet at the address shown on the front of this statement. We must hear from you no later than 60 days after we sent you the first bill on which the error or problem appeared. You can telephone us, but doing so will not preserve your rights.

You do not have to pay any amount in question while we are investigating, but you are obligated to pay the parts of your bill that are not in question.

7. The Hampsens received their credit card bill for $279.45 dated July 25. They noticed that one transaction, a pair of sneakers costing $69, was posted twice. The Hampsens normally pay their balance in full. What should they do in this situation?

   (1) Pay $279.45, and call the store where they bought the sneakers to tell them about the double billing.
   (2) Pay $210.45, and call the credit card company within 60 days to tell them about the double billing.
   (3) Pay $210.45, and write to the credit card company within 60 days to tell them about the double billing.
   (4) Pay $210.45, and call the store where they bought the sneakers and ask them to issue a credit for $69.
   (5) Pay nothing, and write to the credit card company within 60 days to tell them about the double billing.

8. Comparative advantage is the ability to produce goods and services at a lower cost than the cost at which others can produce them.

   When a company has a comparative advantage with a particular product, what is the result?

   (1) The company can advertise its product to a specialized set of consumers.
   (2) The company can sell the product at a lower price than other companies can.
   (3) The company can sell the product at a higher price than other companies can.
   (4) The company can expand its workforce.
   (5) The company can lay off a percentage of its workforce.

Question 9 refers to the following graph.

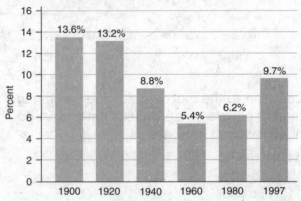

U.S. Foreign-Born Population, 1900–1997

SOURCE: U.S. Bureau of the Census.

9. Which of the following best describes the change in the percentage of foreign-born people in the United States since 1960?

   (1) In 1960, only 6.2 percent of the U.S. population was foreign born.
   (2) Since 1960, the percentage of foreign-born people has been on an upward trend.
   (3) Since 1960, the percentage of foreign-born people has been on a downward trend.
   (4) Since 1960, the percentage of foreign-born people has held steady.
   (5) Since 1960, the percentage of foreign-born people has not exceeded 5 percent.

Questions 10 and 11 refer to the following chart.

Acts of Parliament Directed at the American Colonies

Act	Description
Revenue Act of 1764 (Sugar Act)	Imposed duties (tariffs) on foreign sugar and luxuries to raise money for Great Britain
Quartering Act of 1765	Required colonists to provide food and shelter for British soldiers
Stamp Act of 1765	Required colonists to purchase revenue stamps for all important documents, including legal documents, newspapers, and ads
Declaratory Act of 1766	Asserted the right of Parliament to make laws for the colonies
Townshend Acts of 1767	Imposed new duties on the import of tea, glass, and paper

10. How did the Declaratory Act differ from all the other acts of Parliament shown in the chart?

  (1) It did not involve the quartering of British soldiers.
  (2) It related only to the import of luxury goods.
  (3) It was directed only at the New England colonies.
  (4) It did not impose direct economic costs on the colonists.
  (5) It was enacted long after the other acts of Parliament.

11. The information in this chart would have been most useful for the writing of which of the following documents?

  (1) The Declaration of Independence, which explained why the colonies broke away from Great Britain
  (2) The Articles of Confederation, which established a central government consisting of a congress
  (3) The U.S. Constitution, which established the structure of government for the newly independent nation
  (4) The Federalist Papers, a series of 85 essays written to persuade the states to ratify the Constitution
  (5) Washington's Farewell Address, in which he warned the new nation of policies and practices he thought unwise

12. The civil rights movement of the 1950s and 1960s inspired historians to reinterpret slavery's impact on U.S. society in general and on African Americans in particular. One interpretation that emerged was that slaves and owners were always in conflict and that slavery was destructive. The extent of slavery's destructiveness was debated. Some historians argued that slavery destroyed the culture and self-respect of the slaves and their descendants. Others thought that slaves overcame hardship by developing a unique African American culture that included, among many different things, strong religious and musical traditions.

Based on the paragraph, which of the following statements is an opinion rather than a fact?

  (1) The civil rights movement took place during the middle of the twentieth century.
  (2) The civil rights movement caused historians to take another look at slavery.
  (3) Historians debated slavery's negative effects on slaves and their descendants.
  (4) Slavery destroyed the culture of the slaves, diminishing their self-respect.
  (5) Modern African American culture includes many different forms of music.

Questions 13 through 15 refer to the following paragraph and maps.

Mapmakers have devised many solutions to the problem of projecting the curved surface of Earth onto a flat piece of paper. However, all map projections involve some distortion, and each type of projection has advantages and disadvantages. Two types of projections are shown here.

Mercator Projection

Interrupted Projection

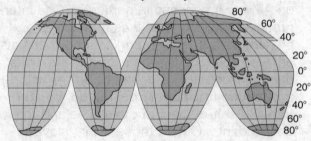

13. Approximately where is there the least distortion on these projections?

(1) at 80° north and south latitude
(2) at 60° north and south latitude
(3) at 40° north and south latitude
(4) at 20° north and south latitude
(5) at 0° latitude

14. What is one of the main differences between the Mercator projection and the interrupted projection?

(1) The Mercator projection distorts the sizes of land masses near the North Pole, and the interrupted projection does not.
(2) The Mercator projection cuts apart the oceans, and the interrupted projection cuts apart the land masses.
(3) The Mercator projection gives an accurate view of the South Pole area, and the interrupted projection does not.
(4) The Mercator projection shows each of the oceans, and the interrupted projection does not.
(5) The Mercator projection shows each of the continents, and the interrupted projection does not.

15. A sailor who needed to plan a rough course for an around-the-world race decided to use the interrupted projection. What was wrong with his decision?

(1) The interrupted projection distorts distances across the continents at mid-latitudes.
(2) The interrupted projection distorts distances across the oceans.
(3) The interrupted projection distorts the shapes of mid-latitude land masses.
(4) The interrupted projection distorts the shapes of polar land masses.
(5) The interrupted projection shows only a few of the world's oceans.

Questions 16 and 17 refer to the following map.

Forced Resettlement of American Indians, 1830s

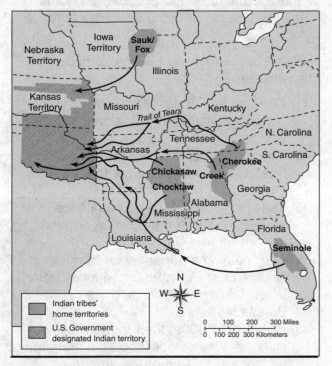

16. Which American Indian tribe was moved the farthest from its tribal lands?

   (1) the Sauk/Fox
   (2) the Cherokee
   (3) the Chickasaw
   (4) the Chocktaw
   (5) the Seminole

17. Which of the following is the most likely reason that American Indians were forcibly relocated in the 1830s?

   (1) Whites wanted lands in the Kansas and Nebraska territory for settlement.
   (2) Whites wanted to take over Indian lands in the eastern states.
   (3) Indians of different tribes wanted to settle in a single Indian territory.
   (4) Indians in the eastern states wanted to look for gold in the West.
   (5) Indians in the eastern states did not want to integrate into white society.

18. During the Neolithic Age (about 8000 B.C. to 3500 B.C.), many societies domesticated plants and animals. One result of animal domestication was a new way of life—pastoralism. In pastoralism, groups of people move from place to place seeking new grazing lands for their animals. Pastoralism has remained the main alternative to settlement agriculture, although in recent times the growth of settled populations has encroached on pastoral lands.

Which of the following is an example of a pastoral society?

   (1) the Bedouin, who are a nomadic herding people of Saudi Arabia
   (2) the Kikuyu, who live on large family farming homesteads in Kenya
   (3) the Amish, who preserve traditional farming methods in the United States
   (4) the Palestinian Arabs, many of whom live in refugee camps
   (5) the mestizos, Mexican people of mixed Native American and European ancestry

19. Once farmers settled beyond the Appalachians in the early 1800s, it became apparent that better transportation of farm produce and trade goods was needed between the East and what is now the Midwest. Constructing decent roads over the Appalachians was one of the first attempts to address this problem.

Which of the following also increased trade between the East and the Midwest?

   (1) dredging deep-water ports on the East Coast
   (2) building the Erie Canal from the Great Lakes to the Hudson River in New York
   (3) prohibiting slavery north of 36° 30' north latitude, the westward extension of Missouri's southern border
   (4) admitting Michigan as a state in 1837
   (5) purchasing Alaska from Russia for $7.2 million

Question 20 refers to the following graph.

Consumer Price Index for Urban Consumers, 1990 and 1999
(1982 to 1984 = 100)

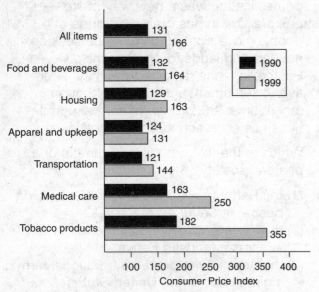

	1990	1999
All items	131	166
Food and beverages	132	164
Housing	129	163
Apparel and upkeep	124	131
Transportation	121	144
Medical care	163	250
Tobacco products	182	355

Consumer Price Index

SOURCE: U.S. Bureau of the Census.

20. Which of the following statements is supported by the data in the graph?

(1) Most of the increased cost of tobacco products was due to increased taxation of these products.
(2) During this period in which the consumer price index rose, wages rose to keep pace with prices.
(3) The cost of food and beverages for an urban consumer almost tripled between 1982–1984 and 1999.
(4) The costs of medical care and tobacco products increased far more than the cost of other items in the 1990s.
(5) Among the items listed, transportation showed the least increase in the period between 1990 and 1999.

21. During the Age of Imperialism (1870 to 1914), the nations of Europe and the United States dominated the political, economic, and cultural life of many countries in Africa, Asia, and Latin America.

Which of the following is an example of imperialism?

(1) Communists under Mao Zedong won control of mainland China after World War II.
(2) Fifteen independent nations, of which Russia is the largest, were formed after the breakup of the Soviet Union.
(3) The United States gained influence over Panama through the building and running of the Panama Canal.
(4) After gaining independence from Great Britain, East Pakistan broke away from West Pakistan and formed the nation of Bangladesh.
(5) In the mid-1800s, the Kingdom of Hungary was established as a monarchy separate from that of the empire of Austria.

22. Areas with average or above average rainfall have humid soils. Humid soils are usually fertile because they contain decaying plant matter. However, humid soils in northern coniferous regions of the United States are not fertile. Acid from the pine needles that cover the ground leaches into the soil, making it unsuitable for agriculture. In the humid, subtropical regions of the southeast, heavy rainfall washes large amounts of minerals from the soil. Growing crops there usually requires heavy use of fertilizers.

Which of the following is a conclusion based on the paragraph rather than a detail?

(1) Humid soils have organic material in them.
(2) Except for soils in northern coniferous regions, humid soils can be used or modified for crops.
(3) The pine needle ground cover of coniferous regions makes the soil acidic.
(4) Rain leaches minerals from the soil in the southeastern United States.
(5) In the southeast, farmers add fertilizers to soil lacking in minerals.

Question 23 and 24 refer to the following passage.

In March 1965, blacks were attacked by state troopers when they first attempted to march from Selma, Alabama, to the state capital, Montgomery, to present Governor Wallace with their complaints about civil rights violations. After several tries, they completed the five-day, 54-mile march along Interstate 80, under the protection of Army troops and the National Guard. Black sharecroppers, who had been evicted from their land for trying to register to vote, built a settlement called Tent City along the highway. The march to Montgomery, which was televised throughout the nation, helped ensure passage of the 1965 Civil Rights Act.

Today that stretch of highway, a national historic trail, is the subject of controversy. In 1998 the local county commission, which has a black majority, approved plans to build a landfill 500 feet off the highway in Lowndes County. Part of the agreement is that the developer will share the revenue with the county, where nearly 40 percent of the people live below the poverty line. The plan has drawn opposition from those who feel that a landfill near the historic highway is an insult. Bob Mants, a former civil rights worker who heads the Lowndes County Friends of the Trail, says, "You can't commemorate it on the one hand and desecrate it on the other." At present, plans for the landfill are on hold as opponents take their case to court.

23. Based on the passage, which of the following statements is an opinion rather than a fact?

(1) The march from Selma to Montgomery helped get the Civil Rights Act of 1965 passed.
(2) Evicted black sharecroppers built Tent City alongside the highway.
(3) It took marchers 5 days to walk the 54 miles between Selma and Montgomery.
(4) Establishing a landfill near a historic site is an insult to the memory of what took place there.
(5) Opponents of the landfill have stopped its progress by taking their case to court.

24. The controversy over the landfill has united blacks and whites on both sides of the issue.

Which values are pitted against one another in this conflict?

(1) individualism versus group welfare
(2) the right to life versus protecting the environment
(3) freedom of speech versus free enterprise
(4) civil rights versus law and order
(5) present-day economic benefit versus respect for the past

Question 25 refers to the following cartoon.

"I THOUGHT HE WAS A MEMBER OF A SPECIAL INTEREST GROUP... BUT I FOUND OUT HE'S ONLY A VOTER!"

© Wayne Stayskal. Reprinted by permission of Wayne Stayskal.

25. With which of the following opinions would the cartoonist be most likely to agree?

(1) People shouldn't have to stand around waiting to see their elected representatives.
(2) Senators should pay attention to special interest groups as well as to voters.
(3) Special interest groups have too much influence with members of Congress.
(4) Senators are nicer to their constituents than are members of the House.
(5) Senators and members of the House of Representatives should work together more closely.

Questions 26 and 27 refer to the map below.

Europe After World War II

26. During World War II, the United States, Great Britain, and the Soviet Union were allied in the fight against Nazi Germany. The Soviet Union had a communist government and the other Allies did not. Toward the end of World War II, the British and Americans approached Germany from the west, as the Soviets approached Germany from the east. Soon Germany surrendered to the Allies.

Based on the paragraph and the map, what was one result of this strategy?

(1) Fighting between communists and non-communists raged in Greece.
(2) Finland became a member of NATO.
(3) Switzerland remained neutral both during and after the war.
(4) Germany was divided into two parts, West Germany and East Germany.
(5) Northern Ireland remained a part of Great Britain, although Ireland became an independent nation.

27. NATO, which stands for the North American Treaty Organization, was a military alliance of noncommunist nations in Europe and North America. The Warsaw Pact was an alliance of communist nations in Europe.

Which of the following is a conclusion based on this information and on the map rather than a detail?

(1) Great Britain was a member of the NATO alliance.
(2) All the Warsaw Pact nations were located in eastern Europe.
(3) Norway was a member of NATO.
(4) Romania was a Warsaw Pact nation.
(5) Austria was neutral after World War II.

28. Constitutional guarantees of fairness and equality under the law, our basic civil liberties, are called due process of law. The Fifth and Fourteenth Amendments state that government shall not deprive anyone of "life, liberty, or property, without due process of law." The Fifth Amendment protects people from actions of the federal government. The Fourteenth, protects people specifically from actions of governments of the individual states.

What is a main difference between the Fifth and Fourteenth Amendments?

(1) The Fifth Amendment applies to adults, and the Fourteenth Amendment, to children.
(2) The Fifth Amendment applies to due process, and the Fourteenth Amendment, to freedom of speech.
(3) The Fifth Amendment applies to liberty, and the Fourteenth Amendment, to property.
(4) The Fifth Amendment applies to the federal government, and the Fourteenth Amendment, to state governments.
(5) The Fifth Amendment applies to life, and the Fourteenth Amendment, to liberty.

Questions 29 and 30 refer to the following map.

The Roman Empire, 500 B.C. to 44 B.C.

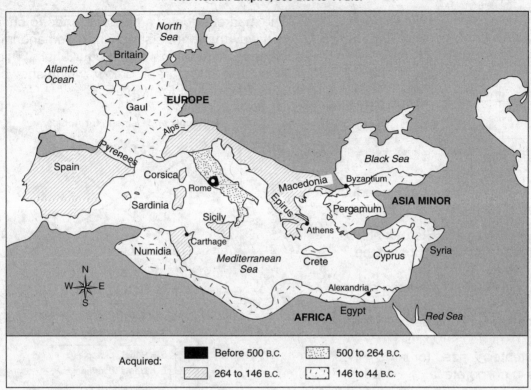

29. During which time period did the Roman Empire gain the most territory in Asia Minor?

   (1) before 500 B.C.
   (2) between 500 and 264 B.C.
   (3) between 264 and 146 B.C.
   (4) between 146 and 44 B.C.
   (5) after 44 B.C.

30. Which of the following conclusions is supported by the information on the map?

   (1) Rome granted citizenship to the Latin-speaking peoples who lived on the Italian peninsula.
   (2) Before 264 B.C., Rome conquered through overland military campaigns; later conquests were made by navies as well.
   (3) Numidia was added to the Roman Empire before the island of Sicily was.
   (4) Corsica, Crete, and Cyprus were conquered by the Romans during the same military campaign.
   (5) Hannibal marched from Carthage to Italy by way of Spain, crossing the Pyrenees into Gaul and the Alps into northern Italy.

Question 31 refers to the following chart.

The Effect of World War II on Industry

Measure	1939	1940	1941
Index of manufacturing output (1939 = 100)	100	116	154
Corporate profits before taxes	$6.4 billion	$9.3 billion	$17 billion
Corporate profits after taxes	$5 billion	$6.5 billion	$9.4 billion

SOURCE: Fute, Gilbert C., and Reese, Jim E. *An Economic History of the United States.*

31. Why did the war have the effect on industry that is indicated by the chart?

    (1) Even before the United States entered the war, corporate profits had increased sharply.
    (2) Manufacturing output increased by over 50 percent in two years.
    (3) The war created a huge demand for military equipment and supplies.
    (4) The war created a need for large increases in corporate tax revenue.
    (5) With men gone to serve as soldiers, more women were employed in factories.

32. The U.S. president has a great deal of influence over foreign policy. In part, this is because international relations often require quick and decisive action, which is best undertaken by an individual. In times of foreign crisis, the public usually rallies to the support of the president, at least at first.

    Which of the following values probably underlies Americans' initial approval of a president's emergency foreign policy actions?

    (1) individualism
    (2) patriotism
    (3) imperialism
    (4) self-expression
    (5) self-sacrifice

Questions 33 and 34 refer to the following paragraph and graph.

The market price of a product tends to change in a way that brings supply and demand into balance, a condition called equilibrium. This is illustrated in the graph below, which shows supply and demand for apples.

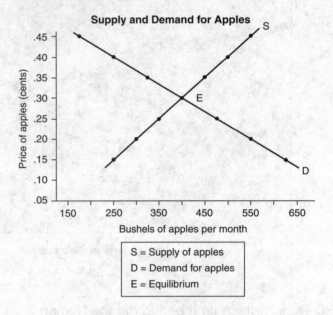

Supply and Demand for Apples

S = Supply of apples
D = Demand for apples
E = Equilibrium

33. According to this graph, what is the market price of apples—also known as the price at equilibrium?

    (1) 45 cents
    (2) 40 cents
    (3) 30 cents
    (4) 20 cents
    (5) 15 cents

34. Which of the following would result if part of the apple crop were destroyed but demand remained the same?

    (1) Supply would increase.
    (2) Supply would remain the same.
    (3) The market price would remain the same.
    (4) The market price would go down.
    (5) The market price would go up.

Questions 35 through 37 refer to the following paragraph and diagram.

Most cases that arise under federal law are tried in the federal court system. The federal court system has several levels of courts and several routes by which cases may be appealed to a higher court.

Routing Cases Through the Federal Court System

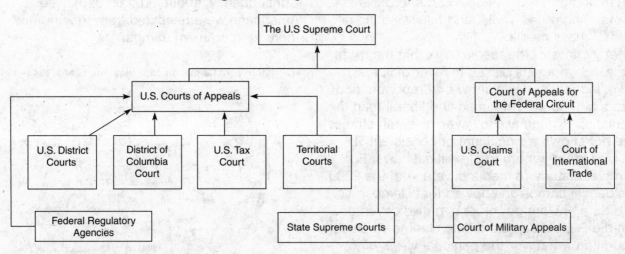

35. If cases are not resolved in any of the lower federal courts, to which court may they eventually, finally be appealed?

    (1) the Supreme Court of the United States
    (2) the United States Court of Appeals
    (3) a state's Supreme Court
    (4) the Court of Appeals for the Federal Circuit
    (5) the Court of Military Appeals

36. A U.S. import-export firm files a lawsuit against a foreign trading company. In which court is the suit most likely to be filed?

    (1) the United States Claims Court
    (2) the United States Court of Appeals
    (3) the Court of International Trade
    (4) the United States Tax Court
    (5) the United States District Court

37. The U.S. Constitution established only the Supreme Court, but it gave Congress the power to create inferior (lower) federal courts. Which is the most likely reason that Congress established other federal courts?

    (1) The justices of the U.S. Supreme Court were not well versed enough in the law to handle all federal cases.
    (2) The volume and variety of federal cases were too great for a single court to handle.
    (3) A system of inferior federal courts gave the United States prestige in the eyes of the rest of the world.
    (4) The Supreme Court was able to both hear original cases and take cases on appeal.
    (5) The Supreme Court's power to interpret the Constitution was established in *Marbury v. Madison*.

Questions 38 and 39 refer to the following passage.

American citizens get most of their political information and news from the mass media—methods of communication that can reach most people and that most people can afford. Newspapers, magazines, radio, and television are all types of mass media.

Many critics of the media think that the mass media's coverage is biased in favor of liberal views. Indeed, surveys show that reporters and editors are more Democratic and liberal than the population in general. However, research studies have not shown a significant or consistent liberal bias in the reporting of political news. For example, a study of media coverage of the 2000 presidential campaign showed that Democratic candidate Al Gore got more negative coverage than did Republican candidate George W. Bush. In addition, whatever the personal views of journalists, a balancing, conservative influence is exerted by media executives and stockholders of media corporations, who are interested in profits.

38. According to the passage, which of the following statements is an opinion?

   (1) The mass media reach most of the U.S. population.
   (2) Newspapers, magazines, radio, and television are all part of the mass media.
   (3) There are more Democrats and liberals among journalists than in the general public.
   (4) The mass media's coverage of political news has a consistent liberal bias.
   (5) Media executives and stockholders tend to exert a conservative influence.

39. Which of the following is most likely to become part of the mass media in the future?

   (1) cellular phones
   (2) personal digital assistants
   (3) the Internet
   (4) pagers
   (5) digital video disks

Question 40 refers to the following paragraph and map.

During World War II, the U.S. government feared that Japanese Americans on the West Coast might pose a danger to American security. Consequently, about 110,000 Japanese Americans were relocated from their homes there to internment camps.

Internment Camps for Japanese Americans, 1942–1945

Military Area (exclusion zone in which Japanese Americans could not live, except in internment camps)

▲ Internment camps

40. Which of the following conclusions is supported by the paragraph and the map?

   (1) More Japanese-American internment camps were located in Arkansas than in any other state.
   (2) Japanese Americans in California lost more property than those in Washington or Oregon.
   (3) There were no internment camps in the states of California, Nevada, Montana, or New Mexico.
   (4) All of the camps were located inland to make it difficult for any Japanese American to communicate with Japanese offshore.
   (5) The government did not have specific evidence that Japanese Americans posed a danger to American security.

Questions 41 through 43 refer to the following passage.

Thousands of years ago, people bartered to meet their needs. For example, if a man caught two fish, he might barter, or exchange, them for a neighbor's basket. Bartering allowed for the exchange of goods and services, but it had disadvantages. First, when two people barter, each must have something the other wants or there is no trade. Second, they must agree on the relative value of the items. Finally, it's not always possible to save something and barter it at a later date. The man with the fish needed to barter it right away or the value of the fish would drop.

Money was invented to solve bartering problems. Money has several advantages over bartering. First, it is a widely accepted way to exchange goods and services. Not everyone will accept a fish or a basket for goods or labor, but everyone will accept money. Second, money allows people to compare the value of goods and services. If one bracelet is priced at $59 and another at $599, it is immediately clear which is worth more. Third, money is a way to store value. Money does not have to be spent right away; it can be saved and spent later.

41. What is bartering?

(1) trading goods and services for other goods and services
(2) stockpiling goods that will increase in value
(3) selling a good or service for a particular amount of money
(4) negotiating the value of a particular good or service
(5) buying a good or service, adding value to it, and reselling it

42. What do bartering and the use of money have in common?

(1) Both necessarily involve trading items for other items.
(2) Both necessarily have time limits on their usefulness.
(3) Both allow for the easy comparison of value.
(4) Both are ways to store value.
(5) Both are ways to exchange goods and services.

43. Which of the following statements is a conclusion from the passage rather than a supporting detail?

(1) Money has several advantages over bartering.
(2) Money is widely accepted in economic transactions.
(3) Money allows for fairly accurate determination of worth.
(4) In bartering, each person must have what the other wants.
(5) In bartering, goods can lose value with time.

Important Political Documents Preceding the Declaration of Independence and the U.S. Constitution

Year	Document	Description
1215	Magna Carta	Limited the power of the English king and granted rights to the nobles
1620	Mayflower Compact	Set rules by which the Pilgrims would govern themselves in Plymouth colony
1628	Petition of Right	Limited the English king's powers further
1636	Great Fundamentals	Established the first basic system of laws in the English colonies, in Massachusetts Bay Colony
1688	English Bill of Rights	Declared that the king rules with the consent of the people's representatives in Parliament; granted ordinary people certain rights

44. Which document first set limits on the British monarch's powers?

(1) the Magna Carta
(2) the Mayflower Compact
(3) the Petition of Right
(4) the Great Fundamentals
(5) the English Bill of Rights

45. What do the Mayflower Compact and the Great Fundamentals have in common?

(1) Both limited the power of the king.
(2) Both granted rights to the nobles.
(3) Both established a parliament.
(4) Both established methods of self-government in English colonies.
(5) Both applied to the government in England.

46. One of the major grievances the American colonists had against the British was that the British taxed the colonists without granting them representation in the British Parliament. Part of the Declaration of Independence is a list of political and economic rights that American colonists complained that the British king had deprived them of.

By which of the following documents were the writers of the Declaration probably most influenced as they drafted their list?

(1) the Magna Carta
(2) the Mayflower Compact
(3) the Petition of Right
(4) the Great Fundamentals
(5) the English Bill of Rights

47. Like the ancient Chinese, the ancient Greeks thought that a sound political system and well-established social relationships were necessary for a stable society. Greek rule was decentralized, and as a result, many political structures coexisted. In contrast, Chinese rule was largely centralized, and a single political system prevailed. The Greeks placed more value on councils, participation, and law; the Chinese, on bureaucracy, hierarchy, and rules.

Based on the paragraph, what did the ancient Greeks and the ancient Chinese have in common in regard to politics and government?

(1) Both emphasized the participation of citizens.
(2) Both governed through a hierarchical bureaucracy.
(3) Both valued a stable political framework for society.
(4) Both had centralized councils.
(5) Both had decentralized political systems.

Question 48 refers to the following chart.

Traffic Delays in the Largest Metropolitan Areas

Metropolitan Area	Annual Hours Delayed per Person	Percent of Workers Not Driving
New York	34	39.3%
Los Angeles	56	12.6%
Chicago	34	23%
Washington, D.C.	46	23.1%
San Francisco	42	23.8%

48. Which of the following statements is a conclusion based on the chart rather than a detail?

(1) Almost 40 percent of workers in the New York area do not use cars to commute.
(2) Los Angeles has the worst traffic delays because such a large percentage of workers drive there.
(3) In Washington the average person spends 46 hours per year delayed in traffic jams.
(4) About one-quarter of workers in the Chicago area do not drive to work.
(5) In San Francisco the average person loses 42 hours per year stuck in traffic.

49. A franchise is a business arrangement in which a large corporation allows an individual or group to operate an outlet, using its well-known name and selling its goods. In return, the franchisee pays an up-front fee and a percent of sales revenues to the corporation.

Which of the following is a franchise?

(1) Middletown General Store, a mom-and-pop operation
(2) General Motors, a corporation that manufactures cars and other products
(3) Dewey & Lopez, an accounting firm run by partners
(4) McDonald's, a chain of fast-food restaurants run by individuals
(5) Get Organized!, a consulting business run out of a person's home

Question 50 refers to the following graph.

Civil War Casualties

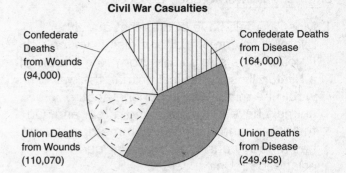

Confederate Deaths from Wounds (94,000)
Confederate Deaths from Disease (164,000)
Union Deaths from Wounds (110,070)
Union Deaths from Disease (249,458)

50. Which of the following conclusions is supported by the data in the graph?

(1) The Confederate Army suffered more casualties than the Union Army.
(2) About the same number of Confederate and Union soldiers died of disease.
(3) About twice as many Civil War soldiers died of disease as died of wounds.
(4) Almost as many civilians died during the Civil War as soldiers.
(5) About twice as many Union soldiers died of wounds as did Confederate soldiers.

Answers and explanations start on page 617.

GED SCIENCE POST-TEST

Directions: You will have 80 minutes to answer 50 questions on the GED Science Test. Choose the one best answer to each question.

1. Most animals have bodies that are either bilaterally symmetrical or radially symmetrical. If you drew a straight line down the middle of a bilaterally symmetrical animal, the two sides would be mirror images of one another. Such animals have a front end and a rear end. On the other hand, a radially symmetrical animal has a body consisting of similar parts arranged around a center.

   Which of the following animals has a radially symmetrical body plan?

   (1) salt marsh greenhead fly

   (2) dogfish

   (3) sea star

   (4) black skimmer

   (5) horseshoe crab

   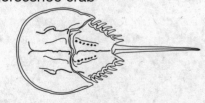

2. In 1969, the U.S. Surgeon General announced that infectious bacterial diseases would soon become a thing of the past because antibiotic drugs had become so effective against them. However, since that time, strains of disease-causing bacteria that are resistant to antibiotics have evolved. Some types of pneumonia and gastrointestinal infections are now untreatable by antibiotics. About 17 million people worldwide still die annually from infectious diseases.

   Why was the U.S. Surgeon General's prediction wrong?

   (1) Antibiotic drugs are not effective against most disease-causing bacteria.
   (2) Infectious diseases are also caused by viruses and parasites.
   (3) Infectious diseases have remained a problem outside the United States.
   (4) Bacteria quickly evolved resistance to antibiotic drugs.
   (5) Some types of pneumonia and gastrointestinal infections can be fatal.

3. If you run too many appliances, like a toaster oven, microwave, and vacuum cleaner, at the same time on the same electrical circuit, the wires can get so hot that they burn away the insulation and cause a fire.

   Which of the following devices would prevent this from happening?

   (1) a smoke detector, which sets off an alarm when triggered by smoke
   (2) a portable fire extinguisher, which is used to put out household fires
   (3) a battery, which provides less voltage than household current
   (4) a switch, a device that is used to open and close an electrical circuit
   (5) a fuse, a strip of wire that melts when it gets too hot, breaking an electrical circuit

Questions 4 through 6 refer to the following map.

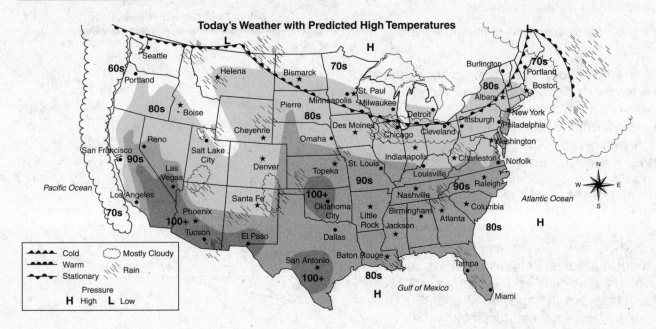

Today's Weather with Predicted High Temperatures

4. What is the high temperature in Tucson?

   (1) 60s
   (2) 70s
   (3) 80s
   (4) 90s
   (5) 100+

5. What is the main difference between the weather in Minneapolis and Chicago?

   (1) It is raining in Minneapolis but cloudy in Chicago.
   (2) It is clear in Minneapolis but there are showers in Chicago.
   (3) It is in the 80s in Minneapolis but in the 90s in Chicago.
   (4) It is in the 90s in Minneapolis but 100+ in Chicago.
   (5) There is a low-pressure system over Minneapolis and a high-pressure system over Chicago.

6. Which of the following statements is supported by the information on the map?

   (1) The weather is clear and sunny in Baton Rouge and Tampa.
   (2) The Northeast is the only region with temperatures in the 70s.
   (3) It is warmer in Oklahoma City than in Santa Fe.
   (4) There is an area of low pressure and a warm front over the Gulf of Mexico.
   (5) In the United States, air masses usually move from west to east.

7. One property of a gas is that its molecules spread out to fill their container.

   Which of the following best illustrates this property of gases?

   (1) A helium balloon rises into the atmosphere.
   (2) A teacher's perfume can be detected at the back of the classroom.
   (3) Rain puddles evaporate more quickly when the sun comes out.
   (4) Water is produced when hydrogen gas is burned in oxygen gas.
   (5) Liquid oxygen is denser than gaseous oxygen.

8. For five years, researchers at the University of Wisconsin Medical School ran an experiment in which they evaluated the hearing of 3,753 people between the ages of 48 and 92. Of the group, 46 percent were nonsmokers, 30.3 percent were former smokers, and 14.7 percent still smoked. The scientists found that smokers were nearly 1.7 times as likely as nonsmokers to suffer hearing loss. The study suggests that age-related hearing loss might be preventable.

   Which of the following statements is most likely to have been the researchers' hypothesis?

   (1) Smoking has been shown to harm health in many different ways.
   (2) People can reduce their chances of developing age-related hearing loss by not smoking.
   (3) The University of Wisconsin study group consisted of 3,753 people between the ages of 48 and 92.
   (4) Of the group, 46 percent were nonsmokers, 30.3 percent used to smoke, and 14.7 percent still smoked.
   (5) Smokers were nearly 1.7 times as likely as nonsmokers to suffer hearing loss.

Question 9 refers to the following graph.

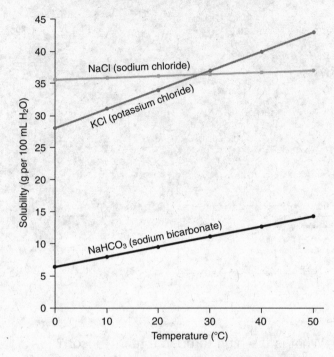

Solubility of Common Compounds in Grams of Solute per 100mL of Water

9. Which of the following statements is supported by the information in the graph?

   (1) About 15 grams of sodium bicarbonate will dissolve in 100 mL of water at 10°C.
   (2) About 30 grams of potassium chloride will dissolve in 100 mL of water at 30°C.
   (3) Sodium chloride shows the greatest increase in solubility with increase in temperature.
   (4) For two compounds shown, solubility increases as temperature increases.
   (5) The amount of water does not affect the solubility of the compounds shown.

10. When removed from the body, large organs live only a few hours or days under cold conditions. Therefore, organ transplants must be performed quickly. Many organs go to waste because the organ cannot be transported to an appropriate patient in the short time available. Unfortunately, it is not yet possible to freeze large organs to preserve them for a longer period. That's because they contain many different types of cells, all of which react differently to freezing. Some cells are even destroyed by the ice crystals that form during freezing.

Which of the following studies is most likely to yield information that might help solve the specific problem of freezing whole organs for transplant?

(1) how the time it takes to locate patients who need organs can be decreased
(2) how the time it takes to transport organs to their destinations can be decreased
(3) how special fluids keep insects alive during subfreezing weather
(4) how radioactive isotopes can be used to diagnose the condition of donated organs
(5) how the long-term success rate of organ donations can be increased

Question 11 refers to the following diagrams.

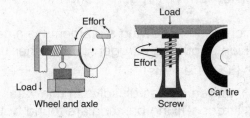

11. What do the wheel and axle and the screw have in common?

(1) Both increase the effort needed to move a load.
(2) Both use ropes to carry the load.
(3) Both involve effort applied with circular motion.
(4) Both involve effort applied with horizontal motion.
(5) Both involve effort applied with vertical motion.

Question 12 refers to the following chart.

Melting and Boiling Points

Element	Melting Point, °F	Boiling Point, °F
Mercury	–38	675
Bromine	19	138
Iron	2,795	5,184
Carbon	6,420	8,720
Gold	1,945	5,379

12. Which of the following statements is supported by the information in the chart?

(1) Mercury and bromine are liquids at room temperature.
(2) Iron has a higher melting point than carbon.
(3) Iron has a higher boiling point than gold.
(4) Mercury, bromine, iron, carbon, and gold are all metals.
(5) Mercury has the highest boiling point of the elements listed.

13. Weathering is the breaking down of rock by rain, frost, wind, and other elements. No transport is involved in weathering. The weathered rock remains in place. Weathering can be physical, involving abrasion—the wearing away of a surface—or changes in temperature. It can be chemical, involving chemical reactions. Or it can be organic, involving the action of living things.

Which of the following is an example of physical weathering?

(1) the cracking of granite from the expansion of freezing water
(2) the breakdown of calcite by reaction with acids in rainwater
(3) the transport of sediment by rivers and glaciers
(4) the transport of sand by the wind
(5) the breakdown of crumbling rock in the soil by burrowing worms

Questions 14 through 17 refer to the following information and diagram.

The processes that circulate nitrogen between the atmosphere, land, and organisms are called the nitrogen cycle.

The Nitrogen Cycle

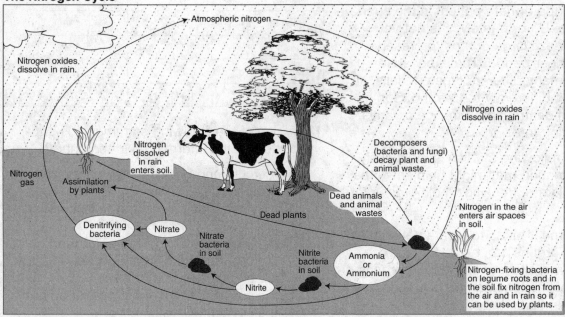

14. Nitrogen-fixing bacteria are found both in the soil and on the roots of legumes like peas and beans. From where do these bacteria get nitrogen?

    (1) ammonia and ammonium
    (2) the air and rainwater in the soil
    (3) plant and animal proteins
    (4) animals and animal wastes
    (5) animal wastes and decaying plants

15. To increase the nitrogen content of the soil, many farmers spread synthetic fertilizers containing nitrogen compounds. What might an organic farmer, who does not use synthetic fertilizers, do to improve the fertility of the soil?

    (1) use atmospheric nitrogen
    (2) compost with plant and animal wastes
    (3) plant more nonleguminous plants
    (4) switch to crops requiring more nitrogen
    (5) switch to crops that grow faster

16. What do denitrifying bacteria do?

    (1) They turn ammonia into nitrites.
    (2) They turn ammonium into nitrates.
    (3) They help plants assimilate nitrates.
    (4) They take in nitrogen gas from the air.
    (5) They return nitrogen gas to the air.

17. Which of the following statements is a conclusion about the nitrogen cycle rather than a supporting statement?

    (1) Nitrogen oxides dissolve in rainwater.
    (2) Nitrogen-fixing bacteria are found both in the soil and on the roots of legumes.
    (3) The recycling of nitrogen through the biosphere involves many complex processes.
    (4) Decomposers break down plant and animal waste, releasing ammonia.
    (5) Nitrite bacteria turn ammonia and ammonium into nitrites.

18. In a fire, hydrocarbon molecules react with oxygen to produce heat and light as well as carbon dioxide and water. This process is called combustion. Air heated by the fire rises, and cool oxygen-rich air flows in below. The movement of air around a fire causes it to flicker. Scientists have found that the flickering of a fire differs from the flickering of all other light sources.

Which of the following devices makes use of this property of fire?

(1) an internal combustion engine
(2) a flame detector
(3) a smoke detector
(4) a dripless candle
(5) an oil burner

19. In 1861, Charles Darwin, a naturalist who formulated the theory of evolution, remarked that the science of geology had made much progress in his lifetime. He wrote, "About thirty years ago there was much talk that geologists ought only to observe and not theorize; and I well remember someone saying that at this rate a man might as well go into a gravel-pit and count the pebbles and describe the colors. How odd it is that anyone should not see that all observation must be for or against some view if it is to be of any service!"

Which of the following statements best summarizes Darwin's view of the role of observation in science?

(1) Observation is the best way to gather facts about any aspect of nature, including geology.
(2) Observation is a useful part of the scientific method as long as it is supported by statistics.
(3) Observation is a good method of gathering information only when experimentation is impossible.
(4) Observation should be used as a method of gathering information only in the field of geology.
(5) Observation is a useful part of the scientific method as long as the results are used to support or disprove a hypothesis.

Question 20 refers to the following paragraph and diagram.

Bernoulli's principle states that the pressure in a fluid decreases as the speed of the fluid increases. An airplane's wing, which is shaped to speed up airflow and thus reduce pressure on the top side of the wing, makes use of this principle.

Bernoulli's Principle

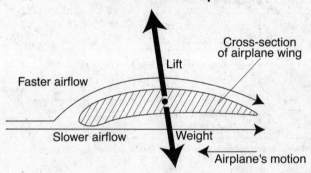

20. Which vertical force holds an airplane up?

(1) Bernoulli's principle
(2) lift
(3) weight
(4) air resistance
(5) airflow

Question 21 refers to the following chart.

Some Major Oil Spills

Year	Description	Gallons (millions)
1979	Blowout of well in Gulf of Mexico oil field	180
1979	Collision of *Atlantic Empress* and *Aegean Captain* in Caribbean	111
1983	Blowout of well in Persian Gulf oil field	180
1989	Grounding of *Exxon Valdez* off Alaska coast	11
1991	Release of oil in Persian Gulf by Iraqi troops at end of Persian Gulf War	240
1996	Grounding of *Sea Empress* off Wales coast	19

SOURCE: *Scientific American Science Desk Reference.* New York, Wiley, 1999

21. What does the person who compiled the data in this chart take for granted that you know?

(1) The worst oil spill on record was deliberately started.
(2) *Atlantic Empress, Aegean Captain, Exxon Valdez,* and *Sea Empress* are oil tankers.
(3) When oil wells blow out, a relatively large oil spill results.
(4) About 11 million gallons of oil were spilled in the *Exxon Valdez* accident.
(5) About 19 million gallons of oil were spilled when the *Sea Empress* ran aground off the coast of Wales.

22. Atoms are composed of protons (positive charge), neutrons (no charge), and electrons (negative charge). Because an atom has an equal number of protons and electrons, it has a total charge of zero.

What would happen if an atom lost an electron?

(1) Its charge would become positive.
(2) Its charge would become negative.
(3) Its charge would remain neutral.
(4) Its neutrons would gain a positive charge.
(5) Its neutrons would gain a negative charge.

23. The life cycle of many plants, including spore-producing plants like ferns, takes place in two generations that alternate: the gametophyte generation and the sporophyte generation. In ferns, the gametophyte is a very small, heart-shaped structure. During the gametophyte generation, sex cells are produced, two of which fuse to produce a zygote. The zygote grows into the sporophyte. In ferns, the sporophyte is the familiar green plant with leaves, stems, and roots. During the sporophyte generation, gametes, which grow into the gametophyte, are produced.

Which of the following conclusions is supported by this information?

(1) Ferns are the only plants that have different forms in alternating generations.
(2) Seed plants reproduce either sexually or asexually.
(3) Most people would not recognize the gametophyte generation of a fern.
(4) Some animal life cycles consist of alternating generations with different forms.
(5) All plants that reproduce sexually have leaves, stems, roots, and flowers.

Question 24 refers to the following graphs.

Elements in Humans and Bacteria

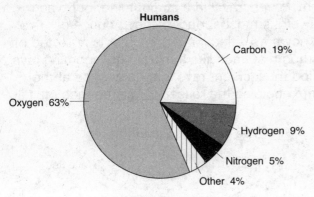

Humans

Carbon 19%
Oxygen 63%
Hydrogen 9%
Nitrogen 5%
Other 4%

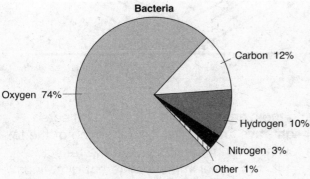

Bacteria

Carbon 12%
Oxygen 74%
Hydrogen 10%
Nitrogen 3%
Other 1%

24. What is one of the main differences between the composition of humans and that of bacteria?

(1) Humans contain nitrogen, and bacteria do not.
(2) Humans contain elements other than oxygen, carbon, nitrogen, and hydrogen and bacteria do not.
(3) Humans contain a higher percentage of oxygen than bacteria do.
(4) Humans contain a higher percentage of hydrogen than bacteria do.
(5) Humans contain a higher percentage of carbon than bacteria do.

25. In the cheese-making process, milk is separated into solid curds and liquid whey through the action of starter bacteria and a curdling agent. The curds are then drained, cooked, pressed, and salted to remove the whey. The final stage of cheese making is ripening. To make Swiss-type cheese, a special type of bacterium is added with the starter bacteria. During ripening, this special bacterium feeds on the lactic acid produced by the other bacteria, and it produces large amounts of carbon dioxide. The gas collects as large bubbles throughout a properly ripened Swiss-type cheese.

What forms the holes in Swiss-type cheese?

(1) lactic acid
(2) starter bacteria
(3) carbon dioxide gas
(4) whey
(5) curds

26. During various periods in Earth's history, average global temperatures have dropped, resulting in ice ages. During an ice age, glaciers cover large regions of Earth. Scientists disagree about what causes ice ages. One theory suggests that there have been long-term changes in Earth's orbit, causing the planet to periodically move farther from the sun. Another theory proposes that a periodic increase in volcanic activity increases the dust in the atmosphere, blocking the sun's rays. Still another theory suggests that changes in Earth's own radiant energy cause ice ages. Yet another theory proposes that changes in the direction of ocean currents causes ice ages.

Which of the following statements is a fact rather than an opinion, hypothesis, or theory?

(1) During an ice age, temperatures drop and ice covers vast areas of Earth.
(2) Changes in Earth's orbit may cause temperature fluctuations and ice ages.
(3) Large amounts of volcanic dust blocking the sun's energy may cause ice ages.
(4) Changes in the Earth's own radiant energy may cause ice ages.
(5) Changes in the direction of ocean currents may cause ice ages.

Questions 27 and 28 refer to the following information.

Vertebrates are animals with backbones. They are grouped into seven classes:

Mammalia. Animals with fur or hair; females produce milk to feed the young; most dwell on land; squirrels are an example.

Aves. Birds, with feathers; most capable of flight; pigeons are an example.

Reptilia. Animals that live mainly on land, with tough skin to withstand dry habitats; snakes are an example.

Amphibia. Animals that develop in water, undergo metamorphosis—a change in body form, and often live as adults on land; salamanders are an example.

Osteichthyes. Fish with a skeleton made of bone, such as tuna.

Agnatha. Jawless fish with a mouth that functions as a suction cup; lampreys are an example.

Chondrichthyes. Fish with skeletons of flexible cartilage rather than of bone; sharks are an example.

27. At Sting Ray City in the Cayman Islands, snorkelers and scuba divers can swim with sting rays, cartilaginous fish with a flattened body and large fins. To which class of vertebrates do sting rays belong?

    (1) Mammalia
    (2) Reptilia
    (3) Amphibia
    (4) Osteichthyes
    (5) Chondrichthyes

28. At a natural history museum, an exhibit shows the life cycle of a frog, from the newly hatched, legless tadpole with gills, to the mature frog with legs and lungs. To which class of vertebrates do frogs belong?

    (1) Mammalia
    (2) Reptilia
    (3) Amphibia
    (4) Osteichthyes
    (5) Agnatha

Question 29 refers to the following paragraph and diagram.

Light waves travel in a straight line, but when they strike most surfaces, they bounce off; this is known as reflection. When light is reflected off a smooth surface like a mirror, the incoming rays, called the incident rays, hit the surface at the same angle as the reflected rays bounce off it.

The Reflection of Light

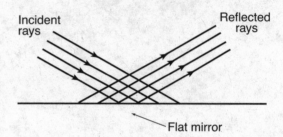

29. In the diagram above, all of the reflected light rays are parallel. Under which of the following circumstances would the reflected light rays travel in many different directions?

    (1) if the source of light were distant
    (2) if the source of light were dim
    (3) if the surface were irregular or rough
    (4) if the surface were perfectly flat
    (5) if the incident rays were parallel

30. In a chemical reaction, the atoms of the reactants are rearranged to form products with different chemical and physical properties. A catalyst is a substance that speeds the rate at which a chemical reaction takes place. The catalyst itself is unchanged at the end of the reaction.

In which of the following reactions is a catalyst at work?

(1) when an acid is neutralized, as when hydrochloric acid is added to sodium hydroxide yielding sodium chloride and water

(2) when food is digested, as when an enzyme in saliva called ptyalin breaks down starch into sugars without itself changing

(3) when nitrogen dioxide is heated, causing the gas to break down and form oxygen and nitrogen monoxide

(4) when copper is oxidized by combining with nitric acid to yield copper nitrate, nitrogen dioxide, and water

(5) when baking soda is heated, causing the sodium bicarbonate to break down, yielding carbon dioxide gas as a byproduct

31. There are an estimated 17 million to 22 million animals in scientific research facilities in the United States. To scientists and many others, animal research provides a way to learn about living organisms, develop treatments for disease, and experiment with genetics, obtaining knowledge that will ultimately benefit people. To others, animal research is a barbaric, outdated practice that should be outlawed.

People who oppose animal research are likely to hold certain values. Which or the following are they most likely to favor?

(1) genetic testing
(2) genetic counseling
(3) animal rights
(4) cloning
(5) individualism

Question 32 refers to the following diagram.

Structure of a Volcano

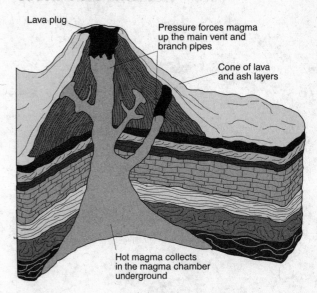

Lava plug

Pressure forces magma up the main vent and branch pipes

Cone of lava and ash layers

Hot magma collects in the magma chamber underground

32. Based on the diagram, what causes a volcano to erupt?

(1) Pressure builds up inside the magma chamber and vent.

(2) Magma flows down toward the underground chamber.

(3) The lava plug at the top of the main vent wears away.

(4) The lava plug at the top of the main vent collapses inward.

(5) The volcano can no longer bear the weight of layers of lava and ash.

Questions 33 and 34 refer to the following diagrams.

Induced Electric Current

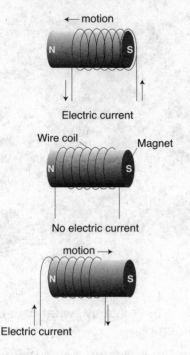

33. What causes an electric current to flow?

   (1) the coil of wire
   (2) the north pole of the magnet
   (3) the south pole of the magnet
   (4) the movement of the magnet
   (5) the shape of the magnet

34. Which of the following statements is supported by the information in the diagram?

   (1) Each magnet has two north poles and two south poles.
   (2) The opposite poles of two magnets attract each other.
   (3) When the magnet changes direction, the current changes direction.
   (4) Batteries as well as moving magnets can induce an electric current.
   (5) Electric current consists of the flow of electrons.

35. Supercomputers are the fastest, most powerful types of computers, performing operations on huge amounts of data at extraordinary speeds. Supercomputers are used in many scientific disciplines, including fluid dynamics, aerodynamics, and nuclear physics.

Which of the following is implied by this information?

   (1) In time, supercomputers will replace personal computers for most business and household uses.
   (2) Supercomputers differ from personal computers only in their speed of operations.
   (3) The computations performed by supercomputers can also be done with electronic calculators.
   (4) The first electronic computer built in 1943, the Colossus, was a supercomputer.
   (5) Fluid dynamics, aerodynamics, and nuclear physics are fields in which large data sets must be analyzed routinely.

36. Drinking too much water can cause a marathon runner to collapse or even die after a race. Here is why: During heavy exercise, blood is diverted to the muscles, so the intestines cannot absorb all the water a runner drinks. Once the race is over, all of the excess water quickly enters the bloodstream, reducing the concentration of salt in the blood. In turn, the brain swells and water is released into the lungs. Although the treatment is simple—adding salt to the blood—the condition is often mistaken for heart trouble because of fluid in the lungs and the circumstances during which the patient collapsed.

Which of the following would help prevent the salt imbalance that leads runners to collapse?

   (1) eating less the day before a marathon
   (2) running the marathon more quickly
   (3) drinking more water than usual during a marathon
   (4) drinking only the amount of water the runner actually loses during a marathon
   (5) carrying one's medical history when running a marathon

Question 37 refers to the following paragraph and diagram.

Herbivores are animals that eat only plants; carnivores are animals that eat animals. Typical herbivore and carnivore teeth patterns are shown below.

Typical Teeth Patterns in Carnivores and Herbivores

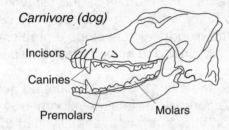

Carnivore (dog)

Incisors

Canines

Premolars

Molars

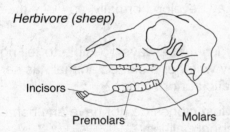

Herbivore (sheep)

Incisors

Premolars

Molars

37. What is the most important difference between the dog's teeth and the sheep's teeth?

    (1) The dog has fewer teeth than the sheep does.
    (2) The dog has molars and the sheep does not.
    (3) The dog has premolars and the sheep does not.
    (4) The dog has incisors and the sheep does not.
    (5) The dog has canines and the sheep does not.

Question 38 refers to the following diagram.

Nuclear Fission

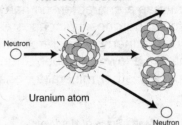

Neutron

Uranium atom

Neutron

38. In the nuclear fission reaction shown above, what is the function of the neutron on the left?

    (1) to split the uranium atom
    (2) to attract the protons in the nucleus of a uranium atom
    (3) to attract the electrons in the nucleus of a uranium atom
    (4) to combine with an atom of uranium
    (5) to neutralize radioactive waste

39. Coevolution is the development, over time, of complementary features in two different species as a result of their interaction. For example, flowering plants are pollinated by insects. The flowers have developed a color or smell that attracts insects and a shape that allows insects to reach the nectar and remove pollen. The insects, in turn, have evolved sensory organs to find the flowers and mouthparts that can reach the nectar. Thus coevolution benefits both species: the insects help the flowering plants reproduce, and the flowering plants provide food for the insects.

Based on the information above, which of the following is a general conclusion, rather than a specific fact?

    (1) Flowering plants and insects frequently interact with one another.
    (2) The shape and color of a flower attract insects.
    (3) The insects get nourishment from the plant's nectar.
    (4) The insects aid in plant reproduction.
    (5) Coevolution provides benefits to both species.

Question 40 refers to the following paragraph and chart.

Each mineral has a characteristic hardness. On the Mohs scale, hardness increases as you go from 1 to 10. A mineral will scratch any other mineral that has a lower number, and be scratched by any other mineral that has a higher number.

Mohs Scale of Hardness

Number	Defining Mineral
1	Talc
2	Gypsum
3	Calcite
4	Fluorite
5	Apatite
6	Orthoclase
7	Quartz
8	Topaz
9	Corundum
10	Diamond

40. A hobbyist has a steel file with a hardness of 6.5. Which of the following minerals will she be able to file?

(1) orthoclase
(2) quartz
(3) topaz
(4) corundum
(5) diamond

Questions 41 and 42 refer to the following passage.

Since 1997, when Dolly the sheep became the first clone, scientists have cloned several other types of mammals, including mice, cows, pigs, and goats. Scientists' first fears, that clones would age rapidly or die of cancer, proved unfounded. However, the clones have often had other problems, such as developmental delays, heart defects, lung problems, and faulty immune systems. Sometimes a clone appears to be normal and then suddenly develops a problem as it matures. According to scientists, the evidence indicates that cloning can introduce random errors into the clone's DNA. The altered genes can halt embryonic or fetal development, kill the clone soon after birth, or eventually lead to major medical problems. On the other hand, the clone may develop normally, as Dolly the sheep has.

41. Why is it not always possible to tell right away whether a cloned animal has serious genetic abnormalities?

(1) Most clones do not have any genetic abnormalities.
(2) Most genetic abnormalities are very minor and do not affect the clone's health.
(3) Some genetic abnormalities do not appear until the clone matures.
(4) Most genetic abnormalities express themselves in ways scientists have never seen before.
(5) Most clones die at the embryo or fetal stages of development.

42. The idea that cloning may cause genetic abnormalities supports which of the following actions?

(1) a ban on human cloning
(2) a ban on genetic research
(3) compulsory genetic testing
(4) compulsory DNA fingerprinting
(5) lifetime quarantine of cloned animals

Question 43 refers to the following graph.

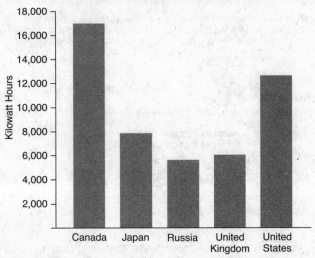

Electricity Consumption per Person, 1995

SOURCE: United Nations Development Programme

43. According to the graph, which of the following nations consumed the least electricity per person in 1995?

(1) Canada
(2) Japan
(3) Russia
(4) United Kingdom
(5) United States

44. The heat of vaporization is the amount of heat energy that is carried away from a liquid for each gram of liquid that the heat vaporizes, or turns into a gas.

In which of the following situations does the heat of vaporization play an important role?

(1) the melting of ice in the palm of your hand
(2) the cooling you feel as sweat evaporates
(3) the burning sensation when you touch very hot water
(4) the cooling effect of drinking ice water on a warm day
(5) the warmth you feel when you rub your hands together

Question 45 refers to the following information.

Animals reproduce in several ways.

Sexual reproduction. The union of an egg and a sperm from a female and a male produces an offspring.

Parthenogenesis. An egg develops without any genetic material from a male.

Self-fertilization. An organism with both male and female sex organs produces an offspring.

Hermaphroditism. Two organisms, both with male and female sex organs, cross-fertilize to produce offspring.

Fragmentation. Parts of an organism break away and form new organisms.

45. To take advantage of good environmental conditions, aphids can produce offspring that develop from the genetic material in their eggs. What type of reproduction is this?

(1) sexual reproduction
(2) parthenogenesis
(3) self-fertilization
(4) hermaphroditism
(5) fragmentation

Question 46 refers to the following diagram.

Ether (C₂H₆O)

```
    H       H
    |       |
H - C - O - C - H
    |       |
    H       H
```

Key

C = Carbon

H = Hydrogen

O = Oxygen

Ethanol (C₂H₅OH)

```
    H   H
    |   |
H - C - C - OH
    |   |
    H   H
```

46. What is the main difference between the hydrocarbons ether and ethanol?

   (1) Ether has carbon, hydrogen, and oxygen atoms, and ethanol has only carbon and hydrogen atoms.
   (2) Ether has three carbon atoms and ethanol has two carbon atoms.
   (3) Ether has one oxygen atom and ethanol has two oxygen atoms.
   (4) The total number of carbon, hydrogen, and oxygen atoms in the two hydrocarbons is different.
   (5) The arrangement of the carbon, hydrogen, and oxygen atoms in the two hydrocarbons is different.

Question 47 refers to the following diagrams.

Amphibian Feet Adaptations

The salamander has strong, flat feet used for digging as well as walking.

The sticky pads on a tree frog's feet allow it to grip branches and leaves.

With its webbed feet, the newt is a good swimmer.

47. Which of the following statements is a conclusion about amphibian feet rather than a supporting statement?

   (1) Feet are adapted to each amphibian's habitat and lifestyle.
   (2) The newt has a webbed foot designed for swimming.
   (3) The salamander's foot is flat and muscular.
   (4) The tree frog's foot enables it to hold on to leaves and branches.
   (5) The salamander uses its feet for walking and digging.

48. A student did an experiment to see how far a ball would roll on different surfaces. He made five different ramps, each with a different surface: a plain pine board, a painted board, a board covered with sandpaper, a board covered with indoor-outdoor carpet, and a board covered with shag carpet. He set up his experiment on a smooth, level floor. To make the ramps, he raised one end of each board with a book. He collected four copies of the science textbook his class was using and set up four of the ramps with these books. He couldn't find a fifth copy of the book, so he used a thinner science study guide to set up the fifth ramp. He rolled a tennis ball down each ramp and measured how far the ball traveled each time. Then he compiled his data and drew conclusions.

Why was the student's experiment flawed?

(1) The student should have used a ball with a smooth surface rather than a tennis ball.
(2) The student should have use books of the same height for all of the ramps.
(3) The student should not have used sandpaper as one of the surfaces.
(4) For a control, the student should have rolled the ball across a piece of wood that was level.
(5) For a control, the student should have rolled the tennis ball across the floor.

49. Sleep may have evolved in humans for several reasons. First, people were unable to hunt, gather food, or travel in the dark, so they were safer from predators asleep in a cave or other shelter. Second, sleep provides an opportunity to repair our body's cells, especially those in the brain. Third, our body temperature is lower during sleep, which conserves energy. Fourth, during deep sleep the pituitary gland releases a growth hormone, so sleep may play a role in growth.

Which of the following is the best title for this paragraph?

(1) Sleep
(2) Sleep and Growth
(3) Our Brains During Sleep
(4) Why We Sleep
(5) The Role of Deep Sleep

Question 50 refers to the following chart.

The Five Largest Asteroids

Name	Average distance from sun (Earth = 1)	Time to orbit sun
Ceres	2.77	4.6 years
Pallas	2.77	4.6 years
Vesta	2.36	3.6 years
Hygeia	3.13	5.5 years
Interamnia	3.06	5.4 years

50. Which of the following statements is supported by the information in the chart?

(1) Ceres, with a diameter of 584 miles, is the largest asteroid in the solar system.
(2) Pallas is further away from the sun than Hygeia is.
(3) Of the five largest asteroids, Vesta has the longest orbital period.
(4) The five largest asteroids are all farther from the sun than Earth is.
(5) Of the five largest asteroids, only Interamnia takes more than five years to orbit the sun.

Answers and explanations start on page 620.

Questions 1 through 5 refer to the following excerpt from an article.

HOW CAN YOU BETTER UNDERSTAND YOUR INTERVIEWER?

It is intrinsic to human nature to take the measure of the people we meet. We do it all the time, automatically. We develop an instinctive way of reading others that is
(5) sometimes the saving of us and at other times can prove to be our undoing. It is this instinct that makes us form instant, lifelong relationships with some people or causes us to give a wide berth to others because
(10) we get a "funny" feeling about them. With some careful consideration and planning, though, these "feelings" can be honed into a useful tool for gauging the personality and character of interviewers and, by extension,
(15) their expectations of potential employees. Let's examine some clues.

Their e-mail. You can tell a lot about your interviewer by his or her e-mail messages. Some interviewers are very warm,
(20) writing in a conversational style, addressing you by your first name. Others are witty, mixing little jokes and humorous remarks in with job-related questions. Still others get right down to business—no chit-chat or
(25) informality. Before you ever meet the interviewer, you begin to form certain "pictures" of the person, based on his or her approach and style. But it still remains for you to check him or her out face-to-face.

(30) **Their office.** Let's begin with the physical setting of interviewers' offices. Some put a desk the size of a 747 between themselves and you. This is a clear message to you to keep your distance. A straight-
(35) backed, rigid chair for the applicant says, "O.K. Let's get down to business, and then you leave so I can get back to mine." Here, you would be advised to adopt a crisp, businesslike style, with brief, professional
(40) answers. And, for heaven's sake, **don't touch that desk!**

Then, there is the homey, comfortable environment—kids' pictures on the desk, executive "toys" around, soft chairs, and a
(45) sofa. There may not even be a desk between the applicant and the interviewer, but rather two chairs grouped around a coffee table. This environment invites more intimacy. It says, "Be yourself. Tell me
(50) about who you are so I can get to know you." Here, your manner, though still professional, should be relaxed and open, more personable. It would be a mistake with this employer to sit ramrod straight
(55) and give cool, truncated responses to the questions.

From "Sizing Up the Interviewer" by Fred Jandt and Mary Nemnich, Indianapolis: JIST Works, 1997.

1. Based on information in the article, at which of the following situations should you be formal at an interview?

   when the interviewer

   (1) calls you by your first name
   (2) asks you how your family is
   (3) offers you coffee and doughnuts
   (4) tells jokes
   (5) sits far away from you

2. With which of the following would the authors most likely agree?

   (1) Interviewers will try to trick you at every turn.
   (2) An inconsiderate interviewer is very common.
   (3) All professional interviewers will be very organized.
   (4) Almost all job interviews are disappointing.
   (5) An interviewee should know how to read cues from an interviewer.

3. What is the purpose of this article?

   (1) to raise awareness about incompetent interviewers
   (2) to describe types of interviewers and how to approach them
   (3) to guarantee a perfect interview with an employer
   (4) to explain how to e-mail an interviewer
   (5) to put a stop to lengthy and formal interviews

4. Which of the following best describes the style in which this excerpt is written?

   (1) friendly and conversational
   (2) technical and dry
   (3) detailed and elaborate
   (4) humorous and wordy
   (5) vague and misleading

5. What shift occurs after the first paragraph?

   (1) mood changes from pessimistic to more optimistic
   (2) focus changes from interviewing to people skills
   (3) tone changes from personal to lecturing
   (4) content changes from general to more specific
   (5) emphasis changes from good interviewers to poor interviewers

Questions 6 through 11 refer to the following piece of nonfiction.

WHAT CRUCIAL MISTAKE DID U.S. AUTOMAKERS MAKE?

The domestic automakers had a huge market share coming into the 1970s but, unfortunately, were upsetting customers left and right. The Detroit auto manufacturers
(5) were able to keep their costs low and profits high in part by producing sub-par cars. Sure, their cars looked nice on the auto dealer's lot, but after a short time in use, many of the U.S.-manufactured cars devel-
(10) oped far more problems than their foreign equivalents. And, to add insult to injury, U.S. auto customers didn't get particularly good customer service when they brought their cars in for needed tune-ups and
(15) repairs.

The chief bean counters and the management of the major U.S. automakers weren't considering the bigger picture when they analyzed their companies' financial
(20) statements during the 1970s. These companies were too focused on their short-term profitability and weren't considering the after-sales service that was required as a result of their initially shoddy products.

(25) Not surprisingly, the U.S. automakers lost tremendous market share at the expense of the best foreign automakers during the 1970s and 1980s. In fact, one of the big four U.S. automakers—Chrysler—
(30) nearly went bankrupt and was saved only because of a government bailout.

In the long run, the Detroit automakers learned the hard way that getting your product right the first time is less costly and
(35) more profitable than retrenching to play catch-up. Customers aren't stupid, and if you continually sell them shoddy merchandise (especially when better merchandise is available from other sources), they won't
(40) come back the next time they're in the market for the products and services you have to offer. What's more, they'll tell others of their lousy experience with your company.

Although the major U.S. automakers
(45) ultimately got their act together in the 1990s and have stopped the erosion of market share, they still feel the financial pain from the millions of customers they alienated and lost to foreign competitors in
(50) the two preceding decades.

From *Small Business for Dummies* by Eric Tyson and Jim Schell, Foster City, Calif.: IDG Books, 2000.

6. Which of the following reasons is given for why U.S. automakers lost business in the 1970s and 1980s?

   (1) They could not afford to make good cars.
   (2) Their cars did not look as attractive as foreign cars.
   (3) They charged too much for their cars.
   (4) They did not offer enough places to get their cars repaired.
   (5) Their cars were not of the highest quality.

7. What do the authors suggest was one of the goals of foreign automakers?

   Foreign automakers

   (1) studied and then improved on the design of U.S. cars
   (2) deliberately underpriced their cars to get a share of the U.S. market
   (3) were initially disinterested in selling to U.S. customers
   (4) wanted to build quality cars with few repair problems
   (5) put short-term profitability above all else

8. What is meant by the phrase "chief bean counters" (line 16)?

   (1) inventory managers
   (2) assembly line workers
   (3) major automakers
   (4) the government
   (5) financial executives

9. This excerpt is most likely taken from what type of reading material?

   (1) a company memo
   (2) a letter to the editor
   (3) a business manual
   (4) a scientific report
   (5) an eyewitness account

10. Which of the following words best describes the authors' tone toward U.S. automakers?

    (1) critical
    (2) proud
    (3) approving
    (4) demeaning
    (5) arrogant

11. Later, the authors advise: "As a small-business owner, remember that if you don't get your product right the first time, you may not have a second chance."

    Based on this information and the excerpt, who did get a second chance?

    (1) U.S. automakers
    (2) foreign automakers
    (3) U.S. auto buyers
    (4) small-business owners
    (5) the government

WHY DOES MARJIE ASK FOR MONEY?

After a while, there was a ring at the back door. The children scampered in from the garden, while Jennie answered the ring.

"Baker," said the man.

(5) "Oh, yes," said Jennie: "wait, I'll get my purse."

I went on writing my letter, only half hearing the sound of Jennie's small-change as she, presumably, paid the baker's man.

(10) In a moment, Marjie was by my side.

"Hallo," I said.

Marjie did not answer.

"Hallo, Marjie," I said. "Have you come to keep me company?"

(15) "Listen," said little Marjie in a whisper, looking over her shoulder. "Listen."

"Yes," I said.

She looked over her shoulder again, as if afraid her mother might come in.

(20) "Will you give me half-a-crown?" whispered Marjie, holding out her hand.

"Well," I said, "what do you want it for?"

"I want it," said Marjie, looking furtively behind her again.

(25) "Would your mummy want you to have it?" I said.

"Give me half-a-crown," said Marjie.

"I'd rather not," I said. "But I'll tell you what, I'll buy you a—"

(30) But Marjie had fled, out of the door, into the kitchen. "She'd rather not," I heard her say to someone.

Presently, Jennie came in, looking upset.

(35) "Oh," she said, "I hope you didn't feel hurt. I only wanted to pay the baker, and I hadn't enough change. He hadn't any either; so just on the spur of the moment I sent Marjie for a loan of half-a-crown till (40) tonight. But I shouldn't have done it. I *never* borrow anything as a rule."

"Well, of course!" I said. "Of course I'll lend you half-a-crown. I've got plenty of change. I didn't understand and I got the (45) message all wrong; I thought she wanted it for herself and that you wouldn't like that."

Jennie looked doubtful. I funked explaining the whole of Marjie's act. It isn't easy to give evidence against a child of (50) five.

"Oh, they never ask for money," said Jennie. "I would never allow them to ask for anything. They never do *that*."

"I'm sure they don't," I said, floundering (55) a bit.

From "The Twins" by Muriel Spark, from the book *The Go-Away Bird and Other Stories* J. B. Lippincott Company.

12. What does Marjie's looking over her shoulder suggest to the narrator?

The narrator thinks Marjie

(1) is imagining what she'll do with the money
(2) has forgotten something in the other room
(3) is shy and lacks confidence
(4) is afraid of the baker
(5) is hoping her mother won't hear her asking for money

13. Which of the following becomes evident during the discussion between Jennie and the narrator?

(1) Jennie knows the narrator wanted to lend her the money.
(2) Jennie can't believe that the narrator wouldn't lend her the money.
(3) Jennie is perplexed when the narrator blames Marjie.
(4) The narrator begins to mistrust Jennie and Marjie.
(5) The narrator and Jennie resolve the misunderstanding.

14. If Jennie were criticized by her boss at work, what would she most likely do?

(1) resent it in silence
(2) discuss it defensively
(3) not take it seriously
(4) argue forcefully
(5) gossip about her boss

15. What kind of relationship do Jennie and the narrator have?

(1) They are cool and indifferent to each other.
(2) They frequently disagree on matters.
(3) They know each other but are not close.
(4) Jennie bosses the narrator around.
(5) Jennie takes advantage of the narrator.

16. Which of the following best describes the situation presented in this excerpt?

(1) uplifting
(2) humorous
(3) sad
(4) uncomfortable
(5) sentimental

Questions 17 through 22 refer to the following excerpt from a short story.

DOES CLEO TAKE ADVANTAGE OF HER FAMILY'S AFFECTION?

He gave them each a copper, too, though he could hardly spare it, what with four of them to feed and Mama wanting yard goods and buttons and ribbons to
(5) keep herself feeling proud of the way she kept her children. Time was, he gave them kisses for toting his bucket. But the day Cleo brazenly said, I don't want a kiss, I want a copper, the rest of them shame-
(10) facedly said it after her. Most times Pa had a struggle to dig down so deep. Four coppers a day, six days a week, was half a day's pay gone up in smoke for candy.

Pa couldn't bring himself to tell Mama.
(15) She would have wrung out of him that Cleo had been the one started it. And Cleo was his eldest. A man who loved his wife couldn't help loving his first-born best, the child of his fiercest passion. When that first-born
(20) was a girl, she could trample on his heart, and he would swear on a stack of Bibles that it didn't hurt.

The sisters put their coppers in their pinafore pockets and skipped back through
(25) the woods.

Midway Cleo stopped and pointed to a towering oak. "You all want to bet me a copper I can't swing by my feet from up in that tree?"

(30) Lily clapped her hands to her eyes. "I doesn't want to bet you," she implored. "I ain't fixing to see you fall."

Serena said severely, "You bust your neck, you see if Mama don't bust it again."

(35) Charity said tremulously, "Cleo, what would us do if our sister was dead?"

Cleo saw herself dressed up fine as Josie Beauchamp, stretched out in a coffin with her sisters sobbing beside it, and Pa
(40) with his Sunday handkerchief holding his tears, and Mama crying, I loved you best, Cleo. I never said it when you were alive. And I'm sorry, sorry, I waited to say it after you were gone.

(45) "You hold my copper, Charity. And if I die, you can have it."

Lily opened two of her fingers and peeped through the crack. "Cleo, I'll give you mine if you don't make me see you
(50) hanging upside down." It was one thing to hear Cleo tell about herself. It was another thing to see her fixing to kill herself.

"Me, too," said Serena, with a little sob,
(55) more for the copper than for Cleo, whom she briefly hated for compelling unnecessary sacrifice.

Reprinted from The Living Is Easy, copyright 1948, 1975 by Dorothy West, by permission of the Feminist Press at the City University of New York, www. feministpress.org.

17. What is the "copper" that Pa gave each of the girls?

    (1) a coin
    (2) a piece of candy
    (3) a hug
    (4) a piece of copper tubing
    (5) a small gift

18. What conflict does Pa feel?

    He wishes

    (1) he had a job that was less demanding
    (2) his children helped with the chores
    (3) his wife cared more about their children
    (4) he could say "no" to his children
    (5) his children were more polite

19. Which of the following best describes Cleo?

    (1) loving
    (2) thoughtful
    (3) bold
    (4) fragile
    (5) serious

20. How do Cleo's sisters respond to her idea for a bet?

    (1) eagerly
    (2) negatively
    (3) indifferently
    (4) angrily
    (5) daringly

21. Which of the following would Cleo probably enjoy?

    (1) jumping from a roof before an audience
    (2) sewing clothes with her mother
    (3) reading a good book
    (4) treating her sisters to candy
    (5) surprising her father with a gift

22. Based on the information in the excerpt, which of the following do you predict would happen next?

    (1) Cleo hangs upside down and gets the coppers.
    (2) Pa scolds Cleo for her behavior.
    (3) Mama punishes the other children for giving in to Cleo.
    (4) Mama finds out that Pa gave coppers to the girls.
    (5) Cleo gets all of her sisters' coppers without having to do anything.

WHAT IS LAVINIA'S OPINION ABOUT CARING FOR ELDERLY PARENTS?

"When he became ill at first, when the strokes led to paralysis, he was very embarrassed for anyone to see him. He was a very proud man. I suppose I didn't (5) have the heart or the will to oppose him, but it seemed natural, after a while, to go on, once I'd started taking care of him. I felt that he'd been through so much physically I didn't want to fight him."

(10) "So you had him all to yourself, then," said Lavinia, as if we had been talking about a date with a movie star. Something in her tone frightened me. Whatever I said would be greeted by this probing incompre- (15) hension.

"There wasn't really anyone else," I went on. "My mother died when I was a baby."

"And no professional help?"

(20) "You have to understand, Lavinia, that for my father, the parish was the community. There weren't social workers and psychologists. There were priests."

"And what did they tell you?"

(25) "I didn't ask. I didn't have to. It was simply assumed that I would step in."

"And you didn't think of going outside for professional help or advice?"

It suddenly occurred to me that Lavinia (30) probably thought me a lunatic or an imbecile. I asked myself the question that Lavinia had just asked me, but my only answer was the stupidest possible one: no, I hadn't thought there was a choice in the (35) matter. It had all seemed exceedingly straightforward. My father was helpless. I would care for him. He wanted me, and I was there. It had all rolled out before me inevitable as a road. I would say to Lavinia (40) that I was very young when he first became ill.

From *Final Payments* by Mary Gordon, New York: Random House, 1978.

23. What reason does the narrator give for taking care of her father?

(1) She was too young to know better.
(2) She wanted to with all her heart.
(3) The priest insisted it was the right thing.
(4) She couldn't find professional help.
(5) It seemed the natural thing to do.

24. When the narrator says, "Something in her
tone frightened me" (lines 12–13), what is
she revealing?

(1) She knows she made the wrong choice.
(2) She realizes Lavinia thinks she is foolish.
(3) She is afraid her father is going to die.
(4) She knows Lavinia will force her to try to
explain her situation.
(5) She is uncomfortable talking to Lavinia.

25. Which of the following is in keeping with the
narrator's character?

(1) running away
(2) standing up for what she wants
(3) exaggerating her situation
(4) pretending to be a saint
(5) doing what is expected of her

26. Which of the following statements best conveys Lavinia's attitude toward life?

(1) Treat others as you would have them treat
you.
(2) Family comes first.
(3) Make things as easy on yourself as
possible.
(4) Subtlety is the best policy.
(5) There are always choices in life.

27. Based on her character as revealed in this
excerpt, how would Lavinia walk through a
crowded room?

(1) pointedly and confidently
(2) carefully and politely
(3) angrily and rudely
(4) shyly and slowly
(5) clumsily and loudly

28. What two qualities are contrasted in this
excerpt?

(1) ignorance and knowledge
(2) pain and pleasure
(3) sincerity and insincerity
(4) needs and wants
(5) self-centeredness and self-sacrifice

DOES THE SPEAKER WORK ALONE?

The Tuft of Flowers

I went to turn the grass once after one
Who mowed it in the dew before the sun.

The dew was gone that made his blade so keen
Before I came to view the leveled scene.

(5) I looked for him behind an isle of trees;
I listened for his whetstone on the breeze.

But he had gone his way, the grass all mown,
And I must be, as he had been—alone,

"As all must be," I said within my heart,
(10) "Whether they work together or apart."

But as I said it, swift there passed me by
On noiseless wing a bewildered butterfly,

Seeking with memories grown dim o'er night
Some resting flower of yesterday's delight.

(15) And once I marked his flight go round and round,
As where some flower lay withering on the ground.

And then he flew as far as eye could see,
And then on tremulous wing came back to me.

I thought of questions that have no reply,
(20) And would have turned to toss the grass to dry;

But he turned first, and led my eye to look
At a tall tuft of flowers beside a brook,

A leaping tongue of bloom the scythe had spared
Beside a reedy brook the scythe had bared.

(25) The mower in the dew had loved them thus,
By leaving them to flourish, not for us,

Nor yet to draw one thought of ours to him,
But from sheer morning gladness at the brim.

The butterfly and I had lit upon,
(30) Nevertheless, a message from the dawn,

That made me hear the wakening birds around,
And hear his long scythe whispering to the ground.

And feel a spirit kindred to my own;
So that henceforth I worked no more alone;

(35) But glad with him, I worked as with his aid,
And weary, sought at noon with him the shade;

And dreaming, as it were, held brotherly speech
With one whose thought I had not hoped to reach

"Men work together," I told him from the heart,
(40) "Whether they work together or apart."

From THE POETRY OF ROBERT FROST edited by Edward Connery Lathem, © 1969 by Henry Holt & Co., LLC.

29. What was the butterfly doing when the speaker first saw it (lines 11–12)?

    (1) escaping the mower
    (2) leading the poet to the river
    (3) looking for a flower from the day before
    (4) showing the poet that it was spring
    (5) resting on a blade of grass

30. Why does the speaker call the flowers "a leaping tongue of bloom" (line 23)?

    because the flowers

    (1) are swaying in the wind
    (2) are the shape and color of a tongue of fire
    (3) survived the mowers' scythe
    (4) seem to be calling out to him
    (5) are about ready to burst open

31. Why did the mower leave the flowers untouched?

    because he

    (1) knew butterflies would look for them
    (2) wanted to leave flowers for the speaker
    (3) got tired and decided to rest
    (4) appreciated their beauty
    (5) neglected to see them

32. What did the tuft of flowers help the speaker understand?

    (1) Spring had finally come.
    (2) He and the mower were kindred spirits.
    (3) Flowers have a beauty all their own.
    (4) Men are by nature distant from each other.
    (5) Nature must be preserved.

33. What type of person does the speaker seem to be?

    (1) humorous
    (2) sad
    (3) thoughtful
    (4) playful
    (5) friendly

34. If music were to accompany this poem, what type of music would be best?

    (1) hip-hop
    (2) quiet classical
    (3) rock 'n' roll
    (4) jazz
    (5) country western

HOW DO THESE PROFESSORS REGARD PEOPLE?

PROFESSOR B: [*Looking at some photos.*] You know what I like best about human beings?

PROFESSOR A: What?

(5) PROFESSOR B: Their feet. Not only are feet durable and sophisticated in their design, they're—well, they're very cute.

STUDENT: Thank you.

PROFESSOR B: [*Referring to photos.*] Can I (10) save these?

STUDENT: Sure.

PROFESSOR A: I have *one* question regarding the human being.

STUDENT: Yes?

(15) PROFESSOR A: Why did you make them so stupid?

DEAN: That's a biased question.

PROFESSOR A: All right, I'll rephrase it: Why didn't you make them smart?

(20) STUDENT: I think they're smart. They've created great civilizations. They've developed magnificent tools and brilliant works of art. Their awareness of the universe is increasing exponentially.

(25) PROFESSOR A: Stop exaggerating. It took them centuries just to come up with the concept of the sandwich. How smart do you have to be to think of putting a piece of meat between two pieces of bread?

(30) STUDENT: But look at what else they've done. Look at what they've done with their languages. Look at English. With only 26 letters, they've built a body of literature with great power, feeling and (35) insight.

PROFESSOR A: So? The creatures on one of the other students' planets created a body of literature that's twice as profound, and with only 17 letters. No (40) wasted, inefficient letters like X or Q. Imagine inventing a letter you can only use if it's followed by a U. What was going on in their heads?

STUDENT: Still, any species that has pro-
(45) duced William Shakespeare . . .

PROFESSOR A: Isn't he the one who wrote, "What a piece of work is man! How noble in reason, how infinite in faculty."

STUDENT: Yes.

(50) PROFESSOR A: What a bunch of self-serving rubbish.

DEAN: You don't expect a good grade just because you created *one* genius do you?

STUDENT: Of course not. The species has (55) also produced Socrates, Freud, Madame Curie, Gandhi, Darwin—

PROFESSOR A: All of whom were resented, misunderstood, ostracized or killed. This is how human beings treat their geniuses.

Excerpt from THE WHOLE SHEBANG by Rich Orloff, reprinted with permission by Bret Adams Ltd., 448 West 44th Street, New York, NY 10036.

35. Who are the professors and the student?

(1) beings from some place other than Earth
(2) people at a university
(3) scientists working for the government
(4) international spies
(5) artists in a workshop

36. Why does the student say, "Thank you" (line 8)?

because the professor

(1) said he is cute
(2) returned his photograph
(3) complimented his creation of humans
(4) has assigned him an easy task
(5) has given him a good grade

37. What evidence does the student offer when the professor suggests he is exaggerating human intelligence?

Humans

(1) are learning more about the universe every day
(2) have created great works of art
(3) have invented tools
(4) have developed languages and produced literature
(5) have invented the sandwich

38. With which of the following statements would Professor A probably agree?

(1) Beauty is in the eye of the beholder.
(2) Nothing is of value unless it is useful.
(3) Variety is the spice of life.
(4) I never met a man I didn't like.
(5) Man's reach should exceed his grasp.

39. What central message is the playwright conveying through the argument between the student and the professors?

(1) Human beings are created equal.
(2) Other civilizations exist.
(3) The human race has both strengths and weaknesses.
(4) Professors are too hard on students.
(5) We must be tolerant of our differences.

40. Later Professor B says, "And what type of organism would let the Marx Brothers make only thirteen movies? They were easily good for another dozen."

Based on this information and the excerpt, how does Professor B compare with Professor A?

Professor B is more

(1) light-hearted
(2) defensive
(3) serious
(4) snobby
(5) accepting

Answers and explanations start on page 623.

GED Math Post-Test Answer Sheet

Part I

1. ① ② ③ ④ ⑤
2. ① ② ③ ④ ⑤
3. ① ② ③ ④ ⑤
4.

5.

6. ① ② ③ ④ ⑤
7. ① ② ③ ④ ⑤
8. ① ② ③ ④ ⑤
9. ① ② ③ ④ ⑤
10. ① ② ③ ④ ⑤
11. ① ② ③ ④ ⑤

12.

13.

14. ① ② ③ ④ ⑤

15. ① ② ③ ④ ⑤
16. ① ② ③ ④ ⑤

17.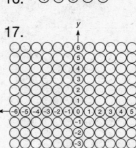

18. ① ② ③ ④ ⑤
19. ① ② ③ ④ ⑤
20. ① ② ③ ④ ⑤

21.

22.

23. ① ② ③ ④ ⑤
24. ① ② ③ ④ ⑤
25. ① ② ③ ④ ⑤

GED Math Post-Test

Part I

Write your answers on the answer sheet provided on page 593. A formulas page is provided on page 611.

Directions: You have 45 minutes to answer 25 questions in Part I of the Math Test. Choose the <u>one best answer</u> to each question. You <u>MAY</u> use your calculator.

<u>Questions 1 and 2</u> refer to the following graph.

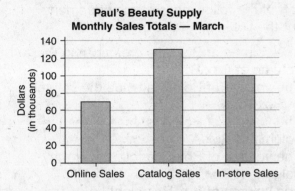

**Paul's Beauty Supply
Monthly Sales Totals — March**

1. Customers of Paul's Beauty Supply can make purchases online, from a catalog, or in the store. <u>About</u> how much more did the company make from catalog sales than from online sales in March?

    (1) $35,000
    (2) $65,000
    (3) $130,000
    (4) $195,000
    (5) $650,000

2. <u>Approximately</u> what fraction of the company's total sales came from in-store sales?

    (1) $\frac{2}{3}$

    (2) $\frac{1}{2}$

    (3) $\frac{1}{3}$

    (4) $\frac{1}{4}$

    (5) $\frac{1}{6}$

3. John needs to replace the boards on a 22-foot section of his fence. He plans to place the boards as shown below.

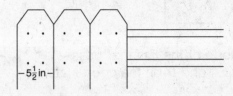

$-5\frac{1}{2}$ in$-$

   If the boards are $5\frac{1}{2}$ <u>inches</u> wide, how many boards should he buy to cover the distance?

    (1)   4
    (2)   33
    (3)   48
    (4)   66
    (5) 121

Question 4 refers to the following graph.

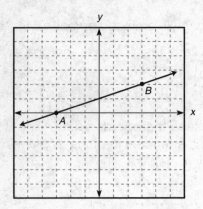

4. What is the slope of the line that passes through points *A* and *B* on the coordinate graph?

   Mark your answer in the circles in the grid on your answer sheet on page 593.

5. What is the value of the expression $3(2x - y) + (3 + x)^2$, when $x = 4$ and $y = 5$?

   Mark your answer in the circles in the grid on your answer sheet on page 593.

6. The dimensions of Box B, shown below, are twice the length of the corresponding dimensions on Box A (not shown).

Which of the following is a true statement about the volumes of the boxes?

(1) The volume of Box A is greater than the volume of Box B.
(2) The volume of Box B is twice the volume of Box A.
(3) The volume of Box B is three times the volume of Box A.
(4) The volume of Box B is four times the volume of Box A.
(5) The volume of Box B is eight times the volume of Box A.

7. At the end of baseball season, 5% of the children enrolled in a local youth baseball program will be chosen to play in the state tournament. If 12 children will be chosen to play in the tournament, how many children are enrolled in the program?

(1) 24
(2) 60
(3) 120
(4) 240
(5) 600

8. A bag contains 12 red, 3 blue, 6 green, and 4 yellow marbles. If a marble is drawn from the bag at random, what is the probability that the marble will be either blue or yellow?

(1) 7%
(2) 12%
(3) 16%
(4) 25%
(5) 28%

9. Fabio has his own computer repair business. He uses the following guidelines to estimate how long a project will take.

Install operating system	1 hour
Replace motherboard	$1\frac{1}{2}$ hours
Install CD-ROM or DVD drive	30 minutes
Upgrade memory	20 minutes
Install hard drive	45 minutes
Install sound card	30 minutes
Install video card	30 minutes

Fabio needs to install a new hard drive and an operating system for a customer. If Fabio charges $65 per hour, what will he charge the customer for the job?

(1) $94.25
(2) $105.00
(3) $110.00
(4) $113.75
(5) $146.25

10. Risa wants to order business cards. A printing company determines the cost (C) to the customer using the following function, where b = the number of boxes of cards and n = number of ink colors.

$C = \$25.60b + \$14.00b(n - 1)$

If Risa orders 4 boxes of cards printed in 3 colors, how much will the cards cost?

(1) $214.40
(2) $168.00
(3) $144.40
(4) $102.40
(5) $56.00

11. Construction plans often call for a diagonal support to strengthen a structure. A section of the plans for the steel frame of a parking structure are shown below.

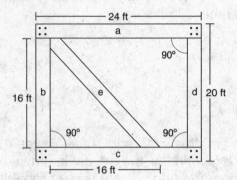

Which of the following expressions could be used to find the approximate length in feet of the beam marked e?

(1) $\frac{1}{2}(8 + 24)(20)$

(2) $\frac{1}{2}(16)(16)$

(3) $\sqrt{16^2 + 16^2}$

(4) $\sqrt{24^2 - 16^2}$

(5) $\sqrt{20^2 - 16^2}$

12. Samantha bought a used mountain bike for $250. She gave the bike a new paint job; replaced the tires, chain, and gear assembly; and sold the bike for 150% of the price she paid. For what amount, in dollars, did she sell the bike?

Mark your answer in the circles in the grid on your answer sheet on page 593.

13. Alice finds that the distance between two landmarks on a map is $6\frac{1}{2}$ inches. If the map scale reads $\frac{3}{4}$ inch = 120 miles, what is the actual distance, in miles, between the two landmarks?

Mark your answer in the circles in the grid on your answer sheet on page 593.

14. Which of the following is a graph of the inequality $-2 \leq x < 4$?

(1)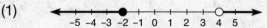

(2)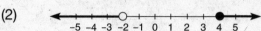

(3)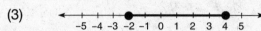

(4)

(5)

Questions 15 and 16 are based on the following figure.

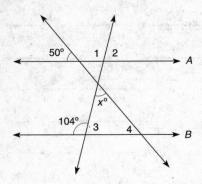

$A \parallel B$

15. What is the measure of ∠2?

    (1) 50°
    (2) 76°
    (3) 104°
    (4) 126°
    (5) 130°

16. What is the value of x?

    (1) 54°
    (2) 76°
    (3) 126°
    (4) 130°
    (5) Not enough information is given.

17. On a coordinate plane, a vertical line is drawn through point (−3,4). On the same plane, a horizontal line is drawn through point (2,−1). At what point on the plane will the two lines intersect?

Mark your answer on the coordinate plane grid on your answer sheet on page 593.

18. The birth weights of the infants born at Midway Hospital on June 1 are listed below. What was the median birth weight of the infants?

7 lb 4 oz	7 lb 13 oz	6 lb 6 oz
7 lb 0 oz	6 lb 12 oz	6 lb 6 oz
7 lb 8 oz		

(1) 6 lb 6 oz
(2) 6 lb 12 oz
(3) 7 lb 0 oz
(4) 7 lb 4 oz
(5) 7 lb 8 oz

19. Evening tickets to a play are $24.50 each. Tickets for the afternoon show are $19 each. Janice wants to buy 6 tickets. Which of the following can be used to find out how much less she will pay if she chooses an afternoon instead of an evening show?

(1) 6($24.50 − $19)
(2) 6($24.50) + 6($19)
(3) $24.50 − $19 + 6
(4) 6($24.50)($19)
(5) 6($24.50) − $19

20. What was Brad's mean score for a round of golf in August if his scores for each round were 78, 86, 82, 81, 82, and 77?

(1) 77
(2) 78
(3) 81
(4) 82
(5) 84

21. In quadrilateral ABCD, side AB is parallel to side CD. Sides AD and BC are not parallel.

What is the area of the figure to the nearest square centimeter?

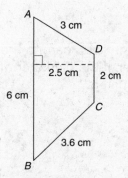

Mark your answer in the circles in the grid on your answer sheet on page 593.

22. A display of canned peaches has a sign that reads "5 cans for $3." At the same rate, how much would the store charge to the nearest cent for 8 cans?

Mark your answer in the circles in the grid on your answer sheet on page 593.

23. The soup can shown below has a circular top and bottom.

12 cm

What is the volume of the soup can, to the nearest cubic centimeter, if the diameter of either base is 6.4 centimeters?

(1)   32
(2) 121
(3) 241
(4) 386
(5) 1543

24. The maximum speed of the space shuttle is 1.66×10^4 miles per hour. What is this number written in standard notation?

(1)   166
(2)   1,660
(3)   16,600
(4)   166,000
(5) 1,660,000

25. $\angle ACD$ is a straight angle. Which of the following is a true statement about the figure?

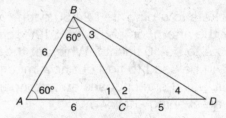

(1) $\triangle ABC$ is a right triangle.
(2) $m\angle 2 = 120°$
(3) $m\angle 3 = 30°$
(4) $m\angle 4 = 60°$
(5) $\triangle BCD$ is an isosceles triangle.

GED MATH POST-TEST ANSWER SHEET
PART II

1. ① ② ③ ④ ⑤
2. ① ② ③ ④ ⑤
3. ① ② ③ ④ ⑤
4. ① ② ③ ④ ⑤
5. ① ② ③ ④ ⑤
6.

```
┌───┬───┬───┬───┬───┐
│   │ / │ / │ / │   │
├───┼───┼───┼───┼───┤
│ · │ · │ · │ · │ · │
├───┼───┼───┼───┼───┤
│ 0 │ 0 │ 0 │ 0 │ 0 │
│ 1 │ 1 │ 1 │ 1 │ 1 │
│ 2 │ 2 │ 2 │ 2 │ 2 │
│ 3 │ 3 │ 3 │ 3 │ 3 │
│ 4 │ 4 │ 4 │ 4 │ 4 │
│ 5 │ 5 │ 5 │ 5 │ 5 │
│ 6 │ 6 │ 6 │ 6 │ 6 │
│ 7 │ 7 │ 7 │ 7 │ 7 │
│ 8 │ 8 │ 8 │ 8 │ 8 │
│ 9 │ 9 │ 9 │ 9 │ 9 │
└───┴───┴───┴───┴───┘
```

7. ① ② ③ ④ ⑤
8. ① ② ③ ④ ⑤

9. ① ② ③ ④ ⑤
10. ① ② ③ ④ ⑤
11. ① ② ③ ④ ⑤

12.

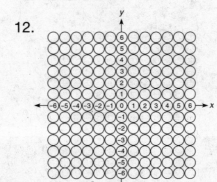

13. ① ② ③ ④ ⑤
14. ① ② ③ ④ ⑤
15. ① ② ③ ④ ⑤
16. ① ② ③ ④ ⑤
17. ① ② ③ ④ ⑤

18.

```
┌───┬───┬───┬───┬───┐
│   │ / │ / │ / │   │
├───┼───┼───┼───┼───┤
│ · │ · │ · │ · │ · │
├───┼───┼───┼───┼───┤
│ 0 │ 0 │ 0 │ 0 │ 0 │
│ 1 │ 1 │ 1 │ 1 │ 1 │
│ 2 │ 2 │ 2 │ 2 │ 2 │
│ 3 │ 3 │ 3 │ 3 │ 3 │
│ 4 │ 4 │ 4 │ 4 │ 4 │
│ 5 │ 5 │ 5 │ 5 │ 5 │
│ 6 │ 6 │ 6 │ 6 │ 6 │
│ 7 │ 7 │ 7 │ 7 │ 7 │
│ 8 │ 8 │ 8 │ 8 │ 8 │
│ 9 │ 9 │ 9 │ 9 │ 9 │
└───┴───┴───┴───┴───┘
```

19. ① ② ③ ④ ⑤
20. ① ② ③ ④ ⑤
21. ① ② ③ ④ ⑤
22. ① ② ③ ④ ⑤
23. ① ② ③ ④ ⑤
24. ① ② ③ ④ ⑤
25. ① ② ③ ④ ⑤

PART II

Write your answers on the answer sheet provided on page 603. A formulas page is provided on page 611.

Directions: You have 45 minutes to answer 25 questions in Part II of the Math Test. Choose the <u>one best answer</u> to each question. You <u>MAY NOT</u> use your calculator.

1. A plastic pipe, 5 feet 9 inches long, is cut into three equal pieces. Assuming no waste when the cuts are made, what is the length of each piece?

   (1) 1 ft 6 in
   (2) 1 ft 8 in
   (3) 1 ft 9 in
   (4) 1 ft 11 in
   (5) 2 ft

<u>Question 2</u> refers to the following diagram.

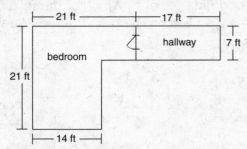

2. The Warners plan to carpet their bedroom and the adjoining hallway as shown in the diagram. What is the area of the bedroom and hallway in square feet?

   (1) 118
   (2) 413
   (3) 462
   (4) 560
   (5) Not enough information is given.

3. Leslie earns a monthly salary of $2230. In July, she will receive a 6% raise. Which of the following expressions could be used to calculate Leslie's new <u>monthly</u> salary?

   (1) 0.06($2230)
   (2) $\dfrac{\$2230}{0.06}$
   (3) 0.06($2230)(12)
   (4) 0.06($2230) + $2230
   (5) $\dfrac{\$2230}{0.06}$ + $2230

4. One number is 12 more than 3 times another number. The sum of the 2 numbers is −20. What are the numbers?

   (1) −2 and −18
   (2) −4 and −16
   (3) −5 and −15
   (4) −6 and −14
   (5) −8 and −12

Questions 5 and 6 refer to the following graph.

The Whitmans are trying to pay off their credit card debt, so they developed the following budget based on their monthly take-home pay.

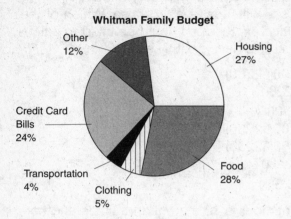

Whitman Family Budget

Other 12%
Housing 27%
Credit Card Bills 24%
Food 28%
Transportation 4%
Clothing 5%

5. If the Whitmans' monthly take-home pay is $2500, <u>about</u> how much do they plan to pay each month on their credit card debt?

(1) $600
(2) $450
(3) $300
(4) $240
(5) Not enough information is given.

6. What <u>fraction</u> of the Whitmans' monthly take-home pay goes toward clothing?

Mark your answers on the circles in the grid on your answer sheet on page 603.

Questions 7 and 8 refer to the following graph.

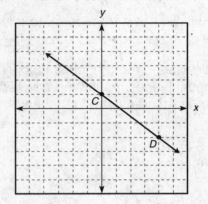

7. The graph of the equation $y = -\frac{3}{4}x + 1$ is a line that passes through points C and D on the coordinate plane. Which of the following points also lies on the graph of the equation?

(1) $(2,0)$
(2) $(3,-1)$
(3) $(5,-3)$
(4) $(8,-5)$
(5) $(10,-6)$

8. Which of the following expressions could be used to find the distance between points C and D?

(1) $\sqrt{(4-0)^2 - (-2-1)^2}$

(2) $\sqrt{(4-0)^2 + (-2-1)^2}$

(3) $\sqrt{(4+0)^2 + (-2+1)^2}$

(4) $\sqrt{(4-1)^2 + (-2-0)^2}$

(5) $\sqrt{(4+-2)^2 + (0+1)^2}$

9. The sum of three consecutive even numbers is 90. What is the greatest number in the series?

(1) 26
(2) 28
(3) 30
(4) 32
(5) 34

10. The three interior angles of $\triangle JKL$ measure 45°, 45°, and 90°. The three interior angles of $\triangle PQR$ measure 45°, 45°, and 90°. Side JK of $\triangle JKL$ measures 4 cm. Based on the given information, which of the following must be a true statement?

(1) $\triangle JKL$ and $\triangle PQR$ are acute triangles.
(2) One side of $\triangle PQR$ measures 4 cm.
(3) The perimeter of $\triangle JKL$ is 12 cm.
(4) $\triangle JKL$ and $\triangle PQR$ are congruent triangles.
(5) $\triangle JKL$ and $\triangle PQR$ are similar triangles.

11. Mike borrowed $400 from his brother for six months. He agreed to pay simple interest at the annual rate of 5%. How much will Mike pay his brother in all at the end of six months?

(1) $10
(2) $120
(3) $410
(4) $500
(5) $520

12. A parallelogram is drawn on a coordinate grid so that three vertices are located at (3,4), (−2,4), and (−4,1). At what coordinates should the fourth vertex be located?

Mark your answer on the coordinate plane grid on your answer sheet on page 603.

13. Eight athletes ran a 1-mile race. The winner's time was 4 minutes 8 seconds. If the median time was 4 minutes 48 seconds, what was the time of the athlete who finished last?

(1) 5 min 28 sec
(2) 5 min 4 sec
(3) 4 min 46 sec
(4) 4 min 28 sec
(5) Not enough information is given.

Questions 14 and 15 refer to the following information.

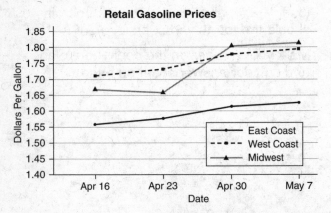

14. On what date and in what location was there the greatest jump in the price of gasoline from one week to the next?

(1) Apr. 23 on the West Coast
(2) Apr. 30 in the Midwest
(3) Apr. 30 on the West Coast
(4) May 7 on the East Coast
(5) May 7 in the Midwest

15. Based on the information in the graph, which of the following is the best prediction of the price per gallon of gasoline on the West Coast for the week following May 7?

(1) $1.64
(2) $1.71
(3) $1.76
(4) $1.82
(5) $1.86

16. A winter coat was marked down 20% from the original price. When the coat still did not sell, the manager reduced the sale price by 25%. If the coat was originally priced at $120, how much was its sale price after two price cuts?

(1) $24
(2) $66
(3) $72
(4) $75
(5) $96

17. Allison made three long-distance calls. According to her phone bill, the calls were 19 minutes, 24 minutes, and 8 minutes in length. If Allison pays 9 cents per minute on all long-distance calls, how much was she billed for the three calls?

(1) $2.70
(2) $4.59
(3) $5.10
(4) $13.77
(5) $15.30

18. Maggie and Colin went in together to buy their friends a wedding gift. Maggie put in $20 less than twice the amount that Colin contributed. Together, they spent $94. How many dollars did Maggie contribute toward the gift?

Mark your answer in the circles in the grid on your answer sheet on page 603.

19. The Northridge Quakes have won 20 games and lost 15. What is the ratio of games won to games played?

(1) 3:4
(2) 3:7
(3) 4:3
(4) 4:7
(5) 4:10

20. Maxine volunteered to make costumes for a school play. Each astronaut costume will require $3\frac{7}{8}$ yards of white fabric. If Maxine needs to make 5 astronaut costumes, how many yards of fabric should she buy?

(1) $4\frac{3}{8}$
(2) $8\frac{7}{8}$
(3) $15\frac{7}{8}$
(4) $19\frac{3}{8}$
(5) $20\frac{1}{4}$

Question 21 refers to the following diagram.

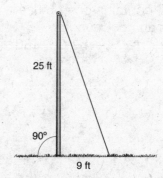

21. To set up a tent, workers place a 25-foot pole in the center of a grassy area as shown in the diagram. A bracing wire is attached to the top of the pole and to a stake 9 feet from the base of the pole. Which of the following represents the length of the bracing wire?

(1) $\sqrt{1156}$
(2) $\sqrt{706}$
(3) $\sqrt{625}$
(4) $\sqrt{256}$
(5) $\sqrt{34}$

22. What is the value of the expression
$-3 \times 5^2 + 2(4 - 18) + 3^3$?

(1) -130
(2) -76
(3) -20
(4) 74
(5) 130

23. The lengths of the sides of $\triangle ABC$ are 6 inches, 8 inches, and 10 inches. Which of the following conclusions must be true?

(1) $\angle C$ is a right angle.
(2) $\triangle ABC$ is an acute triangle.
(3) $\triangle ABC$ contains one obtuse angle.
(4) $\angle A$ is an acute angle.
(5) $m\angle A + m\angle B + m\angle C = 180°$

24. Daniel deposited $\frac{3}{20}$ of his paycheck into his savings account. If Daniel put $150 in savings, what was the amount of his paycheck?

(1) $450
(2) $1000
(3) $2250
(4) $3000
(5) Not enough information is given.

25. A catalog has the following table of shipping charges on its order form.

If your order totals:
Up to $10.00 . . . . . . Add $4.95
$10.01–$25.00 . . . . . Add $5.95
$25.01–$45.00 . . . . . Add $7.95
$45.01–$65.00 . . . . . Add $8.95
$65.01–$95.00 . . . . . Add $9.95
$95.01–$150.00 . . . Add $12.95
Over $150.00 . . . . . Add $14.95

Melinda plans to order a fireplace screen for $34.95 and a rug for $89.90. How much will the items cost plus shipping?

(1) $63.90
(2) $124.85
(3) $137.80
(4) $139.80
(5) $142.75

Answers and explanations begin on page 625.

FORMULAS

AREA of a:

square	Area = side^2
rectangle	Area = length × width
parallelogram	Area = base × height
triangle	Area = $\frac{1}{2}$ × base × height
trapezoid	Area = $\frac{1}{2}$ × (base$_1$ + base$_2$) × height
circle	Area = π × radius^2; π is approximately equal to 3.14.

PERIMETER of a:

square	Perimeter = 4 × side
rectangle	Perimeter = 2 × length + 2 × width
triangle	Perimeter = side$_1$ + side$_2$ + side$_3$

CIRCUMFERENCE of a:

circle	Circumference = π × diameter; π is approximately equal to 3.14.

VOLUME of a:

cube	Volume = edge^3
rectangular solid	Volume = length × width × height
square pyramid	Volume = $\frac{1}{3}$ × (base edge)^2 × height
cylinder	Volume = π × radius^2 × height; π is approximately equal to 3.14.
cone	Volume = $\frac{1}{3}$ × π × radius^2 × height; π is approximately equal to 3.14.

COORDINATE GEOMETRY

Distance between points = $\sqrt{(x_2 - x_1)^2 + (y_2 - y_1)^2}$; (x_1, y_1) and (x_2, y_2) are two points in a plane.

slope of a line $= \dfrac{y_2 - y_1}{x_2 - x_1}$; (x_1, y_1) and (x_2, y_2) are two points on the line.

PYTHAGOREAN RELATIONSHIP

$a^2 + b^2 = c^2$; a and b are legs and c the hypotenuse of a right triangle.

MEASURES OF CENTRAL TENDENCY

mean $= \dfrac{x_1 + x_2 + \ldots + x_n}{n}$, where the x's are the values for which a mean is desired, and n is the total number of values for x.

median = the middle value of an odd number of _ordered_ scores, and halfway between the two middle values of an even number of _ordered_ scores.

SIMPLE INTEREST

interest = principal × rate × time

DISTANCE

distance = rate × time

TOTAL COST

total cost = (number of units) × (price per unit)

Reprinted with permission of the GED Testing Service of the American Council on Education.

LANGUAGE ARTS, WRITING POST-TEST ANSWERS AND EXPLANATIONS

1. **(4) replace hole with whole (Spelling/homonyms)** A *hole* is a place that is dug out of the ground; *whole* means "entire."

2. **(4) change add to adding (Parallel structure)** The verb *add* should end with *-ing* to match *stripping* and *filling*. All the phrases in a series should be in the same form.

3. **(5) Use a brush to paint a clean line (Dangling modifiers)** The original was unclear and wordy. Rewriting the sentence as a command makes it clear that this is a direction for the reader.

4. **(3) is (Verb tense)** The sentence should be in the present tense because the rest of the paragraph is in the present tense.

5. **(2) missed, and go (Comma splices)** Option (2) corrects the comma splice with a logical conjunction.

6. **(3) join paragraphs C and D (Paragraphing)** Both paragraphs C and D are about painting the ceiling and walls.

7. **(2) remove the comma (Overuse of commas)** In a complex sentence, a comma usually is not needed between clauses when the dependent clause follows the independent clause.

8. **(1) disappear magically once you leave (Misplaced modifiers)** What happens magically is that the symptoms disappear, not that you leave work. *Magically* should be placed closer to the part of the sentence that it modifies: symptoms disappearing.

9. **(2) change referred to refers (Verb tense)** The present tense is correct because the statement is still true. Moreover, the verb should, if possible, agree with the tense of the majority of verbs in the passage. With the exception of a few sentences that refer to historical information, most verbs in this passage are in the present tense.

10. **(4) change are recirculated to is recirculated (Subject-verb agreement)** If you mentally omit the phrase *inside the buildings*, it becomes clear that the subject is *air*. The singular subject *air* requires the helping verb *is*.

11. **(1) insert a comma after hand (Comma after introductory element)** A comma should follow an introductory element such as *On the other hand*.

12. **(5) the windows (Pronouns)** The antecedent for the pronoun *they* was unclear; it did not appear until near the end of the sentence. Replacing it with *the windows* makes the meaning clear.

13. **(1) insert a comma after agents (Commas with appositives)** The appositive *including bacteria, viruses, fungi and pollen* is not essential to understanding the noun *biological agents* and therefore should be set off by commas.

14. **(5) move sentence 18 to follow sentence 16 (Logical order /relevance)** The sentence about tobacco smoke interrupts the two sentences (17 and 19) about VOCs and should be moved.

15. **(2) include (Verb forms)** The sentence needs a simple present tense verb.

16. **(1) got (Verb forms)** The sentence correctly uses the past tense of the irregular verb *get*.

17. **(2) sentence 4 (Paragraphing)** Sentences 1–3 give a general introduction to the benefits of the buyers club, and sentences 4–8 discuss discounts in more detail.

18. **(3) assess (Verb tense)** The present tense should be used to match the rest of the paragraph.

19. **(5) customers who live in other states will be (Subordinating ideas)** Option (5) is the most effective combination of the two sentences.

20. **(3) order that (Sentence fragment)** Option (3) joins the independent clause and fragment without unnecessary punctuation or connecting words.

21. **(3) replace they're with their (Spelling/possessives and contractions)** Because the membership fees belong to the customers, the possessive pronoun *their* is correct.

22. **(4) in vacant lots, in parks, or on rooftops (Parallel structure)** In option (4), each noun in the series has an appropriate preposition. Thus, the phrases are in parallel form.

23. **(2) change is to are (Subject-verb agreement)** The verb *are* agrees with the plural subject *gardens*.

24. **(2) insert a comma after garden (Complex sentences)** In a complex sentence, a comma should follow the dependent clause at the beginning of the sentence.

25. **(5) people, and choose (Compound sentences)** Two short, choppy sentences are joined to form a compound sentence using a comma and an appropriate conjunction.

26. **(1) Next, choose a site for the garden. (Topic sentences)** Option (1) is specific enough to be clear and general enough to cover all the details in the paragraph. It also includes a transition from the preceding paragraph.

27. **(5) site, and try (Run-on sentences)** Option (5) corrects a run-on sentence by making it a compound sentence with a comma and coordinating conjunction.

28. **(2) needs (Subject-verb agreement)** The collective noun *group* is singular and requires the verb *needs*. The interrupting phrase *of gardeners* merely comes between the subject and the verb.

29. **(4) exhibit (Verb tense)** The present tense is correct here since the other verbs in the sentence are in the present tense and describe actions that take place habitually.

30. **(5) change face to faces (Subject-verb agreement)** The verb *faces* agrees with the singular subject *Compton Point*.

31. **(3) are attempting (Verb tense)** The present progressive is correct because the phrase *in the process of*, found in the previous sentence, signals an action that is in progress.

32. **(1) Tourism increases both air pollution and litter, which will (Sentence fragment)** Option (1) corrects the sentence fragment by combining it with a complete

sentence and reduces the wordiness found in the original sentences.

33. **(2) remove sentence 11 (Logical order/relevance)** The flyer focuses on the land on Compton Point. This sentence about other areas in the county is irrelevant and should be deleted.

34. **(2) new jobs and the influx of tourism resulting (Subordinating ideas)** Option (2) smoothly combines the two sentences into a complex sentence that contains a compound subject.

35. **(2) change agree to agrees (Subject-verb agreement)** The verb *agrees* agrees with the singular pronoun subject *everyone*.

36. **(5) change road to Road (Capitalization)** All parts of a proper noun must be capitalized.

37. **(5) no correction is necessary (Commas)** The sentence is correct as written.

38. **(1) beans, turning (Sentence structure)** The sentence is correct as written.

39. **(4) began (Verb form)** The simple past tense of *begin* is correct because the sentence refers to the mid-1800s and the information in

the rest of the paragraph is in the past tense. *Begun* is the past participle, which requires a helping verb.

40. **(2) change Explorer to explorer (Capitalization)** *Explorer* is not a formal title, so it should not be capitalized.

41. **(4) insert a comma after XII (Commas with appositives)** The appositive *wife of Louis XII* is helpful but not essential to recognizing Anne of Austria. Thus, the appositive should be set off by commas.

42. **(3) move paragraph C to follow paragraph D (Logical order/ relevance)** Paragraph C discusses later time periods than paragraph D, so paragraph D should come first.

43. **(1) replace affect with effect (Spelling/homonyms)** *Effect*, meaning *result*, is correct. *Affect* means *to influence*.

44. **(2) will continue (Verb tense)** The future tense is correct because the other verb in the paragraph is in the future tense.

45. **(1) Numerous state-of-the-art examining rooms (Subordinating ideas)** Option (1) correctly combines the ideas of

numerous examining rooms and state-of-the-art examining rooms.

46. **(3) October, please (Complex sentences)** A comma should be placed after the dependent clause at the beginning of a complex sentence.

47. **(5) remove sentence 11 (Logical order/relevance)** The paragraph discusses a move that will take place in October, so the fact that it is hard to get appointments during the holiday season is irrelevant.

48. **(4) change Hospital to hospital (Capitalization)** The proper name of the hospital is not mentioned, so it is not necessary to capitalize *hospital*.

49. **(1) change Iv'e to I've (Spelling/contractions)** The apostrophe in a contraction should be placed in the spot where letters are omitted (*I've = I have*).

50. **(5) change you're to your (Spelling/possessives and contractions)** The sentence is about files that belong to you, so the possessive pronoun *your* is required.

Language Arts, Writing Part I Post-Test Planning Chart

Circle the number of the questions that you got correct and total them in the last column of each row.

CONTENT AREA	Correction	Revision	Construction Shift	Correct/Total
Organization (pages 66–83)	14, 33, 47		6, 17, 26, 42	_____/7
Sentence Structure (pages 84–105)	2, 24	5, 20, 22, 25, 27, 38, 46	3, 8, 19, 32, 34, 45	_____/15
Grammar and Usage (pages 106–123)	9, 10, 23, 30, 35	4, 12, 15, 16, 18, 28, 29, 31, 39, 44		_____/15
Mechanics (pages 124–139)	1, 7, 11, 13, 21, 36, 37 40, 41, 43, 48, 49,50			_____/13
Total				_____/50

If you do not have time to review the entire writing unit, you may want to review the sections in which you need the most work.

Language Arts, Writing Post-Test

Part II

Scoring Your Essay

Directions: Ask a friend or family member who is a good writer to read your essay and evaluate it using the checklist below.

	Yes	No
Response to the Prompt		
Does the essay answer the question in the topic?		
Is there a clear main idea?		
Does the essay stay on topic?		
Organization		
Are there an introduction, body, and conclusion?		
Does each body paragraph include a topic sentence and supporting details?		
Does the writing flow smoothly from sentence to sentence and from paragraph to paragraph?		
Development and Details		
Do the topic sentences support the main idea of the essay?		
Are topic sentences supported with specific details and examples?		
Conventions of Edited American English		
Are complete sentences used?		
Does the essay have a variety of sentence structures?		
Do subjects and verbs agree?		
Is it clear what each pronoun refers to?		
Are correct verb forms and tenses used?		
Are all words spelled correctly?		
Is correct punctuation used?		
Are capital letters used correctly?		
Word Choice		
Does the essay use specific and clear language?		
Have all unnecessary words been eliminated?		

Scoring:

Essay scorers read an essay and get an overall impression of it. They do not add up points to get a score. Therefore, you should do the same when looking at your chart. Get a general idea of how you stand. If there are many "yes" answers, you are in good shape. After working through the essay sections of this book, you should succeed on the test. If you have mostly "no" answers, you can still do well, but you will have to practice your writing skills.

The checklist is divided into five areas (notice the bold headings). If you have a lot of "no" answers in a particular area, you should devote extra attention to that area.

Essay Scoring Guide

The following scoring guide is used by the evaluators who read test takers' GED essays. Show this chart to the person who evaluates your essay. Have the evaluator assign a score of 1, 2, 3, or 4 to your essay.

	1 **Inadequate** **Reader has difficulty identifying or following the writer's ideas.**	2 **Marginal** **Reader occasionally has difficulty understanding or following the writer's ideas.**	3 **Adequate** **Reader understands writer's ideas.**	4 **Effective** **Reader understands and easily follows the writer's expression of ideas.**
Response to the Prompt	Attempts to address prompt but with little or no success in establishing a focus.	Addresses the prompt, though the focus may shift.	Uses the writing prompt to establish a main idea.	Presents a clearly focused main idea that addresses the prompt.
Organization	Fails to organize ideas.	Shows some evidence of an organizational plan.	Uses an identifiable organizational plan.	Establishes a clear and logical organization.
Development and Details	Demonstrates little or no development; usually lacks details or examples or presents irrelevant information.	Has some development but lacks specific details; may be limited to listing, repetitions, or generalizations.	Has focused but occasionally uneven development; incorporates some specific detail.	Achieves coherent development with specific and relevant details and examples.
Conventions of Edited American English (EAE)	Exhibits minimal or no control of sentence structure and the conventions of EAE	Demonstrates inconsistent control of sentence structure and the conventions of EAE.	Generally controls sentence structure and the conventions of EAE.	Consistently controls sentence structure and the conventions of EAE.
Word Choice	Exhibits weak and/or inappropriate words.	Exhibits a narrow range of word choice, often including inappropriate selections.	Exhibits appropriate word choice.	Exhibits varied and precise word choice.

Reprinted with permission of the GED Testing Service of the American Council on Education.

A High-Scoring GED Essay

Again, to get a better idea of an effective GED essay, read the sample topic assignment below and the essay on page 616.

TOPIC

What is one important goal you would like to achieve in the next few years?

In your essay, identify that goal. Explain how you plan to achieve it. Use your personal observations, experience, and knowledge to support your essay.

WRITING TEST - PA   CC–135

Write the letter of your essay topic in the box, then fill in the corresponding circle.

TOPIC   Ⓐ Ⓑ ● Ⓓ Ⓔ Ⓕ Ⓖ Ⓗ Ⓘ Ⓙ Ⓚ Ⓛ Ⓜ Ⓝ Ⓞ Ⓟ Ⓠ Ⓡ Ⓢ Ⓣ Ⓤ Ⓥ Ⓦ Ⓧ Ⓨ Ⓩ

This essay scored a 4—the highest score possible. Here is the explanation why.

❑ Classic 5-paragraph essay

❑ Clearly focused main idea

❑ Develops three ideas to explain main idea

❑ Includes specific examples and detail

❑ Varied word choice

❑ Consistent sentence structure, usage, and mechanics

Over the next few years, my main goal is to obtain a college degree from St. Johns University in Collegeville. This goal will be very difficult to obtain and I will need to work hard at it. Three things that will affect the outcome of my goal are; how much money I can raise to pay for it, how much time I am willing to spend studying, and my dedication in training for football.

Before you can register at a college, you must consider how it is going to be paid for. This is especially an issue at St. Johns, because the tuition is around $22,000 a year. This is a huge sum of money. It is not made easier by the fact that my parents will be able to contribute very little towards my education. Thus I am forced to rely on scholarships, grants, and loans from the government and other agencies. I have already taken some action by applying for scholarships, but I will have to apply again next year. I received a $7,500 scholarship from St. Johns and they have also given me some grants. The rest of the money will have to come from student loans and an on campus job.

The next area that will affect my goal is the classroom. This is important because the main point of college is to prepare meself for a successful career. In college, I will need to apply myself and take time to study every night. Sometimes, I may be forced to give up things that I would rather do, but I must if I am going to achieve my goal. I must create a relationship with my professors because they will help.

The third thing is my dedication in training for football. Football is my favorite sport and St. Johns has an excellent football tradition. They have 150 players out for football each year. If I am going to be successful and contribute to the team, I am going to have to be dedicated to training. I must spend twelve hours in the weight room gaining strength and quickness. I believe all of the hard work will pay off.

If I can do these three things, I will successfully complete my goal of graduating from college. If this goal is achieved, I believe I will be well on my way to a successful life.

SOCIAL STUDIES POST-TEST ANSWERS AND EXPLANATIONS

1. **(4) The United States had an unfavorable merchandise balance of trade during the 1990s. (Evaluation)** According to the passage, the balance of trade is the difference between exports and imports. When imports are greater than exports, the balance of trade is unfavorable. Since the graph shows that imports consistently exceeded exports during the 1990s, you can conclude that the merchandise balance of trade was unfavorable during the decade.

2. **(4) the National Rifle Association (Application)** The Second Amendment is one of the strongest arguments the pro-gun lobby has. None of the other organizations is involved with the militia (national guard) or with promoting gun ownership.

3. **(3) Industrialization and urbanization caused many changes in family life in the late 1800s. (Comprehension)** This statement covers the main points of the passage, which discusses the impact of industrialization and urbanization on the American family. The other options are all supporting details.

4. **(1) 0% to 4% (Comprehension)** First find the United States on the map and see what shade it is colored. Then consult the map key to see the percentage of undernourished people that shade represents. The map indicates that the percentage range is 0% to 4%.

5. **(2) a person who heads a relief organization (Application)** World hunger statistics would be of interest to a relief organization, which must decide how to allocate its relief efforts around the world.

6. **(5) Hunger is a major problem in many countries in Africa. (Evaluation)** More than 20 nations in Africa have a very high percentage of undernourished people. The remaining options are not supported by the data on the map.

7. **(3) Pay $210.45, and write to the credit card company within 60 days to tell them about the double billing. (Application)** The instructions have three main points:

(1) the disputed part of the balance ($69) does not have to be paid; (2) the problem must be brought to the credit card company's attention in writing in order for the consumer to keep his or her rights; (3) the credit card company must be notified within 60 days of the billing date. Option (3) is the only option that covers these three elements of the instructions.

8. **(2) The company can sell the product at a lower price than other companies can. (Analysis)** When a company has comparative advantage over other companies in regard to a particular product, that means its cost to produce the product is lower. Therefore, the company can sell the product at a lower price than its competitors can and still make a profit.

9. **(2) Since 1960, the percentage of foreign-born people has been on an upward trend. (Comprehension)** The graph shows that the percentage of foreign-born people has risen since 1960, so this means the foreign-born population is on an upward trend.

10. **(4) It did not impose direct economic costs on the colonists. (Analysis)** With the exception of the Declaratory Act, all of the acts of Parliament shown in the chart cost the colonists money, whether by having to pay import taxes, buy revenue stamps, or use their own resources to shelter British soldiers.

11. **(1) The Declaration of Independence, which explained why the colonies broke away from Great Britain (Application)** The acts of Parliament listed in the chart were several of the grievances the colonists used to justify declaring independence.

12. **(4) Slavery destroyed the culture of the slaves, diminishing their self-respect. (Analysis)** According to the paragraph, this is an opinion, or belief, held by some historians. The other options are all facts stated in the paragraph.

13. **(5) at 0° latitude (Comprehension)** On both of these projections the distortions are greatest near the poles. Along the equator

(0° latitude), the maps look most alike and most similar to a globe; the distortions increase as you go north or south toward the poles.

14. **(1) The Mercator projection distorts the sizes of land masses near the North Pole, and the interrupted projection does not. (Analysis)** Each of these projections takes a different approach to representing a three-dimensional globe in two dimensions. The Mercator "stretches" areas near the poles, increasing their size considerably, which is a problem especially near the North Pole, because there are land masses located there. You can see this because the lines of latitude and longitude are farther apart near the poles than they would be on a globe. (On the globe, the longitude meridians come together at a point at the poles.) The interrupted projection "cuts" the oceans apart near the poles so the land masses—except Antarctica—appear at the correct size. The distortion in the interrupted projection comes not because of the size of the land masses but because the land masses near the poles are cut apart.

15. **(2) The interrupted projection distorts distances across the oceans. (Evaluation)** The interrupted projection was a poor choice because ocean areas are cut apart on the map, making it very difficult to measure distances on an around-the-world voyage.

16. **(5) the Seminole (Comprehension)** The Seminole tribe's home territory was in Florida, which was farthest from the new, government-declared Indian Territory in the Midwest.

17. **(2) Whites wanted to take over Indian lands in the eastern states. (Analysis)** As the population of the United States grew, the need for good land increased. White settlers saw the Indian lands in the eastern portion of the country as an opportunity to expand the settlement options. The U.S. government backed the settlers by forcing the American Indian groups in the region to leave their lands.

18. **(1) the Bedouin, who are a nomadic herding people of Saudi Arabia (Application)** The Bedouin follow a pastoral lifestyle, moving their herds of animals and temporary settlements from place to place in search of good grazing.

19. **(2) building the Erie Canal from the Great Lakes to the Hudson River in New York (Application)** Like roads across the mountains, the Erie Canal provided a transportation route from New York in the East to the Great Lakes in the Midwest. The Great Lakes are all interconnected, and so provided access to the upper Midwest; they also provide direct or canal-mediated access to rivers that flow through the Midwest.

20. **(4) The cost of medical care and tobacco products increased far more than the cost of other items in the 1990s. (Evaluation)** Compared to the price indexes for most other items, the price indexes of medical care and tobacco products increased far more. You can tell this simply by looking at the lengths of the bars.

21. **(3) The United States gained influence over Panama through the building and running of the Panama Canal. (Application)** Among the choices, this is the only example of imperialism— the takeover of aspects of one nation by another. The other options involve either internal events or the independence of one nation from another.

22. **(2) Except for soils in northern coniferous regions, humid soils can be used or modified for crops. (Analysis)** This is a general conclusion based on the details of the paragraph. The remaining options are all supporting details.

23. **(4) Establishing a landfill near a historic site is an insult to the memory of what took place there. (Analysis)** According to the passage, opponents of the landfill believe that building the landfill near the highway would "desecrate" the historic site.

24. **(5) present-day economic benefit versus respect for the past (Evaluation)** Those who favor the landfill think the present economic needs of the Lowndes County population are more important. Those who oppose it think that preserving a historic site without encroaching on it is more important.

25. **(3) Special interest groups have too much influence with members of Congress. (Evaluation)** The cartoonist is using irony in the caption to indicate that he thinks members of Congress treat voters badly, but treat people who represent special interest groups well.

26. **(4) Germany was divided into two parts, West Germany and East Germany. (Analysis)** The Allied armies, approaching Germany from east and west, met in the middle of the country. After Germany surrendered, they divided the country. The map shows that after World War II, Germany was split into East Germany and West Germany and that East Germany was under Soviet influence through the Warsaw Pact and that West Germany was under British, French, and American influence through NATO.

27. **(2) All the Warsaw Pact nations were located in eastern Europe. (Analysis)** Of all the options, this is the only general statement, or conclusion. The remaining options are all details from the map.

28. **(4) The Fifth Amendment applies to the federal government, and the Fourteenth Amendment, to state governments. (Analysis)** According to the passage, this is one of the main differences between the two amendments.

29. **(4) between 146 and 44 B.C. (Comprehension)** First locate Asia Minor on the map and see how it is shaded or patterned. Then consult the map key to see when land in Asia Minor was acquired by the Roman Empire. The map shows that most of the land was acquired between 146 and 44 B.C.

30. **(2) Before 264 B.C., Rome conquered through overland military campaigns; later conquests were made by navies as well. (Evaluation)** The map shows that up to 264 B.C. all of Rome's conquests were located on the Italian peninsula, reachable by land-based military units. After that time, as Rome sought to expand beyond the peninsula, it built navies to help conquer overseas areas.

31. **(3) The war created a huge demand for military equipment and supplies. (Analysis)** The chart shows that there was a substantial increase in manufacturing output between 1939 (when World War II began in Europe) and 1941. Even though the United States did not enter the war until late 1941, industry had already geared up to manufacture and sell military equipment and supplies to the Allies in Europe.

32. **(2) patriotism (Evaluation)** The tendency of the American public to support a president's emergency foreign policy actions is sometimes called the "rally 'round the flag" effect.

33. **(3) 30 cents (Comprehension)** According to the passage, market price is reached under equilibrium conditions—when supply equals demand. According to the graph, this is at 30 cents.

34. **(5) The market price would go up. (Analysis)** When the supply decreases, and demand stays the same, the market price increases. That is because the same number of people want to buy fewer apples. So the people will generally be willing to pay more for the apples.

35. **(1) the Supreme Court of the United States (Comprehension)** According to the passage, cases are appealed to higher level courts; according to the diagram, the Supreme Court is the highest court of appeal.

36. **(3) Court of International Trade (Application)** The word *international* relates to foreign companies. Cases involving foreign companies and foreign trade (imports and exports) are heard in the Court of International Trade.

37. **(2) The volume and variety of federal cases were too great for a single court to handle. (Analysis)** It would be impractical to have just one court handling all cases; the workload would be too great. That was the main reason for the establishment of the lower federal courts.

38. **(4) The mass media's coverage of political news has a consistent liberal bias. (Analysis)** According to the passage, this is an opinion held by critics of the media, although it is not supported by research on bias in political news.

39. **(3) the Internet (Application)** As Internet access becomes more widespread, the Internet will become part of the mass media.

40. **(4) All of the camps were located inland to make it difficult for any Japanese American to communicate with Japanese offshore. (Evaluation)** Since the government considered Japanese Americans on the West Coast a security threat, the entire coast was designated an exclusion zone, and people were moved to camps away from the coast.

41. **(1) trading goods and services for other goods and services (Comprehension)** Bartering is explained and an example of it is given in the first paragraph.

42. **(5) Both are ways to exchange goods and services. (Analysis)** Both bartering and money are means of economic exchange.

43. **(1) Money has several advantages over bartering. (Analysis)** Of all the options, this one is the only general statement, or conclusion. The remaining options are all details from the passage.

44. **(1) the Magna Carta (Comprehension)** The Magna Carta, signed in 1215, was the first document to set limits on the British king's powers.

45. **(4) Both established methods of self-government in the English colonies. (Analysis)** Both the Mayflower Compact and the Great Fundamentals were documents that set forth rules and laws for the self-government of specific English colonies.

46. **(5) the English Bill of Rights (Analysis)** The colonists felt they should be granted the same rights as other British citizens, which were listed in the English Bill of Rights. They used this list to help them draft the grievance section of the Declaration of Independence. None of the other choices relates to the rights the British give its ordinary subjects or refers to Parliament.

47. **(3) Both valued a stable political framework for society. (Analysis)** The paragraph indicates that this was one thing the ancient Chinese and the ancient Greeks had in common. The other options are not shared characteristics.

48. **(2) Los Angeles has the worst traffic delays because such a large percentage of workers drive there. (Analysis)** This is the only generalization, or conclusion, among the options listed. It is based on the facts that Los Angeles has the fewest nondriving workers and the most traffic delays. The remaining options are all details from the chart.

49. **(4) McDonald's, a chain of fast-food restaurants run by individuals (Application)** McDonald's is probably the most famous franchise operation. Its restaurants are owned and operated by franchisees who must run the restaurants according to the strictest procedures and standards.

50. **(3) About twice as many Civil War soldiers died of disease as died of wounds. (Evaluation)** According to the graph, during the Civil War, death from disease claimed about twice the number of lives as death from wounds.

Social Studies Post-Test Planning Chart

Circle the number of the questions that you got correct, and total them in the last column of each row.

CONTENT AREA	Comprehension	Application	Analysis	Evaluation	Correct/Total
U.S. History (pages 166–179)	3, 9, 16	11, 19	10, 12, 17 23, 31	24, 40, 50	_____/13
World History (pages 180–193)	29	18, 21	26, 27, 47	30	_____/7
Civics and Government (pages 194–205)	35, 44	2, 36, 39	28, 37, 38, 45, 46	25, 32	_____/12
Economics (pages 206–217)	33, 41	7, 49	8, 34, 42, 43	1, 20	_____/10
Geography (pages 218–228)	4, 13	5	12, 22, 48	6, 15	_____/8
Total					_____/50

Use this chart to determine your areas of strength and weakness. If you do not have time to review the entire social studies unit of this book, you may want to focus your study on those areas in which you need the most work.

SCIENCE POST-TEST ANSWERS AND EXPLANATIONS

1. **(3) sea star (Comprehension)** Of the five animals shown, only the sea star has a center section from which similar parts radiate. All the other animals are bilaterally symmetrical.

2. **(4) Bacteria quickly evolved resistance to antibiotic drugs. (Evaluation)** In 1969, the Surgeon General did not anticipate that bacteria would evolve to be resistant to the antibiotics that had been so effective until that time.

3. **(5) a fuse, a strip of wire that melts when it gets too hot, breaking an electric circuit (Analysis)** When the wire in a fuse melts, the electricity stops flowing through the circuit because the circuit has been broken. Thus the other wires on the circuit do not have the opportunity to overheat and cause a fire.

4. **(5) 100+ (Comprehension)** First locate Tucson in the southwest section of the United States. Then check the high temperature indication for the Tucson region. It is over 100°F.

5. **(2) It is clear in Minneapolis but there are showers in Chicago. (Analysis)** First locate the two cities on the map. Using the key and the temperature indications, you can see that it is clear in Minneapolis and the high temperature is in the 80s. In Chicago, it is also in the 80s but it is showering there.

6. **(3) It is warmer in Oklahoma City than in Santa Fe. (Evaluation)** The map shows that Oklahoma City has temperatures in the 90s while Santa Fe has temperatures in the 80s. None of the other options is supported by information on the map.

7. **(2) A teacher's perfume can be detected at the back of the classroom. (Application)** This is an example of diffusion, the spreading of gas molecules (perfume vapor) throughout a container (the classroom).

8. **(2) People can reduce their chances of developing age-related hearing loss by not smoking. (Analysis)** Of all the options, this is the only one that is a hypothe-

sis that the researchers could have been testing with their experiment. Option (1) is too general to be a hypothesis for this experiment and is stated more like a conclusion than a hypothesis. All of the other options are facts relating to the study.

9. **(4) For the two compounds shown, solubility increases as temperature increases. (Evaluation)** The graph shows KCl and NaHCO₃ having increased solubility as the temperature rises from 0°C to 50°C. None of the other statements is supported by information in the graph.

10. **(3) how special fluids keep insects alive during subfreezing weather. (Application)** Understanding how insects can survive freezing may be a key to finding a way to freeze organs without destroying them.

11. **(3) Both involve effort applied with circular motion. (Analysis)** The diagrams show that the effort applied to each of these machines is circular.

12. **(1) Mercury and bromine are liquids at room temperature. (Evaluation)** Room temperature is about 70°F. The chart indicates that both mercury and bromine are liquids at that temperature: each has a melting point—the temperature at which it solidifies—well below room temperature; each has a boiling point—the temperature at which it becomes a gas—well above room temperature.

13. **(1) the cracking of granite from the expansion of freezing water (Application)** This is an example of physical weathering because a change of state between liquid and solid is involved. Options (3) and (4) are not examples of weathering because transport is involved.

14. **(2) the air and rainwater in the soil (Comprehension)** According to the diagram, nitrogen-fixing bacteria take nitrogen from both the air and rain found in soil.

15. **(2) compost with plant and animal wastes (Analysis)** According to the diagram, plant and animal waste contains nitrogen com-

pounds that decomposers, including nitrite bacteria and nitrate bacteria, break down. In this way, composting with plant and animal wastes results in the addition of usable forms of nitrogen to the soil. So composting with organic waste (plant and animal materials) would be an alternative to synthetic fertilizers.

16. **(5) They return nitrogen gas to the air. (Comprehension)** The diagram shows that this is the role denitrifying bacteria play in the nitrogen cycle. The arrow points from denitrifying bacteria to the air, specifically to the label atmospheric nitrogen.

17. **(3) The recycling of nitrogen through the biosphere involves many complex processes. (Analysis)** This is a general statement, or conclusion, that is supported by the various details in the diagram. The other statements are details from the diagram.

18. **(2) a flame detector (Application)** Since the flickering of fire is unlike the flickering of other light sources, this fact was used as the basis of the flame detector, which is triggered by the flicker patterns of fire.

19. **(5) Observation is a useful part of the scientific method as long as the results are used to support or disprove a hypothesis. (Comprehension)** According to Darwin's remarks, it is a waste of time to observe phenomena if you do not use what you observe to evaluate your theories.

20. **(2) lift (Comprehension)** As the diagram shows and the paragraph implies, the differing pressures above and below the airplane's wing results in an upward force called lift.

21. **(2) *Atlantic Empress, Aegean Captain, Exxon Valdez*, and *Sea Empress* are oil tankers. (Analysis)** The designer of the chart does not explain that these are ships that were transporting oil; he or she assumes you know that, given the context of the chart.

22. **(1) Its charge would become positive. (Analysis)** If an atom loses an electron, it has more

protons than electrons, and thus it has a net positive charge. (Such an atom is called a positive ion.)

23. **(3) Most people would not recognize the gametophyte generation of a fern. (Evaluation)** This conclusion is supported by the fact that the gametophyte is a small, heart-shaped structure and that the sporophyte generation of the fern is the familiar plant, with roots, stems, and leaves.

24. **(5) Humans contain a higher percentage of carbon than bacteria do. (Analysis)** To find the correct answer, you must check each statement against the graphs to see whether the information in the graphs supports the statement. The graphs show that humans have a higher percentage of carbon than bacteria have.

25. **(3) carbon dioxide gas (Comprehension)** According to the passage, the holes in Swiss-type cheese form when special bacteria feed on lactic acid and produce large bubbles of carbon dioxide.

26. **(1) During an ice age, temperatures drop and ice covers vast areas of Earth. (Analysis)** Of all the options, this is the only one that is a fact. The others are hypotheses or theories about what causes ice ages.

27. **(5) Chondrichthyes (Application)** Two clues tell you that stingrays belong to the class Chondrichthyes. First, they are fish, so they belong to Chondrichthyes, Osteicythyes, or Agnatha. But Agnatha isn't given as a choice. Since stingrays have cartilaginous skeletons, they must be members of Chondrichthyes.

28. **(3) Amphibia (Application)** During its life cycle, the frog undergoes a dramatic change in body form, which is characteristic of amphibians. Also indicative of amphibians, the young frog lives in the water as a tadpole, indicated by its having gills; the adult frog can live in or out of the water, indicated by its having lungs.

29. **(3) if the surface were irregular or rough (Analysis)** If a surface is rough, each light ray will hit the surface at a different angle. Since the angles of incidence vary from ray to ray, the angles of reflection will also vary. In other words, light rays reflecting off of a rough surface travel in all different directions.

30. **(2) when food is digested, as when an enzyme in saliva called ptyalin breaks down starch into sugars without itself changing (Application)** The catalyst is the enzyme ptyalin; you can identify ptyalin as the catalyst, because it aids the chemical reaction of digestion but itself remains unchanged after the reaction. None of the other reactions include a substance that remains unchanged.

31. **(3) animal rights (Evaluation)** People who oppose the use of animals in scientific experiments generally value animal rights, which are predicated on the idea that it is wrong to make animals (usually specifically mammals) suffer.

32. **(1) Pressure builds up inside the magma chamber and vent. (Analysis)** If you examine the diagram, you will see that hot magma wells up into the volcano's cone. You need to infer that when the pressure builds up sufficiently, the volcano explodes, or erupts. None of the other events described would cause a violent explosion from the inside of the volcano.

33. **(4) the movement of the magnet (Analysis)** In the middle drawing, when the magnet is not moving, there is no current; in the top and bottom drawing, when the magnet is moving, there is current. From this you can conclude that the movement of the magnet causes the current to flow.

34. **(3) When the magnet changes direction, the current changes direction. (Evaluation)** Compare the top and bottom drawings. When the magnet moves to the left, the current flows from right to left. When the magnet moves to the right, the current flows from left to right.

35. **(5) Fluid dynamics, aerodynamics, and nuclear physics are fields in which large data sets must be analyzed routinely. (Comprehension)** Since analyzing huge amounts of data quickly is the job of supercomputers, it follows that in the fields in which supercomputers are used, there must be large amounts of data requiring analysis.

36. **(4) drinking only the amount of water the runner actually loses during a marathon (Analysis)** If the runner does not drink more water than she loses during the race, the runner can help prevent the buildup of excess water. The excess water that cannot be absorbed or excreted during strenuous exercise is what causes the salt imbalance, which leads in turn to the harmful symptoms.

37. **(5) The dog has canines and the sheep does not. (Analysis)** If you compare the two diagrams, you will see that the sheep does not have any canines; instead the sheep has a large gap where the canines would be.

38. **(1) to split the uranium atom (Analysis)** The diagram shows that this neutron is used to bombard the uranium atom. This bombardment sets off the fission reaction in which the uranium atom is split; another neutron is released to continue the chain reaction.

39. **(5) Coevolution provides benefits to both species. (Analysis)** Of all the options, this is the only general statement arising out of the supporting details of the passage.

40. **(1) orthoclase (Application)** To find a mineral that the file can scratch, you have to look for one that has a lower number on the Mohs scale than 6.5—the hardness of the file. Orthoclase is the only mineral among the choices with a hardness lower than 6.5.

41. **(3) Some genetic abnormalities do not appear until the clone matures. (Analysis)** According to the passage, genetic abnormalities can show themselves at any stage of development. Thus some animals will appear normal for quite a while before developing problems.

42. **(1) a ban on human cloning (Evaluation)** In addition to the ethical issues raised by cloning humans, the potential for serious health problems due to genetic abnormalities introduced during the cloning process provides another line of argument for those who favor banning human cloning.

43. **(3) Russia (Comprehension)** To find the country with the smallest consumption of electricity per person, look for the shortest bar in the graph.

44. **(2) the cooling you feel as sweat evaporates (Application)** Of the options, this is the only one involving the change from liquid to gas, which results in a loss of heat from the liquid. This heat loss accounts for the cooling effect of sweat.

45. **(2) parthenogenesis (Application)** According to the information given, parthenogenesis occurs when the egg develops without the addition of genetic material from the male. Since the question mentions only eggs but no sperm, parthenogenesis is the best answer.

46. **(5) The arrangement of the carbon, hydrogen, and oxygen atoms in the two hydrocarbons is different. (Analysis)** Although ether and ethanol both have the same number of carbon, hydrogen, and oxygen atoms, the different arrangements of atoms in each compound results in two substances with different properties.

47. **(1) Feet are adapted to each amphibian's habitat and lifestyle. (Analysis)** Of all the options, only Option (1) is a general statement, a conclusion based on the detailed listed in the other options and shown in the diagram.

48. **(2) The student should have use books of the same height for all of the ramps. (Evaluation)** The height of the ramp affects how far the ball rolls. So the height of the ramp should be a controlled variable in this experiment. By using one ramp that is not as high as the others, the student is introducing a second variable into the experiment, which makes his data invalid for the ramp that is lower than the others.

49. **(4) Why We Sleep (Comprehension)** The topic of the paragraph is why sleep evolved in humans, and the paragraph cites several reasons for sleeping. The other options are either too specific or too general.

50. **(4) The five largest asteroids are all farther from the sun than Earth is. (Evaluation)** According to the chart, Earth's distance from the sun is set at 1, so any value greater than one indicates that the asteroid is farther from the sun than Earth is. All the asteroids have distance values of 2 or greater, so they are all farther from the sun than Earth is.

Science Post-Test Planning Chart

CONTENT AREA	Comprehension	Application	Analysis	Evaluation	Correct/Total
Life Science (pages 234–253)	14, 16, 19, 49	1, 10, 27, 28, 45	8, 15, 17, 24, 36, 37, 39, 41, 47	2, 23, 31, 42	_____/22
Earth and Space Science (pages 254–267)	4, 43	13, 40	5, 21, 26, 32	6, 50	_____/10
Physical Science (pages 268–282)	20, 25, 35	7, 18, 30, 44	3, 11, 22, 29, 33, 38, 46	9, 12, 34, 48	_____/18
Total					_____/50

Use this chart to determine your areas of strength and weakness. If you do not have time to review the entire science unit of this book, you may want to focus your study on the areas in which you need the most work.

READING POST-TEST ANSWERS AND EXPLANATIONS

1. **(5) sits far away from you (Comprehension)** When the physical setting indicates distance, the interviewee can pick this up as a cue for formality. "Some put a desk the size of a 747 between themselves and you. This is a clear message to keep your distance."

2. **(5) An interviewee should know how to read cues from an interviewer. (Comprehension)** The article provides specific information on the meaning of an interviewer's e-mail and office set-up. These can be "a useful tool for gauging the personality and character of interviewers."

3. **(2) to describe types of interviewers and how to approach them (Synthesis)** The opening paragraph indicates that this article will examine clues to aid in "gauging the personality and character of interviewers and . . . their expectations of potential employees."

4. **(1) friendly and conversational (Synthesis)** The style of writing includes phrases that sound like spoken conversation between friends: "And, for heaven's sake, don't touch that desk!" "Let's examine some clues." "Still others get right down to business—no chit-chat. . . ."

5. **(4) content changes from general to more specific (Synthesis)** The article begins by discussing human nature—"We develop an instinctive way of reading others . . . that makes us form instant, lifelong relationships with some people. . . ." The article then discusses specifics of an interviewer's e-mail and office set-up.

6. **(5) Their cars were not of the highest quality. (Analysis)** The first paragraph discusses this cause: "The Detroit auto manufacturers were able to keep their costs low and profits high in part by producing sub-par cars." That is why their share of the market suffered.

7. **(4) wanted to build quality cars with few repair problems (Analysis)** The U.S. automakers produced cars with "far more problems than their foreign equivalents." This suggests that quality was a priority for the foreign automakers but not for domestic

automakers looking to "keep their costs low and profits high."

8. **(5) financial executives (Analysis)** A bean counter keeps track of the financial matters of an organization. They "analyzed their companies' financial statements. . . ." As such, they pay attention only to money.

9. **(3) a business manual (Application)** The information and style of writing suggest that it is intended for a general audience of people in business.

10. **(1) critical (Synthesis)** The authors speak negatively of the cars produced by U.S. automakers in the 1970s and 1980s and include comments such as, "to add insult to injury" and "weren't considering the bigger picture."

11. **(1) U.S. automakers (Expanded synthesis)** The last part of the piece explains that U.S. automakers "learned the hard way" and "got their act together."

12. **(5) is hoping her mother won't hear her asking for money (Analysis)** The narrator misinterprets Marjie's actions. She thinks Marjie is asking for money for herself, not her mother. She therefore interprets Marjie's actions as trying to hide her request from her mother.

13. **(3) Jennie is perplexed when the narrator blames Marjie. (Analysis)** When the narrator explains that she thought Marjie wanted the money for herself, "Jennie looked doubtful."

14. **(2) discuss it defensively (Application)** Jennie meets with the narrator directly to try to explain what happened and express concern. However, she misunderstands the narrator's explanation, apologizes for trying to borrow money, and reacts defensively when it is suggested that her daughter would ask for money on her own. Jennie would likely have this same defensive reaction if criticized by a boss.

15. **(3) They know each other but are not close. (Synthesis)** The narrator is staying with Jennie and her family and obviously knows them, yet there is a formal tone to Jennie's explanation about borrowing money, and the

narrator is unable to explain how she misunderstood Marjie and is left "floundering." Those aspects of their relationship help you infer they are not on close, intimate terms.

16. **(4) uncomfortable (Synthesis)** Jennie feels she has to explain why she was going to borrow money from the narrator, and the narrator not only misinterprets Marjie's actions but has a difficult time explaining to Jennie "the whole of Marjie's act." Jennie appears to doubt her and states her children would never ask for money, leaving the narrator "floundering a bit." The entire situation ends with the narrator (and perhaps even the reader) feeling uncomfortable over the situation.

17. **(1) a coin (Analysis)** Pennies were made of copper. The father gives his daughters "Four coppers a day, six days a week . . . half a day's pay."

18. **(4) he could say "no" to his children (Analysis)** Pa is conflicted about giving the girls money that he works so hard for and needs himself.

19. **(3) bold (Synthesis)** Cleo speaks "brazenly" and is the first to ask Pa for money. She bets her sisters that she can hang upside down from a tree.

20. **(2) negatively (Analysis)** The sisters don't want to see Cleo get hurt, and they don't want to lose their money.

21. **(1) jumping from a roof before an audience (Application)** Cleo loves attention. Her challenge of the bet would result in her either winning her sisters' money or gaining attention because she got hurt. Jumping from a rooftop would provide a similar result.

22. **(5) Cleo gets all of her sisters' coppers without doing anything. (Synthesis)** One by one, Cleo's sisters are offering to pay her *not* to take such a chance.

23. **(5) It seemed the natural thing to do. (Comprehension)** The narrator explains to Lavinia, "it seemed natural, after a while, to go on, once I'd started taking care of him."

24. **(4) She knows Lavinia will force her to try to explain her situation. (Comprehension)** The narrator goes on to say, "Whatever I said would be greeted by this probing incomprehension." She knows that Lavinia will not be able to understand her motivation.

25. **(5) doing what is expected of her (Analysis)** Despite the fact that caring for an ill parent is a difficult task, the narrator continued to care for her father because he expected her to and because it seemed like the right thing to do.

26. **(3) Make things as easy on yourself as possible. (Analysis)** Lavinia continues to question why the narrator didn't find someone else or pursue some other alternative that would have released the narrator from the responsibility of caring for her ill father.

27. **(1) pointedly and confidently (Application)** Everything Lavinia says and the manner in which she says it helps you see that she is focused on herself. She would walk through a crowded room with no thought to anyone but herself.

28. **(5) self-centeredness and self-sacrifice (Synthesis)** Lavinia is a shining example of self-centeredness, and the narrator exemplifies self-sacrifice by caring for her father.

29. **(3) looking for a flower from the day before (Comprehension)** The butterfly is looking for a flower from the day before, when the grass was not yet mowed, but the flower was cut down by the mower: "swift there passed me by / . . . a bewildered butterfly, / Seeking . . . / Some resting flower of yesterday's delight."

30. **(2) are the shape and color of a tongue of fire (Analysis)** The poet is comparing flowers and flames. As a tongue of fire seems to leap into the air and is colored red or orange, so is the tuft of flowers.

31. **(4) appreciated their beauty (Comprehension)** The speaker says, "The mower in the dew had loved them thus."

32. **(2) He and the mower were kindred spirits. (Synthesis)** Early in the poem, the narrator feels alone: "And I must be, as he had been—alone." But when he realizes the mower had appreciated the flowers' beauty and intentionally left them uncut, he realizes they share a feeling for the flowers: "and feel a spirit kindred to my own."

33. **(3) thoughtful (Synthesis)** The narrator is very observant of nature and thinks about the meaning of everything he sees—where the butterfly is heading, the patch of flowers that didn't get mowed down, the feelings of the mower, and his relationship to the mower.

34. **(2) quiet classical (Application)** The mood of the poem is peaceful and reflective. This mood is best expressed by quiet classical music.

35. **(1) beings from some place other than Earth (Comprehension)** Human beings are talked about as beings very different from the professors and the student. Also, it is clear that the student has created human beings as a school assignment.

36. **(3) complimented his creation of humans (Comprehension)** The professor has complimented the design and appearance of human feet. Then the student thanks him because he is responsible for their creation.

37. **(4) have developed languages and produced literature (Analysis)** When Professor A tells the student to stop exaggerating and cites the sandwich as an example of how long it takes humans to accomplish something, the student says, "Look at what they've done with their languages. . . . they've built a body of literature with great power, feeling and insight."

38. **(2) Nothing is of value unless it is useful. (Application)** Professor A criticizes the English language because it has too many little-used letters.

39. **(3) The human race has both strengths and weaknesses. (Synthesis)** The student cites accomplishments of humans (artwork, language, literature, and so on) and Professor A cites their shortcomings (length of time to invent even something as simple as a sandwich, useless inventions, inability to recognize genius).

40. **(1) light-hearted (Expanded synthesis)** Professor B comments on the appeal of human feet and the comedy team of the Marx Brothers. He doesn't engage in any of the more serious arguments that Professor A engages in.

Reading Post-Test Evaluation Chart

Circle the number of the questions that you got correct and total them in the last column of each row.

CONTENT AREA	Comprehension	Application	Analysis	Synthesis	Correct/Total
Nonfiction (pages 286–303)	1, 2	9	6, 7, 8	3, 4, 5, 10, 11	____/11
Fiction (pages 304–317)	23, 24	14, 21, 27	12, 15, 17, 18 20, 25, 26	7, 22, 28	____/15
Poetry (pages 318–329)	29, 31	34	30	32, 33	____/6
Drama (pages 330–340)	35, 36	38	37	39, 40	____/6
Total					____/40

Use this chart to determine your areas of strength and weakness. If you do not have time to review the entire reading unit of this book, you may want to focus your study on the areas in which you need the most work.

MATH POST-TEST ANSWERS AND EXPLANATIONS

Part I, page 595

1. **(2) $65,000** About $130,000 was made from catalog sales. About $65,000 was made from online sales. $130,000 − $65,000 = $65,000

2. **(3) $\frac{1}{3}$** About $100,000 was made from in-store sales. To find the total sales, add up the three values. $130,000 + $65,000 + $100,000 = $295,000, which is about $300,000. Working with compatible numbers, $100,000 out of $300,000 is $\frac{1}{3}$, so option (3) is the correct answer.

3. **(3) 48** First you must change the 22 feet into inches. Since there are 12 inches in a foot, multiply $12 \times 22 = 264$ inches. Then divide by $5\frac{1}{2}$ (or 5.5) to find the total number of boards needed to cover the area. $264 \div 5.5 = 48$

4. $\frac{1}{3}$

The coordinates of point A are $(−3,0)$. The coordinates of point B are $(3,2)$. Use the slope formula: $\frac{y_2 − y_1}{x_2 − x_2}$. Substitute the values and solve the equation.
slope $= \frac{2 − 0}{3 − (−3)} = \frac{2}{6}$, or $\frac{1}{3}$

5. **58**

Substitute the values for x and y in the expression. Then simplify the expression using the order of operations.
$3(2 \times 4 − 5) + (3 + 4)^2 =$
$3(3) + 7^2 =$
$9 + 49 = 58$

6. **(5) The volume of Box B is eight times the volume of Box A.** First find the dimensions of Box A. Since they are half of the dimensions of Box B, the side lengths must be 3, 2, and 1.5. Now find the volumes of the two boxes. Use the formula $V = lwh$. The volume of Box B is 72, and the volume of Box A is 9. Since 72 is 8 times larger than 9, option (5) must be the correct answer.

7. **(4) 240** Set up the proportion $\frac{5}{100} = \frac{12}{x}$, where x is the number of children who are enrolled in the program. $12 \times 100 = 1200$, and $1200 \div 5 = 240$

8. **(5) 28%** Probability is the ratio of the number of favorable outcomes to the number of possible outcomes. Add up the numbers of marbles to find out how many marbles are in the bag. $12 + 3 + 6 + 4 = 25$ Therefore, 25 is the number of possible outcomes. 7 marbles are either blue or yellow. 7 is the number of favorable outcomes. $\frac{7}{25} \times \frac{4}{4} = \frac{28}{100} = 28\%$

9. **(4) $113.75** It takes Fabio 45 minutes, or $\frac{3}{4}$ of an hour to install a hard drive. It takes him exactly one hour to install an operating system. It will take him $1\frac{3}{4}$ hours to complete the job. Since he charges $65 per hour, multiply $1\frac{3}{4}$ by $65 to find the total charge. $65 \times 1\frac{3}{4} = 113.75

10. (1) $214.40 Substitute 4 for b and 3 for n into the function. Then solve the equation.
$$C = \$25.60(4) + \$14(4)(3 - 1)$$
$$= \$102.40 + \$112.00$$
$$= \$214.40$$

11. (3) $\sqrt{16^2 + 16^2}$ Beams b, c, and e make a right triangle. Using the Pythagorean relationship, $16^2 + 16^2 = e^2$. Therefore, $e = \sqrt{16^2 + 16^2}$.

12. 375

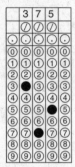

Multiply $250 by 1.5, which equals $375. You cannot grid in the dollar symbol.

13. 1040

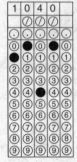

Set up the proportion $\frac{\frac{3}{4}}{120} = \frac{6\frac{1}{2}}{x}$, where x is the number of miles between the two landmarks. $6\frac{1}{2} \times 120 = 780$, and $780 \div \frac{3}{4} = 1040$ mi Note: You could use 6.5 for $6\frac{1}{2}$ and .75 for $\frac{3}{4}$.

14. (4)

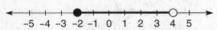

Separate the inequality into two inequalities, $x < 4$ and $-2 \leq x$. To graph $x < 4$, put a blank circle on 4 and draw the line toward the left, where the numbers are less than four. To graph $-2 \leq x$, put a shaded circle on

-2 to show x can equal -2, and draw the line toward the right, where the numbers are greater than -2. The result is option (4).

15. (2) 76° Angle 1 and the angle measuring 104° are corresponding angles. Therefore, $m\angle 1 = 104°$. Angle 1 and $\angle 2$ are supplementary. $180° - 104° = 76°$

16. (1) 54° Angle 3 and the angle measuring 104° are supplementary. Therefore, $m\angle 3 = 180° - 104° = 76°$. Angle 4 and the angle measuring 50° are corresponding: $m\angle 4 = 50°$. Angle 3, angle 4, and x are the interior angles of a triangle. The sum of the interior angles of a triangle is 180°. $50° + 76° + x = 180°$, and so $x = 54°$

17. (−3,−1)

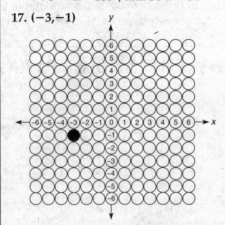

The vertical line is parallel to the y-axis, and all of its points have the x-coordinate -3. The horizontal line is parallel to the x-axis, and all of its points have the y-coordinate -1. Therefore, the coordinates of the point of intersection are $(-3,-1)$.

18. (3) 7 lb 0 oz To find the median, organize the birth weights from least to greatest. Since there are 7 weights, the median will be the fourth one: 7 lb 0 oz.

19. (1) 6($24.50 − $19) The cost of six tickets to an evening show is equal to 6($24.50). The cost of six tickets to an afternoon show is equal to 6($19). The expression 6($24.50) − 6($19) is the same as 6($24.50 − $19), which is equal to the amount Janice would save by going to an afternoon show.

20. (3) 81 The mean is the arithmetic average. Add the scores and divide by the number of scores. $78 + 86 + 82 + 81 + 82 + 77 = 486$, and $486 \div 6 = 81$

21. 10

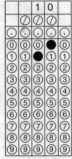

Quadrilateral $ABCD$ is a trapezoid because it has one pair of parallel sides. The bases are the parallel sides, AB and CD. The height is the length 2.5 cm. Use the formula for the area of a trapezoid.
$$A = \tfrac{1}{2} \times (b_1 + b_2) \times h$$
$$= \tfrac{1}{2} \times (6 + 2) \times 2.5$$
$$= \tfrac{1}{2} \times 8 \times 2.5$$
$$= 4 \times 2.5$$
$$= 10 \text{ cm}^2$$

22. 4.8 or 4.80 Set up the proportion $\frac{5}{\$3} = \frac{8}{x}$ where x is the cost of 8 cans of peaches. $3 \times 8 = 24$, and $24 \div 5 = \$4.80$

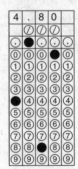

23. (4) 386 To find the volume, use the formula $V = \pi r^2 h$. Since the diameter of the base is 6.4 cm, the radius of the base equals 3.2 cm. Substitute 3.2 for r and 12 for h. $\pi \times 3.2^2 \times 12 \approx 386$ cm^3

24. (3) 16,600 Move the decimal point four places to the right, adding zeros as necessary, or think: 10^4 equals 10,000 and $1.66 \times 10,000$ equals 16,600.

25. (2) $m\angle 2 = 120°$ $m\angle BAC +$
$m\angle ABC + m\angle 1 = 180°$. $60° + 60°$
$+ m\angle 1 = 180°$. Therefore, $m\angle 1 =$
$60°$. Because $\angle ACD$ is a straight
angle, its measure is $180°$.
$180° - m\angle 1 = m\angle 2$
$180° - 60° = 120°$

Part II, page 605

1. **(4) 1 ft 11 in** Change 5 ft 9 in to
   inches: $5 \times 12 = 60$, and $60 + 9 =$
   69 inches. Divide by 3: $69 \div 3 =$
   23 inches. Convert to feet and
   inches. 23 in = 1 ft 11 in

2. **(3) 462** Think of the space as two
   rectangles: 21 ft by 14 ft and 24 ft
   by 7 ft. (Find the length of the
   second rectangle: 21 ft − 14 ft = 7
   ft, and 7 ft + 17 ft = 24 ft.) Use the
   formula Area = length × width:
   $21 \times 14 = 294$ sq ft, and $24 \times 7 =$
   168 sq ft. Combine: $294 + 168 =$
   462 sq ft. Note: There is more
   than one way to divide the room
   into regular figures. You could
   also use a 14 ft by 14 ft square
   and a 38 ft by 7 ft rectangle.

3. **(4) 0.06($2230) + $2230** To find
   the amount of the raise, multiply
   6% (which equals 0.06) by $2230.
   Then add the amount of the
   original salary.

4. **(5) −8 and −12** Let one number
   equal x and the other equal $3x + 12$.
   The sum of the two numbers is
   equal to −20. Solve the equation.
   $x + 3x + 12 = -20$
   $4x + 12 = -20$
   $4x = -32$
   $x = -8$
   If one number is −8, the other
   number is $3(-8) + 12 = -12$.

5. **(1) $600** Find 24% of $2500.
   $2500 \times 0.24 = \$600$ You could
   estimate this answer by thinking
   24% is about $\frac{1}{4}$, and $\frac{1}{4}$ of 2400 is
   $600, so option (1) must be the
   closest choice.

6. $\frac{1}{20}$ **or** $\frac{5}{100}$ Clothing expenses take
   up 5% of the Whitmans take-
   home pay. Change 5% to a fraction. $5\% = \frac{5}{100} = \frac{1}{20}$.

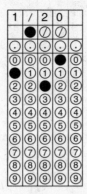

7. **(4) (8,−5)** You can locate each
   point on the grid and compare it
   to the line, or you can substitute
   the x and y values from each
   ordered pair into the equation.
   Only option (4) makes the equation true.
   $y = -\frac{3}{4}x + 1$
   $-5 = -\frac{3}{4}(8) + 1$
   $-5 = -6 + 1$
   $-5 = -5$

8. **(2)** $\sqrt{(4 - 0)^2 + (-2 - 1)^2}$

   Point C is located at (0,1), and
   point D is at (4,−2). Substitute
   these values into the formula for
   finding the distance between
   points.

9. **(4) 32** The three numbers can be
   represented by x, $x + 2$, and
   $x + 4$. Solve the equation.
   $x + x + 2 + x + 4 = 90$
   $3x + 6 = 90$
   $3x = 84$
   $x = 28$
   The three numbers are 28, 30,
   and 32. The question asks for the
   largest of these.

10. **(5) ΔJKL and ΔPQR are similar
    triangles.** Similar triangles have
    the same angle measures. Con-
    gruent triangles have the same
    angle measures and the same
    side lengths. From the given
    information, you cannot know if
    the side lengths are the same, so
    you can only conclude that the
    triangles are similar.

11. **(3) $410** Use the formula Simple
    interest = principal × rate ×
    time. Note that time is expressed
    in terms of a year: 6 months =
    $\frac{1}{2}$ year.
    $i = \$400(0.05)(\frac{1}{2})$
    $= \$10$

The interest is $10, so Mike will
pay back $410 ($400 principal +
$10 interest).

12. **(1,1)**

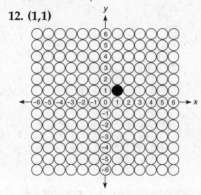

Plot the points given in the problem, and complete the parallelogram. Remember that in a parallelogram, both pairs of opposite
sides are equal and parallel.

13. **(5) Not enough information is
    given.** The median time is the
    middle time. The median does
    not reveal anything about the
    range of the data. You have no
    way of knowing how far behind
    the median the slowest runner
    was.

14. **(2) Apr. 30 in the Midwest** The
    steepest rise on the graph was
    from Apr. 23 to Apr. 30. The
    symbols on this line indicate that
    it represents the Midwest.

15. **(4) $1.82** The prices for the West
    Coast have been rising steadily
    by 2 or 3 cents each week. On
    May 7, the price on the West
    Coast is a little beneath $1.80. If
    it rises 2 or 3 cents, it should be
    at about $1.82 by the following
    week. The question gives no rea-
    son to expect a sudden decline
    in price or a sharp increase.

16. **(3) $72** 20% of $120 is $24.
    Subtract. After the first price cut,
    the price of the coat was $96.
    25% of $96 is $24. Subtract. After
    the second cut, the price of the
    coat was $72.
    You may find it easier to calcu-
    late the discounts using frac-
    tions. The first cut is $\frac{1}{5}$ of the
    price, so divide $120 by 5. The
    second cut is $\frac{1}{4}$, so divide the
    new sale price, $96, by 4.

17. **(2) $4.59** Add the times and multiply by 9 cents.
19 + 24 + 8 = 51 minutes
51 × $0.09 = $4.59

18. **$56**

Let x represent the amount that Colin put in and $2x - \$20$ represent Maggie's contribution. Solve the equation.
$$x + 2x - \$20 = \$94$$
$$3x = \$114$$
$$x = \$38$$
Colin put in $38, and Maggie put in $94 − $38 = $56.

19. **(4) 4:7** The number of games played is the total of the wins and losses (20 + 15 = 35). Write the ratio and simplify. $\frac{20}{35} = \frac{4}{7}$

20. **(4) $19\frac{3}{8}$** Multiply $3\frac{7}{8} \times 5$. $3 \times 5 = 15$, and $\frac{7}{8} \times 5 = 3\frac{5}{8} = 4\frac{3}{8}$ Combine. $15 + 4\frac{3}{8} = 19\frac{3}{8}$ yards

21. **(2) $\sqrt{706}$** Use the Pythagorean relationship: $25^2 + 9^2 = c^2$, so
$$c = \sqrt{25^2 + 9^2} = \sqrt{625 + 81}$$
$$= \sqrt{706}.$$

22. **(2) −76** Use the order of operations.
$-3 \cdot 5^2 + 2(4 - 18) + 3^3$
$-3 \cdot 25 + 2(-14) + 27$
$-75 + (-28) + 27$
-76

23. **(5) $m\angle A + m\angle B + m\angle C = 180°$.** ΔABC is a right triangle, but you have no way of knowing which angle is the right angle, so eliminate option (1). Regardless of the type of triangle, the sum of the measures of the interior angles of a triangle must be 180°, so option (5) is correct.

24. **(2) $1000** There are several ways to approach this problem. The fastest way is to think: If $\frac{3}{20} = \$150$, then $\frac{1}{20}$ must be $50 because $150 ÷ 3 = $50. Therefore, $\frac{20}{20}$ (the whole paycheck) is 20 × $50, or $1000.
Another approach is to solve for x.
$$\frac{3}{20}x = 150$$
$$x = 150 \times \frac{20}{3} = 1000$$

25. **(3) $137.80** Add the items to be purchased. $34.95 + $89.90 = $124.85 Find the shipping charge, and add it to the total. The shipping for an order of $124.85 is $12.95. Add. $124.85 + $12.95 = $137.80

Mathematics Post-Test Planning Chart

Circle the number of the questions that you got correct, and total them in the last column of each row.

CONTENT AREA	Test Portion	Using Procedures	Understanding Concepts	Evaluation Strategies	Correct/Total
Math Basics (pages 346–347)	Part I				
	Part II			22	_____/1
Decimals and Fractions (pages 368–389)	Part I		3	1, 9	
	Part II	25		17, 20, 24	_____/7
Ratio, Proportion, and Percent (pages 390–411)	Part I		12	7, 22	
	Part II	3, 19		6, 11, 16	_____/8
Data Analysis (pages 412–433)	Part I	2	8	18, 20	
	Part II	14		5, 13, 15	_____/8
Measurement (pages 434–449)	Part I	21	13	6, 23	
	Part II	2		1	_____/6
Algebra (pages 450–495)	Part I	5, 19	14, 24	10	
	Part II	9		4, 18	_____/8
Geometry (pages 496–528)	Part I	11, 17	15, 25	4, 16	
	Part II	8, 12, 21	7, 10, 23		_____/12
Total					_____/50

Use this chart to determine your areas of strength and weakness. If you do not have time to review the entire math unit of this book, you may want to focus your study on the areas in which you need the most work.

Language Arts, Writing: Answers and Explanations

Clear and Organized Writing

Lesson 1: Ideas and Paragraphs

Practice 1.1, page 67

A. 1. The pharmacist at the local drugstore is very helpful.
2. No MI
3. Every vote counts, so let your voice be heard and vote!
4. When you are traveling, it's a good idea to mark your luggage clearly.
5. Listening to music can benefit you in many ways.

B. 6. **(3) sentence 4 (Paragraphing)** Sentences 1–3 explain who gets colds and how frequently. Sentences 4–6 are about the causes and prevention of colds.
7. **(4) join paragraphs B and C (Paragraphing)** Sentence 10 in paragraph C is related to the main idea of paragraph B, the prevention of colds.

Practice 1.2, page 69

A. Your topic sentences should be similar to these:
1. Satellites have many different functions in today's world.
2. All signs show that the economy is headed for a slump.
3. The library has adopted a new dress code for employees.

B. 4. **(5) Repetitive strain injury is a painful condition resulting from repeated use of the hands. (Topic sentences)** The original topic sentence is too general. The other options don't tell the central point—what repetitive strain injury is.

5. **(2) A number of factors contribute to repetitive strain injury. (Topic sentences)** This sentence covers the three causes of repetitive strain injury mentioned in the paragraph.

Lesson 2: Logical Order and Relevance

Practice 2, page 71

A. 1. Irrelevant detail: Getting very ill is one bad thing that could happen.

2. Irrelevant detail: Adult students also can use school supplies.
3. Irrelevant detail: This job will be extremely expensive!

B. 4. **(5) no revision is necessary (Logical order/relevance)** The order of the two sentences is logical, as is the placement of the paragraph at the beginning of the letter.
5. **(4) remove sentence 5 (Logical order/relevance)** The information about the secretarial job is not relevant to getting a job in carpentry.
6. **(4) move sentence 9 to follow sentence 7 (Logical order/relevance)** It would be more logical to place sentence 9 right after the first mention of the job.

Lesson 3: Relating Sentences and Paragraphs

Practice 3, page 73

A. Your transitions should be similar to these:
1. Our marketing efforts need to be enhanced. Therefore, we will soon begin another marketing initiative.
2. Sales representatives say that their jobs are extremely demanding. However, the salary is attractive.
3. The marketing director has instructed sales representatives to try some new ideas. For example, sales representatives can give away free samples.
4. A new ad campaign will be launched in just a few weeks. Then we expect sales to increase.

B. 5. **(2) insert however, after the comma (Transitions)** This position is the most logical for the transition. Also, because it is in the middle of a sentence, it should be set off by commas.
6. **(4) restaurant. For example, (Transitions)** Sentence 6 offers an example of the broad menu described in sentence 5.
7. **(1) In addition, having (Transitions)** This option inserts a helpful transition to move the reader smoothly from paragraph B to paragraph C.

Lesson 4: Essay Writing Process: Prewriting

Practice 4.1, page 75

A. The following are sample answers. Your answers may be somewhat different.

Topic 1. Sample main idea: Despite machines, our own abilities are as important as ever.
Sample idea list:
- Ride instead of walking—get lazy and out of shape
- Great medical technology, but still need doctors to diagnose problems
- Can use calculator, but need math skills for everyday decision making like comparison shopping
- Computers can crash—what about old-fashioned handwriting?
- Romance on the Internet

Topic 2. Sample main idea: People overeat for many different reasons.
Sample idea list:
- Loneliness
- Depression
- Boredom
- Too much good food around
- Avoiding homework or other responsibilities
- Has a soothing effect
- Are "comfort foods"
- Can't stay on a diet
- Physiological factors—can't help it
- Poor eating habits
- Lack of knowledge about nutrition

B. **Sample main idea:** The advantages of owning a pet outweigh the disadvantages.
Sample brainstormed ideas:
- Someone to play with
- Security—guard dog, attack cat
- Have to take it on walks, feed it
- Something to love
- Get lots of exercise walking a dog
- Require knowledge to care for
- Expensive when they get sick
- May trigger allergies
- May compete with new baby
- Annoying to have to buy food all the time
- Have to clean fur off the rug when they shed

- Can teach kids about "the birds and the bees"
- Hard to go away for the weekend—need to make arrangements
- Can learn a lot about different breeds
- Easier to take care of than kids

Practice 4.2, page 77

A. Irrelevant ideas: Can vacation with friends, should buy a new suitcase

Here is one way to organize the ideas using an outline.

I. Cheaper
   A. Costs less
   B. Less chance of getting ripped off
II. More relaxing
   A. No planning
   B. No crowds
   C. No negotiating unfamiliar territory
     1. No asking strangers for directions
III. Chance to do things you can do only at home
   A. Can play tourist in your home city
   B. Can see friends
   C. Opportunity to catch up on reading, knitting, other hobbies, home improvement

B. An example of an outline for the topic is given below.
I. Disadvantages of having a pet
   A. Have to do more household chores
     1. Have to take it on walks, feed it
     2. Annoying to have to buy food all the time
     3. Have to clean fur off the rug when they shed
   B. Other inconveniences
     1. Require knowledge to care for
     2. Expensive when they get sick
     3. Hard to go away for the weekend—need to make arrangements
   C. Could be problematic for other people
     1. May trigger allergies
     2. May compete with new baby
II. Advantages of having a pet
   A. A companion
     1. Something to play with
     2. Something to love
   B. Security—guard dog, attack cat
   C. Can teach kids about "the birds and the bees"

D. Get lots of exercise walking a dog
E. Easier to take care of than kids

Practice 5, page 79

A. Sample answers
Introduction:
Although it is often difficult for children to be organized, they have much to gain by making the effort. If you manage to teach your own children to organize their time and belongings, you'll find that there are benefits for yourself as well.
Conclusion:
To sum it up, when children learn to be organized at an early age, they are more proficient at this skill later on, and they are more likely to be successful in school. Moreover, your ability to organize your own time increases. With all these benefits, there's no excuse not to begin teaching your children organizational skills today!
B. Read your draft to a friend or a family member so that you have an audience.

Clear and Organized Writing Practice Questions, page 80

1. **(3) sentence 5 (Paragraphing)** Sentences 1–4 are about the general problem of sleep disruption, whereas sentences 5–8 are about reasons why people don't get enough sleep.
2. **(3) Lack of sleep interferes with concentration. (Topic sentences)** Both studies relate to the impact of lack of sleep on learning.
3. **(1) grades. Similarly, (Transitions)** The sentences are correct as written. All the other options use inappropriate transitions or incorrect punctuation.
4. **(5) remove sentence 13 (Logical order/relevance)** The paragraph is about sleep, not losing weight.
5. **(4) join paragraphs C and D (Paragraphing)** Both paragraphs contain tips for getting more sleep.
6. **(2) sentence 4 (Paragraphing)** Sentences 4–7 contain general rules for stain removal.
7. **(2) Choose the right water temperature for cleaning each stain. (Topic sentences)** This sentence is appropriate since the paragraph

discusses hot, cold, and room-temperature water.
8. **(4) juice, for example, removes (Transitions/Punctuation)** When a transition is placed in the middle of a sentence, commas should both precede and follow it.
9. **(5) remove sentence 15 (Logical order/relevance)** Sentence 15 explains a minor detail and moves away from the main idea of the paragraph.
10. **(4) move sentence 19 to the beginning of paragraph D (Logical order/relevance)** Putting sentence 19 at the beginning of the paragraph lets readers know in advance what point the paragraph will make.
11. **(4) remove sentence 5 (Logical order/relevance)** Sentence 5 is a general statement about HMOs. It is not relevant to the explanation of which insurance carriers are being made available.
12. **(1) insert a comma after However (Transitions/ Punctuation)** A comma should follow a transition.
13. **(4) sentence 9 (Paragraphing)** Sentences 9–11 concern the informational sessions that will introduce the new insurance plans.
14. **(1) move sentence 14 to the end of paragraph C (Logical order/ relevance)** Sentence 14 refers to the card that was mentioned in paragraph C.
15. **(5) no revision is necessary (Logical order/relevance)** The paragraph is logical as written.
16. **(3) move sentence 11 to follow sentence 12 (Logical order/ relevance)** Sentence 11 tells what to do with the spot where there is a leak, so it should follow the information on finding that spot.
17. **(4) The next step is to put the tire and tube back onto the rim. (Topic sentences)** Paragraph C describes the process of putting the tire and tube back on the rim.
18. **(1) The final step is to reinstall the wheel. (Topic sentences)** Paragraph D describes the final step in the process, putting the wheel back on the bike.
19. **(1) replace Moreover, with Then (Transitions)** *Then* is a more appropriate transition for describing steps in a process.

Sentence Structure

Lesson 1: Complete Simple Sentences

Practice 1, page 85

A. The revisions are samples. Your rewrites may differ.
1. F It drives his girlfriend crazy.
2. F As soon as he comes home from work, he gets on the telephone.
3. C
4. F Dave's sister and his best friend like to talk on the telephone, too.

B. 5. **(3) call from (Sentence fragment)** Option (3) joins a sentence fragment to a complete sentence. The other options leave the sentence fragment standing alone or use an unnecessary comma.
6. **(4) insert you before can (Sentence fragment)** Option (4) adds a subject to a sentence fragment, thus creating a complete sentence.
7. **(4) service can (Sentence fragment)** Option (4) joins a sentence fragment to a complete sentence.

Lesson 2: Compound and Complex Sentences

Practice 2.1, page 87

A. 1. It was <u>late, and</u> I was walking home from work.
2. My co-worker, Judy, had offered to drive <u>me, but</u> I had refused.
3. It was a warm <u>night, so</u> I decided to get some fresh air.
4. It was really my choice. I could have taken a <u>cab, or</u> I could have walked.
5. I heard a loud <u>noise, so</u> I ran the last block to my house. Later, I learned that it was only a car backfiring.

B. 6. **(2) remove the comma (Compound sentences)** A comma is required when two independent clauses are joined, not two verbs (*carries . . . gets*).
7. **(3) airlines, but (Compound sentences)** *But* is the most logical coordinating conjunction here. Most travelers on major airlines can check baggage.

8. **(3) insert a comma after <u>advance</u> (Compound sentences)** A comma precedes a coordinating conjunction joining two independent clauses.

Practice 2.2, page 89

A. 1. Most fatal fires occur when a family is asleep.
2. Because a smoke alarm wakes you up, it can allow you to escape.
3. Try to replace the smoke detector's battery before it goes dead.
4. Although smoke detectors cost money, the expense is worth it.

B. 5. **(5) no correction is necessary (Complex sentences)** This complex sentence is correct as written. A comma correctly follows the subordinate clause.
6. **(1) replace <u>Whenever</u> with <u>After</u> (Complex sentences)** *Whenever* is used inappropriately; it does not convey the intended meaning.
7. **(3) up, thank (Complex sentences/Sentence fragments)** Option (3) correctly combines a sentence fragment and an independent clause to form a complex sentence.

Lesson 3: Run-Ons and Comma Splices

Practice 3, page 91

A. There are several possible correct answers. There may be other correct answers in addition to those listed.
1. Jeff just got his driver's license, and he's very excited. OR Jeff just got his driver's license. He's very excited.
2. He bought a car that has a lot of miles on it, so it wasn't very expensive. OR Because he bought a car that has a lot of miles on it, it wasn't very expensive.
3. He doesn't have a lot of free time, but he'd like to take a car trip. OR Although he doesn't have a lot of free time, he'd like to take a car trip.
4. He needs to find out about car insurance, get a good map, and join an auto club.

B. 5. **(2) pictures if you just (Run-on sentences)** Option (2) turns a run-on sentence into a complex sentence by adding a subordinating conjunction.
6. **(2) insert <u>and</u> after the comma (Comma splices)** Option (2) turns a comma splice into a compound sentence by adding a coordinating conjunction.
7. **(2) insert a comma after <u>store</u> (Run-on sentences)** Option (2) turns a run-on sentence into a compound sentence with a coordinating conjunction and a comma.

Lesson 4: Subordinating Ideas

Practice 4, page 93

A. There are several possible answers for each question. Sample answers:
1. Tornadoes and earthquakes can cause a lot of damage.
2. Earthquakes are somewhat common in California, but many Californians do not seem to mind.
3. On May 3, 1999, a tornado in Kansas killed five people and injured one hundred fifty.
4. Tornadoes can occur anywhere in the United States and at any time of year.

B. 5. **(4) repaired up (Subordinating ideas)** Option (4) combines two short, choppy sentences into one smooth sentence.
6. **(1) brought or mailed to (Subordinating ideas)** Option (1) forms a compound predicate and combines two short, choppy sentences into one smooth, effective sentence.
7. **(5) accidents, mishandling, or faulty installation (Subordinating ideas)** Option (5) combines two wordy, repetitive sentences into one smooth, detailed sentence.

Lesson 5: Modifying Ideas

Practice 5, page 95

A. There are several possible answers for each question. Sample answers:
1. Trent's sister, who is also a health professional, encouraged him to become a nurse.

2. When he wakes up the patients to take their blood pressure, they get rather annoyed.
3. He carefully writes their temperature and blood pressure on their charts.
4. Talking with the patients, visitors do not want to leave at 9 P.M.

B. 5. **(3) a person who is not the birth child (Misplaced modifiers)** Option (3) moves the modifier to its correct position.
6. **(3) An agency requires a "home study" (Dangling modifiers)** In the original sentence, it is not clear who is going through an agency.
7. **(4) move frequently to follow Lawyers (Misplaced modifiers)** Option (4) moves the modifier to show that it is the lawyers who frequently handle adoptions, not the parents who frequently ask about it.

Lesson 6: Parallel Structure

Practice 6, page 97

A. 1. Jenna has worked in a factory, in a store, and as a waitress.
2. She would like to put her kids in a better school and to get a better job.
3. She thinks the kids' father is irresponsible, lazy, and uncaring.
4. He doesn't have the time, the energy, or the money to give them what they deserve.

B. 5. **(4) insert more before pleasant (Parallel structure)** Option (4) correctly makes all the adjectives into comparatives (*safer, more comfortable,* and *more pleasant*).
6. **(5) computers, and (Parallel structure)** The original sentence combined single words and clauses in the same series. Option (5) corrects the error by making all items in the series words (*lights, computers,* and *coffee makers*).
7. **(4) change be leaving to leave (Parallel structure)** Option (4) makes all the verbs in the sentence (*punch, press,* and *leave*) parallel.

Lesson 7: Essay Writing Process: Revising Your Sentences

Practice 7.1, page 99

A. Your revised sentences should be similar to the following. The underlined parts show where your revision marks should be:
1. First, write down what you know about your <u>family. Then</u> interview relatives. (Run-on sentence)
2. Videotaping or <u>recording</u> the interviews is a good idea. (Structure not parallel)
3. Ask relatives to provide exact names, dates, <u>and other details.</u> (Structure not parallel)
4. <u>Make</u> copies of documents such as birth certificates and marriage licenses. (Sentence fragment)
5. <u>When older family members are interviewed</u>, they'll often tell you stories you never heard. (Dangling modifier)
6. <u>Carefully</u> record all the information you get and put it in a three-ring binder. (Misplaced modifier)
7. Some people use their computers to do genealogy <u>searches, and</u> they get very good results. (Comma splice; coordinating conjunction needed)
8. However, one must have the time, the patience, and <u>the</u> know-how to use the Internet. (Structure not parallel)
9. If you do decide to learn more about your <u>roots, don't</u> be surprised to find yourself at a huge family reunion. (Comma needed after subordinate clause)
10. The whole process of putting together a family tree and contacting long-lost family members <u>is rewarding</u>. (Sentence fragment)

B. Sample revisions:
It was a beautiful <u>day, and</u> the blue ocean sparkled in the <u>sunlight. It was</u> a perfect day for going to the beach. <u>As Renelle looked</u> across the sand, <u>she saw</u> two little girls building a sandcastle and <u>making</u> a moat next to it. Renelle spread out her towel, anchored it with her shoes and beach bag, and began to read a magazine. Suddenly she heard a voice," Are you going to get in the water, or are you just going to lie there?" Renelle looked <u>up and</u> saw her friend Terry. She laughed softly <u>and got up to greet Terry</u>. Putting on her sandals, <u>she</u> walked <u>with Terry</u> across the burning sand to the water's edge.

Renelle loved going to the beach. <u>It relaxed her and</u> helped her forget about her problems. It didn't cost money like most other forms of entertainment. Most of Renelle's friends also spent a lot of time at the <u>beach, so</u> that was another incentive.

Practice 7.2, page 101

A. Your revised paragraphs should be similar to the following:

Why do people continue to litter? One reason people litter is that they just don't care about others. It doesn't bother them to leave their trash in front of someone else's apartment building, forcing another person to deal with the problem. This inconsiderate attitude is also reflected in the refusal to recycle plastic, glass, and newspapers. People figure that they won't be around in the future when the landfills are used up, so who cares?

¶Another possible reason for littering is low self-esteem. If people don't feel good about themselves, they won't be motivated to keep their environment looking attractive. ~~Low self-esteem can cause many other problems, including depression and lack of self-confidence.~~ People who have high self-esteem believe that it's important to keep their home, the planet Earth, clean and beautiful.

B. Ask a friend or family member to evaluate your work.

Sentence Structure Practice Questions, page 102

1. **(2) remove the comma (Complex sentences)** When an independent clause comes before a subordinate clause in a complex sentence, there is no need to use a comma.
2. **(3) during the day and 62°F (Subordinating ideas)** Option (3) combines two short, choppy

sentences into one smooth sentence.

3. **(4) sun, keep (Complex sentences)** Option (4) combines a subordinate clause sentence fragment and an independent clause to form a complex sentence.

4. **(5) home. Do change (Comma splices)** Option (5) corrects the comma splice by adding a period.

5. **(1) Your home will not cool down any faster (Misplaced modifiers)** *Any faster* should be placed next to the phrase it modifies, *cool down.*

6. **(3) insert a comma after home (Complex sentences)** A comma should be placed after a subordinate clause that begins a complex sentence.

7. **(1) replace Returning with I returned (Sentence fragment)** Option (1) adds a subject to a sentence fragment and corrects the verb form to make a complete sentence.

8. **(1) He claimed that because (Dangling modifiers)** There is not a clear subject for the verb phrase at the beginning of the sentence to modify. By adding the subject *He,* option (1) makes it clear who was claiming that the TV had been used.

9. **(2) angry and frustrated about the (Subordinating ideas)** Option (2) makes one smooth sentence out of two choppy sentences that are not correctly punctuated.

10. **(5) refund or get (Parallel structure)** Option (5) puts both verbs in the same form and is correctly punctuated.

11. **(1) work productively if you (Misplaced modifiers)** This option moves the idea of being productive closer to the word it modifies—*work.* It also reduces wordiness by using the adverb form *productively.*

12. **(4) remove the comma (Compound sentences)** A comma is not required before a coordinating conjunction that joins two verbs.

13. **(2) remove the comma (Complex sentences)** A comma

is not required in a complex sentence when the subordinate clause follows the independent clause.

14. **(3) work or talk (Parallel structure)** Option (3) puts both verbs in the sentence in the same form.

15. **(3) insert a comma after hard (Compound sentences)** A comma is required before the coordinating conjunction that joins the two independent clauses in a compound sentence.

16. **(4) hoaxes designed (Sentence fragments)** Option (4) joins a sentence fragment to an independent clause.

17. **(2) To check a claim like this, contact (Subordinating ideas)** Option (2) combines two choppy sentences into one smooth, effective sentence.

18. **(4) know. This (Comma splices)** Option (4) splits a comma splice into two independent, correct sentences.

19. **(5) remove the comma after safe (Compound sentences)** A comma is not needed in a compound predicate.

Grammar and Usage

Lesson 1: Nouns and Pronouns

Practice 1.1, page 107

A. 1. They
 2. him
 3. it
 4. Her
 5. she
B. 6. **(1) replace me with I (Pronouns)** Bonetta and I is a compound subject, so a subject pronoun is required.
 7. **(5) no correction is necessary (Pronouns)** The sentence is correct as written.
 8. **(2) Walter or me (Pronouns)** The phrase *Walter or me* is an object, so an object pronoun is required.

Practice 1.2, page 109

A. 1. Sally is moving to a small town. Her mother is concerned about the health care options it offers.
 2. Sally tried to reassure her

mother, but it was hard for <u>her mother</u> to believe her. OR for her to believe Sally.
3. C
4. The town has a freestanding clinic where a person can go when <u>he or she is</u> sick. OR where <u>people</u> can go when <u>they</u> are sick.
5. There is also a nearby hospital, and <u>it has</u> a very good reputation.
6. If one is concerned about health care, <u>one</u> should sign up for a good insurance plan. OR If <u>you are</u> concerned about health care, you should sign up for a good insurance plan.
B. 7. **(5) replace one's with their (Pronouns)** The passage is about parents getting angry when their children misbehave. It is written in the third person, so *their* expresses the correct relationship.
8. **(5) parents (Unclear antecedent)** Only option (5) correctly identifies who should be clear about their expectations.
9. **(4) replace them with the group (Pronouns)** The term *play group* is a collective noun, so the plural *them* should not be used to refer to it. In this case, repeating the word *group* is the best way to make the meaning clear.

Lesson 2: Verb Forms and Tenses

Practice 2.1, page 111

A. 1. had ceased
 2. closed
 3. functions
 4. have visited
 5. will open
 6. looks
 7. are thinking
B. 8. **(2) is offering (Verb tenses)** The action is taking place right now, so the present progressive is the correct tense.
9. **(5) no correction is necessary (Verb tense)** The present-tense verb *sign* in the subordinate clause and the future-tense verb *will receive* in the main clause are correct.
10. **(5) change will be amazing to will amaze (Verb tenses)** The verb *will amaze* is in the simple

future tense, which is required in the sentence.

Practice 2.2, page 113

A. 1. came
2. showed
3. had spoken
4. took
5. seen
B. 6. **(5) change begun to began (Verb form)** The action takes place in the past tense, so the verb should be in its past form, *began*. *Begun* is the past participle.
7. **(3) was broken (Irregular verbs)** *Broken* is the correct past participle.
8. **(2) change given to give (Verb form)** The clue word *now* tells you that the action is still true, so the present tense form of *give* is correct.

Lesson 3: Subject-Verb Agreement

Practice 3.1, page 115

A. 1. is
2. become
3. is
4. have
5. seems
6. is
B. 7. **(2) have heard (Subject-verb agreement)** In this sentence the indefinite pronoun *most* is plural ("most of us"). The verb *have heard* agrees with the plural subject.
8. **(4) change start to starts (Subject-verb agreement)** The verb *starts* agrees with the singular subject *plane*.
9. **(3) change conducts to conduct (Subject-verb agreement)** The verb *conduct* agrees with the plural subject *materials*.

Practice 3.2, page 117

A. 1. ~~on the market~~   carry
2. ~~carrying the seal~~   are
3. ~~an important ingredient in many toothpastes~~ strengthens, attacks
4. are
5. offer
6. ~~fluoride and good flavor~~   is
B. 7. **(4) change have to has (Subject-verb agreement)** The verb *has* agrees with the singular subject *state*.

8. **(1) determine (Subject-verb agreement)** The verb *determine* agrees with the compound subject *Wage level and the length of employment*.
9. **(4) change reports to report (Subject-verb agreement)** The verb *report* agrees with the plural subject *workers*.

Lesson 4: Essay Writing Process: Editing

Practice 4, page 119

Sample answers:
A. 1. non-profit organization
2. thousands of
3. substandard
4. dollars
5. as soon as possible
B. If you ever order merchandise from a catalog, you should be aware of your rights. All companies, regardless of what state they are located in, <u>are</u> required to ship your order within 30 days unless they have <u>advertised</u> a different shipping time. If a company is unable to meet the shipping deadline, it must send you an "Option Notice." You can choose to wait longer or get a refund.

Some consumers <u>have complained</u> about receiving merchandise that they did not order. <u>Companies</u> that <u>engage</u> in this practice <u>are breaking</u> the law. <u>If you receive</u> a product you haven't <u>ordered</u>, it is yours to keep.

If you receive a package that <u>has</u> been damaged, don't open it. Write "REFUSED" on the package, and return it to the seller. There's no need to add new postage as long as the package <u>came</u> by regular mail.

C. Have a friend or family member evaluate your work.

Grammar and Usage Practice Questions, pages 120–123

1. **(4) change doesn't to didn't (Verb tenses)** The past tense is required because the second clause in the sentence is discussing what happened in the past.
2. **(1) they (Pronouns)** The antecedent of *they*—*girls*—is clear in the sentence as it is written.
3. **(2) earned (Verb tenses)** The past

tense is correct here because the action happened in the past over the course of a few years.
4. **(5) change is to are (Subject-verb agreement)** The verb *are* agrees with the plural subject *sisters*.
5. **(5) change been to is (Verb tenses)** The main clause needs the present-tense verb *is* because the introductory subordinate clause has a present-tense verb, *face*. *Been* is an incomplete verb form.
6. **(3) change will receive to have received (Verb tenses)** The past perfect is correct here because the point is to find out about other people's past experiences with auto shops, not their predictions about them.
7. **(1) change have picked to pick (Verb tenses)** The simple present tense is needed in this sentence.
8. **(5) change comes to come (Subject-verb agreement)** The verb *come* agrees with the plural subject *specials*.
9. **(4) replace it with the repair job (Pronouns)** The pronoun *it* had no clear antecedent, so replacing it with a noun corrects the sentence.
10. **(3) there are (Subject-verb agreement)** The verb *are* agrees with the plural subject *time* or *mileage limits*.
11. **(3) replace its with their (Pronouns)** The antecedent changes is plural, so the plural possessive *their* should be used.
12. **(4) replace one's with your (Pronouns)** *Your* is used in the rest of the paragraph, so it is appropriate here.
13. **(4) change is to are (Subject-verb agreement)** The pronoun *which* is the subject of a subordinate clause. It refers to the plural noun *calculations*. Therefore, the verb *are*, not *is*, is required.
14. **(1) has increased (Subject-verb agreement)** The interrupting phrase *of taxes* does not change the fact that the subject of the new independent clause is *amount*, which is singular. The verb *has increased* therefore agrees with it.
15. **(2) will credit (Verb tenses)** The future tense indicates an action that will take place at a later

time, which is appropriate in this sentence.

16. **(2) don't (Subject-verb agreement)** The plural indefinite pronoun *many* is the subject of the sentence; the verb *don't* (*don't* = *do* + *not*) agrees with it.

17. **(4) change has to have (Subject-verb agreement)** The verb *have* agrees with the plural subject *people*.

18. **(3) him or her (Pronouns)** The pronouns are objects of the preposition *with*, so the objective forms *him* and *her* are needed.

19. **(5) no correction is necessary (Subject-verb agreement)** The sentence *is* correct as written. The verb *is* agrees with the singular subject *equipment*.

20. **(2) it (Pronouns)** *It* is the proper pronoun to use to refer to a dog.

Mechanics

Lesson 1: Punctuation

Practice 1.1, page 125

A. 1. Train travel is more pleasant than riding a bus, but it can be more expensive.
2. When you're on a train, you can stand up and stretch if you need to.
3. NC
4. Unlike buses, trains sometimes have seats that face each other.
5. Traveling through a scenic area, you may find that your train has a double-decker car that offers a better view.
6. NC
B. 7. **(1) insert a comma after starters (Commas with introductory elements)** A comma is required after an introductory phrase.
8. **(1) dressing, and (Commas in compound sentences)** The comma before the coordinating conjunction *and* is correct in this compound sentence.
9. **(5) no correction is necessary (Comma use)** The sentence uses commas correctly and is correct as written.

Practice 1.2, page 127

A. 1. Kwanzaa is an African American holiday that celebrates culture, community, and family.
2. Kwanzaa, a wintertime holiday, is based on an ancient African harvest celebration.
3. NC
4. Kwanzaa celebrations include rituals such as singing, dancing, drumming, and poetry reading.
5. The family lights one candle every day for each of seven principles: unity, self-determination, responsibility, cooperative economics, purpose, creativity, and faith.
6. NC
B. 7. **(2) remove the comma (Overuse of commas)** The subject and verb of a sentence should not be separated by a comma.
8. **(3) insert a comma after medicines (Commas in a series)** Commas should be placed between items in a series.
9. **(4) children, those ten and up, (Commas with appositives)** You can mentally omit the phrase *those ten and up* and still understand the meaning of *older children*. Therefore, the appositive *those ten and up* should be set off by commas.

Lesson 2: Capitalization

Practice 2, page 129

A. 1. Last spring, I broke my arm in a car accident.
2. My internist, Doctor Claudia McNally, referred me to Waterside.
3. The center's director, Ilana Harris, assigned me a talented physical therapist named Ellie Royce.
4. Ellie studied physical therapy in her native London and used British methods of treatment that relieved my pain quite effectively.
5. She also did therapy with me in the pool at Rainbow Health Club.
6. I finished my treatments just before Labor Day, and I feel

100 percent better, thanks to Ellie.
B. 7. **(2) change Emperors to emperors (Capitalization of titles)** A title should be capitalized only when it comes directly before a person's name or is used in direct address.
8. **(3) change Mountains to mountains (Capitalization of proper nouns)** A geographic feature is capitalized only when it is part of the name of a specific place, like *Rocky Mountains*.
9. **(3) change america to America (Capitalization of proper nouns)** Proper nouns should be capitalized.

Lesson 3: Spelling

Practice 3.1, page 131

A. 1. There's
2. can't, who's, it's
3. we're
4. theirs
5. ours
B. 6. **(5) replace you're with your (Possessives and contractions)** In this sentence, the pronoun in question is showing ownership, so *your* is correct.
7. **(2) change were to we're (Contractions)** *Were* is a verb and is incorrect in this sentence. Rather, an apostrophe should be inserted to create the contraction *we're*, the combined form of *we are*.
8. **(2) replace they're with their (Possessives and contractions)** In this sentence, the pronoun is possessive, so *their* is correct.

Practice 3.2, page 133

A. 1. fourth
2. know
3. whole
4. week
5. affect
6. past
B. 7. **(4) replace fare with fair (Homonyms)** A *fare* is what you pay to get on the subway; *fair* means *just*.
8. **(1) change principal to principle (Homonyms)** A *principal* is the head of a school; *principle* means *a guiding rule*.

9. **(1) replace _affect_ with _effect_ (Homonyms)** _Affect_ is a verb meaning _to influence_; _effect_, which means _result_, is required here.

Lesson 4: Essay Writing Process: Editing

Practice 4, page 135

A. A shorter work day would enable me to accomplish many things that always seem to fall <u>by</u> the wayside. First and most important is spending time with my family. If I had more time, I could be <u>there</u> when my daughter comes home from <u>school</u>. I could help her with her homework, especially for her <u>Spanish</u> class, because <u>that's</u> my native language. Perhaps she would spend less time watching television. I would also like to spend more time with my husband. He works a different shift than I do, and we <u>have</u> trouble coordinating our schedules. If I had a less demanding work schedule, we'd see each other more.

Second, there are many errands that never seem to get done. For instance, it's hard <u>for</u> us to pay bills on time. Once our phone was even cut off! If our lives <u>weren't</u> so busy, we would sit down and take care of our bills when they <u>come</u> in.

Finally, I would continue my education. I dropped out of school at 16 and never got my <u>high school diploma</u>. I was <u>bored</u> and had trouble paying attention. Now that I see the negative <u>effects</u> of not having finished school, I want to get my GED certificate.

B. Have a friend or family member evaluate your work.

Mechanics Practice Questions, pages 136–139

1. **(2) insert a comma after <u>tantrums</u> (Commas in a series)** The phrase _have tantrums_ is the first item in series, so it should be followed by a comma.

2. **(3) understand and show (Overuse of commas)** A comma should not be used between two verbs.

3. **(5) no correction is necessary (Spelling)** All the possessives, contractions, and homonyms in the sentence are spelled correctly.

4. **(4) change <u>are'nt</u> to <u>aren't</u> (Contractions)** The apostrophe in a contraction must be placed in the spot where letters have been removed.

5. **(2) down, consider (Commas with introductory elements)** An introductory subordinate clause should be followed by a comma.

6. **(3) remove the comma (Overuse of commas)** The subject (_One_) and its verb (_is_) should not be separated by a comma.

7. **(3) replace <u>it's</u> with <u>its</u> (Possessives and contractions)** The sentence is about ownership: each time zone has its own standard time. The possessive form _its_ is correct.

8. **(2) change <u>congress</u> to <u>Congress</u> (Capitalization)** The name _Congress_ refers to a specific body of lawmakers and should therefore be capitalized.

9. **(1) insert a comma after <u>example</u> (Comma with introductory elements)** An introductory phrase must be followed by a comma.

10. **(4) remove the comma after time (Overuse of commas)** There is no need to separate the final phrase from the rest of the sentence with a comma.

11. **(4) change <u>center</u> to <u>Center</u> (Capitalization of proper names)** When a proper name consists of more than one word, all the words should be capitalized.

12. **(5) replace <u>when your</u> with <u>when you're</u> (Possessives and contractions)** The sentence is saying, "when you are in the building," so the contraction _you're_ is needed.

13. **(1) replace <u>week</u> with <u>weak</u> (Homonyms)** A _week_ is seven days. _Weak_, meaning _not strong_, is appropriate for this sentence.

14. **(5) no correction necessary (Spelling)** The possessives, contractions, and homonyms in the sentence are all spelled correctly.

15. **(2) register and pay (Overuse of commas)** Two items joined by _and_ do not require a comma unless both are independent clauses.

16. **(4) replace <u>then</u> with <u>than</u> (Spelling)** The word needed in the sentence is _than_, meaning _compared with_. _Then_ means _after that_ or _at that time._

17. **(3) insert a comma after <u>profiling</u> (Commas with appositives)** The phrase _called racial profiling_ is an appositive but is not essential to understanding the sentence. It needs a comma before it (which is already given) as well as one after it.

18. **(2) distinctions, for nonwhites (Commas in compound sentences)** The conjunction _for_ is connecting two independent clauses in a compound sentence, so it must be preceded by a comma.

19. **(2) change <u>illinois</u> to <u>Illinois</u> (Capitalization of proper names)** Names of states should be capitalized.

20. **(2) insert a comma after <u>superintendents</u> (Commas in series)** Three items are listed in the series: _police superintendents, chiefs of police, and other law enforcement officials_. There should be commas separating them.

The GED Essay

Lesson 1: Essay Directions and Prompt

Practice 1, page 143

A. Reasons; causes and/or effects
B. Facts or reasons to explain
C. Your opinion and the reasons for it

Practice 2.1, page 145

A, B, and C. Your idea lists should have ideas that generally stick to the topic. Your brainstormed lists will probably be longer and will likely include off-topic ideas. Be sure that, for each topic, you decide on a main idea that is supported by most of the generated ideas. Cross out any details that do not support that main idea.

Practice 2.2, page 147

A. 1. Main idea statements will vary. Sample: There are several possible causes of stress.
   2. Share your idea map with a friend or family member.

3. Sample outline:

I. Environmental factors
   A. Too much noise
   B. Lots of people bothering you
II. Difficult situations
   A. Big changes like moving to a new home
   B. Waiting for results of a medical test
   C. Something going wrong, like a car breaking down
   D. Money troubles
III. Pressures of school and work
   A. Working too hard
   B. Trying to meet a tight deadline
   C. Taking a test
   D. Being responsible for something important
   B. Have a friend or family member evaluate your work.

Practice 3.1, page 149

A. Sample introductory paragraph:

One job that I would particularly not enjoy is that of a taxi driver. The hours are long, there is no set salary to depend on, and the job is sometimes unsafe.

Sample concluding paragraph:

Although I'm sure that the job of taxi driver has its positive side, that job would not be appropriate for me. My concerns about safety, regular pay, and getting home at a decent hour would cancel out any enjoyment I could get from the work.

B. Sample answers:
1. There are a number of reasons why it's best to avoid eating sugar.
2. Advertising has a negative effect on many people's lives.
3. Here's what you have to do to succeed on the job.
4. Overeating is caused by many different factors.

Practice 3.2, page 151

A. Sample paragraphs:
1. If I had a choice, I would rather live in the country than in the city. First of all, the countryside is beautiful. Who wouldn't feel happy looking at rolling meadows or sitting by a trickling brook? Also, the air is clean and fresh because there are no factories polluting the air.

Finally, the cost of living is lower. Rent, groceries, and other essentials cost less.
2. My father is the most influential person in my life. He's a very caring person, and he always seems to know the right thing to do in a situation. For example, when I was a teenager, I took a job at a fast-food restaurant and then decided I didn't like it. My father urged me not to quit. He said, "Once you start something, you have to finish." I took his advice, and I was glad I did.
3. Winning a lot of money would definitely change my life. The first thing I would do is hire someone to clean our dingy, crowded apartment. Then I'd have time to spend on activities I really enjoy, like going bowling with my friends and reading the newspaper.

B. Sample body paragraphs:

Increased control is the aspect of home ownership that appeals to me the most. For example, homeowners can turn their heat up or down whenever they like, whereas renters are at the mercy of the landlord. Also, owners can hang pictures or build a bookcase without fear. Unreasonable landlords sometimes keep part of the security deposit when they see holes in the walls from pictures. Last, owners don't have to worry about sudden rent increases.

Also, owning a home is a better financial investment than renting. Mortgage payments build equity, whereas rent payments are the equivalent of throwing money away. Furthermore, any small home improvement project, such as painting the bathroom or replacing the lock, benefits the owner and not the landlord. As a result, homeowners have more of an incentive to fix up their homes.

Another advantage of owning a home is more privacy. There's no landlord to check up on a homeowner and comment on the lack of cleanliness. Likewise, there aren't any prospective tenants invading the homeowner's privacy.

C. Show your draft to a friend or family member.

Practice 4.1, page 153

A. Your revised essay should be similar to this:

Most of us are aware of the consequences of speeding, which range from receiving a speeding ticket to getting into an accident. <u>Nonetheless,</u> a quick survey of any highway will show that many drivers exceed the speed limit. Why do people speed?

¶One common reason <u>for speeding</u> is that people do not think they will suffer any consequences. If they have never been stopped by the police or crashed their car, they don't see any reason to worry. <u>Another reason is that</u> people simply need to get somewhere in a hurry. They realize that they are speeding, <u>but</u> they have such a need to arrive on time that they don't care. <u>Their impatience gets the better of them</u>.

¶A final reason is lack of respect for other <u>drivers. One</u> driver who is speeding makes road conditions less safe for everyone. Drivers who act as though they are in the Indy <u>500 have</u> no regard for the safety of others.

We know that people speed because of <u>impatience, lack of fear of the consequences, and lack of respect. Now</u> let's figure out what will make them stop.

B. Have a friend or family member evaluate your work.

Practice 4.2, page 155

A. Your edited essay should be similar to this:

One common reason for speeding is that people do not think they will suffer any consequences. If they have never been stopped by the police or crashed <u>their</u> car, they don't see any reason <u>to</u> worry.

Another reason is that people simply <u>need</u> to get somewhere in a hurry. They realize that they are speeding, but they have such a need to arrive on time that they <u>don't</u> care. <u>Their</u> impatience <u>gets</u> the better of them.

A final reason is lack of respect

for other drivers. <u>One</u> driver who is speeding <u>makes</u> road conditions less safe for everyone. Drivers who act as though they are in the <u>Indy</u> 500 <u>have</u> no regard for the safety of others.

B. Share your work with a friend or family member.

Practice 5, page 157

Share your work with a friend or family member.

SOCIAL STUDIES ANSWERS AND EXPLANATIONS

U.S. History

Lesson 1: Exploration, Colonialism, and the American Revolution

Practice 1, page 167

1. **(4) the Spanish (Comprehension)** According to the map and the key, Spain had the southernmost colony along the east coast of what would eventually become the United States.

2. **(3) The English established several colonies in the New World. (Evaluation)** The map shows several English colonies along the New England coast and in what is now Virginia and Maryland.

3. **(5) Haitian refugees who fled to the U.S. to escape dictatorship. (Application)** Like the early colonists, the Haitian refugees of the mid- and late 1900s came to the United States seeking freedom from political persecution.

4. **(2) increased British taxes and restrictions on the colonies (Analysis)** The fourth sentence of paragraph 4 links increased taxes and restrictions to the outbreak of the American Revolution.

5. **(3) They were concerned about the government becoming tyrannical. (Analysis)** The first amendment guarantees citizens' rights to pressure their government. The framers of the U.S. Constitution did not want government officials to have the power to squelch citizens' concerns and hold arbitrary or tyrannical power over them.

Lesson 2: Westward Expansion and the Civil War

Practice 2, page 169

1. **(5) whether slavery should be permitted in territories in the West (Comprehension)** This is implied in the third and fourth paragraphs of the passage. Option (3) is incorrect because the third paragraph says that Abraham Lincoln promised to halt the spread of slavery, not to end it.

2. **(3) To balance the admission of Missouri, they lobbied to have Maine admitted as a free state. (Application)** The third paragraph of the passage describes how the U.S. government tried to maintain a balance of power between the North and the South by adding states in pairs—one slave state and one free state. Since Missouri was a slave state, the most likely response of Northerners would be to propose the addition of a free state. Maine and Missouri were the 23rd and 24th states to join the United States.

3. **(4) At the end of each of these wars, the nation was reunified. (Application)** The question information indicates that North and South Vietnam were reunited under the Communists at the end of the Vietnam War. The passage implies that at the end of the Civil War, the North and the South again were part of the same (federal) government.

4. **(4) In 1868, many African Americans served in the government of South Carolina. (Analysis)** There are more than 20 African Americans included in this composite photograph of the South Carolina legislature. The other options are opinions or cannot be confirmed by the photograph.

5. **(1) Over the course of Reconstruction, blacks in the South gained and then lost political power. (Evaluation)** The number of African Americans in the composite photograph of the South Carolina state legislature of 1868 indicates that near the beginning of the Reconstruction period, blacks had considerable political power. The last paragraph of the passage on page 168 states that by the 1870s, whites were preventing blacks from exercising their newly won right to vote. This indicates that blacks were losing political power as Reconstruction ended.

Lesson 3: Industrialization, Immigration, and the Progressive Era

Practice 3, page 171

1. **(2) an increase in manufacturing (Comprehension)** By definition, industrialization is related to increased manufacturing.

2. **(3) the development of the Bessemer process, which made it easier to produce steel (Application)** The first paragraph of the passage relates rapid industrialization to the invention of new industrial processes. The Bessemer process was one such process. It made steel more readily available for tools, railroads, construction, and other uses.

3. **(3) cooperation with others to improve worker safety (Evaluation)** The fourth paragraph indicates that union workers pledged to work together (cooperate) for better working conditions. Better working conditions would include improving worker safety.

4. **(5) fairness (Evaluation)** The fifth paragraph discusses the Progressive Era. That reformers were working to improve conditions for poor people and to give people more of a voice in government indicates that fairness was a strong ideal for them.

5. **(1) Northern and Western Europe (Comprehension)** The graph from 1881–1896 shows this to be 61%, indicating that the majority of immigrants during that period came from Northern and Western Europe.

6. **(3) There was a smaller percentage of immigrants from Asia in the late 1800s than in the late 1900s. (Analysis)** The graphs show that 1.5% of immigrants came from Asia in the late 1800s and that 37% came from Asia in the late 1900s. Options (1), (2), and (4) are contradicted by the graphs and option (5) cannot be determined from the graphs.

Lesson 4: The United States as an Emerging World Power

Practice 4, page 173

1. **(3) military/defense (Application)** The building of a naval base indicates that the correct category is "military"; since, as indicated in the question text, Cuba is so close to the United States, the base must be important for defense reasons rather than for the purpose of refueling.

2. **(2) In World War II, the Allies included England, France, and Russia. (Analysis)** It is assumed that you realize that the Allies of World War II included the same major powers as the Allies in World War I. If you don't recognize this unstated assumption, you won't understand who fought whom in World War II.

3. **(4) The New Deal lowered unemployment, but U.S. entry in World War II lowered it further. (Evaluation)** The graph shows a decline in the unemployment rate after the New Deal went into effect in 1934. It shows that unemployment went up in 1938 but then dropped after that and dropped considerably after the U.S. entry into World War II in 1941.

4. **(4) America took a strong leadership role during and after World War II. (Comprehension)** The paragraph focuses on the role the United States played during and after World War II. The other

options are details from the paragraph or they bring up information not included in the paragraph.

Lesson 5: Facing Enduring Challenges

Practice 5, page 175

1. **(5) The two superpowers never actually fought. (Comprehension)** This is implied in the first few sentences of paragraph 1. That the Cold War is defined as a power struggle indicates that military action was not necessarily involved. The third paragraph indicates that the superpowers indeed did not come into direct conflict during the Cold War.

2. **(4) The build-up of nuclear arms increases fear and instability, not peace. (Comprehension)** The statement about peace and stability made by the man on the right in the bottom frame of the cartoon is supposed to be ironic. That he refers to his trembling arms indicates that the situation has made him tense and afraid.

3. **(4) Americans were in complete agreement about pulling out of Vietnam. (Evaluation)** This is an example of a faulty generalization. Paragraph 1 states that even when defeat for South Vietnam seemed fairly certain, a few Americans still wanted to continue contributing to the fighting. Therefore, it is an overstatement to say that Americans were in complete agreement that pulling out of Vietnam was the right thing to do.

4. **(2) the fall of communism in the Soviet Union (Comprehension)** Paragraph 2 implies that the loosening of Soviet control in Eastern Europe and the fall of communism in the Soviet Union itself brought the Cold War to an end, with the diminishment of the communist threat.

5. **(3) petitioning for a city ordinance requiring realtors to sell property to anyone who is able to buy it (Application)** Paragraph 3 states that the aim of the civil rights movement was to end segregation and discrimina-

tion in the United States. Preventing the selective selling of real estate was one important way civil rights activists worked to end discrimination, making decreased segregation possible.

6. **(1) Reliance on technology has increased pollution. (Analysis)** This is a conclusion—a general statement about a topic. The other options are details—facts or examples—that support this conclusion.

U.S. History Practice Questions, pages 176–179

1. **(3) Although the Cherokee adopted many aspects of white culture, they were driven off their ancestral lands. (Analysis)** This statement is the only one with a large enough scope to be considered a conclusion. The other options are details that are either included in, related to, or not based on the time line.

2. **(1) If the government can't protect us from white settlers here, now, how could it protect us from whites moving west in the future? (Evaluation)** This question shows the lack of logic in the government's claim that location was what made it difficult to protect Cherokee rights. Location had nothing to do with the government's lack of protection of Cherokee land in the South. The government did not have the political will to enforce laws protecting the Cherokee. This same lapse would occur again in the early 1900s, leading to the Oklahoma land rush.

3. **(4) equal rights and opportunities for women (Evaluation)** Adams's statements about women not being inferior and her invention of the term *Lordess* clearly indicate that she advocated equality for women.

4. **(3) Delaware, West Virginia, Kentucky, and Missouri (Comprehension)** The map shows that these were all slave states loyal to the Union.

5. **(1) The nation's capital was located nearby. (Evaluation)** If the nation's capital, located

adjacent to the state of Maryland, had been surrounded by Confederate states, it would have been extremely difficult for the U.S. army to defend it. This would have given a great edge to the Confederacy during the Civil War. The other options are untrue, irrelevant, or not verifiable by the map.

6. **(5) to weaken the South by enlisting former slaves in the Union army (Analysis)** This was implied by the text of the Proclamation that is quoted. That the Emancipation Proclamation applied to neither all states or all slave states refutes options (2) and (3). That the Proclamation denounces violence by slaves against former slave owners also refutes option (3). The other options would be nonsensical from Lincoln's perspective.

7. **(1) An Asian American registers to vote and is given a reading test. (Application)** The Voting Rights Act of 1965 applies here, because it prohibited literacy (reading) tests for voting. In the other situations, the Civil Rights acts of 1964 and 1968 would apply.

8. **(3) African Americans were granted the vote soon after the Civil War, but laws enforcing these rights had to be passed a century later. (Comprehension)** This is implied by the passage of the 15th Amendment in 1870 and by the passage of the Voting Rights Act of 1965. Congress would not have passed the later law if the 15th Amendment were being upheld and enforced.

9. **(2) They both prohibited the legal separation of people by race in public places. (Analysis)** Both the 1875 and 1964 civil rights acts banned racial segregation in public places.

10. **(5) The telephone was the greatest electrical invention ever. (Analysis)** This statement is the only opinion. Options (1), (2), and (3) are facts about the invention; option (4) says the scientists admired the invention, which is also a fact.

11. **(2) the framers of the U.S. Constitution (Comprehension)** The clothes of the men in the picture indicate that this cartoon is set in the late 1700s. Impeachment is discussed in the caption. Impeachment was a provision that the framers of the Constitution included in order to prevent the kind of abuse of presidential power carried out by Nixon. It was not discussed in the Declaration of Independence, so option (1) is incorrect.

12. **(2) the pursuit of justice (Evaluation)** By investigating the circumstances of Watergate, Congress was trying to make sure that the nation's laws were carried out.

13. **(4) the escalation and failure of the Vietnam War (Application)** This was the only event that was just prior to the Watergate scandal. The bloodshed and failure of the Vietnam War caused many people to question authority, including the government, and to question decisions made by the government.

14. **(4) 1,000,000 (Comprehension)** The scale on the horizontal axis of the bar graph shows that population is measured in millions. The bar for Cuba stands one unit high. This means that about 1,000,000 people are of Cuban descent.

15. **(2) Mexico (Application)** The bar graph shows that most people in the U.S. who are Hispanic originally came from Mexico. Therefore, Mexico is the most likely nation of origin of the unknown family.

World History

Lesson 1: Early Civilizations

Practice 1, page 181

1. **(3) the Maya (Comprehension)** According to the passage, the Maya recorded their discoveries about mathematics and astronomy in a pictographic writing system. The first two civilizations mentioned did make discoveries about mathematics and astronomy, but they weren't in Central America.

2. **(4) ancient Greece and ancient Rome (Comprehension)** As stated in the passage, the Greek idea of democracy, in which citizens voted, and the representative government as well as the laws of ancient Rome were great influences on the founders of the United States.

3. **(1) Both developed flood control and irrigation technologies to boost food production. (Analysis)** Both ancient Egypt and the civilizations of the Fertile Crescent grew up along rivers. The passage points out that in both areas, people learned to control floods and irrigate fields in order to improve food production.

4. **(3) towns (Analysis)** The food surpluses that result from agriculture mean that not everyone must grow or gather his own food. Therefore, some people are free to live in towns where they can pursue a craft or business in exchange for food from farmers. The other options occur without the gathering together of people in settlements.

5. **(5) ancient Egypt (Application)** Ancient China developed along a great river, the Yellow River. Of the civilizations listed, only ancient Egypt also grew up along a river, the Nile. In both ancient China and ancient Egypt, the river kept the soil rich and damp.

6. **(3) The Yellow River was probably the main trade route between Loyang and Chengchow. (Evaluation)** Not only were rivers the source of water for irrigation, they were a major thoroughfare for the transport of goods. Since both cities are on the Yellow River, trade between them most likely took place by river at that time.

Lesson 2: Feudalism to Nation States

Practice 2, page 183

1. **(4) to protect their noble's land from attack (Comprehension)** According to the passage, the role of the knights in feudal society was to protect their noble's estate, or land.

2. **(3) Spain (Comprehension)** As the passage indicates, of the lands the Muslims conquered, only Spain was in Europe. Thus the only European nation you would expect to have evidence of Muslim culture is Spain.

3. **(2) the migration of people from farms to industrial cities in the 1800s (Application)** Like the migration to the cities in the 1800s, the migration from manors to towns in the late Middle Ages resulted from economic causes. In both migrations, people were seeking better economic opportunities than farming offered.

4. **(1) Roman Catholics accepted the authority of the pope and Protestants did not. (Analysis)** According to the passage, this was one of the main differences between the two branches of Christianity.

5. **(1) accepted legal principles (Evaluation)** Since the manor court did not rely on a written body of legal rulings, its actions were unpredictable. Most people felt they would get a fairer ruling in the royal courts, which were bound by written common law that applied to everyone in the kingdom.

6. **(4) The population of western Europe showed almost constant growth with only brief periods of decline. (Comprehension)** This is the best summary because it contains the main idea (Europe's population rose from 500 to 1500) and important details (two brief periods of decline).

Lesson 3: Expansion and the Global Age

Practice 3, page 185

1. **(5) leading the first around-the-world expedition (Comprehension)** With this expedition, Magellan provided irrefutable proof that the world was round.

2. **(3) to gain economic benefits (Comprehension)** According to the third paragraph of the passage, the main goal of European colonization was economic gain.

3. **(2) Malaya, where the British set up and ran rubber plantations worked by the native peoples (Application)** Of all the options, only Malaya is a colony of economic exploitation rather than of settlement.

4. **(4) war and disease (Analysis)** The third and fifth paragraphs of the passage indicate that war and disease, more than economic exploitation, were primary causes of the population decline among native colonized peoples.

5. **(2) The Dutch had the smallest claim in the Americas in 1700. (Evaluation)** The map shows that by 1700, the Dutch had only a small claim on the northern coast of South America, and the other nations had much larger claims.

Lesson 4: The Age of Revolutions

Practice 4, page 187

1. **(3) the U.S. Declaration of Independence (Comprehension)** According to the passage, the American Revolution and its goals of democracy (as expressed in the Declaration of Independence and the Constitution) were big influences on the French.

2. **(5) Members of the Third Estate owned the least amount of land per person. (Evaluation)** With 98 percent of the population but only 70 percent of the land, the Third Estate owned the least land in proportion to its numbers. Members of the First and Second Estates owned more land in proportion to their percentage of the population.

3. **(1) England had a Parliament, and France did not. (Comprehension)** This contrast is stated in the third paragraph of the passage and was one of the reasons French citizens were dissatisfied with their lack of representation in the monarchy of Louis XVI.

4. **(3) possessing large landholdings (Comprehension)** The last paragraph of the passage on page 186 states that farmland had been the economic mainstay of the aristocracy up until the time of the Industrial Revolution, which began late in the eighteenth century.

5. **(2) A sovereign nation is independent, having the power to control itself. (Analysis)** In the passage, the word *sovereign* is used but not explained; the author takes for granted you know what it means. The remaining options are all stated in the passage.

6. **(5) the Industrial Revolution (Application)** Like the Industrial Revolution, the Information Revolution is an economic revolution that brought about social change. The other revolutions are all political in nature.

Lesson 5: The Twentieth Century

Practice 5, page 189

1. **(1) pay the Allies money to repair war damages (Comprehension)** According to the passage, paying reparations was one of the provisions of the Treaty of Versailles.

2. **(4) the invasion of Poland (Comprehension)** The third paragraph of the passage indicates that to avoid going to war, the Allies permitted Germany to take over, or annex, Austria and Czechoslovakia. However, Germany's invasion of Poland spurred England and France to declare war.

3. **(3) national pride (Evaluation)** The Japanese had a great deal of national pride, which they found difficult to put aside. Thus it took the destruction of two cities and thousands of deaths to overcome their reluctance to surrender.

4. **(5) Both were won by the Allies. (Analysis)** Of the options listed, the fact that the Allies won both wars is the only similarity. Options (1), (3), and (4) are true only of World War II, and option (2) is not true: both wars involved other parts of the world.

5. **(2) The United States sustained only a few civilian casualties. (Analysis)** Because World War II was fought in Europe and Asia, the United States was fortunate in having a negligible number of civilian casualties, in contrast to other nations that played a major role in the war.

6. **(1) the 1812 French invasion of Russia, which failed due to harsh weather and lack of supplies (Application)** Like Napoleon and the French, Hitler and the Germans underestimated the difficulties they would face from the harsh Russian climate, the great distance from home, and the tenacious Russian soldiers and civilians.

World History Practice Questions, pages 190–193

1. **(2) How Germanic Tribes Governed (Comprehension)** The focus of the passage is the minimal government structure of the Germanic tribes.
2. **(3) Cultural differences prevented Muslim assimilation into Hindu society. (Analysis)** This statement is the conclusion of the passage. All the other options are details that relate to this conclusion.
3. **(3) along the Nile River (Comprehension)** The map key gives the dates of each civilization shown on the map. Egypt, Kush, and Axum were the earliest civilizations. They are all located along the Nile River in the northeast part of Africa.
4. **(1) Over 800 years, several civilizations succeeded one another in western Africa. (Evaluation)** The civilizations of Ghana, Mali, and Songhai developed one after the other in the same region of Africa. None of the other options is supported by information on the map.
5. **(5) the League of Nations, formed at the end of WWI to maintain international peace (Application)** The League of Nations was formed for the same purpose and under similar circumstances as the United Nations. In fact, the United Nations was its replacement; the League of Nations had failed to prevent World War II and was disbanded.
6. **(4) The Industrial Revolution started in Great Britain and spread to Europe, but by 1900 the United States was the leading industrialized nation.**

(Comprehension) This summary statement has all the major details from the paragraph—the start of the Industrial Revolution in Great Britain, its spread to Europe, and the lead taken by the United States. The other options either focus too narrowly on a couple of details or are too broad to be an effective summary.

7. **(2) Martin Luther King, Jr., who led peaceful demonstrations to further the cause of civil rights in the United States (Application)** Like Gandhi, King believed that political and social change could be brought about by large numbers of people acting together in peaceful demonstrations and boycotts.
8. **(1) They were led by non-Chinese peoples. (Analysis)** The Yuan government was run by Mongols who invaded China from Mongolia in central Asia and the Ch'ing by Manchus who invaded China from Manchuria, northeast of China.
9. **(3) Portuguese trade in the East Indies grew. (Analysis)** Da Gama's voyage opened up new trading opportunities for the Portuguese. Note from the time line that the Portuguese dominated trade in the East Indies from about 1510 to 1600.
10. **(1) Spanish and Portuguese domination of exploration gave way to that of the Dutch, French, and English. (Evaluation)** According to the time line, most Spanish and Portuguese exploration and conquest took place during the 1500s. From the 1600s on, other nations such as England, France, and the Netherlands increased their activity considerably. The other options are incorrect or cannot be determined from the information in the time line.
11. **(2) Pizarro (Application)** Like Cortés, Pizarro explored on behalf of the Spanish rulers. He conquered the Inca Empire in South America.
12. **(2) The Age of Exploration (Comprehension)** This title describes the era and events

shown. The other options are too narrow, too broad, or simply incorrect.

13. **(4) After the Cold War ended, defense spending began to fall. (Evaluation)** The graph shows defense spending decreasing in the period 1990–1995, after the Cold War ended in 1990. None of the other statements is supported by data on the graph.
14. **(2) Colonies should be economically independent. (Analysis)** Of all the statements, only this one is an opinion. The other statements are facts that are stated in the paragraph.
15. **(1) chivalry, the way of life of European knights that emphasized personal valor and honor (Application)** Both bushido and chivalry were warrior codes of conduct based on values of loyalty, courage, and honor.
16. **(4) recognition of service (Application)** Since the samurai was a warrior whose main role in Japanese society was to serve his lord and since the bushido code emphasized loyalty, a samurai would probably value recognition of service above the other things listed.

Civics and Government

Lesson 1: Levels and Branches of Government

Practice 1, page 195

1. **(1) division of power between national and state governments (Comprehension)** According to the second paragraph of the passage on page 194, a federal form of government divides power between the levels of government.
2. **(5) the State Department (Application)** The State Department is part of the executive branch; its head is a member of the president's cabinet.
3. **(2) Federal judges need not worry about pleasing their constituents in order to be reelected. (Analysis)** Because they do not need to please any constituents in order to be reelected, federal judges can preside without wor-

rying about making unpopular decisions. This leaves them freer to be impartial judges of the law.

4. **(1) abuse of power (Analysis)** Since power is shared among the three branches and the branches can check one another, it becomes difficult for one branch of government to abuse its power.

5. **(3) a member of Congress (Comprehension)** Although this person subscribes to the idea that the government is divided into three branches, he can only think of one of them—the one he belongs to. Since he is probably in the legislative branch, he is likely to be a member of Congress. The way the desks are arranged and the way the man is standing to make his point are visual cues that the setting of the cartoon is Congress.

6. **(1) mutual respect and convenience (Evaluation)** Although in theory each state could insist on its own laws being followed even by residents of other states, in practice that would be too cumbersome. So on many matters, such as driver's licenses, states respect one another's laws because it is convenient to do so.

Lesson 2: Constitutional Government

Practice 2, page 197

1. **(3) elected representatives exercising government power on behalf of citizens (Comprehension)** According to the first paragraph of the passage, the key characteristic of a republic is elected officials governing for the voters.

2. **(4) The details of government would be worked out in the future, as the need arose, within the framework of the Constitution. (Analysis)** The leaders who drafted the Constitution were wise enough to realize that they could not anticipate every eventuality, so instead of trying to cover everything in the Constitution, they made it a general framework within which specific future decisions and laws could be made.

3. **(4) the power of an office, not an individual (Evaluation)** Roosevelt's long tenure worried many people as they saw his power growing with time. To prevent any individual from amassing too much power as president, they favored term limits.

4. **(5) The U.S. Supreme Court declares an Illinois state law unconstitutional. (Application)** The supremacy clause asserts the supremacy of federal law when it conflicts with state law. Therefore the declaring of a state law unconstitutional is an exercise of the supremacy clause.

5. **(1) State governments do not usually act together. (Analysis)** The third and fourth methods of passing a constitutional amendment both require concerted action by state governments. Since there is no structure in place in which state governments can cooperate with one another, it is very difficult for the states to set a potential amendment in motion. The first two methods of amending the Constitution rely on Congress, which meets regularly, to initiate the process.

Lesson 3: The Electoral System

Practice 3, page 199

1. **(3) a majority in the Electoral College (Comprehension)** According to the second paragraph of the passage, a president must have a majority in the Electoral College to be elected.

2. **(1) Exit polls may be inaccurate if the people polled are not representative of the political unit as a whole or if the election is very close. (Evaluation)** It is more likely that a poll will be wrong if an unrepresentative sample is used or if the election is very close. Under those circumstances it is hazardous to call an election based on exit poll results, as was shown in the 2000 presidential election, in which the media gave Florida's vote first to Gore, then to Bush, and only hours later declared the state too close to call.

3. **(5) Two city council members are on a ballot to determine which one will run for mayor as a Democrat. (Application)** A primary is an election to choose among candidates of the same party. The winner of the primary then faces an opponent of another political party in the regular election.

4. **(3) Senate and House candidates received similar proportions of donations from individuals. (Analysis)** Although the amounts raised from PACs and from the candidates themselves differed, both Senate and House candidates received about the same percentage of funds from individual donors, 57% and 54% respectively.

5. **(3) On average, a Senate candidate raises more money than a candidate running for the House. (Evaluation)** Look at the total amount spent by the 108 Senate candidates and the 804 House candidates, and find an average by dividing by the number of candidates who raised the funds. The average Senate campaign raised about $3,000,000 dollars, and the average House campaign, just under $600,000.

Lesson 4: The Role of the Citizen

Practice 4, page 201

1. **(2) the U.S. Constitution (Comprehension)** According to the third paragraph of the passage, the Constitution sets forth the rights of citizens.

2. **(1) resident alien (Application)** Because she moved here permanently as the wife of an American citizen, Louvina is a resident alien and will remain so until she qualifies for citizenship through naturalization.

3. **(3) They would become enemy aliens. (Analysis)** If the country of aliens residing in the United States declares war on the United States, that nation becomes an enemy state, and the aliens become enemy aliens.

4. **(2) privacy (Evaluation)** The protection against unreasonable search and seizure is essentially a

protection of citizens' privacy rights. The government must demonstrate a good reason before it is allowed to search or seize property.

5. **(4) In the United States, voter turnout increases with age. (Analysis)** This is the only statement general enough to be a conclusion. All the other options are details from the graph that support this conclusion.

Civics and Government Practice Questions, pages 202–205

1. **(5) In January 2001, Republicans controlled the 107th Congress by a small margin. (Comprehension)** A good summary includes the main ideas of a chart. In this case, the summary statement includes the number of the Congress and the fact that in January 2001 Republicans had a slim majority (with Vice President Cheney's tie-breaking vote). The other options are either too broad or too specific to be good summaries of the chart.

2. **(2) the Bill of Rights of the U.S. Constitution, guaranteeing citizens certain rights (Application)** Like the Magna Carta, the Bill of Rights of the U.S. Constitution accords citizens certain rights and protections. Note that the scope of the Bill of Rights is broader in that it protects the rights of all citizens, not just a special group, as the Magna Carta did.

3. **(3) a $3,000 contribution to a party fund for TV ads on political issues (Application)** Of all the choices, this is the only donation that is going to a political party fund rather than to a specific candidate, so it is a "soft money" contribution.

4. **(2) People were less aware of soft money because disclosure was not required. (Analysis)** During the 1980s, political parties did not have to reveal the amount and sources of their soft money contributions, so the extent of this type of campaign financing was not generally known. Only when a law was passed requiring disclosure did people become aware of the scale of soft money donations and so began to raise their concerns about the issue.

5. **(4) Perot won a greater percentage of the popular vote than the Electoral College vote in the 1992 election. (Evaluation)** Even though Perot won almost 20 percent of the U.S. popular vote, he did not get any votes in the Electoral College.

6. **(5) The Popular and Electoral Votes (Comprehension)** This is the only option that covers the topic of the paragraph as well as that of the graphs.

7. **(1) The board of election is the county, city, or town office responsible for local voting. (Analysis)** Nowhere in this excerpt from the voter's guide is the board of election defined or explained; the writer assumes that the reader knows what it is.

8. **(2) the National Association of Manufacturers, which lobbies for businesses (Application)** Of all the choices, this is the only group that consists of people with common interests and goals—in this case, manufacturers— working by lobbying to influence government policies. The other choices are either political parties or part of the executive branch.

9. **(2) Most registered voters don't vote. (Comprehension)** Despite the fact that voting is one of the obligations of citizens, in most elections, less than half of the nation's registered voters actually vote.

10. **(3) civic duty (Evaluation)** The cartoonist is appealing to voters to take their civic duty to vote more seriously.

11. **(2) China, where the top leaders of the Communist party control the government (Application)** Of the national governments described, only China is an oligarchy, a government with rule by a small group of people. The other options are not oligarchies; they are either democracies or autocracies.

12. **(1) retribution (Evaluation)** These laws all embody the urge to take revenge on wrongdoers, or to exact retribution. The other principles underlie the modern criminal justice system and other modern legal systems.

13. **(4) 38 (Comprehension)** Look for the map key to determine the symbol for death penalty states. According to the map, 12 states do not have the death penalty, so 38 out of 50 states have the death penalty.

14. **(5) Three of the five states with the lowest homicide rates do not have the death penalty. (Evaluation)** If that argument were correct, then the states with the lowest homicide rates should be death penalty states, but that is not the case. Three states—North Dakota, Iowa, and Massachusetts—that have some of the lowest homicide rates in the nation do not have the death penalty.

15. **(4) The Panama treaties sold out U.S. interests to Panama. (Analysis)** This was an opinion about the Panama treaties, not a fact that could be proved. The word in the passage that signals an opinion is *considered*.

16. **(4) The mayor has ceremonial duties. (Analysis)** In both the mayor-council and the council-manager forms of city government, at least part of the time, the mayor plays a ceremonial role.

Economics

Lesson 1: Basic Economic Concepts

Practice 1, page 207

1. **(2) to convert capital and raw materials into products and services (Comprehension)** According to the first paragraph of the passage, labor transforms capital and raw materials into salable goods.

2. **(5) a plastic material (Application)** A producer good is something used in the production of a finished good. Of all the options, only plastic is a producer good. The remaining options are consumer goods.

3. **(1) When the supply of houses is less than the demand, sellers can**

raise their prices. (Analysis) Because of the law of supply and demand, when the supply of houses is lower than the demand, the sellers have more control over the terms of sale. In that situation, they can raise the asking price. Because there are many potential buyers, the chance is good that the seller will get a good price.

4. **(3) Toys are not critical to a nation's economic and political well-being. (Analysis)** The U.S. government prefers the free-market system; it generally provides price supports only for industries that are extremely important to the nation's welfare, such as agriculture and transportation.

5. **(5) 16 (Comprehension)** On the vertical axis, locate $.30, then see where a horizontal line drawn through .30 meets the sloping demand line. The answer is 16 apples.

6. **(3) As the price of apples rises, Keisha buys fewer apples. (Evaluation)** The demand line on the graph shows that Keisha's apple purchases are related to the price of apples. As the price rises, her demand for apples falls, and she buys fewer apples. None of the other options is supported by the data on the graph.

7. **(3) a bicycle repair shop (Application)** According to the passage, a service business does not produce goods but instead sells services. Of all the options, only a repair shop sells a service; the remaining options are businesses that produce goods for sale.

Lesson 2: The U.S. Economic System

Practice 2, page 209

1. **(5) Monopolies shut out competition. (Comprehension)** When a company has a monopoly on a market, it has great power to squelch competing firms that try to enter the market. This is implied in the last two sentences of the second paragraph of the passage.

2. **(4) rising unemployment (Comprehension)** Of all the eco-nomic factors listed, only high unemployment is associated with recessions, according to the third paragraph of the passage.

3. **(1) Property owners have a stake in the future value of the property. (Analysis)** Since property can increase or decrease in value, its owner is motivated to do things that will maintain or increase its value.

4. **(4) Buying stock in a new company, such as an Internet start-up. (Application)** In general, investing in stocks is riskier than saving money in a bank. Investing in a startup that has no track record of turning a profit is riskier than investing in a big, well-established company like General Motors that has usually been profitable for decades.

5. **(4) Despite ups and downs, the gross domestic product general-ly increases over time. (Evaluation)** Even though the gross domestic product rises and falls with the business cycle, the gen-eral trend shown by the graph is for the gross domestic product to rise over the long term.

6. **(1) They provide capital for businesses to grow. (Analysis)** One of the similarities between saving and investing in stocks is the ultimate use of the money. In both cases, the money provides capital for businesses to start or expand operations.

Lesson 3: The Economy and the U.S. Government

Practice 3, page 211

1. **(5) when revenues exceed expen-ditures (Comprehension)** As implied in the first paragraph of the passage, a budget surplus occurs when the government takes in more tax and other rev-enue than it spends.

2. **(4) cutting the federal income tax (Analysis)** If Congress cut the fed-eral income tax, consumers would have more money to spend. This strategy has been used to stimu-late the economy. The other options would decrease consumer spending or have no direct effect on consumer spending.

3. **(4) the air traffic control system (Application)** Like the federal highway system, the air traffic control system facilitates trans-portation, which is critical for economic activity.

4. **(5) Both affect the amount of money circulating in the econo-my. (Analysis)** Fiscal and mone-tary policies are two tools the government uses to control the money supply. Increasing the money supply by lowering taxes or lowering interest rates stimu-lates the economy, and decreas-ing the money supply slows the economy.

5. **(2) buying government securi-ties (Analysis)** According to the passage, policies that increase the amount of money in circulation are used to stimulate the econo-my. According to the chart, buy-ing government securities is a policy that increases the money supply.

6. **(4) Our complex economy takes time to respond. (Evaluation)** Since the economy is made up of millions of people's actions, any Fed action takes time to have an overall effect that is measurable. In addition, the Fed's actions do not control the economy, they just influence it.

Lesson 4: Labor and Consumer Issues

Practice 4, page 213

1. **(3) wages and benefits (Compre-hension)** According to the first paragraph of the passage, the money a worker earns plus the value of his or her benefits equals total compensation.

2. **(1) Workers must learn skills throughout their lives to be pre-pared for changes in their indus-tries. (Analysis)** This is the con-clusion that the writer comes to after describing the steelworkers who lost their jobs and had to retrain when much of their industry moved overseas.

3. **(3) a woman buying a computer (Application)** Of all the options, this is the only one in which a person is buying something, the definition of a consumer.

4. **(1) All for one and one for all. (Evaluation)** When workers unite in labor unions, all of them together have the power to benefit each of the individual members. Similarly, each member supports the goals of the union as a whole.

5. **(5) in 2000 (Comprehension)** The lower line on the graph shows the number of unemployed. That line is at its lowest point at the year 2000.

6. **(2) As the number of employed civilians rose steadily from 1990 to 2000, the number of unemployed slowly declined. (Evaluation)** The graph shows that the number of employed civilians rose from about 125 million to about 140 million from 1990 to 2000. At the same time, the number of unemployed civilians dropped slightly—by about 1 million.

Economics Practice Questions, pages 214–217

1. **(2) the various types of resources needed for an economy to produce goods and services (Comprehension)** According to the passage, the factors of production include all the resources—natural, human, and man-made—needed to produce products and services.

2. **(5) entrepreneurs (Application)** In a communist nation with centralized economic decision making, there is no place for individual entrepreneurs. The government decides what will be produced and how it will be produced.

3. **(1) an office building (Application)** An office building is a capital resource. The remaining options are natural resources (iron ore and soil), labor (engineer), and an entrepreneur (founder of a publishing business).

4. **(2) In a balanced budget, revenues equal expenditures. (Analysis)** This explanation of a balanced budget is a fact. The remaining options express opinions held by many fiscal conservatives.

5. **(1) About two-thirds of all personal income was earned through work in 2000. (Evaluation)** There are three sources of income from work shown on the graph: wages and salary (55%), other labor (6%), and self-employment (8%). These total 69%, or about two-thirds, of personal income.

6. **(4) an investor (Comprehension)** The man in the plaid shorts represents an investor who buys and sells stock on the stock market.

7. **(4) He is accustomed to stock market ups and downs. (Analysis)** Like the roller coaster in the background, stocks gain and lose value, often precipitously. The investor is calm because he has experienced the ups and downs of the stock market, so a roller coaster ride feels familiar to him.

8. **(3) a person who runs a home day-care center (Application)** This is a person who is running a business out of her home and so is self-employed. Therefore, no federal income tax is withheld from her earnings, and she must pay estimated tax.

9. **(2) individualism (Evaluation)** Individualism is one of the core values of a society with a free enterprise economic system, because each person is free to make his or her own economic decisions.

10. **(3) The United States had a budget surplus in 1998. (Evaluation)** Locate 1998 on the graph. You will see that revenues exceeded expenditures; that is, the government received more money than it spent. When revenues exceed expenditures, a surplus exists.

11. **(2) income tax returns and expense records (Application)** The federal budget is similar to a family budget; it differs primarily in scale. For a family, income tax returns provide documentation of revenues (income), and expense records such as grocery receipts and credit card bills provide a record of expenditures. None of the other options

includes records of both income and expenditures.

12. **(5) The national network of interstate highways is paid for mostly by federal excise taxes. (Comprehension)** Of all the options, this one contains the main details of the paragraph. The remaining options each focus on only one supporting detail.

13. **(1) When cheaper imported goods force out U.S.-made goods, U.S. factory workers often lose their jobs. (Evaluation)** Free trade may benefit the economy as a whole in the long term, but as the economy adapts, some individuals (in this case a factory worker) lose in the short term. The fact that goods are cheaper is not of much interest to someone who is unemployed.

14. **(2) the Federal Trade Commission (Comprehension)** According to the chart, the Federal Trade Commission exists to protect consumers from misleading and/or fraudulent advertising.

15. **(2) There is a shortage of the product. (Analysis)** When the price falls below the equilibrium point, demand for the product increases, and thus the supply decreases, causing a shortage of the product.

16. **(2) what causes high rates of unemployment (Application)** The unemployment rate is a factor in the economy as a whole, so it is a subject of study to a macroeconomist. All the other options relate to the economic actions of individuals or companies, which are not the main interest of a macroeconomist.

17. **(3) As the price per eraser increases, manufacturers supply more erasers. (Analysis)** According to the graph, as prices rise, manufacturers are willing to supply more erasers as they see an opportunity for more profit.

Geography

Lesson 1: Basic Geography Concepts

Practice 1, page 219

1. **(3) Eurasia (Comprehension)** As the first paragraph of the passage on page 218 points out, England and Ireland are part of Europe, and Japan is part of Asia. Europe and Asia are actually one large land mass or continent, Eurasia.
2. **(5) Lines of latitude run east-west, and lines of longitude run north-south. (Analysis)** According to the passage and the maps on page 218, latitude runs east-west and longitude runs north-south.
3. **(3) the latitude and longitude (Evaluation)** Knowing the latitude and longitude of any place on Earth gives the most accurate description of its location because the place is located precisely at the intersection of the latitude and longitude.
4. **(1) by its natural and man-made features (Comprehension)** The natural characteristics of a region, such as rivers and terrain, and its man-made features, such as cities and roads, all factor into a definition of a geographic region.
5. **(4) The United States should be divided into cultural regions rather than states. (Analysis)** According to the passage, this is a point of view held by some geographers. The other options are all facts that can be proved true.
6. **(3) the St. Louis metropolitan region, which includes portions of Missouri and Illinois (Application)** Like New York City, St. Louis is the hub of a large metropolitan region in which people are tied together by common geographic and cultural factors.

Lesson 2: Humans and the Environment

Practice 2, page 221

1. **(3) the move of an individual or population from one geographic area to settle in another (Comprehension)** The first paragraph of the passage on page 220 implies that the key characteristics of migration are the movement of people and their settling in a new place.
2. **(2) the westward movement of the American population from the 1700s to the present (Application)** Because this migration took place (and is still taking place) within the U.S. borders, it is an internal migration. The other options all involve people moving from one country to another.
3. **(1) Urban areas are more densely populated. (Analysis)** One characteristic of the suburbs is sprawl—development over relatively large areas. In contrast, urban areas are usually more compact. Thus an urban area generally has a greater population per unit of land than a suburban area does.
4. **(4) the automobile (Analysis)** Automobiles make it possible for many people to live in the suburbs, where the distances between a home and retail stores and workplaces can be considerable and public transportation may be lacking.
5. **(5) the projected total world population in 2050 (Comprehension)** To answer this question, first locate 9,039,000,000 on the graph. (Note that the figures are given in millions, so you are actually looking for 9,039 million.) It represents a total world population figure. Then look at the bottom axis to see what year that bar represents.
6. **(3) Most of the population growth in the next 50 years will occur in the less developed nations. (Evaluation)** The bar graph shows that the proportion of the world population living in the more developed nations is relatively small, and that it is predicted that it will remain relatively small over the next 50 years. In contrast, the graph predicts that the population in the less developed nations will show much more growth. The remaining options are not supported by the data on the graph.

Lesson 3: Using Resources Wisely

Practice 3, page 223

1. **(1) materials that will never run out or can be replaced if used (Comprehension)** According to the first paragraph of the passage on page 222, a renewable resource can be replaced (for example, replanting a field that's been harvested) or is in endless supply (for example, wind and solar power).
2. **(5) rotating crops (Application)** In crop rotation, a farmer plants different crops in succeeding growing seasons in order to conserve nutrients in the soil. The other options are all examples of a nonsustainable use of a resource, because eventually they cause the resource to be used up.
3. **(2) negotiating in an international forum (Analysis)** An international forum provides a framework for nations to work to resolve conflicts over resource use before the problems escalate.
4. **(4) short-term benefit versus long-term benefit (Evaluation)** Finding and using new oil deposits is a short-term solution to U.S. energy problems because it doesn't solve the underlying problem in the long run. Developing alternative sources of energy requires more investment of time and capital with an uncertain outcome, but it has the potential to help meet long-term U.S. energy needs.
5. **(2) carpool to work and school (Application)** Carpooling saves gas, a nonrenewable resource.
6. **(3) the former U.S.S.R. (Comprehension)** The second column lists current production figures; the highest figure in the column is 25.7, that of the former U.S.S.R.
7. **(1) North America (Analysis)** To answer this question, you must look at the column labeled "Reserves to Production Ratio." This column indicates the relationship between the amount produced annually and the total

amount the region has. The region with the lowest ratio will run out of gas first: this region is North America.

Lesson 4: Maps and Their Uses

Practice 4, page 225

1. **(4) to show how various types of information relate to location (Comprehension)** The first paragraph of the passage on page 224 implies that this is the general, basic purpose of any map.
2. **(2) topographic (Application)** Because the map shows both physical features and political boundaries of present-day France, it is a topographic map.
3. **(4) 325 miles (Comprehension)** First lay the edge of a piece of paper along the imaginary straight line between the two cities. Mark the distance on the paper. Then locate the map scale, which shows the relationship between distance on the map and real distance. Measure the distance you marked on the paper against the map scale. The answer is about 325 miles. (Note that using a piece of paper is far more accurate than using your eyes or your fingers.)
4. **(5) west (Comprehension)** First locate the Loire River and the compass rose on the map. Because, as the question states, the Loire River empties into the Atlantic Ocean, you can see that the river's overall flow is from the east to the west.
5. **(4) Both are on the Seine River. (Analysis)** The map shows that Paris is inland on the Seine, and Le Havre is at the mouth of the Seine.
6. **(3) how agriculture spread in the Americas (Comprehension)** The map key and the labels on the map indicate that the map shows the spread of agriculture.
7. **(2) Both the Andes civilization and Mesoamerica domesticated beans. (Evaluation)** The labels that point out each agricultural center show that in both places, beans were grown. The map either contradicts or does not

include information about the other options.

Geography Practice Questions, pages 226–228

1. **(4) It is possible to feed the human population adequately. (Analysis)** This is an opinion attributed to agriculture experts in the passage. The remaining options are all facts stated in the passage.
2. **(3) People moved from the Northeast and Midwest to the West and South. (Comprehension)** The paragraph does not actually state this, but you can infer it because the paragraph indicates that the total population of the country increased at a lower rate than did the population of specific regions, notably the West and the South. Since that the Northeast and the Midwest lost seats in Congress (and thus residents), and the West and the South gained seats in Congress (and thus residents), you can infer that people moved from the Northeast and Midwest to the South and West.
3. **(2) a visitor to Philadelphia (Application)** This is a special-purpose map designed to help visitors find their way around the airport and locate transportation routes to and from the airport.
4. **(5) Labels for terminals and parking areas are coordinated to provide convenient parking. (Evaluation)** The map shows Terminal E by Lot E, Terminal D by Garage D and so on.
5. **(4) irrigation canals (Comprehension)** Many of the fields that are indicated as belonging to different people are separated from one another by canals.
6. **(1) a town tax assessor's tax map (Application)** Like the king's property map, a town's tax maps show property boundaries. Property ownership in Mesopotamia was a basis for taxation just as it is today in the United States.

7. **(3) the migration of thousands of farm families to other regions (Analysis)** The Dust Bowl and the Great Depression occurred at the same time, so farm families of the Great Plains were doubly hit by bad times. This resulted in one of the largest internal migrations in U.S. history. Many families went west to California.
8. **(5) the spread of the Sahara into the grazing land on its southern border (Application)** The Sahara, the desert that covers much of northern Africa, has been spreading steadily southward into the Sahel, a dry grasslands region that has been overused as grazing land.
9. **(5) Australia/Oceania (Comprehension)** The smallest population figure is 30,000,000, the population of Australia/ Oceania. (Oceania refers to the islands of the Pacific).
10. **(3) Asia (Analysis)** To find the population density of a continent, divide its population by its land area. (You can estimate rather than divide the precise figures.) If you compare the size of each continent given as an option with its population, it is clear that Asia, with its population almost 5 times the size of the continent with the next highest population (which is Africa) is the most densely populated. (Asia has a population density of $3,528,000 \div 17,400 = 203$ people per square mile and Africa has a population density of $761,000 \div 11,700 = 65$ people per square mile.)
    You could also compare the percent of total world population to the percent of Earth for each continent. Europe and Asia are the only two continents that have a greater percent of world population than of Earth. Since Asia boasts a little more than 2 to 1 ratio of total world population to percent of Earth, Asia has the greatest population density. (62.6 to 30.1 is approximately 60 to 30, or 2 to 1)
11. **(4) Together, Asia and Europe account for more than one-third of Earth's land area.**

(Evaluation) Eurasia has about 36.7, or one-third, of the land area on Earth. None of the other options is supported by data in the chart.

12. **(1) The compass direction north does not mean "up" in terms of elevation. (Evaluation)** The student was confusing north and up on the map. The Nile does indeed flow "up" the map to the top of the page, but it is actually flowing *north* and *down* from the mountains of East Africa.

Science Answers and Explanations

Life Science

Lesson 1: Cell Structures and Functions

Practice 1, page 235

1. **(4) the mitochondrion (Comprehension)** According to the diagram's labels, energy is produced in the cell's mitochondria (plural of *mitochondrion*).
2. **(5) Cell walls cannot maintain a plant's shape and rigidity when the plant lacks water. (Analysis)** Even though cell walls contribute to keeping a plant firm and rigid, they cannot do the job without water-filled vacuoles. This conclusion follows from the fact that a plant that lacks water will wilt.
3. **(2) the presence of a nucleus (Evaluation)** According to the passage, the presence of a cell nucleus defines a cell as eukaryotic.
4. **(1) Each time the microscope is improved, scientists can see cell structures more clearly. (Application)** Since cell structures are tiny, the more a cell is magnified, the more detail can be seen.
5. **(2) Oxygen would diffuse from the unicellular organism into the pond water. (Analysis)** Since diffusion is the movement of molecules toward areas of lower concentration, if the organism had more oxygen than the surrounding water did, oxygen would pass out of the organism into the water until the concentrations were equalized.

Lesson 2: Cell Processes and Energy

Practice 2, page 237

1. **(5) carbon dioxide, water, and energy (Comprehension)** According to the equation that summarizes cellular respiration, the products of this process are carbon dioxide, water, and energy.
2. **(1) increasing the amount of light the plants receive each day (Application)** Since light is required for photosynthesis, increasing light is the best choice for increasing the rate of photosynthesis. The other options either would have no effect or would decrease the rate of photosynthesis.
3. **(3) increasing the number of green plants (Analysis)** Since green plants use up carbon dioxide during photosynthesis, increasing the amount of greenery on Earth would help reduce the amount of carbon dioxide in the atmosphere.
4. **(4) carbon dioxide (Comprehension)** According to the diagram, carbon dioxide enters the leaf through openings in the bottom, called stomata (plural form of *stoma*).
5. **(2) Most of a leaf's chloroplasts are found in its palisade cells. (Evaluation)** The diagram shows that most of the leaf's chloroplasts are in the palisade cells. Evidence to support the other choices cannot be found in the diagram.

Lesson 3: Human Body Systems

Practice 3, page 239

1. **(1) the circulatory system (Comprehension)** According to the passage on page 238, the circulatory system transports blood to all the cells of the body.
2. **(3) Both are structures in which substances pass through capillary walls into the blood. (Analysis)** Both alveoli and villi are tiny structures containing capillaries in which substances pass to and/or from the blood. In the alveoli of the respiratory system, oxygen and carbon dioxide pass into and out of blood; in the villi of the digestive system, nutrients pass into the blood.
3. **(5) Veins have valves that allow blood to flow in one direction only. (Evaluation)** Of the five facts given, this is the only one that involves the direction of flow of the blood. Therefore, it helps support Harvey's conclusion that blood in the veins flows toward the heart.
4. **(2) the ureters (Comprehension)** According to the diagram and information, urine flows from the kidneys to the bladder via the ureters.
5. **(3) a patient with a painful kidney stone (Application)** Since a kidney stone forms in the urinary system, the patient is likely to be treated by a urologist.

Lesson 4: Health Issues

Practice 4, page 241

1. **(4) the skin (Comprehension)** As implied by the passage, the skin is one of the first defenses against germs, along with mucous membranes, tears, and stomach acid.

2. **(3) habituation (Application)** Sara's urge to get wine and the fact that she feels no ill effects if she does not, indicate that she is habituated to alcohol. She has a psychological dependence rather than a physical dependence on alcohol. If her dependence were physical, she would feel the effects of skipping her daily drink.

3. **(1) Fats are a more concentrated source of energy than carbohydrates. (Evaluation)** According to the table, carbohydrates provide 4 Calories per gram while fats provide 9 Calories per gram. None of the other statements is supported by the information in the table.

4. **(2) Carbohydrates come from fruits and vegetables as well as from bread and rice. (Analysis)** According to the table, bread and rice are not the only foods that provide carbohydrates; fruits and vegetables (potatoes) also do. Options (1), (3), and (5) are opinions, not facts. Based on the table, option (4) is incorrect, and so is not a fact.

Lesson 5: Reproduction and Heredity

Practice 5, page 243

1. **(1) Both are tall. (Comprehension)** According to the Punnett square, each parent has the same genotype: Tt. The capital letter *T* represents the tallness allele, and the lowercase *t*, the shortness allele. Since tallness is dominant, each parent plant is tall. The paragraph also states that the parent plants are tall.

2. **(2) 1 out of 4 (Analysis)** According to the Punnett square, only one out of four possible combinations yields a short plant (one with two recessive alleles for height: tt).

3. **(4) TT (Application)** If you want to grow only tall plants, then it is better to use purebred tall plants (TT). If you use hybrid tall plants—(Tt) or (tT), in the next generation, you will get some short plants in your garden.

4. **(3) 2 (Comprehension)** According to the passage on page 242, in order to show a recessive trait, an organism must inherit two recessive alleles for the trait. If it inherits only one recessive allele, the dominant form of the trait will show.

5. **(5) Organisms that reproduce sexually produce offspring that have inherited a mix of traits from their parents. (Analysis)** Because they are inheriting a mix of genes from two parents, the offspring of organisms that reproduce sexually are different from the parents and from each other, creating a more diverse population. When an organism reproduces asexually, the offspring are identical to the parent and to each other, which means less diversity in the population.

6. **(2) The black male was actually a hybrid. (Evaluation)** The only way a white rabbit and a black rabbit could produce a white offspring is if the black rabbit is carrying the recessive allele for white fur. That means the black rabbit was actually a hybrid, not purebred as the student had assumed.

Lesson 6: Modern Genetics

Practice 6, page 245

1. **(3) the sequence of base pairs in a gene (Comprehension)** According to the third paragraph of the passage on page 244, particular sequences of base pairs code for particular amino acids, the building blocks of proteins; so, as the paragraph concludes, the order of bases on a gene forms a code for making a particular protein.

2. **(4) a problem with protein synthesis (Analysis)** Since DNA provides the blueprint for protein synthesis, any change in DNA may affect protein synthesis.

3. **(5) Genetically engineered foods are safe for consumers and the environment. (Analysis)** This is an opinion; it is not a fact that can be proved true. All the other statements are facts, based on information given in the paragraph.

4. **(3) so that each daughter cell receives a complete set of DNA (Analysis)** Cell division produces two daughter cells with the identical genetic material, or DNA, as the parent cell. The DNA must be replicated in the parent cell first, so that the daughter cell can receive an exact copy of the parent cell's DNA.

5. **(2) The base guanine pairs only with the base cytosine. (Evaluation)** According to both the diagram and the passage, in DNA sequences, the base guanine always pairs with the base cytosine. (Note that in the diagram, each base is represented by its initial.) The remaining statements are not supported by the passage or the diagram.

6. **(4) identifying a person (Application)** Since each individual has unique DNA, DNA can be used for identification purposes in the same way fingerprints are used. Only in cases involving identical twins will the identification not be certain.

Lesson 7: Evolution and Natural Selection

Practice 7, page 247

1. **(1) traits that make an organism better able to survive in its environment (Comprehension)** According to the passage on page 246, adaptations are traits that some individuals possess that enable them to compete successfully in their environment.

2. **(3) DNA analysis provides more objective data than observation does. (Analysis)** DNA analysis is more objective than observation, because the person doing the observing must interpret what he or she sees.

3. **(1) a frog (Application)** Of all the choices, only the frog has a forelimb like those illustrated in the diagrams. The other organisms are invertebrates; they don't have bones at all.

4. **(4) In penguins, flying birds, humans, and alligators, the forelimbs have evolved to perform different functions. (Evaluation)** Even though the forelimbs of these organisms look alike, they all perform different functions. The arm helps lift and hold things, the penguin's flipper helps it swim, the bird's wing helps it fly, the alligator's foreleg helps it walk.

Lesson 8: Organization of Ecosystems

Practice 8, page 249

1. **(5) the sun (Comprehension)** The ultimate source of energy for all food webs in all ecosystems is the sun. This is implied in paragraph 1.

2. **(3) The populations of hares and seed-eating birds would increase. (Analysis)** With fewer foxes to hunt them, more hares and seed-eating birds would live to reproduce, increasing the populations of these organisms.

3. **(2) an aquarium with aquatic plants and tropical fish (Application)** An aquarium is a humanmade ecosystem with living organisms in balance with one another and their physical environment.

4. **(5) The replacement of oak and hickory forests by red maple forests is an example of succession. (Evaluation)** According to the information, succession is a naturally occurring replacement of one ecosystem by another.

5. **(3) to turn atmospheric nitrogen into compounds plants and animals can use (Comprehension)** According to the information, nitrogen-fixing bacteria in on the roots of plants like peas and beans take nitrogen and use it to form compounds that plants and animals can use.

Life Science Practice Questions pages 250–253

1. **(3) Active transport requires the cell to use energy, and passive transport does not. (Analysis)** According to the information given, the key difference between active and passive transport is the use of the cell's energy.

2. **(5) species interactions in saltwater marshlands (Application)** Of all the choices, this is the only one that involves relationships among organisms and their environment.

3. **(2) Megan's father (Comprehension)** The paragraph indicates that squares stand for males and half-shading represents genetic carriers. Of all the choices, only the square that represents Megan's father is half-shaded, indicating that Megan's father is a carrier of cystic fibrosis.

4. **(5) No one in either family has cystic fibrosis except Cailin. (Evaluation)** Since all the people in this pedigree are healthy (except Cailin), they were probably unaware that some of them were carrying cystic fibrosis, so her disease came as a surprise.

5. **(2) metaphase (Comprehension)** According to the diagram, the chromosomes line up across the middle of the cell during metaphase.

6. **(2) to control the movement of chromosomes (Analysis)** If you examine the diagram, you will see that during anaphase, the chromosomes travel along the spindle fibers to the ends of the cell.

7. **(3) Mitosis occurs in geometric progression: 1 cell, 2 cells, 4 cells, 8 cells, 16 cells, etc. (Evaluation)** This is the best evidence for explaining how bacterial cells can multiply rapidly if the immune system is unsuccessful in fighting off the infection.

8. **(1) if humans needed to make a living there (Application)** Because of the economic needs of people, conservation, not preservation, is the most likely ecological approach.

9. **(4) The fossil record for any given species may be incomplete. (Evaluation)** Because most organisms leave no traces and fossils are found at random, scientists cannot be sure they have a complete fossil record for many species. An incomplete fossil record would also explain why evolution sometimes seems to take place in bursts rather than gradually.

10. **(5) transport and defense (Comprehension)** According to the information, plasma transports nutrients and hormones, and red blood cells transport oxygen. White blood cells defend against infection.

11. **(1) enamel (Comprehension)** The diagram shows that the top surface of the tooth is formed of enamel.

12. **(5) the pulp (Analysis)** When decay reaches the pulp, where the nerve endings are, the tooth becomes extremely painful.

13. **(2) grazing too many cattle on grassland (Application)** Overgrazing of domestic animals like cattle can destroy much plant life in grassland ecosystems. When that happens, the number of cattle the grassland can support decreases.

14. **(1) DNA analysis provides more fundamental, accurate data than does a visual analysis of structures and fossils. (Analysis)** Because DNA analysis involves genetic data at the molecular level, it is a better indicator of the relationships among organisms than visible similarities such as teeth. Thus DNA analysis has caused changes in the way scientists previously classified some organisms.

15. **(3) panting and sweating (Application)** A dog's panting and a human being's sweating are processes that cause loss of body heat through the evaporation of water. In other words, they are body processes that function to cool off an overheated animal.

16. **(5) chronic obstructive lung diseases (Analysis)** If you examine the bar graph, you will see that the only cause of death that had a dramatic doubling from 1980 to 1998 was chronic obstructive lung diseases (such as asthma). In 1980, there were a little over 50,000 deaths from this cause; in 1998, there were slightly more than 100,000 deaths.

17. **(3) The water level in the jar might have gone down because of evaporation. (Evaluation)** Ben should have covered the mouth of the jar so the water would not evaporate. Ben did not control the experiment for other possible causes of a diminishing water level when he did not cover the mouth of the jar. Therefore, his conclusion is flawed.

Earth and Space Science

Lesson 1: Structure of Earth

Practice 1, page 255

1. **(1) changes in Earth's crust (Comprehension)** According to the passage on page 254, the theory of plate tectonics explains how major landforms are created, the continents move, and the seafloor spreads, all of which are changes in Earth's crust.

2. **(3) The inner core is solid, and the outer core is liquid. (Analysis)** As the passage states, both inner and outer core are made mostly of iron; the main difference is that the outer core is liquid and the inner core solid.

3. **(4) destructive margin (Application)** According to the passage, deep ocean trenches are characteristic of destructive margins between oceanic and continental plates.

4. **(5) The west coast of Africa seems to fit into the east coast of the Americas. (Evaluation)** Of the five choices, only this one provides evidence to support the idea that there used to be one continent made up of the pieces that are the continents we know today. The fact that several conti-

nents seem to fit together like the pieces of a jigsaw puzzle suggests that they were once part of one continent.

5. **(4) The continents of North America and Europe are moving apart. (Comprehension)** Since the Atlantic Ocean is getting wider, it follows that the continents on either side of the Atlantic are moving further apart.

6. **(3) A single large landmass called Pangaea existed about 250 million years ago. (Analysis)** The existence of Pangaea is a theory based on evidence, not a fact. All the other choices are facts that can be proved true.

Lesson 2: Earth's Resources

Practice 2, page 257

1. **(5) 152 (Comprehension)** To find the consumption of petroleum in 1999, locate 1999 on the horizontal axis. Then draw a straight vertical line from 1999 to the graph line. Draw a straight horizontal line from that spot on the trend line to the vertical axis to find the approximate number of Btus. Note that Btus are British thermal units, a unit for measuring energy.

2. **(2) World petroleum consumption increased by about 16 quadrillion Btus between 1991 and 1999. (Comprehension)** This is the best summary of the graph because it includes the topic of the graph (world petroleum consumption) and the amount by which consumption changed during the period shown.

3. **(5) Waste not, want not. (Application)** One of the basic approaches of conservationists is to reduce consumption of resources by decreasing waste ("waste not"). If that is done, in the future the resources will still be available ("want not").

4. **(2) Developed nations have started using water more efficiently than they did in the past. (Analysis)** Since population and economic activity are increasing faster than water use in the

developed nations, the most likely reason is that people have learned to conserve water, meaning they use water more efficiently now.

5. **(5) Soil erosion is caused by both natural forces and the actions of people. (Evaluation)** This is the only statement that is supported by the facts in the paragraph.

Lesson 3: Weather and Climate

Practice 3, page 259

1. **(5) southwest to northeast (Comprehension)** The label describes the winds as "westerlies" and the arrows indicate that the winds generally move from the southwest to the northeast. It follows that weather patterns move along with the winds, from southwest to northeast.

2. **(2) The winds in the Northern Hemisphere are a mirror image of those in the Southern Hemisphere. (Analysis)** If you compare the two sets of winds, you will see that those in the Northern Hemisphere are a reflection of those in the Southern Hemisphere as an image is reflected in a mirror.

3. **(5) satellites, which transmit cloud photos and weather data (Application)** Satellite photos of cloud patterns help meteorologists identify hurricanes and follow their paths; weather data helps them follow changes in the intensity of the storm. Thus, the photos and data from satellites help meteorologists make predictions about the development and movement of hurricanes.

4. **(4) global wind and ocean current patterns (Comprehension)** According to the passage, both global wind patterns and ocean currents redistribute heat from the solar heating of Earth.

5. **(4) The highest temperatures in the atmosphere are in the thermosphere. (Evaluation)** According to the chart, the thermosphere has temperatures up to thousands of degrees high—much higher than temperatures in the other layers.

6. (1) the troposphere (Application) As the lowest layer of the atmosphere, the troposphere is where human beings live and work. Even many airplane flights stay within the troposphere.

Lesson 4: Earth in the Solar System

Practice 4, page 261

1. **(5) Mercury (Comprehension)** Revolution refers to the orbit around the sun. Locate the column that shows the planets' revolution period. Then review the data in the column until you find the shortest revolution period. That would be 88 Earth days, which is the time it takes Mercury to travel once around the sun.

2. **(2) Venus (Analysis)** Of all the planets, Venus is closest in size to Earth. Venus's year is also closest in length to Earth's year. These features make Earth and Venus the most similar of the choices given.

3. **(4) Uranus was not clearly visible with the telescopes generally in use at the time. (Analysis)** According to the information given, Herschel made excellent, powerful telescopes, so he probably saw a much sharper image of Uranus than did previous astronomers.

4. **(3) Saturn (Comprehension)** Saturn has 18 moons according to the chart. That is many more than Mercury and Neptune, 2 more than Jupiter, and 1 more than Uranus.

5. **(5) faith in human judgment and decision-making skills (Evaluation)** This is the only value that relates to the possible benefits of sending a crewed mission rather than a robotic mission.

6. **(2) an atom, with a dense nucleus and electrons orbiting the nucleus (Application)** Of all these choices, the structure of the atom is most similar to the structure of the solar system, even though the atom is much tinier.

Lesson 5: The Expanding Universe

Practice 5, page 263

1. **(1) Sirius (Comprehension)** The brightest star as seen from Earth is the one with the lowest apparent magnitude. According to the chart, that is Sirius.

2. **(2) Canopus (Analysis)** Absolute magnitude is the measure of brightness of a star as if it were 32.6 light-years away from Earth. Therefore, the star with the lowest absolute magnitude would be the brightest, if all were seen at 32.6 light-year's distance. Canopus has the lowest absolute magnitude, so it is the brightest of the stars.

3. **(4) In measuring brightness, absolute magnitude takes the star's distance from Earth into account but apparent magnitude does not. (Evaluation)** The apparent magnitude is a measure of how bright the star looks from Earth. (A small close star might look very bright compared with a large distant star.) However, the absolute magnitude is a measure of how bright a star would be if it were a set distance from Earth. These numbers are not necessarily similar, since the apparent magnitude does not take the star's distance into account and the absolute magnitude does.

4. **(2) It is a main-sequence star. (Application)** According to the passage on page 262, stars like the sun have about a 10-billion year life cycle. Since the main-sequence stage is the longest, a star that is about 4.7 billion years old would be a main-sequence star, in the middle of its life cycle.

5. **(5) Pluto should be classified as one of the minor planets. (Analysis)** Options (1), (2), (3), and (4) are factual details about Pluto. Option (5) is not a factual detail about Pluto since scientists no longer classify it as a planet.

Earth and Space Science Practice Questions, page 264–267

1. **(2) The moon and the sun exert the greatest pull on Earth's oceans when these bodies are all in a line. (Evaluation)** According to the paragraph, when the sun, moon, and Earth are in a line, the highest tides, called spring tides, occur. The paragraph also states that tides are caused by the gravitational pull of the moon and the sun on the oceans. Putting this information together, the paragraph supports the idea that the moon and the sun exert their greatest pull on the oceans when these bodies are all in a line, during spring tides. None of the other statements is supported by the paragraph.

2. **(3) Iceland, an island nation in the Atlantic with active volcanoes (Application)** An area with active volcanoes has lots of magma near the surface, so it is ideal for geothermal energy, which is a renewable resource.

3. **(5) 26 percent (Comprehension)** According to the passage, dark matter is matter that does not interact with light, and according to the graph, dark matter may make up 26 percent of the universe.

4. **(5) Ordinary matter is made of the chemical elements. (Analysis)** Of all the statements, only option (5) is a fact that can be proved at this point in time. The other four choices are hypotheses, proposed explanations for things that have been observed but not proved.

5. **(4) tropical-subtropical (Comprehension)** First locate the equator on the map. Then consult the map key to identify the climate represented by the most common color that occurs near the equator.

6. **(1) The continent with the least area of desert-steppe climate is South America. (Evaluation)** To find the answer to this question, you must check each statement against the map. If the map proves the statement is false you can eliminate that statement. If the map doesn't show what the

statement indicates, you can also eliminate that statement. Option (1) is the only statement confirmed by the map.

7. **(1) Temperate-snow zones have higher farm output than other zones, allowing for more food production. (Analysis)** With a large food output, an area can easily support its human population. This not only contributes to the area's wealth, it also frees a good portion of the population to do other work, producing wealth.

8. **(3) when Earth passes between the moon and the sun (Comprehension)** According to the diagrams, a lunar eclipse occurs when the shadow (the umbra) of Earth falls on the moon, which happens when Earth is between the sun and moon.

9. **(4) A lunar eclipse can be seen only at night and a solar eclipse can be seen only during the day. (Evaluation)** The lunar eclipse diagram indicates that a person on the daylight side of Earth would not be able to see the lunar eclipse; only a person on the nighttime side would see it. The solar eclipse diagram indicates that a person on the nighttime side of Earth would not be able to see the eclipse; only a person on the daytime side would see it.

10. **(5) a catalytic converter, a device in the exhaust system of a vehicle that reduces harmful emissions from the engine (Application)** Of all the choices, only this one reduces the harmful pollutants of burning fossil fuel and so would reduce acid rain.

11. **(2) Tornadoes are extremely destructive storms. (Analysis)** Although evidence is given in the last sentence, it is taken for granted and not directly stated that tornadoes are destructive storms. All of the other options are facts actually stated in the paragraph.

12. **(1) The rock cycle is a continuous process of rock formation, destruction, and reformation. (Evaluation)** The diagram is a cycle diagram, which shows a

process that occurs again and again, in this case the formation and destruction of rocks.

13. **(2) sedimentary (Application)** An imprint can only occur in soft material like sand, mud, or silt. The diagram shows that when this material is compacted, sedimentary rock forms. This rock will contain the imprint as a fossil. Note that fossils sometimes also occur in metamorphic rock, but this is not presented as an option.

14. **(2) melted rock (Comprehension)** According to the diagram, igneous, sedimentary, and metamorphic rocks all form magma by melting.

15. **(4) Open-pit mining destroys valuable land. (Analysis)** An open-pit mine destroys a huge area, so it is restricted in many countries in order to prevent large-scale destruction of land.

Physical Science

Lesson 1: Atoms and Molecules

Practice 1, page 269

1. **(1) The sodium atom loses an electron, becoming positively charged, and the chlorine atom gains an electron, becoming negatively charged. (Comprehension)** According to the diagram, the sodium atom gives up an electron to the chlorine atom. With one fewer electron than protons, the sodium becomes a positively charged ion. When the chlorine atom gains an electron, it has one more electron than protons, making it a negatively charged ion. The sodium and chloride ions are attracted to each other, forming an ionic bond.

2. **(5) $C_6H_{12}O_6$ (Application)** According to the passage and the question text, a chemical formula represents the number of atoms of each element in a compound. Chemical symbols, which are letters, represent the elements, followed by subscripts, which represent the number of atoms.

3. **(3) Atoms are neutral in charge, and ions have either a positive or a negative charge. (Analysis)** The

key difference between an atom and an ion is the gain or loss of an electron, which gives it either a negative or a positive charge.

4. **(3) Most of the alpha particles passed right through the gold foil. (Evaluation)** Because most of the alpha particles passed right through the foil without being stopped or deflected, Rutherford concluded that atoms must consist mostly of empty space.

5. **(2) 11 (Application)** The atomic number of sodium refers to how many protons the atom has. An atom has the same number of protons as electrons. Therefore, a sodium atom has 11 electrons.

Lesson 2: Properties and States of Matter

Practice 2, page 271

1. **(1) Melting and boiling (Comprehension)** According to the passage, adding heat to a solid melts the solid, and adding heat to a liquid causes it to boil—or change to a gas.

2. **(2) Solids are usually denser than liquids and gases. (Evaluation)** If you compare the densities of the solids, liquids, and gases in the chart, you will see that the solids are denser than the liquids and the gases.

3. **(1) Water is a unique substance on Earth. (Analysis)** This statement is a conclusion (a general statement) that is supported by the statements that give details about the properties of water.

4. **(3) Antifreeze added to the water in a car's radiator lowers the freezing point below 0°C. (Application)** Adding antifreeze, a solute, to water, a solvent, lowers the freezing point of the solution—the liquid in the radiator.

5. **(5) dusty air (Application)** Of all the options, dusty air is the only one with large suspended particles. Gold and oxygen are elements, not mixtures. Salt water and vinegar are solutions; they have small particles that do not settle out of the mixture.

Lesson 3: Chemical Reactions

Practice 3, page 273

1. **(4) $2Cu + O_2 \rightarrow 2CuO$ (Comprehension)** You can eliminate options (1) and (2) because the product (CuO) is on the left side of the equation rather on than the right side. To determine which of the three remaining alternatives is correct, you must look for the equation that has two copper atoms and two oxygen atoms on the left side to balance the two copper atoms and two oxygen atoms on the right side.

2. **(2) Weigh the reactants, conduct the reaction in a sealed container, and weigh the products. (Evaluation)** This procedure should result in the weights of the reactants and products being equal, because none of the products would escape from the sealed container. The weight measurements would provide evidence for the law of the conservation of mass.

3. **(1) activation energy (Application)** Because the spark starts the gas burning, it is the activation energy necessary to start the reaction.

4. **(3) the time during which the reaction occurs (Comprehension)** The horizontal axis is labeled "Time," so you can eliminate options (4) and (5). The graph shows the progress of the reaction, which takes place over time, not just one instant of the reaction, so you can eliminate options (1) and (2).

5. **(1) Compounds are substances consisting of two or more elements chemically combined in a definite proportion. (Analysis)** The writer of the paragraph takes for granted that you know what a compound is and does not define the term *compound* in the paragraph.

6. **(3) Acids and Bases (Comprehension)** The passage gives an overview of acids and bases and describes what happens when they react with one another.

Lesson 4: The Nature of Energy

Practice 4, page 275

1. **(4) Energy cannot be created or destroyed, but can only change in form. (Comprehension)** According to the third paragraph of the passage, this is the law of conservation of energy.

2. **(3) chemical, electrical, and light energy (Application)** The batteries use chemical energy and convert it to electrical energy, which is converted to light energy in the filament of the light bulb.

3. **(4) power (Application)** Power is the rate at which work is done, or in this case, the rate at which energy is consumed. The wood stove has greater power than the oak tree because it consumes the tree's energy in much less time than it takes the tree to consume the sun's energy.

4. **(2) the relationship between energy and mass (Comprehension)** According to the passage, Einstein's equation explains how energy can be converted to mass, and vice versa.

5. **(2) At the high point of its swing, a pendulum has potential energy. (Evaluation)** The diagram shows that at the high point of its swing, the pendulum has potential energy, the energy of position. The information in the diagram does not support any of the other statements.

6. **(2) The molecules in air are far apart. (Analysis)** Because the molecules of a gas like air are far apart, they are in contact with one another less frequently than are the molecules of a liquid or solid, since liquids and solids are much denser. That is why gases have lower conductivity than liquids and solids do.

Lesson 5: Motion and Forces

Practice 5, page 277

1. **(4) anything that changes the rest or motion of an object (Comprehension)** According to the passage on page 276, this is the definition of a force.

2. **(5) the tendency of an object to remain at rest or in motion (Comprehension)** According to the third paragraph of the passage, inertia is described in Newton's first law of motion as the tendency of objects to remain at rest or keep moving until acted upon by a force.

3. **(2) the International Space Station orbiting Earth (Application)** The key concept regarding centripetal force is circular motion, and the orbit of the space station is the only example of circular motion among the options given.

4. **(3) The momentum of a car decreases when its velocity decreases. (Analysis)** The fifth paragraph of the passage indicates that momentum is defined by multiplying mass and velocity. Slowing a car before a collision decreases the car's momentum. Since, as the passage points out, momentum is a measure of energy of movement, slowing the cars will result in less energy on collision and so less damage to both cars.

5. **(2) an object that has a constant speed (Comprehension)** The graph shows a straight line that slopes upward. According to the paragraph, this type of graph shows an object that is moving at a constant speed.

6. **(3) Some machines simply change the direction of a force. (Evaluation)** According to the information given, a machine is a device that changes the direction OR the size of a force, which means that some machines change only the direction of the force. An example is a simple pulley, which allows you to pull down, rather than up, to lift a load.

Lesson 6: Electricity and Magnetism

Practice 6, page 279

1. **(2) two poles repelling one another (Comprehension)** According to the passage and the diagram, like poles repel each other, so a diagram showing two north poles near one another would show magnetic lines of

force that indicate that the two magnets are being pushed apart.

2. **(1) Copper and aluminum are conductors. (Analysis)** According to the passage, metals are good conductors of electricity, so the metals copper and aluminum would be suitable for electrical wiring.

3. **(4) a flashlight (Application)** According to the passage, direct current is used in battery-operated devices, and the flashlight is the only battery-operated device among the choices.

4. **(5) a transformer (Application)** According to the passage, transformers change the voltage of electric currents. Therefore they would be used to step current up and down for transmission between electric power plants and households.

5. **(3) the light bulb (Comprehension)** According to the passage, devices that are powered by the current are resistors. In the circuit shown, the only device powered by the current is the light bulb.

6. **(4) Disconnecting the light bulb will also stop the current. (Evaluation)** Because electric current needs a complete pathway, or circuit, in order to flow, any break in the circuit will cause the current to stop. Disconnecting the battery isn't the only way to stop the current; disconnecting the light bulb also produces a break in the circuit.

Physical Science Practice Questions, pages 280–282

1. **(2) 5,730 years (Comprehension)** To find the half-life of carbon-14, first locate the element in the left-hand column of the chart, then read across the row until you get to the column that lists half-lives.

2. **(5) Uranium produces radio-active waste that may harm living things for millions of years. (Evaluation)** Radioactive uranium waste is harmful to living things; the chart shows that it persists in the environment for billions of years, since its half-life is so long.

3. **(5) Both involve the transfer of energy through matter or space. (Analysis)** The definition of a wave is given in the first paragraph of the passage. Each of the other options is contradicted by the diagrams of the two types of waves.

4. **(1) A cork in water bobs up and down as waves pass. (Application)** The bobbing cork shows that the particles in a wave do not move far from their original position as the waves pass through the water.

5. **(1) dust motes dancing in a shaft of sunlight (Application)** The dust particles are zigzagging randomly in the air because they are being hit by gas molecules, an example of Brownian motion.

6. **(3) using powdered marble (Analysis)** Powdered marble, with many small particles, has a much greater surface area than an equal mass of marble chunks, thus speeding up the reaction with the sulfuric acid.

7. **(1) As pressure on a gas increases, volume decreases. (Comprehension)** Since the relationship between pressure and volume is an inverse relationship, when one goes up, the other goes down. You can eliminate options (3) through (5) because all involve a change in temperature, which is not part of Boyle's Law.

8. **(4) xenon (Xe) (Comprehension)** Of all the options, only xenon is in the column labeled 18, for Group 18.

9. **(3) Chlorine (Cl) and iodine (I) have similar properties. (Evaluation)** According to the table, both chlorine and iodine are in Group 17. Therefore they must have similar properties.

10. **(1) microwaves (Comprehension)** The diagram of the electromagnetic spectrum shows that the waves with the smallest wavelengths are at the left side of the spectrum; those with the longest wavelength are at the right side. Therefore, microwaves, which are to the right of the waves of the visible spectrum, have a longer wavelength.

11. **(3) People can see only a small portion of the electromagnetic spectrum. (Evaluation)** The diagram shows that the visible part of the spectrum is very small compared to the parts that include gamma rays, X rays, ultraviolet waves, infrared waves, microwaves, and radio waves, none of which we can see.

12. **(2) Its mass remains the same and its weight decreases. (Analysis)** The paragraph points out that mass is the amount of matter an object is made of. As an object travels away from Earth, its mass does not change—it still contains as much matter as it did when on Earth's surface. What does change is its weight, which decreases as the distance from Earth increases because Earth's gravitational pull decreases with distance.

13. **(2) Cold cannot be transferred. (Analysis)** The writer assumes that only heat, not cold, can be transferred, and that is why the can is gaining heat rather than the face gaining cold. All the other options are stated directly in the paragraph.

READING ANSWERS AND EXPLANATIONS

Nonfiction

Lesson 1: Identifying Main Ideas and Supporting Details

Practice 1, page 287

1. **(1) searching for a place to call home (Comprehension)** This feeling is stated directly in the first two lines and in the last paragraph.
2. **(4) the gods (Comprehension)** The second sentence in the second paragraph says, "It was ordained by the deities."
3. **(5) It was simply part of their beliefs to follow the pole. (Comprehension)** The meaning of the pole is explained beginning with the fourth sentence of the second paragraph. The Chickasaws' lack of sorrow at moving because of it is explained at the end of that paragraph.
4. **(3) understands that her sense of search is part of her Chickasaw heritage (Synthesis)** The details about the author's search for a home, combined with the information that "the search for a homeland is part of the Chickasaw migration legend," helps you understand this main idea.
5. **(1) accepts that she is Chickasaw (Analysis)** You can see that the writer is saying that her Chickasaw heritage is an inescapable part of who she is.

Lesson 2: Restating and Summarizing

Practice 2, page 289

1. **(3) lack of proper paperwork (Comprehension)** As the writer discusses the problems, he states that he wants an "itemized list" and "a proper bill of sale."
2. **(3) the car to be repaired free if the cause of the problem is discovered (Comprehension)** This expectation is stated in the fourth point of the letter.
3. **(4) The service and warranty on the customer's car have been unacceptable. (Comprehension)** The letter is a detailed list of the customer's complaints. They can be summed up by saying that both the service and the warranty have not been as promised.

Lesson 3: Applying Ideas

Practice 3, page 291

1. **(1) overcoming a bad habit (Analysis)** The writer advises those trying to break free of credit card debt: "Stick with it until you're free again."
2. **(3) never use the credit cards (Application)** The final paragraph states that using credit cards with low fees and grace periods is fine once your debt is paid. But not using credit cards, especially ones that charge high interest, is the way to see improvement in your finances.
3. **(4) giving up rich foods and losing weight (Application)** Basically, the advice is that you gradually lose your debt by not adding anything to it. This is similar to helping yourself lose weight by not adding to it with rich foods.
4. **(3) Live within your means. (Synthesis)** This statement can be inferred from the advice "Don't borrow any more" and "What I'm against is buying more on your credit cards than you can pay for at the end of the month."

Lesson 4: Relating Cause and Effect

Practice 4, page 293

1. **(4) It affected nearly everyone. (Comprehension)** This answer basically summarizes the meaning of the first two sentences of the passage.
2. **(2) Many people lost the mortgages on their homes. (Comprehension)** This answer is stated in the first paragraph: "men and women who saw their mortgages foreclosed."
3. **(3) low worker incomes (Comprehension)** The second paragraph states, "but the actual cause of the collapse was an unhealthy economy. . . . Most laborers . . . could not afford to buy the automobiles . . . because their incomes were too low."
4. **(3) There was little or no effect. (Analysis)** The writer tells what Herbert Hoover did as president to curb the depression ("loans to businesses and banks"), but then

states, "his efforts proved to be too little and too late."
5. **(5) The depression left people emotionally scarred. (Synthesis)** The first paragraph states, "No one who lived through those years . . . could ever completely forget." The statement about eating mustard that is provided in the question addresses this emotional effect rather than issues related to farmers, workers, the economy, or the number of individuals affected.

Lesson 5: Comparing and Contrasting

Practice 5, page 295

1. **(4) leave some of his possessions behind (Comprehension)** This answer is found in lines 7–8.
2. **(3) They provided milk and pulled wagons. (Comprehension)** The selection states that ". . . cows . . . gave milk all the way to the sink of the Humboldt where they died, having acted as draught animals for several weeks after the oxen had perished."
3. **(1) the provisions of each group of travelers (Analysis)** Each paragraph talks about a different group and what it had to offer the wagon train. For example, "Much in contrast to these men were four batchelors . . . , who had a wagon drawn by four oxen . . . cows following behind."
4. **(2) be happy to have people who could cook and sew (Application)** The writer was interested in assessing how self-sufficient the group could be and what each group could offer the entire wagon train. For example, she writes, "but as he was a wagon maker and his companion a blacksmith by trade and both were accommodating there were always ready hands to 'pry the wheel out of mire.' " On the other hand, she speaks disapprovingly of the southern man who was "insufficiently provisioned."
5. **(2) They must cooperate and work together. (Synthesis)** Throughout the excerpt is evidence that all the travelers depend on each other for animals, food, and physical help,

such as pulling wagons out of the mud.

Lesson 6: Drawing Conclusions

Practice 6, page 297

1. **(2) It is rewarding and one of life's joys. (Analysis)** The passage states that ". . . my teacher's genius, . . . made the first years of my education so beautiful." She also delights in observing and learning from the tadpole.

2. **(5) insightful and grateful (Analysis)** The writer has insight about the connection between herself and the tadpole: "Thus I learned from life itself. At the beginning I was only a little mass of possibilities." The writer is also grateful to her teacher: "nor has she ceased trying . . . to make my life sweet and useful."

3. **(4) show Helen how addition is used in everyday life (Application)** You can apply what you learn in the diary entry: "Thus I learned from life itself. . . . She has never since let pass an opportunity to point out the beauty that is in everything. . . ." The teacher would therefore probably use everyday life situations to teach.

4. **(5) as an anecdote followed by a generalization based on the anecdote (Synthesis)** The writer tells the story of the tadpoles (an anecdote) and relates it to her attitude toward life and learning.

5. **(5) Their development is not entirely smooth. (Synthesis)** The writer describes the tadpole having difficulty after leaping out of the bowl. This is similar to the quotation about "the stony course" of a child's education.

Lesson 7: Determining Tone and Point of View

Practice 7, page 299

1. **(4) the Internet writers (Comprehension)** The writer mentions "Internet sass" and then goes on to say that "you gotta love it" because it keeps its writers "off the street and out of trouble."

2. **(2) The Internet reviews were much more interesting than the** TV show. **(Analysis)** The review states, "They [Internet writers] were taking hours and hours of primetime dross and turning it into decadent, amoral, sharp, electronic gold."

3. **(1) The show was boring. (Comprehension)** The reviewer's main opinion of the show is that it was bad and boring ("non-goings-on of the non-people in the non-house"). Someone yawning certainly supports the idea of boredom.

4. **(3) informal and hip (Synthesis)** Phrases such as "the dude" and "you gotta love it" contribute to an informal and modern, or hip, tone.

5. **(3) someone knowledgeable about the media (Analysis)** The reviewer talks knowledgeably about both television and the Internet.

Nonfiction Practice Questions, pages 300–303

1. **(5) hit a boy in the arm to get his attention (Application)** The writer talks about breaking a ruler over the head of a boy she likes; you can therefore conclude that she would hit a boy in the arm to get his attention. She responds physically and without much thought to consequences.

2. **(2) She was just pretending she didn't want to go to the principal's office. (Analysis)** The circumstances of Brer Rabbit pretending he was afraid to go into the briar patch where he was born and raised are similar to the speaker pretending to be afraid to go to the principal's office.

3. **(4) unusual (Synthesis)** From the different examples of how Frank Doleman behaved (allowing a young girl to play chess in his office and not punishing boys sent to his office), you conclude that he was an unusual principal.

4. **(1) confident (Synthesis)** The additional information you get from the new quotation and the examples of her behavior, plus the overall tone of the excerpt, suggest a confident young girl.

5. **(1) playful yet skilled (Comprehension)** The reviewer gives examples of art that is childlike and has playful qualities. He also speaks about "analysis and rigor"—elements of serious, skilled work.

6. **(3) spare and serious (Analysis)** The reviewer describes art that is "exuberant and lush, even gorgeous." He contrasts this with art that looks the way radical art is supposed to look. You can therefore conclude that he feels radical art looks the opposite, or spare (with little detail) and serious.

7. **(5) to make a new kind of art that is available to everyone (Comprehension)** Lines 19–21 state: "These works do not exclude. This expansiveness is, in fact, essential to LeWitt's radical ambition." Then in lines 32–33, LeWitt is quoted as saying, "Our idea was to re-create art, to start from square one."

8. **(5) respectful (Synthesis)** The reviewer has a positive and admiring attitude toward LeWitt's work and discusses the qualities that make the work successful.

9. **(2) examples of works followed by discussion of artist's philosophy (Synthesis)** The first paragraph cites specific works such as "Splotch" and white cubic sculptures. The second paragraph discusses why LeWitt creates the kind of art he does.

10. **(4) The cost of mandated coverage will lessen the ability of NATS to hire and supply temporary workers. (Comprehension)** This question is basically answered in lines 12–14: "the cost of mandates could weaken the ability of the temporary help industry to act as a 'jobs bridge.'"

11. **(2) Many workers are losing their jobs and need temporary jobs until they find permanent work again. (Comprehension)** The third paragraph explains this reason.

12. **(1) to raise awareness of one side of an issue (Synthesis)** The whole passage—plus knowledge of who Edward A. Lenz is—helps you see that its purpose is to explain the position of the NATS.

13. **(2) Women will not resort to wearing pants or other restrictive men's clothing. (Analysis)** This statement and the lines that follow it help you see that Stanton is saying men can wear their restrictive clothing; women want no part of it.

14. **(5) a cloth worn around the neck (Analysis)** By looking at the context clues—or words around the word *stock*—you can see that it is something worn around the neck.

15. **(2) speak up about current events (Application)** This very direct speech of Stanton's indicates her straight-to-the-point personality. She is not interested in criticism for its own sake, but rather speaks up about issues she strongly believes in.

16. **(1) Women are fighting for the right to vote. (Synthesis)** The phrase "over the horns of bigotry" helps you see that women are fighting for something. The last paragraph of the excerpt helps you see that they are fighting for the right to vote.

Fiction

Lesson 1: Understanding Plot Elements

Practice 1, page 305

1. **(3) swearing that he was telling the truth (Comprehension)** The following statement in the excerpt gives the context and meaning: "It is nevertheless God's own truth, the sacred truth. I repeat it on my soul and my salvation."

2. **(5) confronted him and then asked to be searched (Comprehension)** According to the excerpt, when the harness-maker comes in and repeats his story, the two "abused each other for an hour. At his own request, Maître Hauchecorne was searched."

3. **(4) A peasant is accused of taking a pocket-book. (Synthesis)** As you read the excerpt, you understand that a harness-maker has accused a peasant of taking a pocket-book and the mayor of the town believes the harness-maker.

4. **(4) The harness-maker is higher in social status than the peasant. (Analysis)** The harness-maker is characterized as "a man we can believe." The countryman is referred to as a "peasant."

Lesson 2: Making Inferences

Practice 2, page 307

1. **(1) had always loved her (Comprehension)** In the first paragraph, Josephine recalls her husband's face: "the face that had never looked save with love upon her." The term *save* means "except."

2. **(3) spread her arms out in welcome (Comprehension)** The first paragraph explains that although Josephine knew she would cry at the sight of her dead husband, "that bitter moment" would soon give way to years of freedom, which she welcomed.

3. **(1) she was overcome and thrilled to see her husband (Comprehension)** The doctors assumed that Josephine was so glad to learn her husband had not died in an accident that she was shocked and overjoyed to see him walk in the door.

4. **(2) She was shocked that she would not be free. (Analysis)** There is meaning beneath the surface—much of the excerpt is about Josephine looking forward to the freedom of being without her husband.

Lesson 3: Analyzing Character

Practice 3, page 309

1. **(3) He is frightened about seeing the ghost of his wife. (Comprehension)** This is Yaji's response to his wife supposedly saying that she lies in her grave thinking of him and asking, "Shall I come to meet you?"

2. **(4) untrustworthy (Analysis)** The witch is tricking Yaji. The witch has her own interests at heart when she pretends it is the wife requesting, "Give this witch plenty of money."

3. **(5) neglectful (Expanded synthesis)** Yaji treated his wife poorly when she was alive and does not tend her grave.

Lesson 4: Interpreting Theme

Practice 4, page 311

1. **(3) finds a new explanation (Comprehension)** After his father tells the boy he is dreaming, the boy states, "I decided that it was a magic horse and man that I'd seen."

2. **(2) imaginative (Analysis)** The detailed description of the dream and the boy's insistence on believing in it are signs of his imaginative powers.

3. **(1) He wants to believe his dream. (Analysis)** Most of this excerpt is taken up with the boy's description of the magic of mornings and his dream. He cannot accept the explanation that it was just a dream.

4. **(2) having enough money to pay some bills (Application)** The father is a practical man, a realist—"where were poor people like us going to find big gray stallions?" Therefore, the father is likely to prefer a practical thing like being able to pay bills.

5. **(5) Morning and youth are full of possibility. (Synthesis)** The end of the excerpt states, "I believed that magic hides in the early morning. . . . you might find something so beautiful . . . nothing else in life could ever be better."

Lesson 5: Interpreting Style and Point of View

Practice 5, page 313

1. **(3) He takes things in stride. (Comprehension)** When Coach chides Bobby for having three malts, Bobby jokes with him and then pretends to hide them. Bobby obviously doesn't take Coach seriously.

2. **(4) the actions and speech of the characters (Analysis)** The narrator reports only what can be seen or heard by any observer. As a reader, you don't learn anyone's thoughts or feelings. You must infer them from their actions and speech.

3. **(1) informal (Synthesis)** Throughout the excerpt, people

speak and act quite informally: Daphne washes up in a drinking fountain, Coach speaks with a spoon in his mouth, Bobby jokes with Coach, and so on.

4. **(5) not entirely honest about his feelings (Expanded synthesis)** In his discussion with Daphne, Coach tries to explain his wife's need for an apartment of her own. Yet he sounds a bit hostile and cuts his wife off when she speaks of her apartment. You can conclude he was hiding his real feelings from Daphne.

Fiction Practice Questions, pages 314–317

1. **(4) self-concerned (Analysis)** She "reminds Leroy of Wonder Woman" and is actively interested in bodybuilding but does not seem too concerned with him or his emotional or physical recovery from the accident.

2. **(3) won't be driving his truck for a while (Analysis)** The previous sentence indicates that Leroy probably won't be able to drive his truck again soon. A bird flying home to roost is ready to stay put for a while.

3. **(5) doesn't want to face what to do next (Analysis)** In the excerpt, the statement "He is not sure what to do next" immediately precedes the lengthy discussion of Leroy's craft work, suggesting that crafts are taking up a lot of his time and he is not working on or dealing with the issue of going back to work.

4. **(1) It took some courage. (Comprehension)** The excerpt states that "he was scared as he looked down" and "he had to stop a couple of times in the swaying rigging."

5. **(2) alone (Analysis)** The boy has come to believe that you cannot rely on anyone but yourself. He is alone on the deck and sees the bird alone atop the mast. Even though it needs help, he is not going to help it at first.

6. **(5) loneliness and sense of belonging (Synthesis)** The sailor-boy begins the excerpt believing that everyone must look after

himself. The final sentence of the excerpt states that his adventure leaves him with the belief that "the sky, the ship, the bird and himself were all one."

7. **(4) triumphant (Synthesis)** The mood of the piece rises as the boy climbs the mast to save the bird. At the top, he feels proud of what he has chosen to do and succeeded at doing and feels at one with everything.

8. **(3) start singing again (Analysis)** A clue is given in the phrase "but his parched tongue clove to the roof of his mouth, he could not utter a stave." His mouth, dry from fear, could not utter a note of the song.

9. **(1) panic (Analysis)** Reading those words both alone and in context gives you a sense of Ichabod's panic-stricken haste to get away.

10. **(4) suspenseful (Synthesis)** There is mystery and tension over whether the headless horseman will catch up with Ichabod and, if so, what he will do. The events that are happening and the way they are told create suspense.

11. **(2) too scared to think rationally (Expanded synthesis)** When you realize that Ichabod mistakenly thought he saw a head when it was in reality a pumpkin, you can see that he was letting his fear get the better of his judgment.

12. **(2) reading (Comprehension)** Reading had always been a "gentle thing" to Henry. He is not pleased with the students he has taught, and not interested in the politics and history they bring to interpretations of literature.

13. **(4) a dime a dozen (Comprehension)** Henry thinks of the younger students as "mass produced" undergraduates. In other words, they are all the same.

14. **(1) dissect literature too much and ruin the meaning (Analysis)** Henry views reading as delicate, the meaning comes "whole, unbroken." This is in contrast to the older students,

who overanalyze everything they read ("carve and quarter") and apply their own modern interpretations to it ("stuffed with their political-sexual agendas").

15. **(3) unpleasant (Synthesis)** Henry is critical and dissatisfied with college students. In describing Henry's views, the narrator takes this same unpleasant tone.

16. **(5) disapproving (Synthesis)** Henry is displeased with college students and with college offerings such as the humanities courses taught by his brother. You can conclude that in general he disapproves of the state of college education.

Poetry

Lesson 1: Understanding Rhyme and Rhythm

Practice 1, page 319

1. **(5) Because I kept my feelings secret, it would be painful to look her straight in the eye. (Comprehension)** The speaker expresses that because he hid his love, he dared not gaze, or look, at her.

2. **(4) he deeply feels his failure to speak (Analysis)** Repeating this line emphasizes the importance of what it expresses.

3. **(4) sit and think of a woman he once loved (Application)** In the poem, the speaker dwells on every detail of the past; he is likely to do the same in another situation.

4. **(5) the disruption of the rhyme pattern (Analysis)** Up to the final four lines, each pair of lines rhymed exactly. The breakdown of the rhyme pattern—*tongue/long* and *prove/love* nearly rhyme, but not exactly—is jarring to hear. The disruption therefore helps show how jarring the speaker's undeclared love was to the sounds and even silence of nature.

5. **(1) regretful (Synthesis)** Throughout the poem, the speaker is haunted by the fact that he hid his love because he regrets having done so.

Lesson 2: Interpreting Figurative Language

Practice 2, page 321

1. **(2) rain clouds approaching (Comprehension)** Lines 8–9 state, "... patch of cloud spreads, darkening / Like a water-stain on silk" The following line mentions the coming rain: "... *quickly, before the rain!*"

2. **(3) The rain caused their make-up to run. (Comprehension)** The previous two lines (11 and 12) mention "soaked by the shower" and "drenched." In keeping with this, the girls' makeup is streaked because of the rain.

3. **(2) the wind is so strong that it is blowing spray from the river into the boat (Analysis)** The figurative language helps you "see" the effects of the strong wind by painting a picture of curtains embroidered with white foamy water blown from the river.

4. **(1) quick and easy (Analysis)** A knife cuts through a melon quickly and easily, and that is how cold, wet autumn weather has cut through the warm summer day.

5. **(4) wry and observant (Synthesis)** Throughout the poem the speaker observes and comments what is going on around him with a dryly humorous, or wry, attitude.

Lesson 3: Analyzing Symbols and Images

Practice 3, page 323

1. **(5) things in the pool under the ice (Comprehension)** The speaker lists things she sees under the ice: stones, a rotting log, and fallen leaves.

2. **(4) the speaker's hope for life (Analysis)** The air bubble probably indicates that something is alive and breathing under the ice. This symbolizes her hope for the persistence of life.

3. **(2) relaxed and peaceful (Comprehension)** The poem states, "The beavers thrive somewhere /else, eating" and "they pass without / effort."

4. **(1) the smooth motion of the**

beavers **(Comprehension)** The final stanza states, "they pass without /effort, ... / moving like thoughts / in an unconflicted mind."

5. **(2) contemplative (Synthesis)** The speaker is patient and apparently stands by the beaver pool for a long time, thinking about the beavers.

6. **(3) walking along an empty beach (Application)** Because the speaker obviously gets pleasure out of walking in a quiet winter setting and closely observing nature, you can infer that she would also enjoy walking along an empty beach.

Lesson 4: Interpreting Theme

Practice 4, page 325

1. **(1) The bones used to belong to living people. (Comprehension)** The first line of the poem states that children are picking up bones of the dead.

2. **(5) the dead owner of the house (Synthesis)** Clues throughout the poem help you see who the speaker is: lines 7–10, line 12 ("our gate"), lines 14–16, and lines 19–21.

3. **(4) the wind (Analysis)** Lines 12–13 ("and the windy sky / Cries out a literate despair") compare the sound of the wind to the cries of a person.

4. **(3) a ghost (Comprehension)** Lines 19–21 explain that the children will say it seems a spirit lives in the mansion.

5. **(1) Children don't realize who and what came before them. (Synthesis)** The first two lines state that the children will never know. And later, "least will guess that with our bones / We left much more."

6. **(3) (sad) (Synthesis)** The images of the shuttered mansion and bones and the theme that the dead are left unrecognized lead to a feeling of sadness.

Poetry Practice Questions, pages 326–329

1. **(2) tombstones (Comprehension)** Lines 2–4 explain that the whiteness is the snow and the white is the tombstones.

2. **(1) don't want to disturb the snow (Comprehension)** According to the second stanza the birds "prefer to cut through the sky, / ... / so as to leave the snow alone."

3. **(3) silence (Analysis)** One comparison is based on whiteness, the other on silence: "like one silence fallen upon another / ... / nothing is like a cemetery in the snow!"

4. **(4) It shows that the speaker's belief has strengthened. (Synthesis)** After line 1 the speaker explains why he feels nothing is like a cemetery in the snow. Later he exclaims this to show that after he has considered other possible comparisons, he is even more certain of it.

5. **(5) Some beautiful things are difficult to explain. (Application)** The first two lines show the poet's inability to describe exactly the beauty he is witnessing: "Nothing is like a cemetery in the snow. / What name is there for the whiteness upon the white?"

6. **(1) quiet (Synthesis)** The cemetery and the snow are very quiet images; the poet refers to the silence of the scene.

7. **(2) An unborn fawn is alive in its dead mother. (Comprehension)** Lines 10–11 explain that the side of the dead deer is warm because her fawn was "waiting, / alive, still, never to be born."

8. **(5) It was a night I'll never forget (Application)** The speaker is more or less satisfied with the difficult decision he has made, but clearly was torn over the choices he faced.

9. **(3) think for a while, then make a determined choice (Application)** The speaker "thought hard" and then made a firm decision with no second thoughts.

10. **(5) mindful (Synthesis)** The speaker was observant of what happened, could "hear the wilderness listen," "thought hard," and made a determined decision—all qualities of a mindful person.

11. **(1) to have his son ask him for**

help with everyday things (Comprehension) The son demands a cup of juice from his mother, not from his father: "Not you, / he repeats" referring to his father.

12. **(3) Mothers want to do things for their children. (Analysis)** The speaker realizes this when he sees his wife's reaction to his son's demand and knows that his relationship with his own mother was similar (lines 10–12).

13. **(4) detached (Synthesis)** Even though the speaker is discussing his son's exclusion of him and his own mother's refocused attention away from him, the word choice and straightforwardness of the telling show he is somewhat detached and objective. He seems to be merely commenting on an observation.

14. **(2) grandmother's focus on her grandson (Synthesis)** You can understand that the grandmother has narrowed what she pays attention to—her grandson at the expense of her son—by carefully reading the last three lines.

15. **(3) toward the end of day (Comprehension)** The title of the poem gives a clue—sunset.

16. **(2) Just as we were born and live, sooner or later we will die. (Comprehension)** "Time that made us" refers to birth and life. "Will slay" refers to eventual death.

17. **(1) his lover (Analysis)** The speaker refers to "thee and me" (line 10) and "love in me and thee" (line 12).

18. **(4) If the lovers share their love, then their love will last. (Comprehension)** The poet is stating that if love is expressed, then it has more power than death.

Drama

Lesson 1: Reading Dialogue and Stage Directions

Practice 1, page 331

1. **(4) sit and wait for work (Synthesis)** Ben says, "Anyone would think you're working every day. How often do we do a

job? Once a week?" That is why Ben is reading the paper and Gus gets bored.

2. **(1) He has no outside interests. (Comprehension)** Ben says this in line 12. Even though Gus protests to Ben that he does, he pauses and then responds vaguely by saying, "I've got interests."

3. **(2) paying only partial attention to Gus (Analysis)** Ben is busy reading the paper during this conversation with Gus. This is apparent in stage directions such as "[*lowering the paper*]" and "[BEN *reads*]."

4. **(5) content (Analysis)** Ben may be frustrated by Gus, but he takes his job in stride. Ben says to Gus, "What are you complaining about?" and "I know how to occupy my time, to its best advantage. Then when a call comes, I'm ready."

Lesson 2: Understanding Dramatic Action

Practice 2, page 333

1. **(4) It happened during a fight. (Comprehension)** Tim Casey reports that "Jack knocked Mrs. Fallon's basket into the road, and Bartley made an attack on him with a hayfork" even though that is not exactly what Mrs. Tarpey told him.

2. **(3) It gets the others excited enough to run and tell more people. (Analysis)** Mrs. Tully's comment only adds to the excitement of the people who are listening. James Ryan goes running to tell others.

3. **(4) tell people that Jack Smith is dead (Application)** If Mrs. Tarpey believes Jack Smith's wife was laying out a sheet for the dead, you can conclude that she would think Jack Smith had been killed by Bartley Fallon. Because Mrs. Tarpey ran to tell James Ryan of the fight, you can also apply that knowledge to conclude she would run to tell others that Jack Smith was dead.

Lesson 3: Analyzing Characters

Practice 3, page 335

1. **(3) is impractical and passionate

(Analysis)** Sheila asks Ayamonn to be serious. She says, "We must look well ahead on the road to the future. You lead your life through too many paths instead of treading the one way of making it possible for us to live together."

2. **(4) is chaotic and interesting (Comprehension)** Sheila feels there is "one way of making it possible for us to live together." In response, Ayamonn states that life is "a wide branching flame, grand and good to see" meaning there is more than one path.

3. **(1) They have different ideas about love and life. (Synthesis)** Throughout the dialogue the differences in Sheila's views ("serious," "one way") and Ayamonn's views ("not one thing but many things," "a wide branching flame") add up to this generalization.

4. **(5) poet (Application)** Ayamonn is passionate and obviously loves words. He even speaks poetically to Sheila.

5. **(2) She is fighting her true feelings for Ayamonn because of her mother's feelings. (Expanded synthesis)** Her mother's feelings against Ayamonn help explain why Sheila gets upset when Ayamonn refuses to be practical. She hopes that it will be "possible for us to live together," but her mother has made her question whether Ayamonn is right for her. She becomes upset with him.

Lesson 4: Drawing Conclusions

Practice 4, page 337

1. **(1) John Wright (Comprehension)** Although Mrs. Peters insists they don't know who killed the bird, Mrs. Hale states, "Wright wouldn't like the bird—a thing that sang. She used to sing. He killed that, too. . . . I knew John Wright."

2. **(2) someone who smothers all the joy in a person (Analysis)** Based on Mrs. Hale's comments "No. Wright wouldn't like the bird—a thing that sang. She used to sing. He killed that, too." (lines 37–39), you can conclude that

John Wright was capable of discouraging a person from singing, something that would have made that person happy.

3. **(5) They understand how someone could be driven to murder. (Synthesis)** The two women seem nervous and are evasive about the bird's death. But they are not protecting themselves. You can tell they suspect who might have murdered Wright and what might have driven the person to murder. References to "she," someone who liked to sing but stopped because of Wright ("He killed that, too"), someone who lived in loneliness and had only the bird as pleasure until the bird was killed indicate that the women suspect why this tragedy occurred.

Drama Practice Questions, pages 338–340

1. **(3) She will be forgiven for her misdeeds. (Comprehension)** Sadie says, "You don't understand. I've got to go back and be punished for what I've been," and "I've got to serve my time—then God will forgive me. It's the sacrifice I've got to offer up for the life I've led."

2. **(2) O'Hara thinks Sadie is making a mistake. (Analysis)** O'Hara wants Sadie to get dressed quickly so he can take her away and keep her from going to the penitentiary.

3. **(4) concern for Sadie's welfare (Synthesis)** You can draw this conclusion from O'Hara's lines and reactions throughout the scene. He cares about Sadie and doesn't want her to go to the penitentiary. He replies "brokenly" when she refuses his help.

4. **(1) argue with him (Application)** The fact that O'Hara tries forcibly to make Sadie go with him can be applied to what his reaction would be to the minister. He would most likely be angry enough to argue with Reverend Davidson to save Sadie.

5. **(5) tension (Analysis)** Stage directions indicate tense, wild, angry emotions, such as "She frees herself ferociously; turns on him angrily."

6. **(1) She wasn't perfect, but she worked hard for her children. (Analysis)** Bessie says all of the following: "I worked too hard all my years." "Or was Bessie Berger's children always the cleanest on the block?!" and "Here I'm not only the mother, but also the father. The first two years I worked in a stocking factory for six dollars while Myron Berger went to law school. If I didn't worry about the family who would?"

7. **(3) Life can be better. (Application)** Ralph exclaims that the life his mother had to lead isn't fair. He sees other possibilities and wants to change things: "Gimme the earth in two hands. I'm strong."

8. **(2) An old alarm clock can keep going, but not her aging body. (Analysis)** Bessie is growing older; she brought up her son and did the best she could. Soon her work will be done, and she doesn't have the energy to try to change the world: "A fire burned in *my* heart too, but now it's too late. I'm no spring chicken."

9. **(3) to get the work carving doors (Comprehension)** Fidel wants to learn about this job possibility by talking to Celestina. He knows he has to flatter her to get her to talk with him. Later he tells Berta, "Do you not realize what it means? They will need someone to carve the new doors."

10. **(4) She distrusts Fidel and fears he will hurt her. (Analysis)** Fidel explains he will carve the doors to buy a house for Berta. Fidel asks Berta, "Do you doubt me?" Berta replies that she does doubt him—just as a tree can't trust lightning not to strike it down.

11. **(5) dishonest (Expanded synthesis)** Berta is in love with Fidel but she is not being honest with him about her feelings in this scene.

MATH ANSWERS AND EXPLANATIONS

Math Basics

Lesson 1: Whole Number Review

Practice 1, page 347

1. 4
2. 8
3. 9
4. 1
5. 6
6. 7
7. 3
8. 500
9. 80
10. 1100
11. 12,000
12. 2000
13. 100
14. 100
15. 341
16. 1145

17. 125,391
18. 18, 23, 39, 45
19. 89, 91, 109, 111
20. 909, 932, 1087, 1139
21. 1420, 1425, 1429, 1432
22. 11,098, 12,071, 12,131
23. 15,298, 15,309, 15,356
24. **(4) 50, 48, 45, 40** Arrange weights from heaviest to lightest.
25. **(3) 1,500,000** The digit in the ten thousands column is less than 5, so round down.

Lesson 2: Operations Review

Practice 2.1, page 349

1. 77
2. 100
3. 52
4. 36
5. 190
6. 4078
7. 43
8. 2117
9. 65
10. 114
11. 180
12. 293
13. 483
14. 456
15. 2419
16. 900
17. 11,308
18. 15,185
19. 131,197
20. 30,899

21. **(3) 88**
    $24 + 8 + 56 = 88$
22. **(3) $13**
    $20 - $7 = $13

Practice 2.2, page 351

1. 484
2. 1000
3. 2736
4. 13
5. 105
6. 21

7. 1350
8. 2625
9. 3376
10. 28
11. 15
12. 6
13. 250

14. 44 r3
15. 300
16. 200 r4
17. 150
18. 67,068
19. 538
20. 384

21. 12,011 r8
22. **(4) 96**
    $16 \times 6 = 96$
23. **(4) $75**
    $15 \times \$5 = \$75$
24. **(1) 6**
    $12 \div 2 = 6$

Lesson 3: Distance and Cost Formulas

Practice 3, page 353

1. rate; $d/t = r$
2. distance; $d = rt$
3. time; $d/r = t$
4. price per unit; $c/n = r$
5. cost; $c = nr$
6. number of units; $c/r = n$
7. **$48** $c = nr$
   $4 \times \$12 = \$48$
8. **$36** $c = nr$
   $12 \times \$3 = \$36$
9. **$80** $c/n = r$
   $\$320/4 = \$80$
10. **5** $c/r = n$
    $\$25/\$5 = 5$
11. **$2** $c/n = r$
    $\$20/10 = \$2$
12. **180 miles** $d = rt$
    $60 \times 3 = 180$
13. **200 miles** $d = rt$
    $50 \times 4 = 200$
14. **1 hour** $d/r = t$
    $25/25 = 1$
15. **90 miles per hour** $d/t = r$
    $270/3 = 90$
16. **3 hours** $d/r = t$
    $75/25 = 3$
17. **(1) 32** $c/r = n$
    $\$640/\$20 = 32$
18. **(5) 55** $d/t = r$
    $275/5 = 55$

Lesson 4: Calculators on the GED

Practice 4.1, page 355

1. 153
2. 1187
3. 784
4. 24
5. 27,084
6. 14,442
7. 11,704

8. 54
9. 1580
10. **(2) 26,179**
    $42,920 - 16,741 = 26,179$
11. **(5) $19,900**
    $\$995 \times 20 = \$19,900$

Practice 4.2, page 357

1. 25
2. 18
3. 35
4. 136
5. 125
6. 5%
7. 2
8. 135
9. 5%
10. **(4) $336**
    $\$1680 \times 20\% = \$336$
11. **(1) 5%**
    $\$48 \div \$960 = 5\%$

Lesson 5: Filling in the Standard Grid

Practice 5, page 359

1. 1740
2. 10
3. 994
4. 15
5. 2468
6. 21

Lesson 6: Problem Solving: Estimation

Practice 6, page 361

1. 300 and 260
2. 5000 and 4700
3. 10,000 and 12,000
4. 300 and 330
5. 6000 and 6200
6. 20,000 and 23,000

Your answers may vary.
7. $36 \div 12$
8. $48 \div 8$
9. $45 \div 15$
10. $100 \div 20$
11. $360 \div 4$
12. $450 \div 9$ or $480 \div 8$

13. **(3) 90** $7 + 65 + 19$ rounds to
    $5 + 65 + 20 = 90$ minutes
14. **(5) 1200** 21×55 rounds to $20 \times 60 = 1200$ pounds
15. **(1) 8** 78 rounds to $80 \div 10 = 8$ ounces
16. **(4) 30** $324 \div 11$ rounds to $330 \div 11 = 30$ miles per gallon

Lesson 7: Problem Solving: Set-Up Problems

Practice 7, page 363

1. 46
2. 13
3. 39
4. 10
5. 15
6. 70
7. 11
8. 30
9. 4
10. 2
11. 6
12. 2

13. **(3)** $6 \times 8 \times 7$
14. **(5)** $\$3 \times 2 \times 5$
15. **(4)** $\frac{(\$25 + \$15)}{5}$
16. **(1)** $\frac{\$78 - \$10}{7}$
17. **(5)** $5(\$4 + \$1)$
18. **(1)** $12 \times \$5$

Math Basics Practice Questions, pages 364–367

Part I

1. **(5) 96** Multiply. 12 servings $\times$ 8 ounces = 96
2. **(3) $2092** Add to find the total. $\$839 + \$527 + \$726 = \$2092$
3. **(1) 4** Divide the length of the sample board by the length of the brace you want. 12-foot board ÷ 2-feet per brace = 6 braces per board. Since you can get 6 braces from each board, divide the total number of braces you want by 6: $24 \div 6 = 4$ boards
4. **(2) 21** Use the square root key on your calculator or multiply each answer option by itself to find 441. $\sqrt{441} = 21$
5. **(2) 30,589** Subtract to find the difference in mileage. $70,040 - 39,451 = 30,589$
6. **(3) $656** You can use your calculator. Multiply. $\$3280 \times 20\% = \$656$
7. **(1) $5625** Multiply. $\$125 \times 45 = \$5625$
8. **(3)** $7\left(\frac{180}{3}\right)$ Find the rate per hour: divide distance by time: $\frac{180}{3}$. Then multiply by the number of hours Lydia wants to travel: $7\left(\frac{180}{3}\right)$.
9. **(4)** $\frac{480}{60}$ Use the distance formula to find the time. $d = rt$, so $t = \frac{d}{r}$ or $\frac{480}{60}$
10. **(2) 96** Use the cost formula. $c = nr$ or $n = \frac{c}{r}$. Divide the total cost by price per item to find the number of items. $\$1440 \div 15 = \$96$

11. **(1) $200** Multiply. $25 × 8 = $200

12. **(5) $53** Multiply to find how many dollars each for $5 bills and $1 bills. 7 × $5 = $35 and 18 × $1 = $18 Then add the two amounts. $35 + $18 = $53

13. **(5) Not enough information is given.** Even though the manufacturer recommends changing the oil and filter every 3,500 miles, there is no way of knowing how closely April follows the recommendations.

14. **(1) 134** Divide. 536 ÷ 4 = 134

15. **198** Subtract to find the difference. 636 − 438 = 198

16. **1072** Multiply the payment amount by the number of payments left. $268 × 4 = $1072

Part II

17. **(3) 51, 48, 44, 40** Compare the weights and order them from heaviest to lightest.

18. **(4) 2,350,000** Since the digit to the right of the ten thousands place is less than 5, the digit in the ten thousands place remains the same.

19. **(1) 83** Add. 42 + 18 + 23 = 83

20. **(1) $6** Subtract. $20 − $14 = $6

21. **(2) 60** Round the amounts and add.
8 + 33 + 18 ≈ 10 + 30 + 20 = 60

22. **(4) $\frac{250}{4}$** Divide distance by time to find the rate of speed. 250 ÷ 4 can also be written as $\frac{250}{4}$.

23. **(3) 18** Divide. 144 ÷ 8 = 18

24. **(2) 30** Find a compatible pair and divide. Round 312 to 270 and divide. 270 ÷ 9 = 30 Or round 312 to 300 and 9 to 10. 300 ÷ 10 = 30

25. **(4) 1200** Find a compatible pair and multiply. 33 rounds to 30, and 41 pounds rounds to 40. 30 × 40 = 1200

26. **(3) $9** Find the total and divide by 4. $21 + $15 = $36 Divide. $36 ÷ 4 = $9

27. **(4) $\frac{\$84 - \$8}{9}$** Subtract the amount David paid from the total. Then divide the remaining amount by the number of people in the group.

28. **(5) 260** Multiply rate by time. 65 × 4 = 260

29. **(2) $18** Add the cost of a 1-topping pizza and $2 for each of the 2 additional toppings. $14 + $2 + $2 = $18

30. **(4) 14** Multiply by 2 for each dollar. 2 × 7 = 14

31. **24** Divide the total amount by the amount paid per month. $1800 ÷ $75 = 24

32. **14** Divide the maximum capacity by the number of pages per document. 630 ÷ 45 = 14

Decimals and Fractions

Lesson 1: Decimal Basics

Practice 1, page 369

1. 3.8
2. 6
3. 0.43
4. 0.667
5. 8.1
6. 2.714
7. 0.45
8. 0.08
9. 4.68
10. 1.85
11. 1.029
12. 0.14

13. 5.08, 5.6, 5.8, 5.802
14. 0.1136, 0.115, 0.12, 0.2
15. 4.52, 4.667, 4.8, 14.005
16. 0.8, 0.8023, 0.803, 0.823
17. **(4) 0.6 g, 0.572 g, 0.0785 g** Since none of the weights has a whole number part, compare the tenths places, then the hundredths places.
18. **(5) 1.38** Only options (2) and (5) are rounded to the hundredths place. Since the number in the thousandths place is less than 5, round down.

Lesson 2: Decimal Operations

Practice 2.1, page 371

1. 7.996
2. 10.508
3. 12.26
4. 5.85
5. 7.426
6. 2.11
7. 18.094
8. 5.117
9. 21.32
10. 0.895
11. 3.84
12. 2.35
13. 5.506
14. 21.16
15. 0.645
16. 2.426
17. 0.15
18. 4.88
19. 11.8
20. 14.016
21. 4.522
22. 2.36
23. 17.88
24. 17.225

25. **(2) 22.25** Add the times: 7.2 + 6.8 + 8.25 = 22.25 minutes. You do not need to use the 3-mile distance to solve the problem.

26. **(4) 4.25** Add to find Claudia's total hours for the week: 8.5 + 9.25 + 8.75 + 10 + 7.75 = 44.25. Then subtract 40 to find the number of overtime hours: 44.25 − 40 = 4.25 hours.

27. **(1) 1.8** Add the lengths cut from the pipe: 2.8 + 1.4 = 4.2, and subtract from 6: 6 − 4.2 = 1.8 meters.

28. **(4) $55.26** Add the amounts. $16.98 + $31.78 + $6.50 = $55.26

Practice 2.2, page 373

1. 2.65
2. 12.8
3. 0.496
4. 0.52
5. 3.6
6. 4.09
7. 8.75
8. 3.375
9. 9.6681
10. 24
11. 14.2
12. 15,800
13. 34.1
14. 2.36
15. 0.656
16. 2.64
17. 1.65
18. 4.275
19. 3.696
20. 1.002
21. 0.0072

22. **(5) 15.16** Multiply 3.79 liters by 4. 3.79 × 4 = 15.16 liters
23. **(2) $9.23** Multiply $0.45 × 20.5: $0.45 × 20.5 = $9.225, which rounds to $9.23.
24. **(3) 92.9** Divide to find the average daily miles: 278.7 ÷ 3 = 92.9 miles.
25. **(4) $0.26** Read the table. There are 19 servings in a box of Toasted Oats. Divide: $4.94 ÷ 19 = $0.26.
26. **(2) 50.0** Find the weight in the table and multiply: 12.5 × 4 = 50 ounces.

Lesson 3: Fraction Basics

Practice 3, page 375

1. $\frac{3}{5}$
2. $\frac{2}{4}$, or $\frac{1}{2}$
3. $\frac{2}{3}$
4. $\frac{7}{3}$, or $2\frac{1}{3}$
5. $\frac{7}{2}$, or $3\frac{1}{2}$
6. $\frac{15}{4}$, or $3\frac{3}{4}$
7. $5\frac{2}{3}$
8. $\frac{18}{5}$
9. 4
10. $\frac{47}{9}$
11. $4\frac{3}{4}$
12. $\frac{29}{12}$
13. $4\frac{7}{9}$
14. $\frac{7}{4}$
15. $4\frac{5}{7}$
16. $\frac{57}{10}$
17. $\frac{12}{16}$
18. $\frac{7}{21}$
19. $\frac{48}{60}$
20. $\frac{15}{40}$
21. $\frac{24}{100}$
22. $\frac{3}{4}$
23. $\frac{1}{6}$
24. $\frac{3}{5}$
25. $\frac{13}{15}$
26. $\frac{2}{3}$

27. (1) $\frac{3}{4}$ Of those surveyed, $\frac{18}{24}$ went to at least one movie. Reduce the fraction to lowest terms. $\frac{18 \div 6}{24 \div 6} = \frac{3}{4}$

28. (3) $\frac{40}{100}$ Raise $\frac{2}{5}$ to an equivalent fraction with a denominator of 100 by multiplying both numbers by 20. $\frac{2 \times 20}{5 \times 20} = \frac{40}{100}$

Lesson 4: Fraction Operations

Practice 4.1, page 377

1. $\frac{1}{2}$
2. 1
3. $\frac{1}{3}$
4. $\frac{1}{6}$
5. $\frac{11}{12}$
6. $1\frac{1}{8}$
7. $\frac{3}{10}$
8. $\frac{5}{18}$
9. $3\frac{13}{15}$
10. $1\frac{3}{4}$
11. $8\frac{1}{2}$
12. $11\frac{5}{8}$
13. $21\frac{7}{10}$
14. $7\frac{13}{18}$
15. $12\frac{17}{30}$
16. $2\frac{5}{8}$
17. $42\frac{5}{12}$
18. $22\frac{11}{20}$
19. $5\frac{1}{18}$
20. $11\frac{1}{8}$
21. $3\frac{23}{28}$
22. $1\frac{7}{24}$
23. $2\frac{3}{7}$
24. $8\frac{8}{9}$
25. $\frac{32}{35}$

26. (3) $1\frac{3}{16}$ Add to find the total.
$\frac{5}{16} + \frac{7}{8} = \frac{5}{16} + \frac{14}{16} = \frac{19}{16} = 1\frac{3}{16}$ inches

27. (3) $1\frac{5}{8}$ Subtract to find the difference in the lengths.
$2\frac{7}{8} - 1\frac{1}{4} = 2\frac{7}{8} - 1\frac{2}{8} = 1\frac{5}{8}$ inches

28. (1) $14\frac{3}{8}$ Subtract the amount sold from the amount on the bolt:
$23\frac{1}{4} - 8\frac{7}{8} = 23\frac{2}{8} - 8\frac{7}{8}$
$= 22\frac{10}{8} - 8\frac{7}{8} = 14\frac{3}{8}$ yards.

29. (4) $2\frac{11}{12}$ Add the amounts.
$1\frac{2}{3} + \frac{1}{2} + \frac{3}{4} = 1\frac{8}{12} + \frac{6}{12} + \frac{9}{12} =$
$1\frac{23}{12} = 2\frac{11}{12}$ cups

Practice 4.2, page 379

1. $\frac{1}{6}$
2. $\frac{11}{12}$
3. 14
4. $18\frac{3}{4}$
5. $\frac{7}{8}$
6. $2\frac{5}{32}$
7. $7\frac{14}{15}$
8. $41\frac{1}{4}$
9. $2\frac{1}{32}$
10. 14
11. $1\frac{4}{5}$
12. 48
13. $2\frac{2}{5}$
14. $2\frac{1}{4}$
15. 27
16. 8
17. $9\frac{1}{2}$
18. $\frac{3}{4}$

19. (3) 75 Find $\frac{3}{16}$ of 400. Multiply.
$400 \times \frac{3}{16} = \frac{\overset{25}{\cancel{400}}}{1} \times \frac{3}{\cancel{16}} = \frac{75}{1} = 75$

20. (2) 7 Divide.
$20 \div 2\frac{3}{4} = \frac{20}{1} \div \frac{11}{4} =$
$\frac{20}{1} \times \frac{4}{11} = \frac{80}{11} = 7\frac{3}{11}$
Ignore the remainder since the problem asks how many shirts can be completed.

21. (3) 33 You need to find how many $\frac{2}{3}$ hours there are in 22 hours. Divide.
$22 \div \frac{2}{3} = \frac{22}{1} \div \frac{2}{3} =$
$\frac{22}{1} \times \frac{3}{2} = \frac{\overset{11}{\cancel{22}}}{1} \times \frac{3}{\cancel{2}} = \frac{33}{1} = 33$

22. (4) $37\frac{7}{8}$ Multiply $12\frac{5}{8}$ inches by 3, the number of panels.
$12\frac{5}{8} \times 3 = \frac{101}{8} \times \frac{3}{1} = \frac{303}{8} = 37\frac{7}{8}$

Lesson 5: Solving Problems Using a Calculator

Practice 5, page 381

1. 7.379
2. $2\frac{1}{4}$
3. **$380.10** The calculator display shows [380.1]. To write the cents with two decimal places, add a zero.
4. 42
5. **$84.44** Multiply. $\$95 \times \frac{8}{9} =$ $84.444 = \$84.44$.
6. **$79.74** Divide. $\$956.88 \div 12 =$ 79.74
7. **15 pieces** Divide. $20\frac{5}{8} \div 1\frac{3}{8} =$ 15 pieces
8. **$1,475** Multiply. $\$118,000 \times$ $0.0125 = \$1,475$
9. **$4\frac{1}{4}$ cups** Add. $1\frac{1}{2} + 2\frac{3}{4} = 4\frac{1}{4}$ cups
10. (4) **$194.97** Multiply the cost of a twin quilt by 2 and add the cost of a king-sized quilt. ($\$49.99 \times$ 2) + $94.99 = $194.97
11. (3) **$6.67** Multiply the weight of a queen-sized quilt by $1.20: $5.56 \times \$1.20 = \$6.672$, which rounds to $6.67
12. (5) $\frac{5}{12}$ Think of her take-home pay as 1 whole. Subtract the fractions from the whole.
$1 - \frac{1}{3} - \frac{1}{4} = \frac{5}{12}$ Another approach is to add the fractions: $\frac{1}{3} + \frac{1}{4} = \frac{7}{12}$, and subtract this total from 1.
$1 - \frac{7}{12} = \frac{5}{12}$
13. (3) **24** You need to find $\frac{3}{8}$ of 64. Multiply. $64 \times \frac{3}{8} = 24$ acres

Lesson 6: Filling in the Answer Grid

Practice 6, page 383

Your answers may begin in a different column. You may align your answer on the left or the right, or you may center your answer.

1. **35.6** Add the amounts from the problem.
2. $\frac{2}{3}$ $\frac{\$100}{\$150}$ reduces to $\frac{2}{3}$.

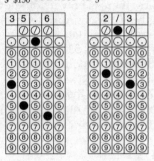

3. $\frac{7}{4}$ **or 1.75** Subtract $7\frac{3}{4}$ from $9\frac{1}{2}$. The difference is $1\frac{3}{4}$, which equals $\frac{7}{4}$. Remember, you must enter mixed numbers as either improper fractions or decimals.
4. **38** Divide 100 by 2.6. You get 38.4615, but you would be able to <u>fill</u> only 38 bottles.

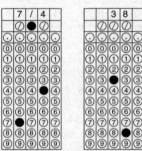

5. $\frac{1}{6}$ The fraction $\frac{3}{18}$ reduces to $\frac{1}{6}$.
6. **25** Divide 12.5 by 0.5.

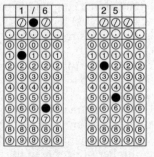

Lesson 7: Problem Solving Fraction and Decimal Equivalencies

Practice 7: page 385

1. **(2) $20.00** Instead of multiplying $80 by 0.25, find $\frac{1}{4}$ of 80.
2. **(4) 480 × 0.3** Find $\frac{3}{10}$ of 480. In this case, "of" indicates multiplication, and the decimal equivalent of $\frac{3}{10}$ is 0.3.
3. **(2) $4\frac{2}{3}$** The decimal part of the calculator display equals the fraction $\frac{2}{3}$.
4. **(4) $18.00** Multiply 12 by 1.5. The decimal 1.5 = $1\frac{1}{2}$. You may be able to find $1\frac{1}{2}$ of $12 mentally: $12 + $6 (half of $12) = $18.
5. **(2) $\frac{3}{4}$** Subtract. $1.875 - 1.125 = 0.75$, which equals $\frac{3}{4}$ inch.
6. **(3) 0.375** Instead of dividing 3 by 8, think: $3 ÷ 8$ means $\frac{3}{8}$, which equals 0.375.

Decimals and Fractions Practice Questions, pages 386–389

Part I

1. **(4) $15\frac{3}{4}$** Subtract.
$$20\frac{1}{2} - 4\frac{3}{4} = 20\frac{2}{4} - 4\frac{3}{4} =$$
$$19\frac{6}{4} - 4\frac{3}{4} = 15\frac{3}{4}$$
2. **(2) $0.25** Divide the cost by the number of servings. $4.69 ÷ 19 ≈ 0.246$, which rounds to $0.25.
3. **(3) $1386.20** To find the amount the 12-month plan will cost a customer, multiply $98.85 by 12 and add $200. ($98.85 × 12) + $200 = $1386.20
4. **(3) $15.42** Multiply using your calculator. Use 10.5 for $10\frac{1}{2}$. $1.469 × 10.5 = $15.4245, which rounds to $15.42.
5. **(2) 2.85** Since the answer choices are decimals, use your calculator. Use decimals instead of fractions: $1\frac{1}{2} = 1.5$, $4\frac{3}{4} = 4.75$, and $2\frac{3}{10} = 2.3$. To find the average, add the three weights and divide the total by 3.
$$\frac{1.5 + 4.75 + 2.3}{3} = \frac{8.55}{3} = 2.85$$
6. **(4) $32\frac{1}{4}$** Divide. $258 ÷ $8 = 32.25, which equals $32\frac{1}{4}$
7. **(3) 57** Subtract $6\frac{1}{4}$ from $20\frac{1}{2}$ and divide the difference by $\frac{1}{4}$. To do the work quickly, use the fraction keys on your calculator or

change the fractions to decimals.
$$20\frac{1}{2} - 6\frac{1}{4} = 14\frac{1}{4}$$
$$14\frac{1}{4} ÷ \frac{1}{4} = 57$$
8. **(4) $90.00** Brand B costs $0.09 more than Brand A, so the school will save $0.09 on each marker. Multiply the savings by 1000. $0.09 × 1000 = $90.00
9. **(2) $3\frac{1}{2}$** Add the times for the appointments.
$$\frac{3}{4} + \frac{3}{4} + 1\frac{1}{4} + \frac{3}{4} = 1\frac{10}{4} =$$
$$3\frac{2}{4} = 3\frac{1}{2}$$
10. **(4) 10** Divide $3\frac{1}{2}$ hours by the amount of time needed for a routine physical.
$$3\frac{1}{2} ÷ \frac{1}{3} = \frac{7}{2} ÷ \frac{1}{3} =$$
$$\frac{7}{2} × \frac{3}{1} = \frac{21}{2} = 10\frac{1}{2}$$
Jennifer can <u>complete</u> 10 physicals. Ignore the fraction remainder.
11. **(5) $\frac{11}{12}$** Write the fraction and reduce it to lowest terms. You can save time by using the fraction key on your calculator, which automatically reduces a fraction to lowest terms.
Enter 5500 $\boxed{a^{b}/_{c}}$ 6000 $\boxed{=}$ $\boxed{11 \quad 12}$ which represents $\frac{11}{12}$.
12. **(3) $7.25** The first hour costs $3.50, and there are $1\frac{1}{2}$ hours left. There are 3 half hours in $1\frac{1}{2}$ hours, so you will pay $3.50 + (3 × $1.25) = $7.25.
13. **$\frac{2}{3}$** Write a fraction and reduce.
$$\frac{56}{84} = \frac{2}{3}$$

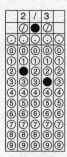

14. **0.84** Subtract to compare.
$3.97 - 3.13 = 0.84$

Part II

15. **(2) $\frac{3}{10}$** Subtract. $250 - 175 = 75$ Thus, 75 out of 250, or $\frac{75}{250}$ have not been loaded. Reduce.
$$\frac{75 ÷ 25}{250 ÷ 25} = \frac{3}{10}$$
16. **(5) (12 × $8.90) + (15 × $7.50)** Multiply the wage for each job by the hours for that job; then add the results.
17. **(1) 285** To find $\frac{3}{4}$ of 380, multiply. Change $\frac{3}{4}$ to .75. $380 × .75 = 285$
18. **(4) $\frac{5}{6}$** To find half of $1\frac{2}{3}$, either multiply by $\frac{1}{2}$ or divide by 2. Both results are the same.
$$1\frac{2}{3} × \frac{1}{2} = \frac{5}{3} × \frac{1}{2} = \frac{5}{6}$$
19. **(5) core box, classic, bevel, cutter** You could change the fractions to decimals to solve the problem, but the quickest method is to rewrite the fractions with a common denominator of 32:
cutter: $\frac{9}{16} = \frac{18}{32}$
core box: $\frac{5}{32}$
classic: $\frac{3}{8} = \frac{12}{32}$
bevel: $\frac{1}{2} = \frac{16}{32}$
Then arrange the like fractions from least to greatest by their numerators.
20. **(2) 50 − (2 × 12.75)** You need to subtract 12.75 from 50 twice. Only option (2) multiplies 12.75 by 2 and then subtracts the result from 50.
21. **(4) 8** Divide. $60 ÷ 7.5 = 8$ days
22. **(4) 150** You need to find $\frac{5}{8}$ of 240. Multiply.
$$240 × \frac{5}{8} = \frac{\overset{30}{240}}{1} × \frac{5}{\underset{1}{8}} = \frac{150}{1} = 150$$
23. **(2) $\frac{1}{2}$** Multiply.
$$\frac{2}{3} × \frac{3}{4} = \frac{\overset{1}{2}}{\underset{1}{3}} × \frac{\overset{1}{3}}{\underset{2}{4}} = \frac{1}{2}$$
24. **(2) 56** Multiply.
$$140 × \frac{2}{5} = \frac{\overset{28}{140}}{1} × \frac{2}{\underset{1}{5}} = \frac{56}{1} = 56$$
25. **(4) 17.9** Maya travels five segments of the route. Add to find the total distance.
$2.4 + 4.3 + 3.6 + 3.6 + 4.0 = 17.9$
26. **(5) 5** Add to find the total amount to be cut off.
$$3\frac{3}{4} + 3\frac{3}{4} = 6\frac{6}{4} = 7\frac{1}{2}$$
Subtract from $12\frac{1}{2}$.
$$12\frac{1}{2} - 7\frac{1}{2} = 5$$
27. **(2) $535.60** Multiply $26.38 by 20 and add $8 to the result.

$26.38 \times 20 = \$527.60$
$\$527.60 + \$8.00 = \$535.60$

28. 80 Divide. $60 \div 0.75 = 80$

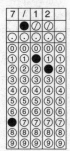

29. $\frac{7}{12}$ Add the fractions and subtract from 1.
$\frac{1}{6} + \frac{1}{4} = \frac{2}{12} + \frac{3}{12} = \frac{5}{12}$
$1 - \frac{5}{12} = \frac{12}{12} - \frac{5}{12} = \frac{7}{12}$

Ratio, Proportion, and Percent

Lesson 1: Using Ratio and Proportion to Solve Problems

Practice 1.1, page 391

1. $\frac{24}{6} = \frac{4}{1}$
2. $\frac{\$250}{\$1500} = \frac{1}{6}$
3. $\frac{180}{15} = \frac{12}{1}$
4. $\frac{12}{30} = \frac{2}{5}$ Add $12 + 18 = 30$ to find the total workers.
5. $\frac{336}{14} = \frac{24}{1}$
6. $\frac{\$1500}{\$2400} = \frac{5}{8}$
7. $\frac{20}{12} = \frac{5}{3}$ Subtract $32 - 20 = 12$ to find the free throws missed.
8. $\frac{14}{24} = \frac{7}{12}$ Add $10 + 14 = 24$ to find the total students.
9. $\frac{1440}{6} = \frac{240}{1}$
10. **(2) 9:11** Write the ratio in fraction form and reduce. $\frac{180}{220} = \frac{9}{11}$
11. **(3) 3 to 10** $\frac{180}{600} = \frac{3}{10}$
12. **(2)** $\frac{1}{3}$ Subtract to find the voters who have made a decision.
$600 - 150 = 450$ Write the ratio and reduce. $\frac{150}{450} = \frac{1}{3}$

13. **(3) 1 to 2** Subtract to find the amount owed. $\$1200 - \$400 = \$800$ Write the ratio and reduce. 400 to 800 = 1 to 2
14. **(5) 8:3** Subtract to find the number of losses. $77 - 56 = 21$ Write the ratio and reduce. $\frac{56}{21} = \frac{8}{3}$

Practice 1.2, page 393

1. 12
2. 45
3. 2.5 or $2\frac{1}{2}$
4. 60
5. $3.71
6. 96
7. 2.1 or $2\frac{1}{10}$
8. 72
9. 12.5 or $12\frac{1}{2}$
10. $8.94
11. 1.25 or $1\frac{1}{4}$
12. 37.5 or $37\frac{1}{2}$
13. 18
14. 32
15. $45.50
16. 28
17. **(2) $1.23**
$\frac{4}{\$0.98} = \frac{5}{x}$
$\$0.98 \times 5 \div 4 = \$1.225$
which rounds to $1.23
18. **(4) 96**
$\frac{5}{8} = \frac{60}{x}$
$8 \times 60 \div 5 = 96$
19. **(2) 23**
$\frac{414}{18} = \frac{x}{1}$
$414 \times 1 \div 18 = 23$
20. **(3) 345**
$\frac{2}{150} = \frac{4.6}{x}$
$150 \times 4.6 \div 2 = 345$
21. **(2)** $6\frac{2}{3}$
Write the proportions using fractions. The process is the same.
$\frac{2\frac{1}{2}}{1\frac{1}{2}} = \frac{x}{4}$
$2\frac{1}{2} \times 4 \div 1\frac{1}{2} = 6\frac{2}{3}$
22. **(1) $155 \times 7 \div 2.5$** Set up the proportion and think about the order of operations you would need to solve for x.
$\frac{155}{2.5} = \frac{x}{7}$
$155 \times 7 \div 2.5 = x$

Lesson 2: Understanding Percents

Practice 2, page 395

1. base = $1000
   part = $200
   rate = 20%

2. base = 80
   part = 72
   rate = 90%
3. base = $13,700
   part = $2,740
   rate = 20%
4. base = $2000
   part = $500
   rate = 25%
5. base = 40
   part = 60
   rate = 150%
   60 is 150% *of* 40. The word *of* indicates that 40 is the base.
6. base = $38
   part = $3.23
   rate = 8.5%
7. base = $900
   part = $135
   rate = 15%
8. base = $10.70
   part = $1.07
   rate = 10%
9. base = 800
   part = 200
   rate = 25%
10. base = 12,500
    part = 5,000
    rate = 40%
11. **(1)** $\frac{9 \times 100}{12}$ Add the wins and losses to find the total games played. Then write the proportion. $\frac{9}{12} = \frac{x}{100}$ To solve the proportion, you need to find the expression that multiplies 9 and 100 and divides by 12. Only option (1) does this.
12. **(4) 50%** Bravo also played 12 games $(6 + 6 = 12)$.
    $\frac{6}{12} = \frac{x}{100}$
    $6 \times 100 \div 12 = 50$
13. **(3) $32** To find 25% of $128, solve the proportion:
    $\frac{x}{\$128} = \frac{25}{100}$
    $\$128 \times 25 \div 100 = \$32$
    Since 25% = $\frac{1}{4}$, you can also find the answer by dividing by 4.

Lesson 3: Using the Percent Formula

Practice 3.1, page 397

1. $5
2. 180
3. 140
4. 95%
5. 25%
6. 3%

7. **17** Since $33\frac{1}{3}\% = \frac{1}{3}$, you can multiply by $\frac{1}{3}$ or divide by 3 to solve the problem.
8. **$60**
9. **200%**
10. **5%**
11. **8%**
12. **$3.91**
13. **$6\frac{1}{2}$% or 6.5%**
14. **$364**
15. **62.5% or $62\frac{1}{2}$%**
16. **72**
17. **(4) 60%** $72 \div 120 = 0.6 = 60\%$
18. **(3) $2,385** $2,250 \times 0.06 = \$135$, and $\$2,250 + \$135 = \$2,385$
19. **(5) $46 × 0.15** $15\% = 0.15$ Multiply the base ($46) by the rate (0.15) to find the part.
20. **(4) 70%** Find what percent $45.50 is of $65 by dividing. $\$45.50 \div \$65 = 0.7$, which equals 70%.
21. **(1) $\frac{\$3 \div 100}{\$50}$** You need to divide the part ($3) by the whole ($50) to find the rate; however, option (4) states $3 ÷ $50 equals 0.06. You still need to change 0.06 to a percent, which you can do by multiplying by 100. If you write a proportion to solve the problem, you will easily see that option (1) is the correct choice.

Practice 3.2, page 399

1. **$175**
2. **280**
3. **6.4**
4. **$200**
5. **30**
6. **$84**
7. **200**
8. **9**
9. **$13.50**
10. **25%**
11. **$75**
12. **$9.30**
13. **900**
14. **90%**
15. **$780**
16. **$3120**
17. **4000**
18. **10%**

19. **(3) $1,230.00** Solve for the base. $\frac{\$369}{0.3} = \$1,230$
20. **(4) $1,200,000** Solve for the base. $\frac{\$72,000}{0.06} = \$1,200,000$
21. **(2) $\frac{160 \times 100}{5}$** Set up the problem as a proportion. $\frac{160}{x} = \frac{5}{100}$ To solve the proportion, you would multiply 160×100 and divide by 5. Only option (2) carries out those operations.
22. **(4) 3600 × 0.2** The base is 3600, the total number who received the application. The part is the unknown number who returned the application. Since 20% = 0.2, you can solve for part by multiplying the base by the rate. 3600×0.2

Lesson 4: Solving Problems Using a Calculator

Practice 4, page 401

1. **$59.80**
2. **$96**
3. **$15.12**
4. **40**
5. **3%**
6. **2080**
7. **25%**
8. **70**
9. **25.2**
10. **79**
11. **2.5% or $2\frac{1}{2}$%**
12. **48**
13. **78%**
14. **$16**
15. **250**
16. **14**
17. **7%**
18. **276**

19. **(4) $8.20** Chanel's order falls between $50.01 and $100. Find 5% of $84. Press: 84 × 5 SHIFT %. The display reads 4.2. Add $4. $4.20 + $4 = $8.20
20. **(1) $0.30** Find the shipping and handling for Jason's order: 8% of $110 = $8.80. Find the shipping and handling for Zola's order. 5% of $90 = $4.50, and $4.50 + $4.00 = $8.50 Find the difference. $8.80 − $8.50 = $0.30
21. **(3) 88%** Press: 3190 ÷ 3625 SHIFT %. The display reads 88.
22. **(5) 15%** Divide strikeouts (63) by at bats (410) and change to percent. Press: 63 ÷ 410 SHIFT %. The display reads 15.36585366, which rounds to 15%.

Lesson 5: Simple Interest

Practice 5, page 403

1. **$360**
2. **$56**
3. **$420**
4. **$480**
5. **$1137.50**
6. **$1998** 8 months = $\frac{2}{3}$ year
7. **$1700**
8. **(5) $1300 + ($1300 × 0.09 × 1.5)** Find the interest by multiplying the amount borrowed ($1300) by the time period in years (1.5) by the interest expressed as a decimal (0.09). To find the amount paid back, the amount borrowed must be added to the interest. Only option (5) shows this series of operations.
9. **(1) $5200** Multiply. $\$8000 \times 0.13 \times 5 = \$5200$
10. **(3) $1545** Find the amount of interest. For the time period, use $\frac{9}{12}$ months, which equals $\frac{3}{4}$, or 0.75. Multiply. $\$1500 \times 0.04 \times 0.75 = \$45$ Add to find the amount paid back. $\$1500 + \$45 = \$1545$
11. **(3) $144** Find the interest for each loan option. Option A: $\$2400 \times 0.12 \times 2.5 = \$720$ Option C: $\$2400 \times 0.09 \times 4 = \$864$ Subtract to find the difference. $\$864 - \$720 = \$144$
12. **(5) $3640** Find the interest she will owe. $\$2800 \times 0.1 \times 3 = \$840$ Add to find the amount she will pay back. $\$2800 + \$840 = \$3640$

Lesson 6: Percent of Change

Practice 6, page 405

1. **50%**
2. **37.5% or $37\frac{1}{2}$%**
3. **200%**
4. **45%**
5. **20%**
6. **32%**
7. **21%**
8. **86%**
9. **420%**
10. **34%**

11. **(3) 60%** Subtract. $\$448 - \$280 = \$168$ Divide by the original weekly pay. $\$168 \div \$280 = 0.6$, which equals 60%.
12. **(2) 25%** Subtract. $\$48 - \$36 = \$12$ Divide by the original price. $\$12 \div \$48 = 0.25$, which equals 25%.
13. **(4) 6%** Subtract. $\$636 - \$600 = \$36$ Divide by the original rent. $\$36 \div \$600 = 0.06$, which equals 6%.
14. **(4) 125%** The wholesale price of the model is $63, and the retail price is $141.75. Subtract. $\$141.75 - \$63 = \$78.75$ Divide by the wholesale price. $\$78.75 \div \$63 = 1.25$, which equals 125%.
15. **(2) 30%** The retail price of the model is $150.50, and the member's price is $105.35. Subtract. $\$150.50 - \$105.35 = \$45.15$ Divide by the retail price. $\$45.15 \div \$150.50 = 0.3$, which equals 30%.

Lesson 7: Problem Solving

Practice 7, page 407

1. **(3) 33%** The number of species affected by road construction is 95. The total number identified (286) is found in the paragraph before the table. $95 \div 286 \approx 0.332 = 33.2\%$, which rounds to 33%.
2. **(4) $\frac{8}{5}$** The number affected by logging is 24, and the number affected by disease is 15. Write the ratio and simplify. $\frac{24}{15} = \frac{8}{5}$
3. **(5) Not enough information is given.** The total number affected by air, water, and soil pollution is 44. You have no way to find the number affected by water pollution only.
4. **(3) $13.55** The discount on the ladder is 30%. $\$32.50 \times 0.3 = \$9.75$ The price of two cans of paint is $\$19 \times 2 = \$38$. At 10% off, the discount on the paint is $\$38 \times 0.1 = \$3.80$. The total discount is $\$9.75 + \$3.80 = \$13.55$.
5. **(5) Not enough information is given.** The discount information does not show the price of either the paint or the brushes.
6. **(4) 3:1** The distance to Niagara Falls (95 miles) is about three times the distance to Finger Lakes (31 miles). The best choice is option (4).

Ratio, Proportion, and Percent
Practice Questions, pages 408–411

Part I

1. **(4) 1:11** Subtract to find the dollars spent on other costs. $\$360,000 - \$30,000 = \$330,000$ Write a ratio and reduce. $\frac{\$30,000}{\$330,000} = \frac{1}{11}$
2. **(1) $\frac{2 \times 50}{5}$** Write a proportion. $\frac{5}{2} = \frac{50}{x}$ To solve it, you need to multiply 2×50 and divide by 5. Only option (1) performs these operations.
3. **(2) $7.56** Find 35% of $5.60. $\$5.60 \times 0.35 = \$1.96$ Add. $\$1.96 + \$5.60 = \$7.56$ Another way to get the answer is to find 135% of $5.60. $\$5.60 \times 1.35 = \$7.56$
4. **(4) $20,000** The current worth of the car ($12,000) is part of the base. Solve for base. $\$12,000 \div 0.6 = \$20,000$

5. **(4) 42** Solve the proportion $\frac{7}{3} = \frac{x}{18}$. $7 \times 18 \div 3 = 42$
6. **(1) 6%** The commission is part of the base. Solve for part. $\$954 \div \$15,900 = 0.06 = 6\%$
7. **(2) 1:6** Add to find the total time spent on the project. $2 + 1\frac{1}{2} + 2 + 3\frac{1}{2} = 9$ hours Write a ratio using decimals and reduce. $\frac{1.5 \div 1.5}{9 \div 1.5} = \frac{1}{6}$
8. **(3) 36%** Add to find the acres used for grains, vegetables, or fruits. $5,200 + 9,200 = 14,400$ Solve for percent. $14,400 \div 40,000 = 0.36 = 36\%$
9. **(5) Not enough information is given.** You can find the total farmland acreage for last year, but you cannot find the number of acres used for dairy production. Without that number, you cannot find the percent.
10. **(1) $\frac{3}{16}$** The total fat is $3 + 13 = 16$ grams. Write the ratio of saturated fat (3 grams) to the total (16 grams). The ratio cannot be simplified.
11. **(2) 10** Write a proportion and solve. $\frac{4}{5} = \frac{x}{12.5}$ $4 \times 12.5 \div 5 = 10$ inches
12. **138** Write a proportion and solve. $\frac{4}{3} = \frac{184}{x}$, and $3 \times 184 \div 4 = 138$ female patients

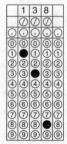

13. **$900** If 20% is the amount of the discount, then the sale price must be 80% of the original price. The sale price is the part, and the original price is the base. Solve for base. $\$720 \div 0.8 = \$900$ Grid in the amount without the dollar sign.

Part II

14. **(2) 40** If the ratio of wins to losses is 5:4, then the ratio of wins to games played is 5:9. Write a proportion and solve. $\frac{5}{9} = \frac{x}{72}$ $5 \times 72 \div 9 = 40$ games won
15. **(3) 192** Add to find the number that did not answer "no." $16\% + 32\% = 48\%$ Find 48% of 400. $400 \times 0.48 = 192$
16. **(5) $\frac{\$24 - \$19}{\$24} \times 100$** To find the percent of decrease, you subtract the lower price from the higher price and divide the difference by the original price. In this case, the original price is $24, the higher price. To change the answer to a percent, you must move the decimal point two places to the right or multiply by 100. Only option (5) shows this series of operations.
17. **(1) 121** When the rate is greater than 100%, the part will be greater than the base. Solve for the part. $55 \times 2.2 = 121$
18. **(4) 18%** There are 6 grams of fat in the roast beef sandwich: $6 \times 9 = 54$ calories in the sandwich from fat. The total calories in the sandwich is 300. Find what percent 54 is of 300. $54 \div 300 = 0.18 = 18\%$
19. **(5) $264** Write a proportion and solve. $\frac{\$8}{\$3} = \frac{\$704}{x}$ $\$3 \times \$704 \div \$8 = \$264$
20. **(3) 175** The 140 employees who have more than 12 days of sick leave are part of the whole workforce. You need to solve for the base. $140 \div 0.8 = 175$
21. **(5) 825** If the ratio of sold to unsold tickets is 11 to 1, then the ratio of sold to total tickets is 11 to 12. Write a proportion and solve. $\frac{11}{12} = \frac{x}{900}$ $11 \times 900 \div 12 = 825$
22. **(4) $2464** Use the formula for finding simple interest: $i = prt$. $\$2200 \times 0.08 \times 1.5 = \$264$ To find the amount in the account at the end of the time, add the interest to the original investment. $\$2200 + \$264 = \$2464$
23. **(1) $410 − ($410 × 0.2)** Once you find the discount by multiplying 0.2 by $410, you will need to subtract the discount

from $410 to find the sale price. Only option (1) shows this sequence of operations.

24. **(5) 330** After changing $2\frac{3}{4}$ to the decimal 2.75, write a proportion and solve. $\frac{0.5}{60} = \frac{2.75}{x}$ $60 \times 2.75 \div 0.5 = 330$

25. **(3) (140 − 91)/140 × 100** There were 140 customers on Sunday, and 91 made a purchase. Therefore, $140 - 91$ did not make a purchase. To find the percent rate, divide the difference by 140, the total number of customers on Sunday (the base). Then move the decimal point two places to the right or multiply by 100 to change the answer to a percent. Only option (3) shows this sequence of operations.

26. **270** Write a proportion and solve. $\frac{9}{14} = \frac{x}{420}$, and $9 \times 420 \div 14 = 270$

27. $\frac{3}{5}$ If she spends 15 hours answering telephones, she spends $40 - 15$, or 25 hours doing other tasks. Write a ratio and reduce. $\frac{15}{25} = \frac{3}{5}$

Data Analysis

Lesson 1: Tables and Pictographs

Practice 1, page 413

1. 9
2. 6%
3. 300

4. 3000
5. **(5) Not enough information is given.** The problem is asking you to find the part, but the table gives only the rate. You have to know two elements of a percent problem in order to solve for the third element.
6. **(3) 84** In 2000, 24% of 3-year-old children could write their own names. Find 24% of 350. $350 \times 0.24 = 84$
7. **(3) 375** There are $7\frac{1}{2}$ car symbols. Each symbol represents 50 cars. Multiply. $7\frac{1}{2} \times 50 = 375$
8. **(1) 75** Compare the symbols for the two rows. There are $1\frac{1}{2}$ more symbols for 8 A.M. to noon than for times after 4:30 P.M. Multiply. $1\frac{1}{2} \times 50 = 75$

Lesson 2: Bar and Line Graphs

Practice 2.1, page 415

1. 50
2. about 15
3. 20%
4. about $20 million
5. Film A
6. 150%
7. **(3) 41** Estimate the values of the bars labeled CDs, Videos, and DVDs. CDs $\approx$ 112, Videos $\approx$ 42, and DVDs $\approx$ 29. Add the values for Videos and DVDs. $42 + 29 = 71$ Subtract this from the value for CDs. $112 - 71 = 41$ You may have chosen different numbers. Even if your result is different, the closest answer choice should be choice (3).
8. **(4) $1000** There were about 50 games sold, so 25 sold for $16 and 25 sold for $24. $(25 \times \$16) + (25 \times \$24) = \$1000$
9. **(4) 14:3** Write a ratio and simplify. $\frac{70}{15} = \frac{14}{3}$
10. **(5) September** Add the 2-day and 5-day permits for each month. Only September's permits equal 80. $60 + 20 = 80$ permits

Practice 2.2, page 417

1. September
2. 270
3. from June to July
4. $10
5. 20%
6. $30

7. **(1) 1930 to 1940** The price of goods decreased over two decades, 1920 to 1940. Note the downward movement of the line. Only the time period 1930 to 1940 is included among the answer options.
8. **(4) $\frac{1}{5}$** The price of the same goods was about $20 in 1970 and $100 in 2000. Write a ratio and simplify. $\frac{\$20}{\$100} = \frac{1}{5}$
9. **(2) 50** There were 390 sales in Store 2 and 340 sales in Store 1 in the sixth week. $390 - 340 = 50$
10. **(3) Week 4** The steepest line segment is for the time period for Week 4 (between Week 4 and Week 5), an increase of 40 sales.

Lesson 3: Circle Graphs

Practice 3, page 419

1. 29%
2. $\frac{2}{25}$
3. $630
4. $30.60
5. heating and air conditioning
6. cooking and refrigeration
7. **(1) 10** According to the graph, a records clerk spends 25%, or $\frac{1}{4}$, of his or her time preparing documents. 25% of 40 hours is 10 hours.
8. **(5) 56%** If 44% of the time is spent on data entry, then $100\% - 44\%$, which equals 56%, is spent on other tasks.
9. **(2) 10%** Add. 3 cents + 7 cents = 10 cents, and 10 cents out of 100 cents is $\frac{10}{100}$, or 10%
10. **(3) $48** 40 cents out of every dollar, or 40%, is spent on public bonds. 40% of $120 is found by multiplying. $\$120 \times 0.4 = \$48$

Lesson 4: Frequency and Central Tendency

Practice 4.1, page 421

1. 57
2. 6
3. 1:2
4. 3:4
5. 46
6. 14%
7. **(2) $\frac{4}{11}$** There are 16 tally marks next to the reason "wrong size." Add the remaining tally marks. $16 + 20 + 3 + 5 = 44$ Write a ratio and reduce. $\frac{16}{44} = \frac{4}{11}$

8. **(4) $33\frac{1}{3}$%** Adding all the tally marks, you find that there were 60 clothing returns in all. Since there are 20 tally marks by "unwanted gift," $\frac{20}{60}$ or $33\frac{1}{3}$ of the total reasons given were "unwanted gift."

9. **(5) Not enough information is given.** You can see that 25 applicants scored from 31 to 45 wpm, but there is no way to determine how many of those scored exactly 40 wpm.

10. **(2) 1:2** To find those who could keyboard above 45 wpm, add. $18 + 12 = 30$ Those keyboarding below 45 wpm are found by adding. $35 + 25 = 60$ Write a ratio and reduce. $\frac{30}{60} = \frac{1}{2}$

Practice 4.2, page 423

1. mean: 80.14
   median: 80
   mode: 82
2. mean: $8,487.17
   median: $8,208.50
   mode: none
3. mean: $4.76
   median: $4.50
   mode: $4.50
4. mean: 309 miles
   median: 300 miles
   mode: none
5. mean: $101.83
   median: $101.81
   mode: none
6. mean: 86
   median: 88
   mode: 88
7. mean: 99.1°
   median: 99°
   mode: 98° and 100°
8. mean: 1.9 inches
   median: 1.8 inches
   mode: none
9. mean: 305
   median: 305
   mode: 305
10. mean: 38.8 hours
    median: 40 hours
    mode: 40 hours
11. **(2) $117,100** Add the amounts in the column labeled "Asking Price," and divide by 6, the number of prices listed.
12. **(4) $116,500** Arrange the selling prices in order: $124,800; $118,400; $116,500; $116,500; $109,000; $103,600. Since the

number of items is even, there are two in the middle: $116,500 and $116,500. Since these are the same amount, the average of the two is also $116,500.

13. **(1) $\frac{790 + 1150 + 662 + 805}{4}$** To find the mean, add the numbers and divide by the number of items in the set. In this case, there are 4 numbers.

14. **(3) $900** The median is the middle amount. Arrange the amounts in order, and find the middle amount.

15. **(2) 14** The mode is the number that occurs most often. Only 14 occurs more than once in the data.

Lesson 5: Probability

Practice 5.1, page 425

1. $\frac{2}{5}$, 0.4, 40%
2. $\frac{3}{10}$, 0.3, 30%
3. $\frac{1}{5}$, 0.2, 20%
4. $\frac{1}{4}$, 0.25, 25%
5. $\frac{1}{3}$, 0.33, $33\frac{1}{3}$%
6. **(3) 50%** There are twelve cards in the deck, and six are diamonds. $\frac{6}{12} = \frac{1}{2} = 50\%$
7. **(1) $\frac{3}{4}$** There are three clubs, so nine are not clubs. $\frac{9}{12} = \frac{3}{4}$
8. **(4) 2 out of 5** Sixteen out of 40 trials resulted in tails. $\frac{16}{40} = \frac{2}{5}$
9. **(5) 1 out of 2** There are two possible outcomes and one favorable outcome (in this case, heads).

Practice 5.2, page 427

1. $\frac{1}{36}$
2. $\frac{1}{4}$
3. $\frac{1}{8}$
4. $\frac{9}{38}$
5. $\frac{1}{16}$
6. $\frac{1}{4}$
7. **(1) $\frac{1}{9}$** The probability of rolling a 5 is $\frac{1}{6}$. Of the six equal sections on the spinner, four are even numbers, so there is a $\frac{4}{6}$, or $\frac{2}{3}$, chance of spinning an even number. Multiply the probability of each outcome.
   $\frac{1}{6} \times \frac{2}{3} = \frac{2}{18} = \frac{1}{9}$
8. **(4) $\frac{1}{6}$** The only numbers that are on both the die and the spinner are 2, 3, and 4. There is a 3 in 6, or $\frac{1}{2}$, chance of getting a 2, 3, or 4

on the dice. No matter which of those numbers you get on the dice, there is a 2 in 6, or $\frac{1}{3}$, chance of getting that number on the spinner. Multiply these probabilities. $\frac{1}{2} \times \frac{1}{3} = \frac{1}{6}$

9. **(4) 1 out of 3** Of the ten cards, 6 are marked with a square; therefore, there is a 6 in 10, or $\frac{3}{5}$, chance of getting a square on the first pick. Now there are only 9 cards left, and 5 are squares: a $\frac{5}{9}$ chance of getting a square on the second pick. Multiply. $\frac{3}{5} \times \frac{5}{9} = \frac{15}{45} = \frac{1}{3}$

10. **(2) 80%** After the five white chips are removed from the bag, the bag contains 10 chips, with 8 green and 2 white. The probability of getting green is $\frac{8}{10}$, which equals 80%.

Lesson 6: Problem Solving

Practice 6, page 429

1. **(3) $\frac{10}{7}$** Using the numbers from the table, the ratio is $\frac{110}{77}$, which reduces to $\frac{10}{7}$.

2. **(3) 43%** The total number who got their pet from a friend or from an animal shelter is 84 + 160 = 244. Find what percent 244 is of 573. $\frac{244}{573} \approx 0.426$, which rounds to 43%.

3. **(1) January** The dotted line represents the temperatures in Boston, and the solid line represents the temperatures in San Francisco. The scale is marked in 10° intervals. Examine the graph to find a month in which the dotted line is two intervals below the solid line. This occurs only in the month of January.

4. **(3) 58°** There isn't a label for the month of May, but you know May is the month after April. Examine the graph. The lines intersect right after April at a point just below 60° on the scale. The only possible correct answer is option (3).

Practice Questions, pages 430–433

Part I

1. **(3) 1997** Only the bar for 1997 falls between 500 and 600 on the scale.
2. **(3) 40%** Estimate the values for 1998 and 1999. Then find the

percent of decrease. For example, suppose you chose the numbers 650 and 390 for 1998 and 1999. Subtract. 650 − 390 = 260 Divide by the original number. 260 ÷ 650 = 0.4 = 40% As long as your original estimates were close to 650 and 390, your percent of decrease should be close to 40%.

3. **(1)** $\frac{3}{100}$ Jim and his friends bought a total of 12 tickets (4 people × 3 tickets). 12 out of 400 = $\frac{12}{400}$ = $\frac{3}{100}$

4. **(5) 50°** Arrange the low temperatures in order: 55°, 53°, 50°, 50°, 49°, and 48°. Find the middle of the list. Since there are two temperatures in the middle and both are 50°, the mean of the two must be 50°.

5. **(3) 1.56** Add the six amounts, and divide by 6. Use your calculator. 0.45 + 0.63 + 1.34 + 3.53 + 2.57 + 0.84 = 9.36, and 9.36 ÷ 6 = 1.56 inches

6. **(4) Woodland Hills** Mentally subtract the low temperature from the high temperature for each area. The greatest difference is in Woodland Hills. 68° − 50° = 18

7. **(4) 1998** Ticket sales showed a relatively constant increase until 1998. In 1998, ticket sales dropped by almost 100,000.

8. **(3) 1997 to 1998** The line graph shows the steepest increase (line rising from left to right) from 1997 to 1998.

9. **(4) 32%** Eight customers chose a mouse pad, and 8 out of 25 = 32%. 8 ÷ 25 = 0.32 = 32%

10. **(1) 1 in 2** 26 of the 52 cards are either hearts or diamonds. $\frac{26}{52}$ = $\frac{1}{2}$

11. **3.5 or** $\frac{7}{2}$ Add the hours, and divide by 6, the number of weeks. 5 + 3.5 + 4 + 1.5 + 7 = 21 hours, and 21 hours ÷ 6 = 3.5 hours

12.

$\frac{2}{5}$ **or 0.4** Only the numbers 4 and 5 are greater than 3. The probability is 2 out of 5, $\frac{2}{5}$, or 0.4.

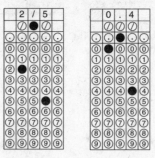

Part II

13. **(2) 41%** You don't need to know exactly how many votes each candidate received. The three candidates who received the smallest percents also received the smallest number of votes. Add. 9% + 14% + 18% = 41%

14. **(4) Bowen and Utley** Since $\frac{3}{5}$ = 60%, look for two candidates whose combined percent is close to 60%. Since 24% + 35% = 59%, the correct answer is option (4).

15. **(5) 5100 × 0.09** Grace Reiner received 9%, which equals 0.09. You know the percent and the base. Multiply to find the part.

16. **(3) March** The lines for both companies cross in March.

17. **(2) 5900** Company A's orders continue to climb at about the same rate. Imagine extending the dotted line to the next month. The line would reach to almost 6000. Option (1) is too high an increase.

18. **(5) Not enough information is given.** The data from the graph shows the number of orders. We have no way of knowing whether the rate of returns at the two companies is the same or different.

19. **(3) 24.5** Use only the Shots Attempted column. Put the numbers in order, and find the middle: 29, 27, 26, 25, 24, 24, 23, 18. The two in the middle are 25 and 24. Find the mean of those numbers. 25 + 24 = 49, and 49 ÷ 2 = 24.5

20. **(4) 10** Use the Shots Made column. The mode is the number that occurs most often. In this case the mode is 10, which occurs three times.

21. **(3)** $\frac{5}{36}$ The probability that a marble is red is $\frac{8}{24}$, or $\frac{1}{3}$. The chance that a marble is white is $\frac{10}{24}$, or $\frac{5}{12}$. Multiply. $\frac{1}{3}$ × $\frac{5}{12}$ = $\frac{5}{36}$

22. **(2)** $\frac{34 + 31 + 42}{3}$ To find the mean, add the three numbers and divide by 3, the number of months in the list. There are 36 employees, but you don't need this number to solve the problem.

23. $\frac{1}{36}$ The probability of rolling one 1 is $\frac{1}{6}$. Multiply to find the chance of rolling two ones. $\frac{1}{6}$ × $\frac{1}{6}$ = $\frac{1}{36}$

24. **210** Arrange the numbers in order, and find the middle number: 305, 276, **210**, 158, 54.

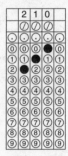

Measurement

Lesson 1: The English System of Measurement

Practice 1.1, page 435

1. 48 in
2. 7 min
3. 72 hr
4. $2\frac{1}{2}$ pt
5. 20 qt
6. $5\frac{1}{2}$ tons
7. 144 in
8. 12 hr
9. 32 c
10. 8 lb
11. 24 ft
12. 7920

13. **(3) 3.75 × 4** 4 qt = 1 gal, so multiply the number of gallons by 4 to find the number of quarts.

14. **(2) 2 ft 3 in** 12 in = 1 ft Divide. 27 ÷ 12 = 2 r3, or 2 ft 3 in

15. **(3) 110** The R612 runs 6 hours. Multiply to convert to minutes: $6 \times 60 = 360$ min. Subtract: $360 - 250 = 110$ min longer.

Practice 1.2, page 437

1. 9 lb 8 oz
2. 10 hr 35 min
3. 16 ft 6 in
4. 1 gal 2 qt
5. 1 yd 6 in
6. 13 lb 14 oz
7. 1 hr 21 min 40 sec
8. 5 ft 10 in
9. 1 min 9 sec
10. **(4) $15\frac{1}{2}$** Use the measurements from the diagram. Notice that some lengths are used more than once. Add. 3 ft 6 in + 3 ft 6 in + 3 ft + 3 ft + 30 in = 12 ft 42 in = 15 ft 6 in = $15\frac{1}{2}$ ft
11. **(2) 6** You need to divide 16 feet by 30 inches. One way is to multiply 16 by 12 to find the number of inches in 16 feet: $16 \times 12 = 192$ inches. Then divide by 30. $192 \div 30 = 6.4$ You can cut 6 full lengths of 30 inches. Ignore the remainder.
12. **(1) 2 qt 10 fl oz** 3 qt = 2 qt 2 pt = 2 qt 1 pt 16 fl oz
Subtract. 2 qt 1 pt 16 fl oz
$$\underline{-\quad\quad 1\text{ pt }6\text{ fl oz}}$$
      2 qt   10 fl oz
13. **(3) 22 lb 8 oz**
Multiply. 3 lb 12 oz
$$\underline{\times\qquad\qquad 6}$$
      18 lb 72 oz
To simplify, divide. Use the fact 1 lb = 16 oz. $72 \div 16 = 4$ r8
18 lb + 4 lb 8 oz = 22 lb 8 oz
14. **(5) 8**
Add.   1 hr 45 min
                2 hr 30 min
$$\underline{+\ 3\text{ hr }45\text{ min}}$$
                6 hr 120 min
Simplify. 120 min $\div$ 60 = 2 hr, so 6 hr 120 min = 6 hr + 2 hr = 8 hr

Lesson 2: The Metric System

Practice 2.1, page 439

1. 5000 m	7. 0.25 g
2. 6 m	8. 30,000 m
3. 4000 mg	9. 75 cl
4. 8000 g	10. 0.05 kg
5. 4050 cl	11. 35.2 *l*
6. 1.5 *l*	12. 1500 cm

13. **(4) 140** There are 100 centimeters in 1 meter.
1.4 m $\times$ 100 = 140 cm
14. **(2) 0.1183** There are 1000 milliliters in 1 liter.
118.3 ml $\div$ 1000 = 0.1183 *l*
15. **(5) 0.5** There are 1000 milligrams in 1 gram.
500 $\div$ 1000 = 0.5 g

Practice 2.2, page 441

1. 27.25 cm	7. 129 cl
2. 22,620 g	8. 2.4 cm
3. 8.18 m	9. 37.5 kg
4. 0.6 *l*	10. 0.25 g
5. 2.22 kg	11. 645 cm
6. 3130 m	12. 200 *l*

13. **(3) 21.1** Convert the two centimeter measures to meters by dividing by 100. 380 cm = 3.8 m and 590 cm = 5.9 m
Add. 3.4 + 5.9 + 8 + 3.8 = 21.1 m
14. **(1) 4.13** Multiply the number of milliliters of soda in a can by the number of cans.
355 ml $\times$ 6 = 2130 ml Convert to liters. 2130 ml $\div$ 1000 = 2.13 *l*
Add the liters of soda and juice. 2.13 *l* + 2 = 4.13 *l*
15. **(2) 625** Convert 2.5 kg to grams. 2.5 $\times$ 1000 = 2500 g Divide. 2500 g $\div$ 4 g = 625 containers
16. **(3) 130** Convert 4.8 meters to centimeters. 4.8 $\times$ 100 = 480 cm Subtract. 480 - 350 = 130 cm
17. **(5) 15.12** Set up a proportion and solve. $\frac{1\text{ cm}}{3.6\text{ km}} = \frac{4.2\text{ cm}}{x}$ 3.6 $\times$ 4.2 $\div$ 1 = 15.12 km

Lesson 3: Using a Calculator

Practice 3, page 443

1. $5\frac{3}{4}$ or 5.75 lb	11. 15 yd 2 ft
2. 42 fl oz	12. 2.335 m
3. 30 sec	13. 3 qt
4. 100 cl	14. 3500 lb
5. $1\frac{1}{4}$ mi	15. 150 mg
6. $18\frac{3}{4}$ or 18.75 lb	16. 1 hr 15 min
7. 920 m	17. 8 fl oz
8. 15 ft 7 in	18. 72 g
9. 92 oz	19. 2 ft
10. 11 m	20. 20 pt

21. **(4) 124** Add the pounds and the ounces on the packages.
1 lb 8 oz + 2 lb 8 oz + 3 lb 12 oz = 6 lb 28 oz Multiply the pounds by 16, the number of ounces in a pound. $6 \times 16 = 96$ oz Add the number of ounces

from the original addition.
96 oz + 28 oz = 124 oz
22. **(3) 16** First change $1\frac{3}{4}$ gallons to cups. Use the decimal equivalent. 1.75 gal $\times$ 4 = 7 qt; 7 qt $\times$ 2 = 14 pt; 14 pt $\times$ 2 = 28 c Divide 28 c by 1.75. 28 $\div$ 1.75 = 16 bowls
23. **(2) 170** You need to divide 40 hours by 14 minutes. First change 40 hours to minutes by multiplying. $40 \times 60 = 2400$ min Divide. 2400 $\div$ 14 $\approx$ 171.4 The closest answer choice is option (2).

Lesson 4: Problem Solving

Practice 4, page 445

1. b	6. a
2. b	7. b
3. a	8. c
4. c	9. a
5. b	10. a

11. **(5) kilograms** Eliminate the choices that are not reasonable. Options (1), (2), and (4) are very small units of weight. Since they are smaller than a pound, the number of any of these units would have to be greater than 100. Option (3) is a unit of length, not weight. Only option (5) makes sense.
12. **(4) centimeters** Option (1) is incorrect because 15.7 inches would be longer than a 12-inch ruler, much longer than the length of a dollar bill. Options (2) and (5) are too large to use to measure a small item. Option (3) is a very small unit of measure. Only option (4) makes sense.
13. **(1) 95 fl oz** You don't need to do any calculations to solve the problem. Options (2), (4), and (5) are very large quantities. Although you can measure juice in cups, you couldn't possibly make 95 cups of juice by adding only $4\frac{1}{2}$ cups of water per can. Option (3) is a very small quantity. Only option (1) makes sense.

Measurement Practice Questions, pages 446–449

Part I

1. **(4) 25** Add and simplify. 5 ft 6 in + 5 ft + 5 ft 6 in + 5 ft + 48 in = 20 ft 60 in = 20 ft + 5 ft = 25 ft

2. **(2) 5** Change 48 inches to 4 feet. Divide 20 feet by 4. 20 ft ÷ 4 = 5 lengths

3. **(4) 14** Subtract. 5 gal − 1½ gal = 3½ gal Convert to quarts by multiplying by 4. 3½ = 3.5 and 3.5 × 4 = 14 qt

4. **(3) 7 lb 13 oz** Multiply and then simplify. 1 lb 9 oz × 5 = 5 lb 45 oz = 5 lb + 2 lb 13 oz = 7 lb 13 oz

5. **(5) 1¼** Add the number of hours Malcom spent updating files this week. 3 hr 15 min + 1 hr 30 min = 4 hr 45 min Subtract from last week's total. 6 hr − 4 hr 45 min = 5 hr 60 min − 4 hr 45 min = 1 hr 15 min, or 1¼ hr

6. **(3) 80** Convert meters to centimeters. 0.8 m × 100 = 80 cm

7. **(3) 3.0** Convert milliliters to liters. 3000 ml ÷ 1000 = 3 *l*

8. **(4) 1** Convert milligrams to grams. 1000 mg ÷ 1000 = 1 g

9. **(3) 25.5** First convert the measurements given in centimeters to meters. 750 cm ÷ 100 = 7.5 m Add the three lengths. 7.5 m + 7.5 m + 10.5 m = 25.5 m

10. **(5) Not enough information is given.** You need to know how much a glass holds in order to find the number of glasses of punch.

11. **(3) 100** Use compatible numbers to find the approximate number of brushings. 1500 mg is approximately 1700 mg, and 1700 and 170 are compatible. Convert milligrams to grams. 1700 mg ÷ 1000 = 1.7 g Then divide to find the approximate number of brushings per tube. 170 g ÷ 1.7 g = 100 brushings

12. **(3) 150** Subtract to find how much plastic is left. 5 m − 3.5 m = 1.5 m Convert to centimeters. 1.5 m × 100 = 150 cm

13. **48.6** Add the amounts. 15.8 kg + 13.5 kg + 19.3 kg = 48.6 kg

14. **80** Convert gallons to cups, since 1 cup = 8 ounces. 1 gal = 4 qt and 1 qt = 4 c, so 1 gal = 16 c Use this information to find how many cups are in 5 gallons. 5 gal = 16 c × 5 = 80 cups

Part II

15. **(4) 11/4** The capacity of the humidifier is given in quarts. Divide by 4 to find the capacity in gallons.

16. **(2) 2 ft 3 in** The width of the humidifier is given as 27 inches. Convert to feet and inches. 27 in ÷ 12 = 2 ft 3 in This is the least amount of space needed for the humidifier.

17. **(2) 4½** Divide the number of minutes by 60 minutes to find the number of hours. 270 ÷ 60 = 4 R30 A remainder of 30 minutes equals ½ hour. 4 R30 = 4½ hours

18. **(5) 175** 3½ in = 3.5 in Set up a proportion and solve.

$$\frac{1 \text{ in}}{50 \text{ mi}} = \frac{3\frac{1}{2} \text{ in}}{x \text{ mi}}, \text{ and}$$

50 × 3.5 ÷ 1 = 175 mi

19. **(4) 64** Convert any weights given in pounds to ounces. 1 lb = 16 oz and 1.5 lb = 1½ lb = 24 oz Add the weights. 16 oz + 20 oz + 24 oz + 4 oz = 64 oz

20. **(3) 8** Convert 2½, or 2.5 gallons, to cups. 2.5 gal = 10 qt = 40 c Divide by 5 cups to find the number of cooking hours the sauce will last. 40 c ÷ 5 c = 8 hr

21. **(4) 99** Find how many patients the doctor can see per hour. 60 min ÷ 20 min = 3 Multiply the number of hours the doctor spends on office visits by the number of patients per hour (3). 33 hr × 3 patients per hr = 99 patients

22. **(5) kilograms** Eliminate option (3), since it is not a unit of weight. Eliminate options (1), (2), and (4), since these are very small units of weight. Kilograms would be the only reasonable unit of measure.

23. **(4) centimeters** Eliminate options (1), (2), and (5), since 28 of these units of length would be too long. Millimeters are too small. Therefore, only option (4) is the correct choice.

24. **(1)** $\frac{(45 + 30)}{15}$ Find how many ounces of beans are needed in all: (45 + 30). Then divide the total by the number of ounces in 1 can of beans. $\frac{(45 + 30)}{15}$

25. **(1) 90 fl oz** Find how many ounces of water are added to 1 can of concentrate. 4.5 c × 8 oz = 36 fl oz Add the amount of concentrate. 36 fl oz + 9 fl oz = 45 fl oz Multiply by 2 to find how much 2 cans would make. 45 fl oz × 2 = 90 fl oz

26. **48** Convert feet to inches by multiplying by 12. 4 ft × 12 in = 48 in

27. **265** Convert hours to minutes. 2.5 hr × 60 min = 150 min Add to find the total amount of time. 150 + 45 + 70 = 265 min

Algebra

Lesson 1: The Number Line and Signed Numbers

Practice 1.1, page 451

1. 5	13. −50
2. 45	14. −11
3. 13	15. 25
4. 1	16. −35
5. 1	17. −11
6. 10	18. 11
7. −3	19. 10
8. 13	20. 75
9. −4	21. 12
10. 2	22. 2
11. −22	23. −1
12. 32	24. −13

25. **(3) 2 + (−5)** The operation starts on +2 and moves 5 units to the left (a negative direction).

26. **(4) 115°** Begin with 92°. Then perform the following operations. 92° + 12° − 5° + 6° − 3° + 13° = 115°

Practice 1.2, page 453

1. 20	15. 6
2. −21	16. −20
3. −48	17. −300
4. 18	18. 2
5. −10	19. −5
6. 3	20. 660
7. −3	21. 12
8. −5	22. −120
9. 2	23. −5
10. −5	24. −12
11. −28	25. 20
12. −3	26. −1
13. −1	27. 0
14. −75	

28. **(2) −7** Substitute the numbers from the spreadsheet for the cells in the expression and solve. Note that A1 is column A, row 1; A3 is column A, row 3; and so on. $\frac{(-3)(7)(-1)}{(3)(-1)} = \frac{21}{-3} = -7$

29. **(3) 2(8) ÷ (−8)** To find the product of two numbers, multiply: 2(8). Then divide by −8, as directed in the problem.

30. **(4) The result is a negative number.** Do not do the calculations. Instead, examine the factors. Since there is an odd number of negative factors, the answer will be negative. This is the only possible option.

Lesson 2: Powers and Roots

Practice 2, page 455

1. 9
2. 4
3. 3 (Although -3 is also a possible answer, you will only be expected to find positive roots on the GED Math Test.)

4. 1
5. 9
6. 7
7. 125
8. $\frac{1}{16}$
9. 16
10. 8
11. $\frac{1}{1000}$
12. 11
13. 6561
14. 1296
15. 12.2
16. 8000
17. 1
18. $\frac{1}{16}$
19. 15.6
20. 10.89
21. 7.5
22. 23.2
23. 1
24. 256

25. **(4) 6^3** To find the volume, you would need to solve the problem $6 \times 6 \times 6$, which can be written as 6^3.

26. **(1) 3^{-3}** Examine the choices. Options (1) and (5) will result in a fraction, a value less than 1. Options (2), (3), and (4) will all have a value greater than 1. Option (1) $3^{-3} = \frac{1}{3^3} = \frac{1}{27}$. Option (5) $2^{-4} = \frac{1}{2^4} = \frac{1}{16}$. Since $\frac{1}{27} < \frac{1}{16}$, option (1) is the correct choice.

Lesson 3: Scientific Notation

Practice 3, page 457

1. 2.3×10^3
2. 4.2×10^{-4}
3. 1.24×10^7
4. 1.432×10^{10}
5. 3.6×10^7
6. 9.5×10^{-3}
7. 5.8×10^{-7}
8. 1.5×10^{11}
9. 9×10^{-9}
10. 0.0005173
11. 3,700,000
12. 480,000,000
13. 0.000017
14. 0.0072
15. 916,000
16. 85,910,000
17. 0.00000956
18. 2.35×10^4
19. 0.000000001
20. 2,670,000,000
21. 3×10^8
22. **(2) 4.356×10^4** In scientific notation, the whole number portion must be a digit from 1 to 9. Option (2) is correct, because the decimal place must be moved 4 places.
23. **(5) $5 \times 9.07 \times 10^{-1}$** In scientific notation, a ton = 9.07×10^{-1} metric tons. Multiply this by 5 to find the equivalent weight of five tons.

Lesson 4: The Order of Operations

Practice 4, page 459

1. 24
2. 1
3. 29
4. 2
5. -1
6. 20
7. 14
8. 55
9. 10
10. 23
11. 161
12. 30
13. 360
14. 4
15. 6

16. **(4) $(1 - 0.75)(28)(30)$** The total cost of the class can be found by multiplying 28 members by $30. Since the foundation pays 75%, or 0.75, the hospital will pay 100% − 75%, or $(1 - 0.75)$. You must multiply the amount the class will cost by the percent that the hospital will pay. Only option (4) performs these operations.
17. **(3) Add 5.** The operations in the brackets must be performed first. Once these are completed, you would multiply by 2 and then add 5. Notice that it is not necessary to find the value of the expression to answer the question.
18. **(2) 28**
$22 + 6[(14 - 5) \div 3(17 - 14)]$
$= 22 + 6[9 \div 3(3)]$
$= 22 + 6[9 \div 9]$
$= 22 + 6[1]$
$= 22 + 6$
$= 28$

Lesson 5: Algebraic Expressions

Practice 5.1, page 461

1. $x - 7$
2. $3x^2 + x$
3. $8x - 10$
4. $-3x - 2y$
5. $\frac{10}{x} - 5$
6. $-8 + 7x$
7. $16x + x - 3y$
8. $x^2 + x^4$
9. $x^2 + \frac{4}{7}$
10. $15 + \sqrt{x} - 6$
11. $x - (y + 13)$
12. $(x + 6)^2$
13. $17 - (2x + y)$
14. $x + \frac{24}{x}$
15. $2x - 15$
16. $4(x - y)$
17. $5(x^2 - 3)$
18. $x(11 - \sqrt{100})$
19. **(4) $\$1500 + \$0.50(x - 2000)$** Let x represent the number of tickets sold. The expression $x - 2000$ is the number of tickets over 2000 sold. Multiply this expression by $0.50 to find the amount donated based on ticket sales, and add $1500. Only option (4) shows this sequence of operations.
20. **(1) $(3x + 4y) \div (2 + z)$** The sum of 3 times a number and 4 times another number is represented by the expression $3x + 4y$. The sum of 2 and a third number is represented by $2 + z$. The first expression is divided by the second. Parentheses are necessary to clarify the order of operations.
21. **(2) $6h + 0.03s$** The correct sequence of operations shows the sum of 6 multiplied by the number of hours ($6h$) and 3% of the sales, or $0.03s$. Only option (2) adds these two expressions.

Practice 5.2, page 463

1. $x^2 + 3x + 2$
2. $19y + 13$
3. $-3x + 54$
4. $6x^3 + 31x^2 + 4$
5. $7y + 14$
6. $3x + 8$
7. $22x - 12$
8. $2y^2 + y + 9$
9. $-5x - 17$
10. $4x - 7$

11. 31
12. 48
13. 8
14. 21
15. 72
16. 80
17. 31
18. −19
19. 9
20. 61
21. **(5) $3x^2 + 4x + 1$** Simplify the expression.

$3x^2 + 3(x - 3) + x + 10$
$= 3x^2 + 3x - 9 + x + 10$
$= 3x^2 + 4x + 1$

22. **(1) $x = 2, y = 3$** Substitute the values in the choices into the expression. Option (1) equals −11.

$4x^2 - 3(y + 6)$
$= 4(2^2) - 3(3 + 6)$
$= 4(4) - 3(9)$
$= 16 - 27$
$= -11$

23. **(2) 20°** You need to convert a Fahrenheit temperature to centigrade.

$C = \frac{5}{9}(F - 32)$
$= \frac{5}{9}(68 - 32)$
$= \frac{5}{9}(36)$
$= 20$

Lesson 6: Algebraic Expressions and the Calculator

Practice 6, page 465

1. 19	11. 57
2. 15.9	12. 36
3. 51	13. 5
4. $16\frac{1}{2}$	14. 24.8
5. 10	15. 54
6. −98	16. −45
7. 74	17. 78
8. 146	18. 108
9. 12	19. 459
10. −76	20. 1430

21. **(2) 36.2** Use the formula stated in the problem.

$P = 2l + 2w$
$= 2(12.5) + 2(5.6)$
$= 25 + 11.2$
$= 36.2$

22. **(5) $-2xy$** Try each expression.

$x + y = -3; -x + y = 7;$
$-x - y = 3; xy = -10;$ and
$-2xy = 20$
The value of option (5) is greatest.

23. **(1) 32**

$x^{-4} = \frac{1}{x^4} = \frac{1}{2^4} = \frac{1}{16}$
and $2 \div \frac{1}{16} = 32$

Lesson 7: Equations

Practice 7.1, page 467

1. $x = 9$	15. $x = 48$
2. $m = 28$	16. $y = -3$
3. $y = -1$	17. $r = 110$
4. $x = -64$	18. $x = 5$
5. $a = 125$	19. $y = -9$
6. $y = -13$	20. $d = -25$
7. $x = 27$	21. $x = 4$
8. $c = 7$	22. $x = -6$
9. $x = -4$	23. $h = 26$
10. $b = -7$	24. $x = 66$
11. $x = 31$	25. $m = -10$
12. $s = -8$	26. $y = 9$
13. $x = 108$	27. $w = -28$
14. $t = 39$	28. $y = 72$

29. **(3) $x + 36 = 77$** Erin's hours (x) plus Kayla's hours (36) = 77 hours.

30. **(4) $2y = 38$** Erin worked twice as many hours as Kayla ($2y$), and Erin worked 38 hours, so $2y = 38$.

31. **(4) 128** A number (x) divided by 4 is 32. Solve for x. $\frac{x}{4} = 32$

$4 \cdot \frac{x}{4} = 4 \cdot 32$
$x = 128$

32. **(5) $12x = -60$** Try −5 for x in each equation. Only option (5) is true when −5 is substituted for x.

$12x = -60$
$12(-5) = -60$
$-60 = -60$

33. **(2) $\$572.18 - c = \$434.68$** When you subtract the check from the amount in the checking account, the result will be the current balance.

Practice 7.2, page 469

1. $x = 50$	11. $x = 6$
2. $y = -2$	12. $r = -5$
3. $m = 2$	13. $y = 11$
4. $x = -4$	14. $b = 4$
5. $y = 6$	15. $x = -1$
6. $z = 2$	16. $h = 20$
7. $m = 3$	17. $x = 9$
8. $x = 4$	18. $z = 4$
9. $p = 7$	19. $b = 3$
10. $s = -2$	20. $n = 7$

21. **(4) $3x + 9 = 6x - 15$** Three times a number = $3x$ and "increased by 9" means to add 9. Six times a number = $6x$, and "15 less" means to subtract 15. The word *is* shows that the two expressions should be connected by the = symbol.

22. **(5) 375** Solve: $3x + x = 500$

$4x = 500$
$x = 125$

The variable x is the number of cards that Travis has. Eric has $3x$, or $3 \cdot 125$, which equals 375.

23. **(1) $4x - 7 = \frac{x}{3} + 15$** Remember that differences and quotients must be written in the order stated in the problem. The difference of four times a number and 7 is $4x - 7$. The quotient of the number and 3 plus 15 is $\frac{x}{3} + 15$.

24. **(1) $54** Solve:

$x + (2x + 12) = \$174$
$3x + 12 = \$174$
$3x = \$162$
$x = \$54$

Lesson 8: Common Algebra Word Problems

Practice 8, page 471

1. 1800 sq ft
2. 10 dimes
3. 24 games
4. 54
5. 8 shirts
6. 59
7. $1100
8. 28 hours
9. **(4) 84** Let x = Wiley's points, $x + 10$ = Sylvia's points, and $x - 6$ = Greg's points. Write and solve an equation:

$x + x + 10 + x - 6 = 226$
$3x + 4 = 226$
$3x = 222$
$x = 74$

Wiley scored 74 points, so Sylvia scored $74 + 10 = 84$ points.

10. **(3) $12** Let x = the price of an adult's ticket and $x - \$6$ = the price of a child's ticket. In the problem the cost of 2 adults' tickets and 4 children's tickets is $48. Write and solve an equation:

$2x + 4(x - 6) = \$48$
$2x + 4x - \$24 = \$48$
$6x - \$24 = \$48$
$6x = \$72$
$x = \$12$

11. **(2) 6** You know that in 12 years Jenny will be twice as old as Tina. Therefore, if you multiply Tina's age in 12 years by 2, it will equal Jenny's age in 12 years. Write and solve an equation:

$$4x + 12 = 2(x + 12)$$
$$4x + 12 = 2x + 24$$
$$2x = 12$$
$$x = 6$$

Lesson 9: Patterns and Functions

Practice 9, page 473

1. 0
2. 41
3. 2
4. 40
5. 23
6. −4
7. 31.25
8. −13
9. 32
10. −5

11. **(2) 49** The number of blocks in each construction equals $2n - 1$, where n is the number in the sequence. The 25th construction would require $2(25) - 1 = 49$ blocks.
12. **(4) 16** Each term is 6 greater than the term before it. The next term in the sequence is 10, and the sixth term is 16.
13. **(2) $c = \$5.00 - \$0.25(n - 1)$** The original price per scarf ($5) is reduced by 25 cents starting with the second scarf.
14. **(2) 1, 5, 9, 13, 17, . . .** Try the numbers 1, 2, and 3 for x in the function. This will result in the first three terms of the pattern: 1, 5, and 9. Only option (2) contains these three terms.

Lesson 10: Function Applications

Practice 10, page 475

1. a. $99
   b. $265
2. a. 5.5 or $5\frac{1}{2}$ hours
   b. 4.25 or $4\frac{1}{4}$ hours
3. a. Plan A
   b. Plan B
4. **(2) $29.50** Use the functions for the two jobs, substituting 30 hours for h.
   Job 1: $P = \$9.75h$
   $\quad = \$9.75(30)$
   $\quad = \$292.50$
   Job 2: $P = \$70 + \$8.40h$
   $\quad = \$70 + \$8.40(30)$
   $\quad = \$70 + \$252$
   $\quad = \$322$
   Subtract. $\$322 - \$292.50 = \$29.50$
5. **(5) Alicia will earn the most at Job 2.** Use the functions to find Alicia's wages at all three jobs based on 40 hours.

Job 1: $P = \$9.75h$
$\quad = \$9.75(40)$
$\quad = \$390$
Job 2: $P = \$70 + \$8.40h$
$\quad = \$70 + \$8.40(40)$
$\quad = \$70 + \$336$
$\quad = \$406$
Job 3: $P = \$380 \cdot \frac{H}{38}$
$\quad = \frac{\$380(40)}{38}$
$\quad = \$400$
Compare the three results. Alicia will earn the most at Job 2.
6. **(2) $19,400** Use the function to calculate the profit.
$P = \$95,000 - \$5,400d$
$\quad = \$95,000 - \$5,400(14)$
$\quad = \$95,000 - \$75,600$
$\quad = \$19,400$

Lesson 11: Inequalities

Practice 11, page 477

1. $x > 4$
2. $x > 7$
3. $x \leq -3$
4. $x \leq 36$
5. $x < -1$
6. $x \geq 5$
7. $x > -8$
8. $x > 4$
9. $x < -7$
10. $x < 2$
11. $x \geq 3$
12. $x < 6$
13. $x \geq 2$
14. $x > -10$
15. $x \leq 3$
16. $x < 21$
17. $x \geq -1$
18. $x < 3$
19. $x < 7$
20. $x \leq 3$

21. $-2 \leq x \leq 2$
22. $-20 < x < 6$
23. $6 < x < 16$
24. $4 \leq x \leq 9$
25. **(1) $s \leq 16$** The perimeter must be less than or equal to 64, so solve the inequality: $4s \leq 64$, which leads to $s \leq 16$.
26. **(4)**

Solve the inequality:
$-4x + 3 < -3x + 5$
$\quad -x < 2$
$\quad\quad x > -2$
To graph the solution $x > -2$, place an open circle at -2 because -2 is not included in the solution. Then extend the line to the right to include all values greater than -2.

Lesson 12: Quadratic Equations

Practice 12, page 479

1. $x^2 + 6x + 8$
2. $x^2 + 2x - 15$

3. $x^2 + 3x - 4$
4. $x^2 - 9x + 18$
5. $x^2 + 6x - 16$
6. $2x^2 - 3x - 2$
7. $x^2 - 14x + 45$
8. $3x^2 + x - 2$
9. $x^2 + 5x - 14$
10. $3x^2 + 14x + 16$
11. $x^2 - x - 30$
12. $x^2 - 13x + 30$
13. $4x^2 + 6x + 2$
14. $x^2 + 5x - 36$
15. $x^2 - 10x + 25$

For questions 16–30, the order of the factors does not matter:
$(2x - 1)(x + 3) = (x + 3)(2x - 1)$

16. $(x + 1)(x + 3)$
17. $(x - 1)(x + 5)$
18. $(x + 2)(x + 6)$
19. $(x - 3)(x + 2)$
20. $(x - 2)(x + 7)$
21. $(x - 4)(x + 3)$
22. $(x - 5)(x + 7)$
23. $(x - 6)(x - 6)$
24. $(x - 7)(x + 1)$
25. $(x - 4)(x + 8)$
26. $(2x - 1)(x + 3)$
27. $(2x - 10)(x + 1)$ or $(2x + 2)(x - 5)$
28. $(x - 5)(x + 10)$
29. $(2x - 1)(2x + 3)$
30. $(x - 7)(x + 8)$
31. **(2) −4 and 5**
   Rewrite the equation as equal to 0. Then factor. $x^2 - x - 20 = 0$
   $\qquad\qquad (x - 5)(x + 4) = 0$
   Determine which values of x will make each factor equal to 0. The solutions 5 and −4 will make the equation true.
32. **(5) $2x^2 + 2x - 24 = 0$** Substitute −4 into each equation. Do not take time to factor and find solutions for each equation. Only option (5) is correct.
   $2x^2 + 2x - 24 = 0$
   $2(-4)^2 + 2(-4) - 24 = 0$
   $2(16) + -8 - 24 = 0$
   $32 - 32 = 0$
33. **(3) 6**
   Factor. $2x^2 - 7x - 30 = 0$
   $\quad (2x + 5)(x - 6) = 0$
   $2x + 5 = 0$ will yield a negative solution. If $x = 6$, the expression $x - 6$ equals 0; therefore, option (3) is correct.

34. (2) x − 10
You know that length × width = area. You need to factor the expression $2x^2 - 27x + 70$, and one of the factors is the length $2x - 7$. $2x^2 - 27x + 70 = (2x - 7)(x - 10)$ The width is $(x - 10)$.

Lesson 13: The Coordinate Plane

Practice 13, page 481

1. (−4,5)
2. (3,6)
3. (0,−3)
4. (6,−7)
5. (−5,0)
6. (−6,−4)
7. (2,0)
8. (7,−2)
9.

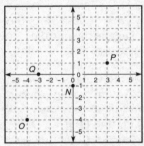

10.

11. **(5) (−1,0)** Plot each point in the answer choices. Only option (5) lies on the line that passes through points A and B.
12. **(1) (−3,−2)** Find the two points discussed in the problem. Then locate the third corner of the triangle, and find the coordinates of the corner. The missing corner is 3 spaces to the left of the origin and 2 spaces down: (−3,−2).

Lesson 14: Linear Equations

Practice 14, page 483

1.

If x =	then y =
−2	2
0	3
2	4

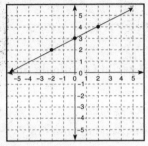

2.

If x =	then y =
−1	2
0	−1
1	−4

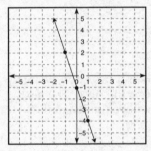

3.

If x =	then y =
1	1
2	0
3	−1

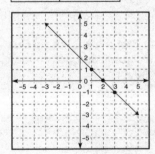

4.

If x =	then y =
0	3
1	1
2	−1

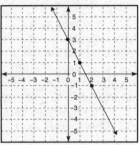

5. **(3) point T and (0,0)** Try the coordinates for points S and T in the equation. Both lie on the graph of the equation. Check the remaining points in the answer choices. Only (0,0) will make the equation $y = \frac{1}{4}x$ true.
6. **(4) y = −4x − 2**
Choose a point on line P, either (−1,2) or (0,−2) and try the point in the equations. If the point works in an equation, try the other point as well. Both points work in only option (4) $y = -4x - 2$.
7. **(2) 2x + 3y = 9** Try the coordinates (−3,5) in each equation. Only option (2) is true.
$$2x + 3y = 9$$
$$2(-3) + 3(5) = 9$$
$$-6 + 15 = 9$$
$$9 = 9$$

Lesson 15: Slope of a Line

Practice 15, page 485

1. 1
2. −2
3. 0
4. $\frac{3}{4}$
5. $-\frac{1}{2}$
6. 0
7. $-\frac{1}{3}$
8. 2
9. −3
10. **(1) line A** Moving from left to right, only lines A and E have a negative slope. Compare the rise to run for both lines. Line A moves down 1 space each time it goes 3 spaces to the right, a ratio of −1 to 3 or $-\frac{1}{3}$.

11. **(2) −2** You have more information than you need. Choose any two points and use the slope formula to solve for the slope. The equation below uses (0,4) and (1,2).

$$\frac{y_2 - y_1}{x_2 - x_1} \qquad \frac{4 - 2}{0 - 1} = \frac{2}{-1} = -2$$

12. **(4) (2,3)** The best way to solve the problem is probably to make a quick sketch. Because the line has a slope of 3, start at point (1,0) and count 3 spaces up and 1 space to the right. You are now at point (2,3), which is option (4). You can check your work using the slope formula.

Lesson 16: Distance Between Points

Practice 16, page 487

1. 5.8
2. 3.6
3. 4.1
4. 4.5
5. 5.4
6. 12.7
7. 9.2
8. 7.1
9. 2.2
10. **(3) 10** Point A is located at (−4,−2) and point C is at (5,3). Use the distance formula:

$$
\begin{aligned}
d &= \sqrt{(x_2 - x_1)^2 + (y_2 - y_1)^2} \\
&= \sqrt{(-4 - 5)^2 + (-2 - 3)^2} \\
&= \sqrt{(-9)^2 + (-5)^2} \\
&= \sqrt{80 + 25} \\
&= \sqrt{106} \approx 10
\end{aligned}
$$

11. **(4) (1,3)** A horizontal segment connects B and C, so you can count spaces to find the distance. The segment is 8 units in length, so the midpoint is 4 units from either B or C. Count 4 spaces and determine the coordinates of the point: (1,3).

12. **(2) 6.3** Point S is located at (−4,−3), and point T is located at (−2,3). Use the distance formula:

$$
\begin{aligned}
d &= \sqrt{(x_2 - x_1)^2 + (y_2 - y_1)^2} \\
&= \sqrt{(-4 - -2)^2 + (-3 - 3)^2} \\
&= \sqrt{(-2)^2 + (-6)^2} \\
&= \sqrt{4 + 36} \\
&= \sqrt{40} \approx 6.3
\end{aligned}
$$

13. **(1) 5** Point S is located at (−4,−3) and the origin on any coordinate grid is at (0,0). Use the distance formula:

$$
\begin{aligned}
d &= \sqrt{(x_2 - x_1)^2 + (y_2 - y_1)^2} \\
&= \sqrt{(-4 - 0)^2 + (-3 - 0)^2} \\
&= \sqrt{(-4)^2 + (-3)^2} \\
&= \sqrt{16 + 9} \\
&= \sqrt{25} \\
&= 5
\end{aligned}
$$

Lesson 17: Special Coordinate Grid Items

Practice 17, page 489

1. **(2,5)** Determine the missing point.

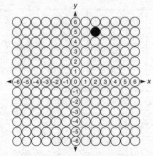

2. **(0,3)** To find the slope, count up 1 and 2 to the right. The next point will be plotted at (0,3).

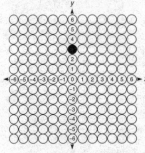

3. **(−2,−4)** Plot the known corners of the rectangle and determine the missing point.

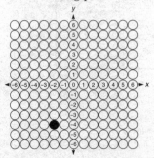

4. **(−1,3)** Start at (4,−6). Count up 9 spaces and 5 to the left.

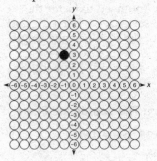

Lesson 18: Problem Solving

Practice 18, page 491

1. **(3) 24** Take each number and divide by 2; then compare to the original number. 24 ÷ 2 is 12, which is 12 less than 24.

2. **(4) $200** Try each number: For example, option (1): If Barbara raised $100, then Matt would have raised $50. To reach a total of $900, Sandra would have to raise $800, which is more than three times $100. Therefore, option (1) is incorrect. Only option (4) works. Barbara raised $200, Matt raised $150, and Sandra raised $600, which is 3 times $200.

3. **(4) 5** Try each option. Since the first package is the middle weight package and the total weight is 15 pounds, the package probably weighs a medium amount. You may want to start in the middle of the answer choices. Option (4) is the only one that works: If the first package weighs 5 pounds, then the second package weighs $2\frac{1}{2}$ pounds, and the third weighs $7\frac{1}{2}$ pounds, for a total of 15 pounds.

4. **(2) 82** You know that the second test is 6 points higher than the first. Add 6 to each score in the answer options. Then add to see whether the two scores would equal 170. Only option (2) works. 82 + 88 = 170

5. **(2) 10** Six years ago Nelson was five times as old as Maria. Start with this fact and work backward. If Nelson was 10 years old six years ago, then Maria was 10 ÷ 5 = 2 years old. Six years later, Nelson was 16 and

Maria was 8. Since 16 is twice 8, option (2) is correct.

6. **(1) −3** Try each option in the equation. Only option (1) works.
$$2x^2 + x - 15 = 0$$
$$2(-3)^2 + -3 - 15 = 0$$
$$2(9) - 3 - 15 = 0$$
$$18 - 18 = 0$$
$$0 = 0$$

7. **(3) 6** Use a calculator for this one. Multiply each answer choice by $15. Then subtract from $440 and divide the difference by $25 to find the number of children's passes. Add the number in the options to the number of passes for adults to see whether the total is 20. Only option (3) works. $15 × 6 = $90, and $440 − $90 = $350. Divide. $350 ÷ $25 = 14 Since 14 + 6 = 20 passes, option (3) is correct.

8. **(3) 20** You know that the distance around is 120 feet. The length added to the width is half the distance around, or 60 feet. Take each answer choice and double it to find the length. Then add. Only option (3) works. 20 ft × 2 = 40 ft, and 20 ft + 40 ft = 60 ft

Algebra Practice Questions, pages 492–495

Part I

1. **(5) −4x − 6** Use the order of operations.
$$6 - 4(x + 3) = 6 - 4x - 12$$
$$= -4x - 6$$

2. **(1) −3**
$$3 + 4x = x - 6$$
$$3x = -9$$
$$x = -3$$

3. **(3) 1.26 × 10⁸** Use your calculator to multiply.
180,000 × 700 = 126,000,000 A number written in scientific notation must have a single-digit whole number. Move the decimal point 8 places to the left and multiply 1.26 by 10 raised to the 8th power.

4. **(4) 4x − y = −7** Try $x = -2$ and $y = -1$ in each equation. Only option (4) is true.
$$4(-2) - (-1) = -7$$
$$-8 + 1 = -7$$
$$-7 = -7$$

5. **(4) $510** Let x = Tom's earnings

and $2x - $150 = $ Jan's earnings.
$$2x - \$150 + x = \$1380$$
$$3x - \$150 = \$1380$$
$$3x = \$1530$$
$$x = \$510$$

6. **(4) D** The coordinates of D are $(-3,-2)$, which make the equation $y = -x - 5$ true.
$$y = -x - 5$$
$$-2 = -(-3) - 5$$
$$-2 = 3 - 5$$
$$-2 = -2$$

7. **(3) $\frac{1}{3}$** Count the rise and run from C to B. The line moves up 3 spaces as it moves 9 to the right. $\frac{3}{9} = \frac{1}{3}$

8. **(1) s ≥ $17,500** Samuel's earnings can be represented by the expression $350 + 0.1s$, where s = total sales. Since Samuel needs to earn at least $2,100, this expression must be greater than or equal to $2,100. Solve.
$$\$350 + 0.1x \ge \$2,100$$
$$0.1x \ge \$1,750$$
$$s \ge \$17,500$$

9. **(2) $5.35** Substitute 24 for n and solve.
$$F = \$3.95 + \$0.10(24 - 10)$$
$$= \$3.95 + \$0.10(14)$$
$$= \$3.95 + \$1.40$$
$$= \$5.35$$

10. **(5) 29** Let x = the first number. The remaining numbers are $x + 2$, $x + 4$, and $x + 6$. Solve.
$$x + (x + 2) + (x + 4) + (x + 6) = 104$$
$$4x + 12 = 104$$
$$4x = 92$$
$$x = 23$$
The numbers are 23, 25, 27, and 29. The problem asks for the largest of these numbers.

11. **(3) 3⁶** 3 × 3 × 3 × 3 × 3 × 3 = 729 The other expressions are less than 400.

12. **(2) 5x − 4 = 8 + 2 + 3x** Translate each part of the problem to numbers and symbols, and connect with the = symbol.

13. **(2) −26** Substitute the given values, and use the order of operations.
$$6(x - y) - 8x = 6(-2 - 5) - 8(-2)$$
$$= 6(-7) + 16$$
$$= -42 + 16$$
$$= -26$$

14. **(3) 31** From 1 to 7, there is a difference of 6. From 7 to 14, there is a difference of 7. From 14 to

22, there is a difference of 8. Add 9 to 22. 22 + 9 = 31

15. **61**

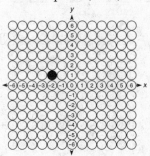

Use the order of operations.
$$4^2 - \frac{3(12 + 2^2)}{6} + 5(4) - 15$$
$$= 64 - \frac{3(12 + 4)}{6} + 5(4) - 15$$
$$= 64 - \frac{3(16)}{6} + 5(4) - 15$$
$$= 64 - \frac{48}{6} + 5(4) - 15$$
$$= 64 - 8 + 20 - 15$$
$$= 61$$

16. **(−2,1)** Choose values, and graph both lines. Or create a table for each linear equation to find values of y when substituting values for x, for example, 0, 1, 2, −1, and −2. The lines intersect at point $(-2,1)$.

Part II

17. **(1) −7x − (8 + y)** Remember, the word *product* indicates multiplication, and the word *sum* indicates addition.

18. **(3) 8 and −3** Either solve by factoring, or try each option in the equation. The correct factoring is:
$$x^2 - 5x - 24 = 0$$
$$(x - 8)(x + 3) = 0$$
$$x = 8 \text{ or } x = -3$$

19. **(2) 4** Write an equation and solve.
$$6x + 6 = 3(x + 6)$$
$$6x + 6 = 3x + 18$$
$$3x = 12$$
$$x = 4$$

20. **(3)** $y = 2x - 3$ Try the given points in the equations in the answer options. Only option (3) is correct.

21. **(2)** $x < 2$ Solve.
$$-2(x - 6) > 8$$
$$-2x + 12 > 8$$
$$-2x > -4$$
$$x < 2$$
Remember to reverse the inequality symbol when you divide both sides by -2 in the last step.

22. **(2) (−5,1)** Point L is 5 spaces to the left of the origin along the x-axis and 1 space above the origin along the y-axis.

23. **(3) 10** Use the distance formula and points $(-3,4)$ and $(3,-4)$.
$$\text{distance} = \sqrt{(x_2 - x_1)^2 + (y_2 - y_1)^2}$$
$$= \sqrt{(-3 - 3)^2 + (4 - -4)^2}$$
$$= \sqrt{-6^2 + 8}$$
$$= \sqrt{36 + 64}$$
$$= \sqrt{100} = 10$$

24. **(3) $18** Let $x =$ Sam's gift and $x =$ Daniel's gift. Celia's gift is $x + \$12$, and Bob's is $\frac{1}{2}(x + \$12)$. Write an equation and solve:
$$x + x + (x + \$12) + \tfrac{1}{2}(x + \$12) = \$81$$
$$x + x + x + \$12 + \tfrac{1}{2}x + \$6 = \$81$$
$$3\tfrac{1}{2}x + \$18 = \$81$$
$$3\tfrac{1}{2}x = \$63$$
$$x = \$18$$

25. **(1)** $x \le 3$ Solve.
$$-7x - 4 \ge x - 28$$
$$-8x \ge -24$$
$$x \le 3$$

26. **(5) 169** Substitute and apply the order of operations.
$$5x^2 - xy + 7y^2 =$$
$$= (5)(3^2) - (3)(-4) + 7(-4)^2$$
$$= (5)(9) - (3)(-4) + 7(16)$$
$$= 45 + 12 + 112$$
$$= 169$$

27. **(3) 8,652** Write an equation and solve. Let $x =$ the votes for the leading candidate.
$$x + \tfrac{1}{3}x + 5,512 = 18,072$$
$$1\tfrac{1}{3}x = 12,560$$
$$x = 9,420 \text{ votes}$$
for the leading candidate Substitute to find the votes for Perez. $\tfrac{1}{3}(9,420) + 5,512 = 8,652$

28. **(2)** $x = -2$ Solve.
$$-4(x + 2) - 10 = 5x$$
$$-4x - 8 - 10 = 5x$$
$$-18 = 9x$$
$$-2 = x$$

29. **(5) $5x + $10(35 − x) = $240** The total value of the $5 bills is $5x$. Since there are 35 bills, the number of $10 bills must be $35 - x$. The value of the $10 bills is $\$10(35 - x)$. The sum of the expression is equal to $240.

30. **(4) 75** Solve.
$$x + x + 1 + x + 2 + x + 3 + x + 4 = 370$$
$$5x + 10 = 370$$
$$5x = 360$$
$$x = 72$$
The numbers are 72, 73, 74, 75, and 76. The fourth number is 75.

31. **4**

Substitute and solve.
$$E = \frac{9r}{i}$$
$$= \frac{9(8)}{18} = \frac{72}{18} = 4$$

32. **(−1,1)** The given points lie in a vertical line. Since the distance between the points is 8 spaces, the midpoint is $(-1,1)$, which is 4 spaces from either point.

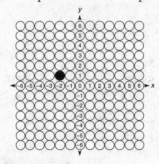

Geometry

Lesson 1: Points, Lines, and Angles

Practice 1, page 497

1. acute
2. obtuse
3. straight
4. acute
5. reflex
6. right
7. acute
8. obtuse

9. **(1) 135°** $m\angle RZS + m\angle QZS = 180°$. Since $\angle RZS$ measure 45°, $\angle QZS$ must measure 135°.

10. **(3) right** Since $m\angle RZQ = 180°$, subtract the two known angles to find the measure of $\angle SZT$. $180° - 45° - 45° = 90°$. Since $\angle SZT$ measures 90°, it is a right angle.

11. **(1) 38°** $\angle AWB + \angle BWC + \angle CWD = \angle AWD$, a straight angle with a measure of 180°. You know that $m\angle AWB = 90°$ and $m\angle CWD = 52°$, so substitute those values in the first equation: $90° + \angle BWC + 52° = 180°$, which leads you to $\angle BWC = °38$.

12. **(3) obtuse** $m\angle AWC$ is greater than the right angle AWB and less than the straight angle AWD. $\angle AWC$ must be obtuse.

Lesson 2: Parallel Lines and Transversals

Practice 2, page 499

All possible answers are shown.
1. $\angle 4$ and $\angle 6$, $\angle 3$ and $\angle 5$
2. $\angle 3$
3. 100°
4. $\angle 1$ and $\angle 7$, $\angle 2$ and $\angle 8$
5. $\angle 2$ and $\angle 4$, $\angle 1$ and $\angle 3$, $\angle 5$ and $\angle 7$, $\angle 6$ and $\angle 8$
6. $\angle 4$
7. **(2) 75°** $\angle 3$ and $\angle 1$ are vertical angles. Therefore, $m\angle 3 = m\angle 1$. Since $\angle 3 = 75°$, then $\angle 1 = 75°$.
8. **(3) They are in the same position from one parallel line to the other.** The transversal and the parallel lines form eight angles. Corresponding angles lie on the same side of the transversal and have the same relationship to the nearest parallel line.
9. **(2) 65°** Angle 7 and $\angle 3$ are corresponding angles, so $m\angle 7 = m\angle 3$; therefore, $m\angle 3 = 115°$. Angle 3 and $\angle 4$ are adjacent angles, which means 115° + $m\angle 4 = 180°$. $m\angle 4 = 65°$
10. **(5) $\angle 8$** Angle 2 and $\angle 8$ are alternate exterior angles. Therefore, they are equal.

Lesson 3: Quadrilaterals

Practice 3, page 501

1. rectangle, square
2. parallelogram, rectangle, square, rhombus

3. trapezoid
4. rectangle, square
5. none
6. rectangle, square, parallelogram, rhombus
7. square, rhombus
8. rectangle, square, parallelogram, rhombus, trapezoid
9. trapezoid
10. square
11. **(4) 140°** Let x = the measure of $\angle H$. $3x + 20° = m\angle F$. The sum of the angles of a quadrilateral is $360°$, so $3x + 20° + x + 90° + 90° = 360°$. Solve the equation. $4x + 200° = 360°$, so $4x = 160°$, $x = 40°$, and $3x + 20° = 140°$
12. **(2)** $EF \parallel GH$ A trapezoid is a quadrilateral with exactly one pair of parallel sides.
13. **(3) 90°** If the opposite sides of a figure are parallel and all four sides are equal, then the figure is either a square or rhombus. Since $\angle T$ is a right angle, the figure is square. Therefore, all the angles measure $90°$.
14. **(4) parallelogram** The quadrilateral has opposite sides that are equal and opposite angles that are equal. It is either a rectangle or a parallelogram. Since the figure has no right angles, it is not a rectangle. The quadrilateral must be a parallelogram.

Lesson 4: Triangles

Practice 4, page 503

1. equilateral, acute
2. scalene, obtuse
3. isosceles, acute
4. 64°
5. 45°
6. 97°
7. **(3) 14** Solve for $\angle BAC$: $m\angle BAC + 55° = 115°$, so $m\angle BAC = 60°$. Solve for $\angle BCA$: $m\angle BCA + 35° = 95°$, so $m\angle BCA = 60°$. If two of the angles of $\triangle ABC$ each measure $60°$, the third angle also measures $60°$. The triangle is equilateral, and all the sides are equal to side AB.
8. **(4) right** $55° + 35° + m\angle D = 180°$. Solve for the missing angle: $m\angle D = 90°$. Therefore, the triangle is a right triangle.
9. **(3) 86°** The angles of a triangle add up to $180°$. $38° + 56° = 94°$,

so the third angle can be found by subtracting $94°$ from $180°$. $180° - 94° = 86°$

Lesson 5: Congruent and Similar Triangles

Practice 5, page 505

1. No
2. Yes
3. Not enough information
4. **(4) 48** Since the triangles are similar, the sides must be proportional. Set up the ratio $\frac{25}{40} = \frac{30}{x}$ where x equals the length of ST. Solve. $x = 48$
5. **(2) 64°** Similar triangles have equal angle measures. If $m\angle S = 68°$, then $m\angle TYX = 68°$. $m\angle TYX + m\angle T + m\angle TXY = 180°$. Substitute and solve. $68° + 48° + m\angle TXY = 180°$, $m\angle TXY = 64°$
6. **(3) 3.2** The two triangles are similar because two of the angle measures in one triangle are equal to two of the angle measures in the other triangle. The side labeled x corresponds to the side with length 4.8. The side of length 2.8 corresponds to the side with length 4.2. Solve the ratio $\frac{x}{4.8} = \frac{2.8}{4.2}$. $x = 3.2$

Lesson 6: Similar Triangle Applications

Practice 6, page 507

1. **(3) 64** Set up a proportion comparing the sign's shadow to the building's shadow and the sign's height to the building's height. $\frac{6}{48} = \frac{8}{x}$ Solve. $x = 64$
2. **(2) 42** The 10-ft pole is 25 ft from the vertex of the angle; the base of the cliff is $80 + 25$, or 105 ft from the vertex of the angle. Set up a proportion. $\frac{105}{25} = \frac{x}{10}$ Solve. $x = 42$
3. **(1)** $\frac{2.5}{22.5} = \frac{1}{x}$ Set up a proportion comparing the meter stick's shadow to the flagpole's shadow and the meter stick's height to the flagpole's height.
4. **(5) 49** Examine the two triangles to find corresponding sides. The 8-ft side of the smaller triangle corresponds to the 28-ft side of the larger triangle. Write a proportion and solve. $\frac{8}{28} = \frac{14}{x}$; $x = 49$

5. **(2) 4** If you imagine a line drawn at the bottom of the frame, you will have two similar triangles. The base of the large triangle is 6 ft, and the base of the small triangle is unknown. The side of the large triangle is 12 ft and the side of the small one is $12 - 4 = 8$ ft. Write a proportion and solve. $\frac{8}{12} = \frac{x}{6}$; $x = 4$

Lesson 7: Perimeter and Area

Practice 7, page 509

1. area: 39 sq units
   perimeter: 30.8 units
2. area: 29.6 sq units
   perimeter: 24.6 units
3. area: 16 sq units
   perimeter: 16 units
4. area: 616 sq units
   perimeter: 109 units
5. area: 640 sq units
   perimeter: 104 units
6. area: 38 sq units
   perimeter: 32 units
7. **(4) 56** The shaded portion is a trapezoid.
   $\frac{1}{2} \times (5 + 9) \times 8 = 56$ sq in
8. **(5) Not enough information is given.** From the measures of the sides, you cannot determine the height of the parallelogram.
9. **(4) 324** Subtract the area of the patio from the area of the entire yard. Both are rectangles, so multiply length and width to find the area.
   $(24 \times 18) - (12 \times 9) = 324$ sq ft
10. **(2) 24** Simply add: $6 + 6 + 6 + 6 = 24$ cm, or multiply by 4: $6 \times 4 = 24$ cm.

Lesson 8: Circles

Practice 8, page 511

1. $C = 62.8$ in, $A = 314$ in^2
2. $C = 12.6$ cm, $A = 12.6$ cm^2
3. $C = 25.1$ m, $A = 50.2$ m^2
4. **(3) 38** Use the formula $C = \pi d$, where $d = 12$. $12(3.14) = 37.7$
5. **(2) 3.14 × 6²** The formula for the area of a circle is $A = \pi r^2$. The radius of a circle is half of the diameter. Half of 12 is 6. Substitute 6 for r and 3.14 for π. $A = 3.14 \times 6^2$
6. **(2) 13.0** The diameter of a circle is twice the radius. $6.5 \times 2 = 13$

7. (3) 19 You need to find the circumference of the 10-point band. First find the diameter, which passes through the inner circle. Add the width of the 10-point band twice and the diameter of the inner circle: $2 + 2 + 2 = 6$ inches. Now you can use the formula for circumference. $6(3.14) = 18.84$, which rounds to 19 inches.

Lesson 9: Volume

Practice 9.1, page 513

1. 160 cubic units
2. 27 cubic units
3. 141 cubic units
4. 420 cubic units
5. 3 cubic units
6. 236 cubic units
7. **(1) 5** $V = lwh$ You know that the length and width of the box both equal 4 and that the volume equals 80. Solve the equation.
$$80 = 4(4)h$$
$$80 = 16h$$
$$5 = h$$
8. **(3) 125** If each edge measures 5 feet, then the figure is a cube. $5^3 = 125$
9. **(4) 17** First, you must find the volume of the pool. The radius of the pool is 6 and the height is 3.
$$V = \pi r^2 h$$
$$\approx 3.14(6^2)(3)$$
$$\approx 3.14(36)(3)$$
$$\approx 339.12$$
Therefore, the volume is about 339. Solve the ratio $\frac{1}{20} = \frac{x}{339}$, where x equals the number of scoops Linda must add.
$20x = 339$; $x = 16.95$, about 17

Practice 9.2, page 515

1. 9 in^3
2. 127 in^3
3. 314 cm^3
4. 480 m^3
5. 11 in^3
6. 1060 cm^3
7. **(4) 480** First, you have to find the volume of the original package. Solve the equation.
$V = \frac{1}{3} \times 10^2 \times 15 = 500$
Then find the volume of the new package. Add 4 to the

length and width of the base, which gives you 14. Now solve the equation.
$V = \frac{1}{3} \times 14^2 \times 15 = 980$
Find the difference of the two volumes. $980 - 500 = 480$
8. **(3) 67** You know that the height of the cone is half of the diameter of the base. Since the radius of the base is also half of the diameter, the radius must equal the height. Therefore, the radius is 4. Now solve the equation.
$V = \frac{1}{3} \times \pi \times 4^2 \times 4 \approx 67$
9. **(5) The volume of B is less than the volume of A.** First, find the volumes of the two figures. Figure A is a rectangular solid. Use the formula $V = lwh$. $4 \times 3 \times 2 = 24$ Figure B is a pyramid. Use the formula $V = \frac{1}{3}e^2 h$.
$\frac{1}{3} \times 3^2 \times 6 = 18$ Now compare the two volumes. Since $24 > 18$, option (5) must be the answer.
10. **(4) 1000** Use the formula $V = \frac{1}{3}\pi r^2 h$: $\frac{1}{3} \times \pi \times 8^2 \times 15 \approx 1,005$, which is about 1000.

Lesson 10: Irregular Figures

Practice 10, page 517

1. $P = 149$ units
   $A = 1040$ sq units
2. $P = 49.7$ units
   $A = 159.25$ sq units
3. $P = 71$ units
   $A = 171$ sq units
4. $V = 185$ cubic units
5. $V = 278$ cubic units
6. $V = 399$ cubic units
7. **(1) 360** Find the volume of the main rectangular slab: $V = lwh$, so $V = 12 \times 8 \times 3 = 288$ cu ft. Find the volume of one of the blocks: $V = lwh$, so $V = 3 \times 3 \times 2 = 18$ cu ft. Multiply by 4, the number of blocks. $18 \times 4 = 72$ cu ft Add the main slab to the blocks. $288 + 72 = 360$ cu ft
8. **(2) 134** The radius of both the cones and the cylinder is 2. The height of one cone is 4 inches. Find the volume of one cone.
$V = \frac{1}{3} \times \pi \times r^2 \times h$
$\approx \frac{1}{3}(3.14)(2^2)(4) \approx 16.7$ cu in
Multiply by 2 to find the volume to both cones. $16.7 \times 2 = 33.4$ cu in Find the volume of the cylinder.
$V = \pi \times r^2 \times h$

$\approx 3.14(2^2)(8) \approx 100.48$ cu in
Add to find the total volume.
$33.4 + 100.48 = 133.88$ cu in, which rounds to 134 cu in

Lesson 11: Pythagorean Relationship

Practice 11, page 519

1. $c = 11.3$ in
2. $c = 15$ yd
3. $c = 2.5$ cm
4. $a = 5.2$ m
5. $b = 8$ mm
6. $a = 17.3$ ft
7. $c = 12.2$ cm
8. $b = 26.0$ in
9. $c = 6.4$ km
10. **(2) 6.7** The distance from A to C is 3 units, and the distance from B to C is 6 units.
$$c^2 = a^2 + b^2$$
$$c^2 = 3^2 + 6^2$$
$$c^2 = 9 + 36$$
$$c^2 = 45$$
$$c = \sqrt{45} \approx 6.7$$
11. **(3) 30** The shorter sides are the legs. Solve for the hypotenuse.
$$c^2 = a^2 + b^2$$
$$c^2 = 18^2 + 24^2$$
$$c^2 = 324 + 576$$
$$c^2 = 900$$
$$c = \sqrt{900} = 30$$
12. **(4) 12.1** The brace divides the rectangle into two right triangles with the brace as the hypotenuse of each. Solve for the hypotenuse of one of the triangles: $c^2 = a^2 + b^2$
$$c^2 = 5^2 + 11^2$$
$$c^2 = 25 + 121$$
$$c^2 = 146$$
$$c = \sqrt{146} \approx 12.08 \text{ which rounds to } 12.1$$
13. **(2) 36**
$$c^2 = a^2 + b^2$$
$$39^2 = 15^2 + b^2$$
$$1,521 = 225 + b^2$$
$$1,296 = b^2$$
$$b = \sqrt{1,296} = 36$$

Lesson 12: Using the Formulas Page

Practice 12, page 521

1. **(5) π (7.5^2)(1.5)** The pond is in the shape of a cylinder, and you need to find the volume. Use the formula: Volume = $\pi \times$ radius^2

× height. The radius is one-half the diameter: $15 \div 2 = 7.5$. The height, in this case, is the depth of 1.5 ft. Volume = $\pi(7.5^2)(1.5)$

2. **(4) $\pi(7.5^2)$** The painting will cover the circular surface that is the bottom of the pond. The measure of the surface is the area. Use the formula: Area = $\pi \times$ radius^2. The radius is one-half of 15, or 7.5. Area = $\pi(7.5^2)$

3. **(4) $\sqrt{3^2 + 2^2}$** The antenna frame is at a right angle to the roof, so the diagonal support becomes the hypotenuse of a right triangle. Use the formula: $c^2 = a^2 + b^2$, and solve for c. $c^2 = 3^2 + 2^2$, so $c = \sqrt{3^2 + 2^2}$

4. **(1) $8^2 - (4^2 \times \pi)$** The shaded portion is equal to the area of the square minus the area of the circle. The area of the square can be found by squaring the side: 8^2. The area of the circle is found by multiplying pi by the radius squared: $A = \pi \times 4^2$. Note that the side of the square equals the diameter of the circle, so the radius of the circle is $8 \div 2 = 4$. The correct option is $8^2 - (4^2 \times \pi)$.

5. **(5) 15(14)(7)** Volume is measured in cubic footage, and a room is rectangular in shape, so you can solve the problem using the formula $V = $ length $\times$ width $\times$ height. 15(14)(7)

6. **(2) 60 + 2(80)** Although the doors are in the shape of a rectangle, there is no molding along the bottom of the door. The correct option combines the 60-inch length with twice the 80-inch height of the doors.

Lesson 13: Using the Calculator

Practice 13, page 523

1. 42 in
2. 195 sq cm
3. 43 cu ft
4. 15.8 cm
5. 37.7 in
6. 3014 cm^3
7. **(4) 520** Use the formulas for finding the area of a rectangle and the area of a triangle. Press: $32 \times 20 - 0.5 \times 20 \times 12 =$ 520.

8. **(2) 35** Use the formula for finding the volume of a cylinder. Press: $3.14 \times 1.5 \boxed{x^2} \times 5 =$ 35.325, which rounds to 35 meters.

9. **(4) 5,056** Use the formula for finding the volume of a rectangular solid. Subtract the volume of Box B from the volume of Box A. Press: $26 \times 12 \times 32 - 22 \times 8 \times 28 =$ 5056.

10. **(3) 608** Use the formula for finding the area of a rectangle. Combine the areas of the two faces. Press: $32 \times 12 + 28 \times 8 =$ 608.

Lesson 14: Problem Solving

Practice 14, page 525

1. **(4) $m\angle 3 + m\angle 6 = 180°$** Lines P and Q are parallel, so AD is a transversal. You know that $\angle 3$ and $\angle 4$ are adjacent supplementary angles, so their sum is 180°. $\angle 4$ and $\angle 6$ are corresponding angles, so they have equal measures. Since the sum of $m\angle 3$ and $m\angle 4$ is 180° and $m\angle 6 = m\angle 4$, the sum of $m\angle 3$ and $m\angle 6$ must be 180° as well.

2. **(1) $m\angle 5 = 60°$** $m\angle ABC$ must equal 60° because the sum of the interior angles of a triangle is 180°, and you know that $\angle BAC$ measures 30° and $\angle ACB$ measures 90°. $180° - 30° - 90° = 60°$ Since lines P and Q are parallel, triangles ABC and ADE are similar. Angle 5, or $\angle ADE$, corresponds to $\angle ABC$; therefore, $\angle 5$ measures 60°.

3. **(4) ΔA and ΔB are not congruent.** The remaining statements could be true under certain circumstances, but there is not enough information to draw any of these conclusions. We know for certain that the two triangles cannot be congruent because they have sides of different lengths.

4. **(2) ΔJKL and ΔQRS are congruent.** We know that the bases of each triangle are the same length (8 units). We know that the triangles share two other sides with the same measure. JK

and RS both measure 5.7 units. We also know that the angles formed by the two sides have the same measure of 46°. By the Side-Angle-Side rule, we can prove the triangles are congruent.

5. **(3) 115°, 115°, and 65°** By the definition of a parallelogram, the opposite angle to the one given must measure 65°. We also know that the remaining two angles must have the same measure and that the sum of the interior angles of this quadrilateral must be 360°. $2x + 65° + 65° = 360°$, and $x = 115°$

6. **(3) 8** You can try each combination of sides in the Pythagorean relationship. Only 6, 8, and 10 will work.
$6^2 + 8^2 = 10^2$
$36 + 64 = 100$
$100 = 100$

Geometry Practice Questions, pages 526–528

1. **(4) $\angle 5$** Line J transverses lines S and T. Lines J and K are not parallel, so $\angle 3$ cannot be equal in measure to the angles numbered 9 through 15. Looking only at transversal J, $\angle 3$ is equal in measure to $\angle 5$ because they are alternate interior angles.

2. **(2) trapezoid** A four-sided figure with only one pair of parallel sides is a trapezoid.

3. **(3) 85°** Angle 10 measures 95°. Since $\angle 14$ corresponds to $\angle 10$, it also measures 95°. Angles 14 and 15 are supplementary angles, so $m\angle 15 = 180° - 95° = 85°$.

4. **(3) 90°** The sum of the interior angle measures of any triangle is 180°. Let $x = $ one of the smaller angles. Let $2x = $ the largest angle.
$2x + x + x = 180°$, so $4x = 180°$, and $x = 45°$, and the largest angle, $2x$, measures 90°.

5. **(5) 224** A closet is in the shape of a rectangular solid. To find the volume, multiply.
$V = lwh = 7(4)(8) = 224$ cubic feet

6. **(3) 45** Write a proportion and solve.
$$\frac{6}{3\frac{1}{2}} = \frac{x}{26\frac{1}{4}}$$
$6 \times 26\frac{1}{4} \div 3\frac{1}{2} = 45$ feet

7. **(5) Not enough information is given.** Since $m\angle 1 = 35°$, you can find $180 - 35° = 145°$. While you can find that the sum of angles 2 and 3 = 145°, there is not enough information to know the measure of either angle 2 or 3 individually.

8. **(2) ΔJKL and ΔLMN are similar.** Solve for the missing angle in each triangle. Angle K measures 42°, and angle M measures 90°. Since the angle measures are equal but the side lengths are not, the triangles are similar.

9. **(2) 500** The distances hiked form a right triangle. The legs are 300 and 400 yards. You must solve for the hypotenuse. You can use the Pythagorean relationship:
$$a^2 + b^2 = c^2$$
$$300^2 + 400^2 = c^2$$
$$90,000 + 160,000 = c^2$$
$$250,000 = c^2$$
$$500 = c$$
You may have noticed that the distances form a large triangle with sides in the 3:4:5 ratio. Therefore, you can see that the hypotenuse of a triangle with legs of 300 and 400 yards is 500 yards.

10. **(4) 168** The volume of the container as drawn in the diagram is $V = lwh = 9(7)(12) = 756$ cu in. If you increase the length by 2 inches, the volume is $11(7)(12) = 924$ cu in. Find the difference. $924 - 756 = 168$ cu in You can solve the problem more easily by multiplying the added length by the width and height. $2(7)(12) = 168$ cu in

11. **(5) $x^2 = 15^2 - 6^2$** Use the Pythagorean Relationship. If $a^2 + b^2 = c^2$ and c is the hypotenuse, then $b^2 = c^2 - a^2$ or $x^2 = 15^2 - 6^2$.

12. **(4) 36** Use the formula for finding the perimeter of a rectangle. Let $3w$ = length.
$$P = 2l + 2w$$
$$96 = 2(3w) + 2w$$
$$96 = 6w + 2w$$
$$96 = 8w$$
$$w = 12$$
Therefore, the width is 12 inches, and the length is $3 \times 12 = 36$ inches.

13. **(3) $\angle 2$ and $\angle 8$** Try each option. Angles 2 and 8 are equal in measure because they are alternate exterior angles.

14. **(1) vertical angles** Vertical angles are formed by intersecting lines. They share the same vertex and are located opposite each other.

15. **(2) $\frac{120}{50} = \frac{AB}{62}$** Set up the proportion in the way that makes sense to you. Then figure out what operations will be necessary to solve it. If you set up the proportion correctly, you will need to multiply 120 and 62 and divide by 50. Look at each proportion in the answer choices. Only option (2) would be solved with this series of operations.

16. **(2) 1,560** You may find it helpful to draw a sketch of the room. Two walls measure 40 by 12 feet. Two measure 25 by 12 feet. Find the total area. $2(40)(12) +$

$2(25)(12) = 960 + 600 = 1,560$

17. **(3) 12,000** Use the formula $V = lwh$. Multiply. $40(25)(12) = 12,000$

18. **(3) 56°** The sum of $\angle 1$ and the angle marked x corresponds to $\angle 2$, a right angle. $m\angle 1$ is 34° because $\angle 1$ is vertical to an angle measuring 34°. $x + 34° = 90°$, so $x = 56°$

19. **24** It may help to make a sketch. The area of the parallelogram is $6(10) = 60$ sq cm. To find the base of the triangle, use the formula for finding the area of a triangle and solve for base. $60 = \frac{1}{2}b(5)$, so $12 = \frac{1}{2}b$, and $24 = b$

20. **164** The sum of supplementary angles is 180°, so $16 + m\angle S = 180°$, and $m\angle S = 164°$.

**GED Formulas page
on the reverse side.**

**You may tear out
for your convenience.**

FORMULAS

AREA of a:

square	Area = side^2
rectangle	Area = length × width
parallelogram	Area = base × height
triangle	Area = $\frac{1}{2}$ × base × height
trapezoid	Area = $\frac{1}{2}$ × (base$_1$ + base$_2$) × height
circle	Area = π × radius^2; π is approximately equal to 3.14.

PERIMETER of a:

square	Perimeter = 4 × side
rectangle	Perimeter = 2 × length + 2 × width
triangle	Perimeter = side$_1$ + side$_2$ + side$_3$

CIRCUMFERENCE of a:

circle	Circumference = π × diameter; π is approximately equal to 3.14.

VOLUME of a:

cube	Volume = edge^3
rectangular solid	Volume = length × width × height
square pyramid	Volume = $\frac{1}{3}$ × (base edge)^2 × height
cylinder	Volume = π × radius^2 × height; π is approximately equal to 3.14.
cone	Volume = $\frac{1}{3}$ × π × radius^2 × height; π is approximately equal to 3.14.

COORDINATE GEOMETRY

Distance between points = $\sqrt{(x_2 - x_1)^2 + (y_2 - y_1)^2}$; (x_1, y_1) and (x_2, y_2) are two points in a plane.

slope of a line $= \dfrac{y_2 - y_1}{x_2 - x_1}$; (x_1, y_1) and (x_2, y_2) are two points on the line.

PYTHAGOREAN RELATIONSHIP

$a^2 + b^2 = c^2$; a and b are legs and c the hypotenuse of a right triangle.

MEASURES OF CENTRAL TENDENCY

mean $= \dfrac{x_1 + x_2 + \ldots + x_n}{n}$, where the x's are the values for which a mean is desired, and n is the total number of values for x.

median = the middle value of an odd number of _ordered_ scores, and halfway between the two middle values of an even number of _ordered_ scores.

SIMPLE INTEREST

interest = principal × rate × time

DISTANCE

distance = rate × time

TOTAL COST

total cost = (number of units) × (price per unit)

Reprinted with permission of the GED Testing Service of the American Council on Education.

Kaplan GED Post-Test Score Conversion Charts

To determine a passing score on the Kaplan GED Post-Tests, you need to meet or exceed a minimum score of 410 on each test AND meet or exceed an average score of 450 on all five of the tests. Scores under 410 are shaded below.

Language Arts, Writing

Correct Answers on Part I	Combined with the Part II, Essay for an Estimated Score2		
	2	3	4
49-50	640	710	800
47-48	560	630	720
45-46	500	570	650
43-44	470	540	630
41-42	460	530	620
39-40	450	520	600
37-38	440	510	590
35-36	430	500	580
33-34	420	490	580
31-32	410	480	570
29-30	410	480	560
27-28	400	470	560
25-26	400	470	550
23-24	390	460	550
21-22	390	460	550
19-20	380	450	540
17-18	380	450	540
15-16	370	440	530
13-14	370	440	520
11-12	360	430	520
9-10	350	420	510
7-8	340	410	500
5-6	310	380	470
3-4	250	320	410
1-2	220	290	380

Social Studies

Correct Answers	Estimated Score
49-50	800
47-48	710
45-46	640
43-44	600
41-42	570
39-40	550
37-38	530
35-36	510
33-34	500
31-32	480
29-30	470
27-28	460
25-26	440
23-24	430
21-22	410
19-20	400
17-18	390
15-16	370
13-14	360
11-12	340
9-10	320
7-8	300
5-6	280
3-4	250
1-2	200

Science

Correct Answers	Estimated Score
49-50	800
47-48	780
45-46	700
43-44	630
41-42	570
39-40	540
37-38	510
35-36	480
33-34	460
31-32	450
29-30	430
27-28	420
25-26	410
23-24	400
21-22	390
19-20	380
17-18	380
15-16	370
13-14	350
11-12	340
9-10	320
7-8	300
5-6	260
3-4	210
1-2	200

Language Arts, Reading

Correct Answers	Estimated Score
39-40	800
37-38	680
35-36	600
33-34	540
31-32	500
29-30	480
27-28	470
25-26	450
23-24	430
21-22	410
19-20	400
17-18	390
15-16	380
13-14	360
11-12	340
9-10	320
7-8	300
5-6	270
3-4	230
1-2	200

Mathematics

Correct Answers	Estimated Score
49-50	800
47-48	750
45-46	690
43-44	630
41-42	580
39-40	540
37-38	530
35-36	510
33-34	500
31-32	480
29-30	470
27-28	450
25-26	440
23-24	430
21-22	410
19-20	400
17-18	390
15-16	380
13-14	360
11-12	350
9-10	330
7-8	300
5-6	280
3-4	250
1-2	200

Have You Passed the Kaplan GED Post-Tests?

Step 1: To determine your score for each test, write the "Number Correct" and the corresponding "Score" in the box below. Check off "Pass" for each test that has a score of 410 or higher.

- If all of your scores are 410 or higher, you have met the minimum score for each test, and you can go on to Step 2.
- If any of your scores are lower than 410, you will need to study more in that test area.

Step 2: To determine your average score for all of the tests, divide the TOTAL Score by 5.

- If the average is 450 or higher, you have passed the GED Post-Tests. CONGRATULATIONS!
- If the average is lower, you need to study more in the test areas with low scores.

	Number Correct	Score	Pass (✔)
Writing			
Reading			
Social Studies			
Science			
Mathematics			
TOTAL			
AVERAGE			

¹These reflect the minimum scores set by the GED Testing Service for the actual test. Individual states may have higher individual test or average scores. Consult your state Department of Adult Education to determine the passing scores for your state. Also, remember that these are practice tests – results on the actual GED will vary. ²On the actual GED Test, you must have an essay score of 2 or higher to pass the Writing Test, no matter what your Part I score is.

INDEX

A

acceleration, 276
action, dramatic, 332–333
action verb, 84
activation energy, 272
acute angle, 496
acute triangle, 502
adaptation, 246
addiction, 240
addition, 348
  of decimals, 370
  of fractions, 376
  of signed numbers, 450
adjacent angles, 498
adjective, proper, 128
advantages and disadvantages, `writing about, 77
agricultural regions, 218
air masses, 258
algebra, problem solving with, 490–491
Algebra section, 341, 450–495
algebra work problems, 470–471
algebraic expressions, 460–465
alleles, 242
Allies, 172, 188
alloy, 270
alternate angles, 498
alternative format questions, 382
alveolus, 238
amendment, 196
American Revolution, 166–167, 186
"amount paid back," in interest problems, 402
analysis, reading
  of character, 308–309
  of characters, 334–335
  of images, 322–323
  of symbols, 322–323
anecdotes, in essay writing, 150
ancient Greece, 180
angle measures, triangles classified by, 502
angle-side-angle (ASA) triangles, 504
angles (geometry), 496–497
  acute, 496
  adjacent, 498
  alternate, 498
  complementary, 496
  corresponding, 498
  obtuse, 496
  vertical, 498

answer grid, filling in, 382–383
answers, reasonable, 360
antecedent-pronoun agreement, 108
antecedents, 106, 108
antibiotics, 240
antibodies, 240
applying ideas, 290–291
appositives, commas with, 126
area, 508–509
  of a circle, 510
  formulas for, 688
aristocracy, 186
arms race, 188
arteries, 238
articles, 196
Articles of Confederation, 166
ASA triangle (angle-side-angle), 504
asexual reproduction, 242
asteroids, 260
atmosphere, 258
atom, 268
atomic bomb, 188
audience, essay, 140
average (numerical), 422
Axis Powers, 172, 188
Aztecs, 180

B

bacteria, 240
banks, 208
bar graphs, 414–417
bargaining, collective, 212
base (measurement), 508
base (percents), 394, 398
Basics, Math, 346–367
benchmarks, and problem solving, 444
benefits, 212
Big Bang, 262
Bill of Rights, 166, 196
biodiversity, 222
biosphere, 248
black hole, 262
body paragraph, 78, 148
boiling point, 270
bonds, covalent and ionic, 268
brain, 238
brainstem, 238
brainstorming, 74, 144

branches of government, 194–195
bronchi, 238
bronchioles, 238
brown dwarfs, 262
budget, 210
business cycle, 208

C

calculator, using, 343, 354–357
    to evaluate algebraic expressions, 464–465
    with formulas, 522–523
    keys on, 354, 356, 464
    for measurements, 442–443
    and solving problems, 380–381, 400–401
canceling fractions, 378
capacity (economics), 208
capacity (volume), 512
capillaries, 238
capitalism, laissez-faire, 208
capitalization, 128–129
carbohydrates, 236, 240
cartographers, 224
cause and effect, relating, 292–293
cell energy, 236–237
cell functions, 234
cell membrane, 234
cell processes, 236–237
cell structures, 234
cell wall, 234
cells, 234
cellular respiration, 236
Central Powers, 172, 188
cerebellum, 238
cerebrum, 238
change, percent of, 404
change sign key, calculator, 464
character, analyzing, 308–309
characters, analyzing, 334–335
charge, electric, 278
Charlemagne, 182
checks and balances, 194
chemical energy, 274
chemical equations, 272
chemical formulas, 268
chemical reactions, 272–273
chemical symbol, 268
child labor, 186
chlorophyll, 236
chromosomes, 244
circle graphs, 418–419

circles, 510–511
    area of, 688
    circumference of, 510, 688
circulatory system, 238
circumference, 510, 688
citizens, role of, 200–201
citizenship, 200
Civics and Government section, 161, 194–205
Civil Rights Movement, 174
Civil War, 168–169
civilizations, early, 180–181
clauses
    independent, 86
    subordinate, 88
Clear and Organized Writing, 66–83
climate and weather, 258–259
codon, 244
cold front, 258
Cold War, 174, 188
collective bargaining, 212
collective nouns, 114
colonialism, 166–167
colonies, 166, 184
comma errors, 126
comma splices, 90–91
commas
    after introductory elements, 124
    with appositives, 126
    in compound sentences, 124
    in a series, 126
    use of, 124–127
common denominators, 376
common noun, 106
communism, 188
comparing
    and contrasting, 294–295
    ideas, 77
    numbers, 368
    values, 346
compass rose, 224
compensation, 212
competition, 206
complementary angle, 496
complete simple sentences, 84–85
complex sentences, 86–89
compound sentences, 86–89
    commas in, 124
compound subject, verb agreement with, 116
compounds, 268
concise vs wordy writing, 118
concluding paragraph, 78, 148

conclusions, drawing, 296–297, 336–337
condensation point, 270
conductor, 278
cones, volume of, 514, 688
Confederacy, 168
confirmation, judicial, 194
conflict, 304
Congress, 194
congruent triangles, 504–505
conjunction, subordinating, 88
consecutive numbers, 470
conservation, 222, 256
conservative margin, 254
constituents, 194
Constitution, U. S., 166, 186
    amendments to, 196
constitutional government, 196–197
contrasting ideas, 77
construction shift questions, 63
constructive margin, 254
consumer goods, 206
consumer issues, 212–213
consumers, 212, 248
consumption, 206
Continental Congress, 166
continents, 218
contour lines, 224
contractions, 130
contrasting and comparing, 294–295
convention, 198
coordinate geometry, 688
coordinate grid items, special, 488–489
coordinate plane, 480–481
coordinating conjunction, 86
core, Earth's, 254
correction questions, 62
corresponding angles, 498
cosmologists, 262
cost formulas, 352
covalent bond, 268
Crusades, 182
crust, Earth's, 254
crystal, 270
cubes, volume of, 512, 688
currency, 210
current
    electric, 278
    ocean, 258
cylinders, volume of, 512, 688
cytoplasm, 234
czar, 188

D

dangling modifier, 94
Data Analysis section, 341, 412–433
data analysis, and problem solving, 428–433
debates, 198
decimal operations, 370–373
decimal system, 368
decimals
    addition of, 370
    division of, 372
    entering measurements as, 442
    and fraction equivalencies, 384–385
    and fractions, 368–389
    multiplication of, 372
    percent to, 394
    subtraction of, 370
    and using the calculator, 380
Declaration of Independence, 166, 186
decrease, percent of, 404
deficit, 210
degrees, 218
demand, supply and, 206
democracy, 180
Democrats, 198
denominators, 374, 376
deoxyribonucleic acid (DNA), 244
dependent events (probability), 426
depression, 208
Depression, Great, 172
destructive margin, 254
details, supporting, 286–287
    using in essay writing, 150
determining
    point of view, 298–299
    tone, 298–299
development, urban, rural and suburban, 220
dialogue, reading, 330–331
diameter, 510
dictatorship, 196
difference (numerical), 348
digestive system, 238
directions, essay, 141
distance, formulas for, 352, 688
distance between points, 486–487
distribution, 206, 220
distributive property, 462
divide, 350
dividend, 350

export, 184
expressions
   evaluating, 462
   simplifying, 462
exterior angles, alternate, 498

F

factoring, solving fractions by, 478
fascism, 172
fats, 240
favorable outcome (probability), 424
FDA (Food and Drug Administration), 210
FDIC (Federal Deposit Insurance Corporation), 210
federal, 194
Federal Deposit Insurance Corporation (FDIC), 210
Federal Reserve System, 210
Federal Trade Commission (FTC), 210
federalism, 194
Fertile Crescent, 180
feudalism, 182–183
Fiction section, 283, 304–317
figurative language, 320–321
figures, irregular (geometry), 516–517
first function keys, calculator, 354
Food and Drug Administration (FDA), 210
food web, 248
forces and motion, 276–277
formal language, 118
formulas
   area, 508
   chemical, 268
   circles, 510
   cost, 352
   distance, 352, 688
   distance between points, 486–487
   page listing, 520–521, 688
   percent, 396–399
   perimeter, 508
   and using the calculator, 522–523
   volume, 512
fossil fuels, 222
fractions
   adding, 376
   basics about, 374–375
   canceling, 378
   and decimals, 368–389, 384–385
   division of, 378
   improper, 374
   inverting, 378
   like, 376

multiplication of, 378
   operations with, 376–379
   percent to, 394
   proper, 374
   raising, 375
   reducing, 375
   subtracting, 376
   terms of, 375
   and using the calculator, 380
fragment, sentence, 84
free enterprise, 208
free market economy, 206
freezing point, 270
French Revolution, 186
frequency table, 420–423
fronts (weather), 258
FTC (Federal Trade Commission), 210
function applications, 474–475
function keys, calculator, 354, 356
function word problems, 474–475
functions
   cell, 234
numerical, 472–473
Functions section, 341

G

galaxies, 262
gases, 270
GED test
   Algebra section, 341, 450–495
   Data Analysis section, 341, 412–433
   filling in standard grid on, 358–359
   Functions section, 341
   Geography section, 218–228
   Government and Civics section, 194–205
   Language Arts section, 61–160, 283–340
   Mathematics section, 341–528
   overview of, vii–viii
   score required to pass, viii
   skills tested on, viii
   Social Studies section, 161
   strategies for taking, ix–xvi
   U.S. History section, 161, 166–179
   using calculator on, 343, 354–357
generating ideas, 74, 144
genes, 242
genetic code, 244
genetic material, 234
genetics, modern, 244–245
genome, 244

red giant, 262

reducing a fraction, 375

reducing to lowest terms, 375

reflex angle, 496

Reformation, 182

regions, 218

regroup (numerical), 348

regular verbs, 110

relating

cause and effect, 292–293

sentences and paragraphs, 72–73

relevance and logical order, 70–71

Renaissance, 182

renewable resources, 222, 256

reparations, 188

reproduction and heredity, 242–243

republic, 196

Republicans, 198

resources, natural, 256–257

nonrenewable, 222, 256

renewable, 222, 256

using wisely, 222–223

respiration, cellular, 236

respiratory system, 238

restating ideas, 288–289

retail, 206

return, 208

revenue, 210

revision, for essay writing, 98–101, 152–155, 156

revision marks, 98

revision questions, 63

revolution, 186–187

rhombus, 500

rhyme, 318–319

rhythm, 318–319

ribonucleic acid (RNA), 244

right angle, 496

right triangle, 502

rise (slope), 484

RNA (ribonucleic acid), 244

Roman conquerors, 180

roots (numerical), 454–455

order of operations for, 458

rounding numbers, 346, 368

run-on sentences, 90–91

run (slope), 484

rural development, 220

Russian Revolution, 188

S

saliva, 238

SAS triangle (side-angle-side), 504

satellites (planetary), 260

saturation, 208

savings and loan associations, 208

scale (map), 224

scalene triangle, 502

scarcity

of goods, 206

of natural resources, 222

Science section, 229–282

content of, 229, vii

Earth Science section, 229, 254–267

Life Science section, 229, 234–253

Physical Science section, 229, 268–282

Space Science section, 229, 254–267

types of questions on, 229

scientific calculator. see calculator, using

scientific notation, 456–457

seceding, 168

second function keys, calculator, 356

semiconductor, 278

Senate, 194

sentence fragment, 84

sentences

complete simple, 84–85

complex, 86–89

compound, 86–89

inverted structure, 116

relating, and paragraphs, 72–73

run-on, 90–91

structure of, 84–105

topic, 68, 148

services, 206

set-up problems, 362–363, 460

settlement, 184

sexual reproduction, 242

sharecropping, 168

side-angle-side (SAS), 504

side lengths, triangles classified by, 502

side-side-side (SSS), 504

signed numbers, 450–453

adding, 450

dividing, 452

multiplying, 452

subtracting, 450–451

similar triangles, 504–505

simple interest problems, solving, 402, 688

simple probability, 424

topic sentence, 68, 148
topographic maps, 224
total cost, formula for, 688
total (numerical), 348
trachea, 238
traits, 242
transform margin, 254
transversals, 498–499
trapezoid, 508, 688
Treaty of Versailles, 188
triangle applications, 506–507
triangles, 502–503
    acute, 502
    area of, 508, 688
    ASA (angle-side-angle), 504
    comparing, 504
    congruent, 504–505
    hypotenuse, 518
    legs, 518
    obtuse, 502
    perimeter of, 508, 688
    right, 502
    SAS (side-angle-side), 504
    scalene, 502
    similar, 504–505
    SSS (side-side-side), 504
twentieth century, 188–189

U

unconstitutional, 194
unemployment, 212
unicellular, 234
Union, 168
unions, 170, 212
units, metric, 438
units of measurement, 434. *see also* Measurement
universe, 262–263
urban development, 220
urban regions, 218
urbanization, 220
U.S., as a world power, 172–173
U.S. Constitution, 166, 186
    amendments of, 196
U.S. economic system, 208–209
U.S. government, 210–211
U.S. history, 161, 166–179
    usage and grammar, 106–123

V

vague vs precise words, 118
values
    comparing, 346
    ordering, 346
variables, 352
    and algebraic expressions, 460
    in interest problems, 402
variations, 246
veins, 238
velocity, 276
verb agreement
    with compound subject, 116
    with simple subject, 114
verb forms, 110–113
verb-subject agreement, 114–117
verb tenses, 110–113
verbs, 84
    action, 84
    helping, 110
    irregular, 112
vertical angles, 498
veto, 194
villi, 238
viruses, 240
vitamins, 240
voltage, 278
volume, 512–515
    of a cone, 514, 688
    of a cube, 512, 688
    of a cylinder, 688
    of a rectangular solid, 688
    of a square pyramid, 688
    units of measurement for, 434

W

wages, 212
warm front, 258
watts, 274
weather and climate, 258–259
weather fronts, 258
weight, 270
Westward Expansion, 168–169
white dwarf, 262
whole number review, 346–351
wholesale, 206
width, units of measurement for, 434